HANDBOOK
of
PSYCHOLOGY

HANDBOOK
of
PSYCHOLOGY

VOLUME 5
PERSONALITY AND SOCIAL PSYCHOLOGY

Theodore Millon
Melvin J. Lerner

Volume Editors

Irving B. Weiner

Editor-in-Chief

John Wiley & Sons, Inc.

Library of Congress Cataloging-in-Publication Data:

Handbook of psychology / Irving B. Weiner, editor-in-chief.
    p.   cm.
    Includes bibliographical references and indexes.
    Contents: v. 1. History of psychology / edited by Donald K. Freedheim — v. 2. Research methods in psychology / edited by John A. Schinka, Wayne F. Velicer — v. 3. Biological psychology / edited by Michela Gallagher, Randy J. Nelson — v. 4. Experimental psychology / edited by Alice F. Healy, Robert W. Proctor — v. 5. Personality and social psychology / edited by Theodore Millon, Melvin J. Lerner — v. 6. Developmental psychology / edited by Richard M. Lerner, M. Ann Easterbrooks, Jayanthi Mistry — v. 7. Educational psychology / edited by William M. Reynolds, Gloria E. Miller — v. 8. Clinical psychology / edited by George Stricker, Thomas A. Widiger — v. 9. Health psychology / edited by Arthur M. Nezu, Christine Maguth Nezu, Pamela A. Geller — v. 10. Assessment psychology / edited by John R. Graham, Jack A. Naglieri — v. 11. Forensic psychology / edited by Alan M. Goldstein — v. 12. Industrial and organizational psychology / edited by Walter C. Borman, Daniel R. Ilgen, Richard J. Klimoski.
    ISBN 0-471-17669-9 (set) — ISBN 0-471-38320-1 (cloth : alk. paper : v. 1)
— ISBN 0-471-38513-1 (cloth : alk. paper : v. 2) — ISBN 0-471-38403-8 (cloth : alk. paper : v. 3)
— ISBN 0-471-39262-6 (cloth : alk. paper : v. 4) — ISBN 0-471-38404-6 (cloth : alk. paper : v. 5)
— ISBN 0-471-38405-4 (cloth : alk. paper : v. 6) — ISBN 0-471-38406-2 (cloth : alk. paper : v. 7)
— ISBN 0-471-39263-4 (cloth : alk. paper : v. 8) — ISBN 0-471-38514-X (cloth : alk. paper : v. 9)
— ISBN 0-471-38407-0 (cloth : alk. paper : v. 10) — ISBN 0-471-38321-X (cloth : alk. paper : v. 11)
— ISBN 0-471-38408-9 (cloth : alk. paper : v. 12)
    1. Psychology. I. Weiner, Irving B.

BF121.H1955 2003
150—dc21

        2002066380

Editorial Board

Handbook of Psychology Preface

Psychology at the beginning of the twenty-first century has become a highly diverse field of scientific study and applied technology. Psychologists commonly regard their discipline as the science of behavior, and the American Psychological Association has formally designated 2000 to 2010 as the "Decade of Behavior." The pursuits of behavioral scientists range from the natural sciences to the social sciences and embrace a wide variety of objects of investigation. Some psychologists have more in common with biologists than with most other psychologists, and some have more in common with sociologists than with most of their psychological colleagues. Some psychologists are interested primarily in the behavior of animals, some in the behavior of people, and others in the behavior of organizations. These and other dimensions of difference among psychological scientists are matched by equal if not greater heterogeneity among psychological practitioners, who currently apply a vast array of methods in many different settings to achieve highly varied purposes.

Psychology has been rich in comprehensive encyclopedias and in handbooks devoted to specific topics in the field. However, there has not previously been any single handbook designed to cover the broad scope of psychological science and practice. The present 12-volume *Handbook of Psychology* was conceived to occupy this place in the literature. Leading national and international scholars and practitioners have collaborated to produce 297 authoritative and detailed chapters covering all fundamental facets of the discipline, and the *Handbook* has been organized to capture the breadth and diversity of psychology and to encompass interests and concerns shared by psychologists in all branches of the field.

Two unifying threads run through the science of behavior. The first is a common history rooted in conceptual and empirical approaches to understanding the nature of behavior. The specific histories of all specialty areas in psychology trace their origins to the formulations of the classical philosophers and the methodology of the early experimentalists, and appreciation for the historical evolution of psychology in all of its variations transcends individual identities as being one kind of psychologist or another. Accordingly, Volume 1 in the *Handbook* is devoted to the history of psychology as it emerged in many areas of scientific study and applied technology.

A second unifying thread in psychology is a commitment to the development and utilization of research methods suitable for collecting and analyzing behavioral data. With attention both to specific procedures and their application in particular settings, Volume 2 addresses research methods in psychology.

Volumes 3 through 7 of the *Handbook* present the substantive content of psychological knowledge in five broad areas of study: biological psychology (Volume 3), experimental psychology (Volume 4), personality and social psychology (Volume 5), developmental psychology (Volume 6), and educational psychology (Volume 7). Volumes 8 through 12 address the application of psychological knowledge in five broad areas of professional practice: clinical psychology (Volume 8), health psychology (Volume 9), assessment psychology (Volume 10), forensic psychology (Volume 11), and industrial and organizational psychology (Volume 12). Each of these volumes reviews what is currently known in these areas of study and application and identifies pertinent sources of information in the literature. Each discusses unresolved issues and unanswered questions and proposes future directions in conceptualization, research, and practice. Each of the volumes also reflects the investment of scientific psychologists in practical applications of their findings and the attention of applied psychologists to the scientific basis of their methods.

The *Handbook of Psychology* was prepared for the purpose of educating and informing readers about the present state of psychological knowledge and about anticipated advances in behavioral science research and practice. With this purpose in mind, the individual *Handbook* volumes address the needs and interests of three groups. First, for graduate students in behavioral science, the volumes provide advanced instruction in the basic concepts and methods that define the fields they cover, together with a review of current knowledge, core literature, and likely future developments. Second, in addition to serving as graduate textbooks, the volumes offer professional psychologists an opportunity to read and contemplate the views of distinguished colleagues concerning the central thrusts of research and leading edges of practice in their respective fields. Third, for psychologists seeking to become conversant with fields outside their own specialty and for persons outside of psychology seeking information about psychological matters, the *Handbook* volumes serve as a reference source for expanding their knowledge and directing them to additional sources in the literature.

The preparation of this *Handbook* was made possible by the diligence and scholarly sophistication of the 25 volume editors and co-editors who constituted the Editorial Board. As Editor-in-Chief, I want to thank each of them for the pleasure of their collaboration in this project. I compliment them for having recruited an outstanding cast of contributors to their volumes and then working closely with these authors to achieve chapters that will stand each in their own right as valuable contributions to the literature. I would like finally to express my appreciation to the editorial staff of John Wiley and Sons for the opportunity to share in the development of this project and its pursuit to fruition, most particularly to Jennifer Simon, Senior Editor, and her two assistants, Mary Porterfield and Isabel Pratt. Without Jennifer's vision of the *Handbook* and her keen judgment and unflagging support in producing it, the occasion to write this preface would not have arrived.

IRVING B. WEINER
Tampa, Florida

Volume Preface

There are probably not many psychologists who have spent much time thinking about creating a handbook. The prevalent reasons for becoming a psychologist—scientific curiosity, the need for personal expression, or the desire for fame and fortune—would be unlikely to bring to mind the idea of generating a handbook. At the same time, most would agree that a handbook can be remarkably useful when the need arises. The chapters can provide the background for a grant proposal, the organization of a course offering, or a place for graduate students to look for a research problem. If presented at the right time, the clearly worthwhile aspects of this otherwise most unlikely endeavor can make it an attractive opportunity; or, at least in retrospect, one could imagine saying, "Well, it seemed like a good idea at the time." Even if there are a few simple and sovereign principles underlying all personality processes and social behavior, they were not consciously present when organizing this volume. Instead, what was terribly salient were the needs and goals of potential users of this volume: What would a reader need to know to have a good understanding of the current theoretical and empirical issues that occupy present-day thinkers and researchers? What could the highly sophisticated investigators who were selected to write the chapters tell the reader about the promising directions for future development? The chapters in this volume provide both thorough and illuminating answers to those questions, and, to be sure, some can be grouped into a few sections based on some common, familiar themes. For those readers who want more information about what chapters would be useful or who are open to being intrigued by the promise of some fascinating new ideas, this is a good time to take a brief glimpse at what the chapters are about.

An immediately pressing question for the editors centered on what content to include and whom to invite for the individual chapters. There are probably many ways to arrive systematically at those decisions, but then there is the intuitive method, which is easier, at least in that it can introduce a slight element of self-expression. The first chapter of this volume is a clear manifestation of the self-expressive mode. It comprises the thoughts of one of this volume's editors and contains a creative series of proposals concerning both the logic and the derivations of employing evolutionary theory as a basis for generating personality attributes, personality being the initial topic of the two major subjects that compose this fifth volume of the 12-volume *Handbook of Psychology*.

Chapters 1 and 2 of this book are subsumed under the general heading of *contexts*. The thought here is that both personality and social psychology, broad though they may be in their own right, should be seen as components of even wider fields of study, namely evolution and culture.

Evolution provides a context that relates to the processes of the *time dimension,* that is, the sequences and progressions of nature over the history of life on earth. Evolutionary theory generates a constellation of phylogenetic principles representing those processes that have endured and continue to undergird the ontogenetic development and character of human functioning. As such, these principles may guide more effective thinking about which functions of personality are likely to have been—and to persist to be—the most relevant in our studies. Similarly, *culture* provides a context that relates to the structure and processes of the *space dimension,* that is, the larger configuration of forces that surround, shape, and give meaning to the events that operate in the more immediate social psychological sphere. The study of culture may explicate the wide constellation of influences within which social behaviors are immersed and that ever so subtly exert direction, transform, and control and regulate even the most prosaic events of ordinary social communications and relationships. A few additional words should be said in elaboration of these two contextual chapters.

Admittedly theoretical and speculative, the paper by Theodore Millon outlines several of what he has deduced as the universal polarities of evolution: first, the core aims of existence, in which the polarities of life preservation are contrasted with life enhancement; second, life's fundamental modes of adaptation, counterposing ecologic accommodation and ecologic modification; third, the major strategies of species replication, setting reproductive nurturance in opposition to reproductive propagation; and fourth, a distinctly human polarity, that of predilections of abstraction, composed of comparative sources of information and their transformational processes. Millon spells out numerous personality implications of these polarities and articulates sources of support from a wide range of psychological literatures, such as humanistic theory and neurobiological research.

Joan G. Miller and Lynne Schaberg, in their contextual chapter, provide a constructively critical review of the failings of mainstream social psychology owing to its culture-free assumption of societal homogeneity. The authors specify a number of reasons why the cultural grounding of basic social-psychological processes have historically been downplayed. No less important is their articulation of the key conceptual formulations that have led to modern cultural psychology. Also notable are the several insights and challenges that stem from this new field. Equally valuable is a thorough review of how cultural research may bear significantly on a range of basic cognitive, emotional, and motivational functions. The authors conclude by outlining the many ways in which ongoing cultural studies can contribute new and useful theoretical constructs, as well as pertinent research questions that may substantially enrich the character, constructs, and range of numerous, more basic social-psychological formulations.

The next set of eight chapters of the volume represent the creative and reflective thinking of many of our most notable theoretical contributors to personology. They range from the genetic and biologic to the interpersonal and factorial. Each contributor is a major player in contemporary personality thought and research.

Before we proceed, a few words should be said concerning the current status of personologic theory. As he wrote in a 1990 book, *Toward a New Personology,* the first editor of this volume commented that the literature of the 1950s and 1960s was characterized by egregious attacks on the personality construct—attacks based on a rather facile and highly selective reading of then-popular research findings. And with the empirical grounding of personality in question and the consequential logic of personologic coherence and behavioral consistency under assault, adherents of the previously valued integrative view of personality lost their vaunted academic respectability and gradually withdrew from active publication. Personality theory did manage to weather these mettlesome assaults, and it began what proved to be a wide-ranging resurgence in the 1970s. By virtue of time, thoughtful reflection, and, not the least, disenchantment with proposed alternatives such as behavioral dogmatism and psychiatric biochemistry, the place of the personality construct rapidly regained its formal solid footing. The alternatives have justly faded to a status consonant with their trivial character, succumbing under the weight of their clinical inefficacy and scholarly boredom. By contrast, a series of widely acclaimed formulations were articulated by a number of contemporary psychological, psychoanalytic, interpersonal,

cognitive, factorial, genetic, social, neurobiologic, and evolutionary theorists. It is to these theorists and their followers that we turn next.

Bringing the primitive and highly speculative genetic thought of the early twentieth century up to date by drawing on the technologies of the recent decade, W. John Livesley, Kerry L. Jang, and Philip Anthony Vernon articulate a convincing rationale for formulating personality concepts and their structure on the basis of trait-heritability studies. In a manner similar to Millon, who grounds his personologic concepts on the basis of a theory of evolutionary functions, Livesley et al. argue that genetic research provides a fundamental grounding for deriving complex trait constellations; these two biologically anchored schemas may ultimately be coordinated through future theoretical and empirical research. The authors contend that most measures of personality reflect heritable components and that the phenotypic structure of personality will ultimately resemble the pattern of an underlying genetic architecture. They assert, further, that etiologic criteria such as are found in genetics can offer a more objective basis for appraising personologic structure than can psychometrically based phenotypic analyses. Moreover, they believe that the interaction of multiple genetic factors will fully account for the complex patterns of trait covariances and trait clusters.

Continuing the thread of logic from evolution to genetics to the neurochemical and physiological, Marvin Zuckerman traces the interplay of these biologically based formulations to their interaction with the environment and the generation of learned behavioral traits. Writing in the spirit of Edward Wilson's concept of *consilience* and its aim of bringing a measure of unity to ostensibly diverse sciences, Zuckerman spells out in considerable detail the flow or pathways undergirding four major personality trait concepts: extroversion/sociability; neuroticism/anxiety; aggression/agreeableness; and impulsivity/sensation seeking. Recognizing that detailed connections between the biological and the personological are not as yet fully developed, Zuckerman goes to great pains, nevertheless, to detail a wide range of strongly supporting evidence, from genetic twin studies to EEG and brain imaging investigations of cortical and autonomic arousal, to various indexes of brain neurochemistry.

Shifting the focus from the biological grounding of personality attributes, Robert F. Bornstein provides a thoughtful essay on both classical psychoanalytic and contemporary models of psychodynamic theory. He does record, however, that the first incarnation of psychoanalysis was avowedly biological, recognizing that Freud in 1895 set out to link psychological phenomena to then-extant models of neural functioning. Nevertheless, the course of analytic theory has evolved in distinctly divergent directions over the past century, although recent efforts have been made to bridge them again to the challenge of modern neuroscience, as Bornstein notes. His chapter spells out core assumptions common to all models of psychoanalysis, such as classical analytic theory, neoanalytic models, object-relations theory, and self psychology, as well as contemporary integrative frameworks. Threads that link these disparate analytic perspectives are discussed, as are the key issues facing twenty-first-century analytic schemas.

No more radical a contrast with psychoanalytic models of personality can be found than in theories grounded in the logical positivism and empiricism that are fundamental to behavioral models, such as those articulated in the chapter by one of its primary exponents, Arthur W. Staats. Committed to a formal philosophical approach to theory development, Staats avers that most personality models lack formal rules of theory construction, possessing, at best, a plethora of different and unrelated studies and tests. Staats's theory, termed *psychological behaviorism*, is grounded in learning principles generated originally in animal research, but more recently put into practice in human behavioral therapy. Like Clark Hull, a major second-generation behavioral thinker, he believes that all behavior is generated from the same primary laws. In his own formulations, Staats explicates a unified model of behavioral personology that is philosophically well structured and provides a program for developing diverse avenues of systematic personality research.

An innovative and dynamic framework for coordinating the cognitive, experiential, learning, and self-oriented components of personology (termed CEST) is presented in the theoretical chapter by Seymour Epstein. The author proposes that people operate through two interacting information-processing modes, one predominantly conscious, verbal, and *rational,* the other predominantly preconscious, automatic, and emotionally *experiential.* Operating according to different rules, it is asserted that the influence of the experiential system on the rational system is akin to what psychoanalysis claims for the role of the unconscious, but it is conceptualized in CEST in a manner more consistent with contemporary evolutionary and cognitive science. Epstein details the application of his CEST model for psychotherapy, notably by pointing out how the rational system can be employed to correct problems generated in the experiential system. Also discussed is the importance of designing research that fully recognizes and encompasses the interplay between these two information-processing systems.

The chapter by Charles S. Carver and Michael F. Scheier represents the current status of their decades-long thought and research on self-regulatory models of personality functioning. Anchored in a sophisticated framework of feedback schemas, the authors emphasize a major facet of personality processing, the system of goals that compose the self, how the patterns of a person's goals are related, and the means by which persons move toward and away from their goals. As a consequence of their research, the authors have come to see that *actions* are managed by a different set of feedback processes than are *feelings.* Aspirations are recalibrated in reasonably predictable ways as a function of experience; for example, successes lead to setting higher goals, whereas failures tend to lower them. Conflicting goals often call for the suppression of once-desired goals, resulting in goal shifts, scaling back, disengagements, and, ultimately, lapses in self-control. Carver and Scheier view their goal as closely related to other contemporary schemas, such as dynamic systems theory and connectionism.

In their richly developed chapter, Aaron L. Pincus and Emily B. Ansell set out to create a new identity for interpersonal theory that recognizes its unique aspects and integrative potential. They suggest that the interpersonal perspective can serve as the basis for integrating diverse theoretical approaches to personality. Given its focus on interpersonal situations, this perspective includes both proximal descriptions of overt behavioral transactions and the covert or intrapsychic processes that mediate those transactions, including the internal mental representations of self and other. In addition to reviewing the work of the major originators (e.g., Sullivan, Leary) and contemporary thinkers in interpersonal theory (e.g., Benjamin, Kiesler), the authors believe that there continues to be a need for a more complete integration of the interpersonal perspective with motivational, developmental, object-relations, and cognitive theories of human behavior. Similarly, they argue for a further identification of those catalysts that stimulate the internalization of relational experiences into influential mental representations.

The current popularity among psychologists of various five-factor formulations of personality in contemporary research is undeniable. Despite the extensive literature in the area, these formulations have not been as thoroughly dissected, critically examined, and explicated as they are in Willem K. B. Hofstee's chapter on the structure of personality traits. The author asserts that concepts such as personality are shaped and defined largely by the operations employed to construct them. Hence, several procedures applied under the rubric of the number five have been employed to characterize trait adjectives describing the structure and composition of the personality concept. Hofstee differentiates four operational modules that constitute the five component paradigms: The first set of operations reflects standardized self-report questionnaires; the second comprises the lexical approach based on selections from a *corpus* of a language; the third relies on a linear methodology employing a principal components analysis of Likert item scales; and the fourth produces rival hierarchical and circumplex models for structuring trait information. Hofstee concludes his chapter by proposing a family of models composed of a hierarchy of generalized semicircumplexes.

Appropriately placed at the conclusion of the social psychology section, Aubrey Immelman's chapter comprises a synthesis of personality and social behavior. It not only examines the history of personality inquiry in political psychology but also offers a far-reaching and theoretically coherent framework for studying the subject in a manner consonant with principles in contextually adjacent fields, such as behavioral neuroscience and evolutionary ecology. Immelman provides an explicit framework for a personality-based risk analysis of political outcomes, acknowledging the role of filters that modulate the impact of personality on political performance. Seeking to accommodate a diversity of politically relevant personality characteristics, he bridges conceptual and methodological gaps in contemporary political study and specifically attempts a psychological examination of political leaders, on the basis of which he imposes a set of standards for personality-in-politics modeling.

By way of confession, the social psychology chapters in this volume were selected for the most part after simply jotting down the first thoughts about what areas to include and who would be good candidates to write the chapters. Fortunately, subsequent scanning of a few well-known introductory texts and prior handbooks did nothing to alter those initial hunches that came so immediately and automatically to mind. For the most part, the vast majority of the chapters cover contemporary perspectives on traditional social psychological issues; however, a few introduce new, highly active areas of inquiry (e.g., justice, close relationships, and peace studies).

At this point, it would be nice to describe the central theme, the deep structure underlying the organization of the social psychology chapters. But, as most readers know, social psychology and social behavior are too broad and varied for that kind of organization to be valid, much less useful. For the past 50 years or so, social psychology has done remarkably well examining the various aspects of social behavior with what Robert Merton termed theories of the midrange—his theory of relative deprivation being a good example.

The social psychology chapters easily fall in to a few categories based on the nature of the issues they address. Four chapters focus on the social context of fundamental psychological structures: social cognitions, emotions, the self concept, and attitudes. These, together with the chapter

on environmental psychology, provide a natural introduction to the social processes and interpersonal dynamics that follow.

In the chapter on social cognition, Galen V. Bodenhausen, C. Neil Macrae, and Kurt Hugenberg, point out that the substance of the chapter contains an excellent review of the available literature describing the types of mental representations that make up the content of social cognitions; how various motives and emotions influence those cognitions; and the recent very exciting work on the nature, appearance, and consequences of automatic as well as more thoughtfully controlled processes. This chapter would be an excellent place for someone to get an overview of the best that is now known about the cognitive structures and processes that shape understanding of social situations and mediate behavioral reactions to them.

No less fundamental are the questions of the sources of people's emotions and how they influence behavior. The chapter by José-Miguel Fernández-Dols and James A. Russell provides a review of the theories and empirical evidence relevant to the two basic approaches to emotions and affect: as modular products of human evolutionary past and as script-like products of human cultural history. Whether one fully accepts their highly creative and brave integration of these two approaches employing the concept of core affect, their lucid description of the best available evidence together with their astute analytic insights will be well worth the reader's time and effort. In addition, it would be remarkably easy to take their integrative theoretical model as the inspiration, or at least starting point, for various lines of critically important research.

Roy F. Baumeister and Jean M. Twenge clearly intend that their readers fully appreciate their observation that the self-concept is intrinsically located in a social processes and interpersonal relations. In fact, as they state, the self is constructed and maintained as a way of connecting the individual organism to other members of the species. It would be easy to view this as a contemporary example of teleological theorizing (i.e., explaining structures and processes referring to a functional purpose); however, the authors go to considerable length to provide evidence explicitly describing the underlying dynamics. This includes issues such as belongingness, social exclusion, and ostracism, as well as the more familiar concerns with conformity and self-esteem. The authors make a good case for their proposition that one of the self's crucial defining functions is to enable people to live with other people in harmony and mutual belongingness.

The notion that people walk around with predispositions to think, feel, and act with regard to identifiable aspects of their world has a long and noble tradition in social psychology. Certainly since Gordon Allport's writings the concept of attitudes and their nature, origins, and behavioral consequences have been at the core of social psychology. To be sure, those issues appear in one form or another throughout most of the chapters in this volume. James M. Olson and Gregory Maio took on the task of presenting what is now known about attitudes in social behavior. This includes the structure of attitudes, the dimensions on which they differ, how they are formed and related to beliefs and values, and their functions in social relations and behavior. Of particular importance is the identification of those issues and questions that should be addressed in future research. For example, the evidence for the distinction between implicit and explicit attitudes opens up several areas worthy of investigation.

Ever since the seminal work of Barker and his colleagues, social psychologists have recognized the importance of considering the built environments as well as sociocultural contexts in arriving at an adequate understanding of human thought, feelings, and actions. In their chapter on environmental psychology, Gabriel Moser and David Uzzell adopt the idea exemplified in Barker's early field research that psychologists must recognize that the environment is a critical factor if they are to understand how people function in the real world. As Moser and Uzzell demonstrate, much has been discovered about the environment-person relationship that falls nicely within the context created by that early work. The authors note that not only do environmental psychologists work in collaboration with other psychologists to understand the processes mediating these relationships, but they also find themselves in collaborative efforts with other disciplines, such as architects, engineers, landscape architects, urban planners, and so on. The common focus, of course, consists of the cognitions, attitudes, emotions, self-concepts, and actions of the social participants.

The next chapters consider the dynamics involved in interpersonal and social processes that lead to changes in people's attitudes and social behavior.

Recognizing the important distinction between implicit and explicit attitudes, in their chapter on persuasion and attitude change Richard E. Petty, S. Christian Wheeler, and Zakary L. Tormala report that as yet there is no way to change implicit attitudes. Their main contribution consists of presenting the evidence and theories relevant to changing explicit attitudes. After a relatively brief discussion of the currently influential elaboration likelihood model, their chapter is organized around the important distinction between processes that involve relatively automatic low-effort reactions from the target person and those that engage the target's thoughts and at times behavioral reactions. The distinction between high- and low-effort processes of attitude change

provides a comfortable and rather meaningful framework for organizing processes as seemingly disparate as affective priming, heuristic-based reactions, role playing, dissonance, information integration, and so on.

Andrzej Nowak, Robin R. Vallacher, and Mandy E. Miller's chapter on social influence and group dynamics has several noteworthy features, one of which is the range of material that they have included. The chapter is so nicely composed and lucidly written that the reader may not easily appreciate the wide range of material, both theory and evidence, that is being covered. For example, the chapter begins with the more traditionally familiar topics such as obedience and reactance, moves on to what is known about more explicit efforts to influence people's behavior, and then addresses the interpersonal processes associated with group pressure, polarization, and social loafing. All that is pretty familiar to most psychologists. However, the authors finally arrive at the most recent theoretical perspectives involving cellular automata that naturally lend themselves to the use of computer simulations to outline the implicit axiomatic changes in complex systems. What an amazing trip in both theories and method! Is it possible that what the authors identify as the press for higher order coherence provides a coherent integration of the entire social influence literature?

The transition from these initial chapters to those remaining can be roughly equated with the two dominant concerns of social psychologists. Up to this point, the chapters were most concerned with basic social psychological processes: scientific understanding of the interpersonal processes and social behavior. The remaining chapters exemplify social psychologists' desire to find ways to make the world a better place, where people treat each other decently or at least are less cruel and destructive. Three of these chapters consider the social motives and processes that are involved in people helping and being fair to one another, whereas the last three examine harmful things that can happen between individuals and social groups, ranging from acts of prejudice to open warfare. The last chapter offers an introduction to what is now known about achieving a peaceful world.

In their chapter on altruism and prosocial behavior, C. Daniel Batson and Adam A. Powell offer a most sophisticated analysis of the relevant social psychological literature. On the basis of his research and theoretical writings, Batson is the most cited and respected psychological expert on prosocial behavior. In this chapter he discusses the evidence for four sources of prosocial behavior. After providing an analysis of the sources of these prosocial motives—enlightened self-interest, altruism, principalism, and collectivism—he then takes on the task of discussing the points of possible conflict and cooperation among them. One might argue with his evidence for the ease with which the principalist motives—justice and fairness—can be corrupted by self-interest, and thus his conclusion is that prosocial behavior can be most reliably based on altruistic (i.e., empathy-based) motives. I suspect, however, that Kurt Lewin would have been very pleased with this highly successful example of the potential societal value of good social psychological theory.

Leo Montada, in the chapter on justice, equity, and fairness in human relations, provides a very content-rich but necessarily selective review of what is known about how justice appears in people's lives, the various aspects of justice, and their social and individual sources, as well as interpersonal consequences. At the same time that he leads the reader through a general survey of the justice literature, he provides the reader with highly sophisticated insights and critical analyses. It is clear from the outset of this chapter that Montada is a thoroughly well-informed social scientist approaching one of the fundamental issues in human relations: how and why people care about justice in their lives, what forms that concern takes, and how important those are concerns in shaping how they treat one another.

Margaret S. Clark and Nancy K. Grote's chapter can be viewed as the integration of several literatures associated with close relationships, friendships, and marriages—romantic and familial. They focus on the social-psychological processes associated with "good relationships": those that they define as fostering members' well-being. This chapter provides the most recent developments in Clark's important distinction between communal and exchange relationships and includes the report of an important longitudinal study examining the relationship between conflict and fairness in close relationships. They find that conflict in a relationship leads to increased concern with issues of fairness that then lead the participants even further from the important communal norms based on mutual concern for one another's welfare.

Kenneth L. Dion's chapter on prejudice, racism, and discrimination looks at various aspects of the darker side of interpersonal relations. In the first section of the chapter, Dion leads the reader to a very thoughtful and complete review of the various explanations for prejudice, racism, and discrimination. Beginning with the classic and contemporary versions of the authoritarian personality theories, he discusses just-world, belief congruence, and ambivalence literatures. Dion does a masterful job of leading the reader through the more recently developed distinction between automatic and controlled processes, as well as social dominance theory and multicomponent approaches to intergroup attitudes. But that is only the beginning. Reflecting his own earlier research interests, Dion devotes the second section of his chapter to the psychology of the victim of prejudice and discrimination. This section integrates the most recent findings in this highly active and productive area of inquiry. Dion describes the research that has given the familiar self-fulfilling prophecy notion in social psychology new meaning and has provided compelling new insights into the very important ways victims respond to their unfair treatment.

The chapter by John F. Dovidio, Samuel L. Gaertner, Victoria M. Esses and Marilynn B. Brewer examines the social-psychological processes involved in interpersonal and intergroup relations. This includes both the sources of social conflict and those involved in bringing about harmony and integration. The origins of the important work reported in this chapter can be traced to the initial insights of European social psychologists who recognized that when people they think in terms of "we" rather than "I," there is a strong tendency also to react in terms of "us" versus "them" (i.e., in-group vs. out-group). The consequences, of course, include favoring members of the in-group and discriminating against members of the salient out-groups. After describing what is known about the psychological processes involved in these biased reactions, the authors then consider those processes that can preclude or overcome those destructive biases and promote harmony and social integration.

Joseph de Rivera's chapter takes a similar path, by first focusing on those social-psychological processes involved in aggression and violence, and then with that as background presenting his recommendations concerning how positive peace can be promoted. For de Rivera this does not simply mean an absence of open conflict, but rather a benevolent and supportive environment, as well as societal norms, that promote individual processes involving harmony and well-being. In describing the various means for generating a global culture of peace, he also makes the case for the importance of individual's personal transformation in creating and maintaining a culture of peace. De Rivera offers the reader a highly sophisticated use of the social-psychological research and theory to arrive at specific recommendations for solving, arguably, the most important issues of our lives: the achievement of a peaceful, caring, nurturing social environment. Ambitious? Yes. But de Rivera generates the framework of his own perspective out of the best of what social science has to offer.

We trust the readers of this volume on personality and social psychology will find the chapters it contains to be both provocative and illuminating. It has been an honor and a joy to edit a book written by so many able, inspiring, and cooperative authors, whom we thank personally for their thoughtful and stimulating contributions.

THEODORE MILLON
MELVIN J. LERNER

Contents

PART ONE
CONTEXTS

PART TWO
PERSONALITY

Contributors

Emily B. Ansell
Department of Psychology
Pennsylvania State University
University Park, Pennsylvania

C. Daniel Batson, PhD
Department of Psychology
University of Kansas
Lawrence, Kansas

Roy F. Baumeister, PhD
Department of Psychology
Case Western Reserve University
Cleveland, Ohio

Galen V. Bodenhausen, PhD
Department of Psychology
Northwestern University
Evanston, Illinois

Robert F. Bornstein, PhD
Department of Psychology
Gettysburg College
Gettysburg, Pennsylvania

Marilynn B. Brewer, PhD
Department of Psychology
The Ohio State University
Columbus, Ohio

Charles S. Carver, PhD
Department of Psychology
University of Miami
Coral Gables, Florida

Margaret S. Clark, PhD
Department of Psychology
Carnegie Mellon University
Pittsburgh, Pennsylvania

Kenneth L. Dion, PhD
Department of Psychology
University of Toronto
Toronto, Ontario, Canada

John F. Dovidio, PhD
Department of Psychology
Colgate University
Hamilton, New York

Seymour Epstein, PhD
Psychology Department
University of Massachusetts at Amherst
Amherst, Massachusetts

Victoria M. Esses, PhD
Department of Psychology
University of Western Ontario
London, Ontario, Canada

José-Miguel Fernández-Dols
Facultad de Psicologia
Universidad Autonoma de Madrid
Madrid, Spain

Samuel L. Gaertner, PhD
Department of Psychology
University of Delaware
Newark, Delaware

Nancy K. Grote, PhD
Department of Social Work
University of Pittsburgh
Pittsburgh, Pennsylvania

Willem K. B. Hofstee, PhD
University of Groningen
Groningen, The Netherlands

Kurt Hugenberg, MA
Department of Psychology
Northwestern University
Evanston, Illinois

Aubrey Immelman, PhD
Department of Psychology
Saint John's University
Collegeville, Minnesota

Kerry L. Jang, PhD
Department of Psychiatry
University of British Columbia
Vancouver, British Columbia, Canada

W. John Livesley, PhD, MD
Department of Psychiatry
University of British Columbia
Vancouver, British Columbia, Canada

C. Neil Macrae, PhD
Department of Psychological and Brain Science
Dartmouth College
Hanover, New Hampshire

Gregory R. Maio, PhD
Department of Psychology
University of Wales
Cardiff, United Kingdom

Joan G. Miller, PhD
Institute for Social Research
University of Michigan
Ann Arbor, Michigan

Mandy E. Miller, JD
Department of Psychology
Florida Atlantic University
Boca Raton, Florida

Theodore Millon, PhD, DSc
Institute for Advanced Studies in Personology
    and Psychopathology
Coral Gables, Florida

Leo Montada, PhD
Department of Psychology
University of Trier
Trier, Germany

Gabriel Moser, PhD
Institute of Psychology
Université René Descartes—Paris 5
Boulogne-Billancourt, France

Andrzej Nowak, PhD
Center for Complex Systems
University of Warsaw
Warsaw, Poland

James M. Olson, PhD
Department of Psychology
University of Western Ontario
London, Ontario, Canada

Richard E. Petty, PhD
Department of Psychology
Ohio State University
Columbus, Ohio

Aaron L. Pincus, PhD
Department of Psychology
Pennsylvania State University
University Park, Pennsylvania

Adam A. Powell, MBA, MA
Department of Psychology
University of Kansas
Lawrence, Kansas

Joseph de Rivera, PhD
Department of Psychology
Clark University
Worcester, Massachusetts

James A. Russell, PhD
Department of Psychology
Boston College
Chestnut Hill, Massachusetts

Lynne Schaberg, PhD
Department of Psychology
University of Michigan
Ann Arbor, Michigan

Michael F. Scheier, PhD
Department of Psychology
Carnegie Mellon University
Pittsburgh, Pennsylvania

Arthur W. Staats, PhD
Department of Psychology
University of Hawaii
Honolulu, Hawaii

Zakary L. Tormala, MA
Department of Psychology
Ohio State University
Columbus, Ohio

Jean M. Twenge, PhD
Department of Psychology
San Diego State University
San Diego, California

David Uzzell, PhD
Department of Psychology
University of Surrey
Guildford, United Kingdom

Robin R. Vallacher, PhD
Department of Psychology
Florida Atlantic University
Boca Raton, Florida

Philip A. Vernon, PhD
Department of Psychiatry
University of British Columbia
Vancouver, British Columbia, Canada

S. Christian Wheeler, PhD
Graduate School of Business
Stanford University
Stanford, California

Marvin Zuckerman, PhD
Department of Psychology
University of Delaware
Newark, Delaware

PART ONE

CONTEXTS

CHAPTER 1

Evolution: A Generative Source for Conceptualizing the Attributes of Personality

THEODORE MILLON

In the last year of the twentieth century, voters elected a group of Kansas school board members who supported the removal of the concept of evolution from the state's science curriculum, an act that indicated the extent to which evolutionary ideas could incite intense emotional, if not irrational opposition on the part of unenlightened laymen. Retrospectively appalled by their prior action, in the following year Kansan voters rescinded their perverse judgment and chose new board members who intended to restore the concept.

The theory of evolution was reinstated not because the electors of Kansas, a most conservative and religious state, suddenly became agnostic, but because they realized that rejecting the idea would deny their children the necessity of remaining in touch with one of the fundamentals of modern science; they realized that this could, in effect, allow their children to fall behind, to be bereft of a basic science, and to be both a misinformed and misguided generation. Their children could become embarrassingly backward in a time of rapidly changing technology.

Might not the same ambivalence be true of our own field, one composed of ostensibly sophisticated and knowledgeable scientists? Might we not be so deeply mired in our own traditions (scholarly religions?) that we are unable to free ourselves from the habit of seeing our subject from no vantage point other than those to which we have become accustomed? Are we unable to recognize that behavior, cognition, the unconscious, personality—all of our traditional subjects—are merely diverse manifestations of certain common and deeper principles of functioning, processes, and mechanisms that have evolved either randomly or adaptively through history and time? Do we psychologists have a collective phobia about laws that may represent the fundamental origins of our traditional subjects? Does the search for and application of such laws push our emotional buttons, perhaps run hard against our habitual blinders, so much so as to prevent us from recognizing their value as a potential generative source that may more fully illuminate our science?

PERSONOLOGY'S RELATIONSHIP TO OTHER SCIENCES

It is the intent of this chapter to broaden our vistas, to furnish both a context and a set of guiding ideas that may enrich our studies. I believe it may be wise and perhaps even necessary to go beyond our current conceptual boundaries in psychology, more specifically to explore carefully reasoned, as well as intuitive hypotheses that draw their laws and principles if not their substance from contextually adjacent sciences such as evolution. Not only may such steps bear new conceptual fruits, but they may also provide a foundation that can undergird and guide our own discipline's explorations. Much of personology, no less psychology as a whole, remains adrift, divorced from broader spheres of scientific knowledge; it is isolated from firmly grounded if not universal principles, leading us to continue building the patchwork quilt of concepts and data domains that characterize our field. Preoccupied with but a small part of the larger puzzle of nature or fearful of accusations of reductionism, we may fail to draw on the rich possibilities to be found in parallel realms of scientific pursuit. With few exceptions, cohering concepts that would connect our subject domain to those of its sister sciences in nature have not been adequately developed.

It appears to me that we have become trapped in (obsessed with?) horizontal refinements. A search for integrative schemas and cohesive constructs that link its seekers closely to relevant observations and laws developed in other scientific fields is needed. The goal—albeit a rather ambitious one—is to refashion our patchwork quilt of concepts into a well-tailored and aesthetically pleasing tapestry that interweaves the diverse forms in which nature expresses itself (E. O. Wilson, 1998).

What sphere is there within the psychological sciences more apt than personology to undertake the synthesis of nature? Persons are the only organically integrated system in the psychological domain, evolved through the millennia and inherently created from birth as natural entities rather than culture-bound and experience-derived gestalts. The intrinsic cohesion of nature's diverse elements that inheres in persons is not a rhetorical construction, but rather an authentic substantive unity. Personological features may often be dissonant and may be partitioned conceptually for pragmatic or scientific purposes, but they are segments of an inseparable physicochemical, biopsychosocial entity.

To take this view is not to argue that different spheres of scientific inquiry must be collapsed or even equated, but rather that there may be value in seeking a single, overarching conceptual system that interconnects ostensibly diverse subjects such as physics, biology, and psychology (Millon, 1990; E. O. Wilson, 1998). Arguing in favor of establishing explicit links between these domains calls for neither a reductionistic philosophy, nor a belief in substantive identicality, nor efforts to so fashion the links by formal logic. Rather, one should aspire to their substantive concordance, empirical consistency, conceptual interfacing, convergent dialogues, and mutual enlightenment.

A few words should be said concerning the undergirding framework used to structure an evolutionary context for a personology model. Parallel schemas are almost universally present in the literature; the earliest may be traced to mid–nineteenth-century philosophers, most notably Spencer (1855) and Haeckel (1874). More modern but equally speculative systems have been proposed by keen and broadly informed observers such as Edward Wilson (1975), Cosmides and Tooby (1987, 1989) and M. Wilson and Daley (1992), as well as by empirically well-grounded methodologists, such as Symons (1979, 1992) and D. M. Buss (1989, 1994). Each of

their proposals fascinates either by virtue of its intriguing portrayals or by the compelling power of its logic or its data. Their arguments not only coordinate with but also are anchored to observations derived specifically from principles of modern physical and biological evolution. It is these underpinnings of knowledge on which the personological model presented in this chapter has been grounded and from which a deeper and clearer understanding may be obtained concerning the nature of both normal and pathological personality functioning.

On the Place of Theory in Personology

The following discussion is conjectural, if not overly extended in its speculative reach. In essence, it seeks to explicate the structure and styles of personality with reference to deficient, imbalanced, or conflicted modes of evolutionary survival, ecological adaptation, and reproductive strategy. Whatever one's appraisal of these conjectures, the model that follows may best be approached in the spirit in which it was formulated—an effort to provide a context for explicating the domains of personological science in the hope that it can lead to a clearer understanding of our subject. All sciences have organizing principles that not only create order but also provide the basis for generating hypotheses and stimulating new knowledge. A contextual theory not only summarizes and incorporates extant knowledge, but is heuristic—that is, it has "systematic import," as Hempel (1965) has phrased it, in that it may originate and develop new observations and new methods.

It is unfortunate that the number of theories that have been advanced to "explain" personality is proportional to the internecine squabbling found in the literature. However, and ostensibly toward the end of pragmatic sobriety, those of an antitheory bias have sought to persuade the profession of the failings of premature formalization, warning that one cannot arrive at the desired future by lifting science by its own bootstraps. To them, there is no way to traverse the road other sciences have traveled without paying the dues of an arduous program of empirical research. Formalized axiomatics, they say, must await the accumulation of so-called hard evidence that is simply not yet in. Shortcutting the route with ill-timed systematics, they claim, will lead us down primrose paths, preoccupying attentions as we wend fruitlessly through endless detours, each of which could be averted by our holding fast to an empiricist philosophy and methodology.

No one argues against the view that theories that float, so to speak, on their own, unconcerned with the empirical domain, should be seen as the fatuous achievements they are and the travesty they make of the virtues of a truly coherent conceptual system. Formal theory should not be pushed far beyond the data, and its derivations should be linked at all points to established observations. However, a theoretical framework can be a compelling instrument for coordinating and giving consonance to complex and diverse observations—if its concepts are linked to relevant facts in the empirical world. By probing beneath surface impressions to inner structures and processes, previously isolated facts and difficult-to-fathom data may yield new relationships and expose clearer meanings. Scientific progress occurs when observations and concepts elaborate and refine previous work. However, this progression does not advance by brute empiricism alone, by merely piling up more descriptive and more experimental data. What is elaborated and refined in theory is understanding, an ability to see relations more plainly, to conceptualize categories and dimensions more accurately, and to create greater overall coherence in a subject—to integrate its elements in a more logical, consistent, and intelligible fashion.

A problem arises when introducing theory into the study of personality. Given our intuitive ability to "sense" the correctness of a psychological insight or speculation, theoretical efforts that impose structure or formalize these insights into a scientific system will often be perceived as not only cumbersome and intrusive, but alien as well. This discomfiture and resistance does not arise in fields such as particle physics, in which everyday observations are not readily available and in which innovative insights are few and far between. In such subject domains, scientists not only are quite comfortable, but also turn readily to deductive theory as a means of helping them explicate and coordinate knowledge. It is paradoxical but true and unfortunate that personologists learn their subject quite well merely by observing the ordinary events of life. As a consequence of this ease, personologists appear to shy from and hesitate placing trust in the obscure and complicating, yet often fertile and systematizing powers inherent in formal theory, especially when a theory is new or different from those learned in their student days.

Despite the shortcomings in historic and contemporary theoretical schemas, systematizing principles and abstract concepts can "facilitate a deeper seeing, a more penetrating vision that goes beyond superficial appearances to the order underlying them" (Bowers, 1977). For example, pre-Darwinian taxonomists such as Linnaeus limited themselves to apparent similarities and differences among animals as a means of constructing their categories. Darwin was not seduced by appearances. Rather, he sought to understand the principles by which overt features came about. His classifications were based not only on descriptive qualities, but also on explanatory ones.

On the Place of Evolutionary Theory in Personology

It is in both the spirit and substance of Darwin's explanatory principles that the reader should approach the proposals that follow. The principles employed are essentially the same as those that Darwin developed in seeking to explicate the origins of species. However, they are listed to derive not the origins of species, but rather the structure and style of personalities that have previously been generated on the basis of clinical observation alone. Aspects of these formulations have been published in earlier books (Millon, 1969, 1981, 1986, 1990; Millon & Davis, 1996); they are anchored here, however, explicitly to evolutionary and ecological theory. Identified in earlier writings as a biosocial learning model for personality and psychopathology, the theory we present seeks to generate the principles, mechanisms, and typologies of personality through formal processes of deduction.

To propose that fruitful ideas may be derived by applying evolutionary principles to the development and functions of personological traits has a long (if yet unfulfilled) tradition. Spencer (1870), Huxley (1870), and Haeckel (1874) offered suggestions of this nature shortly after Darwin's seminal *Origins* was published. The school of *functionalism,* popular in psychology in the early part of this century, likewise drew its impetus from evolutionary concepts as it sought to articulate a basis for individual difference typologies (McDougall, 1932).

In recent decades, numerous evolution-oriented psychologists and biologists have begun to explore how the human mind may have been shaped over the past million years to solve the problems of basic survival, ecological adaptation, and species replication and diversification. These well-crafted formulations are distinctly different from other, more traditional models employed to characterize human functioning.

The human mind is assuredly sui generis, but it is only the most recent phase in the long history of organic life. Moreover, there is no reason to assume that the exigencies of life have differed in their essentials among early and current species. It would be reasonable, therefore—perhaps inevitable—that the study of the functions of mind be anchored to the same principles that are universally found in evolution's progression. Using this anchor should enable us to build a bridge between the human mind and all other facets of natural science; moreover, it should provide a broad blueprint of *why* the mind engages in the functions it does, as well as what its essential *purposes* may be, such as pursuing parental affection and protection, exploring the rationale and patterns of sexual mating, and specifying the styles of social communication and abstract language.

In recent times we have also seen the emergence of sociobiology, a new science that has explored the interface between human social functioning and evolutionary biology (E. O. Wilson, 1975, 1978). The common goal among both sociobiological and personological proposals is the desire not only to apply analogous principles across diverse scientific realms, but also to reduce the enormous range of behavioral and trait concepts that have proliferated through modern history. This goal might be achieved by exploring the power of evolutionary theory to simplify and order previously disparate personological features. For example, all organisms seek to avoid injury, find nourishment, and reproduce their kind if they are to survive and maintain their populations. Each species displays commonalities in its adaptive or survival style. Within each species, however, there are differences in style and differences in the success with which its various members adapt to the diverse and changing environments they face. In these simplest of terms, differences among personality styles would be conceived as representing the more-or-less distinctive ways of adaptive functioning that an organism of a particular species exhibits as it relates to its typical range of environments. Disorders of personality, so formulated, would represent particular styles of maladaptive functioning that can be traced to deficiencies, imbalances, or conflicts in a species' capacity to relate to the environments it faces.

A few additional words should be said concerning analogies between evolution and ecology on the one hand and personality on the other. During its life history, an organism develops an assemblage of traits that contribute to its individual survival and reproductive success, the two essential components of fitness formulated by Darwin. Such assemblages, termed *complex adaptations* and *strategies* in the literature of evolutionary ecology, are close biological equivalents to what psychologists have conceptualized as personality styles and structures. In biology, explanations of a life history strategy of adaptations refer primarily to biogenic variations among constituent traits, their overall covariance structure, and the nature and ratio of favorable to unfavorable ecological resources that have been available for purposes of extending longevity and optimizing reproduction. Such explanations are not appreciably different from those used to account for the development of personality styles or functions.

Bypassing the usual complications of analogies, a relevant and intriguing parallel may be drawn between the phylogenic evolution of a species' genetic composition and the ontogenic development of an individual organism's adaptive strategies (i.e., its personality style, so to speak). At any point in time, a species possesses a limited set of genes that serve as trait potentials. Over succeeding generations, the frequency distribution of these genes will likely change in their relative proportions depending on how well the traits they undergird contribute to the species' "fittedness" within its varying ecological habitats. In a similar fashion, individual organisms begin life with a limited subset of their species' genes and the trait potentials they subserve. Over time the *salience* of these trait potentials—not the proportion of the genes

themselves—will become differentially prominent as the organism interacts with its environments. It "learns" from these experiences which of its traits fit best (i.e., most optimally suit its ecosystem). In phylogenesis, then, actual gene frequencies change during the generation-to-generation adaptive process, whereas in ontogenesis it is the *salience* or prominence of gene-based traits that changes as adaptive learning takes place. Parallel evolutionary processes occur—one within the life of a species, and the other within the life of an organism. What is seen in the individual organism is a shaping of latent potentials into adaptive and manifest styles of perceiving, feeling, thinking, and acting; these distinctive ways of adaptation, engendered by the interaction of biological endowment and social experience, comprise the elements of what is termed *personality styles*. It is a formative process in a single lifetime that parallels gene redistributions among species during their evolutionary history.

Two factors beyond the intrinsic genetic trait potentials of advanced social organisms have a special significance in affecting their survival and replicability. First, other members of the species play a critical part in providing postnatal nurturing and complex role models. Second, and no less relevant, is the high level of diversity and unpredictability of their ecological habitats. This requires numerous, multifaceted, and flexible response alternatives that are either preprogrammed genetically or acquired subsequently through early learning. Humans are notable for unusual adaptive pliancy, acquiring a wide repertoire of styles or alternate modes of functioning for dealing with both predictable and novel environmental circumstances. Unfortunately, the malleability of early potentials for diverse learnings diminishes as maturation progresses. As a consequence, adaptive styles acquired in childhood and usually suitable for comparable later environments become increasingly immutable, resisting modification and relearning. Problems arise in new ecological settings when these deeply ingrained behavior patterns persist, despite their lessened appropriateness; simply stated, what was learned and was once adaptive may no longer fit. Perhaps more important than environmental diversity, then, is the divergence between the circumstances of original learning and those of later life, a schism that has become more problematic as humans have progressed from stable and traditional to fluid and inconstant modern societies.

From the viewpoint of survival logic, it is both efficient and adaptive either to preprogram or to train the young of a species with traits that fit the ecological habitats of their parents. This wisdom rests on the usually safe assumption that consistency if not identicality will characterize the ecological conditions of both parents and their offspring. Evolution is spurred when this continuity assumption fails to hold—when formerly stable environments undergo significant change. Radical shifts of this character could result in the extinction of a species. It is more typical, however, for environments to be altered gradually, resulting in modest, yet inexorable redistributions of a species' gene frequencies. Genes that subserve competencies that proved suited to the new conditions become proportionately more common; ultimately, the features they engender come to typify either a new variant of or a successor to the earlier species.

All animal species intervene in and modify their habitats in routine and repetitive ways. Contemporary humans are unique in evolutionary history, however, in that both the physical and social environment has been altered in precipitous and unpredictable ways. These interventions appear to have set in motion consequences not unlike the "equilibrium punctuations" theorized by modern paleontologists (Eldredge & Gould, 1972). This is best illustrated in the origins of our recent borderline personality epidemic (Millon, 1987):

> Central to our recent culture have been the increased pace of social change and the growing pervasiveness of ambiguous and discordant customs to which children are expected to subscribe. Under the cumulative impact of rapid industrialization, immigration, urbanization, mobility, technology, and mass communication, there has been a steady erosion of traditional values and standards. Instead of a simple and coherent body of practices and beliefs, children find themselves confronted with constantly shifting styles and increasingly questioned norms whose durability is uncertain and precarious. Few times in history have so many children faced the tasks of life without the aid of accepted and durable traditions. Not only does the strain of making choices among discordant standards and goals beset them at every turn, but these competing beliefs and divergent demands prevent them from developing either internal stability or external consistency. (p. 363)

Murray has said that "life is a continuous procession of explorations . . . learnings and relearnings" (1959). Yet, among species such as humans, early adaptive potentials and pliancies may fail to crystallize because of the fluidities and inconsistencies of the environment, leading to the persistence of what some have called immature and unstable styles that fail to achieve coherence and effectiveness.

Lest the reader assume that those seeking to wed the sciences of evolution and ecology find themselves fully welcome in their respective fraternities, there are those who assert that "despite pious hopes and intellectual convictions, [these two disciplines] have so far been without issue" (Lewontin, 1979). This judgment is now both dated and overly severe, but numerous conceptual and methodological impediments do face those who wish to bring these fields of biological inquiry into fruitful synthesis—no less employing them to construe the styles of personality. Despite such concerns, recent developments bridging ecological and evolutionary theory are well underway, and hence do offer some justification for extending their principles to human styles of adaptation.

To provide a conceptual background from these sciences and to furnish a rough model concerning the styles of personality, four domains or spheres of evolutionary and ecological principles are detailed in this chapter. They are labeled *existence, adaptation, replication,* and *abstraction.* The first relates to the serendipitous transformation of random or less organized states into those possessing distinct structures of greater organization; the second refers to homeostatic processes employed to sustain survival in open ecosystems; the third pertains to reproductive styles that maximize the diversification and selection of ecologically effective attributes; and the fourth, a distinctly human phenomenon, concerns the emergence of competencies that foster anticipatory planning and reasoned decision making.

What makes evolutionary theory and ecological theory as meritorious as I propose them to be? Are they truly coextensive with the origins of the universe and the procession of organic life, as well as human modes of adaptation? Is extrapolation to personality a conjectural fantasy? Is there justification for employing them as a basis for understanding normal and pathological behaviors?

Owing to the mathematical and deductive insights of our colleagues in physics, we have a deeper and clearer sense of the early evolution and structural relations among matter and energy. So too has knowledge progressed in our studies of physical chemistry, microbiology, evolutionary theory, population biology, ecology, and ethology. How odd it is (is it not?) that we have only now again begun to investigate—as we did at the turn of the last century—the interface between the basic building blocks of physical nature and the nature of life as we experience and live it personally. How much more is known today, yet how hesitant are people to undertake a serious rapprochement? As Barash (1982) has commented:

> Like ships passing in the night, evolutionary biology and the social sciences have rarely even taken serious notice of each other, although admittedly, many introductory psychology texts give an obligatory toot of the Darwinian horn somewhere in the first chapter . . . before passing on to discuss human behavior as though it were determined only by environmental factors. (p. 7)

Commenting that serious efforts to undergird the behavioral sciences with the constructs and principles of evolutionary biology are as audacious as they are overdue, Barash (1982) notes further:

> As with any modeling effort, we start with the simple, see how far it takes us, and then either complicate or discard it as it gets tested against reality. The data available thus far are certainly suggestive and lead to the hope that more will shortly be forthcoming, so that tests and possible falsification can be carried out. In the meanwhile, as Darwin said when he first read Malthus, at least we have something to work with! (p. 8)

The role of evolution is most clearly grasped when it is paired with the principles of ecology. So conceived, the so-called procession of evolution represents a series of serendipitous transformations in the structure of a phenomenon (e.g., elementary particle, chemical molecule, living organism) that appear to promote survival in both its current and future environments. Such processions usually stem from the consequences of either random fluctuations (such as mutations) or replicative reformations (e.g., recombinant mating) among an infinite number of possibilities—some simpler and others more complex, some more and others less organized, some increasingly specialized and others not. Evolution is defined, then, when these restructurings enable a natural entity (e.g., species) or its subsequent variants to survive within present and succeeding ecological milieus. It is the continuity through time of these fluctuations and reformations that comprises the sequence we characterize as evolutionary progression.

THREE UNIVERSAL POLARITIES OF EVOLUTION

As noted in previous paragraphs, *existence* relates to the serendipitous transformation of states that are more ephemeral, less organized, or both into those possessing greater stability, greater organization, or both. It pertains to the formation and sustenance of discernible phenomena, to the processes of evolution that enhance and preserve life, and to the psychic polarity of *pleasure and pain. Adaptation* refers to homeostatic processes employed to foster survival in open ecosystems. It relates to the manner in which extant phenomena adapt to their surrounding ecosystems, to the mechanisms employed in accommodating to or in modifying these environments, and to the psychic polarity of *passivity* and *activity. Replication* pertains to reproductive styles that maximize the diversification and selection of ecologically effective attributes. It refers to the strategies utilized to replicate ephemeral organisms, to the methods of maximizing reproductive propagation and progeny nurturance, and to the psychic polarity of *self* and *other.* These three polarities have

forerunners in psychological theory that may be traced back to the early 1900s.

Some Historical Notes

A number of pre–World War I theorists proposed polarities that were used as the foundation for understanding a variety of psychological processes. Although others formulated parallel schemas earlier than he, I illustrate these conceptions with reference to ideas presented by Sigmund Freud. He wrote in 1915 what many consider to be among his most seminal works, those on metapsychology and in particular, the paper entitled "The Instincts and Their Vicissitudes." Speculations that foreshadowed several concepts developed more fully later both by himself and by others were presented in preliminary form in these papers. Particularly notable is a framework that Freud (1915/1925) advanced as central to understanding the mind; he framed these polarities as follows:

> Our mental life as a whole is governed by three polarities, namely, the following antitheses:
>
> • Subject (ego)-Object (external world)
> • Pleasure-Pain
> • Active-Passive
>
> The three polarities within the mind are connected with one another in various highly significant ways.
>
> We may sum up by saying that the essential feature in the vicissitudes undergone by instincts is their subjection to the influences of the three great polarities that govern mental life. Of these three polarities we might describe that of activity-passivity as the biological, that of the ego-external world as the real, and finally that of pleasure-pain as the economic, respectively. (pp. 76–77, 83)

Preceding Freud, however, aspects of these three polarities were conceptualized and employed by other theorists—in France, Germany, Russia, and other European nations as well as in the United States. Variations of the polarities of active-passive, subject-object, and pleasure-pain were identified by Heymans and Wiersma in Holland, McDougall in the United States, Meumann in Germany, Kollarits in Hungary, and others (Millon, 1981; Millon & Davis, 1996).

Despite the central role Freud assigned these polarities, he failed to capitalize on them as a coordinated system for understanding patterns of human functioning. Although he failed to pursue their potentials, the ingredients he formulated for his tripartite polarity schema were drawn upon by his disciples for many decades to come, seen prominently in the progressive development from instinct or drive theory, in which pleasure and pain were the major forces, to ego psychology, in which the apparatuses of activity and passivity were central constructs, and, most recently, to self-psychology and object relations theory, in which the self-other polarity is the key issue (Pine, 1990).

Forgotten as a metapsychological speculation by most, the scaffolding comprising these polarities was fashioned anew by this author in the mid-1960s (Millon, 1969). Unacquainted with Freud's proposals at the time and employing a biosocial-learning model anchored to Skinnerian concepts, I constructed a framework similar to Freud's "great polarities that govern all of mental life." Phrased in the terminology of learning concepts, the model comprised three polar dimensions: *positive versus negative* reinforcement (pleasure-pain); *self-other* as reinforcement source; and the instrumental styles of *active-passive*. I (Millon, 1969) stated:

> By framing our thinking in terms of *what* reinforcements the individual is seeking, *where* he is looking to find them and *how* he performs we may see more simply and more clearly the essential strategies which guide his coping behaviors.
>
> These reinforcements [relate to] whether he seeks primarily to achieve positive reinforcements (pleasure) or to avoid negative reinforcements (pain).
>
> Some patients turn to others as their source of reinforcement, whereas some turn primarily to themselves. The distinction [is] between *others* and *self* as the primary reinforcement source.
>
> On what basis can a useful distinction be made among instrumental behaviors? A review of the literature suggests that the behavioral dimension of activity-passivity may prove useful. . . . Active patients [are] busily intent on controlling the circumstances of their environment. . . . Passive patients . . . wait for the circumstances of their environment to take their course . . . reacting to them only after they occur. (pp. 193–195)

Do we find parallels within the disciplines of psychiatry and psychology that correspond to these broad evolutionary polarities?

In addition to the forerunners noted previously, there is a growing group of contemporary scholars whose work relates to these polar dimensions, albeit indirectly and partially. For example, a modern conception anchored to biological foundations has been developed by the distinguished British psychologist Jeffrey Gray (1964, 1973). A three-part model of temperament, matching the three-part polarity model in most regards, has been formulated by the American psychologist Arnold Buss and his associates (Buss & Plomin 1975, 1984). Circumplex formats based on factor analytic studies of mood and arousal that align well with the polarity schema have been published by Russell (1980) and Tellegen (1985). Deriving inspiration from a sophisticated analysis of neuroanatomical substrates, the highly resourceful American psychiatrist Robert Cloninger (1986, 1987) has deduced a threefold schema that is coextensive with major elements of the model's three polarities. Less oriented to biological foundations, recent advances in both interpersonal and psychoanalytic theory have likewise exhibited strong parallels to one or more of the three polar dimensions. A detailed review of these and other parallels has been presented in several recent books (e.g., Millon, 1990; Millon & Davis, 1996).

The following pages summarize the rationale and characteristics of the three-part polarity model. A few paragraphs draw upon the model as a basis for establishing attributes for conceptualizing personality patterns.

Aims of Existence

The procession of evolution is not limited just to the evolution of life on earth but extends to prelife, to matter, to the primordial elements of our local cosmos, and, in all likelihood, to the elusive properties of a more encompassing universe within which our cosmos is embedded as an incidental part. The demarcations we conceptualize to differentiate states such as nonmatter and matter, or inorganic and organic, are nominal devices that record transitions in this ongoing procession of transformations, an unbroken sequence of re-formed elements that have existed from the very first.

We may speak of the emergence of our local cosmos from some larger universe, or of life from inanimate matter, but if we were to trace the procession of evolution backward we would have difficulty identifying precise markers for each of these transitions. What we define as life would become progressively less clear as we reversed time until we could no longer discern its presence in the matter we were studying. So, too, does it appear to theoretical physicists that if we trace the evolution of our present cosmos back to its ostensive origins, we would lose its existence in the obscurity of an undifferentiated and unrecoverable past. The so-called Big Bang may in fact be merely an evolutionary transformation, one of an ongoing and never-ending series of transitions.

Life Preservation and Life Enhancement: The Pain-Pleasure Polarity

The notion of open systems is of relatively recent origin (Bertalanffy, 1945; Lotka, 1924; Schrodinger, 1944), brought to bear initially to explain how the inevitable consequences of the second law of thermodynamics appear to be circumvented in the biological realm. By broadening the ecological field so as to encompass events and properties beyond the local and immediate, it becomes possible to understand how living organisms on earth function and thrive, despite seeming to contradict this immutable physical law (e.g., solar radiation, continuously transmitting its ultimately exhaustible supply of energy, temporarily counters the earth's inevitable thermodynamic entropy). The *open system* concept has been borrowed freely and fruitfully to illuminate processes across a wide range of subjects. In recent decades it has been extended, albeit speculatively, to account for the evolution of cosmic events. These hypotheses suggest that the cosmos as known today may represent a four-dimensional "bubble" or set of "strings" stemming either from the random fluctuations of an open meta-universe characterized primarily by entropic chaos or of transpositions from a larger set of dimensions that comprise the properties of an open mega-universe—that is, dimensions beyond those we apprehend (Millon, 1990).

By materializing new matter from fluctuations in a larger and unstable field—that is, by creating existence from non-existence (cold dark matter)—any embedded open system might not only expand, but also form entities displaying anti-entropic structure, the future survival of which is determined by the character of parallel materializations and by the fortuitous consequences of their interactions (including their ecological balance, symbiosis, etc.). Beyond fortuitous levels of reciprocal fitness, some of these anti-entropic structures may possess properties that enable them to facilitate their own self-organization; that is to say, the forms into which they have been rendered randomly may not only survive, but also be able to amplify themselves, to extend their range, or both, sometimes in replicated and sometimes in more comprehensive structures.

Recent mathematical research in both physics and chemistry has begun to elucidate processes that characterize how structures "evolve" from randomness. Whether one evaluates the character of cosmogenesis, the dynamics of open chemical systems, or repetitive patterns exhibited among weather movements, it appears that random fluctuations assume sequences that often become both self-sustaining and recurrent. In chemistry, the theory of dissipative (free energy) structures (Prigogine 1972, 1976) proposes a principle called *order through fluctuation* that relates to self-organizational dynamics; these fluctuations proceed through sequences that not only maintain the integrity of the system but are also self-renewing. According to the theory, any open system may evolve when fluctuations exceed a critical threshold, setting in motion a qualitative shift in the nature of the system's structural form. Similar shifts within evolving systems are explained in pure mathematics by what has been termed *catastrophic theory* (Thom, 1972); here, sudden switches from

one dynamic equilibrium state to another occur instantaneously with no intervening bridge. As models portraying how the dynamics of random fluctuation drive prior levels of equilibrium to reconstitute themselves into new structures, both catastrophe and dissipative theories prove fruitful in explicating self-evolving morphogenesis—the emergence of new forms of existence from prior states.

There is another equally necessary step to existence, one that maintains "being" by protecting established structures and processes. Here, the degrading effects of entropy are counteracted by a diversity of safeguarding mechanisms. Among both physical and organic substances, such as atoms and molecules, the elements comprising their nuclear structure are tightly bound, held together by the strong force that is exceptionally resistant to decomposition (hence the power necessary to split the atom). More complicated organic structures, such as plants and animals, also have mechanisms to counter entropic dissolution—that is to say, to maintain the existence of their lives.

Two intertwined strategies are required, therefore: one to achieve existence, the other to preserve it. The aim of one is the enhancement of life—creating and then strengthening ecologically survivable organisms; the aim of the other is the preservation of life—avoiding circumstances that might terminate (entropically decompose) it. Although I disagree with Freud's concept of a death instinct (Thanatos), I believe he was essentially correct in recognizing that a balanced yet fundamental biological bipolarity exists in nature, a bipolarity that has its parallel in the physical world. As he wrote in one of his last works, "The analogy of our two basic instincts extends from the sphere of living things to the pair of opposing forces—attraction and repulsion—which rule the inorganic world" (Freud, 1940, p. 72). Among humans, the former may be seen in life-enhancing acts that are attracted to what we experientially record as pleasurable events (positive reinforcers), the latter in life-preserving behaviors oriented to repel events experientially characterized as painful (negative reinforcers). More is said of these fundamental if not universal mechanisms of countering entropic disintegration in the next section.

To summarize, the aims of existence reflects a to-be or not-to-be issue. In the inorganic world, *to be* is essentially a matter of possessing qualities that distinguish a phenomenon from its surrounding field—*not* being in a state of entropy. Among organic beings, *to be* is a matter of possessing the properties of life as well as being located in ecosystems that facilitate the enhancement and preservation of that life. In the phenomenological or experiential world of sentient organisms, events that extend life and preserve it correspond largely to metaphorical terms such as pleasure and pain; that is to say, recognizing and pursuing positive sensations and emotions, on the one hand, and recognizing and eschewing negative sensations and emotions, on the other.

Although there are many philosophical and metapsychological issues associated with the nature of pain and pleasure as constructs, it is neither our intent nor our task to inquire into them here. That they recur as a polar dimension time and again in diverse psychological domains (e.g., learned behaviors, unconscious processes, emotion, and motivation, as well as their biological substrates) has been elaborated in another publication (Millon, 1990). In this next section, I examine their role as constructs for articulating attributes that may usefully define personality.

Before we proceed, let us note that a balance must be struck between the two extremes that comprise each polarity; a measure of integration among the evolutionary polarities is an index of normality. Normal personality functioning, however, does not require equidistance between polar extremes. Balanced but unequal positions emerge as a function of temperamental dispositions, which, in their turn, are modified by the wider ecosystems within which individuals develop and function. In other words, there is no absolute or singular form of normal personality. Various polar positions and the personality attributes they subserve result in diverse *styles of normality,* just as severe or marked imbalances between the polarities manifest themselves in diverse *styles of abnormality* (Millon & Davis, 1996).

Moreover, given the diverse and changing ecological milieus that humans face in our complex modern environment, there is reason to expect that most persons will develop multiple adaptive styles, sometimes more active, sometimes less so, occasionally focused on self, occasionally on others, at times oriented to pleasure, at times oriented to the avoidance of pain. Despite the emergence of relatively enduring and characteristic styles over time, a measure of adaptive flexibility typifies most individuals: Persons are able to shift from one position on a bipolar continuum to another as the circumstances of life change.

Personality Implications

As noted, an interweaving and shifting balance between the two extremes that comprise the pain-pleasure polarity typifies normal personality functioning. Both of the following personality attributes should be met in varying degrees as life circumstances require. In essence, a synchronous and coordinated personal style would have developed to answer the question of whether the person should focus on experiencing only the enhancement of life versus concentrating his or her efforts on ensuring its preservation.

Avoiding Danger and Threat: The Life Preservation Attribute. One might assume that an attribute based on the avoidance of psychic or physical pain would be sufficiently self-evident not to require specification. As is well known, debates have arisen in the literature as to whether normal personality functioning represents the absence of mental disorder—that is, the reverse side of the mental illness or abnormality coin. That there is an inverse relationship between health and disease cannot be questioned; the two are intimately connected both conceptually and physically. On the other hand, to define a healthy personality solely on the basis of an absence of disorder does not suffice. As a single attribute of behavior that signifies both the lack of (e.g., anxiety, depression) and an aversion to (e.g., threats to safety and security) pain in its many and diverse forms does provide a foundation upon which other, more positively composed attributes may rest. Substantively, however, positive personal functioning must comprise elements beyond mere nonnormality or abnormality. And despite the complexities of personality, from a definitional point of view normal functioning does preclude nonnormality.

Turning to the evolutionary aspect of pain avoidance, that pertaining to a distancing from life-threatening circumstances, psychic and otherwise, we find an early historical reference in the writings of Herbert Spencer, a supportive contemporary of Darwin. In 1870 Spencer averred:

> Pains are the correlative of actions injurious to the organism, while pleasures are the correlatives of actions conducive to its welfare.
>
> Those races of beings only can have survived in which, on the average, agreeable or desired feelings went along with activities conducive to the maintenance of life, while disagreeable and habitually avoided feelings went along with activities directly or indirectly destructive of life.
>
> Every animal habitually persists in each act which gives pleasure, so long as it does so, and desists from each act which gives pain. . . . It is manifest that in proportion as this guidance approaches completeness, the life will be long; and that the life will be short in proportion as it falls short of completeness.
>
> We accept the inevitable corollary from the general doctrine of Evolution, that pleasures are the incentives to life-supporting acts and pains the deterrents from life-destroying acts. (pp. 279–284)

More recently, Freedman and Roe (1958) wrote:

> We . . . hypothesize that psychological warning and warding-off mechanisms, if properly studied, might provide a kind of psychological-evolutionary systematics. Exposure to pain, anxiety, or danger is likely to be followed by efforts to avoid a

repetition of the noxious stimulus situation with which the experience is associated. Obviously an animal with a more highly developed system for anticipating and avoiding the threatening circumstance is more efficiently equipped for adaptation and survival. Such unpleasant situations may arise either from within, in its simplest form as tissue deprivation, or from without, by the infliction of pain or injury. Man's psychological superstructure may be viewed, in part, as a system of highly developed warning mechanisms. (p. 458)

As for the biological substrate of pain signals, Gray (1975) suggests two systems, both of which alert the organism to possible dangers in the environment. Those mediating the behavioral effects of unconditioned (instinctive?) aversive events are termed the fight-flight system (FFS). This system elicits defensive aggression and escape and is subserved, according to Gray's pharmacological inferences, by the amygdala, the ventromedial hypothalamus, and the central gray of the midbrain; neurochemically, evidence suggests a difficult-to-unravel interaction among aminobutyric acids (for example, gamma-ammobutyric acid), serotonin, and endogenous opiates (for example, endorphins). The second major source of sensitivity and action in response to pain signals is referred to by Gray as the behavioral inhibition system (BIS), consisting of the interplay of the septal-hippocampal system, its cholinergic projections and monoamine transmissions to the hypothalamus, and then on to the cingulate and prefrontal cortex. Activated by signals of punishment or nonreward, the BIS suppresses associated behaviors, refocuses the organism's attention, and redirects activity toward alternate stimuli.

Harm avoidance is a concept proposed by Cloninger (1986, 1987). As he conceives the construct, it is a heritable tendency to respond intensely to signals of aversive stimuli (pain) and to learn to inhibit behaviors that might lead to punishment and frustrative nonreward. Those high on this dimension are characterized as cautious, apprehensive, and inhibited; those low on this valence would likely be confident, optimistic, and carefree. Cloninger subscribes essentially to Gray's behavioral inhibition system concept in explicating this polarity, as well as the neuroanatomical and neurochemical hypotheses Gray proposed as the substrates for its pain-avoidant mechanisms.

Shifting from biological-evolutionary concepts, we may turn to proposals of a similar cast offered by thinkers of a distinctly psychological turn of mind. Notable here are the contributions of Maslow (1968), particularly his hierarchical listing of needs. Best known are the five fundamental needs that lead ultimately to self-actualization, the first two of which relate to our evolutionary attribute of life preservation. Included in the first group are the *physio-logical needs* such as air, water, food, and sleep, qualities of the ecosystem

essential for survival. Next, and equally necessary to avoid danger and threat, are what Maslow terms the *safety needs*, including the freedom from jeopardy, the security of physical protection and psychic stability, as well as the presence of social order and interpersonal predictability.

That pathological consequences can ensue from the failure to attend to the realities that portend danger is obvious; the lack of air, water, and food are not issues of great concern in civilized societies today, although these are matters of considerable import to environmentalists of the future and to contemporary poverty-stricken nations.

It may be of interest next to record some of the psychic pathologies that can be traced to aberrations in meeting this first attribute of personality. For example, among those termed *inhibited* and *avoidant personalities* (Millon, 1969, 1981), we see an excessive preoccupation with threats to one's psychic security—an expectation of and hyperalertness to the signs of potential rejection—that leads these persons to disengage from everyday relationships and pleasures. At the other extreme of the polarity attribute, we see those of a risk-taking attitude, a proclivity to chance hazards and to endanger one's life and liberty, a behavioral pattern characteristic of those we contemporaneously label *antisocial personalities*. Here there is little of the caution and prudence expected in the normal personality attribute of avoiding danger and threat; rather, we observe its opposite, a rash willingness to put one's safety in jeopardy, to play with fire and throw caution to the wind. Another pathological style illustrative of a failure to fulfill this evolutionary attribute is seen among those variously designated as masochistic and self-defeating personalities. Rather than avoid circumstances that may prove painful and self-endangering, these nonnormal personality styles set in motion situations in which they will come to suffer physically, psychically, or both. Either by virtue of habit or guilt absolution, these individuals induce rather than avoid pain for themselves.

Seeking Rewarding Experiences: The Life Enhancement Attribute.   At the other end of the existence polarity are attitudes and behaviors designed to foster and enrich life, to generate joy, pleasure, contentment, fulfillment, and thereby strengthen the capacity of the individual to remain vital and competent physically and psychically. This attribute asserts that existence and survival call for more than life preservation alone—beyond pain avoidance is what we have chosen to term *pleasure enhancement*.

This attribute asks us to go at least one step further than Freud's parallel notion that life's motivation is chiefly that of "reducing tensions" (i.e., avoiding or minimizing pain), maintaining thereby a steady state, if you will, a homeostatic balance and inner stability. In accord with my view of evolution's polarities, I would assert that normal humans are also driven by the desire to enrich their lives, to seek invigorating sensations and challenges, to venture and explore, all to the end of magnifying if not escalating the probabilities of both individual viability and species replicability.

Regarding the key instrumental role of "the pleasures," Spencer (1870) put it well more than a century ago: "Pleasures are the correlatives of actions conducive to [organismic] welfare. . . . the incentives to life-supporting acts" (pp. 279, 284). The view that there exists an organismic striving to expand one's inherent potentialties (as well as those of one's kin and species) has been implicit in the literature of all times. That the pleasures may be both sign and vehicle for this realization was recorded even in the ancient writings of the Talmud, where it states: "everyone will have to justify himself in the life hereafter for every failure to enjoy a legitimately offered pleasure in this world" (Jahoda, 1958, p. 45).

As far as contemporary psychobiological theorists are concerned, brief mention will be made again of the contributions of Gray (1975, 1981) and Cloninger (1986, 1987). Gray's neurobiological model centers heavily on activation and inhibition (active-passive polarities) as well as on signals of reward and punishment (pleasure-pain polarity). Basing his deductions primarily on pharmacological investigations of animal behavior, Gray has proposed the existence of several interrelated and neuroanatomically grounded response systems that activate various positive and negative affects. He refers to what he terms the *behavioral activation system* (BAS) as an approach system that is subserved by the reward center uncovered originally by Olds and Milner (1954). Ostensibly mediated at brain stem and cerebellar levels, it is likely to include dopaminergic projections across various striata and is defined as responding to conditioned rewarding and safety stimuli by facilitating behaviors that maximize their future recurrence (Gray, 1975). There are intricacies in the manner with which the BAS is linked to external stimuli and its anatomic substrates, but Gray currently views it as a system that subserves signals of reward, punishment relief, and pleasure.

Cloninger (1986, 1987) has generated a theoretical model composed of three dimensions, which he terms *reward dependence*, *harm avoidance*, to which I referred previously, and *novelty seeking*. Proposing that each is a heritable personality disposition, he relates them explicitly to specific monoaminergic pathways; for example, high reward dependence is connected to low noradrenergic activity, harm avoidance to high serotonergic activity, and high novelty seeking to low dopaminergic activity. Cloninger's reward dependence dimension reflects highs and lows on the positive-gratifying-

pleasure valence, whereas the harm avoidance dimension represents highs and lows on the negative-pain-displeasure valence. Reward dependence is hypothesized to be a heritable neurobiological tendency to respond to signals of reward (pleasure), particularly verbal signals of social approval, sentiment, and succor, as well as to resist events that might extinguish behaviors previously associated with these rewards. Cloninger portrays those high on reward dependence to be sociable, sympathetic, and pleasant; in contrast, those low on this polarity are characterized as detached, cool, and practical. Describing the undergirding substrate for the reward-pleasure valence as the *behavior maintenance system* (BMS), Cloninger speculates that its prime neuromodulator is likely to be norepinephrine, with its major ascending pathways arising in the pons, projecting onward to hypothalamic and limbic structures, and then branching upward to the neocortex.

Turning again to pure psychological formulations, both Rogers (1963) and Maslow (1968) have proposed concepts akin to my criterion of enhancing pleasure. In his notion of "openness to experience," Rogers asserts that the fully functioning person has no aspect of his or her nature closed off. Such individuals are not only receptive to the experiences that life offers, but they are able also to use their experiences in expanding all of life's emotions, as well as in being open to all forms of personal expression. Along a similar vein, Maslow speaks of the ability to maintain a freshness to experience, to keep up one's capacity to appreciate relationships and events. No matter how often events or persons are encountered, one is neither sated nor bored but is disposed to view them with an ongoing sense of awe and wonder.

Perhaps less dramatic than the conceptions of either Rogers and Maslow, I believe that this openness and freshness to life's transactions is an instrumental means for extending life, for strengthening one's competencies and options, and for maximizing the viability and replicability of one's species. More mundane and pragmatic in orientation than their views, this conception seems both more substantive theoretically and more consonant a rationale for explicating the role the pleasures play in undergirding reward experience and openness to experience.

As before, a note or two should be recorded on the pathological consequences of a failure to possess an attribute. These are seen most clearly in the personality disorders labeled *schizoid* and *avoidant*. In the former there is a marked hedonic deficiency, stemming either from an inherent deficit in affective substrates or the failure of stimulative experience to develop attachment behaviors, affective capacity, or both (Millon, 1981, 1990). Among those designated avoidant personalities, constitutional sensitivities or abusive life experiences have led to an intense attentional sensitivity to psychic pain and a consequent distrust in either the genuineness or durability of the pleasures, such that these individuals can no longer permit themselves to chance experiencing them, lest they prove again to be fickle and unreliable. Both of these personalities tend to be withdrawn and isolated, joyless and grim, neither seeking nor sharing in the rewards of life.

Modes of Adaptation

To come into existence as an emergent particle, a local cosmos, or a living creature is but an initial phase, the serendipitous presence of a newly formed structure, the chance evolution of a phenomenon distinct from its surroundings. Although extant, such fortuitous transformations may exist only for a fleeting moment. Most emergent phenomena do not survive (i.e., possess properties that enable them to retard entropic decomposition). To maintain their unique structure, differentiated from the larger ecosystem of which they are a part, and to be sustained as a discrete entity among other phenomena that comprise their environmental field requires good fortune and the presence of effective modes of adaptation. These modes of basic survival comprise the second essential component of evolution's procession.

Ecological Accommodation and Ecological Modification. The Passive-Active Polarity

The second evolutionary stage relates to what is termed the *modes of adaptation;* it is also framed as a two-part polarity. The first may best be characterized as the mode of ecological accommodation, signifying inclinations to passively fit in, to locate and remain securely anchored in a niche, subject to the vagaries and unpredictabilities of the environment, all acceded to with one crucial proviso: that the elements comprising the surroundings will furnish both the nourishment and the protection needed to sustain existence. Although based on a somewhat simplistic bifurcation among adaptive strategies, this passive and accommodating mode is one of the two fundamental methods that living organisms have evolved as a means of survival. It represents the core process employed in the evolution of what has come to be designated as the plant kingdom: a stationary, rooted, yet essentially pliant and dependent survival mode. By contrast, the second of the two major modes of adaptation is seen in the lifestyle of the animal kingdom. Here we observe a primary inclination toward ecological modification, a tendency to change or rearrange the elements comprising the larger milieu, to intrude upon otherwise quiescent settings, a versatility in shifting from one

niche to another as unpredictability arises, a mobile and interventional mode that actively stirs, maneuvers, yields, and at the human level substantially transforms the environment to meet its own survival aims.

Both modes—passive and active—have proven impressively capable to both nourishing and preserving life. Whether the polarity sketched is phrased in terms of accommodating versus modifying, passive versus active, or plant versus animal, it represents at the most basic level the two fundamental modes that organisms have evolved to sustain their existence. This second aspect of evolution differs from the first stage, which is concerned with what may be called *existential becoming,* in that it characterizes modes of being: how what has become endures.

Broadening the model to encompass human experience, the active-passive polarity means that the vast range of behaviors engaged in by humans may fundamentally be grouped in terms of whether initiative is taken in altering and shaping life's events or whether behaviors are reactive to and accommodate those events.

Much can be said for the survival value of fitting a specific niche well, but no less important are flexibilities for adapting to diverse and unpredictable environments. It is here again where a distinction, although not a hard and fast one, may be drawn between the accommodating (plant) and the modifying (animal) mode of adaptation, the former more rigidly fixed and constrained by ecological conditions, the latter more broad-ranging and more facile in its scope of maneuverability. To proceed in evolved complexity to the human species, we cannot help but recognize the almost endless variety of adaptive possibilities that may (and do) arise as secondary derivatives of a large brain possessing an open network of potential interconnections that permit the functions of self-reflection, reasoning, and abstraction. But this takes us beyond the subject of this section of the chapter. The reader is referred elsewhere (Millon 1990) for a fuller discussion of active-passive parallels in wider domains of psychological thought (for example, the "ego apparatuses" formulated by Hartmann (1939) or the distinction between classical and operant conditioning in the writings of Skinner (1938, 1953).

Normal or optimal functioning, at least among humans, appears to call for a flexible balance that interweaves both polar extremes. In the first evolutionary stage, that relating to existence, behaviors encouraging both life enhancement (pleasure) and life preservation (pain avoidance) are likely to be more successful in achieving survival than actions limited to one or the other alone. Similarly, regarding adaptation, modes of functioning that exhibit both ecological accommodation and ecological modification are likely to be more successful than is either by itself. Nevertheless, it does appear that the two advanced forms of life on earth—plants and animals—have evolved by giving precedence to one mode rather than both.

Personality Implications

As with the pair of criteria representing the aims of existence, a balance should be achieved between the two criteria comprising modes of adaptation, those related to ecological accommodation and ecological modification, or what I have termed the passive-active polarity. Healthy personality functioning calls for a synchronous and coordinated style that weaves a balanced answer to the question of whether one should accept what the fates have brought forth or take the initiative in altering the circumstances of one's life.

Abiding Hospitable Realities: The Ecologically Accommodating Attribute.   On first reflection, it would seem to be less than optimal to submit meekly to what life presents, to adjust obligingly to one's destiny. As described earlier, however, the evolution of plants is essentially grounded (no pun intended) in environmental accommodation, in an adaptive acquiescence to the ecosystem. Crucial to this adaptive course, however, is the capacity of these surroundings to provide the nourishment and protection requisite to the thriving of a species.

Could the same be true for the human species? Are there not circumstances of life that provide significant and assured levels of sustenance and safekeeping (both psychic and physical?) And if that were the case, would not the acquisition of an accommodating attitude and passive lifestyle be a logical consequence? The answer, it would seem, is yes. If one's upbringing has been substantially secure and nurturant, would it not be not normal to flee or overturn it?

We know that circumstances other than those in infancy and early childhood rarely persist throughout life. Autonomy and independence are almost inevitable as a stage of maturation, ultimately requiring the adoption of so-called adult responsibilities that call for a measure of initiative, decision making, and action. Nevertheless, to the extent that the events of life have been and continue to be caring and giving, is it not perhaps wisest, from an evolutionary perspective, to accept this good fortune and let matters be? This accommodating or passive life philosophy has worked extremely well in sustaining and fostering those complex organisms that comprise the plant kingdom. Hence passivity, the yielding to environmental forces, may be in itself not only unproblematic, but where events and circumstances provide the pleasures of life and protect against their pains, positively

adaptive and constructive. Accepting rather than overturning a hospitable reality seems a sound course; or as it is said, "If it ain't broke, don't fix it."

Often reflective and deliberate, those who are passively oriented manifest few overt strategies to gain their ends. They display a seeming inertness, a phlegmatic lack of ambition or persistence, a tendency toward acquiescence, a restrained attitude in which they initiate little to modify events, waiting for the circumstances of their environment to take their course before making accommodations. Some persons may be temperamentally ill-equipped to rouse or assert themselves; perhaps past experience has deprived them of opportunities to acquire a range of competencies or confidence in their ability to master the events of their environment; equally possible is a naive confidence that things will come their way with little or no effort on their part. From a variety of diverse sources, then, those at the passive end of the polarity engage in few direct instrumental activities to intercede in events or generate the effects they desire. They seem suspended, quiescent, placid, immobile, restrained, listless, waiting for things to happen and reacting to them only after they occur.

Is passivity a natural part of the repertoire of the human species, does agreeableness serve useful functions, and where and how is it exhibited? A few words in response to these questions may demonstrate that passivity is not mere inactivity but a stance or process that achieves useful gains. For example, universal among mammalian species are two basic modes of learning: the *respondent* or *conditioned* type and the *operant* or *instrumental* type. The former is essentially a *passive* process, the simple pairing of an innate or reflexive response to a stimulus that previously did not elicit that response. In like passive fashion, environmental elements that occur either simultaneously or in close temporal order become connected to each other in the organism's repertoire of learning, such that if one of these elements recurs in the future, the expectation is that the others will follow or be elicited. The organisms do not have to do anything active to achieve this learning; inborn reflexive responses and environmental events are merely associated by contiguity.

Operant or instrumental learning, in contrast, represents the outcome of an active process on the part of the organism, one that requires an effort and execution on its part that has the effect of altering the environment. Whereas respondent conditioning occurs as a result of the passive observation of a conjoining of events, operant conditioning occurs only as a result of an active modification by the organism of its surroundings, a performance usually followed by a positive reinforcer (pleasure) or the successful avoidance of a negative one (pain). Unconditioned reflexes, such as a leg jerk in reaction to a knee tap, will become a passively acquired conditioned respondent if a bell is regularly sounded prior to the tap, as will the shrinking reflex of an eye pupil passively become conditioned to that bell if it regularly preceded exposure to a shining light.

The passive-active polarity is central to formulations of psychoanalytic theory. Prior to the impressively burgeoning literature on self and object relations theory of the past two decades, the passive-active antithesis had a major role in both classical instinct and post–World War II ego schools of analytic thought. The contemporary focus on self and object is considered in discussions of the third polarity, that of self-other. However, we should not overlook the once key and now less popular constructs of both instinct theory and ego theory. It may be worth noting, as well as of special interest to the evolutionary model presented in this chapter, that the beginnings of psychoanalytic metapsychology were oriented initially to instinctual derivatives (in which pleasure and pain were given prominence), and then progressed subsequently to the apparatuses of the ego (Hartmann, 1939; Rapaport, 1953)—where passivity and activity were centrally involved.

The model of activity, as Rapaport puts it, is a dual one: First, the ego is strong enough to defend against or control the intensity of the id's drive tensions; or second, through the competence and energy of its apparatuses, the ego is successful in uncovering or creating in reality the object of the id's instinctual drives. Rapaport conceives the model of passivity also to be a dual one: First, either the ego gradually modulates or indirectly discharges the instinctual energies of the id; or second, lacking an adequately controlling apparatus, the ego is rendered powerless and subject thereby to instinctual forces. Translating these formulations into evolutionary terms, effective actions by the ego will successfully manage the internal forces of the id, whereas passivity will result either in accommodations or exposure to the internal demands of the id.

Turning to contemporary theorists more directly concerned with normal or healthy personality functioning, the humanistic psychologist Maslow (1968) states that "self-actualized" individuals accept their nature as it is, despite personal weaknesses and imperfections; comfortable with themselves and with the world around them, they do not seek to change "the water because it is wet, or the rocks because they are hard" (p. 153). They have learned to accept the natural order of things. Passively accepting nature, they need not hide behind false masks or transform others to fit distorted needs. Accepting themselves without shame or apology, they are equally at peace with the shortcomings of those with whom they live and relate.

Where do we find clinical states of personality functioning that reflect failures to meet the accommodating-agreeable attribute?

One example of an inability to leave things as they are is seen in what is classified as the histrionic personality disorder. These individuals achieve their goals of maximizing protection, nurturance, and reproductive success by engaging busily in a series of manipulative, seductive, gregarious, and attention-getting maneuvers. Their persistent and unrelenting manipulation of events is designed to maximize the receipt of attention and favors, as well as to avoid social disinterest and disapproval. They show an insatiable if not indiscriminate search for stimulation and approval. Their clever and often artful social behaviors may give the appearance of an inner confidence and self-assurance; beneath this guise, however, lies a fear that a failure on their part to ensure the receipt of attention will in short order result in indifference or rejection—hence their desperate need for reassurance and repeated signs of approval. Tribute and affection must constantly be replenished and are sought from every interpersonal source. As they are quickly bored and sated, they keep stirring up things, becoming enthusiastic about one activity and then another. There is a restless stimulus-seeking quality in which they cannot leave well enough alone.

At the other end of the polarity are personality maladaptations that exhibit an excess of passivity, failing thereby to give direction to their own lives. Several personality disorders demonstrate this passive style, although their passivity derives from and is expressed in appreciably different ways. Schizoid personalities, for example, are passive owing to their relative incapacity to experience pleasure and pain; without the rewards these emotional valences normally activate, they are devoid of the drive to acquire rewards, leading them to become apathetically passive observers of the ongoing scene. Dependent personality styles typically are average on the pleasure-pain polarity, yet they are usually as passive as schizoids. Strongly oriented to others, they are notably weak with regard to self. Passivity for them stems from deficits in self-confidence and competence, leading to deficits in initiative and autonomous skills, as well as a tendency to wait passively while others assume leadership and guide them. Passivity among so-called obsessive-compulsive personalities stems from their fear of acting independently, owing to intrapsychic resolutions they have made to quell hidden thoughts and emotions generated by their intense self-other ambivalence. Dreading the possibility of making mistakes or engaging in disapproved behaviors, they became indecisive, immobilized, restrained, and thereby passive. High on pain and low on both pleasure and self, individuals with masochistic personality styles operate on the assumption that they dare not expect nor deserve to have life go their way; giving up any efforts to achieve a life that accords with their true desires, they passively submit to others' wishes, acquiescently accepting their fate. Finally, narcissistic personality styles, especially high on self and low on others, benignly assume that good things will come their way with little or no effort on their part; this passive exploitation of others is a consequence of the unexplored confidence that underlies their self-centered presumptions.

Mastering One's Environment: The Ecologically Modifying Attribute. The active end of the adaptational polarity signifies the taking of initiative in altering and shaping life's events. Such persons are best characterized by their alertness, vigilance, liveliness, vigor, forcefulness, stimulus-seeking energy, and drive. Some plan strategies and scan alternatives to circumvent obstacles or avoid the distress of punishment, rejection, and anxiety. Others are impulsive, precipitate, excitable, rash, and hasty, seeking to elicit pleasures and rewards. Although specific goals vary and change from time to time, actively aroused individuals intrude on passing events and energetically and busily modify the circumstances of their environment.

Neurobiological research has proven to be highly supportive of the activity or arousal construct ever since Papez (1937), Moruzzi and Magnum (1949), and MacLean (1949, 1952) assigned what were to be termed the reticular and limbic systems' both energizing and expressive roles in the central nervous system.

First among historic figures to pursue this theme was Ivan Pavlov. In speaking of the basic properties of the nervous system, Pavlov referred to the strength of the processes of excitation and inhibition, the equilibrium between their respective strengths, and the mobility of these processes. Although Pavlov's (1927) theoretical formulations dealt with what Donald Hebb (1955) termed a *conceptual nervous system,* his experiments and those of his students led to innumerable direct investigations of brain activity. Central to Pavlov's thesis was the distinction between strong and weak types of nervous systems.

Closely aligned to Pavlovian theory, Gray (1964) has asserted that those with weak nervous systems are easily aroused, non–sensation-seeking introverts who prefer to experience low rather than high levels of stimulation. Conversely, those with strong nervous systems would arouse slowly and be likely to be sensation-seeking extroverts who find low stimulation levels to be boring and find high levels to be both exciting and pleasant.

Akin also to the active modality are the more recent views of Cloninger (1986, 1987). To him, novelty-seeking is a heritable tendency toward excitement in response to novel stimuli or cues for reward (pleasure) or punishment relief (pain), both of which leading to exploratory activity. Consonant with its correspondence to the activity polarity, individuals who are assumed to be high in novelty-seeking may be characterized in their personality attributes as impulsive, excitable, and quickly distracted or bored. Conversely, those at the passive polarity or the low end of the novelty-seeking dimension may be portrayed as reflective, stoic, slow-tempered, orderly, and only slowly engaged in new interests.

Turning from ostensive biological substrates to speculative psychological constructs, de Charms (1968) has proposed that "man's primary motivational propensity is to be effective in producing changes in his environment" (p. 269). A similar view has been conveyed by White (1959) in his concept of *effectance,* an intrinsic motive, as he views it, that activates persons to impose their desires upon environments. De Charms (1968) elaborates his theme with reference to man as *Origin* and as *Pawn,* constructs akin to the active polarity on the one hand and to the passive polarity on the other; he states this distinction as follows:

> That man is the origin of his behavior means that he is constantly struggling against being confined and constrained by external forces, against being moved like a pawn into situations not of his own choosing. . . . An Origin is a person who perceives his behavior as determined by his own choosing; a Pawn is a person who perceives his behavior as determined by external forces beyond his control. . . . An Origin has strong feelings of personal causation, a feeling that the locus for causation of effects in his environment lies within himself. The feedback that reinforces this feeling comes from changes in his environment that are attributable to personal behavior. This is the crux of personal causation, and it is a powerful motivational force directing future behavior. (pp. 273–274)

Allport (1955) argued that history records many individuals who were not content with an existence that offered them little variety, a lack of psychic tension, and minimal challenge. Allport considers it normal to be pulled forward by a vision of the future that awakened within persons their drive to alter the course of their lives. He suggests that people possess a need to invent motives and purposes that would consume their inner energies. In a similar vein, Fromm (1955) proposed a need on the part of humans to rise above the roles of passive creatures in an accidental if not random world. To him, humans are driven to transcend the state of merely having been created; instead, humans seek to become the creators, the active shapers of their own destiny. Rising above the passive and accidental nature of existence, humans generate their own purposes and thereby provide themselves with a true basis of freedom.

Strategies of Replication

In their mature stage, organisms possess the requisite competencies to maintain entropic stability. When these competencies can no longer adapt and sustain existence, organisms succumb inexorably to death and decomposition. This fate does not signify finality, however. Prior to their demise, all ephemeral species create duplicates that circumvent their extinction, engaging in acts that enable them to transcend the entropic dissolution of their members' individual existences.

If an organism merely duplicates itself prior to death, then its replica is doomed to repeat the same fate it suffered. However, if new potentials for extending existence can be fashioned by chance or routine events, then the possibility of achieving a different and conceivably superior outcome may be increased. And it is this co-occurrence of random and recombinant processes that does lead to the prolongation of a species' existence. This third hallmark of evolution's procession also undergirds another of nature's fundamental polarities, that between self and other.

Reproductive Nurturance and Reproductive Propagation: The Other-Self Polarity

At its most basic and universal level, the manifold varieties of organisms living today have evolved, as Mayr (1964) has phrased it, to cope with the challenge of continuously changing and immensely diversified environments, the resources of which are not inexhaustible. The means by which organisms cope with environmental change and diversity are well known. Inorganic structures survive for extended periods of time by virtue of the extraordinary strength of their bonding. This contrasts with the very earliest forerunners of organic life. Until they could replicate themselves, their distinctive assemblages existed precariously, subject to events that could put a swift end to the discrete and unique qualities that characterized their composition, leaving them essentially as transient and ephemeral phenomena. After replicative procedures were perfected, the chemical machinery for copying organismic life, the DNA double helix, became so precise that it could produce perfect clones—*if* nothing interfered with its structure or its mechanisms of execution. But the patterning and processes of complex molecular change are not immune to accident. High temperatures and radiation dislodge and rearrange atomic structures, producing what are termed

mutations, alterations in the controlling and directing DNA configuration that undergirds the replication of organismic morphology.

Despite the deleterious impact of most mutations, it is the genetic variations to which they give rise that have served as one of the primary means by which *simple* organisms acquire traits making them capable of adapting to diverse and changing environments. But isomorphic replication, aided by an occasional beneficent mutation, is a most inefficient if not hazardous means of surmounting ecological crises faced by complex and slowly reproducing organisms. Advantageous mutations do not appear in sufficient numbers and with sufficient dependability to generate the novel capabilities required to adapt to frequent or marked shifts in the ecosystem. How then did the more intricate and intermittently reproducing organisms evolve the means to resolve the diverse hazards of unpredictable environments?

The answer to this daunting task was the evolution of a recombinant mechanism, one in which a pair of organisms exchange their genetic resources: They develop what we term *sexual mating*. Here, the potentials and traits each partner possesses are sorted into new configurations that differ in their composition from those of their origins, generating thereby new variants and capabilities, of which some may prove more adaptive (and others less so) in changing environments than were their antecedents. Great advantages accrue by the occasional favorable combinations that occur through this random shuffling of genes.

Recombinant replication, with its consequential benefits of selective diversification, requires the partnership of two parents, each contributing its genetic resources in a distinctive and species-characteristic manner. Similarly, the attention and care given the offspring of a species' matings are also distinctive. Worthy of note is the difference between the mating parents in the degree to which they protect and nourish their joint offspring. Although the investment of energy devoted to upbringing is balanced and complementary, rarely is it identical or even comparable in either devotion or determination. This disparity in reproductive investment strategies, especially evident among nonhuman animal species (e.g., insects, reptiles, birds, mammals), underlies the evolution of the male and female genders, the foundation for the third cardinal polarity I propose to account for evolution's procession.

Somewhat less profound than that of the first polarity, which represents the line separating the enhancement of order (existence-life) from the prevention of disorder (nonexistence-death), or that of the second polarity, differentiating the adaptive modes of accommodation (passive-plant) from those of modification (active-animal), the third polarity, based on distinctions in replication strategies, is no less fundamental in that it contrasts the maximization of reproductive propagation (self-male) from that of the maximization of reproductive nurturance (other-female).

Evolutionary biologists (Cole, 1954; Trivers, 1974; E. O. Wilson, 1975) have recorded marked differences among species in both the cycle and pattern of their reproductive behaviors. Of special interest is the extreme diversity among *and* within species in the number of offspring spawned and the consequent nurturing and protective investment the parents make in the survival of their progeny. Designated the *r-strategy* and *K-strategy* in population biology, the former represents a pattern of propagating a vast number of offspring but exhibiting minimal attention to their survival; the latter is typified by the production of few progeny followed by considerable effort to assure their survival. Exemplifying the r-strategy are oysters, which generate some 500 million eggs annually; the K-strategy is found among the great apes, which produce a single offspring every 5 to 6 years.

Not only do species differ in where they fall on the r- to K-strategy continuum, but *within* most animal species an important distinction may be drawn between male and female genders. It is this latter differentiation that undergirds what has been termed the self- versus other-oriented polarity, implications of which are briefly elaborated in the following discussion.

Human females typically produce about four hundred eggs in a lifetime, of which no more than twenty to twenty-five can mature into healthy infants. The energy investment expended in gestation, nurturing, and caring for each child, both before and during the years following birth, is extraordinary. Not only is the female required to devote much of her energies to bring the fetus to full term, but during this period she cannot be fertilized again; in contrast, the male is free to mate with numerous females. And should her child fail to survive, the waste in physical and emotional exertion not only is enormous, but also amounts to a substantial portion of the mother's lifetime reproductive potential. There appears to be good reason, therefore, to encourage a protective and caring inclination on the part of the female, as evident in a sensitivity to cues of distress and a willingness to persist in attending to the needs and nurturing of her offspring.

Although the male discharges tens of millions of sperm on mating, this is but a small investment, given the ease and frequency with which he can repeat the act. On fertilization, his physical and emotional commitment can end with minimal consequences. Although the protective and food-gathering efforts of the male may be lost by an early abandonment of a mother and an offspring or two, much more may be gained by investing energies in pursuits that achieve the wide reproductive spread of his genes. Relative to the female of the species, whose best strategy appears to be the care and comfort of child and kin—that is, the K-strategy—the male is likely to be reproductively more prolific by maximizing self-propagation—that is, adopting the r-strategy. To focus primarily on self-replication may diminish the survival probabilities of a few of a male's progeny, but this occasional reproductive loss may be well compensated for by mating with multiple females and thereby producing multiple offspring.

In sum, males lean toward being self-oriented because competitive advantages that inhere within themselves maximize the replication of their genes. Conversely, females lean toward being other-oriented because their competence in nurturing and protecting their limited progeny maximizes the replication of their genes.

The consequences of the male's r-strategy are a broad range of what may be seen as self- as opposed to other-oriented behaviors, such as acting in an egotistical, insensitive, inconsiderate, uncaring, and minimally communicative manner. In contrast, females are more disposed to be other-oriented, affiliative, intimate, empathic, protective, communicative, and solicitous (Gilligan, 1982; Rushton, 1985; E. O. Wilson, 1978).

Personality Implications

As before, I consider both of the following criteria necessary to the definition and determination of a full personality characterization. I see no necessary antithesis between the two. Humans can be both self-actualizing and other-encouraging, although most persons are likely to lean toward one or the other side. A balance that coordinates the two provides a satisfactory answer to the question of whether one should be devoted to the support and welfare of others (the underlying philosophy of the "Democrats") or fashion one's life in accord with one's own needs and desires (the underlying philosophy of the "Republicans").

Constructive Loving: The Other-Nurturing Attribute. As described earlier, recombinant replication achieved by sexual mating entails a balanced although asymmetrical parental investment in both the genesis and the nurturance of offspring. By virtue of her small number of eggs and extended pregnancy, the female strategy for replicative success among most mammals is characterized by the intensive care and protection of a limited number of offspring. Oriented to reproductive nurturance rather than reproductive propagation, most adult females, at least until recent decades in Western society, bred close to the limit of their capacity, attaining a reproductive ceiling of approximately 20 viable births.

By contrast, not only are males free of the unproductive pregnancy interlude for mating, but they may substantially increase their reproductive output by engaging in repetitive matings with as many available females as possible.

The other-versus-self antithesis follows from additional aspects of evolution's asymmetric replication strategy. Not only must the female be oriented to and vigilant in identifying the needs of and dangers that may face each of her few offspring, but it is reproductively advantageous for her to be sensitive to and discriminating in her assessment of potential mates. A bad mating—one that issues a defective or weak offspring—has graver consequences for the female than for the male. Not only will such an event appreciably reduce her limited reproductive possibilities and cause her to forego a better mate for a period of time, but she may exhaust much of her nurturing and protective energies in attempting to revitalize an inviable or infertile offspring. By contrast, if a male indulges in a bad mating, all he has lost are some quickly replaceable sperm, a loss that does little to diminish his future reproductive potentials and activities.

Before we turn to other indexes and views of the self-other polarity, let us be mindful that these conceptually derived extremes do not evince themselves in sharp and distinct gender differences. Such proclivities are matters of degree, not absolutes, owing not only to the consequences of recombinant "shuffling" and gene "crossing over," but also to the influential effects of cultural values and social learning. Consequently, most normal individuals exhibit intermediate characteristics on this as well as on the other two polarity sets.

The reasoning behind different replication strategies derives from the concept of inclusive fitness, the logic of which we owe to the theoretical biologist W. D. Hamilton (1964). The concept's rationale is well articulated in the following quote (Daly & Wilson, 1978):

> Suppose a particular gene somehow disposes its bearers to help their siblings. Any child of a parent that has this gene has a one-half of probability of carrying that same gene by virtue of common descent from the same parent bearer. . . . From the gene's point of view, it is as useful to help a brother or sister as it is to help the child.
>
> When we assess the fitness of a . . . bit of behavior, we must consider more than the reproductive consequences for the individual animal. We must also consider whether the reproductive prospects of any kin are in any way altered. *Inclusive fitness is a sum of the consequences for one's own reproduction plus the consequences for the reproduction of kin multiplied by the degree of relatedness of those kin* [italics added].
>
> An animal's behavior can therefore be said to serve a strategy whose goal is the maximization of inclusive fitness. (pp. 30–31)

Mutual support and encouragement represents efforts leading to reciprocal fitness—a behavioral pattern consonant with Darwin's fundamental notions. Altruism, however, is a form of behavior in which there is denial of self for the benefit of others, a behavioral pattern acknowledged by Darwin himself as seemingly inconsistent with his theory (1871, p. 130). A simple extrapolation from natural selection suggests that those disposed to engage in self-sacrifice would ultimately leave fewer and fewer descendants; as a consequence, organisms motivated by self-benefiting genes would prevail over those motivated by other-benefiting genes, a result leading to the eventual extinction of genes oriented to the welfare of others. The distinguished sociobiologist E. O. Wilson states the problem directly: "How then does altruism persist?" (1978, p. 153). An entomologist of note, Wilson had no hesitation in claiming that altruism not only persists, but also is of paramount significance in the lives of social insects. In accord with his sociobiological thesis, he illustrates the presence of altruism in animals as diverse as birds, deer, porpoises, and chimpanzees, which share food and provide mutual defense—for example, to protect the colony's hives, bees enact behaviors that lead invariably to their deaths.

Two underlying mechanisms have been proposed to account for cooperative behaviors such as altruism. One derives from the concept of inclusive fitness, briefly described in preceding paragraphs; E. O. Wilson (1978) terms this form of cooperative behavior *hard-core altruism,* by which he means that the act is "unilaterally directed" for the benefit of others and that the bestower neither expects nor expresses a desire for a comparable return. Following the line of reasoning originally formulated by Hamilton (1964), J. P. Rushton (1984), a controversial Canadian researcher who has carried out illuminating r-K studies of human behavior, explicates this mechanism as follows:

> Individuals behave so as to maximize their inclusive fitness rather than only their individual fitness; they maximize the production of successful offspring by both themselves and their relatives. . . . Social ants, for example, are one of the most altruistic species so far discovered. The self-sacrificing, sterile worker and soldier ants . . . share 75% of their genes with their sisters and so by devoting their entire existence to the needs of others . . . they help to propagate their own genes. (p. 6)

The second rationale proposed as the mechanism underlying other-oriented and cooperative behaviors Wilson terms *soft-core altruism* to represent his belief that the bestower's actions are ultimately self-serving. The original line of reasoning here stems from Trivers's (1971) notion of reciprocity, a thesis suggesting that genetically based dispositions to cooperative behavior can be explained without requiring the assumption of kinship relatedness. All that is necessary is that the performance of cooperative acts be mutual—that is, result in concurrent or subsequent behaviors that are comparably beneficial in terms of enhancing the original bestower's survivability, reproductive fertility, or both.

E. O. Wilson's (1978) conclusion that the self-other dimension is a bedrock of evolutionary theory is worth quoting:

> In order to understand this idea more clearly, return with me for a moment to the basic theory of evolution. Imagine a spectrum of self-serving behavior. At one extreme only the individual is meant to benefit, then the nuclear family, next the extended family (including cousins, grandparents, and others who might play a role in kin selection), then the band, the tribe, chiefdoms, and finally, at the other extreme, the highest sociopolitical units. (p. 158)

Intriguing data and ideas have been proposed by several researchers seeking to identify specific substrates that may relate to the other-oriented polarities. In what has been termed the *affiliation-attachment drive,* Everly (1988), for example, provides evidence favoring an anatomical role for the cingulate gyrus. Referring to the work of Henry and Stephens (1977), MacLean (1985), and Steklis and Kling (1985), Everly concludes that the ablation of the cingulate eliminates both affiliative and grooming behaviors. The proximal physiology of this drive has been hypothesized as including serotonergic, noradrenergic, and opoid neurotransmission systems (Everly, 1988; Redmond, Maas, & Kling, 1971). MacLean (1985) has argued that the affiliative drive may be phylogenically coded in the limbic system and may undergird the concept of family in primates. The drive toward other-oriented behaviors, such as attachment, nurturing, affection, reliability, and collaborative play, has been referred to as the "cement of society" by Henry and Stevens (1977).

Let us move now to the realm of psychological and social proposals. Dorothy Conrad (1952) specified a straightforward list of constructive behaviors that manifest "reproductive nurturance" in the interpersonal sphere. She records them as follows:

Has positive affective relationship: The person who is able to relate affectively to even one person demonstrates that he is potentially able to relate to other persons and to society.

Promotes another's welfare: Affective relationships make it possible for the person to enlarge his world and to act for the benefit of another, even though that person may profit only remotely.

Works with another for mutual benefit: The person is largely formed through social interaction. Perhaps he is most completely a person when he participates in a mutually beneficial relationship (pp 456–457)

More eloquent proposals of a similar prosocial character have been formulated by the noted psychologists Maslow, Allport, and Fromm.

According to Maslow, after humans' basic safety and security needs are met, they next turn to satisfy the belonging and love needs. Here we establish intimate and caring relationships with significant others in which it is just as important to give love as it is to receive it. Noting the difficulty in satisfying these needs in our unstable and changing modern world, Maslow sees the basis here for the immense popularity of communes and family therapy. These settings are ways to escape the isolation and loneliness that result from our failures to achieve love and belonging.

One of Allport's criteria of the *mature personality,* which he terms a warm relating of self to others, refers to the capability of displaying intimacy and love for a parent, child, spouse, or close friend. Here the person manifests an authentic oneness with the other and a deep concern for his or her welfare. Beyond one's intimate family and friends, there is an extension of warmth in the mature person to humankind at large, an understanding of the human condition, and a kinship with all peoples.

To Fromm, humans are aware of the growing loss of their ties with nature as well as with each other, feeling increasingly separate and alone. Fromm believes humans must pursue new ties with others to replace those that have been lost or can no longer be depended upon. To counter the loss of communion with nature, he feels that health requires that we fulfill our need by a brotherliness with mankind and a sense of involvement, concern, and relatedness with the world. And with those with whom ties have been maintained or reestablished, humans must fulfill their other-oriented needs by being vitally concerned with their well-being as well as fostering their growth and productivity.

In a lovely coda to a paper on the role of evolution in human behavior, Freedman and Roe (1958) wrote:

> Since his neolithic days, in spite of his murders and wars, his robberies and rapes, man has become a man-binding and a time-binding creature. He has maintained the biological continuity of his family and the social continuity of aggregates of families. He has related his own life experiences with the social traditions of those who have preceded him, and has anticipated those of his progeny. He has accumulated and transmitted his acquired goods and values through his family and through his organizations. He has become bound to other men by feelings of identity and by

shared emotions, by what clinicians call empathy. His sexual nature may yet lead him to widening ambits of human affection, his acquisitive propensities to an optimum balance of work and leisure, and his aggressive drives to heightened social efficiency through attacks on perils common to all men. (p. 457)

The pathological consequences of a failure to embrace the polarity criterion of *others* are seen most clearly in the personality maladaptations termed *antisocial* and *narcissistic* disorders. Both personalities exhibit an imbalance in their replication strategy; in this case, however, there is a primary reliance on self rather than others. They have learned that reproductive success as well as maximum pleasure and minimum pain is achieved by turning exclusively to themselves. The tendency to focus on self follows two major lines of development.

In the narcissistic personality maladaptive style, development reflects the acquisition of a self-image of superior worth. Providing self-rewards is highly gratifying if one values oneself or possesses either a real or inflated sense of self-worth. Displaying manifest confidence, arrogance, and an exploitive egocentricity in social contexts, this individual believes he or she already has all that is important—him- or herself.

Narcissistic individuals are noted for their egotistical self-involvement, experiencing primary pleasure simply by passively being or attending to themselves. Early experience has taught them to overvalue their self-worth; this confidence and superiority may be founded on false premises, however—it may be unsustainable by real or mature achievements. Nevertheless, they blithely assume that others will recognize their special-ness. Hence they maintain an air of arrogant self-assurance, and without much thought or even conscious intent, benignly exploit others to their own advantage. Although the tributes of others are both welcome and encouraged, their air of snobbish and pretentious superiority requires little confirmation either through genuine accomplishment or social approval. Their sublime confidence that things will work out well provides them with little incentive to engage in the reciprocal give and take of social life.

Those clinically designated as antisocial personalities counter the indifference or the expectation of pain from others; this is done by actively engaging in duplicitous or illegal behaviors in which they seek to exploit others for self-gain. Skeptical regarding the motives of others, they desire autonomy and wish revenge for what are felt as past injustices. Many are irresponsible and impulsive, behaviors they see as justified because they judge others to be unreliable and disloyal. Insensitivity and ruthlessness with others are the primary means they have learned to head off abuse and victimization.

In contrast to the narcissistic form of maladaptation, the antisocial pattern of self-orientation develops as a form of protection and counteraction. These styles turn to themselves first to avoid the depredation they anticipate, and second to compensate by furnishing self-generated rewards in their stead. Learning that they cannot depend on others, individuals with these personality styles counterbalance loss not only by trusting themselves alone, but also by actively seeking retribution for what they see as past humiliations. Turning to self and seeking actively to gain strength, power, and revenge, they act irresponsibly, exploiting and usurping what others possess as just reprisals. Their security is never fully assured, however, even when they have aggrandized themselves beyond their lesser origins.

In both narcissistic and antisocial personality styles, we see maladaptations arising from an inability to experience a constructive love for others. For the one, there is an excessive self-centeredness; for the other, there is the acquisition of a compensatory destructiveness driven by a desire for social retribution and self-aggrandizement.

Realizing One's Potentials: The Self-Actualizing Attribute.   The converse of other-nurturance is not self-propagation, but rather the lack of other-nurturance. Thus, to fail to love others constructively does not assure the actualization of one's potentials. Both may and should exist in normal, healthy individuals. Although the dimension of self-other is arranged to highlight its polar extremes, it should be evident that many if not most behaviors are employed to achieve the goals of both self- and kin reproduction. Both ends are often simultaneously achieved; at other times one may predominate. The behaviors comprising these strategies are driven, so to speak, by a blend of activation and affect—that is, combinations arising from intermediary positions reflecting both the life enhancement and life preservation polarity of pleasure-pain, interwoven with similar intermediary positions on the ecological accommodation and ecological modification polarity of activity-passivity. Phrasing replication in terms of the abstruse and metaphorical constructs does not obscure it, but rather sets this third polarity on the deeper foundations of existence and adaptation, foundations composed of the first two polarities previously described.

At the self-oriented pole, Everly (1988) proposes an autonomy-aggression biological substrate that manifests itself in a strong need for control and domination as well as in hierarchical status striving. According to MacLean (1986), it appears that the amygdaloid complex may play a key role in driving organisms into self-oriented behaviors. Early studies of animals with ablated amygdalas showed a notable increase in their docility (Kluver & Bucy, 1939), just as nonhuman primates have exhibited significant decreases in social hierarchy status (Pribram, 1962). Although the evidence remains somewhat equivocal, norepinephrine and dopamine seem to be the prime neurotransmitters of this drive; the testosterone hormone appears similarly implicated (Feldman & Quenzar, 1984).

Regarding psychological constructs that parallel the notion of self-actualization, their earliest equivalent was in the writings of Spinoza (1677/1986), who viewed development as that of becoming what one was intended to be and nothing other than that, no matter how exalted the alternative might appear to be.

Carl Jung's (1961) concept of individuation shares important features with that of actualization in that any deterrent to becoming the individual one may have become would be detrimental to life. Any imposed "collective standard is a serious check to individuality," injurious to the vitality of the person, a form of "artificial stunting."

Perhaps it was my own early mentor, Kurt Goldstein (1939), who first coined the concept under review with the self-actualization designation. As he phrased it, "There is only one motive by which human activity is set going: the tendency to actualize oneself" (1939, p. 196).

The early views of Jung and Goldstein have been enriched by later theorists, notably Fromm, Perls, Rogers, and Maslow.

Focusing on what he terms the sense of identity, Fromm (1955) spoke of the need to establish oneself as a unique individual, a state that places the person apart from others. Further—and it is here where Fromm makes a distinct self-oriented commitment—the extent to which this sense of identity emerges depends on how successful the person is in breaking "incestuous ties" to one's family or clan. Persons with well-developed feelings of identity experience a feeling of control over their lives rather than a feeling of being controlled by the lives of others.

Perls (1969) enlarged on this theme by contrasting self-regulation versus external regulation. Normal, healthy persons do their own regulating, with no external interference, be it the needs and demands of others or the strictures of a social code. What we must actualize is the true inner self, not an image we have of what our ideal selves should be. That is the "curse of the ideal." To Perls, each must be what he or she really is.

Following the views of his forerunners, Maslow (1968) stated that self-actualization is the supreme development and use of all our abilities, ultimately becoming what we have the potential to become. Noting that self-actuals often require detachment and solitude, Maslow asserted that such persons are strongly self-centered and self-directed, make up their own minds, and reach their own decisions without the need to gain social approval.

In like manner, Rogers (1963) posited a single, overreaching motive for the normal, healthy person—maintaining, actualizing, and enhancing one's potential. The goal is not that of maintaining a homeostatic balance or a high degree of ease and comfort, but rather to move forward in becoming what is intrinsic to self and to enhance further that which one has already become. Believing that humans have an innate urge to create, Rogers stated that the most creative product of all is one's own self.

Where do we see failures in the achievement of self-actualization, a giving up of self to gain the approbation of others? Two maladaptive personality styles can be drawn upon to illustrate forms of self-denial.

Those with *dependent personalities* have learned that feeling good, secure, confident, and so on—that is, those feelings associated with pleasure or the avoidance of pain—is provided almost exclusively in their relationship with others. Behaviorally, these persons display a strong need for external support and attention; should they be deprived of affection and nurturance, they will experience marked discomfort, if not sadness and anxiety. Any number of early experiences may set the stage for this other-oriented imbalance. Dependent individuals often include those who have been exposed to an overprotective training regimen and who thereby fail to acquire competencies for autonomy and initiative; experiencing peer failures and low self-esteem leads them to forego attempts at self-assertion and self-gratification. They learn early that they themselves do not readily achieve rewarding experiences; these experiences are secured better by leaning on others. They learn not only to turn to others as their source of nurturance and security, but also to wait passively for others to take the initiative in providing safety and sustenance. Clinically, most are characterized as searching for relationships in which others will reliably furnish affection, protection, and leadership. Lacking both initiative and autonomy, they assume a dependent role in interpersonal relations, accepting what kindness and support they may find and willingly submitting to the wishes of others in order to maintain nurturance and security.

A less benign but equally problematic centering on the wishes of others and the denial of self is seen in what is termed clinically as the obsessive-compulsive personality. These persons display a picture of distinct other-directedness—a consistency in social compliance and interpersonal respect. Their histories usually indicate having been subjected to constraint and discipline when they transgressed parental strictures and expectations. Beneath the conforming other-oriented veneer, they exhibit intense desires to rebel and assert their own self-oriented feelings and impulses. They are trapped in an ambivalence; to avoid intimidation and punishment they have learned to deny the validity of their own wishes and emotions and instead have adopted as true the values and precepts set forth by others. The disparity they sense between their own urges and the behaviors they must display to avoid condemnation often leads to omnipresent physical tensions and rigid psychological controls.

Readers who have reached this final paragraph on the basic three polarities that undergird all physical forms and organic species should have a foundation to move onto our next series of polarities, those which are distinctly human—that is, these polarities relate to personality attributes found almost exclusively in the human species that set us off from all earlier forms of evolution and that pertain to the higher powers and adaptive functions of *abstraction* and their constituent cognitive modes.

THE DISTINCTLY HUMAN POLARITIES OF EVOLUTION

This group of personality attributes incorporates the sources employed to gather knowledge about the experience of life and the manner in which this information is registered and transformed. Here, we are looking at *styles of cognizing*—differences (first) in what people attend to in order to learn about life, and (second) how they process information: what they do to record this knowledge and make it useful to themselves.

Predilections of Abstraction

The cognitive features of intelligence are judged by me to be central elements in personological derivations. Comprising the fourth and most recent stage of evolution, they comprise the reflective capacity to transcend the immediate and concrete, they interrelate and synthesize the diversity of experience, they represent events and processes symbolically, they weigh, reason, and anticipate; in essence, they signify a quantum leap in evolution's potential for change and adaptation.

Cognitive differences among individuals and the manner in which they are expressed have been much overlooked in generating and appraising personality attributes. With an occasional notable exception or two, little of the recent so-called revolution in cognitive science that has profoundly affected contemporary psychology has impacted the study of personology. Historically, the realms of intellect, aptitude, and ability have not been considered to be personality-related spheres of study.

In my view, personology should be broadened to encompass the *whole person,* an organically unified and unsegmented totality. Consequently, cognitive dimensions and their various styles not only should be included, but also may have a significance equal to that of other functions as a source of personality attributes (Millon, 1990). Unfortunately, the various features comprising cognitive abstraction have only rarely been included as components in personality-oriented concepts and appraisals.

Emancipated from the real and present, unanticipated possibilities and novel constructions may routinely be created cognitively. The capacity to sort, to recompose, to coordinate, and to arrange the symbolic representations of experience into new configurations is in certain ways analogous to the random processes of recombinant replication, but processes enabling manipulation of abstractions are more focused and intentional. To extend this rhetorical liberty, replication is the recombinant mechanism underlying the adaptive progression of phylogeny, whereas abstraction is the recombinant mechanism underlying the adaptive progression of ontogeny. The powers of replication are limited, constrained by the finite potentials inherent in parental genes. In contrast, experiences, abstracted and recombined, are infinite.

Over one lifetime, innumerable events of a random, logical, or irrational character transpire, are construed, and are reformulated time and again—some of which prove more and others less adaptive than their originating circumstances may have called forth. Whereas the actions of most nonhuman species derive from successfully evolved genetic programs, activating behaviors of a relatively fixed nature suitable for a modest range of environmental settings, the capabilities of both implicit and intentional abstraction that characterize humans give rise to adaptive competencies that are suited to radically divergent ecological circumstances, circumstances that themselves may be the result of far-reaching acts of symbolic and technological creativity.

Although what underlies our self- versus other-oriented attributes stems from differential replication strategies, the conscious state of knowing self as distinct from others is a product of the power of abstraction, the most recent phase of evolution's procession. The reflective process of turning inward and recognizing self as an object—no less to know oneself, and further, to know that one knows—is a uniqueness found only among humans. Doubling back on oneself, so to speak, creates a new level of reality, consciousness that imbues self and others with properties far richer and more subtle than those that derive from strategies of reproductive propagation and nurturance alone.

The abstracting mind may mirror outer realities but reconstructs them in the process, reflectively transforming them into subjective modes of phenomenological reality, making external events into a plastic mold subject to creative designs. Not only are images of self and others emancipated from direct sensory realities, becoming entities possessing a life of their own, but contemporaneous time may also lose its immediacy and impact. The abstracting mind brings the past effectively into the present, and its power of anticipation brings the future into the present as well. With past and future embedded in the here and now, humans can encompass at once not only the totality of our cosmos, but also its origins and nature, its evolution, and how they have come to pass. Most impressive of all are the many visions humans have of life's indeterminate future, where no reality as yet exists.

Four polarities constitute this distinctly human abstraction function. The first two pairs refer to the information sources that provide cognitions. One set of contrasting polarities addresses the orientation either to look outward, or external-to-self, in seeking information, inspiration, and guidance, versus the orientation to turn inward, or internal-to-self. The second set of abstraction polarities contrasts predilections for either direct observational experiences of a tangible, material, and concrete nature with those geared more toward intangible, ambiguous, and inchoate phenomena.

The third and fourth set of abstraction polarities relate to cognitive processing—that is, the ways in which people evaluate and mentally reconstruct information and experiences after they have been apprehended and incorporated. The first of these sets of cognitive polarities differentiates processes based essentially on ideation, logic, reason, and objectivity from those that depend on emotional empathy, personal values, sentiment, and subjective judgments. The second set of these polarities reflects either a tendency to make new information conform to preconceived knowledge, in the form of tradition-bound, standardized, and conventionally structured schemas, versus the opposing inclination to bypass preconceptions by distancing from what is already known and instead to create innovative ideas in an informal, open-minded, spontaneous, individualistic, and often imaginative manner.

Cognitive functions are consonant with our earlier biosocial formulations concerning the architecture of human functioning (Millon, 1990) because we see cognitive processes to be an essential component of our fourfold model regarding how organisms approach their environments. Beyond the driving motivational elements of personality style (as in my formulation of the personality disorders), or the factorial structure of personality (e.g., as explicated in the Big Five model), we seek to conjoin all components of personality style by linking and integrating the various expressions and functions of personality into an overarching and coherent whole.

Several polar dimensions have been proposed through the years as the basis for a schema of cognitive styles. Contrasting terms such as *leveling* versus *sharpening, narrow* versus *broad, analytic* versus *synthetic, constricted* versus *flexible, inductive* versus *deductive, abstract* versus *concrete,* and *convergent* versus *divergent* have been used to illustrate the stylistic differences among cognitive functions. Although each of these pairs contributes to distinctions of importance in describing cognitive processes, few were conceptualized with *personality* differences in mind, although some may prove productive in that regard.

As noted above, the model formulated by the author separates cognitive activities into two superordinate functions. The first pertains to the contrasting origins from which cognitive data are gathered, or what may be termed *information sources;* the second pertains to the methods by which these data are reconstructed by the individual, or what we label *transformational processes.* These two functions—the initial gathering and subsequent reconstruction of information—are further subdivided into two polarities each. As is elaborated later in this chapter, the sources of information are separated into (a) *external* versus *internal* and (b) *tangible* versus *intangible.* Transformational processes are divided into (a) *ideational* versus *emotional* and (b) *integrative* versus *imaginative.* The resulting four personality attributes are by no means exhaustive. Rather surprisingly, they turn out to be consonant with a model formulated in the 1920s by Jung (1971a).

Sources of Information

Information may be seen as the opposite of entropy. What energy or nutrients are to physical systems, information is to cognitive systems. A physical system sustains itself by sucking order, so to speak, from its environs, taking in energy or nutrients and transforming them to meet tissue needs; a cognitive system does something similar by sucking information from its environs—that is, taking in data and transforming them to meet its cognitive needs. In much the same way as any other open system, a cognitive structure needs to maintain itself as an integrated and cohesive entity. In the physical world, the integrity of a system is achieved by making adaptations that preserve and enhance the physical structure, thereby precluding the entropic dissipation of its ordered elements. Similarly, a cognitive system achieves its integrity through a variety of preserving and enhancing adaptations that reduce the likelihood of events that may diminish the order and coherence of its knowledge base.

Moreover, an open cognitive system is purposefully focused, as is a physical system. Just as a physical system must be selective about its nutrition sources in order to find those suitable to meet its tissue needs, so, too, must a cognitive system be selective about information sources, choosing and processing particular raw inputs according to specific cognitive goals. A cognitive system can no more process random input than a physical system can ingest random material. Hence, information (negative entropy) must be acquired selectively rather than randomly or diffusely; some sources of information will be heeded and others ignored or suppressed.

Coherence may be optimized by adopting and maintaining a preferred and regular information source, thereby ensuring a consistent confirmatory bias in favor of a cognitive structure's world view and organizational architecture. Conversely, a cognitive structure that is exposed to dissonant or contradictory sources or that heeds diverse or multitudinous sources ultimately may be challenged successfully or may be exhausted beyond its ability to maintain coherence. In other words, burdensome processing and discordant sources are likely to result in increasing cognitive entropy. A more structured and coherent focus that strengthens and confirms prior sources of information becomes useful in ensuring optimal cognitive survivability.

External Versus Internal Orientation Polarity: The Extraceptive and Intraceptive Attributes.   In light of the preceding argument, we see two primary stimulative sources of information, that which originates external to the self and that which originates internally. Whether this polar cognitive orientation is termed external versus internal, extraceptive versus intraceptive, or extraversing versus introversing, each polarity provides a replicable reservoir for cognitive information—a selectively narrowed wellspring of knowledge to which the person will continue to be exposed.

A few lines paraphrasing Jung, the originator of the extraversing-introversing dimension, may be of value in highlighting core features of the externally oriented preference. Extraversion, from Jung's view, was centered in an interest in the external object noted by a ready acceptance of external happenings, a desire to influence and be influenced by external events, a need to join in, and the capacity not only to endure the bustle and noise of every kind, but actually find them enjoyable (Jung, 1971a).

Similarly, Jung clearly states a view paralleling ours in what we have termed the internal orientation. To Jung, the introverted person is "not forthcoming"; he or she "retreats before the external object." Such an individual is aloof from external happenings and does not join in. Self-communings are a pleasure and the introverted individual experiences his or her own world as a safe harbor, a "carefully tended and walked-in garden, closed to the public and hidden from prying eyes." The internally oriented person's own company is best. One who is internally oriented feels at home in one's own world, a place where changes are made only by oneself. Most significantly, the best work of such individuals is done

with their own resources, on their own initiative, and in their own way (Jung, 1971b).

Tangible Versus Intangible Disposition Polarity: The Realistic and Intuitive Attributes.   Information, whether its source is internal or external to the self, can be classified in numerous ways. A core distinction can be drawn between information that is tangible versus that which is intangible. By *tangible* we mean identifiable by human sensory capacities, well-defined, distinctive, recognizable, and knowable—referring to phenomena that are concrete, factual, material, realistic, or self-evident. In contrast, information that is termed *intangible* takes in phenomena that lack an intrinsically distinctive order and structural clarity; they are inherently ambiguous, abstract, insubstantial, vague, mysterious, and obscure. Such phenomena usually can be fathomed only by means that are unknown, unconscious, and percipient, or by glimmerings into their diffuse and elusive nature that are materially tenuous or psychical in form.

The readiness of some individuals to be receptive to information that is well-structured and tangible, and of others to receive information that is obscure and intangible, constitutes, in our view, a fundamental difference in cognitive style that is of appreciable personological significance. Although Jung's language is only tangentially formulated in cognitive terms, close parallels can be seen between the polarity presented here and that offered by Jung in his distinction between Sensing and Intuiting. As Jung (1933) wrote decades ago:

> Here we should speak of sensation when sense impressions are involved, and of intuition if we are dealing with a kind of perception which cannot be traced back directly to conscious sensory experience. Hence, I define sensation as perception via conscious sensory functions, and intuition as perception via the unconscious. (pp. 538–539)

Favoring tangible, structured, and well-defined sources of information that call upon one's five senses will no doubt correlate with a wide range of associated behaviors, such as choosing actions of a pragmatic and realistic nature, preferring events in the here and now, and attending to matters calling for facts and quantitative precision.

Jung conceived what we would term the *tangible disposition* as the fact-minded men in whom intuition is "driven into the background by actual facts." In contrast, those preferring the intangible, unstructured, and ambiguous world of information are likely to be inspired by possibilities, by challenges, and potentials of an abstract, connotative, and symbolic character, as well as by matters that depend on mystery and speculation. In Jung's words, "for these persons, actual reality counts only insofar as it harbors possibilities, regardless of the way things are in the actual present" (Jung, 1971b, p. 539).

Transformational Processes

The first two pairs of cognitive functions were grouped according to attributes that signify choices among the sources and styles of *gathering* information. These next two pairs of attribute polarities represent amplification preferences and transformational processes, referring to what is done to information after it has been received. Cognitive science has articulated a number of concepts related to the registering, encoding, and organizing of life experiences. These concepts pertain to various questions, such as *Through what cognitive mode will information be received and amplified—intellective or affective?* and *How shall information be organized; will it be assimilated into preformed memory systems or will it be recast through imagination into novel schemas?* Although individuals may be positioned on several other continua or polarities—for example, convergent versus divergent, serial versus hierarchical, primary versus secondary, verbal versus visual—it is the author's view that the most fruitful cognitive distinctions relevant to personality are the pairs selected in this and the following section.

Ideational Versus Emotional Preference Polarity: The Intellective and Affective Attributes. Stated simply, there are essentially two pathways through which experiences pass once recorded by our consciousness or by our senses, if they are of sufficient magnitude to activate an encoded response. The first pathway accentuates information that is conceptual and logical, eliciting a reasoned judgment that signifies in an articulate and organized way that the registered experience makes sense—that is, it is rationally consistent and coherent. The second pathway resonates an emotional response, a subjective feeling reaction, signaling in a somewhat diffuse and global way that the registered event was experienced either as affectively neutral, clearly positive, or distinctly negative.

The ideational pole indicates a preference and elaboration of experience in light of reason and logic. Although life events may derive from internal or external sources and may be of a tangible or intangible nature, the interpretive and evaluative process is inclined toward and augments the objective and impersonal, as events are amplified by means of critical reason and intensified by the application of rational and judicious thought. By diminishing affective engagements—reducing the unruly emotional input of others or the upsetting effects of one's own affective state—the preference is to sustain and strengthen a high degree of cognitive logic and cohesion. Objective analysis and affective detachment

protect against unwanted incursions upon intellectual rationality, but often at the price of promoting processes that tend to be rigid, overcontrolled, and unyielding.

In contrast, experiences processed and amplified emotionally activate subjective states, such as liking versus disliking, feeling good versus feeling bad, comfort versus discomfort, attracted versus repelled, valuing versus devaluing, and so on. Through empathic resonance, the route of enhanced affectivity inclines the individual to record not so much what other people think but rather how they feel. The individual who inclines toward the affective attribute uses *feeling vibrations* to learn more from the melodic tone that words convey than from their content or logic. The usual modality for those who exhibit an affective bent is that of a subjective reality, a series of more-or-less gut reactions composed of either global or differentiated positive or negative moods. For the most part, the affective amplification style indicates individuals who evince modest introspective analyses, who show an open and direct empathic response to others, and who have a subconscious susceptibility to the emotional facets of experience in as pure a manner as possible.

Integrating Versus Innovating Bias Polarity: The Assimilative and Imaginative Attributes. The second cognitive transformational polarity addresses the question of whether new information is shaped to fit preformed memory schemas (integrated within preexisting cognitive systems), or is organized through the imagination to be cast into innovative and creative forms. Evolutionary theory suggests that the best course may be to reinforce (cognitive) systems that have proved stable and useful. On the other hand, progress will not be made unless promising new possibilities are explored. A beneficial tension in evolution clearly exists between conservation and change, between that of adhering to the habitual and that of unleashing the creative. These two contrasting cognitive biases demonstrate the two options—integrating experiences into already established systems versus exploring innovative ways to structure them.

Assimilators are akin in certain features to persons with well-structured memory systems to which they routinely attach new cognitive experiences. Disposed to operate within established perspectives, assimilators integrate new information to fit previous points of view, exhibiting thereby a high degree of dependability and consistency, if not rigidity, in their functioning. Typically, such people are predictable, conventional, orderly, systematic, decisive, methodical, exacting, formal, disciplined, conscientious, faithful, loyal, and devoted. Hence, in evolutionary terms, the integrating polarity leads to continuity and tradition, or to the maintenance of existing levels of cognitive entropy; this cognitive style

Russell, J. A. (1980). A circumplex model of affect. *Journal of Personality and Social Psychology, 39,* 1161–1178.

Schrodinger, E. (1944). *What is life?* Cambridge, UK: Cambridge University Press.

Skinner, B. F. (1938). *The behavior of organisms: An experimental analysis.* New York: Appleton.

Skinner, B. F. (1953). *Science and human behavior.* New York: Macmillan.

Spencer, H. (1855). *Principles of psychology.* London: Longman, Brown, Green.

Spencer, H. (1870). *The principles of psychology.* London: Williams and Norgate.

Spinoza, B. de (1986). *Ethics: On the correction of understanding.* London: Dent. (Original work published 1677)

Steklis, H., & Kling, A. (1985). Neurobiology of affiliation in primates. In M. Reite & T. Fields (Eds.), *The psychobiology of attachment and separation.* Orlando, FL: Academic Press.

Symons, D. (1979). *The evolution of human sexuality.* New York: Oxford University Press.

Symons, D. (1992). On the use and misuse of Darwinism in the study of human behavior. In J. Barkow, L. Cosmides, & J. Tooby (Eds.), *The adapted mind* (pp. 137–159). New York: Oxford University Press.

Tellegen, A. (1985). Structure of mood and personality and their relevance to assessing anxiety, with an emphasis on self-report. In A. H. Tuma & J. Maser (Eds.), *Anxiety and the anxiety disorders* (pp. 681–706). Hillsdale, NJ: Erlbaum.

Thom, R. (1972). *Structural stability and morphogenesis.* Reading, MA: Benjamin.

Trivers, R. L. (1971). The evolution of reciprocal altruism. *Quarterly Review of Biology, 46,* 35–57.

Trivers, R. L. (1974). Parental investment and sexual selection. In B. Campbell (Ed.), *Sexual selection and the descent of man 1871–1971.* Chicago: Aldine.

White, R. W. (1959). Motivation reconsidered: The concept of competence. *Psychological Review, 66,* 297–323.

Wilson, E. O. (1975). *Sociobiology: The new synthesis.* Cambridge, MA: Harvard University Press.

Wilson, E. O. (1978). *On human nature.* Cambridge, MA: Harvard University Press.

Wilson, E. O. (1998). *Consilience: The unity of knowledge.* New York: Knopf.

Wilson, M., & Daly, M. (1992). The man who mistook his wife for a chattel. In J. Barkow, L. Cosmides, & J. Tooby (Eds.), *The adapted mind* (pp. 289–322). New York: Oxford University Press.

CHAPTER 2

Cultural Perspectives on Personality and Social Psychology

JOAN G. MILLER AND LYNNE SCHABERG

During much of its past, psychology represented a culturally grounded enterprise that took into account the constitutive role of cultural meanings and practices in human development. Yet, as recent historical accounts make clear (Jahoda, 1993), this attention to culture was muted during the twentieth century, with psychology dominated by an idealized physical-science model of explanation. This has given rise to the enigma that psychologists find it "difficult to keep culture in mind," noted by Cole (1996):

> On the one hand, it is generally agreed that the need and ability to live in the human medium of culture is one of the central characteristics of human beings. On the other hand, it is difficult for many academic psychologists to assign culture more than a secondary, often superficial role in the constitution of our mental life. (p. 1)

From this type of perspective, which dominates the field, culture is seen as at most affecting the display of individual psychological processes, but not as impacting qualitatively on their form.

However, although culture thus remains in a peripheral role in the contemporary discipline, recent years have seen a reemergence of interest in cultural approaches and an increased recognition of their importance to psychological theory. As reflected in the interdisciplinary perspective of cultural psychology (e.g., Cole, 1990; Greenfield, 1997; J. G. Miller, 1997; Shweder, 1990), culture and psychology are coming to be understood as mutually constitutive processes. It is recognized that human development occurs in historically grounded social environments that are structured by cultural meanings and practices. Cultural meanings and practices are themselves understood to be dependent on the subjectivity of communities of intentional agents. By affecting individuals' understandings and intentions, cultural meanings and practices, in turn, are recognized to have a qualitative impact on the development of psychological phenomena and to be integral to the formulation of basic psychological theory.

The goal of the present chapter is to highlight some of the insights for understanding personality and social psychology that emerge from a consideration of the cultural grounding of psychological processes. The first section of the chapter considers factors that have contributed to the downplaying of culture in mainstream social psychology and the assumptions that guided some of the earliest research in the traditions of cross-cultural psychology. In the second section, consideration is given to key conceptual developments underlying cultural psychology, recent empirical findings that illustrate the existence of cultural variation in basic social psychological processes, and challenges for future theory and research. In conclusion, consideration is given to the multiple contributions of a cultural perspective in psychology.

APPROACHES TO CULTURE IN MAINSTREAM SOCIAL PSYCHOLOGY AND IN EARLY CROSS-CULTURAL PSYCHOLOGY

The present section provides an overview of shifts in the role accorded to culture in psychological theory over time, and it outlines some of the changing conceptual understandings and disciplinary practices that are affecting these shifts. The first section considers factors that are contributing to the tendency to assign cultural considerations a relatively peripheral role both in social psychology and more generally in the larger discipline. The second section provides an overview of some of the earliest traditions of cultural research in social psychology, highlighting respects in which this research, although groundbreaking in many respects, did not seriously challenge this tendency to downplay the importance of culture in psychology. Finally, attention turns to the core assumptions of cultural psychology, assumptions that highlight the need to accord culture a more integral role in basic psychological theory.

Downplaying of Culture in Mainstream Social Psychology

Signs of the peripheral theoretical role accorded to cultural considerations in social psychology may be seen in its being downplayed in major social psychological publications. Textbooks typically either leave the construct of culture theoretically undefined, treat it as the same as the objective environment or social ecology, or approach it in an eclectic way that lacks conceptual clarity. Likewise, basic theory tends to be presented without any reference to cultural considerations. Culture is treated merely as a factor that influences the universality of certain psychological effects but not as a process that must be taken into account to explain the form of basic psychological phenomena. One example of such a stance can be found in Higgins and Kruglanski's (1996) recent handbook on basic principles of social psychology: The only citations for *culture* in the index—with only one exception—refer to pages within the single chapter on cultural psychology by Markus, Kitayama, and Heiman (1996), rather than to any of the other 27 chapters of the volume. In the following discussion, we argue that this downplaying of culture in social psychology reflects to a great degree the tendency to conceptualize situations in culture-free terms, the embrace of an idealized natural-science model of explanation, and the default assumption of cultural homogeneity that dominates the field.

Culture-Free Approach to Situations

A key contribution of social psychology—if not its signature explanatory feature—is its recognition of the power of situations to impact behavior. Such a stance is reflected, for example, in a series of classic studies; salient examples include the Milgram conformity experiment, which demonstrated that to conform with the orders of an experimenter,

individuals were willing to inflict a harmful electric shock on a learner (Milgram, 1963), as well as the prison experiment of Zimbardo and his colleagues (Haney, Banks, & Zimbardo, 1973), which demonstrated that individuals who had been thrust into the role relationships of guards and prisoners in a simulated prison behaved in ways that reflected these positions, with the guards behaving abusively and the prisoners becoming passive. It also may be seen in recent lines of inquiry on such topics as individuals' limited conscious access to their cognitive processes, priming effects, and the mere exposure effect (Bargh, 1996; Bornstein, Kale, & Cornell, 1990; Zimbardo, Banks, Haney, & Jaffe, 1973). Social psychological work of this type has shown that contexts affect behavior in ways that do not depend on conscious mediation and that may even violate individuals' conscious expectations and motivational inclinations.

Supplementing this focus on the power of situations to affect behavior, it has also been documented that individual differences influence the meaning accorded to situations. This attention to individual differences is evident not only in work on personality processes but also in the attention given to cognitive and motivational schemas as sources of individual variability in behavior. Individual difference dimensions, however, typically are accorded a secondary role to situational influences within social psychological theory. They are believed to affect the display of certain basic psychological dimensions, but they are not often implicated in normative models of psychological phenomena. To give a representative example of such a stance, the theory of communal and exchange relationships has been forwarded to distinguish qualitatively between relationships that are based on need versus those based on exchange considerations (Mills & Clark, 1982). In this model, individual differences are invoked only in a descriptive sense (i.e., to distinguish between persons who are more or less likely to adopt each type of orientation) and not in a theoretical sense (that is, to identify distinctive approaches to relationships beyond those specified in the original conceptual model).

The crucial point is that the approach to situations that dominates social psychological inquiry treats contexts as presenting one most veridical structure that can be known through inductive or deductive information processing. No consideration is given to the possibility that culture is necessarily implicated in the definition of situations or that cultural presuppositions constitute prerequisites of what is considered objective knowledge. It is assumed that variability in judgment arises from differences in the information available to individuals or from differences in their information-processing abilities, resulting in certain judgments' being more or less cognitively adequate or veridical than others

(Nisbett & Ross, 1980). Evidence that individuals from different cultural backgrounds maintain contrasting systems of belief, value, or meaning—and that they interpret situations in contrasting ways—tends to be assimilated to an individual difference dimension. It is viewed as implying that individual differences in attitudes, understandings, or available information may relate to cultural group membership, but not as implying that there is a need to give any independent weight to cultural meanings and practices per se in explanation.

In maintaining the present realist approach to situations and in adopting explanatory frameworks focused on factors in the situation and in the person, cultural considerations are downplayed in theoretical importance. It is assumed that cultural information may substitute for or shortcut individual information processing: The individual comes to learn about the world indirectly through acquiring the knowledge disseminated in the culture. As such, culture is viewed as providing information redundant with that which individuals could obtain by themselves through direct cognitive processing. Wells (1981), for example, maintains that enculturation processes are nonessential to individual knowledge acquisition:

> It is difficult for anyone who has raised a child to deny the pervasive influence of socialized processing that surely surfaces as causal schemata originate through secondary sources such as parents . . . Even though socialized processing may be an important determinant of knowledge about causal forces at one level, it nevertheless begs the question. How is it that the parents knew an answer? The issue is circular. That is precisely the reason that one must consider a more basic factor–namely original processing. (p. 313)

From the present type of perspective, cultural knowledge is seen as necessary neither to account for the nature of individual knowledge nor to evaluate its adequacy.

Natural Science Ideals of Explanation

The tendency to downplay the importance of culture in social psychological theory also derives from the field's embrace of an idealized physical-science model of explanation. Although social psychology makes use of multiple normative models of scientific inquiry, it has typically treated physical science models of scientific inquiry as the ideal approach. This has affected both the goals and methods of inquiry in ways that have tended to marginalize cultural approaches.

In terms of explanatory goals, the foremost aim of psychological explanation has been to identify universal laws of behavior. Adopting the criteria of parsimony and of predictive power as the hallmarks of a successful explanation,

psychological inquiry has been conceptualized as involving the identification of deep structural explanatory mechanisms that (it is assumed) underlie overt behavior. Higgins and Kruglanski (1996) outline this vision for social psychological inquiry:

> A discovery of lawful principles governing a realm of phenomena is a fundamental objective of scientific research . . . A useful scientific analysis needs to probe beneath the surface. In other words, it needs to get away from the 'phenotypic' manifestations and strive to unearth the 'genotypes' that may lurk beneath. . . . We believe in the scientific pursuit of the nonobvious. But less in the sense of uncovering new and surprising phenomena than in the sense of probing beneath surface similarities and differences to discover deep underlying structures. (p. vii)

From this perspective, the assumption is made that fundamental psychological processes are timeless, ahistorical, and culturally invariant, with the principles of explanation in the social sciences no different from those in the natural or physical sciences.

From the present physical-science view of explanation, cultural considerations tend to be regarded as noise; they are consequently held constant in order to focus on identifying underlying processes. Malpass (1988) articulates this type of position:

> Cultural differences are trivial because they are at the wrong level of abstraction, and stand as 'medium' rather than 'thing' in relation to the objects of study. The readily observable differences among cultural groups are probably superficial, and represent little if any differences at the level of psychological processes. (p. 31)

According to this perspective, an explanation that identifies a process as dependent on culturally specific assumptions is regarded as deficient. To discover that a phenomenon is culturally bound is to suggest that the phenomenon has not as yet been fully understood and that it is not yet possible to formulate a universal explanatory theory that achieves the desired goals of being both parsimonious and highly general.

Another consequence of the present physical-science model of explanation is that social psychology has tended to privilege laboratory-based methods of inquiry and to be dismissive of what is perceived to be the inherent lack of methodological control of cultural research. Skepticism surrounds the issue of whether sufficient comparability can be achieved in assessments made in different cultural contexts to permit valid cross-cultural comparisons. Equally serious concerns are raised that methodological weaknesses are inherent in the qualitative methods that are frequently involved in assessment of cultural meanings and practices. In particular, because such measures are at times based on analyses undertaken by single ethnographers or similar methods, measures used in cultural assessment are seen as characterized by limited reliability and validity, as well as by heavy reliance on interpretive techniques.

It is notable that the adoption within social psychology of a physical-science ideal of explanation also promotes disciplinary insularity. Although there is considerable openness to the integration of biologically based conceptual models and methodologies—a trend seen in the growing interest in neuroscience—there is little or no interest in integrating the theoretical insights and empirical findings from other social science fields, such as anthropology. Rather, the body of knowledge developed within anthropology becomes difficult for social psychologists to assimilate. Thus, for example, psychologists typically treat the findings of anthropological research as merely descriptive or anecdotal, with little attention even given to such findings as a source of hypotheses that might be subject to further testing through controlled social psychological procedures. A situation is then created in which the findings of cultural variability in human behavior (which have been widely documented within anthropology) as well as anthropological tools of interpretive methodological inquiry tend to be given little or no attention in social psychological inquiry.

Default Assumption of Cultural Heterogeneity

Finally, the downplaying of the importance of cultural considerations in social psychology also stems from the tendency to assume a universalistic cultural context in recruitment of research participants and in formulation of research questions. This type of stance has led to skewed population sampling in research. As critics (Reid, 1994) have charged, the field has proceeded as though the cultural context for human development is homogeneous; consequently, research has adopted stances that treat middle-class European-American research populations as the default or unmarked subject of research:

> Culture . . . has been assumed to be homogenous, that is, based on a standard set of values and expectations primarily held by White and middle-class populations. . . . For example, in developmental psychology, *children* means White children (McLoyd, 1990); in psychology of women, *women* generally refers to White women (Reid, 1988). When we mean other than White, it is specified. (p. 525)

In this regard, slightly over a decade ago, it was observed that fewer than 10% of all hypothesis testing research undertaken

in social psychology involved samples drawn from two or more cultures (Pepitone & Triandis, 1987). Likewise, a review conducted of more than 14,000 empirical articles in psychology published between 1970 and 1989 yielded fewer than 4% centering on African Americans (Graham, 1992).

However, it is not only these skewed sampling practices but also the resulting skewed knowledge base brought to bear in inquiry that contributes to the downplaying of the importance of cultural considerations. Commonly, research hypotheses are based on investigators' translations of observations from their own experiences into testable research hypotheses. In doing this, however, researchers from non–middle-class European-American backgrounds frequently find themselves having to suppress intuitions or concerns that arise from their own cultural experiences. As reflected in the following account by a leading indigenous Chinese psychologist (Yang, 1997), the present type of stance may give rise to a certain sense of alienation among individuals who do not share the so-called mainstream cultural assumptions that presently dominate the field:

> I found the reason why doing Westernized psychological research with Chinese subjects was no longer satisfying or rewarding to me. When an American psychologist, for example, was engaged in research, he or she could spontaneously let his or her American cultural and philosophical orientations and ways of thinking be freely and effectively reflected in choosing a research question, defining a concept, constructing a theory and designing a method. On the other hand, when a Chinese psychologist in Taiwan was conducting research, his or her strong training by overlearning the knowledge and methodology of American psychology tended to prevent his or her Chinese values, ideas, concepts and ways of thinking from being adequately reflected in the successive stages of the research process. (p. 65)

It has been suggested, in this regard, that to broaden psychological inquiry to be sensitive to aspects of self emphasized in Chinese culture, greater attention would need to be paid to such presently understudied concerns as filial piety, impression management, relationship harmony, and protection of face (Hsu, 1963, 1985; Yang, 1988; Yang & Ho, 1988). Taking issues of this type into account, researchers of moral development, for example, have challenged the Kohlbergian claim that a concern with human rights fully captures the end point of moral development (Kohlberg, 1969, 1971); such researchers have uncovered evidence to suggest that within Chinese cultural populations, the end point of moral development places greater emphasis on *Ch'ing* (human affection or sentiment) as well as on the Confucian value of *jen* (love, human-heartedness, benevolence, and sympathy; Ma, 1988, 1989).

As a consequence of its tendency to privilege considerations emphasized in European-American cultural contexts, psychology in many cases has focused on research concerns that have a somewhat parochial character, as Moscovici (1972) has argued in appraising the contributions of social psychology:

> . . . The real advance made by American social psychology was . . . in the fact that it took for its theme of research and for the content of its theories the issues of *its own* society. Its merit was as much in its techniques as in translating the problems of American society into sociopsychological terms and in making them an object of scientific inquiry. (p. 19)

In proceeding with a set of concepts that are based on a relatively narrow set of cultural experiences, psychological research then has tended to formulate theories and research questions that lack adequate cultural inclusiveness and instead are based on the experiences of highly select populations.

Summary

Despite its concern with social aspects of experience and with units of analysis, such as groups, that are larger than individuals, social psychological inquiry has tended to downplay cultural factors. This downplaying, as we have seen, reflects in part the field's tendency to give weight both to situational and individual difference considerations, while according no independent explanatory force to cultural factors. Equally, it reflects the field's embrace of natural-science models of explanation, which emphasize generality as the hallmark of a successful explanation and controlled experimentation as the most adequate approach to scientific inquiry. Finally, in both its sampling practices and in its consideration of research questions, social psychology has privileged a middle-class European-American outlook that gives only limited attention to the perspectives and concerns of diverse cultural and subcultural populations.

Early Research in Cross-Cultural Psychology

Although cultural considerations have tended to be accorded little importance in social psychological theory, there exists a long-standing tradition of research in cross-cultural psychology that has consistently focused attention on them. The scope of work in cross-cultural psychology is reflected in the vast body of empirical research that has been conducted. Empirical work from this perspective is extensive enough to fill the six-volume first edition of the *Handbook of Cross-Cultural Psychology* (Triandis & Lambert, 1980), as well as

numerous textbooks and review chapters (e.g., Berry, Poortinga, Segall, & Dasen, 1992; Brislin, 1983).

Research in cross-cultural psychology shares many of the conceptual presuppositions of mainstream psychology—which explains, at least in part, why it has not fundamentally posed a challenge to the mainstream discipline (see discussion in Shweder, 1990; J. G. Miller, 2001a). These assumptions involve a view of culture as an independent variable affecting psychological processes understood as a dependent variable. From such a perspective, culture is seen as affecting the display or level of development of psychological processes, but not their basic form—a stance similar to the assumption in mainstream social psychology that culture has no impact on fundamental psychological phenomena. Research in cross-cultural psychology also assumes an adaptive approach to culture that is consonant with the view of the environment emphasized in mainstream psychology. Naturally occurring ecological environments are viewed as presenting objective affordances and constraints to which both individual behavior and cultural forms are adapted.

A major thrust of work in cross-cultural psychology has been to test the universality of psychological theories under conditions in which there is greater environmental variation than is present in the cultural context in which the theories were originally formulated. Brief consideration of early cross-cultural research in the traditions of culture and personality, culture and cognition, and individualism-collectivism highlights both the groundbreaking nature of this work as well as the limited extent to which it challenges the core theoretical presuppositions of the mainstream discipline.

Culture and Personality

The research tradition of culture and personality constituted an interdisciplinary perspective that generated great interest and inspired extensive research throughout the middle years of the twentieth century (e.g., LeVine, 1973; Shweder, 1979a, 1979b; Wallace, 1961; J. W. Whiting & Child, 1953; B. B. Whiting & Whiting, 1975). Although many of the classic assumptions of this perspective were subject to challenge, and although interest in this viewpoint diminished after the 1980s, work in culture and personality has served as an important foundation for later work on culture and the development of self.

Some of the earliest work in the tradition of culture and personality adopted a critical case methodology to test the generality of psychological theories. For example, in a classic example of this type of approach, Malinowski tested the universality of the Oedipus complex against case materials from the Trobriand Islands (1959). In contrast to the Freudian modes of self-construal, Markus and Kitayama did not adopt all of the assumptions of the individualism-collectivism framework as developed by early cross-cultural psychologists. In contrast to such theorists, for example, they were concerned with the cultural psychological agenda of identifying insights for basic psychological theory of cultural variation (e.g., identifying new culturally based forms of motivation), rather than with the cross-cultural agenda of applying existing psychological theories in diverse cultural contexts (e.g., identifying cultural variation in the emphasis placed on internal vs. external locus of control, as specified by Rotter's framework). They tended to eschew the use of scale measures of individualism-collectivism; they also did not draw some of the global contrasts made within much work within this framework, such as devaluation of the self in collectivism or of relationships in individualism (see discussion in Kitayama, in press; J. G. Miller, 2002). However, in part as a reflection of the interest in the distinction between independent versus interdependent self-construals introduced by Markus and Kitayama (1991), the number of investigators concerned with individualism and collectivism has grown in recent years, with many investigators drawing on this framework to further the cultural psychological agenda of broadening basic psychological theory (e.g., Greenfield & Cocking, 1994; Greenfield & Suzuki, 1998), and other investigators in social psychology drawing on the framework to further the original agenda of theorists such as Triandis to develop a universal, ecologically based framework to explain psychological variation on a worldwide scale (e.g., Oyserman, Coon, & Kemmelmeier, 2002).

In terms of criticisms, the tradition of cross-cultural research on individualism is limited in its emphasis on testing the generality of existing psychological theories in diverse cultural contexts, and in its inattention to examining the degree to which such theories themselves may be culturally bound and take somewhat contrasting forms in different cultural contexts. This stance represents perhaps the most central reason that mainstream psychologists have tended to view the findings of research on individualism-collectivism as primarily descriptive in nature rather than to view them as contributing to basic psychological theory (e.g., Shweder, 1990). The framework of individualism-collectivism has also been subject to criticism for its global view of culture: Much work in this tradition fails to account for subtleties in cultural meanings and practices, and it has also been criticized for the somewhat stereotypical nature of its portrayal of these two cultural systems (e.g., Dien, 1999). Thus, for example, as numerous theorists have noted (e.g., Markus & Kitayama, 1991; J. G. Miller, 1994, 2002; Rothbaum, Pott, Azuma, Miyake, &

Weisz, 2000), much work on individualism-collectivism has failed to recognize that concerns with self have importance in collectivist cultures rather than only in individualistic cultures—although they may take somewhat contrasting forms in the two cultural contexts, just as concerns with relationships have importance but may take different forms in the two cultural contexts. Finally, methodological criticisms have been directed at the widespread use of attitudinal scale measures in work in this tradition (e.g., Kitayama, 2002), with theorists noting the many problems associated with the limited ability of individuals to report on the orientations emphasized in their culture and with the inattention to everyday cultural practices, artifacts, and routines that has characterized much work in this tradition with its reliance on attitudinal indexes of culture.

The individualism-collectivism framework has made major and enduring contributions to understanding culture and society in ecological terms. Work in this tradition has been of great value in providing insight into processes of modernization and cultural change, and it has assisted in modeling how both factors in the physical environment and social structural considerations affect psychological outcomes. The broad framework of individualism-collectivism has also proven useful heuristically as a source of initial research hypotheses, with this distinction embraced—at least in a limited way—not only by investigators concerned with the more universalistic agenda of cross-cultural psychology, but also by some theorists identified more explicitly with cultural psychology (e.g., Greenfield & Suzuki, 1998).

Culture and Cognitive Development

Early work on culture and cognitive development was theoretically diverse and international in character, drawing on Piagetian as well as Vygotskiian viewpoints among others. Within Piagetian viewpoints, cross-cultural research was undertaken to test the presumed universality of cognitive developmental theory (Dasen, 1972; Dasen & Heron, 1981). This work involved administering standard Piagetian cognitive tests in different cultures after translating the tests and making minor modifications to ensure their ecological validity. Likewise, in the domain of moral development, Kohlbergian measures of moral judgment were administered in a large number of cultural settings after only minor changes in research protocols were made, such as substituting local names for those originally in the text (e.g., Edwards, 1986; Kohlberg, 1969; Snarey, 1985). The findings on Piagetian tasks suggested that in certain African settings, cognitive development proceeds at a slower rate than that observed in

Geneva, with the highest level of formal operations generally not obtained. Likewise, cross-cultural Kohlbergian research indicated that populations not exposed to higher levels of education do not reach the highest (postconventional) stage of moral judgment. Results of this type were generally interpreted as reflecting the cognitive richness of the environment that resulted in more advanced cognitive development in certain cultures over others. They were also interpreted as supporting the universality of cognitive developmental theory. It was concluded that culture is nonessential in development, in that the sequence and end point of developmental change are culturally invariant (e.g., Piaget, 1973).

Inspired by Vygotsky and other Soviet investigators (e.g., Vygotsky, 1929, 1934/1987; 1978; Luria, 1928, 1976), theorists in the early sociocultural tradition of cross-cultural research on cognitive development proceeded by undertaking experiments in diverse cultural settings. However, in contrast to cognitive developmental viewpoints, they assumed that cognitive development has a formative influence on the emergence of basic psychological processes. Rather than viewing development as proceeding independently of cultural learning, cultural learning was assumed to be necessary for development to proceed. Vygotskiian theory and related sociocultural approaches emphasized the importance of tool use in extending cognitive capacities. From this perspective, cultural transmission was assumed to be essential, with cognitive development involving the internalization of the tools provided by the culture. Among the key cultural tools assumed to transform minds were literacy and formal schooling, through their assumed effects of providing individuals exposure to abstract symbolic resources and giving rise to modes of reasoning that are relatively decontextualized and not directly tied to practical activity (e.g., Goody, 1968). In viewing cultural processes as a source of patterning of thought, work in the sociocultural tradition shared many assumptions with and may be considered part of cultural psychology. However, at least in its early years, research in this tradition focused on establishing the universality of basic cognitive processes; this linked it closely to other contemporary traditions of cross-cultural cognitive developmental research.

The earliest traditions of cross-cultural experimental research undertaken by sociocultural theorists resembled those of Piagetian researchers in both their methods and their findings. After making only minor modifications, experimental tests were administered to diverse cultural populations. These populations were selected to provide a contrast in the cultural processes thought to influence cognitive development, such as literacy and schooling (e.g., Bruner, Olver, & Greenfield, 1966; Cole, Gay, Glick, & Sharp, 1971). Results revealed

that individuals who were illiterate or who lacked formal education scored lower in cognitive development, failing to show such features as abstract conceptual development or propositional reasoning, which appeared as end points of cognitive development in Western industrialized contexts. Such findings supported a "primitive versus modern mind" interpretation of cultural differences, in which it was assumed that the cognitive development of certain populations remains arrested at lower developmental levels. This type of argument may be seen, for example, in the conclusion drawn by Greenfield and Bruner (1969) in drawing links between such observed cross-cultural differences and related differences found in research contrasting cognition among mainstream and minority communities within the United States:

> . . . As Werner (1948) pointed out, 'development among primitive people is characterized on the one hand by precocity and, on the other, by a relatively early arrest of the process of intellectual growth.' His remark is telling with respect to the difference we find between school children and those who have not been to school. The latter stabilize earlier and do not go on to new levels of operation. The same 'early arrest' characterizes the differences between 'culturally deprived' and other American children.
>   . . . Some environments 'push' cognitive growth better, earlier, and longer than others. . . . Less demanding societies—less demanding intellectually—do not produce so much symbolic embedding and elaboration of first ways of looking and thinking. (p. 654)

From this perspective, the impact of culture on thought was assumed to be highly general, with individuals fully internalizing the tools provided by their culture and that resulting in generalized cultural differences in modes of thought.

Later experimental research in the sociocultural tradition challenged these early conclusions about global differences in thought and about the transformative impact of cultural tools on minds. Programs of cross-cultural research were undertaken that focused on unpacking the complex cognitive processes that are tapped in standard cognitive tests and in assessing these components under diverse circumstances (Cole & Scribner, 1974). Thus, for example, rather than using the multiple objects that tended to be employed in Piagetian seriation tasks, with their extensive memory demands, researchers employed fewer objects in memory procedures. Also, processes such as memory were assessed in the context of socially meaningful material, such as stories, rather than merely in decontextualized ways, such as through the presentation of words. These and similar modifications showed that cognitive performance varied depending on features of the implications of features of the context (Bronfenbrenner, 1979). However, they also are limited in treating the context exclusively in objective terms, as presenting affordances and constraints that are functional in nature. In such frameworks, which have tended to be adopted in both mainstream and cross-cultural psychology, culture is seen as nonessential to interpretation or construction of reality. In contrast, within symbolic approaches, cultural systems are understood as bearing an indeterminate or open relationship to objective constraints rather than being fully determined by objective adaptive contingencies. Within symbolic approaches to culture, it is recognized that cultural meanings serve not merely to represent reality, as in knowledge systems, or to assume a directive function, as in systems of social norms. Rather, they are seen as also assuming constitutive or reality-creating roles. In this latter role, cultural meanings serve to create social realities, whose existence rests partly on these cultural definitions (Shweder, 1984). This includes not only cases in which culturally based social definitions are integral to establishing particular social institutions and practices (e.g., marriage, graduation, etc.) but also cases in which such definitions form a key role in creating psychological realities. Thus, it is increasingly recognized that aspects of psychological functioning (e.g., emotions) depend, in part, for their existence on cultural distinctions embodied in natural language categories, discourse, and everyday practices. For example, the Japanese emotional experience of *amae* (Doi, 1973; Yamaguchi, 2001) presupposes not only the concepts reflected in this label but also norms and practices that support and promote it. As an emotional state, *amae* involves a positive feeling of depending on another's benevolence. At the level of social practices, *amae* is evident not only in caregiver-child interactions in early infancy (Doi, 1973, 1992), but also in the everyday interactions of adults, who are able to presume that their inappropriate behavior will be accepted by their counterparts in close relationships (Yamaguchi, 2001).

The significance of a symbolic view of culture for the development of cultural psychology was in its complementing the attention to meaning-making heralded by the cognitive revolution. It became clear that not only were meanings in part socially constructed and publicly based, but they also could not be purely derived merely by inductive or deductive processing of objective information. Culture, then, in this way became an additional essential factor in psychological explanation, beyond merely a focus on objective features of the context and subjective features of the person.

Incompleteness Thesis

Finally, and most critically, the theoretical grounding of cultural psychology emerged from the realization of the necessary role of culture in completion of the self, an insight that has been termed the *incompleteness thesis* (Geertz, 1973; T. Schwartz, 1992). This stance does not assume the absence of innate capacities or downplay the impact of biological influences as a source of patterning of individual psychological processes. However, without making the assumption that psychological development is totally open in direction, with no biological influences either on its initial patterning or on its subsequent developmental course, this stance calls attention to the essential role of culture in the emergence of higher-order psychological processes. Individuals are viewed not only as developing in culturally specific environments and utilizing culturally specific tools, but also as carrying with them, in their language and meanings systems, culturally based assumptions through which they interpret experience. Although there has been a tendency within psychology to treat this culturally specific input as noise that should be filtered out or controlled in order to uncover basic features of psychological functioning, the present considerations suggest that it is omnipresent and cannot be held constant or eliminated. Rather, it is understood that the culturally specific meanings and practices that are essential for the emergence of higher-order psychological processes invariably introduce a certain cultural-historical specificity to psychological functioning, as Geertz (1973) once noted:

> We are . . . incomplete or unfinished animals who complete or finish ourselves through culture—and not through culture in general but through highly particular forms of it. (p. 49)

From the present perspective, it is assumed that whereas an involuntary response may proceed without cultural mediation, culture is necessary for the emergence of higher-order psychological processes. Wertsch (1995) articulates this point:

> Cultural, institutional, and historical forces are 'imported' into individuals' actions by virtue of using cultural tools, on the one hand, and sociocultural settings are created and recreated through individuals' use of mediational means, on the other. The resulting picture is one in which, because of the role cultural tools play in mediated action, it is virtually impossible for us to act in a way that is not socioculturally situated. Nearly all human action is mediated action, the only exceptions being found perhaps at very early stages of ontogenesis and in natural responses such as reacting involuntarily to an unexpected loud noise. (p. 160)

Thus, for example, whereas involuntary physiological reactions may be elicited by situational events, whether they become interpreted and experienced in emotional terms depends in part on such input as culturally based theories regarding the nature, causes, and consequences of emotions, cultural routines for responding to emotions, natural language categories for defining emotions, and a range of other sociocultural processes.

This assumption of the interdependence of psychological and cultural processes represents the central idea of cultural psychology. Notably, the term *cultural psychology* was selected by theorists to convey this central insight that psychological processes need to be understood as always grounded in particular socio-cultural-historical contexts that influence their form and patterning, just as cultural communities depend for their existence on particular communities of intentional agents. The present considerations then lead to the expectation that qualitative differences in modes of psychological functioning will be observed among individuals from cultural communities characterized by contrasting self-related sociocultural meanings and practices.

Summary

Among the key conceptual insights giving rise to cultural psychology were the emergence of a view of the individual as actively contributing meanings to experience and an understanding of culture as a symbolic system of meanings and practices that cannot be explained exclusively in functional terms as mapping onto objective adaptive constraints. Crucial to the field's development was that it also came to be recognized that higher-order psychological processes depend for their emergence on individuals' participation in particular sociocultural contexts, and thus that culture is fundamental to the development of self.

Select Overview of Empirical Research in Cultural Psychology

The present section examines representative examples of empirical studies that embody this core insight regarding the cultural grounding of psychological processes, an insight that is central to the many traditions of work in cultural psychology (e.g., Cole, 1990, 1996; Markus et al., 1996; J. G. Miller, 1997; Shweder, 1990; Shweder et al., 1998). Although the overview presented here is necessarily highly selective and incomplete, it serves to illustrate ways in which cultural research is offering new process explanations of psychological phenomena as well as identifying fundamental variability in the forms that psychological processes assume.

Sociocultural Traditions of Research

The discussion here makes reference to findings from a diverse range of related viewpoints that have derived from the work of such major cultural theorists as Vygotsky (1978, 1981a, 1981b), Leontiev (1979a, 1979b), Luria (1979, 1981), Bakhtin (1986), and Bourdieu (1977) among others; their work is reflected in the many contemporary traditions of research in sociocultural psychology (e.g., Cole, 1988, 1990; Rogoff, 1990; Valsiner, 1988, 1989; Wertsch, 1979, 1991). Central to theoretical work within this tradition is an emphasis on the mediated nature of cognition. Human behavior is seen as dependent on cultural tools or on other mediational means, with language recognized as one of the most central of these cultural supports. Embodying a broad lens, sociocultural approaches focus on understanding human activity at phylogenetic, historical, ontogenetic, and microgenetic levels, with cultural practices and activities viewed in terms of their place in larger sociopolitical contexts.

Considerable research in this area focuses on documenting how interaction with cultural tools and participation in everyday cultural activities leads to powerful domain-specific changes in thought. In work on everyday cognition (see review in Schliemann, Carraher, & Ceci, 1997), it has been shown, in fact, that everyday experiences can produce changes that represent an advance on those produced by schooling. For example, Scribner (1984) documented that individuals who work as preloaders in a milk factory and have less formal education than do white-collar workers are able to solve a simulated loading task more rapidly than do white-collar workers through using a more efficient perceptual solution strategy as contrasted with a slower enumerative approach. Likewise, in a growing body of research on expertise, it has been revealed, for example, that compared with novice adult chess players, child chess experts use more complex clustering strategies in organization and retrieval of chess information; they are also more proficient in their memory for chess pieces (Chi, Glaser, & Farr, 1998). Similar effects have equally been shown to occur in the solving of math problems among expert versus novice abacus users (Stigler, 1984).

It is important to note that sociocultural research is also providing new process models of the nature of everyday cognition. For example, recent research on situated cognition has challenged the view of learning as a distinct activity or as an end in itself set off from daily life and has emphasized its embeddedness in everyday activities and social contexts (Lave, 1988, 1993; Lave & Wenger, 1991). Research has revealed, for example, that in contrast to the forms of instruction that occur in formal school settings, learning in everyday situations is more oriented toward practical problems. In part as a result, individuals tend to be more motivationally involved in tasks and spontaneously to search for and generate more flexible task solutions in everyday situations than they do in formal school contexts.

practices affect the degree to which particular emotions are *hypercognized* (in the sense that they are highly differentiated and implicated in many everyday cultural concepts and practices) versus *hypocognized* (in that there is little cognitive or behavioral elaboration of them; Levy, 1984). Even universal emotions, it has been observed, play contrasting roles in individual experience in different cultural settings. For example, whereas in all cultures both socially engaged feelings (e.g., friendliness, connection) and socially disengaged feelings (e.g., pride, feelings of superiority) may exist, among the Japanese only socially engaged feelings are linked with general positive feelings, whereas among Americans both types of emotions have positive links (Kitayama, Markus, & Kurokawa, 2000).

Cross-cultural differences have also been observed in emotion categories as well as in individuals' appraisals of emotions. Thus, variation in emotion concepts has been documented not only in the case of culturally specific categories of emotion, such as the concept of *amae* among the Japanese (Russell & Yik, 1996; Wierzbicka, 1992), but also among such assumed basic emotions as anger and sadness (Russell, 1991, 1994). It has been shown that Turkish adults make systematically different appraisals of common emotional experiences than do Dutch adults, whose cultural background is more individualist (Mesquita, 2001). Thus, as compared with Dutch adults' appraisals, Turkish adults tend to categorize emotions as more grounded in assessments of social worth, as more reflective of reality than of the inner subjective states of the individual, and as located more within the self-other relationship than confined within the subjectivity of the individual.

Notably, work on culture and emotions is also providing evidence of the open relationship that exists between physiological and somatic reactions and emotional experiences. For example, research has revealed that although Minangkabu and American men show the same patterns of autonomic nervous system arousal to voluntary posing of prototypical emotion facial expressions, they differ in their emotional experiences (Levenson, Ekman, Heider, & Friesen, 1992). Whereas the Americans tend to interpret their arousal in this type of situation in emotional terms, Minangkabu tend not to experience an emotion in such cases, because it violates their culturally based assumptions that social relations constitute an essential element in emotional experience.

Finally, important cultural influences on the mental health consequences of affective arousal are also being documented. For example, various somatic experiences—such as fatigue, loss of appetite, or agitation—that are given a psychological interpretation as emotions by European-Americans tend not to be interpreted in emotional terms but rather as purely physiological events among individuals from various Asian, South American, and African cultural backgrounds (Shweder, Much, Mahapatra, & Park, 1997). It is notable that such events tend to be explained as originating in problems of interpersonal relationships, thus requiring some form of nonpsychological form of intervention for their amelioration (Rosaldo, 1984; White, 1994).

Motivation

Whereas early cross-cultural research was informed exclusively by existing theoretical models, such as Rotter's framework of internal versus external locus of control (Rotter, 1966), recent work is suggesting that motivation may assume socially shared forms. This kind of focus, for example, is reflected in the construct of *secondary control,* which has been identified among Japanese populations, in which individuals are seen as demonstrating agency via striving to adjust to situational demands (Morling, 2000; Morling, Kitayama, & Miyamoto, 2000; Weisz et al., 1984). Equally, work in India has also pointed to the existence of joint forms of control, in which the agent and the family or other social group are experienced as together agentic in bringing forth certain outcomes (Sinha, 1990).

In another related area of work on motivation, research is highlighting the positive affective associations linked with fulfillment of role-related responsibilities. This type of documentation notably challenges what has been the assumption informing much psychological theory—that behavior is experienced as most agentic when it is freely chosen rather than socially constrained and that social expectations are invariably experienced as impositions on individual freedom of choice. For example, behavioral research on intrinsic motivation has documented that Asian-American children experience higher intrinsic motivation for an anagrams task that has been selected for them by their mothers than for one that they have freely chosen (Iyengar & Lepper, 1999). In contrast, it is shown that European-American children experience greater intrinsic motivation when they have selected such a task for themselves.

Further support for this view that agency is compatible with meeting role expectations may be seen in attributional research, which has documented that Indian adults indicate that they would want to help as much and derive as much satisfaction in helping when acting to fulfill norms of reciprocity as when acting in the absence of such normative expectations (J. G. Miller & Bersoff, 1994). Such a trend contrasts with that observed among Americans, who assume that greater satisfaction is associated with more freely chosen helping. These kinds of results challenge prevailing models of communal relationships, which assume that a concern with obligation detracts from a concern with being responsive to the others' needs (Mills & Clark, 1982). They also challenge models of self-determination, which assume that internalization involves a greater sense of perceived autonomy (Deci & Ryan, 1985). Rather, it appears that in certain collectivist cultures individuals may experience their behavior as demanded by role requirements, while also experiencing themselves as strongly endorsing, choosing to engage in, and deriving satisfaction from the behavior.

In turn, work in the area of morality, relationships, and attachment highlights the need to expand current conceptualizations of motivation. For example, research in the domain of morality with both Hindu Indian populations (Shweder, Mahapatra, & Miller, 1990) as well as with orthodox religious communities within the United States (Jensen, 1997) has documented forms of morality based on concerns with divinity that are not encompassed in existing psychological theories of morality, with their exclusive stress on issues of justice, individual rights, and community (e.g., Kohlberg, 1971; Turiel, 1983). Furthermore, work on moralities of community have documented the highly individualistic cultural assumptions that inform Gilligan's morality of caring framework (Gilligan, 1982), with its emphasis on the voluntaristic nature of interpersonal commitments. Cross-cultural work conducted on the morality of caring among Hindu Indian populations and cross-cultural work conducted utilizing Kohlbergian methodology have uncovered the existence of forms of duty-based moralities of caring that although fully moral in character, differ qualitatively in key respects from those explained within Gilligan's framework (J. G. Miller, 1994, 2001b; Snarey & Keljo, 1991).

In terms of relationship research, a growing cross-cultural literature on attachment is suggesting that some of the observed variation in distribution of secure versus nonsecure forms of attachment arises at least in part from contrasting cultural values related to attachment, rather than from certain cultural subgroups' having less adaptive styles of attachment than others. For example, research conducted among Puerto Rican families suggests that some of the greater tendency of children to show highly dependent forms of attachment reflects the contrasting meanings that they place on interdependent behavior (Harwood, Miller, & Irizarry, 1995). Thus, an analysis of open-ended responses of mothers revealed that compared with European-American mothers, Puerto Rican mothers viewed dependent behavior relatively positively as evidence of the child's relatedness to the mother. Suggesting that present dimensions of attachment may not be fully capturing salient concerns for Puerto Rican mothers, this work further demonstrated that Puerto Rican mothers spontaneously emphasized other concerns—such as display of respect and of tranquility—that are not tapped by present attachment formulations.

In other research, recent work on attachment among Japanese populations highlights the greater emphasis on indulgence of the infant's dependency and on affectively based rather than informationally oriented communication in Japanese versus American families (Rothbaum, Weisz, Pott, Miyake, & Morelli, 2000). In contrast to the predictions of attachment theory, however, such forms of parenting are not linked with maladaptive outcomes; rather, these parenting styles have positive adaptive implications, in fitting in with the cultural value placed on *amae,* an orientation that involves presuming upon another's dependency and plays an important role in close relationships throughout the life cycle. Such research has pointed out that the common finding that Japanese attachment more frequently takes what are considered as insecure or overly dependent forms reflects biases in present conceptions of attachment, which fail to take into account the concerns with interdependence in the Japanese context. Furthermore, it is noted that methodologically, the attachment research paradigm presents a separation context that is much rarer and thus much more stressful for Japanese than for American infants. Equally, it is suggested that (rather than treat the individual as the unit of attachment) to fully capture Japanese attachment-related concerns would require treating the individual-caregiver unit rather than the individual alone as the object of attachment assessment, with a focus on how well individuals can anticipate each other's responses.

Summary

Work in cultural psychology is not only documenting cultural variability in psychological outcomes, but is also focused on uncovering respects in which this variation has theoretical implications in pointing to the implicit cultural underpinnings of existing psychological effects, as well as respects in which psychological theory needs to be conceptually expanded to account for culturally diverse modes of psychological functioning. We have seen specifically that cultural work is highlighting the culturally mediated nature of cognition through individuals' participation in everyday cultural practices and use of culturally specific tools; such work has also uncovered the existence of contrasting culturally based cognitive styles, as well as extensive cultural variation in basic psychological processes involving the self, emotions, and motivation.

research that is informed by in-depth understandings of different cultural communities will become more common in psychology in the future. As the field becomes increasingly international and culturally diverse, investigators will be able to bring to their research cultural sensitivities and concerns contrasting with those presently dominating the discipline.

There is equally a need for future research on culture to become increasingly interdisciplinary, with investigators taking into account the conceptual and methodological insights of anthropological and sociolinguistic research traditions and avoiding the present insularity that results from ignoring or dismissing work from different disciplinary viewpoints. This neglect can yield findings considered to have relatively little importance from the perspective of the other traditions. However, given the overlap in concerns across these research traditions and given their contrasting strengths, greater interdisciplinary exchange can only serve to enhance progress in the field.

Summary

To enhance the quality of existing cultural research, it is important for investigators to go beyond dichotomous frameworks for understanding cultural differences, such as the global dimensions of individualism-collectivism. These types of frameworks fail to capture the complexity of individual cultural systems, portraying cultures in ways that are overly static, uniform, and isolated. Effort must be made to develop more nuanced views of culture through attending to everyday cultural activities and practices as well as to symbolic culture and ecological dimensions of contexts. Additionally, attention must be given both to individual differences and to cultural influences—the assumption should not be made that individual differences map directly onto cultural variation. Finally, the sensitivity of cultural research stands to be enhanced through researchers' working to gain a greater understanding of the specific cultural communities which they study.

CONCLUSION

In conclusion, the present examination of culture in social psychological theory highlights the importance of recognizing that culture is part of human experience and needs to be an explicit part of psychological theories that purport to predict, explain, and understand that experience. What work in culture aims to achieve, and what it has already accomplished in many respects, is more than to lead investigators to treat psychological findings and processes as limited in generality. Rather than leading to an extreme relativism that precludes

comparison, work in this area holds the promise of leading to the formulation of models of human experience that are increasingly culturally inclusive. By calling attention to the cultural meanings and practices that form the implicit context for existing psychological effects, and by broadening present conceptions of the possibilities of human psychological functioning, work in cultural psychology is contributing new constructs, research questions, and theoretical insights to expand and enrich basic psychological theory.

REFERENCES

Adorno, T., Frenkel-Brunswick, E., Levinson, D. J., & Sanford, R. N. (1950). *The authoritarian personality*. New York: Harper & Brothers.

Bakhtin, M. M. (1986). *Speech genres and other late essays* (V. W. McGee, Trans.). Austin: University of Texas Press.

Bargh, J. A. (1996). Automaticity in social psychology. In E. T. Higgins & A. Kruglanski (Eds.), *Social psychology: Handbook of basic principles* (pp. 169–183). New York: Guilford Press.

Benedict, R. (1932). Configurations of culture in North America. *American Anthropologist, 34,* 1–27.

Benedict, R. (1946). *The chrysanthemum and the sword*. Boston: Houghton Mifflin.

Berry, J. W., Poortinga, Y. H., Segall, M. H., & Dasen, P. R. (1992). *Cross-cultural psychology: Research and applications*. Cambridge, UK: Cambridge University Press.

Bornstein, R. F., Kale, A. R., & Cornell, K. R. (1990). Boredom as a limiting condition on the mere exposure effect. *Journal of Personality and Social Psychology, 42,* 239–247.

Bourdieu, P. (1977). *Outline of a theory of practice* (R. Nice, Trans.). Cambridge, UK: Cambridge University Press.

Brislin, R. W. (1983). Cross-cultural research in psychology. *Annual Review of Psychology, 34,* 363–400.

Bronfenbrenner, U. (1979). *The ecology of human development: Experiments by nature and design*. Cambridge, MA: Harvard University Press.

Bruner, J. S. (1990). *Acts of meaning*. Cambridge, MA: Harvard University Press.

Bruner, J. S., Olver, R. R., & Greenfield, P. M. (1966). *Studies in cognitive growth: A collaboration at the Center for Cognitive Studies*. New York: Wiley.

Chi, M. T. H., Glaser, R., & Farr, M. (1988). *The nature of expertise*. Hillsdale, NJ: Erlbaum.

Cole, M. (1988). Cross-cultural research in the sociohistorical tradition. *Human Development, 31*(3), 137–152.

Cole, M. (1990). Cultural psychology: A once and future discipline? In J. J. Berman (Ed.), *Nebraska Symposium on Motivation: Vol. 38. Cross-cultural perspectives* (pp. 279–335). Lincoln: University of Nebraska Press.

Cole, M. (1996). *Cultural psychology: A once and future discipline.* Cambridge, MA: Harvard University Press.

Cole, M., & Engestroem, Y. (1995). Mind, culture, person: Elements in a cultural psychology [Comment]. *Human Development, 38*(1), 19–24.

Cole, M., Gay, J., Glick, J., & Sharp, D. W. (1971). *The cultural context of learning and thinking.* New York: Basic Books.

Cole, M., & Scribner, S. (1974). *Culture and thought: A psychological introduction.* New York: Wiley.

Cousins, S. D. (1989). Culture and self-perception in Japan and the United States. *Journal of Personality and Social Psychology, 56,* 124–131.

Crystal, D. S., & Stevenson, H. W. (1991). Mothers' perceptions of children's problems with mathematics: A cross-national comparison. *Journal of Educational Psychology, 83*(3), 372–376.

Dasen, P. R. (1972). Cross-cultural Piagetian research: A summary. *Journal of Cross-Cultural Psychology, 7,* 75–85.

Dasen, P. R., & Heron, A. (1981). Cross-cultural tests of Piaget's theory. In H. C. Triandis & A. Heron (Eds.), *Handbook of cross-cultural psychology, Vol. 4: Developmental psychology* (pp. 295–342). Boston: Allyn & Bacon.

Deci, E. L., & Ryan, R. M. (1985). *Intrinsic motivation and self-determination in human behavior.* New York: Plenum Press.

Dien, D. S. (1999). Chinese authority-directed orientation and Japanese peer-group orientation: Questioning the notion of collectivism. *Review of General Psychology, 3*(4), 372–385.

Diener, E., & Diener, M. (1995). Cross-cultural correlates of life satisfaction and self-esteem. *Journal of Personality & Social Psychology, 68*(4), 653–663.

Diener, E., Diener, M., & Diener, C. (1995). Factors predicting the subjective well-being of nations. *Journal of Personality Psychology, 69*(5), 851–864.

Doi, T. (1973). *Anatomy of dependence.* Tokyo: Kodansha International Press.

Doi, T. (1992). On the concept of *amae. Infant Mental Health Journal, 13,* 7–11.

Edwards, C. (1986). Cross-cultural research on Kohlberg's stages: the basis for consensus. In S. Modgil & C. Modgil (Eds.), *Kohlberg: Consensus and controversy* (pp. 419–430). Philadelphia: Falmer Press.

Festinger, L. (1957). *A theory of cognitive dissonance.* Stanford, CA: Stanford University Press.

Fromm, E. (1941). *Escape from freedom.* New York: Farrar & Rinehart.

Gabrenya, W. K., Jr., & Hwang, K.-K. (1996). Chinese social interaction: Harmony and hierarchy on the good earth, *The handbook of Chinese psychology* (pp. 309–321). Hong Kong: Oxford University Press.

Geertz, C. (1973). *The interpretation of cultures.* New York: Basic Press.

Gilligan, C. (1982). *In a different voice: Psychological theory and women's development.* Cambridge, MA: Harvard University Press.

Goody, J. (Ed.). (1968). *Literacy in traditional societies.* New York: Cambridge University Press.

Gorer, G. (1955). *Exploring English character.* New York: Criterion Books.

Gorer, G., & Rickman, J. (1962). *The people of Great Russia.* New York: W. W. Norton.

Graham, S. (1992). Most of the subjects were White and middle class: Trends in published research on African Americans in selected APA journals, 1970–1989. *American Psychologist, 47*(5), 629–639.

Greenfield, P. M. (1997). Culture as process: Empirical methods for cultural psychology. In J. W. Berry, Y. H. Poortinga, & J. Pandey (Eds.), *Handbook of cross-cultural psychology: Vol. 1. Theory and method* (2nd ed., pp. 301–346). Boston: Allyn & Bacon.

Greenfield, P. M., & Bruner, J. S. (1969). Culture and cognitive growth. In D. A. Goslin (Ed.), *Handbook of socialization theory and research* (pp. 633–657). Chicago: Rand-McNally.

Greenfield, P. M., & Cocking, R. R. (Eds.). (1994). *Cross-cultural roots of minority child development.* Hillsdale, NJ: Erlbaum.

Greenfield, P. M., & Suzuki, L. (1998). Culture and human development: Implications for parenting, education, pediatrics, and mental health. In I. E. Sigel & K. A. Renninger (Eds.), *Handbook of child psychology* (Vol. 4, pp. 1059–1109). New York: Wiley.

Gudykunst, W. B., Yoon, Y., & Nishida, S. (1987). The influence of individualism-collectivism on perceptions of communication in ingroup and outgroup relationships. *Communication Monographs, 54,* 295–306.

Haney, C., Banks, C., & Zimbardo, P. (1973). Interpersonal dynamics in a simulated prison. *International Journal of Criminology and Penology, 1,* 69–97.

Harwood, R. L., Miller, J. G., & Irizarry, N. L. (1995). *Culture and attachment : Perceptions of the child in context.* New York: Guilford Press.

Heath, S. B. (1983). *Ways with words: Language, life, and work in communities and classrooms.* Cambridge, UK: Cambridge University Press.

Heine, S. J., & Lehman, D. R. (1997). Culture, dissonance, and self-affirmation. *Personality & Social Psychology Bulletin, 23*(4), 389–400.

Heine, S. J., & Morikawa, S. (2000). [Cultural differences in motivated reasoning biases]. Unpublished raw data, University of British Columbia.

Heine, S. H., Lehman, D. R., Markus, H. R., & Kitayama, S. (1999). Is there a universal need for positive self-regard? *Psychological Review, 106*(4), 766–794.

Herzog, A. R., Franks, M. M., Markus, H. R., & Holmberg, D. (1998). Activities and well-being in older age: Effects of self-concept and educational attainment. *Psychology & Aging, 13*(2), 179–185.

Higgins, E. T., & Kruglanski, A. W. (1996). *Social psychology: Handbook of basic principles.* New York: Guilford Press.

Hofstede, G. (1980). *Culture's consequences.* Beverly Hills, CA: Sage.

Honigmann, J. J. (1954). *Culture and personality.* New York: Harper and Row.

Hsu, F. L. K. (1963). *Clan, caste and club.* New York: van Nostrand.

Hsu, F. L. K. (1985). The self in cross-cultural perspective. In A. J. Marsella, G. DeVos, & F. L. K. Hsu (Eds.), *Culture and self: Asian and western perspectives* (pp. 24–55). London: Tavistock.

Inkeles, A. (1974). *Becoming modern: Individual change in six developing countries.* Cambridge, MA: Harvard University Press.

Irwin, M. H., & McLaughlin, D. H. (1970). Ability and preference in category sorting by Mano schoolchildren and adults. *Journal of Social Psychology, 82,* 15–24.

Iyengar, S. S., & Lepper, M. R. (1999). Rethinking the value of choice: A cultural perspective on intrinsic motivation. *Journal of Personality & Social Psychology, 76*(3), 349–366.

Jahoda, G. (1993). *Crossroads between culture and mind: Continuities and change in theories of human nature.* Cambridge, MA: Harvard University Press.

Jensen, L. A. (1997). Different worldviews, different morals: America's culture war divide. *Human Development, 40*(6), 325–344.

Ji, L.-J., Peng, K., & Nisbett, R. E. (2000). Culture, control, and perception of relationships in the environment. *Journal of Personality & Social Psychology, 78*(5), 943–955.

Jourard, S. M. (1965). *Personal adjustment: An approach through the study of healthy personality.* New York: Macmillan.

Kanagawa, C., Cross, S. E., & Markus, H. R. (2001). "Who am I?": The cultural psychology of the conceptual self. *Personality and Social Psychology Bulletin, 27*(1), 1557–1564.

Kardiner, A. (1945). *Psychological frontiers of society.* New York: Columbia University Press.

Kashima, Y., Siegal, M., Tanaka, K., & Kashima, E. S. (1992). Do people believe behaviours are consistent with attitudes? Towards a cultural psychology of attribution processes. *British Journal of Social Psychology, 31*(2), 111–124.

Kim, M.-S., Sharkey, W. F., & Singelis, T. M. (1994). Relationship between individuals' self-construals and perceived importance of interactive constraints. *International Journal of Intercultural Relations, 18,* 117–140.

Kitayama, S. (2002). Culture and basic psychological processes: Toward a system view of culture: Comment on Oyserman et al. (2002). *Psychological Bulletin, 128*(1), 89–96.

Kitayama, S., Markus, H. R., & Kurokawa, M. (2000). Culture, emotion, and well-being: Good feelings in Japan and the United States. *Cognition & Emotion, 14*(1), 93–124.

Kohlberg, L. (1969). Stage and sequence: The cognitive-developmental approach to socialization. In D. A. Goslin (Ed.), *Handbook of socialization theory* (pp. 347–380). Chicago: Rand-McNally.

Kohlberg, L. (1971). From is to ought: How to commit the naturalistic fallacy and get away with it in the study of moral development. In T. Mischel (Ed.), *Cognitive development and epistemology* (pp. 151–236). New York: Academic Press.

Kusserow, A. S. (1999). De-homogenizing American individualism: Socializing hard and soft individualism in Manhattan and Queens. *Ethos, 27*(2), 210–234.

Lave, J. (1988). *Cognition in practice: Mind, mathematics, and culture in everyday life.* Cambridge, UK: Cambridge University Press.

Lave, J. (1993). The practice of learning. In S. Chaiklin & J. Lave (Eds.), *Understanding practice: Perspectives on activity and context* (pp. 3–32). Cambridge, UK: Cambridge University Press.

Lave, J., & Wenger, E. (1991). *Situated learning: Legitimate peripheral participation.* Cambridge, UK: Cambridge University Press.

Leontiev, A. N. (1979a). The problem of activity in psychology. In J. V. Wertsch (Ed.), *The concept of activity in Soviet psychology* (pp. 37–71). Armonk, NY: M. E. Sharpe.

Leontiev, A. N. (1979b). Sign and activity. In J. V. Wertsch (Ed.), *The concept of activity in Soviet psychology* (pp. 241–255). Armonk, NY: M. E. Sharpe.

Levenson, R. W., Ekman, P., Heider, K., & Friesen, W. V. (1992). Emotion and autonomic nervous system activity in the Minangkabau of West Sumatra. *Journal of Personality and Social Psychology, 62,* 972–988.

LeVine, R. A. (1973). *Culture, behavior and personality.* Chicago: Aldine.

Levy, R. I. (1984). Emotion, knowing, and culture. In R. A. Shweder & R. A. LeVine (Eds.), *Culture theory: Essays on mind, self, and emotion* (pp. 214–237). Cambridge, UK: Cambridge University Press.

Lillard, A. (1998). Ethnopsychologies: Cultural variations in theories of mind. *Psychological Bulletin, 123,* 1–32.

Luria, A. R. (1928). The problem of the cultural development of the child. *Journal of Genetic Psychology, 35,* 493–506.

Luria, A. R. (1976). *Cognitive development: Its cultural and social foundations.* Cambridge, MA: Harvard University Press.

Luria, A. R. (1979). *The making of the mind: A personal account of Soviet psychology.* Cambridge, MA: Harvard University Press.

Luria, A. R. (1981). *Language and cognition* (J. V. Wertsch, Ed. & Trans.). New York: Wiley.

Lutz, C., & White, G. (1986). The anthropology of emotions. *Annual Review of Anthropology, 15,* 405–436.

Ma, H. K. (1988). The Chinese perspective on moral judgment development. *International Journal of Psychology, 23,* 201–227.

Ma, H. K. (1989). Moral orientation and moral judgment in adolescents in Hong Kong, Mainland China, and England. *Journal of Cross-Cultural Psychology, 20,* 152–177.

Malinowski, D. (1959). *Sex and repression in savage society.* New York: Meridan Books.

Malpass, R. S. (1988). Why not cross-cultural psychology?: A characterization of some mainstream views. In M. H. Bond (Ed.), *The cross-cultural challenge to social psychology: Cross-cultural research and methodology series* (pp. 29–35). Beverly Hills, CA: Sage.

Markus, H. R., & Kitayama, S. (1991). Culture and the self: Implications for cognition, emotion, and motivation. *Psychological Review, 98*(2), 224–253.

Markus, H. R., Kitayama, S., & Heiman, R. J. (1996). Culture and "basic" psychological principles. In E. T. Higgins & A. W. Kruglanski (Eds.), *Social psychology: Handbook of basic principles* (pp. 857–913). New York: Guilford Press.

Markus, H. R., Mullally, P. R., & Kitayama, S. (1997). Selfways: Diversity in modes of cultural participation. *In The conceptual self in context: Culture, experience, self-understanding* (pp. 13–61). New York: Cambridge University Press.

Matsumoto, D. (1999). Culture and self: An empirical assessment of Markus and Kitayama's theory of independent and interdependent self-construals. *Asian Journal of Social Psychology, 2,* 289–310.

McLoyd, V. (1990). The impact of economic hardship on Black families and children: Psychological distress, parenting, and socioemotional development. *Child Development: Special Issue: Minority children, 61*(2), 311–346.

Mead, M. (1928). *Coming of age in Samoa.* New York: Morrow.

Mead, M. (1939). *From the South Seas.* New York: Morrow.

Mesquita, B. (2001). Emotions in collectivist and individualist contexts. *Journal of Personality and Social Psychology, 80*(1), 68–74.

Milgram, S. (1963). The behavioral study of obedience. *Journal of Abnormal and Social Psychology, 67,* 467–472.

Miller, J. G. (1984). Culture and the development of everyday social explanation. *Journal of Personality & Social Psychology, 46*(5), 961–978.

Miller, J. G. (1987). Cultural influences on the development of conceptual differentiation in person description. *British Journal of Developmental Psychology, 5*(4), 309–319.

Miller, J. G. (1994). Cultural diversity in the morality of caring: Individually oriented versus duty-based interpersonal moral codes. *Cross-Cultural Research, 28*(1), 3–39.

Miller, J. G. (1997). Theoretical issues in cultural psychology. In J. W. Berry, Y. H. Poortinga, & J. Pandey (Eds.), *Handbook of cross-cultural psychology: Vol. 1. Theory and method* (2nd ed., pp. 85–128). Boston: Allyn & Bacon.

Miller, J. G. (2001a). The cultural grounding of social psychological theory. In A. Tesser & N. Schwarz (Eds.), *Blackwell Handbook of Social Psychology: Vol. 1. Intrapersonal processes* (pp. 22–43). Malden, MA: Blackwell.

Miller, J. G. (2001b). Culture and moral development. In D. Matsumoto (Ed.), *The handbook of culture and psychology* (pp. 151–169). New York: Oxford University Press.

Miller, J. G. (2002). Bringing culture to basic psychological theory: Beyond individualism and collectivism: Comment on Oyserman et al. (2002). *Psychological Bulletin, 128*(1), 97–109.

Miller, J. G., & Bersoff, D. M. (1994). Cultural influences on the moral status of reciprocity and the discounting of endogenous motivation [Special issue]. *Personality and Social Psychology Bulletin: The self and the collective, 20*(5), 592–602.

Miller, P. (1986). Teasing as language socialization and verbal play in a white working-class community. In B. B. Schieffelin & E. Ochs (Eds.), *Language socialization across cultures* (pp. 199–212). New York: Cambridge University Press.

Mills, J., & Clark, M. (1982). Communal and exchange relationships. In L. Wheeler (Ed.), *Review of personality and social psychology* (pp. 121–144). Beverly Hills, CA: Sage.

Morling, B. (2000). "Taking" an aerobics class in the U.S. and "Entering" an aerobics class in Japan: Primary and secondary control in a fitness context. *Asian Journal of Social Psychology, 3,* 73–85.

Morling, B., Kitayama, S., & Miyamoto, Y. (2000). Control and adjustment as two modes of constructing social situations: A comparison between Japan and the U.S. Manuscript submitted for publication.

Moscovici, S. (1972). Society and theory in social psychology. In J. Israel & H. Tajfel (Eds.), *The context of social psychology: A critical assessment* (pp. 17–69). New York: Academic Press.

Nisbett, R. E., & Cohen, D. (1996). *Culture of honor: The psychology of violence in the South.* Boulder, CO: Westview Press.

Nisbett, R. E., & Ross, L. (1980). *Human inference: Strategies and shortcomings of social judgment.* Englewood Cliffs, NJ: Prentice Hall.

Ochs, E., & Schieffelin, B. B. (1984). Language acquisition and socialization: Three developmental stories and their implications. In R. A. Shweder & R. A. LeVine (Eds.), *Culture theory: Essays on mind, self, and emotion* (pp. 276–320). Cambridge, UK: Cambridge University Press.

Oyserman, D., Coon, H., & Kemmelmeier, M. (2002). Rethinking individualism and collectivism: Evaluation of theoretical assumptions and meta-analyses. *Psychological Bulletin, 128*(1), 3–72.

Peng, K., & Nisbett, R. E. (1999). Culture, dialectics, and reasoning about contradiction. *American Psychologist, 54*(9), 741–754.

Pepitone, A., & Triandis, H. C. (1987). On the universality of social psychological theories. *Journal of Cross-Cultural Psychology, 18,* 471–499.

Piaget, J. (1973). Need and significance of cross-cultural studies in genetic psychology. In J. W. Berry & P. R. Dasen (Eds.), *Culture and cognition: Readings in cross-cultural psychology* (pp. 299–309). London: Methuen.

Reid, P. T. (1988). Racism and sexism: Comparisons and conflicts. In P. Katz & D. Taylor (Eds.), *Eliminating racism: Profiles in controversy* (pp. 203–221). New York: Plenum Press.

Reid, P. T. (1994). The real problem in the study of culture. *American Psychologist, 49*(6), 524–525.

Rogoff, B. (1990). *Apprenticeship in thinking: Cognitive development in social context.* New York: Oxford University Press.

Rogoff, B. (1996). Developmental transitions in children's participation in sociocultural activities. In M. H. Arnold Sameroff (Ed.), *The five to seven year shift: The age of reason and responsibility* (pp. 273–294). Chicago: University of Chicago Press.

Rosaldo, M. A. (1984). Toward an anthropology of self and feeling. In R. A. Shweder & R. A. LeVine (Eds.), *Culture theory : Essays on mind, self, and emotion* (pp. 137–157). New York: Cambridge University Press.

Ross, M. (1989). Relation of implicit theories to the construction of personal histories. *Psychological Review, 96,* 341–357.

Rothbaum, F., Pott, M., Azuma, H., Miyake, K., & Weisz, J. (2000). The development of close relationships in Japan and the United States: Paths and symbiotic harmony and generative tension. *Child Development, 71*(5), 1121–1142.

Rothbaum, F., Weisz, J., Pott, M., Miyake, K., & Morelli, G. (2000). Attachment and culture: Security in the United States and Japan. *American Psychologist, 55*(10), 1093–1104.

Rotter, J. G. (1966). Generalized expectancies for internal versus external locus of control of reinforcement. *Psychological Monographs: General and Applied, 80* (Whole No. 609).

Russell, J. A. (1991). Culture and the categorization of emotions. *Psychological Bulletin, 110,* 426–450.

Russell, J. A. (1994). Is there universal recognition of emotion from facial expression? A review of the cross-cultural studies. *Psychological Bulletin, 115*(1), 102–141.

Russell, J. A., & Yik, M. S. M. (1996). Emotion among the Chinese. In M. H. Bond (Ed.), *The handbook of Chinese psychology* (pp. 166–188). Hong Kong: Oxford University Press.

Sahlins, M. (1976). *Culture and practical reason.* Chicago: University of Chicago Press.

Schliemann, A., Carraher, D., & Ceci, S. (1997). Everyday cognition. In J. W. Berry, Y. H. Poortinga, & J. Pandey (Eds.), *Handbook of cross-cultural psychology: Vol. 2. Basic processes and human development* (2nd ed., pp. 177–216). Needham Heights, MA: Allyn & Bacon.

Schwartz, S. H. (1994). Beyond individualism and collectivism: New cultural dimensions of values. In U. Kim, H. C. Triandis, C. Kagitcibasi, S.-C. Choi, & G. Yoon (Eds.), *Individualism and collectivism: Theory, method, and applications* (pp. 85–122). Newbury Park, CA: Sage.

Schwartz, T. (1981). The acquisition of culture. *Ethos, 9,* 4–17.

Schwartz, T. (1992). Anthropology and psychology: An unrequited relationship. In T. Schwartz, G. M. White, & C. Lutz (Eds.), *New directions in psychological anthropology* (pp. 324–349). New York: Cambridge University Press.

Schwartz, T., White, G. M., & Lutz, C. (Eds.). (1992). *New directions in psychological anthropology.* Cambridge, UK: Cambridge University Press.

Scribner, S. (1984). Studying working intelligence. In B. Rogoff & J. Lave (Eds.), *Everyday cognition: Its development in social context* (pp. 9–40). Cambridge, MA: Harvard University Press.

Scribner, S., & Cole, M. (1981). *The psychology of literacy.* Cambridge, MA: Harvard University Press.

Sharp, D., Cole, M., & Lave, C. (1979). Education and cognitive development: The evidence from experimental research. *Monographs of the Society for Research on Child Development, 44*(1–2).

Shore, B. (1996). *Culture in mind: Cognition, culture and the problem of meaning.* New York: Oxford University Press.

Shweder, R. A. (1975). How relevant is an individual difference theory of personality? *Journal of Personality, 43*(3), 455–484.

Shweder, R. A. (1979a). Rethinking culture and personality theory Part I: A critical examination of two classical postulates. *Ethos,* 255–278.

Shweder, R. A. (1979b). Rethinking culture and personality theory: Pt 2. A critical examination of two more classical postulates. *Ethos, 7,* 255–278.

Shweder, R. A. (1984). Anthropology's romantic rebellion against the enlightenment, or there's more to thinking than reason and evidence. In R. A. Shweder & R. A. LeVine (Eds.), *Culture theory: Essays on mind, self, and emotion* (pp. 27–66). Cambridge, UK: Cambridge University Press.

Shweder, R. A. (1990). Cultural psychology: What is it? In J. W. Stigler, R. A. Shweder, & G. Herdt (Eds.), *Cultural psychology: Essays on comparative human development* (pp. 27–66). New York: Cambridge University Press.

Shweder, R. A., & Bourne, E. J. (1984). Does the concept of the person vary cross-culturally? In R. A. Shweder & R. A. Levine (Eds.), *Culture theory: Essays on mind, self, and emotion* (pp. 158–199). New York: Cambridge University Press.

Shweder, R. A., Goodnow, J., Hatano, G., LeVine, R. A., Markus, H., & Miller, P. (1998). The cultural psychology of development: One mind, many mentalities. In W. Damon (Ed.), *Handbook of child psychology* (Vol. 1, pp. 865–937). New York: Wiley.

Shweder, R. A., & LeVine, R. A. (1984). *Culture theory : Essays on mind, self, and emotion.* Cambridge, UK: Cambridge University Press.

Shweder, R. A., Mahapatra, M., & Miller, J. (1990). Culture and moral development. In J. W. Stigler, R. A. Shweder, & G. Herdt (Eds.), *Cultural psychology: Essays on comparative human development* (pp. 130–204). New York: Cambridge University Press.

Shweder, R. A., Much, N. C., Mahapatra, M., & Park, L. (1997). The "big three" of morality (autonomy, community, divinity) and the "big three" explanations of suffering. In A. M. Brandt (Ed.), *Morality and health* (pp. 119–169). New York: Routledge.

Sinha, D. (1990). The concept of psycho-social well being: Western and Indian perspectives. *National Institute of Mental Health and Neurosciences Journal, 8,* 1–11.

Snarey, J. R. (1985). Cross-cultural universality of social-moral development: A critical review of Kohlbergian research. *Psychological Bulletin, 97*(2), 202–232.

Snarey, J. R., & Keljo, K. (1991). In a Gemeinschaft voice: The cross-cultural expansion of moral development theory, *Handbook of moral behavior and development* (pp. 395–424). Hillsdale, NJ: Erlbaum.

Spindler, G. D. (Ed.). (1980). *The making of psychological anthropology.* Berkeley: University of California Press.

Spiro, M. E. (1958). *Children of the kibbutz.* Cambridge, MA: Harvard University Press.

Spiro, M. E. (1965). Religious systems as culturally constituted defense mechanisms. In M. E. Spiro (Ed.), *Context and meaning in cultural anthropology* (pp. 100–113). New York: Free Press.

Spiro, M. E. (1982). *Oedipus in the Trobriands.* Chicago: University of Chicago Press.

Stevenson, H. W., & Lee, S.-Y. (1990). Contexts of achievement: A study of American, Chinese, and Japanese children. *Monographs of the Society for Research in Child Development.* Chicago: University of Chicago Press.

Stigler, J. W. (1984). "Mental abacus": The effect of abacus training on Chinese children's mental calculation. *Cognitive Psychology, 16,* 145–176.

Strauss, C. (1992). What makes Tony run? Schemas as motives reconsidered, *Human motives and cultural models* (pp. 197–224). New York: Cambridge University Press.

Strauss, C., & Quinn, N. (1997). *A cognitive theory of cultural meaning.* New York: Cambridge University Press.

Suh, E. (2000). Culture, identity consistency, and subjective well-being. Manuscript submitted for publication, University of California, Irvine.

Swann, W. B., Wenzlaff, R. M., Krull, D. S., & Pelham, B. W. (1992). Allure of negative feedback: Self-verification strivings among depressed persons. *Journal of Abnormal Psychology, 101,* 293–306.

Triandis, H. C. (1972). *The analysis of subjective culture.* New York: Wiley.

Triandis, H. C. (1980). Values, attitudes, and interpersonal behavior. In H. E. Howe & M. M. Page (Eds.), *Nebraska symposium on motivation, 1979* (pp. 195–259). Lincoln: University of Nebraska Press.

Triandis, H. C. (1988). Collectivism vs individualism: A reconceptualization of a basic concept in cross-cultural social psychology. In G. K. Verma & C. Bagley (Eds.), *Cross-cultural studies of personality, attitudes and cognition* (pp. 60–95). London: MacMillan.

Triandis, H. C. (1989). The self and social behavior in differing cultural contexts. *Psychological Review, 96,* 506–520.

Triandis, H. C. (1990). Cross-cultural studies of individualism and collectivism. In J. Berman (Ed.), *Nebraska symposium on motivation* (pp. 41–133). Lincoln: University of Nebraska Press.

Triandis, H. C. (1994). *Culture and social behavior.* New York: McGraw-Hill.

Triandis, H. C. (1996). The psychological measurement of cultural syndromes. *American Psychologist, 51*(4), 407–415.

Triandis, H. C., & Lambert, W. E. (Eds.). (1980). *Handbook of cross-cultural psychology: Vol. 1. Perspectives.* Boston: Allyn & Bacon.

Turiel, E. (1983). *The development of social knowledge: Morality and convention.* Cambridge, UK: Cambridge University Press.

Valsiner, J. (Ed.). (1988). *Child development within culturally structured environments: Social coconstruction and environmental guidance in development.* (Vol. 2). Norwood, NJ: Ablex.

Valsiner, J. (Ed.). (1989). *Child development in cultural context.* Toronto, Canada: Hogrefe and Huber.

Vygotsky, L. S. (1929). The problem of the cultural development of the child, Pt. 2. *Journal of Genetic Psychology, 36,* 414–436.

Vygotsky, L. S. (1978). *Mind in society: The development of higher psychological processes.* Cambridge, MA: Harvard University Press.

Vygotsky, L. S. (1981a). The genesis of higher mental functions. In J. V. Wertsch (Ed.), *The concept of activity in Soviet psychology* (pp. 144–188). Armonk, NY: M. E. Sharpe.

Vygotsky, L. S. (1981b). The instrumental method in psychology. In J. V. Wertsch (Ed.), *The concept of activity in Soviet psychology* (pp. 134–143). Armonk, NY: M. E. Sharpe.

Vygotsky, L. D. (1987). *Thinking and speech.* New York: Plenum Press. (Original work published 1934)

Wallace, A. F. C. (1961). *Culture and personality.* New York: Random House.

Weisz, J. R., Rothbaum, F. M., & Blackburn, T. C. (1984). Standing out and standing in: The psychology of control in America and Japan. *American Psychologist, 39,* 955–969.

Wells, G. (1981). Lay analyses of causal forces on behavior. In J. H. Harvey (Ed.), *Cognition, social behavior and the environment.* Hillsdale, NJ: Erlbaum.

Werner, H. (1948). *Comparative psychology of mental development.* New York: Science Editions.

Wertsch, J. V. (Ed.). (1979). *The concept of activity in Soviet psychology.* Armonk, NY: M. E. Sharpe.

Wertsch, J. V. (1991). *Voices of the mind: A sociocultural approach to mediated action.* Cambridge, MA: Harvard University Press.

Wertsch, J. V. (1995). Sociocultural research in the copyright age. *Culture and Psychology, 1,* 81–102.

Wierzbicka, A. (1992). Talking about emotions: Semantics, culture and cognition. *Cognition & Emotion, 6,* 285–319.

White, G. M. (1994). Affecting culture: Emotion and morality in everyday life. In S. Kitayama & H. R. Markus (Eds.), *Emotion and culture: Empirical studies of mutual influence* (pp. 219–240). Washington, DC: American Psychological Association.

Whiting, B. B., & Edwards, C. P. (1988). *Children of different worlds: The formation of social behavior.* Cambridge, MA: Harvard University Press.

Whiting, B. B., & Whiting, J. W. (1975). *Children of six cultures: A psycho-cultural analysis.* Cambridge, MA: Harvard University Press.

Whiting, J. W., & Child, I. (1953). *Child training and personality.* New Haven, CT: Yale University Press.

Witkin, H. A., & Berry, J. W. (1975). Psychological differentiation in cross-cultural perspective. *Journal of Cross-Cultural Psychology, 6,* 4–87.

Yamaguchi, S. (2001). Culture and control orientations. In D. Matsumoto (Ed.), *The handbook of culture and psychology* (pp. 223–243). New York: Oxford University Press.

Yang, K.-S. (1997). Indigenizing westernized Chinese psychology. In M. H. Bond (Ed.), *Working at the interface of culture: Eighteen lives in social science.* London: Routledge.

Yang, K.-S. (1988). Chinese filial piety: A conceptual analysis. In K. S. Yang (Ed.), *The psychology of the Chinese people: An indigenous perspective* (pp. 39–73). Taipei, Taiwan: Kuei-Kuan. (In Chinese)

Yang, K. S., & Ho, D. Y. F. (1988). The role of the *yuan* in Chinese social life: A conceptual and empirical analysis. In A. C. Paranjpe, D. Y. F. Ho, & R. W. Rieber (Eds.), *Asian contributions to psychology* (pp. 263–281). New York: Praeger.

Zimbardo, P. G., Banks, W. C., Haney, C., & Jaffe, D. (1973, April 8). The mind is a formidable jailer: A Pirandellian prison. *The New York Times Magazine,* pp. 38–60.

PART TWO

PERSONALITY

CHAPTER 3

Genetic Basis of Personality Structure

W. JOHN LIVESLEY, KERRY L. JANG, AND PHILIP A. VERNON

Until recently, the study of personality was handicapped by the lack of a systematic taxonomy of constructs to represent individual differences. A confusing array of constructs and measures was available, and different measures of purportedly the same construct often showed little correspondence. This diversity hindered the development of a systematic understanding of individual differences. Recently, the situation began to change with emerging agreement about some of the major dimensions of personality. Broad traits such as neuroticism-stability, extraversion-introversion, and psychoticism-constraint are identified in most analyses of personality traits and part of most descriptive systems. There is also agreement about the way personality is organized. Models based on trait concepts assume that traits differ along a dimension of breadth or generalization and that traits are hierarchically organized, with global traits such as neuroticism subdividing into a set of more specific traits such as anxiousness and dependence (Goldberg, 1993; Hampson, John, & Goldberg, 1986).

Within this framework, attention has focused particularly on the five major factors as a parsimonious taxonomy of personality traits (Goldberg, 1990). Lexical analyses of the natural language of personality description (Digman, 1990; Goldberg, 1990) and subsequent psychometric studies of personality inventories (Costa & McCrae, 1992) have converged in identifying five broad factors typically labeled extraversion or surgency, agreeableness, conscientiousness, emotional stability versus neuroticism, and intellect, culture, or openness. It is widely assumed that this structure is transforming our understanding of personality and that the higher-order structure of personality is becoming more clearly delineated. Enthusiasm for the emergent structure, although understandable because it promises to bring coherence to a field characterized more by conceptual and theoretical debate than by substantive findings, tends to minimize confusions that still exist regarding the number and content of higher-order domains (Zuckerman, 1991, 1995, 1999; Zuckerman, Kulhman, Joireman, Teta, & Kraft, 1993) and nature of the assumed hierarchical arrangement of traits.

These problems remain unresolved despite numerous attempts to explicate personality structure, partly because the methods used incorporate subjective elements regarding choice of analytic strategies and data interpretation, and partly because personality concepts are inherently fuzzy, a factor that contributes to interpretive problems. In this chapter, we examine the contribution that behavioral genetic approaches can make to explicating the structure of personality and resolving issues of the number and content of phenotypic and psychometric analyses. However, numerous psychometric studies have not resolved these problems, raising the possibility that studies of phenotypes alone may not be sufficient.

The problem with phenotypic analyses is their reliance on constructs that are by their nature fuzzy and imprecise. This is illustrated by the confusion noted about the components of extraversion (Depue & Collins, 1999; Watson & Clark, 1997). Conceptions of extraversion include sociability or affiliation (includes agreeableness, affiliation, social recognition, gregariousness, warmth, and social closeness), agency (surgency, assertion, endurance, persistence, achievement, social dominance, ascendancy, ambitiousness), activation (liveliness, talkativeness, energy level, activity level, activity level), impulsive–sensation seeking (impulsivity, sensation seeking, excitement seeking, novelty seeking, boldness, risk taking, unreliability, disorderliness, adventurousness, thrill and adventure seeking, monotony avoidance, boredom susceptibility), positive emotions (positive affect, elatedness, enthusiasm, exuberance, cheerfulness, merriness, joviality), and optimism (Depue & Collins, 1999).

This list reveals the problems faced by attempts to delineate phenotypic structure. Not only does the content of extraversion differ across models, but the definition of each basic or lower-order trait may also differ across models and measures. Moreover, the meaning of putatively distinct traits overlaps so that facet traits defining a given domain shade into each other and into facet traits defining other domains. This fuzziness is probably an inevitable consequence of using natural language concepts that evolved to capture socially significant behaviors that are multidetermined. It adds to concerns that the taxonomies of phenotypic traits may not represent natural cleavages in the way behavior is organized nor reflect underlying etiological structures.

This fuzziness contributes to the considerable variability in personality phenotypes so that minor variations in measures and samples influence the number and contents of factors. The problem is compounded by the fact that many decisions about methodology and analytic strategies have an arbitrary component. More objective criteria are needed to guide decisions on the number of higher-order domains and the location of lower-order or basic traits within domains and to define a systematic set of basic traits. Phenotypic analyses are concerned primarily with describing trait covariation. This evokes the oft-voiced criticism of the five-factor approach—it is descriptive rather than explanatory. The basic problem of *why* traits are related to each other is not considered. An understanding of etiology of trait covariance, especially genetic etiology, would provide a conceptual foundation for current models. At each level of the trait hierarchy,

traits and behaviors, including test items, could be grouped according to a shared etiology. Etiology would provide an additional criterion to supplement the usual psychometric criteria such as proposed by Costa and McCrae (1997) to guide decisions on the number and content of domains. Identification of a robust model of personality structure would be facilitated by evidence that a given phenotypic structure reflects the genetic architecture of personality traits. Unfortunately there are few studies of the genetic architecture underlying multiple personality traits compared to studies of phenotypic structure. Evidence that a given phenotypic structure parallels genotypic structure would support the validity and generalizability of the structure.

HERITABILITY

The foundation for an etiological understanding of personality structure and for a behavioral genetic approach is provided by evidence that genetic influences account for approximately 40–60% of the variance for virtually all personality traits, with most of the remaining variance being explained by nonshared environmental effects (Bouchard, 1999; Loehlin & Nicholls, 1976; Plomin, Chipeur, & Loehlin, 1990). The broad traits of extraversion and neuroticism have received most attention. The data from several twin studies yield heritability estimates of approximately 60% for extraversion and 50% for neuroticism. Loehlin (1992) also examined multiple personality scales organized according to the five-factor framework. Estimates of about 40% heritability were obtained for each domain. Subsequent studies using the NEO-PI-R yielded heritability estimates of 41% for neuroticism, 53% for extraversion, 41% for agreeableness, and 40% for conscientiousness (Jang, Livesley, Vernon, & Jackson, 1996; see also Bergeman et al., 1993; Jang, McCrae, Angleitner, Riemann, & Livesley, 1998). Nonadditive genetic effects accounted for 61% the variance in openness to experience.

Although the evidence points to a significant genetic component to personality traits, it has been suggested that traits could be divided into temperament traits that have a substantial heritable component and character traits that are largely environmental in origin. If this is the case and environmental factors give rise to distinct traits, the role of genetic criteria in clarifying trait structure would be limited. The evidence does not, however, support the proposal. Putatively characterological traits such as openness to experience are as heritable as so-called temperament traits. Moreover, molecular genetic studies have found significant allelic associations between so-called character traits such as cooperativeness and self-directedness as assessed using the Temperament and Character Inventory and the 5-HTTLPR allele (Hamer, Greenberg, Sabol, & Murphy, 1999).

To date, a self-report measure of personality that has no genetic influence has not been identified (Plomin & Caspi, 1998). The qualification should be added that heritability studies have relied largely on self-report measures—alternative methods of assessment may yield different results. However, this was not the case with the few studies using other methods (Heath, Neale, Kessler, Eaves, & Kendler, 1992; Riemann, Angleitner, & Strelau, 1997). Riemann and colleagues (1997), for example, reported a twin study conducted in Germany and Poland that compared assessments of the five factors using self-report questionnaires with peer ratings. Estimates of heritability based on self-report were similar to those reported by other studies. The peer ratings also showed evidence of heritability, although estimates were lower than those obtained from self-reports. Multivariate genetic analyses showed that the same genetic factors contributed to self-report and peer ratings. These results suggest that findings of a heritable component to all self-report measures are likely to generalize to other methods of measurement.

Evidence of heritability alone, however, is not sufficient to justify the use of behavioral genetic criteria to clarify trait structure. It is possible that environmental factors that account for about 50% of the variance have a substantial effect on trait covariation. If this were the case, the finding that traits are genetically related would be of less value in clarifying personality structure. The evidence, however, suggests that the phenotypic structure of traits closely parallels the underlying genetic architecture (Livesley, Jang, & Vernon, 1998; Loehlin, 1987)—a point that is discussed in detail later in this chapter.

It should be noted, however, that information about heritability merely explains the variance in a single trait as opposed to the covariance between traits. Such information has limited value in explicating personality structure. As Turkheimer (1998) argued, all individual differences in behavior are heritable and ". . . the very ubiquity of these findings make them a poor basis for reformulating scientists' conceptions of human behavior" (p. 782). Nevertheless, information on heritability forms the foundation for understanding of the etiology of personality. The major contribution of behavior genetics to understanding personality structure, however, comes from multivariate genetic analyses that elucidate the genetic structure underlying multiple traits (Carey & DiLalla, 1994). Multivariate analyses extend univariate analysis of the genetic and environmental influences on a trait to evaluate genetic and environmental components of the covariation between two or more traits (DeFries & Fulker, 1986). It is this

extension that promises to contribute to personality theory by explicating the etiological basis for trait covariance by evaluating the degree to which different traits are influenced by the same genetic and environmental factors. This issue is central to resolving some of the problems of personality description and structure.

THE ETIOLOGICAL BASIS OF COVARIANCE

The phenotypic covariation between two traits may be due to pleiotropy—that is, the degree to which the traits share a common genetic influence, environmental effects common to both traits, or both. The degree to which two variables have genetic and environmental effects in common is indexed by genetic (r_G) and environmental correlation coefficients (r_E). These statistics are interpreted as any other correlation coefficient and they may be subjected to other statistical procedures such as factor analysis (Crawford & DeFries, 1978). Genetic and environmental correlation coefficients are readily estimated from data obtained from monozygotic (MZ) and dizygotic (DZ) twin pairs.

The calculation of the genetic correlation is similar to that used to estimate the heritability of a single variable. A higher within-pair correlation for MZ twins than for DZ twins suggests the presence of genetic influences because the greater similarity is directly attributable to the twofold increase in genetic similarity in MZ versus DZ twins. In the multivariate case, a common genetic influence is suggested when the MZ cross-correlation (the correlation between one twin's score on one of the variables and the other twin's score on the other variable) exceeds the DZ cross-correlation.

The phenotypic correlation (r_p) between two variables (traits), x and y, is expressed by the following equation:

$$r_p = (h_x \cdot h_y \cdot r_g) + (e_x \cdot e_y \cdot r_e) \qquad (3.1)$$

where the observed or phenotypic correlation, (r_p), is the sum of the extent to which the same genetic (r_g) and/or environmental factors (r_e) influence each variable, weighted by the overall influence of genetic and environmental causes on each variable (h_x, h_y, e_x, e_y, respectively). The terms h and e are the square roots of heritability and environmental effect (h^2 and e^2) for variables x and y, respectively.

It should be noted that a genetic correlation describes *statistical pleiotropism*—that is, the extent to which allelic effects on trait predict allelic effects on the other trait. As Carey (1987) pointed out, statistical pleiotropism is not to be confused with *biological pleiotropism* in which two variables factor. Factor analysis of the ratings yielded the familiar five factors. Some researchers concluded from such studies that trait structure merely reflects the effects of semantic biases on person perceptions (Shweder, 1975). Ratings of strangers must contain bias due to implicit personality theory because they cannot be influenced by the true personalities of the targets. It is also likely that self-reports and ratings of well-known targets incorporate a similar bias. For example, two observers may agree that a person is sociable but disagree on the extent of his or her sociability. The observer assigned a higher rating for sociability is also likely to assign a higher rating for cheerfulness and talkativeness. Thus, part of the covariance of these traits may be attributable to systematic biases in person perception that lead to correlated errors in individual judgments. If this is the case, similarities in structure between genetic covariance and nonshared environmental covariance could reflect the biasing effects of implicit personality theory on the latter.

To test for this bias, self-report twin data were supplemented with cross-observer correlations on the NEO-PI-R. This allowed the computation of two matrices of nonshared environmental covariance. The first estimated the covariance due to implicit personality theory bias alone. Factorial analysis of this matrix yielded the familiar five factors. Comparison with normative structure yielded congruence coefficients of .81, .45, .81, .89, and .85 for Neuroticism, Extraversion, Openness, Agreeableness, and Conscientiousness, respectively. The second matrix of nonshared environmental covariance estimated was free from systematic bias. Factor analysis of this "unbiased" matrix with targeted rotations to the normative NEO-PI-R factors produced low congruence coefficients at .53, .68, .22, .61, and .80 for Neuroticism, Extraversion, Openness, Agreeableness, and Conscientiousness, respectively. Subsequent factor analysis of this matrix yielded two factors. The first resembled a broad form of Conscientiousness with salient loading of the facets Activity, Order, Dutifulness, Achievement Striving, Self-Discipline, and (low) Impulsiveness. The second factor was defined by the facets Warmth, Gregariousness, Positive Emotions, Openness to Feelings, Altruism, and Tender-Mindedness. This combination of Extraversion and Agreeableness facets resembles the Love axis of the Interpersonal Circumplex (Wiggins, 1979). The other interpersonal axis—Dominance—does not appear to be influenced by the nonshared environment. Assertiveness did not load on either factor.

These results suggest that when the conventional estimates of nonshared environmental covariances are decomposed into implicit personality theory bias and true nonshared effects, much of the resemblance to the five-factor structure appears attributable to bias. Overall, these studies point to the conclusion that genetic factors are largely responsible for the observed pattern of trait covariation.

THE HIERARCHICAL STRUCTURE OF PERSONALITY

Beyond problems with the content of personality taxonomies, there are also uncertainties about the nature of the proposed hierarchical structure of traits and the relationship between higher- and lower-order traits. Factor analytic studies provide consistent evidence that specific traits are organized into more global entities. Lexical studies also show that natural language reflects this structure. Substantial agreement exists among individuals in judgments of trait breadth (Hampson et al., 1986). Despite this evidence, the nature and origins of the hierarchy are unclear. This is clearly a problem that requires explanation.

Fundamental differences exist among models on the way the personality hierarchy is conceptualized. The lexical approach seems to consider the higher-order domains to be lexical categories that impose structure on personality descriptors by organizing them into clusters that are not necessarily discrete or equally important (Saucier & Goldberg, 1996). The lexical structure "provides a framework for description, but not necessarily for explanation" (Saucier & Goldberg, 1996, p. 24–25). Saucier and Goldberg also asserted that *"as a representation of phenotypes based on natural language, the Big Five structure is indifferent and thus complementary to genotypic representations of causes, motivations, and internal personality dynamics"* (p. 42). The higher-order terms do not appear, therefore, to have any significance beyond that of description.

Traits psychologists, including other five-factor theorists, make different assumptions. For Allport (1961), a trait is "a neuropsychic structure" (p. 347) and therefore an explanatory concept. Eysenck also adopted this approach: Traits have heritable biological basis. Similarly, the five-factor model assumes that traits are "endogenous basic tendencies" with a substantial heritable component (McCrae & Costa, 1996, p. 72). For Eysenck and Costa and for McCrae, traits are explanatory as well as descriptive. In contrast to the lexical approach, the five-factor model assumes that domains are equally important and equal in breadth.

Assumptions that trait theories make about the psychobiological basis for the higher-order domains initially created uncertainty about the status of the lower-order traits. Most research effort has been directed toward understanding higher-order factors and little attention has been paid to parsing these domains into more specific components. Until recently, it was unclear whether the lower-order traits were merely facets of the higher-order traits or distinct entities with their own etiology. The use of the term *facet* to describe the lower-order traits, a convention adopted by Costa and McCrae, implies that they are merely exemplars or components of a more fundamental global trait. In this sense, the facet traits can be understood in terms of the domain sampling approach used in test construction in which facets are merely arbitrary ways to subdivide global traits to ensure adequate domain sampling. Identification of general genetic factors that have a broad influence on personality phenotypes also raises questions about the significance of the lower-order or facet traits—in particular, whether these traits are heritable simply because of their association with the broader domains or whether they are also subject to specific genetic influences. Clarification of this issue is critical to constructing an explanatory account of personality structure.

Heritability of Lower-Order Traits

If lower-order traits are only subcomponents of broader traits, all variance in a facet apart from error variance should be explained by the variance in the global trait. Recently, however, behavioral genetic research has suggested that lower-order traits have a distinct heritable component (Jang et al., 1998; Livesley et al., 1998). These studies estimated whether lower-order traits have a unique genetic basis when the heritable component of higher-order traits is removed from them. Jang and colleagues (1998) partialled out all of the common variance due to each of higher-order Neuroticism, Extraversion, Openness, Agreeableness, and Conscientiousness scales from the 30 facet scales of the NEO-PI-R. When the residual variances on the facets were subjected to heritability analyses, a substantial genetic influence remained. Additive genetic effects accounted for 25 to 65% of the reliable specific variance, with most heritabilities ranging from .20 to .35 (see Table 3.3).

When these values were corrected for unreliability, the values increased to the usual range observed for personality traits. The implication is that these traits are not merely facets of more general traits, but rather distinct heritable entities.

A similar approach was used to study the residual heritability of the 18 traits underlying personality disorder (Livesley et al., 1998). Factor scores were computed for the four factors described previously. A standardized residual score for each scale was computed by regressing the four factor scores on each of the 18 basic traits. Monozygotic twin correlations were higher that the dizygotic twin correlations for all 18 traits. Estimates of the heritability of the residual trait scores showed substantial residual heritability for 11 of

TABLE 3.3   Heritability Estimates, Retest Reliabilities, and Relative Reliabilities of Revised NEO Personality Inventory Residual Facet Scores

Domain and Facet Scale	h^2	c^2	e^2	r_u	h^2/r_u
Neuroticism					
Anxiety	0.25	—	0.75	0.58	0.43
Hostility	0.21	—	0.79	0.53	0.40
Depression	0.25	—	0.75	0.50	0.50
Self-Consciousness	0.29	—	0.71	0.54	0.54
Impulsiveness	0.27	—	0.73	0.59	0.46
Vulnerability	0.26	—	0.74	0.56	0.46
Extraversion					
Warmth	0.23	—	0.77	0.60	0.38
Gregariousness	0.28	—	0.72	0.71	0.39
Assertiveness	0.29	—	0.71	0.72	0.40
Activity	0.27	—	0.73	0.70	0.39
Excitement Seeking	0.36	—	0.64	0.69	0.52
Positive Emotions	0.30	—	0.70	0.63	0.48
Openness					
Fantasy	0.25	—	0.75	0.60	0.42
Aesthetics	0.37	—	0.63	0.72	0.51
Feelings	0.26	—	0.74	0.57	0.46
Actions	0.34	—	0.66	0.69	0.49
Ideas	0.33	—	0.67	0.69	0.48
Values	0.35	—	0.65	0.71	0.49
Agreeableness					
Trust	0.31	—	0.69	0.62	0.50
Straightforwardness	0.25	—	0.75	0.56	0.45
Altuism	—	0.20	0.80	0.50	—
Compliance	0.26	—	0.74	0.54	0.48
Modesty	—	0.26	0.74	0.64	—
Tendermindedness	0.28	—	0.72	0.64	0.44
Conscientiousness					
Competence	0.11	—	0.89	0.44	0.25
Order	0.26	—	0.74	0.69	0.38
Dutifulness	0.28	—	0.72	0.43	0.65
Achievement Striving	—	0.26	0.74	0.54	—
Self-Discipline	0.28	—	0.72	0.61	0.46
Deliberation	—	0.18	0.82	0.71	—

the 18 basic traits that ranged from .26 for Intimacy Problems to .48 for Conduct Problems.

These studies, in contrast to studies of phenotypic structure, point to the significance of the lower-order traits. Although these traits have tended to be neglected in personality research, they appear to be important for understanding personality. This suggests that a bottom-up approach to personality structure would provide additional information to complement that provided by the traditional top-down approach of the three- and five-factor models that identify the higher-order domains first and then seek to define an appropriate complement of facet traits. Before considering these issues in greater depth, it is important to recognize a limitation of the methods used. The regression method does not model genetic effects directly, and the results need to be replicated using multivariate genetic analyses. This introduces another feature of behavioral genetic analyses that is pertinent to

TABLE 3.4   Multivariate Genetic Analysis (independent pathways model) of the NEO-PI-R Neuroticism Facets on a Sample of German and a Sample of Canadian Twins

Facet Scale	Common Genetic Factors		Common Nonshared Environmental Factors		Variable-specific Factors	
	1	2	1	2	A	E
Canadian Sample						
Anxiety	.48	.27	.50	.30	.30	.56
Hostility	.65	—	.29	.21	—	.67
Depression	.45	.43	.59	.26	.23	.38
Self-Consciousness	.42	.35	.42	.24	.37	.57
Impulsivity	.36	—	.78	—	.50	—
Vulnerability	.47	.40	.40	.21	.28	.57
German Sample						
Anxiety	.46	.34	.29	.46	.36	.51
Hostility	.66	—	.76	—	—	—
Depression	.47	.45	.33	.46	.22	.45
Self-Consciousness	.35	.44	.22	.35	.40	.60
Impulsivity	.24	—	.19	—	.57	.77
Vulnerability	.43	.42	.33	.49	.28	.46

Note.   All parameters are significant at $p < .05$.

dimensions. These conclusions are, however, based on a single study using only a single measure of personality. Replication is clearly needed, given the results' significance for understanding trait structure. The conclusions are, however, similar to those drawn from a study of personality disorder traits (Livesley & Jang, 2000).

Personality Disorder Traits

Livesley and Jang (2000) investigated the etiological structure of personality disorder by fitting independent and common pathways models to the 18 lower-order traits of personality disorder assessed by administering the DAPP to a volunteer sample of 686 twin pairs. Each trait consists of two or more specific traits so that a total of 69 specific traits define the 18 basic traits. The 18 traits in turn define four higher-order factors. Thus the DAPP system incorporates three levels of construct (higher-order factors, lower-order traits, and specific traits) whereas the NEO-PI-R has only two levels (domains and facets). This makes it possible to explore the genetic architecture of personality in more detail. For example, the basic trait of Anxiousness is defined by four specific traits: trait anxiety, guilt proneness, rumination, and indecisiveness. Each basic trait represents a single phenotypic factor. If personality is inherited as a few genetic dimensions represented by the four higher-order factors, a single genetic dimension should underlie each basic trait that is shared by other traits constituting the higher-order factor. Evidence of a genetic effect specific to each trait would be provided by

evidence that the 18 basic traits are composed of two or more genetic dimensions.

A one-factor common pathways model did not provide a satisfactory fit for any of the 18 basic traits. On the other hand, an independent pathways model postulating a single genetic dimension explained the covariation among specific traits for 12 of the 18 basic trait scales: Anxiousness, Cognitive Dysregulation, Compulsivity, Conduct Problems, Identity Problems, Insecure Attachment, Intimacy Problems, Oppositionality, Rejection, Stimulus Seeking, Submissiveness, and Suspiciousness. The results of model fitting for illustrative scales are provided in Table 3.5. For three of these scales, Intimacy Problems, Rejection, and Stimulus Seeking, the common genetic dimension accounted for little of the variance for one or more of the specific trait scales, indicating that a specific genetic factor influenced these traits. Two genetic dimensions were found to underlie four scales: Affective Lability, Narcissism, Restricted Expression, and Social Avoidance. Three common genetic dimensions contributed to Callousness (see Table 3.5).

Multivariate analyses of normal and disordered personality traits suggest that multiple genetic and environmental factors influence the covariant structure of traits. They also confirm the findings of the regression analyses that many lower-order traits are influenced by one or more genetic dimensions specific to those traits. Finally, in both sets of analyses, the common pathways model did not provide a better fit to the data than did the independent pathways model. This suggests that the general genetic dimensions found by Livesley and colleagues (1998) and others by factor analyzing matrices of genetic correlations do not influence each trait through a latent phenotypic variable, but rather exert a direct influence on each trait.

IMPLICATIONS FOR PERSONALITY STRUCTURE

The studies described in the previous section reveal a complex genetic basis for personality. Multiple genetic dimensions differing in the breadth of their effects contribute to personality phenotypes (Jang et al., 1998; Livesley et al., 1998; Livesley & Jang, 2000). Some are relatively specific dimensions that influence single phenotypic traits, whereas others have broader effects influencing multiple phenotypically distinct but covarying traits. Consequently, many traits appear to be influenced by multiple genes and gene systems. Similarly, trait covariation seems to arise from multiple genetic effects. Genetic effects on traits appear to be direct rather than mediated by higher-order entities. These findings require replication. Nevertheless they appear to challenge

TABLE 3.5 Illustrative Scales: Multivariate Genetic Analyses of the DAPP-DQ Facet Scales

	A1	A2	A3	E1	E2	A	C	E
$\chi^2 = 52.45$, $df = 54$, $p = .53$								
Rejection								
Rigid Cognitive Style	—	—	—	.43	—	.38	—	.56
Judgmental	.13	—	—	.46	—	.34	—	.57
Interpersonal Hostility	.46	—	—	.31	—	.34	—	.51
Dominance	.53	—	—	—	—	.40	—	.61
$\chi^2 = 90.63$, $df = 84$, $p = .22$								
Restricted Expression								
Self-Disclosure	.55	.30	—	.12	.49	.33	—	.49
Affective Expression	.31	.58	—	.21	.56	—	—	.45
Angry Affects	.24	.38	—	.75	—	.49	—	—
Positive Affects	.40	.51	—	—	.46	.33	—	.52
Self-Reliance	.55	.15	—	.17	.50	.23	—	.59
$\chi^2 = 154.48$, $df = 166$, $p = .73$								
Callousness								
Contemptuousness	.36	.27	.42	.28	.15	.44	—	.57
Egocentrism	.28	.36	.28	.46	.21	.47	—	.48
Exploitation	.26	.54	.43	.35	.18	—	—	.51
Irresponsibility	.40	.33	.23	.22	.23	.40	—	.65
Lack of Empathy	.53	.20	.16	.33	.23	.26	—	.65
Remorselessness	.42	.16	.34	—	.76	.32	—	—
Sadism	.36	—	.66	.27	.14	.40	—	.65

models of personality positing links between specific genetically based neurotransmitter systems and specific personality traits. They also suggest a different conception of the trait hierarchies from that assumed by many trait taxonomies.

Hierarchical Structure

Factor analyses of genetic correlations and the modeling studies cited in the previous section identified general genetic factors that account for trait covariation. The model-fitting analyses also confirmed conclusions based on regression analyses that lower-order traits are not merely components of higher-order traits, but rather are distinct etiological entities. It appears that each basic or facet trait is influenced by general and specific genetic factors. Genetic dimensions that affect multiple traits appear to influence each trait directly rather than indirectly through a higher-order phenotypic entity. This raises questions about the basis for the hierarchy consistently identified by factor analytic studies and the conceptual status of higher-order constructs like neuroticism and extraversion and their role in theories of individual differences.

Although the facets delineating each of the five-factor domains covary due to shared genetic effects, it is not necessary to invoke a higher-order latent construct to explain this covariation. This raises the possibility that higher-order constructs such as neuroticism merely represent the pleiotropic action of genes. If this is the case, neuroticism and other higher-order domains are not entities that are distinct from the specific traits that delineate them. They are not traits in Allport's sense of distinct phenotypic entities with an underlying biology, but rather heuristic devices that represent clusters of traits that covary because of a common genetic effect. This is consistent with the conception of domains as lexical categories (Saucier & Goldberg, 1996). Nevertheless, facet traits defining domains such as neuroticism and extraversion overlap sufficiently to justify grouping them into an overall global measure.

The model of trait structure implied by these findings differs from that of traditional trait theories. With traditional models in which lower-order traits are nested within a few higher-order factors, it follows that any statement about the higher-order factor applies to all subordinate traits. This is not the case with the model proposed because each basic trait has its own specific etiology. A second difference is that traditional hierarchical models seem to assume that trait taxonomies are similar to any classification based on set theory principles. At each level in the hierarchy, categories are assumed to be exhaustive and exclusive (Simpson, 1961). *Exhaustiveness* means that trait categories exist to classify all subordinate traits, whereas *exclusiveness* refers to the principle that each subordinate feature can be classified into only one superordinate trait. Considerable effort has been expended in attempts to delineate a structure with these properties. Indeed, this is the reason for debate on number and content of domains. It also explains Costa and McCrae's insistence that domains are equal in breadth. If they are not, the five-factor model is open to the criticism that the model is not sufficiently parsimonious, as argued by Eysenck. This theoretical structure is understandable if trait taxonomies are conceptualized only as lexical structures. It is possible, however, that traits at the biological level are not organized in the systematic way proposed by the five-factor model.

There are no a priori reasons to assume that all basic traits must be organized into a hierarchy or that each higher-order domain is equally broad and defined by an equal number of facets as hypothesized by the five-factor model. An equally plausible model is that traits are organized into clusters that differ in the number of basic traits that they subsume and that the hierarchy is incomplete, with some specific traits showing minimal degrees of covariation. This structure is illustrated by the findings regarding the structure of the higher-order dimension of compulsivity identified in studies of personality disorder traits (Livesley et al., 1998). Pathways models identified a single genetic dimension underlying the specific traits that define this construct. Factor analyses show that it is consistently not related to other traits—hence, the three phenotypic traits that delineate compulsivity from separate higher-order factors. Compulsivity is, however, a trait narrower than other higher-order domains. It appears to represent a distinct basic or lower-order trait based on a single genetic dimension that does not have a hierarchical relationship with other basic traits.

Basic-Level Traits: Defining the Basic Unit of Personality

The idea that personality is inherited as a few genetic modules with broad effects and a large number of modules with more specific effects focuses attention on the significance of lower-order or basic traits. These findings are similar to evaluations of hierarchical models of cognitive ability that also provide evidence that specific abilities are heritable (Casto, DeFries, & Fulkner, 1995; Pedersen, Plomin, Nesselroade, & McClearn, 1992). Basic traits do not appear to be specific exemplars of the higher-order traits that they define or blends of two or more factors (Hofstee, DeRaad, & Goldberg, 1992). Rather, they are discrete genetic entities with their own biological basis. This suggests that personality models that reduce traits to a few global domains do not reflect the genetic architecture of normal or disordered personality. As noted earlier, personality research has tended to neglect these traits in favor of more global dimensions. Yet evidence of specificity of genetic effects suggests that the basic traits are the fundamental building blocks of personality that are more

important for understanding personality than are the global constructs that have traditionally been the focus of research and explanation. This approach again raises the question of how basic traits should be conceptualized and defined, as well as which criteria are relevant to defining domains.

Costa and McCrae (1998) noted the challenges of delineating a comprehensive set of basic traits. The specificity of genetic effects also reveals the challenge involved because of the large number of genetic dimensions that are likely to be involved. A genetic perspective does, however, provide a definition of a basic dimension that could facilitate the identification and assessment of these traits. The usual psychometric criteria used to develop homogeneous scales could be supplemented with the genetic criterion that a basic trait scale represents a single specific genetic dimension. With this approach, items assessing a basic trait would form a genetically homogeneous unit as opposed to a factorially homogeneous unit. Items could then be selected according to their correlation with the underlying genetic dimension. Thus items forming a scale would share the same general and specific genetic etiology. With this approach, the goal would be to use behavioral genetic techniques to bring about definitions of the phenotype that correspond to what Farone, Tsuang, and Tsuang (1999) refer to as "genetically crisp categories" (p. 114).

An example of this approach is provided by a study of the genetic structure of the Eysenck Personality Questionnaire (Heath, Eaves, & Martin, 1989). This instrument has three broad scales composed of 21 to 25 items that assess Neuroticism, Extraversion, and Psychoticism. Heath and colleagues extracted a common genetic and environmental factor for Neuroticism and Extraversion, indicating that these items are etiologically homogeneous. In contrast, little evidence was found for a common genetic factor for the Psychoticism items. Subsequent analyses showed that the items formed into two distinct genetic factors: paranoid attitudes and hostile behavior. The results of such a systematic evaluation of item etiology could be used to form etiologically homogeneous scales.

This approach could be used either to develop new scales or modify existing scales so that they resemble the underlying genetic architecture more closely. This could be achieved by applying differential weights that index the influence of specific genetic and environmental influences on different traits. In this way, questions about the phenotypic structure of personality are addressed, and scales could be constructed so that they do not reflect competing genetic and environmental influences.

The estimation of genetic and environmental factor scores is a relatively new and active area of research. Sham et al. (2001) recently described a method that permits these genetic factor scores to be computed. Their method uses the following equation:

$$y = \gamma \Sigma^{-1} x \qquad (3.2)$$

where y = factor score for the common genetic factor, $\tilde{a}$ = the factor loadings of each variable on the genetic factor of interest (i.e., the column vector of estimated path coefficients that represent the correlations between the common genetic or environmental factor and the observed measures), Σ^{-1} = correlation matrix between all of the variables (i.e., the inverse of the correlation matrix of the observed measures), and x = each person's score or response to each of the variables (i.e., column vector of observed values on the measures). Other methods are also available to compute genetic and environmental factor scores (Thomis et al., 2000).

Domain Content

As discussed earlier, the facet structure of several five-factor domains is still unclear. The same behavioral genetic approach used to define and measure basic trait scales could also be applied to the delineation of domain content. The unity of a domain is demonstrated by evidence that a single common genetic factor influences all the facets composing the domain. This approach could be used to clarify the location of impulsivity within the higher-order structure. The five-factor model locates impulsivity in Neuroticism, whereas Eysenck places it within Extraversion. As noted earlier, the bivariate correlations of this facet with other Neuroticism facets assessed with the NEO-PI-R are lower than correlations between other facets. Etiological data could be used to relocate impulsivity with other traits with which it shares a common etiology. Alternatively the item content could be changed based on genetic and environmental etiology so that correlations with the other Neuroticism facets are increased (of the loadings on the common factors are increased). In the case of the DAPP scales, impulsivity is part of the phenotypic trait of stimulus seeking along with sensation seeking and recklessness. Multivariate genetic analyses showed that a single common genetic factor underlies this dimension that is defined by sensation seeking and recklessness (see Table 3.5). Impulsivity has a low loading on the factor and a substantial specific heritable component. It appears that impulsivity as defined within the DAPP structure is a specific heritable entity and not the result of interaction between extraversion and constraint or psychoticism as suggested by Depue and Collins (1999) or extraversion and psychoticism as suggested by Gray (1970, 1973, 1987; Pickering & Gray, 1999), although it is consistent with Gray's argument that impulsivity is a fundamental dimension of temperament.

The findings of behavioral genetic studies of personality structure also have implications for attempts to identify the putative genes for personality. Most molecular genetic studies of personality use an analytic strategy that correlates a *total* personality trait score such as Neuroticism with variations in the candidate allele (Lesch et al., 1996). As the studies described show, the total scale score confounds multiple genetic and environmental effects and reduces the power to detect putative loci. The use of etiological factor scores that index the proportions of the personality phenotype directly attributable to specific genetic and environmental effects (Boomsma, 1996; Sham et al., 2001; Thomis et al., 2000) could reduce these confounds.

UNIVERSALITY OF TRAIT STRUCTURE

Most models of personality traits including Eysenck's three-factor model (Eysenck & Eysenck 1992), the five-factor model, and diagnostic categories of personality disorder proposed in the *DSM-IV* (American Psychiatric Association, 1994) assume that the taxonomies proposed reflect a universal structure. This assumption is also assumed to apply to the measures developed to assess these constructs. The only differences that these models of personality (and their measures) permit between cultures and other groups (e.g., gender) are quantitative in nature; they typically mean differences in trait levels or severity. If these assumptions are correct, we should find that the etiological architecture of personality is also invariant across cultures and other basic groupings. We discuss this idea with respect to cross-cultural comparisons and the effects of gender.

Cross-Cultural Comparisons

Multiple studies show that the observed factorial structure of scales such as the NEO-PI-R is stable across cultures. For example, McCrae and Costa (1997) reported that the five-factor structure is consistent across samples from the United States, Western Europe, and Asia (see also Costa & McCrae, 1992; McCrae et al., 2000). The issue of cross-cultural stability also applies to etiological structure. Earlier, we described fitting an independent pathways model to the six facets defining NEO-PI-R domains in independent samples of German and Canadian twins. The universality of genetic effects can be evaluated by testing the equivalence of the genetic and environmental structures across independent samples. It is possible to test whether: (a) the same genetic and environmental factors influenced the Canadian and German samples; and (b) whether these factors influenced each sample to the same

TABLE 3.6   Model-Fitting Statistics

Model	Canadian Sample				German Sample			
	χ^2	p	RMSEA	AIC	χ^2	p	RMSEA	AIC
Neuroticism								
1[a]	199.91	.00	.040	−64.09	216.56	.00	.039	−47.44
2[b]	172.11	.00	.036	−79.89	149.82	.07	.019	−102.18
3[c]	151.12	.00	.029	−88.88	135.86	.15	.015	−104.14
4[d]	144.88	.03	.029	−83.12	131.14	.13	.016	−96.86
5[e]	145.12	.03	.030	−82.88	130.40	.14	.014	−97.60
6[f]	210.86	.00	.043	−61.14	220.57	.00	.038	−51.43

Note. All models specified additive genetic and nonshared environmental factors unique to each facet. [a]$df = 132$, one common additive and one common nonshared environmental factor. [b]$df = 126$, one common additive and two common nonshared environmental factors. [c]$df = 120$, two common additive and two common nonshared environmental factors. [d]$df = 114$, two common additive and three common nonshared environmental factors. [e]$df = 114$, three additive and two nonshared environmental factors. [f]$df = 136$, common pathways model.

degree. Two tests of equivalency were applied. The first evaluated equivalency of model *form* by testing the hypothesis that the same kind and number of genetic parameters are required to explain the data across the two samples. Sample differences are hypothesized to be limited to differences in the magnitude of the genetic and environmental influence exerted on a domain's facet scales. If equivalence of model form was supported across the samples, the next step was to evaluate the *magnitude* of genetic and environmental influences across samples. This was accomplished by applying a model with the same parameters to both samples. That is, the model specified the same number and type of factors in both samples and identical and constrained the factor loadings to be identical.

The results of tests of model form and magnitude for NEO-PI-R Neuroticism are shown in Table 3.6. The same number and types of genetic and environmental influences (two additive genetic and two nonshared environmental common factors) were identified in both samples, suggesting that the structure of neuroticism was similar across the samples. When the factor loadings on the common factors from the German sample were made to be the same as those on the Canadian sample (and vice versa), the model no longer fit the data. The results suggested that the primary differences between the German and Canadian samples were limited to the magnitude rather than kind of genetic and environmental effects supporting the claim that the factorial structure of the NEO-PI-R facets is universal.

Gender Differences

Personality tests are usually constructed to minimize gender-based differences by eliminating items whose intercorrelations with the other items can be attributable to gender and

eliminating items evoking marked gender differences in endorsement. The approach yields scales that are applicable to both females and males but it overlooks the possibility of gender differences in the etiology. Behavioral genetic methods may be used to determine whether the same genetic and environmental factors influence personality measure scores in males and females and whether the etiological architecture underlying the factorial structure of a personality measure is the same in males and females.

The first question can be answered by fitting sex-limitation models to personality data (Neale & Cardon, 1992). This is accomplished by fitting a simple extension of the usual heritability model that uses data from same- and opposite-sex twin pairs to test whether the same genetic factors operate in males and females. In this case, gender differences are limited to differences in the magnitude of genetic and environmental influences. Another form of sex-limited gene expression occurs when *different* genes control the expression of a trait that is measured in the same way in males and females. With this form of sex-limitation, it is also possible to determine whether the same genes are present in both sexes but only expressed in one sex. This is evaluated by comparing the similarities of opposite-sex DZ twin pairs with same-sex DZ pairs. Sex-specific genetic influences are suggested when the similarity of opposite-sex pairs is significantly less than the similarities of male or female DZ pairs. The difference in the correlation is attributable to the gender composition of each zygosity group. When the same and opposite-sex DZ correlations are similar, gender differences are not indicated.

Only a few studies have investigated sex-limited gene expression in normal personality. The most notable is Finkel and McGue's (1997) study that showed that the *same* genetic loci influence 11 out of the 14 scales of Multidimensional Personality Questionnaire (MPQ; Tellegen, 1982) in males and females. The heritable influences on the remaining three

TABLE 3.7   Intrapair Twin Correlations (Pearson's *r*)

| | Canadian Sample | | | | | German Sample | | | | |
| | MZ | | DZ | | | MZ | | DZ | | |
NEO-FFI Domain	M	F	M	F	M-F	M	F	M	F	M-F
Neuroticism	.41	.53	.22	.35	.13	.49	.52	.36	.20	.15
Extraversion	.50	.49	.34	.30	.23	.57	.57	.34	.25	.17
Openness	.63	.51	.28	.36	.20	.57	.50	.44	.26	.10
Agreeableness	.50	.46	.14	.33	.26	.43	.42	.37	.10	.10
Conscientiousness	.47	.50	.28	.38	.01	.57	.46	.40	.23	.05
Sample sizes (pairs)	102	165	61	129	73	104	425	38	163	68

traits—Alienation, Control, and Absorption—indicated that the genetic influences were gender-specific. Jang, Livesley, and Vernon (1998) reported some evidence for sex-limited gene expression in 18 traits delineating personality disorder measured by the DAPP. All dimensions except Submissiveness in males, and Cognitive Dysfunction, Compulsivity, Conduct Problems, Suspiciousness, and Self-Harm in females were significantly heritable. Sex-by-genotype analyses suggested that the genetic influences underlying all but four DAPP dimensions (Stimulus Seeking, Callousness, Rejection, Insecure Attachment) were specific to each gender, whereas environmental influences were the same in both genders across all dimensions. Furthermore, the four higher-order dimensions derived from the 18 basic traits (Livesley et al., 1998) were also heritable across sex, and genetic effects were in common to both genders; the exception was Dissocial Behavior, which was not heritable in females.

Such evidence of sex-limited effects challenges the assumed universality of trait taxonomies. However, it could be argued that the results based on the DAPP and MPQ are atypical. The DAPP is a specialized scale designed primarily to assess personality dysfunction. The scale does not cover such areas of normal personality as Openness to Experience (Jang & Livesley, 1999; Schroeder et al., 1992) because abnormal variants of Openness are not included in clinical descriptions of personality disorder. The MPQ, unlike other scales, routinely reveals nonadditive genetic effects due to dominance (Waller & Shaver, 1994). This suggests that it may assess content different from that tested by scales such as the NEO-PI-R, which reveals genetic effects that are additive (e.g., Jang et al., 1998).

A more appropriate evaluation of the assumption of universality would be to examine sex-limited gene expression on a major model of personality such as the five-factor model. Evaluation of whether the same genes are present across different samples is similar to the evaluation of cross-cultural effects. Jang, Livesley, Riemann, and Angleitner (in press) applied sex-limitation models to NEO-FFI data

obtained from the Canada and German twin samples described earlier. Two general models were fit to the data. The first specified additive genetic and nonshared environmental influences for females and males and a male-specific genetic factor. The second tested whether heritable influences common to males and females were the same across the two samples. Table 3.7 reports the intrapair twin correlations for each zygosity group in each sample. The MZ male and MZ female correlations exceed their respective DZ correlations, suggesting the presence of heritable influences on each NEO-FFI domain in each sample. Of particular interest is the comparison between the DZ opposite-sex correlations and the same-sex DZ correlations. In both samples, the DZ opposite-sex correlation for Conscientiousness was near zero, suggesting the presence of differential gender effects. The final form of the best-fitting model is presented in Table 3.8. The results suggest that genetic and environmental influences common to males and females influence four of the five FFM domains. The exception was Conscientiousness, for which gender-specific additive genetic influences operate. However, the external events and experiences specific to each twin—nonshared environmental influences—are common to males and females. The results also suggest that the type and magnitude of genetic and environmental influence were the same across the two groups, supporting the notion that the five-factor model as assessed by the NEO-FFI is applicable to different cultures and genders.

This study has several limitations. The first is that the sample sizes are rather small in both samples, especially male DZ twin pairs and opposite-sex pairs. The twin covariances associated with these two zygosity types, especially the opposite-sex pairs, are crucial for the validity of the analyses. The availability of relatively few twin pairs calls into question the stability of the correlations and thus the detection of sex-limited genes—as was obtained for Conscientiousness. Second, the study used the NEO-FFI, the short form of the NEO-PI-R. The full scale might produce different results because long versions of these scales sample domains more

these findings (Flory et al., 1999; Gelernter, Kranzler, Coccaro, Siever, & New, 1998; Hamer et al., 1999; Herbst, Zonderman, McCrae, & Costa, 2000). Gustavsson et al. (1999) also failed to replicate these findings using the Karolinska Scales of Personality.

These inconsistencies can be attributed to conceptual and measurement issues. The early studies in particular were often based on a conceptual model that assumed that personality is influenced by relatively few genes, each accounting for substantial variance. As noted, the evidence does not support this approach. There has also been a tendency to assume that each trait was linked a specific neurotransmitter system. More recently, however, attention has focused on pleiotropic effects by investigating the possibility that a given polymorphism influences several traits. Work on the serotonin transporter gene, for example, suggests that it is not associated with a single trait but rather has a pleiotropic relationship with Neuroticism and Agreeableness. Studies on humans and primates suggest that altered serotonin activity is related to negative emotional states such as depression, anxiety, and hostility, and to social behaviors such as dominance, aggression, and affiliation with peers (Graeff, Guimaraes, De Andrade, & Deakin, 1996; Knutson et al., 1998; Murphy et al., 1998). Knutson and colleagues (1998) found that administration of the specific serotonin reuptake inhibitor, paroxetine, decreased negative affect and increased social affiliation in normal human subjects. Lesch and colleagues (1996) reported that individuals carrying the 5-HTTLPR-S allele had increased total scores on NEO-PI-R Neuroticism and the facets of Anxiety, Angry Hostility, Depression, and Impulsiveness. The allele accounted for 3 to 4% of the total variance in these scales. Unexpectedly, the allele was also associated with a *decreased* NEO-PI-R Agreeableness score. Greenberg et al. (1999) recently replicated these findings. Hamer et al. (1999) showed that 5-HTTLPR-S genotypes were significantly associated with increased Harm Avoidance (which correlates .66 with NEO-PI-R Neuroticism) and decreased Self-Directedness (correlated −.64 with NEO-PI-R Neuroticism), Reward Dependence, and Cooperativeness (shown to correlate .43 and .66 with NEO-PI-R Agreeableness). These effects accounted for .80%, 1.98%, .97%, and 2.60% of the total variance in these scores, respectively. Mazzanti et al. (1998), Peirson et al. (2000), and Benjamin et al. (2000) have reported replications.

Measurement problems contributing to inconsistent findings include the use of measures with less-than-optimal psychometric properties and the use of relatively broad personality constructs. Comparison of the dopamine–novelty seeking and serotonin-neuroticism studies suggests that the serotonin-neuroticism literature is less ambiguous than the dopamine–novelty seeking literature. These differences appear to be related to scale properties. Inconsistent findings may also be due to the confounding of genetic and environmental influences on the phenotypes. As we have tried to show, many constructs and scales are etiologically heterogeneous.

Twin studies estimating statistical pleiotropy could contribute to molecular genetic studies by identifying traits that are etiologically homogeneous units and etiologically related. Molecular genetic work could then be used to confirm these associations by identifying the actual genes that account for trait covariance. This would provide the strongest basis for revising personality models and allocating traits to etiologically related domains.

CONCLUSIONS

The thesis of this chapter is that behavioral genetic approaches promise to provide an additional perspective that may help to resolve some of the more intractable problems in delineating and conceptualizing personality structure. The evidence reviewed suggests an alternative perspective on the trait structure of personality that complements traditional conceptions. Although trait theory has largely concentrated on mapping personality in terms of broad global traits, the evidence suggests that personality is inherited as a large number of genetic dimensions that have relatively specific effects on personality phenotypes and a smaller number of genetic dimensions that have broader effects, perhaps through a modulating influence on related dispositions. These dimensions with broader effects appear to account for some of the observed covariation among traits. They do not appear, however, to exert these effects through higher-order phenotypic structures, but rather through a direct influence on each basic trait. We assume that these common features are more likely to involve modulating functions or common mechanisms that regulate each trait in a given cluster.

These tentative conclusions suggest the need to reconsider traditional models of the hierarchical structure of personality in which traits are organized into broad domains due to the effects on broad dispositions. Instead, the organization of traits into clusters is assumed to arise from the pleiotropic effects of genetic dimensions that affect multiple traits. Under these circumstances, it is conceivable that not all traits are organized into clusters of covarying features, but rather remain relatively distinct characteristics. Nor is it inevitable the traits are hierarchically organized in similar ways across domains. That is, it is possible that the symmetrical hierarchical structure avidly sought by trait theorists and students of psychopathology does not reflect the way personality is organized at a genetic level. An equally feasible structure would involve considerable differences in complexity across domains. Some domains may consist of a relatively large number of traits, whereas others may consist of only one or two genetically homogeneous traits. These assumptions are consistent with the lexical view of Saucier and Goldberg (1996), who argued that the five domains are merely a convenient way of organizing lower-order traits and that there is no inherent reason to assume that domains are equal in breadth or in pervasiveness.

Although behavioral genetic analyses show that environmental factors exert a considerable influence on personality, they do not appear to influence the structural relationships among traits to any appreciable extent. Instead, environmental factors appear to exert a more contemporaneous effect on trait expression. The nature of these factors and the way that they function remain important topics of research.

REFERENCES

Allport, G. W. (1961). *Pattern and growth in personality*. New York: Holt, Reinhart and Winston.

Almagor, M., Tellegen, A., & Waller, N. G. (1995). The big seven model: A cross-cultural replication and further exploration of the basic dimensions of natural language trait descriptors. *Journal of Personality and Social Psychology, 69,* 300–307.

American Psychiatric Association (1994). *The diagnostic and statistical manual for mental disorders* (4th ed.). Washington, DC: Author.

Ashton, M. C., Lee, K., Vernon, P. A., & Jang, K. L. (2000). Fluid intelligence, crystallized intelligence, and the Openness/Intellect factor. *Journal of Research in Personality, 34,* 198–207.

Avia, M. D., Sanz, J., Sanchez-Bernardos, M. L., Martinez-Arias, M. R. Silva, & Graña, (1995). The five-factor model—II. Relations of the NEO-PI with other personality variables. *Personality and Individual Differences, 19,* 81–97.

Baker, L. A., & Daniels, D. (1990). Nonshared environmental influences and personality differences in adult twins. *Journal of Personality and Social Psychology, 58,* 103–110.

Benjamin, J., Greenberg, B., & Murphy, D. L. (1996). Mapping personality traits related to genes: Population and family association between the D4 dopamine receptor and measures of novelty seeking. *Nature Genetics, 12,* 81–84.

Benjamin, J., Osher, Y., Lichtenberg, P., Bachner-Melman, R., Gritsenko, I., Kotler, M., Belmaker, R. H., Valsky, V., Drendel, M., & Ebstein, R. P. (2000). An interaction between the catechol O-methyltransferase and serotonin transporter promoter region polymorphisms contributes to Tridimensional Personality Questionnaire persistence scores in normal subjects. *Neuropsychobiology, 41,* 48–53.

Bergeman, C. S., Chipeur, H. M., Plomin, R., Pederson, N. L., McClearn, G. E., Nesselroade, J. R., Costa, P. T., & McCrae, R. R. (1993). Genetic and environmental effects on openness to experience, agreeableness, and conscientiousness: An adoption/twin study. *Journal of Personality, 61,* 159–179.

Boomsma, D. I. (1996). Using multivariate genetic modeling to detect pleiotropic quantitative trait loci. *Behavior Genetics, 26,* 161–166.

Bouchard, T. J. (1999). Genes, environment, and personality. In S. J. Ceci & W. M. Williams (Eds.), *The nature-nurture debate: The essential readings. Essential readings in developmental psychology* (pp. 97–103). Malden, MA: Blackwell.

Carey, G. (1987). Is extraversion a unitary trait? *Behavior Genetics, 17,* 619.

Carey, G., & DiLalla, D. L. (1994). Personality and psychopathology: Genetic perspectives. *Journal of Abnormal Psychology, 103,* 32–43.

Caspi, A., & Bem, D. J. (1990). Personality continuity and change across the life course. In L. A. Pervin (Ed.), *Handbook of personality: Theory and research.* New York: Guilford.

Casto, S. D., DeFries, J. C., & Fulker, D. W. (1995). Multivariate genetic analysis of Wechsler Intelligence Scale for Children—Revised (WISC–R) factors. *Behavior Genetics, 25,* 25–32.

Cloninger, C. R. (1987). A systematic method for clinical description and classification of personality variants: A proposal. *Archives of General Psychiatry, 44,* 573–588.

Cloninger, C. R., Adolfsson, R., & Svrakic, N. M. (1996). Mapping genes for human personality. *Nature Genetics, 12,* 3–4.

Cloninger, C. R., Svrakic, D. M., & Przybeck, T. R. (1993). A psychobiological model of temperament and character. *Archives of General Psychiatry, 50,* 975–990.

Costa, P. T., & McCrae, R. R. (1985). *Manual for the NEO Personality Inventory.* Odessa, FL: Psychological Assessment Resources.

Costa, P. T., & McCrae, R. R. (1992). *Revised NEO Personality Inventory (NEO-PI-R) and the NEO Five-Factor Inventory (NEO-FFI) professional manual.* Odessa, FL: Psychological Assessment Resources.

Costa, P. T., & McCrae, R. R. (1995). Domains and facets: Hierarchical personality assessment using the Revised NEO Personality Inventory. *Journal of Personality Assessment, 64,* 21–50.

Costa, P. T., & McCrae, R. R. (1997). Longitudinal stability of adult personality. In R. Hogan & J. A. Johnson (Eds.), *Handbook of personality psychology* (pp. 269–290). San Diego, CA: Academic Press.

Costa, P. T., & McCrae, R. R. (1998). Six approaches to the explication of facet-level traits: Examples from conscientiousness. *European Journal of Psychology, 12,* 117–134.

Crawford, C. B., & DeFries, J. C. (1978). Factor analysis of genetic and environmental correlation matrices. *Multivariate Behavioral Research, 13,* 297–318.

DeFries, J. C., & Fulker, D. W. (1986). Multivariate behavioral genetics and development: An overview. *Behavior Genetics, 16,* 1–10.

Depue, R. A., & Collins, P. F. (1999). Neurobiology of the structure of personality: Dopamine, facilitation of incentive motivation, and extraversion. *Behavioral and Brain Sciences, 22,* 491–569.

Digman, J. M. (1990). Personality structure: Emergence of the five-factor structure. *Annual Review of Psychology, 41,* 417–440.

Digman, J. M., & Inouye, J. (1986). Further specification of the five robust factors of personality. *Journal of Personality and Social Psychology, 50,* 116–123.

Draycott, S. G., & Kline, P. (1995). The Big Three or the Big Five—the EPQ-R vs. the NEO-PI: A research note, replication and elaboration. *Personality and Individual Differences, 18,* 801–804.

Ebstein, R. P., Gritsenko, I., & Nemanov, L. (1997). No association between the serotonin transporter gene regulatory region polymorphism and the tridimensional personality questionnaire (TPQ) temperament of harm avoidance. *Molecular Psychiatry, 2,* 224–226.

Ebstein, R. P., Novick, O., & Umansky, R. (1996). D4DR exon III polymorphism associated with the personality trait of novelty seeking in normal human volunteers. *Nature Genetics, 12,* 78–80.

Ebstein, R. P., Segman, R., & Benjamin, J. (1997). 5–HT2C (HTR2C) serotonin receptor gene polymorphism associated with the human personality trait of reward dependence: Interaction with dopamine D4 receptor (D4DR) and dopamine D3 (D3DR) polymorphisms. *American Journal of Medical Genetics, 74,* 65–72.

Eysenck, H. J. (1991). Dimensions of personality: 16, 5 or 3? Criteria for a taxonomic paradigm. *Personality and Individual Differences, 12,* 773–790.

Eysenck, H. J. (1992). A reply to Costa and McCrae: P or A and C—the role of theory. *Personality and Individual Differences, 13,* 867–868.

Eysenck, H. J., & Eysenck, S. B. G. (1992). *Manual for the Eysenck Personality Questionnaire–Revised.* San Diego, CA: Educational and Industrial Testing Service.

Farone, S. V., Tsuang, M. T., & Tsuang, D. W. (1999). *Genetics of mental disorders.* New York: Guilford Press.

Finkel, D., & McGue, M. (1997). Sex differences and nonadditivity in heritability of the Multidimensional Personality Questionnaire Scales. *Journal of Personality and Social Psychology, 72,* 929–938.

Flory, J .D., Manuck, S. B., Ferrell, R. E., Dent, K. M., Peters, D. G., & Muldoon, M. F. (1999). Neuroticism is not associated with the serotonin transporter (5–HTTLR) polymorphism. *Molecular Psychiatry, 4,* 93–96.

Gelernter, J., Kranzler, H., Coccaro, E. F., Siever, L. J., & New, A. S. (1998). Serotonin transporter protein gene polymorphism and personality measures in African American and European American subjects. *American Journal of Psychiatry, 155,* 1332–1338.

Goldberg, L. R., (1990). An alternative "description of personality": The Big-Five factor structure. *Journal of Personality and Social Psychology, 59,* 1216–1229.

Goldberg, L. R. (1993). The structure of phenotypic personality traits. *American Psychologist, 48,* 26–34.

Gough, H. G. (1989). The California Psychological Inventory. In C. S. Newmark (Ed.), *Major psychological assessment instruments* (Vol. 2, pp. 67–98). Needham Heights, MA: Allyn & Bacon.

Graeff, F. G., Guimaraes, F. S., De Andrade, T. G., & Deakin, J. F. (1996). Role of 5–HT in stress, anxiety, and depression. *Pharmacology, Biochemistry, and Behavior, 54,* 129–141.

Gray, J. A. (1970). The psychophysiological basis of intraversion-extraversion. *Behavior Research and Therapy, 8,* 249–266.

Gray, J. A. (1973). Causal theories of personality and how to test them. In J. R. Royce (Ed.), *Multivariate analysis and psychological theory,* (pp. 409–463). London: Academic Press.

Gray, J. A. (1987). The neuropsychology of emotion and personality. In S. M. Stahl & S. D. Iversen (Eds.), *Cognitive neurochemistry* (pp. 171–190). Oxford, England: Oxford University Press.

Greenberg, B. D., Tolliver, T. J., Huang, S. J., Li, Q., Bengel, D., & Murphy, D. L. (1999). Genetic variation in the serotonin transporter promoter region affects serotonin uptake in human blood platelets. *American Journal of Medical Genetics, 88,* 83–87.

Gustavsson, J. P., Nöthen, M. M., Jonsson, E. G., Neidt, H., Forslund, K., Rylander, G., Mattila-Evenden, M., Sedvall, G. C., Propping, P., & Åsberg, M. (1999). No association between serotonin transporter gene polymorphisms and personality traits. *American Journal of Medical Genetics, 88,* 430–436.

Hamer, D. H., Greenberg, B. D., Sabol, S. Z., & Murphy, D. L. (1999). Role of serotonin transporter gene in temperament and character. *Journal of Personality Disorders, 13,* 312–328.

Hampson, S. E., John, O. P., & Goldberg, L. R. (1986). Category breadth and hierarchical structure in personality: Studies of asymmetries in judgments of trait implications. *Journal of Personality and Social Psychology, 51,* 37–54.

Hansenne, M., & Ansseau, M. (1999). Harm avoidance and serotonin. *Biological Psychology, 51,* 77–81.

Heath, A. C., Eaves, L. J., & Martin, N. G. (1989). The genetic structure of personality: III. Multivariate genetic item analysis of the EPQ scales. *Personality and Individual Differences, 10,* 877–888.

Heath, A. C., Neale, M. C., Kessler, R. C., Eaves, L. J., & Kendler, K. S. (1992). Evidence for genetic influences on personality from self-reports and informant ratings. *Journal of Personality and Social Psychology, 63,* 85–96.

Herbst, J. H., Zonderman, A. B., McCrae, R. R., & Costa, P. T. (2000). Do the dimensions of the Temperament and Character Inventory map a simple genetic architecture? Evidence from molecular genetics and factor analysis. *American Journal of Psychiatry, 157,* 1285–1290.

Hetherington, E. M., Reiss, D., & Plomin, R. (Eds.) (1994). *Separate social worlds of siblings: The impact of nonshared environment on development.* Hillsdale, NJ: Lawrence Erlbaum.

Hofstee, W. K., deRaad, B., & Goldberg, L. R. (1992). Integration of the Big Five and circumplex approaches to trait structure. *Journal of Personality and Social Psychology, 63,* 146–163.

Jackson, D. N. (1984). *The Personality Research Form.* Ontario, Canada: Sigma Assessment Systems.

Jang, K. L., & Livesley, W. J. (1999).Why do measures of normal and disordered personality correlate? A study of genetic comorbidity. *Journal of Personality Disorders, 13,* 10–17.

Jang, K. L., Livesley, W. J., Riemann, R., & Angleitner, A. (in press). The Five-Factor Model of personality: A behavioural genetic analysis of gender across cultures. *Personality and Individual Differences.*

Jang, K. L., Livesley, W. J., Vernon, P. A., & Jackson, D. N. (1996). Heritability ofpersonality disorder traits: A twin study. *Acta Psychiatrica Scandinavica, 94,* 438–444.

Jang, K. L., McCrae, R. R., Angleitner, A., Riemann, R., & Livesley, W. J. (1998). Heritability of facet-level traits in a cross-cultural twin study: Support for a hierarchical model of personality. *Journal of Personality and Social Psychology, 74,* 1556–1565.

Jang, K. L., Vernon, P. A., & Livesley, W. J. (2000). Personality disorder traits, family environment, and alcohol misuse: A multivariate behavioural genetic analysis. *Addiction, 95,* 873–888.

John, O. P., & Srivastava, S. (1999). The big five trait taxonomy: History, measurement, and theoretical perspectives. In L. A. Pervin & O. P. John (Eds.), *Handbook of Personality* (pp. 102–138). New York: Guilford.

Katsuragi, S., Kunugi, A. S., Sano, A., Tsutsumi, T., Isogawa, K., Nanko, S., & Akiyoshi, J. (1999). Association between serotonin transporter gene polymorphism and anxiety-related traits. *Biological Psychiatry, 45,* 368–370.

Kendler, K. S., & Karkowski-Shuman, L. (1997). Stressful life events and genetic liability to major depression: Genetic control of exposure to the environment? *Psychological Medicine, 27,* 539–547.

Knutson, B., Wolkowitz, O. M., Cole, S. W., Chan, T., Moore, E. A., Johnson, R. C., Terpstra, J., Turner, R. A., & Reus, V. I. (1998). Selective alteration of personality and social behavior by serotonergic intervention. *American Journal of Psychiatry, 155,* 373–379.

Lake, R. I. E., Eaves, L. J., Maes, H. H., Heath, A. C., & Martin, N. G. (2000). Further evidence against the environmental transmission of individual differences in neuroticism from a collaborative study of 45,850 twins and relatives on two continents. *Behavior Genetics, 30,* 223–233.

Lesch, K. P., Bengel, D., Heils, A., Zhang Sabol, S., Greenberg, B. D., Petri, S., Benjamin, J., Muller, C. R., Hamer, D. H., &

Murphy, D. L. (1996). Association of anxiety-related traits with a polymorphism in the serotonin transporter gene regulatory region. *Science, 274,* 1527–1530.

Livesley, W. J. (1986). Trait and behavioral prototypes of personality disorder. *American Journal of Psychiatry, 143,* 728–732.

Livesley, W. J., & Jackson, D. N. (in press). *Manual for the dimensional assessment of personality pathology.* Port Huron, MI: Sigma Press.

Livesley, W. J., Jackson, D. N., & Schroeder, M. L. (1992). Factorial structure of traits delineating personality disorders in clinical and general population samples. *Journal of Abnormal Psychology, 101,* 432–440.

Livesley, W. J., & Jang, K. L. (2000). Toward an empirically based classification of personality disorder. *Journal of Personality Disorders, 14,* 137–151.

Livesley, W. J., Jang, K. L., & Vernon, P. A. (1998). The phenotypic and genetic architecture of traits delineating personality disorder. *Archives of General Psychiatry, 55,* 941–948.

Loehlin, J. C. (1987). Heredity, environment, and the structure of the California Psychological Inventory. *Multivariate Behavioral Research, 22,* 137–148.

Loehlin, J. C. (1992). *Genes and environment in personality development.* Newbury Park, CA: Sage.

Loehlin, J. C., & Nicholls, R. C. (1976). *Heredity, environment, and personality.* Austin: University of Texas Press.

Lykken, D. T., McGue, M., & Tellegen, A. (1987). Recruitment bias in twin research: The rule of two-thirds reconsidered. *Behavior Genetics, 17,* 343–362.

Magnus, K., Diener, E., Fujita, F., & Pavot, W. (1993). Extraversion and neuroticism as predictors of objective life events: A longitudinal analysis. *Journal of Personality and Social Psychology, 65,* 1046–1053.

Malhotra, A. K., Goldman, D., Ozaki, N., & Breier, A. (1996). Lack of association between polymorphisms in the 5–HT-sub(2A) receptor gene and the antipsychotic response to clozapine. *American Journal of Psychiatry, 153,* 1092–1094.

Mazzanti, C. M., Lappalainen, J., Long, J. C., Bengel, D., Naukkarinen, H., Eggert, M., Virkkunen, M., Linnoila, M., Goldman, D. (1998). Role of the serotonin transporter promoter polymorphism in anxiety-related traits. *Archives of General Psychiatry, 55,* 936–940.

McArdle, J. J., & Goldsmith, H. H. (1990). Alternative common factor models for multivariate biometric analyses. *Behaviour Genetics, 20,* 569–608.

McCrae, R. R., & Costa, P. T. (1985a). Comparison of EPI and psychoticism scales with measures of the five-factor model of personality. *Personality and Individual Differences, 6,* 587–597.

McCrae, R. R., & Costa, P. T. (1985b). Updating Norman's "adequacy taxonomy": Intelligence and personality dimensions in natural language and in questionnaires. *Journal of Personality and Social Psychology, 49,* 710–721.

McCrae, R. R., & Costa, P. T. (1986). Clinical assessment can benefit from recent advances in personality psychology. *American Psychologist, 41,* 1001–1003.

McCrae, R. R., & Costa, P. T. (1996). Toward a new generation of personality theories: Theoretical contexts for the five-factor model. In J. S. Wiggins (Ed.), *The five factor model of personality* (pp. 51–87). New York: Guilford.

McCrae, R. R., Costa, P. T., & Piedmont, R. L. (1993). Folk concepts, natural language, and psychological constructs: The California Psychological Inventory and the five factor model. *Journal of Personality, 61,* 1–26.

McCrae, R. R., & Costa, P. T., Jr. (1997). Personality trait structure as a human universal. *American Psychologist, 52,* 509–516.

McCrae, R. R., Costa, P. T., Jr., Ostendorf, F., Angleitner, A., Hrebickova, M., Avia, M. D., Sanz, J., Sanchez-Bernardos, M. L., Kusdil, M. E., Woodfield, R., Saunders, P. R., & Smith, P. B. (2000). Nature over nurture: Temperament, personality, and life span development. *Journal of Personality and Social Psychology, 78,* 173–186.

McCrae, R. R., Jang, K. L., Livesley, W. J., Riemann, R., & Angleitner, A. (in press). The five-factor model of personality: A behavioural genetic analysis of gender across cultures. *Personality and Individual Differences.*

McCrae, R. R., & John, O. P. (1992). An introduction of the five-factor model and its applications. *Journal of Personality, 60,* 175–215.

Moos, R. H., & Moos, B. S. (1974). *Manual for the Family Environment Scale.* Palo Alto, CA: Consulting Psychologists Press.

Murphy, D. L., Andrews, A. M., Wichems, C. H., Li, Q., Tohda, M., & Greenberg, B. (1998). Brain serotonin neurotransmission: An overview and update with an emphasis on serotonin subsystem heterogeneity, multiple receptors, interactions with other neurotransmitter systems, and consequent implications for understanding the actions of serotonergic drugs. *Journal of Clinical Psychiatry, 59,* 4–12.

Neale, M. C., & Cardon, L. R. (1992). *Methodology for genetic studies of twins and families.* Dordrecht, Netherlands: Kulwer Academic Press.

Ono, Y., Manki, H., Yomishura, K., Muramatsu, T., Higuchi, S., Yagi, G., Kanba, S., & Asai, M. (1997). Association between dopamine D4 receptor (D4DR) exon III polymorphism and novelty seeking in Japanese subjects. *American Journal of Genetics, 47,* 501–503.

Passini, F. T., & Norman, W. T. (1966). A universal conception of personality structure? *Journal of Personality and Social Psychology, 4,* 44–49.

Paunonen, S. V., & Jackson, D. N. (1996). The Jackson Personality Inventory and the Five factor model of personality. *Journal of Research in Personality, 30,* 42–59.

Pedersen, N. L., Plomin, R., Nesselroade, J. R., & McClearn, G. E. (1992). A quantitative genetic analysis of cognitive abilities during the second half of the life span. *Psychological Science, 3,* 346–353.

Peirson, A. R., Heuchert, J. W., Thomala, L., Berk, M., Plein, H., & Cloninger, C. R. (2000). Relationship between serotonin and the Temperament and Character Inventory. *Psychiatry Research, 89,* 29–37.

Pickering, A. D., & Gray, J. A. (1999). The neuroscience of personality. In L. A. Pervin & O. P. John (Eds.), *The handbook of personality* (pp. 277–299). New York: Guilford.

Plomin, R., & Caspi, A. (1998). DNA and personality. *European Journal of Personality, 12,* 387–407.

Plomin, R., Chipeur, H. M., & Loehlin, J. C. (1990). Behavior genetics and personality. In L. A. Pervin (Ed.), *Handbook of personality: Theory and research.* New York: Guilford.

Plomin, R., & Daniels, D. (1987). Children in the same family are very different, but why? *Behavioral and Brain Sciences, 10,* 44–59.

Plomin, R., DeFries, J. C., & McClearn, G. E. (1990). *Behavioral genetics: A primer* (2nd ed.). New York: W. H. Freeman.

Plomin, R., DeFries, J. C., McClearn, G. E., & McGuffin, P. (Eds.). (2000). *Behavioral genetics: A primer* (3rd ed.). New York: W. H. Freeman.

Pogue-Geile, M., Ferrell, R., Deka, R., Debski, T., & Manuck, S. (1998). Human novelty seeking personality traits and dopamine D4 receptor polymorphisms: A twin and genetic association study. *American Journal of Medical Genetics, 81,* 44–48.

Poulton, R. G., & Andrews, G. (1992). Personality as a cause of adverse life events. *Acta Psychiatrica Scandinavica, 85,* 35–38.

Reiss, D., Neiderhiser, J. M., Hetherington, E. M., & Plomin, R. (2000). *The relationship code: Deciphering genetic and social influences on adolescent development.* Cambridge, MA: Harvard University Press.

Riemann, R., Angleitner, A., & Strelau, J. (1997). Genetic and environmental influences on personality: A twin study. *Journal of Personality, 65,* 449–476.

Rinne, T., Westenberg, H. G. M., den Boer, J. A., & van den Brink, W. (2000). Serotonergic blunting to meta-chlorophenylpiperazine (m-CPP) highly correlates with sustained childhood abuse in impulsive and autoaggressive female borderline patients. *Biological Psychiatry, 47,* 548–556.

Saucier, G., & Goldberg, L. R. (1996). The language of personality: Lexical perspectives on the five-factor model. In J. S. Wiggins (Ed.), *The five factor model of personality* (pp. 21–50). New York: Guilford.

Saudino, K. J., Pedersen, N. L., Lichtenstein, P., & McClearn, G. E. (1997). Can personality explain genetic influences on life events? *Journal of Personality and Social Psychology, 72,* 196–206.

Schroeder, M. L., Wormworth, J. A., & Livesley, W. J. (1992). Dimensions of personality disorder and their relationships to the big five dimensions of personality. *Psychological Assessment: A Journal of Consulting and Clinical Psychology, 4,* 47–53.

Sham, P. C., Sterne, A., Purcell, S., Cherny, S., Webster, M., Rijsdijk, F., Asherson, P., Ball, D., Craig, I., Eley, T., Goldberg, D., Gray, J., Mann, A., Owen, M., & Plomin, R. (2001). Genesis. Creating a composite index of the vulnerability to anxiety and depression in a community-based sample of siblings. *Twin Research, 3,* 316–322.

Shweder, R. A. (1975). How relevant is an individual difference theory of personality? *Journal of Personality, 43,* 455–484.

Simpson, C. G. (1961). *Principles of animal taxonomy.* New York: Columbia University Press.

Tellegen, A. (1982). *Brief manual for the Differential Personality Questionnaire.* Unpublished manuscript, University of Minnesota, Minneapolis.

Tellegen, A. (1985). Structures of mood and personality and their relevance to assessing anxiety with an emphasis on self-report. In A. H. Tuma & J. D. Maser (Eds.), *Anxiety and the anxiety disorders* (pp. 681–706). Hillsdale, NJ: Erlbaum.

Thomis, M. A., Vlietnick, R. F., Maes, H. H., Limkie, C. J., van Leemputte, M., Claessens, A. L., Marchal, G., & Beunen, G. P. (2000). Predictive power of individual genetic and environmental factor scores. *Twin Research, 3,* 99–108.

Turkheimer, E. (1998). Heritability and biological explanation. *Psychological Review, 105,* 782–791.

Turkheimer, E., & Waldron, M. (2000). Nonshared environment: A theoretical, methodological, and quantitative review. *Psychological Bulletin, 126,* 78–108.

Vandenbergh, D. J., Zonderman, A. B., Wang, J., Uhl, G. R., & Costa, P. T. (1997). No association between Novelty Seeking and dopamine D4 receptor (DRD4) exon III seven repeat alleles in Baltimore Longitudinal Study of aging participants. *Molecular Psychiatry, 2,* 417–419.

Vernon, P. A., Lee, D., Harris, J. A., & Jang, K. L. (1996). Genetic and environmental contributions to individual differences in alcohol expectancies. *Personality and Individual Differences, 21,* 183–187.

Waller, N. G., & Shaver, P. R. (1994). The importance of nongenetic influences on romantic love styles: A twin-family study. *Psychological Science, 5,* 268–274.

Watson, D., & Clark, L. A. (1997). Extraversion and its positive emotional core. In R. Hogan & J. A. Johnson (Eds.), *Handbook of personality psychology* (pp. 767–793). San Diego, CA: Academic Press.

Widiger, T. A. (1993). The DSM-III-R categorical personality disorder diagnoses: A critique and alternative. *Psychological Inquiry, 4,* 75–90.

Wiggins, J. S. (1979). A psychological taxonomy of trait-descriptive terms: The interpersonal domain. *Journal of Personality and Social Psychology, 37,* 395–412.

Zuckerman, M. (1991). *Psychobiology of personality.* Cambridge, England: University of Cambridge Press.

Zuckerman, M. (1994). An alternative five-factor model for personality. In C. F. Halverson, Jr. & G. A. Kohnstamm (Eds.), *The developing structure of temperament and personality from infancy to adulthood* (pp. 53–68). Hillsdale, NJ: Lawrence Erlbaum.

Zuckerman, M. (1995). Good and bad humors: Biochemical bases of personality and its disorders. *Psychological Science, 6,* 325–332.

Zuckerman, M. (1999). *Vulnerability to psychopathology: A biosocial model.* Washington, DC: American Psychological Association.

Zuckerman, M., Kuhlman, D. M., Joireman, J., Teta, P., & Kraft, M. (1993). A comparison of three structural models for personality: The Big Three, the Big Five, and the Alternative Five. *Journal of Personality and Social Psychology, 65,* 757–768.

CHAPTER 4

Biological Bases of Personality

MARVIN ZUCKERMAN

Whether we speak of mice or men, every member of a species is the same as other members in many respects but different in others. One task of personality psychology is to describe the basic behavioral differences and discover their origins. Description of personality is usually in terms of observable traits, and various models have been proposed to classify them. Biology has confronted a similar task in the classification of species (taxonomy). Taxonomy has been based on phenomenal and functional similarities and differences but more recently has been moving in the direction of using evolutionary analyses to define species in terms of their ancestries. Psychology still depends on phenomenal similarities and differences. As the genome reveals its secrets, both fields will eventually turn to DNA for the classification task.

There are two basic pathways for the second task, the search for the sources of individual differences. These are shown in Figure 4.1. One pathway is the biological beginning in behavioral genetics. Genes make proteins into neurons, and neurons are organized into brain and nervous systems.

Neurons operate through chemical neurotransmitters and the enzymes that govern their production and catabolism, as well as through hormones produced in other loci. This is the biochemical level. Differences in neurochemical makeup result in differences in neural activity and reactivity or physiology. Physiological differences affect conditionability, both of the classical and operant types. Individuals differ in both their conditionability and their sensitivities to conditioned stimuli associated with reward and punishment.

The second pathway begins with the largest social unit, culture. Cultures are subdivided into specific societies defined by geography or class groupings defined by wealth, occupation, and education. Neighborhood provides the more proximal influences on behavior. The family of origin and peers transmit the influences of society, albeit with individual variations on modal mores, values, and behavior patterns. Observational learning combined with social reinforcement is the mechanism of influence at the next level. At this point there is a convergence of the pathways because the different

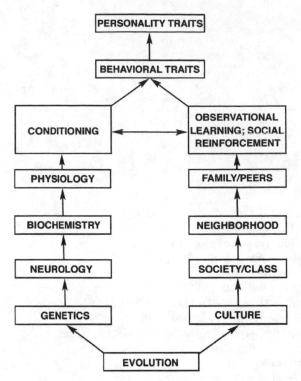

Figure 4.1 Two pathways to individual differences in personality: the biological and the social.

mechanisms of learning combine to produce behavioral traits. These traits are usually specific to certain types of situations. Depending on their generality and strength they combine to form what we call *personality traits*.

Both of these pathways have a historical origin in the evolutionary history of the species. Genetic changes account for the origin and changes (over long periods of time) in the species. Cultures represent the collective solutions of the human species to the basic demands of evolution: survival and reproduction. Cultural evolution is more rapid than biological evolution. Significant changes can occur within a generation, as with the sudden impact of computer technology on the current generation.

This chapter describes the biological pathway up to, but not including, conditioning. For each of four dimensions of personality I describe theory and research at each level of analysis along this pathway starting at the top (physiology). At the genetic level I describe primarily the studies of molecular genetics that link specific genes to traits. The biometric genetic studies are covered in the chapter by Livesly, Jang, and Vernon in this volume. The molecular studies link genes more directly to the neurological and biochemical levels on the way up to personality traits. An analysis of this type was conducted a decade ago (Zuckerman, 1991). Advances occur rapidly in the neurosciences. Ten years is equivalent to at least several decades in the social sciences. I have made an attempt to survey the changes since my last attempt. In a chapter I can hope only to highlight some of these advances and will reserve a more thorough review for a revision of my 1991 book. My approach draws heavily on comparative studies of other species as any psychobiological model must do (Gosling, 2001; Zuckerman, 1984, 1991), but I cannot do so within the constraints of a single chapter. I will limit comparative studies to those in which there are clear biological markers in common between animal and human models.

TEMPERAMENT AND PERSONALITY TRAITS

Researchers of temperament in children and behavioral traits in other species have typically included certain dimensions like emotionality, fearfulness, aggressiveness, approach versus withdrawal (in reactions to novel stimuli), general activity, playfulness, curiosity, sociability versus solitariness, and inhibition versus impulsivity (Strelau, 1998). From the 1950s through the 1970s personality trait classification was dominated by two models: Eysenck's (1947) three-factor theory (extraversion, neuroticism, and psychoticism) and Cattell's (1950) 16-factor model. Eysenck's (1967) model was biologically based with an emphasis on genetics, physiology, and conditioning. Gray's (1982, 1987) model is a bottom-up model that starts with behavioral traits in animals and extrapolates to human personality. He places his three behavioral dimensions (anxiety, impulsivity, fight-flight) within the axes of Eysenck's dimensions, but not lying on the axes of those dimensions or being precise equivalents of them.

The first five-factor model originated in lexical studies of trait-descriptive adjectives in language done in the 1960s (Norman, 1963; Tupes & Christal, 1961) with its roots in a much earlier study by Fiske (1949). Interest in this model reawakened in the 1980s (Digman & Inouye, 1986; Goldberg, 1990; Hogan, 1982; McCrae & Costa, 1985). Most of these studies used adjective rating scales. The translation of the model into a questionnaire form (NEO-PI-R; Costa & McCrae, 1992a) increased the use of the scales by personality investigators. The five factors incorporated in this tests are labeled extraversion, neuroticism, agreeableness, conscientiousness, and openness to experience. The five factors have been replicated in studies in many countries although with some differences—particularly on the last factor, openness. The enthusiasts for the Big Five insist it is the definitive and final word on the structure of personality (Costa & McCrae, 1992b), although critics regard this claim as premature (Block, 1995; Eysenck, 1992; Zuckerman, 1992). One of the criticisms of the model is its atheoretical basis in contrast to Eysenck's development of his factors from theory as well as empirical factor analytic studies of questionnaire content. However, recent studies in behavior genetics have used the model, and some of the data from earlier studies has been translated into the form of these five factors (Loehlin, 1992).

Two recent models have been derived from biosocial theories. Based on factor analyses of scales used in psychobiological studies of temperament and personality, Zuckerman and Kuhlman developed a five-factor model dubbed the *alternative five* (Zuckerman, Kuhlman, & Camac, 1988; Zuckerman, Kuhlman, Thornquist, & Kiers, 1991). This model was translated into a five-factor questionnaire (Zuckerman-Kuhlman Personality Questionnaire, or ZKPQ) on the basis of item and factor analyses (Zuckerman, Kuhlman, Joireman, Teta, & Kraft, 1993). The five factors are sociability, neuroticism-anxiety, impulsive sensation seeking, aggression-hostility, and activity. This model was used as the framework for a volume on the psychobiology of personality (Zuckerman, 1991).

Cloninger (1987) developed a personality model for both clinical description and classification of personality. The theory is biologically based and, like Zuckerman's, uses the monoamine neurotransmitters as fundamental determinants of personality differences. The factors included in the most recent version of his questionnaire include novelty seeking, harm avoidance, reward dependence, persistence, cooperativeness, persistence, self-directedness, and self-transcendence (Cloninger, Przybeck, Svrakic, & Wetzel, 1994). Much of the recent psychobiological research in personality and psychopathology has used Cloninger's system and questionnaires.

Builders of personality trait models often give different names to what are essentially the same traits. But even if one goes by the trait labels alone there are obvious similarities in what are considered the basic personality traits. Extraversion and neuroticism appear in nearly every system. Of course, one cannot take their equivalence for granted until empirical studies are done of their correlational relatedness.

Zuckerman et al. (1993) compared Eysenck's Big Three, Costa and McCrae's Big Five, and Zuckerman and Kuhlman's Alternative Five in a factor-analytic study. A four-factor solution accounted for two thirds of the variance. The first factor was clearly extraversion, and the second was neuroticism with representative scales from all three questionnaires highly loading on their respective factors. The third factor consisted of Eysenck's psychoticism and Zuckerman and Kuhlman's impulsive sensation seeking at one pole and the NEO conscientiousness at the other. The fourth factor was defined by NEO agreeableness at one pole and ZKPQ aggression-hostility at the other. The analysis did not yield a fifth factor, possibly because of a lack of representative

markers in the three tests. Activity loaded on the extraversion factor, and openness loaded on the agreeableness factor.

Zuckerman and Cloninger (1996) compared the scales of the ZKPQ with those of Cloninger's Temperament and Character Inventory (TCI). ZKPQ impulsive sensation seeking was highly correlated with TCI novelty seeking ($r = .68$), ZKPQ neuroticism-anxiety with TCI harm-avoidance ($r = .66$), ZKPQ aggression-hostility with TCI cooperativeness ($r = -.60$), and ZKPQ activity with TCI persistence ($r = .46$). These scales showed convergent and discriminant cross validity, but the other scales in both tests had weaker correlations and correlated equally with several measures on the other scales. In Cloninger's model there is no specific scale for extraversion or sociability.

The personality systems described thus far have been developed using factor analyses of trait dimensions. Many personologists have developed typologies on a rational-theoretical basis. Freud (1914/1957), Erikson (1963), and Maslow (1954) described personality types based on their developmental theories, each stressing the adult expressions of types derived from earlier stages of development. No valid methods of assessment were developed to operationalize these theories, although many clinicians continue to use them to describe personality differences among patients or others.

More recently, Millon and Everly (1985) defined eight types based on the interactions of four primary sources of reinforcement and two kinds of instrumental behavior patterns (active and passive). Some of the resultant types resemble different poles of the standard dimensions of personality. Sociable and introversive personality types resemble the two poles of the extraversion dimension; the inhibited type resembles neuroticism; and the cooperative types sounds like agreeableness. The model was developed as a way of integrating personality development of psychopathology, particularly the personality disorders. It has been described as a biosocial theory but has not as yet been widely used in psychobiological research.

The examination of the biosocial bases of personality in this chapter will be organized around four basic personality factors, derived mostly from factor analytic studies, which are the same or quite similar across these studies, have some similarity to traits described in studies of temperament and animal behavior, and have been used in correlational studies of traits and psychobiology in humans. The four traits are extraversion/sociability, neuroticism/anxiety, aggression/agreeableness, and impulsivity/sensation seeking/psychoticism. Although activity is a widely used trait in studies of children and animals, it has not been widely used in studies of humans except for the pathological extreme of hyperactivity

If the stimulus attribute had been intensity, these kinds of results might be compatible with Eysenck's theory of increased sensitivity of introverts to low-intensity stimuli. But the evolutionary type of explanation offered by Stelmack for the greater survival significance of low-frequency sounds is not convincing.

Recent studies have focused on the P300 EP component, many using the "odd-ball" paradigm in which the participant listens with eyes closed to a sequence of tones in which one tone is presented frequently and another one (the oddball) rarely. The rare tone is the signal for some task. These are usually vigilance tasks on which extraverts' performances and EP reactions are expected to decline more rapidly than those for introverts. However, when the task is made less montonous or response requirements are high, the differences may disappear or even be reversed with larger EP amplitudes in extraverts (Stenberg, 1994).

The intensity of the stimulus is another factor in the I-E difference. Brocke, Tasche, and Beauducel (1997) found that introverts showed larger P3 reactions to a 40-db stimulus, whereas extraverts showed a larger amplitude of P3 in response to a 60-db stimulus. Introverts' EP amplitudes decreased going from 40 db to 60 db, whereas extraverts increased going from the less intense to the more intense stimulus. These effects were a function of the impulsivity component rather than the sociability component of the E scale used in the study. The results of studies that vary the experimental conditions suggest that attention and inhibition may be the basic mechanisms governing the nature of the relationship between E and cortical EPs. Responses at the brain-stem level are probably less susceptible to these mechanisms, and Eysenck's theory does involve the brain stem and other points along the reticulocortical arousal system in I and E.

Stelmack and Wilson (1982) found that extraverts had longer latencies for the EP subcortical wave V (inferior colliculus) for stimulus intensity levels up to but not including 90 db. The direction of the finding was confirmed in a second experiment (Stelmack, Campbell, & Bell, 1993) and in a study by Bullock and Gilliland (1993). Different doses of caffeine and levels of task demand were used in the latter study, but the differences between extraverts and introverts held across all levels of caffeine and task demand. The results support Eysenck's theory more strongly than those using cortical EPs, which seem more susceptible to stimulus, task, and background arousal factors. A study by Pivik, Stelmack, and Bylsma (1988), however, suggested that Eysenck's arousal-inhibition hypothesis may not be broad enough. These researchers measured the excitability of a spinal motoneuronal reflex in the leg and found that extraverts showed reduced motoneuronal excitability as measured by reflex recovery functions. These results show that the inhibitory properties of the nervous system related to E may extend well below the reticulocortical level.

Another line of EP research is based on Gray's (1982, 1987) model of personality. Gray proposed that impulsivity, a dimension close to extraversion, is related to sensitivity to signals (conditioned stimuli) of reward whereas anxiety, close to neuroticism, is related to sensitivity to signals of punishment. This model suggests that the learned biological significance of stimuli, in addition to the intensity of stimulation, governs the strength of reaction to them.

Bartussek, Diedrich, Naumann, and Collet's (1993) results supported the theory by showing a stronger EP response (P2, N2) of extraverts than introverts to tones associated with reward (winning money) but no differences in tones associated with punishment (losing money). In a later experiment, however, extraverts showed larger P3 EP amplitudes to stimuli associated with *both* reward and punishment compared to neutral stimuli (Bartussek, Becker, Diedrich, Naumann, & Maier, 1996).

DePascalis and his colleagues also presented findings supporting Gray's theory. In one study they used a questionnaire scale developed more directly from Gray's theory measuring the approach tendency (DePascalis, Fiore, & Sparita, 1996). Although they found no effect for E itself, the participants scoring high on the approach scale had higher EP (P6) amplitudes in response to stimuli (words) associated with winning than to those associated with losing, and the reverse was true for low-approach motive subjects.

Eysenck's and Gray's theories have also been tested using peripheral autonomic measures of activity like the electrodermal activity (EDA), or skin conductance (SC), heart rate (HR), and blood pressure (BP). These are only indirect measures of cortical activity and reactivity because they occur in the autonomic nervous system (ANS) and are controlled by limbic system centers, which in Eysenck's model are associated more closely with neuroticism than with E. The results in relation to E are similar to those obtained with more direct cortical measures. Reviews by Smith (1983) and Stelmack (1990) showed mixed and inconclusive findings relating tonic EDA arousal to E, but some evidence of stronger SC responses of introverts than extraverts in response to low-to-moderate-intensity stimuli and stronger responses of extraverts in response to high-intensity stimulation. Tonic (base-level) measures of HR (Myrtek, 1984) and BP (Koehler, Scherbaum, Richter, & Boettcher, 1993) are unrelated to E. Young children rated as shy and inhibited had higher and less variable HRs, and a high HR at 21 months is the same behavior pattern at 48 months (Kagan, Reznick, &

Snidman, 1988). Shyness and inhibition, however, are traits that are a mixture of introversion and neuroticism or anxiety; therefore, the correlation with HR could be due to the anxiety component rather than to E.

Eysenck's model for the trait of extraversion produced a great deal of research in the area of psychophysiology. But psychophysiology has its problems as a branch of neuroscience. Both tonic and phasic psychophysiological measures are highly reactive to environmental conditions. Tonic levels can vary as a function of reactions to the testing situation itself, and phasic reactions depend on the specific qualities of stimulation such as intensity and novelty. It is not surprising that the relationships of physiological measures with personality traits often interact with these stimulus characteristics in complex ways. Eysenck's theory based on optimal levels of stimulation has received some support. Those based on differences in basal arousal levels are beginning to receive some support from PET studies, although the earlier results with EEG measures remain problematic.

Monoamines

The monoamine neurotransmitter systems in the brain have been the focus of most biosocial theories of personality. The reasons are the evidence of their involvement in human emotional and cognitive disorders and basic emotional and motivational systems in other species. Much of the work with humans has been correlational, comparing basal levels of the neurotransmitters, as estimated from levels of their metabolites in cerebrospinal fluid (CSF), blood, or urine, to personality traits as measured by questionnaires. Of these sources CSF is probably the best because the CSF is in direct contact with the brain. But the indirect relationship of these indicators with brain levels of activity (which can differ in different brain loci) and the fact that some of the metabolites in plasma and urine are produced in the peripheral nervous system make the putative measures of brain amine activity problematic. New imaging methods may eventually overcome these problems by directly viewing the monoamine activities in the brain itself. Added to these problems of validity of measurement is the use of small numbers of subjects in most studies, as well as the use of subjects with certain types of disorders rather than normal subjects. The ethical constraints of giving drugs that affect activity in the brain systems is another barrier, although some of the more recent studies have used such drugs in normals.

The freedom of investigators to experiment directly with the brain in other species has given us a fairly coherent picture of the emotional and motivational functions of the monoamine systems in the brain, and bottom-up theorists

have used these findings to extend animal models to human motivations and personality (Gray, 1982, 1987; Mason, 1984; Panksepp, 1982; Soubrié, 1986; Stein, 1978). Top-down theorists have drawn on these findings from the comparative research but have attempted to reconcile them with the relevant research on humans, including clinical and personality studies (Cloninger, Svrakic, & Prszybeck, 1993; Depue & Collins, 1999; Netter, Hennig, & Roed, 1996; Rammsayer, 1998; Zuckerman, 1991, 1995). The problem with building a bridge from two banks is to make it meet in the middle. With these caveats let us first examine the case for extraversion.

The primary monoamines in the brain are norepinephrine, dopamine, and serotonin. The first two are labeled catecholamines because of the similarities in their structures. Serotonin is an indoleamine. These are not independent neurotransmitter systems because activity in one may affect activity in another. Serotonin, for example, may have antagonistic effects on the catecholamines. These kinds of interaction must be kept in mind because most studies relate one neurotransmitter to one personality trait. Some models suggest that this kind of isomorphism of trait and transmitter is the rule. This is a new kind of phrenology based on biochemistry rather than bumps on the head.

To understand the human research one needs to know the pathways of biosynthesis and catabolism (breakdown) of the monoamines because some experiments block the precursors of the transmitter to see its effect on behavior and most use metabolite products of the catabolism to gauge activity in the systems. Figure 4.2 is a simplified diagram showing the

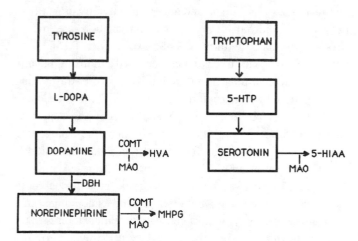

Figure 4.2 Biosynthesis and breakdown of the monoamines dopamine, norepinephrine, and serotonin.
Note. COMT = catechol-O-methyltransferase; MAO = monoamine oxidase; HVA = homovanillic acid; DBH = dopamine ß-hydroxylase; MHPG = 3-methoxy-4-hydroxyphenylglycol; 5-HIAA = 5-hydroxyindoleacetic acid. From *Psychobiology of personality,* p. 177, by M. Zuckerman, 1991, Cambridge: Cambridge University Press. Copyright 1991 by Cambridge University Press. Reprinted by permission.

stages of production of the monoamines and some of the enzymes (DBH, COMT, MAO) involved in the conversions from one stage to another. The metabolite for dopamine is homovanillic acid (HVA), for norepinephrine it is 3-methoxy-4-hydroxyphenylglycol (MHPG), and for serotonin it is 5-hydroxyindoleacetic acid (5-HIAA).

Theorists are in fair agreement on the role of dopaminergic systems in motivation based on studies of other species: approach and sensitivity to stimuli associated with reward (Crow, 1977; Gray, 1982, 1987; Stein, 1978); foraging and exploration and positive emotions like hope, desire, and joy in humans (Panksepp, 1982; Zuckerman, 1991); and novelty or sensation seeking in animals and humans (Bardo, Donohew, & Harrington, 1996; Cloninger et al., 1993; Le Moal, 1995; Zuckerman, 1984, 1991). I have proposed that the activity of the mesolimbic dopamine system is related to a broad approach trait that includes extraversion, sensation seeking, and impulsivity (Zuckerman, 1991). Considering that dopaminergic reactivity is also related to aggression and sexuality in many species, it is also possible that the third dimension of personality, low socialization, or psychoticism, may also be involved. Gray's (1987) model linked dopamine and reward sensitivity with impulsivity, a dimension related to high E, P, and N, although his more recent remarks (Gray, 1999) suggest that he is linking dopamine more closely with the P dimension because of this transmitter's involvement in schizophrenia.

Depue and Collins (1999) defined a broad view of extraversion with two main factors: interpersonal engagement, or affiliation and warmth, and agency, which includes social dominance, exhibitionism, and achievement motivation. Positive affect and positive incentive motivation are more strongly associated with the agentic extraversion factor. Impulsivity and sensation seeking are regarded as constituting an emergent factor representing a combination of extraversion and constraint (a dimension related to Eysenck's P and Costa and McCrae's conscientiousness). The "lines of causal neurobiological influence" are suggested to lie along the orthogonal dimensions of extraversion and constraint rather than along the dimension of impulsive sensation seeking. Although Depue and Collins say that this structural system does not mean that positive incentive motivation and its dopaminergic basis are related only to extraversion, the expectation is that they will be more strongly related to agentic extraversion than to impulsive sensation seeking or constraint.

Only a few correlational studies of monoamine CSF metabolites and personality traits were done prior to 1991 (Zuckerman, 1991), and they generally showed few significant relationships between the dopamine metabolite HVA and either extraversion or sensation seeking. This is still the case with studies that simply correlate CSF levels of HVA with questionnaire measures of extraversion, even when there is sufficient power to detect weak relationships (Limson et al., 1991). In fact, the Limson et al. study failed to find any correlations between CSF metabolites of serotonin (5-HIAA), norepinephrine (MHPG), norepinephrine itself, and Dopac and any of the personality measures assessed by the Minnesota Multiphasic Personality Inventory (MMPI), Eysenck Personality Questionnaire (EPQ), or Cloninger's Temperament Character Inventory (TCI). As with psychophysiological measures, levels of neurotransmitter activity in a resting basal state are not sensitive to variations in personality, at least as the latter is measured in self-report questionnaires. However, studies that attempt to potentiate or attenuate activity in neurotransmitters with agonists or antagonists have yielded some significant findings in regard to personality, even though they typically use very small sample sizes.

Depue, Luciana, Arbisi, Collins, and Leon (1994) challenged the dopamine system with bromocriptine, a potent agonist at D_2 receptor sites, and measured the effects using inhibition of prolactin secretion and activation of eye-blink rate, two measures of dopamine activation. The correlations between Positive Emotionality (PE) and baselline measures of the dopamine activity indicators were small and insignificant, but they found significant correlations between the putative measures of dopamine response to the agonist and the PE (an extraversion type measure) factor from Tellegen's MPQ. Rammsayer (1998, 1999) challenged Depue et al.'s interpretation of their findings as indicative of higher dopamine reactivity in high-PE persons (extraverts) than in lows, suggesting that the prolactin response would indicate just the reverse (i.e., higher reactivity in the low-PE persons). The disagreements on the meaning of the data are too complicated to elucidate here.

Rammsayer's interpretation of the findings is supported by PET measures of higher cerebral blood flow to the dopamine-rich basal ganglia areas in introverts than in extraverts (Fischer, Wik, & Fredrikson, 1997); but another PET study found no relationship between E and dopamine binding in the basal ganglia (N. S. Gray, Pickering, & Gray, 1994), and still another found a positive relationship with E (Haier et al., 1987). The first two of these studies used normal controls as subjects whereas the Haier et al. study used patients with Generalized Anxiety Disorder, a possible confounding factor.

Rammsayer, Netter, and Vogel (1993), using an inhibiter of tyrosine hydroxlase, thereby blockading dopamine synthesis, found no difference between introverts and extraverts in either baseline dopamine or reactivity to the blockading agent. Despite the lack of difference in dopaminergic activity or reactivity, they found that reaction time performance was markedly impaired in introverts but not in extraverts by the dopamine blockading agent. In another study, using a chemical that selectively blocks D_2 receptors and inhibits dopamine neurons in the limbic and cortical regions of the brain, Rammsayer (1998) again found a detrimental effect on reaction (liftoff) time in introverts but not in extraverts. The agent that was used caused a marked decrease in alertness and cortical arousal, but this effect was equivalent in introverts and extraverts. Both this finding and the performance findings would seem to contradict Eysenck's arousal explanation for the differences between introverts and extraverts. That theory would predict a more detrimental effect in extraverts because they supposedly start with a lower level of cortical arousal. But the results also raise the question, What is the source of the performance differences between introverts and extraverts if they do not differ in dopamine activity or reactivity?

The answer might lie in the interactions of dopaminergic and other neurotransmitters or hormones or, at another level, in the genetics of the dopaminergic receptors. Considerable interest has developed in a gene associated with the dopamine receptor 4 (DRD4). Allelic variations in this gene have been associated with novelty or sensation seeking, but not with extraversion (Ebstein, Nemarov, Klotz, Gritsenko, & Belmaker, 1997; Ebstein et al., 1996).

Simple correlative studies have found no relationship between serotonin or norepinephrine and E or other personality variables measured by questionnaires given to adult subjects. A study using CSF from newborns in predicting temperamental traits found that infants born with low levels of the serotonin metabolite 5-HIAA showed low sociability at 9 months of age (Constantino & Murphy, 1996). Retest reliability for 5-HIAA in neurologically normal infants was very high ($r = .94$).

A study of adults with depressive disorder treated with either a noradrenergic or a serotonergic reuptake inhibiter, which increase activity in those systems, showed that there were significant increases in measures of E and gregariousness (sociability) in those treated with these drugs (Bagby, Levitan, Kennedy, Levitt, & Joffe, 1999). The change in E was correlated with the change in depression severity, but the change in sociability was not. Although the result with sociability probably represents a change of state rather than the preillness trait, serotonin and norepinephrine might play some role in the trait as well. Studies of serotonin transporter genes have not shown any relationship to E, although they have to

other personality traits (Hamer, Greenberg, Sabol, & Murphy, 1999; Jorm, Henderson, Jacomb, Croft, & Easteal, 1997).

Monoamine Oxidase

Monoamine oxidase (MAO) is an enzyme involved in the catabolic deamination of monoamines. Evidence using selective monoamine inhibitors suggests that MAO-Type B, assayed from blood platelets in humans, is preferentially involved in the catabolic breakdown of dopamine more than the other two brain monoamines, norepinephrine and dopamine (Murphy, Aulakh, Garrick, & Sunderland, 1987). Although no direct correlation of platelet and brain MAO has been found, indirect assessments and the effects of MAO inhibitors on depression, as well as a large body of behavioral data, suggest that there must be a connection, if only one limited to certain brain areas. Platelet MAO is normally distributed in the human population, is highly reliable although it increases in brain and platelets with age, and is lower in men than in woman at all ages, and variations are nearly all genetic in origin. Unlike other biochemical variables it does not vary much with changes in state arousal. Thus, MAO has all of the characteristics of a biological trait.

Low levels of MAO-B taken from umbilical cord blood samples in newborn infants were related to arousal, activity, and good motor development (Sostek, Sostek, Murphy, Martin, & Born, 1981). High levels of the enzyme were related to sleep time and general passivity. The relationship with motor development is particularly suggestive of development of the dopamine-influenced basal ganglionic areas of the brain involved in motor coordination. In a study of monkeys living in a colony in a natural environment, low-platelet MAO was related to high sociability, activity, dominance, and sexual and aggressive activity, a broad array of E-type traits described by Depue and Collins (1999) as agentic extraversion. However, in human correlative studies the results relating MAO-B to questionnaire-measured extraversion have been inconsistent (Zuckerman, 1991). The enzyme has more consistently correlated (inversely) with the trait of sensation seeking. But using reported behavioral indices of sociability in college students, low MAO was related to sociability and high MAO to social insolation (Coursey, Buchsbaum, & Murphy, 1979).

Hormones

The hormone testosterone (T) is produced by both men and women but is 8 to 10 times as high in men as in women. Plasma T is highly heritable (66%) in young adult males and moderately heritable (41%) in females (Harris, Vernon, & Boomsa, 1998). In rats T has reward effects in the nucleus accumbens, the major site of dopaminergic reward. Administration of a dopamine receptor blocker eliminates the rewarding effects of T in rats, suggesting that its rewarding effects are mediated by an interaction with dopamine in the mesolimbic system (Packard, Schroeder, & Gerianne, 1998).

The hormone T affects personality traits and may account in part for many of the personality trait differences between men and women. Men and women do not differ on the pure sociability or affiliative type of extraversion, but they do on the agentic type, which includes dominance, assertiveness, surgency, and self-confidence. To the extent that sensation seeking is associated with extraversion, it is with the agentic type.

Daitzman and Zuckerman (1980) found that T in young males was positively correlated with sociability and extraversion, as well as with dominance and activity and inversely with responsibility and socialization, indicating an association with the agentic type of extraversion. Windle (1994) also found that testosterone was associated with a scale measuring behavioral activation, characterized by boldness, sociability, pleasure seeking, and rebelliousness. Dabbs (2000) also found that T is associated with a type of extraversion characterized by high energy and activity levels and lower responsibility.

Summary

Eysenck's theory relating cortical arousal to extraversion has been extensively tested using the EEG and, in more recent times, the brain scanning methods. The EEG studies yielded mixed results in which the sources of differences between studies were not clearly apparent. Two cerebral blood flow studies did confirm that extraverts were cortically underaroused related to introverts in female subjects but not in males. Studies measuring cortical arousability have also not clarified the picture. Apparently, experimental conditions affecting attention or inhibition may confound the relationship with E. Some more consistent results have been obtained from EP studies of responses at subcortical levels in which conscious attention is less of a factor. Although Eysenck's theory is confined to cortical arousal and reactivity, differences between introverts and extraverts have been found at lower levels of the central nervous system, even in a spinal motoneuronal reflex.

Theories of the biochemical basis of extraversion have focused on the monoamine neurotransmitters, particularly dopamine. Simple correlational studies between the monoamine metabolites and trait measures of E have not yielded significant findings, although there is some evidence that drugs that increase noradrenergic or serotonergic activity in depressed patients also increase their extraversion and sociability. This may be an indirect effect of the reduction in depression rather than a direct effect on E. The enzyme MAO-B is involved in regulation of the monoamines, particularly dopamine. Low levels of MAO have been related to arousal and activity in newborn human infants and to sociable behavior in adult humans and monkeys. These results suggest that a dysregulation of the dopamine system may be a factor in extraversion even in its earliest expression in the behavior of newborns. The hormone testosterone is related to E, but more so to E of the agentic type, which is the type characterized by dominance, assertiveness, surgent affect, high energy levels, activity, and irresponsibility, rather than simple sociability and interest in social relationships. This distinction between the two types of E has been hypothesized to be crucial for the relationship between dopamine and E as well (Depue & Collins, 1999).

NEUROTICISM/ANXIETY/HARM AVOIDANCE

Although the broad trait of neuroticism/anxiety includes other negative emotions, such as depression, guilt, and hostility, and character traits such as low self-esteem, neuroticism and anxiety are virtually indistinguishable as traits. Neuroticism is highly correlated with measures of negative affect, but when the negative affect was broken down into anxiety, depression, and hostility components, anxiety had the highest correlation, and hostility the lowest, with the N factor while depression was intermediate (Zuckerman, Joireman, Kraft, & Kuhlman, 1999). Hostility had a higher relationship to a factor defined by aggression.

Eysenck (1967) assumed a continuity between N as a personality trait and anxiety disorders. Indeed, N is elevated in all of the anxiety and depressive mood disorders, and longitudinal studies show that the trait was evident in most persons before they developed the symptoms of the clinical disorder (Zuckerman, 1999). In the first half of the twentieth century, when little was known about the role of the limbic system in emotions, the biological basis of neuroticism and anxiety trait was related to overarousal or arousability of the sympathetic branch of the autonomic nervous system. Such arousal is apparent in state anxiety elicited by anticipation of some kind of aversive stimulus or conditioned stimuli associated with aversive consequences.

Autonomic overarousal is apparent in the primary symptoms of many anxiety disorders. On the assumption of continuity between the N trait and these disorders, it was expected that autonomic arousal, as assessed by peripheral measures such as heart rate (HR), breathing rate (BR), blood pressure (BP), and electrodermal activity (EDA), would be correlated with N. In Eysenck's (1967) theory, N was ultimately based on reactivity of the limbic system, which regulates the ANS, but he did not distinguish particular pathways, structures, or neurotransmitters within that system that were involved in N. Some theories did not even make a distinction between cortical and autonomic arousal in emotions. Eysenck felt that there was some correlation between the two kinds of arousal because of collaterals between the limbic and ascending reticulocortical system. Gray (1982) and others, extrapolating from experimental studies of animals, delineated specific limbic systems involved in anxiety and the neurotransmitters involved in these systems. Neuroimaging studies have attempted to extend these brain models to humans.

Autonomic Arousal

Large-scale studies of the relationship between cardiovascular measures, either in resting levels of activity or reactivity to stressful experimental situations, and Measures of N failed to reveal any significant relationships (Fahrenberg, 1987; Myrtek, 1984). On the assumption that high cardiovascular activity put high-N subjects at risk for cardiovascular disease, Almada et al. (1991) investigated the relation between measures of N and subsequent health history in nearly 2,000 men. N was not associated with systolic BP or serum cholesterol but was associated with cigarette smoking and alcohol consumption. When tobacco and alcohol consumption were held constant there was no relationship between N and cardiovascular disease. Similar studies have failed to find any relationships between electrodermal activity and N or trait anxiety (Fahrenberg, 1987; Hodges, 1976; Naveteur & Baque, 1987).

Given the fact that many anxiety disorders do show elevated heart rate and electrodermal reactivity, how can we explain the lack of correlation with N? The answer may lie in the difference between generalized anxiety disorder (GAD) and panic disorder (PD), agoraphobia (Ag), and obsessive-compulsive disorder (OCD). Whereas the latter (PD, Ag, OCD) show elevated basal HRs and frequent spontaneous SCRs, GAD patients show little evidence of this kind of autonomic arousal (Zuckerman, 1991). Their anxiety is expressed cognitively (worry) and in symptoms of muscle tension such as fatigue. In contrast, PD, Ag, and OCD patients complain of autonomic symptoms, such as accelerated heart rate, even when they are not experiencing an actual panic attack (Zuckerman, 1999). Most persons who are high on N probably represent subclinical GAD disorder rather than the other types of anxiety disorders.

Brain Arousal

Studies of general cortical arousal using the EEG have historically focused on E, but some of these studies found interactions with N. These effects were inconsistent; some found higher and some reported lower arousal for high-N persons. Application of PET methods has not shown any association of general cortical or limbic arousal with N in situations that were not emotionally provoking (Fischer et al., 1997; Haier et al., 1987). Similar results are seen in anxiety patients; but when anxiety is provoked in patients by presenting them with feared stimuli, increased activity is seen in areas like the orbitofrontal cortex, insular cortex, temporal cortex, and anterior cingulate (Breier et al., 1992; Rauch et al., 1995). These studies identify an anxiety pathway in humans (orbitofrontal-frontal to cingulate to temporal lobe and amygdala) already established in animals, but they do not show a preexisting sensitivity of this pathway in normals scoring high in N. Another study of anxiety patients in non-stimulated conditions, which did use normal controls, found that whole brain blood flow did not distinguish anxiety patients from normals but did find a negative correlation between a depression scale and caudate activation. The previously mentioned study by Canli et al. (2001) found that in a small sample of normal women N correlated with increased brain activation to negative pictures (relative to activation by positive pictures) in left-middle frontal and temporal gyri and reduced activation in the right-middle frontal gyrus. Taken together, the clinical studies and this last study of normals suggests that whole brain activation does not vary with N-Anx, but given negative emotional provocation there may be a reactive disposition in frontal cortex of high-N persons that activates a pathway through the orbitofrontal cortex around the cingulum to the temporal lobe and amygdala.

Davis (1986) argued that the central nucleus of the amygdala is a major center where the input of fear-provoking stimuli is organized and where output to various intermediate nuclei organizes the entire range of behavioral, autonomic, and neurotransmitter reactions involved in panic or fear. A recent MRI study (van Elst, Woermann, Lemieux, & Trimble, 1999) found an enlargement of left and right amygdala volumes in epileptic patients with dysthymia (a chronic kind of neurotic depression). Amygdala volume within the group did not correlate with trait or state anxiety but did correlate positively with a depression inventory. Because anxiety and depression are usually highly correlated and both correlate highly with N, it is not clear why depression alone was related to amygdala volume.

Monoamines

Much of the recent exploration of the role of the monoamines in N-Anx have been based on Cloninger's (1987) biosocial model of personality and therefore used his scale of Harm

Avoidance (HA) instead of the N or anxiety trait scales used by other investigators. HA, however, is not a pure scale of the N factor but lies between the E and N dimensions, constituting a measure of introverted neuroticism. It is defined in the same way that Gray defines trait anxiety: a sensitivity to cues associated with punishment and nonreward (frustration) and a tendency to avoid them.

Gray's (1982) model suggests that norepinephrine in the dorsal ascending noradrenergic system (DANA) originating in the locus coeruleus is the major neurotransmitter involved in anxiety, although high levels of serotonin may mediate the behavioral inhibition that is associated with high levels of anxiety. Redmond (1977), from a psychiatric viewpoint, sees the DANA as an alarm system at lower levels and a panic provoker at high levels of activity. In contrast to these two theorists, Cloninger, Svrakic, and Przybeck (1993) proposed that high levels of serotonin activity underlie the trait of HA whereas norepinephrine activity is related to another trait called Reward Dependence.

In patients there has been little evidence of higher levels of the norepinephrine metabolite MHPG in anxiety patients compared to normals, although a more recent study by Spivak et al. (1999) showed higher levels of MHPG in plasma of patients with combat-related posttraumatic stress disorder than in controls.

The alpha-2 receptor functions as a homeostatic regulator of the norepinephrine systems, tuning them down when excessive neurotransmitter levels are detected in the synapse. Yohimbine is a antagonist to this receptor and therefore potentiates the activity of the norepinephrine system, just as a broken thermostat results in an overheated room. Yohimbine increases MHPG levels and provokes panic attacks in patients with panic disorders, although it does not have these effects in normal controls (Charney & Heninger, 1986). Cameron et al. (1996) replicated a previous result finding a decreased number of alpha-2 receptors in panic disorder. One might extrapolate that MHPG should correlate with N or anxiety over the range in normals and other patient groups. However, as noted earlier, high N in normals may resemble GAD more than panic disorder. Heinz, Weingarten, Hommer, Wolkowitz, and Linnoila (1999) reported a high correlation between CSF MHPG and an anxiety scale in a combined group of abstinent alcoholics and normals. A stress resistant group, defined by N and similar measures, had lower plasma MHPG after a mild stressor than did a nonresistant (high-N) group (de Leeuwe, Hentschel, Tavenier, & Edelbroek, 1992). Norepinephrine may be one of the factors underlying N, but it may be the dysregulation of norepinephrine by a lack of the receptors needed for this and a consequent tendency to be unable to cope with stress, rather than the basal level of activity in the norepinephrine system, which is related to N.

Cloninger's biosocial theory of personality proposes that the trait of harm avoidance is related to behavioral inhibition mediated by serotonergic activity in the brain. Earlier studies showed no correlation between between CSF levels of the serotonin metabolite, 5-HIAA, and N. A more recent study has found a positive correlation between CSF 5-HIAA and N but in a sample of depressed patients (Roy, 1999). Constantino and Murphy's (1996) study of the prediction of infant temperament from CSF levels of 5-HIAA showed no relationships between this metabolite and emotionality, soothability, or activity in infants.

Studies of normals using serotonin challenges, drugs that stimulate serotonergic activity, and indirect measures of serotonin response in normals have yielded mixed results including both positive (Gerra et al., 2000; Hansenne & Ansseau, 1999), nonsignificant (Ruegg et al., 1997), and a negative relationship (Mannuck et al., 1998) with N. The first three of these studies used the HA scale, whereas the last used the N scale, but with a much larger number of normal subjects than in the other studies. Serotonin seems to be implicated in harm avoidance, but the nature of that relationship is open to question. As with other neurotransmitters, the personality-relevant aspects of serotonin may have more to do with receptor number and sensitivity than with basal levels of transmitter activity.

Hormones

Daitzman and Zuckerman (1980) found that testosterone (T) in males correlated negatively with various MMPI indexes of anxiety, depression, and neuroticism; that is, subjects with neurotic tendencies were low on T. Dabbs, Hopper, and Jurkovic (1990) reported a significant negative correlation between T and N in one study, but this was not replicated in another larger study of males; and in an even larger study of over 5,000 veterans T was not correlated with any MMPI indexes of trait anxiety or N. In still another study Dabbs et al. report significant negative correlations between T and a measure of pessimism in both males and females. T reflects both trait and state characteristics; that is, it is affected by immediate stressful experiences, particularly those involving success or defeat in competitive activities (Dabbs, 2000). The relationship with pessimism may reflect a history of defeat and consequent expectations for future failures. This depressive attitude may underlie negative relationships with N if any such relationships do exist.

Cortisol is one of the end products of activation of the hypothalamic-pituitary adrenocortical (HYPAC) system, a stress-reactive hormonal system. Like T, cortisol reactivity has both trait and state characteristics. Elevated cortisol is associated with major depressive disorder as a trait but is found in anxiety disorders only when activated by an immediate stressor.

Molecular Genetics

Lesch, Bengal, Hells, and Sabol (1996) found an association between a serotonin transporter gene (5-HTTLPR) and the trait of neuroticism, as assessed by three different scales including the NEO N scale and Cloninger's TCI harm avoidance scale. Individuals with either one or two copies of the short form had higher N scores than individuals homozygous for the long variant of the gene. The association was limited to the N factor of the NEO and the harm avoidant factor of the TCI; none of the other factors in these test was associated with the genetic variant. However, in a second study by this group (Hamer, Greenberg, Sabol, & Murphy, 1999) the association of the gene with harm avoidance was weaker, and associations were found with TCI traits of cooperativeness and self-directiveness.

Several other studies have not been able to replicate the relationship between the gene variants and N or harm avoidance. This is a common outcome in the hunt for specific genes associated with personality traits or types of psychopathology, even when studies have adequate power and use good methodology. Population differences may account for some of these failures. Even in the studies that are significant the particular gene accounts only for a small portion of the genetic variance. In the Lesch et al. study the 5-HTT polymorphism accounted for 3% to 4% of the total variance for the trait and 7% to 9% of the genetic variance, and 10 to 15 more genes were estimated to be involved. If there is any replication of a gene-trait association, that finding should not be immediately dismissed by subsequent failures of replication, particularly if the finding has a theoretical basis. In this case Cloninger's theory has suggested the involvement of serotonin in harm avoidance.

The short form of the gene, which is associated with high neuroticism, reduces serotonin uptake and therefore increases serotonergic transmission. Reduced uptake has been associated with anxiety in animal and human models, but paradoxically the serotonin uptake inhibitors are therapeutic agents in depressive disorders and several forms of anxiety disorders. These drugs could achieve their results through the inhibitory effects of serotonin on other systems such as the noradrenergic ones.

Summary

A sudden intense surge in anxiety is characterized by arousal of the sympathetic branch of the autonomic nervous system as expressed in elevated heart and breathing rates, blood pressure, sweating, and other signs of activation of this system. This led to the expectation that N or trait anxiety would be related to measures of these indicators either in the basal state or in reaction to stress. Research has generally failed to support this correlational hypothesis. EEG and brain scan studies also fail to reveal a difference in arousal levels as a trait distinguishing high- and low-N individuals. However, PET scan studies, done primarily on patients with anxiety disorders in reaction to fearful stimuli, show heightened reactivity of frontal, insular, and temporal cortex and anterior cingulate to such stimuli. Evidence from studies of animals has implicated the amygdala as a center for organization of the fear response, but brain imaging studies in humans have not yet supplied evidence for this localization.

Much of the research on other species identifies activation of the dorsal ascending noradrenergic system originating in the locus coeruleus as an alarm system activating the entire cortex in states of fear or anxiety. Reactivity of this system is a characteristic of panic disorders during panic attacks compared to the reactions of other types of anxiety disorders and normal controls. Correlational studies of norepinephrine metabolites and N-type trait measures in the basal state have not found a relationship, but at least one study has found a relationship between N and reactivity of a norepinephrine metabolite and response to stress. A hypothesized relationship with the monoamine serotonin has also shown no relationship with N in the basal state and no consistent findings relating N to reactions to drugs that stimulate serotonergic activity. Initial findings of a relationship between a serotonin transporter gene and N-type scales have not been replicated. Hormones like testosterone and cortisol show similar negative findings in the basal state and few findings relating N to reactivity to stress.

The research attempting to find a biological basis for N has had a disappointing outcome, particularly in view of the positive results in experimental research with animals and with humans that suffer from anxiety and mood disorders. Longitudal research has shown that N is a personality precursor of these disorders, so why does N not show relationships with some of the same biological indicators that characterize the disorders? There may be a kind of threshold effect so that the dysregulation of neurotransmitter systems characteristic of the disorders only emerges at some critical level of persistent stress that is not reproducible in controlled laboratory studies.

PSYCHOTICISM/IMPULSIVITY/SENSATION SEEKING/CONSCIENTIOUSNESS/CONSTRAINT

The third major personality factor goes under a variety of names depending on the various trait classification systems. Our factor analyses of personality scales have shown that

Eysenck's psychoticism scale is one of the best markers for the dimension that consists of scales for impulsivity and sensation seeking at one pole and scales for socialization, responsibility, and restraint at the other pole (Zuckerman et al., 1988, 1991, 1993). In a three-factor solution this factor also includes aggression and capacity to inhibit aggression, but in a four- or five-factor solution aggression and hostility versus agreeableness form a separate factor (Zuckerman et al., 1993). This chapter is organized by the four-factor model.

Cortical Arousal and Arousability

At the time the original studies were done relating conditioning to arousal and the construct "strength of the nervous system" to extraversion, E was measured by scales with two components: E and Impulsivity (Imp). In a theoretical shift, not receiving much attention, Eysenck and Eysenck (1985) reassigned Imp to the P rather than the E dimension. Although nearly all the earlier arousal and conditioning studies focused on E, it was shown that the relationship of E to conditionability (introverts more conditionable than extraverts) depended on the Imp component of E rather than the sociability component (Barratt, 1971; Eysenck & Levey, 1972). A later study showed that classical eyelid conditoning was related most closely to a specific type of Imp, the tendency to act quickly on impulse without thinking or planning. This is the type of Imp, called *narrow impulsivity* (IMPn), that constitutes a subscale of the older E scale. It is also the type of Imp that has been combined with sensation seeking in the latest ImpSS scale. Conditionability is thought to be a function of arousal; the more aroused a person is, the more conditionable he or she is thought to be. Could this mean that cortical arousal is related to the third dimension (P), including sensation seeking and IMPn, rather than the first (E) dimension of personality? A PET study found negative correlations between P and glucose use in cortex and in thalamic and cingulate areas of the limbic system (Haier et al., 1987). Low cortical and autonomic arousal is a characteristic of the psychopathic (antisocial) personality, which may represent an extreme manifestation of the P dimension of personality (Zuckerman, 1989).

Evidence for a relationship between cortical arousal (EEG) and P and IMPn was found by some investigators (Goldring & Richards, 1985; O'Gorman & Lloyd, 1987); high P and impulsive subjects were underaroused. Sensation seeking, however, was not related to tonic arousal. Instead, sensation seeking—particularly that of the disinhibitiory type—has been consistently related to a particular measure of cortical arousability called *augmenting-reducing* (A-R, Buchsbaum, 1971).

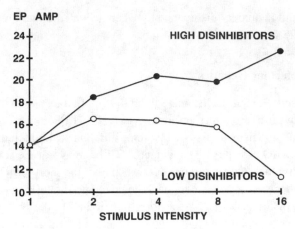

Figure 4.3 Mean visual evoked potential amplitudes (P1-N1) at five levels of light intensity for low and high scorers on the disinhibition subscale of the Sensation Seeking Scale.
From "Sensation seeking and cortical augmenting-reducing," by M. Zuckerman, T. T. Murtaugh, and J. Siegel, 1974, *Psychophysiology*, 11, p. 539. Copyright 1974 by the Society for Psychophysiological Research. Reprinted by permission.

A-R asseses the relationship of cortical reactivity, measured as a function of the relationship between the cortical EP and stimulus intensity for any given individual. A strong positive relationship between the amplitude of the EP and the intensity of stimuli is called augmenting, and a negative or zero relationship is called reducing. A-R differences are most often observed at the highest intensities of stimulation, where the reducers show a marked EP reduction and the augmenters continue to show increased EP amplitude. There is an obvious relevance of this measure to Pavlov's (1927/1960) construct of "strength of the nervous system," based on the nervous system's capacity to respond to high intensities of stimulation without showing transmarginal inhibition.

Figure 4.3 shows the first study of the relationship between the Disinhibition (Dis) subscale of the SSS and amplitude of the visual EP. Those scoring high on Dis displayed an augmenting pattern, and those scoring low on this scale showed a strong reducing pattern, particularly at the highest intensity of stimulation. This study was followed by many others, some using visual and others using auditory stimuli. Replications were frequent, particularly for the auditory EP (Zuckerman, 1990, 1991). Replications continue to appear (Brocke, Beauducel, John, Debener, & Heilemann, 2000; Stenberg, Rosen, & Risberg, 1990). A-R has also been found to be related to Imp, particularly cognitive impulsiveness (Barratt, Pritchard, Faulk, & Brandt, 1987).

The A-R model has been extended to other species and used as a biological marker for behavioral traits in animals resembling those in high and low human sensation seekers and impulsive and constrained persons. Cats who showed the augmenting pattern were active, exploratory, and approached rather than withdrew from novel stimuli. Augmenting cats adapted easily to novel situations, were responsive to a simple reward task, but were poor at learning to inhibit responses where they were only reinforced for low rates of response (Hall, Rappaport, Hopkins, Griffin, & Silverman, 1970; Lukas & Siegel, 1977; Saxton, Siegel, & Lukas, 1987).

Siegel extended this paradigm to a study of two genetically selected strains of rats, one actively avoidant or more aggressive and the other passive and frozen in reaction to shock (Siegel, Sisson, & Driscoll, 1993). The first strain consistently showed the augmenting EP pattern, and the second showed the reducing. Other behavioral characteristics of these strains were consistent with the human model of impulsive sensation seeking: The augmenting strain was aggressive, more willing to ingest alcohol, had high tolerance for barbituates, and self-administered higher intensities of electrical stimulation in reward areas of the limbic brain than the reducing strain.

Biochemical reactions suggested the basis for behavioral differences in characteristics of stress-reactive neurotransmitter and hormonal responses. Under stress, the augmenting strain showed more dopaminergic activity in the prefrontal cortex of brain, whereas the reducers had a stronger reaction in the hypothalamic-pituitary-adrenal cortex (HYPAC) stress pathway including increased serotonergic activity and corticotropin releasing factor in the hypothalamus and adrenocorticotropic hormone in the pituitary gland. Dopamine is a neurotransmitter implicated in action tendencies and theorized to be the basis of novelty and sensation seeking. Dopamine release would explain the active avoidance patterns that were the basis for selecting the two strains. Conversely, serotonin activity is associated with behavioral inhibition.

Monoamines

The animal model described earlier suggests that sensation seeking and related traits in humans may be associated positively with dopaminergic and negatively with serotonergic reactivity. Indirect evidence of this association comes from patients with Parkinson's disease (PD), in which dopamine is depleted 75% in ventral tegmental neurons. A study of personality of PD patients showed that the PD patients were significantly lower on novelty seeking than controls but did not differ from them on harm avoidance or reward dependence (Menza, Golbe, Cody, & Forman, 1993). The PD patients were more depressed than controls, but depression did not correlate with novelty seeking scores.

Simple correlations between sensation seeking and dopamine and serotonin metabolites (HVA and 5-HIAA) assayed from CSF reveal no correlations between these metabolites and sensation seeking or the P scale or impulsivity scales (Ballenger et al., 1983; Limson et al., 1991). However, the correlational study by Ballenger et al. found a significant negative correlation between norepinephrine in the CSF and sensation seeking. A significant correlation was found between P and dopamine D2 binding in left and right basal ganglia in a PET study of a small group of normal subjects (Gray, Pickering, & Gray, 1994).

An experimental study by Netter, Hennig, and Roed (1996) used drugs that stimulate (agonist) or inhibit (antagonist) activity in the serotonergic and dopaminergic systems and measured their effects on hormonal, emotional-state, and behavioral reactions. Their findings suggested a low responsivity of the serotonergic system in high sensation seekers, but no association of dopaminergic response to an agonist and sensation seeking. However, craving for nicotine was increased by a dopamine agonist in high sensation seekers, suggesting that dopamine stimulation may induce more approach behavior in high than in low sensation seekers. Experiments in which nicotine or amphetamine is given to participants high or low in sensation seeking or novelty seeking showed that the high sensation/novelty seekers had more intense "highs" or subjective effects in response to these drugs than did low sensation seekers (Hutchison, Wood, & Swift, 1999; Perkins, Wilson, Gerlach, Broge, & Grobe, 2000). The effect for nicotine was most intense for nonsmokers, and the study on amphetamine did not use persons with a drug history. These special reactions of high sensation/novelty seekers to the novel drugs suggests some sensitivity to these dopamine agonists, perhaps in the receptors.

Another study by the German group found that the disinhibition type of sensation seeking and impulsivity, as well as aggression, were correlated with a response to a serotonin antagonist indicating low serotonergic responsivity in impulsive sensation seekers (Hennig et al., 1998).

Monoamine Oxidase

Fairly consistent negative relationships have been found between sensation seeking and MAO. A survey of results in 1994 showed low but significant negative correlations between platelet MAO and sensation seeking trait in 9 of 13 groups, and in 11 of 13 groups the correlations were negative in sign. The gender and age differences in sensation seeking are consistent with the gender and age differences in MAO described previously. Low MAO levels are characteristic of disorders characterized by impulsive, antisocial behavior including antisocial and borderline personality disorders, alcoholism and heavy drug abuse, pathological gambling disorder, bipolar relationship between the P dimension and dopaminergic reactivity although animal and clinical research would support such a relationship.

High levels of testosterone and low levels of cortisol have been associated with disinhibition and psychopathic traits. But high levels of testosterone have also been associated with sociability and low levels with neuroticism, as discussed in previous sections. There is no necessary one-to-one relationship between biological and personality traits. Neurotransmitters like dopamine and hormones like testosterone may be related to two or more of the basic dimensions of personality or to a higher order dimensions like approach or inhibition.

Personality in the third dimension shows a high degree of heritability compared to other major dimensions. A specific gene, the dopamine receptor D4, has been associated with the trait of novelty seeking, although replication has been spotty. The association is supported by animal and clinical studies. Disorders characterized by impulsivity like opiate abuse, pathological gambling disorder, and attention-deficit-hyperactivity disorder share the same form of the gene as found in high novelty seekers. Mice with the gene removed show decreases in exploration and responses to novel situations. The third dimension of personality has been a rich lode of biological findings from the psychophysiological down to the most basic genetic level.

AGGRESSION/HOSTILITY/ANGER/ AGREEABLENESS

Problems of definition confuse the fourth dimension of personality. Aggression refers to behavior, hostility to attitude, and anger to emotion. One can be aggressive without being hostile or angry, as in certain kinds of competition; or one can be chronically hostile and angry without expressing the negative attitude and feelings in overt aggression. One may be disagreeable without being aggressive or being aware of hostile attitudes or anger. Hostility without aggression is more closely associated with the N factor whereas aggression, with or without hostility, is more closely associated with this fourth factor.

Another source of differences is in the way aggression is expressed. Aggression in other species is classified by the source or context of the aggression: predatory, intermale, fear-induced, maternal, sex-related, instrumental, territorial, or merely irritable (Volavka, 1995). Human aggression is more often characterized by the form of expression. For instance, the widely used Buss-Durkee (1957) Hostility Scale (BDHS) classifies aggression as assault, indirect hostility, verbal hostility, irritability, negativism, resentment, and suspicion.

A new form of the scale has reduced the number of subscales to four, using factor analyses: physical aggression, verbal aggression, anger, and hostility (Buss & Perry, 1992). Although the subscales are moderately intercorrelated, quite different results have been found for the different subscales of the test in biological studies. Another important distinction in the literature is whether aggression is impulsive. The impulsive type of aggression seems more biologically rooted than instrumental types of aggression, but this confounds two different dimensions of personality.

Although aggression and hostility are correlated in tests and life, they are separated in two of the major trait classification systems. Eysenck's system includes negative feelings like anger (moodiness) in neuroticism, but aggression and hostility are at the core of the psychoticism dimension. Costa and McCrae (1992a) have angry-hostility as a facet of neuroticism but regard aggression as the obverse of agreeableness. My colleagues and I found that hostility and anger load more highly on N and aggression on P in a three-factor model, but all three correlate with a common factor in a five-factor analysis (Zuckerman et al., 1991).

Aggression has been defined by several methods, including self-report ratings or questionnaires, observer or ratings by others, and life-history variables like membership in groups characterized by violent acts or crimes. Aggression is not a socially desirable trait and this may limit the usefulness of self-report methods in some settings. Laboratory observations may be too specific to the experimental conditions. Persons who committed a violent crime, like murder, may differ depending on how characteristic their violent behavior was before they committed the crime. All methods have methodological problems, but in spite of this there are certain consistencies in results across methods in the literature.

Cortical Arousal and Arousability

Early studies of the EEG in abnormal populations, like violent criminals, used crude qualitative judgments of the EEG records as "abnormal" or "normal" (Volavka, 1995). EEG abnormalities included diffused or focal slowing, spiking or sharp waves in certain areas, and generalized paroxysmal features resembling minor epileptic seizures. The incidence of abnormal records found in samples of prisoners convicted of homicides and habitually violent prisoners was quite high (50–65%) compared to nonviolent prisoners or normal controls (about 5–10%; Volavka, 1995). However, some other studies found no differences between violent and nonviolent offenders.

Studies using quantitative methods showed EEG slowing in offenders, including slowing of alpha activity and an excess of slow wave (theta) activity. Volavka (1995) pointed out that these results could be due to a variety of factors including developmental retardation, brain injuries, decreased arousal level, cortical disinhibition, or genetic factors. Actually, twin research suggests that most of the activity in spectrum parameters of the EEG is genetically determined (Lykken, 1982).

One limitation of most of these earlier studies was that only prisoners referred for neuropsychiatric evaluation were used. A study by Wong, Lumsden, Fenton, and Fenwick (1994) selected subjects from a population of prisoners who had all been rated for violent behavior, and 70% had received EEG assessment. The prisoners were divided into three groups based on their history of violence. Going from the lowest to the highest violent groups, the percentages of abnormal EEG's were, respectively, 26%, 24%, and 43%. The most frequent EEG characteristics differentiating the most violent from the less violent groups was focalized EEG abnormalities, particularly in the temporal lobes. Twenty percent of the most violent patients showed abnormal temporal lobe readings compared to 2% to 3% in the other two groups. Computerized tomography (CT) scans confirmed the high incidence of temporal lobe abnormalities in the most violent group.

The cortical EP has also been used to study cortical arousability. A study comparing detoxified alcoholic patients with and without histories of aggression found lower amplitudes of the P300 in the aggressive group (Branchey, Buydens-Branchey, & Lieber, 1988). Aggressive alcoholics often have other characteristics, such as impulsivity and alcoholism, which might have produced the weaker P300 signal. Another study found that impulsive aggressive subjects screened from a college student population also showed lower P300 amplitudes at frontal electrode sites (Gerstle, Mathias, & Stanford, 1998). Still another study showed that a drug that reduced frequency of aggressive acts among prisoners with a history of impulsive aggression also increased the amplitude of the P300 in this group (Barratt, Stanford, Felthous, & Kent, 1997). This effect of the drug was not found in a group of prisoners who had committed premeditated murders. A reduced P300, particularly in the frontal lobes, may be symptomatic of a weakened inhibition from the frontal lobes and may account for the impulsive aspect of the aggression.

Visual imaging methods have been used in the study of violent behavior. Two structural methods are computed tomography (CT) and magnetic resonance imaging (MRI). MRI yields better images for precise assessment of brain structure. PET is used to assess brain activity in specific areas of brain including regions not accessible by ordinary EEG methods. Mills and Raine (1994) reviewed 15 studies of structural brain imaging (MRI, CT) and 5 studies using PET and regional CBF. Subject groups were violent prisoners, convicted murderers, pedophiles, incest offenders, property offenders, and, in some studies, normal controls. Property offenders were regarded as controls for violent offenders. Sexual offenders were not necessarily violent. Nine of the 15 studies using CT or MRI showed some type of structural abnormality, about evenly divided between frontal and temporal or frontotemporal deficits. Frontal abnormalities characterized the violent offenders and frontotemporal the sexual offenders, according to the authors of the review. However, most studies used small samples. The two studies of violent offenders using large samples (Ns of 128 and 148) found no particular localization of abnormalities (Elliot, 1982; Merikangus, 1981). The only study using MRI with any kind of N (another had only 2 cases) found evidence of temporal lobe lesions in 5 of 14 violent patients (Tonkonogy, 1990). The large study by Wong et al. (1994), not included in the review, found that 55% of the most violent group had abnormal CT findings, and 75% of these were temporal lobe findings. Contrary to the hypothesis of Mills and Raine, temporal lobe lesions alone seem to be characteristic of violent patients. More MRI studies are needed to clarify the issue of localization.

The temporal lobe overlays the amygdala and has connections with it. Animal lesion and stimulation studies have found sites in the amygdala that inhibit and others that trigger aggression. Total amygdalectomies in monkeys produce a drop in the dominance hierarchy and an inability to defend against aggression from other monkeys. The comparative data suggest loci for aggression in the amygdala.

Mills and Raine reviewed five PET studies, but of these only one had a near-adequate number of subjects (3 had less than 10) and another compared child molesters with controls. The one study remaining compared 22 murderers with 22 normals and found selective prefrontal dysfunction in the group of murderers (Raine et al., 1994). Temporal lobe damage and functional hypofrontality are not unique to violent offenders but are also found in patients with schizophrenia.

Cardiovascular Arousal and Arousability

Numerous studies show that persons who score high on hostility scales show greater anger and cardiovascular arousal, especially blood pressure, in response to stress or perceived attack than do low hostile persons. As an example, a recent study found that among participants who were deliberately harassed in an experiment, the high hostile group who was harassed showed enhanced and prolonged blood pressure, heart rate, forearm blood flow and vascular resistance, and increased norepinephrine, testosterone, and cortisol

Short time periods of prediction may confound environmental-developmental interactions that could mask the influence of endogenous levels of T. Windle and Windle (1995), in a retrospective longitudinal study, examined the adult levels of plasma T in four groups: (a) those who were aggressive only in childhood; (b) those who became aggressive as adults; (c) those who were aggressive in both childhood and adulthood (continuity); and (d) those who were low in aggression in childhood and adulthood. Adult onset and continuity (in aggressiveness) groups had higher T levels as adults than the other two groups. Other than aggressiveness, the high-T adult groups had higher rates of antisocial personality and a history of various signs of antisocial behavior. Was the high level of T in these groups a product of their history or a sign of an earlier level of T that affected the development of these behaviors? The authors admit that it is impossible to answer this question.

High levels of cortisol are associated with stress and inhibition and low levels with impulsivity and sensation seeking, as noted previously. In baboons dominant and aggressive males usually have low levels of cortisol and subordinate and nonaggressive primates have higher levels of cortisol. As with testosterone, cortisol varies considerably with recent and long-term patterns of experience such as winning or losing in fights. Low levels of cortisol have been found in psychopathic, violent offenders (Virkkunen, 1985), but high levels of cortisol are positively associated with hostility as measured by hostility questionnaires (Keltikangas, Räikkönen, & Adlercreutz, 1997; Pope & Smith, 1991). Chronic feelings of hostility are often associated with anxiety and depression, but the type of impulsive aggression seen in antisocial personality represents a brief state of anger in a generally unemotional personality.

Genetics

Behavior genetic studies of general hostility scales or aggression in children have shown significant heritabilities. However, it is possible that some aspects of hostility or aggression may be more heritable than others. A twin study of adult males using the BDHS revealed heritabilities ranging from 28% for verbal hostility to 47% for assault (Coccaro, Bergeman, Kavoussi, & Seroczynski, 1997). Verbal hostility is the most common form and yet it had the least heritability and the strongest environmental influence. An analysis of the genetic influence on the correlations among the scales that the assault scale had different underlying influences than the other scales which shared a common genetic influence. With the exception of the assault scale the genetic influence underlying the scales is of a nonadditive type suggesting

Mendelian dominant or recessive or epistatic mechanisms. If it is the former, there is the likelihood of finding a gene of major effect in the general trait of aggression, apart from physical assault type.

The MAO type-A gene has become a likely candidate for this trait. Aggression in male mice is heightened by deletion of the MAO-A gene (Cases et al., 1995), and a mutation in the gene in a large Dutch family has been linked to mild retardation and impulsive aggressive behavior (Bruner, Nelsen, Breakfield, Ropers, & van Oost, 1993). The mutation is rare, but the gene has a wide range of alleles varying in repeat length. Subjects with one form, in contrast to those with another form, had lower scores on an index of aggression/impulsivity and the Barratt impulsiveness scale (Manuck, Flory, Ferrell, Mann, & Muldoon, 2000). The life history of aggression only approached significance and the BDHS did not show significant differences between allele groups. Apparently, the impulsivity was more salient than the aggressiveness in the combination. Consistent with the association between low serotonin and aggression in the finding that the allele group with the higher impulsive aggression score also showed less response to a serotonergic challenge test.

Just as the findings on the MAO-A gene suggest one source of the link between serotonin and aggression, another gene has been found that suggests a genetic mechanism for the association of norepinephrine with aggression. The adrenergic-2A receptor gene (ADRA2A) plays a role in modulating norepinephrine release in the locus coeruleus. Alleles of this gene were associated with scales for hostility and impulsivity in a younger student sample and impulsivity alone in an older sample (Comings et al., 2000).

Summary

Extreme violence has been associated with EEG evidence of cortical abnormality usually in the form of an excess of slow wave activity (underarousal) or focalized EEG abnormalities in the temporal lobes. Brain scans have confirmed the temporal lobe abnormalities and also found an equal incidence of frontal lobe abnormalities. A reduced P300 cortical EP response has also been found in prisoners with a history of extremely violent behavior. The reduced activity and reactivity in the frontal lobes may reflect a deficit in inhibitory capacity, which is part of the executive function of these lobes. The abnormal activity of the temporal lobe may be symptomatic of abnormal amygdala function because this lobe is in close proximity to the underlying amygdala. An MRI study has revealed temporal lobe lesions in about one third of violent patients. Hostility or anger proneness is related to a high level of cardiovascular, noradrenergic, and testosterone and cortisol response to stress or perceived attack. Suppressed hostility can lead to cardiovascular disease.

Among the monoamines, serotonin deficit is most highly associated with impulsive aggression. However, low serotonin is associated with depression and suicide as well as aggression and homicide, another example of the multiple trait associations of biological markers. Lack of emotional and behavioral control is the likely consequence of serotonin deficit. Depletion of tryptophan, the precursor of serotonin in the production chain, increases aggressive responses and angry and hostile feelings in laboratory experiments. Augmentation of serotonin, through reuptake inhibitors, can reduce aggression in aggression-prone persons.

Unlike depression, in which both serotonin and norepinephrine depletions are seen, brain norepinephrine (from CSF) tends to be positively correlated with aggressive tendencies in monkeys and humans. However, low levels of peripheral levels of the catecholamines norepinephrine and epinephrine are also related to aggressiveness. We need to distinguish between the type of aggression that occurs in states of high emotional arousal and the cold type of aggression more characteristic of the psychopath. The latter type may be reflected in the low levels of peripheral catecholamine reactivity.

Testosterone is associated with aggression based on behavioral records, but results using self-report measures of hostility or aggression are less conclusive. Prisoners with either histories of extremely violent crimes or characterized by aggression in prison show high levels of testosterone. Testosterone is increased by victory in competitive contests and sexual stimulation and decreased by defeat, raising the old "chicken or egg" problem of causation. The influence of testosterone during development may be mediated by its influence on physique in male adolescents where it is associated with a more muscular mesomorhpic body build. Low cortisol levels are found in aggressive types and are also influenced by the outcomes of fights.

Aggression trait is moderately heritable, but its heritability depends on the form it takes. Assaultive aggression is moderately heritable but verbal aggression is only weakly heritable. The gene for MAO of the A type has been linked to aggression in a human family study. Deletion of the MAO-A gene in mice increases their aggressivity, suggesting that the gene is involved in the inhibition or regulation of aggression.

CONCLUSIONS

Wilson (1998) described *consilience* as a quality of science that links knowledge across disciplines to create a common background of explanation. Personality psychology, extending from social psychology at the higher level to biopsychology at the more fundamental level, provides a daunting challenge to consilience. The introduction to this chapter presented a model of levels along the biological and social pathways leading up to a merger in personality traits.

Such a levels approach suggests a goal of reductionism, a pejorative term for critics of science and many scientists as well. The artist is contemptuous of the critic's attempts to reduce his or her art to a textual formula, and the social scientist may resent the presumptuous intrusion of the biological scientist into his or her own complex type of explanation. Wilson, however, views reductionism as a natural mode of science:

> The cutting edge of science is reductionism, the breaking apart of nature into its natural constituents. . . . It is the search strategy employed to find points of entry into otherwise impenetrably complex systems. Complexity is what interests scientists in the end, not simplicity. Reductionism is the way to understand it. The love of complexity without reductionism makes art; the love of complexity with reductionism makes science. (pp. 58–59)

Later, Wilson (1998) admits that reductionism is an oversimplification that may sometimes be impossible. At each level of organization the phenomena may require new laws and principles that cannot be predicted from those at more general levels. My view is that this is always true for levels that involve an interaction between biological traits or genes and experience in the social environment. A learned association cannot be reduced to a *specific* set of neural events, at least not in the complex brain of a higher organism. It is not inconceivable, however, that the difference in *general* neural events that make an association more likely in one individual than another is not only explicable but also essential for a complete understanding of the event. Consilience is more possible at the borders of two levels, and this is where the breakthroughs are most likely to take place. As Wilson puts it, "The challenge and the cracking of thin ice are what gives science its metaphysical excitement" (p. 60).

This chapter was organized around a top-down approach, starting with four broad classes of personality traits that are empirically identifiable across several systems of trait description: extraversion/sociability, neuroticism/anxiety, impulsiveness/conscientousness, and aggression/agreeableness. One way to bypass the complex social determinants of these traits in human societies is to look for appropriate animal models and biological links between behavior in these species and our own. This approach has identified certain biological markers for analogous behavioral traits such as the monoamine neurotransmitters and enzymes like MAO that regulate them; hormones like testosterone and cortisol; psychophysiological characteristics such as augmenting/ reducing of the cortical evoked potential; brain structure and physiology as assessed by brain imaging methods in humans and lesion and stimulation studies in other species; and molecular genetic studies that link genes, biological mechanisms, and behavioral and personality traits.

Simple-minded reductionism would expect one personality or behavioral trait to be associated with one brain structure, one neurotransmitter, one hormone, one physiological pattern of reactivity, and one gene in both humans and other animals. The chapter is organized by personality traits, but if one reads across the traits it is clear that this neat kind of phrenological isomorphism is not the rule. Evolution may have shaped the nervous system around behavioral mechanisms necessary for adaptation, but evolution did not select for personality traits. The tendency to explore, forage, and approach novel but nonthreatening objects or creatures is part of that adaptation and is important in survival, as is competitive and defensive aggression, cooperation, and even altruism.

If we reverse direction and work up from the biological mechanisms to the personality trait and behavioral levels the fourfold classification at the top becomes blurred. Monoamine reactivities, MAO, testosterone, cortisol, and reactivity of cortical EPs to stimulus variation are related to sociability and sensation seeking, impulsivity and aggression, asocialization, neuroticism, anxiety, and inhibition, but in no simple one-to-one manner. Low levels of serotonergic activity are related to both depression and impulsive aggression producing both violent and impulsive homicides and suicides, sometimes in the same person. Is it the impulsivity, the aggression, or the neuroticism that is related to a serotonin deficiency? High levels of testosterone are related to sociability and social dominance, disinhibitory sensation seeking, aggressivity, asocialization, and low levels to neuroticism and agreeableness. Low levels of MAO are related to sensation seeking, impulsivity, asocial tendencies, and sociability.

Personality traits may be orthogonal, but biological traits do not respect these boundaries. It is almost as if the functional biology of the organism is organized around two basic traits: approach (including sociability, impulsivity, sensation seeking, and aggression) and inhibition/avoidance (or neuroticism/anxiety at the personality trait level). The comparative psychologist Schneirla (1959) put this idea into a postulate: "For all organisms in early ontogenetic stages, low intensities of stimulation tend to evoke approach reactions, high intensities withdrawal reactions" (p. 3). In evolved or more mature organisms Schneirla used the terms "seeking" and "avoidance" in place of "approach" and withdrawal." The latter terms convey the idea of reflexive or tropistic

mechanisms, whereas the former imply learned behavior. Approach-withdrawal describes a basic dimension of temperament and inhibition/shyness another in infant scales of temperament. These individual differences in infants may represent two biologically based dimensions found in other species, and they may develop into more diffentiated characteristics in adult humans.

Genetic dissection is one method of defining the boundaries of biological influence in traits. If both biological and behavioral traits are included in biometric or molecular genetic studies, the genetic covariance between the genetic and the other two can be determined. Rarely are genetic, biological, and behavioral traits all included in one study.

A biosocial approach cannot ignore the complex interactions between biological traits and environmental experiences. In both animals and humans the levels of the hormones testosterone and cortisol influence behavioral interactions with the environment but are in turn influenced by the outcomes of these interactions. There is no reason to think that similar interactions do not occur for the monoamine neurotransmitters. All of these systems are regulated by internal mechanisms. For instance, if there is overactivity in a system, regulators like MAO may catabolize the excess neurotransmitter. There may be more trait stability in the regulator than in the transmitter itself. After repeated experiences, however, there may be changes in the activity of a biological system that are relatively enduring if not irreversible. Environment may even influence the effect of genes by affecting their release. Given the constant interaction between the biological and environmental pathways (Figure 4.1), reductionism of one to the other is impossible. It would be like describing the biological activity of the lungs in the absence of oxygen, the digestive organs in the absence of food, or, using a more relevant analogy, the brain in the absence of stimulation.

Psychology emerged from the biological sciences more than a century ago, although its origins were forgotten by those who wanted a science that would emulate physics and those who wanted to cut all connections with the biological sciences. Fifty years ago, when I entered the field, the founder of behaviorism, Watson, had declared that the outcome of personality was entirely a matter of life experience (conditioning) and had nothing to do with genetics, and Skinner had declared the irrelevancy of the brain in behavior. Despite Freud's own view that the mysteries of the psyche would one day be understood in terms of biology, his followers advocated an environmental determinism that put the entire weight of explanation on society, the family, and early experience. These early prophets of our science are now historical footnotes, and the science is more cognitive and biosocial with new cross disciplines like cognitive neuroscience emerging. The changes are in large measure due to the rapid advances in the neurosciences that have opened new, unforeseen vistas in psychology. Further progress will also procede apace with the development of new methodolo gies and the refinement of current ones.

Behavior genetics has challenged the radical environmentalist position by showing that nearly all personality traits and even some broad attitudinal traits have a significant degree of genetic determination. It is becoming a truism that genes interact with environment throughout life. But the precise nature of this complex interaction remains obscure. Genes do not make personality traits; they make proteins. The development of molecular behavioral genetics will help solve some of these problems. When we know some of the major genes involved with a personality trait and what these genes make and influence in the nervous system, we will be in a better position to define the biological mechanisms that lie between gene and behavior. Knowing the gene-biological trait link is not sufficient until we can understand the way the biological mechanism interacts with the environment, or more specifically the brain-behavior relationship.

Until recent decades the study of the brain was limited to peripheral measures like the EEG. The brain-imaging methods are only in their infancy but are already influencing the course of our science. The ones like PET or the more effective fMRI can tell us exactly what is happening in the brain after the presentation of a stimulus or condition, as well as where it is happening. The expensiveness of these methods has limited their use to medical settings and to clinical populations. Studies of personality in normals are rare and incidental to the objectives of clinical studies. They usually involve small numbers of subjects with a consequent unreliability of findings. Sooner or later the application of these methods to the study of personality dimensions in nonclinical populations will help to understand exactly what a personality predisposition is in the brain. Longitudinal studies starting with genetic and neurochemical markers and tracking the fate of individuals with these markers through life will enable us to predict both normal variant outcomes and psychopathology.

REFERENCES

Almada, S. J., Zonderman, A. B., Shekelle, R. B., Dyer, A. R., Daviglus, M. L., Costa, P. T., & Stamler, J. (1991). Neuroticism and cynicism and risk of death in middle-aged men: The Western Electric Study. *Psychosomatic Medicine, 53,* 165–175.

Archer, J. (1991). The influence of testosterone on human aggression. *British Journal of Psychology, 82,* 1–28.

Archer, J., Birring, S. S., & Wu, F. C. W. (1998). The association between testosterone and aggression in young men: Empirical findings and a meta-analysis. *Aggressive Behavior, 24,* 411–420.

Åsberg, M. (1994). Monoamine neurotransmitters in human aggressiveness and violence: A selected review. *Criminal Behaviour and Mental Health, 4,* 303–327.

Auerbach, J., Faroy, M., Kahanna, M., Ebstein, R., Geller, V., Levine, J., & Belmaker, H. (1998, October). *Dopamine D4 receptor and serotonin transporter promoter in the determination of infant temperament.* Poster presented at 12th Occasional Temperament Conference, Philadelphia.

Bagby, R. M., Levitan, R. D., Kennedy, S. H., Levitt, A. J., & Joffe, R. T. (1999). Selective alteration of personality in response to noradrenergic and serotonergic antidepressant medication in a depressed sample: Evidence on non-specificity. *Psychiatry Research, 86,* 211–216.

Ballenger, J. C., Post, R. M., Jimerson, D. C., Lake, C. R., Murphy, D. L., Zuckerman, M., & Cronin, C. (1983). Biochemical correlates of personality traits in normals: An exploratory study. *Personality and Individual Differences, 4,* 615–625.

Bardo, M. T., Donohew, R. L., & Harrington, N. G. (1996). Psychobiology of novelty seeking and drug seeking behavior. *Behavioural Brain Research, 77,* 23–43.

Barratt, E. S. (1971). Psychophysiological correlates of classical differential eyelid conditioning among subjects selected on the basis of impulsivity and anxiety. *Biological Psychiatry, 3,* 339–346.

Barratt, E. S., Pritchard, W. S., Faulk, D. M., & Brandt, M. E. (1987). The relationship between impulsiveness subtraits, trait anxiety, and visual N100-augmenting-reducing: A topographic analysis. *Personality and Individual Differences, 8,* 43–51.

Barratt, E. S., Stanford, M. S., Felthous, A. R., & Kent, T. A. (1997). The effects of phenytoin on impulsive and premeditated aggression: A controlled study. *Journal of Clinical Psychopharmacology, 17,* 341–349.

Bartussek, D., Becker, G., Diedrich, O., Naumann, E., & Maier, S. (1996). Extraversion, neuroticism, and event-related brain potentials in response to emotional stimuli. *Personality and Individual Differences, 20,* 301–312.

Bartussek, D., Diedrich, O., Naumann, E., & Collet, W. (1993). Introversion-extraversion and event-related potential (ERP): A test of J. A. Gray's theory. *Personality and Individual Differences, 14,* 565–574.

Benjamin, J., Ebstein, R. P., & Belmaker, R. (1997). Personality genetics. *Israel Journal of Psychiatry and Related Sciences, 34,* 270–280.

Benjamin, J., Li, L., Patterson, C., Greenberg, B. D., Murphy, D. L., & Hamer, D. H. (1996). Population and familial association between the D4 dopamine receptor gene and measures of sensation seeking. *Nature Genetics, 12,* 81–84.

Bergman, B., & Brismar, B. (1994). Hormone levels and personality traits in abusive and suicidal male alcoholics. *Alcoholism: Clinical and Experimental Research, 18,* 311–316.

Berman, M., Gladue, B., & Taylor, S. (1993). The effects of hormones, Type A behavior pattern, and provocation on aggression in men. *Motivation and Emotion, 17,* 125–138.

Block, J. (1995). A contrarian view of the five-factor approach to personality description. *Psychological Bulletin, 117,* 187–215.

Bogaert, A. F., & Fisher, W. A. (1995). Predictors of university men's number of sexual partners. *Journal of Sex Research, 32,* 119–130.

Branchey, M. H., Buydens-Branchey, L., & Lieber, C. S. (1988). P3 in alcoholics with disordered regulation of aggression. *Psychiatry Research, 25,* 49–58.

Breen, R. B., & Zuckerman, M. (1999). "Chasing" in gambling behavior: Personality and cognitive determinants. *Personality and Individual Differences, 27,* 1097–1111.

Breier, A., Buchanan, R. W., Elkashef, A., Munson, R. C., Kirkpatrick, B., & Gellad, F. (1992). Brain morphology and schizophrenia: A magnetic resonance imaging study of limbic, prefrontal cortex and caudate structures. *Archives of General Psychiatry, 49,* 921–924.

Brocke, B., Beauducel, A., John, R., Debener, S., & Heilemann, H. (2000). Sensation seeking and affective disorders: Characteristics in the intensity dependence of acoustic evoked potentials. *Neuropsychobiology, 41,* 24–30.

Brocke, B., Tasche, K. G., & Beauducel, A. (1997). Differential effort reactivity and state control. *Personality and Individual Differences, 22,* 447–458.

Brown, G. L., Ebert, M. H., Gover, P. F., Jimerson, D. C., Klein, W. J., Bunney, W. E., & Goodwin, F. K. (1982). Aggression, suicide, and serotonin: Relationships to CSF amine metabolites. *American Journal of Psychiatry, 139,* 741–746.

Bruner, H. G., Nelsen, M., Breakefield, X. O., Ropers, H. H., & van Oost, B. A. (1993). Abnormal behavior associated with a point mutation in the structural gene for monoamine oxidase-A. *Science, 262,* 578–580.

Buchsbaum, M. S. (1971). Neural events and the psychophysical law. *Science, 172,* 502.

Bullock, W. A., & Gilliland, K. (1993). Eysenck's arousal theory of introversion-extraversion: A converging measures investigation. *Journal of Personality and Social Psychology, 64,* 113–123.

Buss, A. H., & Durkee, A. (1957). An inventory for assessing different kinds of hostility. *Journal of Consulting Psychology, 21,* 343–349.

Buss, A. H., & Perry, M. (1992). The aggression questionnaire. *Journal of Personality and Social Psychology, 63,* 452–459.

Cameron, O. G., Smith, C. B., Neese, R. M., Hill, E. M., Hollingsworth, P. J., Abelson, J. A., Hariharan, M., & Curtis, G. C. (1996). Platelet alpha2-adrenoreceptors, catecholamines, hemodynamic variables, and anxiety in panic patients and their asymptomatic relatives. *Psychosomatic Medicine, 58,* 289–301.

Campbell, A., Muncer, S., & Odber, J. (1997). Aggression and testosterone: Testing a bio-social model. *Aggressive Behavior, 23* 229–238.

Canli, T., Zhao, Z., Desmond, J. E., Kang, E., Gross, J., & Gabrieli, J. D. E. (2001). An fMRI study of personality influences on brain reactivity to emotional stimuli. *Behavioral Neuroscience, 115,* 33–42.

Carrigan, P. M. (1960). Extraversion-introversion as a dimension of personality: A reappraisal. *Psychological Bulletin, 57,* 329–360.

Cases, O., Seif, L., Grimsby, J., Gaspar, P., Chen, K., Pournin, S., Muller, U., Aguet, M., Babinet, C., Shih, J. C., & Demaeyer, E. (1995). Aggressive behavior and altered amounts of brain serotonin and norepinephrine in mice lacking MAO-A. *Science, 268,* 1763–1766.

Castro, I. P., Ibanez, A., Torres, P., Sáiz-Ruiz, J., & Fernández-Piqueras, J. (1997). Genetic association study between pathological gambling and a fundamental DNA polymorphism at the D4 receptor gene. *Pharmacogenetics, 7,* 345–348.

Cattell, R. B. (1950). *Personality: A systematic, theoretical, and factual study.* New York: McGraw-Hill.

Charney, D. S., & Heninger, G. R. (1986). Abnormal regulation of noradrenergic function in panic disorders. *Archives of General Psychiatry, 43,* 1042–1054.

Cleare, A. J., & Bond, A. J. (1995). The effects of tryplophan depletion and enhancement on subjective and behavioral aggression in normal male subjects. *Psychopharmacology, 118,* 72–81.

Cleare, A. J., & Bond, A. J. (1997). Does central serotonergic function correlate inversely with aggression? A study using d-fenfluramine in healthy subjects. *Psychiatry Research, 69,* 89–95.

Cloninger, C. R. (1987). A systematic method for clinical classification of personality. *Archives of General Psychiatry, 44,* 573–588.

Cloninger, C. R., Svrakic, D. M., & Przybeck, T. R. (1993). A psychobiological model of temperament and character. *Archives of General Psychiatry, 50,* 975–990.

Coccaro, E. F., Bergeman, C. S., Kavoussi, R. J., & Seroczynski, A. D. (1997). Heritability of aggression and irritability: A twin study of the Buss-Durkee aggression scales in adult male subjects. *Biological Psychiatry, 41,* 273–284.

Coccaro, E. F., Kavoussi, R. J., Sheline, Y. I., Berman, M. E., & Csernansky, J. G. (1997). Impulsive aggression in personality disorder correlates with platelet 5-HT-sub(2A) receptor binding. *Neuropsychopharmacology, 16,* 211–216.

Coccaro, E. F., Lawrence, T., Trestman, R., Gabriel, S., Klai, H. M., & Siever, L. (1991). Growth hormone responses to intravenous clonidine challenge correlates with behavioral irritability in psychiatric patients and healthy volunteers. *Psychiatry Research, 39,* 129–139.

Comings, D. E., Johnson, J. P., Gonzalez, N. S., Huss, M., Saucier, G., McGue, M., & MacMurray, J. (2000). *Psychiatric Genetics, 10,* 39–42.

Constantino, J. N., & Murphy, D. L. (1996). Monoamine metabolites in "leftover" newborn human cerebrospinal fluid: A potential resource for biobehavioral research. *Psychiatry Research, 65,* 129–142.

Costa, P. T., Jr., & McCrae, R. R. (1992a). *Revised NEO Personality Inventory (NEO-PI-R).* Odessa, FL: Psychological Assessment Resources.

Costa, P. T., Jr., & McCrae, R. R. (1992b). Four ways five factors are basic. *Personality and Individual Differences, 13,* 653–665.

Coursey, R. D., Buchsbaum, M. S., & Murphy, D. L. (1979). Platelet MAO activity and evoked potentials in the identification of subjects biologically at risk for psychiatric disorders. *British Journal of Psychiatry, 134,* 372–381.

Crow, T. J. (1977). Neurotransmitter related pathways: The structure and function of central monoamine neurons. In A. N. Davison (Ed.), *Biochemical correlates of brain structure and function* (pp. 137–174). New York: Academic Press.

Dabbs, J. M., Jr. (2000). *Heroes, rogues, and lovers.* New York: McGraw-Hill.

Dabbs, J. M., Jr., Carr, T. S., Frady, R. L., & Riad, J. K. (1995). Testosterone, crime, and misbehavior among 692 male prison inmates. *Personality and Individual Differences, 18,* 627–633.

Dabbs, J. M., Hopper, C. H., & Jurkovic, G. J. (1990). Testosterone and personality among college students and military veterans. *Personality and Individual Differences, 11,* 1263–1269.

Daitzman, R. J., & Zuckerman, M. (1980). Personality, disinhibitory sensation seeking and gonadal hormones. *Personality and Individual Differences, 1,* 103–110.

Daitzman, R. J., Zuckerman, M., Sammelwitz, P. H., & Ganjam, V. (1978). Sensation seeking and gonadal hormones. *Journal of Biosocial Science, 10,* 401–408.

Davis, M. (1986). Pharmacological and anatomical analysis of fear conditioning using the fear-potentiated startle paradigm. *Behavioral Neuroscience, 100,* 814–824.

De Pascalis, V. F., Fiore, A. D., & Sparita, A. (1996). Personality, event-related potential (ERP) and heart rate (HR): An investigation of Gray's theory. *Personality and Individual Differences, 20,* 733–746.

Depue, R. A., & Collins, P. F. (1999). Neurobiology of the structure of personality: Dopamine, facilitation of incentive motivation, and extraversion. *Behavioral and Brain Sciences, 22,* 491–569.

Depue, R. A., Luciana, M., Arbisi, P., Collins, P., & Leon, A. (1994). Dopamine and the structure of personality: Relationship of agonist induced dopamine activity to positive emotionality. *Journal of Personality and Social Psychology, 67,* 485–498.

Digman, J. M., & Inouye, J. (1986). Further specification of the five robust factors of personality. *Journal of Personality and Social Psychology, 50,* 116–123.

Dougherty, D. M., Bjork, J. M., Marsh, D. M., & Moeller, F. G. (1999). Influence of trait hostility on tryptophan depletion-induced laboratory aggression. *Psychiatry Research, 88,* 227–232.

Dulawa, S. C., Grandy, D. K., Low, M. J., Paulus, M. P., & Geyer, M. A. (1999). Dopamine (D4) receptor knock-out mice exhibit reduced exploration of novel stimuli. *Journal of Neuroscience, 19,* 9550–9556.

Ebmeier, K. P., Deary, I. J., O'Carroll, R. E., Prentice, N., Moffoot, A. P. R., & Goodwin, G. M. (1994). Personality associations with the uptake of the cerebral blood flow marker-super(99m) Tc-Examtazime estimated with single photon emission tomography. *Personality and Individual Differences, 17,* 587–595.

Ebstein, R. P., & Belmaker, R. H. (1997). Saga of an adventure gene: Novelty seeking, substance abuse and the dopamine D4 receptor (D4DR) exon III repeat polymorphism. *Molecular Psychiatry, 2,* 381–384.

Ebstein, R. P., Nemarov, L., Klotz, I., Gritsenko, I., & Belmaker, R. H. (1997). Additional evidence for an association between the dopamine D4 receptor (D4DR) exon III repeat polymorphism and the human personality trait of novelty seeking. *Molecular Psychiatry, 2,* 472–477.

Ebstein, R. P., Novick, O., Umansky, R., Priel, B., Osher, Y., Blaine, D., Bennett, E. R., Nemanov, L., Katz, M., & Belmaker, R. H. (1996). Dopamine D4 receptor (D4DR) exon III polymorphism associated with the human personality trait novelty seeking. *Nature Genetics, 12,* 78–80.

Ekelund, J., Lichtermann, D., Jaervelin, M. R., & Peltonen, L. (1999). Association between novelty seeking and type 4 dopamine receptor gene in a large Finnish sample. *American Journal of Psychiatry, 156,* 1453–1455.

Elliot, F. A. (1982). Neurological findings in adult minimal brain dysfunction and the dyscontrol syndrome. *Journal of Nervous and Mental Disease, 179,* 680–687.

van Elst, L. T., Woermann, F. G., Lemieux, L., & Trimble, M. R. (1999). Amygdala enlargement in dysthymia: A volumetric study of patients with temporal lobe epilepsy. *Biological Psychiatry, 46,* 1614–1623.

Erikson, E. H. (1963). *Childhood and society.* New York: Norton.

Eysenck, H. J. (1947). *Dimensions of personality.* New York: Praeger.

Eysenck, H. J. (1967). *The biological basis of personality.* Springfield, IL: Charles C. Thomas.

Eysenck, H. J. (1983). A biometrical-genetic analysis of impulsive and sensation seeking behavior. In M. Zuckerman (Ed.), *Biological bases of sensation seeking, impulsivity and anxiety* (pp. 1–27). Hillside, NJ: Erlbaum.

Eysenck, H. J. (1992). Four ways five factors are not basic. *Personality and Individual Differences, 13,* 667–673.

Eysenck, H. J., & Eysenck, M. W. (1985). *Personality and individual differences: A natural science approach.* New York: Plenum Press.

Eysenck, H. J., & Levey, A. (1972). Conditioning, introversion-extraversion and the strength of the nervous system. In V. D. Nebylitsyn & J. A. Gray (Eds.), *Biological bases of individual behavior* (pp. 206–220). New York: Academic Press.

Eysenck, S. B. G., & Eysenck, H. J. (1963). On the dual nature of extraversion. *British Journal of Social and Clinical Psychology, 2,* 46–55.

Fahrenberg, J. (1987). Concepts of activation and arousal in the theory of emotionality. (Neuroticism): A multivariate conceptualization. In J. Strelau & H. J. Eysenck (Eds.), *Personality dimensions and arousal* (pp. 99–120). New York: Plenum Press.

Finn, P. R., Young, S. N., Pihl, R. O., & Ervin, F. R. (1998). The effects of acute plasma tryptophan manipulation on hostile mood: The influence of trait hostility. *Aggressive Behavior, 24,* 173–185.

Fischer, H., Wik, G., & Fredrikson, M. (1997). Extraversion, neuroticism and brain function: A PET study of personality. *Personality and Individual Differences, 23,* 345–352.

Fishbein, D. H., Dax, E. M., Lozovsky, D. B., & Jaffe, J. H. (1992). Neuroendocrine responses to a glucose challenge in substance abusers with high and low levels of aggression, impulsivity, and antisocial personality. *Neuropsychobiology, 25,* 106–114.

Fiske, D. W. (1949). Consistency of factorial structures for personality ratings from different sources. *Journal of Abnormal and Social Psychology, 44,* 329–344.

Freud, S. (1957). Various papers. In J. Strachey (Ed.), *The standard edition of the complete psychological works of Sigmund Freud.* London: Hogarth Press. (Original work published 1914)

Fulker, D. W., Eysenck, S. B. G., & Zuckerman, M. (1980). The genetics of sensation seeking. *Journal of Personality Research, 14,* 261–281.

Gale, A. (1983). Electroencephalographic studies of extraversion-introversion: A case study in the psychophysiology of individual differences. *Personality and Individual Differences, 4,* 371–380.

Gallagher, J. E., Yarnell, J. W., Sweetnam, P. M., Elwood, P. C., & Stansfield, S. A. (1999). Anger and incident heart disease in the Caerphilly study. *Psychosomatic Medicine, 61,* 446–453.

Gerra, G., Zaimovic, A., Timpano, M., Zambelli, U., Delsignore, R., & Brambilla, F. (2000). Neuroendocrine correlates of temperamental traits in humans. *Psychoneuroendocrinology, 20,* 479–496.

Gerstle, J. E., Mathias, C. W., & Stanford, M. S. (1998). Auditory P300 and self-reported impulsive aggression. *Progress in Neuropsychopharmacology and Biological Psychiatry, 22,* 575–583.

Gladue, B. A. (1991). Aggressive behavioral characteristics, hormones, and sexual orientation in men and women. *Aggressive Behavior, 17,* 313–326.

Goldberg, L. R. (1990). An alternative description of personality: The big-five factor structure. *Journal of Personality and Social Psychology, 59,* 1216–1229.

Goldring, J. F., & Richards, M. (1985). EEG spectral analysis, visual evoked potentials and photic-driving correlates of personality and memory. *Personality and Individual Differences, 6,* 67–76.

Gosling, S. D. (2001). From mice to men: What can we learn about personality from animal research? *Psychological Bulletin, 127,* 45–86.

Gray, J. A. (1982). *The neuropsychology of anxiety: An enquiry into the functioning of the septohippocampal system.* New York: Oxford University Press.

Gray, J. A. (1987). The neuropsychology of emotion and personality. In S. M. Stahl, S. D. Iverson, & E. C. Goodman (Eds.), *Cognitive neurochemistry* (pp. 171–190). Oxford, UK: Oxford University Press.

Gray, J. A. (1999). But the schizophrenic connection. . . . *Behavioral and Brain Sciences, 22,* 523–524.

Gray, N. S., Pickering, A. D., & Gray, J. A. (1994). Psychoticism and dopamine D2 binding in the basal ganglia using single photon emission tomography. *Personality and Individual Differences, 17,* 431–434.

Guilford, J. P. (1975). Factors and factors of personality. *Psychological Bulletin, 82,* 802–814.

Haier, R. J., Sokolski, K., Katz, M., & Buchsbaum, M. S. (1987). The study of personality with positron emission tomography. In J. Strelau & H. J. Eysenck (Eds.), *Personality dimensions and arousal* (pp. 251–267). New York: Plenum Press.

Hall, R. A., Rappaport, M., Hopkins, H. K., Griffin, R. B., Silverman, J. (1970). Evoked response and behavior in cats. *Science, 170,* 998–1000.

Halpern, C. T., Udry, J. R., Campbell, B., & Suchindran, C. (1993). Relationships between aggression and pubertal increases in testosterone: A panel analysis of adolescent males. *Social Biology, 40,* 8–24.

Hansenne, M., & Ansseau, M. (1999). Harm avoidance and serotonin. *Biological Psychology, 51,* 71–81.

Hamer, D. H., Greenberg, B. D., Sabol, S. Z., & Murphy, D. L. (1999). Role of the serotonin transporter gene in temperament and character. *Journal of Personality Disorders, 13,* 312–328.

Harris, J. A., Rushton, J. P., Hampson, E., & Jackson, D. N. (1996). Salivary testosterone and self-report aggression and pro-social personality characteristics in men and women. *Aggressive Behavior, 22,* 321–331.

Harris, J. A., Vernon, P. A., & Boomsa, D. I. (1998). The heritability of testosterone: A study of Dutch adolescent twins and their parents. *Behavior Genetics, 28,* 165–171.

Heath, A., Cloninger, C., & Martin, N. (1994). Testing a model for the genetic structure of personality: A comparison of the personality systems of Cloninger and Eysenck. *Journal of Personality and Social Psychology, 66,* 702–775.

Heinz, A., Weingarten, H. G. D., Hommer, D., Wolkowitz, O. M., & Linnoila, M. (1999). Severity of depression in abstinent alcoholics is associated with monoamine metabolites and dehydroepiandrosterone-sulfate concentration. *Psychiatry Research, 89,* 97–106.

Hennig, J., Kroeger, A., Meyer, B., Prochaska, H., Krien, P., Huwe, S., & Netter, P. (1998). Personality correlates of +/− Pinodel induced decreases in prolactin. *Pharmacopsychiatry, 31,* 19–24.

Hodges, W. F. (1976). The psychophysiology of anxiety. In M. Zuckerman & C. D. Spielberger (Eds.), *Emotions and anxiety: New concepts, methods and applications* (pp. 175–194). Hillsdale, NJ: Erlbaum.

Hogan, R. (1982). A socioanalytic theory of personality. In M. M. Page (Ed.), *Personality: Current theory and research: Nebraska Symposium on motivation* (pp. 55–89). Lincoln: University of Nebraska Press.

Hur, Y., & Bouchard, T. J., Jr. (1997). The genetic correlation between impulsivity and sensation seeking traits. *Behavior Genetics, 27,* 455–463.

Hutchison, K. E., Wood, M. D., & Swift, R. (1999). Personality factors moderate subjective and psychophysiological responses to d-amphetamine in humans. *Experimental and Clinical Psychopharmacology, 7,* 493–501.

Johnson, D. L., Wiebe, J. S., Gold, S. M., Andreason, N. C., Hichwa, R. D., Watkins, G. L., & Ponton, L. L. B. (1999). Cerebral blood flow and personality: A positron emission tomography study. *American Journal of Psychiatry, 156,* 252–257.

Jönsson, E. G., Nöthen, M. M., Gustavsson, J. P., Neidt, H., Forslund, K., Mattila-Evenden, M., Rylander, G., Propping, P., & Åsberg, M. (1998). Lack of association between dopamine D4 receptor gene and personality traits. *Psychological Medicine, 28,* 985–989.

Jorm, A. F., Henderson, A. S., Jacomb, P. A., Croft, L., & Easteal, S. (1997). Quantitative trait loci for neuroticism: An allele association study with the serotonin receptor (HTR2) and monoamine oxidase A (MAOA) genes. *Personality and Individual Differences, 22,* 287–290.

Kagan, J., Reznick, J. S., & Snidman, N. (1988). Biological bases of childhood shyness. *Science, 240,* 167–171.

Keltikangas, J. L., Räikkönen, K., & Adlercreutz, H. (1997). Response of the pituitary adrenal axis in terms of Type A behaviour, hostility and vital exhaustion in healthy middle-aged men. *Psychology and Health, 12,* 533–542.

Klinteberg, B., Oreland, L., Hallman, J., Wirsen, A., Levander, S. E., & Schalling, D. (1991). Exploring the connections between platelet monoamine oxidase (MAO) activity and behavior: Relationships with performance in neuropsychological tasks. *Neuropsychobiology, 23,* 188–196.

Knuston, B., Wolkowitz, O. M., Cole, S. W., Chan, T., Moore, E. A., Johnson, R. C., Terpstra, J., Turner, R. A., & Reus, V. I. (1998). Selective alteration of personality and social behavior by serotonergic intervention. *American Journal of Psychiatry, 155,* 373–379.

Koehler, T., Scherbaum, N., Richter, R., Boettcher, S. (1993). The relationship between neuroticism and blood pressure reexamined: An investigation of a nonclinical sample of military conscripts. *Psychotherapy and Psychosomatics, 60,* 100–105.

Kotler, M., Cohen, H., Segman, R., Gritsenko, I., Nemanov, L., Lerer, B., Kramer, I., Zer-Zion, M., Kletz, I., & Ebstein, R. P. (1997). Excess dopamine D4 receptor (D4DR) exon III seven repeat allele in opioid-dependent subjects. *Molecular Psychiatry, 2,* 251–254.

Lawler, K. A., Kline, K., Seabrook, E., Krishnamoorthy, J., Anderson, S. F., Wilcox, Z. C., Craig, F., Adlin, R., & Thomas, S. (1998). Family history of hypertension: A psychophysiological analysis: *International Journal of Psychophysiology, 28,* 207–222.

de Leeuwe, J. N., Hentschel, U., Tavenier, R., & Edelbroek, P. (1992). Prediction of endocrine stress reactions by means of personality variables. *Psychological Reports, 70,* 791–802.

Le Moal, M. (1995). Mesocorticolimbic dopaminergic neurons. Functional and regulatory roles. In F. E. Bloom & D. J. Kupfer (Eds.), *Psychopharmacology: The fourth generation of progress* (pp. 283–294). New York: Raven Press.

Lesch, K. P., Bengel, D., Heils, A., & Sabol, S. Z. (1996). Association of anxiety-related traits with a polymorphism in the serotonin transporter gene regulatory region. *Science, 274,* 1527–1531.

Lidberg, L., Levander, S. E., Schalling, D., & Lidberg, Y. (1978). Urinary catecholamines, stress, and psychopathy: A study of arrested men awaiting trial. *Psychosomatic Medicine, 40,* 116–125.

Limson, R., Goldman, D., Roy, A., Lamparski, D., Ravitz, B., Adinoff, B., & Linnoila, M. (1991). Personality and cerebrospinal monoamine metabolites in alcoholics and normals. *Archives of General Psychiatry, 48,* 437–441.

Loehlin, J. C. (1992). *Genes and environment in personality development.* Newbury Park, CA: Sage.

Lukas, J. H., & Siegel, J. (1977). Cortical mechanisms that augment or reduce evoked potentials in cats. *Science, 196,* 73–75.

Lykken, D. T. (1982). Research with twins: The concept of emergenesis. *Psychophysiology, 19,* 361–373.

Magnusson, D. (1987). Individual development in interactional perspective. In D. Magnusson (Ed.), *Paths through life.* Hillsdale, NJ: Erlbaum.

Manuck, S. B., Flory, J. D., Ferrell, R. E., Mann, J. J., & Muldoon, M. F. (2000). A regulatory polymorphism of the monoamine oxidase-KA gene may be associated with variability in aggression, impulsivity, and central nervous system serotonergic responsivity. *Psychiatry Research, 95,* 9–23.

Mannuck, S. B., Flory, J. D., McCaffery, J. M., Matthews, K. A., Mann, J. J., & Muldoon, M. F. (1998). Aggression, impulsivity, and central nervous system serotonergic responsivity in a nonpatient sample. *Neuropsychopharmacology, 19,* 287–299.

Maslow, A. H. (1954). *Motivation and personality.* New York: Harper and Row.

Mason, S. T. (1984). *Catechoamines and behavior.* Cambridge, UK: Cambridge University Press.

Mathew, R. J., Weinman, M. L., & Barr, D. L. (1984). Personality and regional cerebral blood flow. *British Journal of Psychiatry, 144,* 529–532.

Matthews, G., & Amelang, M. (1993). Extraversion, arousal theory and performance: A study of individual differences in EEG. *Personality and Individual Differences, 14,* 347–363.

McCrae, R. R., & Costa, P. T., Jr. (1985). Updating Norman's "Adequate taxonomy": Intelligence and personality dimensions in natural languages and in questionnaires. *Journal of Personality and Social Psychology, 49,* 710–721.

Menza, M. A., Golbe, L. I., Cody, R. A., & Forman, N. E. (1993). Dopamine-related personality traits in Parkinson's disease. *Neurology, 43*(3, Pt. 1), 505–508.

Merikangus, J. R. (1991). The neurology of violence. In J. R. Merikangus (Ed.), *Brain behavior relationships* (pp. 155–186). Lexington, MA: Lexington Books.

Miller, S. B., Dolgoy, L., Friese, M., & Sita, A. (1998). Parental history of hypertension and hostility moderate cardiovascular responses to interpersonal conflict. *International Journal of Psychophysiology, 28,* 193–206.

Millon, T., & Everly, G. S., Jr. (1985). *Personality and its disorders.* New York: Wiley.

Mills, S., & Raine, A. (1994). Neuroimaging and aggression. *Journal of Offender Rehabilitation, 21,* 145–158.

Moss, H. B., Yao, J. K., & Panzak, G. L. (1990). Serotonergic responsivity and behavioral dimensions in antisocial personality disorder with substance abuse. *Biological Psychiatry, 28,* 325–338.

Murphy, D. L., Aulakh, C. S., Garrick, N. A., & Sunderland, T. (1987). Monoamine oxidase inhibitors as antidepressants: Implications for the mechanism of action of antidepressants and the psychobiology of the affective disorders and some related disorders. In H. Y. Meltzer (Ed.), *Psychopharmacology: The third generation of progress* (pp. 545–552). New York: Raven Press.

Myrtek, M. (1984). *Constitutional psychophysiology.* London: Academic Press.

Naveteur, J., & Baque, E. F. (1987). Individual differences in electrodermal activity as a function of subject's anxiety. *Personality and Individual Differences, 8,* 615–626.

Netter, P., Hennig, J., & Roed, I. S. (1996). Serotonin and dopamine as mediators of sensation seeking behavior. *Neuropsychobiology, 34,* 155–165.

Netter, P., Hennig, J., & Rohrmann, S. (1999). Psychobiological differences between the aggression and psychoticism dimension. *Pharmacopsychiatry, 32,* 5–12.

Norman, W. T. (1963). Toward an adequate taxonomy of personality attributes: Replicated factor structure. *Journal of Abnormal and Social Psychology, 66,* 574–583.

O'Carroll, R. E. (1984). Androgen administration to hypogonadal and eugonadal men: Effects on measures of sensation seeking, personality and spatial ability. *Personality and Individual Differences, 5,* 595–598.

O'Gorman, J. G. (1984). Extraversion and the EEG I: An evaluation of Gale's hypothesis. *Biological Psychology, 19,* 95–112.

O'Gorman, J. G., & Lloyd, J. E. M. (1987). Extraversion, impulsiveness, and EEG alpha activity. *Personality and Individual Differences, 8,* 169–174.

Ono, Y., Manki, H., Yoshimura, K., Muramatsu, T., Muzushina, H., Higuchi, S., Yagi, G., Kanba, S., & Masahiro, A. (1997). Association between dopamine D4 receptor (D4DR) exon III polymorphism and novelty seeking in Japanese subjects. *American Journal of Medical Genetics (Neuropsychiatric Genetics), 74,* 501–503.

Packard, M. G., Schroeder, J. P., & Gerianne, M. A. (1998). Expression of testosterone conditioned place preference is blocked by peripheral or intra-accumbens injection of ∂-Flupenthixol. *Hormones and Behavior, 34,* 39–47.

Panksepp, J. (1982). Toward a general psychobiological theory of emotions. *The Behavioral and Brain Sciences, 5,* 407–422.

Pavlov, I. P. (1960). *Conditioned reflexes: An investigation of the physiological activity of the cerebral cortex* (G. V. Anrep, Trans.). New York: Dover. (Original work published 1927)

Perkins, K. A., Wilson, A., Gerlach, D., Broge, M., & Grobe, E. (2000). Greater sensitivity to subjective effects of nicotine in nonsmokers high in sensation-seeking. *Experimental and Clinical Psychopharmacology, 8,* 462–471.

Persky, H., Dresisbach, L., Miller, W. R., O'Brien, C. P., Khan, M. A., Lief, H., Charney, N., & Strauss, D. (1982). The relation of plasma androgen levels to sexual behaviors and attitudes of women. *Psychosomatic Medicine, 44,* 305–319.

Pivik, R. T., Stelmack, R. M., & Bylsma, F. W. (1988). Personality and individual differences in spinal motoneuronal excitability. *Psychophysiology, 25,* 16–24.

Pope, H. G., & Katz, D. L. (1994). Psychiatric and medical effects of anabolic-androgenic steroid use: A controlled study of 160 athletes. *Archives of General Psychiatry, 51,* 375–382.

Pope, M. K., & Smith, T. W. (1991). Cortisol secretion in high and low cynically hostile men. *Psychosomatic Medicine, 53,* 386–392.

Räikkönen, K., Matthews, K. A., Flory, J. D., & Owens, J. F. (1999). Effects of hostility on ambulatory blood pressure and mood during daily living in healthy adults. *Health Psychology, 18,* 44–53.

Raine, A., Buchsbaum, M. S., Stanley, J., Lottenberg, S., Abel, L., & Stoddard, J. (1994). Selective reductions in prefrontal glucose in murderers. *Biological Psychiatry, 36,* 365–373.

Rammsayer, T. H. (1998). Extraversion and dopamine: Individual differences in response to changes in dopamine activity as a possible biological basis of extraversion. *European Psychologist, 3,* 37–50.

Rammsayer, T. H. (1999). Dopamine and extraversion: Differential responsivity may be the key. *Behavioral and Brain Sciences, 22,* 535–536.

Rammsayer, T. H., Netter, P., & Vogel, W. H. (1993). A neurochemical model underlying differences in reaction times between introverts and extraverts. *Personality and Individual Differences, 14,* 701–712.

Rauch, S. L., Savage, C. R., Alpert, N. M., Miguel, E. C., Baer, L., Breiter, H. C., Fischman, A. J., Manzo, P. A., Moretti, C., & Jenike, M. A. (1995). A positron emission tomographic study of simple phobia. *Archives of General Psychiatry, 52,* 20–28.

Redmond, D. E., Jr. (1977). Alterations in the function of the nucleus locus coeruleus. A possible model for studies of anxiety. In I. Hanan & E. Usdin (Eds.), *Animal models in psychiatry and neurology* (pp. 293–305). New York: Pergamon Press.

Redmond, D. E., Jr., Murphy, D. L., & Baulu, J. (1979). Platelet monoamine oxidase activity correlates with social affiliative and agonistic behaviors in normal rhesus monkeys. *Psychosomatic Medicine, 41,* 87–100.

Roy, A. (1999). CSF 5-HIAA correlates with neuroticism in depressed patients. *Journal of Affective Disorders, 52,* 247–249.

Ruegg, R. G., Gilmore, J., Ekstrom, R. D., Corrigan, M., Knight, B., Tancer, M., Leatherman, M. E., Carson, S. W., & Golden, R. N. (1997). Clomipramine challenge responses covary with the tridimensional personality questionnaire scores in healthy subjects. *Biological Psychiatry, 42,* 1123–1129.

Salvador, A., Suay, F., Martinez, S. S., Simon, V. M., & Brain, P. F. (1999). Correlating testosterone and fighting in male participants in judo contests. *Physiology and Behavior, 68,* 205–209.

Saxton, P. M., Siegel, J., & Lukas, J. H. (1987). Visual evoked potential augmenting-reducing slope in cats—2: Correlations with behavior. *Personality and Individual Differences, 8,* 511–519.

Schneirla, T. C. (1959). An evolutionary and developmental theory of biphasic processes underlying approach and withdrawal. In M. J. Jones (Ed.), *Nebraska Symposium on motivation* (Vol. 7, pp. 1–42). Lincoln: University of Nebraska Press.

Seeman, P. (1995). Dopamine receptors: Clinical correlates. In F. E. Bloom & D. J. Kupfer (Eds.), *Psychopharmacology: The fourth generation of progress* (pp. 295–302). New York: Raven Press.

Siegel, J., Sisson, D. F., & Driscoll, P. (1993). Augmenting and reducing of visual evoked potentials in Roman high- and low-avoidance rats. *Physiology and Behavior, 54,* 707–711.

Smith, B. D. (1983). Extraversion and electrodermal activity: Arousability and the inverted U. *Personality and Individual Differences, 4,* 411–419.

Smith, T. W., & Gallo, L. C. (1999). Hostility and cardiovascular reactivity during marital interaction. *Psychosomatic Medicine, 61,* 436–445.

Sostek, A. J., Sostak, A. M., Murphy, D. L., Martin, E. B., & Born, W. S. (1981). Cord blood amine oxidase activities relate to arousal and motor functioning in human newborns. *Life Sciences, 28,* 2561–2568.

Soubrié, P. (1986). Reconciling the role of central serotonin neurons in human and animal behavior. *Behavioral and Brain Sciences, 9,* 319–364.

Spivak, B., Vered, Y., Graff, E., Blum, I., Mester, R., & Weizman, A. (1999). Low platelet-poor plasma concentrations of serotonin in patients with combat-related posttraumatic stress disorder. *Biological Psychiatry, 45,* 840–845.

Stein, L. (1978). Reward transmitters: Catecholamines and opioid peptides. In M. A. Lipton, A. DiMascio, & K. F. Killam (Eds.), *Psychopharmacology: A generation of progress* (pp. 569–581). New York: Raven Press.

Stelmack, R. M. (1990). Biological bases of extraversion: Psychophysiological evidence. *Journal of Personality, 58,* 293–311.

Stelmack, R. M., Campbell, K. B., & Bell, I. (1993). Extraversion and brainstem auditory evoked potentials during sleep and wakefulness. *Personality and Individual Differences, 14,* 447–453.

Stelmack, R. M., & Wilson, K. G. (1982). Extraversion and the effects of frequency and intensity on the auditory brainstem evoked response. *Personality and Individual Differences, 3,* 373–380.

Stenberg, G. (1994). Extraversion and the P300 in a visual classification task. *Personality and Individual Differences, 16,* 543–560.

Stenberg, G., Rosen, I., & Risberg, J. (1990). Attention and personality in augmenting/reducing of visual evoked potentials. *Personality and Individual Differences, 11,* 1243 1254.

Stenberg, G., Wendt, P. E., & Risberg, J. (1993). Regional blood flow and extraversion. *Personality and Individual Differences, 15,* 547–554.

Strelau, J. (1987). Personality dimensions based on arousal theories: Search for integration. In J. Strelau & H. J. Eysenck (Eds.), *Personality dimensions and arousal* (pp. 269–286). New York: Plenum Press.

Strelau, J. (1998). *Temperament: A psychological perspective.* New York: Plenum.

Strelau, J., & Eysenck, H. J. (Eds.). (1987). *Personality dimensions and arousal.* New York: Plenum Press.

Suarez, E. C., Kuhn, C. M., Schanberg, S. M., Williams, R. B., Jr., & Zimmermann, E. A. (1998). Neuroendocrine, cardiovascular, and emotional responses of hostile men: The role of interpersonal challenge. *Psychosomatic Medicine, 60,* 78–88.

Swanson, J. M., Sunohara, G. A., Kennedy, J. L., Regino, R., Fineberg, E., Wigal, T., Lerner, M., Williams, L., La Hoste, G. J., & Wigal, S. (1998). Association of the dopamine receptor (DRD4) gene with a refined phenotype of attention deficit disorder (ADHD): A family-based approach. *Molecular Psychiatry, 3,* 38–41.

Thornquist, M. H., & Zuckerman, M. (1995). Psychopathy, passive-avoidance learning and basic dimensions of personality. *Personality and Individual Differences, 19,* 525–534.

Tonkonogy, J. M. (1990). Violence and the temporal lobe lesion: Head CT and MRI data. *Journal of Neuropsychiatry, 3,* 189–196.

Tremblay, R. E., Schaal, B., Boulerice, B., Arseneault, L., Soussignan, R. G., Paquette, D., & Laurent, D. (1998). Testosterone, physical aggression, dominance, and physical development in early adolescence. *International Journal of Behavioral Development, 22,* 753–777.

Tupes, E. C., & Christal, R. E. (1961). *Recurrent personality factors based on trait ratings.* (USAF ASD Tech. Rep. No. 61–97). Lockland Air Force Base, TX: U.S. Air Force.

Virkkunen, M. (1985). Urinary free cortisol secretion in habitually violent offenders. *Acta Psychiatrica Scandinavica, 72,* 40–44.

Volavka, J. (1995). *Neurobiology of violence.* Washington, DC: American Psychiatric Press.

Wang, S., Mason, J., Charney, D., & Yehuda, R. (1997). *Biological Psychiatry, 41,* 145–151.

Wilson, E. O. (1998). *Consilience: The unity of knowledge.* New York: Vintage Books.

Windle, M. (1994). Temperamental inhibition and activation: Hormonal and psychosocial correlates and associated psychiatric disorders. *Personality and Individual Differences, 17,* 61–70.

Windle, R. C., & Windle, M. (1995). Longitudinal patterns of physical aggression: Associations with adult social, psychiatric, and personality functioning and testosterone levels. *Development and Psychopathology, 7,* 563–585.

Wong, M. T. H., Lumsden, J., Fenton, G. W., & Fenwick, P. B. C. (1994). Electroencephalography, computed tomography and

psychoanalysis are unique to the psychodynamic framework: No other theories of personality accept these three premises in their purest form.

Primacy of the Unconscious

Psychodynamic theorists contend that the majority of psychological processes take place outside conscious awareness. In psychoanalytic terms, the activities of the mind (or *psyche*) are presumed to be largely unconscious, and unconscious processes are thought to be particularly revealing of personality dynamics (Brenner, 1973; Fancher, 1973). Although aspects of the *primacy of the unconscious* assumption remain controversial (see Kihlstrom, 1987; McAdams, 1997), research on implicit learning, memory, motivation, and cognition has converged to confirm this basic premise of psychoanalysis (albeit in a slightly modified form). Many mental activities are only imperfectly accessible to conscious awareness—including those associated with emotional responding, as well as more mundane, affectively neutral activities such as the processing of linguistic material (see Bornstein & Pittman, 1992; Greenwald & Banaji, 1995; Schacter, 1987; Stadler & Frensch, 1998). Whether unconscious processes are uniquely revealing of personality dynamics is a different matter entirely, and psychologists remain divided on this issue.

It is ironic that the existence of mental processing outside awareness—so controversial for so long—has become a cornerstone of contemporary experimental psychology. In fact, in summarizing the results of cognitive and social research on automaticity, Bargh and Chartrand (1999) recently concluded that evidence for mental processing outside of awareness is so pervasive and compelling that the burden of proof has actually reversed: Rather than demonstrate unconscious influences, researchers must now go to considerable lengths to demonstrate that a given psychological process is at least in part under conscious control. This conclusion represents a rather striking (and counterintuitive) reversal of prevailing attitudes regarding the conscious-unconscious relationship throughout much of the twentieth century.

Psychic Causality

The second core assumption of psychodynamic theory is that nothing in mental life happens by chance—that there is no such thing as a random thought, feeling, motive, or behavior (Brenner, 1973). This has come to be known as the principle of *psychic causality*, and it too has become less controversial over the years. Although few psychologists accept

the principle of psychic causality precisely as psychoanalysts conceive it, most theorists and researchers agree that cognitions, motives, emotional responses, and expressed behaviors do not arise randomly, but always stem from some combination of identifiable biological and/or, psychological processes (Rychlak, 1988).

Although few psychologists would argue for the existence of random psychological events, researchers do disagree regarding the underlying processes that account for such events, and it is here that the psychodynamic view diverges from those of other perspectives. Whereas psychoanalysts contend that unconscious motives and affective states are key determinants of ostensibly random psychological events, psychologists with other theoretical orientations attribute such events to latent learning, cognitive bias, motivational conflict, chemical imbalances, or variations in neural activity (e.g., see Buss, 1991; Danzinger, 1997). The notion that a seemingly random event (e.g., a slip of the tongue) reveals something important about an individual's personality is in its purest form unique to psychoanalysis.

Critical Importance of Early Experiences

Psychoanalytic theory is not alone in positing that early developmental experiences play a role in shaping personality, but the theory is unique in the degree to which it emphasizes childhood experiences as determinants of personality development and dynamics. In its strongest form, psychoanalytic theory hypothesizes that early experiences—even those occurring during the first weeks or months of life—set in motion personality processes that are to a great extent immutable (see Emde, 1983, 1992). In other words, the events of early childhood are thought to create a trajectory that almost invariably culminates in a predictable set of adult character traits (Eagle, 1984; Stern, 1985). This is especially of events that are outside the normal range of experience (i.e., very positive or very negative).

The psychodynamic hypothesis that the first weeks or months of life represent a *critical period* in personality development contrasts with those of alternative theories (e.g., cognitive), which contend that key events in personality development occur somewhat later, after the child has acquired a broad repertoire of verbal and locomotive skills. Freud's notion of a critical early period in personality development—coupled with his corollary hypothesis that many of the most important early experiences involve sexual frustration or gratification—was (and is) highly controversial. It helped create a decades-long divergence of psychoanalysis from mainstream developmental psychology, which has only recently begun to narrow (Emde, 1992).

THE EVOLUTION OF PSYCHOANALYSIS: GAZING ACROSS THREE CENTURIES

Many psychodynamic ideas—including the core assumptions just discussed—predated Freud's work and were anticipated by eighteenth and nineteenth century philosophers (Ellenberger, 1970; Hilgard, 1987). Nonetheless, psychoanalytic theory as an independent school of thought was conceived just over 100 years ago, with the publication of Breuer and Freud's (1895/1955) *Studies on Hysteria.* Since that time, the history of psychoanalysis can be divided into four overlapping phases: classical psychoanalytic theory, neo-analytic models, object relations theory and self psychology, and contemporary integrative models. Each phase introduced a novel approach to human development and personality.

Classical Psychoanalytic Theory

Given Freud's background in neurology, it is not surprising that the first incarnation of psychoanalytic theory was avowedly biological. In his early writings, Freud (1895/1966, 1900/1958a) set out to explain psychological phenomena in terms that could be linked to extant models of neural functioning (an ironic goal to say the least, given that psychoanalysis developed in part to explain "neurological" symptoms that had no identifiable neurological basis, such as hysterical blindness and hysterical paralysis).

Because the core principles of classical psychoanalytic theory developed over more than 40 years, there were numerous revisions along the way. Thus, it is most accurate to think of classical psychoanalytic theory as a set of interrelated models, which were often (but not always) consistent with and supportive of each other: the drive model, the topographic model, the psychosexual stage model, and the structural model.

The Drive Model

One consequence of Freud's determination to frame his theory in quasi-biological terms is that the earliest version of psychoanalytic *drive theory* was for all intents and purposes a theory of energy transformation and tension reduction (Breuer & Freud, 1895; Freud, 1896/1955c). Inborn (presumably inherited) instincts were central to the drive model, and most prominent among these was the sex drive, or libido. Freud's interest in (some might say obsession with) sexual impulses as key determinants of personality development and dynamics was controversial during his lifetime, and remains so today (e.g., see Torrey, 1992). At any rate, during the earliest phase of psychoanalytic theory, personality was seen as a by-product of the particular way in which sexual impulses were expressed in an individual.

Freud never fully renounced the drive concept, even after he shifted the emphasis of psychoanalytic theory from inborn instincts to dynamic mental structures with no obvious biological basis (Greenberg & Mitchell, 1983). The concept of cathexis—investment of libidinal (or psychic) energy in an object or act—remained central to psychoanalytic theory even as the drive model waned in influence. As his career drew to a close during the 1930s, Freud (1933/1964a, 1940/1964b) continued to use the concept of cathexis to account for a wide range of psychological processes, from infant-caregiver bonding and infantile sexuality to group behavior and parapraxes (i.e., "Freudian slips").

As the concept of cathexis became reified in classical psychoanalytic theory, so did the companion concepts of fixation (i.e., lingering investment of psychic energy in objects and activities from an earlier developmental period), and regression (i.e., reinvestment of psychic energy in an earlier stage of development, usually under stress). As should become apparent, the concept of cathexis gradually faded from view, but the concepts of fixation and regression continue to be widely discussed and used to explain a wide range of issues related to personality development and dynamics.

The Topographic Model

At the same time as Freud was refining the drive theory, he was elaborating his now-famous *topographic model* of the mind, which contended that the mind could usefully be divided into three regions: the conscious, preconscious, and unconscious (Freud, 1900/1958a, 1911/1958b). Whereas the conscious part of the mind was thought to hold only information that demanded attention and action at the moment, the preconscious contained material that was capable of becoming conscious but was not because attention (in the form of psychic energy) was not invested in it at that time. The unconscious contained anxiety-producing material (e.g., sexual impulses, aggressive wishes) that were deliberately repressed (i.e., held outside of awareness as a form of self-protection). Because of the affect-laden nature of unconscious material, the unconscious was (and is) thought to play a more central role in personality than are the other two elements of Freud's topographic model. In fact, numerous theories of personality ascribe to the notion that emotion-laden material outside of awareness plays a role in determining an individual's personality traits and coping style (see Hogan, Johnson, & Briggs, 1997; Loevinger, 1987).

The terms *conscious, preconscious,* and *unconscious* continue to be used today in mainstream psychology, and research has provided a surprising degree of support for this tripartite approach in the areas of memory and information processing (Bucci, 1997; Stein, 1997; Westen, 1998). Consciousness is indeed linked with attentional capacity, and studies show that a great deal of mental processing (including perceptual processing) occurs preconsciously (Bornstein, 1999b; Erdelyi, 1985). As noted earlier, the existence of a dynamic unconscious remains controversial, with some researchers arguing that evidence favoring this construct is compelling (Westen, 1998), and others contending that "unconscious" processing can be accounted for without positing the existence of a Freudian repository of repressed wishes and troubling urges and impulses (Kihlstrom, 1987, 1999).

Perhaps the most troubling aspect of the topographic model—for Freud and for contemporary experimentalists as well—concerns the dynamics of information flow (i.e., the mechanisms through which information passes among different parts of the mind). Freud (1900/1958a, 1915/1957, 1933/1964a) used a variety of analogies to describe information movement among the conscious, preconscious, and unconscious, the most well-known of these being his *gatekeeper* (who helped prevent unconscious information from reaching conscious awareness), and *anteroom* (where preconscious information was held temporarily before being stored in the unconscious). Contemporary researchers (e.g., Baddeley, 1990) have coined terms more scientific than those Freud used (e.g., *central executive, visuospatial scratch pad*), but in fact they have not been much more successful than Freud was at specifying the psychological and neurological mechanisms that mediate intrapsychic information flow.

The Psychosexual Stage Model

Freud clung to the drive model (and its associated topographic framework) for several decades, in part because of his neurological background, but also because the drive model helped him bridge the gap between biological instincts and his hypothesized stages of development. By 1905, Freud had outlined the key elements of his *psychosexual stage model,* which argued that early in life humans progress through an invariant sequence of developmental stages, each with its own unique challenge and its own mode of drive (i.e., sexual) gratification (Freud, 1905/1953, 1918/1955a). Freud's psychosexual stages—oral, anal, Oedipal, latency, and genital—are well known even to nonpsychoanalytic psychologists. So are the oral, anal, and Oedipal (or phallic) character types associated with fixation at these stages (Fisher & Greenberg, 1996). From a personality perspective, the psychosexual stage model marks a turning point in the history of psychoanalysis because it was only with the articulation of this

TABLE 5.1 The Psychosexual Stage Model

Stage	Age Range	Developmental Task	Associated Character Traits
Oral	0–18 months	Moving from infantile dependency toward autonomy and self-sufficiency	Dependency
Anal	18–36 months	Learning to exercise control over one's body, one's impulses, and other people	Obsessiveness
Oedipal	5–6 years	Mastering competitive urges and acquiring gender role related behaviors	Competitiveness
Latency	6 years–puberty	Investing energy in conflict-free (nonsexual) tasks and activities	—
Genital	Puberty onward	Mature sexuality (blending of sexuality and intimacy)	—

Note. Dashes indicate that no associated character traits exist (fixation in the latency and genital periods does not play a role in classical psychoanalytic theory).

model that personality moved from the periphery to the center of psychoanalytic theory.

Table 5.1 illustrates the basic organization of Freud's (1905/1953) psychosexual stage model. Frustration or overgratification during the infantile, oral stage was hypothesized to result in oral fixation, and an inability to resolve the developmental issues that characterize this period (e.g., conflicts regarding dependency and autonomy). The psychosexual stage model further postulated that the orally fixated (or oral dependent) person would (a) remain dependent on others for nurturance, protection, and support; and (b) continue to exhibit behaviors in adulthood that reflect the oral stage (i.e., preoccupation with activities of the mouth, reliance on food and eating as a means of coping with anxiety). Research supports the former hypothesis, but has generally failed to confirm the latter (Bornstein, 1996).

A parallel set of dynamics (i.e., frustration or overgratification during toilet training) were assumed to produce anal fixation and the development of an anal character type. Because toilet training was viewed by Freud as a struggle for control over one's body and impulses, the anally fixated individual was thought to be preoccupied with issues of control, and his or her behavior would thus be characterized by a constellation of three traits, sometimes termed the *anal triad:* obstinacy, orderliness, and parsimony (Masling & Schwartz, 1979). Fixation during the Oedipal stage was presumed to result in a personality style marked by aggressiveness, competitiveness, and a concern with status and influence (Fisher & Greenberg, 1996; Juni, 1992).

Empirical studies have yielded mixed results with respect to the anal and Oedipal stages. Studies support the existence of an anal triad, but they do not support the critical role of toilet training in the ontogenesis of these traits (Kline, 1981). Similarly, research offers only mixed support for the concept of an Oedipal personality type and offers little evidence for the Oedipal dynamic as Freud conceived it (Fisher & Greenberg, 1996; Masling & Schwartz, 1979).

The Structural Model

Ultimately, Freud recognized certain explanatory limitations in the topographic model (e.g., the model's inability to account for certain forms of psychopathology), and as a result he developed an alternative, complementary framework to explain normal and abnormal personality development. Although the *structural model* evolved over a number of years, the theoretical shift from topography to structure is most clearly demarcated by Freud's (1923/1961) publication of *The Ego and the Id,* wherein he described in detail the central hypothesis underlying the structural model: the notion that intrapsychic dynamics could be understood with reference to three interacting mental structures called the id, ego, and superego. The *id* was defined as the seat of drives and instincts (a throwback to the original drive model), whereas the *ego* represented the logical, reality-oriented part of the mind, and the *superego* was akin to a conscience, or set of moral guidelines and prohibitions (Brenner, 1973). Figure 5.1 illustrates the sequence of development of the id, ego, and superego in Freud's structural model.

According to the structural model, personality is derived from the interplay of these three psychic structures, which differ in terms of power and influence (Freud, 1933/1964a, 1940/1964b). When the id predominates, an impulsive, stimulation-seeking personality style results. When the superego is strongest, moral prohibitions inhibit impulses, and a restrained, overcontrolled personality ensues. When the ego (which serves in part to mediate id impulses and superego prohibitions) is dominant, a more balanced set of personality traits develop. Table 5.2 summarizes the psychodynamic conceptualization of personality in Freud's structural model, as well as within the drive, topographic, and psychosexual stage models.

From 1923 until his death in 1939, Freud spent much of his time elaborating the key principles and corollaries of the structural model, and he extended the model to various areas of individual and social life (e.g., humor, mental errors, cultural dynamics, religious belief). He also made numerous

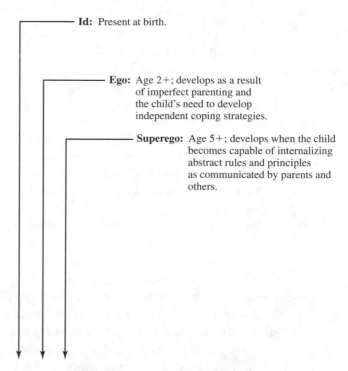

Id: Present at birth.

Ego: Age 2+; develops as a result of imperfect parenting and the child's need to develop independent coping strategies.

Superego: Age 5+; develops when the child becomes capable of internalizing abstract rules and principles as communicated by parents and others.

Figure 5.1 Development of the id, ego, and superego in classical psychoanalytic theory.

efforts to link the structural model to his earlier work in order to form a more cohesive psychodynamic framework. For example, Freud (and other psychoanalysts) hypothesized that oral fixation was characterized in part by a prominent, powerful id, whereas Oedipal fixation was characterized by strong investment in superego activities. At the time of his death, Freud was actively revising aspects of the structural model (Fancher, 1973; Gay, 1988), and it is impossible to know how the model would have developed had Freud continued his work. This much is certain, however: During the decades wherein Freud explicated details of the structural model of the mind, he altered it in myriad ways, and in doing so he laid the foundation for several concepts that—many years later—became key elements of modern psychoanalytic theory.

TABLE 5.2 Conceptions of Personality Within Classical Psychoanalytic Theory

Model	Conception of Personality
Drive	Personality traits as drive (instinct) derivatives.
Topographic	Unconscious (repressed) material is a primary determinant of personality.
Psychosexual	Fixation at a particular psychosexual stage leads to an associated character type.
Structural	Id-ego-superego dynamics determine personality traits and coping strategies.

Neo-Analytic Models

Following Freud's 1909 Clark University lectures, psychoanalysis attracted large numbers of adherents from within the medical and lay communities. At first, these adherents followed Freud's ideas with little questioning and minimal resistance. By the early 1920s, however, competing schools of psychoanalytic thought were beginning to emerge both in Europe and in America. At first, the growth of these alternative psychodynamic frameworks was inhibited by Freud's strong personality and by the immense international popularity of psychoanalytic theory (Hilgard, 1987; Torrey, 1992). It was only upon Freud's death in 1939 that competing psychoanalytic perspectives blossomed into full-fledged theories in their own right.

By the mid-1940s, the discipline had splintered into an array of divergent theoretical perspectives. This splintering process, which has continued (albeit in a somewhat abated form) to the present day, is summarized graphically in Figure 5.2. As Figure 5.2 shows, each post-Freudian psychodynamic model was rooted in classical psychoanalytic theory, but each drew upon ideas and findings from other areas of psychology as well.

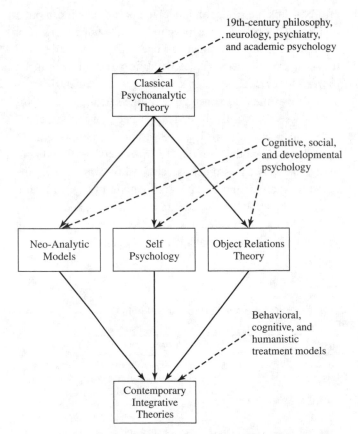

Figure 5.2 Evolution of psychodynamic models of personality; arrows indicate the influence of earlier theories/perspectives on later ones.

TABLE 5.3   Neo-Analytic Models of Personality

Theorist	Key Assumption	Key Terms/Concepts
Adler	Family dynamics (especially birth order) are primary determinants of personality.	Striving for superiority, inferiority complex
Erikson	Social interactions between individual and significant others are key in personality development.	Psychosocial stages, developmental crises
Fromm	Personality is best understood with reference to prevailing social and political (as well as intrapsychic) forces.	Authoritarianism
Horney	Infantile dependency-powerlessness is key to personality.	Basic anxiety
Jung	Personality is shaped by spiritual forces as well as by biological and social variables.	Archetypes, collective unconscious
Sullivan	Personality can only be conceptualized within the context of an individual's core relationships.	Personifications, developmental epochs

Several neo-analytic theories became particularly influential in the decades following Freud's death. Among the most important of these were Jung's (1933, 1961) analytical psychology, Erikson's (1963, 1968) psychosocial theory, Sullivan's (1947, 1953) interpersonal theory, and the quasi-dynamic models of Adler (1921, 1923), Fromm (1941, 1947), and Horney (1937, 1945). These theories shared a Freudian emphasis on intrapsychic dynamics, childhood experiences, and unconscious processes as determinants of personality and psychopathology. However, each neo-analytic theorist rejected the classical psychoanalytic emphasis on sexuality as a key component of personality, and each theory sought to supplant sexuality with its own unique elements. Key features of the most prominent neo-analytic models are summarized in Table 5.3.

Each neo-analytic model in Table 5.3 attained a loyal following during its heyday, but for the most part these neo-analytic models are no longer influential in mainstream psychology. To be sure, aspects of these neo-analytic theories continue to be discussed (and on occasion isomorphically rediscovered by other personality theorists). However, with the exceptions of Erikson and Sullivan, the neo-analytic theories summarized in Table 5.3 have comparatively few adherents today, and they do not receive much attention within the clinical and research communities.

Erikson's (1963, 1968) psychosocial approach continues to have a strong impact on personality and developmental research (Franz & White, 1985). Sullivan's (1953, 1956) interpersonal theory not only helped lay the groundwork for object relations theory and self psychology (described later in this chapter), but continues to influence developmental research on adolescence (Galatzer Levy & Cohler, 1993), as well as psychodynamic writing on treatment of severe pathology (Kernberg, 1984; Millon, 1996).

Object Relations Theory and Self Psychology

Although the influence of most neo-analytic models has waned, two other psychodynamic frameworks that evolved out of Freud's work—*object relations theory* and *self psychology*—remain very much a part of mainstream psychoanalytic theory and practice. Both frameworks developed out of early work in *ego psychology,* an offshoot of the classical model; this model updated Freud's thinking on the role of the ego in personality development. Where Freud had conceptualized the ego primarily in terms of its reality-testing and defensive functions, ego psychologists posited that the ego plays another equally important role in intrapsychic life—setting goals, seeking challenges, striving for mastery, and actualizing potential (Hartmann, 1964). Within this line of thinking, the ego was seen as an autonomous, conflict-free structure, rather than an entity that simply responded to the demands of id, superego, and the external world. Ego psychologists' reconceptualization of the ego set the stage for object relations theory and self psychology.

Object Relations Theory

Although there are several distinct variants of object relations theory (see Greenberg & Mitchell, 1983), they share a core belief that personality can be analyzed most usefully by examining mental representations of significant figures (especially the parents) that are formed early in life in response to interactions taking place within the family (Gill, 1995; Winnicott, 1971). These mental representations (sometimes called *introjects*) are hypothesized to serve as templates for later interpersonal relationships, allowing the individual to anticipate the responses of other people and draw reasonably accurate inferences regarding others' thoughts, feelings, goals, and motivations (Sandler & Rosenblatt, 1962). Mental representations of the parents—parental introjects—also allow the individual to carry on an inner dialogue with absent figures. This inner dialogue helps modulate anxiety and enables the person to make decisions consistent with values and beliefs acquired early in life (Fairbairn, 1952; Jacobson, 1964).

One of the most prominent object relations models of personality today is Blatt's (1974, 1991) anaclitic-introjective framework. Blending psychoanalytic theory with research in cognitive development, Blatt postulated that the structure of an individual's parental introjects play a key role in personality development and dynamics. When introjects are weak (or even absent), an anaclitic personality configuration results, characterized by dependency, insecurity, and feelings of helplessness and emptiness. When introjects are harsh and demanding, an introjective personality configuration is produced, characterized by feelings of guilt, failure, worthlessness, and self-loathing. A plethora of studies have shown that Blatt's anaclitic-introjective distinction helps predict risk for psychopathology and physical illness, the form that psychopathology and illness will take, the kinds of stressful events that are likely to be most upsetting to the individual, and the types of interventions that will effect therapeutic change most readily (Blatt & Homann, 1992; Blatt & Zuroff, 1992).

Self Psychology

Self psychologists share object relations theorists' emphasis on mental representations as the building blocks of personality. However, self psychologists contend that the key introjects are those associated with the self, including *selfobjects* (i.e., representations of self and others that are to varying degrees merged, undifferentiated, and imperfectly articulated). Self psychology developed in part in response to analysts' interest in treating severe personality disorders and other treatment-resistant forms of psychopathology (Goldberg, 1980; Kohut, 1971). The development of self psychology was also aided by a recognition that the knowledge base of analytic theory and practice could be enriched if greater attention were paid to the ontogenesis of the self in the context of early child-caregiver relationships (see Mahler, Pine, & Bergman, 1975).

The most widely known self psychology framework was first described by Kohut (1971, 1977). Kohut postulated that empathic and supportive early interactions resulted in the construction of a secure, cohesive *autonomous self,* with sufficient resources to deal with the stresses and challenges of intimacy. In contrast, disturbances in infant-caregiver interactions were hypothesized to result in damage to the self along with impairments in evocative constancy (i.e., the ability to generate stable mental images of self and absent others) and an inability to tolerate true intimacy with others. A variety of narcissistic disorders result from damage to the self—and although these narcissistic disorders range in severity from moderate to severe, all reflect the individual's inability to maintain a cohesive sense of self, except when recapitulating specific (often destructive) interaction patterns. Empirical data testing Kohut's model are less plentiful than those assessing various object relations frameworks, but studies offer indirect support for Kohut's contention that early difficulties within the infant-caregiver unit result in subsequent character pathology and may predict the form that character pathology will take (Galatzer-Levy & Cohler, 1993; Masling & Bornstein, 1993).

Contemporary Integrative Models

Object relations theory and self psychology have revived academic psychologists' interest in psychodynamic ideas during the past several decades, in part because they represent natural bridges between psychoanalytic theory and research in other areas of psychology (e.g., cognitive, social, developmental; see Barron, Eagle, & Wolitzky, 1992; Masling & Bornstein, 1994; Shapiro & Emde, 1995). While object relations theory and self psychology continue to flourish, a parallel stream of theoretical work has developed that focuses on integrating psychodynamic models of personality with ideas and findings from competing clinical frameworks.

As Figure 5.1 shows, contemporary integrative psychodynamic models draw from both object relations theory and self psychology (and to some extent, from classical psychoanalytic theory as well). Unlike most earlier psychodynamic theories, however, these integrative frameworks utilize concepts and findings from other schools of clinical practice (e.g., cognitive, behavioral, humanistic) to refine and expand their ideas. Some integrative models have gone a step further, drawing upon ideas from neuropsychology and psychopharmacology in addition to other, more traditional areas.

There are almost as many integrative psychodynamic models as there are alternative schools of psychotherapeutic thought. Among the most influential models are those that link psychodynamic thinking with concepts from cognitive therapy (Horowitz, 1988; Luborsky & Crits-Christoph, 1990), behavioral therapy (Wachtel, 1977), and humanistic-existential psychology (Schneider & May, 1995). Other integrative models combine aspects of psychoanalysis with strategies and principles from family and marital therapy (Slipp, 1984). Needless to say, not all analytically oriented psychologists agree that these integrative efforts are productive or desirable. Moreover, the question of whether these integrative frameworks are truly psychoanalytic or have incorporated so many nonanalytic principles as to be something else entirely is a matter of considerable debate within the psychoanalytic community.

PSYCHOANALYTIC PERSONALITY THEORIES: BRINGING ORDER TO CHAOS

Given the burgeoning array of disparate theoretical perspectives, a key challenge confronting psychodynamic theorists involves finding common ground among contrasting viewpoints. Although there are dozens of psychodynamically oriented models of personality in existence today, all these models have had to grapple with similar theoretical and conceptual problems. In the following sections, I discuss how contemporary psychodynamic models have dealt with three key questions common to all personality theories.

Personality Processes and Dynamics

Three fertile areas of common ground among psychodynamic models of personality involve motivation, mental structure and process, and personality stability and change.

Motivation

With the possible exception of the radical behavioral approach, every personality theory has addressed in detail the nature of human motivation—that set of unseen internal forces that impel the organism to action (see Emmons, 1997; Loevinger, 1987; McAdams, 1997). Although classical psychoanalytic theory initially conceptualized motivation in purely biological terms, the history of psychoanalysis has been characterized by an increasing emphasis on psychological motives that are only loosely based in identifiable physiological needs (Dollard & Miller, 1950; Eagle, 1984).

During the 1940s and 1950s, evidence from laboratory studies of contact-deprived monkeys (Harlow & Harlow, 1962) and observational studies of orphaned infants from World War II (Spitz, 1945, 1946) converged to confirm that human and infrahumans alike have a fundamental need for *contact comfort* and sustained closeness with a consistent caregiver. Around this time, developmental researchers were independently formulating theories of infant-caregiver attachment that posited a separate need to relate to the primary caregiver of infancy and specified the adverse consequences of disrupted early attachment relationships (Ainsworth, 1969, 1989; Bowlby, 1969, 1973).

Object relations theorists and self psychologists integrated these developmental concepts and empirical findings into their emerging theoretical models, so that by the late 1960s most psychodynamic psychologists assumed the existence of one or more psychological drives related to contact comfort (e.g., Kernberg, 1975; Kohut, 1971; Winnicott, 1971). Theorists emphasized the critical importance of interactions that take place within the early infant-caregiver relationship, not only because these interactions determined the quality of contact comfort available to the infant, but also because positive interactions with a nurturing caregiver were necessary for the construction of a cohesive sense of self (Kohut, 1971; Mahler et al., 1975); stable, benevolent introjects (Blatt, 1974, 1991);

and useful mental models of self-other interactions (Main, Kaplan, & Cassidy, 1985).

Mental Structure and Process

Along with psychoanalysts' recognition that mental images of self and others were key building blocks of personality came a change in the way the structures and processes of personality were conceptualized. Terms like *introject, schema,* and *object representation* gradually took their place alongside those of Freud's structural model as cornerstones of psychoanalytic theory and therapy (Bornstein, 1996; Greenberg & Mitchell, 1983). Analysts recognized that in addition to mental images of self and others, a key derivative of early relationships was the formation of *internal working models* of self-other interactions (sometimes identified as *scripts*). This alternative conceptualization of the nature of mental structure not only enabled psychodynamic theorists to derive new treatment approaches (especially for working with character-disordered patients), but also helped connect psychodynamic models with research in attachment theory and social cognition (Galatzer-Levy & Cohler, 1993; Masling & Bornstein, 1994).

This language shift not only was due to theoretical changes, but also reflected a need to develop a psychoanalytic terminology that was less abstract and closer to the day-to-day experience of psychoanalytic patients. In fact, close analysis of psychoanalytic discourse during the early days of object relations theory indicated that this terminological evolution was already underway, regardless of the fact that some newfound language was only gradually becoming formalized within the extant psychoanalytic literature.

In this context, Mayman (1976) noted that at any given time, a psychoanalytic theorist or practitioner may use several different levels of discourse to communicate theoretical concepts. At the top of this framework is psychoanalytic metapsychology—the complex network of theoretical concepts and propositions that form the infrastructure of psychoanalysis. Metapsychological terms are often abstract, rarely operationalizable, and typically used in dialogue with other theorists and practitioners. The concepts of libido and selfobject are examples of language most closely associated with psychoanalytic metapsychology.

The middle-level language of psychoanalysis incorporates the constructs used by theorists and practitioners in their own day-to-day work. It is the language in which psychoanalysts conceptualize problems and communicate informally—the kind of language likely to turn up in the heart of a case study or in a set of clinical notes. The terms *oral dependent* and *sublimation* are examples of the middle-level language of psychoanalysis.

The bottom level of psychoanalytic language centers on the experience-near discourse that characterizes therapist-patient exchanges within an analytic session. Less formal than Mayman's (1976) middle-level language, this experience-near discourse is intended to frame psychoanalytic concepts in a way that resonates with a patient's personal experience without requiring that he or she have any understanding of psychoanalytic metapsychology. When an analyst discusses a patient's "aggressive impulses" or "sibling rivalry," that analyst has translated an abstract concept into experience-near terms.

Thus, like most personality theorists, psychoanalysts today conceptualize mental structures and processes on several levels simultaneously. Unfortunately, it has taken psychoanalytic psychologists a long time to develop an experience-near language for day-to-day work—longer perhaps than it has taken psychologists in other areas. On the positive side, however, in recent years psychoanalytic theorists have addressed this issue more openly and systematically than have theorists from other theoretical backgrounds (e.g., see Horowitz, 1991; Kahn & Rachman, 2000).

Personality Stability and Change

The parallel conceptualization of psychoanalytic concepts in relational terms introduced a fundamentally new paradigm for thinking about continuity and change in personality development and dynamics. In addition to being understood in terms of a dynamic balance among id, ego, and superego, stability in personality was now seen as stemming from continuity in the core features of key object representations (including the self-representation; see Blatt, 1991; Bornstein, 1996). In this context, personality change was presumed to occur in part because internalized representations of self and other people changed as a result of ongoing inter- and intra-personal experiences (Schafer, 1999).

This alternative framework influenced psychoanalytic theories of normal personality development and led to a plethora of studies examining the intrapsychic processes involved in therapeutic resistance, transference, and cure (Blatt & Ford, 1994; Luborsky & Crits-Christoph, 1990). It also called theorists' attention to the critical importance of present-day experiences in moderating long-term psychodynamic processes. One important consequence of newfound concepts of personality stability and change was a continuing shift from past to present in the study of psychodynamics (Spence, 1982).

Insight, Awareness, and Coping

As noted earlier, a key tenet of all psychodynamic models is that unconscious processes are primary determinants of thought, emotion, motivation, and behavior. To the degree that people have only limited introspective access to these under-lying causes, they have only limited control over these processes as well. In part as a consequence of their emphasis on unconscious processes, psychodynamic theorists are unanimous in positing that a certain degree of self-deception is characteristic of both normal and abnormal functioning: Not knowing why we are driven to behave in a certain way, but needing to explain our behavior to ourselves, we generate explanations that may or may not have anything to do with the real causes of behavior (e.g., see Bornstein, 1999b). Moreover, when feelings, thoughts, and motivations produce anxiety (including guilt), we invoke coping strategies called *ego defenses* to minimize these negative reactions and to hide them from ourselves (Cramer, 2000).

The once-radical notion of defensive self-deception is now widely accepted among psychoanalytic and nonpsychoanalytic psychologists alike. Research in social cognition (attribution theory in particular) confirms that systematic, predictable distortions in our perceptions of self and others are a normal part of everyday life (Kihlstrom, 1987; Robins & John, 1997). Although the language of attribution theory differs substantially from that of psychoanalysis, scrutiny reveals a remarkable degree of convergence between these two frameworks. Moreover, researchers have begun to bridge the gap between these ostensibly divergent theoretical perspectives, uncovering a surprising degree of overlap in the process.

One area in which psychodynamic models of defensive self-deception diverge from social psychological models of this phenomenon is in the explanations of why these distortions occur. Although both models agree that these distortions stem largely (but not entirely) from self-protective processes, only psychoanalytic theories explicitly link these distortions to an identifiable set of unconsciously determined strategies termed ego defenses. Social cognitive researchers have tended to favor explanatory models that emphasize limitations in the human information-processing apparatus and mental shortcuts that arise from the need to process multiple sources of information simultaneously as key factors in our cognitive biases and distortions of self and others (Robins & John, 1997). Recent work in terror management theory represents a potential bridge between psychodynamic and social-cognitive work in this area, insofar as the terror management theory model specifies how distortions in inter- and intrapersonal perception simultaneously reflect defensive processes and information-processing limitations (Pyszczynski, Greenberg, & Solomon, 1999).

Ironically, the concept of the ego defense—now central to psychodynamic models of personality—did not receive much attention during the theory's formative years. In fact, Janet paid greater attention to the defense concept than Freud did

(Perry & Laurence, 1984), and in certain respects Janet's position regarding this issue has turned out to be more accurate than Freud's has (see Bowers & Meichenbaum, 1984). Evidence suggests that a conceptualization of defensive activity as narrowing of consciousness may be more valid and heuristic than is the classic psychoanalytic conceptualization of defense in terms of exclusion (or *barring*) of material from consciousness (Cramer, 2000; cf. Erdelyi, 1985).

Although Freud discussed certain ego defenses (e.g., repression, projection, sublimation) in his theoretical and clinical writings, it was not until Anna Freud's (1936) publication of *The Ego and the Mechanisms of Defense* that any effort was made to create a systematic, comprehensive listing of these defensive strategies. Most of the ego defenses discussed by A. Freud continue to be discussed today, although some have fallen out of favor, and new ones have been added as empirical research on defenses began to appear following A. Freud's (1936) seminal work.

In the decades following A. Freud's (1936) publication, several alternative methods for conceptualizing ego defenses were offered. The most influential of these are summarized in Table 5.4. As Table 5.4 shows, differences among the individual defense, defense style, and defense cluster models have less to do with the way that specific defensive processes are conceptualized and more to do with how these processes are organized and relate to one another. Each approach to conceptualizing and organizing ego defenses has its own associated measurement strategy (technique), its own research base, and its own adherents within the discipline.

The combined influences of unconscious processes and ego defenses raise the unavoidable question of whether within the

TABLE 5.4 **Perspectives on Ego Defenses**

Perspective	Key Contributors	Key Terms
Individual defenses	S. Freud, A. Freud	Specific defenses: Repression Projection Denial Sublimation Displacement
Defense style approach	Ihilevich & Gleser	Defense styles: Reversal Projection Principalization Turning against object Turning against self
Defense levels-clusters	Vaillant	Defense levels-clusters: Adaptive-mature Maladaptive-immature Image distorting Self-sacrificing

Note. Detailed discussions of these three perspectives are provided by Cramer (2000), Ihilevich & Gleser (1986, 1991), and Vaillant (1986).

psychodynamic framework humans are seen as inherently irrational creatures. Like most questions in psychoanalysis, this one has more than one answer. On the one hand, humans are indeed irrational—driven by forces they do not understand, their thoughts and feelings are distorted in ways they cannot control. On the other hand, humans are as rational as can be expected given the constraints of their information-processing skills, their need to cope with and manage anxiety, and the adaptations necessary to survive in an unpredictable, threatening world. Within the psychodynamic framework, all humans are irrational, but most are irrational in a rational way.

Normal and Pathological Functioning

As any psychologist knows, all humans may be irrational, but some are more irrational than others. Like most personality theorists, psychoanalysts see psychopathology as reflected in a greater-than-expected degree of self-destructive, self-defeating (i.e., irrational) behavior (Millon, 1996). In most psychodynamic frameworks, psychopathology is also linked with increased self-deception, decreased insight into the underlying causes of one's behavior, and concomitant limitations in one's ability to modify dysfunctional interaction patterns and alter self-defeating responses (Eagle, 1984).

Psychodynamic models conceptualize psychopathology in terms of three general processes: (a) low ego strength, (b) maladaptive ego defenses, and (c) dysfunctional introjects. Low ego strength contributes to psychopathology because the ego cannot execute reality testing functions adequately; intra- and interpersonal distortions increase. Maladaptive defenses prevent the individual from managing stress and anxiety adequately leading to higher levels of self-deception, increased perceptual bias, and decreased insight. Dysfunctional introjects (including a distorted or deficient self-representation) similarly lead to inaccurate perceptions of self and others, but they also foster dysfunctional interaction patterns and propagate problematic interpersonal relationships.

A key premise of the psychoanalytic model of psychopathology is that psychological disorders can be divided into three broad levels of severity (Kernberg, 1970, 1975). The classic conceptualization of this three-level framework invokes the well-known terms *neurosis, character disorder,* and *psychosis.* In most instances, neuroses are comparatively mild disorders which affect only a few areas of functioning (e.g., phobias). Character disorders are more pervasive, long-standing disorders associated with problematic social relationships, distorted self-perception, and difficulties with impulse control (e.g., borderline personality disorder). Psychoses are characterized by severely impaired reality testing

TABLE 5.5   Levels of Psychopathology in Psychodynamic Theory

Level	Ego Strength	Ego Defenses	Introjects
Neurosis	High	Adaptive-mature (displacement, sublimation)	Articulated-differentiated and benign
Character disorder	Variable	Maladaptive-immature (denial, projection)	Quasi-articulated, malevolent, or both
Psychosis	Low	Maladaptive-immature or nonexistent	Unarticulated-undifferentiated and malevolent

and low levels of functioning in many areas of life (e.g., schizophrenia).

Although this tripartite model is both theoretically heuristic and clinically useful, it is important not to overgeneralize regarding differences among different levels of functioning. There are great variations in both severity and chronicity within a given level (e.g., certain neuroses may be more debilitating than an ostensibly more severe personality disorder). In addition, there is substantial comorbidity—both within and between levels—so that a disordered individual is likely to show multiple forms of psychopathology (Bornstein, 1998; Costello, 1995).

As Table 5.5 shows, all three dimensions of intrapsychic dysfunction—low ego strength, maladaptive defenses, and dysfunctional introjects—can be mapped onto the tripartite psychopathology model. In this respect, the model represents an integrative framework that links different psychodynamic processes and connects the psychoanalytic model with contemporary diagnostic research. Although the term *neurosis* is rarely used today in mainstream psychopathology research, perusal of contemporary diagnostic frameworks (including the *DSM-IV;* APA, 1994) confirms that the tripartite model has had a profound influence on the way practitioners conceptualize and organize psychological disorders (see also Masling & Bornstein, 1994, and Millon, 1996, for discussions of this issue).

PSYCHOANALYSIS AND CONTEMPORARY PSYCHOLOGY: RETROSPECT AND PROSPECT

Psychodynamic models of personality occupy a unique place in contemporary psychology. On the one hand, they continue to be roundly criticized—perceived by those within and outside the discipline as untested and untestable and denigrated by skeptics as a quasi-phrenological pseudoscience that has hindered the progress of both scientific and clinical psychology. On the other hand, Freud's theory continues to fascinate many, occupying a central place in undergraduate and graduate psychology texts and influencing in myriad ways our

(1950, 1954), who developed a detailed theoretical framework linking specific psychodynamic processes with predictable physiological sequelae and illness states. When Sifneos (1972) articulated his empirically grounded, psychoanalytically informed model of alexithymia (i.e., an inability to verbalize emotions), the stage was set for the development of a truly psychoanalytic health psychology. The key hypotheses of Sifneos's approach—that unverbalized emotions can have myriad destructive effects on the body's organ systems—helped lay the groundwork for several ongoing health psychology research programs that are to varying degrees rooted in psychodynamic concepts. Research on health and hardiness (Kobasa, 1979), stress and coping (Pennebaker & O'Heeron, 1984), emotional disclosure and recovery from illness (Spiegel, Bloom, Kraemer, & Gottheil, 1989), and the "Type C" (cancer-prone) personality (Temoshok, 1987) are all based in part in psychodynamic models of health and illness.

The Opportunities and Challenges of Neuroscience

Some of the first contemporary efforts to integrate psychoanalytic principles with findings from neuroscience involved sleep and dreams (Hobson, 1988; Winson, 1985). Although the language of Freudian dream theory is far removed from that of most neuropsychological models, work in this area has revealed a number of heretofore unrecognized convergences between the psychodynamics and neurology of dreaming. In fact, contemporary integrative models of dream formation now incorporate principles from both domains, setting the stage for extension of this integrative effort to other aspects of mental life.

Neuroimaging techniques such as the computerized axial tomography (CAT) scan, the positron-emission tomography (PET) scan, and magnetic resonance imaging (MRI) have begun to play a leading role in this ongoing psychoanalysis-neuroscience integration. Just as neuroimaging techniques have allowed memory researchers to uncover the neural underpinnings of previously unseen encoding and retrieval processes, functional magnetic resonance imaging (fMRI) have enabled dream researchers to record on-line visual representations of cortical activity associated with different sleep stages and experiences.

Two psychodynamically relevant issues now being studied via fMRI (functional MRI) and other neuroimaging techniques are unconscious processes (e.g., implicit perception and learning) and psychological defenses (Schiff, 1999; Walla, Endl, Lindinger, & Lang, 1999). In general, evidence suggests that implicit processes are centered in mid- and hindbrain regions to a greater degree than are explicit processes—a finding that dovetails with Freud's own hypotheses as well as with recent evolutionary interpretations of psychodynamic principles (Slavin & Kriegman, 1992). Neuroimaging studies of defensive mental operations are still in their infancy, but preliminary findings suggests that the process of biasing and distorting previously-encoded information involves predictable patterns of cortical (and possibly subcortical) activation.

CONCLUSION: THE PSYCHOLOGY OF PSYCHODYNAMICS AND THE PSYCHODYNAMICS OF PSYCHOLOGY

Despite their limitations, psychodynamic models of personality have survived for more than a century, reinventing themselves periodically in response to new empirical findings, theoretical shifts in other areas of psychology, and changing social and economic forces. Stereotypes notwithstanding, psychodynamic models have evolved considerably during the twentieth century and will continue to evolve during the first decades of the twenty-first century as well.

For better or worse, psychoanalytic theory may be the closest thing to an overarching field theory in all of psychology. It deals with a broad range of issues—normal and pathological functioning, motivation and emotion, childhood and adulthood, individual and culture—and although certain features of the model have not held up well to empirical testing, the model does have tremendous heuristic value and great potential for integrating ideas and findings in disparate areas of social and neurological science.

More than a century ago, Freud (1895b) speculated that scientists would be resistant to psychoanalytic ideas because of the uncomfortable implications of these ideas for their own functioning. Whether or not he was correct in this regard, it is true that psychodynamic models of personality provide a useful framework for examining ourselves and our beliefs. Clinical psychologists have long used psychoanalytic principles to evaluate and refine their psychotherapeutic efforts. Scientists have not been as open to this sort of self-scrutiny. There is, however, a burgeoning literature on the biases and hidden motivations of the scientist (Bornstein, 1999a; Mahoney, 1985), and psychodynamic models of personality may well prove to contribute a great deal to this literature.

REFERENCES

Adler, A. (1921). *Understanding human nature.* New York: Fawcett.

Adler, A. (1923). *The practice and theory of individual psychology.* London: Routledge & Kegan Paul.

Ainsworth, M. D. S. (1969). Object relations, dependency, and attachment: A theoretical review of the infant-mother relationship. *Child Development, 40,* 969–1025.

Ainsworth, M. D. S. (1989). Attachments beyond infancy. *American Psychologist, 44,* 709–716.

Alexander, F. (1950). *Psychosomatic medicine.* New York: W. W. Norton.

Alexander, F. (1954). *The scope of psychoanalysis.* New York: Basic Books.

American Psychiatric Association (1994). *Diagnostic and statistical manual of mental disorders* (4th ed.). Washington, DC: Author.

Baddeley, A. (1990). *Human memory: Theory and practice.* Needham Heights, MA: Allyn and Bacon.

Bargh, J. A., & Chartrand, T. L. (1999). The unbearable automaticity of being. *American Psychologist, 54,* 462–479.

Barron, J. W., Eagle, M. N., & Wolitzky, D. L. (Eds.). (1992). *Interface of psychoanalysis and psychology.* Washington, DC: American Psychological Association.

Blatt, S. J. (1974). Levels of object representation in anaclitic and introjective depression. *Psychoanalytic Study of the Child, 29,* 107–157.

Blatt, S. J. (1991). A cognitive morphology of psychopathology. *Journal of Nervous and Mental Disease, 179,* 449–458.

Blatt, S. J., & Ford, R. Q. (1994). *Therapeutic change.* New York: Plenum Press.

Blatt, S. J., & Homann, E. (1992). Parent-child interaction in the etiology of dependent and self-critical depression. *Clinical Psychology Review, 12,* 47–91.

Blatt, S. J., & Zuroff, D. C. (1992). Interpersonal relatedness and self-definition: Two prototypes for depression. *Clinical Psychology Review, 12,* 527–562.

Bornstein, R. F. (1993). Implicit perception, implicit memory, and the recovery of unconscious material in psychotherapy. *Journal of Nervous and Mental Disease, 181,* 337–344.

Bornstein, R. F. (1996). Beyond orality: Toward an object relations/interactionist reconceptualization of the etiology and dynamics of dependency. *Psychoanalytic Psychology, 13,* 177–203.

Bornstein, R. F. (1998). Reconceptualizing personality disorder diagnosis in the *DSM-V:* The discriminant validity challenge. *Clinical Psychology: Science and Practice, 5,* 333–343.

Bornstein, R. F. (1999a). Objectivity and subjectivity in psychological science: Embracing and transcending psychology's positivist tradition. *Journal of Mind and Behavior, 20,* 1–16.

Bornstein, R. F. (1999b). Source amnesia, misattribution, and the power of unconscious perceptions and memories. *Psychoanalytic Psychology, 16,* 155–178.

Bornstein, R. F. (2001). The impending death of psychoanalysis. *Psychoanalytic Psychology, 18,* 3–20.

Bornstein, R. F., & Masling, J. M. (Eds.). (1998). *Empirical perspectives on the psychoanalytic unconscious.* Washington, DC: American Psychological Association.

Bornstein, R. F., & Pittman, T. S. (Eds.). (1992). *Perception without awareness: Cognitive, clinical, and social perspectives.* New York: Guilford Press.

Bowers, K. S. (1984). On being unconsciously informed and influenced. In K. S. Bowers & D. Meichenbaum (Eds.), *The unconscious reconsidered* (pp. 227–272). New York: Wiley.

Bowers, K. S., & Meichenbaum, D. (1984). *The unconscious reconsidered.* New York: Basic Books.

Bowlby, J. (1969). *Attachment.* New York: Basic Books.

Bowlby, J. (1973). *Separation: Anxiety and anger.* New York: Basic Books.

Brenner, C. (1973). *An elementary textbook of psychoanalysis.* New York: Anchor Books.

Breuer, J., & Freud, S. (1955). Studies on hysteria. In J. Strachey (Ed. & Trans.), *The standard edition of the complete psychological works of Sigmund Freud* (Vol. 2, pp. 1–305). London: Hogarth. (Original work published 1893)

Bucci, W. (1997). *Psychoanalysis and cognitive science: A multiple code theory.* New York: Guilford Press.

Buss, D. M. (1991). Evolutionary personality psychology. *Annual Review of Psychology, 42,* 459–491.

Costello, C. G. (1995). *Personality characteristics of the personality disordered.* New York: Wiley.

Cramer, P. (2000). Defense mechanisms in psychology today: Further processes for adaptation. *American Psychologist, 55,* 637–646.

Crews, F. C. (Ed.). (1998). *Unathorized Freud: Doubters confront a legend.* New York: Viking Press.

Danzinger, K. (1997). *Naming the mind.* Beverly Hills, CA: Sage.

Deutsch, F. (1922). Psychoanlayse und Organkrankheiten. *International Journal of Psychoanalysis, 8,* 290–306.

Deutsch, F. (1924). Zur Bildung des Konversions Symptoms. *International Journal of Psychoanalysis, 10,* 380–392.

Dollard, J., & Miller, N. E. (1950). *Personality and psychotherapy.* New York: McGraw-Hill.

Duberstein, P. R., & Masling, J. M. (Eds.). (2000). *Psychodynamic perspectives on sickness and health.* Washington, DC: American Psychological Association.

Eagle, M. N. (1984). *Recent developments in psychoanalysis.* New York: McGraw-Hill.

Eagle, M. N. (1996). Attachment research and psychoanalytic theory. In J. M. Masling & R. F. Bornstein (Eds.), *Psychoanalytic perspectives on developmental psychology* (pp. 105–149). Washington, DC: American Psychological Association.

Eagle, M. N. (2000). A critical evaluation of current conceptions of transference and countertransference. *Psychoanalytic Psychology, 17,* 24–37.

Ellenberger, H. (1970). *The discovery of the unconscious.* New York: Basic Books.

Emde, R. N. (1983). The prerepresentational self and its affective core. *Psychoanalytic Study of the Child, 38,* 165–192.

Schafer, R. (1999). Recentering psychoanalysis. *Psychoanalytic Psychology, 16,* 339–354.

Schiff, N. D. (1999). Neurobiology, suffering, and unconscious brain states. *Journal of Pain Management, 17,* 303–304.

Schneider, K. J., & May, R. (1995). *The psychology of existence.* New York: McGraw-Hill.

Shapiro, T., & Emde, R. N. (Eds.). (1995). *Research in psychoanalysis: Process, development, outcome.* Madison, CT: International Universities Press.

Sifneos, P. (1972). *Short-term psychotherapy and emotional crisis.* Cambridge, MA: Harvard University Press.

Slavin, M. O., & Kriegman, D. (Eds.). (1992). *The adaptive design of the human psyche: Psychoanalysis, evolutionary theory, and the therapeutic process.* New York: Guilford Press.

Slipp, S. (1984). *Object relations: A dynamic bridge between individual and family treatment.* New York: Jason Aronson.

Spence, D. P. (1982). *Narrative truth and historical truth: Meaning and interpretation in psychoanalysis.* New York: W. W. Norton.

Spiegel, D., Bloom, J. R., Kraemer, H. C., & Gottheil, E. (1989). Effect of psychosocial treatment on survival of patients with metastatic breast cancer. *The Lancet, 114,* 888–891.

Spitz, R. A. (1945). Hospitalism. *Psychoanalytic Study of the Child, 1,* 53–74.

Spitz, R. A. (1946). Hospitalism: A follow-up report on investigation described in Volume 1, 1945. *Psychoanalytic Study of the Child, 2,* 113–117.

Stadler, M. A., & Frensch, P. A. (Eds.). (1998). *Handbook of implicit learning.* Beverly Hills, CA: Sage.

Stein, D. J. (Ed.). (1997). *Cognitive science and the unconscious.* Washington, DC: American Psychiatric Press.

Stern, D. (1985). *The interpersonal world of the infant.* New York: Basic Books.

Sullivan, H. S. (1947). *Conceptions of modern psychiatry.* New York: W. W. Norton.

Sullivan, H. S. (1953). *The interpersonal theory of psychiatry.* New York: W. W. Norton.

Sullivan, H. S. (1956). *Clinical studies in psychiatry.* New York: W. W. Norton.

Temoshok, L. (1987). Personality, coping style, emotion, and cancer: Toward an integrative model. *Cancer Surveys, 6,* 545–567.

Torrey, E. F. (1992). *Freudian fraud: The malignant effect of Freud's theory on American thought and culture.* New York: HarperCollins.

Vaillant, G. E. (Ed.) (1986). *Empirical studies of ego mechanisms of defense.* Washington, DC: American Psychiatric Press.

Wachtel, P. (1977). *Psychoanalysis and behavior therapy.* New York: Basic Books.

Walla, P., Emdl, W., Lindinger, G., & Lang, W. (1999). Implicit memory within a word recognition task: An event-related potential study in human subjects. *Neuroscience Letters, 16,* 129–132.

Westen, D. (1998). Unconscious thought, feeling, and motivation: The end of a century-long debate. In R. F. Bornstein & J. M. Masling (Eds.), *Empirical perspectives on the psychoanalytic unconscious* (pp. 1–43). Washington, DC: American Psychological Association.

Winnicott, D. W. (1971). *Playing and reality.* Middlesex, UK: Penguin.

Winson, J. (1985). *Brain and psyche: The biology of the unconscious.* New York: Doubleday.

CHAPTER 6

A Psychological Behaviorism Theory of Personality

ARTHUR W. STAATS

This chapter has several aims. One is that of considering the role of behaviorism and behavioral approaches in the fields of personality theory and measurement. A second and central aim is that of describing a particular and different behavioral approach to the fields of personality theory and personality measurement. A third concern is that of presenting some of the philosophy- and methodology-of-science characteristics of this behavioral approach relevant to the field of personality theory. A fourth aim is to characterize the field of personality theory from the perspective of this philosophy and methodology of science. And a fifth aim is to project some developments for the future that derive from this theory perspective. Addressing these aims constitutes a pretty full agenda that will require economical treatment.

BEHAVIORAL APPROACHES AND PERSONALITY

Behavioral approaches to personality might seem of central importance to personology because behaviorism deals with learning and it is pretty generally acknowledged that learning affects personality. Moreover, behaviorist theories were once the models of what theory could be in psychology. But certain features militate against behaviorism's significance for the field of personality. Those features spring from the traditional behaviorist mission.

Traditional Behaviorism and Personality

One feature is behaviorism's search for *general* laws. That is ingrained in the approach, as we can see from its strategy of discovering learning-behavior principles with rats, pigeons, dogs, and cats—for the major behaviorists in the first and second generation were animal psychologists who assumed that those learning-behavior principles would constitute a complete theory for dealing with any and all types of human behavior. John Watson, in behaviorism's first generation, showed this, as B. F. Skinner did later. Clark Hull (1943) was quite succinct in stating unequivocally about his theory that "all behavior, individual and social, moral and immoral, normal and psychopathic, is generated from the same primary laws" (p. v). Even Edward Tolman's goal, which he later

135

admitted was unreachable, was to constitute through animal study a general theory of human behavior. The field of personality, in contrast, is concerned with individual differences, with humans, and this represents a schism of interests.

A second, even more important, feature of behaviorism arises in the fact that personality as conceived in personology lies within the individual, where it cannot be observed. That has always raised problems for an approach that placed scientific methodology at its center and modeled itself after logical positivism and operationism. Watson had decried as mentalistic the inference of concepts of internal, unobservable causal processes. For him personality could only be considered as the sum total of behavior, that is, as an observable effect, not as a cause. Skinner's operationism followed suit. This, of course, produced another, even wider, schism with personology because personality is generally considered an internal process that *determines* external behavior. That is the raison d'être for the study of personality.

Tolman, who along with Hull and Skinner was one of the most prominent second-generation behaviorists, sought to resolve the schism in his general theory. As a behaviorist he was concerned with how conditioning experiences, the independent variable, acted on the organism's responding, the dependent variable. But he posited that there was something in between: the intervening variable, which also helped determine the organism's behavior. Cognitions were intervening variables. Intelligence could be an intervening variable. This methodology legitimated a concept like personality.

However, the methodology was anathema to Skinner. Later, Hull and Kenneth Spence (1944) took the in-between position that intervening variables should be considered just logical devices, not to be interpreted as standing for any real psychological events within the individual. These differences were played out in literature disputes for some time. That was not much of a platform for constructing psychology theory such as personology. The closest was Tolman's consideration of personality as an intervening variable. But he never developed this concept, never stipulated what personality is, never derived a program of study from the theory, and never employed it to understand any kind of human behavior. Julian Rotter (1954) picked up Tolman's general approach, however, and elaborated an axiomatic theory that also drew from Hull's approach to theory construction. As was true for Hull, the axiomatic construction *style* of the theory takes precedence over the goal of producing a theory that is useful in confronting the empirical events to which the theory is addressed.

To exemplify this characteristic of theory, Rotter's social learning has no program to analyze the psychometric instruments that stipulate aspects of personality, such as intelligence, depression, interests, values, moods, anxiety, stress, schizophrenia, or sociopathy. His social learning theory, moreover, does not provide a theory of what personality tests are and do. Nor does the theory call for the study of the learning and functions of normal behaviors such as language, reading, problem-solving ability, or sensorimotor skills. The same is true with respect to addressing the phenomena of abnormal behavior. For example, Rotter (1954) described the Minnesota Multiphasic Personality Inventory (MMPI) but in a very conventional way. There are no analyses of the different personality traits measured on the test in terms of their behavioral composition or of the independent variables (e.g., learning history) that result in individual differences in these and other traits. Nor are there analyses of how individual differences in traits affect other people's responses to the individuals or of how individual differences in the trait in turn act on the individual's behavior. For example, a person with a trait of paranoia is more suspicious than others are. What in behavioral terms does being suspicious consist of, how is that trait learned, and how does it have its effects on the person's behavior and the behavior of others? The approach taken here is that a behavioral theory of personality must analyze the phenomena of the field of personality in this manner. Rotter's social learning theory does not do these things, nor do the other social learning theories.

Rather, his theory inspired academic studies to test his formal concepts such as expectancy, need potential, need value, freedom of movement, and the psychological situation. This applied even to the personality-trait concept he introduced, the *locus of control*—whether people believe that they themselves, others, or chance determines the outcome of the situations in which the individuals find themselves. Although it has been said that this trait is affected in childhood by parental reward for desired behaviors, studies to show that differential training of the child produces different locus-of-control characteristics remain to be undertaken. Tyler, Dhawan, and Sinha (1989) have shown that there is a class difference in locus of control (measured by self-report inventory). But this does not represent a program for studying learning effects even on that trait, let alone on the various aspects of personality.

The social learning theories of Albert Bandura and Walter Mischel are not considered here. However, each still carries the theory-oriented approach of second-generation behaviorism in contrast to the phenomena-oriented theory construction of the present approach. For example, there are many laboratory studies of social learning theory that aim to show that children learn through imitation. But there are not programs to study individual differences in imitation, the cause of such differences, and how those differences affect individual differences in important behaviors (e.g., the ability to copy letters, learn new words, or accomplish other actual learning tasks of the child). Bandura's approach actually began in a loose social learning framework. Then it moved toward a behavioral approach several years later, drawing on the approach to be described here as well as the approach of Skinner, and later it moved toward including a more cognitive terminology. Mischel (1968) first took a Watsonian-Skinnerian approach to personality and assessment, as did other radical behaviorists. He later abandoned that position (Mischel, 1973) but, like the other social learning theorists, offered no program for study stipulating what personality is, how it is learned, how it functions, and how personality study relates to psychological measurement.

When all is said and done, then, standard behaviorism has not contributed a general and systematic program for the study of personality or personality measurement. It has features that interfere with doing so. Until they are overcome in a fundamental way (which Tolmanian social learning approaches did not provide), those features represent an impassable barrier.

Behavior Therapy and Personality

The major behaviorists such as Hull, Skinner, and Tolman were animal learning researchers. None of them analyzed the learning of functional human behaviors or traits of behavior. Skinner's empirical approach to human behavior centered on the use of his technology, that is, his operant conditioning apparatus. His approach was to use this "experimental analysis of behavior" methodology in studying a simple, repetitive response of a subject that was automatically reinforced (and recorded). That program was implemented by his students in studies reinforcing psychotic patients, individuals with mental retardation, and children with autism with edibles and such for pulling a knob. Lovaas (1977), in the best developed program among this group, did not begin to train his autistic children in language skills until after the psychological behaviorism (PB) program to be described had provided the foundation. Although Skinner is widely thought to have worked with children's behavior, that is not the case. He constructed a crib for infants that was air conditioned and easy to clean, but the crib had no learning or behavioral implications or suggestions. He also worked with programmed learning, but that was a delimited technology and did not involve behavior analyses of the intellectual repertoires taught, and the topic played out after a few years. Skinner's experimental analysis of behavior did not indicate how to research functional human behaviors or problems of behavior or how they are learned.

Behavior Therapy

The original impetus for the development of behavior therapy (which in the present usage includes behavior modification, behavior analysis, cognitive behavior therapy, and behavior

assessment) does not derive from Hull, Skinner, Tolman, or Rotter, although they and Dollard and Miller (1950) helped stimulate a general interest in the possibility of applications. One of the original sources of behavior therapy came from Great Britain, where a number of studies were conducted of simple behavior problems treated by using conditioning principles, either classical conditioning or reinforcement. The learning framework was not taken from an American behaviorist's theory but from European developments of conditioning principles. As an example, Raymond (see Eysenck, 1960) treated a man with a fetish for baby carriages by classical conditioning. The patient's many photographs of baby carriages were presented singly as conditioned stimuli paired with an aversive unconditioned stimulus. Under this extended conditioning the man came to avoid the pictures and baby carriages. The various British studies using conditioning were collected in a book edited by Hans Eysenck (1960). Another of the foundations of behavior therapy came from the work of Joseph Wolpe. He employed Hull's theory nominally and loosely in several endeavors, including his systematic desensitization procedure for treating anxiety problems. It was his procedure and his assessment of it that were important.

A third foundation of behavior therapy came from my PB approach that is described here. As will be indicated, it began with a very broad agenda, that of analyzing human behavior generally employing its learning approach, including behaviors in the natural situation. Its goal included making analyses of and treating problems of specific human behavior problems of interest to the applied areas of psychology. Following several informal applications, my first published analysis of a behavior in the naturalistic situation concerned a journal report of a hospitalized schizophrenic patient who said the opposite of what was called for. In contrast to the psychodynamic interpretation of the authors, the PB analysis was that the abnormal behavior was learned through inadvertent reinforcement given by the treating doctors. This analysis suggested the treatment—that is, not to reinforce the abnormal behavior, the opposite speech, on the one hand, and to reinforce normal speech, on the other (Staats, 1957). This analysis presented what became the orientation and principles of the American behavior modification field: (a) deal with actual behavior problems, (b) analyze them in terms of reinforcement principles, (c) take account of the reinforcement that has created the problem behavior, and (d) extinguish abnormal or undesirable behavior through nonreinforcement while creating normal behavior by reinforcement.

Two years later, my long-time friend and colleague Jack Michael and his student Teodoro Ayllon (see Ayllon & Michael, 1959), used this analysis of psychotic behavior and these principles of behavior modification to treat behavioral symptoms in individual psychotic patients in a hospital. Their study provided strong verification of the PB behavior modification approach, and its publication in a Skinnerian journal had an impact great enough to be called the "seeds of the behavioral revolution" by radical behaviorists (Malott, Whaley, & Malott, 1997, p. 175). Ayllon and Michael's paper was written as though this approach derived from Skinnerian behaviorism and this error was repeated in many works that came later. For example, Fordyce (see 1990) followed Michael's suggestion both in using the PB principles and in considering his pain theory to be Skinnerian.

The study of child behavior modification began similarly. Following my development of the behavior modification principles with simple problems, I decided that a necessary step was to extend behavior analysis to more complex behavior that required long-term treatment. At UCLA (where I took my doctoral degree in general experimental and completed clinical psychology requirements) I had worked with dyslexic children. Believing that reading is crucially important to human adjustment in our society, I selected this as a focal topic of study—both remedial training as well as the original learning of reading. My first study—done with Judson Finley, Karl Minke, Richard Schutz, and Carolyn Staats—was exploratory and was used in a research grant application I made to the U.S. Office of Education. The study was based on my view that the central problem in dyslexia is motivational. Children fail in learning because their attention and participation are not maintained in the long, effortful, and nonreinforcing (for many children) learning task that involves thousands and thousands of learning trials. In my approach the child was reinforced for attending and participating, and the training materials I constructed ensured that the child would learn everything needed for good performance. Because reading training is so extended and involves so many learning trials, it is necessary to have a reinforcing system for the long haul, unlike the experimental analysis of behavior studies with children employing simple responses and M&Ms. I thus introduced the token reinforcer system consisting of poker chips backed up by items the children selected to work for (such as toys, sporting equipment, and clothing). When this token reinforcer system was adopted for work with adults, it was called the token economy (see Ayllon & Azrin, 1968) and, again, considered part of Skinner's radical behaviorism.

With the training materials and the token reinforcement, the adolescents who had been poor students became attentive, worked well, and learned well. Thus was the token methodology born, a methodology that was to be generally applied. In 1962 and 1964 studies we showed the same effect with preschool children first learning to read. Under reinforcement their attention and participation and their learning of reading was very good, much better than that displayed by the usual four-year-old. But without the extrinsic reinforcement, their learning behavior deteriorated, and learning stopped. In reporting this and the treatment of dyslexia (Staats, 1963; Staats & Butterfield, 1965; Staats, Finley, Minke, & Wolf, 1964; Staats & Staats, 1962), I projected a program for using these child behavior modification methods in studying a wide variety of children's (and adults') problems. The later development of the field of behavior modification showed that this program functioned as a blueprint for the field that later developed. (The Sylvan Learning Centers also use methods similar to those of PB's reading treatments, with similar results.)

Let me add that I took the same approach in raising my own children, selecting important areas to analyze for the application of learning-behavior principles to improve and advance their development as well as to study the complex learning involved. For example, in 1960 I began working with language development (productive and receptive) when my daughter was only several months old, with number concepts at the age of a year and a half, with reading at 2 years of age. I have audiotapes of this training with my daughter, which began in 1962 and extended for more than 5 years, and videotapes with my son and other children made in 1966. Other aspects of child development dealt with as learned behaviors include toilet training, counting, number operations, writing, walking, swimming, and throwing and catching a ball (see Staats, 1996). With some systematic training the children did such things as walk and talk at 9 months old; read letters, words, sentences, and short stories at 2.5 years of age; and count unarranged objects at 2 years (a performance Piaget suggested was standard at the age of 6 years). The principles were also applied to the question of punishment, and I devised time-out as a mild but effective punishment, first used in the literature by one of my students, Montrose Wolf (Wolf, Risely, & Mees, 1964).

Traditional behaviorism was our background. However, the research developed in Great Britain and by Wolpe and by me and a few others constituted the foundation for the field of behavior therapy. And this field now contains a huge number of studies demonstrating that conditioning principles apply to a variety of human behavior problems, in children and adults, with simple and complex behavior. There can be no question in the face of our behavior therapy evidence that learning is a centrally important determinant of human behavior.

The State of Personality Theory and Measurement in the Field of Behavior Therapy

Behaviorism began as a revolution against traditional psychology. The traditional behaviorist aim in analyzing psychology's studied phenomena was to show behaviorism's superiority and that psychology's approach should be abandoned. In radical behaviorism no recognition is given still that work in traditional psychology has any value or that it can be useful in a unification with behaviorism. This characteristic is illustrated by the Association of Behavior Analysis's movement in the 1980s to separate the field from the rest of psychology. It took a PB publication to turn this tide, but the isolationism continues to operate informally. Radical behaviorism students are not trained in psychology, or even in the general field of behaviorism itself. While many things from the "outside" have been adopted by radical behaviorism, some quite inconsistent with Skinner's views, they are accepted only when presented as indigenous developments. Radical behaviorism students are taught that all of their fundamental knowledge arose within the radical behaviorism program, that the program is fully self-sufficient.

Psychological behaviorism, in conflict with radical behaviorism, takes the different view: that traditional psychology has systematically worked in many areas of human behavior and produced valuable findings that should not be dismissed sight unseen on the basis of simplistic behaviorist methodological positions from the past. Psychology's knowledge may not be complete. It may contain elements that need to be eliminated. And it may need, but not include, the learning-behavior perspective and substance. But the PB view has been that behaviorism has the task of using traditional psychology knowledge, improving it, and behaviorizing it. In that process, behaviorism becomes *psychologized* itself, hence the name of the present approach. PB has aimed to discard the idiosyncratic, delimiting positions of the radical behaviorism tradition and to introduce a new, unified tradition with the means to effect the new developments needed to create unification.

An example can be given here of the delimiting effect of radical behaviorism with respect to psychological measurement. Skinner insisted that the study of human behavior was to rest on his experimental analysis of behavior (operant conditioning) methodology. Among other things he rejected self-report data (1969, pp. 77–78). Following this lead, a general position in favor of direct observation of specific behavior, not signs of behavior, was proposed by Mischel, as well as Kanfer, and Phillips, and this became a feature of the field of behavioral assessment. The view became that psychological tests should be abandoned in favor of Skinner's experimental analysis of behavior methodology, an orientation that could not yield a program for unification of the work of the fields of personality and psychological measurement with behavior therapy, behavior analysis, and behavioral assessment.

It may be added that PB, by contributing foundations to behavior therapy, had the anomalous effect of creating enthusiasm for a radical behaviorism that PB in good part rejects.

For example, PB introduced the first general behavioral theory of abnormal behavior and a program for treatment applications (see Staats, 1963, chaps. 10 & 11), as well as a foundation for the field of behavioral assessment:

> Perhaps [this] rationale for learning [behavioral] psychotherapy will also have to include some method for the assessment of behavior. In order to discover the behavioral deficiencies, the required changes in the reinforcing system [the individual's emotional-motivational characteristics], the circumstances in which stimulus control is absent, and so on, evaluational techniques in these respects may have to be devised. Certainly, no two individuals will be alike in these various characteristics, and it may be necessary to determine such facts for the individual prior to beginning the learning program of treatment.
>
> Such assessment might take a form similar to some of the psychological tests already in use. . . . [H]owever, . . . a general learning rationale for behavior disorders and treatment will suggest techniques of assessment. (Staats, 1963, pp. 508–509)

At that time there was no other broad abnormal psychology-behavioral treatment theory in the British behavior therapy school, in Wolpe's approach, or in radical behaviorism. But PB's projections, including creation of a field of behavioral assessment, were generally taken up by radical behaviorists. Thus, despite its origins within PB (as described in Silva, 1993), the field of behavioral assessment was developed as a part of radical behaviorism. However, the radical behaviorism rejection of traditional psychological measurement doomed the field to failure.

That was quite contrary to the PB plan. In the same work that introduced behavioral assessment, PB unified traditional psychological testing with behavior assessment. Behavior analyses of intelligence tests (Staats, 1963, pp. 407–411) and interest, values, and needs tests (Staats, 1963, pp. 293–306) were begun. The latter three types of tests were said to measure what stimuli are reinforcing for the individual. MacPhillamy and Lewinsohn (1971) later constructed an instrument to measure reinforcers that actually put the PB analysis into practice. Again, despite using traditional rating techniques that Skinner (1969, pp. 77–78) rejected, they replaced their behavioral assessment instrument in a delimiting radical behaviorism framework. Thus, when presented in the radical behaviorism framework, this and the other behavioral assessment works referenced earlier were separated from the broader PB framework that included the traditional tests of intelligence, interests, values, and needs and its program for general unification (Staats, 1963, pp. 304–308).

The point here is that PB's broad-scope unification orientation has made it a different kind of behaviorism in various fundamental ways, including that of making it a behaviorism with a personality. The PB theory of personality is the only one that has been constructed on the foundation of a set of learning-behavior principles (Staats, 1996). Advancing in successive works, with different features than other personality theories, only in its later version has the theory of personality begun to arouse interest in the general field of behavior therapy. It appears that some behavior therapists are beginning to realize that behaviorists "have traditionally regarded personality, as a concept, of little use in describing and predicting behavior" (Hamburg, 2000, p. 62) and that this is a liability. Making that realization general, along with understanding how this weakens the field, is basic in effecting progress.

As it stands, behavior therapy's rejection of the concept of personality underlies the field's inability to join forces with the field of psychological measurement. This is anomalous because behavior therapists use psychological tests even while rejecting them conceptually. It is anomalous also because Kenneth Spence (1944), while not providing a conceptual framework for bringing behaviorism and psychological testing together, did provide a behavioral rationale for the utility of tests. He said that tests produce R-R (response-response) laws—in which a test score (one response) is used to predict some later performance (the later response). It needs to be added that tests can yield knowledge of behavior in addition to prediction as we will see.

This, then, is the state of affairs at present. Not one of the other behavioral approaches—radical behaviorism, Hullian theory, social learning theory, cognitive-behavioral theory—has produced or projected a program for the study of personality and its measurement. That is a central reason why traditional psychology is alienated from behaviorism and behavioral approaches. And that separation has seriously disadvantaged both behaviorism and traditional psychology.

THE STATE OF THEORY IN THE FIELD OF PERSONALITY

Thus far a critical look has been directed at the behaviorism positions with respect to the personality and psychological testing fields. This is not to say that those two fields are fulfilling their potential or are open to unification with any behavioral approach. Just as behaviorism has rejected personality and psychological measurement, so have the latter rejected behaviorism. Part of this occurs because traditional behaviorism does not develop some mutuality of interest, view, or product. But the fields of psychological testing and personality have had a tradition that considers genetic heredity as the real explanation of individual differences. Despite lip service

to the contrary, these fields have never dealt with learning. So there is an ingrained mutual rejection. Furthermore, the lack of a learning approach has greatly weakened personality theory and measurement, substantively as well as methodologically, as I will suggest.

To continue, examination of the field of personology reveals it to be, at least within the present philosophy-methodology, a curiosity of science. For this is a field without guidelines, with no agreement on what its subject matter—personality—is and no concern about that lack of stipulation. It is accepted that there will be many definitions in the operating field. The only consensus, albeit implicit, is that personality is some process or structure within the individual that is a *cause* of the individual's behavior. Concepts of personality range from the id, ego, and superego of Sigmund Freud, through the personal constructs of George Kelly and Carl Rogers's life force that leads to the maintenance and enhancement of self, to Raymond B. Cattell's source traits of sociability, intelligence, and ego strength, to mention a very few.

Moreover, there is no attempt to calibrate one concept of personality with respect to another. In textbooks each personality theory is described separately without relating concepts and principles toward creating some meaningful relationships. There are no criteria for evaluating the worth of the products of the field, for comparing them, for advancing the field as a part of science. Each author of a theory of personality is free to pursue her or his own goals, which can range from using factor analytic methods by which to establish relationships between test items and questionnaires to running pigeons on different schedules of reinforcement. There will be little criticism or evaluation of empirical methods or strategies. All is pretty much accepted as is. There will be no critical consideration of the kind of data that are employed and evaluation of what the type of data mean about the nature of the theory. Other than psychometric criteria of reliability and validity, there will be no standards of success concerning a test's provision of understanding of the trait involved, what causes the trait, or how it can be changed. Also, the success of a personality theory will not be assessed by the extent to which it provides a foundation for constructing tests of personality, therapies, or procedures for parents to employ. It is also not necessary that a personality theory be linked to other fields of study.

Moreover, a theory in this field does not have the same types of characteristics or functions as do theories in the physical sciences. Those who consider themselves personality theorists are so named either because they have created one of the many personality theories or because they have studied and know about one or more of the various existent theories. They are not theorists in the sense that they work on the various personality theories in order to improve the theory level of the field. They are not theorists in the sense that they study their field and pick out its weaknesses and errors in order to advance the field. They do not analyze the concepts and principles in different theories in order to bring order into the chaos of unrelated knowledge. They do not, for example, work on the large task of weaving the theories together into one or more larger, more advanced, and more general and unified theories that can then be tested empirically and advanced.

An indication of the mixed-up character of the field of personality theory is the inclusion of Skinner's experimental analysis of behavior as a personality theory in some textbooks on personality theory. This is anomalous because Skinner has rejected the concept of personality, has never treated the phenomena of personality, has had no program for doing so, and his program guides those who are radical behaviorists to ignore the fields of personality and its measurement. His findings concerning schedules of reinforcement are not used by personologists, nor are his students' findings using the experimental analysis of behavior with human subjects nor his philosophy-methodology of science. His approach appears to be quite irrelevant for the field. What does it say about the field's understanding of theory that the irrelevance of his theory does not matter? From the standpoint of the philosophy and methodology of PB, the field of personality is in a very primitive state as a science.

To some extent the following sections put the cart before the horse because I discuss some theory needs of the field of personality before I describe the approach that projects those needs. That approach involves two aspects: a particular theory and a philosophy-methodology. The latter is the basis for the projections made in this section. This topic needs to be developed into a full-length treatment rather than the present abbreviation.

The Need for Theorists Who Work the Field

One of the things that reveals that the field of personality theory is not really part of a fully developed science is the lack of systematic treatment of the theories in the field. Many study the theories of the field and their empirical products. But that study treats the field as composed of different and independent bodies of knowledge to be learned. There is not even the level of integration of study that one would find in humanities, such as English literature and history, where there is much comparative evaluating of the characteristics of different authors' works.

If the field of personality theory is to become a real scientific study, we need theorists who *work* the field. Theories have

certain characteristics. They contain concepts and principles, and the theories deal with or derive from certain empirical data. And those concepts, principles, and data vary in types and in functions. With those differences, theories differ in method and content and therefore in what they can do and thus how they fit together or not. We need theorists who study such things and provide knowledge concerning the makeup of our field. What can we know about the field without such analysis?

We need theorists who work the field in other ways also. For example, two scientific fields could be at the same level in terms of scientific methods and products. One field, however, could be broken up by having many different theorists, each of whom addresses limited phenomena and does so in idiosyncratic theory language, with no rules relating the many theories. This has resulted in competing theories, much overlap among theories and the phenomena they address, and much redundancy in concepts and principles mixed in with real differences. This yields an unorganized, divided body of knowledge. Accepting this state provides no impetus for cooperative work or for attaining generality and consensus.

The other hypothetical field has phenomena of equal complexity and difficulty, and it also began with the same unorganized growth of theory. But the field devoted part of its time and effort in working those theories, that is, in assessing what phenomena the various theories addressed, what their methods of study were, what types of principles and concepts were involved, and where there was redundancy and overlap, as well as in comparing, relating, and unifying the different theory-separated islands of knowledge. The terms for the concepts and principles were standardized, and idiosyncrasy was removed. The result was a simpler, coherent body of knowledge that was also more general. That allowed people who worked in the field to speak the same language and to do research and theory developments in that language in a way that everyone could understand. In turn, researchers could build on one another's work. That simplifying consensus also enabled applied people to use the knowledge better.

It can be seen that although these two sciences are at the same level with respect to much of their product, they are quite different with respect to their theory advancement and operation. The differences in the advancement of knowledge in science areas along these lines have not been systematically considered in the philosophy of science. There has not been an understanding that the disunified sciences (e.g., psychology) operate differently than do the unified sciences (e.g., physics) that are employed as the models in the philosophy of science. Thus, there has been no guide for theorists to *work* the fields of personality theory and psychological testing to produce the more advanced type of knowledge. So this remains a crying need.

We Need Theory Constructed in Certain Ways and With Certain Qualities and Data

We need theorists to work the field of personality. And they need to address certain tasks, as exemplified earlier and later. This is only a sample; other characteristics of theory also need to be considered in this large task.

Commonalities Among Theories

In the field of personality theory there is much commonality, overlap, and redundancy among theories. This goes unrecognized, however, because theorists are free to concoct their own idiosyncratic theory language. The same or related phenomena can be given different names—such as ego, self, self-concept, and self-efficacy—and left alone as different. Just in terms of parsimony (an important goal of science), each case of multiple concepts and unrecognized full or partial redundancy means that the science is unnecessarily complex and difficult, making it more difficult to learn and use. Unrecognized commonality also artificially divides up the science, separating efforts that are really relevant. Personality theorists, who are in a disunified science in which novelty is the only recognized value, make their works as different as possible from those of others. The result is a divided field, lacking methods of unification.

We need theorists who work to remove unnecessary theory elements from our body of knowledge, to work for simplicity and standardization in theory language. We need to develop concepts and principles that everyone recognizes in order to build consistency and consensus. It is essential also for profundity; when basic terms no longer need to be argued, work can progress to deeper levels.

Data of Theories and Type of Knowledge Yielded

A fundamental characteristic of the various theories in personality is that despite overlap they address different sets of phenomena and their methods of data collection are different. For example, Freud's theory was drawn to a large extent from personal experience and from the stated experiences of his patients. Carl Rogers's data was also drawn from personal experience and clinical practice. Gordon Allport employed the *lexical approach,* which involved selecting all the words from a dictionary that descriptively labeled different types of human behavior. The list of descriptive words was whittled down by using certain criteria and then was organized into categories, taken to describe traits of personality. This methodology rests on large numbers of people, with lay knowledge, having discriminated and labeled different

characteristic behaviors of humans. Raymond Cattell used three sources of data. One consisted of life records, as in school or work. Another source was self-report in an interview. And a third could come from objective tests on which the individual's responses could be compared to the responses of others. These data could be subjected to factor analytic methods to yield groupings of items to measure personality traits.

What is not considered systematically to inform us about the field is that the different types of data used in theories give those theories different characteristics and qualities. To illustrate, a theory built only on the evanescent and imprecise data of personal and psychotherapy experience—limited by the observer's own concepts and flavored by them—is unlikely to involve precisely stated principles and concepts and findings. Moreover, any attempt by the client to explain her behavior on the basis of her life experience is limited by her own knowledge of behavior and learning and perhaps by the therapist's interpretations. The naturalistic data of self-description, however, can address complex events (e.g., childhood experiences) not considered in the same way in an experimental setup. Test-item data, as another type, can stipulate behaviors while not including a therapist's interpretations. However, such items concern how individuals are, not how they got that way (as through learning).

Let us take as an example an intelligence test. It can predict children's performance in school. The test was constructed to do this. But test data do not tell us how "intelligence" comes about or what to do to increase the child's intelligence. For in constructing the test there has been no study of the causes of intelligence or of how to manipulate those causes to change intelligence. The theory of intelligence, then, is limited by the data used. Generally, because of the data on which they rest, tests provide predictive variables but not explanatory, causal variables. Not understanding this leads to various errors.

The data employed in some theories can be of a causal nature, but not in other theories. Although data on animal conditioning may lack other qualities, it does deal with cause-effect principles. Another important aspect of data used involves breadth. How many different types of data does a theory draw on or stimulate? From how many different fields of psychology does the theory draw its data? We should assess and compare theories on the types of data on which they are based. Through an analysis of types of data we will have deeper knowledge of our theories, how they differ, how they are complementary, the extent to which they can be developed to be explanatory as well as predictive, and also how they can or cannot be combined in organizing and unifying our knowledge.

Precision of Theories

There are also formal differences in theories in terms of other science criteria, for example, in the extent of precision of statement. A known example of imprecision was that of Freud's *reaction formation*. If the person did not do as predicted, then the reaction formation still allowed the theory always to be "right." Another type of difference lies in the precision or vagueness of definition of concepts. Hull aimed to define his *habit strength* concept with great precision. Rogers's concept of the life force does not have such a precise definition. Science is ordinarily known for its interest in considering and assessing its theory tools with respect to such characteristics. The field of personality needs to consider its theories in this respect.

Unifying and Generality Properties of Theories

Hans Eysenck showed an interest in applications of conditioning principles to problems of human behavior. He also worked on the measurement of personality, in traits such as intelligence and extroversion-introversion. Moreover, he also had interest in variations in psychic ability as shown in experiments in psychokinisis. (During a six-month stay at the Maudsley Hospital in 1961, the author conveyed the spread of our American behavioral applications and also argued about psychic phenomena, taking the position that selecting subjects with high "psychic" ability abrogated the assumptions for the statistics employed.) Theorists vary in the number of different research areas to which they address themselves. And that constitutes an important dimension; other things equal, more general theories are more valuable than narrow theories.

Another property of a theory is that of unifying power. The example of Eysenck can be used again. That is, although he was interested in behavior therapy, personality measurement, and experimental psychic ability, he did not construct a theory within which these phenomenal areas were unified within a tightly reasoned set of interrelated principles. Both the generality *and* the unifying power of theories are very important.

Freud's psychological theory was more general than Rogers's. For example, it pertains to child development, abnormal psychology, and clinical psychology and has been used widely in those and other fields. And Freud's theory—much more than other theories that arise in psychotherapy—also was high in the *goal* of unification. John Watson began behaviorism as a general approach to psychology. The behavioral theories of personality (such as that of Rotter, and to some extent the other social learning theories) exhibit some generality and unification. The present theory, PB, has the most generality and unification aims of all. None of the personality theories, with the exception of the present one, moreover, has a systematic program for advancing further in generality and unification.

In general, there are no demands in the field of personality to be systematic with respect to generality or unification, and there are no attempts to evaluate theories for success in attaining those goals. Again, that is different from the other more advanced, unified sciences. That is unfortunate, for the more a theory of personality has meaning for the different areas of psychology, employs products of those fields, and has implications for those fields, the more valuable that theory can be.

This view of the field of personality and its personality theories is a byproduct of the construction of the theory that will be considered in the remaining sections. The perspective suggests that the field of personality will continue to stagnate until it begins to *work* its contents along the lines proposed.

PERSONALITY: THE PSYCHOLOGICAL BEHAVIORISM THEORY

More than 45 years ago, while still a graduate student at UCLA, I began a research program that for some years I did not name, then called social behaviorism, later paradigmatic behaviorism, and finally PB. I saw great importance in the behaviorism tradition as a science, in fundamental learning principles, and in experimentation. But I saw also that the preceding behaviorisms were incompletely developed, animal oriented, and too restricted to laboratory research. They also contained fundamental errors and had no plan by which to connect to traditional psychology, to contribute to it, and to use its products. Very early in the research program I began to realize that animal conditioning principles are not sufficient to account for human behavior and personality. In my opinion a new behavioral theory was needed, it had to focus on human behavior systematically and broadly, it had to link with traditional psychology's treatments of many phenomena of human behavior, and it had to include a new philosophy and methodology.

Basic Developments

The early years of this program consisted of studies to extend, generally and systematically, conditioning principles to samples of human behavior. This was a new program in behaviorism. Some of the studies were informal, some were formal publications, and many involved theoretical analyses of behaviors—experimental, clinical, and naturalistic—that had been described in the psychology literature. One of the goals was to advance progressively on the dimension of simple-complex with respect to behavior. The low end of the dimension involved establishment of basic principles, already begun with the animal conditioning principles. But those principles had to be verified with humans, first with simple behaviors and laboratory control. Then more and more complex behaviors had to be confronted, with the samples of behavior treated becoming more *representative* of life behaviors. The beginning of this latter work showed convincingly the relevance of learning-behavior principles for understanding human behavior and progressively indicated that new human learning principles were needed to deal with complex human behavior. Several areas of PB research are described here as historical background and, especially, to indicate how the theory of personality arose in an extended research-conceptual development.

Language-Cognitive Studies

My dissertation studied how subjects' verbal responses to problem-solving objects were related to the speed with which they solved the problem. It appeared that people learn many word labels to the objects and events of life. When a situation arises that involves those objects and events, the verbal responses to them that individuals have learned will affect their behavior. The research supported that analysis.

There are various kinds of labeling responses. A child's naming the letters of the alphabet involves a labeling repertoire. Studies have shown that children straightforwardly learn such a repertoire, as they do in reading numbers and words. The *verbal-labeling repertoire* is composed of various types of spoken words controlled by stimulus events. The child learns to say "car" to cars as stimulus events, to say "red" to the stimulus of red light, to say "running" to the visual stimulus of rapidly alternating legs that produce rapid movement, and to say "merrily" to people happily reveling. Moreover, the child learns these verbal labeling responses—like the nouns, adjectives, verbs, and adverbs just exemplified—in large quantities, so the verbal-labeling repertoire becomes huge. This repertoire enables the person to describe the many things experienced in life, but it has other functions as well. As discussed later, this and the other language repertoires are important components of intelligence.

As another aspect of language, the child also learns to make different motor responses to a large number of words. The young child learns to look when hearing the word "look," to approach when hearing the word "come," to sit when told the word "sit," and to make a touching response when told to "touch" something. The child will learn to respond to many words with motor responses, constituting the *verbal-motor*

repertoire. This repertoire enables the person to follow directions. It is constituted not only of a large number of verbs, but also of adverbs, nouns, adjectives, and other grammatical elements. For example, most people could respond appropriately to the request to "Go quickly, please, to the top-left drawer of my dresser and bring me the car keys" because they have learned motor responses to the relevant words involved. Important human skills involve special developments of the verbal-motor subrepertoire. As examples, ballet dancers, violinists, NFL quarterbacks, mechanics, and surgeons have special verbal-motor repertoires that are essential parts of their special skills.

Another important part of language is the *verbal-association repertoire.* When the word *salt* is presented as a stimulus in a word-association task, a common response is *pepper* or *water.* However, an occasional person might respond by saying *wound* or *of the earth* or something else that is less usual. Years ago it was believed that differences in associations had personality implications, and word-association tests were given with diagnostic intent. Analysis of word associations as one of the subrepertoires of the language-cognitive repertoire suggests more definitively and specifically that this constitutes a part of personality. Consider a study by Judson, Cofer, and Gelfand (1956). One group of subjects learned a list of words that included the sequence *rope, swing,* and *pendulum.* The other group learned the same list of words, but the three words were not learned in sequence. Both groups then had to solve a problem by constructing a pendulum from a light rope and swinging it. The first group solved the problem more quickly than did the second. Thus, in the present view the *reasoning ability* of the two groups depended on the word associations they had learned.

Word associates are central to our grammatical speech, the logic of our speech and thought, our arithmetic and mathematical knowledge, our special area and general knowledge, our reasoning ability, our humor, our conversational ability, and our intelligence. Moreover, there are great individual differences in the verbal-association repertoire such that it contributes to differences on psychological tests. Additional repertoires are described in the PB theory of language-cognition (see Staats, 1968, 1971, 1975, 1996).

Emotional-Motivational Studies

An early research interest of PB concerned the emotional property of words. Using my *language conditioning* method I showed subjects a visually presented neutral word (nonsense syllable) paired once each with different auditorily presented words, each of which elicited an emotional response, with one group positive emotion and with another group negative in a classical conditioning procedure. The results of a series of experiments have showed that a stimulus paired with positive or negative emotional words acquires positive or negative emotional properties. Social attitudes, as one example, are emotional responses to people that can be manipulated by language conditioning (Staats & Staats, 1958). To illustrate, in a political campaign the attempt is made to pair one's candidate with positive emotional words and one's opponent with negative emotional words. That is why the candidate with greater financial backing can condition the audience more widely, giving great advantage.

Skinner's theory is that emotion (and classical conditioning) and behavior (and operant conditioning) are quite separate, and it is the operant behavior that is what he considers important. In contrast, PB's basic learning-behavior theory states that the two types of conditioning are intimately related and that both are important to behavior. For one thing, a stimulus is reinforcing because it elicits an emotional response. Thus, as a stimulus comes to elicit an emotional response through classical conditioning, it gains potential as a reinforcing stimulus. My students and I have shown that words eliciting a positive or negative emotional response will function as a positive or negative reinforcer. In addition, the PB learning-behavior theory has shown that a stimulus that elicits a positive or negative emotional response will also function as a positive or negative incentive and elicit approach or avoidance behavior. That is a reason why emotional words (language) guide people's behavior so ubiquitously. An important concept from this work is that humans learn a very large repertoire of emotion-eliciting words, the *verbal-emotional repertoire*. Individual differences in this repertoire widely affect individual differences in behavior (see Staats, 1996).

One other principle should be added for positive emotional stimuli: They are subject to motivational (deprivation-satiation) variations. For example, food is a stimulus that elicits a positive emotional response on a biological basis; however, the size of the response varies according to the extent of food deprivation. That also holds for the reinforcement and incentive effect of food stimuli on operant behavior. These three effects occur with stimuli that elicit an emotional response through biology (as with food) or through learning, as with a food word.

The human being has an absolutely gargantuan capacity for learning. And the human being has a hugely complex learning experience. The result is that in addition to biologically determined emotional stimuli, the human *learns* a gigantic repertoire that consists of stimuli that elicit an emotional response, whether positive or negative. There are many varieties of stimuli—art, music, cinema, sports, recreations, religious, political, manners, dress, and jewelry stimuli—that are operative for humans. They elicit emotion on a learned basis. As a consequence, they can also serve as motivational stimuli and act as reinforcers and incentives. That leads to a conclusion that individual differences in the quantity and type of emotional stimuli will have great significance for personality and human behavior.

Sensorimotor Studies

Following its human-centered learning approach, PB studied sensorimotor repertoires in children. To illustrate, consider the sensorimotor response of speech. Traditional developmental norms state that a child generally says her first words at the age of 1 year, but why there are great individual differences is not explained, other than conjecturing that this depends on biological maturation processes. In contrast, PB states that speech responses are learned according to reinforcement principles, but that reinforcement depends on prior classical conditioning of positive emotion to speech sounds (Staats, 1968, 1996). I employed this theoretical analysis and learning procedures in accelerating the language development of my own children, in naturalistic interactions spread over a period of months, but adding up to little time expenditure. Their speech development accelerated by three months, which is 25% of the usual 12-month period (Staats, 1968). I have since validated the learning procedures with parents of children with retarded speech development. Lovaas (1977) has used this PB framework. Psychological behaviorism also systematically studied sensorimotor skills such as standing, walking, throwing and catching a ball, using the toilet, writing letters, paying attention, counting objects, and so on in systematic experimental-longitudinal research (see Staats, 1968, 1996).

In this theory of child development, PB pursued its goal of unification with traditional psychology, in this case with the field of child development. The PB position is that the norms of traditional child developmentalists provide valuable knowledge. But this developmental conception errs in assuming biological determination and in ignoring learning. Prior to my work, the reigning view was that it was wasteful or harmful to attempt to train the child to develop behaviors early. For example, the 4-year-old child was said to be developmentally limited to an attention span of 5 min to 15 min and thus to be incapable of formal learning. We showed that such preschoolers can attend well in the formal learning of reading skills for 40-min periods if their work behaviors are reinforced (Staats et al., 1964). When not reinforced, however, they do not attend. My later research showed that children *learn progressively* to attend and work well for longer periods by having been reinforced for doing so.

Rather than being a biologically determined cognitive ability, attention span is actually a learned behavior. The same is true with the infant's standing and walking, the development of both of which can be advanced by a little systematic training. The child of 2 years also can be straightforwardly trained to count unarranged objects (Piaget said 6 years). Writing training can be introduced early and successfully, as can other parts of the sensorimotor repertoire. I also developed a procedure for potty training my children (see Staats, 1963) that was later elaborated by Azrin and Foxx (1974). Such findings have changed society's view of child development.

What emerges from this work is that the individual *learns* the sensorimotor repertoire. Without the learning provided in the previous cases, children do not develop the repertoires. Moreover, the human sensorimotor repertoire is, again, vast for individuals. And over the human community it is infinitely varied and variable. There are skills that are generally learned by all, such as walking and running. And there are skills that are learned by only few, such as playing a violin, doing surgery, or acting as an NFL quarterback. As such there are vast individual differences among people in what sensorimotor skills are learned as well as in what virtuosity.

Additional Concepts and Principles

Human Learning Principles

As indicated earlier, a basic assumption of traditional behaviorism is that the animal learning principles are the necessary and sufficient principles for explaining human behavior. Psychological behaviorism's program has led to the position that while the animal conditioning principles, inherited through evolution, are indeed necessary for explaining human behavior, they are far from sufficient. I gained an early indication of that with my research on the language conditioning of attitudes, and later findings deepened and elaborated the principles.

What the traditional behaviorists did not realize is that human learning also involves principles that are unique to humans—*human* learning principles. The essential, new feature of these principles is that much of what humans learn takes place on the basis of what they have learned before. For example, much human learning can occur only if the individual has first learned language. Take two children, one of whom has learned a good verbal-motor repertoire and one of whom has not. The first child will be able to follow directions and therefore will be able to learn many things the second child cannot because many learning tasks require the following of directions. The goodness of that verbal-motor repertoire distinguishes children (as we can see on any intelligence test for

children). In PB, language is considered a large repertoire with many important learning functions. Learning to count, to write, to read, to go potty, to form attitudes, to have logic and history and science knowledge and opinions and beliefs, to be religious, to eat healthily and exercise, and to have political positions are additional examples in which language is a foundation. A child of 18 months can easily learn to name numbers of objects and then to count if that child has previously learned a good language repertoire (see Staats, 1968). On the other hand, a child of 3 years who has not learned language will not be able to learn those number skills. The reason for the difference is not some genetic difference in the goodness of learning. Rather, the number learning of the child is built on the child's previous language learning. It is not age (biology) that matters in the child's learning prowess; it is what the child has already learned.

Cumulative-Hierarchical Learning

Human learning is different from basic conditioning because it typically involves learning that is based on repertoires that have been previously learned. This is called *cumulative-hierarchical learning* because of the building properties involved—the second learning is built on the first learning but, in turn, provides the foundation for a third learning. Multiple levels of learning are typical when a fine performance is involved. Let us take the learning of the language repertoire. When the child has a language repertoire, the child can then learn to read. When the child has a reading repertoire, the child can learn more advanced number operations, after which the child can learn an algebra repertoire, which then is basic in learning additional mathematics repertoires, which in turn enable the learning of physics. Becoming a physicist ordinarily will involve in excess of 20 years of cumulative-hierarchical learning.

Cumulative-hierarchical learning is involved in all the individual's complex characteristics. A sociopath—with the complex of language-cognitive, emotional-motivational, and sensorimotor repertoires this entails—does not spring forth full-blown any more than being a physicist. Understanding the sociopathic personality, hence, requires understanding the cumulative-hierarchical learning of the multiple repertoires that have been involved.

The Basic Behavioral Repertoire: A Cause as Well as an Effect

And that brings us to another concept developed in PB, that is, the basic behavioral repertoire (BBR). The BBRs are those repertoires that provide the means by which later learning can occur, in the cumulative-hierarchical learning process. In providing foundations for further learning, the three major BBRs—the emotional-motivational, language-cognitive, and sensorimotor—also grow and elaborate through cumulative-hierarchical learning.

The learning of the basic behavioral repertoires changes the individual. The BBRs thus act as independent variables that determine what the individual experiences, how the individual behaves, and what the individual learns. The cumulative-hierarchical learning of such repertoires is fundamental in child development; in fact, the PB theory is that the study of that learning should be the primary objective of this field, as it should be in the field of personality.

The Concept of Personality

It is significant in comparing the PB theory to other personality theories to note differences in such things as the type of data involved and the specificity, precision, systematicity, and empirical definition of principles and concepts. It is such characteristics that determine the functions that a theory can have. Another characteristic of the PB approach concerns the schism between traditional psychology and traditional behaviorism. Traditional psychology infers personality as a unique internal process or structure that determines the individual's unique behavior. That makes study of personality (and related concepts) very central. Traditional behaviorism, in opposition, and according to its fundamental methodology, cannot accept an inferred concept as the cause of behavior. So, while almost every personologist considers learning to be important in personality, traditional behaviorism, which should be concerned with how learning affects personality, cannot even consider the topic. The schism leaves personality theories incomplete and divides psychology.

The PB Definition of Personality

The PB program has led to the development of a theory of personality that can resolve that schism in a way that is valuable to both sides. The PB definition of personality is that it is composed of the three basic behavioral repertoires that the individual has learned. That definition harmonizes with behaviorism, for the PB program is to study the behaviors in those repertoires and how they are learned, as well as how they have their effects on the individual's characteristic behavior. At the same time, that definition is very compatible with the traditional view of personality as an internal process or structure that determines behavior. As such, the PB concept of personality can link with traditional work on personality, including personality tests, and can also contribute to

advancement of that work. How the three BBRs compose personality is described next.

The Emotional-Motivational Aspects of Personality

There are many concepts that refer to human emotions, emotional states, and emotional personality traits. As examples, it may be said that humans may feel the responses of joy or fear, may be in a depressed or euphoric state, and may be optimistic or pessimistic as traits. The three different emotional processes are not usually well defined. PB makes explicit definitions. First, the individual can experience specific, ephemeral emotional responses depending on the appearance-cessation of a stimulus. Second, multiple emotion-eliciting events can yield a series of related emotional responses that add together and continue over time; this constitutes an emotional state. Third, the individual can learn emotional responses to sets of stimuli that are organized—like learning a positive emotional response to a wide number of religious stimuli. That constitutes an emotional-motivational trait (religious values); that is, the individual will have positive emotional responses to the stimuli in the many religious situations encountered. And that emotional-motivational trait will affect the individual's behavior in those many situations (from the reinforcer and incentive effects of the religious stimuli). For these reasons the trait has generality and continuity. There are psychological tests for *traits* such as interests, values, attitudes, and paranoid personality. There are also tests for *states* such as anxiety and depression and moods. And there are also tests for single emotional responses, such as phobias or attitudes.

Personality theories usually consider emotion. This is done in idiosyncratic terminology and principles. So how one theory considers emotion is not related to another. Theories of emotion at the personality level are not connected to studies of emotion at more basic levels. Many psychological tests measure emotions, but they are not related to one another. Psychological behaviorism provides a systematic framework theory of emotion that can deal with the various emotional phenomena, analyze many findings within the same set of concepts and principles, and thus serve as a unifying overarching theory. Psychological behaviorism experimentation has shown that interest tests deal with emotional responses to occupation-related stimuli, that attitude tests deal with emotional responses to groups of people, and that values tests deal with emotional responses to yet other stimuli, unifying them in the same theory.

In the PB theory, beginning with the basic, the individual has emotional responses to stimuli because of biological structure, such as a positive emotional response to food stimuli, certain tactile stimuli, warm stimulation when cold, and vice versa, and a negative emotional response to aversive, harmful stimuli of various kinds. Conditioning occurs when any neutral stimulus is paired with one of those biological stimuli and comes to elicit the same type of emotional response. Conditioning occurs also when a neutral stimulus is paired with an emotion-eliciting stimulus (e.g., an emotional word) that has gained this property through learning. The human has a long life full of highly variable, complex experiences and learns an exceedingly complex emotional-motivational repertoire that is an important part of personality. People very widely have different emotional learning. Not everyone experiences positive emotional responses paired with religious stimuli, football-related stimuli, or sex-related stimuli. And different conditioning experiences will produce different emotional-motivational repertoires. Because human experience is so variegated, with huge differences, everyone's hugely complex emotional-motivational personality characteristics are unique and different.

That means, of course, that people find different things reinforcing. What is a reward for one will be a punishment for someone else. Therefore, people placed in the same situation, with the same reinforcer setup, will learn different things. Consider a teacher who compliments two children for working hard. For one child the compliment is a positive reinforcer, but for the other child it is aversive. With the same treatment one child will learn to work hard as a consequence, whereas the other will work less hard. That is also true with respect to incentives. If one pupil has a positive emotional response to academic awards and another pupil does not, then the initiation of an award for number of books read in one semester will elicit strong reading behavior in the one but not in the other. What is reinforcing for people and what has an incentive effect for them strongly affects how they will behave. That is why the emotional BBR is an important personality cause of behavior.

The Language-Cognitive Aspects of Personality

Each human normally learns a huge and fantastically complex language repertoire that reflects the hugely complex experience each human has. There is commonality in that experience across individuals, which is why we speak the same language and can communicate. But there are gigantic individual differences as well (although research on language does not deal with those). Those differences play a central role in the individual differences we consider in the fields of personality and personality measurement.

To illustrate, let us take intelligence as an aspect of personality. In PB theory intelligence is composed of basic behavioral repertoires, largely of a language-cognitive nature but including important sensorimotor elements also. People differ in intelligence not because of some biological quality, but because of the basic behavioral repertoires that they have learned. We can see what is specifically involved at the younger age levels, where the repertoires are relatively simple. Most items, for example, measure the child's verbal-motor repertoire, as in following instructions. Some items specifically test that repertoire, as do the items on the Stanford-Binet (Terman & Merrill, 1937, p. 77) that instruct the child to "Give me the kitty [from a group of small objects]" and to "Put the spoon in the cup." Such items, which advance in complexity by age, also test the child's verbal-labeling repertoire. The child can only follow instructions and be "intelligent" if he or she has learned the names of the things involved.

The language-cognitive repertoires also constitute other aspects of personality, for they are important on tests of language ability, cognitive ability, cognitive styles, readiness, learning aptitude, conceptual ability, verbal reasoning, scholastic aptitude, and academic achievement tests. The tests, considered to measure different facets of personality, actually measure characteristics of the language-cognitive BBR. The self-concept also heavily involves the verbal-labeling repertoire, that is, the labels learned to the individual's own physical and behavioral stimuli. People differ in the labels they learn and in the emotional responses elicited by those verbal labels. We can exemplify this using an item on the MMPI (Dahlstrom & Welsh, 1960, p. 57): "I have several times given up doing a thing because I thought too little of my ability." Individuals who have had different experience with themselves will have learned different labels to themselves (as complex stimuli) and will answer the item differently. The self-concept (composed of learned words) is an important aspect of personality because the individual reasons, plans, and decides *depending on those words.* So the learned self-concept plays the role of a cause of behavior. As another example, the "suspiciousness" of paranoid personality disorder heavily involves the learned verbal-labeling repertoire. This type of person labels the behaviors of others negatively in an atypical way. The problem is that the unrealistic labeling affects the person's reasoning and behavior in ways that are not adjustive either for the individual or for others.

These examples indicate that what are traditionally considered to be parts of personality are conceived of in PB as parts of the learned language-cognitive BBR.

The Sensorimotor Aspects of Personality

Traditionally, the individual's behavior is not considered as a part of personality. Behavior is unimportant for the personologist. Everyone has the ability to behave. It is personality that is important, for personality determines behavior. Even when exceptional sensorimotor differences are clearly the focus of attention, as with superb athletes or virtuoso musicians, we explain the behavior with personality terms such as "natural athlete" or "talent" or "genius" each of which explains nothing.

Psychological behaviorism, in contrast, considers sensorimotor repertoires to constitute learned personality traits in whole or part. And there are very large individual differences in such sensorimotor repertoires. Part of being a physically aggressive person, for example, involves sensorimotor behaviors for being physically aggressive. Being a natural athlete, as another example, involves a complex set of sensorimotor skills (although different body types can be better suited for different actions). Being dependent, as another example, may also involve general deficits in behavior skills. Moreover, sensorimotor repertoires impact on the other two personality repertoires. For example, a person recognized for sensorimotor excellence in an important field will display language-cognitive and emotional-motivational characteristics of "confidence" that have been gained from that recognition.

A good example of how sensorimotor repertoires are part of personality occurred in a study by Staats and Burns (1981). The Mazes and Geometric Design tests of the Wechsler Preschool and Primary Scale of Intelligence (WPPSI) (Wechsler, 1967) were analyzed into sensorimotor repertoire elements. That analysis showed that children learn that repertoire—of complex visual discrimination and other sensorimotor skills—when exposed to learning to write the letters of the alphabet. The expectation, thus, is that children trained to write letters will thereby acquire the repertoire by which to be "intelligent" on the Mazes and Geometric Design tests, as confirmed in our study. As other examples, on the Stanford-Binet (Terman & Merrill, 1937) the child has to build a block tower, complete a line drawing of a man, discriminate forms, tie a knot, trace a maze, fold and cut a paper a certain way, string beads a certain way, and so on. These all require that the child have the necessary sensorimotor basic behavioral repertoire. This repertoire is also measured on developmental tests. This commonality shows that tests considered measures of different aspects of personality actually measure the same BBR. Such an integrative analysis would be central in conceptualizing the field and the field needs many such analyses.

The sensorimotor repertoire also determines the individual's experiences in ways that produce various aspects of personality. For example, the male who acquires the skills of a ballet dancer, painter, carpenter, center in the NBA, symphony violinist, auto mechanic, hair dresser, professional boxer, architect, or opera singer will in the learning and practice of those skills have experiences that will have a marked affect on his other personality repertoires. Much emotional-motivational and language-cognitive learning will take place, and each occupational grouping will as a result have certain common characteristics.

As final examples, being physically aggressive is generally seen as an aspect of personality, a part of some inner psychological process. However, a person cannot be physically aggressive without the sensorimotor skills for being so. It is true that more is involved than just those skills. But those sensorimotor skills are an important part. Likewise, part of a person's being caring and nurturing resides in the sensorimotor skills for being so. A person cannot be a "natural" athlete without having learned the repertoire of sensorimotor skills that enables him or her to learn new sports easily, rapidly, gracefully, and very well. One cannot be a mechanical, athletic, artistic, or surgical genius, or a musical or dance virtuoso, without the requisite sensorimotor repertoire. Are sensorimotor differences part of personality? And are those differences learned? The PB theory answer to both questions is yes.

The PB analyses that show tests measure BBRs provide a whole new way of viewing psychological tests, with a large new agenda for research, as will be indicated.

Definition of the Personality Trait

The personality trait is thus a particular feature of one or more of the three basic behavioral repertoires. Traits involve complex repertoires. For example, liking a religious song involves an isolated emotion. But if the person also has a positive emotional response to many religious stimuli—to the stated beliefs, history, rituals, holidays, personages, and tenets of religion, generally and particularly—this constitutes a personality trait, an important part of the emotional-motivational BBR (as well as of language-cognitive and sensorimotor repertoires). That emotional-motivational repertoire will have general effects on the individual's behavior, life experiences, and further learning, both for normal and abnormal traits.

In PB the personality trait, as a complex repertoire of responses, is considered a universe from which the various situations of life sample. To illustrate, the individual's language repertoire includes many different behaviors. A question like "How much are two and two?" is a life situation that samples the language-cognitive repertoire in eliciting the one response "Four." Many items on intelligence tests *sample* individuals' language repertoires. That sample is representatives of how rich that particular universe is. The entire universe is the total BBR, that is, the personality repertoire.

Personality traits are constituted of particular repertoires that produce types of experience, learning, and behavior. For

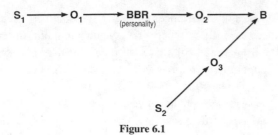

Figure 6.1

example, a person with a trait of religiosity will display coincident knowledge (language) of religious material, will experience religious situations with positive emotion and be motivated by such situations, as well as exhibit the specialized ritualistic behaviors of the religion.

The Principles of the Personality Theory

Figure 6.1 schematizes and makes more explicit the concepts and principles of the PB theory of personality. Personality is composed of the individual's basic behavioral repertoires. As a consequence of previous learning, depicted as S_1, the individual learns BBRs. At a later time the individual is confronted with an environmental situation, S_2, which elicits (samples) elements from the individual's BBRs. Those elements make up the individual's behavior (B) in that situation. Personality does not equate with the individual's behavior. For example, many individuals learn words that are never uttered. So the individual's language-cognitive BBR can never be ascertained from observing behavior; the individual's potential for behavior is greater than that which is exhibited.

Traditional behaviorism never established how biology works its effects in the explanation of behavior. In contrast, in PB's personality theory the individual's biological character plays an important role at different times. First, the learning of the basic behavioral repertoires takes place by virtue of the brain and peripheral nervous system, muscles, tendons, emotional response organs, and such. The organic state at the time of learning is thus an important independent variable. This includes permanent biological conditions such as brain damage as well as ephemeral biological conditions such as those of deprivation-satiation, illness, and drug and alcohol effects. These biological conditions that are influential at the time of learning the BBRs are designated as O_1.

In addition, however, at the time the individual experiences a later situation certain biological conditions, O_2, are operating in ways that affect the state of the individual's BBRs. For the BBRs to be operative they have to be retained (remembered). Any temporary conditions, such as drugs or a fever, that effect the brain mechanisms that house the BBRs will be important, as will more permanent conditions such as brain damage that has deleted BBRs in whole or part. In addition, the biological mechanism plays a third role. Even though the individual has retained the BBRs, other biological conditions, O_3, may affect the ability of S_2, the later situation, to elicit them. For example, the individual's sensory systems may be affected by drugs or other organic conditions that limit or distort the sensory responses, as occurs with a person who because of poor hearing cannot respond emotionally to a touching dialogue in a movie.

In this theoretical conception environmental conditions play two roles in the determination of the individual's behavior. Separating these environmental events enables a more explicit consideration of both environmental and biological effects on personality and behavior. In both of these ways the definition of personality becomes more explicit. Several additional specifications can be added.

Plasticity and Continuity in Personality

There has been an issue of whether individuals behave the same across time and situations or whether their behavior is situationally determined. Watson's behaviorism raised the issue, which was argued to a stalemate in his era. Mischel's 1968 book revivified the contest by arguing for the situational determinism position and against the conception that the individual has a personality that acts across situations. A number of pro and con works were then published until, as generally happens in such issues, interest for the moment was exhausted. A deeper analysis can be made, however, that can resolve the issue.

To begin, Figure 6.1 has various implications. Behavior is certainly situational, for the situation does indeed play an important role in selecting the elements of behavior displayed in that situation. For example, people generally act boisterously at a football game or wrestling match and sedately in a place of worship, a library, or a museum.

But there is generality to personality also. A particular BBR over time can be relevant to various situations, and the individual's behavior can thereby show characteristic features across those situations. For example, a person with a large repertoire of skilled singing behaviors will have learned a repertoire whose elements are called out in many later environmental situations. Compared to others the individual will sing more generally and more skillfully than others lacking that repertoire. Clearly that will be a characteristic, general, and stable feature of the individual's behavior, considered to reflect a personality trait.

Personality typically produces stability over time and situations. For example, a person who has learned positive values (emotion) to positions on the conservative side of many political-social-economic events (issues) will tend to display conservative behavior in the books and magazines that are read, the television programs that are watched, the lectures that are attended, the church that is attended, the voting choices that are made, the person who is married, the opinions that are expressed, and so on. As this example shows, a general trait—emotional-motivational, language-cognitive, or sensorimotor—promulgates additional trait development by ensuring additional experience of the same type that originally produced the BBR. In the abnormal area, for example, once the individual has learned negative emotional responses to people generally, the individual will display negative behaviors (such as suspicion) to people. They in turn will typically respond in negative ways that will further condition the individual to have negative emotional responses to people. That can become a general, deep, and continuing abnormal trait.

Stability in personality is produced in these ways. Thus, the BBRs, once formed, tend to ensure continuity of experience, learning, and behavior. But personality can also exhibit change. For the process of personality development never ends. Learning goes on for the whole life span. In unusual cases something may happen to change a fundamental direction in life. To illustrate, a conservative, conventional man may experience the horrors and immorality of war and thereby read things and participate in activities and meet people he otherwise would not. And these continuing experiences may ultimately provide him with new BBRs—new personality traits—that change his behavior drastically. The cumulative-hierarchical learning involved smacks of a chaos theory effect.

The Multilevel Nature of the Theory and the Implications

Simplification is a goal of science, and oversimplification is common. The traditional approach to personality involves this; that is, personality is conceptually simpler than myriad behaviors. Specification of personality, thus, could make it unnecessary to study all those behaviors. Furthermore, if one takes personality to be the cause of behavior, one need only study personality and not all the other fields of psychology, like animal learning principles and cognitive things (such as language), child development, social interaction principles, educational psychology, and so on.

But PB differs here. Explaining human behavior is not considered a two-level task, with one basic theory level, the study of personality, which explains the second level, behavior. Psychological behaviorism says that psychology is divided into fields that have a general hierarchical relationship

with one another. The field of animal learning is basic to a field like developmental psychology because much of development depends on learning. The field of developmental psychology, on the other hand, is basic to the field of personality because important aspects of personality develop in childhood. In turn, knowledge of personality is relevant to psychological measurement, abnormal psychology, and clinical and educational psychology.

This multilevel relationship has many exceptions, and there is a bidirectional exchange between areas (levels). But the present position is that a personality theory that does not take into account the various major fields (levels) of psychology can only be a part theory. Learning, for example, is important to personality, as most personologists would agree. That being the case, the field should demand that a personality theory indicate how it links to and draws from the study of learning. The same is true of the fields of child development, experimental psychology (in studying language-cognition, emotion-motivation, and sensorimotor behavior), biology, and social interaction. Personality theory on the other side should be basic to personality measurement and to abnormal, clinical, educational, and industrial psychology. Personality theories should be evaluated comparatively for the extent to which they have a program for drawing from and contributing to the various fields of psychological knowledge (see Staats, 1996, for PB's most advanced statement of its multilevel approach.)

The traditional oversimplified view of the study of personality needs change that broadens and deepens its scope as well as its analytic powers.

PERSONALITY THEORY FOR THE TWENTY-FIRST CENTURY

The PB theory of personality says the phenomena of personality—what it is, how it is learned, and the effects it has—are complex and require a theory capable of dealing with that complexity. And that complex theory suggests many more things to do than the traditional approach envisages. For one thing, there is a large task of specifying what the personality repertoires are, how they are learned, and how they operate. Psychological behaviorism says it has begun the study, but the task is huge, and the program for the twenty-first century must be suitably huge. It should be added that PB, while showing the task to be more complex than traditionally considered, provides a foundation that simplifies the task. For all the studies made within its framework will be related and meaningful to one another. They all add together and advance toward explaining personality. Doing that permits research becoming progressively more profound, unimpeded by the necessity of arguing perennially about basics. The fact is the traditional framework allows for a seeming simplicity; personality theories can be created that are simple, but they have very little scope. Worse, however, the traditional framework allows for the creation of an infinity of such approaches to personality, all of them unrelated. The result is a large and chaotic fund of unrelated knowledge, set forth in many different and competing theory languages, impossible to work with as a student, researcher, or practitioner. This constitutes irresolvable complexity. And the framework only guides the field to multiply its complexity with new and unrelated works. Generally, there is no advancement of knowledge in terms of parsimony, profundity, organization, non-redundancy, relatedness, and explanatory value.

Some of the implications of the PB theory of personality for study in the twenty-first century will be sketched.

Biology and Personality

Biological characteristics do indeed play an important role in human behavior and in individual differences in behavior. But in the present view, without a good conception of personality, biological research is presently not of the type needed. The traditional search is for the biological mechanisms that produce personality traits, which PB considers the wrong path. Rather, the PB position is that the individual's biology provides the *mechanism* by which the learning of the BBRs can take place, be stored, and be selectively activated by the stimuli of the later environmental situations the individual encounters. Biological studies of various kinds are needed to specify the biological events involved in these processes.

Learning and Personality

While biological conditions are the most basic level of study proposed, it is the field of learning that is the most important basic level. Anomalously, however, especially since most every personologist would agree that personality is in good measure learned, personologists generally have not studied how learning-behavior principles are involved in the acquisition or function of personality. There seems to be an implicit view that learning is not that much different for people except in extreme cases.

The PB position, on the contrary, is that the personality repertoires are learned, that there are wide individual differences in the learning conditions involved, and that those differences produce infinitely varied personality characteristics. Psychological behaviorism says that the first major task of a personality theory is formulating a basic theory of learning-behavior and a theory of human learning. No other existing personality theory does this.

Human Learning and Personality

The basic animal-conditioning principles are not sufficient for dealing with the learning of personality. There have been studies, long since abandoned, employing human subjects that dealt with more complex learning situations and produced principles such as mediated generalization, sensory preconditioning, and verbal associations. But there has not been a conceptual framework to guide the field to study what is necessary, that is, to study how humans learn complex, functional repertoires in an advancing cumulative-hierarchical way. There has been no systematic goal of studying the basic behavioral repertoires that are important to humans. Although there are research fields that study language, emotion, and sensorimotor behavior, these fields do not systematically address how these behaviors are important for human adjustment. Studies should be conducted that indicate how such repertoires function to (a) change the individual's experience, (b) change the individual's behavior, and (c) change the individual's ability to learn. Such knowledge is needed to provide foundations for advancing the study of personality. For constructing theory, personology needs fundamental knowledge of cumulative-hierarchical learning, the BBRs, their content, and how the BBRs work to affect experience, learning, and behavior.

Developmental Psychology

Some of the theories of personality include reference to how personality develops in childhood. Freud's psychoanalytic theory initiated this and has had great influence on some other personality theories in this respect. But Freud's theory of learning was lacking: He had no understanding of human learning principles or what is learned via those principles, no concepts of the BBRs, how they are learned, how important they are for further learning of personality, and so on. So his treatment (and others in this tradition) of child development in personality formation had to be limited and lacking.

The PB position is that the learning experiences of childhood set the individual's basic personality (BBRs) to a great extent so that what follows typically continues in the same line of development. This conceptual position and its empirical findings indicate that the field of child development should be an essential study. The focus of the field in the PB view should become the study of the central BBRs that are learned in childhood—a large agenda. This position recognizes the value of traditional research, such as longitudinal study of behavioral development, but also sets new avenues of research. To illustrate, it is important to know that children stand unaided at the age of 6 months and walk at the age of 1 year. But that type of knowledge needs to be joined with a behavioral analysis of the behavior involved, how the behavior is learned, and what the function of the behavior is in later development.

Moreover, research needs to be conducted with respect to how repertoires are learned in a cumulative-hierarchical manner to constitute progressively more complex entities that constitute personality. Language development, for example, needs progressive study from the time when the repertoires are simple to the time when they are more complex, both in their features that are general to most children as well as in features personal to individuals. The manner in which different repertoires in language provide the springboards for later learning needs study. To illustrate, the verbal-motor repertoire (by which the child follows directions) is elaborated throughout childhood. How is that BBR basic in the learning of elements in other language, sensorimotor, and emotional repertoires? Such very essential subject matter is not being studied today.

This is to say that the theory of personality as BBRs projects a new framework for research in developmental psychology that will make developmental psychology fundamental for the fields of personality and personality measurement (see Staats, 1966).

Social Psychology

The basic principles of learning behavior and the human learning principles pertain to single individuals. But much learning of humans and much human behavior occur in social interaction. While learning and behavior follow the basic principles, principles of social interaction can be abstracted that are useful in understanding personality formation and function.

Take the child's learning of the personality repertoires. Very central elements are formed in the parent-child interactions. And that process will be influenced greatly by the BBRs the child learns to the parent (as a stimulus object), as well as the reverse. To illustrate, the parent ordinarily provides for the child's needs, which means the presentation of positive emotional stimuli (food, warmth, caresses) paired with the parent. The parent comes thereby to elicit a very positive emotional response (love) in the child. And that is important to the child's further learning, for the more positive emotion the parent elicits, the more effective the parent will be in promoting the child's learning. That follows from PB's social psychological principle that the stronger a person

elicits a positive emotional response in another individual the more effective the person will be as a reinforcing and directive stimulus for the individual. That means that the parent who is more loved will be more effective in rewarding the child for a desired behavior or in admonishing the child for an undesirable behavior. The more loved parent will also be a stronger "incentive" for the child to follow in learning via imitation. Moreover, generalization will occur to other people so the child has learned a general personality trait.

The point is that the PB framework calls for research that concerns how social interaction principles (see Staats, 1996) are involved in personality formation and function.

Personality Tests and Measurement

There is not room in this chapter to deal with the nature of the field of psychological measurement as a science. However, it shares the same weakness as the field of personality already described and repairing those weaknesses calls for many studies of different types, including linking psychological measurement to other fields of psychology, such as that of learning. Traditional behaviorism never made sense of how the concepts and methods of psychological testing are related to behaviorism concepts and methods (see Skinner, 1969, pp. 77–78). The conceptual gap between the two sets of knowledge is just too wide. To understand tests and test construction methods in behavioral terms, it is necessary to have the concepts and principles of a behavioral theory of personality, so the developments made by PB are necessary for bridging the gap. PB introduces the position that tests can provide information about behavior and personality.

Let me begin by making a behavioral analysis of test construction methods, in a manner that answers the question of why psychological tests can predict later behavior. Traditionally, tests are thought to predict behavior because they measure an unobservable process-entity of personality. Rather, tests can predict behavior because that is what they are constructed to do. That is, the test constructor first gathers a group of items. But in test construction only those items that do predict the behavior of interest are retained. Sometimes the test constructor first selects items without any justifying rationale. Sometimes, however, the test constructor first selects items that are believed to be measures of the personality trait. But this selection difference does not matter, for in both cases the test constructor discards and retains items on the basis of which ones relate to (predict) the behavior of interest.

The next question is why items are related to behaviors. Some, influenced by radical behaviorism, have assumed that the test item and the predicted behavior are, and should be, the same. However, in most cases that is not true. One real reason for item-behavior relationships is that the test measures an element of a BBR or the verbal labeling of that repertoire. For example, we would find that a group of people who affirmatively answered the item "I am an excellent athlete" would also display more athletic ability than would a group who answered negatively. The two behaviors are in the same repertoire. People generally learn to describe their own behavior with some accuracy (but there are variations in that respect).

It can also be the case that a test, because of how it was constructed, measures a BBR that is *necessary* for the learning of the predicted behavior. Intelligence tests are a prime example. Behavioral analysis of IQ test items reveals that many test whether the child has the language-cognitive elements. Most of the items, for example, test for the child's verbal-motor repertoire that is necessary for following instructions. Others test the number concept repertoire, the counting and other arithmetic repertoires, and the verbal-labeling repertoire. The manner in which items on the WPPSI (Wechsler, 1967) measure aspects of the sensorimotor repertoire has been described earlier. Why do such items predict later school performance? The answer is that the items measure basic behavioral repertoires the child *needs* to be successful in learning materials that are later presented in school. So the items correlate with school performance.

Other tests measure the emotional-motivational BBR. Consider an interest test. Constructing the test involves gathering a number of items together that are thought to represent a range of interests that are occupationally relevant. But the important part involves the standardization procedures. The items are given to different occupational groups, and those that distinguish the groups are retained and organized (keyed). When the test is used, it can be ascertained whether the individual answers the items in a manner that is like some particular occupational group. What does this mean in the PB analysis? The answer is that the items measure emotional responses (indicated, e.g., by like-dislike) to different life stimuli. So the individual's test responses reveal life stimuli to which the individual has positive and negative emotional responses. Remember that those life stimuli the individual likes or dislikes will also serve as positive or negative reinforcers and incentives. Thus, if the individual has emotional responses to life stimuli that are like people who are successful in some occupation, then the individual should be happy in that same work situation. Moreover, the individual should be reinforced by that work and be attracted to it incentively. That means that other things equal, the individual should work harder in the job, study relevant material more, and so on. That is why interest tests predict job success.

It is important to bridge the psychological testing–behaviorism gap, for unifying the two traditions produces new knowledge. For example, in terms of the present theory of personality, the various existent psychological tests are an invaluable source of knowledge for defining the basic behavioral repertoires. PB's basic experimental studies, developmental studies, and behavior therapy studies have been important avenues of definition. But the manner in which psychological tests have been constructed means that their items measure elements of BBRs that constitute aspects of personality. The extensive work of behaviorally analyzing the items of psychological tests can be expected to tell us much about the content of personality (see Staats, 1996). And, as indicated, those analyses will then yield directives for conducting research on how the BBRs involved are learned and how they function in producing the individual's behavior. We have already trained children to be more intelligent (Staats & Burns, 1981) by training them in basic behavioral repertoires. In addition, interest and values (see Staats, 1996) tests have been shown to measure aspects of the learned emotional-motivational BBR. Those findings merely open the way.

Other positive avenues of development emerge from the conceptual unification of tests and PB theory. For one thing, the unified theory enables us to understand what tests are. That should be valuable in constructing tests. The approach provides an avenue for defining in objective, stipulable terms just what personality is. That should be valuable in using tests, namely, that test items—not just total scores—when analyzed behaviorally, describe the content of personality traits of the individual. This conception of tests, moreover, says that tests can yield more than prediction; they can describe the contents of personality traits and thus the nature of the individual's BBR being measured. With study of how people come to learn those personality traits we will have knowledge on how to avoid doing things that will give children undesirable traits, while doing things to give them desirable traits. And behaviorally-analyzed tests will also give specific information regarding what remedial treatment needs to do.

Many studies are needed that analyze existing tests in terms of the behavioral repertoires they assess, as already demonstrated in PB experiments. With that knowledge tests could be compared to one another in a way that would make sense of the field. At present tests are independent entities; they are not related to each other. Many tests of different aspects of personality are actually redundant and share types of items (e.g., interest, values, and needs tests, on the one hand, and fears, anxiety, and stress tests, on the other).

The field of testing does not relate itself to the content areas of psychology or to personality theories. The analysis of tests in terms of BBRs provides a means for doing so. Studying how the repertoires on tests are learned and function will lead to studies that are relevant in different areas of psychology. There is a vast amount of research to be conducted within this framework. The results of that research will help organize the presently chaotic knowledge of the field. That research will help relate the field of testing to the other fields of psychology. That research will render theoretically meaningful many works that exist in this field. And the knowledge produced should also enable the field to construct better tests.

Abnormal Psychology

The PB position is that a theory of personality should contain principles and concepts for formulating a theory of abnormal psychology. Freud's psychoanalytic theory was composed to have that potentiality, and this was elaborated in others works. Radical behaviorism has not produced such a theory, nor has the traditional behavioral field.

Psychological behaviorism, however, began a new development in behaviorism when it analyzed the opposite speech of the schizophrenic patient (Staats, 1957). Not only was the abnormal symptom considered as a behavior, but the analysis also indicated how the symptom was learned and how it could be extinguished and replaced with normal behavior. In the early presentation of PB (see Staats, 1963) one chapter was devoted to further formulation of its theory of abnormal behavior. This theory was employed in the social learning theory of abnormal behavior (Bandura, 1968) and in later behavioral works of various kinds. However, the PB theory was developed a good deal further after its theory of personality was systematically formulated (Staats, 1975) and then further extended (Staats, 1989, 1996).

The PB theory of abnormal behavior follows the theory of personality schematized in Figure 6.1. However, each term in the causal circumstances can be normal or abnormal and result in abnormal behavior. With respect to biological conditions, O_1, O_2, and O_3 may be abnormal in some way. For example, because of organic conditions a child with Down syndrome does not learn normally and will display deficits in the BBRs and thus not behave normally in various life situations, such as school. The same is true of the O^2 and O^3. When they are abnormal, they will produce abnormal behavior.

In addition, the behavioral variables in the schematized theory of personality can be either normal or abnormal. In this case abnormal can mean either deficits in what should be or inappropriate conditions that should not occur. The original learning, for example, S_1, may be deficit or inappropriate and produce deficit or inappropriate BBRs that will result in deficit or inappropriate behavior in later situations such that the individual will be diagnosed as abnormal. The deficit or inappropriate conditions can also occur in S_2 and produce behavior that will be judged as abnormal.

The task is to analyze, for the various diagnostic categories, these various behavioral or organic conditions that produce abnormal behavior. Each such analysis constitutes a theory of the disorder involved that can be employed by therapists or parents. For example, if the deficit or inappropriate conditions occur at S_1, the analysis can be used to instruct parents how to see to it that the child does not develop abnormal BBRs. The analysis will also provide the practitioner with knowledge about how to correct the abnormal conditions and treat the behavior disorder after it has occurred. For example, PB works have presented analyses of developmental disorders, developmental reading disorder, autism, and mental retardation (Staats, 1996). In addition, PB theories of depression, the anxiety disorders (phobic disorder, generalized anxiety disorder, panic disorder, obsessive-compulsive disorder, and posttraumatic stress disorder) have also been presented. Various other behavior therapists have produced other analyses of behavior disorders that use elements from PB theory. However, typically they do not employ the full approach, and there remains a general need to stipulate the elements of abnormal BBRs further, how they are learned, and how they have their effects in a general theory of abnormal behavior.

The PB theory of abnormal behavior takes the position that traditional descriptions of categories of abnormal behavior (see DSM-IV; American Psychiatric Association, 1994) are valuable. PB analyses of behavior disorders yield extensive implications for research that PB suggests for the twenty-first century. So, in addition to those already made, many analyses of the various behavior disorders are needed. Such analyses need to be empirically verified, their implications for prevention and treatment assessed, and their implications for test construction exploited. Centrally, research is needed that gathers observations of the development of abnormal behavior through learning that, strangely enough, have never been made.

Application of the Personality Theory

From the beginning the PB position has been that basic and applied work should be closely related in psychology but presently are not. For example, the field of animal learning has ceased providing useful information to the various areas of human study because the field needs input from those areas concerning important things to study. As an example in the other direction, a personality theory in the PB view should have implications for the improvement of psychology's fields of practice. To illustrate, my own personal experience has exposed me to cases of disadvantageous parenting that resulted from following psychoanalytic theory or traditional developmental (biologically oriented) theory. Such cases of applied failure represent disconfirmation of the theory. A good theory should yield good applications. An important part of PB's development, thus, has been directed toward practice, as will be briefly mentioned.

Clinical Applications

The analysis of the opposite speech of the schizophrenic patient contained clinical directives. The analysis said that the opposite speech was learned and maintained via the inadvertent reinforcement provided by the professional staff (Staats, 1957). That analysis led directly to applications (Ayllon & Michael, 1959). As another example, PB's token reinforcer system was employed as the token economy in dealing with hospitalized psychotic patients (Ayllon & Azrin, 1968). Psychological behaviorism analyses and reinforcement methods have been used to train mentally retarded children (Bijou, 1965; Birnbrauer, Bijou, Wolf, & Kidder, 1965) and autistic children (Lovaas, 1977), to toilet train children (Azrin & Foxx, 1974), and to treat juvenile delinquents in different settings (see Staats & Butterfield, 1965; Wolf, et al., 1976). Wolf, Risely, and Mees (1964) used the PB approach of working in the naturalistic situation, including PB's time-out procedure, in their seminal study to treat an autistic child's behavior problems. Many of the other extensions of PB's methods, as suggested for a wide variety of children's problems (see Staats, 1963; Staats & Butterfield, 1965; Staats & Staats, 1962) were accomplished by others, creating the body of works contributed to the establishment of the field of behavior analysis. As another example, the PB theory of language provided a basis for understanding why traditional verbal psychotherapy could be used to change behavior therapeutically laying a foundation for the field of cognitive behavior therapy (Staats, 1972). Radical behaviorism, however, rejected for some 16 years. Finally, verbal therapy was later accepted as though it were a derivative of radical behaviorism (Hamilton, 1988; Hayes & Wilson, 1994). Additional projections of clinical research and treatment have been outlined based on the additional developments of PB (Staats, 1996, chap. 8).

Educational Psychology Applications

The PB research on reading and treatment of nonreading has already been mentioned. Reading was conceptualized as a later elaboration of the language-cognitive BBR. Learned on the foundation of the repertoires of language, it is a complex repertoire that requires long-term training and a huge number of training trials. The subrepertoires of reading, when they have been acquired, serve various learning functions for the individual in later school learning (Staats, 1975). The PB theory of reading focuses on this extensive learning and denies the existence of biological defects responsible for learning disabilities such as dyslexia because the children have normal intelligence, which means normal language BBRs. PB research and analysis thus states the definitive principle that if the child has developed normal language, then the child has all the cognitive ability needed to learn reading perfectly well because no additional abilities are required for reading (see Staats, 1975).

Dyslexia arises because there is inadequate reinforcement to maintain the child's attention and participation in the long task. I designed the token reinforcer system to solve the motivation problem by providing reinforcement for the child's attention and participation. The system works widely, as shown by its use in the multitude of studies and programs designed to treat reading and other developmental academic disorders (see Burns & Kondrick, 1998; Sulzer-Azeroff & Mayer, 1986). The Sylvan Learning Centers enterprise by its use of the token reinforcer system validates the system as well as the PB theories of developmental academic disorders (see Staats, 1963, 1968, 1975, 1996). The PB theories of the various academic repertoires (reading, writing, counting, number operations, math) provide the foundation for deriving a large body of additional research to understand school learning and to solve the problems of school learning. The educational field's absorption with cognitive psychology stands in the way of the vast research and application that would advance education so much.

CONCLUSION

The PB theory of personality is set in a general theory that goes from the study of basic learning, including the biology of that learning, through the multiple levels of study that provide its principles and concepts. The theory of personality, thus, is sunk into general psychology, making connections to various fields in psychology. It is specific, objective, and empirical. It draws widely on various areas of study, and it has implications for conducting large amounts of additional research and application in various areas and fields of study. The theory provides a philosophy of science and methodology of theory construction. This is the only theory of personality that claims it can be employed to establish or to change personality, a claim that if fulfilled would have enormous importance. It is the only theory that is unified and has comprehensive scope—sorely needed developments for the field and psychology generally. It is a theory that ties together personality and personality measurement on a broad front. And it projects new areas and topics of research. An important need for the twenty-first century is to compare this theory with others as part of the general comparison and evaluation of personality theories called for by PB. Another is to exploit the theory in the various areas of theoretical analysis and empirical research it suggests.

REFERENCES

American Psychiatric Association. (1994). *Diagnostic and statistical manual of mental disorders* (4th ed.). Washington, DC: Author.

Ayllon, T. & Azrin, N. H. (1968). *The token economy.* New York: Appleton-Century-Crofts.

Ayllon, T., & Michael, J. (1959). The psychiatric nurse as a behavioral engineer. *Journal of the Experimental Analysis of Behavior, 2,* 323–334.

Azrin, N. H., & Foxx, R. M. (1974). *Toilet training in less than a day.* New York: Simon and Schuster.

Bandura, A. (1968). A social learning interpretation of psychological dysfunction. In P. London & D. Rosenhan (Eds.), *Foundations of abnormal psychology.* New York: Holt, Rinehart, and Winston.

Bijou, S. (1965). Experimental studies of child behavior, normal and deviant. In L. Krasner & L. P. Ullman (Eds.), *Research in behavior modification* (pp. 56–81). New York: Holt, Rinehart, and Winston.

Birnbrauer, J. S., Bijou, S. W., Wolf, M. M., & Kidder, J. D. (1965). Programmed instruction in the classroom. In L. Krasner & L. P. Ullmann (Eds.), *Case studies in behavior modification* (pp. 358–363). New York: Holt, Rinehart, and Winston.

Burns, G. L., & Kondrick, P. A. (1998). Psychological behaviorism's reading therapy program: Parents as reading therapists for their children reading disability. *Journal of Learning Disabilities, 31,* 278–285.

Dahlstrom, W. G., & Welsh, G. S. (1960). *An MMPI handbook: A guide for use in clinical practice and research.* Minneapolis: University of Minnesota Press.

Dollard, J., & Miller, N. E. (1950). *Personality and psychotherapy.* New York: McGraw-Hill.

Eysenck, H. J. (Ed.). (1960). Behavior therapy and the neuroses. New York: Pergamon Press.

Fordyce, E. E. (1990). Learned pain: Pain as behavior. In J. J. Bonica (Ed.), *The management of pain* (2nd ed., pp. 291–300). Philadelphia: Lea Febiger.

Hamburg, S. R. (2000). Review of *Handbook of personality: Theory and research. Child and Family Behavior Therapy, 22,* 62–66.

Hamilton, S. A. (1988). Behavioral formulation of verbal behavior in psychotherapy. *Clinical Psychology Review, 8,* 181–194.

Hayes, S. C., & Wilson, K. G. (1994). Acceptance and commitment therapy: Altering the verbal support for experiential avoidance. *Behavior Analyst, 17,* 289–303.

Hull, C. L. (1943). Principles of behavior. New York: Appleton-Century-Crofts.

Judson, A. J., Cofer, C. N., & Gelfand, S. (1956). Reasoning as an associative process. II. "Direction" in problem solving as a function of prior reinforcement of relevant responses. *Psychological Reports, 2,* 501–507.

Lovaas, O. I. (1977). *The autistic child.* New York: Irvington.

MacPhillamy, D., & Lewinsohn, P. (1971). *The pleasant events schedule.* Eugene: University of Oregon Press.

Malott, R. W., Whaley, D. L., & Malott, M. E. (1997). *Elementary principles of behavior.* Upper Saddle River, NJ: Prentice Hall.

Mischel, W. (1968). *Personality and assessment.* New York: Wiley.

Mischel, W. (1973). Toward a cognitive social learning reconceptualization of personality. *Psychological Review, 80,* 252–283.

Raymond, M. J. (1960). Case of fetishism treated by aversion therapy. In H. J. Eysenck (Ed.), *Behaviour therapy and the neuroses* (pp. 208–217). New York: Pergamon Press.

Rotter, J. (1954). *Social learning and clinical psychology.* New York: Prentice Hall.

Silva, F. (1993). *Psychometric foundations of behavioral assessment.* New York: Sage.

Skinner, B. F. (1969). *Contingencies of reinforcement.* New York: Appleton-Century-Crofts.

Spence, K. W. (1944). The nature of theory construction in contemporary psychology. *Psychological Review, 51,* 47–68.

Staats, A. W. (1957). Learning theory and 'opposite speech.' *Journal of Abnormal and Social Psychology, 55,* 268–269.

Staats, A. W. (1963). *Complex human behavior.* New York: Holt, Rinehart, and Winston.

Staats, A. W. (1968). *Learning, language, and cognition.* New York: Holt, Rinehart, and Winston.

Staats, A. W. (1971). *Child learning, intelligence and personality.* New York: Harper and Rowe.

Staats, A. W. (1972). Language behavior therapy. *Behavior Therapy, 3,* 165–192.

Staats, A. W. (1975). *Social behaviorism.* Homewood, IL: Dorsey Press.

Staats, A. W. (1989). *Personality and abnormal behavior.* Unpublished manuscript.

Staats, A. W. (1996). *Behavior and personality.* New York: Springer.

Staats, A. W., & Burns, G. L. (1981). Intelligence and child development: What intelligence is, how it is learned, and functions. *Genetic Psychology Monographs, 104,* 237–301.

Staats, A. W., & Butterfield, W. H. (1965). Treatment of non-reading in a culturally-deprived juvenile delinquent: An application of reinforcement principles. *Child Development, 36,* 925–942.

Staats, A. W., Finley, J. R., Minke, K. A., & Wolf, M. M. (1964). Reinforcement variables in the control of unit reading responses. *Journal of the Experimental Analysis of Behavior, 7,* 139–149.

Staats, A. W., & Staats, C. K. (1958). Attitudes established by classical conditioning. *Journal of Abnormal and Social Psychology, 57,* 37–40.

Staats, A. W., & Staats, C. K. (1962). Comparisons of the development of speech and reading with implications for research. *Child Development, 33,* 841–846.

Sulzer-Azeroff, B., & Mayer, G. R. (1986). *Achieving educational excellence and behavioral strategies.* New York: Holt, Rinehart, and Winston.

Terman, L. M., & Merrill, M. A. (1937). *Measuring intelligence.* Boston: Houghton Mifflin.

Tyler, F. B., Dhawan, N., & Sinha, Y. (1989). Cultural contributions to constructing locus of control attributions. *Genetic, Social, and General Psychology Monographs, 115,* 205–220.

Wechsler, D. (1967). *Wechsler Preschool and Primary Scale of Intelligence.* New York: Psychological Corporation.

Wolf, M. M., Phillips, E. L., Fixsen, D. I., Braukmann, C. J., Kirigin, K. A., Willner, A. G., & Schumaker, J. B. (1976). Achievement place: The teaching family model. *Child Care Quarterly, 5,* 92–101.

Wolf, M. M., Risely, T., & Mees, H. (1964). Application of operant conditioning procedures to the behavior problems of an autistic child. *Behavior Research and Therapy, 1,* 305–312.

CHAPTER 7

Cognitive-Experiential Self-Theory of Personality

SEYMOUR EPSTEIN

Cognitive-experiential self-theory (CEST) is a broadly integrative theory of personality that is compatible with a variety of other theories, including psychodynamic theories, learning theories, phenomenological self-theories, and modern cognitive scientific views on information processing. CEST achieves its integrative power primarily through three assumptions. The first is that people process information by two independent, interactive conceptual systems, a preconscious *experiential system* and a conscious *rational system.* By introducing a new view of the unconscious in the form of an experiential system, CEST is able to explain almost everything that psychoanalysis can and much that it cannot, and it is able to do so in a scientifically much more defensible manner. The second assumption is that the experiential system is emotionally driven. This assumption permits CEST to integrate the passionate phallus-and-tooth unconscious of psychoanalysis with the "kinder, gentler" affect-free unconscious of cognitive science (Epstein, 1994). The third assumption is that four

basic needs, each of which is assumed in other theories to be the one most fundamental need, are equally important according to CEST.

In this chapter, I review the basic assumptions of CEST, summarize the research conducted to test the theory, and note the implications of the theory for research and psychotherapy.

TWO INFORMATION-PROCESSING SYSTEMS

According to CEST, humans operate by two fundamental information-processing systems: a rational system and an experiential system. The two systems operate in parallel and are interactive. CEST has nothing new to say about the rational system, other than to emphasize the degree to which it is influenced by the experiential system. CEST does have a great deal to say about the experiential system. In effect, CEST introduces a new system of unconscious processing in the experiential system that is a substitute for the unconscious system in psychoanalysis. Although like psychoanalysis, CEST emphasizes the unconscious, it differs from psychoanalysis in its conception of how the unconscious operates. Before proceeding further, it should be noted that the word *rational* as used in the *rational system* refers to a set of

This chapter includes material from several other chapters and articles as well as new information. The research reported here was supported by National Institute of Mental Health (NIMH) Research Grant MH 01293 and NIMH Research Scientist Award 5 KO5 MH 00363.

analytical principles and has no implications with respect to the reasonableness of the behavior, which is an alternative meaning of the word.

It is assumed in CEST that everyone, like it or not, automatically constructs an implicit theory of reality that includes a self-theory, a world-theory, and connecting propositions. An implicit theory of reality consists of a hierarchical organization of schemas. Toward the apex of the conceptual structure are highly general, abstract schemas, such as that the self is worthy, people are trustworthy, and the world is orderly and good. Because of their abstractness, generality, and their widespread connections with schematic networks throughout the system, these broad schemas are normally highly stable and not easily invalidated. However, should they be invalidated, the entire system would be destabilized. Evidence that this actually occurs is provided by the profound disorganization following unassimilable experiences in acute schizophrenic reactions (Epstein, 1979a). At the opposite end of the hierarchy are narrow, situation-specific schemas. Unlike the broad schemas, the narrower ones are readily susceptible to change, and their changes have little effect on the stability of the personality structure. Thus, the hierarchical structure of the implicit theory allows it to be stable at the center and flexible at the periphery. It is important to recognize that unlike other theories that propose specific implicit or heuristic rules of information processing, it is assumed in CEST that the experiential system is an organized, adaptive system, rather than simply a number of unrelated constructs or so-called cognitive shortcuts (e.g., Tversky & Kahneman, 1974). As it is assumed in CEST that the experiential system in humans is the same system by which nonhuman animals adapt to their environments, it follows that nonhuman animals also have an organized model of the world that is capable of disorganization. Support for this assumption is provided by the widespread dysfunctional behavior that is exhibited in animals when they are exposed to emotionally significant unassimilable events (e.g., Pavlov, 1941).

Unlike nonhuman animals, humans have a conscious, explicit theory of reality in their rational system in addition to the model of reality in their experiential system. The two theories of reality coincide to different degrees, varying among individuals and situations.

Comparison of the Operating Principles of the Two Systems

The experiential system in humans is the same system with which other higher order animals have adapted to their environments over millions of years of evolution. It adapts by learning from experience rather than by logical inference,

TABLE 7.1 Comparison of the Experiential and Rational Systems

Experiential System	Rational System
1. Holistic.	1. Analytic.
2. Emotional; pleasure-pain oriented (what feels good).	2. Logical; reason oriented (what is sensible).
3. Associationistic connections.	3. Cause-and-effect connections.
4. Outcome oriented.	4. Process oriented.
5. Behavior mediated by vibes from past experience.	5. Behavior mediated by conscious appraisal of events.
6. Encodes reality in concrete images, metaphors, and narratives.	6. Encodes reality in abstract symbols, words, and numbers.
7. More rapid processing; oriented toward immediate action.	7. Slower processing; oriented toward delayed action.
8. Slower to change; changes with repetitive or intense experience.	8. Changes more rapidly; changes with speed of thought.
9. More crudely differentiated; broad generalization gradient; categorical thinking.	9. More highly differentiated; dimensional thinking.
10. More crudely integrated; dissociative, organized in part by emotional complexes (cognitive-affective modules).	10. More highly integrated.
11. Experienced passively and preconsciously; seized by our emotions.	11. Experienced actively and consciously; in control of our thoughts.
12. Self-evidently valid: "Seeing is believing."	12. Requires justification via logic and evidence.

Note. Adapted from Cognitive-experiential self-theory: An integrative theory of personality by S. Epstein, 1991, in R. C. Curtis, editor, *The relational self: Theoretical convergences in psychoanalysis and social psychology,* New York: Guilford. Adapted by permission.

which is the exclusive domain of the rational system. The experiential system operates in a manner that is preconscious, automatic, rapid, effortless, holistic, concrete, associative, primarily nonverbal, and minimally demanding of cognitive resources (see Table 7.1 for a more complete comparison of the two systems). It encodes information in two ways: as memories of individual events, particularly events that were experienced as highly emotionally arousing, and also in a more abstract, general way.

Although the experiential system is a cognitive system, its operation is intimately related to the experience of affect. It is, in fact, inconceivable that a conceptual system that learns from experience would not be used to facilitate positive affect and avoid negative affect. According to CEST, the experiential system both influences and is influenced by affect. Not only does the experiential system direct behavior in a manner anticipated to achieve pleasurable outcomes and to avoid unpleasurable ones, but the cognitions themselves are influenced by affect. As noted previously, the experiential conceptual system, according to CEST, is emotionally driven. After this is recognized, it follows that the affect-free unconscious proposed by cognitive scientists is untenable. The automatic, preconscious experiential conceptual system that regulates everyday behavior is of necessity an emotionally driven, dynamic unconscious system. Because affect determines what is attended to and what is reinforced, without affect there would be neither schemas nor motivation in the experiential system, and, therefore, no experiential system. It follows that CEST is as much an emotional as a cognitive theory.

In contrast to the experiential system, the rational system is an inferential system that operates according to a person's understanding of the rules of reasoning and of evidence, which are mainly culturally transmitted. The rational system, unlike the experiential system, has a very brief evolutionary history. It operates in a manner that is conscious, analytical, effortful, relatively slow, affect-free, and highly demanding of cognitive resources (see Table 7.1).

Which system is superior? At first thought, it might seem that it must be the rational system. After all, the rational system, with its use of language, is a much more recent evolutionary development than is the experiential system, and it is unique to the human species. Moreover, it is capable of much higher levels of abstraction and complexity than is the experiential system, and it makes possible planning, long-term delay of gratification, complex generalization and discrimination, and comprehension of cause-and-effect relations. These attributes of the rational system have been the source of humankind's remarkable scientific and technological achievements. Moreover, the rational system can understand the operation of the experiential system, whereas the reverse is not true.

On the other side of the coin, carefully consider the following question: If you could have only one system, which would you choose? Without question, the only reasonable choice is the experiential system. You could exist with an experiential system without a rational system, as the existence of nonhuman animals testifies, but you could not exist with only a rational system. Even mundane activities such as crossing a street would be excessively burdensome if you had to rely exclusively on conscious reasoning. Imagine having to estimate your walking speed relative to that of approaching vehicles so that you could determine when to cross a street. Moreover, without a system guided by affect, you might not even be able to decide whether you should cross the street. Given enough alternative activities to consider, you might remain lost in contemplation at the curb forever.

The experiential system also has other virtues, including the ability to solve some kinds of problems that the rational system cannot. For example, by reacting holistically, the experiential system can respond adaptively to real-life problems that are too complex to be analyzed into their components. Also, there are important lessons in living that can be learned directly from experience and that elude articulation and logical analysis. Moreover, as our research has demonstrated, the experiential system is more strongly associated with the ability to establish rewarding interpersonal relationships, with creativity, and with empathy than is the rational system (Norris & Epstein, 2000b). Most important is that the experiential system has demonstrated its adaptive value over millions of years of evolution, whereas the rational system has yet to prove itself and may yet be the source of the destruction of the human species as well as all other life on earth.

Fortunately, there is no need to choose between the systems. Each has its advantages and disadvantages, and the advantages of one can offset the limitations of the other. Besides, we have no choice in the matter. We are they, and they are us. Where we do have a choice is in improving our ability to use each and to use them in a complementary manner. As much as we might wish to suppress the experiential system in order to be rational, it is no more possible to accomplish this than to stop breathing because the air is polluted. Rather than achieving control by denying the experiential system, we lose control when we attempt to do so: By being unaware of its operation, we are unable to take its influence into account. When we are in touch with the processing of the experiential system, we can consciously decide whether to heed or discount its influence. Moreover, if, in addition, we understand its operation, we can begin to take steps to improve it by providing it with corrective experiences.

How the Experiential System Operates

As noted, the operation of the experiential system is intimately associated with the experience of affect. For want of a better word, I shall use the word *vibes* to refer to vague feelings that may exist only dimly (if at all) in a person's consciousness. Stating that vibes often operate outside of awareness is not meant to imply that people cannot become aware of them. Vibes are a subset of feelings, which include other feelings that are more easily articulated than vibes, such as those that accompany standard emotions. Examples of negative vibes are vague feelings of agitation, irritation, tension, disquietude, queasiness, edginess, and apprehension. Examples of positive vibes are vague feelings of well-being, gratification, positive anticipation, calmness, and light-heartedness.

When a person responds to an emotionally significant event, the sequence of reactions is as follows: The experiential system automatically and instantaneously searches its memory banks for related events. The recalled memories and feelings influence the course of further processing and of behavioral tendencies. If the recalled feelings are positive, the person automatically thinks and has tendencies to act in ways anticipated to reproduce the feelings. If the recalled feelings are negative, the person automatically thinks and has tendencies to act in ways anticipated to avoid experiencing the feelings. As this sequence of events occurs instantaneously and automatically, people are normally unaware of its operation. Seeking to understand their behavior, they usually succeed in finding an acceptable explanation. Insofar as they can manage it without too seriously violating reality considerations, they will also find the most emotionally satisfying explanation possible. This process of finding an explanation in the rational system for what was determined primarily by the experiential system and doing so in a manner that is emotionally acceptable corresponds to what is normally referred to as rationalization. According to CEST, such rationalization is a routine process that occurs far more often than is generally recognized. Accordingly, the influences of the experiential system on the rational system and its subsequent rationalization are regarded, in CEST, as major sources of human irrationality.

The Four Basic Needs

Almost all of the major theories of personality propose a single, most basic need. CEST considers the four most often proposed needs as equally basic. It is further assumed in CEST that their interaction plays an important role in behavior and can account for paradoxical reactions that have eluded explanation by other theoretical formulations.

Identification of the Four Basic Needs

In classical Freudian theory, before the introduction of the death instinct, the one most basic need was the pleasure principle, which refers to the desire to maximize pleasure and minimize pain (Freud, 1900/1953). Most learning theorists make a similar implicit assumption in their view of what constitutes reinforcement (e.g., Dollard & Miller, 1950). For other theorists, such as object-relations theorists, most notably Bowlby (1988), the most fundamental need is the need for relatedness. For Rogers (1951) and other phenomenological psychologists, it is the need to maintain the stability and coherence of a person's conceptual system. For Allport (1961) and Kohut (1971), it is the need to enhance self-esteem. (For a more thorough discussion of these views, see Epstein, 1993.) Which of these views is correct? From the perspective of CEST, they are all correct, because each of the needs is basic—but they are also all incorrect because of their failure to recognize that the other needs are equally fundamental. They are equally fundamental in the sense that each can dominate the others.

Moreover, there are equally serious consequences, including disorganization of the entire personality structure, when any one of the needs is insufficiently fulfilled.

Interactions Among the Basic Needs

Given four equally important needs that can operate simultaneously, it follows that behavior is determined by the combined influence of those needs that are activated in a particular situation. An important adaptive consequence of such influence is that the needs serve as checks and balances against each other. When any need is fulfilled at the expense of the others, the intensity of the others increases, thereby increasing the motivation to satisfy the other needs. However, under certain circumstances the frustration of a need may be so great that frustration of the other needs is disregarded, which can have serious maladaptive consequences. As is shown next, these assumptions about the interaction of basic needs can resolve some important, otherwise paradoxical findings.

The finding that normal people characteristically have unrealistic self-enhancing and optimistic biases (Taylor & Brown, 1988) has evoked considerable interest because it appears to contradict the widely held assumption that reality awareness is an important criterion of mental health. From the perspective of CEST, this finding does not indicate that reality awareness is a false criterion of mental health, but only that it is not the only criterion. According to CEST, a compromise occurs between the need to realistically assimilate the data of reality into a stable, coherent conceptual system and the need to enhance self-esteem. The result is a modest self-enhancing bias that is not unduly unrealistic. It suggests that normal individuals tend to give themselves the benefit of the doubt in situations in which the cost of slight inaccuracy is outweighed by the gain in positive feelings about the self. Note that this assumes that the basic need for a favorable pleasure-pain balance is also involved in the compromise.

There are more and less effective ways of balancing basic needs. A balance that is achieved among equally unfulfilled competing needs is a prescription for chronic distress—not good adjustment. Whereas poorly adjusted people tend to fulfill their basic needs in a conflictual manner, well-adjusted people fulfill their basic needs in a synergistic manner, in which the fulfillment of one need contributes to rather than conflicts with the fulfillment of the other needs. They thereby maintain a stable conceptual system, a favorable pleasure-pain balance, rewarding interpersonal relationships, and a high level of self-esteem.

Let us first consider an example of a person who balances her basic needs in a synergistic manner and then consider an opposite example. Mary is an emotionally stable, happy person with high self-esteem who establishes warm, rewarding relationships with others. She derives pleasure from helping others. This contributes to her self-esteem, as she is proud of her helpful behavior and others admire and appreciate her for it. As a result, Mary's behavior also contributes to favorable relationships with others. Thus, Mary satisfies all her basic needs in a harmonious manner.

Now, consider a person who fulfills his basic needs in a conflictual manner. Ralph is an unhappy, unstable person with low self-esteem who establishes poor relationships with others. Because of his low self-esteem, Ralph derives pleasure from defeating others and behaving in other ways that make him feel momentarily superior. Not surprisingly, this alienates people, so he has no close friends. Because of his low self-esteem and poor relationships with others, he anticipates rejection, from which he protects himself by maintaining a distance from people. His low self-esteem and poor relationships with others contribute to feelings of being unworthy of love as well as to an unfavorable pleasure-pain balance. Because his conceptual system is failing to fulfill its function of directing his behavior in a manner that fulfills his basic needs, it is under the stress of potential disorganization, which he experiences in the form of anxiety. The more his need for enhancing his self-esteem is thwarted, the more he acts in a self-aggrandizing manner, which exacerbates his problems with respect to fulfilling his other basic needs.

Imbalances in the Basic Needs as Related to Specific Psychopathologies

Specific imbalances among the basic needs are associated with specific mental disorders. For present purposes, it will suffice to present some of the more obvious examples.

Paranoia with delusions of grandeur can be understood as a compensatory reaction to threats to self-esteem. In a desperate attempt to buoy up self-esteem, paranoid individuals disregard their other needs. They sacrifice their need to maintain a favorable pleasure-pain balance because their desperate need to maintain their elevated self-esteem is continuously threatened. They sacrifice their need to maintain relationships because their grandiose behavior alienates others who do not appreciate being treated as inferiors and who are repelled by their unrealistic views. The situation is somewhat more complicated with respect to their need to realistically assimilate the data of reality into a coherent, stable, conceptual system. They sacrifice the reality aspect of this need but not the coherence aspect. In both of these respects they are similar to paranoid individuals with delusions of persecution, considered in the next example.

Paranoia with delusions of persecution can be understood as a desperate attempt to defend the stability of a person's conceptual system and, to a lesser extent, to enhance self-esteem.

By viewing their problems in living as resulting from persecution by others, paranoid people with delusions of persecution can focus all their attention and resources on defending themselves. Such focus and mobilization provide a highly unifying state that serve as an effective defense against disorganization. Delusions of persecution also contribute to self-esteem because the perception of the persecutors as powerful or prestigious, which is invariably the case, implies that the target of the persecution must also be important. The basic needs that are sacrificed are the pleasure principle, as being persecuted is a terrifying experience, and the need for relatedness, as others are either viewed as enemies or repelled by the unrealistic behavior.

Schizophrenic disorganization can be understood as the best bargain available for preventing extreme misery under desperate circumstances in which fulfillment of the basic needs is seriously threatened. Ultimate disorganization is a state devoid of conceptualization and (relatedly) therefore of feelings. Although its anticipation is dreaded, its occurrence corresponds to a state of nonbeing, a void in which there are neither pleasant nor unpleasant feelings (Jefferson, 1974). Thus, what is gained is a net improvement in the pleasure-pain balance (from a negative to a zero value). What is sacrificed are the needs to maintain the stability of the conceptual system, to maintain relatedness, and to enhance self-esteem.

The Four Basic Beliefs

The four basic needs give rise to four corresponding basic beliefs, which are among the most central constructs in a personal theory of reality. They therefore play a very important role in determining how people think, feel, and behave in the world. Moreover, as previously noted, because of their dominant and central position and their influence on an entire network of lower-order beliefs, should any of them be invalidated, the entire conceptual system would be destabilized. Anticipation of such disorganization would be accompanied by overwhelming anxiety. The disorganization, should it occur (as previously noted) would correspond to an acute schizophrenic reaction.

The question may be raised as to how the four basic needs give rise to the development of four basic beliefs. Needs, or motives, in the experiential system, unlike those in the rational systems, always include an affective component. They therefore determine what is important to a person at the experiential level and what a person is spontaneously motivated to pursue or avoid. Positive affect is experienced whenever a need is fulfilled, and negative affect is experienced whenever the fulfillment of a need is frustrated. Because people wish to experience positive affect and to avoid negative affect, they automatically attend to whatever is associated with the fulfillment or frustration of a basic need. As a result, they develop implicit beliefs associated with each of the basic needs. Let us examine this idea in greater detail.

Depending on a person's history in fulfilling the need to maximize pleasure and minimize pain, a person tends to develop a basic belief about the world along a dimension varying from benign to malevolent. Thus, if a person experienced an environment that was predominantly a source of pleasure and security, the person will most likely develop the basic belief that the world is a good place in which to live. If a person has the opposite experiences, the person will tend to develop the opposite basic belief. The basic belief about the benignity versus malevolence of the world is the core of a network of related beliefs, including optimistic versus pessimistic views about future events.

Corresponding to the basic need to represent the data of reality in a stable and coherent conceptual system is a basic belief about the world that varies along a dimension of meaningful versus meaningless. Included in the network of related beliefs are beliefs about the predictability, controllability, and justness of the world versus its unpredictability, uncontrollability, and lack of justice. Corresponding to the basic need for relatedness is a basic belief about people that varies along a dimension from helpful and trustworthy to dangerous and untrustworthy. Included in the network of related beliefs are beliefs about the degree to which people are loving versus rejecting and trustworthy versus untrustworthy. Corresponding to the basic need for self-enhancement is a basic belief about the self that varies along a dimension from worthy to unworthy. Included in the network of related beliefs are beliefs about how competent, moral, worthy of love, and strong the self is compared to how incompetent, immoral, unworthy of love, and weak it is.

Interaction of the Experiential and Rational Systems

As previously noted, according to CEST, the experiential and rational systems operate in parallel and are interactive.

The Influence of the Experiential System on the Rational System

As the experiential system is the more rapidly reacting system, it is able to bias subsequent processing in the rational system. Because it operates automatically and preconsciously, its influence normally occurs outside of awareness. As noted previously, this prompts people to search for an explanation in their conscious rational system, which often results in rationalization. Thus, even when people believe their thinking is completely rational, it is often biased by their experiential processing.

The biases that influence conscious, rational thinking in everyday life are, for the most part, adaptive, as the experiential system operates according to schemas learned from past experience. In some situations, however, the experientially determined biases and their subsequent rationalizations are highly maladaptive. An extreme case is the life-long pursuit of "false goals." Such goals are false in the sense that their achievement is followed by disappointment and sadness, rather than by the anticipated happiness, enhanced self-esteem, or security that was the reason for their pursuit. It is noteworthy that the achievement of a false goal is experientially disappointing although at the rational level, it is viewed as a significant achievement about which the individual is proud. The following passage from Tolstoi (1887), in which he describes his thoughts during a period of depression, provides a poignant example of such a reaction:

When I thought of the fame which my works had gained me, I used to say to myself, 'Well, what if I should be more famous than Gogol, Pushkin, Shakespeare, Moliere—than all the writers of the world—well, and what then? I could find no reply. Such questions demand an answer, and an immediate one; without one it is impossible to live, but answer there was none.

My life had come to a sudden stop. I was able to breathe, to eat, to drink, to sleep. I could not, indeed, help doing so; but there was no real life in me. I had not a single wish to strive for the fulfillment of what I could feel to be reasonable. If I wished for something, I knew beforehand, that were I to satisfy the wish, nothing would come of it, I should still be dissatisfied.

Such was the condition I had come to, at the time when all the circumstances of my life were preeminently happy ones, and when I had not yet reached my fiftieth year. I had a good, a loving, and a well-beloved wife, good children, a fine estate, which, without much trouble on my part, continually increased my income; I was more than ever respected by my friends and acquaintances; I was praised by strangers, and could lay claim to having made my name famous . . .

The mental state in which I then was seemed to me summed up into the following: my life was a foolish and wicked joke played on me by I knew not whom . . .

Had I simply come to know that life has no meaning, I could have quietly accepted it as my allotted position. I could not, however, remain thus unmoved. Had I been like a man in a wood, about which he knows that there is no issue, I could have lived on; but I was like a man lost in a wood, and, who, terrified by the thought, rushes about trying to find a way out, and though he knows each step can only lead him farther astray, can not help running backwards and forwards.

Two features of Tolstoi's situation are of particular interest. One is that he experiences deep despair after achieving his life goals. This suggests that his achievements, although viewed as successes in his rational system, failed to fulfill a basic need or needs in his experiential system. His success, therefore, can be said to be success at the rational level but failure at the experiential level. This raises the question of what the deeply frustrated need in his experiential system might be. In the absence of additional information, it is, of course, impossible to know, and one can only speculate. One possibility within the framework of CEST is that the frustrated need was for unconditional love in early childhood. Such a need, of course, cannot be satisfied by material rewards or accomplishments.

The other interesting observation is that Tolstoi is distressed not only because of his feelings of emptiness and meaninglessness, but that, try as he might, he cannot solve the problem of why he should be unhappy when all the conditions of his life suggest that he should be happy. It follows from CEST that the reason he cannot solve his problem, despite his considerable intelligence and motivation, is that he believes it exists in his rational system when in fact it exists in his experiential system. Moreover, assuming the speculation about frustration of unconditional love in childhood is true, its early, preverbal occurrence and its remoteness from the kinds of motives normally present in the rational systems of adults can help account for Tolstoi's inability to articulate the source of his distress.

The influence of the experiential system on the rational system can be positive as well as negative. As an associative system, the experiential system can be a source of creativity by suggesting ideas that would not otherwise be available to the linear-processing rational system. Because the experiential system is a learning system, it can be a source of useful information, which can be incorporated into the rational system. Most important is that the experiential system can provide a source of passion for the rational system that it would otherwise lack. The result is that intellectual pursuits can be pursued with heart, rather than as dispassionate intellectual exercises.

The Influence of the Rational System on the Experiential System

As the slower system, the rational system is in a position to correct the experiential system. It is common for people to reflect on their spontaneous, impulsive thoughts, recognize they are inappropriate, and then substitute more constructive ones. For example, in a flash of anger an employee may have the thought that he would like to tell off his boss, but on further reflection may decide this course of action would be most unwise. To investigate this process, we conducted an experiment in which people were asked to list the first three thoughts that came to mind in response to reading a variety of provocative situations. The first thought was often counterproductive and

in the mode of the experiential system, whereas the third thought was usually corrective and in the mode of the rational system.

The rational system can also influence the experiential system by providing the understanding that allows a person to train the experiential system so that its initial reactions are more appropriate. That is, by understanding the operating principles of the experiential system as well as its schemas, it is possible to determine how that system can be improved; this can be accomplished in a variety of ways, the most obvious of which is by disputing the maladaptive thoughts in the experiential system, a procedure widely utilized by cognitive therapists. As the experiential system learns directly from experience, another procedure is to provide real-life corrective experiences. A third procedure is to utilize imagery, fantasy, and narratives for providing corrective experiences vicariously.

The rational system can influence the experiential system in automatic, unintentional ways as well as by its intentional employment. As the experiential system operates in an associative manner, thoughts in the rational system can trigger associations and thereby emotions in the experiential system. For example, a student attempting to solve a mathematics word problem may react to the content with conscious thoughts that produce associations in the experiential system; the associations then elicit emotional reactions that interfere with performance. In this illustration, we have an interesting cycle of the rational system's influencing the experiential system, which in turn influences the rational system.

Another unintentional way in which the rational system can influence the experiential system is through repetition of thoughts or behavior in the rational system. Through such repetition, thoughts and behavior that were originally under rational control can become habitualized or *proceduralized,* with the control shifting from the rational to the experiential system (Smith & DeCoster, 2000). An obvious advantage to this shift in control is that the thought and behavior require fewer cognitive resources and can occur without conscious awareness. Potential disadvantages are that the habitual thoughts and behavior are under reduced volitional control and are more difficult to change. Although this can be desirable for certain constructive thoughts and behaviors, it is problematic when the thoughts and behavior are counterproductive.

The Lower and Higher Reaches of the Experiential System

The experiential system operates at different levels of complexity. Classical conditioning is an example of the operation of the experiential system at its simplest level. In classical conditioning, a conditioned, neutral stimulus (the CS), such as a tone, precedes an unconditioned stimulus (the UCS), such as food. Over several trials, a connection is formed between the conditioned and unconditioned stimulus, so that the conditioned stimulus evokes a conditioned response (the CR), such as salivation, that originally occurred only to the UCS. This process illustrates the operation of several of the attributes of the experiential system, including associative processing, automatic processing, increased strength of learning over trials, affective influence (e.g., emotional significance of the UCS), and arbitrary outcome-orientation (e.g., reacting to the CS independent of its causal relation to the UCS). The CS is also responded to holistically, as the animal reacts not only to the tone, but to the entire laboratory context.

A more complex operating level of the experiential system is exhibited in heuristic processing. In an article that has had a widespread influence on understanding decisional processes, Tversky and Kahneman (1974) introduced the concept of *heuristics,* which they defined as cognitive shortcuts that people use naturally in making decisions in conditions of uncertainty. They and other cognitive psychologists have found such processing to be a prevalent source of irrational reactions in a wide variety of situations. For example, people typically report that the protagonists in specially constructed vignettes would become more upset following arbitrary outcomes preceded by acts of commission than by acts of omission, by near than by far misses, by free than by constrained behavior, and by unusual than by usual acts. As they respond as if the protagonist's behavior were responsible for the arbitrary outcomes, their thinking is heuristic in the sense that it is based on simple associative reasoning rather than on cause-and-effect analysis.

A vast amount of research on heuristic processing (see review in Fiske & Taylor, 1991) has produced results that are highly consistent with the principles of experiential processing. Although the data-driven views on heuristic processing derived from social-cognitive research and the theory-driven views of CEST have much in common, the two approaches differ in three important respects. One is that CEST attributes heuristics to the normal mode of operation of an organized conceptual system, the experiential system, that is contrasted with an alternative organized conceptual system, the rational system. The second is that heuristic processing and the experiential system in CEST are embedded in a global theory of personality. The third is that heuristic processing, according to CEST, has withstood the test of time over millions of years of evolution, and is considered to be primarily adaptive. In contrast to these views, social cognitive psychologists, such as Kahneman and Tversky (1973) and Nisbett and Ross (1980), regard heuristics as individual "cognitive tools" that

are employed within a single conceptual system that includes both associative (experiential) and analytical (rational) reasoning. These theorists further regard heuristics as quirks in thinking that although sometimes advantageous are common sources of error in everyday life, and therefore are usually desirable to eliminate. It is of interest in this respect to note how resistant some of these blatantly nonrational ways of processing have been to elimination by training. From the perspective of CEST, given the intrinsically compelling nature of experiential processing and its highly adaptive value in most situations in everyday life, such resilience is to be expected.

Although the experiential system encodes events concretely and holistically, it is nevertheless able to generalize, integrate, and direct behavior in complex ways, some of which very likely involve a contribution by the rational system. It does this through prototypical, metaphorical, symbolic, and narrative representations in conjunction with the use of analogy and metaphor. Representations in the experiential system are also related and generalized through their associations with emotions. It is perhaps through processes such as these that the experiential system is able to make its contributions to empathy, creativity, the establishment of rewarding interpersonal relationships, and the appreciation of art and humor (Norris & Epstein, 2000b).

PSYCHODYNAMICS

Psychodynamics, as the term is used here, refers to the interactions of implicit motives and of implicit beliefs and their influence on conscious thought and behavior. The influence on conscious thought and behavior is assumed to be mediated primarily by vibes. Two major sources of vibes that are important sources of maladaptive behavior are early-acquired beliefs and needs.

The Influence of Early-Acquired Beliefs on Maladaptive Behavior

As you will recall, according to CEST, the implicit beliefs in a person's experiential system consist primarily of generalizations from emotionally significant past experiences. These affect-laden implicit beliefs correspond to schemas about what the self and other people are like and how one should relate to them. Particularly important sources of such schemas are experiences with mother and father figures and with siblings. The schemas exist in varying degrees of generality. At the broadest level is the basic belief about what people in general are like, as previously discussed. At a more specific level are views about particular categories of people, such as authority figures, maternal figures, mentors, and peers. Such implicit beliefs, both broader and narrower ones, exert a strong influence on how people relate to others, particularly to those who provide cues that are reminders of the original generalization figures. The influence of the schemas is mediated by the vibes automatically activated in cue-relevant situations.

It is understandable why implicit beliefs that contribute to a person's happiness and security are maintained. But why should implicit beliefs that appear to contribute only to misery also be maintained? Why do they not extinguish as a result of the negative affect following their retrieval? According to the pleasure principle, they should, of course. They do not because of the influence of the need to maintain the stability of one's conceptual system (Epstein & Morling, 1995; Hixon & Swann, 1993; Morling & Epstein, 1997; Swann, 1990). Depending on circumstances, the need for stability can override the pleasure principle. But how exactly does this operate? What do people actually do that prevents their maladaptive beliefs acquired in an earlier period from being extinguished when they are exposed to corrective experiences in adulthood?

There are three things people do or fail to do that serve to maintain their maladaptive implicit beliefs. First, they tend to perceive and interpret events in a manner that is consistent with their biasing beliefs. Biased perceptions and interpretations allow individuals to experience events as verifying a belief even when on an objective basis they should be disconfirming it. For example, an offer to help or an expression of concern can be perceived as an attempt to control one, and an expression of love can be viewed as manipulative. Second, people often engage in self-verifying behavior, such as by provoking counterbehavior in others that provides objective confirmation of the initial beliefs. For example, a person who fears rejection in intimate relationships may behave with aggression or withdrawal whenever threatened by relationships advancing toward intimacy. This predictably provokes the other person to react with counteraggression or withdrawal, thereby providing objective evidence confirming the belief that people are rejecting. Third, people fail to recognize the influence of their implicit beliefs and associated vibes on their behavior and conscious thoughts, which prevents them from identifying and correcting their biased interpretations and self-verifying behavior. As a result, they attribute the consequences of their maladaptive behavior to unfavorable circumstances or, more likely, to the behavior of others. In the event that after repeated failed relationships, they should consider the possibility that their own behavior may play a role, they are at a loss to understand in what way this could be true, as they can cite objective evidence to support their biased views. You will recall that an important maxim in CEST is that a failure to recognize the operation of one's experiential system means that one will be controlled by it.

There is an obvious similarity between the psychoanalytic concept of transference and the view in CEST that people's relationships are strongly influenced by generalizations from early childhood experiences with significant others. Psychoanalysts have long emphasized the importance of transference relations in psychotherapy. They have observed that their patients, after a period in therapy, react to the analyst as if the analyst were a mother or a father figure. They encourage the development of such transference reactions with the aim of providing a corrective emotional experience. Through the use of this procedure as well as by interpreting the transference, the analyst hopes to eliminate the tendency of the patient to establish similar relationships with others. Although this procedure is understandable from the perspective of CEST, it is fraught with danger, as the patient may become overly dependent on the therapist and the therapist, despite the best of intentions, may provide a destructive rather than a corrective experience. Moreover, working through a transference relationship—even when successful—may not be the most efficient way of treating inappropriate generalizations. Nevertheless, for present purposes, it illustrates how generalizations from early childhood tend to be reproduced in later relationships, including those with therapists, and how appropriate emotional experiences can correct maladaptive generalizations.

Although there are obvious similarities between the concepts of transference in psychoanalysis and of generalization in CEST, there are also important differences. Generalization is a far broader concept, which, unlike transference, is not restricted to the influence of relationships with parents. Rather, it refers to the influence of all significant childhood relationships, including in particular those with siblings as well as with parents. Schemas derived from childhood experiences are emphasized in CEST because later experiences are assimilated by earlier schemas. Also, generalizations acquired from childhood experiences are likely to be poorly articulated (if articulated at all) in the rational system. Their influence, therefore, is likely to continue to be unrecognized into adulthood.

The Influence of Early-Acquired Motives on Maladaptive Behavior

Much of what has been said about implicit beliefs in the experiential system can also be applied to implicit needs. Like implicit beliefs, implicit needs or motives are acquired from emotionally significant experiences. They are also maintained for similar reasons. As previously noted, when people experience a positive or negative event, they automatically acquire a behavioral tendency or motive to reproduce the experience if it was favorable and to avoid experiencing it if it was unfavorable. The stronger the emotional response and the more often it occurs in the same or similar situations, the greater the strength of the motive. Although this learning procedure is adaptive most of the time, it is maladaptive when past conditions are unrepresentative of present ones. One such condition is when a child has experiences involving the deep thwarting of one or more basic needs. For example, if the need to maintain self-esteem is deeply frustrated in childhood, the child will acquire a sensitivity to threats to self-esteem and a corresponding compulsion to protect himself or herself from such threats in the future. *Sensitivities,* in CEST, refer to areas of particular vulnerability, and *compulsions* refer to rigid, driven behavioral tendencies with the aim of protecting oneself from sensitivities. Such sensitivities and compulsions are considered in CEST to be major sources of maladaptive behavior.

The following case history illustrates the operation of a sensitivity and compulsion. In this and other case histories, names, places, and details are altered to protect the anonymity of the protagonists. Ralph was the oldest child in a family that included three other children. He was extremely bright and far outshone his siblings in academic performance. However, rather than being appreciated for it, he was resented by both his parents and siblings. When he eagerly showed his mother the excellent grades on his report card, she would politely tell him that she was busy at the moment and would like to look at it later, when she had more time. Not infrequently, she would forget to do so. It gradually became evident to Ralph that she was more upset than pleased with his accomplishments, so he stopped informing her about them.

The mother's behavior can be understood in terms of her own background. She had been deeply resentful, as a child, when her mother expressed admiration for the accomplishments of her brighter sibling and ignored her own accomplishments. Thus, her automatic reaction to cues that reminded her of such experiences was to have unpleasant vibes accompanied by resentful thoughts. Consequently, although she meant to be a good mother to Ralph, her experiential reactions undermined her conscious intent. Being unaware of her underlying experiential reactions, she could not help but react as she did. Moreover, over time she found objective reasons for considering him as her least favored child. Little did she realize that his resentful and reticent attitude toward her and others were reactions to her own behavior toward him. She simply regarded him as a stubborn, difficult child by nature.

As a result of his experience in the family, Ralph developed feelings of being unlovable and unworthy and felt depressed much of the time. As an adult, he devoted his energy to bolstering his self-esteem by working extremely hard at becoming a successful businessman. He succeeded at this to a remarkable extent, becoming wealthy at an early age. Yet despite his success and accumulation of material things that other people admired, happiness eluded him. He continued to feel unlovable and depressed no matter what his possessions were and no matter that he had a wife and children who tried hard to please him. When his wife praised the children for their accomplishments, he became resentful toward her and the children. He spent less and less time with his family and increasingly immersed himself in his business. He also began to accuse his wife and children of not loving him and said that was the reason he was spending so little time with them. In his eyes, he was the victim of rejection, not its perpetrator. The result was that he increasingly alienated his family, which verified for him that they did not love him. He became convinced that his wife would ask him for a divorce, and rather than be openly rejected by her, he asked her for a divorce first. He was sure she would be pleased to oblige, and he was extremely relieved when she protested that she did not want a divorce. She said that she wanted more than anything else for them to work together to improve their relationship. This gave a great boost to Ralph, and he tried to the best of his ability to be a more attentive husband and father. This was no easy task for him, particularly as he had no insight into the role his own behavior played in his distressing relationships with his family. It remains to be seen if he will succeed. From the perspective of CEST, it is doubtful that he will unless he gains insight into the influence of his experiential system.

This case illustrates the development, operation, and consequences of a sensitivity and compulsion. Of further interest is that it illustrates the transference of sensitivities and compulsions across generations. The mother's sensitivity was to being outshone intellectually, and her compulsion was to get back in some way or other at whomever activated the sensitivity. In this case it was her own son, who provided cues reminiscent of her childhood experiences with her brighter sibling. Lest you blame the mother, consider that her reactions occurred automatically, outside of her awareness, and that she was no less a victim than was Ralph.

Ralph had three related sensitivities: threat to his self-esteem, lack of appreciation for his accomplishments, and rejection by a loved one. His compulsive reaction in response to the first sensitivity was to attempt to increase his self-esteem by becoming an outstanding success in business and thereby gaining the admiration of others. His compulsive reaction to the second sensitivity was again to gain the admiration of others for his success and material possessions. His compulsive reaction to the third sensitivity was to withdraw from and reject the members of his family before they rejected him. Not surprisingly, his compulsive reactions interfered with rather than facilitated gaining the love he so desperately desired.

RESEARCH SUPPORT FOR THE CONSTRUCT VALIDITY OF CEST

Research generated by a variety of dual-process theories other than CEST has produced many findings consistent with the assumptions in CEST (see review in Epstein, 1994, and articles in Chaiken & Trope, 1999). As a review of this extensive literature is beyond the scope of this chapter, here I confine the discussion to studies my associates and I specifically designed to test assumptions in CEST. Three kinds of research are reviewed: research on the operating principles of the experiential system, research on the interactions within and between the two systems, and research on individual differences in the extent and efficacy in the use of the two systems.

Research on the Operating Principles of the Experiential System

For some time, my associates and I have been engaged in a research program for testing the operating principles of the experiential system. One of our approaches consisted of adapting procedures used by Tversky and Kahneman and other cognitive and social-cognitive psychologists to study heuristic, nonanalytical thinking through the use of specially constructed vignettes (for examples of this research by others, see Fiske & Taylor, 1991; Tversky & Kahneman, 1974, 1983; Kahneman, Slovic, & Tversky, 1982).

Irrational Reactions to Unfavorable Arbitrary Outcomes

People in everyday life often react to arbitrary, unintended outcomes as if they were intentionally and causally determined. Thus, they view more favorably the proverbial bearer of good than of evil tidings despite knowing full well that the messenger is not responsible for the message. Such behavior is an example of outcome-oriented processing. It is the typical way the experiential system reacts to events—by associating outcomes with the stimuli that precede the outcomes, as in classical conditioning.

As an example of the kinds of vignettes we used, one of them described a situation in which two people, as the result of unanticipated heavy traffic, arrive at an airport 30 minutes after the scheduled departure of their flights. One learns that her flight left on time, and the other learns that her flight just

left. Tversky and Kahneman (1983) found that people typically reported that the one who barely missed her flight would be more upset than the other protagonist would be, although from a rational perspective it should not matter at all as both were equally inconvenienced and neither was responsible for the outcome. We modified Tversky and Kahneman's experiment by having the participants respond from three perspectives: how they believed most people would react; how they themselves would react based on how they have reacted to similar situations in the past, and how a completely logical person would react (Epstein, Lipson, Holstein, & Huh, 1992). The first two perspectives were considered to be mainly under the jurisdiction of the experiential system and the third to be mainly under the jurisdiction of the rational system. In order to control for and examine the influence of each of the perspectives on the effect of subsequent perspectives, we counterbalanced the order of presentation of the perspectives.

The findings supported the following hypotheses: There are two different modes of information processing, experiential and rational; the experiential system is an associative system that automatically relates outcomes to preceding situations and behavior, treating them as if they are causally related, even when the relation is completely arbitrary; the rational system is an analytical system that judges cause-and-effect relations according to logical rules; and the systems are interactive, with each influencing the other. Support for the last hypothesis is of particular interest, as it supports the important assumption in CEST that the prevalence of irrational thinking in humans can be attributed largely to the influence of their automatic, preconscious experiential processing on their conscious analytical thinking.

In research on arbitrary outcomes in which we varied the affective consequences of the outcomes, the results supported the assumption in CEST that the degree of experiential relative to rational influence varies directly with the intensity of the affect that is implicated (Epstein et al., 1992). What we found is that the greater the emotional intensity of the outcomes, the more the responses reflected experiential (vs. rational) processing.

The Ratio-Bias Phenomenon

Imagine that you are told that on every trial in which you blindly draw a red jellybean from a bowl containing red and white jellybeans, you will receive two dollars. To make matters more interesting, you are given a choice between drawing from either of two bowls that offer the same 10% odds of drawing a winning bean. One contains one red jellybean and nine white ones; the other contains 10 red jellybeans and 90 white ones. Which bowl would you choose to draw from, and how much would you pay for the privilege of drawing from the bowl of your choice, rather than having the choice decided by the toss of a coin? When people are simply asked how they would behave, almost all say they would have no preference and would not pay a cent for a choice between two equal probabilities. Yet when they are placed in a real situation, most willingly pay small sums of money for the privilege of drawing from the bowl with more red jellybeans (Kirkpatrick & Epstein, 1992). This difference in response to the verbally presented and the real situation can be explained by the greater influence of the experiential than the rational system in real situations with emotionally significant consequences compared to simulated situations without consequences. According to CEST, the experiential system is particularly reactive to real experience, whereas the rational system is uniquely responsive to abstract, verbal representations.

This jellybean experimental situation, otherwise referred to as the *ratio-bias experimental paradigm,* is particularly interesting with respect to CEST because it pits experiential against rational processing. The conflict between the two modes of processing arises because the experiential system is a concrete system that is less responsive to abstractions such as ratios than to the numerousness of objects. Comprehension of numerousness, unlike comprehension of ratios, is an extremely fundamental ability that is within the capacity of 3-year-old children and nonhuman animals (Gallistel & Gelman, 1992).

Even more impressive than the irrational behavior exhibited by people paying for the privilege of choosing between bowls that offer equal probabilities are the results obtained when unequal probabilities are offered by the bowls. If our reasoning is correct, a conflict between the two systems can be established by having one bowl probability-advantaged and the other numerousness-advantaged. In one study, the probability-advantaged bowl always contained 1 in 10 red jellybeans, whereas the numerousness-advantaged bowl offered between 5 and 9 red jellybeans out of 100 jellybeans, depending on the trial (Denes-Raj & Epstein, 1994). Under these circumstances, many adults made nonoptimal responses by selecting the numerousness-advantaged bowl against the better judgment of their rational thinking. For example, they often chose to draw from the bowl that contained 8 of 100 (8%) in preference to the one that contained 1 of 10 (10%) red jellybeans. Some sheepishly commented that they knew it was foolish to go against the probabilities, but somehow they felt they had a better chance of drawing a red jellybean when there were more of them. Of additional interest, participants made nonoptimal responses only to a limited degree, thereby suggesting a compromise between the two

systems. Thus, although many selected a numerousness-advantaged 8% option (8 of 100 red jellybeans) over a 10% probability-advantaged one (1 of 10 red jellybeans), almost no one selected a 5% numerousness-advantaged option (5 of 100 red jellybeans) over a 10% probability-advantaged option (1 of 10 red jellybeans). Apparently, most people preferred to behave according to their experiential processing only up to a point of violating their rational understanding. To be sure, there were participants who always responded rationally. What was impressive about the study, however, was the greater number who responded irrationally despite knowing better (in their rational systems).

To determine whether children who have not had formal training in ratios have an intuitive understanding of ratios, we conducted a series of studies in which we examined children's responses to the ratio-bias experimental paradigm (Yanko & Epstein, 2000). We were also interested in these studies in determining whether children who have only an intuitive understanding of ratios exhibit compromises between the two systems. We found that children without formal knowledge of ratios had only a rudimentary comprehension of ratios. They responded appropriately to differences between ratios only when the magnitude of the differences was large. Like adults, children exhibited compromises, but their compromises were more in the experiential direction. For example, many children but no adults selected a 5% numerousness-advantaged bowl over a 10% probability-advantaged one. However, very few of the same children selected a 2% numerousness-advantaged bowl over a 10% probability-advantaged one.

We also used the ratio-bias experimental paradigm to test the assumption in CEST that the experiential system responds to visual imagery in a way similar to the way it does to real experience (Epstein & Pacini, 2001). We presented participants in an experimental group with a verbal description of the ratio-bias experimental paradigm after training them to vividly visualize the situation. Participants in the control group were given only the verbal description. In support of the assumption, the visual-imaging group but not the control group exhibited the ratio-bias phenomenon in a manner similar to what we have repeatedly found in real situations but not in simulated situations.

The overall results from the many studies we conducted with the ratio-bias paradigm (Denes-Raj & Epstein, 1994; Denes-Raj, Epstein, & Cole, 1995; Kirkpatrick & Epstein, 1992; Pacini & Epstein, 1999a, 1999b; Yanko & Epstein, 2000) provided support for the following assumptions and hypotheses derived from CEST. There are two independent information-processing systems. Sometimes they conflict with each other, but more often they form compromises. With increasing maturation from childhood to adulthood, the balance of influence between the two processing systems shifts in the direction of increased rational dominance. The experiential system is more responsive than is the rational system to imagery and to other concrete representations than the rational system, whereas the rational system is more responsive than is the experiential system to abstract representations. Engaging the rational system in children who do not have formal knowledge of ratios by asking them to give the reasons for their responses interferes with the application of their intuitive understanding of ratios, resulting in a deterioration of performance.

We have also used the ratio-bias phenomenon to elucidate the thinking of people with emotional disorders. In a study of depressed college students (Pacini, Muir, & Epstein, 1998), the ratio-bias phenomenon helped to clarify the paradoxical *depressive-realism phenomenon* (Alloy & Abramson, 1988). The phenomenon refers to the finding that depressed participants are more rather than less accurate than are nondepressed participants in judging contingencies between events. We found that the depressed participants made more optimal responses than did their nondepressed counterparts only when the stakes for nonoptimal responding were inconsequential. When we raised the stakes, the depressed participants responded more experientially and the control participants responded more rationally, so that the groups converged and no longer differed. We concluded that the depressive-realism phenomenon can be attributed to an overcompensatory reaction by subclinically depressed participants in trivial situations to a more basic tendency to behave unrealistically in emotionally significant situations. We further concluded that normal individuals tend to rely on their less demanding experiential processing when incentives are low, but increasingly engage their more demanding rational processing as incentives are increased.

The Global-Evaluation Heuristic

The *global-person-evaluation heuristic* refers to the tendency of people to evaluate others holistically as either good or bad people rather than to restrict their judgments to specific behaviors or attributes. Because the global-person-evaluation heuristic is consistent with the assumption that holistic evaluation is a fundamental operating principle of the experiential system (see Table 7.1), it follows that global-person-evaluations tend to be highly compelling and not easily changed. The heuristic is particularly important because of its prevalence and because of the problems that arise from it—such as when jurors are influenced by the attractiveness of a defendant's appearance or personality in judging his or her guilt. An interesting example of this phenomenon was provided in the hearing of Clarence Thomas for appointment to the United States Supreme Court. The testimony by Anita Hill about the obscene sexual advances she alleged he made to her was discredited in the eyes of several senators because of the favorable testimony by employees and acquaintances about his character and behavior. It seemed inconceivable to the senators that an otherwise good person could be sexually abusive.

We studied the global-person-evaluation heuristic (reported in Epstein, 1994) by having participants respond to a vignette adapted from a study by Miller and Gunasegaram (1990). In the vignette, a rich benefactor tells three friends that if each throws a coin that comes up heads, he will give each $100. The first two throw a heads, but Smith, the third, throws a tails. When asked to rate how each of the protagonists feels, most participants indicated that Smith would feel guilty and the others would feel angry with him. In an alternative version with reduced stakes, the ratings of guilt and anger were correspondingly reduced. When asked if the other two would be willing, as they previously had intended, to invite Smith to join them on a gambling vacation in Las Vegas, where they would share wins and losses, most participants said they would not "because he is a loser." These responses were made both from the perspective of how the participants reported they themselves would react in a real situation and how they believed most people would react. When responding from the perspective of how a completely logical person would react, most participants said a logical person would recognize that the outcome of the coin tosses was arbitrary, and they therefore would not hold it against Smith. They further indicated that a logical person would invite him on the gambling venture.

This study indicates that people tend to judge others holistically by outcomes, even arbitrary ones. It further indicates that people intuitively recognize that there are two systems of information processing that operate in a manner consistent with the principles of the experiential and rational systems. It also supports the hypotheses that experiential processing becomes increasingly dominant with an increase in emotional involvement and that people overgeneralize broadly in judging others on the basis of outcomes over which the person has no control, even though they know better in their rational system.

Conjunction Problems

The Linda conjunction problem is probably the most researched vignette in the history of psychology. It has evoked a great deal of interest among psychologists because of its paradoxical results. More specifically, although the solution to the Linda problem requires the application of one of the simplest and most fundamental principles of probability theory, almost everyone—including people sophisticated in statistics—gets it wrong. How is this to be explained? As you might suspect by now, the explanation lies in the operating principles of the experiential system.

Linda is described as a 31-year-old woman who is single, outspoken, and very bright. In college she was a philosophy major who participated in antinuclear demonstrations and was concerned with issues of social justice. How would you rank the following three possibilities: Linda is a feminist, Linda is a bank teller, and Linda is a feminist and a bank teller? If you responded like most people, you ranked Linda as being a feminist *and* a bank teller ahead of Linda's being just a bank teller. In doing so, you made what Tversky & Kahneman (1982) refer to as a *conjunction fallacy*, and which we refer to as a conjunction error (CE). It is an error or fallacy because according to the conjunction rule, the occurrence of two events cannot be more likely than the occurrence of only one of them.

The usual explanation of the high rate of CEs that people make is that they either do not know the conjunction rule or they do not think of it in the context of the Linda vignette. They respond instead, according to Tversky and Kahneman, by the representativeness heuristic, according to which being both a bank teller and a feminist is more representative of Linda's personality than being just a bank teller.

In a series of studies on conjunction problems, including the Linda problem (Donovan & Epstein, 1997; Epstein, Denes-Raj, & Pacini, 1995; Epstein & Donovan, 1995; Epstein, Donovan, & Denes-Raj, 1999; Epstein & Pacini, 1995), we concluded that the major reason for the difficulty of the Linda problem is not an absence of knowledge of the conjunction rule or a failure to think of it. We demonstrated that almost all people have intuitive knowledge of the conjunction rule, as they apply it correctly in natural contexts, such as in problems about lotteries. Nearly all of our participants, whether or not they had formal knowledge of the conjunction rule, reported that winning two lotteries, one with a very low probability of winning and the other with a higher probability, is less likely than is winning either one of them (Epstein et al., 1995). This finding is particularly interesting from the perspective of CEST because it indicates that the experiential system (which knows the conjunction rule intuitively) is sometimes smarter than the rational system (which may not be able to articulate the rule). We also found that when we presented the conjunction rule among other alternatives, thereby circumventing the problem of whether people think of it in the context of the Linda problem, most people selected the wrong rule. They made the rule fit their responses to the Linda problem rather than the reverse, thereby demonstrating the compelling nature of experiential processing and its ability to dominate analytical thinking in certain situations.

The conclusions from our series of studies with the Linda problem can be summarized as follows:

- The difficulty of the Linda problem cannot be fully accounted for by the misleading manner in which it is presented, for even with full disclosure about the nature of the problem and the request to treat it purely as a probability problem, a substantial number of participants makes CEs. Apparently, people tend to view the Linda problem as a personality problem rather than as a probability problem, no matter what they are told.

- The difficulty of the Linda problem can be explained by the rules of operation of the experiential system, which is the mode employed by most people when responding to it. Thus, people tend to reason associatively, concretely, holistically, and in a narrative manner rather than abstractly and analytically when responding to the problem. For example, a number of participants explained their responses that violated the conjunction rule by stating that Linda is more likely to be a bank teller and a feminist than just a feminist because she has to make a living.

- The essence of the difficulty of the Linda problem is that it involves an unnatural, concrete presentation, where an unnatural presentation is defined as one that differs from the context in which a problem is normally presented. We found that concrete presentations facilitate performance in natural situations (in which the two processing systems operate in synchrony) and interfere with performance in unnatural situations (in which the two systems operate in opposition to each other).

- Processing in the experiential mode is intrinsically highly compelling and can override processing in the rational mode even when the latter requires no more effort. Thus, many people, despite knowing and thinking of the conjunction rule, nevertheless prefer a representativeness solution.

- Priming intuitive knowledge in the experiential system can facilitate the solution to problems that people are unable initially to solve intellectually.

Interaction Between the Two Processing Systems

An important assumption in CEST is that the two systems are interactive. Interaction occurs simultaneously as well as sequentially. Simultaneous interaction was demonstrated in the compromises between the two systems observed in the studies of the ratio-bias phenomenon. Sequential interaction was demonstrated in the study in which people listed their first three thoughts and in the studies of conjunction problems, in which presenting concrete, natural problems before abstract problems facilitated the solution of the abstract problems.

There is also considerable evidence that priming the experiential system subliminally can influence subsequent responses in the rational system (see review in Bargh, 1989). Other evidence indicates that the form independent of the content of processing in the rational system can be influenced by priming the experiential system. When processing in the experiential mode is followed by attempts to respond rationally, the rational mode itself may be compromised by intrusions of experiential reasoning principles (Chaiken & Maheswaren, 1994; Denes-Raj, Epstein, & Cole, 1995; Edwards, 1990; Epstein et al., 1992).

Sequential influence does not occur only in the direction of the experiential system influencing the rational system. As previously noted, in everyday life sequential processing often proceeds in the opposite direction, as when people react to their irrational, automatic thoughts with corrective, rational thoughts. In a study designed to examine this process, we instructed participants to list the first three thoughts that came to mind after imagining themselves in various situations described in vignettes (reported in Epstein, 1994). The first response was usually a maladaptive thought consistent with the associative principle of the experiential system, whereas the third response was usually a more carefully reasoned thought in the mode of the rational system. As an example, consider the responses to the following vignette, which describes a protagonist who fails to win a lottery because she took the advice of a friend rather than follow her own inclination to buy a ticket that had her lucky number on it. Among the most common first thoughts were that the friend was to blame and that the participant would never take her advice again. By the third thought, however, the participants were likely to state that the outcome was due to chance and no one was to blame.

Interaction Between the Basic Needs

You will recall that a basic assumption in CEST is that behavior often represents a compromise among multiple basic needs. This process is considered to be particularly important, as it provides a means by which the basic needs serve as checks and balances against each other, with each need constrained by the influence of the other needs. To test the assumption about compromises, we examined the combined influence of the needs for self-enhancement and self-verification. Swann and his associates had previously demonstrated that the needs for

enhancement and verification operate sequentially, with the former tending to precede the latter (e.g., Swann, 1990; Hixon & Swann, 1993). We wished to demonstrate that they also operate simultaneously, as manifested by compromises between them. Our procedure consisted of varying the favorableness of evaluative feedback and observing whether participants had a preference for feedback that matched or was more favorable to various degrees than their self-assessments (Epstein & Morling, 1995; Morling & Epstein, 1997). In support of our hypotheses, participants preferred feedback that was only slightly more favorable than their own self-assessments, consistent with a compromise between the need for verification and the need for self-enhancement.

Research on Individual Differences

Individual Differences in the Intelligence of the Experiential System

If there are two different systems for adapting to the environment, then it is reasonable to suspect that there are individual differences in the efficacy with which people employ each. It is therefore assumed in CEST that each system has its own form of intelligence. The question remains as to how to measure each. The intelligence of the rational system can be measured by intelligence tests, which are fairly good predictors of academic performance. To a somewhat lesser extent, they also predict performance in a wide variety of activities in the real world, including performance in the workplace, particularly in situations that require complex operations (see reviews in Gordon, 1997; Gottfredson, 1997; Hunter, 1983, 1986; Hunter & Hunter, 1984). However, intelligence tests do not measure other kinds of abilities that are equally important for success in living, including motivation, practical intelligence, ego strength, appropriate emotions, social facility, and creativity.

Until recently, there was no measure of the intelligence of the experiential system; one reason for this is that the concept of an experiential system was unknown. Having established its theoretical viability, the next step was to construct a way of measuring it, which resulted in the Constructive Thinking Inventory (CTI; Epstein, 2001). The measurement of experiential intelligence is based on the assumption that experiential intelligence is revealed by the adaptiveness of the thoughts that tend to spontaneously occur in different situations or conditions.

People respond to the CTI by reporting on a 5-point scale the degree to which they have certain common adaptive and maladaptive automatic or spontaneous thoughts. An example of an item is *I spend a lot of time thinking about my mistakes, even if there is nothing I can do about them* (reverse scored).

The CTI provides a Global Constructive Thinking scale and six main scales, most of which have several facets, or subscales. The six main scales are Emotional Coping, Behavioral Coping, Categorical Thinking, Esoteric Thinking, Naive Optimism, and Personal Superstitious Thinking. The main scales all have high internal-consistency reliability coefficients and evidence for their validity in numerous studies. They are predictive of a wide variety of criteria related to success in living. A review of the extensive literature supporting the construct validity of the CTI is beyond the scope of this chapter, but is available elsewhere (Epstein, 2001). For present purposes, it will suffice to note that favorable CTI scores have been found to be significantly associated with performance in the workplace and in the classroom, social competence, leadership ability, ability to cope with stress, emotional adjustment, physical well-being, and an absence of drug and alcohol abuse.

The relation of constructive thinking to intellectual intelligence is of considerable interest for theoretical as well as practical reasons. According to CEST, the experiential and rational systems operate independently, each by its own set of principles (see Table 7.1). One would therefore expect the intelligence or efficacy of the two processing systems to be independent. This is exactly what we have repeatedly found in several studies that have compared scores on the Global CTI scale with measures of intellective intelligence (Epstein, 2001). Of additional interest, constructive thinking and intellectual intelligence were found to exhibit opposite courses of development across the life span. Constructive thinking is at its nadir in adolescence, when intellectual intelligence is at its peak, and it gradually increases throughout most of the adult years when intellectual intelligence is gradually declining. Unlike intellectual intelligence, constructive thinking is only negligibly related to academic achievement tests. Yet it adds significant variance in addition to the contribution of intellectual intelligence to the prediction of performance in the classroom, as indicated by grades received and class rank (Epstein, 2001). Apparently, good constructive thinkers are able to capitalize on their knowledge and obtain appropriate recognition for their achievements, whereas poor constructive thinkers are more likely to engage in counterproductive behavior such as antagonizing their teachers, resulting in their being downgraded.

Individual Differences in Rational and Experiential Thinking Styles

If people process information by two different systems, the extent to which they employ each should be an important personality variable. To investigate this aspect of personality, we constructed a self-report test, the Rational-Experiential Inventory (REI). The REI has main scales of rational and experiential processing. Each of the main scales has subscales of self-assessed effectiveness and of frequency in use of the thinking style.

The REI scales have internal-consistency reliabilities of .87–.90 for the main scales and .79–.84 for the subscales. There is considerable evidence in support of their construct validity. The major findings from several studies (Epstein et al., 1996; Norris & Epstein, 2000a, 2000b; Pacini & Epstein, 1999b; Pacini, Muir, & Epstein, 1998; Rosenthal & Epstein, 2000) can be summarized as follows:

- In support of the assumption in CEST of independent rational and experiential processing systems, the two main scales are independent.

- In support of the inclusion of the subscales, they exhibit factorial, discriminant, and convergent validity.

- The rational and experiential scales are coherently associated with objective measures of heuristic processing. As expected, the relation of the rational scale with heuristic processing is inverse, and the relation of the experiential scale with heuristic processing is direct.

- Although the rational and experiential main scales are uniquely associated with some variables, they make independent, supplementary contributions to the prediction of other variables. The rational scale is more strongly positively associated than is the experiential scale with intellectual performance, as measured by SAT scores and grade point average, and with adjustment, including measures of ego strength and self-esteem, and with measures of openness, conscientiousness, favorable beliefs about the self and the world, and physical well-being. The rational scale is more strongly negatively associated than the experiential REI scale with measures of neuroticism, depression, anxiety, stress in college life, subtle racism, extreme conservatism, alcohol abuse, and naive optimism. The experiential scale is more strongly positively associated than the rational scale with measures of extroversion, agreeableness, favorable interpersonal relationships, empathy, creativity, emotionality, sense of humor, and art appreciation, and it is more strongly negatively associated than the rational system with distrust and intolerance.

When introducing a new measure, it is important to demonstrate that the measure provides information that is not readily available from existing instruments. In order to determine whether the REI is redundant with more standard personality measures, we conducted a study (Pacini & Epstein, 1999b) in which we compared the REI to the NEO Five-Factor Inventory (NEO-FFI; Costa & McCrae, 1989), the most popular measure of the Big Five personality traits.

The two inventories contributed independent, supplementary variance to the prediction of many of the same variables and unique variance to the prediction of other variables. Moreover, when the five NEO-FFI scales were entered into a regression equation as predictors of the REI scales, they accounted for only 37% of the variance of the Rationality scale and 11% of the variance of the Experientiality scale. This is of interest not only because it demonstrates that the REI is mainly independent of the NEO-FFI, but also because of the information it provides about the NEO-FFI. It suggests that the NEO-FFI mainly measures attributes associated with the rational system and is relatively deficient in measuring attitudes and behavior associated with preconscious, automatic information processing.

Consistent with gender stereotypes, women report significantly greater appreciation of and engagement in experiential processing than men, and men report greater appreciation of and engagement in rational processing. However, the mean gender differences are small, and there is a great deal of overlap between the groups.

Given fundamentally different ways of processing information, it might reasonably be expected that people with different thinking styles would be receptive to different kinds of messages. To test this hypothesis, Rosenthal and Epstein (2000) conducted a study with the REI in which they compared the reactions of women with high scores on rationality and low scores on experientiality with women with the opposite pattern. The groups were subdivided according to whether they received messages on the danger of breast cancer and the importance of self-examination in the form of information designed to appeal to the rational or the experiential mode of information processing. The rational message emphasized actuarial and other objective information, whereas the experiential message included personal appeals and vivid individual cases. The dependent variable was the intention to regularly conduct breast self-examinations. Both groups reported a greater intention to conduct breast examinations when the message they received matched their own thinking style.

Individual Differences in Basic Beliefs About the Self and the World

The Basic Beliefs Inventory (BBI; Catlin & Epstein, 1992) is a self-report questionnaire that measures the four basic beliefs proposed in CEST. It includes a global scale of overall favorability of basic beliefs and separate scales for measuring each of the basic beliefs. The internal-consistency reliabilities (coefficients alpha) of the scales are between .77 to .91. The scales are moderately intercorrelated with a median correlation of .42, thereby justifying combining them into an overall scale of favorability of beliefs as well as considering them individually.

You will recall that according to CEST, a person's basic beliefs are primarily derived from emotionally significant personal experiences. To test this hypothesis, Catlin and Epstein (1992) examined the relations of scores on the BBI and self-reports of two kinds of highly significant emotional experiences. The two kinds of experiences were extreme life events, such as loss of a loved one, and the quality of relationships with parents during early childhood. In support of hypothesis, both kinds of experiences were significantly and coherently related to basic beliefs. Often, the two kinds of experience made independent, supplementary contributions to the prediction of the same basic belief. Of additional interest, the self-reported quality of childhood relationships with parents moderated the influence of extreme life events on basic beliefs.

Summary and Conclusions Regarding Research Support for CEST

In summary, the program of research on CEST has provided impressive support for its construct validity. The following basic assumptions of CEST have all been verified: There are two independent information-processing systems that operate in parallel by different rules. The systems are interactive, with each influencing the other, and the interaction occurs both sequentially and simultaneously. The influence of experiential processing on rational processing is of particular importance, as it identifies a process by which people's automatic, preconscious, experiential processing routinely biases their conscious rational thinking. The experiential system is an associative, rapid, concretist, primarily nonverbal system that is intrinsically highly compelling to the extent that it can override the rational system, leading people to "behave against their better judgment."

When people are aware of the maladaptive thoughts generated by their automatic experiential processing, they often correct the thoughts through more deliberative reasoning in their rational systems. There are reliable individual differences in the efficacy or intelligence of the experiential system. The intelligence of the experiential system is independent of the intelligence of the rational system and is more strongly associated with a variety of indexes of success in living than is the intelligence of the rational system. Included are work success, social facility, absence of drug and alcohol abuse, and mental and physical well-being. There are reliable individual differences in experiential and rational thinking styles. The two thinking styles exhibit coherent patterns of relations with a variety of criterion variables. There are also reliable individual differences in the four basic beliefs proposed by CEST. As the basic beliefs influence behavior simultaneously in the form of compromises, they serve as checks and balances against each other.

IMPLICATIONS OF COGNITIVE-EXPERIENTIAL SELF-THEORY FOR PSYCHOTHERAPY AND RESEARCH

Implications for Psychotherapy

For psychotherapy to be effective, it is necessary according to CEST for changes to occur in the experiential system. This is not meant to imply that changes in the rational system are of no importance, but rather to suggest that changes in the rational system are therapeutic only to the extent that they facilitate changes in the experiential system.

There are three basic ways of producing changes in the experiential system. These include the use of the rational system to correct and train the experiential system, the provision of emotionally significant corrective experiences, and communicating with the experiential system in its own medium—namely fantasy, imagery, metaphor, concrete representations, and narratives. These three approaches provide a unifying framework for a wide variety of approaches in psychotherapy, including insight approaches, cognitive-behavioral approaches, and experiential approaches, including gestalt therapy and psychosynthesis (Epstein, 1994, 1998).

Using the Rational System to Correct the Experiential System

The rational system has an important advantage over the experiential system in that it can understand the experiential system, whereas the reverse is not true. Thus, one way the rational system can be used to improve the functioning of the experiential system is by teaching people to understand the operation of their experiential systems. Almost everyone is aware of having conflicts between the heart and the head as well as having unbidden distressing thoughts that they can not consciously control. These are not deep, dark, inaccessible thoughts, but rather ones of which people are acutely aware. Beginning with a discussion of such reactions, it should not be difficult to convince people that they operate by two independent systems. The next step is to teach them about the operating principles of the experiential system and the manner in which it influences their behavior and biases their conscious thought. They then can be helped to understand that their problems are almost always in their automatic experiential processing, not in their conscious thinking. Not

only is such knowledge useful for correcting and training the experiential system, but it also provides a useful foundation for the other two approaches.

One of the important advantages of clients' recognizing that their problems lie primarily in their experiential and not their rational systems is that it reduces resistance and defensiveness because they no longer have to defend the reasonableness of their behavior. For example, if a client engages in excessive rational discourse and feels compelled to defend his or her behavior as reasonable, the therapist can remind the client that the experiential system does not operate by logic. Rather, what is important is to uncover the maladaptive beliefs and needs in the experiential system and ultimately change them in a constructive way.

Uncovering implicit beliefs in the experiential system can be accomplished in several ways. One way is by noting repetitive behavior patterns, and in particular becoming aware of sensitivities, compulsions, and ego-alien behavior, and becoming aware of the situations in which they arise. A second way is by using fantasy to vicariously explore reactions to different situations. A third way is by attending to emotional reactions, vibes, and the kinds of automatic thoughts that instigate them.

Emotional reactions are particularly revealing according to CEST because they provide a royal road to the important schemas in people's implicit theories of reality. They do this in two ways. First, whenever an event elicits a strong emotional response, it indicates that a significant schema in a person's implicit theory of reality has been implicated. Accordingly, by noting the events that elicit emotional responses, some of the more important schemas in a person's theory of reality can be determined. Second, emotions can be used to infer schemas through knowledge of the relation between specific thoughts and specific emotions (e.g., Averill, 1980; Beck, 1976; Ellis, 1973; Epstein, 1983, 1984; Lazarus, 1991). This relation has been well documented by the clinical observations of cognitive-behavioral therapists (e.g., Beck, 1976; Ellis, 1973) and by research that has examined the relation of thoughts and emotions in everyday life (e.g., Averill, 1980; Epstein, 1983). It follows from the relation of automatic thoughts to emotions that people who characteristically have certain emotions characteristically spontaneously think in certain ways. For example, angry people can be assumed to have the implicit belief that people often behave badly and deserve to be punished, frightened people can be assumed to have the implicit belief that the world is dangerous and they should be prepared for flight, and sad people can be assumed to have the implicit belief that they have sustained an irreplaceable loss, or that they are inadequate, bad, or unloveworthy people, and there is nothing they can do about it.

The most obvious way in which the rational system can be used to correct maladaptive feelings and behavior is by detecting and disputing the automatic thoughts that precede the feelings and behavior, a technique widely practiced by cognitive-behavioral therapists (e.g., Beck, 1976; Ellis, 1973). Clients can be taught to attend to the automatic thoughts that immediately precede troublesome emotions and behavior. By recognizing these thoughts as destructive and repeatedly substituting more constructive ones, they often can change the maladaptive emotions and behavior that had been instigated by the thoughts.

Another way that people can employ their rational system to correct their experiential processing is by understanding the value of real-life corrective emotional experiences. Clients can be helped to understand how their biased interpretations and habitual reaction tendencies—particularly those involving sensitivities and compulsions—have served to maintain their maladaptive reactions in the past, and how changing them can allow them to have and learn from potentially corrective experiences.

The rational system can also be employed to teach people about the rules of operation of the two systems, the weaknesses and strengths of each system, and the importance of using the two systems in a supplementary manner. They should understand that neither system is superior to the other, and that each has certain advantages and limitations. They should appreciate that each processing mode can provide useful guidance and each can lead one astray when not checked by the other. As an example of how the two systems can be used together when making an important decision, a client can be told to ask him- or herself, "How do I feel about doing this, what do I think about doing it, and considering both, what should I do?" In evaluating the wisdom of behaving according to one's feelings, it is helpful to consider the influence of past experiences on current feelings (particularly when sensitivities are implicated), and to consider how appropriate the past experiences are as a guide for reacting to the present situation.

Learning Directly from Emotionally Significant Experiences

As its name implies, the essence of the experiential system is that it is a system that learns from experience. It follows that the most direct route for changing maladaptive schemas in the experiential system is to provide corrective experiences. One way to accomplish this is through the relationship between client and therapist. This procedure is particularly emphasized in psychoanalytic transference relationships. Another way to learn directly from experience is by having corrective emotionally significant experiences in everyday life. As

previously noted, it can be very useful in this respect for clients to gain insight into their biasing interpretations and self-verifying behavior. In the absence of such insight, potentially corrective experiences can be misinterpreted in a way that makes them contribute to the reinforcement rather than extinction of their destructive thoughts and behavior patterns. Having emphasized the contribution of insight, a caveat is in order concerning valuing it too highly and considering it a necessary condition for improvement. Although insight can be very useful, it is not a necessary condition for improvement. It is quite possible for change to occur in the experiential system in the absence of intellectual understanding of the process, which, of course, is the way nonhuman animals as well as people who are not in therapy normally learn from experience. Many a novel has been written about cures through love. In fact, for clients who are nonintellectual, corrective experiences in the absence of insight may be the only way to proceed in therapy. In the absence of recognizing the limited value of intellectual insight, there is the danger that therapists will insufficiently attend to the experiential aspects of therapy.

Communicating with the Experiential System in Its Own Medium

Communicating with the experiential system in its own medium refers to the use of association, metaphor, imagery, fantasy, and narrative. Within the scope of this chapter, it is impossible to discuss all of these procedures or even to discuss any in detail. It is important to recognize in this regard that there is no single kind of therapy that is specific to CEST. Rather, CEST is an integrative personality theory that provides a framework for placing into broad perspective a variety of therapies. For present purposes, it will suffice to present both a simple and a more complicated example of how communication with the experiential system in its own medium can be used therapeutically.

The simple example concerns a person who under the guidance of a therapist visualizes a situation to learn how he might react to the situation in real life. The procedure is based on the assumption that the experiential system reacts to visualized events in a similar way as to real events, an assumption supported by research expressly designed to test it (Epstein & Pacini, 2001).

Robert exhibited a life pattern of ambivalence about getting married. Recently, the woman he had been dating for several years gave him an ultimatum. She demanded that either he pronounce his intention to marry her or she would leave him. Robert loved her dearly, but he did not feel ready for marriage. He had always assumed he would settle down and raise a family, but somehow whenever he came to the point of committing himself, something went wrong with the relationship, and he and his partner parted ways. At first, Robert attributed the partings to failings in his partners, but after repeated reenactments, it occurred to him that he might be ambivalent about marriage. Because this made no sense to him, he decided to seek the help of a therapist. The therapist instructed and trained Robert to vividly imagine being married and coming home to his wife and children after work. When he had the scene clearly in mind, he was asked to carefully attend to his feelings. To his surprise, he felt irritated and burdened when his wife greeted him at the door and the children eagerly began relating the events of the day. The therapist then instructed Robert to imagine another scene in which he had the very same feelings. His mind turned to his childhood, and he had an image of taking care of his younger siblings when his parents went out for entertainment. He deeply resented having to take care of them frequently and not being able to play with his peers. The result was that he learned to dislike interacting with children at the experiential level, but had never articulated this feeling at the rational level.

As an adult, although Robert believed in his conscious, rational mind that he wanted to get married and raise a family, in his experiential mind, the thought of being in the company of children produced unpleasant vibes. He and his therapist discussed whether he should follow his heart or his mind. In order to help him to decide, the therapist pointed out that following his heart would be the path of least resistance. He added that if Robert decided to follow his mind, it would be important for him to work on overcoming his negative feelings toward children. When Robert decided that is what he wanted to do, he was given an exercise to practice in fantasy that consisted of scenes in which Robert engaged in enjoyable activities with children. He was also encouraged to visualize whatever occasions he could remember from his childhood in which he enjoyed being with his siblings. He was given other scenes to imagine, including being pleased with himself for behaving as a better parent to his imaginary children than his parents had behaved to him.

The more complex example is taken from a book by Alice Epstein (1989) in which she described her use of fantasy and other procedures designed to communicate with her experiential system. She attributed a surprisingly rapid reorganization of her personality to this procedure. She also believed that the change in her feelings that accompanied the change in her personality contributed to a dramatic recovery from a life-threatening illness against all odds.

Alice began psychotherapy after receiving a diagnosis of terminal cancer and being informed that she would not likely live more than three months. The statistics at that time of her diagnosis on the outcome of a metastasized hypernephroma, the form of kidney cancer that she had, indicated that no more than 4 in 1000 cases experienced remission from the disease, let alone cure. Now, many years after that diagnosis, Alice has no detectable signs of cancer and has been considered cured for more than 15 years. Whether her belief that the psychotherapy actually saved her life is correct is not at issue here. What is of primary interest is the rapid resolution of deep-seated problems through the use of fantasy that usually require a prolonged period of intensive psychotherapy. However, given increasing evidence of the relation of emotions to the immune system, it would be unwise to summarily reject her belief that her psychological recovery contributed to her physical recovery. It is possible that the experiential system has a relation to physical well-being much stronger than orthodox medicine recognizes.

The following is one of the early fantasies described by Alice in her book: In the session preceding the fantasy, she had expressed hostility toward her mother for her mother's behavior to her during a period of extended turmoil in the household. During that period, the mother surprisingly gave birth to Alice's younger sister after denying being pregnant and attributing the change in her appearance to a gain in weight from eating too much. During the same period, the mother's mother, who shared the household with the family, and to whom the mother was deeply attached, was dying of cancer. After the session in which Alice Epstein (1989) expressed her hostility to her mother, she experienced a prolonged feeling of isolation and loneliness that lasted until she reported and discussed the following fantasy with her therapist.

My therapist and I decided to try the same technique to try to understand my intense discomfort at being alone. Visualizing isolation was much more difficult than visualizing pain. After many attempts that we both rejected as trivial, I finally caught the spirit of what I was experiencing. I saw some figures with shrouds—very unclear. Then as they took on a more distinct form, I saw that they were witches standing around a fire. My therapist told me to ask them to come over to talk to us. They were frightening to me in the light of the fire, but they were more horrible as they came closer. They laughed at me and started to poke at me with their sticks. The visualization was so real and their presence was so chilling to me that I burst into tears over the interaction with them.

My therapist told me to ask them what I could do to get rid of the awful fear of isolation. Finally they revealed their price. It was that I make a sacrifice so that they could become beautiful and mingle with other people. When I heard their price I began to tremble. In an almost inaudible voice I whispered, 'They want my children so they can turn them into witches like them, but I'll never do it. I'll never give them my children!'

My therapist then told me to destroy them, but I told him that I couldn't possibly do it. He urged me to try to turn my fear to wrath, to try to imagine a creature that could help me. The image that came to me was a white winged horse. He told me to mount the horse and to supply myself with a weapon that would destroy them. I refused to kill them myself, but said that the wings of the horse would fan the flames of their fire, which would turn back on them and destroy them.

There was only one problem with this scenario—the horse and I were one now and I couldn't get airborne. The wings were so heavy that I couldn't flap them hard enough to catch the breeze. The harder I tried, the more I failed and the more the witches laughed at me. My therapist . . . told me that another horse who loved the first horse very much would join her and together they would destroy the witches. The other horse flew above me and made a vacuum into which I could take off. Once in the air, I flew effortlessly and fanned the fire into a huge blaze. The witches ran here and there trying to avoid the flames but in the end they were consumed by the fire.

I practiced the scene over and over again until it became easy, but I never enjoyed it. I liked to fly, but I felt sorry for the witches, no matter how mean they were to me. My therapist felt that it was a mistake to feel sympathy for them because they would take advantage of any mercy that I displayed. He felt they would use any deception and illusion they could to control me. I was not so sure but I did agree with him that I must assume the right to soar into the world and be free of their influence. After the session, my therapist and I discussed the meaning of the images. Although I had begun with the concept of isolation in mind, I knew that the witches related to my mother, particularly the way she would poke at me and shame me. They probably represented my fear of isolation if I did not acquiesce to her demands. My therapist added that in destroying the witches I was only destroying the hostile part of our relationship, the witch part of it, and leaving the loving part intact. This was necessary for me to be free, autonomous, and no longer ensnared by fear of abandonment.

The concept that I had a great deal of conflict between the need for association and the need for autonomy was not new. I believed I had to buy affection and that no one would love me if I were myself, i.e., if I attended to my own wants. I knew also that I felt that I had to carry the burden of being responsible for my mother's well-being, that she would die at some level if I broke the bond with her. (pp. 45–47)

There are several aspects of this fantasy that warrant further comment. First, it is noteworthy that the only aspect that reached awareness before the fantasy was an enduring feeling of loneliness and isolation. The source of the feeling and its associations remained unconscious until they were dealt with at the experiential level and perhaps assimilated at the rational level.

Second, the insight represented in the fantasy—namely, that Alice had a conflict between autonomy and relatedness—was not new to her. As she noted, she had been consciously aware of this conflict before. What, then, did the fantasy accomplish? What it accomplished was to produce a vicarious corrective emotional experience that had a profound effect at the experiential level. The previous intellectual insight in the absence of involvement of the experiential system had accomplished little. To make a therapeutic contribution, the same information had to be felt and processed experientially.

Third, the fantasy provided useful diagnostic clues for the psychotherapist. Alice, apparently, could not free herself from the hold of the bad mother figure until a loving figure supported her independence, after which she could soar freely. This suggested that what she needed to resolve her conflict was to be convinced at a compelling experiential level that it is possible to be autonomous and loved at the same time. This was duly noted by her therapist, who made a point of encouraging its implementation in her family, as well as supporting it himself in the therapeutic relationship.

Fourth, the fantasy illustrates the usefulness of vicarious symbolic experience as a therapeutic tool. Alice spontaneously began to practice in fantasy enjoying the feeling of soaring freely into space, and as a result she was able to gain a newfound freedom without guilt or fear of abandonment. What she learned through the fantasy at a deep experiential level suggests a therapeutic technique that may be more generally useful—namely, the practice in symbolic form of coping with a deep-seated problem that cannot be resolved by intellectual insight. Of additional general value of this example of a spontaneous fantasy is that it indicates how such fantasies can provide diagnostic information that can be useful in therapy.

There is, of course, no way of knowing the extent to which the use of fantasy relative to other factors, such as having a highly supportive environment, played in Alice's rapid progress. It is very likely that both contributed. However, it should be considered in this respect that the equally favorable environment before the therapy was insufficient to resolve Alice's conflict between autonomy and relatedness. As she reported, the love and affection that were abundantly available to her from her husband, her children, her extended family, and her deeply caring friends could not penetrate, so long as she felt that the price of love was the sacrifice of autonomy. Having developed a lifelong pattern of self-sacrifice in order to maintain relationships, she had no way of learning before therapy that it was unnecessary.

Implications for Research

If there are two different information-processing systems, it can only be a source of confusion to conduct research as if there were only one, which is the customary practice. As an example, given the existence of two different systems, it is meaningless to investigate "the" self-concept because a person's self-concept in one system may not conform to the self-concept in the other system. Moreover, the difference between the two self-concepts can be of considerable importance in its own right. The problem of treating the two self-concepts as if there were only one has been particularly evident in research on self-esteem, in which individuals are typically classified as high or low in self-esteem based on self-report questionnaires. Yet if there are *two* self-concepts, then it is quite possible for people to be high in self-esteem in one system and low in the other. For example, a person might be high in self-esteem in the rational system, as measured by a self-report test, yet low in self-esteem in the experiential system, as inferred from behavior (Savin-Williams & Jaquish, 1981).

There has been much disagreement concerning whether elevating students' self-esteem by treating them as successful no matter what their performance is desirable or undesirable. In order to resolve this issue, from the perspective of CEST it is necessary to recognize that high self-esteem at the conscious, rational level may coexist with low self-esteem at the experiential level. It is one thing to teach students to consciously believe they have high self-regard and another to have them acquire the quiet confidence that comes from feelings of mastery and competence that are a consequence of real accomplishment. The former in the absence of the latter can be considered to be no more than self-deception and a potential source of disillusionment in the future. It follows that not only is it important to examine self-esteem separately in each of the two systems, but it is equally important to conduct research on their convergence. What is obviously true of self-esteem in this respect is equally true of other personality variables, including basic needs and beliefs.

Although the importance of four basic needs and corresponding beliefs is emphasized in CEST, this is not meant to imply that lower-level beliefs and needs are not also very important. Recently, social and personality psychologists have emphasized midlevel motivational constructs (e.g., Emmons, 1986; Markus & Nurius, 1986; Mischel & Shoda, 1995). It is assumed in CEST that personality is hierarchically organized, with broad, basic needs subsuming midlevel motives, which in turn subsume narrower, situation-specific motives. It would

therefore be desirable to examine the organization of such needs and beliefs, and to determine in particular the kinds of relations the different levels establish with each other, as well as with other variables. It might reasonably be expected that the lowest-order needs and beliefs are most strongly associated with situationally specific behaviors, and the higher-order beliefs and needs are more strongly associated with broad dispositions, or traits. The higher-order beliefs and needs can also be expected to be more weakly but more extensively associated with narrow behavioral tendencies. Midlevel motives can be expected to have relations that fall in between those of the higher- and lower-order needs. A particularly important hypothesis with regard to CEST is that higher-order needs and beliefs are more resistant to change than are lower-order needs and beliefs, but should they be changed they have greater effects on the overall personality structure. Moreover, any major changes, including positive changes, are disorganizing and anxiety-producing because of the basic need to maintain the stability of the conceptual system.

Although considerable research has recently been conducted on midlevel needs that has demonstrated their theoretical importance and predictive value (e.g., Emmons, 1986; Markus & Nurius, 1986; Mischel & Shoda, 1995), the question remains as to how the midlevel needs can best be designated and measured. The most thorough and compelling list of midlevel needs to date still appears to be the list proposed by Henry A. Murray (1938) many years ago. It is interesting from the perspective of CEST that Murray measured midlevel needs both explicitly via direct self-report and implicitly through the use of the Thematic Apperception Test (TAT; Murray, 1943). A more psychometrically advanced procedure for measuring the Murray midlevel needs at the explicit level has since become available in the form of the Edwards Personal Preference Schedule (Edwards, 1959).

There is a need for research to further explore the TAT as a measure of implicit needs and to also examine additional measures of implicit needs. Included could be older procedures such as word association and sentence completion, as well as promising new procedures such as priming techniques and subthreshold measures (see Bargh & Chartrand, in press, for a review of such techniques). It would be interesting to relate the various implicit measures to each other to determine whether they have enough in common to combine them into an overall measure. The implicit measure (or measures) of needs could then be related to explicit measures of needs, and both could be related to external criteria. Through such procedures it should be possible to determine in what ways implicit and explicit measures are similar and different. It could also be determined whether they contribute in a supplementary way to the prediction of the same variables and whether the degree to which they coincide in individuals is an important personality variable, as assumed in CEST. It would be informative to determine what kinds of combinations of implicit needs usually result in compromises, what kinds usually result in conflict, and how this differs among individuals. Such research would not only be of theoretical importance, but would also have important implications for the diagnosis of sources of distress and for therapy.

Although considerable research has been done with the CTI that has supported its construct validity (see review in Epstein, 2001), there are many areas that could profit from further research with it. One such area is the predictive value of the CTI for success in a variety of work situations that have not yet been investigated. It would be interesting, for example, to conduct a study comparing the contribution of intellectual intelligence, as measured by a standard intelligence test, and experiential intelligence, as measured by the CTI, for predicting performance in graduate school and beyond. A hypothesis derived from CEST and consistent with previous research (Epstein, 2001) is that intellectual intelligence is a stronger predictor of grades and scores on paper-and-pencil tests, whereas constructive thinking is a stronger predictor of practical performance. The latter could be indicated by demonstrations of research productivity and creativity, by length of time to complete the PhD degree, and by successful professional performance after obtaining the PhD degree.

As noted previously, with the aid of a newly constructed instrument, the Rational-Experiential Inventory (REI; Epstein et al., 1996; Norris & Epstein, 2000a, 2000b; Pacini & Epstein, 1999b), it is possible to study the effects of individual differences in processing in each of the two modes. Of particular interest is the independent contribution of each of the modes for predicting well-being and performance in different kinds of activities. Although a promising beginning has been made in this area, there is a need for more extensive research, particularly with the use of objective rather than self-reported dependent variables.

An important area of research with both practical and theoretical implications is the relation of the two thinking styles to receptivity to different kinds of messages. The one research project that has been completed on this issue (Rosenthal & Epstein, 2000) has produced interesting results consistent with CEST and suggests that it is a promising area for further research. It remains to be determined how each of the processing styles—separately and in combination—is related to receptivity to messages regarding politics, advertising, and health-related behaviors such as smoking and sexual risk-taking.

An area of particular theoretical and practical importance is the influence of the experiential system on the rational system. As previously noted, this relation can account for the paradoxical irrationality exhibited by humans despite their unique capacity for rational reasoning. The influence of experiential on rational processing is assigned an extremely important role in CEST, equivalent to the influence of the Freudian unconscious in psychoanalysis. It is therefore important from the perspective of CEST to conduct further research to demonstrate the influence of experiential on rational processing under various conditions. Relatedly, it is important to test the hypotheses that such influence is often mediated by feelings, the identification of which, accordingly, can be helpful as a first step in controlling the influence of the experiential on the rational system.

Research is needed on the positive contributions of experiential processing to creativity, wisdom, and physical and mental well-being. It is important in this respect to determine how people can most effectively influence and learn from their experiential systems by communicating with these systems in their own medium, as illustrated in the case history that was presented. You will recall that Alice, by practicing soaring freely and unaided in fantasy, was able to accept the belief, at a deep experiential level, that it is possible to be an autonomous being without fear of rejection in a way that intellectual insight was unable to accomplish. It will be interesting to determine how effective such symbolic rehearsal is more generally as a way of resolving deep-seated conflicts at the experiential level.

SUMMARY AND CONCLUSIONS

Cognitive-experiential self-theory (CEST) is a psychodynamic global theory of personality that substitutes a different kind of unconscious processing for the Freudian unconscious. Unlike the maladaptive Freudian unconscious, the unconscious of CEST is an adaptive, associative learning system. It is the same system with which higher-order animals have increasingly effectively adapted to their environments over millions of years of evolution. Because it is a system that learns from experience, it is referred to as the *experiential system*. In addition to an experiential system, humans uniquely have a *rational system*. The rational system is a logical, inferential system that operates with the aid of language. The experiential system can account for the widespread irrationality in the thinking of humans despite their unique capacity for reasoning rationally by recognizing that it biases conscious thinking automatically and outside of awareness.

The operating principles of the experiential system were described and contrasted with those of the rational system. Although the systems are independent in the sense that they operate by different rules, they nevertheless are highly interactive. The two systems usually operate in synchrony and produce compromises between them, but sometimes they conflict with each other, resulting in what are commonly referred to as conflicts between the heart and the head. A research program was described that provided support for many of the assumptions in CEST. The implications of CEST were discussed for psychotherapy and psychological research.

It was noted that neither system is superior to the other. They are simply different ways of understanding the world and behaving in it. The experiential system is intimately associated with emotions and adapts by learning from outcomes. The rational system is a affect-free and adapts by logical inference. Each has its advantages and disadvantages. Although the rational system is responsible for remarkable achievements in science and technology, it is less well suited for everyday living than is the experiential system. Moreover, the experiential system can intuitively and holistically solve some problems that are beyond the capacity of the analytical, rule-based reasoning of the rational system (Hammond, 1996). The experiential system is also a source of some of humankind's most desirable attributes, including the capacity for passion, compassion, love, creativity, and appreciation of aesthetics. However, it is also a source of serious difficulties, including superstitious thinking, prejudice, violence, and—perhaps most important—undermining people's ability to think rationally. Thus, the experiential system is a mixed blessing; it is difficult to live with it, but it would be impossible to live without it.

REFERENCES

Alloy, L. B., & Abramson, L. Y. (1988). Depressive realism: Four theoretical perspectives. In L. B. Alloy (Ed.), *Cognitive processes in depression* (pp. 167–232). New York: Guilford Press.

Allport, G. W. (1961). *Pattern and growth in personality*. New York: Holt, Rinehart, and Winston.

Averill, J. R. (1980). A constructionist view of emotion. In R. Plutchik & H. Kellerman (Eds.), *Emotion, theory, research, and experience: Vol. 1. Theories of emotion*. New York: Academic Press.

Bargh, J. A. (1989). Conditional automaticity: Varieties of automatic influence in social perception and cognition. In J. S. Uleman & J. A. Bargh (Eds.), *Unintended thought* (pp. 3–51). New York: Guilford Press.

Bargh, J. A., & Chartrand, T. L. (in press). Studying the mind in the middle: A practical guide to priming and automaticity research. In H. Reis & C. Judd (Eds.), *Research methods in the social sciences*. New York: Cambridge University Press.

Beck, A. T. (1976). *Cognitive therapy and the emotional disorders*. New York: International Universities Press.

Bowlby, J. (1988). *A secure base*. New York: Basic Books.

Catlin, G., & Epstein, S. (1992). Unforgettable experiences: The relation of life-events to basic beliefs about the self and world. *Social Cognition, 10,* 189–209.

Chaiken, S., & Maheswaren, D. (1994). Heuristic processing can bias systematic processing: Effects of resource credibility, argument ambiguity, and task importance on attitude adjustment. *Journal of Personality and Social Psychology, 66,* 460–473.

Chaiken, S., & Trope, Y. (1999). *Dual-process theories in social psychology*. New York: Guilford Press.

Costa, P. T., & McCrae, R. R. (1989). *NEO/FFI: Manual Supplement*. Odessa, FL: Psychological Assessment Resources.

Denes-Raj, V., & Epstein, S. (1994). Conflict between experiential and rational processing: When people behave against their better judgment. *Journal of Personality and Social Psychology, 66,* 819–829.

Denes-Raj, V., Epstein, S., & Cole, J. (1995). The generality of the ratio-bias phenomenon. *Personality and Social Psychology Bulletin, 10,* 1083–1092.

Dollard, J., & Miller, N. E. (1950). *Personality and psychotherapy: An analysis in terms of learning, thinking, and culture*. New York: McGraw-Hill.

Donovan, S., & Epstein, S. (1997). The difficulty of the Linda conjunction problem can be attributed to its simultaneous concrete and unnatural presentation, and not to conversational implicature. *Journal of Experimental Social Psychology, 33,* 1–20.

Edwards, A. L. (1959). *Manual for Edwards Personal Preference Schedule* (Rev. ed). New York: Psychological Corporation.

Edwards, K. (1990). The interplay of affect and cognition in attitude formation and change. *Journal of Personality and Social Psychology, 59,* 202–216.

Ellis, A. (1973). *Humanistic psychotherapy*. New York: McGraw-Hill.

Emmons, R. A. (1986). Personal strivings: An approach to personality and subjective wellbeing. *Journal of Personality and Social Psychology, 51,* 1058–1068.

Epstein, A. (1989). *Mind, fantasy, and healing*. New York: Delacorte. (This book is out of print, but copies can be obtained from Amazon.com or from Balderwood Books, 37 Bay Road, Amherst, MA 01002 by enclosing a check for $18.00, which includes postage.)

Epstein, S. (1979a). Natural healing processes of the mind: Pt. 1. Acute schizophrenic disorganization. *Schizophrenic Bulletin, 5,* 313–321.

Epstein, S. (1983). A research paradigm for the study of personality and emotions. In M. M. Page (Ed.), *1982 Nebraska Symposium on motivation: Personality—Current theory and research* (pp. 91–154). Lincoln: University of Nebraska Press.

Epstein, S. (1984). Controversial issues in emotion theory. In P. Shaver (Ed.), *Annual review of research in personality and social psychology* (pp. 64–87). Beverly Hills, CA: Sage.

Epstein, S. (1987). Implications of cognitive self-theory for psychopathology and psychotherapy. In N. Cheshire & H. Thomae (Eds.), *Self, symptoms and psychotherapy* (pp. 43–58). New York: Wiley.

Epstein, S. (1990). Cognitive-experiential self-theory. In L. Pervin (Ed.), *Handbook of personality theory and research: Theory and research* (pp. 165–192). New York: Guilford.

Epstein, S. (1993). Emotion and self-theory. In M. Lewis & J. Haviland (Eds.), *The handbook of emotions* (pp. 313–326). New York: Guilford.

Epstein, S. (1994). Integration of the cognitive and the psychodynamic unconscious. *American Psychologist, 49,* 709–724,

Epstein, S. (1998). *Constructive thinking: The key to emotional intelligence.* Westport, CT: Praeger.

Epstein, S. (2001). *Manual for the Constructive Thinking Inventory.* Lutz, FL: Psychological Assessments Resources.

Epstein, S., Denes-Raj, V., & Pacini, R. (1995). The Linda problem revisited from the perspective of cognitive-experimental self-theory. *Personality and Social Psychology Bulletin, 11,* 1124–1138.

Epstein, S., & Donovan, S. (1995). [Is the Linda problem a true conjunction problem? Implications from frequency versus probability versions and individual differences in analytical style.] Unpublished raw data.

Epstein, S., Donovan, S., & Denes-Raj, V. (1999). The missing link in the paradox of the Linda conjunction problem: Beyond knowing and thinking of the conjunction rule, the intrinsic appeal of heuristic processing. *Personality and Social Psychology Bulletin, 25,* 204–214.

Epstein, S., Lipson, A., Holstein, C., & Huh, E. (1992). Irrational reactions to negative outcomes: Evidence for two conceptual systems. *Journal of Personality and Social Psychology, 62,* 328–339.

Epstein, S., & Morling, B. (1995). Is the self motivated to do more than enhance and verify itself? In M. H. Kernis (Ed.), *Efficacy, agency, and self-esteem* (pp. 9–29). New York: Plenum Press.

Epstein, S., & Pacini, R. (1995). [The Linda problem: A true conjunction problem, or does the conjunction rule not apply to multiple attributes in a single person?] Unpublished raw data.

Epstein, S., & Pacini, R. (2001). A comparison of the influence of imagined and unimagined verbal information on intuitive and analytical information processing. *Imagination, Cognition, and Personality, 20,* 195–216.

Epstein, S., Pacini, R., Denes-Raj, V., & Heier, H. (1996). Individual differences in intuitive-experiential and analytical-rational thinking styles. *Journal of Personality and Social Psychology, 71,* 390–405.

Fiske, S. T., & Taylor, S. E. (1991). *Social cognition* (2nd ed.). New York: McGraw-Hill.

Freud, S. (1953). *The interpretation of dreams.* In J. Strachey (Ed. & Trans.), *The standard edition of the complete psychological works of Sigmund Freud* (Vols. 4 & 5). London: Hogarth. (Original work published 1900)

Gallistel, C. R., & Gelman, R. (1992). Preverbal and verbal counting and computation. *Cognition, 44,* 43–74.

Gordon, R. A. (1997). Everyday life as an intelligence test [Special issue]. *Intelligence, a Multidisciplinary Journal, 24,* 203–320.

Gottfredson, L. S. (1997). Why g matters: The complexity of everyday life [Special issue]. *Intelligence, a Multidisciplinary Journal, 24,* 79–132.

Hammond, K. R. (1996). *Human judgment and Social policy.* New York: Oxford University Press.

Hixon, J. G., & Swann, W. B. (1993). When does introspection bare fruit? Self-reflection, self-insight, and interpersonal choices. *Journal of Personality and Social Psychology, 64,* 35–43.

Hunter, J. E. (1983). *Overview of validity generalization for the U.S. Employment Service* (USES Test Research Report No. 43). Washington, DC: U.S. Department of Labor, Employment, and Training Administration.

Hunter, J. E. (1986). Cognitive ability, cognitive aptitudes, job knowledge, and job performance. *Journal of Vocational Behavior, 29,* 340–362.

Hunter, J. E., & Hunter, R. F., (1984). Validity and utility of alternative predictors of job performance. *Psychological Bulletin, 96,* 72–98.

Jefferson, L. (1974). *These are my sisters.* Garden City, NY: Anchor Press.

Kahneman, D., Slovic, P., & Tversky, A. (1982). *Judgment under uncertainty: Heuristics and biases.* New York: Cambridge University Press.

Kahneman, D., & Tversky, A. (1973). On the psychology of prediction. *Psychological Review, 80,* 237–251.

Kirkpatrick, L. A., & Epstein, S. (1992). Cognitive-experiential self-theory and subjective probability: Further evidence for two conceptual systems. *Journal of Personality and Social Psychology, 63,* 534–544.

Kohut, H. (1971). *The analysis of the self.* New York: International Universities Press.

Lazarus, R. (1991). *Emotion and adaptation.* New York: Oxford University Press.

Markus, H., & Nurius, P. (1986). Possible selves. *American Psychologist, 41,* 954–969.

Miller, D. T., & Gunasegaram, S. (1990). Temporal order and the perceived mutability of events: Implications for blame assignment. *Journal of Personality and Social Psychology, 59,* 1111–1118.

Mischel, W., & Shoda, Y. (1995). A cognitive-affective system theory of personality: Reconceptualizing situations, dispositions, dynamics, and invariance in personality structure. *Psychological Review, 102,* 246–268.

Morling, B., & Epstein, S. (1997). Compromises produced by the dialectic between self-verification and self-enhancement. *Journal of Personality and Social Psychology, 73,* 1268–1283.

Murray, H. A. (1938). *Explorations in personality.* New York: Oxford University Press.

Murray, H. A. (1943). *Thematic Apperception Test manual.* Cambridge, MA: Harvard University Press.

Nisbett, R., & Ross, L. (1980). *Human inference: Strategies and shortcomings of social judgment.* Englewood Cliffs, NJ: Prentice Hall.

Norris, P., & Epstein, S. (2000a). *The measurement of analytical and intuitive thinking styles with a short form of the Rational-Experiential Inventory.* Manuscript submitted for publication.

Norris, P., & Epstein, S. (2000b). [Objective and subjective correlates of rational and experiential thinking styles]. Unpublished raw data.

Pacini, R., & Epstein, S. (1999a). The interaction of three facets of concrete thinking in a game of chance. *Thinking and Reasoning, 5,* 303–325.

Pacini, R., & Epstein, S. (1999b). The relation of rational and experiential information processing styles to personality, basic beliefs, and the ratio-bias phenomenon. *Journal of Personality and Social Psychology, 76,* 972–987.

Pacini, R., Muir, F., & Epstein, S. (1998). Depressive realism from the perspective of cognitive-experiential self-theory. *Journal of Personality and Social Psychology, 74,* 1056–1068.

Pavlov, I. P. (1941). *Conditioned reflexes in psychiatry* (W. H. Gannt, Trans.). Madison, CT: International Universities Press.

Rogers, C. R. (1951). *Client-centered therapy: Its current practice, applications, and theory.* Boston: Houghton Mifflin.

Rosenthal, L., & Epstein, S. (2000). *Rational and experiential thinking styles as related to receptivity to messages syntonic and dystonic with thinking style.* Unpublished manuscript, University of Massachusetts at Amherst.

Savin-Williams, R. C., & Jaquish, G. A. (1981). The assessment of adolescent self-esteem: A comparison of methods. *Journal of Personality, 49,* 324–335.

Smith, E. R., & DeCoster, J. (2000). Dual-process models in social and cognitive psychology: Conceptual integration and links to underlying memory systems. *Personality and Social Psychology Review, 4,* 108–131.

Swann, W. B., Jr. (1990). To be known or to be adored: The interplay of self-enhancement and self-verification. In R. M. Sorrentino & E. T. Higgins (Eds.), *Handbook of motivation and cognition: Foundations of social behavior* (Vol. 2, pp. 408–448). New York: Guilford.

Taylor, S. E., & Brown, J. D. (1988). Illusion and wellbeing: A social psychological perspective on mental health. *Psychological Bulletin, 103,* 193–210.

Tolstoi, L. (1887). *My confession.* New York: Crowell.

Tversky, A., & Kahneman, D. (1974). Judgment under uncertainty: Heuristics and biases. *Science, 185,* 1124–1131.

Tversky, A., & Kahneman, D. (1982). Judgments of and by representativeness. In D. Kahneman, P. Slovic, & A. Tversky (Eds.), *Judgment under uncertainty: Heuristics and biases.* New York: Cambridge University Press.

Tversky, A., & Kahneman, D. (1983). Extensional versus intuitive reasoning: the conjunction fallacy in probability judgment. *Psychological Review, 90,* 293–315.

Yanko, J., & Epstein, S. (2000). [The intuitive knowledge of ratios in children without formal training in ratios and the interference produced by requesting explanations.] Unpublished raw data.

CHAPTER 8

Self-Regulatory Perspectives on Personality

CHARLES S. CARVER AND MICHAEL F. SCHEIER

Personality is a difficult concept to pin down. By necessity it is a very broad concept because personality impinges on virtually all aspects of human behavior. This breadth is viewed differently by different theorists, however. As a result, many different approaches have been taken to thinking about and conceptualizing personality. The diversity in focus among the chapters in the first part of this volume attests very clearly to that fact.

We were both trained as personality psychologists. Throughout our careers, however, our research interest has focused on a set of issues regarding the structure of behavior. These issues link the concept of personality and its functioning to a set of themes that might be regarded as representing the psychology of motivation. Our interest in how behavior occurs has taken us into a number of specific research domains—most recently health-related behavior and responses to stress (Carver & Scheier, 2001; Scheier, Carver, & Bridges, 2001). However, these specific explorations have almost always occurred in service to a more general interest in the structure of behavior.

What we mean by "the structure of behavior" is reflected in the issues underlying questions such as these: What is the most useful way to think about how people create actions from their intentions, plans, and desires? Once people have decided to do something, how do they stay on course? What is the relation between people's values and their actions?

Preparation of this chapter was facilitated by grants CA64710, CA64711, CA62711, CA78995, and CA84944 from the National Cancer Institute, and grants HL65111 and HL65112 from the National Heart, Lung, and Blood Institute.

What processes account for the existence of feelings as people make their way through the world?

As we have tried to address such questions, we have consistently returned to the idea that people are self-regulatory entities. That is, human behavior is an attempt to make something occur in action that is already held in mind. Similarly, affects serve as self-regulatory controls on what actions take place and with how much urgency.

The self-regulatory principles we emphasize in our writings were not conceived as being a model of personality. However, the principles do turn out to provide an interesting *perspective* on personality. They suggest some implications about how personality is organized and expressed in people's actions. These principles also point to some of the issues that are involved in successfully negotiating the world. The principles we emphasize deal most explicitly with the "process" aspect of personality—the functions that make everyone a little bit alike—but they can also be seen to have implications for the individual differences that are part of personality psychology.

This chapter is organized as a series of conceptual themes that reflect this self-regulatory perspective on personality. We start with basic ideas about the nature of behavior and some of the processes by which we believe behavior is regulated. We then turn to emotion—how we think it arises and a way in which two classes of affects differ from each other. This leads to a discussion of the fact that people sometimes are unable to do what they set out to do and of what follows from that problem. The next sections are more speculative and reflect emerging themes in thinking about behavior. They deal with dynamic systems, connectionism, and catastrophe theory as models for behavior and how such models may influence how people such as ourselves view self-regulation.

BEHAVIOR AS GOAL DIRECTED AND FEEDBACK CONTROLLED

The view we take on behavior begins with the concept of goal and the process of feedback control, ideas we see as intimately linked. Our focus on goals is in line with a growing re-emergence of goal constructs in personality psychology (e.g., Austin & Vancouver, 1996; Elliott & Dweck, 1988; Miller & Read, 1987; Pervin, 1989), constructs known by a variety of labels such as *current concern* (Klinger, 1975, 1977), *personal strivings* (Emmons, 1986), *life task* (Cantor & Kihlstrom, 1987), and *personal project* (Little, 1983). The goal construct is at its core very simple. Yet these theories all emphasize that it has room for great diversity and individualization. For example, any life task can be achieved in diverse

ways. People presumably choose paths for achieving a given life task that are compatible with other aspects of their life situation (e.g., many concerns must usually be managed simultaneously) and with other aspects of their personality.

Two goal constructs that differ somewhat from those named thus far are the *possible self* (Markus & Nurius, 1986) and the *self-guide* (Higgins, 1987, 1996). These constructs were intended to bring a dynamic quality to conceptualization of the self-concept. In contrast to traditional views, but consistent with other goal frameworks, possible selves are future oriented. They concern how people think of their as-yet-unrealized potential, the kind of people they might become. Self-guides similarly reflect dynamic aspects of the self-concept.

Despite differences among these various constructs (see Austin & Vancouver, 1996; Carver & Scheier, 1998), they are the same in many ways. All include the idea that goals energize and direct activities; all implicitly convey the sense that goals give meaning to people's lives (cf. Baumeister, 1989). Each theory emphasizes the idea that understanding the person means in part understanding the person's goals. Indeed, the view represented by these theories often implies that the self consists partly of the person's goals and the organization among them.

Feedback Processes

How are goals used in behaving? We believe that goals serve as reference values for feedback loops (Wiener, 1948). A feedback loop, the unit of cybernetic control, is a system of four elements in a particular organization (cf. MacKay, 1956; Miller, Galanter, & Pribram, 1960). The elements are an input function, a reference value, a comparator, and an output function (see Figure 8.1).

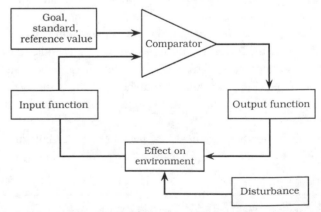

Figure 8.1   Schematic depiction of a feedback loop, the basic unit of cybernetic control. In such a loop a sensed value is compared to a reference value or standard, and adjustments are made in an output function (if necessary) to shift the sensed value in the appropriate direction.

An input function is a sensor. Think of it as perception. The reference value is a bit of information specified from within the system. Think of it as a goal. A comparator is something that makes continuous or repeated comparisons between the input and the reference value. The comparison yields one of two outcomes: values being compared either are or are not discriminably different from one another. Following the comparison is an output function. Think of this as behavior (although the behavior sometimes is internal). If the comparison yielded "no difference," the output function remains whatever it was. If the comparison yielded "discrepancy," the output changes.

There are two kinds of feedback loops, corresponding to two kinds of goals. In a discrepancy-reducing loop (a *negative* feedback loop), the output function is aimed at diminishing or eliminating any detected discrepancy between input and reference value. It yields conformity of input to reference. This conformity is seen in the attempt to approach or attain a valued goal.

The other kind of feedback loop is a discrepancy-enlarging loop (a *positive* feedback loop). The reference value here is not one to approach, but one to avoid. Think of it as an "anti-goal." An example is a feared possible self. Other examples would be traffic tickets, public ridicule, and the experience of being fired from your job. This loop senses present conditions, compares them to the anti-goal, and tries to enlarge the discrepancy. For example, a rebellious adolescent who wants to be different from his parents senses his own behavior, compares it to his parents' behavior, and tries to make his own behavior as different from theirs as possible.

The action of discrepancy-enlarging processes in living systems is typically constrained in some way by discrepancy-reducing loops (Figure 8.2). To put it differently, avoidance behaviors often lead into approach behaviors that are compatible with the avoidance. An avoidance loop creates pressure to increase distance from the anti-goal. The movement away occurs until it is captured by the influence of an approach loop. This loop then serves to pull the sensed input into its orbit. The rebellious adolescent, trying to be different from his parents, soon finds other adolescents to *conform* to, all of whom are actively deviating from their parents.

Our use of the word *orbit* in the last paragraph suggests a metaphor that may be useful for those to whom these concepts do not feel very intuitive. You might think of feedback processes as metaphorically equivalent to gravity and antigravity. The discrepancy-reducing loop exerts a kind of gravitational pull on the input it is controlling, pulling that input closer to its ground zero. The discrepancy-enlarging loop has a kind of antigravitational push, moving sensed values ever farther away. Remember, though, that this is a metaphor. More is involved here than a force field.

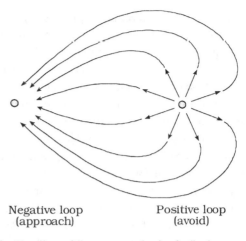

Figure 8.2 The effects of discrepancy-enlarging feedback systems are often constrained by discrepancy-reducing feedback systems. A value moves away from an undesired condition in an avoidance loop and then comes under the influence of an approach loop, moving toward its goal value. *Source:* From C. S. Carver and M. F. Scheier, *On the Self-Regulation of Behavior,* copyright 1998, Cambridge University Press. Reprinted with permission.

Note that situations are often more complex than the one in Figure 8.2 in that there often are several potential values to move toward. Thus, if several people try to deviate from a mutually disliked reference point, they may diverge from one another. For example, one adolescent trying to escape from his parents' values may gravitate toward membership in a rock band, whereas another may gravitate toward the army. Presumably, the direction in which the person moves will depend in part on the fit between the available reference values and the person's preexisting values, and in part on the direction the person takes initially to escape from the anti-goal.

Feedback processes have been studied for a long time in a variety of physical systems (cf. Wiener, 1948). With respect to living systems, they are commonly invoked regarding physiological systems, particularly those that maintain the equilibriums that sustain life. We all know of the existence of homeostatic systems that regulate, for example, temperature and blood pressure. It is a bit of a stretch to go from homeostatic maintenance processes to intentional behavior, but the stretch is not as great as some might think (see Miller et al., 1960; MacKay, 1956; Powers, 1973).

One key to this extrapolation is the realization that reference values for feedback loops need not be static. They can change gradually over time, and one can be substituted quickly for another. Thus, a feedback system need not be purely homeostatic. It can be highly dynamic—chasing (and avoiding) moving targets and changing targets. This is not too far from a description (albeit a very abstract one) of the events that make up human life.

Some years ago we argued that the comparator of a psychological feedback process is engaged by self-focused

that person's actions. Values are the source of intentions to take certain patterns of actions, and those programmatic action plans are realized in an extended series of sequences of movement. This view also provides for a mechanism by which the actions themselves take place, which is not typically the case in models of personality.

Multiple Paths to High-Level Goals, Multiple Meanings from Concrete Acts

This hierarchy also has implications for several further issues in thinking about behavior (for more detail see Carver & Scheier, 1998, 1999a). In this view, goals at a given level can often be attained by a variety of means at lower levels. This addresses the fact that people sometimes shift radically the manner in which they try to reach a goal when the goal itself has not changed. This happens commonly when the emergent quality that is the higher order goal is implied in several lower order activities. For example, a person can be helpful by writing a donation check, picking up discards for a recycling center, volunteering at a charity, or holding a door open for someone else.

Just as a given goal can be obtained via multiple pathways, so can a specific act be performed in the service of diverse goals. For example, you could buy someone a gift to make her feel good, to repay a kindness, to put her in your debt, or to satisfy a perceived holiday-season role. Thus, a given act can have strikingly different meanings depending on the purpose it's intended to serve. This is an important subtheme of this view on behavior: Behavior can be understood only by identifying the goals to which behavior is addressed. This is not always easy to do, either from an observer's point of view (cf. Read, Druian, & Miller, 1989) or from the actor's point of view.

Goals and the Self

Another point made by the notion of hierarchical organization concerns the fact that goals are not equivalent in their importance. The higher you go into the organization, the more fundamental to the overriding sense of self are the qualities encountered. Thus, goal qualities at higher levels would appear to be intrinsically more important than those at lower levels.

Goals at a given level are not necessarily equivalent to one another in importance, however. In a hierarchical system there are at least two ways in which importance accrues to a goal. The more directly an action contributes to attainment of some highly valued goal at a more abstract level, the more

important is that action. Second, an act that contributes to the attainment of several goals at once is thereby more important than an act that contributes to the attainment of only one goal.

Relative importance of goals returns us again to the concept of self. In contemporary theory the self-concept has several aspects. One is the structure of knowledge about your personal history; another is knowledge about who you are now. Another is the self-guides or images of potential selves that are used to guide movement from the present into the future. As stated earlier, a broad implication of this view is that the self— indeed, personality—consists partly of a person's goals.

FEEDBACK LOOPS AND CREATION OF AFFECT

We turn now to another aspect of human self-regulation: emotion. Here we add a layer of complexity that differs greatly from the complexity represented by hierarchicality. Again, the organizing principle is feedback control. But now the control is over a different quality.

What are feelings, and what makes them exist? Many have analyzed the information that feelings provide and situations in which affect arises (see, e.g., Frijda, 1986; Lazarus, 1991; Ortony, Clore, & Collins, 1988; Roseman, 1984; Scherer & Ekman, 1984). The question we address here is slightly different: What is the internal mechanism by which feelings arise?

Velocity Control

We have suggested that feelings arise within the functioning of another feedback process (Carver & Scheier, 1990). This process operates simultaneously with the behavior-guiding process and in parallel to it. One way to describe this second function is to say that it is checking on how well the behavior loop is doing at reducing its discrepancies. Thus, the input for this second loop is a representation of the rate of discrepancy reduction in the action system over time. We focus first on discrepancy-reducing loops and turn later to enlarging loops.

We find an analogy useful here. Because action implies change between states, think of behavior as analogous to distance. If the action loop deals with distance, and if the affect-relevant loop assesses the progress of the action loop, then the affect loop is dealing with the psychological equivalent of velocity, the first derivative of distance over time. To the extent that the analogy is meaningful, the perceptual input to this loop should be the first derivative over time of the input used by the action loop.

This input does not in itself create affect because a given rate of progress has different affective consequences under different circumstances. As in any feedback system, this input is compared against a reference value (cf. Frijda, 1986, 1988). In this case, the reference is an acceptable or desired rate of behavioral discrepancy reduction. As in other feedback loops, the comparison checks for a deviation from the standard. If there is one, the output function changes.

We suggest that the result of the comparison process in this loop (the error signal generated by its comparator) appears phenomenologically in two forms. One is a nonverbal sense of confidence or doubt (to which we turn later). The other is affect, feeling, a sense of positivity or negativity.

Research Evidence

Because this idea is relatively novel, we should devote some attention to whether any evidence supports it. Initial support came from Hsee and Abelson (1991), who arrived independently at the velocity hypothesis. They conducted two studies of velocity and satisfaction. In one, participants read descriptions of paired hypothetical scenarios and indicated which they would find more satisfying. For example, they chose whether they would be more satisfied if their class standing had gone from the 30th percentile to the 70th over the past 6 weeks, or if it had done so over the past 3 weeks. Given positive outcomes, they preferred improving to a high outcome over a constant high outcome; they preferred a fast velocity over a slow one; and they preferred fast small changes to slower larger changes. When the change was negative (e.g., salaries decreased), they preferred a constant low salary to a salary that started high and fell to the same low level; they preferred slow falls to fast falls; and they preferred large slow falls to small fast falls.

We have since conducted a study that conceptually replicates aspects of these findings but with an event that was personally experienced rather than hypothetical (Lawrence, Carver, & Scheier, in press). We manipulated success feedback on an ambiguous task over an extended period. The patterns of feedback converged such that block 6 was identical for all subjects at 50% correct. Subjects in a neutral condition had 50% on the first and last block, and 50% average across all blocks. Others had positive change in performance, starting poorly and gradually improving. Others had negative change, starting well and gradually worsening. All rated their mood before starting and again after block 6 (which they did not know ended the session). Those whose performances were improving reported mood improvement, whereas those whose performances were deteriorating reported mood deterioration, compared to those with a constant performance.

Another study that appears to bear on this view of affect was reported by Brunstein (1993). It examined subjective well-being among college students over the course of an academic term, as a function of several perceptions, including perception of progress toward goals. Of particular interest at present, perceived progress at each measurement point was strongly correlated with concurrent well-being.

Cruise Control Model

Although the theory may sound complex, the system we have proposed functions much the same as another device that is well known to many people: the cruise control on a car. If you are moving too slowly toward a goal, negative affect arises. You respond to this condition by putting more effort into your action, trying to speed up. If you are going faster than you need to, positive affect arises, and you pull back effort and coast. A car's cruise control is very similar. You come to a hill, which slows you down. The cruise control responds by feeding the engine more gas to bring the speed back up. If you pass the crest of a hill and roll downhill too fast, the system pulls back on the gas, which eventually drags the speed back down.

This analogy is intriguing because it concerns regulation of the very quality that we believe the affect system is regulating: velocity. It is also intriguing that the analogy incorporates a similar asymmetry in the consequences of deviating from the set point. That is, both in a car's cruise control and in human behavior, going too slow calls for investing greater effort and resources. Going too fast does not. It calls only for pulling back on resources. That is, the cruise control does not apply the brakes; it just cuts back on the gasoline. In this way it permits the car to coast gradually back to its velocity set point. In the same fashion, people do not respond to positive affect by trying to make it go away, but just by easing off.

Does positive affect actually lead people to withdraw effort? We are not aware of data that bear unambiguously on the question. To do so, a study must assess coasting with respect to the same goal as lies behind the affect. Many studies that might otherwise be seen as relevant to the question created positive affect in one context and assessed its impact on another task (see, e.g., Isen, 2000). The question thus seems to remain open, and to represent an important area for future work (for broader discussion of relevant issues see Carver, in press).

Affect from Discrepancy-Enlarging Loops

Thus far we have restricted ourselves to issues that arise in the context of approach. Now we turn to attempts to avoid a point of comparison, attempts to not-be or not-do: discrepancy-enlarging loops.

Our earlier discussion should have made it clear that behavior regarding avoidance goals is just as intelligible as behavior regarding approach goals. We think the same is true of the affective accompaniments to behavior. Our model rests on the idea that positive affect comes when a behavioral system is doing well at what it is organized to do. Thus far we have considered only systems organized to close discrepancies. There seems no obvious reason, however, why the principle should not apply just as well to systems organized to enlarge discrepancies. If the system is doing well at what it is organized to do, positive affect should arise. If it is doing poorly at what it is organized to do, negative affect should arise.

That much would seem to be fully comparable across the two types of systems. But doing well at moving toward an incentive is not exactly the same experience as doing well at moving away from a threat. Both have the potential to induce positive feelings, by doing well. Both also have the potential to induce negative feelings, by doing poorly. Yet the two positives may not be quite the same as each other, nor the negatives quite the same as each other.

Our view of this difference derives partly from the insights of Higgins and his colleagues (Higgins, 1987, 1996). Following their lead, we suggest that the affect dimension relating to discrepancy reduction is (in its purest form) the dimension that runs from depression to elation (Figure 8.4). The affect that relates to discrepancy enlargement is (in its purest form) the dimension from anxiety to relief or contentment. As Higgins and his colleagues have noted, dejection-related and agitation-related affect may take several forms, but these two dimensions capture the core qualities behind those two classes of affect. Similarly, Roseman (1984) has argued that joy and sadness are related to appetitive (moving-toward) motives, whereas relief and distress are related to aversive (moving-away-from) motives.

Merging Affect and Action

Theories about emotion typically emphasize the idea that emotion is related to action. How do affect and action relate in this model? We see the regulation provided by these systems as forming a two-layered array, with both simultaneously at work (Carver & Scheier, 1998, 1999a, 1999b). The two layers are analogous to position and velocity controls in a two-layered engineering control system (e.g., Clark, 1996). Such a two-layered system in engineering has the quality of responding both quickly and accurately (without undue oscillation). There is reason to believe that the simultaneous functioning of the two layers has the same broad consequence for human behavior.

Another way of addressing the relation between affect and action is to ask about the nature of the output of the affect loop. Earlier we described affect as reflecting the error signal of a loop that has as input a perception of rate of progress. The resulting output thus must be an adjustment in rate of progress. This output therefore has a direct link to behavior because it means changing its pace.

What does it mean to adjust the rate of progress? In some cases it means literally changing velocity. If you are behind, go faster. Some adjustments are less straightforward. The rates of many behaviors in which personality–social psychologists are interested are not defined in terms of literal pace of motion. Rather, they are defined in terms of choices among actions, even potential *programs* of action. For example, increasing your rate of progress on a reading assignment may mean choosing to spend a weekend working rather than playing. Increasing your rate of manifestation of kindness means choosing to perform an action that reflects that value. Thus, adjustment in rate must often be translated into other terms, such as concentration or reallocation of time and effort.

Despite this complexity in implementing changes in rate, it should be apparent from this description that the action system and the velocity system are presumed to work in concert with one another. Both are involved in the flow of action. They influence different aspects of the action, but both are

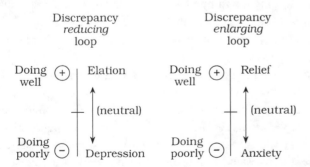

Figure 8.4 Two affect-creating systems and the affective dimensions we believe arise from the functioning of each. Discrepancy-reducing systems are presumed to yield affective qualities of sadness or depression when progress is well below standard and happiness or elation when progress is above standard. Discrepancy-enlarging systems are presumed to yield anxiety when progress is below standard and relief or contentment when progress is above standard. *Source:* From C. S. Carver and M. F. Scheier, *On the Self-Regulation of Behavior,* copyright 1998, Cambridge University Press. Reprinted with permission.

always involved. Thus, this view incorporates clear links between behavior and affect.

Comparison with Biological Models of Bases of Affect

It is useful to compare this model with the group of biologically focused theories mentioned earlier in the chapter. As indicated earlier, those theories assume that two separate systems regulate approach and avoidance behavior. Many assume further that the two systems also underlie affect. Given cues of impending reward, the activity of the approach system creates positive feelings. Given cues of impending punishment, the avoidance system creates feelings of anxiety.

Data from a variety of sources fit this picture. Of particular relevance is work by Davidson and collaborators involving electroencephalography (EEG) recordings assessing changes in cortical activation in response to affective inducing stimuli. Among the findings are these: Subjects exposed to films inducing fear and disgust (Davidson, Ekman, Saron, Senulis, & Friesen, 1990) and confronted with possible punishment (Sobotka, Davidson, & Senulis, 1992) show elevations in *right* frontal activation. In contrast, subjects with a chance to obtain reward (Sobota et al., 1992), subjects presented with positive emotional adjectives (Cacioppo & Petty, 1980), and smiling 10-month olds viewing their approaching mothers (Fox & Davidson, 1988) show elevations in *left* frontal activation. From findings such as these, Davidson (1992a, 1992b) concluded that neural substrates for approach and withdrawal systems (and thus positive and negative affect) are located in the left and right frontal areas of the cortex, respectively.

Thus far the logic of the biological models resembles the logic of our model. At this point, however, there is a divergence. The key question is what regulatory processes are involved in—and what affects result from—failure to attain reward and failure to receive punishment. Gray (1987b, 1990) holds that the avoidance system is engaged by cues of punishment and cues of frustrative nonreward. It thus is responsible for negative feelings in response to either of these types of cues. Similarly, Gray holds that the approach system is engaged by cues of reward or cues of escape from (or avoidance of) punishment. It thus is responsible for positive feelings in response to either of these types of cues. In his view, then, each system creates affect of one hedonic tone (positive in one case, negative in the other), regardless of its source. This view is consistent with a picture of two unipolar affective dimensions, each linked to a distinct behavioral system. Others have taken a similar position (see Cacioppo, Gardner, & Berntson, 1999; Lang, 1995; Lang, Bradley, & Cuthbert, 1990; Watson, Wiese, Vaidya, & Tellegen, 1999).

Our position is different. We argue that both approach and avoidance systems can create affects of both hedonic tones because affect is a product of doing well or doing poorly. We think that the frustration and eventual depression that result from failure to attain desired goals involve the approach system (for similar predictions see Clark, Watson, & Mineka, 1994, p. 107; Cloninger, 1988, p. 103; Henriques & Davidson, 1991). A parallel line of reasoning suggests that relief, contentment, tranquility, and serenity relate to the avoidance system rather than to the approach system (see Carver, 2001).

Less information exists about the bases of these affects than about anxiety and happiness. Consider first relief-tranquility. We know of two sources of evidence, both somewhat indirect. The first is a study in which people worked at a laboratory task and experienced either goal attainment or lack of attainment (Higgins, Shah, & Friedman, 1997, Study 4). Participants first were given either an approach orientation to the task (to try to attain success) or an avoidance orientation (to try to avoid failing). After the task outcome (which was manipulated), several feeling qualities were assessed. Among persons given an avoidance orientation, success caused an elevation in calmness, and failure caused an elevation in anxiety. These effects on calmness and anxiety did not occur, however, among those who had an approach orientation. This pattern suggests that calmness is linked to doing well at avoidance, rather than doing well at approach.

Another source is data reported many years ago by Watson and Tellegen (1985). In their analysis of multiple samples of mood data, they reported "calm" to be one of the 10 best markers (inversely) of negative affect (which was defined mostly by anxiety) in the majority of the data sets they examined. In contrast, "calm" never emerged as one of the top markers of positive affect in those data sets. This suggests that these feelings are linked to the functioning of a system of avoidance.

The same sources also provide information on the momentary experience of sadness. In the study by Higgins et al. (1997), failure elevated sadness and success elevated cheerfulness among persons with an approach orientation. These effects did not occur, however, among participants who had an avoidance orientation. The pattern suggests that sadness is linked to doing poorly at approach, rather than doing poorly at avoidance. Similarly, Watson and Tellegen (1985) reported "sad" to be one of the 10 best markers (inversely) of the factor that they called positive affect in the majority of the data sets they examined. In contrast, "sad" never emerged as one of the top markers of negative affect in those data sets. This pattern suggests that sad feelings are linked to the functioning of a system of approach.

This issue clearly represents an important difference among theoretical viewpoints (Carver, 2001). Just as clearly, it is not yet resolved. It seems likely that it will receive more attention in the near future.

RESPONDING TO ADVERSITY: PERSISTENCE AND GIVING UP

In describing the genesis of affect, we suggested that one process yields two subjective experiences as readouts: affect and a sense of confidence versus doubt. We turn now to confidence and doubt—expectancies for the immediate future. We focus here on the behavioral and cognitive manifestations of the sense of confidence or doubt.

One likely consequence of momentary doubt is a search for more information. We have often suggested that when people experience adversity in trying to move toward goals, they periodically interrupt efforts in order to assess in a more deliberative way the likelihood of a successful outcome (e.g., Carver & Scheier, 1981, 1990, 1998). In effect, people suspend the behavioral stream, step outside it, and evaluate in a more deliberated way. This may happen once or often. It may be brief, or it may take a long time. In this assessment people presumably depend heavily on memories of prior outcomes in similar situations. They may also consider such things as additional resources they might bring to bear, alternative approaches that might be taken, and social comparison information (Wills, 1981; Wood, 1989).

These thoughts sometimes influence the expectancies that people hold. When people retrieve "chronic" expectancies from memory, the information already *is* expectancies—summaries of the products of previous behavior. In some cases, however, the process is more complex. People bring to mind possibilities for changing the situation and evaluate their consequences. This is often done by briefly playing the possibility through mentally as a behavioral scenario (cf. Taylor & Pham, 1996). Doing so can lead to conclusions that influence expectancies ("If I try doing it this way instead of that way, it should work better" or "This is the only thing I can see to do, and it will just make the situation worse").

It seems reasonable that this mental simulation engages the same mechanism as handles the affect-creation process during actual overt behavior. When your progress is temporarily stalled, playing through a confident and optimistic scenario yields a higher rate of progress than is currently being experienced. The affect loop thus yields a more optimistic outcome assessment than is being derived from current action. If the scenario is negative and hopeless, it indicates a further reduction in progress, and the loop yields further doubt.

Behavioral Manifestations

Whether stemming from the immediate flow of experience or from a more thorough introspection, people's expectancies are reflected in their behavior. If people expect a successful outcome, they continue exerting effort toward the goal. If doubts are strong enough, the result is an impetus to disengage from effort, and potentially from the goal itself (Carver & Scheier, 1981, 1990, 1998, 1999a; see also Klinger, 1975; Kukla, 1972; Wortman & Brehm, 1975). This theme—divergence in behavioral response as a function of expectancies—is an important one, applying to a surprisingly broad range of literatures (see Carver & Scheier, 1998, chap. 11).

Sometimes the disengagement that follows from doubt is overt, but sometimes disengagement takes the form of mental disengagement—off-task thinking, daydreaming, and so on. Although this can sometimes be useful (self-distraction from a feared stimulus may allow anxiety to abate), it can also create problems. Under time pressure, mental disengagement can impair performance, as time is spent on task-irrelevant thoughts. Consistent with this, interactions between self-focus and expectancies have been shown for measures of performance (Carver, Peterson, Follansbee, & Scheier, 1983; Carver & Scheier, 1982).

Often, mental disengagement cannot be sustained, as situational cues force the person to reconfront the problematic goal. In such cases, the result is a phenomenology of repetitive negative rumination, which often focuses on self-doubt and perceptions of inadequacy. This cycle is both unpleasant and performance-impairing.

Is Disengagement Good or Bad?

Is the disengagement tendency good or bad? Both and neither. On the one hand, disengagement (at some level, at least) is an absolute necessity. Disengagement is a natural and indispensable part of self-regulation (cf. Klinger, 1975). If people are ever to turn away from unattainable goals, to back out of blind alleys, they must be able to disengage, to give up and start over somewhere else.

The importance of disengagement is particularly obvious with regard to concrete, low-level goals: People must be able to remove themselves from literal blind alleys and wrong streets, give up plans that have become disrupted by unexpected events, even spend the night in the wrong city if they miss the last plane home. Disengagement is also important, however, with regard to more abstract and higher level goals. A vast literature attests to the importance of disengaging and moving on with life after the loss of close relationships (e.g., Orbuch, 1992; Stroebe, Stroebe, & Hansson, 1993; Weiss, 1988).

People sometimes must be willing to give up even values that are deeply embedded in the self if those values create too much conflict and distress in their lives.

However, the choice between continued effort and giving up presents opportunities for things to go awry. It is possible to stop trying too soon, thereby creating potentially serious problems for oneself (Carver & Scheier, 1998). It is also possible to hold on to goals too long, thereby preventing oneself from taking adaptive steps toward new goals. But both continued effort and giving up are necessary parts of the experience of adaptive self-regulation. Each plays an important role in the flow of behavior.

Hierarchicality and Importance Can Impede Disengagement

Disengagement is sometimes precluded by situational constraints. However, a broader aspect of this problem stems from the idea that behavior is hierarchically organized, with goals increasingly important higher in the hierarchy, and thus harder to disengage from.

Presumably, disengaging from concrete values is often easy. Lower order goals vary, however, in how closely they link to values at a higher level, and thus in how important they are. To disengage from low-level goals that are tightly linked to higher level goals causes discrepancy enlargement at the higher level. These higher order qualities are important, even central to one's life. One cannot disengage from them, disregard them, or tolerate large discrepancies between them and current reality without reorganizing one's value system (Greenwald, 1980; Kelly, 1955; McIntosh & Martin, 1992; Millar, Tesser, & Millar, 1988). In such a case, disengagement from even very concrete behavioral goals can be quite difficult.

Now recall again the affective consequences of being in this situation. The desire to disengage was prompted by unfavorable expectancies. These expectancies are paralleled by negative affect. In this situation, then, the person experiences negative feelings (because of an inability to make progress toward the goal) and is unable to do anything about the feelings (because of an inability to give up). The person simply stews in the feelings that arise from irreconcilable discrepancies. This kind of situation—commitment to unattainable goals—seems a sure prescription for distress.

Watersheds, Disjunctions, and Bifurcations Among Responses

An issue that bears some further mention is the divergence in the model of the behavioral and cognitive responses to favorable versus unfavorable expectancies. We have long argued

for a psychological watershed among responses to adversity (Carver & Scheier, 1981). One set of responses consists of continued comparisons between present state and goal, and continued efforts. The other set consists of disengagement from comparisons and quitting. Just as rainwater falling on a mountain ridge ultimately flows to one side of the ridge or the other, so do behaviors ultimately flow to one of these sets or the other.

Our initial reason for taking this position stemmed largely from several demonstrations that self-focused attention creates diverging effects on information seeking and behavior as a function of expectancies of success. We are not the only ones to have emphasized a disjunction among responses, however. A number of others have done so, for reasons of their own.

Kukla (1972) proposed an early model that emphasized the idea of a disjunction in behavior. Another such model is the reactance–helplessness integration of Wortman and Brehm (1975): the argument that threats to control produce attempts to regain control and that perceptions of loss of control produce helplessness. Brehm and his collaborators (Brehm & Self, 1989; Wright & Brehm, 1989) developed an approach to task engagement that resembles that of Kukla (1972), but their way of approaching the description of the problem is somewhat different. Not all theories about persistence and giving up yield this dichotomy among responses. The fact that some do, however, is interesting. It becomes more so a bit later on.

SCALING BACK ASPIRATIONS AND RECALIBRATION OF THE AFFECT SYSTEM

The preceding sections dealt with the creation of affect and confidence and the concomitant effects on behavior. By implication, the time frames under discussion were quite narrow. In this section we broaden our view somewhat and indicate an important way in which reference values change across longer periods of time. These particular changes are changes in the *stringency* of the goals being sought after. We consider this issue both with respect to the reference values underlying the creation of affect and with respect to the goals of behavior.

Shifts in Velocity Standards

Reference values used by the affect system presumably can shift through time and experience. That is, as people accumulate experience in a given domain, adjustments can occur in the pacing that they expect and demand of themselves. There is a recentering of the system around the past experience, which occurs via shifts in the reference value (Carver & Scheier, 2000).

Consider first upward adjustments. As an example, a person who gains work-related skills often undertakes greater challenges, requiring quicker handling of action units. Upward adjustment of the rate standard means that the person now will be satisfied only with faster performance. Such a shift has the side effect of decreasing the potential for positive affect and increasing the potential for negative affect because there now is more room to fail to reach the rate standard and less room to exceed it. Recall, however, that the shift was induced by a gain in skills. The change in skill tends to counter the shift in regions of potential success and failure. Thus, the likelihood of negative affect (vs. positive affect or no affect) remains fairly constant.

Now consider a downward adjustment. For example, a person whose health is failing may find that it takes longer to get things done than it used to. This person will gradually come to use less stringent rate standards. A lower pace will then begin to be more satisfying. One consequence of this downward shift of standard is to increase the potential for experiencing positive affect and to decrease the potential for negative affect because there now is less room for failing to reach the rate standard and more room for exceeding it. The failing health, however, tends to counter the shift in regions of potential success and failure. Again, then, the net result is that the likelihood of negative affect (vs. positive and neutral) remains fairly constant.

Mechanism of Shift

Such changes in comparison value do not happen quickly or abruptly. Shifting the reference value downward is not people's first response when they have trouble maintaining a demanding pace. First, they try harder to keep up. Only more gradually, if they continue to lag behind, does the rate-related standard shift to accommodate. Similarly, the immediate response when people's pace exceeds the standard is not an upward shift in reference value. The more typical response is to coast for a while. Only when the overshoot is frequent does the standard shift upward.

We believe that adjustments in these standards occur automatically and involuntarily, but slowly. Such adjustments *themselves* appear to reflect a self-corrective feedback process (Figure 8.5). This feedback process is slower than the ones focused on thus far, involving a very gradually accumulating shift. It resembles what Solomon (1980; Solomon & Corbit, 1974) described as the long-term consequences of an opponent process system (see also Helson, 1964, regarding the concept of adaptation level).

As an illustration, assume for the moment that a signal to adjust the standard occurred every time there was a signal to

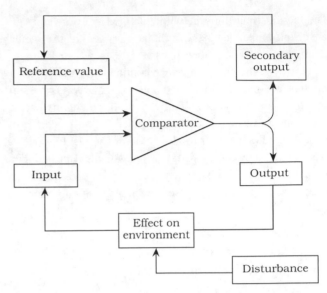

Figure 8.5 A feedback loop (in this case, the postulated velocity loop) acts to create change in the input function, to shift it toward the reference value. Sometimes an additional process is in place as well (gray lines), which adjusts the reference value in the direction of the input. This additional process is presumed to be weaker or slower; thus, the reference value is stable relative to the input value.   *Source:* From C. S. Carver and M. F. Scheier, *On the Self-Regulation of Behavior,* copyright 1998, Cambridge University Press. Reprinted with permission.

change output, but that the former was much weaker than the latter—say, 5% of the latter. If so, it would take a fairly long time for the standard to change. Indeed, as long as the person deviated from the standard in both directions (under and over) with comparable frequency, the standard would never change noticeably, even over an extended period. Only with repeated deviation in the same direction could there be an appreciable effect on the standard.

This view has an interesting implication for affective experience across an extended period. Such shifts in reference value (and the resultant effects on affect) would imply a mechanism within the organism that prevents both the too-frequent occurrence of positive feeling and the too-frequent occurrence of negative feeling. That is, the (bidirectional) shifting of the rate criterion over time would tend to control pacing such that affect continues to vary in both directions around neutral, roughly as before. The person thus would experience more or less the same range of variation in affective experience over long times and changing circumstances (see Myers & Diener, 1995, for evidence of this). The organization would function as a gyroscope serving to keep people floating along within the framework of the affective reality with which they are familiar. It would provide for a continuous recalibration of the feeling system across changes in situation. It would repeatedly shift the balance point of a psychic teeter-totter so that rocking both up and down remains possible.

Scaling Back on Behavioral Goals

The principle of gradual adjustment of a standard also operates at the level of behavioral goals (Carver & Scheier, 1981, 1998). Sometimes progress is going poorly, expectancies of success are dim, and the person wants to quit. Rather than quit altogether, the person trades this goal for a less demanding one. This is a kind of limited disengagement in the sense that the person is giving up the first goal while adopting the lesser one. However, this limited disengagement keeps the person engaged in activity in the domain he or she had wanted to quit. By scaling back the goal—giving up in a small way—the person keeps trying to move ahead—thus *not* giving up, in a larger way.

Small-scale disengagement occurs often in the context of moving forward in broader ways. A particularly poignant example comes from research on couples in which one partner is becoming ill and dying from AIDS (Moskowitz, Folkman, Collette, & Vittinghoff, 1996). Some healthy participants initially had the goal of overcoming their partner's illness and continuing active lives together. As the illness progressed and it became apparent that that goal would not be met, it was not uncommon for the healthy partners to scale back their aspirations. Now the goal was, for example, to do more limited activities during the course of a day. Choosing a more limited and manageable goal ensures that it will be possible to move toward it successfully. The result was that even in those difficult circumstances the person experienced more success than would otherwise have been the case and remained engaged behaviorally with efforts to move forward.

How does the scaling back of goals within a domain occur? We believe that the answer is the same as in the case of affect: If the loop's output function is inadequate at moving the input toward the standard, a second (slower-acting) process moves the standard toward the input. The scaling back of behavioral goals thus would involve the same structural elements as are involved in the recalibration of the affect system.

CONFLICT AND RESTRAINT

In thinking about the self-regulation of behavior, another set of issues to be considered concerns the existence of conflict. Conflict arises whenever two incompatible goals are held simultaneously and both are salient (see also Carver & Scheier, 1998, 1999b). It sometimes is possible to move toward two goals simultaneously, but sometimes moving toward one interferes with one's ability to move toward the other. For example, the woman who wants to develop her career and also spend time with her family faces a conflict imposed by

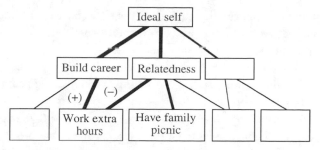

Figure 8.6 Conflict arises when two desired goals are incompatible for some reason. For example, by working extra hours in order to further a career aspiration, this woman may at the same time be having an adverse influence (indicated by the opposite-direction arrow) on another goal that is also related to her ideal self—spending time maintaining a sense of relatedness with her family.

the limited number of hours in the day and days in the week (Figure 8.6). The effort to attain one (e.g., further the career by working extra hours) can interfere with efforts to attain the other (by removing the time available for family activities).

Given this structure, the experience of conflict naturally produces negative feelings, as movement toward one of the goals is impeded. If movement toward the active goal is rapid (relative to the reference velocity) as movement toward the other goal is stifled, the person may have mixed feelings, feelings relating to each of the two goal values. It is no surprise that people typically try to balance their conflicting desires so that both goals are partly attained. It is also no surprise that this strategy often feels unsatisfying, as the person "almost" keeps up with goals in both domains but keeps up fully with neither of them.

Often there is no structural basis for viewing one goal as intrinsically more valuable than the other (as in Figure 8.6). Sometimes, however, one goal has a kind of primacy because it is reflected in an explicitly formulated intention to override efforts to move toward the other goal. Sometimes the tendencies involved are mental; sometimes they are behavioral. Often, the attempt to override works for a while (sometimes a long while), but sometimes it fails.

Ironic Processes in Mental Control

One literature bearing on this theme was developed by Wegner (e.g., 1994) and his colleagues. The study that began this work was simple. Some people were told not to think of a white bear for 5 minutes. Then they were told to think about the bear. When the thought was permitted, it came more frequently than it did for people who had not had to suppress the thought first. Something about trying not to think of the bear seemed to create pressure to think of it.

This study was followed by others. Most of this research looked not at rebounds, but at what goes on during people's attempts to control their thoughts. The data consistently indicate that an instruction to exert mental control yields better control if the person has no other demands. If something else is going on, however (e.g., if the person is trying to remember a 9-digit number), the instruction backfires, and people tend to do the opposite of what they are trying to do.

Wegner (1994) interprets this as follows: Trying to suppress a thought engages two processes. An intentional process tries to suppress. An ironic monitoring process looks for the occurrence of whatever is being suppressed. If it finds it, it increases the effort of the first mechanism. The ironic monitor is sensitive, but it is automatic and does not require much in the way of mental resources. The intentional process requires more resources. Thus, any reduction in mental resources (e.g., being distracted by a second thought or task) disrupts the intentional process more than it disrupts the ironic monitor. The monitor, searching for lapses, in effect invites those lapses to occur.

This theory also applies to the opposite pattern—attempts to concentrate. In this case, the intentional process concentrates, and the ironic process looks for the occurrence of distractions. As in the first case, if the person's mental resources are stretched thin, the ironic process seems to invite the undesired thought into consciousness. In this case, the thought is a distraction.

This research indicates that trying hard to do something (or suppress something) gets much harder when your mental resources are stretched thin. Not only does it get harder, but you may even begin to do the opposite of what you are trying to do.

Lapses in Self-Control

Another important literature bearing on this set of issues concerns what Baumeister and Heatherton (1996) termed self-regulatory failure, which we will term lapse in self-control. The potential for this kind of event arises when someone has both the desire to do something (e.g., overindulge in food or drink) and also the desire to restrain that impulse. Self-control of this sort is often especially hard, and sometimes the restrained impulse breaks free.

Consider binge eating as an example. The binge eater wants to eat but also wants to restrain that desire. If self-control lapses, the person stops trying to restrain the desire to eat, lets himself or herself go, and binges.

In characterizing the decision to quit trying to restrain, Baumeister and Heatherton noted that restraint is hard work and that mental fatigue plays a role; however, giving up the restraint attempt rarely requires that the person reach a state of total exhaustion. Rather, there is a point where the person

has had enough and stops trying to control the impulse. We have suggested that confidence about resisting the impulse plays a role in whether the person stops trying (Carver & Scheier, 1998). The confident person continues the struggle to restrain. The person whose confidence has sagged is more likely to give up.

Muraven, Tice, and Baumeister (1998) have extended this line of thought to argue that self-control is a resource that not only is limited but also can become depleted by extended self-control efforts. When the resource is depleted, the person becomes vulnerable to a failure of self-control. This view also suggests that there is a shared pool of self-control resources, so that exhausting the resource with one kind of self-control (e.g., concentrating very hard for many hours on a writing assignment) can leave the person vulnerable to a lapse in a different domain (e.g., eating restraint).

It seems worthwhile to compare the cases considered in this section (lapses in self-control) with those described just earlier (mental control). Both sections dealt with efforts at self-control. In many ways the situations are structurally quite similar. Each is an attempt to override one process by another, which falters when mental resources are depleted. There even is a resemblance between the "overdoing" quality in the previously restrained behavior in Baumeister and Heatherton's cases and the rebound quality in Wegner's research.

One difference is that the cases emphasized by Baumeister and Heatherton explicitly involve desires that direct the person in opposing directions. In most cases studied by Wegner, there is no obvious reason why the suppressed thought (or the distractor) would be desirable. This difference between cases seems far from trivial. Yet the similarities in the findings in the two literatures are striking enough to warrant further thought about how the literatures are related.

DYNAMIC SYSTEMS AND SELF-REGULATION

Recent years have seen the emergence in the psychological literature of new (or at least newly prominent) ideas about how to conceptualize natural systems. Several labels attach to these ideas: chaos, dynamic systems theory, complexity, catastrophe theory. A number of introductions to this body of thought have been written, some of which include applications to psychology (e.g., Brown, 1995; Gleick, 1987; Thelen & Smith, 1994; Vallacher & Nowak, 1994, 1997; Waldrop, 1992). These themes are of growing interest in several areas of psychology, including personality–social psychology. In this section we sketch some of the themes that are central to this way of thinking.

Nonlinearity

Dynamic systems theory holds that the behavior of a system reflects all the forces operating on (and within) it. It also emphasizes that the behavior of a complex system over any period but a brief one is very hard to predict. One reason for this is that the system's behavior may be influenced by these forces in nonlinear ways. Thus, the behavior of the system—even though highly determined—can appear random.

Many people are used to thinking of relationships between variables as linear. But some relationships clearly are not. Familiar examples of nonlinear relationships are step functions (ice turning to water and water turning to steam as temperature increases), threshold functions, and floor and ceiling effects. Other examples of nonlinearity are interactions. In an interaction the effect of one predictor on the outcome differs as a function of the level of a second predictor. Thus the effect of the first predictor on the outcome is not linear.

Many personality psychologists think in terms of interactions much of the time. Threshold effects and interactions are nonlinearities that most of us take for granted, though perhaps not labeling them as such. Looking intentionally for nonlinearities, however, reveals others. For example, many psychologists now think that many developmental changes are dynamic rather than linear (Goldin-Meadow & Alibali, 1995; Ruble, 1994; Siegler & Jenkins, 1989; Thelen, 1992, 1995; van der Maas & Molenaar, 1992).

Sensitive Dependence on Initial Conditions

Nonlinearity is one reason for the difficulty in predicting complex systems. Two more reasons why prediction over any but the short term is difficult is that you never know all the influences on a system, and the ones you do know you never know with total precision. What you think is going on may not be quite what's going on. That difference, even if it is small, can be very important.

This theme is identified with the phrase *sensitive dependence on initial conditions*. This means that a very small difference between two states of affairs can lead to divergence and ultimately to an absence of relation between the paths that are taken later on. The idea is (partly) that a small initial difference between systems causes a difference in what they encounter next, which produces slightly different outcomes (Lorenz, 1963). Through repeated iterations, the systems diverge, eventually moving on very different pathways. After a surprisingly brief period they no longer have any noticeable relation to one another.

How does the notion of sensitive dependence on initial conditions relate to human behavior? Most generally, it suggests that a person's behavior will be hard to predict over a long period except in general terms. For example, although you might be confident that Mel usually eats lunch, you will not be able to predict as well what time, where, or what he will eat on the second Friday of next month. This does not mean Mel's behavior is truly random or unlawful (cf. Epstein, 1979). It just means that small differences between the influences you think are affecting him and the influences that *actually* exist will ruin the predictability of moment-to-moment behavior.

This principle also holds for prediction of your own behavior. People apparently do not plan very far into the future most of the time (Anderson, 1990, pp. 203–205), even experts (Gobet & Simon, 1996). People seem to have goals in which the general form is sketched out but only a few steps toward it have been planned. Even attempts at relatively thorough planning appear to be recursive and "opportunistic," changing—sometimes drastically—when new information becomes known (Hayes-Roth & Hayes-Roth, 1979).

The notion of sensitive dependence on initial conditions fits these tendencies. It is pointless (and maybe even counterproductive) to plan too far ahead too fully (cf. Kirschenbaum, 1985), because chaotic forces in play (forces that are hard to predict because of nonlinearities and sensitive dependence) can render much of the planning irrelevant. Thus, it makes sense to plan in general terms, chart a few steps, get there, reassess, and plan the next bits. This seems a perfect illustration of how people implicitly take chaos into account in their own lives.

Phase Space, Attractors, and Repellers

Another set of concepts important to dynamic-systems thinking are variations on the terms *phase space* and *attractor* (Brown, 1995; Vallacher & Nowak, 1997). A phase diagram is a depiction of the behavior of a system over time. Its states are plotted along two (sometimes three) axes, with time displayed as the progression of the line of the plot, rather than on an axis of its own. A phase space is the array of states that the system occupies across a period of time. As the system changes states from one moment to the next, it traces a trajectory within its phase space—a path of the successive states it occupies across that period.

Phase spaces often contain regions called attractors. Attractors are areas that the system approaches, occupies, or tends toward more frequently than other areas. Attractors exert a metaphorical gravitational pull on the system, bringing

For example, two mutually inhibitory nodes cannot both be highly active at the same time. Thus they constrain one another. Constraints among multiple nodes are settled out during the repeated updating of activation levels.

This idea of multiple constraint satisfaction is now having a substantial impact on how people in social psychology think about a variety of topics (Kunda & Thagard, 1996; Read, Vanman, & Miller, 1997; Schultz & Lepper, 1996). It is an idea that has a great deal of intuitive appeal. It captures well the introspective sense that people come to conclusions and decisions not by weighing the evidence, exactly, but rather by letting the evidence sort itself until it reaches a degree of internal consistency. The conclusion then pops into mind.

Another term that goes along with this picture is *self-organization* (e.g., Prigogine & Stengers, 1984). The idea behind this label is that multiple causal forces which have no intrinsic relation to each other can cause the spontaneous emergence of some property of the system as a whole that does not otherwise exist. The term is used to describe emergent qualities in a variety of scientific disciplines. A number of people have begun to invoke it as a basis for emergent properties in dynamic systems (Nowak & Vallacher, 1998; Prigogine & Stengers, 1984).

Self-Organization and Self-Regulation

Some would argue that models of self-organization in dynamic systems represent a serious challenge to the viability of the type of self-regulatory model with which we began. That is, it might be asserted that behavior only *seems* to be self-regulated—that behavior instead self-organizes from among surrounding forces, like foam appearing on roiling surf.

Do feedback processes actually reflect self-organization—a haphazard falling together of disparate forces? Or are there structures in the nervous system (and elsewhere) in living systems that carry out true feedback functions? In considering the relation between the two sets of ideas, it is of interest that MacKay (1956) anticipated the principle of self-organization many years ago when he described a system of feedback processes that could evolve its own goals (see also Beer, 1995; Maes & Brooks, 1990). Thus, MacKay found the principle of self-organization to be useful, but he found it useful explicitly within the framework of a self-regulatory model.

Our view is, similarly, that the concepts of attractors and trajectories within phase space complement the idea that behavior is guided by feedback processes but do not replace it (Carver & Scheier, in press). There do appear to be times and circumstances in which forces converge—unplanned—and induce acts to occur that were not intended beforehand. However, there also seem to be clear instances of intentionality in behavior and its management.

It is of interest in this regard that contemporary cognitive psychologists often assume the existence of both bottom-up organizational tendencies and top-down directive tendencies (see, e.g., Holyoak & Spellman, 1993; Shastri & Ajjanagadde, 1993; Sloman, 1996; Smolensky, 1988). That view would seem to fit a picture in which self-organization of action *can* occur, but where actions can also be planned and executed systematically, from the top down. Similar two-mode models of regulation have also appeared in several literatures in personality-social psychology (Chaiken & Trope, 1999). In short, there seems to be some degree of consensus that human experience is part self-organization and part self-regulation.

Even when the focus is on planful behavior, the two kinds of models seem to complement each other in a different way. The feedback model provides a mechanism through which goal-directed action is managed, which the phase-space model lacks. The phase-space model suggests ways of thinking about how multiple goals exist and how people shift among those multiple goals over time, an issue that is not dealt with as easily in terms of feedback processes.

That is, think of the landscape of chaotic attractors, but with many different basins rather than just two or three. This seems to capture rather well the sense of human behavior. No basin in this system ever becomes a point attractor. Behavior tends toward one goal and then another, never being completely captured by any goal. The person does one thing for a while, then something else. The goals are all predictable—in the sense that they all influence the person—and the influence is highly predictable when aggregated across time. But the shifts from one to another occur unpredictably (thus being chaotic).

CATASTROPHE THEORY

Another set of ideas that has been around for some time but may be reemerging in influence is catastrophe theory, a mathematical model that bears on the creation of discontinuities, bifurcations, or splittings (Brown, 1995; Saunders, 1980; Stewart & Peregoy, 1983; van der Maas & Molenaar, 1992; Woodcock & Davis, 1978; Zeeman, 1977). A catastrophe occurs when a small change in one variable produces an abrupt (and usually large) change in another variable.

An abrupt change implies nonlinearity. This focus on nonlinearity is one of several themes that catastrophe theory shares with dynamic systems theory, though the two bodies of thought have different origins (and are seen by some as quite different from each other—see Kelso, 1995, chap. 2). The similarity is nicely expressed in the statement that the discontinuity in catastrophe theory reflects "the sudden disappearance of one attractor and its basin, combined with the dominant emergence of another attractor" (Brown, 1995, p. 51).

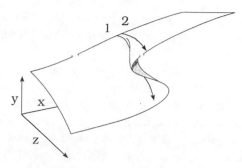

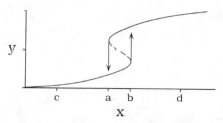

Figure 8.9 Three-dimensional depiction of a cusp catastrophe. Variables x and z are predictors, and y is the system's "behavior," the dependent variable. The catastrophe shows sensitive dependence on initial conditions. Where z is low, points 1 and 2 are nearly the same on x. If these points are projected forward on the surface (with increases in z), they move in parallel until the cusp begins to emerge. The lines are then separated by the formation of the cusp and project to completely different regions of the surface. *Source:* From C. S. Carver and M. F. Scheier, *On the Self-Regulation of Behavior,* copyright 1998, Cambridge University Press. Reprinted with permission.

Figure 8.10 A cusp catastrophe exhibits a region of hysteresis (between values a and b on the x axis), in which x has two stable values of y (the solid lines) and one unstable value (the dotted line that cuts backward in the middle of the figure). The region represented by the dotted line repels trajectories, whereas the stable regions (those surrounding values c and d on the x-axis) attract trajectories. Traversing the zone of hysteresis from the left of this figure results in an abrupt shift (at value b on the x-axis) from the lower to the upper portion of the surface (right arrow). Traversing the zone of hysteresis from the right of this figure results in an abrupt shift (at value a on the x-axis) from the upper to the lower portion of the surface (left arrow). Thus, the disjunction between portions of the surface occurs at two different values of x, depending on the starting point. *Source:* From C. S. Carver and M. F. Scheier, *On the Self-Regulation of Behavior,* copyright 1998, Cambridge University Press. Reprinted with permission.

Though several types of catastrophe exist (Brown, 1995; Saunders, 1980; Woodcock & Davis, 1978), the one receiving most attention regarding behavior is the cusp catastrophe, in which two variables influence an outcome. Figure 8.9 portrays its three-dimensional surface. X and z are predictors, and y is the outcome. At low values of z, the surface of the figure shows a roughly linear relationship between x and y. As x increases, so does y. As z increases, the relationship between x and y becomes less linear. It first shifts toward something like a step function. With further increase in z, the x-y relationship becomes even more clearly discontinuous—the outcome is either on the top surface or on the bottom. Thus, changes in z cause a change in the way x relates to y.

Another theme that links catastrophe theory to dynamic systems is the idea of sensitive dependence on initial conditions. The cusp catastrophe displays this characteristic nicely. Consider the portion of Figure 8.9 where z has low values and x has a continuous relation to y (the system's behavior). Points 1 and 2 on x are nearly identical, but not quite. Now track these points across the surface as z increases. For a while the two paths track each other closely, until suddenly they begin to be separated by the fold in the catastrophe. At higher levels of z, one track ultimately projects to the upper region of the surface, the other to the lower region. Thus, a very slight initial difference results in a substantial difference farther along.

Hysteresis

The preceding description also hinted at an interesting and important feature of a catastrophe known as hysteresis. A simple characterization of what this term means is that at some levels of z, there is a kind of fold-over in the middle of the x-y

relationship. A region of x exists in which more than one value of y exists. Another way to characterize hysteresis is that two regions of this surface are attractors and one is a repeller (Brown, 1995). This unstable area is illustrated in Figure 8.10. The dashed-line portion of Figure 8.10 that lies between values a and b on the x-axis—the region where the fold is going backward—repels trajectories (Brown, 1995), whereas the areas near values c and d attract trajectories. To put it more simply, you cannot be on the dashed part of this surface.

Yet another way of characterizing hysteresis is captured by the statement that the system's behavior depends on the system's recent history (Brown, 1995; Nowak & Lewenstein, 1994). That is, as you move into the zone of variable x that lies between points a and b in Figure 8.10, it matters which side of the figure you are coming from. If the system is moving from point c into the zone of hysteresis, it stays on the bottom surface until it reaches point b, where it jumps to the top surface. If the system is moving from d into the zone of hysteresis, it stays on the top surface until it reaches point a, where it jumps to the bottom surface.

An Application of Catastrophe Theory

How does catastrophe theory apply to the human behaviors of most interest to personality and social psychologists? Several applications of these ideas have been made in the past decade or so, and others seem obvious candidates for future study (for broader discussion see Carver & Scheier, 1998, chap. 16).

One interesting example concerns what we believe is a bifurcation between engagement in effort and giving up. Earlier we pointed to a set of theories that assume such a

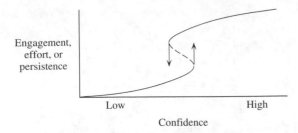

Figure 8.11 A catastrophe model of effort versus disengagement. *Source:* From C. S. Carver and M. F. Scheier, *On the Self-Regulation of Behavior,* copyright 1998, Cambridge University Press. Reprinted with permission.

disjunction (Brehm & Self, 1989; Kukla, 1972; Wortman & Brehm, 1975). In all those models (as in ours), there is a point at which effort seems fruitless and the person stops trying. Earlier, we simply emphasized that the models all assumed a discontinuity. Now we look at the discontinuity more closely and suggest that the phenomena addressed by these theories may embody a catastrophe.

Figure 8.11 shows a slightly relabeled cross section of a cusp catastrophe similar to that in Figure 8.10. This figure displays a region of hysteresis in the engagement versus disengagement function. In that region, where task demands are close to people's perceived limits to perform, there should be greater variability in effort or engagement, as some people are on the top surface of the catastrophe and others are on the bottom surface. Some people would be continuing to exert efforts at the same point where others would be exhibiting a giving-up response.

Recall that the catastrophe figure also conveys the sense that the history of the behavior matters. A person who enters the region of hysteresis from the direction of high confidence (who starts out confident but confronts many contradictory cues) will continue to display engagement and effort, even as the situational cues imply less and less basis for confidence. A person who enters that region from the direction of low confidence (who starts doubtful but confronts contradictory cues) will continue to display little effort, even as the cues imply a greater basis for confidence.

This model helps indicate why it can be so difficult to get someone with strong and chronic doubts about success in some domain of behavior to exert real effort and engagement in that domain. It also suggests why a confident person is so rarely put off by encountering difficulties in the domain where the confidence lies. To put it in terms of broader views about life in general, it helps show why optimists tend to stay optimistic and pessimists tend to stay pessimistic, even when the current circumstances of the two sorts of people are identical (i.e., in the region of hysteresis).

It is important to keep in mind that the catastrophe cross section (Figure 8.11) is the picture that emerges under catastrophe theory *only once a clear region of hysteresis has begun to develop.* Farther back, the model is more of a step function. An implication is that to see the fold-over it is important to engage the variable that is responsible for bringing out the bifurcation in the surface (i.e., axis z in Figure 8.9).

What is the variable that induces the bifurcation? We think that in the motivational models under discussion—and perhaps more broadly—the control parameter is *importance*. Importance arises from several sources, but there is a common thread among events seen as important. They demand mental resources. We suspect that almost any strong pressure that demands resources (time pressure, self-imposed pressure) will induce bifurcating effects.

CONCLUDING COMMENT

In this chapter we sketched a set of ideas that we think are important in conceptualizing human self-regulation. We believe that behavior is goal directed and feedback controlled and that the goals underlying behavior form a hierarchy of abstractness. We believe that experiences of affect (and of confidence vs. doubt) also arise from a process of feedback control, but a feedback process that takes into account temporal constraints. We believe that confidence and doubt yield patterns of persistence versus giving up and that these two responses to adversity form a dichotomy in behavior. These ideas have been embedded in our self-regulatory viewpoint for some time.

We have also recently begun to consider some newer ideas, addressed in the latter parts of the chapter. In those sections we described ideas from dynamic systems theory, connectionism, and catastrophe theory. We suggest that they represent useful tools for the analysis and construal of behavior. Our view is that they supplement rather than replace the tools now in use (though not everyone will agree on this point). We see many ways in which those ideas mesh with the ideas presented earlier, though space constraints limited us to discussing that integration only briefly.

In thinking about the structure of behavior, we have tried to draw on ideas from disparate sources while continuing to follow the thread of the logical model from which we started. The result is an aggregation of principles that we think have a good deal to say about how behavioral self-regulation takes place. In so doing, they also say something about personality and how it is manifested in people's actions.

The conceptual model presented here is surely not complete, and many avenues exist for further discussion and indeed further conceptual development. For example, this chapter included little attention to the issue of how new goals are added to people's hierarchies or of how to think about growth and change over time (but see Carver & Scheier, 1998, 1999a, 1999b). Similarly, the concepts addressed here bear in several ways on problems in behavior and behavior change, though space constraints prevent us from describing them in detail. For example, we suspect that many problems in people's lives are, at their core, problems of disengagement versus engagement and the failure to disengage adaptively (Carver & Scheier, 1998). As another example, it may be useful to conceptualize problems as less-than-optimal adaptations in a multidimensional phase space, which require some jostling to bounce the person to a new attractor (Hayes & Strauss, 1998). These are all areas in which more work remains to be done.

These are just some of the ways in which we think the family of ideas described here will likely be explored in the near future. Further analyses of the self-regulation of behavior are likely to produce insights that transform the models from which the insights grew. As the models change, so will our understanding of motivational processes and of how human beings function as coherent, autonomous units. This we take to be one of the core pursuits of personality psychology.

REFERENCES

Anderson, J. R. (1990). *The adaptive character of thought.* Hillsdale, NJ: Erlbaum.

Austin, J. T., & Vancouver, J. B. (1996). Goal constructs in psychology: Structure, process, and content. *Psychological Bulletin, 120,* 338–375.

Baumeister, R. F. (1989). The problem of life's meaning. In D. M. Buss & N. Cantor (Eds.), *Personality psychology: Recent trends and emerging directions* (pp. 138–148). New York: Springer-Verlag.

Baumeister, R. F., & Heatherton, T. F. (1996). Self-regulation failure: An overview. *Psychological Inquiry, 7,* 1–15.

Beer, R. D. (1995). A dynamical systems perspective on agent-environment interaction. *Artificial Intelligence, 72,* 173–215.

Brehm, J. W., & Self, E. A. (1989). The intensity of motivation. *Annual Review of Psychology, 40,* 109–131.

Brown, C. (1995). *Chaos and catastrophe theories.* Thousand Oaks, CA: Sage.

Brunstein, J. C. (1993). Personal goals and subjective well-being: A longitudinal study. *Journal of Personality and Social Psychology, 65,* 1061–1070.

Cacioppo, J. T., Gardner, W. L., & Berntson, G. G. (1999). The affect system has parallel and integrative processing components: Form follows function. *Journal of Personality and Social Psychology, 76,* 839–855.

Cacioppo, J. T., & Petty, R. E. (1980). The effects of orienting task on differential hemispheric EEG activation. *Neuropsychologia, 18,* 675–683.

Cantor, N., & Kihlstrom, J. F. (1987). *Personality and social intelligence.* Englewood Cliffs, NJ: Prentice Hall.

Carver, C. S. (1979). A cybernetic model of self-attention processes. *Journal of Personality and Social Psychology, 37,* 1251–1281.

Carver, C. S. (2001). Affect and the functional bases of behavior: On the dimensional structure of affective experience. *Personality and Social Psychology Review, 5,* 345–356.

Carver, C. S. (in press). Pleasure as a sign you can attend to something else: Placing positive feelings within a general model of affect. *Cognition and Emotion.*

Carver, C. S., & Humphries, C. (1981). Havana daydreaming: A study of self-consciousness and the negative reference group among Cuban Americans. *Journal of Personality and Social Psychology, 40,* 545–552.

Carver, C. S., Lawrence, J. W., & Scheier, M. F. (1999). Self-discrepancies and affect: Incorporating the role of feared selves. *Personality and Social Psychology Bulletin, 25,* 783–792.

Carver, C. S., Peterson, L. M., Follansbee, D. J., & Scheier, M. F. (1983). Effects of self-directed attention on performance and persistence among persons high and low in test anxiety. *Cognitive Therapy and Research, 7,* 333–354.

Carver, C. S., & Scheier, M. F. (1981). *Attention and self-regulation: A control-theory approach to human behavior.* New York: Springer-Verlag.

Carver, C. S., & Scheier, M. F. (1982). Outcome expectancy, locus of attributions for expectancy, and self-directed attention as determinants of evaluations and performance. *Journal of Experimental Social Psychology, 18,* 184–200.

Carver, C. S., & Scheier, M. F. (1990). Origins and functions of positive and negative affect: A control-process view. *Psychological Review, 97,* 19–35.

Carver, C. S., & Scheier, M. F. (1998). *On the self-regulation of behavior.* New York: Cambridge University Press.

Carver, C. S., & Scheier, M. F. (1999a). Themes and issues in the self-regulation of behavior. In R. S. Wyer, Jr. (Ed.), *Advances in social cognition* (pp. 1–105). Mahwah, NJ: Erlbaum.

Carver, C. S., & Scheier, M. F. (1999b). Several more themes, a lot more issues: Commentary on the commentaries. In R. S. Wyer, Jr. (Ed.), *Advances in social cognition* (Vol. 12, pp. 261–302). Mahwah, NJ: Erlbaum.

Carver, C. S., & Scheier, M. F. (2000). Autonomy and self-regulation. *Psychological Inquiry, 11,* 284–291.

Carver, C. S., & Scheier, M. F. (2001). Optimism, pessimism, and self-regulation. In E. C. Chang (Ed.), *Optimism and pessimism: Implications for theory, research, and practice* (pp. 31–51). Washington, DC: American Psychological Association.

Carver, C. S., & Scheier, M. F. (in press). Control processes and self-organization as complementary principles underlying behavior. *Personality and Social Psychology Review.*

Chaiken, S. L., & Trope, Y. (Eds.). (1999). *Dual-process theories in social psychology.* New York: Guilford.

Clark, L. A., Watson, D., & Mineka, S. (1994). Temperament, personality, and the mood and anxiety disorders. *Journal of Abnormal Psychology, 103,* 103–116.

Clark, R. N. (1996). *Control system dynamics.* New York: Cambridge University Press.

Cloninger, C. R. (1987). A systematic method for clinical description and classification of personality variants. *Archives of General Psychiatry, 44,* 573–588.

Cloninger, C. R. (1988). A unified biosocial theory of personality and its role in the development of anxiety states: A reply to commentaries. *Psychiatric Developments, 2,* 83–120.

Davidson, R. J. (1992a). Anterior cerebral asymmetry and the nature of emotion. *Brain and Cognition, 20,* 125–151.

Davidson, R. J. (1992b). Prolegomenon to the structure of emotion: Gleanings from neuropsychology. *Cognition and Emotion, 6,* 245–268.

Davidson, R. J., Ekman, P., Saron, C. D., Senulis, J. A., & Friesen, W. V. (1990). Approach–withdrawal and cerebral asymmetry: Emotional expression and brain physiology I. *Journal of Personality and Social Psychology, 58,* 330–341.

Deci, E. L., & Ryan, R. M. (1985). *Intrinsic motivation and self-determination in human behavior.* New York: Plenum.

Deci, E. L., & Ryan, R. M. (2000). The "what" and "why" of goal pursuits: Human needs and the self-determination of behavior. *Psychological Inquiry, 11,* 227–268.

Depue, R. A., & Iacono, W. G. (1989). Neurobehavioral aspects of affective disorders. *Annual Review of Psychology, 40,* 457–492.

Depue, R. A., Krauss, S. P., & Spoont, M. R. (1987). A two-dimensional threshold model of seasonal bipolar affective disorder. In D. Magnusson & A. Öhman (Eds.), *Psychopathology: An interactional perspective* (pp. 95–123). Orlando, FL: Academic Press.

Elliott, E. S., & Dweck, C. S. (1988). Goals: An approach to motivation and achievement. *Journal of Personality and Social Psychology, 54,* 5–12.

Emmons, R. A. (1986). Personal strivings: An approach to personality and subjective well being. *Journal of Personality and Social Psychology, 51,* 1058–1068.

Epstein, S. (1979). The stability of behavior: I. On predicting most of the people much of the time. *Journal of Personality and Social Psychology, 37,* 1097–1126.

Fowles, D. C. (1980). The three arousal model: Implications of Gray's two-factor learning theory for heart rate, electrodermal activity, and psychopathy. *Psychophysiology, 17,* 87–104.

Fox, N. A., & Davidson, R. J. (1988). Patterns of brain electrical activity during facial signs of emotion in 10-month old infants. *Developmental Psychology, 24,* 230–236.

Frijda, N. H. (1986). *The emotions.* Cambridge, England: Cambridge University Press.

Frijda, N. H. (1988). The laws of emotion. *American Psychologist, 43,* 349–358.

Gleick, J. (1987). *Chaos: Making a new science.* New York: Viking Penguin.

Gobet, F., & Simon, H. A. (1996). The roles of recognition processes and look-ahead search in time-constrained expert problem solving: Evidence from grand-master-level chess. *Psychological Science, 7,* 52–55.

Goldin-Meadow, S., & Alibali, M. W. (1995). Mechanisms of transition: Learning with a helping hand. In D. Medin (Ed.), *The psychology of learning and motivation* (Vol. 33, pp. 115–157). San Diego, CA: Academic Press.

Gray, J. A. (1982). *The neuropsychology of anxiety: An enquiry into the functions of the septo-hippocampal system.* New York: Oxford University Press.

Gray, J. A. (1987a). Perspectives on anxiety and impulsivity: A commentary. *Journal of Research in Personality, 21,* 493–509.

Gray, J. A. (1987b). *The psychology of fear and stress.* Cambridge, England: Cambridge University Press.

Gray, J. A. (1990). Brain systems that mediate both emotion and cognition. *Cognition and Emotion, 4,* 269–288.

Greenwald, A. G. (1980). The totalitarian ego: Fabrication and revision of personal history. *American Psychologist, 35,* 603–618.

Hayes, A. M., & Strauss, J. L. (1998). Dynamic systems theory as a paradigm for the study of change in psychotherapy: An application to cognitive therapy for depression. *Journal of Consulting and Clinical Psychology, 66,* 939–947.

Hayes-Roth, B., & Hayes-Roth, F. (1979). A cognitive model of planning. *Cognitive Science, 3,* 275–310.

Helson, H. (1964). *Adaptation-level theory: An experimental and systematic approach to behavior.* New York: Harper & Row.

Henriques, J. B., & Davidson, R. J. (1991). Left frontal hypoactivation in depression. *Journal of Abnormal Psychology, 100,* 535–545.

Higgins, E. T. (1987). Self-discrepancy: A theory relating self and affect. *Psychological Review, 94,* 319–340.

Higgins, E. T. (1996). Ideals, oughts, and regulatory focus: Affect and motivation from distinct pains and pleasures. In P. M. Gollwitzer & J. A. Bargh (Eds.), *The psychology of action: Linking cognition and motivation to behavior* (pp. 91–114). New York: Guilford.

Higgins, E. T., Shah, J., & Friedman, R. (1997). Emotional responses to goal attainment: Strength of regulatory focus as moderator. *Journal of Personality and Social Psychology, 72,* 515–525.

Higgins, E. T., & Tykocinski, O. (1992). Self-discrepancies and biographical memory: Personality and cognition at the level of psychological situation. *Personality and Social Psychology Bulletin, 18,* 527–535.

Holyoak, K. J., & Spellman, B. A. (1993). Thinking. *Annual Review of Psychology, 44,* 265–315.

Hsee, C. K., & Abelson, R. P. (1991). Velocity relation: Satisfaction as a function of the first derivative of outcome over time. *Journal of Personality and Social Psychology, 60,* 341–347.

Isen, A. M. (2000). Positive affect and decision making. In M. Lewis & J. M. Haviland-Jones (Eds.), *Handbook of emotions* (2nd ed., pp. 417–435). New York: Guilford.

Kelly, G. A. (1955). *The psychology of personal constructs.* New York: W. W. Norton.

Kelso, J. A. S. (1995). *Dynamic patterns: The self-organization of brain and behavior.* Cambridge, MA: MIT Press.

Kirschenbaum, D. S. (1985). Proximity and specificity of planning: A position paper. *Cognitive Therapy and Research, 9,* 489–506.

Klinger, E. (1975). Consequences of commitment to and disengagement from incentives. *Psychological Review, 82,* 25.

Klinger, E. (1977). *Meaning and void: Inner experience and the incentives in people's lives.* Minneapolis: University of Minnesota Press.

Kukla, A. (1972). Foundations of an attributional theory of performance. *Psychological Review, 79,* 454–470.

Kunda, Z., & Thagard, P. (1996). Forming impressions from stereotypes, traits, and behaviors: A parallel-constraint-satisfaction theory. *Psychological Review, 103,* 284–308.

Lang, P. J. (1995). The emotion probe: Studies of motivation and attention. *American Psychologist, 50,* 372–385.

Lang, P. J., Bradley, M., & Cuthbert, B. (1990). Emotion, attention, and the startle reflex. *Psychological Review, 97,* 377–395.

Lawrence, J. W., Carver, C. S., & Scheier, M. F. (in press). Velocity toward goal attainment in immediate experience as a determinant of affect. *Journal of Applied Social Psychology.*

Lazarus, R. S. (1991). *Emotion and adaptation.* New York: Oxford University Press.

Little, B. R. (1983). Personal projects: A rationale and methods for investigation. *Environment and Behavior, 15,* 273–309.

Lorenz, E. N. (1963). Deterministic nonperiodic flow. *Journal of Atmospheric Science, 20,* 130–141.

MacKay, D. M. (1956). Towards an information-flow model of human behaviour. *British Journal of Psychology, 47,* 30–43.

Maes, P. (1994). Modeling adaptive autonomous agents. *Artificial Life, 1,* 135–162.

Maes, P., & Brooks, R. A. (1990). Learning to coordinate behaviors. *Proceedings of the American Association of Artificial Intelligence* (pp. 796–802). Los Alto, CA: Kaufmann.

Mahoney, M. J. (1991). *Human change processes: The scientific foundations of psychotherapy.* New York: Basic Books.

Markus, H., & Nurius, P. (1986). Possible selves. *American Psychologist, 41,* 954–969.

McIntosh, W. D., & Martin, L. L. (1992). The cybernetics of happiness: The relation of goal attainment, rumination, and affect. In M. S. Clark (Ed.), *Review of personality and social psychology: Volume 14. Emotion and social behavior* (pp. 222–246). Newbury Park, CA: Sage.

Melton, R. J. (1995). The role of positive affect in syllogism performance. *Personality and Social Psychology Bulletin, 21,* 788–794.

Millon, K. J., Tesser, A., & Millon, M. G. (1988). The effects of a threatening life event on behavior sequences and intrusive thought: A self-disruption explanation. *Cognitive Therapy and Research, 12,* 441–458.

Miller, G. A., Galanter, E., & Pribram, K. H. (1960). *Plans and the structure of behavior.* New York: Holt, Rinehart, & Winston.

Miller, L. C., & Read, S. J. (1987). Why am I telling you this? Self-disclosure in a goal-based model of personality. In V. J. Derlega & J. Berg (Eds.), *Self-disclosure: Theory, research, and therapy* (pp. 35–58). New York: Plenum.

Moskowitz, J. T., Folkman, S., Collette, L., & Vittinghoff, E. (1996). Coping and mood during AIDS-related caregiving and bereavement. *Annals of Behavioral Medicine, 18,* 49–57.

Muraven, M., Tice, D. M., & Baumeister, R. F. (1998). Self-control as a limited resource: Regulatory depletion patterns. *Journal of Personality and Social Psychology, 74,* 774–789.

Myers, D. G., & Diener, E. (1995). Who is happy? *Psychological Science, 6,* 10–19.

Nowak, A., & Lewenstein, M. (1994). Dynamical systems: A tool for social psychology. In R. R. Vallacher & A. Nowak (Eds.), *Dynamical systems in social psychology* (pp. 17–53). San Diego, CA: Academic Press.

Nowak, A., & Vallacher, R. R. (1998). *Dynamical social psychology.* New York: Guilford.

Orbuch, T. L. (Ed.). (1992). *Close relationship loss: Theoretical approaches.* New York: Springer-Verlag.

Ortony, A., Clore, G. L., & Collins, A. (1988). *The cognitive structure of emotions.* Cambridge, England: Cambridge University Press.

Pervin, L. A. (Ed.). (1989). *Goal concepts in personality and social psychology.* Hillsdale, NJ: Erlbaum.

Powers, W. T. (1973). *Behavior: The control of perception.* Chicago: Aldine.

Prigogine, I., & Stengers, I. (1984). *Order out of chaos: Man's new dialogue with nature.* New York: Random House.

Read, S. J., Druian, P. R., & Miller, L. C. (1989). The role of causal sequence in the meaning of action. *British Journal of Social Psychology, 28,* 341–351.

Read, S. J., Vanman, E. J., & Miller, L. C. (1997). Connectionism, parallel constraint satisfaction processes, and Gestalt principles: (Re)introducing cognitive dynamics to social psychology. *Review of Personality and Social Psychology, 1,* 26–53.

Roseman, I. J. (1984). Cognitive determinants of emotions: A structural theory. In P. Shaver (Ed.), *Review of personality and social psychology* (Vol. 5, pp. 11–36). Beverly Hills, CA: Sage.

Ruble, D. N. (1994). A phase model of transitions: Cognitive and motivational consequences. In M. Zanna (Ed.), *Advances in experimental social psychology* (Vol. 26, pp. 163–214). San Diego, CA: Academic Press.

Ryan, R. M., & Deci, E. L. (2000). Self-determination theory and the facilitation of intrinsic motivation, social development, and well being. *American Psychologist, 55,* 68–78.

Saunders, P. T. (1980). *An introduction to catastrophe theory.* Cambridge, England: Cambridge University Press.

Scheier, M. F., & Carver, C. S. (1983). Self-directed attention and the comparison of self with standards. *Journal of Experimental Social Psychology, 19,* 205–222.

Scheier, M. F., Carver, C. S., & Bridges, M. W. (2001). Optimism, pessimism, and psychological well-being. In E. C. Chang (Ed.), *Optimism and pessimism: Implications for theory, research, and practice* (pp. 189–216). Washington, DC: American Psychological Association.

Scherer, K. R., & Ekman, P. (Eds.). (1984). *Approaches to emotion.* Hillsdale, NJ: Erlbaum.

Schultz, T. R., & Lepper, M. R. (1996). Cognitive dissonance reduction as constraint satisfaction. *Psychological Review, 103,* 219–240.

Shastri, L., & Ajjanagadde, V. (1993). From simple associations to systematic reasoning: A connectionist representation of rules, variables, and dynamic bindings using temporal synchrony. *Behavioral and Brain Sciences, 16,* 417–494.

Siegler, R. S., & Jenkins, E. A. (1989). *How children discover new strategies.* Hillsdale, NJ: Erlbaum.

Sloman, S. A. (1996). The empirical case for two forms of reasoning. *Psychological Bulletin, 119,* 3–22.

Smith, E. R. (1996). What do connectionism and social psychology offer each other? *Journal of Personality and Social Psychology, 70,* 893–912.

Smolensky, P. (1988). On the proper treatment of connectionism. *Behavioral and Brain Sciences, 11,* 1–23.

Sobotka, S. S., Davidson, R. J., & Senulis, J. A. (1992). Anterior brain electrical asymmetries in response to reward and punishment. *Electroencephalography and Clinical Neurophysiology, 83,* 236–247.

Solomon, R. L. (1980). The opponent-process theory of acquired motivation: The costs of pleasure and the benefits of pain. *American Psychologist, 35,* 691–712.

Solomon, R. L., & Corbit, J. D. (1974). An opponent-process theory of motivation: III. Temporal dynamics of affect. *Psychological Review, 81,* 119–145.

Stewart, I. N., & Peregoy, P. L. (1983). Catastrophe theory modeling in psychology. *Psychological Bulletin, 94,* 336–362.

Stroebe, M. S., Stroebe, W., & Hansson, R. O. (Eds.). (1993). *Handbook of bereavement: Theory, research, and intervention.* Cambridge, England: Cambridge University Press.

Taylor, S. E., & Pham, L. B. (1996). Mental stimulation, motivation, and action. In P. M. Gollwitzer & J. A. Bargh (Eds.), *The psychology of action: Linking cognition and motivation to behavior* (pp. 219–235). New York: Guilford.

Thagard, P. (1989). Explanatory coherence. *Behavioral and Brain Sciences, 12,* 435–467.

Thelen, E. (1992). Development as a dynamic system. *Current Directions in Psychological Science, 1,* 189–193.

Thelen, E. (1995). Motor development: A new synthesis. *American Psychologist, 50,* 79–95.

Thelen, E., & Smith, L. B. (1994). *A dynamic systems approach to the development of cognition and action.* Cambridge, MA: MIT Press.

Tomarken, A. J., Davidson, R. J., Wheeler, R. E., & Doss, R. C. (1992). Individual differences in anterior brain asymmetry and fundamental dimensions of emotion. *Journal of Personality and Social Psychology, 62,* 676–687.

Vallacher, R. R., & Nowak, A. (Eds.). (1994). *Dynamical systems in social psychology.* San Diego, CA: Academic Press.

Vallacher, R. R., & Nowak, A. (1997). The emergence of dynamical social psychology. *Psychological Inquiry, 8,* 73–99.

Vallacher, R. R., & Wegner, D. M. (1985). *A theory of action identification.* Hillsdale, NJ: Erlbaum.

van der Maas, H. L. J., & Molenaar, P. C. M. (1992). Stagewise cognitive development: An application of catastrophe theory. *Psychological Review, 99,* 395–417.

Waldrop, M. (1992). *Complexity: The emerging science at the edge of order and chaos.* New York: Simon & Schuster.

Watson, D., & Tellegen, A. (1985). Toward a consensual structure of mood. *Psychological Bulletin, 98,* 219–235.

Watson, D., Wiese, D., Vaidya, J., & Tellegen, A. (1999). The two general activation systems of affect: Structural findings, evolutionary considerations, and psychobiological evidence. *Journal of Personality and Social Psychology, 76,* 820–838.

Wegner, D. M. (1994). Ironic processes of mental control. *Psychological Review, 101,* 34–52.

Weiss, R. S. (1988). Loss and recovery. *Journal of Social Issues, 44,* 37–52.

Wiener, N. (1948). *Cybernetics: Control and communication in the animal and the machine.* Cambridge, MA: MIT Press.

Wills, T. A. (1981). Downward comparison principles in social psychology. *Psychological Bulletin, 90,* 245–271.

Wood, J. V. (1989). Theory and research concerning social comparisons of personal attributes. *Psychological Bulletin, 106,* 231–248.

Woodcock, A., & Davis, M. (1978). *Catastrophe theory.* New York: E. P. Dutton.

Wortman, C. B., & Brehm, J. W. (1975). Responses to uncontrollable outcomes: An integration of reactance theory and the learned helplessness model. In L. Berkowitz (Ed.), *Advances in experimental social psychology* (Vol. 8, pp. 277–336). New York: Academic Press.

Wright, R. A., & Brehm, J. W. (1989). Energization and goal attractiveness. In L. A. Pervin (Ed.), *Goal concepts in personality and social psychology* (pp. 169–210). Hillsdale, NJ: Erlbaum.

Zeeman, E. C. (1977). *Catastrophe theory: Selected papers 1972–1977.* Reading, MA: Benjamin.

CHAPTER 9

Interpersonal Theory of Personality

AARON L. PINCUS AND EMILY B. ANSELL

INTERPERSONAL FOUNDATIONS FOR AN INTEGRATIVE THEORY OF PERSONALITY

The origins of the interpersonal theory of personality we discuss in the present chapter are found in Sullivan's (1953a, 1953b, 1954, 1956, 1962, 1964) interpersonal theory of psychiatry. Extensions, elaborations, and modifications have consistently appeared over the last 50 years, with landmark works appearing in each successive decade (see Table 9.1). Given this clear line of theoretical development, it might seem puzzling that in a discussion of the scope of interpersonal theory held at a recent meeting of the Society for Interpersonal Theory and Research (SITAR), it was pointed out that psychology's expanding focus on interpersonal functioning has rendered study of interpersonal processes so fundamental that interpersonal theory risks an identity crisis (Gurtman, personal communication, June 20, 2000). In our opinion, both promising and perplexing aspects of this identity crisis are respectively reflected in two growing bodies of literature. The former body recognizes the integrative and synthetic potential of interpersonal theory to complement and enhance many other theoretical approaches to the study of personality (e.g., Benjamin, 1996c; Kiesler, 1992), whereas the latter body focuses on interpersonal functioning without any recognition of interpersonal theory.

Explicit efforts have been made toward integration of interpersonal theory and *cognitive theory* (e.g., Benjamin, 1986; Benjamin & Friedrich, 1991; Carson, 1969, 1982; Safran, 1990a, 1990b; Tunis, Fridhandler, & Horowitz, 1990), *attachment theory* (e.g., Bartholomew & L. Horowitz, 1991; Benjamin, 1993; Birtchnell, 1997; Florsheim, Henry, & Benjamin, 1996; Pincus, Dickinson, Schut, Castonguay, & Bedics, 1999; Stuart & Noyes, 1999), *contemporary psychodynamic theory* (e.g., Benjamin, 1995; Benjamin & Friedrich, 1991; Heck & Pincus, 2001; Lionells, Fiscalini, Mann, & Stern, 1995; Pincus, 1997; Roemer, 1986), and *evolutionary theory* (e.g., Hoyenga, Hoycnga, Walters, & Schmidt, 1998; Zuroff, Moskowitz, & Cote, 1999). Although it might be argued that such efforts could lead to identity diffusion of interpersonal theory, we believe this points to the fundamental integrative potential of an interpersonal theory of personality. In contrast, efforts at integrating interpersonal theory with social psychological theories of human interaction and social cognition appear to be lagging despite the initial works of Carson (1969) and Wiggins (1980). We note continued expansion of a significant social psychological literature on interpersonal behavior, such as self-verification and self-confirmation theories (e.g., Hardin & Higgins, 1996; Swann & Read, 1981) and interpersonal expectancies (e.g., Neuberg, 1996), that does not incorporate interpersonal theory as reviewed here. Remarkably, recent reviews of interpersonal functioning (Reis, Collins, & Berscheid, 2000; Snyder & Stukas, 1999) did not cite any of the literature reviewed for the present chapter on interpersonal theory,

TABLE 9.1   Landmark Publications in Interpersonal Theory

1950s	1960s	1970s	1980s	1990s
Sullivan (1953a)	Schaefer (1961)	Benjamin (1974)	Wiggins (1980)	Benjamin (1996b)
Sullivan (1953b)	Sullivan (1962)	McLemore & Benjamin (1979)	Anchin & Kiesler (1982)	Wiggins & Trapnell (1996)
Sullivan (1954)	Lorr & McNair (1963)	Wiggins (1979)	Wiggins (1982)	Kiesler (1996)
Sullivan (1956)	Sullivan (1964)		Kiesler (1983)	Wiggins & Trobst (1999)
Leary (1957)	Lorr & McNair (1965)		Benjamin (1984)	
Schaefer (1959)	Carson (1969)		Horowitz & Vitkus (1986)	

nor do interpersonal theorists regularly recognize the social psychological literature on interpersonal interaction in their work (cf. Kiesler, 1996).

Thus, the current state of affairs compels interpersonal theorists to take the next step in defining the interpersonal foundations for an integrative theory of personality. The initial integrative efforts provide a platform to refine the scope of interpersonal theory, and the areas in which integration is lacking indicate that further development is necessary. The goal of this chapter is to begin to forge a new identity for interpersonal theory that recognizes both its unique aspects and integrative potential; in this chapter, we also suggest important areas in need of further theoretical development and empirical research.

THE INTERPERSONAL SITUATION

> I had come to feel over the years that there was an acute need for a discipline that was determined to study not the individual organism or the social heritage, but the interpersonal situations through which persons manifest mental health or mental disorder. (Sullivan, 1953b, p. 18)
>
> Personality is the relatively enduring pattern of recurrent interpersonal situations which characterize a human life. (Sullivan, 1953b, pp. 110–111)

These statements are remarkably prescient, as much of psychology in the new millenium seems devoted in one way or another to studying interpersonal aspects of human existence. To best understand how this focus has become so fundamental to the psychology of personality (and beyond), we must clarify what is meant by an *interpersonal situation.* Perhaps the most basic implication of the term is that the expression of personality (and hence the investigation of its nature) focuses on phenomena involving more than one person—that is to say, *some form of relating is occuring* (Benjamin, 1984; Kiesler, 1996; Mullahy, 1952). Sullivan (1953a, 1953b) suggested that individuals express "integrating tendencies" that bring them together in the mutual pursuit of both satisfactions (generally a large class of biologically grounded needs) and security (i.e., self-esteem and anxiety-free functioning).

These integrating tendencies develop into increasingly complex patterns or *dynamisms* of interpersonal experience. From infancy onward through six developmental epochs these dynamisms are encoded in memory via age-appropriate learning. According to Sullivan, interpersonal learning of social behaviors and self-concept is based on an *anxiety gradient* associated with interpersonal situations. All interpersonal situations range from rewarding (highly secure) through various degrees of anxiety and ending in a class of situations associated with such severe anxiety that they are dissociated from experience. Individual variation in learning occurs when maturational limits affect the developing a person's understanding of cause-and-effect logic and consensual symbols such as language (i.e., Sullivan's prototaxic, parataxic, and syntaxic modes of experience), understanding of qualities of significant others (including their "reflected appraisals" of the developing person), as well as their understanding of the ultimate outcomes of interpersonal situations characterizing a human life. Thus, Sullivan's concept of the interpersonal situation can be summarized as the experience of a pattern of relating self with other associated with varying levels of anxiety (or security) in which learning takes place that influences the development of self-concept and social behavior. This is a very fundamental human experience for psychology to investigate, and it is a significant aspect of the efforts to integrate interpersonal theory with cognitive, attachment, psychodynamic, and evolutionary theories previously noted.

Sullivan (1954) described three potential outcomes of interpersonal situations. Interpersonal situations are resolved when integrated by mutual complementary needs and reciprocal patterns of activity, leading to "felt security" and probable recurrence. A well-known example is the resolution of an infant's distress by provision of tender care by parents. The infant's tension of needs evokes complementary parental needs to provide care (Sullivan, 1953b). Interpersonal situations are continued when needs and patterns of activity are not initially complementary, such that tensions persist and covert processing of possible alternative steps toward resolution emerge, leading to possible negotiation of the relationship (Kiesler, 1996). Finally, interpersonal situations are frustrating when needs and actions are not complementary and no resolution can be found, leading to an increase in anxiety and likely disintegration of the situation.

For Sullivan, the interpersonal situation underlies genesis, development, mutability, and maintenance of personality. The continuous patterning and repatterning of interpersonal experience in relation to the vicissitudes of satisfactions and security in interpersonal situations gives rise to lasting conceptions of self and other (Sullivan's "personifications") as well as to enduring patterns of interpersonal relating. To us, the interpersonal situation is at the core of an interpersonal theory of personality. The power of interpersonal experiences to create, refine, and change personality as Sullivan conceived is the foundation of an interpersonal theory of personality that has been elaborated in the last half century by a wide range of theoretical, empirical, and clinical efforts.

A comprehensive theory of personality includes contemporaneous analysis emphasizing present description and developmental analysis emphasizing historical origins as well as the continuing significance of past experience on current functioning (Millon, 1996). Consistent with these approaches, the fundamental aspects of an interpersonal theory of personality should include (a) a delineation of what is meant by *interpersonal,* (b) the systematic description of interpersonal behavior, (c) the systematic description of reciprocal interpersonal patterns, (d) articulation of processes and structures that account for enduring patterns of relating, and (e) motivational and developmental principles. In our opinion, interpersonal theorists have reached greater consensus on contemporaneous description than on developmental concepts. This consensus may be due in part to ambiguity in the meaning of the term *interpersonal.*

THE INTERPERSONAL AND THE INTRAPSYCHIC

Where are interpersonal situations to be found? Millon's (1996) distinction between contemporaneous and developmental analysis alludes to the dichotomy of the interpersonal and the intrapsychic. Specifically, current description evokes a view of the reciprocal behavior patterns of two persons engaged in resolving, negotiating, or disintegrating their present interpersonal situation. In this sense, we might focus on what can be observed to transpire between them. In contrast, developmental analysis implies that there is something relatively stable that a person brings to each new interpersonal situation. Such enduring influences might be considered to reside within the person—that is, they are *intrapsychic.* The dichotomous conception of the interpersonal and the intrapsychic as two sets of phenomena—one residing between

people and one residing within a person—may have at times led interpersonal theorists to focus more attention on contemporaneous analysis with perhaps greater hesitancy to elaborate on developmental influences. In our opinion, however, we must include developmental concepts if we are to be comprehensive, and this in turn requires examination of intrapsychic structures and processes. As it turns out, Sullivan would not be opposed to such efforts.

Greenberg and Mitchell (1983) point out that Sullivan's interpersonal theory of psychiatry was largely a response to Freud's strong emphasis on drive-based intrapsychic aspects of personality. Because of Sullivan's opposition to drives as the source of personality structuralization, there is a risk of simplifying interpretation of interpersonal theory as focusing solely on what occurs outside the person, in the world of observable interaction. Mitchell (1988) points out that Sullivan was quite amenable to incorporating the intrapsychic into interpersonal theory because he viewed the most important contents of the mind to be the consequence of lived interpersonal experience. For example, Sullivan (1964) states, ". . . everything that can be found in the human mind has been put there by interpersonal relations, excepting only the capabilities to receive *and elaborate* the relevant experiences" (p. 302; see also Stern, 1985, 1988).

Mitchell (1988) specifies several concepts associated with the dichotomization of interpersonal and intrapsychic, including perception versus fantasy and actuality versus psychic reality. Sullivan clearly viewed fantasy as fundamental to interpersonal situations. He defined psychiatry as the "study of the phenomena that occur in configurations made up of two or more people, all but one of whom may be more or less completely illusory" (Sullivan, 1964, p. 33). These illusory aspects of the interpersonal situation involve mental structures—that is, personifications of self and others. Sullivan (1953b) was forceful in asserting that personifications are elaborated organizations of past interpersonal experience, stating ". . . I would like to make it forever clear that the relation of the personifications to that which is personified is always complex and sometimes multiple; and that personifications are not adequate descriptions of that which is personified" (p. 167). Sullivan also saw subjective meaning (i.e., psychic reality) as highly important. For example, Mitchell (1988) points out that Sullivan's conception of parataxic integration involves subjective experience of the interpersonal situation influenced by intrapsychic structure and process. Sullivan (1953a) describes parataxic integrations as occurring "when, beside the interpersonal situation as defined within the awareness of the speaker, there is a concomitant interpersonal situation quite different as to its principle integrating tendencies, of which the speaker is more or less completely unaware" (p. 92). In discussing the data of psychiatry, Sullivan (1964) asserted that "human behavior, including the verbal report of subjective appearances (phenomena), is the actual matter of observation" (p. 34).

Thus, we can assert that interpersonal theory is not strictly an interactional theory emphasizing observable behavior; rather, the term *interpersonal* is meant to convey a sense of primacy, a set of fundamental phenomena important for personality development, structuralization, function, and pathology. It is not a geographic indicator of locale: It is not meant to generate a dichotomy between what is inside the person and what is outside the person. From a Sullivanian standpoint, the intrapsychic is intrinsically interpersonal, derived from the registration and elaboration of interactions occurring in the interpersonal field (Mitchell, 1988). As we will see, however, descriptions of observable interpersonal behavior and patterns of relating have generated far more consensus among interpersonal theorists than have elaboration of intrapsychic processes and concepts.

DESCRIBING INTERPERSONAL BEHAVIOR

The emphasis on interpersonal functioning in Sullivan's work stimulated efforts to develop orderly and lawful conceptual and empirical models describing interpersonal behavior. The goal of such work was to obtain a taxonomy of interpersonal behavior—"to obtain categories of increasing generality that permit description of behaviors according to their natural relationships" (Schaefer, 1961, p. 126; see also Millon, 1991, for a general discussion of taxonomy in classification of personality and psychopathology). In contemporary terms, such systems are referred to as structural models, which can be used to conceptually systematize observation and covariation of variables of interest. If sufficiently integrated with rich theory, such models can even be considered nomological nets (Benjamin, 1996a; Gurtman, 1992).

There have been two distinct but related empirical approaches to the development of structural models describing interpersonal functioning. We refer to these as the *individual differences approach* and the *dyadic approach* (Pincus, Gurtman, & Ruiz, 1998). These authors pointed out that although each approach has unique aspects, the approaches converge in that they assert that the best structural model of interpersonal behavior takes the form of a circle or *circumplex* (Gurtman & Pincus, 2000; Pincus et al., 1998; Wiggins & Trobst, 1997). The geometric properties of circumplex models give rise to unique computational methods for assessment and research (Gurtman, 1994, 1997, 2001; Gurtman &

Balakrishnan, 1998; Gurtman & Pincus, in press) that are not reviewed here. In the present chapter, circumplex models of interpersonal behavior are used to anchor description of theoretical concepts. The development of circumplex models of interpersonal behavior has significantly influenced contemporary developments in interpersonal theory, and vice versa (Pincus, 1994).

The Individual Differences Approach

The *individual differences approach* focuses on qualities of the individual, (e.g., personality traits) that are assumed to give rise to behavior that is generally consistent over time and across situations (Wiggins, 1997). From a relational standpoint, this approach involves behavior which is also generally consistent across interpersonal situations, giving rise to the individual's *interpersonal style* (e.g., Lorr & Youniss, 1986; Pincus & Gurtman, 1995; Pincus & Wilson, 2001), and in cases of psychopathology, an individual's *interpersonal diagnosis* (Kiesler, 1986; Leary, 1957; McLemore & Benjamin, 1979; Wiggins, Phillips, & Trapnell, 1989).

The individual differences approach led to the empirical derivation of a popular structural model of interpersonal traits, problems, and behavioral acts often referred to as the *Leary circle* (Freedman, Leary, Ossorio, & Coffey, 1951; Leary, 1957) or the *Interpersonal Circle* (IPC; Kiesler, 1983; Pincus, 1994; Wiggins, 1996). Leary and his associates at the Kaiser Foundation Psychology Research Group observed interactions among group psychotherapy patients and asked, "What is the subject of the activity, e.g., the *individual* whose behavior is being rated, doing to the object or objects of the activity?" (Freedman et al., 1951, p. 149). This context-free cataloging of all individuals' observed interpersonal behavior eventually led to an empirically derived circular structure based on the two underlying dimensions of dominance-submission on the vertical axis and nurturance-coldness on the horizontal axis (see Figure 9.1).

The IPC model is a geometric representation of individual differences in a variety of interpersonal domains, including interpersonal traits (Wiggins, 1979, 1995), interpersonal problems (Horowitz, Alden, Wiggins, & Pincus, 2000), verbal and nonverbal interpersonal acts (Gifford, 1991; Kiesler, 1985, 1987), and covert interpersonal impacts (Kiesler, Schmidt, & Wagner, 1997; Wagner, Keisler, & Schmidt, 1995). Thus, all qualities of individual differences within these domains can be described as blends of the circle's two underlying dimensions. Blends of dominance and nurturance can be located along the 360° perimeter of the circle. Interpersonal qualities close to one another on the perimeter are conceptually and statistically similar, qualities at 90°

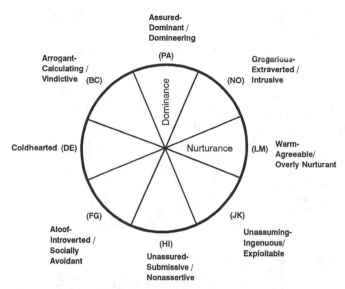

Figure 9.1   The Interpersonal Circle (IPC).

are conceptually and statistically independent, and qualities 180° apart are conceptual and statistical opposites. Although the circular model itself is a continuum without beginning or end (Carson, 1969, 1996; Gurtman & Pincus, 2000), any segmentalization of the IPC perimeter to identify lower-order taxa is potentially useful within the limits of reliable discriminability. The IPC has been segmentalized into sixteenths (Kiesler, 1983), octants (Wiggins, Trapnell, & Phillips, 1988), and quadrants (Carson, 1969).

Although the IPC represents a model of functioning in which the individual is presumed to be in many possible interpersonal situations, the model itself is monadic. The IPC structure does not include specific structural or contextual references to the interacting other. Most often, it is used to describe qualities of the individual interacting with a "generalized other" (Mead, 1932; Sullivan, 1953a, 1953b), such as the "hostile-dominant patient" interacting with a generic "psychotherapist" (e.g., Gurtman, 1996; Horowitz, Rosenberg, & Kalehzan, 1992).

The Dyadic Approach

In contrast to the individual differences approach, a second approach assumes that the basic unit of analysis for the study of interpersonal functioning was the dyad. As is the case for the IPC, there is a long history of theoretical and empirical conceptualizations of dyadic interpersonal functioning. At the same time that Leary and his colleagues were investigating individual differences in interpersonal behavior, Schaefer (1959, 1961) began investigating mother-child dyads in an effort to develop a structural model of interpersonal behavior. His methods were similar, but he emphasized the specific

dyad as the basic unit of observation: "For maternal behavior, the universe [of content] is the behavior of the mother directed toward an individual child, excluding all other behaviors of the mother" (Schaefer, 1961, p. 126). His work showed a remarkable convergence with Leary (1957)—both investigators found that a two-dimensional circular model best represented interpersonal behavior. As with the IPC, the horizontal dimension was love-hostility. However, the vertical dimension differed, and was labeled *autonomy,* ranging from autonomy-granting to controlling. Given a dyadic focus, Schaefer (1961) also derived a complementary circular model of children's behavior in reaction to mothers. Although this early model failed to parallel his maternal behavior model, the notion that parent-like interpersonal behaviors and childlike interpersonal behaviors may be distinguished from each other was an important advance that led to the development of a second prominent circular model of interpersonal behavior from a dyadic point of view.

Structural Analysis of Social Behavior (SASB; Benjamin, 1974, 1984, 1996a, 1996b, 2000) is a complex three-plane circumplex that operationally defines interpersonal and intrapsychic interactions (see Figure 9.2). The dimensions underlying SASB include autonomy (i.e., enmeshment-differentiation on the vertical axis), affiliation (i.e., love-hate on the horizontal axis), and interpersonal focus (i.e., parent like transitive actions towards others represented by the top circle, childlike intransitive reactions to others represented by the middle circle, and introjected actions directed toward the self represented by the bottom circle). Benjamin (1996c) described the development of SASB as an effort "to combine the prevailing clinical wisdom about attachment with the descriptive power of the circumplex as Schaefer had envisioned it" (p. 1204). The unique multiplane structure of SASB also incorporates Sullivan's concept of *introjection—* that is, the expected impact of interpersonal situations on the self-concept—by proposing a third corresponding circle that reflects how one relates to self.

By separating parent-like and childlike behaviors into two planes, SASB incorporates both the vertical dimension of Schaefer's model (control vs. emancipate) and that of the IPC (dominate vs. submit). The transitive surface represents the former, whereas the intransitive surface opposes submission with autonomy-taking. Thus, according to circumplex geometry, controlling and autonomy-granting are opposite interpersonal actions, whereas submitting and autonomy-taking are opposite interpersonal reactions (Lorr, 1991). Dominance and submission are placed at comparable locations on different surfaces to reflect the fact that they are complementary positions rather than opposites. Thus, SASB expands interpersonal description by including taxa reflecting friendly

TRANSITIVE:
Action Toward Other
Identification

INTRANSITIVE:
Reaction to Other
Recapitulation

INTROJECT
Relation to Self
Introjection

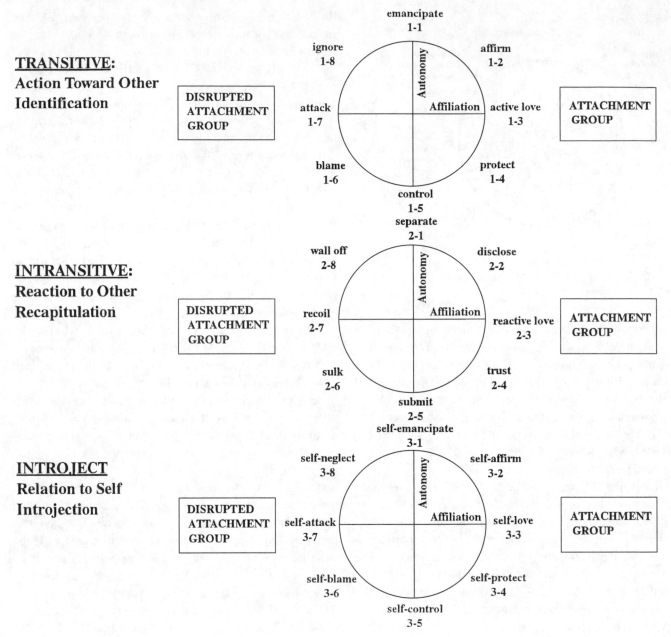

Figure 9.2   Structural Analysis of Social Behavior (SASB).

and hostile differentiation (e.g., affirming, ignoring) not defined within the IPC structure, as well as describing the introjected relationship with self. Although the vertical dimensions and complexity of SASB set it apart from the IPC, the same geometric assumptions are applicable. Interpersonal behaviors located along the perimeters of the SASB circles (identified as *clusters* in SASB terminology) represent blends of the basic dimensions with the same geometric relations among clusters on each surface.

To complete the description, we note that attachment concepts have been incorporated into the SASB structure

(Benjamin, 1993, 1996a, Florsheim et al., 1996; Henry, 1994). Boxes in Figure 9.2 denote that interpersonal elements on the right side of the circles (affirm-disclose, reciprocal love, protect-trust) represent the attachment group (AG). Interpersonal elements on the left side of the circles (blame-sulk, attack-recoil, ignore-wall off) represent the disrupted attachment group (DAG).

Using this expanded taxonomy, SASB describes a dyadic interpersonal unit—that is, a real or internalized relationship—rather than the qualities of a single interactant. For example, psychotherapy research using SASB has focused on the therapist-patient dyad as the unit of investigation (e.g., Henry, Schacht, & Strupp, 1990). Despite these differences, we view the structural models derived from the individual differences and dyadic approaches to be highly convergent in many respects, and they should be viewed as complementary approaches rather than mutually exclusive competitors (e.g., Pincus, 1998; Pincus & Wilson, 2001).

INTERPERSONAL RECIPROCITY AND TRANSACTION

The notion of reciprocity in human relating is reflected in a wide variety of psychological concepts including repetition compulsion (Freud, 1914, 1920), projective identification (Grotstein, 1981), core conflictual relational themes (Luborsky & Crits-Cristoph, 1990), self-fulfilling prophecies (Carson, 1982), vicious circles (Millon, 1996), self-verification seeking (Swann, 1983), and object-relational enactments (Kernberg, 1976), to name a few. If we assume that an interpersonal situation involves two or more people relating to each other in ways that bring about social and self-related learning, this implies that something is happening that is more than mere random activity. Reciprocal relational patterns create an interpersonal field (Wiggins & Trobst, 1999) in which various transactional influences impact both interactants as they resolve, negotiate, or disintegrate the interpersonal situation. Within this field, interpersonal behaviors tend to pull, elicit, invite, or evoke *restricted classes* of responses from the other, and this is a continual, dynamic transactional process. Thus, an interpersonal theory of personality emphasizes *field-regulatory* processes over *self-regulatory* or *affect-regulatory* processes (Mitchell, 1988).

Sullivan (1948) initially conceived of reciprocal processes in terms of basic conjunctive and disjunctive forces that lead either to resolution or to disintegration of the interpersonal situation. He further developed this in the "theorem of reciprocal emotions," which states that "integration in an interpersonal situation is a process in which (1) complementary needs are resolved (or aggravated); (2) reciprocal patterns of activity are developed (or disintegrated); and (3) foresight of satisfaction (or rebuff) of similar needs is facilitated" (Sullivan, 1953b, p. 129). Kiesler (1983) pointed out that although this theorem was a powerful interpersonal assertion, it lacked specificity, and "the surviving general notion of complementarity was that actions of human participants are redundantly interrelated (i.e., have patterned regularity) in some manner over the sequence of transactions" (p. 198).

Leary's (1957) "principle of reciprocal interpersonal relations" provided a more systematic declaration of the patterned regularity of interpersonal behavior, stating "interpersonal reflexes tend (with a probability greater than chance) to initiate or invite reciprocal interpersonal responses from the 'other' person in the interaction that lead to a repetition of the original reflex" (p. 123). Learning in interpersonal situations takes place in part because social interaction is reinforcing (Leary, 1957). Carson (1991) referred to this as an interbehavioral contingency process whereby "there is a tendency for a given individual's interpersonal behavior to be constrained or controlled in more or less predictable ways by the behavior received from an interaction partner" (p. 191).

Describing Reciprocal Interpersonal Patterns

Structural models of interpersonal behavior such as the IPC and SASB have provided conceptual anchoring points and lexicons upon which more systematic description of the patterned regularity of reciprocal interpersonal processes can be articulated (e.g., Benjamin, 1974; Carson, 1969; Kiesler, 1983).

The Interpersonal Circle

Carson (1969) focused on the notion of interpersonal complementarity as the patterned regularity between two people that contributed to "felt security." This notion is directly related to Sullivan's conception of a resolved interpersonal situation as an outcome in which both persons' needs are met via reciprocal patterns of activity leading to its likely recurrence. Anchoring his propositions within the IPC system, Carson first proposed that complementarity was based on the social exchange of status and love, as reflected in reciprocity for the vertical dimension (i.e., dominance pulls for submission; submission pulls for dominance) and correspondence for the horizontal dimension (friendliness pulls for friendliness; hostility pulls for hostility).

Kiesler's (1983) seminal paper on complementarity significantly expanded these IPC-based conceptions in several ways. First, he recognized the continuous nature of the circular model's descriptions of behavior, and he noted that because all interpersonal behaviors are blends of dominance and nurturance, the principles of reciprocity and correspondence could be employed to specify complementary points along the entire IPC perimeter. Thus, beyond the cardinal points of the IPC, it was asserted that (for example) hostile dominance pulls for hostile submission, friendly dominance pulls for friendly submission, and so forth, which can be further described by the lower-level taxa in these segments of the model. Second, Kiesler also incorporated Wiggins' (1979, 1980, 1982) conception of the IPC as a formal geometric model into his description of complementarity, whereby the distance from the center of the circle represents a dimension of intensity. That is, complementarity involves both the class of behaviors and their strength. Reciprocity on dominance, correspondence on nurturance, and equivalent intensity thus define complementary behaviors.

In addition, Kiesler (1983, 1996) defined two other broad classes of reciprocal interpersonal patterns anchored by the IPC model. When reciprocal interpersonal patterns meet one of the two rules of complementarity, he referred to this situation as an *acomplementary pattern*. In such a case, interactants may exhibit correspondence with regard to nurturance or reciprocity with regard to dominance, but not both. When interactants exhibit neither reciprocity on dominance nor correspondence on nurturance, he referred to this situation as an *anticomplementary pattern*. In Kiesler's (1996) discussion of these three reciprocal patterns of interpersonal behavior, it is clear that they relate rather directly to the types of outcomes of interpersonal situations suggested by Sullivan. Complementary reciprocal patterns are considered to promote relational stability—that is, such interpersonal situations are resolved, they are mutually reinforcing, and they are recurring. Acomplementary patterns are less stable and instigate negotiation (e.g., toward or away from greater complementarity). Finally, anticomplementary patterns are the most unstable and lead to avoidance, escape, and disintegration of the interpersonal situation.

SASB

After developing his two circular models of maternal and child behavior, Schaefer (1961) suggested that relationships between the two surfaces could be the basis for articulating a *theory of influence* of maternal behavior on child behavior, stating

> Bowlby (1951) has pointed out that both European and American investigators agree that the quality of parental care has great importance to the development of the child. Less agreement exists about how specific patterns of parent behavior are related to specific patterns of child behavior. One obstacle to the understanding of such relationships has been a lack of knowledge of *the interrelations of the concepts within each universe* [italics added]. For the purpose of discussion, let us accept the conceptual models presented here and attempt to develop hypotheses concerning *the relationship of the two models* [italics added]. (pp. 143–144)

Benjamin (1974, 1984, 1996a, 1996b) has extended Schaefer's proposition by formally articulating a class of reciprocal interpersonal patterns defined by intersurface

relationships within the SASB model, referred to as *SASB predictive principles*. The main predictive principles are complementarity, similarity, opposition, antithesis, and introjection, although others may be logically deduced (Schacht, 1994). It is important to note that these principles are not mutually exclusive from those anchored in the IPC model. The first four listed can also be articulated using the IPC. Complementarity implies the very same conditions for an interpersonal situation in both models with content (i.e., differing taxa) being the point of descriptive distinction. As Kiesler (1983) noted, similarity and opposition are specific forms of an acomplementary pattern as defined on the IPC. Antithesis is a form of anticomplementarity from the IPC perspective, again distinctly described using the SASB lexicon. Only introjection cannot be at least partially specified within the IPC model.

Complementarity is based on the relations between transitive and intransitive SASB surfaces; it reflects the typical transactional so-called pulls, bids, or invitations that influence dyadic interactants. It is defined when both members of a dyad are focused on the same person and exhibit comparable amounts of affiliation and autonomy. These can be identified by the numbers indicating the SASB surface (1, 2, or 3) and the cluster (1 through 8) as indicated in Figure 9.2. For example, a therapist focuses on her patient and empathically communicates that she notices an emotional shift (1-2: affirm). In response, the patient focuses on himself and tells the therapist of the associated perceptions, cognitions, wishes, fears, or memories associated with his current affective state (2-2: disclose). All possible complementary positions are marked by taxa appearing in the same locations on surface one and surface two (i.e., attack-recoil, blame-sulk, control-submit, protect-trust, active love-reactive love, affirm-disclose, emancipate-separate, and ignore-wall off). Like the continuous nature of the IPC, the SASB model has several versions, differing in their level of segmentalization and thus precision in terms of their descriptive taxa and predictive principles.

Similarity is exhibited when an individual imitates or acts like someone else—that is, they occupy the same points on the same SASB surface. Imitation, modeling, and observational learning (Bandura, 1977) are important mechanisms in social learning theories that can be described by similarity. However, similarity has a different meaning if it is exhibited by two interactants in an interpersonal situation. If two people rigidly maintain similar positions at the same time, the situation will be rather unproductive—negotiation must occur for there to be much progress. A familiar example is a couple planning their weekend. If both attempt to control (demand their way), there is a power struggle. If both submit, little is accomplished as the pattern of *What do you want to do?—I don't know, I'll do whatever you want* cycles and stalls. In an occupational relationship, both boss and employee tend to focus on the employee. The boss controls (in a friendly, neutral, or hostile way) and the employee complies in kind (i.e., complementarity). In contrast, an employee who consistently tries to boss the boss (i.e., similarity) will not be an employee for long!

Points 180° apart describe opposition on each SASB surface. Opposing transitive actions are attack and active love, blame and affirm, control and emancipate, and protect and ignore. Opposing intransitive reactions are recoil and reactive love, sulk and disclose, submit and separate, and trust and wall off. Opposing introjected actions are self-attack and self-love, self-blame and self-affirm, self-control and self-emancipate, and self-protect and self-neglect.

The complementary point of an opposite is its antithesis. Given a particular transitive or intransitive behavior, the antithesis is identified by first locating the behavior's opposite on the same surface, and then identifying its complement. That is, antithetical points differ in interpersonal focus and are 180° apart. Due to the impact of complementarity (i.e., a bid or invitation), the antithesis is the response that pulls for maximal change in an interpersonal relationship. For example, a psychotherapy patient treated by the first author would frequently sulk (2-6) when she experienced the therapist as not understanding or supporting her (e.g., *I don't know why I come here, this isn't helping me*). Rather than complement this with blame (1-6; e.g., *If you don't try to tolerate not getting exactly what you want from me, this won't work*), the antithetical affirming (1-2) response was enacted, (e.g., *I can see that something I have done or failed to do has left you feeling pretty upset*). The complement of affirm (1-2) is disclose (2-2). The patient would often visibly relax and communicate her frustration and disappointment. Thus, the antithesis of sulk (2-6) is affirm (1-2). Other antithetical pairs are emancipate and submit, active love and recoil, protect and wall off, control and separate, blame and disclose, attack and reactive love, and ignore and trust.

Introjection is based on the relations between the transitive and introject SASB surfaces and describes the circumstance where an individual treats him- or herself as he or she has been treated by important others. This reflects Sullivan's view that important aspects of an individual's self-concept are derived from reflected appraisals of others. That is, the person comes to conceptualize and treat himself in accordance with the ways important others have related to him or her. Common patterns often seen in psychotherapy include depressed patients who recall chronic blame and criticism from parents and now chronically self-blame, and patients with borderline personalities who were physically or sexually abused as children (perpetrator attack) and who now chronically self-attack via cutting or burning. As with complementarity, all introjected positions are marked by clusters in the same location but reflect the pairing of transitive and introject surface descriptors. These include attack and self-attack, blame and self-blame, control and self-control, protect and self-protect, active love and self-love, affirm and self-affirm, emancipate and self-emancipate, and ignore and self-neglect.

It is important to note that reciprocal interpersonal patterns anchored in either the IPC or SASB are neither inherently good nor inherently bad; they are value-free. In addition, we have tried to present them in their simplest form—as descriptors of behavior patterns that can be observed in interpersonal situations. A taxonomy of reciprocal interpersonal patterns is fundamental to contemporaneous analysis to account for transactional influences occurring in the interpersonal field and to developmental analysis to account for the enduring patterning of interpersonal situations that characterize a human life.

Contemporaneous Analysis of Human Transaction

In examining the immediate interpersonal situation, we may now use the taxonomies of interpersonal behavior and reciprocal interpersonal patterns to provide a contemporaneous analysis of human transaction. The most central pattern discussed previously is that of complementarity, and it is this reciprocal interpersonal pattern that anchors most theoretical discussions of interpersonal interaction. If we are to regard interpersonal behavior as influential or field regulatory, there must be some basic goals toward which our behaviors are directed. Sullivan (1953b) viewed the personification of the self to be a dynamism that is built up from the positive reflected appraisals of significant others, allowing for relatively anxiety-free functioning and high levels of felt security and self-esteem. The self-dynamism tends to be self-perpetuating due to both our awareness and organization of interpersonal experience (input), and the field-regulatory influences of interpersonal behavior (output). Sullivan proposed that both our enacted behaviors and our perceptions of others' behaviors toward us are strongly affected by our self-concept. When we interact with others, we are attempting to define and present ourselves and trying to negotiate the kinds of interactions and relationships we seek from others. Sullivan's (1953b) theorem of reciprocal emotion and Leary's (1957) principle of reciprocal interpersonal relations have led to the formal view that what we attempt to regulate in the interpersonal field are the responses of the other. "Interpersonal behaviors, in a relatively unaware, automatic, and unintended fashion, tend to invite, elicit, pull, draw, or entice from inter-actants restricted classes of reactions that are reinforcing of, and consistent with, a person's proffered self-definition" (Kiesler, 1983, p. 201; see also Kiesler, 1996). To the extent that individuals can mutually satisfy their needs for interaction that are congruent with their self-definitions (i.e., complementarity), the interpersonal situation remains integrated (resolved). To the extent that this fails, negotiation or disintegration of the interpersonal situation is more probable.

As noted previously, interpersonal theory includes intrapsychic elements. The contemporaneous description of the interpersonal situation utilizing either the IPC or SASB to delineate behavior and reciprocal patterns is not limited to the observable behaviors occurring between two people. Thus, interpersonal complementarity (or any other reciprocal pattern) should not be conceived of as some sort of stimulus-response process based solely on overt actions and reactions (Pincus, 1994). A comprehensive account of the contemporaneous interpersonal situation must somehow bridge the gap between the interpersonal (or overt) and the intrapsychic (or covert). Interpersonalists have indeed proposed many concepts and processes that clearly imply a rich and meaningful intrapsychic life (Kielser, 1996; Pincus, 1994), including personifications, selective inattention, and parataxic distortions (Sullivan, 1953a, 1953b), covert impacts (Kiesler et al., 1997), expectancies of contingency (Carson, 1982), fantasies and self-statements (Brokaw & McLemore, 1991), and cognitive interpersonal schemas (Foa & Foa, 1974; Safran, 1990a, 1990b; Wiggins, 1982). We agree with Safran's (1992) conclusion that the "ongoing attempt to clarify the relationship between interpersonal and intrapsychic levels is what is needed to fully realize the transtheoretical implications of interpersonal theory" (p. 105). Much of the field is moving in this direction, as the relationship between the interpersonal and the intrapsychic is a common entry point for current integrative efforts (e.g., Benjamin, 1995; Florshiem et al., 1996, Tunis et al., 1990).

Kiesler's (1986, 1988, 1991, 1996) *interpersonal transaction cycle* provides the most articulated discussion of the relations among overt and covert interpersonal behavior within interpersonal situations. He proposes that the basic components of an interpersonal transaction are (a) Person X's covert experience of Person Y, (b) Person X's overt behavior toward Person Y, (c) Person Y's covert experience in response to Person X's action, and (d) Person Y's overt behavioral response to Person X. These four components are part of an ongoing transactional chain of events cycling toward resolution, further negotiation, or disintegration. Within this process, overt behavioral output serves the purpose of regulating the interpersonal field via elicitation of complementary

overt responses in the other. The structural models of interpersonal behavior specify the range of descriptive taxa, whereas the motivational conceptions of interpersonal theory give rise to the nature of regulation of the interpersonal field. For example, dominant or controlling interpersonal behavior (e.g., *Do it this way!*) communicates a bid for status (e.g., *I am an expert*) that impacts the other in ways that elicit either complementary (e.g., *Can you show me how?*) or noncomplementary (e.g., *Quit bossing me around!*) responses in an ongoing cycle of reciprocal causality, mediated by covert and subjective experience.

In our opinion, the conceptions of covert processes mediating behavioral exchange have been a weak link in the interpersonal literature, reflecting much less consensus among theorists than do the fundamental dimensions and circular nature of structural models. The diverse conceptualizations proposed have not been comprehensively related to developmental analyses, nor have their influences on the observable interpersonal field been fully developed. In a significant step forward, Kiesler (1996) has synthesized many concepts (i.e., emotion, behavior, cognition, and fantasy) in developing the construct referred to as the *impact message* (see also Kiesler et al., 1997). Impact messages are fundamental covert aspects of the interpersonal situation, encompassing feelings (e.g., elicited emotions), action tendencies (pulls to do something; i.e., *I should calm him down* or *I should get away*), perceived evoking messages (i.e., subjective interpretations of the other's intentions, desires, affect states, or perceptions of interpersonal situation), and fantasies (i.e., elaborations of the interaction beyond the current situation). Kiesler and his colleagues view the link between the covert and overt aspects of the interpersonal situation to be emotional experience. Impact messages are part of a "transactional emotion process that is peculiarly essential to interpersonal behavior itself" (Kiesler, 1996, p. 71). Impact messages are registered covertly by Person X in response to Person Y's interpersonal behavior, imposing complementary demands on the behavior of Person X through elicited cognition, emotion, and fantasy. Notably, the underlying structure of impact messages parallels that of the IPC (Kiesler et al., 1997; Wagner et al., 1995), allowing for description of covert processes that are on a metric common with the description of overt interpersonal behavior.

In summary, contemporaneous analysis of the interpersonal situation accounts for the patterned regularity of interactions by positing that interpersonal behavior typically evokes a class of covert responses (impact messages) that mediate cycles of overt behavior—that is, patterned relational behavior occurs, in part, due to the field-regulatory influences of interpersonal behavior on covert experience and the subsequent mediation of overt action by evoked covert experience. In our opinion, this is only part of the story. Covert responses are intrapsychic phenomena that give rise to subjective experience. It is clear that the nature of such covert responses—that is, feelings, action tendencies, interpretations, and fantasies—are not evoked completely in the moment due to interpersonal behavior of another, but rather arise in part from enduring organizational tendencies of the individual, as the following example illustrates.

Parataxic Integration of Interpersonal Situations

The covert impact messages evoked within a contemporaneous interpersonal transaction cycle are primarily associated with the overt behaviors of the interactants. It is assumed that interactants are generally aware of such covert experience, as the development of the self-report Impact Message Inventory (Kiesler & Schmidt, 1993) suggests. However, Sullivan (1953a) also suggested that other integrating tendencies—beyond those that are encoded within the proximal interpersonal field—often influence the interpersonal situation. Such *parataxic distortions* may play a more or less significant role in the covert experience of one or the other person in an interpersonal situation.

Clinical Example

A psychotherapy patient treated by the first author entered her therapy session genuinely distraught and depressed. She reported that a person she labeled "an important friend" had ignored her during a recent social gathering and failed to attend a small celebration of her birthday. This was certainly no surprise to me, as this fellow had consistently behaved in an unreliable and invalidating manner toward my patient. However, it again appeared to be a surprise to her, and her disappointment was profound. The immediate interpersonal situation with this patient was quite familiar, and I decided our alliance was now sufficiently established to allow for an empathic effort to confront her continued unrealistic expectations of this fellow and to further examine how her attachment to him seemed to leave her vulnerable to ongoing disappointments.

I responded by saying, "I can understand that what has happened over the weekend has left you hurt, but I wonder why it is that despite repeated similar experiences with this 'friend,' you continue to remain attached to him and hope he will give you what you want? It seems to leave you very vulnerable." My patient responded with sullen withdrawal, curtly remarking, "Now you're yelling at me just like my mother always does!"

I am fairly certain that had the session been videotaped, there would be no increase in the decibel level of my voice during the intervention. And, an internal scan of my reaction to her report suggested helpful intent rather than countertransferential punitiveness. Nonetheless, my patient's response clearly communicated that I was now berating her and putting her down, and that therapy was not supposed to go this way. This continued for several months—any effort I made to examine my patient's contributions to her difficulties was rebuffed in a similar way. This continued to shape my therapeutic responses, leaving me hesitant to venture in this direction when my patient reported interpersonal difficulties. In other words, the repertoire of therapeutic behaviors I could provide became more and more limited by my patient's rather rigid behaviors in our relationship. In Kiesler's (1988) terminology, I was "hooked."

Several things are apparent from this example. First, using interpersonal structural models to describe the contemporaneous therapeutic transaction, we would see that the relationship was often characterized by *noncomplementary* responses and by a movement away from an integrated therapeutic relationship. I would try to direct her attention toward herself in an empathic way, and in response my patient would withdraw and threaten to leave. Second, my patient's response of sullen withdrawal was, however, quite *complementary* to her subjective experience of me as blaming and punishing. And third, the dynamic interaction between the overt and the covert aspects of our therapeutic transactions continuously exerted field-regulatory influence that allowed the therapy to continue. Too much "yelling and blaming" on my part would lead to a quick termination. My patient did not seem particularly aware of her bids to get me to back off, instead insisting she wanted my help with her depression and interpersonal difficulties.

In our opinion, this example highlights the challenges ahead for fully developing an integrative interpersonal theory of personality. In bridging the interpersonal and the intrapsychic, there are several limitations to contemporaneous analysis, three of which we discuss further in the next section.

Some Comments on Interpersonal Complementarity

The Locus of Influence

Safran (1992) is correct in pointing out that interpersonal theory's bridge between the overt and the covert requires further development. It is possible that many interpersonal situations generate undistorted, proximal field-regulatory influences—that is, covert experience generally is consistent with overt experience and impact messages reflect reasonably accurate encoding of the interpersonal bids proffered by the interactants. Thus, all goes well, the interpersonal situation is resolved, and the relationship is stable. However, this is clearly not always the case, as the previous example suggests. When covert experience is inconsistent with the field-regulatory bids communicated via overt behavior, it is our contention that subjective experience takes precedence. That is, the locus of complementarity is internal and covert experience is influenced to a greater or lesser degree by enduring tendencies to elaborate incoming data in particular ways. The qualities of the individual that give rise to such tendencies have yet to be well articulated within interpersonal theory. Interpersonal theory can easily accommodate the notion that individuals exhibit tendencies to organize their experience in certain ways (i.e., they have particular interpersonal schemas, expectancies, fantasies, etc.), but there has been relatively little consensus on how these tendencies develop and how they impact the contemporaneous interpersonal situation.

The Problem of Complementarocentricity

Complementarocentricity can be defined as the tendency to place complementarity at the center of interpersonal theory and research. In our opinion, this overemphasis has limited the growth of theory. Three examples of complementarocentricity are as follows:

1. What does failure to find empirical support for interpersonal complementarity mean? When empirical studies do not confirm the existence of complementarity, investigators often label it "a failure to statistically support complementarity" (e.g., Orford, 1986). Even when empirical investigations do find significant results (e.g., Gurtman, 2001), they are not indicative of 100% lawfulness. In our opinion, the answer to our question is that other reciprocal interpersonal patterns are also occurring in the interpersonal situation(s) under investigation.

2. In perhaps the most influential articulation of complementarity, Kiesler (1983) defined all reciprocal patterns in relation to complementarity. That is, other forms of reciprocal interpersonal patterns are said to take either acomplementary or anticomplementary forms. We wonder if this has inadvertently promoted complementarity as a more fundamental reciprocal interpersonal pattern than it actually should be.

3. In his encyclopedic review of complementarity theory and research, Kiesler (1996) presented 11 propositions to define and clarify the nature of, scope, and generizability

of complementarity, and nine counterpoints to Orford's (1986) famous critique of complementarity. In this work, Kiesler summarized important contributions by many interpersonalists emphasizing situational, personological, and intrapsychic moderators of complementarity (e.g., see Tracey, 1999), and suggested that significant attention be directed toward articulating when and under what conditions complementarity should and should not be expected to occur. Although this is exceptionally important, it continues to reflect complementarocentric thinking in that what is not recognized is that Kiesler's (1996) 11 propositions, nine counterpoints, and continuing investigation of moderators serve to *decentralize* complementarity as the fundamental reciprocal interpersonal pattern by suggesting that its occurrence is more limited and contextualized. For example, consider Proposition 11 regarding "appropriate situational parameters" from Kiesler (1996): "The condition of complementarity is likely to obtain and be maintained in a dyadic relationship only if the following conditions are operative: a) the two participants are peers, b) are of the same gender, c) the setting is unstructured, and d) the situation is reactive (the possibility of reciprocal influence exists)" (p. 104). Considered alone, complementarity is thus suggested to be most applicable to understanding the unstructured interactions of same-sex peers. This is certainly important, but is perhaps not the core phenomenon of interest for a comprehensive theory of personality.

The Problem of Motivation

The two core theoretical assertions associated with interpersonal complementarity are Sullivan's theorem of reciprocal emotion and Leary's principle of reciprocal interpersonal relations. With regard to the former, we suggest that interpersonal theorists have overemphasized Sullivan's first point (i.e., complementary needs are resolved or aggravated) and underemphasized his second point (i.e., reciprocal patterns of activity are developed or disintegrated). It is important to note that the needs involved are left undefined, and that the nature of satisfaction in the Sullivanian system involves a global sense of felt security marked by the absence of anxiety. Leary's principle provided an important extension in its emphasis on interpersonal influence and reinforcement that shapes the nature of ongoing interpersonal situations. But to what end? What is behavior's purpose? Traditionally, the cornerstone of complementarity has been the assertion that behavior is enacted to invite self-confirming reciprocal responses from others. We believe this has also been overemphasized in the interpersonal literature.

We agree that reciprocal interpersonal influence, reinforcement, and gratification are central to understanding human personality. This is reflected in the large number of psychological concepts that in some way reflect the notion of reciprocity. That is, individuals develop some consistently sought-after relational patterns and some strategies for achieving them. However, we do not believe that a single superordinate motive such as self-confirmation will succeed in comprehensively explaining how personality develops and is expressed.

Summary

Our discussion of interpersonal reciprocity and transaction has highlighted many of the unique strengths of interpersonal theory, as well as areas in which significant development and synthesis are necessary. In our view, interpersonal theory emphasizes relational functioning in understanding personality; this emphasis has led to the development of well-validated structural models that provide anchors to systematically describe interpersonal behavior and the patterned regularity of human transaction. Interpersonal theory has also emphasized field-regulatory aspects of personality in addition to the more traditional drive, self, and affect-regulatory foci of most theories of personality. The combination of descriptive structural models and clear focus on the interpersonal situation provides a rich nomological net that has had a significant impact in psychology, particularly with regard to the classification of personological and psychopathological taxa and the contemporaneous analysis of human transactions and relationships. However, we also feel that the future of interpersonal theory will require continuing efforts to address (a) the intrapsychic or covert structures and processes involved in human transaction, (b) the overemphasis on complementarity as the fundamental reciprocal interpersonal pattern in human relationship, (c) the overemphasis on self-confirmation as the fundamental motive of interpersonal behavior, and (d) the lack of a comprehensive developmental theory to complement its strength in contemporaneous analysis.

THE FUTURE OF INTERPERSONAL THEORY

We believe the future of interpersonal theory is bright. Addressing the four major issues previously noted will require interpersonal theorists to continue efforts at integrating interpersonal theory's nomological net with the wisdom contained in the cognitive, psychodynamic, and attachment literature. Fortunately, this is already beginning to take place.

Benjamin (1993, 1995, 1996a, 1996b) has initiated this with her interpersonal "gift of love" theory that integrates the descriptive precision of the SASB model with intrapsychic, motivational, and developmental concepts informed by attachment, cognitive, and object-relations theories.

Interpersonal Theory and Mental Representation

We have previously asked the question *Where are interpersonal situations to be found?* Our answer is that they are found both in the proximal relating of two persons and also in the minds of individuals. There are now converging literatures that suggest mental representations of self and other are central structures of personality that significantly affect perception, emotion, cognition, and behavior (Blatt, Auerbach, & Levy, 1997). Attachment theory refers to these as *internal working models* (Bowlby, 1969; Main, Kaplan, & Cassidy, 1985), object-relations theory refers to these as *internal object relations* (Kernberg, 1976), and cognitive theory refers to these as *interpersonal schemas* (Safran, 1990a). Notably, theorists from each persuasion have observed the convergence in these concepts (Blatt & Maroudas, 1992; Bretherton & Munholland, 1999; Collins & Read, 1994; Diamond & Blatt, 1994; Fonagy, 1999; Safran & Segal, 1990; Westen, 1992). Benjamin (1993, 1996a, 1996b) has also proposed that mental representations of self and other are central to the intrapsychic interpersonal situation. She refers to these as *important people or their internalized representations,* or *IPIR*s. Thus, whether referred to as internal working models, internal object relations, interpersonal schemas, or IPIRs, psychological theory has converged in identifying mental representations of self and other as basic structures of personality.

In our opinion, the fundamental advantage of integrating conceptions of dyadic mental representation into interpersonal theory is the ability to import the interpersonal field (Wiggins & Trobst, 1999) into the intrapsychic world of the interactants (Heck & Pincus, 2001). What we are suggesting is that an interpersonal situation can be composed of a proximal interpersonal field in which overt behavior serves important communicative and regulatory functions, as well as an internal interpersonal field that gives rise to enduring individual differences in covert experience through the elaboration of interpersonal input.

In addition, Benjamin's conception of IPIRs retains interpersonal theory's advantage of descriptive precision based on the SASB model (Pincus et al., 1999). Benjamin (1993, 1996a, 1996b) proposes that the same reciprocal patterns that describe the interactions of actual dyads may be used to describe internalized relationships (mental representations of self and other) on the common metric articulated by the SASB model (see also Henry, 1997). In our view, this adds explanatory power for interpersonal theory to account for individuals' enduring tendencies to organize interpersonal information in particular ways. Although the concept of the *impact message* is extremely useful in identifying the classes of covert cognitive, affective, and behavioral experiences of individuals, it does not necessarily account for the nature of individual differences in covert experiences. Benjamin's IPIRs provide a way to account for the unique and enduring organizational tendencies that people bring to interpersonal situations—experiences that may underlie their covert feelings, impulses, interpretations, and fantasies in relation to others. Interpersonal theory proposes that overt behavior is mediated by covert processes. Psychodynamic, attachment, and cognitive theories converge with this assertion, and they suggest that dyadic mental representations are key influences on the subjective elaboration of interpersonal input. In our opinion, Benjamin has advanced interpersonal theory by incorporating mental representations explicitly into the conception of the interpersonal situation.

Returning briefly to our clinical example, recall that the patient consistently came into therapy reporting disappointments in her interpersonal relations. In telling her sad stories, she communicated her need to be consoled and nurtured. When she was asked to reflect on her own contributions to her disappointments, she became sullen and withdrawn. This reaction was a bid at negotiation, communicating a threat to leave in an effort to reestablish a reciprocal pattern of satisfying responses from her therapist. Why was this happening, given that the therapist attempted to provide recognition and consolation of her hurt feelings? Despite good therapeutic intentions, efforts to focus her attention on her own patterns seemed unhelpful. There was a clue in her report of her subjective covert experience. When the therapist turned the focus toward the patient's contributions to her relational difficulties, he was experienced as similar to her *mother*. The proximal interpersonal field was no longer the primary source of her experience. There was now a second, parataxic integration of the situation that led to a covert experience that was driven by previous lived interpersonal experiences that now influenced the patient's subjective experience; this became the primary mediating influence on her overt behavior. Despite her requests for help and consistent attendance in therapy, the patient was having difficulty organizing her experience of the therapist independently of her maternal IPIR. In our view, this example demonstrates that noncomplementary reciprocal interpersonal responses in the proximal interpersonal field may indicate significantly divergent experiences within the internal interpersonal field that can

best be described by integrating interpersonal theory's structural models with concepts of mental representation.

Development and Motivation

Adding conceptions of dyadic mental representation is not sufficient for a comprehensive interpersonal theory of personality. Sullivan (1964), Stern (1988), and others have suggested that the contents of the mind are in some way the elaborated products of lived interpersonal experience. A comprehensive interpersonal theory must account for how lived interpersonal experience is associated with the development of mental representation. In our opinion, Benjamin has provided the only comprehensive developmental approach to evolve from interpersonal theory.

Using SASB as the descriptive anchor (Figure 9.2), Benjamin (1993, 1996a, 1996b) has proposed three developmental *copy processes* that describe the ways in which early interpersonal experiences are internalized. The first is *identification,* which is defined as treating others as one has been treated; this is associated with the transitive SASB surface. To the extent that individuals strongly identify with early caretakers (typically parents), there will be a tendency to act toward others in ways that copy how important others have acted toward the developing person. The second copy process is *recapitulation,* which is defined as maintaining a position complementary to an IPIR; this is associated with the intransitive SASB surface and can be described as reacting *as if* the IPIR were still there. The third copy process is *introjection,* which is defined as treating the self as one has been treated. This is associated with the introject SASB surface and is related to Sullivan's conceptions of "reflected appraisals" as a source of self-personification.

Identification, recapitulation, and introjection are not incompatible with Kiesler's conception of covert impact messages. In fact, we suggest that the proposed copy processes can help account for individual differences in covert experience by providing developmental hypotheses regarding the origins of a person's enduring tendencies to experience particular feelings, impulses, cognitions, and fantasies in interpersonal situations. For the patient described earlier, it seems that her experience of the therapist as yelling and blaming reflects (in part) recapitulation of her relationship with her mother. This in turn leads to a parataxic distortion of the proximal interpersonal field in therapy and noncomplementary overt behavior.

Although the copy processes help to describe possible pathways in which past interpersonal experience is internalized into mental structures (IPIRs), it is still insufficient to explain *why* early IPIRs remain so influential. The answer to this question requires a discussion of motivation. Whereas Sullivan's legacy has led many interpersonal theorists to posit self-confirmation as the core motive underlying human transaction, Benjamin (1993) proposed a fundamental shift toward the establishment of attachment as the fundamental interpersonal motivation. In doing so, she has provided one mechanism to account for the enduring influence of early experience on mental representation and interpersonal behavior. Although a complete description of attachment theory is beyond the scope of the present chapter, we agree that attachment to proximal caregivers in the early years of life is both an evolutionary imperative (e.g., Belsky, 1999; Bowlby, 1969; Simpson, 1999) and a primary organizing influence on early mental representation (Beebe & Lachmann, 1988a, 1988b; Bowlby, 1980; Stern, 1985).

Infants and toddlers must form attachments to caregivers in order to survive. Benjamin has suggested that the nature of the early interpersonal environment will dictate what must be done to establish attachments. These early attachment relationships can be described using the SASB model's descriptive taxa, predictive principles, and copy processes. The primacy of relationships to IPIRs is thus associated with the need to maintain attachment to them even when not immediately present. Benjamin (1993) refers to this as maintaining "psychic proximity" to IPIRs. The need to maintain psychic proximity is organized around wishes for love and connectedness (secure attachment or AG on the SASB model), as well as fears of rejection and loss of love (disrupted attachment or DAG on the SASB model). The primacy of early attachment patterns and mental representations influencing current experience is consistent with psychodynamic and attachment theories. Bowlby (1980) suggested that internal working models act conservatively; thus, assimilation of new experience into established schemas is typical (see also Stern, 1988). Benjamin (1996a) suggested that "psychic proximity fulfills the organizing wish to receive love from the IPIR . . . acting like the IPIR, acting like the IPIR were present, or treating the self as would the IPIR can bring about psychic proximity" (p. 189).

Returning again to the patient described earlier, it was clear that she was ambivalently but strongly attached to her mother. She consistently experienced blame any time she attempted to convey interpersonal disappointments or bad feelings. Anything that disrupted her mother's sense of control over the world was met with the accusation that the patient was being selfish and immature—and that it was the patient's fault, so her feelings were not valid. In addition, she was told that if she didn't stop causing so much trouble, her parents might divorce. It became clear that the patient had internalized a critical maternal IPIR. Whenever the patient was asked about her experience of self, she would inevitably begin her response with "My mother says that I am . . . ," or "My mother says it's bad for me to feel this way." When the therapist would try to explore the patient's contributions to her interpersonal difficulties, it evoked recapitulation. Despite affirming and affiliative efforts on the part of the therapist, the patient had a difficult time accommodating the new interpersonal input; instead she covertly experienced psychic proximity to the critical maternal IPIR and responded in kind. She experienced the therapeutic interpersonal situation as if the maternal IPIR were present, and she needed to back down rather than own her disappointments. To do otherwise would risk her attachment to her mother, painful as it was.

Concluding Propositions

Benjamin's developmental and motivational extensions of interpersonal theory provide some of the richest advances to date. We see her work, along with Kiesler's recent integration of emotion theory into the interpersonal transaction cycle, as solid evidence that interpersonal theory as originally conceived of by Sullivan has a vital and promising future as a fundamental and integrative approach to personality. In this vein we would like to close this chapter with a further extension of these contemporary works.

Interpersonal theorists are interested in understanding why certain reciprocal interpersonal patterns become prominent for an individual. Benjamin has made an important start by suggesting that a basic human motivation is attachment and that the interpersonal behaviors and reciprocal interpersonal patterns (described by interpersonal theory's unique structural models) that help achieve attachment become fundamental to personality through internalization of relationships (characterized by the copy processes). She posits that the wish for attachment and the fear of its loss are universal, and that positive early environments lead to secure attachments and normal behavior (i.e., AG). If the developing person is faced with achieving attachment in a toxic early environment, behavior will be abnormal (DAG), but will develop in the service of attachment needs and be maintained via internalization.

We would like to extend this further in an effort to generate an interpersonal theory of personality that more broadly addresses issues of basic human motivation. It is our contention that the maturational trajectory of human life allows us to conceptualize many developmentally salient motives that may function to mediate and moderate current interpersonal experience. That is, *reciprocal interpersonal patterns develop in concert with emerging motives that take developmental priority,* thus expanding the goals that underlie their formation and maintenance. We can posit core issues likely to elicit the activation of central reciprocal patterns and their associated IPIRs, potential developmental deficits associated with early experiences, and unresolved conflicts that continue to influence the subjective experience of self and others. The output of such intrapsychic structures and processes for individuals are those consistently sought-after relational patterns and their typical strategies for achieving them (i.e., proximal and internal field regulation). These become the basis for the recurrent interpersonal situations that characterize a human life.

It is our view that what catalyzes and reinforces identification, recapitulation, and introjection is the organizing power of developmental achievements and traumatic stressors. Although interpersonalists have discussed differential "evoking power" of behavior due to situational constraints and the quality of interactions (i.e., moderators of complementarity), we believe such evoking power is limited in comparison to the catalyzing effects of major personality developments and their underlying motivational influences. At different points in personality development, certain motives become a priority. Perhaps initially the formation of attachment bonds and security are primary motivations; but later, separation-individuation, self-esteem, mastery of unresolved conflicts, and identity formation may become priorities (see Table 9.2). If we are to understand the reciprocity seeking, field-regulatory strategies individuals employ, we must learn what interpersonal behaviors and patterns were required to achieve particular developmental milestones. In this way, we see that what satisfies a need or achieves an important goal for a given individual is strongly influenced by his or her developmental history. In addition to developmental achievements, traumatic learning may also catalyze the internalization of patterns associated with coping responses to early loss of an attachment figure, severe physical illness in childhood, sexual or physical abuse, and so on.

Integrating the developmental and traumatic catalysts for internalization of reciprocal interpersonal patterns allows

TABLE 9.2   Some Possible Catalysts of Internalization

Developmental Achievements	Traumatic Learning
Attachment	Early loss of attachment figure
Security	Childhood illness or injury
Separation-individuation	Physical abuse
Positive affects	Sexual abuse
Gender identity	
Resolution of Oedipal issues	
Self-esteem	
Self-confirmation	
Mastery of unresolved conflicts	
Identity formation	

for greater understanding of current behavior. If individuals have the goal of individuating the self in the context of a current relationship in which they feel too enmeshed, they are likely to employ strategies that have been successful in the past. Some individuals have internalized hostile forms of differentiation such as walling off, whereas others have internalized friendly forms of differentiation such as asserting their opinions in an affiliative manner. The overt behavior of the other is most influential as it activates a person's expectancies, wishes, and fears associated with current goals, needs, and motives; this will significantly influence their covert experience of impact messages. In our opinion, the most important goals, needs, and motives of individuals are those that are central to personality development.

A brief example highlights this point and provides some clues as to why individuals may repeat maladaptive interpersonal behaviors over and over. Another psychotherapy patient treated by the first author was severely sexually and emotionally abused by multiple family members while she was growing up. The predictive principle of *opposition* to what she experienced as a child characterized her transitive actions towards others in the present. In all dealings with others she was hyper-loving and hyper-protective, even when clearly to her detriment. She compulsively exhibited such behaviors, even when treated badly by others. In therapy, it became clear that she counteridentified with her perpetrators and chronically exhibited the opposite pattern in order to maintain a conscious sense of individuation. It was as if she were saying, "If I allow myself to become even the slightest bit angry or blaming, it will escalate and I'll be just like those who hurt me in the past." Unfortunately, although she could shed tears for the victims of the holocaust and the victims of the recent epidemic of school shootings, she could not do so for herself. She had also introjected her early treatment within the family and continued to self-injure and ignore her own needs and basic human rights. Thus, although she consciously behaved in ways that individuated her from her abusers, she also abused and neglected herself in ways that unconsciously maintained attachment to her abusive IPIRs (see Table 9.3).

We end this chapter with a bit of speculation. A broader taxonomy of reciprocal interpersonal patterns such as SASB predictive principles and copy processes, combined with a theory of personality development and motivation, can be the basis for understanding both personality and its pathology. Obviously this approach could take many forms. From the contemporary interpersonal perspective developed in this chapter, a basic approach would be an open system with consideration of IPIR-Goal linkages associated with fundamental developmental achievements and traumatic learning. We could also

TABLE 9.3   Interpersonal Analysis of Ms. W's Behavior

IPIRs	Motive, Goal	Copy Process	Predictive Principle	Overt Behavior
Brothers & mother	Individuation	(Counter-) identification	Opposition	Hyper-loving & protective
Brothers & mother	Attachment, psychic proximity	Introjection	Introjection	Self-attacking, self-neglecting

consider individual differences in the influence of certain copy processes, such that personalities are classified as highly recapitulating, highly introjective, and so on. Similarly, we could consider individual differences in the tendency to enact certain reciprocal interpersonal patterns, such that personalities are differentiated by their tendencies to exhibit oppositional, complementary, antithetical, similar, or introjected behaviors. Although these final thoughts are purely speculative, we wish to emphasize our hope that the ideas presented throughout this chapter provide the interpersonal foundations for an integrative theory of personality.

REFERENCES

Anchin, J. C., & Kiesler, D. J. (1982). *Handbook of interpersonal psychotherapy*. New York: Pergamon.

Bandura, A. (1977). *Social learning theory*. Englewood Cliffs, NJ: Prentice Hall.

Bartholomew, K., & Horowitz, L. M. (1991). Attachment styles among young adults: A test of a four-category model. *Journal of Personality and Social Psychology, 61,* 226–244.

Beebe, B., & Lachmann, F. M. (1988a) Mother-infant mutual influence and precursors of psychic structure. In A. Goldberg (Ed.), *Frontiers in self psychology: Vol. 3. Progress in self psychology* (pp. 3–25). Hillsdale, NJ: Analytic Press.

Beebe, B., & Lachmann, F. M. (1988b) The contribution of mother infant mutual influence to the origins of self- and object representations. *Psychoanalytic Psychology, 5,* 305–337.

Belsky, J. (1999). Modern evolutionary theory and patterns of attachment. In J. Cassidy & P. R. Shaver (Eds.), *Handbook of attachment:Theory, research, and clinical applications* (pp. 141–161). New York: Guilford.

Benjamin, L. S. (1974). Structural analysis of social behavior. *Psychological Review, 81,* 392–425.

Benjamin, L. S. (1984). Principles of prediction using Structural Analysis of Social Behavior. In A. Zucker, J. Aronoff, & J. Rubin (Eds.), *Personality and the prediction of behavior* (pp. 121–173). New York: Academic Press.

Benjamin, L. S. (1986). Adding social and intrapsychic descriptors to Axis I of DSM-III. In T. Millon & G. Klerman (Eds.), *Contemporary directions in psychopathology. Towards DSM-IV* (pp. 599–638). New York: Guilford.

Benjamin, L. S. (1993). Every psychopathology is a gift of love. *Psychotherapy Research, 3,* 1–24.

Benjamin, L. S. (1995). Good defenses make good neighbors. In H. Conte & R. Plutchik (Eds.), *Ego defenses: Theory and measurement* (pp. 38–78). New York: Wiley.

Benjamin, L. S. (1996a). An interpersonal theory of personality disorder. In J. Clarkin & M. Lenzenweger (Eds.), *Major theories of personality disorder* (pp. 141–220). New York: Guilford.

Benjamin, L. S. (1996b). *Interpersonal diagnosis and treatment of personality disorder* (2nd ed.). New York: Guilford.

Benjamin, L. S. (1996c). Introduction to the special section on Structural Analysis of Social Behavior. *Journal of Consulting and Clinical Psychology, 64,* 1203–1212.

Benjamin, L. S. (2000). Use of structural analysis of social behavior for interpersonal diagnosis and treatment in group therapy. In A. P. Beck & C. M. Lewis (Eds.), *The process of group psychotherapy: Systems for analyzing change* (pp. 381–412). Washington, DC: American Psychological Association.

Benjamin, L. S., & Friedrich, F. J. (1991). Contributions of Structural Analysis of Social Behavior (SASB) to the bridge between cognitive science and a science of object relations. In M. Horowitz (Ed.), *Person schemas and maladaptive interpersonal patterns* (pp. 379–412). Chicago: University of Chicago Press.

Birtchnell, J. (1997). Attachment in an interpersonal context. *British Journal of Medical Psychology, 70,* 265–279.

Blatt, S. J., Auerbach, J. S., & Levy, K. N. (1997). Mental representations in personality development, psychopathology, and the therapeutic process. *Review of General Psychology, 1,* 351–374.

Blatt, S. J., & Maroudas, C. (1992). Convergence of psychoanalytic and cognitive behavioral theories of depression. *Psychoanalytic Psychology, 9,* 157–190.

Bowlby, J. (1951). *Maternal care and mental health*. Geneva, Switzerland: World Health Organization.

Bowlby, J. (1969). *Attachment and loss: Vol. 1. Attachment*. New York: Basic Books.

Bowlby, J. (1980). *Attachment and loss: Vol. 3. Loss: Sadness and depression*. New York: Basic Books.

Bretherton, I., & Munholland, K. A. (1999). Internal working models in attachment relationships: A construct revisited. In J. Cassidy & P. R. Shaver (Eds.), *Handbook of attachment: Theory, research, and clinical applications* (pp. 89–114). New York: Guilford.

Brokaw, D. W., & McLemore, C. W. (1991). Interpersonal models of personality and psychopathology. In D. G. Gilbert & J. J. Connolly (Eds.), *Personality, social skills, and psychopathology: An individual differences approach. Perspectives on individual differences* (pp. 49–83). New York: Plenum Press.

Carson, R. C. (1969). *Interaction concepts of personality.* Chicago: Aldine.

Carson, R. C. (1982). Self-fulfilling prophecy, maladaptive behavior, and psychotherapy. In J. C. Anchin & D. J. Kiesler (Eds.), *Handbook of interpersonal psychotherapy* (pp. 64–77). New York: Pergamon.

Carson, R. C. (1991). The social-interactional viewpoint. In M. Hersen, A. Kazdin, & A. Bellack (Eds.), *The clinical psychology handbook* (2nd ed., pp. 185–199). New York: Pergamon.

Carson, R. C. (1996). Seamlessness in personality and its derangements. *Journal of personality assessment, 66,* 240–247.

Collins, N. L., & Read, S. J. (1994). Cognitive representations of attachment: The structure and function of working models. In K. Bartholomew & D. Perlman (Eds.), *Attachment processes in adulthood: Vol. 5. Advances in personal relationships* (pp. 53–90). London: Jessica Kingsley.

Diamond, D., & Blatt, S. J. (1994). Internal working models of attachment and psychoanalytic theories of the representational world: A comparison and critique. In M. Sperling & W. H. Berman (Eds.), *Attachment in adults: Theory, assessment, and treatment* (pp. 72–94). New York: Guilford.

Florsheim, P., Henry, W. P., & Benjamin, L. S. (1996). Integrating individual and interpersonal approaches to diagnosis: The structural analysis of social behavior and attachment theory. In F. Kaslow (Ed.), *Handbook of relational diagnosis* (pp. 81–101). New York: Wiley.

Freud, S. (1914). *Remembering, repeating and working through.* Standard Edition, Volume 12, pp. 145–156. New York: Norton.

Freud, S. (1920). *Beyond the pleasure principle.* Standard Edition, Volume 18, pp. 1–64. New York: Norton.

Foa, U. G., & Foa, E. B. (1974). *Societal structures of the mind.* Springfield, IL: Charles C. Thomas.

Fonagy, P. (1999). Psychoanalytic theory from the viewpoint of attachment theory and research. In J. Cassidy & P. R. Shaver (Eds.), *Handbook of attachment: Theory, research, and clinical applications* (pp. 595–624). New York: Guilford.

Freedman, M. B., Leary, T. F., Ossorio, A. G., & Coffey, H. S. (1951). The interpersonal dimension of personality. *Journal of Personality, 20,* 143–161.

Gifford, R. (1991). Mapping nonverbal behavior on the Interpersonal Circle. *Journal of Personality and Social Psychology, 61,* 856–867.

Greenberg, J. R., & Mitchell, S. A. (1983). *Object relations in psychoanalytic theory.* Cambridge, MA: Harvard University Press.

Grotstein, J. S. (1981). *Splitting and projective identification.* Northvale, NJ: Jason Aronson.

Gurtman, M. B. (1992). Construct validity of interpersonal personality measures: The interpersonal circumplex as a nomological net. *Journal of Personality and Social Psychology, 63,* 105–118.

Gurtman, M. B. (1994). The circumplex as a tool for studying normal and abnormal personality: A methodological primer. In S. Strack & M. Lorr (Eds.), *Differentiating normal and abnormal personality* (pp. 243–263). New York: Springer.

Gurtman, M. B. (1996). Interpersonal problems and the psychotherapy context: The construct validity of the Inventory of Interpersonal Problems. *Psychological Assessment, 8,* 241–255.

Gurtman, M. B. (1997). Studying personality traits: The circular way. In R. Plutchik & H. R. Conte (Eds.), *Circumplex models of personality and emotions* (pp. 81–102). Washington, DC: American Psychological Association.

Gurtman, M. B. (2001). Interpersonal complementarity: Integrating interpersonal measurement with interpersonal models. *Journal of Counseling Psychology, 48,* 97–110.

Gurtman, M. B., & Balakrishnan, J. D. (1998). Circular measurement redux: The analysis and interpretation of interpersonal circle profiles. *Clinical Psychology: Science and Practice, 5,* 344–360.

Gurtman, M. B., & Pincus, A. L. (2000). Interpersonal Adjective Scales: Confirmation of circumplex structure from multiple perspectives. *Personality and Social Psychology Bulletin, 26,* 374–384.

Gurtman, M. B., & Pincus, A. L. (in press). The circumplex model: Methods and research applications. In J. A. Schinka & W. F. Velicer (Eds.), *Comprehensive handbook of psychology: Vol. 2. Research methods in psychology.* New York: Wiley.

Hardin, C. D., & Higgins, E. T. (1996). Shared reality: How social verification makes the subjective objective. In R. M. Sorrentino & E. T. Higgins (Eds.), *Handbook of motivation and cognition: The interpersonal context* (pp. 29–84). New York: Guilford.

Heck, S. A., & Pincus, A. L. (2001). Agency and communion in the structure of parental representations. *Journal of Personality Assessment, 76,* 180–184.

Henry, W. P. (1994). Differentiating normal and abnormal personality: An interpersonal approach based on the Structural Analysis of Social Behavior. In S. Strack & M. Lorr (Eds.), *Differentiating normal and abnormal personality* (pp. 316–340). New York: Springer.

Henry, W. P. (1997). Interpersonal case formulation: Describing and explaining interpersonal patterns using the structural analysis of social behavior. In T. D. Eells (Ed.), *Handbook of psychotherapy case formulation* (pp. 223–259). New York: Guilford.

Henry, W. P., Schacht, T. E., & Strupp, H. H. (1990). Patient and therapist introject, interpersonal process, and differential psychotherapy outcome. *Journal of Consulting and Clinical Psychology, 58,* 768–774.

Horowitz, L. M., Alden, L. E., Wiggins, J. S., & Pincus, A. L. (2000). *IIP-64/IIP-32 professional manual.* San Antonio, TX: The Psychological Corporation.

Horowitz, L. M., Rosenberg, S. E., & Kalehzan, B. M. (1992). The capacity to describe other people clearly: A predictor of interpersonal problems and outcome in brief dynamic psychotherapy. *Psychotherapy Research, 2,* 37–51.

Horowitz, L. M. & Vitkus, J. (1986). The interpersonal basis of psychiatric symptoms. *Clinical Psychology Review, 6,* 443–469.

Hoyenga, K. B., Hoyenga, K. T., Walters, K., & Schmidt, J. A. (1998). Applying the interpersonal circle and evolutionary theory to gender differences in psychopathological traits. In L. Ellis & L. Ebertz (Eds.), *Males, females, and behavior: Towards biological understanding* (pp. 213–241). Westport, CT: Praeger.

Kernberg, O. (1976). *Object relations theory and clinical psychoanalysis.* New York: Jason Aronson.

Kiesler, D. J. (1983). The 1982 interpersonal circle: A taxonomy for complementarity in human transactions. *Psychological Review, 90,* 185–214.

Kiesler, D. J. (1985). *The 1982 interpersonal circle: Acts version.* Unpublished manuscript, Virginia Commonwealth University, Richmond.

Kiesler, D. J. (1986). The 1982 interpersonal circle: An analysis of *DSM-III* personality disorders. In T. Millon & G. L. Klerman (Eds.), *Measures of personality and social psychological attitudes* (pp. 161–194). San Diego, CA: Academic Press.

Kiesler, D. J. (1987). *Revised Check List of Psychotherapy Transactions.* Richmond: Virginia Commonwealth University.

Kiesler, D. J. (1988). *Therapeutic metacommunication: Therapist impact disclosure as feedback in psychotherapy.* Palo Alto, CA: Consulting Psychological Press.

Kiesler, D. J. (1991). Interpersonal methods of assessment and diagnosis. In C. R. Snyder & D. R. Forsyth (Eds.), *Handbook of social and clinical psychology: The health perspective* (pp. 438–468). Elmsford, NY: Pergamon.

Kiesler, D. J. (1992). Interpersonal circle inventories: Pantheoretical applications to psychotherapy research and practice. *Journal of Psychotherapy Integration, 2,* 77–99.

Kiesler, D. J. (1996). *Contemporary interpersonal theory and research: Personality, psychopathology, and psychotherapy.* New York: Wiley.

Kiesler, D. J., & Schmidt, J. A. (1993). *The Impact Message Inventory: Form IIA Octant Scale version.* Palo Alto, CA: Mind Garden.

Kiesler, D. J., Schmidt J. A., & Wagner, C. C. (1997). A circumplex inventory of impact messages: An operational bridge between emotion and interpersonal behavior. In R. Plutchik and H. Contes (Eds.), *Circumplex models of personality and emotions* (pp. 221–244). Washington, DC: American Psychological Association.

Leary, T. (1957). *Interpersonal diagnosis of personality.* New York: Ronald Press.

Lionells, M., Fiscalini, J., Mann, C. H., & Stern, D. B. (1995). *Handbook of interpersonal psychoanalysis.* Hillsdale, NJ: Analytic Press.

Lorr, M. (1991). A redefinition of dominance. *Personality and Individual Differences, 12,* 877–879.

Lorr, M. & McNair, D. M. (1963). An interpersonal behavior circle. *Journal of Abnormal and Social Psychology, 67,* 68–75.

Lorr, M. & McNair, D. M. (1965). Expansion of the interpersonal behavior circle. *Journal of Personality and Social Psychology, 2,* 68–75.

Lorr, M., & Youniss, R. P. (1986). *The Interpersonal Style Inventory.* Los Angeles: Western Psychological Services.

Luborsky, L., & Crits-Christoph, P. (1990). *Understanding transference: The Core Conflictual Relationship Theme method.* New York: Basic Books.

Main, M., Kaplan, N., & Cassidy, J. (1985). Growing points of attachment theory and research. *Monographs of the Society for Research in Child Development, 50,* 66–104.

McLemore, C. W., & Benjamin, L. S. (1979). Whatever happened to interpersonal diagnosis? *American Psychologist, 34,* 17–34.

Mead, G. H. (1932). *Mind, self, and society.* Chicago: University of Chicago Press.

Millon, T. (1991). Classification in psychopathology: Rationale, alternatives, and standards. *Journal of Abnormal Psychology, 100,* 245–261.

Millon, T. (1996). *Disorders of personality: DSM-IV and beyond.* New York: Wiley.

Mitchell, S. A. (1988). The intrapsychic and the interpersonal: Different theories, different domains, or historical artifacts? *Psychoanalytic Inquiry, 8,* 472–496.

Mullahy, P. (1952). *The contributions of Harry Stack Sullivan.* Northvale, NJ: Jason Aronson.

Neuberg, S. L. (1996). Social motives and expectancy-tinged social interactions. In R. M. Sorrentino & E. T. Higgins (Eds.), *Handbook of motivation and cognition: The interpersonal context* (pp. 225–261). New York: Guilford.

Orford, J. (1986). The rules of interpersonal complementarity: Does hostility beget hostility and dominance, submission? *Psychological Review, 93,* 365–377.

Pincus, A. L. (1994). The interpersonal circumplex and the interpersonal theory: perspective on personality and its pathology. In S. Strack & M. Lorr (Eds.) *Differentiating normal and abnormal personality* (pp. 114–136). New York: Springer.

Pincus, A. L. (1997, August). *Beyond complementarity: An object-relations perspective.* Paper presented at the symposium of the American Psychological Association Annual Convention, Chicago, IL.

Pincus, A. L., (1998, June). *Parental representations and interpersonal traits.* Paper presented at the meeting of Society for Interpersonal Theory and Research. Snowbird, UT.

Pincus, A. L., Dickinson, K. A., Schut, A. J., Castonguay, L. G., & Bedics, J. (1999). Integrating interpersonal assessment and adult attachment using SASB. *European Journal of Psychological Assessment, 15,* 206–220.

Pincus, A. L., & Gurtman, M. B. (1995). The three faces of interpersonal dependency: Structural analyses of self-report dependency measures. *Journal of Personality and Social Psychology, 69,* 744–758.

Pincus, A. L., Gurtman, M. B., & Ruiz, M. A. (1998). Structural Analysis of Social Behavior (SASB): Circumplex analyses and structural relations with the Interpersonal Circle and the five-factor model of personality. *Journal of Personality and Social Psychology, 74,* 1629–1645.

Pincus, A. L., & Wilson, K. (2001). Interpersonal variability in dependent personality. *Journal of Personality, 69,* 223–252.

Reis, H. T., Collins, W. A., & Berscheid, E. (2000). The relationship context of human behavior and development. *Psychological Bulletin, 126,* 844–872.

Roemer, W. W. (1986). Leary's circle matrix: A comprehensive model for the statistical measurement of Horney's clinical concepts. *American Journal of Psychoanalysis, 46,* 249–262.

Safran, J. D. (1990a). Towards a refinement of cognitive therapy in light of interpersonal theory: I. Theory. *Clinical Psychology Review, 10,* 87–105.

Safran, J. D. (1990b). Towards a refinement of cognitive therapy in light of interpersonal theory: II. Practice. *Clinical Psychology Review, 10,* 107–121.

Safran, J. D. (1992). Extending the pantheoretical applications of interpersonal inventories. *Journal of Psychotherapy Integration, 2,* 101–105.

Safran, J. D., & Segal, Z. V. (1990). *Interpersonal process in cognitive therapy.* New York: Basic Books.

Schacht, T. E. (1994). SASB and clinical psychology: Further hypotheses. *Psychological Inquiry, 5,* 324–326.

Schaefer, E. S. (1959). A circumplex model for maternal behaviors. *Journal of Abnormal and Social Psychology, 59,* 226–235.

Schaefer, E. S. (1961). Converging conceptual models for maternal behavior and child behavior. In J. C. Glidwell (Ed.), *Parental attitudes and child behavior* (pp. 124–146). Springfield, IL: Charles C. Thomas.

Simpson, J. A. (1999). Attachment theory in modern evolutionary perspective. In J. Cassidy & P. R. Shaver (Eds.), *Handbook of attachment: Theory, research, and clinical applications* (pp. 115–140). New York: Guilford.

Snyder, M., & Stukas, A. A. (1999). Interpersonal processes: The interplay of cognitive, motivational, behavioral activities in social interaction. *Annual Review of Psychology, 50,* 273–303.

Stern, D. N. (1985). *The interpersonal world of the infant.* New York: Basic Books.

Stern, D. N. (1988). The dialectic between the "interpersonal" and the "intrapsychic": With particular emphasis on the role of memory and representation. *Psychoanalytic Inquiry, 8,* 505–512.

Stuart, S. & Noyes, R. (1999). Attachment and interpersonal communication in somatization. *Psychosomatics, 40,* 34–43.

Sullivan, H. S. (1948). The meaning of anxiety in psychiatry and life. *Psychiatry, 11,* 1–13.

Sullivan, H. S. (1953a) *Conceptions of modern psychiatry.* New York: Norton.

Sullivan, H. S. (1953b). *The interpersonal theory of psychiatry.* New York: Norton.

Sullivan, H. S. (1954). *The psychiatric interview.* New York: Norton.

Sullivan, H. S. (1956). *Clinical studies in psychiatry.* New York: Norton.

Sullivan, H. S. (1962). *Schizophrenia as a human process.* New York: Norton.

Sullivan, H. S. (1964). *The fusion of psychiatry and social science.* New York: Norton.

Swann, W. B., Jr. (1983). Self-verification: Bringing social reality into harmony with the self. In J. Suls & A. F. Greenwald (Eds.), *Psychological perspectives on the self* (Vol. 2, pp. 33–66). Hillsdale, NJ: Erlbaum.

Swann, W. B., & Read, S. J. (1981). Acquiring self-knowledge: The search for feedback that fits. *Journal of Personality and Social Psychology, 41,* 1119–1128.

Tracey, T. J. G. (1999). *Moderators of complementarity: Not all examinations of complementarity are equivalent or valid.* Paper presented at the meeting of Society for Interpersonal Theory and Research, Madison, WI.

Tunis, S. L., Fridhander, B. M., & Horowitz, M. J. (1990). Identifying schematized views of self with significant others: Convergence of quantitative and clinical methods. *Journal of Personality and Social Psychology, 59,* 1279–1286.

Wagner, C. C., Kiesler, D. J., & Schmidt, J. A. (1995). Assessing the interpersonal transaction cycle: Convergence of action and reaction interpersonal circumplex measures. *Journal of Personality and Social Psychology, 69,* 938–949.

Westen, D. (1992). Social cognition and social affect in psychoanalysis and cognitive psychology: From regression analysis to analysis of regression. In J. W. Barron, M. N. Eagle, & D. L. Wolitsky (Eds.), *Interface of psychoanalysis and psychology* (pp. 375–388). Washington, DC: American Psychological Association.

Wiggins, J. S. (1979). A psychological taxonomy of trait-descriptive terms: The interpersonal domain. *Journal of Personality and Social Psychology, 37,* 395–412.

Wiggins, J. S. (1980). Circumplex models of interpersonal behavior. In L. Wheeler (Ed.), *Review of personality and social psychology* (Vol. 1, pp. 265–293). Beverly Hills, CA: Sage.

Wiggins, J. S. (1982). Circumplex models of interpersonal behavior in clinical psychology. In P. C. Kendall & J. N. Butcher (Eds.), *Handbook of research methods in clinical psychology* (pp. 183–221). New York: Wiley.

Wiggins, J. S. (1995). *Interpersonal adjective scales: Professional manual.* Odessa, FL: Psychological Assessment Resources.

Wiggins, J. S. (1996). An informal history of the interpersonal circumplex tradition. *Journal of Personality Assessment, 66,* 217–233.

Wiggins, J. S. (1997). In defense of traits. In R. Hogan, J. A. Johnson, & S. R. Briggs (Eds.), *Handbook of personality psychology* (pp. 95–115). San Diego, CA: Academic Press.

Wiggins, J. S., Phillips, N., & Trapnell, P. (1989). Circular reasoning about interpersonal behavior: Evidence concerning some untested assumptions underlying diagnostic classification. *Journal of Personality and Social Psychology, 56,* 296–305.

Wiggins, J. S., & Trapnell, P. D. (1996). A dyadic interactional perspective on the five-factor model. In J. S. Wiggins (Ed.), *The five-factor model of personality: Theoretical perspective* (pp. 88–162). New York: Guilford Press.

Wiggins, J. S., Trapnell, P. D. & Phillips, N. (1988). Psychometric and geometric characteristics of the revised Interpersonal Adjective Scales (IAS-R). *Multivariate Behavioral Research, 23,* 17–30,

Wiggins, J. S., & Trobst, K. K. (1997). When is a circumplex an "interpersonal circumplex"? The case of supportive actions. In R. Plutchik & H. R. Conte (Eds.), *Circumplex models of personality and emotions* (pp. 57–80). Washington, DC: American Psychological Association.

Wiggins, J. S., & Trobst, K. K. (1999). The fields of interpersonal behavior. In L. A. Pervin and O. P. John (Eds.), *Handbook of personality theory and research* (2nd ed., pp. 653–670). New York: Guilford.

Zuroff, D. C., Moskowitz, D. S., & Cote, S. (1999). Dependency, self-criticism, interpersonal behaviour and affect: Evolutionary perspectives. *British Journal of Clinical Psychology, 38,* 231–250.

CHAPTER 10

Structures of Personality Traits

WILLEM K. B. HOFSTEE

Operations reshape concepts. Over the past decades, the very concept of personality has been subject to implicit redefinition through a set of operations labeled the *Big Five taxonomy* or the *five-factor model* of personality. In a restricted sense, the number five refers to the finding that most of the replicable variance of trait-descriptive adjectives in some Western languages is caught by five principal components whose varimax rotations are named extraversion, agreeableness, conscientiousness, emotional stability, and intellect (or openness to experience, autonomy, imagination, and so on, depending on operational variations). In a wider sense, however, the five-dimensional (5-D) approach has come to represent no less than a paradigm—in particular, a revival of the individual-differences or trait conception of personality. For an evaluation of its status and future perspectives, a systematic analysis of its operational credentials is in order.

A first module of the set of operations that constitute the 5-D paradigm consists of the questionnaire construction of personality, whereby someone's personality is defined through his or her own answers, or more exceptionally through the answers given by third persons, to standardized questions. The questionnaire approach is not confined to the 5-D tradition, but it has to a significant extent been taken over by that paradigm (the megamerger impressing some as monopolistic). Is there a viable alternative to the questionnaire method, and if so, would it change our view of personality?

A second, more specific, operational module contains ways of choosing personality descriptors. The general guiding principle in this module is the lexical approach that consists of selecting items from a corpus of language, particularly a dictionary of that language. The distinguishing characteristic of the lexical approach is its purposely inductive nature, in contrast to approaches in which the descriptor base is deduced from particular trait constructs, for example, neuroticism. Again, the leading question is about the impact of these operations on our conception of personality.

A third operational characteristic consists of reliance on the linear model, particularly, principal component analysis (PCA) of Likert item scales. This is probably the most

The author is greatly indebted to Lewis R. Goldberg, Gerard Saucier, and Jos M. F. Ten Berge for their incisive comments on a draft of this chapter.

constitutive operation of the paradigm, if only because the number of five dimensions is intimately connected with it. The merits or demerits of PCA as such (if that problem makes sense at all) are not in order here. Clearly, however, other methods—notably, methods advocated under the label of person-oriented approach—yield concepts of personality that differ from the 5-D trait paradigm.

A fourth set of operations contains models for structuring, interpreting, and communicating trait information. The major rivals are the hierarchical and the circumplex models of personality structure. Their common point of departure is simple structure. On the one hand, simple structure is a primitive case of the circumplex in that trait variables are assigned to the factor on which they load highest, thus, to circle segments that are 90 deg wide with the factor poles as bisectrices. On the other, simple structure may be viewed as a primitive case of hierarchical structure containing two levels: factors at the top and trait variables at the bottom. But from there on, ways separate. I judge structure models by their capacity to produce clear and communicable trait concepts; their underlying mechanics, however, should be allowed to be intricate and may stretch the mind.

After discussing the structure models that have been proposed or implied in the 5-D context, I conclude with sketching a family of models that may serve as a base for capturing personality structure. It consists of a hierarchy of generalized semicircumplexes, with one general p component of personality at the top, and including two-dimensional circumplex, giant three, 5-D, and other dimensional structures. The joint structure responds to the greatest challenge in personality assessment, which is to deal with its dominating evaluative component in a realistic manner.

CONSTRUCTING PERSONALITY THROUGH QUESTIONNAIRES

Under the 5-D paradigm, what does it mean to say that a person is extraverted? In the typical case, it means that this individual has given answers to a number of standard questions regarding himself or herself and that these answers have been summarized into a score under the hopefully adequate label of extraversion—rather than, for example, surgency or sociability, which are related but not the same. This is not to suggest that a ready alternative to the questionnaire approach is available; rather, it functions as a tacit presupposition in trait psychology taken generally. However, there is an obvious alternative to the individual himself

or herself as a responder, namely, others who know the person well.

The Hegemony of Questionnaires

The association between personality and questionnaires is not merely a matter of fashion or a historical coincidence. To assess someone's personality, we have to ask questions about it—to the person himself or herself, to third parties who know the person well, to expert observers. Between the investigator or practitioner on the one hand and the person on the other, there is an indispensable assessor. So-called behavior observations, for example, are not objective in the way they would be if behavior recordings were translated into a score without the intervention of an observer; they represent answers to questions put to a human assessor. Moving from asking questions to applying a questionnaire is a small step: A systematic approach to personality requires standard questions, and thus a questionnaire. Using an unstructured interview, for example, means obtaining answers to an imperfectly standardized set of questions.

One seeming exception is self-report, in which person and assessor coincide. Failure to distinguish between the two roles, however, would amount to denying that the assessor could be someone else, thereby abandoning personality as an intersubjective phenomenon. Another more interesting apparent exception to questionnaire use is expert clinical diagnosis, in which practitioner and assessor coincide. In the first place, however, that process may be reconstructed in part as giving answers to more or less standardized questions about the person that the diagnostician has learned to ask to himself or herself. Second and more fundamental, the diagnostician could have been another individual. By virtue of that exchangeability, a case can be made for maximizing the intersubjective character of diagnoses. Actually using a standardized set of questions (e.g., a personality questionnaire phrased in the third person singular) to guide and articulate one's diagnostic impressions would contribute to that end. This is not to deny the heuristic element in clinical diagnosis, or in any other applied setting, but to document the central place of asking questions to third persons in the systematic study of personality.

The reason for the primacy of questionnaires may of course be sought in a tendency of students of personality to take things easy: There is nothing more convenient than giving a self-report questionnaire to a client or applicant. But more valid reasons may be brought forward. There is a tension between the concepts of "test" and "personality." Surely, we may decide to assess a person's typical intelligent behavior by means of a questionnaire (e.g., Goff & Ackerman, 1992), or test the maximal introversion of which he or she is capable (see Riemann, 1997), but neither of these crossovers has appeared to be adequate or promising. Ability and tests of maximal performance, and personality and assessments of typical behavior, are associated in a nonarbitrary manner (Hofstee, 2001).

Are Questionnaires There to Stay?

The prime product of the 5-D paradigm consists of questionnaires, including most notably the Neopersonality incentives-PI-R and NEO-FFI (Costa & McCrae, 1992), and includes many other questionnaires and trait adjective lists; the model has thus given a significant boost to the questionnaire construction of personality. I have argued in brief that the relation between personality traits and the questionnaire operationalization is intimate. Should one be happy with the prospect of such an essentially monomethod definition of personality, and if not, can alternatives be foreseen?

Asking questions to third persons in order to assess personality implies a social definition of it. Surely, the field has moved beyond the stage at which personality was deemed to be merely in the eye of the beholder; cumulative behavior-genetic research (see, e.g., chapter by Livesley, Jang, & Vernon in this volume; Loehlin, 1992) has put an end to that subjective conception of traits. But the dominant conception of personality remains social in the sense of intersubjective rather than objective. Buss (1996) made a virtue of this need by explaining the Big Five as elementary social mechanisms; for example, Factor III represents the need of the perceiver to know whether the other person can be depended upon. Most students of personality, however, would have hesitations with this subordination of personality to social psychology, especially if that bondage is a side effect of a dominant operational approach.

The scientific emancipation of a subjective or intersubjective concept appears to hinge upon the discovery of objective indicators that cover the concept well. If we wish to establish how much of a fever we run, we do not use a Likert scale but measure it with a thermometer. If we want to gauge an applicant's intelligence, we apply a test rather than asking questions to the applicant or even to a number of third persons. If the latter example is more problematic than the first, that is because there may be doubt regarding the coverage of the concept of intelligence by an IQ score. In the same vein, one may have doubts about the thermometer scale as a measure of outdoor temperature and prefer a formula that includes sunshine, humidity, and wind force. But once a certain level of coverage is secured, a return to sheer subjectivity would count as regressive. Are adequate objective indicators of personality traits in sight?

Probably the most promising indicators of personality are genes. According to estimates based on behavior-genetic research, genetic patterns will be capable of covering some 40% of the trait variance. That degree of coverage is not enough; we would not accept a thermometer that is only 40% valid. But before discarding the prospect, one should realize that the figure of .4 is heavily attenuated. An indicator need not and should not predict the error components in subjective assessments of temperature or extraversion. Heredity coefficients in the order of .4 should thus be divided by an estimate of the proportion of valid variance in questionnaire scores.

The first source of error in the self-reports that have almost invariably been used in behavior-genetic studies of personality is lack of agreement between assessors. The highest agreement coefficients between self and other in assessing personality (Hendriks, 1997; McCrae & Costa, 1987) are in the order of .7. Unless it is assumed that self is a systematically better assessor than other or vice versa, that figure may be taken as an estimate of the rater reliability of a single respondent, and some 30% of the questionnaire variance is rater error. Second, some 20% of the variance results from lack of internal consistency of the questionnaire scale, assuming alpha reliabilities in the order of .8; and third, a comparable error component results from temporal instability. Taking all these independent sources of error into account, one is left wondering how the heredity coefficients can reach .4 at all (Hofstee, 1994a).

The ironic conclusion from this crude analysis of error components in questionnaire variance is that the perspective of molecular-genetic diagnosis of personality traits cannot at all be discarded: It may well appear that whatever valid variance remains in questionnaire data can be accounted for to a satisfactory extent by genetic configurations. However, the analysis also points to the conditions for such a development. To establish links between genes and phenotypic personality traits, the assessment of the latter will have to be much more valid than it has been up to now (see also Bouchard, 1993). The central element of that program is discussed in the next paragraphs. Another aspect—optimizing the internal consistency of questionnaire data—is treated in the section on the linear approach to personality.

Definitions of Personality by Self and Others

Self-report fosters a conception of personality whereby the individual knows best how he or she is. With self-report *questionnaires,* the situation is more complicated. Standardized questions aim at comparing personalities rather than capturing unique and emergent characteristics. McAdams's (1992) criticism of the Big Five approach as a psychology of the stranger is correct in that sense (although other phrasings might be preferred if the value of scientific objectivity is stressed); it would be even more correct if the emphasis in Big Five research were on other-report rather than self-report. Self-report questionnaires embody a discordant blend of subjective and intersubjective accents.

In preparing an earlier (Hofstee, 1994a) paper on the topic, I met with unexpectedly ardent arguments in favor of self-report from prominent American Big Five researchers, the essence of which is documented in that paper. One argument pertained to personal secrets, whose content, however, would not be central to personality in most definitions. (A person might be said to be secretive, but that trait hardly even makes sense from the person's own point of view.) Another argument was that a person might sit in a corner over a large number of consecutive parties but still consider himself or herself to be extraverted, which would be all that counts. In practice, however, most witnesses would start worrying whether that person were still in contact with reality (which is again different from the question about introversion or extraversion). In the abstract, actors are at liberty to entertain a subjective definition of personality, but in real life it does not carry them very far. The intersubjective viewpoint is not merely a matter of scientific style; it is in touch with what people think of personality.

If the intersubjective viewpoint is accepted as a proper perspective on personality and if idiosyncrasies in self-report are seen as a source of error among other sources of error, the consequence for personality research and practice is as straightforward as it is revolutionary: Multiple assessors are needed to achieve acceptable reliability and validity; self-reports, being single by definition, are inevitably deficient. Self is of course acceptable as an assessor among others; self-ratings might even contribute more to the common variance than others' ratings do. But in any case, the road toward an eventual objective, genetic diagnosis of personality, will have to be paved with multiple assessors; good intentions will not be enough.

THE FUTURE OF THE FIVE-DIMENSIONAL MODEL

Will genetic fingerprinting in due time describe personality in terms of extraversion, agreeableness, conscientiousness, emotional stability, and some version of Factor V? In other words, will the 5-D model survive the developments that most readers may expect to witness in their lifetimes (whether they like it or not)? At the moment of writing this, the answer can hardly be unequivocal; even the question may appear to need rephrasing.

In an extensive reanalysis of several data sets, Saucier (2002a) found a three-dimensional structure containing agreeableness, conscientiousness, and extraversion to be more replicable across samples than a 5-D structure, especially in peer ratings, which in the present reasoning are more germane than self-ratings. So we might end up with a subset. Using a comparable three-dimensional solution, Krueger (2000) showed that the additive-genetic structure underlying the Multidimensional Personality Questionnaire (Tellegen, 1982) corresponded closely to the phenotypic structure. On the other hand, Jang, McCrae, Angleitner, Riemann, & Lively (1998) demonstrated that specific factors beyond the first five have nonzero heritability coefficients.

Even supposing reliable and valid assessments of phenotypic personality traits, a routine search for indicators of, for example, conscientiousness would require enormous samples just for tracing additive polygenetic effects; for interactions, the required sizes would rise exponentially (for a discussion of strategies of molecular-genetic research on personality, see Plomin & Caspi, 1998). At the turn of the century, attempts to trace genetic polymorphisms that explain personality showed the familiar picture of high initial expectations followed by failing replications (e.g., Herbst, Zonderman, McCrae, & Costa, 2000). According to a possibly more feasible scenario, large principal components of personality traits may be expected to reappear as an aggregate result of studies searching for single genes to explain specific patterns of deviant behavior (see, e.g., Brunner, Nelen, Breakfield, Roppers, & Van Oost, 1993). Assuming continuity between the range of normal behavior and deviant extremes, the aggregate structure of a large number of such specific patterns would resemble the 5-D structure. In the process, such taxonomies of phenotypic traits would receive a status comparable to mineralogical classifications; the chemistry of individual differences would be located at the DNA level.

Decades ago, Carlson (1971) found that personality was spelled in either of two ways: social or clinical. The questionnaire conception of personality is arguably social-psychometric by its methodological nature. If the genetic approach becomes dominant, a clinical reconstruction will regain momentum; individual differences within the normal range will be seen as mitigations and moderations of personality defects constituting the chemical elements. Meanwhile, an enormous amount of work has to be done, and 5-D questionnaires filled out by several third persons and self are instrumental in that labor.

THE LEXICAL BASE OF THE FIVE-DIMENSIONAL MODEL

A basic motive of researchers involved in the 5-D paradigm is to give a systematic and comprehensive, or at least representative, account of personality traits. An accompanying notion is that the field is characterized by a proliferation (John, 1990) of concepts and instruments, which frustrates the progress of the science of personality. The signature of the 5-D paradigm is empiricist and, in a sense, antitheoretical: If theorists, in this context, are individuals bent on disseminating their idiosyncratic concepts of personality, then their collective but uncoordinated action is responsible for a chaotic state of affairs in which thousands of unrelated concepts and their operationalizations form a market rather than a science. The 5-D conception is thus a taxonomy intended to end all idiosyncratic taxonomies.

To lift personality out of its chaotic state, an Archimedean point was needed. The most obvious candidate for a point of departure at the descriptive or phenotypic (Goldberg, 1993b) level is the lexicon. Like genetics, it provides a finite set of elements on the base of which a taxonomy may be built and proliferation may be counteracted. This section contains a discussion of the lexical point of departure, its variations, and its consequences. An analysis of the different shapes of the Factor V and their operational antecedents serves as an illustration.

The Lexical Axiom

What is usually referred to as the lexical hypothesis is more like an axiom. It states that people wish to talk about whatever is important and that the terms in which they talk may be found in the lexicon. The first and central part of that statement is not a hypothesis that is subject to empirical confirmation or disconfirmation; it introduces a heuristic that may or may not appear to be fertile. The second part is definitely false as no dictionary is ever complete; however, it is unproblematic because most dictionaries contain far more words than most people care to use or even understand, and hardly if ever omit common terms.

An objection that is seldom voiced although it is obvious enough is that the reverse of the lexical axiom does not necessarily hold true: People may well be talking about *unim*portant things most of the time. There is something to be said for the idea that the language of normal personality does not serve much of a purpose. However, PCA (see the next section) capitalizes on redundancies among variables. That method thus retroactively introduces a corollary of the lexical axiom, namely, that redundancy is indicative of real

importance. For playful purposes, we may seek rare and sophisticated terms or combinations of terms; at the level of common components, however, we mean business. Of course, this corollary, in its turn, may or may not be judged credible.

A reverse objection is that common language is not subtle enough for scientific purposes. One may philosophize at length about this proposition, which is as metaphysical as the lexical axiom itself. The historic rebuttal, however, was delivered by Digman (1990; Digman & Inouye, 1986), who recovered the Big Five structure in questionnaires, that is, in instruments designed by experts. In a similar vein, I (Hofstee, 1999) asked 40 clinicians to score a prototypical personality disorder with which they were familiar on the items of the Five-Factor Personality Inventory (FFPI; Hendriks, Hofstee, & De Raad, 1999). These items do not contain any technical terms or pathological content. Nonetheless, very distinct and extreme profiles in 5-D terms resulted, again indicating that expert categories may be well represented by ordinary language.

In principle, the lexical approach both reflects and fosters a lay definition of personality; in practice, however, the effect seems to be slight. Thus, at low conceptual costs 5-D research has succeeded in bringing a considerable measure of order to the anarchy of phenotypic traits. Any serious investigator proposing a new trait concept would now be well advised to investigate whether it has incremental validity over an optimal linear combination of the five factors; existing concepts are better understood in that framework. An example is typical intellectual engagement (Goff & Ackerman, 1992), which appears to be a label for a mixture of Factors V and III; another is the familiar concept of sociability, blending Factors I and II. As I argue later, there is nothing against using dedicated labels for blends if they are distinguished from variables that do carry considerable specific variance. But even if taken liberally, the five factors represent a taxonomic breakthrough, part of which may be credited to the lexical approach.

Operationalizations of the Lexical Approach

There is no unique and cogent operationalization of the lexical approach. It pertains to single personality-relevant words, under the tacit supposition that words do not interact, so that the meaning of any trait combination can be represented by a linear function of them. That supposition is patently false in the case of *oxymora* like "amiably inimical" or "quietly exuberant," joinings of opposite terms whose meaning cannot be accounted for in a linear fashion; however, there are reasons to be wary of such seductions of literary language. In any case, the search for single words is a defining characteristic of the lexical approach. But the question of how to select the single words has no straightforward answer; a number of decisions must be made.

A first decision concerns grammatical categories. Most investigators, from Galton (1884) on, have concentrated on adjectives (for an overview, see De Raad, 2000; Saucier, Hampson, & Goldberg, 2000). Goldberg (1982) and De Raad (1992) have studied type nouns, alphabetically running from ace to zombie in American English, but there is a consensus that this category does not add much (cf. extraverted vs. an extravert) or consists of invectives that have uses other than describing personality. A more interesting addition to adjectives are personality-descriptive verbs, which run from abandon to yield (not counting zap, zip, and zigzag) in English, denoting acts that would be more characteristic of one person than another. De Raad's (1992) analyses of personality verbs and nouns, however, do not result in novel content over the factors found in adjectives. The focus on adjectives does not recoil significantly on the implicit definition of personality.

A second set of operations consists of exclusion categories, for example, moods (e.g., sad), body characteristics (e.g., fat), social relations (e.g., subordinate), attitudes (e.g., progressive), and effects (e.g., famous). These exclusions are unproblematic because the categories are outside the domain of personality traits. Two other categories, however, deserve special consideration. One is called mere evaluations (e.g., good). In the language of personality, content and evaluation are intimately connected: On the one hand, neutral content is hard to find; on the other, mere evaluation is equally scarce. Tellegen (1993), in particular, has argued against excluding this category and has shown that it contains variance over and above the five factors (Almagor, Tellegen, & Waller, 1995). Thus, the 5-D model entertains a conception of personality that is somewhat sterilized with respect to evaluation.

The other problematic category is one that is invariably included, containing adjectives denoting intelligence, capabilities, talents, erudition, and the like—thus, the kind of maximum-performance traits that have traditionally been distinguished from typical-behavior traits. This inclusion is not an automatic consequence of the lexical approach; Ostendorf (1990), for example, sharply distinguished between temperament and character on the one hand, and skills and talents on the other, before joining the two sets of traits under the heading of dispositions. One could simply state that the 5-D approach has opted for the broader of the two definitions of personality, including not only temperamental or stylistic aspects (most notably Factors I, extraversion-introversion, and IV, emotional stability vs. neuroticism) and character (most notably Factors II, agreeableness, and III, conscientiousness), but also intellect, erudition, and the like (Factor V; see Hofstee, 1994b). However, I voice some reservations regarding that inclusive choice when discussing Factor V later.

A final operation consists of the exclusion of technical, highly metaphorical, and otherwise difficult terms. As I argued earlier, that procedure is probably not very consequential with respect to the scientific concept of personality, even though the literary loss is considerable. In constructing the FFPI, however, Hendriks (1997) went one step further and retained only items that were found perfectly comprehensible by students of lower professional education. Of the 1,045 brief expressions (e.g., Wants to be left alone) that made up the pool from which the items were chosen, 34% met this criterion. In a set of 195 trait-descriptive adjectives carefully selected to cover the factors of the 5-D model, only 14% did. It is a sobering thought that the founding studies of the 5-D model could not have been meaningfully carried out with these respondents. Furthermore, this sharpening of the comprehensibility criterion does appear to have consequences for the content of Factor V, as is shown next.

The Credentials of the Fifth Factor

The most spectacular vindication of the 5-D model has been brought forward by Ostendorf (1990). In the introduction to his study, Ostendorf related that he viewed the model with great skepticism at first, as the available American studies were based on very small samples of trait variables that had been composed using very subjective criteria (Ostendorf, 1990, p. 9). Not only this initial skepticism, but also the fact that the replication was completely independent, started from scratch, and was carried out in another language, added to the credibility of the 5-D model. Ostendorf, however, expressly included ability adjectives; consequently, his Factor V is a clear intellect factor defined by such terms.

In our Dutch lexical project, subjects were asked whether an adjective would fit in the framing sentence "he/she is [adjective] by nature" (cf. Brokken, 1978) in order to determine an adjective's prototypicality as a trait descriptor. Adjectives like dull, gifted, capable, brilliant, one-sided, idiotic, sharp, and ingenious received very low prototypicality ratings (along with other categories of terms, most notably social-effect adjectives like horrible, commonplace, and captivating). In a selection of terms used by De Raad (1992) to establish the replicability of the 5-D model in the Dutch language, terms with low prototypicality were excluded; consequently, no clear fifth factor appeared. In a Dutch-German-American comparison (Hofstee, Kiers, De Raad, Goldberg, & Ostendorf, 1997), the correspondence between the American and German structures was higher than the match of either with the Dutch structure, especially with regard to Factor V.

Plagued with feelings of intellectual inferiority, we took drastic steps to better our lives. In constructing the item pool for the FFPI (Hendriks et al., 1999), we expressly added 266 intellect items over the 1,045 constructed to cover the five Dutch factors (see Hendriks, 1997, p. 19f). However, only two of these 266 were judged to be perfectly comprehensible by our students of lower professional education, who did not connect to words like reflect, analyze, and contemplate. In a PCA of the whole item pool, based on responses of more sophisticated subjects, typical intellect items like Thinks ahead, Uses his/her brains, Sees through problems, Learns quickly, Is well-informed, and their counterparts had sizable secondary or even primary loadings on Factor III, conscientiousness; pure markers of V(−) were items like Follows the crowd, Copies others, and Does what others do. Consequently, Factor V(+) was interpreted as autonomy. We were thus unsuccessful in our attempts to arrive at an intellect factor. The autonomy interpretation of Factor V reappears in Italian data (see De Raad, Perugini, & Szirmák, 1997).

A powerful competitor—if only by virtue of the widespread use of the NEO-PI-R (Costa & McCrae, 1992)—to the intellect conception of Factor V is its interpretation as openness to experience. That construct does not come out of the lexical approach; in fact, McCrae (1990, 1994) has used it repeatedly to argue the deficiency of that approach. The consequent problem with such constructs, however, is that they do not share the taxonomic status that is awarded by the lexical paradigm. Furthermore, many of the NEO items in general, and of the openness to experience scales in particular, would not pass the comprehensibility test that was outlined earlier. Brand (1994) predicted that both intellect and openness to experience would correlate substantially with measured intelligence (*g*) over the whole intellectual range of the population. A special reason may be that subjects of modest IQ would reject such items because they do not understand them, and thus receive low scores.

Distinguishing Personality from Ability

The 5-D model seems to have contributed to a shifting emphasis from a narrow to a broad conception of personality. That shift can hardly be objected to as such. Not only are both intelligence and other personality traits stable and psychologically relevant, but they also combine with each other. An intelligent extravert may be found eloquent; a dull one may be judged to be loudmouthed. In the study on 5-D profiles of prototypical personality disorders (Hofstee, 1999) referred to earlier, the narcissistic and antisocial profiles were relatively

close together, but that must be because the FFPI's Factor V has little to do with intellect: Sizable differences between the two would be expected on measured intelligence (Millon, personal communication, September 29, 1999). For a proper assessment of personality, the inclusion of intelligence is indispensable.

There is no good reason, however, to contaminate typical behavior and maximum performance. On the contrary, there are good reasons to separate the operations. One is that objective measurement of intelligence is more scientific than its assessment, however intersubjective that assessment may be. Another is that methods are not neutral: Abilities and tests of maximum performance are as closely associated as are stylistic traits and assessments of typical behavior. To include ability items in questionnaires can only obscure the view on intelligence.

With respect to concepts of temperament and character, state-of-the-art assessment would include a 5-D questionnaire as a baseline instrument, and novel concepts would have to prove their added value against that background. According to the same principle of parsimony, however, 5-D factors have to prove their added value over measured intelligence. Precisely because personality and intelligence belong together, objective measures of intelligence should be included in investigating the structure of personality. In view of the scientific primacy of intelligence, its variance should be partialled out of the questionnaire scores. While in the process, attitudinal factors, which are out of bounds in most definitions of personality, should be removed in the same manner. They, too, are empirically correlated with certain versions of Factor V, particularly with openness to experience (Saucier, 2002a). With these corrections, it is entirely conceivable that little would remain of Factor V.

THE LINEAR APPROACH TO THE CONCEPT OF PERSONALITY

The "Magical Number Five," in the words of Goldberg (1992b), is intricately connected with applying PCA to large numbers of trait variables. Forerunners have been pinpointed, most notably Tupes and Christal's (1961/1992) analyses. However, Tupes and Christal's denomination of the fifth factor in terms of culture is now obsolete. On the other hand, if the magical number had been found to be six, one could have referred to another Cattellian's (Pawlik, 1968) set consisting of I Extraversion, II Cooperativeness, III Deliberate Control, IV Emotionality, V Independence of Opinion, and VI Gefühlsbetontheit (which is difficult to translate; the order in which the factors appear has been adjusted to the present context). These examples of imperfect historical fit could easily be expanded upon. The five factors owe their consolidation and impact to analyses of large data matrices that did not become possible until the last decades of the twentieth century.

This section starts with setting out the strongest possible case for PCA by presenting a classical (see Horst, 1965) rationale for it. Next, it examines the grounds for the magical number five. It then considers the so-named person-centered approach as an alternative to PCA in certain contexts.

The Case for Principal Component Analysis

Applying PCA to a scores matrix is the logical consequence of performing item analysis. In the general case, the aim of item analysis is to maximize the internal consistency of one or more scales based on the items; the exception whereby items are weighted by their predictive validity is outside the present scope. The basic idea of item analysis may be expressed as follows: The investigator is aware that each single item, carefully chosen as it may be, is an imperfect operationalization of whatever construct it represents. But the investigator has no better criterion against which to gauge the validity of the item than the total score on the set of equivalent items. Item analysis is thus a bootstrapping operation.

Carrying this basic idea to its logical consequence proceeds as follows: At the first step, items are weighted according to their association with the total score. Discarding items on that basis would amount to arbitrarily assigning a zero weight. That may be defensible in extreme cases where it is evident for substantive reasons—albeit post hoc—that the item does not belong in the set. In the general case, however, all items would be retained.

By virtue of assigning weights to the items, however, the total score has been replaced by a weighted sum. The implicit rationale is that this weighted sum is a better approximation of the underlying construct than was the unweighted sum. So the logical second step would be to assign item weights according to their association with the weighted sum. Thus an iteration procedure has been started, the endpoint of which is reached when convergence of weights and of weighted sums occurs. At that point, the weighted total score is the first principal component of the item scores (Horst, 1965). If the item set is multidimensional, more than one principal component is obtained, but the reasoning is essentially the same.

Thus a particularly strong argument in favor of PCA is that it is logically inevitable. Also, since the days of computer scoring, any practical objections against calculating weighted sums have disappeared: Sooner than applying 10 hand-scoring keys to a 5-D questionnaire (five keys for positive items and five for negative items), one would put the item scores on electronic file anyway.

Raw-Scores PCA

The present argument does not prejudice in favor of PCA as it is usually conceived, namely, PCA of z scores or correlation matrices. Rather, it refers to raw-scores PCA, with deviation scores and their covariance matrices, or standardized scores and their correlations, as special cases. Raw-scores PCA should be performed on bipolar scores; for example, scores on a five-point scale should be coded as -2, -1, 0, $+1$, and $+2$: We (Hofstee, 1990; Hofstee & Hendriks, 1998; Hofstee, Ten Berge, & Hendriks, 1998) have argued that a bipolar representation of personality variables is appropriate, as they tend to come in pairs of opposites. Thinking in terms of all-positive numbers is a habit imported from the abilities and achievement domain, where it does not make sense to assign a negative score.

Raw-scores PCA implies an absolute-scale interpretation of the Likert scale, rather than the conventional interval-scale interpretation. These alternative interpretations have subtle consequences for our conception of personality. The first of these concerns the reference point. With relative, interval-scale scoring, the population mean is the reference point. For desirable traits, that reference point is at the positive side of the scale midpoint (0), and vice versa. Thus a person with a score of $+.8$ on a socialness scale with a population mean of $+1.1$ (most people being found social), would be said to be somewhat asocial, albeit in a relative sense, which however is the only available interpretation when using interval scaling. The unthinking adoption of interval scales from the domain of intelligence and achievement may lead to a bleak view of humankind, whereby a sizable proportion of the population is judged more or less deviant. A poor comfort is that the proportion is a bit less than 50% because the raw-score distribution is not symmetric. Taking the scale midpoint seriously solves the problem; it prevents a positive judgment from being translated into something unfavorable and vice versa, based on an inappropriate convention.

The second way in which absolute and interval scale conceptions differ concerns spread. Using a five-point scale, most items have standard deviations close to 1, as the prevalent responses are -1 and $+1$; thus the difference between absolute and interval scaling is not dramatic in this respect. But extremely favorable and unfavorable items obtain smaller standard deviations. The effect of standard PCA and interval scoring procedures is to increase their impact on the total score. It would seem that this is also an unintended consequence rather than a deliberate effect.

In sum, item scoring through weights obtained by raw-scores PCA deserves more consideration than it has received so far. The standard objection to treating scores on a Likert scale as absolute is that strong assumptions would be imposed on the data. I am unable to see the validity of that argument. So-called weak models may in fact be very strong: To assume that the midpoint of a personality scale has no meaning and, consequently, that respondents' evaluations can be reversed, is about as strong as hypothesizing, for example, that a large proportion of the population cannot be trusted. At the very least, the absolute conception of Likert-scale scores is no more indefensible than the interval conception.

A Review of the Grounds for the Number Five

A way to obtain many principal components is to analyze matrices with large numbers of variables, in this case single trait descriptors. Earlier, limitations on computing capacity virtually prevented the number of trait variables from being much larger than the 35 employed by Tupes and Christal (1961/1992). With the expanding power of computers, however, it became feasible to analyze the very large numbers of variables that were needed to justify claims of representativeness if not exhaustiveness. However, the sorcerer's apprentice problem then becomes keeping the number of factors from getting out of hand. With hundreds of variables, it will take many factors to get down to the time-honored "eigenvalue 1" threshold; for example, the 20th factor in Ostendorf's (1990) PCA of 430 traits still has an eigenvalue of 3.

Hofstee et al. (1998) proposed a more stringent criterion based on the alpha reliability of principal components, which is approximately $1 - 1/E$ with large numbers of variables, E being the eigenvalue of that principal component. Setting the minimum alpha at .75, an "eigenvalue 4" threshold results ($E = 1$ gives $\alpha = 0$). Using this criterion, Ostendorf (1990) should still have set the dimensionality of the personality sphere at about 14 rather than 5; with even larger numbers of traits, the dimensionality would only increase. There can be no doubt that the 5-D model discards linear composites of traits that are of sufficient internal consistency, and would add to the number of dimensions. It is of interest to note that the most prominent 5-D questionnaire, Costa and McCrae's (1992) NEO-PI-R, in fact postulates 30 dimensions rather than 5, as each of the 30 subscales is deemed to have specific variance in their hierarchical model. (The five second-order factors do not add to the dimensionality, as they are linear combinations of six subscales at a time.)

An entirely valid pragmatic reason to restrict the number of factors is parsimony. The first principal component is the linear combination of traits that explains a maximum of variance; the second maximizes the explained variance in the residual, and so on. Consecutive factors thus follow the law of diminishing returns. Next, the scree test acts on the amount of drop in eigenvalue between consecutive factors; it thus signals points of increasingly diminishing returns. Using the scree test, Brokken (1978) retained 6 principal components in a set of 1,203 trait adjectives; Ostendorf (1990) retained 5. However, the scree test does not offer a unique solution; Ostendorf, for example, could have opted for an 8-factor solution on that basis. Neither PCA nor the scree test dictates the number of five.

Does replicability of factors provide a cogent criterion for the dimensionality of the space? That depends on how the term is understood. If one and the same large trait list were administered to large samples from the same population, the number of replicable factors would in all likelihood exceed five. At the other extreme, when independent, "emic" replications of the lexical approach in different languages are undertaken, the number tends to be in the order of three (De Raad et al., 1997; Saucier et al., 2000) rather than five, Ostendorf's replication being an exception. Saucier, Hampson, and Goldberg list 18 points on which such studies might diverge and recommend methodological standardization. A familiar objection is that standardization leads to premature closure of the issue: Not only would the outcome depend on arbitrary choices, but moreover one could not tell anymore what makes a difference and what does not. It would be preferable to use these points for studies on whether and how the number varies in function of differences in approach.

In sum, the number five takes on the character of a point estimate in a Bayesian credibility function on an abscissa that runs from 0 to some fairly large number, with the bulk of the density stacked up between 3 and 7. As with other empirical constants, the uncertainty does not so much result from random error as from the interplay of diverging arguments and specifications. In any case, the number should be taken with a grain of salt.

The Person-Centered or Typological Approach

A familiar critique of trait psychology is that it loses the individual from sight (see, e.g., Block, 1995; Magnusson, 1992). A set of alternative operations is available under labels such as type or person-centered approach; it comprises Q-sorts in preference to Likert scales, longitudinal designs to assess the dynamics of personality, and cluster analysis of persons rather than PCA of variables. Recent empirical studies (e.g., Asendorpf & Van Aken, 1999; Robins, John, Caspi, Moffit, & Stouthamer-Loeber, 1996) concentrate on the three "Block" types: resilient, overcontrolled, and undercontrolled.

I document the relativeness of the opposition between the person-centered and variable-centered paradigms (see also Millon, 1990) but try to do justice to a real difference in their ranges of application.

Persons in Principal Component Analysis

Unlike factor analysis proper, in which factor scores are hardly more than an afterthought, PCA offers a fairly symmetric treatment of individuals and variables. One could rotate a matrix of scores on principal components to simple structure and characterize individuals by the person factor on which they had their highest score. In an even closer approximation to the person-centered approach, factors and loadings may be rescaled such that individuals receive loadings and variables receive factor scores. That is not precisely the same thing as performing Q-factor analysis, as the scores still become standardized per variable instead of per individual as in Q-analysis; but the two operations would be mathematically identical in the case of raw-score PCA. If the argument in favor of raw-score PCA is accepted, the difference between variable-centered and person-centered analysis reduces to a set of scaling constants and rotation criteria being applied to one matrix rather than another, which is hard to get excited about.

Variables and Types

An orthodox typological solution may be viewed as a binary matrix of persons by types with one 1 per row, representing the type to which that person is assigned, and 0 scores in the remaining cells. At the other extreme, each person could be given a score for each type on a continuous scale, representing the extent to which that person corresponds with that type, thereby treating the types as continuous variables. The orthodox solution could be reconstructed from that matrix by selecting the highest score per row and dichotomizing accordingly. Intermediate, liberalized typological solutions (Millon, 1990) could also be derived, most notably through matrix-wise dichotomization of the continuous scores. In the liberalized solution, some persons would appear to be assigned to more than one type, whereas some others would fail to meet the threshold for any type at all. The types would no longer be orthogonal in the way they are forced to be according to the orthodox solution; so one could correlate the types, factor analyze them, and the like.

To those who would find this methodological play with types improper, there is a perfectly serious answer. In the ideal case, a diagnosis is performed by an infinite number of independent experts. Experts do not agree perfectly in all cases.

Thus the sum or average of even their orthodox typological solutions would give precisely the kind of matrix of continuous scores introduced in the earlier argument. In a scientific (in the sense of intersubjective) conception of types, the continuous matrix is the primitive case, not the binary matrix. The primitive case arises not because types (or even personality variables in general) are necessarily continuous as such, but because of the tacit third dimension of the matrix.

Q-Sorts and Likert Scales

Investigators working in the person-centered paradigm prefer ipsative scores, as they would represent intra-individual rather than interindividual comparisons. Varieties of ipsative scoring are row standardization, which fixes the means and standard deviations, and forced distribution, whereby all moments are fixed. Q-sorts automatically result in forced-distribution scores (unless the number of items in the "most applicable" to "least applicable" categories is not fixed, in which case, however, the method is indistinguishable from using a Likert scale).

Like orthodox typologies, ipsative scores may be constructed from continuous "interactive" scores, in this case by standardizing over variables or by forcing a distribution on them. One might object that Q-sorts are different in principle from Likert-scale scores, but that remains to be seen. In the first place, judges need not respond the way we instruct them to. If I am asked, by way of intra-individual comparison, whether I am (or John is) more reliable than friendly, I may well respond against the background of people in general; it could even be argued that the question is meaningless without that background. Conversely, when confronted with a standard personality questionnaire, intra-individual considerations might well enter into my response process. It is thus arguable that all responding is interactive. In the second place, Q-sorts are *used* to compare people, therefore, interindividually: If John is said to be of Type A whereas Mary is not, the intra-individual level is automatically surpassed.

The *effect* of ipsatization is to remove interindividual differences in elevation and spread (and skewness, kurtosis, and so on) of the responses. The operation thus implies a view of personality in which such individual differences have no place. Surprisingly, that view appears to be shared by some unadulterated trait researchers, most notably Goldberg (1992a) and Saucier (1992; see, however, Saucier, 2002a). Their rationale, however, has nothing to do with an emphasis on intra-individual differences. Rather, they use ipsatization of Likert-scale data to remove differences in scale usage, in other words, response sets. Whatever the rationale is, the implication needs to be examined in detail.

Removing differences in elevation and spread prevents one person from having more traits than another, as well as from being more extreme. Correcting for elevation is quite defensible in the special case where the variable set is completely balanced (i.e., consists of opposites like reliable and unreliable). Except in a fairly poetic manner, it hardly makes sense for a person to be both more X and un-X than another; it is more parsimonious to attribute such a response pattern to excentric scale use, traditionally denoted as the acquiescent response set. Hofstee et al. (1998; see also Ten Berge, 1999) presented ways to correct for excentric responding. However, if the variables set is not balanced, correcting for elevation removes content and social desirability variance. In the most elementary case, John is prevented from being both more friendly and reliable than Mary. That consequence is infelicitous.

The person-centered approach is thus subject to an irony of fate: An intention (a proper approach to personality) materializes into an operation (ipsative scoring) that appears to cradle aversive implications (for the very concept of personality). Ipsatization would do the job in a strictly idiographic approach, but that condition is not fulfilled: By virtue of the fact that one and the same method and vocabulary is applied to more than one person, interindividual comparison automatically creeps in. It may make sense to separate ipsative and normative components of a scores matrix by representing the latter as a vector containing the person means. Discarding that vector, however, has the effect of flattening the concept of personality. Essentially the same argument applies to individual differences in spread (and other moments of the score distribution).

Dynamics

Analytically, a dynamic approach to personality, as advocated by person-centered investigators, may mean either of two things: taking the time or growth dimension into account, and interpreting traits as an intra-individual pattern, therefore, in a nonlinear fashion. The dynamic approach thus stands in opposition to an orthodox trait approach, which is static and linear.

However, dynamics are easily accommodated in the individual-differences paradigm. A chronological series of assessments pertaining to an individual may be conceived as an extension of the scores vector. In a multiple prediction of some criterion, the question then becomes whether, for example, last year's emotional stability has incremental validity over today's. Alternatively, a (fitted) growth curve may be represented by its first derivative representing growth speed, its second derivative representing growth acceleration, and so on, in addition to the overall score of that individual.

Again, the derivatives function as extra traits. Similarly, pattern interpretation may be represented by introducing extra predictors, in this case, moderator or interaction terms formed by multiplication of predictors. Thoroughbred trait psychologists would argue that growth and pattern scores cannot be expected to have incremental validity, but that is not an objection of principle. What this brief analysis shows is that the two paradigms are not ideologically incompatible but appear to consist of different generalized expectations regarding the relevance of growth and moderator terms.

A final wording of the moderator issue is whether single predictors may receive different weights according to the individual in question; thus, whether Mary's emotional stability may be less relevant in predicting her performance as a pursuit plane pilot than is John's. Again, there is no a priori reason why the weights should be uniform. A technical problem is that the Pearson correlation is undefined in the single case; however, raw-score association coefficients like Gower's (1971) and Zegers and Ten Berge's (1985) can do the job. Their application to the single case also gives a precise expression to the otherwise elusive idea of intra-individual trait structure. The Gower coefficient for the general case is the mean of the single-case coefficients; it thus writes interindividual structure as the mean of intra-individual structures, thereby joining two paradigms of personality that are usually brought in opposition to each other. This integration is still another reason for taking raw scores seriously. An empirical problem, however, is that individual weights may be extremely unstable. However, the same holds for intra-individual structure.

Ranges of Application

After digesting a number of red herrings, what remains is a matter of conventional preference. The trait psychologist represents the person as a vector of scores on a continuous scale, whereas the typologist would prefer a single qualification on a binary (applicable vs. not applicable) scale. Taking a sophisticated trait model incorporating growth and moderator effects, the person-centered approach is a special or degenerate case of it, and can therefore not be psychometrically superior in any respect. To justify the type approach, a different perspective should be adopted. To that end, I distinguish between a context of prediction and a context of communication.

Given the same basic materials, there can be no reasonable doubt that the trait approach is superior in a predictive context. On the one hand, typing consists of discarding information that is potentially valid. On the other, it introduces dynamic predictor terms whose empirical status is highly dubious; therefore, even an orthodox trait approach may be expected to do better upon cross validation.

Ironically, the 5-D approach meets with ambivalence from the side of its very proponents in predictive respects. McCrae and Costa (1992) and Jang and others (1998) have emphasized the incremental validity of the 30 subscales of the NEO-PI-R (Costa & McCrae, 1992) over its five factor scales, thereby implicitly questioning the 5-D model as an adequate representation of personality. The psychometric value of such arguments, however, is quite limited. Principle component analysis capitalizes on the common variance in the predictor set; successive residuals follow the law of diminishing returns. So does validity, unless in some magical and unintended way specific variance would be more valid than common variance.

The value of the type approach is to be found at a different, pragmatic level, at which personality is a subject of communication between a diagnostician and a therapist (in the wide sense of someone who is going to work with the individual, possibly the individual him- or herself). Human discourse and cognition being what they are, it makes little sense in that context to exchange vectors of continuous scores. Professional communication is better served by an attempt to capture the essence of the individual's personality in a vivid and suggestive picture. To insist on using a trait paradigm in this context is to ignore the human element at the receiving end of a communication.

In the end, the two sets of operations appear to refer to different conceptions of personality-in-context rather than personality-in-vitro. The trait approach is geared toward automated predictive procedures in which substantive considerations do not even surface. The type approach caters to human receivers of personality information. Which of the two scripts is appropriate in a particular case is difficult to say in abstract terms. A personnel selection situation, for example, may be conceived in predictive as well as in communicative terms; the same goes for a clinical intake situation. The emphasis here is on distinguishing the scripts: Predicting on the basis of types and communicating in terms of traits are both arguably deficient.

HIERARCHICAL AND CIRCUMPLEX STRUCTURES

In a hierarchical model, trait concepts are seen as specifications of broader traits, which in turn may be grouped under the heading of supertraits. In a circumplex model, trait variables appear as combinations of each other; they form a network in which all concepts define each other in a recursive manner, without subordination or superordination. In mixed models, all variables and factors are equal, but some are more equal than others because they explain more variance or are assigned privileged status for conventional reasons.

This section contains an evaluation of trait taxonomies that have been proposed or implied, and it works its way toward a family model that may be acceptable by way of integration. However, it should be kept in mind that taxonomies are subject to contradictory demands, namely, conceptual and communicative simplicity on the one hand, and adequate coverage of empirical reality on the other.

The Principal Component Analysis Plus Varimax Taxonomic Model

In its elementary form, the Big Five structure consists of a varimax rotation of the first five principal components taken from a large heterogeneous set of trait adjectives (see, e.g., Ostendorf, 1990). Whether this result is intended as a model in any proper sense is irrelevant, as it evidently functions like one: People receive scores on the Big Five, and these scores are interpreted as their personality structure—specifically, an orthogonal structure according to which these factors vary independently over persons.

Goldberg (1993a) articulated that the model in question may be viewed as hierarchical: Items specify scales, and scales specify factors. This argument presupposes simple structure, but that condition is not fulfilled. A concomitant and very widespread notion is that the Big Five are "broad" (in the sense of fuzzy) factors of personality.

The Implicit Assumption of Simple Structure

Simple structure, in which each variable loads on only one factor and factors exhaust the common variance would be hierarchical indeed: Each variable would be a specification of only that factor; a particular factor could legitimately and meaningfully be interpreted in terms of the variables that load on it. The interpretation would not surreptitiously introduce other variance common to some subset of the variables in question.

In empirical practice, however, variable structures are so overwhelmingly complex—as opposed to simple—that the hierarchical model functions as an obstacle to proper conceptualization: The practice of interpreting factors on the basis of their highest loading items, which *would* be appropriate under simple structure, is quite erroneous if the condition is not fulfilled. For to the extent that some of the highest loading items share other common variance, factor interpretations become contaminated. For example, an extraversion factor easily receives a social interpretation (sociability, social extraversion, and the like; for an overview, see Digman, 1990) because many high-loading items have positive secondary loadings on agreeableness.

The Alleged Broadness of Factors

Under conditions of actual simple structure, factors could be called broad in a hierarchical sense, as they capture the common variance of a number of variables. Even then, factors are not broad in a conceptual sense but rather more narrow than variables, as their internal consistency is higher and their angular position in the trait space is thus more fixed. A *g* factor of intelligence, for example, is not a broadband but a high-fidelity measure of some latent trait. A fortiori, there is nothing broad about a Big Five factor based on a particular domain of trait variables. For lack of actual simple structure, it does not encompass a sizable number of lower level items or scales. The meaning of a factor, even if latent, is much more precise in a psychometric sense than is the meaning of the variables on which it is based. In that domain of variables, a set of five rotated principal components covers more variance than does any other set of five linear combinations, but "broadness" is an inappropriate and misleading term for that.

In another terminology, to view the Big Five as broad factors is to treat them as a circumplex structure. In a regular two-dimensional circumplex, the plane is sliced into a number of angular segments (e.g., 12 segments). Variables within a segment form a homogeneous set. A special case is simple structure, in which "mixed" segments are empty, as in Figure 10.1, panel A. The actual situation, however, is closer to panel B, amounting to a circumplex with four segments, of which two are well filled. These segments contain very heterogeneous sets of variables; two of those variables may even be orthogonal to each other. The very specific meaning of the factor is thus not adequately captured by the broad array of variables that have their primary loading on it.

Marker Variables

The interpretation problem would be solved if stable marker variables could be found, that is, trait terms that load exclusively on one factor. Goldberg (1992a) presented such sets of psychometric synonyms, for example, extraverted, talkative, assertive, verbal, bold, and five other terms for the positive pole of the extraversion factor. A minor problem with this interpretation strategy is that markers for some factor poles are difficult to find, for example, markers for emotional stability. A major problem is that marker sets appear to be no longer orthogonal in fresh samples or upon translation. Any two homogeneous sets of traits may be expected to correlate positively if both are desirable or if both are undesirable, negatively if they are opposite in that respect; neutral sets hardly exist. Orthogonal sets may be selected in a sample, but they will regress to obliqueness upon cross validation. On the basis of a large-scale study, Saucier (2002b) has developed marker scales that appear to be robustly orthogonal within his several data sets and might thus defy the present analysis. Still, one would have to wait and see how they do in another laboratory, for example, when transported abroad.

The obliqueness problem (see, e.g., Block, 1995) cannot be answered by the truism that varimax-rotated factors are by definition orthogonal. The missed point is that they have no interpretation—not because they are broad or fuzzy, but because any interpretation in terms of sets of variables is biased. To interpret a Big Five factor properly, one would have to perform and communicate a suppression operation, such as the following: Factor I is what remains of extraversion after suppressing any connotation of agreeableness or socialness that may be associated with it, however firmly; Factor V is a residue of intellect or openness to experience after subtracting a virtually indissoluble tinge of energy, which rather belongs to Factor I. That is a bit much to ask.

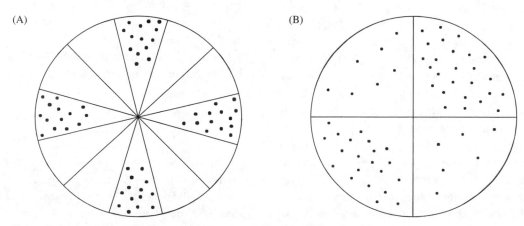

Figure 10.1   Prototypical simple-structure (A) and semicircumplex (B) configurations.

In conclusion, the PCA plus varimax set of operations leads to an inadequate representation of personality. The argument is not that traits are correlated, in any metaphysical sense: For purely predictive purposes, linear regression of criteria on orthogonal factors is a perfectly defensible approach. What was stressed is the conceptual risk of starting to talk in Big Five terms, either among experts or with others. Conceivably, we could keep our mouths shut, but in practice that is too high a price to pay.

The PCA plus varimax model has been imported into personality from the domain of intelligence research. The question arises whether it is appropriate in that domain. I (Hofstee, 1994c) have argued that it is not. The empirical structure of intelligence variables is an *n*-dimensional simplex (the all-positive quadrant of an *n*-dimensional sphere) characterized by positive manifold and lack of simple structure. Treating it as an orthogonal simple structure gives rise to biased conceptualizations of the underlying dimensions and inadequate representation of the domain. Essentially the same objection holds for the domain of personality.

The Double Cone Model

A seminal attempt at a specific structure model of personality in the 5-D framework is Peabody and Goldberg's (1989) double cone, based on Peabody's (1984; see also De Boeck, 1978) work on separating descriptive and evaluative aspects of trait terms. It focuses on the first three Factors; the smaller factors IV, emotional stability, and V, intellect, are treated as separate axes orthogonal to the sphere that is formed by the bigger three: I Extraversion, II Agreeableness, and III Conscientiousness.

The double cone model may be envisaged as follows: Take a globe with desirability as its north-south axis, so that all desirable traits are on the northern hemisphere and their undesirables opposites are on the southern hemisphere in the antipode positions. Apply an orthogonal rotation to the Factors I, II, and III such that their angular distances to the desirability axis become equal, namely, 54.7 deg with cosine 1/3. Draw a parallel of latitude at 35.3 deg (close to Kyoto and Oklahoma City) through the positive endpoints of the Factors I, II, and III, and another one (close to Sydney and Montevideo) through the negative endpoints. Connect each possible pair of antipode points on the two circles by a vector. Together, these vectors form the double cone. The model represents empirical trait variables by their projection on the closest model vector.

The double cone was designed to embody a particular taxonomic principle, informally referred to by insiders as the

Peabody plot and named chiasmic structure by Hofstee and Arends (1994). A classical example of a chiasm is

| Thrifty | Generous |
| Stingy | Extravagant |

In Peabody's reasoning, this configuration arises by pitting a content contrast (i.e., not spending vs. spending) against a social desirability contrast (thrifty and generous vs. stingy and extravagant). In the double cone model, chiasmic structure recurs in the shape of Xs that are formed by vertical slicings through the center of the double cone. On the Northern circle, we would have thrifty and generous at opposite longitudes; on the southern hemisphere, stingy and extravagant. More generally, descriptive and evaluative aspects are represented by longitude and latitude, respectively.

Evaluation of the Double Cone Model

The model is readily generalized to five dimensions, although it loses some of its aesthetic appeal in the process: Take all 10 subsets of 3 out of the 5 factors, that is, the I × II × III, I × II × IV, through III × IV × V subsets, and treat each of these spheres in the manner just sketched. The generalized double cone thus consists of a Gordian knot of 10 three-dimensional double cones in the 5-D space sharing their vertical (desirability) axis, or 10 pairs of latitude circles. There is no valid reason why the range of the chiasmic structural principle should be restricted to a particular subset of three dimensions. But the model easily passes the generalizability test.

It is not entirely clear whether the algorithm for analyzing the data as used by Peabody and Goldberg (1989) is consistent with the model. Via Peabody (1984), the reader is referred to an algorithm proposed by De Boeck (1978). De Boeck's procedure, however, sets the I, II, and III dimensions orthogonal to the desirability axis, rather than at 54.7 deg. Still, it is certainly possible to design an algorithm that would be consistent with the double-cone model.

The next question, however, concerns fit. That may be tested by assessing the quality of chiasms that are generated by the model. Hofstee and Arends (1994, Table 1) present chiasms derived from Peabody and Goldberg's (1989) materials. An example is

| Forceful | Peaceful |
| Quarrelsome | Submissive |

The content contrasts in this and in other examples are not convincing. The reasons are not hard to find. First and most important, the cone structure supposes an angular distance of only 109.5 deg between terms that should form a content contrast, like forceful-peaceful and quarrelsome-submissive. Second, 5-D factors have different angles with the desirability vertical axis: II+, agreeableness, for example, is much further north than is I+, extraversion. When these angular distances are forced to be equal, as in the model, content contrasts become contaminated by a desirability contrast. In the example, peaceful is more desirable than forceful; therefore, to the extent that they are at all judged opposite, that is partly an artifact of a desirability difference.

It is fair to conclude that the double cone does not model the underlying principle of chiasmic structure in an optimal way. One could refine the model, but there is no need to do so: Hofstee and Arends (1994) showed that the Abridged Big Five circumplex (AB5C; see Hofstee, De Raad, & Goldberg, 1992) model to be discussed later can account for chiasmic structure, and generates credible chiasms:

Daring	Cautious
Reckless	Timid

In two experiments, participants judged content contrasts taken from AB5C chiasms to be superior over double cone contrasts. This is not to say that chiasmic structure exists: Hofstee and Arends reiterate a point already taken by Peabody (1967) himself, namely, that desirability and content cannot be separated. So the best one can do is create a chiasmic illusion, as in the previous example. The algorithm goes as follows: Take a particular circumplex; draw a diameter separating desirable from undesirable traits; select two traits on different sides of the diameter but close to it and to each other, for example, cautious (slightly desirable) and timid (slightly undesirable); together with their opposites, they create the chiasmic illusion. It arises because in this case the alleged content contrast is formed by two terms with an angular distance that is only slightly less than 180 deg, instead of 109.5 deg as according to the double cone model.

Do Chiasms Have a Future?

The double cone model was shown to be generalizable; it may be possible to design a refined version by widening the angle between content opposites, amounting to oblique rotation. The more basic questions that remain, are What is the taxonomic status of the underlying principle of chiasmic structure? and What does it do to our conception of personality?

Whatever the refined model would be, it would focus on traits that are close to the equator of a hypersphere whose vertical axis is desirability: The model would focus on fairly neutral traits. They form a small minority, so the focus would be on a counterrepresentative subset of personality variables. On the one hand, there is something venerable (to use Saucier's, 1994, term) to such a value-free approach; personality psychologists, like everybody else, would prefer practicing a discipline that is not submerged in extrascientific values. On the other, desirability is not fruitfully considered as a mere response set or other artifact that is to be separated from content: Hofstee and Arends (1994) emphasized that even in the classical example of chiasmic structure cited earlier, stinginess is not merely undesirable thrift, but an asocial version of it, whereas generousness differs from extravagance in being prosocial; therefore, the evaluation contrast is in fact one of content, as in the AB5C model. So the most realistic conclusion is that chiasmic structure and related models cannot be central to the concept of personality, even though they may have their place in specific contexts (see Saucier, 1994; Saucier, Ostendorf, & Peabody, 2001).

Central features of the double cone model, however, appear to be valuable by themselves. One is the "circular pattern" (Peabody & Goldberg, 1989, p. 556), as opposed to simple structure, that is embodied in the model. Another is orienting the trait space toward desirability as its reference axis. These points are taken up later when developing an integrative family of structure models.

Generalized Circumplexes

In circumplex models, traits are assigned to segments of a circle and are thus represented by their projection on the bisectrix of that segment. Circumplexes picture tissues or networks of traits: Contrary to hierarchies, circumplexes have no superordinate and subordinate concepts. Eysenck and Rachman (1965), for example, represented Hippocrates' melancholic, choleric, sanguinic, and phlegmatic types as mixtures of the positive and negative poles of neuroticism and extraversion; presumably, however, Hippocrates would have preferred a rotation by which an extravert is a mixture of the choleric and sanguinic types, neuroticism is what melancholics and cholerics have in common, and so on. Circles enjoy full freedom of rotation.

Circles generalize to spheres, and spheres generalize to hyperspheres—particularly, in this context, to the 5-D hypersphere. An early example of a 3-D structure is Heymans's (1929) temperament cube. Not until the end of the twentieth century, however, did 5-D researchers (Hofstee et al., 1992; Saucier, 1992) construct circumplexes of more than two dimensions.

Heymans's Cube

Heymans (1929) constructed a network model with three dimensions—emotionality, primary versus secondary function (comparable to extraversion-introversion), and activity—forming the axes of a cube. Types are located at each of the eight vertices of the cube, among which are the four Hippocratic types; for example, the sanguinic type is at the vertex where low emotionality, primary function, and high activity meet.

Heymans tended to conceive the temperament space as unipolar: The type characterized by the absence of emotionality, activity, and secondary function is named amorphous. One amendment therefore is to move the origin of the trait space to the center of the cube. Next, it is difficult to conceive of activity and primary function as orthogonal; different dimensions (and types) would be chosen in a contemporary three-dimensional model. Finally, one would prefer rounding the cube to a sphere. On the one hand, it is thus gratifying to note that time has not stood still, and that Heymans's cube is now obsolete by reasonable standards. On the other, it is equally gratifying to recognize Heymans's model as a forerunner of the generalized circumplexes that did not appear until the end of the twentieth century.

Saucier's Rhombicuboctahedron

Saucier (1992) presented an integration of interpersonal and mood circumplexes and the Big Five Factors I, II, and IV. He drew attention to the fact that simple structure does not materialize in these domains; many variables are interstitial in that they are closer to the bisectrix of the angle between two factors than to the factors themselves. When simple structure is nonetheless imposed, interstitial variables are likely to be assigned to different factors by different investigators, even though the positions of variables and factors are closely comparable. Saucier constructed 6 bipolar scales as benchmarks for the interstitial positions, in addition to the 3 bipolar factor markers: a I+II+ versus I−II− scale (friendly vs. unfriendly), a I+II− versus I−II+ scale (dominant vs. submissive), and so on. He depicted the resulting trait structure as a rhombicuboctahedron, a prism showing the 18 (i.e., $2 \times [3 + 6]$) unipolar benchmarks as facets.

Saucier's model may be alternatively conceived as an abridged three-dimensional circumplex, depicted by three orthogonal circles based on two of the three factors at a time. Each circle contains two bisectrices of the angles between the factor axes; in the model, a variable is represented by its projection on the vector (out of 9 bipolar or 18 unipolar vectors) to which it is closest. This representation has the advantage that it is easily carried to the fifth dimension (discussed later). Saucier showed that the I × II × IV sphere was the most interstitially structured of all 10 spheres that are contained in the 5-D hypersphere; that difference, however, is quite relative in view of the many mixtures involving Factors III or V.

Like Wiggins's (1980) two-dimensional interpersonal circumplex, Saucier's model uses octants, which are 45 deg wide, corresponding to a correlation of .707. Therefore, the variables assigned to such a segment may still form a fairly heterogeneous set. Hofstee et al. (1992) distinguished traits that had their primary loading on one factor and their secondary loading on another (e.g., I+II+; sociable, social) and traits with a reverse pattern (II+I+; merry, cheerful). This strategy amounts to slicing up a circle into 12 clock segments of 30 deg, corresponding to a correlation of .866. A reason for making these finer distinctions is that 30 deg is about the angular distance at which vectors are still given the same substantive interpretation (Haven & Ten Berge, 1977). If this amendment is worked into Saucier's model, it becomes identical to a three-dimensional version of the abridged circumplex.

The Abridged Big Five Circumplex Model

The AB5C model consists of the 10 circumplex planes that are based on 2 of the 5 factors at a time. Thus, variables are represented by their projections on the closest plane or, more precisely, on the closest of the 6 bipolar clock vectors (running from 12 o'clock to 6 o'clock, 1 to 7, and so on) in that plane. The hypersphere contains large empty spaces between the model planes, so it may look as if the abridgement is rather drastic. However, varimax rotation puts the variables as close to the planes as possible; Hofstee et al. (1992) showed that it does a better job at this than at maximizing simple structure, which is putting the variables as close to the single factors as possible. Thus, representing traits by their two highest loadings seems acceptable; a model including tertiary loadings is entirely conceivable, but it would be much more complex and add very little.

More aptly than by a spatial configuration, the AB5C tissue is depicted by a table using the 10 factor poles (I+, I−, II+, II−, and so on) as both warp and weft, the column denoting the primary loading, and the row, the secondary loading of the traits assigned to a cell. Of the 100 cells in that table, the 10 combinations of the positive and negative poles of the same factor are void; the remaining 90 contain the unipolar facets generated by the model. The gain over the simple-structure model is enormous. That model accommodates only relatively pure factor markers, that is, traits assigned to the 10 diagonal (I+I+ to V−V−) cells of the table. If simple structure would in fact materialize, most if not all of the variables would be found in those cells. If, on the other hand, the empirical structure is essentially circumplex, only 11.1% of the variables would find their way to the diagonal cells. In Hendriks's (1997) analysis of 914 items, 105 (11.5%) ended up in those cells. That illustration is as dramatic as is the percentage of variables that would have to be discarded in a proper application of the simple-structure model.

In the discussion of the person-centered approach, I introduced a distinction between the contexts of prediction and communication. Against that background, it should be noted that the predictive gain of the off-diagonal AB5C facets over the five principal components is nil, as the facets are linear combinations of the components. However, they do serve conceptual, interpretive, and communicative purposes. An individual's profile of scores on the FFPI, for example, may be typified by that person's single most characteristic facet; thus, for example, a person whose highest score is on factor V+ and whose second highest score is on III+ may be characterized by the cluster of expressions and adjectives that form the V+III+ facet (Knows what he/she is talking about, Uses his/her brains, Sees through problems, and the many other items listed by Hendriks, 1997, for this "Tight Intelligence" facet). One or more of these catch phrases should be more effective than presenting a 5-D profile or even the subset based on the scores in question ("This person is primarily someone who Thinks quickly [V+], and secondarily someone who Does things according to plan [III+]"). Furthermore, at the theoretical level the AB5C model accounts for a large number of concepts that do not coincide with the five Factors but are quite adequately reconstructed as their mixtures.

Another way to document the flexibility of the AB5C design is in noting that it incorporates features of both oblique rotation and cluster analysis on an orthogonal basis. Oblique rotation as such does not solve the simple-structure problem when the configuration of variables is essentially circumplex. However, the insertion of oblique model vectors enables one to capture relatively homogeneous clusters of traits. That function is also served by cluster analysis procedures, but they lose sight of the dimensional fabric of the structure and the recursive definitions of clusters.

With respect to predictive purposes, the loss incurred by adopting the AB5C model is quite limited. First, the principal components base maximizes the internal consistency of the facets (Ten Berge & Hofstee, 1999), which should be beneficial to their validity. Second, if factors beyond the

Big Five are needed to increase validity, the model is easily extended to include those factors. That would be more efficient than including separate scales for each additional specific concept.

Undoing Hierarchies

The traditional design of questionnaires is hierarchical: Items are grouped into subscales, subscales into scales. From the manuals of such questionnaires (see, e.g., Costa & McCrae, 1992) it is easily verified that subscales actually form a network; they have substantial secondary correlations with scales other than the one they are assigned to. Upon analyzing the single items of a questionnaire, a similar tissue pattern would arise; items would appear to have all sorts of promiscuous relationships, inviting circumplex analysis of the data.

Generalized (beyond two dimensions) circumplex analysis would proceed as follows: First, the item scores are subjected to PCA. The maximum number of principal components would be the number of subscales or facets (e.g., 30 in the case of the NEO-PI-R). Note that these 30 principal components extract more variance by definition than traditional scoring does. (In practice, it would soon become apparent that only a part of these principal components should be retained because the redundancies in the item tissue are captured by fewer components than the number of subscales.)

At the scale level, the optimal strategy is to proceed from the first m principal components, m being the number of superordinate scales (e.g., 5), as they make more efficient use of the data than do traditional scale scores. If, for reasons of continuity, the original interpretations of the scales are to be simulated, target rotations of the m principal components toward these scales could be carried out. If the original scales are conceived to be orthogonal, as in 5-D questionnaires, the optimal approximation procedure would be a simultaneous orthogonal target rotation of the m principal components towards the set of m scales. That procedure conserves internal consistency (Ten Berge & Hofstee, 1999); consequently, the average coefficient alpha of the rotated principal components is maximal. Most notably, it is automatically higher than the average alpha of the original scales.

Subscales of traditional questionnaires are very short; therefore, they are unreliable or consist of asking essentially the same question over and again, which is annoying to respondents and introduces unintended specific variance. If they are to be retained, their quality can be improved to a considerable extent by estimating subscale scores on the basis of (maximally) as many principal components as are postulated relatively socially desirable), and/or a Situations effect (e.g., a personnel selection context gives rise to elevated scores), and/or some interaction effect, but not a Persons or individual differences effect. The *p* component concerns the latter.

Carrying out the slight rotation, if needed, to align the first principal component in any particular data set with the desirability variable should prove helpful in solving the vexing problem of indeterminate rotational positions of components. Saucier (2002a) has already documented that varimax rotation does not help in this respect: Across data sets, the positions of unrotated principal components were at least as replicable as were varimaxed components. Among the principal components, the first is by far the most replicable one. Across differently composed sets of variables, however, part of this stability gets lost (as discussed earlier). Anchoring *p* at the desirability values, which are external to the studies, should enhance replicability.

The *p*-oriented model produces another taxonomic lever, namely, a measure of the representativeness of a set of personality traits or items, in the shape of the correlation between the first principal component of the set and the desirability variable. In a set overloaded with fairly neutral extraversion-introversion items attracting the first principal component, that correlation would be clearly below unity. In a heterogeneous set of neutral items, the desirability variable would be unstable, again lowering the correlation. In the spirit of the lexical axiom, such sets would be judged insufficiently representative. The proposed measure simulates that judgment.

The Two-Dimensional Level

Upon extracting *p*, a residual remains in the shape of a matrix of part scores. The first principal component of that residual matrix comes close to the second principal component of the original scores, at least in a representative set of variables. Taking *p* as the ordinate, a 45-deg counterclockwise rotation of the two components including *p* will produce an X structure, or a flat version of the double cone. The upper and lower segments contain the most unambiguously positive and negative, or consonant, traits; the left and right segments contain the most relatively neutral and discordant traits. The abridged semicircumplex structure at this level contains two bipolar facet vectors running from 11 o'clock to 5 o'clock and from 1 to 7 in addition to the 12 to 6 *p* vector; the relatively neutral traits are left unaccounted for by the model, as their projections on the vectors will be very low.

Substantively, the plane would resemble, but not be identical to, the interpersonal circumplex (Wiggins, 1980), the I × II or Agreeableness × Extraversion slice of the 5-D

structure, Digman's (1997) α × β plane, and the like. In a perfectly representative set of traits as defined earlier, the model plane would be identical to the plane formed by the first two (rotated) principal components; this property makes it a good candidate for a canonical or reference structure. Its suitability for that purpose is enhanced by the absence of rotational freedom at this level: The positions of the model vectors are indirectly prescribed by the desirability values of the traits. Theoretical criteria, as in the interpersonal circumplex, or the simple-structure criterion as in 5-D models, are insufficiently capable of serving that reference function.

In the rationale of the semicircumplex model, the transition from one *p* dimension to two dimensions means a spreading of the desirability component, in the manner of the unfolding of a fan. The primordial one becomes diluted in the process, like the *g* factor of intelligence does when it is spread over two or more dimensions. Following elementary rules of parsimony, the transition should not be made lightly; the burden of proof is on those who take the step. Psychometrics offers an adequate procedure for this proof: More-dimensional assessments of personality should be shown to have sufficient incremental validity over the *p* component. This requirement implies that an assessment of *p*, as a baseline variable, would have to be part of any empirical study of personality.

Incremental validity of variables other than *p* would necessarily imply that variance orthogonal to it, thus neutral variance, is valid. This implication bridges the present family of models and those that capitalize on neutral variance, like Peabody's (1984) and Saucier's (1994; Saucier et al., 2001). In fact, the latter model is the complement of the Semi-Circumplex, at the present and subsequent dimensional levels; it fills in what the present model leaves empty. Although the basic assumption—potential incremental validity of neutral variance—is thus necessarily the same, a strategic difference remains at the executive level. In the semicircumplex approach, neutral variance is assessed indirectly, by suppressing the *p* variance from consonant traits rather than directly, as in Saucier (1994). The reason was given earlier: Discordant personality concepts are difficult to handle.

Semicircumplex Spheres and Hyperspheres

The three-dimensional member of the model family arises as follows: Add the second principal component of the matrix of residual scores (after removing *p*); retain the vertical orientation so that a globe is formed with the positive traits on the northern hemisphere and the negative traits on the southern one; perform an orthogonal rotation of the three axes

A Family Model of Trait Structure 251

including p so that they become equidistant (the angles being 54.7 deg, with cosine $\sqrt{1/3}$; further constraints are discussed later) from the vertical axis. All this is in correspondence with the double cone model. Now form three slices (circumplexes) by taking two rotated axes at a time. The projection of p on these tilted planes has the 12 o'clock to 6 o'clock direction, and the 3 o'clock and 9 o'clock positions are on the equator. Additional model vectors are constructed running from 11 to 5 and from 1 to 6, as in the two-dimensional member of the model family.

The central positions in this structure are taken by the 12 to 6 vectors—to be labeled I/II, I/III, and II/III—that are the bisectrices of the right angle between the two rotated principal components forming the circumplex. The I, II, and III axes themselves merely guard the boundaries of the model structure; as such, they have no place or name in the model. The central model vectors appear to be close to p, namely, at a distance of 35.3 deg (with cosine .816 or $\sqrt{2/3}$; generally, $\sqrt{2/n}$, where n is the number of dimensions). Note that this oblique structure arises as a side effect of an orthogonal rotation, not through some more liberal oblique rotation procedure as such. The central model vectors are thus much more saturated with desirability than are the factors themselves; at all dimensional levels of the model, they share exactly $\sqrt{2}$ as much variance with p as do the orthogonal factors.

What is new about this structure is that mixtures or blends of factors have stolen the central place that used to belong to the factors. Instead of being derivatives, the bisectrices of the factor pairs have become the central concepts. This play of musical chairs comes about because of the closer association of the central vectors with p, which entitles them to their position. In passing, the model resolves the uneasiness of inserting orthogonal axes into an essentially oblique structure; it rigorously defines oblique axes without giving up the convenience of an orthogonal base. The only price is that the number of musical chairs has to be increased, from four dimensions onward: There are $n(n-1)/2$ central vectors, with n the number of dimensions or factors. However, that extension will be welcomed by those who have always wondered whether five is all there is. The model has shaken off the last remnants of simple-structure thinking. Parenthetically, I note that the model is equally appropriate in other domains, notably, intelligence.

With four dimensions, the rotated factors are at an angle of 60 deg with respect to the p factor; the central model vectors are at 45 deg from that pivot. With five dimensions, the factors are at 63.4 deg, and the central vectors are at 50.7 deg. Still, the model rotation maximizes the sum of the correlations of the central axes with p, and in that sense minimizes their average neutrality. Conversely, any other orthogonal

rotation of these dimensions (e.g., varimax) is inferior in this respect: It takes in more neutral traits, which are less representative of the domain.

With three or more dimensions, the model leaves freedom of spin. A three-dimensional structure, for example, may be rotated around its vertical p-axis without violating the model. For reasons of continuity, this freedom may be used for maximizing the correspondence of the rotated factors with the current varimax factors, particularly, the 5-D model factors. This amounts to some lowering of the positive poles of the current dimensions I and III toward the hyperequator, and some lifting of the others. One may speculate, for example, that the American lexical extraversion factor loses its aggressive connotation and moves in the direction of sociability. However, it is difficult to gauge what the substantive effects of the joint rotation will be on all the versions in all the different languages (see, e.g., Saucier et al., 2000) that have been proposed. The labels of the 5-D model are probably used in a manner vague enough to permit this twisting. (Agreeableness and conscientiousness, in particular, do not even fit their present axes; see Hofstee et al., 1992.)

From the three-dimensional level on, there is some redundancy between model vectors at different levels. At the top level, there is the one vector. At the second level, two additional bipolar vectors appear, which satisfy the requirement of being 30 deg removed from p. At the third, we find three semicircumplexes with three model vectors each; at the fourth, there are 6×3 at the fifth, the AB5SC model with 30 vectors appears; in general, at the nth level from 3 on, there are $1.5n(n-1)$ vectors specific to that level. In successively adding levels, the cumulative number of model vectors thus becomes 1, 3, 12, 30, and 60. From the third level on, it appears impossible to rotate the central vectors in such a way that all the additional vectors stay at least 30 deg away from the ones at the second level. Thus some vectors would have indistinguishable interpretations.

One strategy would be to settle for a particular dimensionality of the trait space. That would prevent overlap and would simplify things in general. The foremost drawback is that from three dimensions onward the most central trait concepts would be missed. Furthermore, that strategy would only stir up the debate on the dimensionality of the trait space, to which there is no cogent solution; it would thus frustrate the attainment of a canonical structure rather than contribute to it. The other, preferable, strategy is to adopt the model family as a whole, including as many (or as few) levels as will appear to be needed, and deleting concepts at lower levels that are virtual clones of those at higher levels. The foreseeable result of this strategy is maximal convergence of structures at each level, and maximal efficiency in communicating about

McCrae, R. R., & Costa, P. T., Jr. (1987).Validation of the five-factor model of personality across instruments and observers. *Journal of Personality and Social Psychology, 52,* 81–90.

McCrae, R. R., & Costa, P. T., Jr. (1992). Discriminant validity of NEO-PIR facet scales. *Educational and Psychological Measurement, 52,* 229–237.

Millon, T. (1990). The disorders of personality. In L. A. Pervin (Ed.), *Handbook of personality: Theory and research* (pp. 339–370). New York: Guilford.

Ostendorf, F. (1990). *Sprache und Persönlichkeitsstruktur: Zur Va-lidität des Fünf-Faktoren-Modells der Persönlichkeit* [Language and personality structure: On the validity of the five-factor model of personality]. Regensburg, Germany: S. Roderer Verlag.

Pawlik, K. (1968). *Dimensionen des Verhaltens* [Dimensions of behavior]. Bern, Switzerland: Huber.

Peabody, D. (1967). Trait inferences: Evaluative and descriptive aspects. *Journal of Personality and Social Psychology Monograph, 7* (4, Whole No. 644).

Peabody, D. (1984). Personality dimensions through trait inferences. *Journal of Personality and Social Psychology, 46,* 384–403.

Peabody, D., & Goldberg, L. R. (1989). Some determinants of factor structures from personality-trait descriptors. *Journal of Personality and Social Psychology, 57,* 552–567.

Plomin, R., & Caspi, A. (1998). DNA and personality. *European Journal of Personality, 12,* 387–407.

Riemann, R. (1997). *Persönlichkeit: Fähigkeiten oder Eigenschaften?* [Personality: Capabilities or traits?]. Lengerich, Germany: Pabst Science.

Robins, R. W., John, O. P., Caspi, A., Moffit, T. E., & Stouthamer-Loeber, M. (1996). Resilient, overcontrolled, and undercontrolled boys: Three replicable personality types. *Journal of Personality and Social Psychology, 70,* 157–171.

Saucier, G. (1992). Benchmarks: Integrating affective and interpersonal circles with the Big-Five personality factors. *Journal of Personality and Social Psychology, 62,* 1025–1035.

Saucier, G. (1994). Separating description and evaluation in the structure of personality attributes. *Journal of Personality and Social Psychology, 66,* 141–154.

Saucier, G. (2002a). What is more replicable than the Big Five? Broader-factor structures from English lexical descriptors. Manuscript submitted for publication.

Saucier, G. (2002b). Orthogonal markers for orthogonal factors: The case of the Big Five. *Journal of Research in Personality, 36,* 1–31.

Saucier, G., Hampson, S. E., & Goldberg, L. R. (2000). Cross-language studies of lexical personality factors. In S. E. Hampson (Ed.), *Advances in personality psychology* (Vol. 1, pp. 1–36). London: Routledge.

Saucier, G., Ostendorf, F., & Peabody, D. (2001). The non-evaluative circumplex of personality adjectives. *Journal of Personality, 69,* 537–582.

Tellegen, A. (1982). *Brief manual for the Multidimensional Personality Questionnaire.* Unpublished manuscript, University of Minnesota, Minneapolis.

Tellegen, A. (1993). Folk concepts and psychological concepts of personality and personality disorder. *Psychological Inquiry, 4,* 122–130.

Ten Berge, J. M. F. (1999). A legitimate case of component analysis of ipsative measures and partialling the mean as an alternative to ipsatization. *Multivariate Behavioral Research, 34,* 89–102.

Ten Berge, J. M. F., & Hofstee, W. K. B. (1999). Coefficients α and reliabilities of unrotated and rotated components. *Psychometrika, 64,* 83–90.

Tupes, E. C., & Christal, R. E. (1956/1992). Recurrent personality factors based on trait ratings. Technical Report No. ASD-TR-61-97, US Air force, Lackland Air Force Base, TX; *Journal of Personality, 60,* 225–251.

Wiggins, J. S. (1980). Circumplex models of interpersonal behavior. In L. Wheeler (Ed.), *Review of personality and social psychology* (Vol. 1, pp. 265–294). Beverly Hills, CA: Sage.

Zegers, F. E., & Ten Berge, J. M. F. (1985). A family of association coefficients for metric scales. *Psychometrika, 50,* 17–24.

PART THREE
SOCIAL PSYCHOLOGY

CHAPTER 11

Social Cognition

GALEN V. BODENHAUSEN, C. NEIL MACRAE, AND KURT HUGENBERG

Sociality is a hallmark of human functioning. Indeed, the survival and success of our evolutionary ancestors depended on their ability to form coordinated bands of interdependent actors (e.g., Leakey, 1978). The benefits of group living allowed a band to succeed where an individual might fail (e.g., Axelrod & Hamilton, 1981). Although our species has come a long way from the harsh and precarious conditions present during early hominid evolution, human beings continue to be utterly dependent on one another for their survival and well-being. It is therefore quite reasonable to assume that human cognitive and motivational tendencies were shaped by the demands of group living (e.g., Brewer, 1997; Seyfarth & Cheney, 1994). Some have claimed that our capacities for reasoning and our other higher mental functions may owe their very existence to the constraints imposed by sociality on human survival and reproductive success (Byrne, 2000). Our most fundamental concerns depend crucially on our ability to understand the characteristics, motivations, and intentions of others; according to Cummins (1998, p. 37), "the evolution of mind emerges as a strategic arms race in which the weaponry is ever-increasing mental capacity to represent and manipulate internal representations of the minds of others." This capacity to understand the minds of others is so central to successful human functioning that when it is compromised, the consequences are often devastating (e.g., Baron-Cohen, 1995). How the mind understands the social world within

which it functions is therefore a matter of central importance in psychology. It is this question that is at the center of theory and research on social cognition.

Social cognition refers to the cognitive structures and processes that shape our understanding of social situations and that mediate our behavioral reactions to them. At its core, the fundamental assumption of social cognition research is the idea that internal mental representations of other persons and of social situations play a key causal role in shaping behavior. The central task of social cognition research is thus to provide a specification of the nature of these mental structures and the processes that operate on them. A simple, generic depiction of the theoretical space within which social cognition researchers work is provided in Figure 11.1. Stated at the most general level, a social cognition analysis incorporates a consideration of (a) the informational cues that are currently experienced in the social environment; (b) mental representations that are constructed on the basis of current or previous experience; (c) the ways these representations are manipulated and the processes through which they influence other aspects of attention and cognition; and (d) the decisions, judgments, intentions, and behaviors that result from the application of these processes. The distinction between representation and process is more a matter of convenience than it is a reflection of a clear theoretical dissociation between considerations of mental structure and mental process.

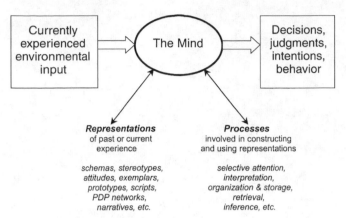

Figure 11.1   A schematic overview of the core assumptions of the social cognition perspective.

In fact, as we shall see, many social-cognitive theories consist of propositions that link representational assumptions with particular processing tendencies that are assumed to be inherent within the representational format.

In taking seriously the role of mental events in mediating social behavior, social cognition theorists part company from the radical behaviorists, who view the mind as a black box having little if any theoretical relevance to an understanding of the factors controlling and directing behavior. However, the form of mentalism embodied in contemporary social cognition research also parts company from the early structuralists, who took the data provided by introspection to be the primary phenomena of psychological inquiry. Indeed, one of the cornerstones of social cognition is the recognition that the mind may be largely unaware of what it is doing; quite commonly, social perceivers may have very little introspective access to the cognitive processes that give rise to their behavioral reactions (Nisbett & Wilson, 1977). These metatheoretical commitments create some methodological challenges for social cognition researchers of social cognition. On one hand, it is assumed that mental events have central, causal importance in shaping social behavior. One the other hand, it is also assumed that people may not be able to provide accurate self-reports concerning the nature of these mental events. As a result, social-cognitive researchers have devoted considerable effort to the development and adaptation of methodologies for studying mental processes that do not rely upon introspection. Before commencing with our survey of social-cognitive theory and research, we begin with a brief consideration of the methodological underpinnings of this work.

The obvious difficulties of explicitly studying mental events without falling prey to the potential biases and limitations of self-report measures have led to innovations in both the measurement and manipulation of social-cognitive processes. Two broad classes of process measures that do not rely on introspection have been developed. The first class consists of chronometric techniques that measure the speed with which a task can be performed (for a review, see Fazio, 1990). Building on classic chronometric methods for analyzing mental processes (e.g., Donders, 1868; Sperling, 1960; Sternberg, 1966), these techniques bring the workings of the mind into the scientific sphere by focusing on a directly observable property of mental events (i.e., their duration). Through carefully constructed experimental situations, it becomes possible to use participants' response times to derive inferences about a number of theoretically important issues, such as determining the nature of mental associations (e.g., Bargh & Chartrand, 2000) and identifying the subsystems or component stages of a more general process (e.g., Lingle & Ostrom, 1979). The second class of process measures consists of techniques focusing on memory performance (for a review, see Srull, 1984). Through the study of aspects of performance such as omissions, intrusions, and the serial ordering of freely recalled material, or the error rates observed in recognition memory, inferences can be drawn concerning both mental structure and process (e.g., Jacoby, 1998; Srull, 1981). Techniques such as these do not require any insight on the part of participants into the workings of their own minds; moreover, they are unlikely to be influenced by concerns about social desirability that can often contaminate self-report data.

Another important methodological approach has involved the development of experimental manipulations that are designed either to activate or to interfere with hypothesized mental structures, processes, or both (for a review, see Bargh & Chartrand, 2000). For example, priming techniques can be used to study nonconscious biases in social perception (e.g., Bargh & Pietromonaco, 1982; Devine, 1989). In one version of this kind of research, general concepts (such as *Blacks*) are activated outside of perceivers' conscious awareness, and the consequences for social perception and memory are examined. If subsequent impressions of an ambiguous social target are more in line with the subliminally activated concept (e.g., more stereotypical of African Americans), then one can conclude that stereotypical associations can be activated and applied in a manner that is automatic and unintentional. Along similar lines, the imposition of secondary tasks can be used to study the efficiency or the resource dependency of the mental processes mediating social responses (e.g., Gilbert, Pelham, & Krull, 1988; Macrae, Milne, & Bodenhausen, 1994). Relatively automatic mental processes occur efficiently (i.e., they do not require much in the way of attentional resources for their successful deployment) and hence will not be disrupted by the imposition of a secondary task. This very brief methodological sampler is merely meant to offer a taste of the general spirit within which social cognition research is conducted. The creativity with which researchers have gone about mapping the workings of the social mind testifies to the possibility of approaching the subject with a respectable measure of scientific rigor and objectivity, unhampered by the limitations of introspective methods.

The study of the social mind inevitably proceeds from a set of (often implicit) assumptions about its fundamental character. The major theoretical precursors of contemporary social cognition research lie in the seminal research on social perception and attribution conducted by such pioneers as Asch (1946) and Heider (1958). Embodied within these historical approaches is a view of the human mind as largely rational and even—in its own naive way—scientific. Attributional models such as Heider's were grounded in the assumption that perceivers seek out cues pertaining to issues such as the controllability, foreseeability, or desirability of others' behavior; perceivers then use these cues to logically derive assumptions about their mental states and about the reasons for their observed behavior. Classic models of impression formation (e.g., Anderson, 1965) assumed that social perceivers ascertain the likelihood that various characteristics or traits apply to a given target, and they then assess the favorableness of these traits, combining them into a composite impression in a manner dictated by familiar expectancy-value models of human judgment. Contemporary social-cognitive research calls this optimistic view of humans as rational actors into question and suggests a set of alternative metaphors. We mention several of these newer metaphors here, as a way to anticipate many of the major themes of the rest of this review.

- *Humans as automatons.* Whereas classic social-psychological theories emphasized the role of rational analysis and active reasoning in guiding human behavior, much of contemporary social cognition research has emphasized the role of automatic and implicit processes in shaping social conduct. This work certainly casts into doubt the assumption of pervasive rationality, and it suggests that in many (if not most) circumstances, we may be the slaves of mental processes that occur outside the realm of our ratiocinations.

- *Humans as motivated tacticians.* Even when engaging in active thought, there is ample reason to believe that people seek out and use mental shortcuts rather than engage in a thorough and systematic analysis of relevant data. Because of the inherent limitations of our attentional capacity (Miller, 1956) and epistemic motivation (Simon, 1967), humans are likely to be quite strategic in allocating their mental resources to the tasks confronting them (Fiske & Taylor, 1991). A major theme of the research we review in this chapter concerns the specification of the conditions under which social cognition will be likely to be relatively more analytical versus superficial.

- *Humans as intuitive lawyers.* Whereas an intuitive scientist would be expected to be a truth-seeker, objectively seeking and using data concerning the state of the social environment, an abundant research literature shows that social cognition actually is subject to a wide range of powerful motivational biases. Rather than seeking to know the world as it is, we often see the world in the way we want it to be (e.g., Kunda, 1990). Much as a lawyer manipulates the available facts in a manner that is most flattering to a preferred conclusion, social perceivers also often show a rather shameless partiality in their dealings with the evidence relevant to their judgments, impressions, and choices.

- *Humans as affect-driven agents.* The historical metaphor of the rational actor leaves relatively little room for the world of emotions, moods, and other feeling-states that form the real-life context of all social thought and action. In recent years, the importance of affective states in influencing social cognition and social behavior has been undeniably established (e.g., Forgas, 2001). It has thus become clear that affect is of integral importance in shaping the character of social cognition. In the remainder of this chapter, we trace the developments that have led researchers toward new conceptions of the social mind.

MENTAL REPRESENTATION: STRUCTURE AND PROCESS

With the advent of powerful technologies for studying the functioning of the brain *in vivo,* there have been many important advances in our understanding of the neural basis of information processing (e.g., Gazzaniga, 2000). Nevertheless, there continues to be a sizable gap between our understanding of the low-level functioning of the central nervous system and the development of a satisfying theoretical account for the higher-order mental phenomena that are the focus of social cognition research. To fill the gap, theorists have hypothesized the existence of mental structures such as schemas and associative networks that can provide a relatively parsimonious account of how information is organized and used to meet the demands of a complex social world. These hypothetical representational constructs are best thought of as metaphors that capture theoretically or empirically important properties of social information processing. Although in a literal sense the nervous system may not contain schemas or other sorts of hypothesized mental structures, such constructs can be scientifically useful to the extent that they capture some important behavior is encountered (e.g., *won the citywide chess tourna-ment*), it is assumed to be linked directly to the central concept (*Tina*) by a relatively strong node, because it fits with precon-ceptions about this target quite well. However, when an in-consistent behavior is encountered (e.g., *got confused trying to figure out the subway system*), it is assumed to be linked to the central concept in a more tenuous way because it does not really fit with the general image of the target. However, the in-congruity embodied in the inconsistent behavior is assumed to provoke efforts to resolve the confusion by thinking about how the inconsistent behavior might make sense in light of other known facts. This triggers the formation of inter-item associations among the different behavior nodes. Thus, al-though inconsistent behaviors are likely to be less strongly linked to the central person concept than are consistent behav-iors, the inconsistent behaviors are actually *more* likely to be linked to a variety of other behavior nodes. As a result, the in-consistent behaviors tend to be more memorable on average because they tend to have more associative links with other items, producing a greater number of pathways through which activation can spread into them and draw them into working memory.

We have presented only the most general statement of how associative network models have been applied in the domain of social memory. Specific theoretical approaches have been much more elaborate in their assumptions—although they still share the key core assumptions that we have outlined. This general approach has been used to predict a wide and impressive array of empirical phenomena concerning social memory, including the serial order of information retrieval in free recall (e.g., Srull, 1981) and the influence of different processing goals and levels of attentional capacity on the probability of recalling inconsistent versus consistent infor-mation (e.g., Srull, Lichtenstein, & Rothbart, 1983; for a comprehensive review, see Wyer & Srull, 1989). Research in these and several other topic areas confirm the explanatory power of the relatively simple assumptions embodied in the associative network approach.

Schemas

A rather different view of the nature of human understanding emerged in Continental philosophy (particularly the ideas of Kant). From this perspective, simple associations are inade-quate to account for the complexity of human cognition. Instead, it is assumed that knowledge is organized into more elaborately structured conceptual representations. This ap-proach to mental representation is epitomized in schema theories.

Originally introduced prominently into psychology by Bartlett (1932), schema theories focus on the role played by generic knowledge structures that organize a person's un-derstanding of a particular domain. A schema can be thought of as a subjective theory (Markus & Zajonc, 1985) that is for-mulated to account for the generalities of one's experience. The elements of the schema are typically thought to be orga-nized by more than simple association. For example, spatial, temporal, logical, and causal relations constrain and provide coherence to the schematic structure. To take a simple exam-ple, a *face* schema consists not only of a set of elements that are associated with faces (e.g., eyes, nose, mouth), but also of rules about the spatial relations among these elements. This general understanding of what faces are like is assumed to have been abstracted from experience with numerous specific faces over time. In addition to this inductive pathway to schema formation, it is often assumed that schemas can be learned in a more top-down manner. For example, most schoolchildren could, one hopes, articulate a rather detailed *mammal* schema, although they have most likely not induced its elements by observing particular instances. Instead, they have learned directly what the core elements of the schema are and how these elements are related to one another.

The elements contained in a schema often function like variables that can take a variety of values, provided that they adhere to the fundamental constraints of the schema. For ex-ample, there is a range of acceptable colors and shapes that eyes can take, but they must invariably be located above the nose, contain a pupil and an iris, and so on. This observation points to the fundamental function of schemas: They serve as templates for understanding experience by providing preor-ganized, general-purpose understandings that can be adapted to the particulars of the current situation via *instantiation*. It is assumed that schemas will be activated spontaneously in situations in which they are relevant, and that this activation occurs in an all-or-none fashion. Thus, unlike the associative network models (in which some nodes in a network can be active while others are not), schema models assume that if any part of the schema has been activated, then the rest of the schema will also be activated.

Schemas are thought to fulfill a variety of functions (for a review, see Bodenhausen, 1992). Most notably, they provide a basis for making inferences about unspecified elements of a stimulus or situation, and they can guide the interpretation of ambiguous features as well. Activated schemas also tend to guide the processes of perception and memory toward infor-mation that is relevant to the particular schema. One famous demonstration of the operation of schemas was provided by Bransford and Franks (1971), who showed that memory for ambiguous verbal stimuli (e.g., *the notes were sour because the seam was split*) was substantially enhanced when a relevant schema was activated that would allow for the disambiguation of the sentence (in this example, *bagpipe*). As Bartlett (1932) emphasized in his seminal writings, schemas also serve an important function in facilitating the reconstruction of the past. Schematic inferences undoubtedly do contribute to our memories for past experiences in important ways.

In many situations, competing schemas may be potentially applicable, and the understanding one gains of the situation may be substantially altered depending upon which schema is activated to parse the situation. Consider the famous case of Kitty Genovese, a New York resident who was brutally murdered in 1964. After observing Ms. Genovese being chased, screaming, by an unknown man, many witnesses failed to activate and apply the correct schema (i.e., *homicidal maniac pursuing victim*) and instead applied a quite mistaken one (e.g., *teenagers engaging in horseplay*). The failure of other bystanders to take action only served to underscore the plausibility of the erroneous interpretation. Clearly, the meaning of observed behavior can take on a very different meaning—and obliges very different behavioral reactions—depending upon which schema is invoked. Research by Shotland and Straw (1976) subsequently showed that when people observe an ambiguous situation in which a man is harassing a woman on the street, they often assume by default that it is a lover's quarrel and fail to take any steps to help the woman. Only when this schema was rendered inapplicable (by the woman's exclaiming, "I don't know you!") did people perceive the situation as one in which they should intervene. Research such as this underscores the importance of understanding the conditions under which particular schemas will be applied.

Sometimes a relevant schema is activated because it fits the current situation unambiguously. But when there is any ambiguity and competing schemas can each afford some degree of fit to the situation, then the schema that is applied is likely to be the one that most accessible (Bruner, 1957). Accessibility, in turn, is a function of relevance of the contending schemas to the perceiver's chronically and momentarily active goals, as well as the recency and frequency with which each of the competing schemas has been used. As such, schemas that are goal-relevant or that have been recently or frequently used will be much more likely to be applied. Dodge (1993) has shown, for example, that some boys have a chronically accessible schema for parsing social interactions, in which they assume that the behavior of others toward them is motivated by hostile intentions and disrespect. When confronted with ambiguous behavior, they consistently assume the worst. These schema-based impressions then lead to hostile reactions. Perhaps unsurprisingly, these same boys have a tendency to show poor social adjustment and are at higher risk for delinquency. In addition to dispositional biases in the accessibility of schemas, situational factors can prompt certain schemas to become more accessible. The

expansive literature on priming effects is built on the realization that schemas that have been activated in unrelated contexts may continue to exert an influence on social cognition because their previous use has rendered them momentarily accessible (e.g., Higgins, 1996).

Schema theory has been applied in a wide variety of topical domains. One domain in which schematic models have been especially influential is gender. Bem (1981) proposed a gender schema theory, which asserts that cultural conventions regarding gender become a sort of lens through which perceptions of others are filtered. Bem (1993, p. 154) explains that the gender-schematic person "has a readiness to superimpose gender-based classification on every heterogeneous collection of human possibilities that presents itself." In one of the most well-known studies of this phenomenon, Bem (1981) first identified individuals who were or were not gender schematic (i.e., based on their sex-role attitudes, they either did or did not appear to possess an internalized schema for gender appropriateness that was consistent with prevailing cultural conventions). Then she presented them with lists of concepts (animals, verbs, clothing) to learn, in a randomly mixed order. An important aspect of this study was that some of the concepts were pretested as being conventionally masculine (e.g., gorilla, hurling, trousers), some were conventionally feminine (e.g., butterfly, blushing, bikini), and some had no gender connotations (e.g., ant, stepping, sweater). The order in which these concepts were recalled in a memory task revealed that gender-schematic individuals were far more likely than were aschematic persons to cluster the concepts together in terms of their gender connotations, consistent with the idea that a gender schema guided the way the information was interpreted and organized in the minds of the gender-schematic participants.

Gender is but one of many domains in which the schema construct has been invoked to account for the regularities of social cognition. Person schemas, event schemas, self schemas, role schemas, and many others have been proposed (for a review, see Fiske & Taylor, 1991). The appeal of schema theory as opposed to associative network models of mental representation appears to lie in the recognition that the stimuli of the social world are often quite complex, and the assumptions of structured organization contained within schema models seems more appropriate for capturing this complexity, compared to the comparatively simple structural assumptions underlying network models. Moreover, the emphasis of schema approaches on processes of selective attention and organization of social information has an undeniable resonance with many phenomena of long-standing interest to social cognition researchers. Nevertheless, schematic models have been criticized as being too loose and theoretically underspecified (e.g., Alba & Hasher, 1983; Fiske & Linville, to be called *automatic* or *implicit* social cognition and have been the subject of a massive amount of recent research.

The contrast between conscious, effortful, controlled mental processes on one hand and unconscious, automatic ones on the other became a prominent issue in cognitive psychology largely due to influential papers by Posner and Snyder (1974), Shiffrin and Schneider (1977), and Hasher and Zacks (1979), yet there is quite a history of interest in the extent to which the mind might be operating in ways unknown to the conscious self. For example, researchers interested in human performance have long been interested in the processes involved in skill acquisition, whereby an initially novel task that requires considerable effort and attention becomes relatively automatic with practice (e.g., Fitts & Posner, 1967). After they become automated, skills can be triggered and used without much involvement of the conscious mind. In a different vein, psychoanalytically oriented researchers have been interested in how unconscious motivations might shape processes of perception and cognition (e.g., Erdelyi, 1974). Cognitive research of this sort addresses profound questions concerning who is running the show. Does the conscious self call the shots, or is the brain going about its business without much interference from the conscious thinker? In this section, we first review research on automatic aspects of social cognition, and then we consider the case that can be made for the capacity of the conscious mind to control and regulate processes of social cognition. Finally, we consider some of the ways in which automatic and effortful processes can interact to determine jointly the course of perception, thought, and action.

Automatic Social Cognition

The foundations for social-psychological treatments of the issue of automaticity have been established in the work of Bargh (e.g., 1982; Bargh & Chartrand, 1999; Bargh & Ferguson, 2000). Synthesizing the insights emerging from disparate research areas touching on the issue of automaticity, Bargh (1994) argued that the notion of automatic mental processes is complex and multifaceted. He argued that the term has been used to refer to four distinct qualities of information processing: *awareness, intention, efficiency,* and *control.* That is, a process tends to be considered automatic if it (a) occurs without the person's awareness, (b) occurs without the person's intention, (c) occurs with great efficiency and does not require much mental capacity, or (d) occurs in a manner that is difficult to prevent or stop. Not all four criteria are necessary for a process to be considered automatic. When one or more of these characteristics is present, the relevant process is often deemed to be relatively automatic.

A particularly compelling and influential demonstration of the implicit operation of the mind was provided by Warrington and Weiskrantz (1968). Their research documented that individuals suffering from anterograde amnesia, who are unable to consciously recollect their recent experiences, nevertheless showed a clear benefit from that experience in the performance of indirect tests of memory, such as completing word fragments. Although these patients have no explicit memory for the words they saw during a study period, they nevertheless were better able to complete word fragments when the corresponding word had indeed been previously studied. This research clearly indicates that memories can be quite influential even when there is no conscious awareness of the relevant prior episodes.

Social cognition researchers have sought to investigate the role of awareness in social cognition in several ways. One approach has simply been to demonstrate that individuals are often unable to articulate accurately the factors that are important in shaping their behavioral choices (e.g., Nisbett & Wilson, 1977). This fact obviously implies that people are generally unaware of the processes at work behind the scenes in the preconscious mind. Another approach to documenting that some processes occur without awareness has been adopted in research on priming. The basic idea of priming research is quite straightforward. Individuals are exposed to a task or environmental context that is designed to activate a particular mental representation. Then a second, ostensibly unrelated task is performed, and the researcher seeks to determine whether the previously activated representation exerts any influence on information processing in the second task. Research of this sort conclusively demonstrates that concepts that have been activated in one context can continue to influence social cognition in subsequent, unrelated contexts, by virtue of their enhanced accessibility (Higgins, 1996). A common effect of such priming is that subsequently encountered information is assimilated toward the activated concept. For example, Srull and Wyer (1979) showed that activating hostile concepts in a language-processing task caused participants to form more negative impressions of an ambiguous social target in a subsequent impression formation task, compared to participants who never had the hostile concepts activated in the initial task. It is typically assumed that this assimilation process occurs because the fortuitously activated concepts are used to disambiguate later information, and the perceiver is presumed to be oblivious to the fact that it is occurring.

Perhaps the best evidence that priming effects occur without the perceiver's awareness comes from research that employs subliminal priming techniques. In this research, concepts are activated by exposing participants to extremely brief stimulus presentations (see Bargh & Chartrand, 2000, for procedural details). Although perceivers are unable to describe the stimuli to which they have been exposed, they nevertheless show evidence of priming effects. We have already described one experiment by Devine (1989) that showed that subliminal activation of words associated with the African American stereotype caused perceivers to view an ambiguously aggressive target as more hostile, compared to individuals who had not been primed with the stereotypic concepts. Similar findings have been reported by other researchers (e.g., Bargh & Pietromonaco, 1982), confirming that priming effects can occur outside of the perceiver's conscious awareness.

It is usually assumed that for these assimilative priming effects to occur, not only must the relevant concept be accessible, but it must also be applicable (Higgins, 1996). In line with this proposition, Banaji, Hardin, and Rothman (1993) demonstrated that priming gender stereotypes resulted in more stereotypical impressions of ambiguous targets, but only when the target was a member of the relevant gender group—that is, activating masculine concepts resulted in the perception of ambiguous male targets in a more stereotypical manner, but it largely did not affect perceptions of female targets. Conversely, activating feminine concepts resulted in perceiving ambiguous female targets in a more stereotypical manner, but it did not affect perceptions of male targets. Although priming effects do operate under the constraints of applicability, the processes involved in using or failing to use activated concepts as a basis for disambiguating social targets appears to operate largely without any awareness on the perceiver's part.

It is not inevitably the case that priming results in assimilation to the primed concepts. For example, Herr (1986) demonstrated that when activated concepts are sufficiently extreme, they can produce contrast effects. A *contrast effect* is said to occur when an object is judged more extremely in the direction opposite to the activated concept. For example, if an ambiguous target were judged to be significantly *less* hostile after an African American stereotype had been activated (compared to an unprimed control group), this would constitute a contrast effect. The mechanism producing contrast effects involves using the activated concept as a comparison standard rather than as an interpretive frame. Thus, in the case of Herr's research, for example, the target person is compared to the activated standard and is consequently seen as relatively less hostile, given the extremity of the standard. The question of whether contrast effects occur automatically has been a matter of continuing theoretical dispute (e.g., Martin, Seta, & Crelia, 1990; Stapel & Koomen, 1998).

Another hallmark of automatic processing is the occurrence of unintended effects. The assimilative priming effects just reviewed certainly meet this criterion of automaticity, because it is clearly not the case that individuals intend to use subliminally activated concepts to guide subsequent impressions. Another domain providing compelling evidence for unintended aspects of impression formation is research on spontaneous trait inferences. The question at stake in this research concerns whether social perceivers spontaneously infer that observed behavior implies that the actor has a corresponding personality trait. In historical models of this process of dispositional inference (e.g., Jones & Davis, 1965), it was typically assumed that perceivers engage in a fairly extensive deductive reasoning process to determine the trait implications of observed behavior, comparing the effects of the observed behavior with the simulated effects of not performing it or of performing an alternative option. In contrast, more recent research on spontaneous trait inferences suggests that perceivers automatically infer the trait implications of behavioral information, even if that is not their conscious intention. For example, Winter and Uleman (1984) presented participants with behavioral descriptions (e.g., *Billy hit the ballerina*) and subsequently asked participants to recall the presented descriptions with the aid of cues. The cues were either semantically related to the theme of the description (e.g., *dance*) or were related to the trait implications of the behavior (e.g., *hostile*). Cued recall performance was markedly better when trait cues were available. In a different paradigm, Uleman, Hon, Roman, and Moskowitz (1996) showed that people spontaneously made trait inferences when processing behavioral descriptions, even when such inferences actually impaired performance of their focal task. In this paradigm, participants read behavioral descriptions on a computer screen. Immediately after the presentation of a description, a word appeared on the screen and participants had to indicate whether that exact word had appeared in the preceding sentence. When the target word was a trait that was implied by the behavioral description, reaction times were slower and error rates were higher than they were when the same target words followed similar descriptions that did not imply the traits in question. This kind of evidence suggests that fundamental aspects of social perception can occur quite spontaneously, without any conscious instigation on the part of the perceiver.

Trait inferences are but one manifestation of unintended social cognition. In a growing program of research, Bargh and colleagues have shown that without the formation of any conscious intention, primed or salient stimuli can trigger spontaneous behavior (e.g., Bargh, Chen, & Burrows, 1996). For example, Bargh et al. showed that activating stereotypes about elderly persons resulted in slower rates of walking. Similarly, Chen and Bargh (1997) showed that subliminal presentation of African American (as compared with European American) faces resulted in more hostile behavior in a subsequent verbal game played with an unprimed partner. Moreover, the unprimed partner's behavior also became more hostile as a consequence, showing that self-fulfilling prophecies can emerge in a very automatic manner—even when participants are unaware that stereotypical concepts have even been activated and have formed no conscious intention to act in a manner consistent with these concepts. Although the precise mechanisms responsible for these fascinating effects have not been isolated, the very existence of the phenomenon provides a potent demonstration of the potential automaticity of not only social thought, but also interpersonal interaction.

A principal advantage of automatic reactions lies in the fact that they are largely not dependent on the availability of processing resources. Because of the great efficiency with which they unfold, automatic processes do not require much investment of attentional capacity or perceiver motivation. Whereas novice drivers can find it harrowing to coordinate all of the requisite activities (shifting gears, monitoring traffic, steering, braking, etc.), after the process has been automated, not only can these tasks be easily performed, but the driver may also have sufficient reserve capacity available for singing along with the stereo or engaging in mobile phone conversations. Empirical confirmation of the resource-conserving properties of automatic mental processes was provided in a series of experiments by Macrae, Milne, and Bodenhausen (1994). In one of their studies, they asked participants to engage in two tasks simultaneously: a visual impression-formation task that involved reading personality descriptions of four different persons, and an audio task that involved listening to a description of the geography and economy of Indonesia. For half of the participants, stereotypes were activated in the impression-formation task (by providing information about a social group to which each target belonged). Some of the personality information was consistent with stereotypes about the relevant group, and the rest was irrelevant to such stereotypes. One might expect that giving these participants an additional piece of information to integrate would simply make their task all that much harder—but in fact, the introduction of the stereotype provided a framework that participants could spontaneously use to organize their impressions, making the process of impression formation much more automatic and efficient. As a consequence, participants who knew about the group memberships of the social targets not only recalled more information about the targets (as revealed in a free recall measure), they also learned more information about Indonesia (as revealed in a multiple-choice test). The automatic reactions triggered by stereotype activation provided a clear functional benefit to perceivers by making the process of impression formation more efficient, thereby freeing up attentional resources that could be devoted to the other pressing task.

When automatic effects of these sorts occur without awareness, intention, or much attentional investment, is there any hope of preventing them or stopping them after they start? In the realm of automatic stereotyping effects, Bargh (1999) has argued that the prospects for controlling such effects are slim to none. Indeed, the final hallmark of an automatic process is its imperviousness to control. In line with Bargh's assertion, the previously described research of Devine (1989) showed that even low-prejudice individuals who disavow racist stereotypes are still prone to showing automatic effects of stereotype activation. Similarly, Dunning and Sherman (1997) found that implicit gender stereotyping occurred independently of participants' level of sexism. However, other research has begun to suggest that at least some of the time, it may be possible to develop control over automatic processes. Uleman et al. (1996), for example, found that with practice, people could learn to avoid making spontaneous trait inferences. Similarly, it seems that egalitarian individuals can also learn to control automatic stereotyping effects, at least under some circumstances (e.g., Wittenbrink, Judd, & Park, 1997). It is toward the processes through which mental control can be achieved that we now turn our attention.

Controlled Social Cognition

The process of controlling thought and action, at least in relatively novel and unpracticed domains, requires attention. Whereas automatic processes occur efficiently and thus require little expenditure of mental resources, effortful, controlled processes come with an attentional price to pay. Moreover, controlled processes typically require intentional deployment, and they occur in a manner that is at least partially accessible to the conscious mind. Whereas many computational processes of implicit cognition are regarded to be massively parallel, attention and consciousness represent a processing bottleneck that results in highly selective and serial information processing (e.g., Simon, 1994). As Simon notes, connecting one's motives to one's thought processes requires a system that can cope with the constraints imposed by limitations of attentional capacity.

Attentional capacity has turned out to be a major theoretical construct in social cognition research (for a review, see Sherman, Macrae, & Bodenhausen, 2001) precisely because it plays such a fundamental role in determining whether it will be possible for the perceiver to engage in controlled processing. Without sufficient mental resources, automatic mental processes are presumed to operate in an unchecked manner, and it is difficult or impossible for perceivers to impose their will and exercise control over the workings of their own minds. Early theorizing about attentional capacity assumed a simple, unitary structure to the mental resources that are used in conscious, controlled information processing. However, advances in cognitive neuroscience have made it possible to identify a more differentiated set of working memory resources (e.g., Roberts, Robbins, & Weiskrantz, 1998). Baddeley (1998) proposed that there are three principal facets to working memory, each with a limited capacity for holding information: a phonological buffer, a visuospatial sketch pad, and a central executive. It is the latter resource that is most important to social-cognitive theorizing, because it is the central executive that governs the conscious planning, execution, and regulation of behavior. When these executive resources are in ample supply, individuals are generally able to exercise a considerable degree of control over their conscious thought processes and behavioral responses; when these finite resources have been usurped by other ongoing processes, however, the resulting executive dysfunction can put perceivers in the position of failing to produce intended patterns of thinking and responding. Under this circumstance, thought and action will be dictated more by potent automatic reactions than by the force of the conscious will.

Research on mental control has undergone a dramatic resurgence in the past decade (for an excellent sampling of research topics, see Wegner & Pennebaker, 1993). Wegner's research on thought suppression has been a major impetus for this explosion of research attention (e.g., Wegner, 1994; Wenzlaff & Wegner, 2000). In this research, the prospects for mental self-control have been investigated by providing participants with a self-regulatory injunction to consciously pursue (e.g., *don't think about white bears* or *don't be sexist*). Success is measured simply by the number of times the unwanted response is generated, and success rates can be considerable—provided that the person has ample attentional resources. However, if a cognitive load is imposed on the person (e.g., a secondary task must be completed simultaneously, such as rehearsing an eight-digit number), not only are unwanted responses likely to emerge, but they are also likely to occur with even greater frequency than they would if the person had never tried to suppress them in the first place (i.e., a *rebound effect*).

Wegner (1994) proposed a theoretical account for this state of affairs; his account rests on the assumption that mental control reflects the operation of two separate processes. A *monitoring process* is responsible for checking to see whether undesired responses (e.g., sexist thoughts) are occurring. If it

should detect such responses, an *operating process* is triggered that serves to squelch the unwanted response by finding an acceptable substitute response (e.g., thoughts about a target's occupation rather than her gender). Crucial to his model are two additional assumptions. First, the monitoring process can do its work in a relatively automatic manner, but must of necessity keep active in memory (even if only at a relatively low level) a representation of the undesirable response so that it can be recognized if it should appear. Thus, the monitoring process ironically keeps an unwanted thought or response salient in the perceiver's mind. This recurrent activation of the undesired target stimulus is not a big problem, so long as the operating process can counteract the unwanted response whenever it does exceed the threshold necessary for conscious awareness. However, a second assumption of the model is that the operating process is relatively effortful and requires sufficient attentional resources. Hence, if these resources are being depleted by other tasks (e.g., rehearsing a digit string), the enhanced accessibility created as a byproduct of the monitoring process cannot be effectively checked, and the stage is set for rebound effects.

These assumptions have been explored in the domain of stereotype suppression by several researchers. In the contemporary social world, it has become largely taboo to respond to many stigmatized social groups in terms of negative stereotypes and prejudices that have historically been prevalent. In the previous section, we reviewed several pieces of evidence suggesting that stereotypes can exert numerous automatic effects on information processing. If so, what are the prospects for success when perceivers strive to follow the dictates of cultural injunctions against thinking discriminatory thoughts about these stigmatized groups? In an initial demonstration, Macrae, Bodenhausen, Milne, and Jetten (1994) showed that individuals who strive to prevent stereotypical reactions from entering their thoughts can succeed as long as they are actively pursuing that objective. However, consistent with the implications of Wegner's ironic model of mental control, this process rendered the unwanted thoughts hyper-accessible, and Macrae et al. found that after the suppression motivation had dissipated, rebound effects emerged when subsequent members of the stereotyped group were encountered. That is, participants reported even more stereotypical reactions to the subsequent group members than did individuals who had never engaged in any previous stereotype suppression. These findings confirm that intentionally suppressing stereotypes ironically involves repeatedly priming them, albeit at relatively low levels—and this in turn renders the stereotypes all the more accessible. If the operating process that is commissioned to direct attention away from unwanted thoughts should be compromised either by the imposition of a cognitive load or by the dissipation of the motivation required for its activity (being a relatively effortful, controlled process), this in turn can lead to rebound effects.

Additional ironic implications of stereotype suppression were uncovered in subsequent research. For example, trying not to think stereotypical thoughts about an elderly target resulted in better memory for the most stereotypical characteristics displayed by the target (Macrae, Bodenhausen, Milne, & Wheeler, 1996). Moreover, these effects are not limited to situations in which an overt, external requirement for thought suppression is imposed; even when suppression motivation was self-generated in a relatively spontaneous manner, ironic effects were observed to result (Macrae, Bodenhausen, & Milne, 1998). Other research suggests that rebound effects of this sort are more likely to emerge in high-prejudice persons (Monteith, Spicer, & Toomen, 1998) and in situations in which the perceiver is unlikely to have chronically high levels of suppression motivation (Wyer, Sherman, & Stroessner, 2000). These qualifications are quite consistent with general idea that even the process of mental control itself is subject to some degree of automation. With practice, the initial effortfulness of stereotype suppression may be replaced by relative efficiency.

Another form of controlled processing that has received considerable attention from social cognition researchers is judgmental correction. When perceivers suspect that their judgments have been contaminated by unwanted or inappropriate biases, they may take steps to adjust their judgments in a manner that will remove the unwanted influence (e.g., Wilson & Brekke, 1994). Whereas the initial processes that produced the bias are likely to be automatic ones, the processes involved in correcting for them are usually considered to be effortful. Hence, they require perceiver motivation and processing capacity for their deployment. One particularly noteworthy domain in which such hypotheses have been investigated is research on person perception. In particular, it has long been established that people are susceptible to a *correspondence bias,* in which they tend to perceive the behavior of others to be a reflection of corresponding internal dispositions—even when there are clear and unambiguous situational constraints on the behavior (e.g., Jones & Harris, 1967; Gilbert & Malone, 1995). The previously described research on spontaneous trait inference is consistent with the idea that people often immediately assume that behavior reflects the actor's dispositions. In an influential theoretical assessment of this bias, Gilbert (e.g., 1998) proposed that dispositional inferences involve three distinct stages. In the *categorization* stage, the observed behavior is construed in terms of its trait implications (e.g., *Hannah shared her dessert with her brother* could be categorized as *kind*). Then

the inferred trait is ascribed to the actor in the *characterization* stage. Both of these stages are assumed to be relatively automatic —that is, they occur spontaneously, efficiently, and without intention. In a third *correction* stage, individuals may consider the situational constraints that might have influenced the behavior (e.g., *Mommy threatened Hannah with retribution if she failed to share her dessert*) and adjust their dispositional inferences accordingly (e.g., *perhaps Hannah isn't so kind after all*). This correction process is assumed to be a controlled activity that requires motivation and processing capacity for its execution.

In numerous experiments, Gilbert and colleagues have pursued the implications of this model by demonstrating that situational constraints are often not taken into account when perceivers are given a taxing mental task to perform that occupies their central executive resources (e.g., rehearsing a random digit string). For example, when watching a nervous-looking woman, people spontaneously assume that she is an anxious person; only subsequently do they correct this initial assumption in light of the fact that she is in an anxiety-provoking situation (e.g., a job interview). If they have to watch the seemingly nervous person while rehearsing a digit string, they still automatically infer the trait of anxiety, but they no longer engage in corrective adjustments in light of the situational constraint. This pattern of results is quite consistent with the idea that correction is a controlled, resource-dependent process. When attentional resources are diminished, the automatic tendencies of the system remain unchecked by more effortful control mechanisms.

A more general treatment of the nature of correction processes has been provided by Wegener and Petty (1997) in their flexible correction model. According to this model, correction processes operate on the basis of lay theories about the direction and extent of biasing influences. When people suspect that they may have fallen prey to some untoward influence, they rely on their intuitive ideas about the nature of the bias to make compensatory corrective adjustments. For example, if they believe that their judgments of a particular person have been assimilated to stereotypes about the person's gender group, then they would adjust those judgments in the opposite direction to make them less stereotypical in nature. Conversely, if they believe that their judgment of a target has been contrasted away from a salient standard of comparison, they will make adjustments that result in judgments in which the target is seen as more similar to the comparison standard. Several points are important to keep in mind with regard to this correction process. First, it requires that the perceiver detect the biasing influence before the process can initiate (Stapel, Martin, & Schwarz, 1998; Strack & Hannover, 1996). Many automatic biasing influences are likely to be subtle and hence escape detection; as a result, no correctional remedy is pursued. Second, as a controlled process, it is likely to require motivation and attentional capacity for its successful execution. Third, if correctional mechanisms are to result in a less biased judgment, the perceiver must have a generally accurate lay theory about the direction and extent of the bias. Otherwise, corrections could go in the wrong direction, they could go insufficiently in the right direction, or they could go too far in the right direction, leading to overcorrection. Indeed, many examples of overcorrection have been documented (see Wegener & Petty, 1997, for a review), indicating that even when a bias is detected *and* capacity and motivation are present, controlled processes are not necessarily effective in accurately counteracting automatic biases.

Wegner and Bargh (1998) categorize several ways in which automatic and controlled mental processes interact with one another. The examples we have just described fall into the category of *regulation*—when a controlled process overrides an automatic one. When an automatic process overrides a controlled one, as in the rebound effect, *intrusion* is said to occur. Controlled processes can also launch automatic processes that subserve the achievement of the actor's momentary intentions, and this is termed *delegation*. For example, delegation would be said to occur if a conscious goal to go to the shopping mall triggered the many automatic aspects of driving behavior. Conversely, automatic processes can serve an *orienting* function in which they launch controlled processes, as in Wegner's model of mental control: When the automatic monitoring process detects an unwanted thought, it triggers the more effortful operating process to banish the thought from conscious awareness. Finally, controlled processes can be transformed into automatic processes via *automatization,* as when perceivers become so skilled at suppressing stereotypes that it happens automatically, and automatic processes can be transformed into controlled processes via *disruption,* as when one starts thinking too much about the steps involved in a well-learned task and subsequently performs the task more poorly.

In many ways, the tension between automatic and controlled processes has become the heart of social cognition research. Most contemporary social cognition research programs are oriented toward this issue in a fundamental way. One of the key insights to emerge from this research is that our perceptions of and reactions to the social world are often shaped by rapid, automatic processes over which we commonly exercise very little control. By virtue of their very automaticity, the impressions that are constructed on this basis often have the phenomenological quality of being direct representations of objective reality. We feel, for example, that

Mary is objectively *a kind and caring person* rather than recognize the role that our own biases (e.g., gender stereotypes) may have played in shaping this necessarily subjective interpretation. It may be possible to exercise control over these processes. If we pause long enough to entertain the possibility that our perceptions of the world may contain systematic biases, we can engage in suitable corrective action. This action, however, requires awareness, motivation, and attentional capacity. Without them, we may function more like automatons than like the rational agents we often fancy ourselves to be.

SOCIAL COGNITION IN CONTEXT: MOTIVATIONAL AND AFFECTIVE INFLUENCES

A common question asked of social cognition researchers is *How is social cognition different from "regular" cognition?* A common answer to this question is that whereas cognitive psychologists often study cognitive processes in a manner that is divorced from the real-life contexts in which these mechanisms operate, social-cognition researchers muddy the waters by attempting to add back some of the real-life context into their experiments. In real life, our mental processes occur within a complex framework of motivations and affective experiences. Whereas most cognitive psychology experiments attempt to eliminate the role played by these factors, social cognition researchers have had to increasingly recognize that an understanding of how the social mind works must include a consideration of how basic processes of perception, memory, and inference are influenced by motivation and emotion.

There have been a series of interesting debates in social psychology that take the form of questioning whether a particular phenomenon can be explained in purely cognitive terms, or whether one must invoke motivational processes in order to account for it. One case in point is the tendency for people to form negative stereotypes about minority groups. This phenomenon has been studied for quite a long time, and many explanations for it focus on the perceiver's motivations that are gratified by engaging in stereotyping of this sort. For instance, maybe perceivers derive feelings of superior self-worth by looking down on members of other groups (e.g., Adorno, Frenkel-Brunswik, Levinson, & Sanford, 1950) or by viewing their own group as positively distinct from other groups (Tajfel & Turner, 1986). Alternatively, negative stereotypes might arise in order to forestall feelings of guilt about social inequality (Jost & Banaji, 1994). Could the tendency to stereotype minority groups negatively ever be explained in purely cognitive terms, without appealing to these

better if we could avoid it. Thus, our need to know the social world inevitably involves a tension between accuracy and defensive motives (e.g., Taylor & Brown, 1988). Defensive motives reflect our desire to see ourselves and our social worlds in desirable, positive ways and to avoid unflattering or threatening realities. This tension is reflected in research examining the perceiver's need to feel like a reasonable, rational agent. Although previously described research has suggested that people often apply stereotypes as a sort of default, only going beyond a stereotypical impression when accuracy motivation is high and need for closure is low, there are some cases in which this tendency may be undermined by a different set of concerns.

Sometimes individuals may be reluctant to apply stereotypes in their judgments of others because such stereotypes are considered socially undesirable or inaccurate. As reviewed in the previous section, this kind of situation can motivate effortful attempts to suppress stereotypes or otherwise correct for their influence on judgments. More generally, people may be reluctant to render judgments about others unless they feel they have a defensible basis for doing so (e.g., Yzerbyt, Leyens, & Corneille, 1998). For example, if presented with a male versus female target (e.g., just a picture and no other information) and asked to judge the person's suitability for an engineering job, judges would probably be very reluctant to rely on sexist stereotypes. Under these circumstances, they would very likely feel that they were not entitled to judge the person. However, if given a résumé to go along with the photo, perhaps containing evaluatively mixed credentials, they may then feel entitled to judge (and might very well rely on their sexist stereotypes under this circumstance). In a different vein, some individuals typically do not rely on social stereotypes because they do not view persons (or groups) as having very stable, enduring qualities (Levy, Stroessner, & Dweck, 1998). For these persons, simply knowing a person's group membership does not seem like a very informative basis for forming impressions, so they must satisfy their epistemic motivations by seeking out other kinds of data. Perceivers thus must balance their tendency to use simplifying generalizations with their desire to feel that they have a valid and reasonable basis for judging others. This latter desire can derive as much from defensive as from epistemic motivations.

Perhaps the most classic example of a defensive motive is the desire for self-enhancement. People want to think well of themselves and avoid confronting their own shortcomings. This powerful motivation has been examined in innumerable psychological studies (for a review, see Pittman, 1998). The obvious implication for social cognition is that people are motivated to form self-serving impressions, and this tendency

has been documented in many ways. To pick but one example, it has been found that people are more likely to activate and apply negative stereotypes when self-enhancement needs have been aroused by a recently experienced threat to self-esteem (Spencer, Fein, Wolfe, Fong, & Dunn, 1998). As previously noted, one fundamental motivation for prejudice and stereotyping may be the fact that their application can provide a mechanism whereby the perceiver can feel superior to others (e.g., Fein & Spencer, 1997). In addition to economizing cognition, stereotyping thus can simultaneously gratify other motivational constraints.

In addition to wanting to feel superior to others, we also want to feel impervious to harm and to believe that the world is fair and just. The phenomenon of "blaming the victim" (e.g., Lerner, 1998) is one important by-product of these profound needs. If bad things can happen to good people, this has disturbing implications for our senses of safety and justice. Consequently, we may come to view the victims of unfortunate circumstances as possessing qualities that precipitated or otherwise can explain their unhappy fate. Lerner argues that these beliefs often operate in a primitive, implicit manner in shaping our impressions and blame reactions, rather than through a more conscious application of deductive reasoning. Seen in this light, applying negative stereotypes to members of socially disadvantaged groups can be seen as a way of bolstering our sense that the existing system of social inequality is just and appropriate (see also Jost & Banaji, 1994).

Perhaps the greatest threat to our sense of safety and invulnerability comes from the recognition of our own mortality. Research on terror management (e.g., Pyszczynski, Greenberg, & Solomon, 1999) suggests that we have a fundamental motivation to defend ourselves against confronting our own eventual demise. One strategy for coping with this unpleasant reality lies in the creation and maintenance of broader worldviews that imbue life with a sense of meaning and purpose that extend beyond the life of the individual. In a series of studies, it has been shown that reminding people of their own mortality results in the motivation to bolster one's cultural worldview. One way in which this can be accomplished is by disparaging individuals who threaten or contradict one's worldview, such as the members of other social groups (Schimel et al., 1999). Given the wide array of defensive motivations that are addressed by forming negative and hostile impressions of out-groups, the enduring manifestations of intergroup conflict around the world may seem all the more intractable.

Research of this sort shows that although accurate perceptions are important to attainment of control, other powerful needs operate, pushing us toward perceiving the world in ways we want it to be (Kunda, 1990; MacCoun, 1998). Fortunately for the social perceiver, given the often-considerable ambiguity of social stimuli, the need to feel that one has accurate knowledge can often be met while simultaneously pursuing the need to feel good about oneself. But just what mechanisms are available to produce the desired self-serving impressions and judgments? There are many such mechanisms. First, perceivers may selectively attend to stimuli in ways that provide desired outcomes. In one recent demonstration, Mussweiler, Gabriel, and Bodenhausen (2000) showed, for example, that when put in the threatening position of having been outperformed by another person, people tend to strategically focus on aspects of their own identity that serve to differentiate them from the upward comparison standard. For example, a European American woman who is outperformed by an Asian woman may activate self-definitions in which her ethnicity is more salient. People generally find similar others to be more relevant bases for social comparison, so by emphasizing an aspect of her identity that differentiates her from a potential comparison standard, she renders that standard less diagnostic for self-evaluation. Use of this identity differentiation strategy is indeed associated with greater positive affect and enhanced situational self-esteem following an upward comparison.

A particularly powerful demonstration of motivated selectivity in the use of identity dimensions was provided by Sinclair and Kunda (1999). In their research, they presented individuals with evaluative feedback that ostensibly came from a source that was simultaneously a member of both a positively stereotyped and a negatively stereotyped group. For example, the participants were either praised or criticized by an African American doctor. Having been criticized, participants were motivated to discredit the evaluator, and they tended to activate African American stereotypes while at the same time inhibiting doctor stereotypes. Conversely, having been praised, participants were motivated to imbue the evaluator with credibility, so they tended to activate doctor stereotypes while simultaneously inhibiting African American stereotypes. This research suggests an important mechanism whereby desired conclusions can be reached: By inhibiting stimulus dimensions that could challenge the preferred impression, perceivers do not have to face their unwanted implications. Selective attention is clearly a hallmark of motivated social cognition.

Perceivers can also selectively sample from their memories in order to reach desired conclusions. For example, Sanitioso, Kunda, and Fong (1990) showed that after receiving information indicating that introverts (or, alternatively, extroverts) are more likely to enjoy positive academic and social outcomes, people selectively recalled past behaviors that were consistent with the desirable characteristic. There are many ways in which we selectively construct autobiographical memories in order to confirm our desired beliefs about ourselves (e.g., Ross & Wilson, 2000). Similar processes may operate in our perceptions of others. That is, we may selectively remember the "facts" differently about liked versus disliked others, giving the benefit of the doubt to those toward whom we feel an affinity by recalling their most favorable moments; however, when we pause to think about those to whom we feel enmity, we may conjure up episodes when they were at their worst. Moreover, if confronted with an irrefutable set of facts, perceivers always have the option of explaining the facts in different ways. For instance, a liked individual (or group) will be assumed to be more responsible for a positive event than a disliked entity would be, whereas negative events may be seen as more situationally caused for liked (versus disliked) social entities (e.g., Pettigrew, 1979; Regan, Straus, & Fazio, 1974). Further, the perceived trait implications of a behavior can depend critically on whether we are motivated to think well or ill of the actor. An ambiguously aggressive behavior may be seen as disgraceful hostility when performed by an African American, yet the same behavior may be seen as a playful interaction when performed by a European American (e.g., Sagar & Schofield, 1980). Again, the inherent ambiguity of many social events lends itself to creative and selective interpretations and reconstructions.

Perceivers can also apply differential evidentiary standards, depending on the desirability of the implied conclusion. Naturally, a more stringent criterion of proof is required for unwanted or unpleasant conclusions compared to pleasing ones (Ditto & Lopez, 1992). That is to say, if an initial consideration of the evidence supports a desired conclusion, we may be quite content to stop, but if the initial implications are displeasing, we may sort through the evidence much more extensively and subject the counterevidence to our desired conclusions to particularly harsh scrutiny. In this way, effortful reasoning can be engaged in the service of producing desired impressions and judgments. We also may estimate the likelihood of events at least partially in terms of their desirability. This form of wishful thinking appears to be a ubiquitous source of bias in belief-based reasoning (McGuire, 1960). However, the fact that our expectations tend to covary with our desires can also reflect the simultaneous operation of a mechanism whereby desires are constrained by reality—that is, just as we may want to think that desirable events are more probable, we may also determine what it is that we desire in part by assessing its attainability.

It is thus evident that the wily social perceiver has many strategies for getting what he or she wants. Via selective attention, memory, and interpretation, the world can be seen as a flattering, safe, desirable place. These positive biases may provide important coping resources for us (Taylor & Brown, 1988). However, it is important to recognize there are always some reality constraints in operation when we perceive the social environment. It is only when a suitable justification can be constructed that the perceiver is free to indulge in these positive illusions. Given the typical degree of ambiguity in social reality and the range of motivational strategies that are available, it may only rarely be the case that reality constraints are completely impervious to the distorting influence of defensive motives.

Social-Adjustive Motivation

The need for belonging and interpersonal acceptance is another powerful motivational force acting on social perceivers, as decades of research on normative social influence have documented (e.g., Baron, Kerr, & Miller, 1992). A major implication of this body of research is that social perceivers will be motivated to perceive the world in ways that win them acceptance and approval and that make them feel like worthy members of their social groups. One major component of this tendency is simple conformity to the impressions and judgments of others. For instance, hearing information that condones or criticizes prejudice can influence the types of attitudes that an individual expresses (e.g., Blanchard, Lilly, & Vaughn, 1991). One might argue that such an effect merely reflects simple compliance with clear situational demands and does not necessarily reflect motivated distortion of the person's true inner judgments and impressions. However, similar findings have emerged even when relevant social norms are activated in very subtle and indirect ways, and when there is no audience that will be aware of whether the person conformed or failed to conform to the apparent social consensus (Wittenbrink & Henley, 1996).

There is also interesting evidence that belongingness needs can direct social attention and memory. Gardner, Pickett, and Brewer (2000) had participants engage in interactions in a computer chat room. The nature of the interaction was manipulated so that the participants would have social acceptance or rejection experiences. Following social rejection, belongingness needs were expected to be activated and to guide subsequent information processing. After the chat room experience, all participants read a diary that contained information about both social and individual events. As expected, in a subsequent memory task, the individuals who had experienced exclusion in the chat room were significantly more likely to remember the social information contained in the diary. This finding confirms the long-standing claim that

the momentary needs and goals of the person are likely to play an important directive role in social cognition (e.g., Bruner, 1957; Jones & Thibaut, 1958; Klinger, 1975). The pursuit of belonging is just one of many possible goals that can serve this directive function, and a recent focus of empirical attention has been on the mechanisms through which goals guide cognition down a path toward desired outcomes (e.g., Bargh & Barndollar, 1996; Gollwitzer, 1990).

Affective States

The study of emotion is intimately tied up with the study of motivation. Just as the perceiver's motives can influence the extent and direction of social cognition, so too do affective states play a regulatory role in shaping the course of social information processing. Moods and other emotional states can direct memory toward affectively congruent material (e.g., Forgas, 1995), influence which dimensions and attributes of objects are salient (e.g., Niedenthal, Halberstadt, & Innes-Ker, 1999), and lead perceivers to interpret ambiguous social stimuli in a manner that is consistent with the implications of their affect (e.g., Keltner, Ellsworth, & Edwards, 1993). Affective states can influence the perceived likelihood of events (e.g., Johnson & Tversky, 1983) and can themselves be used as information directing judgments when perceivers interpret their affect as being a reaction to the object of judgment (e.g., Clore, Schwarz, & Conway, 1994).

In keeping with major themes of the present review, affective and arousal states have also been hypothesized to influence attentional capacity and epistemic motivation. Thus, they may play a role in determining the extent to which social impressions are based primarily on relatively automatic, immediate reactions or instead are based on more controlled, analytic assessments. Evidence consistent with these possibilities has emerged in many domains of social cognition, including the study of stereotyping. For example, several studies suggest that happiness is associated with a tendency to think less extensively about the social environment. Instead, happy people often appear content to rely on their generic knowledge about social groups rather than taking the trouble to engage in extensive individuation of particular group members (e.g., Bodenhausen, Kramer, & Süsser, 1994; Park & Banaji, 2000; for a review, see Bodenhausen, Mussweiler, Gabriel, & Moreno, 2001). Happiness may confer a sense of confidence in initial top-down impressions that makes effortful thought processes seem subjectively unnecessary. Fluctuations in arousal can also influence information-processes resources and thereby moderate the extent of reliance upon stereotypical generalizations. For example, Bodenhausen (1990) showed that stereotype-based discrimination covaried with circadian fluctuations in mental energy. When "early birds" were tested in the morning, they showed little evidence of reliance on stereotypes, but later in the day they were much more likely to render stereotypical judgments. Conversely, "night owls" were highly likely to make stereotypical judgments in the morning, but not in the afternoon or evening. These findings suggest that low levels of circadian arousal represent a risk factor for intergroup discrimination because perceivers will lack the mental resources to marshal the effort necessary for forming more individuated impressions. At the other end of the spectrum, it is also the case that excessive amounts of arousal can prompt greater reliance on stereotypes, presumably by disrupting attentional processes (e.g., Kim & Baron, 1988).

One emerging trend in the literature on affect and social cognition is the examination and comparison of the effects of integral versus incidental sources of affect (e.g., Bodenhausen et al., 2001). Most of the previous research has focused on moods and other affective states that were triggered in contexts unrelated to the current information-processing situation. This incidental affect can be contrasted with feelings and emotions that arise in reaction to the present situation itself. This latter, *integral affect*, comes in two important varieties. *Chronic integral affect* refers to enduring feelings one has about the individual(s), group(s), or setting present when an interaction is transpiring, whereas *episodic integral affect* refers to momentary feelings triggered in a particular interaction. For example, if one has a fear of dentists, a trip to the dentist's office will be imbued with chronic negative integral affect; however, if this particular trip happens to go very well, the episodic integral affect may end up being quite positive. The affective dynamics of social behavior are very likely to involve both of these kinds of integral affect, as well as the incidental affective background of moods that are brought into an interaction from previous unrelated events. Whereas a rich set of theory and data has emerged to study the incidental side of the picture, the role of integral affect in social cognition is only beginning to be explored (e.g., Moreno & Bodenhausen, 2001; Perrott & Bodenhausen, 2002). In any case it is clear that the affective and motivational context of social cognition will continued to be explored with great vigor as researchers attempt to reunite thinking and doing with feeling and wanting.

CONCLUSION

There have been many debates about the appropriate definition of *social cognition*—many reflect attempts to circumscribe the content domain or topics that fall within its purview.

In our view, social cognition is not so much a topic area as a general perspective that can be applied to virtually any social psychological topic in which one is interested. In keeping with this perspective, we have reviewed the central conceptual themes of social cognition research, including the form and nature of mental representations, the automatic and effortful use of such representations, and the ways in which these processes are modulated by the motivational and affective context within which they occur. Although we produced examples of the use of these general principles from a limited number of topic areas (often focusing on stereotyping as a prototypical example), they could be (and have been) applied in a host of content domains, including group decision making, interpersonal conflict, relationship development, social influence, political judgment, marketing and consumer behavior, academic and athletic performance, and countless others. The fruitfulness of these various applications shows that much explanatory power can be gained when psychologists explore the workings of the so-called black box, using objectively observable aspects of task performance to derive and test inferences about how the mind goes about its business. Inevitably, much of that business is social in nature. The business of studying social cognition is to unravel the mysteries of our socially embedded minds.

REFERENCES

Adorno, T. W., Frenkel-Brunswik, E., Levinson, D. J., & Sanford, R. N. (1950). *The authoritarian personality.* New York: Harper.

Alba, J. W., & Hasher, L. (1983). Is memory schematic? *Psychological Bulletin, 93,* 203–231.

Anderson, N. H. (1965). Averaging versus adding as a stimulus combination rule in impression formation. *Journal of Experimental Psychology, 70,* 394–400.

Asch, S. E. (1946). Forming impressions of personality. *Journal of Abnormal and Social Psychology, 41,* 1230–1240.

Axelrod, R., & Hamilton, W. D. (1981). The evolution of cooperation. *Science, 211,* 1390–1396.

Baddeley, A. D. (1998). *Human memory: Theory and practice.* Boston: Allyn and Bacon.

Banaji, M. R., Hardin, C., & Rothman, A. J. (1993). Implicit stereotyping in person judgment. *Journal of Personality and Social Psychology, 65,* 272–281.

Bargh, J. A. (1982). Attention and automaticity in the processing of self-relevant information. *Journal of Personality and Social Psychology, 43,* 425–436.

Bargh, J. A. (1994). The four horsemen of automaticity: Awareness, intention, efficiency, and control in social cognition. In R. S. Wyer, Jr., & T. K. Srull (Eds.), *Handbook of social cognition* (2nd ed., Vol. 1, pp. 1–40). Mahwah, NJ: Erlbaum.

Bargh, J. A. (1999). The cognitive monster: The case against the controllability of automatic stereotype effects. In S. Chaiken & Y. Trope (Eds.), *Dual process theories in social psychology* (pp. 361–382). New York: Guilford.

Bargh, J. A., & Barndollar, K. (1996). Automaticity in action: The unconscious as the repository of chronic goals and motives. In P. M. Gollwitzer & J. A. Bargh (Eds.), *The psychology of action: Linking cognition and motivation to behavior* (pp. 457–481). New York: Guilford.

Bargh, J. A., & Chartrand, T. L. (1999). The unbearable automaticity of being. *American Psychologist, 54,* 462–479.

Bargh, J. A., & Chartrand, T. L. (2000). The mind in the middle: A practical guide to priming and automaticity research. In H. T. Reis & C. M. Judd (Eds.), *Handbook of research methods in social and personality psychology* (pp. 253–285). Cambridge, England: Cambridge University Press.

Bargh, J. A., Chen, M., & Burrows, L. (1996). Automaticity of social behavior: Direct effects of trait construct and stereotype activation on action. *Journal of Personality and Social Psychology, 71,* 230–244.

Bargh, J. A., & Ferguson, M. J. (2000). Beyond behaviorism: On the automaticity of higher mental processes. *Psychological Bulletin, 126,* 925–945.

Bargh, J. A., & Pietromonaco, P. (1982). Automatic information processing and social perception: The impact of trait information presented outside of conscious awareness on impression formation. *Journal of Personality and Social Psychology, 43,* 437–449.

Baron, R. S., Kerr, N. L., & Miller, N. (1992). *Group process, group decision, group action.* Pacific Grove, CA: Brooks Cole.

Baron-Cohen, S. (1995). *Mindblindness: An essay on autism and theory of mind.* Cambridge, MA: MIT Press.

Bartlett, F. A. (1932). *A study in experimental and social psychology.* New York: Cambridge University Press.

Bem, S. L. (1981). Gender schema theory: A cognitive account of sex typing. *Psychological Review, 88,* 354–364.

Bem, S. L. (1993). *The lenses of gender: Transforming the debate on sexual inequality.* New Haven, CT: Yale University Press.

Blanchard, F. A., Lilly, T., & Vaughn, L. A. (1991). Reducing the expression of racial prejudice. *Psychological Science, 2,* 101–105.

Bodenhausen, G. V. (1990). Stereotypes a judgmental heuristics: Evidence of circadian variations in discrimination. *Psychological Science, 1,* 319–322.

Bodenhausen, G. V. (1992). Information-processing functions of generic knowledge structures and their role in context effects in social judgment. In N. Schwarz & S. Sudman (Eds.), *Context effects in social and psychological research* (pp. 267–277). New York: Springer-Verlag.

Bodenhausen, G. V., Kramer, G. P., & Süsser, K. (1994). Happiness and stereotypic thinking in social judgment. *Journal of Personality and Social Psychology, 66,* 621–632.

Bodenhausen, G. V., Mussweiler, T., Gabriel, S., & Moreno, K. N. (2001). Affective influences on stereotyping and intergroup relations. In J. P. Forgas (Ed.), *Handbook of affect and social cognition* (pp. 319–343). Mahwah, NJ: Erlbaum.

Bransford, J. D., & Franks, J. J. (1971). The abstraction of linguistic ideas. *Cognitive Psychology, 2,* 331–350.

Brewer, M. B. (1997). On the social origins of human nature. In C. McGarty & S. A. Haslam (Eds.), *The message of social psychology* (pp. 54–62). Oxford, England: Blackwell.

Bruner, J. S. (1957). On perceptual readiness. *Psychological Review, 64,* 123–152.

Byrne, R. W. (2000). Evolution of primate cognition. *Cognitive Science, 24,* 543–570.

Cacioppo, J. T., Petty, R. E., Feinstein, J. A., & Jarvis, W. B. G. (1996). Dispositional differences in cognitive motivation: The life and times of individuals varying in the need for cognition. *Psychological Bulletin, 119,* 197–253.

Chaiken, S., & Trope, Y. (Eds.). (1999). *Dual process theories in social psychology.* New York: Guilford.

Chen, M., & Bargh, J. A. (1997). Nonconscious behavioral confirmation processes: The self-fulfilling consequences of automatic stereotype activation. *Journal of Experimental Social Psychology, 33,* 541–560.

Clore, G. L., Schwarz, N., & Conway, M. (1994). Affective causes and consequences of social information processing. In. R. S. Wyer, Jr., & T. K. Srull (Eds.), *Handbook of social cognition* (2nd ed., Vol. 2, pp. 323–417). Hillsdale, NJ: Erlbaum.

Cummins, D. D. (1998). Social norms and other minds: The evolutionary roots of higher cognition. In D. D. Cummins & C. Allen (Eds.), *The evolution of mind* (pp. 30–50). New York: Oxford University Press.

Devine, P. G. (1989). Stereotypes and prejudice: Their automatic and controlled components. *Journal of Personality and Social Psychology, 56,* 5–18.

Ditto, P. H., & Lopez, D. F. (1992). Motivated skepticism: Use of differential decision criteria for preferred and nonpreferred conclusions. *Journal of Personality and Social Psychology, 34,* 568–584.

Dodge, K. A. (1993). Social-cognitive mechanisms in the development of conduct disorder and depression. *Annual Review of Psychology, 44,* 559–584.

Donders, F. C. (1868). Die Schnelligkeit psychischer Processe [The speed of mental processes]. *Archiv für Anatomie und Wissenschaftliche Medizin,* 657–681.

Dovidio, J. F., Evans, N., & Tyler, R. B. (1986). Racial stereotypes: The contents of their cognitive representations. *Journal of Experimental Social Psychology, 22,* 22–37.

de Dreu, C. K. W., Koole, S. L., & Oldersma, F. L. (1999). On the seizing and freezing of negotiator inferences: Need for cognitive closure moderates the use of heuristics in negotiation. *Personality and Social Psychology Bulletin, 25,* 348–362.

Dunning, D., & Sherman, D. A. (1997). Stereotypes and tacit inference. *Journal of Personality and Social Psychology, 73,* 459–471.

Edwards, J. A., & Weary, G. (1993). Depression and the impression-formation continuum: Piecemeal processing despite the availability of category information. *Journal of Personality and Social Psychology, 64,* 636–645.

Erdelyi, M. H. (1974). A new look at the New Look: Perceptual defense and vigilance. *Psychological Review, 81,* 1–25.

Fazio, R. H. (1986). How do attitudes guide behavior? In R. M. Sorrentino & E. T. Higgins (Eds.), *Handbook of motivation and cognition* (pp. 204–243). New York: Guilford.

Fazio, R. H. (1990). A practical guide to the use of response latency in social psychological research. In C. Hendrick & M. S. Clark (Eds.), *Research methods in personality and social psychology* (pp. 74–97). Newbury Park, CA: Sage.

Fein, S., & Spencer, S. J. (1997). Prejudice as self-image maintenance: Affirming the self through derogating others. *Journal of Personality and Social Psychology, 73,* 31–44.

Fiedler, K. (1991). The tricky nature of skewed frequency tables: An information loss account of distinctiveness-based illusory correlations. *Journal of Personality and Social Psychology, 60,* 24–36.

Fiske, S. T., & Dépret, E. (1996). Control, interdependence, and power: Understanding social cognition in its social context. In W. Stroebe & M. Hewstone (Eds.), *European review of social psychology* (Vol. 7, pp. 31–61). New York: Wiley.

Fiske, S. T., & Linville, P. W. (1980). What does the schema concept buy us? *Personality and Social Psychology Bulletin, 6,* 543–557.

Fiske, S. T., & Taylor, S. E. (1991). *Social cognition.* New York: McGraw-Hill.

Fitts, P. M., & Posner, M. I. (1967). *Human performance.* Belmont, CA: Brooks Cole.

Forgas, J. P. (1995). Mood and judgment: The affect infusion model. *Psychological Bulletin, 117,* 39–66.

Forgas, J. P. (Ed.). (2001). *Handbook of affect and social cognition.* Mahwah, NJ: Erlbaum.

Gardner, W. L., Pickett, C. L., & Brewer, M. B. (2000). Social exclusion and selective memory: How the need to belong influences memory for social events. *Personality and Social Psychology Bulletin, 26,* 486–496.

Gazzaniga, M. S. (Ed.). (2000). *The new cognitive neurosciences* (2nd ed.). Cambridge, MA: MIT Press.

Gilbert, D. T. (1998). Ordinary personology. In D. T. Gilbert, S. T. Fiske, & G. Lindzey (Eds.), *Handbook of social psychology* (4th ed., Vol. 2, pp. 89–150). New York: McGraw-Hill.

Gilbert, D. T., & Malone, P. S. (1995). The correspondence bias. *Psychological Bulletin, 117,* 21–30.

Gilbert, D. T., Pelham, B. W., & Krull, D. S. (1988). On cognitive busyness: When person perceivers meet persons perceived. *Journal of Personality and Social Psychology, 54,* 733–739.

Gollwitzer, P. M. (1990). Action phases and mindsets. In E. T. Higgins & R. M. Sorrentino (Eds.), *Handbook of motivation and cognition* (Vol. 2, pp. 53–92). New York: Guilford.

Hamilton, D. L., & Gifford, R. K. (1976). Illusory correlation in interpersonal perception: A cognitive basis of stereotypic judgments. *Journal of Experimental Social Psychology, 12,* 392–407.

Hamilton, D. L., & Sherman, J. W. (1994). Stereotypes. In R. S. Wyer, Jr., & T. K. Srull (Eds.), *Handbook of social cognition* (2nd ed., Vol. 2, pp. 1–68). Mahwah, NJ: Erlbaum.

Hasher, L., & Zacks, R. T. (1979). Automatic and effortful processes in memory. *Journal of Experimental Psychology: General, 108,* 356–388.

Hastie, R. (1980). Memory for behavioral information that confirms or contradicts a personality impression. In R. Hastie, T. M. Ostrom, E. B. Ebbesen, R. S. Wyer, Jr., & D. E. Carlston (Eds.), *Person memory: The cognitive basis of social perception* (pp. 141–172). Hillsdale, NJ: Erlbaum.

Heider, F. (1958). *The psychology of interpersonal relations.* New York: Wiley.

Herr, P. M. (1986). Consequences of priming: Judgment and behavior. *Journal of Personality and Social Psychology, 51,* 1106–1115.

Higgins, E. T. (1996). Knowledge activation: Accessibility, applicability, and salience. In E. T. Higgins & A. W. Kruglanski (Eds.), *Social psychology: Handbook of basic principles* (pp. 133–168). New York: Guilford.

Jacoby, L. L. (1998). Invariance in automatic influences of memory: Toward a user's guide for the process-dissociation procedure. *Journal of Experimental Psychology: Learning, Memory, & Cognition, 24,* 3–26.

Johnson, E. J., & Tversky, A. (1983). Affect generalization and the perception of risk. *Journal of Personality and Social Psychology, 45,* 20–31.

Jones, E. E., & Davis, K. E. (1965). From acts to dispositions: The attribution process in person perception. In L. Berkowitz (Ed.), *Advances in experimental social psychology* (Vol. 2, pp. 220–266). New York: Academic Press.

Jones, E. E., & Harris, V. A. (1967). The attribution of attitudes. *Journal of Experimental Social Psychology, 3,* 1–24.

Jones, E. E., & Thibaut, J. W. (1958). Interaction goals as bases of inference in interpersonal perception. In R. Tagiuri & L. Petrullo (Eds.), *Person perception and interpersonal behavior* (pp. 151–178). Palo Alto, CA: Stanford Unviersity Press.

Jost, J. T., & Banaji, M. R. (1994). The role of stereotyping in system justification and the production of false consciousness. *British Journal of Social Psychology, 33,* 1–27.

Kashima, Y., Woolcock, J., & Kashima, E. S. (2000). Group impressions as dynamic configurations: A tensor product model of impression formation and change. *Psychological Review, 107,* 914–942.

Srull, T. K. (1981). Person memory: Some tests of associative storage and retrieval models. *Journal of Experimental Psychology: Human Learning and Memory, 7,* 440–462.

Srull, T. K. (1984). Methodological techniques for the study of person memory and social cognition. In R. S. Wyer, Jr., & T. K. Srull (Eds.), *Handbook of social cognition* (1st ed., Vol. 2, pp. 1–72). Hillsdale, NJ: Erlbaum.

Srull, T. K., Lichtenstein, M., & Rothbart, M. (1983). Associative storage and retrieval processes in person memory. *Journal of Experimental Psychology: Learning, Memory, and Cognition, 11,* 316–345.

Srull, T. K., & Wyer, R. S., Jr. (1979). The role of category accessibility in the interpretation of information about persons: Some determinants and implications. *Journal of Personality and Social Psychology, 37,* 1660–1672.

Srull, T. K., & Wyer, R. S., Jr. (1983). The role of control processes and structural constraints in models of memory and social judgment. *Journal of Experimental Social Psychology, 19,* 497–521.

Stapel, D. A., & Koomen, W. (1998). When stereotype activation results in (counter)stereotypical judgments: Priming stereotype-relevant traits and exemplars. *Journal of Experimental Social Psychology, 34,* 136–163.

Stapel, D. A., Martin, L. L., & Schwarz, N. (1998). The smell of bias: What instigates correction processes in social judgments? *Personality and Social Psychology Bulletin, 24,* 797–806.

Sternberg, S. (1966). High speed scanning in human memory. *Science, 153,* 652–654.

Strack, F., & Hannover, B. (1996). Awareness of influence as a precondition for implementing correctional goals. In P. M. Gollwitzer & J. A. Bargh (Eds.), *The psychology of action: Linking motivation and cognition to behavior* (pp. 579–596). New York: Guilford.

Tajfel, H., & Turner, J. C. (1986). The social identity theory of intergroup behavior. In S. Worchel & W. G. Austin (Eds.), *Psychology of intergroup relations* (pp. 7–24). Chicago: Nelson-Hall.

Taylor, S. E., & Brown, J. D. (1988). Illusion and well-being: A social psychological perspective on mental health. *Psychological Bulletin, 103,* 193–210.

Tversky, A., & Kahneman, D. (1974). Judgment under uncertainty: Heuristics and biases. *Science, 185,* 1124–1131.

Uleman, J. S., Hon, A., Roman, R. J., & Moskowitz, G. B. (1996). On-line evidence for spontaneous trait inferences at encoding. *Personality and Social Psychology Bulletin, 22,* 377–394.

Warrington, E. K., & Weiskrantz, L. (1968). New method of testing long-term retention with special reference to amnesic patients. *Nature, 277,* 972–974.

Wegener, D. T., & Petty, R. E. (1997). The flexible correction model: The role of naïve theories of bias in bias correction. In M. Zanna (Ed.), *Advances in experimental social psychology* (Vol. 29, pp. 141–208). San Diego, CA: Academic Press.

Wegner, D. M. (1994). Ironic processes of mental control. *Psychological Review, 101,* 34–52.

Wegner, D. M., & Bargh, J. A. (1998). Control and automaticity in social life. In D. T. Gilbert, S. T. Fiske, & G. Lindzey (Eds.), *Handbook of social psychology* (4th ed., Vol. 1, pp. 446–496). New York: McGraw-Hill.

Wegner, D. M., & Pennebaker, J. W. (Eds.). (1993). *Handbook of mental control.* Englewood Cliffs, NJ: Prentice Hall.

Wenzlaff, R. M., & Wegner, D. M. (2000). Thought suppression. *Annual Review of Psychology, 51,* 59–91.

Wilson, T. D., & Brekke, N. (1994). Mental contamination and mental correction: Unwanted influences on judgments and evaluations. *Psychological Bulletin, 116,* 117–142.

Winter, L., & Uleman, J. S. (1984). When are social judgments made? Evidence for the spontaneousness of trait inferences. *Journal of Personality and Social Psychology, 47,* 237–252.

Wittenbrink, B., & Henley, J. R. (1996). Creating social reality: Informational social influence and the content of stereotypic beliefs. *Personality and Social Psychology Bulletin, 22,* 598–610.

Wittenbrink, B., Judd, C. M., & Park, B. (1997). Evidence for racial prejudice at the implicit level and its relationship with questionnaire measures. *Journal of Personality and Social Psychology, 72,* 262–274.

Wyer, N., Sherman, J. W., & Stroessner, S. J. (2000). The roles of motivation and ability in controlling the consequences of stereotype suppression. *Personality and Social Psychology Bulletin, 26,* 13–25.

Wyer, R. S., Jr., & Carlston, D. E. (1994). The cognitive representation of persons and events. In R. S. Wyer, Jr., & T. K. Srull (Eds.), *Handbook of social cognition* (2nd ed., Vol. 1, pp. 41–98). Mahwah, NJ: Erlbuam.

Wyer, R. S., Jr., & Srull, T. K. (1989). *Memory and cognition in its social context.* Mahwah, NJ: Erlbaum.

Yzerbyt, V. Y., Leyens, J.-P., & Corneille, O. (1998). The role of naïve theories of judgment in impression formation. *Social Cognition, 16,* 56–77.

CHAPTER 12

Emotion, Affect, and Mood in Social Judgments

JOSÉ-MIGUEL FERNÁNDEZ-DOLS AND JAMES A. RUSSELL

In everyday conversation, Spaniards occasionally describe someone as being *emocionado(a)*. To be *emocionado* means to be emotional, but this translation is misleadingly simple. Whereas English speakers use the phrases *to be emotional* and *to have an emotion* largely interchangeably, Spaniards make a clear distinction between *estar emocionado* and *sentir una emoción*. *Emocionado* is perhaps better rendered into American English metaphorically as "to be touched" or "to be moved" (as a psychological state); *emocionado* can be used in either positive or negative contexts. Spaniards recognize different expressive behaviors for *emocionado* and *emoción,* even when both occur in a positive context. For example, a Spanish journalist described two medal winners on an Olympic podium, one smiling and the other crying. The journalist described the smiling woman as *alegre* (joyful) and the crying woman as *emocionada* (Fernández-Dols & Ruiz-Belda, 1995). *Emocionado* is an emotional state distinct from specific emotions such as anger or joy. In fact, as early as 1921, Gregorio Marañón, a Spanish doctor, pointed to Spaniards' use of *emocionado* as a recognition of the nonspecific nature of visceral changes in emotion (Ferrandiz, 1984). If *emocionado* denotes an emotional state not recognized clearly in English, Spanish may segment emotional experience in a subtler way than does English.

Ethnographers' and historians' descriptions of remote or past cultures reveal many more examples of different ways of talking about emotion. For example, Tahitians lack the word *sadness* entirely (Levy, 1973). Even where a similar word

exists, it may cover different experiences—just as the English word *sadness* has covered different experiences during different historical periods (Barr-Zisowitz, 2000).

Another observation from the ethnographic record is vast differences even when an emotion word appears the same. Consider two societies, both of whom have words easily translatable as anger. In *Never in Anger,* Briggs (1970) describes an Utku family in the Canadian Arctic; the Utku smile and laugh off situations that would make most of us angry. They endure with patience and humor situations that would drive us to fury. The clearest case of an Utku's anger recorded by Briggs was particularly telling. A group of visiting Kapluna (White) sports fishermen borrowed a canoe and damaged it. It was one of only two canoes the Utku band possessed. The fishermen later asked to borrow the other canoe. Damage to this second canoe would endanger the future livelihood of Briggs's Utku family. Briggs was the interpreter, and she refused the fisherman's request, becoming overtly angry with them. The Utku elder for whom she was translating did not react with anger toward the fishermen, who were to be shown indulgence and forgiven, as a child would be. But he did react with *ningaq* to Briggs. He found her angry outburst so inappropriate that she was ostracized for several months. The Utku never see anger (*ningaq*) as justified. The Utku believe that angry feelings, by themselves, with no mediation, can harm others or even kill them. For an Utku, to experience *ningaq* is to experience oneself as unjustifiably harboring murderous feelings—this in a society in which kindness and tolerance are expected of all adults and are even considered to define what it means to be a mature functioning human (Kaplunas—White people—are suspected of being descended from dogs and to have the minds of children).

Our second case comes from the Ilongot, a group indigenous to the Philippines and studied by Michelle Rosaldo (1980). Their word commonly translated as anger is *liget*. A young man is restless, frustrated, mulling over past insults. He is envious of the privileges of his elders and the successes of his peers. His liget mounts and weighs down on him. There will likely be other such young men, competing, envious of one another, and heavy with frustration and boredom. Led by an elder man, a small group of such youths conducts a raiding party, sometimes against a known enemy, but more often against a random victim (man, woman, or child). During the raid, the young men beat their heads to increase their *liget*. The *liget* mounts and weighs on them. It is felt as heavy and oppressive, an unrelieved yearning. Finally, the victim is selected and killed (it does not particularly matter by whom). The young men rush at the victim, slashing and mutilating. The victim's head is severed, and one youth throws the head in the air. Now the *liget* is felt as "burning joy." The young men feel lightened, freed from the heavy burden. Filled with *liget,* the party is intent on mutilation. They slash, mutilate, and toss heads. They then raid the home of the victim, destroying property. As they return to their homes, to keep their *liget* hot, they drink hot drinks. They return in triumph as men.

QUESTIONS ARISE FROM CULTURAL DIFFERENCES

Whatever the validity of these specific observations, these and many more like them have been important in the psychology of emotion. For one, reactions to such observations reveal diverse assumptions. One reaction to claims of this sort has been to conclude that emotions among Spaniards, Tahitians, Ilongot, and Utku are different from emotions in English-speaking societies. Another reaction has been to conclude that perhaps each language has a different way of describing emotions (but that does not mean that the emotions themselves are different). Another reaction has been to conclude that emotional experience is culture-specific but that emotions are not. Yet another reaction is to dismiss much of the ethnographic and historical evidence as concerning mere talk—nothing important for those who would study emotion.

When confronted with claims of cultural and historical differences in the concept of sadness or with anecdotes of cultural variability of anger, psychologists must face difficult

questions: Is anger of the Utku the same emotion as anger in the Ilongot? How could that sameness be empirically tested? What, if anything, is the anger behind the manifest differences? Is anger universal? Or could it be a cultural artifact? Answers to such questions follow predictable theoretical positions on fundamental issues such as what is real and what is not, what are legitimate topics in science, and what is the relationship between mind and body and between language and reality.

The issues raised by reports of cultural differences have not been settled by available evidence. There is no consensus on such matters. Or even on how they could be settled. Instead, different researchers assume different positions, based on deeply held philosophical assumptions. These often-unvoiced assumptions then guide scientific theorizing, dividing the field into camps that each pursue different goals with different methods. For example, an approach to emotions as universal natural entities independent of language and culture stems from (or resonates with) a basic philosophical position that could be labeled as *ontological realism*. In contrast, an approach to emotions as cultural products created through language stems from (or resonates with) a philosophical position that could be labeled as *nominalism*. Psychological theorists may not endorse all the traditional consequences of their philosophical assumptions, and most theorists introduce ways to accommodate data grounded on other assumptions. Nevertheless, exposure of these philosophical assumptions can help us understand some of the sources of strength and weakness in current research on emotion.

In this chapter, we first outline four philosophical positions (in necessarily overly simplified and stark terms) that seem to underlie different research programs on emotion and that center on the issue of the relation between language and reality. (Does language accurately describe reality? Influence reality? Constitute reality? Or does everyday language conceal and obscure reality?) We then explore one way that these research programs might be integrated.

Ontological Realism

The ontological realist assumes that words such as *anger* and *sadness* are simply labels for preexisting entities. Emotions are like rivers or lakes or other things in the natural world. They are self-contained and distinct from any other thing. They have a concrete localization inside human beings and other animals ("inside" nowadays often means "in the brain"). With scientific effort, emotions will be isolated, localized, measured, and manipulated. From this point of view, it would not be surprising if each specific emotion were discovered to correspond to a single neural center, neural circuit, peptide, or some other specific physical entity.

Emotions existed long before culture or language. At best, language can provide labels for different emotions. Of course, different languages provide different labels, but these point to the same preexisting reality: Just as *luna* and *moon* are different labels for the same entity, so are *anger, ningaq,* and *liget* just different labels for the same entity. Language is useful only in providing labels, and most talk about emotion is of little interest to the scientist and can often obscure or conceal reality behind the words, as in romantic or metaphoric talk about the moon.

Nominalism

Nominalism is thought by some to have started with the medieval philosopher Ockham, who broke with many of the philosophical assumptions of his contemporaries. Ockham taught that there exist only individual events and things (such as Briggs's reaction that day to the Kapluna fishermen). Individual events or things (even those called by the same name) do not share with each other some Platonic essence. Names for general classes of events or things (e.g., *emotion* or *anger*) are therefore misleading. Sometimes some events look similar enough for an observer to group them together and give them a common name—hence nominalism. Through language, people can name general groups of these individual events and talk about the type in general. Nevertheless, such groupings are always arbitrary, in the sense that the only thing real is the individual. A nominalist position is thus skeptical about any claims about reality outside individual events and words themselves.

In a modern version of nominalism, the emphasis is on the role of words. Words differ from one society to the next or one historical era to the next, and that is the reality to be analyzed. As words, *anger, liget,* and *ningaq* are important in their own right, rather than as labels for a common entity (Harre, 1986). An extreme version of this approach asserts that these words lack any denotation. Instead, they are simply cultural practices (e.g., Lutz, 1988). Another version would be the belief that there do exist individual events, but these individual events take on the meaning of *anger, liget,* or *ningaq* only by being labeled. For example, one approach to emotion words is to study them only as part of discourse and focus on pragmatics of their use. (What is the consequence, in Utku society, of accusing someone of being *ningaq?*) Emotion words, as part of discourse, create an object (the emotion) that exists only in the context of the speaker's construed social reality: Words create a cultural, idiosyncratic illusion that is the emotion itself. *Anger, liget,* and *ningaq* are therefore not comparable and cannot be understood outside the culture in which they fulfill an important role in the regulation of everyday interaction. From this point of view, much of the psychology of emotion is the imposition of a Western construction on other cultures, which ignores the implicit symbolic structure that gives shape and meaning to each potential candidate for the label *emotion* in that culture (Shweder & Haidt, 2000).

Conceptualism

A conceptualist position shares with ontological realism its assumption that emotion words refer to a nonlinguistic reality, its interest in that reality rather than in words, and its skepticism about the ability of language to reveal that reality. The conceptualist, however, takes such words as *anger* and *liget* as concepts rather than as labels for entities. There are many ways to construe reality. Thus, any inference to emotions as independent, real entities, while possible, is suspect. The nature of the reality so conceptualized is the focal question. For example, one might hold that when people use an emotion word, they are pointing to a physiological, behavioral, or situational event—something observable—and not to any emotional entity. The scientist's job is to search for an objective account of the actual processes commonly conceptualized as *anger, liget,* or *ningaq.* Behaviorist, functionalist, and situationist approaches to emotion arise from this philosophical background.

Formalism

The formal approach treats emotion words as formal objects, much like numbers or logical operators. As in the nominalist approach, the focus is again on language, although in this case it is on the semantics rather than pragmatics of language. *Emotion* and *emoción* are first and foremost words. What are the necessary and sufficient features for *emotion* and *emoción?* Or for *anger, liget,* or *ningaq?* These terms may have both common and distinguishing features, which would reveal universal and language-specific aspects of these words, respectively. Rather than simply assume that *anger = liget = ningaq,* the researcher seeks to provide a formal analysis of each word. Words are linguistic phenomena, parts of a particular language. Each specific language is a cultural product, but language in general has universal aspects.

DIFFERENT RESEARCH PROGRAMS ON EMOTION

The study of emotion is guided by deep assumptions that resonate with old philosophical debates. The result is that different and apparently incompatible research programs have arisen that provide different frameworks for research and applications in the field. From one program to the next, there is no agreement about the meaning and scientific usefulness of words such as *anger, sadness,* and the like or even of *emotion* itself. In this section we describe several of these programs. Although we emphasize the philosophical assumptions guiding each program, we do not imply that individual theorists endorse these philosophies explicitly, consistently, or exclusively.

Emotions as Entities

The Facial Expression Program

Ontological realism comes close to the philosophical assumptions of the person in the street and remains the dominant position in the psychology of emotion. (See Lillard, 1998, for a discussion of the ontological realist assumptions of the concept of mind.) Emotions are natural entities. By "natural," we mean that emotions are now viewed as biological products of evolution. By "entity," we mean (a) that an emotion could, at least in principle, be isolated from its surrounding context (i.e., from its eliciting stimulus and behavioral and physiological consequences) and still be the emotion that it is and (b) that an emotion has causal powers (fear causes flight and love makes one care for the loved one). Thus, in the days of faculty psychology, emotion was a faculty.

The ontological position can be seen in much of the research conducted on emotion, but its major theoretical representatives today were inspired by Silvan Tomkins (1962, 1963). Tomkins was a psychiatrist with a vast range of interests and a formidable intellectual curiosity. Tomkins's influence on two creative, enthusiastic scientists, Carroll Izard and Paul Ekman, was a powerful tool in spreading his ideas. Together, they created the Facial Expression Program (FEP; Russell & Fernández-Dols, 1997), arguably the most influential network of assumptions, theories, and methods in the psychology of emotion. The FEP combined ontological assumptions about emotion with modern scientific concerns about the evolutionary origins, neural mechanisms, and precise physiological correlates of emotion.

In this framework, the kinds of cultural differences with which we began are acknowledged. Ekman (1972) named his own theory *neurocultural.* Culture influences the observable elements surrounding emotion, but not the unobservable emotion itself. Members of different societies learn to have different emotions in given situations: A food that produces pleasure in one society can produce disgust in another. And society regulates (through display rules) the observable manifestations of each emotion: A society might believe that boys should show a brave face even when sad or frightened. These cultural differences are not taken to challenge the reality or universality of the emotions themselves.

Izard and Ekman traced their intellectual roots to Charles Darwin. Darwin's *Expression of the Emotions in Man and Animals* was an extended argument for human evolution and against the then-popular belief that most muscles of the human face were God's creations designed exquisitely for the expression of emotion (Montgomery, 1985). Darwin's strategy was to show that expressions are not simply expressions at all but vestiges of formerly instrumental actions. (A facial expression of anger with bared teeth does not simply express anger but is a genetically transmitted habit of baring the teeth when preparing to bite.) Emotions and movements (expressions) were described according to the everyday categorization of nineteenth-century English society. Darwin was a great empirical scientist, but his views on emotion were commonsense assumptions in the tradition of academic treatises of the seventeenth and eighteenth centuries. His three *principles of expression* do not mention emotion, and his book is focused mostly on the physiology of expression.

In the hands of Izard and Ekman the emphasis shifted back to facial movements as genuine expressions and even more to the emotions expressed. Darwin's research became the search for universal entities (now called basic emotions) behind human faces. His findings of similar *movements* across cultures, ages, and species became a finding of similar *emotions* across cultures, ages, and species. Ekman and Izard transformed Darwin's vague and open-ended list of emotions (e.g., meditation, hunger, determination, love, low spirits, despair) into a closed list of basic emotions. Ekman (1972) included happiness, fear, sadness, anger, surprise, and disgust and more recently added contempt (Ekman & Friesen, 1986) and shame (Keltner, 1995). Basic emotions are prepackaged neural programs that can be detected in all human beings as well as in other species. Other emotions, such as love, jealousy, shame, *emocionado, liget,* or *ningaq* are blends, mixtures, subcategories, or synonyms of the basic emotions.

Although different theorists have proposed somewhat different theories, a list of the prototypical principles of the FEP would include the following:

1. There is a closed (although revisable) list of basic emotions.

2. Basic emotions are discrete entities.

3. Basic emotions are genetically determined and universal.

4. Each basic emotion produces a coherent and unique pattern of facial and vocal signals, conscious experience, instrumental action, and physiological changes.

5. All emotions other than the basic ones are subcategories or mixtures of the basic emotions.

6. Signals for basic emotions are recognized by any normal human being.

7. Voluntary facial expressions are deceptive and culturally determined.

The FEP stimulated the gathering of a vast quantity of data, much of it aimed at establishing one fact: Across a range of ages and cultures, human beings can attribute the same emotions to select facial configurations. But this fact (assuming it is a fact; cf. Russell, 1994) would establish only one of the basic principles of the FEP. For example, research has not yet shown that an allegedly universally recognized facial expression is a manifestation in all human societies of the very emotion recognized. Indeed, available data make this assumption doubtful (see Camras; 2000; Fernández-Dols & Ruiz-Belda, 1997; Fridlund, 1994).

The FEP has generated much valuable data on how people associate emotion names with facial expressions and on physiological or vocal patterns of those said to have those emotions. Curiously, no data have been gathered to establish the existence of anger, fear, and other basic emotions beyond the facial configurations, vocal and physiological patterns, and so on from which the emotion is inferred—that is, beyond the emotion's observable manifestations. Instead, the emphasis has been on the importance (in Darwinian terms, the *adaptiveness*) of emotion. This approach is reminiscent of another argument in the ontological tradition: Anselm's ontological argument for the existence of God, by which the meaning of the word *God* implies the necessity of his existence. By definition, God is perfect, but nonexistence would be an imperfection and therefore a contradiction. Emotions are important (adaptive), but a nonexistent entity could not be important.

Appraisal Theories

The clearest candidate for the research program that is replacing FEP as dominant in the psychology of emotion today is known as appraisal theory. Appraisal theory (see Frijda, 1986; Lazarus, 1991; Scherer, Schorr, & Johnstone, 2001) shares with FEP the assumption that emotions are adaptive entities that have evolved to respond quickly to recurring important circumstances. Appraisal theories can be thought of as a development of FEP in which emphasis is put on a cognitive step between those circumstances and the emotion (event → appraisal → emotion). (Some versions of appraisal theory assume that appraisals are a part of the emotion). An appraisal provides an explanation for (a) which situations

elicit which emotions and (b) individual differences in the stimulus-response link. (For example, if you appraise dogs as threats, then, for you, dog → threat → fear; but if you like dogs, then dog → good → happy.) The main question then becomes the nature of appraisal. In the earliest versions, appraisal was a simple evaluation (Arnold, 1960). In later versions, appraisals became increasingly complex and took into account a person's plans, beliefs, desires, values, and so on (Lazarus, 1991).

One appraisal theorist, Smith (Smith & Kirby, 2001), noted the ontological assumptions of appraisal theories. These theories generally share with FEP assumptions about emotions as entities, but they also began by assuming that appraisals are also entities (which are capable of producing emotions). This ontological predisposition can be seen in the primary method used: If a subject could label an appraisal with a word such as *threat* or *good*, then these specific appraisals were assumed to exist and to trigger the emotion. Smith and Kirby called for more circumspect inferences from such methods and for the use of methods that focus on the actual processes that constitute appraisals.

Concluding Comment

The ontological approach has been an enormous success—indeed, sometimes a victim of its own successes. For example, data generated by the FEP unveiled extraordinary complexity within "basic" emotions. Facial, vocal, and instrumental behavior, as well as cognitive appraisal, subjective experience, and physiological changes all show much more variability within each emotion than anticipated (Ortony & Turner, 1990; Smith & Scott, 1997). Further, these separate components do not correlate with each other as highly as anticipated (Lang, 1994). As a second example, the ontological approach has relied heavily on human judgment studies (e.g., in the studies on recognition of emotion from faces or in questionnaire studies on appraisal). This method did not yield the simple patterns anticipated, but it did pave the way for the study of a completely different topic: the cognitive representation of emotion.

Emotion as Discourse

A very different reaction to observations about cultural differences comes from a loosely related group known as social constructionists (e.g., Averill, 1982; Harré, 1986; Kemper, 1978; Lutz, 1988; Parkinson, 1995). Social constructionist ideas show the influence of nominalism and focus on discourse about emotion. They also emphasize cultural differences in the observable antecedents and consequences of emotions—but then these differences were acknowledged by such ontological realists as Ekman (1972). In contrast, the social constructionist takes the role of culture to be deeper, extending to emotion itself.

Return to the Ilongot's *liget* and Utku's *ningaq*. A nominalist would argue that instances of *liget* and *ningaq* are merely similar enough for an observer to give them a common name (*anger*). The word *anger* admits the head-hunting Ilongot youth and the Utku elder who ostracized Briggs. But this judgment is in the eye of the beholder—in this case, an outsider's third-person point of view. There is no entity shared by the Ilongot youth and the Utku elder. Further, there is no entity shared by different examples of *liget* within Ilongot society, or shared by different examples of *ningaq* within Utku society, or shared by different examples of anger within an English-speaking society. Nothing, that is, except the label.

It is clear that the causes and consequences of *liget* differ from those of *ningaq*. For the social constructionist, there is a difference as well in the conscious subjective experiences of the Ilongot youth's *liget* and of the Utku elder's *ningaq*. The two experiences are similar in some ways, but they differ in other ways and do not share any essence. Although the Utku elder might share with the Ilongot youth some of the same raw ingredients (and this remains to be demonstrated), he experiences *ningaq* rather than *liget* or *anger*. To experience *ningaq* is to experience something that human beings should not experience. In contrast, to experience *liget* is to experience the most important force in life, something vital to life. For an Ilongot, to feel *liget* and to head-hunt as a result are the most natural thing.

An analogy may make the nominalist position clearer. Consider a baby nursing, a Jew celebrating a seder at Passover, and a gourmand savoring a meal at Maxim's in Paris. The word *eating* admits all three experiences, yet their experiences are quite different. They might have some of the same lip movements, physiological processes, and raw sensations. However, the meaning given to the behaviors, physiological changes, and sensations would be different. Experience is a complex web of associations that draws on expectations, history, norms of what is proper, and so on. Suppose that we give the Utku elder and the Ilongot youth a meal at Maxim's. The experiences would be different again. Imagine the Utku elder being engaged in Ilongot head-hunting. He would likely experience this state as abnormal and unnatural. In contrast, the Ilongot youth experiences himself in line with his ancestors as doing something completely natural, almost inevitable.

Some social constructionists view terms such as *liget, ningaq,* and *anger* are names for interpretative schemas or scripts (Shweder, 1994). Emotional experience is based on a narrative constructed with the help of this cultural script, which gives meaning to the experience. By sharing a script, members of a society create similar narratives. Sometimes narratives in different societies are similar enough to an outside observer that they can all be called by the same name. People form widely applicable concepts and talk about them in general. From this view, emotional experiences are cultural products. To be sure, physiological changes, facial movements, and actions are also real and might even be universal, but these tend to be viewed as raw ingredients, devoid of inherent meaning.

The nominalist perspective is easy to apply to the experiences of those most foreign to us, but it applies equally to our own emotions. In his study of road rage in Los Angeles, Katz (1999) emphasized that road rage fits a highly regular narrative that shapes the driver's experience in a characteristic way (although to an external observer road rage can be as mysterious and frightening as the Ilongots' *liget*). When cut off by another driver, the driver becomes morally outraged, insults the other driver (even though the other driver cannot hear the insult), makes obscene gestures, and feels the need to retaliate in order to teach the offender a lesson (sometimes thereby increasing the danger).

Emotion as Process

A line of thinking about emotion that resembles a conceptualist philosophical stance began with William James. James wrote disparagingly of thinking of emotions as entities or of giving credence to distinctions embedded in everyday language (such as anger vs. irritation vs. annoyance, etc.). His view opened the door to asking about the actual process that occurs when an emotion is said to occur. He suggested that the actual process is quite different from what is suggested by common sense. James famously argued that bodily changes (e.g., crying, running) produce rather than follow the experience of emotion.

Marañon (1924, 1950) tested James's hypothesis about the role of bodily changes in the experience of emotion. Marañon injected epinephrine (adrenalin) into 210 hospital patients. He observed two different results. Some (29%) of the patients reported a strong "genuine" emotion, but most (71%) reported an "as-if" emotion. That is, they felt as if they were having an emotion but denied having any real emotion. Marañon concluded that James's hypothesis was not confirmed. Instead, Marañon suggested that different reactions to the same epinephrine-induced bodily changes were related to a patient's specific medical condition, such as hyperthyroidism.

Cantril and Hunt (1932) challenged Marañon's interpretation by replicating his study with 22 students and professors without medical problems. They found a similar split between reports of genuine and as-if emotions. Cantril and Hunt pointed not to medical conditions, but to the unique situational circumstances of each subject. In cases of genuine emotion, the subject's current situation bore a "logical relationship" to the emotion reported; in cases of as-if-emotion, no such situation was present. Landis and Hunt (1934) also replicated Marañon's experiment, this time with psychiatric patients, and obtained similar results. Landis and Hunt therefore concluded that emotion was influenced by "environmental" factors and "higher intellectual and perceptual functions."

Cantril (1934) placed subjects in four successive negative situations (e.g., watching photographs of mutilated war victims or hearing sudden loud noises as the lights were unexpectedly turned off). Subjects went through the four situations in different orders. Each was injected four times, getting a placebo for the first three trials and epinephrine for the fourth. In comparison with the placebo, epinephrine increased the subjects' ratings of their emotional reactions in fear situations but decreased their rated emotional reaction in disgust situations. Cantril suggested that "the awareness of some object or situation around which the emotion is intellectually organized is the immediate cause for the emotional experiences" (p. 578), and that "the quality of an emotion is primarily dependent upon the attitude aroused in the [subject] by the stimulus" (p. 579). In this way, Cantril, Hunt, and Landis moved away from a view in which emotion is an entity triggered by a stimulus and defined by bodily changes, as assumed in early ontological theories. They moved toward a view in which emotion depends not just causally but logically on a complex situation intellectually organized in the context of bodily arousal.

An interesting development of this view was Nina Bull's (1951) attitude theory of emotion. Bull begins with a simple framework: Situations elicit actions. Action consists of two successive stages: (a) a preparatory phase and (b) a consummatory movement (e.g., fight or flight). The first stage is a motor attitude or action readiness and includes involuntary changes in posture and in various organs. This phase has both a direct and an indirect consequence: The direct consequence is the particular action (the second stage) for which the first phase prepares. The indirect consequence is a feeling. It is this feeling that is usually known as emotion. The feeling of an emotion is thus an epiphenomenon of the sequence in which a motor attitude becomes action. Although Bull shares with ontological thinkers the attempt to identify the one event that is the emotion, she also moved in the direction of thinking of emotion as something that can be understood only in terms of a process that necessarily includes both situation and action. Indeed, unless the feeling of the emotion is

equated with the emotion itself, there is no emotion per se within Bull's theory of emotion.

Schachter (1964) further articulated and developed this perspective in his two-factor theory of emotion. Schachter's specific ideas were an application of Lewinian principles (Ross & Nisbett, 1991): Emotion is the result of a tension between environmental constraints and cognitive construals. The environmental constraints were both situational (mainly others' behaviors) and internal (nonspecific arousal). The cognitive construals were originally cognitive labels but shortly afterward became attributions (Nisbett & Schachter, 1966). Schachter's theory of emotion dominated the study of emotion in social psychology for several decades. The combination of nonspecific arousal and (mis)attribution inspired important theoretical models of aggression (e.g., Zillmann & Bryant, 1974), helping (e.g., Piliavin, Piliavin, & Rodin, 1975), interpersonal attraction (e.g., Dutton & Aron, 1974), environmental behavior (e.g., Anderson & Anderson, 1984), and attitude change (e.g., Zanna & Cooper, 1974). Mandler (1984) developed a related theory of emotion that dominated the study of emotion in cognitive psychology around the same time.

Ginsburg and Harrington (1996) recently proposed an account of emotion along more purely conceptualist lines. The concept of emotion refers to an action in a context. The context has two structural features. The first is hierarchical: a broad system of events and social relationships that are necessary to give meaning to the action. The second feature of the context is linear; that is, it includes a sequence of actions unfolding over time. Prior actions lead to (or, in Lewinian terms, create a channel for) subsequent actions. Actions also alter bodily state and felt experience. The entire sequence of actions in context with its accompanying bodily and mental state is construed (conceptualized) as emotion. In this way, there is no emotion in addition to the action in context. No single event within the sequence can be equated with emotion.

Ginsburg and Harrington described the proper study of emotion as descriptive. They suggested creating natural histories of specific emotional episodes. In turn, these emotional episodes are to be understood as a subsystem of larger and more complex systems. The search for universal entities is abandoned in favor of an exhaustive description of such systems relevant for a particular culture.

Formal Definitions for Emotion Terms

Much philosophical work on emotion has been aimed at a formal analysis of emotion terms. Solomon's (1976) inspired analysis was a precursor to appraisal theories. Wierzbicka's (1992, 1999) linguistic analysis provides a formal framework for any word in any language. She developed a contemporary version of an ancient philosophical dream: the creation of a universal language based on fundamental concepts indispensable for thought. Wierzbicka developed a list of universal semantic primitives (*I, you, someone, something, know, good, bad, maybe, feel,* etc.). These, together with a minigrammar specifying the rules of their combination, constitute a universal language. This universal language can then be used to analyze any emotion word in any language. The interesting result of her analyses so far is that emotion words (*anger, liget, ningaq*) and *emotion* itself have all been found to be culture-specific but, nevertheless, definable in terms of her universal semantic primitives, especially *feel, good,* and *bad.* Even words with a similar etymology, such as *emotion,* the Italian *emozione,* and the Spanish *emoción,* have not been found to be equivalent.

Psychologists have also offered formal analyses of the emotion lexicon, although they are limited to the English language. Oatley and Johnson-Laird (1990) defined *emotion* as a disjunctive set of five semantic primitives: happy, sad, fear, anger, and disgust. Any emotion term is then defined by reference to one or more of these five. This approach clearly also has ties to the position of ontological realism. Ortony, Clore, and Collins (1988), in contrast, define all English emotion terms as referring to a valenced reaction to an event. Differences between terms are defined by cognitive differences in interpreting that event (along the lines of appraisal theories). Their approach has ties to a conceptualist perspective.

An alternative formal analysis began with Wittgenstein and entered psychology largely through the work of Rosch (e.g., Rosch, 1978, 1987). This analysis is skeptical of the classical search for necessary and sufficient features to define such everyday words as *emotion* or *anger.* Various nonclassical alternatives have been proposed (e.g., Fehr & Russell, 1984), but all share the idea that membership in the category labeled by a word is a matter of degree and that the border between members and nonmembers is fuzzy.

TOWARD INTEGRATION

No one research program has been able to achieve consensus. The persistence of competing and possibly incommensurate programs is frustrating, but at the same time fascinating and potentially useful. Differences force us to question assumptions and to notice ignored questions. Competing approaches thus create the grounds for a qualitative shift in our understanding of emotion. This shift might take the form of an integration of two or more of the various paradigms or even of a revolutionary change in our understanding of emotion. In

this chapter we offer neither a revolutionary theory nor even a complete integration of available paradigms, but we do offer the beginnings of one possible integration. We describe a new descriptive framework deliberately built on all of these paradigms.

So far, we have perhaps overemphasized the limitations of these various paradigms. Their longevity indicates that each addresses some aspect of the topic. All of them have made substantial contributions to the understanding of emotion. Indeed, all of them are necessary for raising—if not answering—essential questions about those very important events that are labeled *emotion.*

We also believe that all can be integrated within a common framework. What has prevented integration in the past is the assumption that each of these research programs is dealing with the same thing, namely, emotion. If the word *emotion* denoted a homogeneous, well-defined set of events, then different theories of emotion would, indeed, be in direct conflict with each other over the same territory. Scientific analysis would long ago have settled major disputes. If, instead, emotion is a heterogeneous, poorly defined mix of qualitatively different events (originally grouped together by our hunter-gatherer ancestors and modified with each era to suit cultural concerns), then different theories could be about different topics within that loose domain. Selected evidence could easily find support for each such theory.

We therefore begin by abandoning *emotion* as a scientific term. It remains here only as an everyday term and as a figurehead, a convenient symbol for the general domain of study, but it is not allowed to set the boundary for the set of events that any theory in this domain must explain. In fact, our proposed integrative framework extends beyond the traditional boundaries of emotion by including such states as fatigue, drowsiness, and calm. It is especially important to underscore that abandoning *emotion* as a scientific term does not mean abandoning the study of those very real and very important events now called *emotion.*

Abandoning *emotion* as a scientific term allows us to borrow from each of the established research programs on emotion (as diagrammed in Figure 12.1). Programs based on an ontological realist position embody the traditional scientific search for basic entities that underlie all the varied manifest differences in a domain. They rightly emphasize empirical examination of physiological and behavioral details. Programs based on a nominalist position emphasize the uniqueness and complexity of each emotion event and of emotional experience. They also emphasize the role of meaning systems shared by members of a culture. Unique events are understood (both by a scientist and a nonscientist) through the mediation of concepts (which are mental processes that

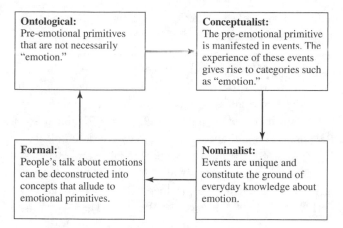

Ontological:
Pre-emotional primitives that are not necessarily "emotion."

Conceptualist:
The pre-emotional primitive is manifested in events. The experience of these events gives rise to categories such as "emotion."

Formal:
People's talk about emotions can be deconstructed into concepts that allude to emotional primitives.

Nominalist:
Events are unique and constitute the ground of everyday knowledge about emotion.

Figure 12.1 Four research programs on emotion.

group or order unique events). Programs based on a conceptualist stance hold that nonscientists and scientists alike hold conceptualizations of reality. The history of science teaches that common-sense conceptualizations can be improved and ultimately replaced with scientifically honed ones. And programs based on a formalist position suggest possible alternative universal primitives (such as *feel, good,* and *bad*) and bolster our claim that *emotion* is a heterogeneous cluster of events.

CORE AFFECT AS A POINT OF DEPARTURE

Next, we search for primitive entities. One reason that basic emotions are ill suited to serve as emotion primitives has been established by research from the basic emotions perspective: They are too complex. For example, they typically consist of separable components (Izard, 1977) and are directed at an object (i.e., one fears, loves, hates, or is angry with *something*). Oatley and Johnson-Laird (1987) pointed out that an emotional primitive should be free of this something (the object) because of the cognitive involvement that the object implies. Curiously, then, our search for emotional primitives begins with moods and other simple feelings that lack an object. In this way, Oatley and Johnson-Laird created an important new theory based on a categorical perspective.

Here we explore that same approach but from a dimensional perspective. The goal in dimensional studies is to find what is common to various emotions, moods, and related states. Methods have included multivariate analyses of self-reported feelings, introspection, the semantic differential, and various biological techniques. This research has regularly found such broad dimensions as pleasure-displeasure and activation-deactivation. We refer to any state that can be defined simply as some combination of these two dimensions as *core affect.*

Core affect is similar to Thayer's (1986) activation, Watson and Tellegen's (1985) affect, and Morris's (1989) mood; it is also translatable into the everyday term *feeling.* In its most primitive form, core affect is free-floating. That is, it lacks an object. For example, one can feel anxious (unpleasant activation) about nothing in particular and without knowing why one feels that way. Core affect thus fits the ontological requirements for a primitive, elemental, and simple emotional ingredient. Biological research has often found that the most basic levels of emotional behavior are better conceptualized as dimensions than as discrete emotions (Cabanac 1990; Caccioppo, Gardner, & Berntson, 1999; Davidson, 1992a, 1992b; Gray, 1994; Lang, 1979; Rozin, 1999; Shizgal & Conover, 1996; Thayer, 1996). For example, in their review of studies on the peripheral physio-logical changes in emotion, Cacioppo, Berntson, Larsen, Poehlmann, & Ito, (2000) emphasized the existence of a primitive and fast response categorizing stimuli as hospitable or hostile (see also Carver, 2001).

More formally, core affect is that neurophysiological state consciously accessible as the simplest raw feelings evident in (but not limited to) moods and emotions, such as feeling good or bad, energized or enervated. In line with nominalist ideas, core affect does not correspond with any word in a natural language (just as the physicist's concept of force cannot be easily translated into lay terms). Core affect consists of all possible combinations of pleasure-displeasure and activation-deactivation and therefore includes states that would not be called emotions, such as calm, fatigue, or drowsiness. Indeed, a person is always in some state of core affect, which can be extreme, mild, or even neutral. Core affect is part of most psychological processes.

Specifically, core affect is one part of those events people call *emotion* (and which we call emotional episodes). Self-reports of emotion persistently yield two large general factors interpretable as pleasure and arousal (e.g., Russell & Mehrabian, 1977; Watson & Clark, 1992). Furthermore, the manipulation of arousal by drugs influences self-reported discrete emotions (Cooper, Zanna, & Taves, 1978; Gerdes, 1979; Schachter & Latané, 1964; Schachter & Wheeler, 1962). Feldman Barrett and Russell (2000) explored this hypothesis further in a study of self-reported emotions. In one condition participants were asked to describe how they currently felt. In a second condition they were asked to search their memory for the very last time they had an emotion. In the third condition they were asked to search their memories for a strong, clear emotion. In all three conditions the pleasure and arousal dimensions accounted for substantial variance in the intensity of self-reported emotions. However, as the event to be described became more restricted to clearer and stronger cases of emotion, the amount of variance accounted for declined, though not to zero. For example, the variance accounted for by pleasure and arousal in a scale of anger was .80, .63, and .68 in the three conditions, respectively. Thus, pleasure and arousal remained a part of strong, clear emotions, but other components played a larger role.

Core affect also guides behavior. Core affect leads us to expose ourselves to affect-congruent situations (Bower & Forgas, 2000), thereby playing a role in action preparation and behavioral choice. Pleasure-displeasure influences our way of assessing resources when planning or deciding on action. Pleasure and displeasure are thus not restricted to emotional behavior and are currently found in the explanation of different kinds of action, including aggression (Berkowitz, 1993), eating (Pinel, Assanand, & Lehman, 2000), sex (Abramson, & Pinkerton, 1995), and drug abuse (Solomon, 1977). The dimension of arousal is one's state of readiness for action. For example, feeling enthused (high pleasure and arousal) gives a person a sense of optimism in choosing goals and plans. Arousal has been the basic component of the most popular situationist theory of emotion in social psychology (Schachter, 1964). The existence of core affect complements rather than contradicts the characterization of emotions as action patterns, provided that action patterns too are thought to be parts of rather than the whole of or essential to emotion.

Core affect provides a way of comparing qualitatively different scenarios by representing them on a single dimension, thereby solving a common human problem: The events encountered and the choices available are often qualitatively different. Occasionally, one chooses between the larger and smaller dessert, but more often the choice is between two qualitatively different options: dessert or a film. The dimension of pleasure-displeasure is a psychological currency that provides a yardstick for such comparisons (e.g., Mellers, 2000).

A final advantage of thinking in terms of core affect is that the psychology of emotion is more easily integrated with the rest of psychology. The concept of emotion has led writers to think of emotions as stemming from a separate faculty. In contrast, the concept of core affect is compatible with a growing body of evidence that links it to other psychological processes. For example, core affect has been found to guide cognitive processes such as attention, perception, thinking, judgment, mental simulation, and retrieval from memory (e.g., Baron, 1987; Blaney, 1986; Bower, 1992; Eich, 1995; Forgas, 1995; Forgas, Bower, & Krantz, 1984; Izard, Wehmer, Livsey, & Jennings, 1965; Mayer, Gaschke, Braverman, & Evans, 1992; Schiffenbauer, 1974). Pleasure and displeasure facilitate the accessibility of positive and negative material respectively; the more pleasant core affect is, the more positive are evaluative judgments (Schwarz & Clore, 1988) and the more

optimistic is one's simulation of the future (Sanna, 1998). Arousal could also have a similar effect; high or low arousal facilitates the accessibility of high and low arousal material respectively (Clark, Milberg, & Ross, 1983; for a dissenting opinion see Bower & Forgas, 2000). Core affect also influences the quality and type of cognitive processing. Arousal affects the quality of cognitive performance (Humphreys & Revelle, 1984) and attention selectivity (Easterbrook, 1959; Eysenck, 1982). Pleasure affects heuristic processing and problem solving (see Aspinwall, 1998; Isen, 1993; Lerner & Keltner, 2000; Niedenthal, Halberstadt, & Setterlund, 1997; Park & Banaji, 2000; Schwarz & Bless, 1991).

A VOCABULARY FOR A SCIENTIFIC FRAMEWORK FOR EMOTION

Core affect is not simply another term for *emotion,* and a variety of additional concepts are needed to deal with those events called *emotion.* Some of these new concepts are generated by thinking in terms of core affect, and others are simply borrowed from other branches of psychology. Core affect is thus a departure point for a new vocabulary in the study of emotion. It can be used to define some common terms and to generate a set of secondary concepts that covers various emotion-related events.

Mood is defined as prolonged core affect without an object, and *affect regulation* is any attempt to alter core affect directly. Individuals typically (though not always) seek pleasure and avoid displeasure. Individuals also seek a level of arousal appropriate to the task at hand (e.g., looking for pleasant relaxation when stressed, but for excitement when bored). Exercise, coffee, cigarettes, looking for particular companions, and listening to music are at least in part ways of regulating core affect.

Affective Quality

Just as the objects and events in our perceptual world emerge into consciousness already interpreted, they emerge affectively interpreted. Core affect should be distinguished from the affective qualities of the stimuli we perceive on at least two grounds. First, unlike core affect, which is objectless, affective quality is linked to a particular stimulus. Second, phenomenologically, core affect resides in the person who feels it, whereas affective quality resides in the stimulus; it is the odor that is pleasant (a fragrance) or unpleasant (a stench). Although core affect and affective quality are usually linked, each can change without the other: Core affect can be altered chemically, and a depressed patient can acknowledge that something is pleasant but report no changes in actual core affect. Various terms from the literature (e.g., *evaluation, affective judgment, affective appraisal, affective reaction,* or *primitive emotion*) are similar to the perception of affective quality (see Cacioppo et al., 1999; Zajonc, 1980, 2000). Several experiments suggest that an initial perception of affective quality of a stimulus takes place automatically within 25 ms of encountering the stimulus (Bargh, 1997; Bargh, Chaiken, Govender, & Pratto, 1992; Bargh, Chaiken, Raymond, & Hymes, 1996; Fazio, Sanbonmatsu, Powell, & Kardes, 1986).

Attribution

People seek the cause of any change in core affect that they experience. They attribute core affect to someone or something or some condition. In this way, core affect takes on an object: One moves from simply feeling bad to grieving over the loss of a friendship. Attributions are complex perceptual-cognitive processes and entail the possibility of misattribution. Although the object typically is an obvious thing or event, it can be invented (fear of ghosts), hallucinated, remembered, or anticipated. The object is a psychological construction that includes past and future.

Motive

Attributing core affect to an object becomes a *motive* for action—for example, attributing negative core affect (displeasure) to a deprivation (e.g., attributing discomfort to the lack of a cigarette constitutes a motive to smoke). Motives may or may not result in action.

Liking and Disliking

These everyday concepts include both occurrent (actual, brief) events and dispositions to those events. An occurrent instance of liking (e.g., tasting a novel soup and liking it) is the experience of pleasure attributed to the liked object (the soup). A person's disposition to like something (e.g., Joe likes soup) is that person's tendency to derive pleasure from that thing.

Categories of Emotion

Core affect, perception of affective quality, and the corresponding attributions to an object describe a huge variety of phenomena usually called *emotion*. Nevertheless, a dimensional affect system should also explain all these cases in which psychologists and laypeople prefer to speak in terms of specific categories such as *fear, sadness,* and so on.

Categorization is a basic cognitive process. Rather than consider each event encountered as unique (as we are encouraged to do by the nominalists), people group them together on the basis of perceived similarity. Thus, one notes a resemblance between some actual event and a stored representation of a group of events. On one theory, an emotion category is mentally represented by a script of the components of that emotion, unfolding in a causally linked sequence (Fehr & Russell, 1984; Fischer, 1991; Lakoff, 1987; Russell, 1991; Russell & Fehr, 1994). Categories are also linked to one another in a complex net of associations, and categorization is implicated in the perception of emotion both in others and in self.

Emotional Episode

Our term that comes closest to *emotion* is *emotional episode.* It is any actual event that resembles the mental representation of an emotion category sufficiently to count as a member of that category. Resemblance is a matter of degree, and no sharp boundary separates members from nonmembers. We define a *prototypical emotional episode* as an emotional episode for which the resemblance is especially close. Our notion of emotional episode as a pattern among simpler ingredients (including those already described, such as core affect and attribution) is congruent with much current conceptual and empirical analysis of emotion as the integration of simpler components through a process of attribution (Bem, 1972; Blascovich, 1990; Higgins, 1987; Keltner, Locke, & Audrain, 1998; Öhman, 1999; Olson, 1990; Schachter, 1964; Weiner, 1985).

An emotional episode typically begins with a real or imaginary event, which has a perceived *affective quality.* (This initial estimate of affective quality is included in appraisal theories, usually as a first evaluative step; Arnold, 1960; Smith & Ellsworth, 1985.) Core affect changes and prompts an *attributional process.* In most cases, the eliciting event is readily identified, but ambiguous cases can give rise to misattributions (Nisbett & Schachter, 1966). Whatever event is identified as the cause is thereby seen as the source of current core affect—and therefore as a problem to be solved or an opportunity to be seized. Behavior follows accordingly.

Emotional Meta-experience

It is one thing to undergo an emotional episode, another to notice that this is happening. Emotional meta-experience is the perception of oneself as having a specific emotion. It is similar to what is commonly called subjective emotional experience. The prefix "meta-" draws attention to the notion that the raw data (affect core, affective quality, action, somatic sensations, attribution, etc.) on which emotional meta-experience is based are themselves consciously accessible experiences. On this account, to perceive oneself as "angry" is a complex process of self-categorization based on the everyday category of anger. The hypothesis of emotional meta-experience fits well with recent findings that conscious emotional feelings follow and monitor rather that precede other emotional ingredients (e.g., Gray, 1999; LeDoux, 1996; Öhman, 1999).

THE UNIVERSAL AND THE CULTURAL

In the debate between universalists and cultural relativists, the psychology of emotion inherited a version of the perennial nature-nurture controversy. As long as this question is posed about the heterogeneous cluster called *emotion,* more debate than resolution can be expected. When *emotion* is replaced with the variety of concepts proposed here, we hope that a resolution is nearer. In this chapter, we have come down squarely both on the side of nature and on the side of nurture. In principle, every psychological event is a joint product of genetic and epigenetic influences. In searching for elementary processes, we sought those whose existence appears to be as much a part of a universal human nature as possible. We offered core affect (and the specific dimensions of pleasure and arousal), perception of affective quality, attribution, categorization, and so on as candidates. Specific outcomes of some of these universal processes, however, might show variability caused by epigenetic factors. For instance, the event to which core affect is attributed and the affective quality perceived in a specific stimulus might show measurable epigenetic variability.

Emotional episodes are patterns among these ingredients and might show more variability caused by epigenetic influences. Behavior, for example, draws on prepackaged modules that are coupled or decoupled to suit the specific antecedent event and one's goals, plans, social role, norms, values, and so forth. An emotional episode in response to frustration will bear a family resemblance to all human responses to frustration. Still, it might more typically resemble the script for *liget* among the Ilongot, but more the script for *ningaq* among the Utku. As a consequence, concepts formed in one society can be expected to differ from those formed in another (Russell, 1991).

On our account, emotional meta-experience (although hypothesized to be a universal process) allows the greatest cultural diversity in content. For example, the concept of *emocionado* is available and readily accessible for Spaniards. They are easily able to conceptualize, label, and report states that resemble *emocionado*. Perhaps all persons experience a core affect combined with thoughts and behaviors that do not fit well into a specific emotion category, but Spaniards experience this state in terms of *emocionado*. Doing so places that state within a culture-specific network of meaning. In contrast, a person who lacks this concept might also have the same raw ingredients but would, nevertheless, not experience the resulting Gestalt in the same way.

A COMPARISON OF CORE AFFECT WITH EMOTION

Emotion is an old and rich term that refers to a variety of fascinating phenomena that are not as closely related to each other as one might think. The gap between emotion and nonemotion is fuzzier and smaller than was once thought. As a consequence, the psychology of emotion is fragmented into many largely independent areas. Research even on a supposedly single emotion is fragmented. For example, research on fear includes clinical research on anxiety, social psychological research on the effect of fear on attitude change, and experimental research on fear as a basic emotion; each of these areas has its own traditions. Articles in one tradition rarely reference an article in another. These considerations suggest any number of strategies for the future. One suggestion is to take stock of the ecology of emotion events. Another is to move to a much lower level of analysis. Fear, sadness, and the like consist of components that can be studied in their own right. A search for patterns among the components would replace assumption with empirically established patterns.

Our proposal of a new framework and vocabulary for research on emotion should not be understood as a new theory about emotion but as an outline for the integration of old theories. The concept of *emotional episode* has several advantages over the old concept of *emotion*. It encourages the study of individual components and thus allows researchers to explain and include in their theories the huge variability of emotional behavior, expression, experience, and physiology that has been uncovered in research on basic emotions. Behavior probably does not divide naturally into two qualitatively different classes, the emotional and the nonemotional. Core affect, affective quality, and attribution all occur outside emotional episodes as well.

Unlike "basic emotions," which are self-contained entities, emotional episodes consist of ingredients that can be shaped in a variety of ways. For example, Bugental (2000) proposed that socialization is not simply a general process of social influence but an acquisition of effective procedures (algorithms) for solving problems in five specific domains (attachment, power in hierarchies, mating, coalitions in groups, and reciprocity).

Effective procedures in one domain may be unrelated to those in another. Considered to be emotional episodes, love and jealousy involve not just such processes as core affect and attribution but also these specific algorithms for social life—roles, strategies, tactics, stances, norms—that shape behavior and social interaction in a dynamic way.

Although an amalgam of prior theories, our framework results in a picture of emotional life different from what is currently available. The events highlighted in previous paradigms—prototypical emotion episodes, discourse about emotion, concepts—all occur and are important. Nevertheless, rather than incompatible approaches to one thing, they are interacting parts of a larger system. This system also includes many other related parts, such as moods, evaluations, and unattributed core. Whatever the fate of our specific framework, a new study of emotion that goes beyond current assumptions promises to yield an even richer field than we see today.

REFERENCES

Abramson, P. R., & Pinkerton, S. D. (1995). Introduction: Nature, nurture and in between. In P. R. Abramson & S. D. Pinkerton (Eds.), *Sexual nature, sexual culture* (pp. 1–14). Chicago: University of Chicago Press.

Anderson, C. A., & Anderson, D. C. (1984). Ambient temperature and violent crime: Test of the linear and curvilinear hypotheses. *Journal of Personality and Social Psychology, 46,* 91–97.

Arnold, M. B. (1960). *Emotion and personality.* New York: Columbia University Press.

Aspinwall, L. G. (1998). Rethinking the role of positive affect in self-regulation. *Motivation and Emotion, 22,* 1–32.

Averill, J. R. (1982). *Anger and aggression: An essay on emotion.* New York: Springer-Verlag.

Bargh, J. A. (1997), The automaticity of everyday life. In R. S. Wyer, Jr. (Ed.), *The automaticity of everyday life: Advances in social cognition* (Vol. 10, pp. 1–61). Mahwah, NJ: Lawrence Erlbaum.

Bargh, J. A., Chaiken, S., Govender, R., & Pratto, F. (1992). The generality of the automatic attitude activation effect. *Journal of Personality and Social Psychology, 62,* 893–912.

Bargh, J. A., Chaiken, S., Raymond, P., & Hymes, C. (1996). The automatic evaluation effect: Unconditionally automatic attitude activation with a pronunciation task. *Journal of Experimental Social Psychology, 32,* 185–210.

Baron, R. A. (1987). Interviewer's mood and reactions to job applicants: The influence of affective states on applied social judgements. *Journal of Applied Social Psychology, 17,* 911–926.

Barr-Zisowitz, C. (2000). "Sadness"—Is there such a thing? In M. Lewis & J. M. Haviland-Jones (Eds.), *Handbook of emotions* (2nd ed., pp. 607–622). New York: Guilford.

Bem, D. J. (1972). Self-perception theory. In L. Berkowitz (Ed.), *Advances in Experimental Social Psychology* (Vol. 6, pp. 1–62). San Diego, CA: Academic.

Berkowitz, L. (1993). Towards a general theory of anger and emotional aggression: Implications of the cognitive-neoassociationistic perspective for the analysis of anger and emotion. In R. S. Wyer, Jr., & T. K. Srull (Eds.), *Perspectives on anger and emotion* (pp. 1–46). Hillsdale, NJ: Lawrence Erlbaum.

Blaney, P. H. (1986). Affect and memory: A review. *Psychological Bulletin, 99,* 229–246.

Blascovich, J. (1990). Individual differences in physiological arousal and perception of arousal: Missing links in Jamesian notions of arousal-based behaviors. *Personality and Social Psychology Bulletin, 16,* 665–675.

Bower, G. H. (1992). How might emotions affect learning? In S. A. Christianson (Ed.), *The handbook of emotion and memory* (pp. 3–31). Hillsdale, NJ: Lawrence Erlbaum.

Bower, G. H., & Forgas, J. P. (2000). Affect, memory, and social cognition. In E. Eich, J. F. Kihlstrom, G. H. Bower, J. P. Forgas, & P. M. Niedenthal (Eds.), *Cognition and emotion* (pp. 87–168). New York: Oxford University Press.

Briggs, J. (1970). *Never in anger: Portrait of an Eskimo family.* Cambridge, MA: Harvard University Press.

Bugental, D. B. (2000). Acquisition of the algorithms of social life: A domain-based approach. *Psychological Bulletin, 126,* 187–219.

Bull, N. (1951). *The attitude theory of emotion.* New York: Nervous and Mental Disease Monographs.

Cabanac, M. (1990). Taste: The maximization of multidimensional pleasure. In E. D. Capaldi & T. L. Pawley (Eds.), *Taste, experience, and feeding* (pp. 28–42). Washington DC: American Psychological Association.

Cacioppo, J. T., Berntson, G. G., Larsen, J. T., Poehlmann, K. M., & Ito, T. A. (2000). The psychophysology of emotion. In M. Lewis & J. M. Haviland-Jones (Eds.), *Handbook of emotions* (2nd ed., pp. 173–191). New York: Guilford.

Cacioppo, J. T., Gardner, W. L., & Berntson, G. G. (1999). The affect system: Form follows function. *Journal of Personality and Social Psychology, 76,* 839–855.

Camras, L. A. (2000). Surprise! Facial expressions can be coordinative motor structures. In M. D. Lewis and I. Granic (Eds.), *Emotion, development, and self-organization: Dynamic systems approaches to emotional development* (pp. 100–124). New York: Cambridge University Press.

Cantril, H. (1934). The roles of the situation and adrenalin in the induction of emotion. *The American Journal of Psychology, 46,* 568–579.

Cantril, H., & Hunt, W. A. (1932). Emotional effects produced by the injection of adrenalin. *The American Journal of Psychology, 44,* 300–307.

Carver, C. S. (2001). Affect and the functional bases of behavior: On the dimensional structure of affective experience. *Personality and Social Psychology Bulletin, 5,* 345–356.

Clark, M. S., Milberg, S. & Ross J. (1983). Arousal cues arousal-related material in memory. *Journal of Verbal Learning and Verbal Behavior, 22,* 633–649.

Cooper, J., Zanna, M. P., & Taves, P. A. (1978). Arousal as a necessary condition for attitude change following induced compliance. *Journal of Personality and Social Psychology, 36,* 1101–1106.

Davidson, R. J. (1992a). Emotion and affective style: Hemispheric substrates. *Psychological Science, 3,* 39–43.

Davidson, R. J. (1992b). A prolegomenon to the structure of emotion: Gleanings from neuropsychology. *Cognition and Emotion, 6,* 245–2658.

Dutton, D. G., & Aron, A. P. (1974). Some evidence for heightened sexual attraction under conditions of high anxiety. *Journal of Personality and Social Psychology, 30,* 510–517.

Easterbrook, J. A. (1959). The effects of emotion on cue utilization and the organization of behavior. *Psychological Review, 66,* 183–201.

Eich, E. (1995). Searching for mood dependent memory. *Psychological Science, 6,* 67–75.

Ekman, P. (1972). Universals and cultural differences in facial expression of emotion. In J. R. Cole (Ed.), *Nebraska Symposium on motivation* (Vol. 19, pp. 207–283). Lincoln: University of Nebraska Press.

Ekman, P., & Friesen, W. V. (1986). A new pan cultural expression of emotion. *Motivation and Emotion, 10,* 159–168.

Eysenck, M. W. (1982). Attention and arousal. New York: Springer-Verlag.

Fazio, R. H., Sanbonmatsu, D. M., Powell, M. C., & Kardes, F. R. (1986). On the automatic activation of attitudes. *Journal of Personality and Social Psychology, 50,* 229–238.

Fehr, B., & Russell, J. A. (1984). Concept of emotion viewed from a prototype perspective. *Journal of Experimental Psychology: General, 113,* 464–486.

Feldman-Barrett, L., & Russell, J. A. (2000). Unpublished raw data. [Pleasure and arousal in self-reports of emotion]

Fernández-Dols, J. M., & Ruiz-Belda, J. A. (1995). Expression of emotion versus expressions of emotion. In J. A. Russell, J. M. Fernández-Dols, A. S. R. Manstead, J. C. & Wellenkamp (Eds.), *Everyday conceptions of emotion: An introduction to the psychology, anthropology and linguistics of emotion* (pp. 505–522). Dordrech, The Netherlands: Kluwer Academic.

Fernández-Dols, J. M., & Ruiz-Belda, M, A. (1997). Spontaneous facial behavior during intense emotional episodes: Artistic truth and optical truth. In J. A. Russell & J. M. Fernández-Dols (Eds.), *The psychology of facial expression* (pp. 255–274). New York: Cambridge University Press.

Ferrandiz, A. (1984). *La Psicología de G. Marañón* [The psychology of G. Marañón]. Madrid, Spain: Ediciones de la Universidad Complutense.

Fischer, A. H. (1991). *Emotion scripts: A study of the social and cognitive faces of emotion.* Leiden, The Netherlands: DSWO.

Forgas, J. P. (1995). Mood and judgment: The affect infusion model (AIM). *Psychological Bulletin, 117,* 39–66.

Forgas, J. P., Bower, G. H., & Krantz, S. (1984). The influence of mood on perceptions of social interactions. *Journal of Experimental Social Psychology, 20,* 497–513.

Fridlund, A. J. (1994). *Human facial expression: An evolutionary view.* San Diego, CA: Academic.

Frijda, N. H. (1986). *The emotions.* Cambridge, England: Cambridge University Press.

Gerdes, E. P. (1979). Autonomic arousal as a cognitive cue in stressful situations. *Journal of Personality, 47,* 677–711.

Ginsburg, G. P., & Harrington, M. E. (1996). Bodily states and context in situated lines of action. In R. Harré & W. G. Parrott (Eds.), *The emotions: Social, cultural and biological dimensions* (pp. 229–258). London: Sage.

Gray, J. A. (1994). Three fundamental emotion systems. In P. Ekman & R. J. Davidson (Eds.), *The nature of emotion* (pp. 243–247). New York: Oxford University Press.

Gray, J. A. (1999). Cognition, emotion, conscious experience and the brain. In T. Dalgleish & M. J. Power (Eds.), *Handbook of cognition and emotion* (pp. 83–102). Chichester, England: Wiley.

Harré, R. (1986). *The social construction of emotions.* Oxford, England: Blackwell.

Higgins, E. T. (1987). Self-discrepancy theory: A theory relating self and affect. *Psychological Review, 94,* 319–340.

Humphreys, M. S., & Revelle, W. (1984). Personality, motivation, and performance: A theory of the relationship between individual differences and information processing. *Psychological Review, 91,* 153–184.

Isen, A. M. (1993). Positive affect and decision making. In M. Lewis & J. M. Haviland (Eds.), *Handbook of emotions.* (pp. 261–278). New York: Guilford.

Izard, C. E. (1977). *Human emotions.* New York: Plenum.

Izard, C. E., Wehmer, G. M., Livsey, W., & Jennings, J. R. (1965). Affect, awareness, and performance. In S. S. Tomkins & C. E. Izard (Eds.), *Affect, cognition, and personality* (pp. 2–41). New York: Springer-Verlag.

Katz, J. (1999). *How emotions work.* Chicago: University of Chicago Press.

Keltner, D. (1995). Signs of appeasement: Evidence for the distinct displays of embarrassment, amusement and shame. *Journal of Personality and Social Psychology, 68,* 441–454.

Keltner, D., Locke, K. D., & Audrain, P. C. (1998). The influence of attribution on the relevance of negative feelings to personal satisfaction. *Personality and Social Psychology Bulletin, 19,* 21–29.

Kemper, T. D. (1978). *A social interactional theory of emotions.* New York: Wiley.

Lakoff, G. (1987). *Women, fire, and dangerous things.* Chicago: University of Chicago Press.

Landis, C., & Hunt, W. A. (1934). Adrenalin and emotion. *Psychological Review, 39,* 467–485.

Lang, P. J. (1979). A bio-informational theory of emotion imagery. *Psychophysiology, 16,* 495–512.

Lang, P. J. (1994). The varieties of emotional experience: A meditation on James-Lange theory. *Psychological Review, 101,* 211–221.

Lazarus, R. S. (1991). *Emotion and adaptation.* New York: Oxford University Press.

LeDoux, J. (1996). *The emotional brain.* New York: Touchstone.

Lerner, J. S., & Keltner, D. (2000). Beyond valence: Toward a model of emotion-specific influences on judgment and choice. *Cognition and Emotion, 14,* 473–493.

Levy, R. I. (1973). *Tahitians.* Chicago: University of Chicago Press.

Lillard, A. (1998). Ethnopsychologies: Cultural variations in theories of mind. *Psychological Bulletin, 123,* 3–32.

Lutz, C. A. (1988). *Unnatural emotions: Everyday sentiments on a Micronesian atoll and their challenge to Western theory.* Chicago: University of Chicago Press.

Mandler, G. (1984). *Mind and body: Psychology of emotion and stress.* New York: Norton.

Marañón, G. (1924). Contribution a l'étude de l'action émotive de l'adrenaline. *Revue Française d'Endocrinologie, 2,* 301–325. [A study of the emotional effects of epinephrine]

Marañón, G. (1950). The psychology of gesture. *The Journal of Nervous and Mental Disease, 112,* 469–497.

Mayer, J. D., Gaschke, Y. N., Braverman, D. L., & Evans, T. W. (1992). Mood-congruent judgment is a general effect. *Journal of Personality and Social Psychology, 63,* 119–132.

Mellers, B. A. (2000). Choice and the relative pleasure of consequences. *Psychological Bulletin, 126,* 910–924.

Montgomery, W. (1985). Charles Darwin's thought on expressive mechanisms in evolution. In G. Zivin (Ed.), *The development of expressive behavior: Biology-environment interactions* (pp. 27–49). Orlando, FL: Academic.

Morris, W. N. (1989). *Mood: The frame of mind.* New York: Springer.

Niedenthal, P. M., Halberstadt, J. B., & Setterlund, M. B. (1997). Being happy and seeing "happy": Emotional state mediates visual word recognition. *Cognition and Emotion, 11,* 403–432.

Nisbett, R. E., & Schachter, S. (1966). Cognitive manipulation of pain. *Journal of Experimental Social Psychology, 2,* 227–236.

Oatley, K., & Johnson-Laird, P. N. (1987). Towards a cognitive theory of emotions. *Cognition and Emotion, 1,* 29–50.

Oatley, K., & Johnson-Laird, P. N. (1990). Semantic primitives for emotions. *Cognition and Emotion, 4,* 129–143.

Öhman, A. (1999). Distinguishing unconscious form conscious emotional processes: Methodological considerations and theoretical implications. In T. Dalgleish & M. J. Power (Eds.), *Handbook*

of cognition and emotion (pp. 321–352). Chichester, England: Wiley.

Olson, J. M. (1990). Self-inference processes in emotion. In J. M. Olson & M. P. Zanna (Eds.), *Self-inference processes: The Ontario Symposium* (Vol. 6, pp. 17–41). Hillsdale, NJ: Lawrence Erlbaum.

Ortony, A., Clore, G. L., & Collins, A. (1988). *The cognitive structure of emotions.* Cambridge, England: Cambridge University Press.

Ortony, A., & Turner, T. J. (1990). What's basic about basic emotions? *Psychological Review, 97,* 315–331.

Park, J., & Banaji, M. R. (2000). Mood and heuristics: The influence of happy and sad states on sensitivity and bias in stereotyping. *Journal of Personality and Social Psychology, 78,* 1005–1023.

Parkinson, B. (1995). *Ideas and realities of emotion.* London: Routledge.

Piliavin, I. M., Piliavin, J. A., & Rodin, J. (1975). Costs, diffusion, and the stigmatised victim. *Journal of Personality and Social Psychology, 32,* 429–438.

Pinel, J. P. J., Assanand, S., & Lehman, D. R. (2000). Hunger, eating and ill health. *American Psychologist, 55,* 1105–1116.

Rosaldo, M. Z. (1980). *Knowledge and passion: Ilongot notions of self and social life.* Cambridge, England: Cambridge University Press.

Rosch, E. H. (1978). Principles of categorization. In E. H. Rosch & B. B. Lloyd (Eds.), *Cognition and categorization* (pp. 27–71). Hillsdale, NJ: Lawrence Erlbaum.

Rosch, E. H. (1987). Wittgenstein and categorization research in cognitive psychology. In M. Chapman & M. Dixon (Eds). *Meaning and the growth of understanding: Wittgenstein's significance for developmental psychology* (pp. 151–166). Berlin, Germany: Springer-Verlag.

Ross, L., & Nisbett, R. E. (1991). *The person and the situation: Perspectives of social psychology.* New York: McGraw-Hill.

Rozin, P. (1999). Preadaptation and the puzzles and properties of pleasure. In D. Kahneman, E. Diener, & N. Schwarz (Eds.), *Well-being: The foundations of hedonic psychology* (pp. 109–133). New York: Russell Sage Foundation.

Russell, J. A. (1991). Culture and the categorization of emotion. *Psychological Bulletin, 110,* 426–450.

Russell, J. A. (1994). Is there universal recognition of emotion from facial expression? A review of the cross-cultural studies. *Psychological Bulletin, 115,* 102–141.

Russell, J. A., & Fehr, B. (1994). Fuzzy concepts in a fuzzy hierarchy: Varieties of anger. *Journal of Personality and Social Psychology, 67,* 186–205.

Russell, J. A., & Fernández-Dols, J. M. (1997). What does a facial expression mean? In J. A. Russell & J. M. Fernández-Dols (Eds.), *The psychology of facial expression* (pp. 3–30). New York: Cambridge University Press.

Russell, J. A., & Mehrabian, A. (1977). Evidence for a three-factor theory of emotions. *Journal of Research in Personality, 11,* 273–294.

Sanna, L. J. (1998). Defensive pessimism and optimism. *Cognition and Emotion, 12,* 635–665.

Schachter, S. (1964). The interaction of cognitive and physiological determinants of emotional state. In L. Berkowitz (Ed.), *Advances in Experimental Social Psychology,* (Vol. 1, pp. 48–81). New York: Academic.

Schachter, S., & Latané, B. (1964). Crime, cognition, and the autonomic nervous system. In D. Levine (Ed.), *Nebraska Symposium on motivation* (Vol. 12, pp. 221–275). Lincoln: University of Nebraska Press.

Schachter, S., & Wheeler, L. (1962). Epinephrine, chlorpromazine, and amusement. *Journal of Abnormal and Social Psychology, 65,* 121–128.

Scherer, K. R., Schorr, A., & Johnstone, T. (Eds.). (2001). *Appraisal processes in emotion: Theory, methods, research.* New York: Oxford University Press.

Schiffenbauer, A. (1974). Effect of observer's emotional state on judgments of the emotional state of others. *Journal of Personality and Social Psychology, 30,* 31–35.

Schwarz, N., & Bless, H. (1991). Happy and mindless, but sad and smart? The impact of affective states on analytic reasoning. In J. P. Forgas (Ed.), *Emotion and social judgements* (pp. 55–71). Oxford, England: Pergamon.

Schwartz, N., & Clore, G. L. (1988). How do I feel about it? The informative function of affective states. In K. Fiedler & J. P. Forgas (Eds.). *Affect, cognition, and social behavior* (pp. 44–62). Toronto, Ontario, Canada: Hogrefe.

Shizgal, P., & Conover, K. (1996). On the neural computation of utility. *Current Directions in Psychological Science, 5,* 37–43.

Shweder, R. A. (1994). "You are not sick, you are just in love": Emotion as an interpretative system. In P. Ekman, & R. J. Davidson (Eds.), *The nature of emotion: Fundamental questions* (pp. 32–44). New York: Oxford University Press.

Shweder, R. A., & Haidt, J. (2000). The cultural psychology of emotions: Ancient and new. In M. Lewis & J. M. Haviland-Jones (Eds.), *Handbook of emotions* (2nd ed., pp. 397–414). New York: Guilford.

Smith, C. A., & Ellsworth, P. C. (1985). Patterns of cognitive appraisal in emotion. *Journal of Personality and Social Psychology, 48,* 813–838.

Smith, C. A., & Kirby, L. D. (2001). Affect and cognitive appraisal processes. In J. P. Forgas (Ed.), *Handbook of affect and social cognition* (pp. 75–92). Mahwah, NJ: Lawrence Erlbaum.

Smith, C. A., & Scott, H. S. (1997). A componential approach to the meaning of facial expressions. In J. A. Russell & J. M. Fernandez-Dols (Eds.), *The psychology of facial expression* (pp. 229–254). New York: Cambridge University Press.

Solomon, R. C. (1976). *The passions.* Notre Dame, IN: University of Notre Dame Press.

Solomon, R. L. (1977). Addiction. In J. D. Maser & M. E. P. Seligman (Eds.), *Psychopathology: Experimental models* (pp. 66–103). San Francisco: Freeman.

Thayer, R. E. (1986). Activation-Deactivation Check List: Current overview and structural analysis. *Psychological Reports, 58,* 607–614.

Thayer, R. E. (1996). *The origin of everyday moods: Managing energy, tension, and stress.* New York: Oxford University Press.

Tomkins, S. S. (1962). *Affect, imagery, consciousness: Vol. 1. The positive affects.* New York: Springer.

Tomkins, S. S. (1963). *Affect, imagery, consciousness: Vol. 2. The negative affects* New York: Springer.

Watson, D., & Clark, L. A. (1992). Affects separable and inseparable: On the hierarchical arrangement of the negative affects. *Journal of Personality and Social Psychology, 62,* 489–505.

Watson, D., & Tellegen, A. (1985). Toward a consensual structure of mood. *Psychological Bulletin, 98,* 219–235.

Weiner, B. (1985). An attributional theory of achievement motivation and emotion. *Psychological Review, 92,* 548–573.

Wierzbicka, A. (1992). Defining emotion concepts. *Cognitive Science, 16,* 539–581.

Wierzbicka, A. (1999). *Emotions across languages and cultures.* New York: Cambridge University Press.

Zajonc, R. B. (1980). Feeling and thinking: Preferences need no inferences. *American Psychologist, 35,* 151–175.

Zajonc, R. B. (2000). Feeling and thinking. In J. P. Forgas (Ed.), *Feeling and thinking* (pp. 31–58). New York: Cambridge University Press.

Zanna, M. P., & Cooper, J. (1974). Dissonance and the pill: An attribution approach to studying the arousal properties of dissonance. *Journal of Personality and Social Psychology, 29,* 703–709.

Zillmann, D., & Bryant, J. (1974). Effect of residual excitation on the emotional response to provocation and delayed aggressive behavior. *Journal of Personality and Social Psychology, 30,* 782–791.

CHAPTER 13

Attitudes in Social Behavior

JAMES M. OLSON AND GREGORY R. MAIO

Popular culture seems obsessed with the concept of attitude. Entering the word *attitude* into an Internet search engine generates many listings, including "Art with Attitude," "Animals with Attitude," "Attitude Bikes," and "Spice Girls—Spicy Attitude." Moreover, the importance of attitude is frequently cited in promotional media (e.g., gym posters), self-help books (e.g., Russell-McCloud, 1999; Ryan, 1999), and even large-scale business conferences (e.g., Wal-Mart Canada, 1997). All of these examples support (albeit indirectly) Gordon Allport's (1935) famous assertion that attitude is one of the most indispensable constructs in social psychology.

In this chapter, we review social psychological research and theory about attitudes. In the first portion of the chapter, we define attitudes and compare this construct to other important social psychological constructs. Next, we discuss different theories about the psychological structure of attitudes, focusing on the theories' implications for measuring attitudes and the evidence supporting or refuting them. Third, we

examine the psychological functions served by attitudes. Fourth, we consider the relations among attitudes and between attitudes and higher-order constructs such as ideologies. Fifth, we identify important ways in which attitudes vary. Sixth, we address briefly how attitudes form. Seventh, we discuss the effects of attitudes on information processing. Finally, we consider the relation between attitudes and behavior.

WHAT ATTITUDES ARE AND WHAT ATTITUDES ARE NOT

When they define *attitudes,* social psychologists focus on the tendency to like or dislike an attitude object or behavior. That is, attitudes are defined as tendencies to *evaluate* objects favorably or unfavorably (Bem, 1970; Eagly & Chaiken, 1993; Fazio, 1990; Olson & Zanna, 1993; Petty, Wegener, & Fabrigar, 1997; Wood, 2000). Attitudes can be directed toward any identifiable object in our environment, including groups of people (e.g., ethnic groups), controversial issues (e.g., legalized abortion), and concrete objects (e.g., pizza). In fact, the potentially unlimited range of attitude objects sometimes causes confusion about the relations between attitudes and other social psychological constructs. For example, there is conceptual overlap between attitudes and values, which are abstract ideals that people consider to be important guiding principles in their lives (e.g., freedom; Rokeach, 1973; Schwartz, 1992). The *importance* component of values makes them distinct from attitudes (Feather, 1995; Maio & Olson, 1998), because positive attitudes do not imply that the targets are important guiding principles in life.

One fundamental attribute of attitudes is that they are subjective—that is, they reflect how a person sees an object and not necessarily how the object actually exists. Consequently, attitudes should be considered a part of the subjective self, which is the stream of thoughts, feelings, and actions that govern how someone lives (James, 1890).

STRUCTURE OF ATTITUDES

The relevance of attitudes to the subjective self suggests that attitudes may be connected to thoughts, feelings, and actions. This hypothesis raises the question of how attitudes are structured in the human mind. Understanding the mental structure of attitudes is potentially as important to attitude research as identifying the structure of DNA was to biological research. Uncovering the internal structure of attitudes can facilitate our understanding of how attitudes form, strengthen, and change.

In this section, we describe four well-established perspectives on attitude structure and their implications for attitude measurement. Two perspectives focus on the content of attitudes. These perspectives examine how attitudes may express more elemental psychological constructs, such as beliefs and emotions. The other two perspectives examine the dimensionality of attitudes—that is, these theories consider precisely how attitudes summarize positivity and negativity toward the attitude object. After reviewing attitude content and dimensionality, we describe some alternative attitude measures and the concept of implicit attitudes.

Attitude Content

Two perspectives have dominated research on the content of attitudes: the three-component model and the expectancy-value model. For both models, we describe their chief characteristics, implications for attitude measurement, and supporting evidence.

Three-Component Model

Guiding Assumptions   The three-component model hypothesizes that attitudes express people's beliefs, feelings, and past behaviors regarding the attitude object (Zanna & Rempel, 1988). For example, people might form a positive attitude toward eating spaghetti because spaghetti tastes good (affective component) and they believe that spaghetti is nutritious (cognitive component). Moreover, through the process of self-perception (Bem, 1972; Olson, 1992), people may decide that they like spaghetti because they can recall eating it often (behavioral component). Thus, this model suggests that people have positive attitudes toward an object when their beliefs, feelings, and behaviors express favorability toward an object, whereas people have negative attitudes toward an object when their beliefs, feelings, and behaviors express unfavorability toward the object.

We think it important to note, however, that the three-component view also regards attitudes as being distinct from the beliefs, feelings, and behaviors that influence them—following the adage that the whole is not simply the sum of its parts (Eagly & Chaiken, 1998; Zanna & Rempel, 1988). The attitude per se is a net evaluation of an attitude object; people can experience this evaluation when they encounter the attitude object, and they can store their attitude as a statement in memory (e.g., *ice cream is good*). Similarly, the attitude object can evoke the component beliefs, feelings, and behaviors, and the components can be subjectively represented in memory. Nonetheless, these components are more circumscribed in their focus. Beliefs are perceived associations between an object and its attributes, which may be evaluative in nature (e.g., *ice cream is fattening*); feelings are experiences of pleasant or unpleasant mood, which may be evoked by particular objects (e.g., *ice cream makes me relaxed*); and behaviors are overt acts that involve approaching or avoiding the object in some way (e.g., *I buy ice cream often*).

Measurement   The three-component model indicates that it is possible to obtain measures of overall attitudes without attempting to assess attitude-relevant beliefs, feelings, and behaviors. For example, attitudes are frequently measured using an attitude thermometer, which asks participants to use a thermometer-like scale to indicate the extent to which they feel favorable versus unfavorable toward the attitude object (Campbell, 1971; Haddock, Zanna, & Esses, 1993; Maio, Bell, & Esses, 1996; Wolsko, Park, Judd, & Wittenbrink, 2000). Using this scale, people can indicate a general evaluation, which may be derived from attitude-relevant beliefs, feelings, behaviors, or some combination of all three.

Nonetheless, such measures do not utilize the three-component model as rigorously as do measures that assess directly the attitude-relevant beliefs, feelings, and behaviors. Breckler (1984) provided an excellent example of the direct assessment of attitude-relevant beliefs, feelings, and behaviors. His research measured attitudes toward snakes and used a variety of verbal and nonverbal indicators. The verbal measures asked participants to rate (using self-report scales) their beliefs, feelings, and past behaviors toward snakes. The nonverbal measures assessed attitude-relevant affect and behavior, using recordings of participants' heart rate and behavior in the presence of a live snake. The verbal and nonverbal measures for each component were then aggregated to form overall indices for each attitude component.

Open-ended measures offer another method for assessing the three components of attitudes. These measures ask participants to list their beliefs, feelings, and behaviors regarding the attitude object (Esses & Maio, 2002; Haddock & Zanna, 1998). Participants then rate the valence of each response by using a semantic-differential scale. This approach makes it necessary for respondents to indicate responses that are accessible to them, rather than simply rate agreement with responses that the researcher presents (Esses & Maio, 2002).

Evidence In support of the three-component model, research has found that people's beliefs, feelings, and behaviors toward an attitude object are correlated but distinct. For example, Breckler (1984) found that people's beliefs, feelings, and behaviors toward snakes were moderately correlated when the components were assessed using verbal and nonverbal measures in a context in which a snake was present. His use of verbal *and* nonverbal measures provides a good test of the three-component model, because this technique corrects for the systematic measurement error that would occur if either technique were used alone. (In fact, the components were highly intercorrelated when verbal items alone were used in the absence of a snake.)

Using primarily pen-and-paper measures, additional research has examined the distinction between the cognitive and affective components, and such research has found moderate correlations for attitudes toward a large variety of objects (e.g., birth control, blood donation, microwaves; Breckler & Wiggins, 1989; Crites, Fabrigar, & Petty, 1994; Haddock & Zanna, 1998). Further, Trafimow and Sheeran (1998) found that attitude-relevant feelings and beliefs were clustered separately in memory.

Given the evidence that the cognitive and affective components are distinct, attitudes in different domains may be uniquely related to one or the other component. Consistent with this prediction, cognitive responses are strong predictors of attitudes toward a variety of controversial issues (e.g., capital punishment, legalized abortion, nuclear weapons; Breckler & Wiggins, 1991; Crites et al., 1994), whereas affective responses are strong predictors of attitudes toward blood donation (Breckler & Wiggins, 1989), intellectual pursuits (e.g., literature, math; Crites et al., 1994), smoking (Trafimow & Sheeran, 1998), and politicians (Glaser & Salovey, 1998).

Belief-Based Attitudes

Guiding Assumptions It is also possible to view attitudes as evaluative responses to an object that are influenced by beliefs alone (e.g., McGuire, 1960; Wyer, 1970). From this perspective, it is important to understand exactly how beliefs are interrelated and how beliefs are linked to affective responses. For example, a message might argue that it is good to reduce waste, and therefore that people should recycle waste. The message is persuasive if the message recipient accepts both the premise of the argument (i.e., reducing waste is good) and the implied link between the premise and the conclusion (i.e., recycling will reduce waste). Notice that the evaluative nature of the premise (reducing waste is good) introduces an evaluative bias into the conclusion—that is, people should become more *favorable* toward recycling because of its desirable implications for reducing waste. In this manner, attitudes can be evoked by beliefs (i.e., premises) that are evaluative in nature.

The notion that attitudes reflect the acceptance or rejection of evaluative premises is central to the well-known expectancy-value perspective on attitudes (e.g., the *theory of reasoned action;* Fishbein & Ajzen, 1975). According to this approach, an attitude is the sum of all of the evaluative beliefs regarding the attitude object. For instance, if people believe that recycling is easy and that recycling helps the environment, people should hold a positive attitude toward recycling. This attitude is positive because both beliefs link positively valued attributes to the behavior. Of course, beliefs are rarely held with absolute certainty. For example, a person may be only 70% certain that recycling is easy, but also be 100% certain that recycling helps the environment. According to the expectancy-value model, beliefs have less impact on attitudes when they are less certain. This reasoning is frequently summarized in a well-known equation: $A = \Sigma b_i e_i$, where A is the total attitude toward the attitude object, b_i is the subjective belief that the object possesses attribute i (e.g., the probability that recycling helps the environment), and e_i is the evaluation of attribute i (e.g., the positive value attached to the environment).

Measurement   The expectancy-value model prescribes a method for measuring attitudes: Participants must first consider a list of potential attributes of an attitude object and then for each attribute rate (a) the probability that the object possesses the attribute, and (b) the desirability of the attribute. In most research, the probability ratings are made using scales from −3 (*very improbable*) to +3 (*very probable*) or from 0 (*not at all*) to 1 (*definitely*). The evaluative ratings are made using evaluative scales from −3 (e.g., *very bad*) to +3 (e.g., *very good*). To derive the overall attitude, the product of the probability and evaluative ratings is computed for each attribute, and the products are summed across all of the attributes.

The expectancy-value model is also compatible with an open-ended thought-listing procedure for measuring attitudes. In this procedure, participants list their beliefs about the attributes of the attitude object, and they rate the desirability of each attribute. An overall index of attitude is then obtained by summing the desirability ratings. The thought-listing procedure does not require probability ratings because it elicits attributes that participants perceive as being highly associated with the attitude object (Esses, Haddock, & Zanna, 1993; Esses & Zanna, 1995).

Evidence   Research has examined the utility of the expectancy-value model by testing whether people's reports of their own attitudes are correlated with the summed products of the attitude-relevant expectancies and values. Results indicate that there are at least moderate correlations between attitudes and the expectancy-value products (e.g., Budd, 1986; van der Pligt & de Vries, 1998), although there have been statistical and methodological criticisms of these findings (e.g., Bagozzi, 1984; Sparks, Hedderley, & Shepherd, 1991).

To test the expectancy-value model directly, it is necessary to examine experimentally the causal impact of beliefs and evaluations on attitudes. Fortunately, studies of persuasion have yielded some support for the idea that persuasive messages influence evaluative beliefs, which influence attitudes (e.g., Maio, Bell, et al., 1996), although this effect may occur only when people are motivated and able to process persuasive messages in a systematic manner (Chaiken, Liberman, & Eagly, 1989; Petty & Cacioppo, 1986; E. P. Thompson, Kruglanski, & Spiegel, 2000).

Reconciling the Three-Component and Belief-Based Models

The comprehensiveness of the expectancy-value model is challenged by the findings noted earlier—that affect and past behavior predict attitudes independently of beliefs. This challenge can be met by the argument that affective reactions and past behaviors are simply different types of beliefs about the attitude objects. For example, the three-component model suggests that people may form a positive attitude toward an object that makes them feel happy. The expectancy-value model can account for this process by suggesting that people *believe* that the object makes them happy and *value* their own happiness—the effect of happiness is reduced to an expectancy-value product. Nevertheless, affective beliefs and behavioral beliefs are made salient only by considering the three-component model. Thus, at the very least, the three-component model spurs the expectancy-value formulation to consider different types of beliefs.

On the other hand, the three-component model would be more compelling if the relations between the three attitude components and attitudes fell into a discernible pattern that could be explained by prior theory. Discovering such a pattern is difficult, partly because there is conflicting evidence for some attitude objects. For example, Esses et al. (1993) found that affect played the greatest unique role in predicting attitudes toward two groups (French Canadian and native people), whereas beliefs about out-group values played the greatest unique role in predicting attitudes toward two other groups (Pakistani and homosexual people). These researchers also obtained evidence that the relative dominance of emotions and cognitions depended on individual differences and situational factors.

These findings indicate that there is a need for theory describing when one component should be more influential than another. Such a theory would need to consider evidence that the roles of affect and cognition may depend on the psychological functions fulfilled by attitudes (see Maio & Olson, 2000). For example, affective reactions may be stronger predictors of attitude when the attitude object has a hedonic purpose than when the object has a utilitarian purpose (Kempf, 1999). In addition, attitudes toward social partners become more imbued with affect as people get older and when they are diagnosed with a critical illness—conditions that presumably increase the importance of close affective ties with others (Carstensen, Isaacowitz, & Charles, 1999).

It is also important to consider that affect and cognition may have different processing requirements. For example, affective associations may be more accessible (Verplanken, Hofstee, & Janssen, 1998) and they may be processed more easily (Reeder & Pryor, 2000). Perhaps the ease of affective processing explains why (a) affective reactions exert a stronger influence on attitudes when there is a conflict between affect and cognition (Lavine, Thomsen, Zanna, & Borgida, 1998), (b) affect has a stronger influence on mental representations of others in general (Jussim, Nelson, Manis, & Soffin,

1995), and (c) affect is more closely related to the importance attached to social values (Maio & Olson, 1998).

The Dimensionality of Attitudes

The three-component model and the expectancy-value model describe the manner in which attitudes are related to beliefs, feelings, and behavior. Neither model, however, specifies precisely how attitudes summarize positivity and negativity in memory. There are two prominent perspectives on this question: the unidimensional model and the bidimensional model.

Unidimensional Model

Guiding Assumptions   The traditional perspective regards attitudes as being unidimensional evaluations, which express sentiments ranging from extreme unfavorability toward the attitude object to extreme favorability toward the attitude object. In other words, the unidimensional perspective assumes that attitudes can take the form of (a) favorability, (b) unfavorability, or (c) neither favorability nor unfavorability toward the attitude object. Thus, a person may feel either positively or negatively about the object, but not both at the same time.

Measurement   The most common measures of attitudes are based on the unidimensional perspective. These measures include bipolar semantic-differential scales, which are anchored by a negative adjective at one end (e.g., *bad*) and a positive adjective at the other end (e.g., *good*). For example, respondents could be asked to rate their attitude toward censorship using a 7-point scale from -3 (*very unfavorable*) to $+3$ (*very favorable*), with 0 (*neither favorable nor unfavorable*) in between. Respondents may be given many semantic differential scales, anchored by different adjective pairs (e.g., *good* vs. *bad; negative* vs. *positive*). To yield an overall index of attitudes, responses are averaged across the scales.

Another common procedure uses Likert-like scales. This technique utilizes many statements expressing varying degrees of favorability or unfavorability toward the attitude object. Examples might be *Censorship unfairly restricts access to information* and *Censorship is necessary to keep obscene material from children*. People respond to each item on a scale from -2 (*strongly disagree*) to $+2$ (*strongly agree*). To yield an overall index of attitudes, responses to the items that imply unfavorability toward the attitude object are reverse coded (e.g., $+2$ changes to -2), and responses to all items are then averaged.

Evidence   To some extent, the unidimensional model is supported by findings that unidimensional measures of attitude exhibit substantial criterion validity. That is, semantic-differential and Likert scales yield attitude scores that predict behavior (Ajzen & Fishbein, 1977; Kraus, 1995). In addition, the unidimensional model is consistent with Judd and Kulik's (1980) observation that people are faster at identifying their agreement or disagreement with extreme attitude positions than with neutral attitude positions. These researchers argued that this result should occur if people easily represent strong positivity (without any negativity) and strong negativity (without any positivity) in their minds.

Bidimensional Model

Guiding Assumptions   The bidimensional model rejects the notion that attitudes exist only on a single evaluative continuum from negativity to positivity. Instead, the bidimensional model suggests that attitudes subsume an evaluative tendency that varies in positivity and a separate evaluative tendency that varies in negativity. Consequently, attitudes can take the form of (a) favorability, (b) unfavorability, (c) neither favorability nor unfavorability, and (d) both favorability and unfavorability toward the attitude object.

Measurement   To measure attitudes from the bidimensional perspective, the positive and negative responses must be assessed separately. Kaplan (1972) suggested that any single semantic-differential scale could be split to yield separate positive and negative dimensions. For example, researchers could use a semantic-differential scale from -3 (*very bad*) to 0 (*neutral*) and a semantic-differential scale from 0 (*neutral*) to 3 (*very good*), rather than use a single semantic-differential scale from -3 (*very bad*) to 3 (*very good*). In this manner, separate negative and positive dimension scores are obtained. This approach prevents ambiguous neutral responses (Kaplan, 1972). That is, in single semantic-differential and Likert items, neutrality may stem from an absence of both positivity and negativity toward the attitude object, or it may stem from the simultaneous presence of both positivity and negativity; the split scales can differentiate between these two types of neutrality.

Split scales may be unnecessary when an attitude measure includes many items that assess both positive and negative attributes of the attitude object. For example, open-ended measures of attitude ask participants to list their beliefs about an attitude object and the emotions that the object elicits in them (see Esses & Maio, 2002; Haddock & Zanna, 1998). Using a traditional semantic-differential scale, participants then rate the valence of each response. This approach enables respondents to indicate some beliefs and emotions that are positive and some beliefs and emotions that are negative. Using this technique, a positive-dimension score can be derived from the sum or average of the positive ratings, and a negative-dimension score can be derived from the sum or average of the negative ratings (Bell, Esses, & Maio, 1996; Maio, Esses, & Bell, 2000).

Separation of the positive and negative dimensions enables the calculation of *ambivalence,* which is the simultaneous existence of positivity and negativity toward the attitude object (Kaplan, 1972; Olson & Zanna, 1993). Ambivalence is calculated using formulas that are designed to assess the extent to which there are high amounts of positivity *and* negativity rather than a high amount of positivity or negativity alone (e.g, Bell et al., 1996; Priester & Petty, 1996; M. M. Thompson, Zanna, & Griffin, 1995). We find it interesting, however, that the scores derived from these formulas exhibit only moderate correlations with subjective self-reports of ambivalence (approximately $r = .40$; Priester & Petty, 1996). Thus, although the objective and subjective measures possess some convergent validity, they must be tapping psychological processes that are at least somewhat distinct.

Evidence   If the bidimensional view is valid, people's favorability toward an attitude object should at least sometimes be largely unrelated to their unfavorability toward the object. In contrast, the unidimensional view suggests that there should be a strong negative correlation between positivity and negativity. In support of the bidimensional view, past research has found only moderate negative correlations between positivity and negativity, across a variety of attitude objects (e.g., different ethnic groups; Bell et al., 1996; Kaplan, 1972; I. Katz & Hass, 1988; M. M. Thompson et al., 1995; cf. Jonas, Diehl, & Brömer, 1997).

Cacioppo, Gardner, and Berntson (1997) observed that positivity and negativity toward an object do not change in parallel: (a) There is a tendency for people to initially possess more positivity than negativity toward attitude objects, and (b) positivity increases more slowly than does negativity. Therefore, it is plausible that positivity and negativity summarize different mental processes. Also, if the positive and negative dimensions are distinct, they should exhibit somewhat different correlations with other variables. Unfortunately, researchers have not yet systematically examined this issue.

Finally, if the bidimensional view is valid, the simultaneous existence of positivity and negativity (i.e., ambivalence) should have unique psychological consequences that are not predicted by the unidimensional model. And, indeed, researchers have found unique consequences of ambivalence (see the section on characteristics of attitudes later in this chapter).

Reconciling the Unidimensional and Bidimensional Perspectives

Despite the empirical support for the bidimensional view, it should be noted that most researchers have not examined the correlations between positivity and negativity while simultaneously controlling random *and* systematic measurement error. Failure to control for both sources of error can artifactually decrease the magnitude of the observed correlation (Green, Goldman, & Salovey, 1993), leaving the impression that the positive and negative dimensions are less strongly related than they actually are.

Even if future evidence supports the bidimensional model, it is plausible that the unidimensional model and bidimensional model are valid at different psychological levels. For instance, the bidimensional model may apply to attitude formation, in which people perceive the attitude object on both positive and negative dimensions; these dimensions might then be integrated to form a single, unidimensional evaluation (see Cacioppo et al., 1997). Alternatively, the unidimensional model may lose predictive validity as knowledge about the attitude object becomes more complex, because it becomes difficult to integrate the object's positive and negative attributes.

Neither perspective on attitude dimensionality explicitly considers implications of the fact that people can be made aware of many different exemplars of the attitude object, in addition to many attributes of each exemplar (Lord & Lepper, 1999). For example, when thinking of their attitude toward cheese, people can imagine the most recent type of cheese that they ate (e.g., fresh brie vs. processed cheese slices). The reported attitude will depend on which exemplar is retrieved because different exemplars are often associated with different attributes and evaluations. Thus, it is likely that attitudes subsume many different exemplars of the attitude object in addition to the varied attributes of the exemplars.

Alternative Attitude Measures

Past researchers have most often measured attitudes using self-report scales. An important limitation of self-report scales is that they are affected by tendencies to respond in a socially desirable manner (Paulhus, 1991). For example, people might be reluctant to report prejudice against ethnic groups because of the social stigma attached to prejudicial attitudes.

To overcome this problem, various techniques have been developed. For example, the bogus pipeline procedure (Jones & Sigall, 1971) deceives participants into believing that the researcher can detect their true feelings about an attitude object, after which participants are asked to report their attitude toward the attitude object. This technique has been shown to reduce social desirability in responses to simple self-report attitude measures (Roese & Jamieson, 1993).

Another approach involves assessing participants' physiological responses to attitude objects. Unfortunately, many physiological measures are incapable of distinguishing positive and negative affective reactions (e.g., skin conductance, papillary response; Petty & Cacioppo, 1983; Guglielmi, 1999). Positive and negative evaluations can be distinguished, however, using facial electromyography (EMG) recordings (Cacioppo, Petty, Losch, & Kim, 1986), which detect the relative amount of electrical activity in the muscles that control smiling and frowning.

Two other psychophysiological techniques show considerable promise. One technique detects a specific pattern of electrical activity in the centroparietal region of the brain (amplitude of the late positive potential: Cacioppo, Crites, & Gardner, 1996; Gardner, Cacioppo, Crites, & Berntson, 1994), whereas the other examines the frequency and latency of eye blinks for attitude objects (Ohira, Winton, & Oyama, 1998). Future research should test whether these techniques are more closely linked to one attitude component (e.g., affect) than to others and whether the techniques yield support for separate positive and negative dimensions in evaluations.

Implicit Attitudes

Another limitation of most self-report measures of attitudes is that they assess only explicit attitudes, which are consciously retrievable from memory. As discussed in Petty's chapter on attitude change, explicit, conscious attitudes may differ in numerous ways from implicit, nonconscious attitudes (Greenwald & Banaji, 1995; Wilson, Lindsey, & Schooler, 2000). Thus, it is useful to measure directly the nonconscious attitudes.

Several techniques are available to accomplish this goal. One approach involves extracting self-report, attitude-relevant information without relying directly on participants' conscious determination of their attitude. For example, researchers can calculate participants' attitudes from their responses to open-ended measures, even though these measures do not directly ask participants to report their attitudes. Other measures circumvent respondents' inferential processes more strongly by recording behavior that occurs outside of participants' conscious control. For example,

researchers can unobtrusively measure participants' nonverbal and verbal behaviors toward other people as an indication of liking (e.g., Fazio, Jackson, Dunton, & Williams, 1995; Word, Zanna, & Cooper, 1974). Because people have difficulty consciously monitoring such behaviors, their behaviors may often reveal attitudes of which the participants are unaware (see Dovidio, Kawakami, Johnson, Johnson, & Howard, 1997).

The most common measures of implicit attitudes use elaborate priming techniques (e.g., Dovidio et al., 1997; Fazio et al., 1995; Greenwald, McGhee, & Schwartz, 1998). For example, Fazio et al.'s (1995) "bona fide pipeline" presents participants with a target attitude object and asks participants to classify subsequently presented adjectives as being good or bad. Theoretically, positive evaluations should be activated in memory after viewing an attitude object that evokes a positive attitude. This priming of positive affect should cause participants to be faster at classifying positive adjectives (e.g., nice, pleasant) than at classifying negative adjectives (e.g., disgusting, repugnant). In contrast, after viewing an attitude object that evokes a negative attitude, participants should be slower at classifying positive adjectives than at classifying negative adjectives. Indeed, evidence from several studies suggests that the latency to classify positive versus negative adjectives is affected by the prior presentation of a liked or disliked attitude object, particularly when participants hold a strong attitude toward the attitude object (Fazio, 1993; Fazio, Sanbonmatsu, Powell, & Kardes, 1986; cf. Bargh, Chaiken, Govender, & Pratto, 1992). Moreover, attitude scores can be derived from the speed of responding to the positive versus negative adjectives following the positive versus negative primes, and these attitude scores predict attitude-relevant behavior toward the attitude object (Fazio et al., 1995). Greenwald et al.'s (1998) "implicit association test" similarly relies on facilitating versus inhibiting effects of evaluation on task performance. An interesting issue is whether such measures of implicit attitudes can be adapted to test the models of attitude content and attitude dimensionality.

ATTITUDE FUNCTIONS

Although models of attitude structure are useful for describing ways in which attitudes may be represented in memory, these models do not address attitude functions, which are the psychological motivations that attitudes fulfill (Olson & Zanna, 1993). Understanding the functions of attitudes should clarify why people bother to form and maintain attitudes, as well as how underlying motivations influence the valence and structure of attitudes.

Two early theoretical statements are the best-known models of attitude function (D. Katz, 1960; Smith, Bruner, & White, 1956). Smith et al. (1956) suggested that attitudes serve three functions: object appraisal, social adjustment, and externalization. *Object appraisal* refers to the ability of attitudes to summarize the positive and negative attributes of objects in our environment; *social adjustment* is served by attitudes that help us to identify with people whom we like and to dissociate from people whom we dislike; and *externalization* is fulfilled by attitudes that defend the self against internal conflict. D. Katz (1960) proposed four attitude functions, which overlap with those proposed by Smith et al. (1956): knowledge, utility, value expression, and ego defense. The *knowledge* function represents the ability of attitudes to summarize information about attitude objects; the *utilitarian* function exists in attitudes that maximize rewards and minimize punishments obtained from attitude objects; the *value-expressive* function exists in attitudes that express the self-concept and central values (e.g., equality, freedom; Maio & Olson, 1998; Rokeach, 1973; Schwartz, 1992); and the *ego-defensive* function protects self-esteem.

The object-appraisal function (which combines aspects of the utilitarian and knowledge functions) perhaps best explains why people form attitudes in the first place. This function implies that attitudes classify objects in the environment for the purposes of action. Moreover, it can be argued that *all* strong attitudes simplify interaction with the environment in this way, regardless of whether the attitudes imply favorability or unfavorability toward the attitude object.

Two important themes have emerged in research on attitude functions since these early theoretical statements. First, as just noted, evidence suggests that strong attitudes fulfill an object-appraisal function. Second, a distinction between instrumental attitudes (serving a utilitarian function) and symbolic attitudes (serving a value-expressive function) appears to be useful. In the following sections, we describe the evidence regarding these observations.

Object Appraisal

In their description of the object-appraisal function, Smith et al. (1956) hypothesized that attitudes are energy-saving devices, because attitudes make attitude-relevant judgments faster and easier to perform. Two programs of research have directly supported this reasoning while suggesting important caveats. First, Fazio (1995, 2000) argued that the object-appraisal function should be more strongly served by attitudes that are spontaneously activated from memory when the object is encountered than by attitudes that are not spontaneously retrieved. This prediction is based on the assumption that activated attitudes guide relevant judgments and behavior, whereas dormant attitudes have little effect during judgment and behavior processes. Consistent with this hypothesis is that highly accessible attitudes (either measured via response latency or manipulated via repeated attitude expression) have been shown to increase the ease with which people make attitude-relevant judgments. For example, people who have accessible attitudes toward an abstract painting have been shown to be subsequently faster at deciding whether they prefer the painting over another painting; they also exhibit less physiological arousal during these preference decisions than do people who have less accessible attitudes (see Fazio, 2000).

Another program of research has revealed that the strength of the object-appraisal motivation is influenced by levels of the need for closure, which is a "desire for a definite answer on some topic, *any* answer as opposed to confusion and ambiguity" (Kruglanski, 1989, p. 14). Of course, the object-appraisal function reflects the notion that attitudes can provide such answers because attitudes help people to make decisions about attitude objects. Consequently, a high need for closure should increase the desire to form and maintain attitudes. Kruglanski (1996) has tested this hypothesis using an individual difference measure of need for closure and situational manipulations of the need for closure (which involve imposing or withdrawing situational pressures to resolve uncertainty). As expected, the effects of need for closure on attitude change depended on whether participants had already formed an attitude toward the assigned topic. If participants had already formed an attitude, those who were high in need for closure were less persuaded by new information than were participants who were low in need for closure. In contrast, if participants had not yet formed an attitude, those who were high in need for closure were more persuaded by new information than were participants who were low in need for closure. Thus, the need for closure was associated with a tendency to form and maintain attitudes.

Instrumental Versus Symbolic Attitudes

Numerous researchers have argued for a distinction between instrumental (or utilitarian) and symbolic (or value-expressive) attitudes (e.g., Herek, 1986; Prentice, 1987; Sears, 1988). Instrumental attitudes classify attitude objects according to their ability to promote self-interest, whereas symbolic attitudes express concerns about self-image and personal values (Herek, 1986; Sears, 1988). This distinction has been used to understand attitudes toward many social groups (e.g., homosexual persons, persons with HIV, African Americans; Herek, 2000; Reeder & Pryor, 2000; Sears, 1988), consumer objects (Ennis & Zanna, 2000; Prentice, 1987; Shavitt, 1990), altruistic behaviors (Maio & Olson, 1995; Snyder, Clary, & Stukas, 2000), and political issues (Kinder & Sears, 1985; Lavine & Snyder, 2000).

At least three lines of research support this distinction. First, some attitude *objects* elicit attitudes that are associated primarily with one or the other of these functions. For example, Shavitt (1990) found that people's thoughts about air conditioners and coffee focus on the utility of the objects, whereas thoughts about greeting cards and flags tend to focus on the objects' capacity to symbolize the self and social values.

Second, evidence indicates that people are more persuaded by messages containing arguments that match the instrumental or symbolic functions of their attitudes than by messages containing arguments that do not match the functions of their attitudes. For example, Shavitt (1990) found that instrumental ads for instrumental products (e.g., an air conditioner) were more persuasive than were symbolic ads for instrumental products. Similarly, Snyder and DeBono (1985) found that low self-monitors (who typically possess instrumental attitudes) were more persuaded by instrumental ads for various products (e.g., whiskey, cigarettes) than were high self-monitors (whose attitudes typically fulfill social adjustive functions). Also, Prentice (1987) found that participants who attached high importance to symbolic values (e.g., mature love, self-respect) and symbolic possessions (e.g., family heirlooms) were less persuaded by messages that contained instrumental arguments than by messages that contained symbolic arguments. Presumably, these match effects occurred because people scrutinize arguments that match the function of their attitude more carefully than they scrutinize arguments that do not match the function of their attitude (Petty & Wegener, 1998). As a result, match effects occur only when the persuasive arguments are strong, but not when the persuasive arguments are weak (Petty & Wegener, 1998).

Finally, the distinction between instrumental and symbolic attitudes improves the measurement of attitudes and the prediction of behavior. Regarding attitude measurement, many studies have shown that attitudes toward ethnic groups are related to beliefs about the group members' values, over and above beliefs about the group members' implications for personal well-being (e.g., Esses et al., 1993; I. Katz & Hass, 1988; see also Schwartz & Struch, 1989). Also, when an attitude serves a symbolic function, personal values enhance the prediction of attitude-relevant behavior over and above beliefs about the positive or negative instrumental attributes of

the behavior and perceptions of group norms (Beck & Ajzen, 1991; Maio & Olson, 1995). Values exhibit weaker relations to attitudes and behaviors that serve utilitarian functions (Kristiansen & Zanna, 1988; Maio & Olson, 1994, 1995; cf. Maio & Olson, 2000).

ATTITUDES AND HIGHER-ORDER CONSTRUCTS

Attitudes do not, of course, exist in isolation from each other or from other constructs. For example, people who favor social assistance payments to the poor may on average possess positive attitudes toward other social welfare programs such as national health care and subsidized housing. The positive attitudes toward all of these programs may in turn arise because the person attaches high importance to the social value of helpfulness. Such relations among attitudes and values may have implications for stability and change in attitudes. In this section, we consider how attitudes are structurally and functionally related to each other and how sets of attitudes may be related to higher-order constructs such as values and ideologies.

Interattitude Structure

Heider's (1958) balance theory is one of the earliest models of relations between attitudes. This theory examined a situation in which a person (P) holds a positive or negative attitude toward another person (O), and both people (P and O) hold a positive or negative attitude toward a particular object (X). According to Heider, such P-O-X triads are *balanced* when P likes O and they hold the same (positive or negative) attitude toward X, or when P dislikes O and they hold different attitudes toward X. A state of *imbalance* occurs when P likes O and they hold different attitudes toward X, or when P dislikes O and they hold the same attitude toward X. In other words, balance exists when a person agrees with someone whom he or she likes, or when a person disagrees with someone whom he or she dislikes.

Heider (1958) predicted that unbalanced states create an unpleasant tension, which causes people to prefer balanced states. Subsequent research documented that participants report more discomfort with hypothetical unbalanced triads than with hypothetical balanced triads (e.g., Jordan, 1953). Individuals can convert unbalanced states to balanced states by using three strategies: Change the attitude toward O or X (*attitude change*), change the beliefs about O's attitude (*belief change*), or focus on some aspect of O or X that balances the triad (*differentiation*). In cases in which attitude change is the selected route to imbalance reduction, Heider did not indicate whether the attitude toward O or the attitude toward X is more likely to change.

Osgood and Tannenbaum's (1955) congruity theory addressed this latter issue by proposing that attitudes toward both O and X would change in the face of imbalance. In addition, these researchers predicted that the amount of attitude change would depend on the extremity of each attitude, such that the more extreme attitude would change the least. (Balance theory did not consider the role of attitude extremity.) These predictions have received some support (e.g., Tannenbaum, 1966), with important exceptions (e.g., Tannenbaum & Gengel, 1966).

Relations Between Attitudes, Values, and Ideologies

Attitudes and Values

Not only are different attitudes interconnected, but they may also be related to other, higher-order constructs such as values. The capacity of attitudes to express values is highlighted by theories describing the value-expressive function of attitudes (e.g., Herek, 1986; D. Katz, 1960) and by measures that specifically include value-relevant beliefs in the assessment of attitude components (e.g., Esses et al., 1993). In addition, Rokeach's (1973) seminal theory of values emphasized the role of values in driving attitudes. He suggested that a relatively small set of social values underlie most attitudes. Consistent with this reasoning, rankings of the importance of values have been shown to predict a large variety of attitudes and behavior (e.g., Maio, Roese, Seligman, & Katz, 1996). Moreover, priming a value makes accessible a variety of value-relevant attitudes, but priming value-relevant attitudes does not make accessible a variety of values (Gold & Robbins, 1979; Thomsen, Lavine, & Kounios, 1996), suggesting that values are above attitudes in the hierarchical network of attitudes, beliefs, and values.

The potential centrality of values is also reflected in Rosenberg's (1960, 1968) evaluative-cognitive consistency theory. According to this theory, people strive for consistency between their attitudes and social values. This pursuit of consistency is similar to the pursuit of balance in P-O-X triads. Specifically, people seek consistency across a series of person-value-object (P-V-X) triads or *bands*. Each band contains the person's attitude toward the attitude object (e.g., censorship), the person's belief in the importance of a particular value (e.g., freedom), and the perceived relation between the attitude object and the value (e.g., censorship threatens freedom). Moreover, for any given attitude object, the number of bands equals the number of relevant values, such that the bands differ only in their referent values (e.g.,

P-V_1-X, P-V_2-X, P-V_3-X). Rosenberg (1960) suggested that people are unlikely to restore consistency by changing personal values because each value can be relevant to many attitudes. Thus, changing a value may balance triads for one attitude object, but could also create imbalance in other triads. Consistent with this reasoning, Rosenberg observed that people were more likely to change their beliefs about the relations between an attitude object and relevant values than to change the values themselves.

Attitudes and Ideologies

Attitudes may also express ideologies, which are clusters of thematically related values and attitudes (Converse, 1964; McGuire, 1985). Liberalism and conservatism are well-known ideologies. Liberal ideologies encompass attitudes and values that promote universal rights and benevolence, whereas conservative ideologies encompass attitudes and values that promote freedom and self-enhancement (e.g., Kerlinger, 1984).

If the liberal-conservative dimension is a valid means for sorting political attitudes, then people should tend to endorse either conservative attitudes or liberal attitudes, but not both. Yet people's actual endorsement of liberal and conservative attitudes does not follow this simple pattern (Converse, 1964; Fleishman, 1986). Multidimensionality is most evident among people who lack expertise in political issues (Lavine, Thomsen, & Gonzales, 1997; Lusk & Judd, 1988). Researchers have found at least two distinct ideological dimensions within political attitudes: attitudes toward moral regulation versus individual freedom, and attitudes toward compassion versus competition (e.g., Ashton, Esses, & Maio, 2001; Boski, 1993).

There has been recent interest in ideologies from researchers examining nonpolitical attitudes as well. For example, researchers in the area of intergroup attitudes have examined several ideological dimensions, including multiculturalism versus color blindness (Wolsko et al., 2000) and individualism versus communalism (I. Katz & Hass, 1988). Diverse ideologies have also been examined in studies of attitudes toward gender roles (Spence, 1993), body weight and obesity (Quinn & Crocker, 1999), ways of life (de St. Aubin, 1996), and violence (Cohen & Nisbett, 1994).

At present, there is little evidence documenting precisely how attitudes express broad values and ideologies. For example, values may occasionally function as post hoc justifications for attitudes, rather than as their psychological basis (Kristiansen & Zanna, 1988). When causal influences of values and ideologies do occur, the effects may be indirect or direct. In an indirect effect, values and ideologies influence a specific attitude indirectly through other attitudes, whereas a direct effect occurs when people perceive the value itself as relevant to their attitude (Maio & Olson, 1994, 1995). The latter, direct process may be more likely when the value and the reasons for its importance have been consciously articulated (Maio & Olson, 1998).

CHARACTERISTICS OF ATTITUDES

Attitudes vary along numerous dimensions, or *characteristics,* that have significant implications for information processing, persistence, and behavior. A continuing issue in the literature on attitude has been the relations among these dimensions; some researchers have argued that the various characteristics are distinct and should be treated as independent, but other researchers have argued that the characteristics are interdependent and should be treated as manifestations of a smaller set of constructs. In this section, we briefly describe these dimensions and address the controversy surrounding the interrelations among them.

Extremity

Attitude extremity is the oldest and most basic dimension of attitudes. *Extremity* refers to the extent to which the attitude deviates from a neutral midpoint—that is, the extent to which the individual's evaluation is strongly favorable or strongly unfavorable. Extreme attitudes (compared to moderate attitudes) are more resistant to influence (e.g., Osgood & Tannenbaum, 1955), more likely to be projected onto others (e.g., Allison & Messick, 1988), and more likely to predict behavior (e.g., Fazio & Zanna, 1978). Attitude theorists have generally assumed that extreme attitudes develop over time, often resulting from actions that publicly commit the individual to his or her position.

Direct-Indirect Experience

Attitudes can be based on direct, personal experience with the attitude object, or they can be based on indirect information from others about the object. For example, students' attitudes toward chemistry courses can be based on their own experiences with previous chemistry courses or on things they have heard from others who have taken chemistry courses. Researchers have found that attitudes based on direct experience (compared to those based on indirect experience) are more confidently held (e.g., Fazio & Zanna, 1978), more stable over time (e.g., Doll & Ajzen, 1992), more resistant to influence (e.g., Wu & Shaffer, 1987), and more likely to predict behavior (e.g., Fazio & Zanna, 1981). Presumably, these effects of direct experience reflect that we trust our own senses more than we do others' reports, which increases confidence in attitudes based on direct experience.

Accessibility

Accessibility refers to the ease of activation (activation potential) of a construct (Higgins, 1996). Highly accessible attitudes are evaluations that come to mind quickly and spontaneously when the attitude object is encountered. Accessibility depends at least in part on the frequency with which the attitude has been activated in the recent past. Researchers have found that highly accessible attitudes (compared to less accessible attitudes) are more resistant to change (e.g., Bassili, 1996), more likely to influence perceptions of attitude-relevant events (e.g., Houston & Fazio, 1989), and more likely to predict behavior (e.g., Fazio & Williams, 1986). These effects of accessibility presumably reflect that highly accessible attitudes are always activated by the attitude object, so they exert an impact (compared to low accessibility attitudes, which are more likely to remain dormant).

Embeddedness

Attitude *embeddedness* (also called working knowledge) refers to the amount of attitude-relevant information, such as beliefs and experiences, that is linked to the attitude (Scott, 1968; Wood, 1982). The more information that comes to mind when one encounters the attitude object, the more embedded is the attitude. Highly embedded attitudes are more resistant to change (e.g., Wood, Rhodes, & Biek, 1995), more likely to influence perceptions of attitude-relevant stimuli (e.g., Vallone, Ross, & Lepper, 1985), and more predictive of behavior (e.g., Kallgren & Wood, 1986) than are attitudes with low embeddedness. These effects of embeddedness presumably reflect that attitudes based on a lot of information are held more confidently and provide the individual with many bits of knowledge to counteract the potential influence of new information. Also, embedded attitudes can be more accessible than are attitudes low in embeddedness (see Wood et al., 1995).

Evaluative Consistency

Evaluative consistency refers to the degree of consistency between the overall attitude (the evaluation) and one of its components (cognitive, affective, or behavioral information). Evaluative consistency occurs when the favorability of the overall evaluation of the object is similar to (a) the favorability implied by the individual's beliefs about the object (evaluative-cognitive consistency), (b) the favorability implied by the individual's feelings toward the object (evaluative-affective consistency), or (c) the favorability implied by the individual's behavioral experience with the object (evaluative-behavioral consistency). Most past research has examined evaluative-cognitive consistency (see Eagly & Chaiken, 1993, 1998). Attitudes that are high in evaluative consistency are more stable (e.g., Rosenberg, 1968), more resistant to change (e.g., Chaiken & Baldwin, 1981), more likely to influence information processing (e.g., Chaiken & Yates, 1985), and more likely to predict behavior (e.g., Chaiken, Pomerantz, & Giner-Sorolla, 1995) than are attitudes that are low in evaluative consistency. These effects of evaluative consistency probably reflect—at least in part—that consistent attitudes yield similar evaluative reactions to the object regardless of the situational salience of attitude components. Consistent attitudes might also be held more confidently and be more accessible than are inconsistent attitudes (see Chaiken et al., 1995).

Ambivalence

Ambivalence refers to the simultaneous presence of conflicting positive and negative elements within an attitude (Bell et al., 1996; Kaplan, 1972; I. Katz & Hass, 1988; M. M. Thompson et al., 1995). Ambivalence can occur between elements of the same component of an attitude, such as when people possess both positive and negative feelings about a minority group (intracomponent ambivalence), or between two components of an attitude, such as when people possess negative beliefs but positive feelings about junk food (intercomponent ambivalence). Attitudes that are ambivalent are likely also to be low in evaluative consistency, but the constructs are distinct: Low consistency refers to discrepancies between the overall evaluation and one component, whereas ambivalence refers to discrepancies between elements of a component or between components (Maio et al., 2000). Ambivalent attitudes have been shown (compared to nonambivalent attitudes) to be easier to change (e.g., Armitage & Conner, 2000) and to be less predictive of behavior (e.g., Lavine et al., 1998). Ambivalent attitudes have also been shown to polarize judgments when one of the conflicting elements is made more salient than another. For example, MacDonald and Zanna (1998) showed that individuals with ambivalent attitudes toward feminists made either more favorable or more unfavorable judgments about a feminist job applicant, depending on whether positive or negative information was made salient, whereas individuals with nonambivalent but equally extreme attitudes were not affected by the salience of positive or negative information. Ambivalent attitudes are hypothesized to have these polarizing effects because such attitudes contain both positive and negative information; priming can make available one or the other

category of information, which then influences judgments. There is also some evidence that ambivalent attitudes are less accessible than are nonambivalent attitudes (Bargh et al., 1992), which might explain in part why the former are more pliable and less predictive of behavior (Armitage & Conner, 2000).

Strength: An Integrative Concept?

The characteristics of attitudes discussed to this point overlap in several ways. First, they all tend to influence the degree to which attitudes are stable, resist change, affect the perception of attitude-relevant stimuli, and influence behavior. Also, the characteristics tend to be interrelated. For example, attitudes based on direct experience tend to be more extreme, less ambivalent, and more accessible; evaluatively consistent attitudes tend to be more accessible and less ambivalent; ambivalent attitudes tend to be less extreme and less accessible; and so on.

Intuitively, all of these characteristics reflect the extent to which attitudes are *important* to individuals (Krosnick, 1989) or are held with *conviction* (Abelson, 1988). The term *attitude strength* has become a common label for this quality (e.g., Petty & Krosnick 1995). Theorists have linked many attitude characteristics with strength, including extremity, intensity, certainty, importance, embeddedness, direct experience, accessibility, conviction, evaluative consistency, ambivalence, and vested interest (see Bassili, 1996; Krosnick & Abelson, 1992; Raden, 1985). Each of these characteristics incorporates aspects of subjective certainty, personal importance, and significant psychological and behavioral consequences.

Given the conceptual overlap among these various characteristics, theorists have wondered whether the variables represent more-or-less-interchangeable terms for attitude strength—in other words, whether the characteristics form a single dimension ranging from weak to strong attitudes. The most common way to investigate this issue has been to measure numerous characteristics and conduct a factor analysis of the data. If a single factor emerged, the unidimensional attitude strength notion would be supported, whereas if multiple factors emerged, a more complex framework would be suggested. Such studies have generally supported the multidimensional view (e.g., Abelson, 1988; Krosnick, Boninger, Chuang, Berent, & Carnot, 1993), although the precise structures of the factors emerging from the analyses have been inconsistent. Based on these data, the most common conclusion has been that the various characteristics should be viewed as distinct but related constructs (e.g., Krosnick et al., 1993; Raden, 1985).

Bassili (1996) proposed a distinction between "operative" and "meta-attitudinal" measures of attitude strength. Operative measures reflect ongoing processes that are related to attitude strength, whereas meta-attitudinal measures reflect the individual's conscious judgments about qualities that are related to the strength of his or her attitude. For example, response latency is an operative measure—it unobtrusively reveals the accessibility of the evaluation (one feature of attitude strength). In contrast, a subjective judgment of the importance of the attitude is a meta-attitudinal measure—it reflects a conscious judgment about a strength-related feature. In two studies, operative and meta-attitudinal measures of attitude strength were obtained from participants and used to predict resistance to influence and stability (two presumed consequences of attitude strength). Results showed that the operative measures predicted the criteria better than did the meta-attitudinal measures. Bassili concluded that operative measures of attitude strength are more valid than meta-attitudinal measures.

ATTITUDE FORMATION

Where do attitudes come from? How do they develop? As described in the earlier section on attitude structure, attitudes can be based on cognitive, affective, and behavioral information. Each of these possible avenues of attitude formation is discussed in the following section; a biological perspective on attitude formation is also introduced.

It is important to note that the psychological processes involved in attitude formation can also lead to attitude change (i.e., the alteration of an existing attitude to a different evaluative position), and that theories of attitude formation are also theories of attitude change. Because there is another chapter in this volume dedicated entirely to attitude change (see the chapter by Petty in this volume), we describe the mechanisms involved in attitude formation only briefly here.

Cognitive Processes

One crucial source of attitudes is cognitive information about the target—that is, beliefs about the attributes of the target. Indeed, as discussed in the section of this chapter on attitude structure, beliefs play a prominent role in both major models of attitude content. Knowledge about an object can come either from direct experience with the object or from indirect sources such as parents, peers, and the media. As already noted, attitudes based on direct experience tend to be stronger than are attitudes derived from indirect information.

The best-known theory of attitude formation based on cognitive beliefs is the *theory of reasoned action* (Fishbein & Ajzen, 1975), which is an expectancy-value model in which salient (i.e., highly accessible) beliefs are hypothesized to combine additively to form the overall evaluation of the target (attitude toward the target). As noted earlier in the chapter, many researchers have documented a strong relation between attitudes and expectancy-value products (e.g., Budd, 1986; van der Pligt & de Vries, 1998). This model of attitudes is based on a conception of humans as rational, deliberate thinkers who base their attitudes and behavior on information about the positive and negative consequences of various actions.

Affective Processes

Individuals' evaluations of targets can also be based on how the target makes them feel—that is, on the emotions or affect aroused by the target. Indeed, as noted in this chapter's section on attitude structure, affect sometimes predicts attitudes better than does cognition (e.g., see Esses et al., 1993). Of course, affect and cognition are often (or even usually) consistent with one another because these processes are mutually interdependent (e.g., knowledge can influence feelings, and feelings can guide thoughts).

Although affect toward objects can spring from beliefs about those objects, there are a number of processes that can result in affect's becoming associated with an object independently of cognition (i.e., independently of information about the characteristics of the object). These processes are discussed in detail in the section entitled "Low-Effort Attitude Change Processes" in the chapter on attitude change (see the chapter by Petty in this volume), so we only mention them here briefly. One process is classical conditioning, which occurs when a stimulus comes to evoke a response that it did not previously evoke, simply by being paired with another stimulus that already evokes that response. For example, the receptionist at a dental office might come to evoke negative affect for patients who are very fearful of dental work. Although a conditioning perspective on attitudes has been around for many years in social psychology (e.g., Staats & Staats, 1958), the past decade has continued to see very sophisticated studies documenting conditioning effects on attitudes (e.g., Cacioppo, Marshall-Goodell, Tassinary, & Petty, 1992).

A second process through which affect can become linked to objects without necessary cognitive mediation is mere exposure. The *mere exposure effect* (Zajonc, 1968) occurs when repeated, simple exposure to an object (i.e., exposure without reinforcement feedback) leads to more favorable feelings toward the object. For example, an abstract painting that initially evokes confusion might come to be liked over time—simply because the painting is more familiar. The results of several fascinating studies have shown that conscious recognition that stimuli are familiar is not necessary for the mere exposure effect to occur (e.g., Moreland & Beach, 1992), nor, in fact, is conscious *perception* of the object—subliminal exposures can increase liking for a stimulus (e.g., Bornstein & D'Agostino, 1992).

Behavioral Processes

A third potential source of attitudes is behavioral information—specifically, knowledge of one's previous actions toward a target. This knowledge can influence attitudes through a variety of processes, including dissonance arousal and self-perception processes. From the perspective of dissonance theory (Festinger, 1957), knowing that one has acted favorably or unfavorably toward a target will *motivate* an individual to evaluate the target in a manner consistent with those actions (e.g., Cooper & Fazio, 1984). From the perspective of self-perception theory (Bem, 1972), individuals might logically *infer* that their attitudes are consistent with their actions (e.g., Olson, 1992). Thus, an effect of past behavior on attitudes may reflect both cognitive and affective processes.

In a recent paper, Albarracin and Wyer (2000) reported several studies in which they cleverly tested the effects of knowledge about past behavior by leading participants to believe that they had expressed either support for or opposition to a particular position without being aware of it. Because participants had not actually engaged in such behavior, the research tested directly the effects of *believing* that one has behaved in a certain fashion. Results showed that participants reported attitudes that were consistent with the alleged past behavior and that subsequent behavior toward the target also tended to be consistent with the alleged prior action. Thus, behavioral information had a direct effect on attitudes and subsequent behavior.

Biological Processes

Social psychologists have directed little attention to biological processes in attitude formation. A few biological issues have been examined, including physiological concomitants of attitudes (e.g., Cacioppo & Petty, 1987), the impact of certain drugs on attitudes and persuasion (e.g., MacDonald, Zanna, & Fong, 1996), and the role of physiological arousal in specific attitudinal phenomena (e.g., Zanna & Cooper, 1974). In general, however, biological processes have been neglected by attitude researchers.

A provocative biological perspective on attitudes concerns the role of genetic factors. The field of behavioral genetics has begun to influence social psychologists, including attitude researchers. It is extremely unlikely, of course, that there are direct, one-to-one connections between genes and attitudes (e.g., a gene that causes attitudes toward capital punishment). Nevertheless, genes could establish general predispositions that shape environmental experiences in ways that increase the likelihood of an individual's developing specific traits and attitudes. For example, children who are naturally small for their age might be picked on by other children more than their larger peers are, with the result that the smaller children might develop anxieties about social interaction, resulting in consequences for their attitudes toward social events.

Arvey, Bouchard, Segal, and Abraham (1989) found that approximately 30% of the observed variance in job satisfaction in their sample of identical twins raised apart was attributable to genetic factors. Thus, respondents' attitudes toward their jobs appeared to be partly inherited. In addition, Eaves, Eysenck, and Martin (1989) reported the results of two surveys involving almost 4,000 pairs of same-sex twins. A variety of social attitudes were assessed, including those toward crime, religion, race, and lifestyle. Heritability estimates for individual items ranged from 1% to 62%, with a median of 39%.

But *how* do genes impact attitudes? What are some specific, genetically influenced characteristics that can systematically bias environmental experience so as to induce particular attitudes? Tesser (1993) identified several possibilities, including intelligence, temperament, and sensory structures. Olson, Vernon, Harris, and Jang (2001) measured some potential mediators of attitude heritability, including physical characteristics and personality factors, in a study of more than 300 pairs of same-sex twins. Most of these possible mediators were themselves highly heritable in the sample of twins, and multivariate analyses showed that several of the variables correlated at a genetic level with attitudes that were heritable. For example, the personality trait of sociability yielded a significant heritability coefficient and significant genetic correlations with five of the six heritable attitude measures. These data suggest that the heritability of sociability (see Zuckerman, 1995) might account in part for the heritable components of some attitudes.

Tesser (1993) hypothesized that attitudes that are highly heritable might have a biological basis that makes attitude change difficult, which could lead individuals to develop psychological defenses to protect the attitudes. For example, *niche building* might occur (see Plomin, DeFries, & Loehlin, 1977), such that individuals seek out environments that are compatible with their highly heritable attitudes. Tesser (1993; Tesser & Crelia, 1994) tested this idea in several ingenious ways. In all of his studies, attitudes that had been shown by Eaves et al. (1989) to have either high or low heritability coefficients were studied. In one study, individuals were found to provide answers more quickly for high than for low heritability attitudes. In another study, individuals were found to be less affected by conformity pressure when reporting high than when reporting low heritability attitudes. In a third study, interpersonal similarity on high heritability attitudes was shown to affect liking for others more than did similarity on low heritability attitudes. Finally, in two studies, individuals found agreement feedback more reinforcing when the agreement occurred for highly heritable attitudes than when it occurred for less heritable attitudes. These findings suggest that attitude strength is positively correlated with attitude heritability (see also Olson et al., 2001).

ATTITUDES AND INFORMATION PROCESSING

One of the fundamental functions of attitudes, as discussed earlier, is the object-appraisal function, which refers to the capacity of attitudes to facilitate both the identification of objects and the rapid appraisal of the objects' implications for the self. This function underscores that attitudes influence how objects are perceived and how information about those objects is processed. In this section we review research on the effects of attitudes on information processing. The theme of this section is *selectivity*—attitudes tend to facilitate the processing of information that is consistent with them and to inhibit the processing of inconsistent information.

Selective Attention

Festinger (1957) proposed in his *dissonance theory* that people want to believe that their decisions and attitudes are correct. Whereas individuals attend in an unbiased way to information prior to making decisions or forming attitudes, Festinger argued that after attitudes are formed, they motivate people to pay attention to consistent information and avoid inconsistent information. Early tests of this *selective exposure hypothesis* yielded little support (see Freedman & Sears, 1965), but researchers gradually identified boundary conditions for the effect (see Frey, 1986). For example, the utility, novelty, and salience of consistent versus inconsistent information must be controlled so that the effects of attitudinal consistency can be tested clearly. Researchers have documented selective attention in the laboratory (e.g., Frey & Rosch, 1984) and in field settings (e.g., Sweeney &

Gruber, 1984), and there is evidence that individuals with repressing-avoidance defensive styles may exhibit selective attention to consistent information more than do individuals with ruminative-approach defensive styles (Olson & Zanna, 1979).

There is also some evidence of a broader form of selective attention, which relates to the existence of strong attitudes per se. Specifically, Roskos-Ewoldsen and Fazio (1992) showed that objects toward which individuals have highly accessible attitudes (whether positive or negative) are more likely to attract attention than are objects toward which individuals have less accessible attitudes. Presumably, this selectivity effect is not motivated by a desire to believe one's attitudes to be correct, but rather by the functional value of quickly attending to objects that personal experience has shown to be potentially rewarding or punishing.

Selective Perception

Many researchers have shown that attitudes influence the perception or interpretation of attitude-relevant information, with the effect generally of interpreting information as more supportive of one's attitudes than is actually the case. For example, Vidmar and Rokeach (1974) found that viewers' perceptions of the television show *All in the Family* were related to their racial attitudes: Low-prejudice viewers saw the bigoted character of Archie Bunker as the principal target of humor and sarcasm in the show, whereas high-prejudice viewers saw Archie sympathetically and considered his liberal son-in-law Mike to be the principal target of humor and sarcasm. Similarly, Lord, Ross, and Lepper (1979) found that individuals' attitudes toward capital punishment predicted their assessments of the quality of two alleged scientific studies, one supporting and one questioning the deterrence value of the death penalty: Participants evaluated the study that apparently supported their own view more favorably than they evaluated the study that apparently disconfirmed their view. Houston and Fazio (1989) replicated this study and showed that the biasing effect of attitudes on the interpretation of information was significant only when the attitudes were highly accessible (see also Fazio & Williams, 1986; Schuette & Fazio, 1995). In another domain, Vallone et al. (1985) found that individuals' evaluations of the media coverage of an event were biased by their relevant attitudes (see also Giner-Sorolla & Chaiken, 1994).

If there is a general bias to perceive the world as consistent with one's attitudes, then existing attitudes might reduce the ability of perceivers to detect that the attitude object has changed. Indeed, Fazio, Ledbetter, and Towles-Schwen (2000) have documented such an effect and related it to attitude accessibility. Specifically, attitudes tended to interfere with participants' ability to perceive change in an attitude target, and this effect was stronger for highly accessible attitudes than for less accessible attitudes. In another set of studies, Stewart, Vassar, Sanchez, and David (2000) showed that participants' attitudes toward women's and men's societal roles influenced whether they individuated male or female targets more: Individuals with traditional sex-role attitudes individuated male targets more than they did female targets, whereas individuals with nontraditional sex-role attitudes individuated female targets more than they did male targets.

Selective Memory

Attitudes have long been thought to influence memory and learning of attitude-related information. A variety of processes could contribute to selective memory, including paying more attention to attitudinally consistent information (but see Roberts, 1985), finding it easier to store attitudinally consistent information, and finding it easier to retrieve attitudinally consistent information from memory. Early studies (e.g., Levine & Murphy, 1943) indicated that individuals learned and recalled information that was consistent with their attitudes better than they did information that was inconsistent with their attitudes. Subsequent researchers, however, had difficulty obtaining significant selective memory effects and questioned the reliability of the phenomenon (e.g., Greenwald & Sakumura, 1967).

In a comprehensive and detailed review and meta-analysis of research on attitude-memory effects, Eagly, Chen, Chaiken, and Shaw-Barnes (1999) concluded that the hypothesized attitude congeniality effect (i.e., information congenial with one's attitudes is more memorable than is uncongenial information) has been small in magnitude and inconsistent across studies. Especially worrisome was evidence that the effect has grown weaker in more recent experiments (compared to earlier experiments), because the recent studies have generally used more rigorous methods. It appears that selective memory may be a phenomenon weaker than selective attention and selective perception.

Perhaps the clearest evidence of selective memory has been obtained in studies testing whether individuals use their attitudes as clues for searching memory (i.e., studies specifically testing selective search and retrieval effects, as opposed to selective learning and memory in general). Ross (1989) reviewed a number of studies showing that people used their attitudes as clues for searching memory, reconstructing past events, or both. For example, Ross, McFarland, and Fletcher (1981) exposed respondents to one of two messages that had previously been shown to have reliable persuasive effects in

opposite directions. In an apparently separate study, respondents exposed to the persuasive message provided reports of the frequency with which they had performed a number of behaviors in the past month, including some behaviors related to the target of the persuasive message. Respondents reported more frequent behaviors consistent with the attitude promoted in their message than with the attitude promoted in the opposing message. Presumably, respondents used their newly formed attitudes to search their memories and to reconstruct their behaviors in the previous month.

Attitude Polarization

Attitudes guide information processing in another way—namely, they guide spontaneous thinking about the attitude object. Tesser (1978) showed that simply thinking about an attitude object tended to polarize the evaluation even in the absence of any new information. For example, simply thinking about a person who was either likable or unlikable led to stronger evaluations (positive for the likable target, negative for the unlikable partner) than did a control condition in which participants performed a distracting task. Presumably, the existing attitude led participants to generate thoughts that were consistent with it. This interpretation is supported by findings that polarization effects are stronger when the individual is knowledgeable about the attitude object and when the existing attitude is high in evaluative-cognitive consistency (see Chaiken & Yates, 1985).

ATTITUDES AND BEHAVIOR

We discussed earlier how attitudes fulfill various functions for individuals, including the rapid appraisal of attitude objects (object-appraisal function), the approach of rewarding objects and the avoidance of punishing objects (utilitarian function), the expression of underlying values and identity (value-expressive function), and so on. All of these hypothesized functions are predicated in part on the assumption that individuals behave in ways that are consistent with their attitudes—in other words, on the assumption that attitudes influence action. In this final section, we review some of the literature on attitude-behavior consistency.

The hypothesized strong relation between attitudes and behavior has sometimes proven difficult to document. For example, Wicker (1969) reviewed 30 studies that examined attitude-behavior consistency and concluded that there was "little evidence to support the postulated existence of stable, underlying attitudes within the individual which influence both his verbal expressions and his actions" (p. 75). Fortunately, since that time, researchers have identified several factors that influence attitude-behavior consistency, and the appropriate conclusion seems to be that measures of attitudes and behavior are closely related in some circumstances but not in others. We outline these factors in the following sections.

Compatibility of Attitude and Behavior Measures

An important conceptual advance came from Fishbein and Ajzen's (1975) theory of reasoned action. These theorists distinguished between attitudes toward objects and attitudes toward behaviors—a distinction that can also be viewed as general attitudes versus specific attitudes. Hypothetically, attitudes toward objects should influence the favorability of the *class* of behaviors related to the object, whereas attitudes toward behaviors should influence the favorability of those specific behaviors.

The point made by Fishbein and Ajzen was that for there to be a strong relation between measures of attitudes and behavior, the measures must be *compatible* (or congruent) in terms of their *specificity*: Measures of general attitudes (toward objects) predict general or broad behavior measures (encompassing the class of relevant behaviors, also called *multiple act behavioral criteria*), whereas measures of specific attitudes (toward behaviors) predict specific behavior measures (the single, focal behavior). Single behaviors can be specified along four dimensions: action (e.g., giving money), target (e.g., to a homeless person), context (e.g., on the street), and time (e.g., at lunchtime today). To predict single behaviors maximally, the measure of attitude should correspond on as many dimensions of specification as possible. For example, a measure of the individual's attitude toward *giving money to a homeless person on the street at lunchtime today* would be the best predictor of this specific behavior, whereas measures of attitudes that corresponded only on the action dimension (attitudes toward *giving money*) or only on the target dimension (attitudes toward *homeless people*) would rarely yield strong correlations. Many early researchers inappropriately used general attitude measures (e.g., participants' attitudes toward an ethnic group) to try to predict specific behavior measures (e.g., how participants behaved toward a particular member of the ethnic group in a particular setting at a particular time). When measures of attitudes and behavior have been highly compatible in terms of their specificity, attitude-behavior correlations have been substantial (see Ajzen & Fishbein, 1977; Kraus, 1995).

The impact of another kind of compatibility on attitude-behavior consistency was investigated by Lord, Lepper, and Mackie (1984). These researchers proposed a "typicality

effect," such that attitudes toward a social group would predict individuals' behavior toward typical members of the group better than the same attitudes would predict behavior toward atypical members of the group. Results showed that individuals' attitudes toward gay men predicted how they behaved toward a gay man who closely matched the stereotype better than the same attitudes predicted how they behaved toward a gay man who differed substantially from the stereotypical image of gay men. Thus, compatibility between group stereotypes and individual group members influences whether attitudes toward the group predict behavior toward those individual members (see also Blessum, Lord, & Sia, 1998).

Nature of the Behavior

Certain kinds of behavior are more predictable from attitudes than are other kinds of behavior. In particular, attitudes are hypothesized to guide only *volitional* actions—behaviors that individuals are free to perform or to not perform. When strong external incentives or constraints exist regarding an action, attitudes may not play much role in determining behavior. For example, politeness norms may cause people to say hello to coworkers whom they dislike. This conceptual point—that social pressures often guide behavior—was recognized in the theory of reasoned action (Fishbein & Ajzen, 1975) by including subjective norms as a determinant of behavioral intentions that was distinct from attitudes. *Subjective norms* refer to individuals' perceptions that other people who are important to them want them to act in certain ways.

Researchers have identified several factors, including the nature of the behavior, that influence the degree of impact that attitudes and norms exert on behavior. For example, Ybarra and Trafimow (1998) showed that increasing the accessibility of individuals' *private self* cognitions (i.e., assessments of the self by the self) led participants to place more weight on attitudes than on perceived norms in behavioral choices, whereas increasing the accessibility of individuals' *collective self* cognitions (assessments of the self by other people and reference groups) led participants to place more weight on perceived norms than on attitudes in behavioral choices. Presumably, these findings reflected that attitudes derive from personal preferences, whereas norms derive from other people.

Ajzen (1985, 1991) proposed a revision to the theory of reasoned action, which he labeled the *theory of planned behavior* (for a review, see Conner & Armitage, 1998). This model includes *perceived behavioral control* as another determinant of intentions and behavior, distinct from both attitudes and subjective norms. The construct of perceived

(see Tyler & Smith, 1998). Family and close relationships (see the chapter by Clark & Grote in this volume) are built upon positive attitudes, encompassing such concepts as love, trust, caring, and intimacy. Positive attitudes encourage good communication, which is the basis of effective relationships.

Research on consumer behavior is one of the clearest examples of the application of social psychological findings on attitudes (e.g., Cialdini, 1993; Reardon, 1991), with topics ranging from advertising to purchasing behavior. Finally, research on expectancies (see Olson, Roese, & Zanna, 1996) has shown that expectancies influence information processing and behavior. One of the principal sources of expectancies is attitudes—we expect good things from positively evaluated objects and bad things from negatively evaluated objects. These attitude-induced expectancies can lead to errors in information processing, biased hypothesis-testing, and self-fulfilling prophesies (see Olson et al., 1996).

CONCLUSIONS

Many issues and questions must be addressed in future research on attitudes in social behavior. One important issue is the internal structure of attitudes, including the dimensionality of attitudes and the conditions under which different components of attitudes are more influential than are other components. A related issue is the distinction between implicit attitudes and explicit attitudes (or between implicit and explicit measures of attitudes), including the question of which sorts of behavior are best predicted by each type of attitude (measure). The connections between attitudes and broader constructs like values and ideologies also need to be clarified. Turning to a different domain, the role of biological factors in attitude formation and change seems likely to receive more attention over the next decade. Finally, the connection between attitudes and behavior will continue to interest social psychologists, with models of attitude-behavior consistency becoming increasingly complex. For example, prediction may be improved by simultaneously taking into account attitudes toward all of the different behavioral options in a setting.

In closing, the evidence described in this chapter supports the importance of the construct of attitude. Because of their broad evaluative nature, attitudes may potentially reflect diverse beliefs, feelings, and behaviors. In addition, these evaluations serve a number of attitude functions and vary on several characteristics (e.g., ambivalence, certainty). Most important is that attitudes influence a wide variety of important social behaviors. Indeed, no matter what the setting, personal evaluations play a role in information processing and in behavior. The obsession of popular culture with the concept of attitude, noted at the outset of this chapter, is comprehensible when the ubiquity of attitudes is recognized.

REFERENCES

Abelson, R. P. (1988). Conviction. *American Psychologist, 43,* 267–275.

Ajzen, I. (1985). From intentions to actions: A theory of planned behavior. In J. Kuhl & J. Beckman (Eds.), *Action-control: From cognition to behavior* (pp. 11–39). Heidelberg, Germany: Springer.

Ajzen, I. (1991). The theory of planned behavior. *Organizational Behavior and Human Decision Processes, 50,* 179–211.

Ajzen, I., & Fishbein, M. (1977). Attitude-behavior relations: A theoretical analysis and review of empirical research. *Psychological Bulletin, 84,* 888–918.

Ajzen, I., Timko, C., & White, J. B. (1982). Self-monitoring and the attitude-behavior relation. *Journal of Personality and Social Psychology, 42,* 426–435.

Albarracin, D., & Wyer, R. S., Jr. (2000). The cognitive impact of past behavior: Influences on beliefs, attitudes, and future behavioral decisions. *Journal of Personality and Social Psychology, 79,* 5–22.

Allison, S. T., & Messick, D. M. (1988). The feature-positive effect, attitude strength, and degree of perceived consensus. *Personality and Social Psychology Bulletin, 14,* 231–241.

Allport, G. W. (1935). Attitudes. In C. Murchison (Ed.), *Handbook of social psychology* (pp. 798–844). Worcester, MA: Clark University Press.

Armitage, C. J., & Conner, M. (2000). Attitude ambivalence: A test of three key hypotheses. *Personality and Social Psychology Bulletin, 26,* 1421–1432.

Arvey, R. D., Bouchard, T. J., Segal, N. L., & Abraham, L. M. (1989). Job satisfaction: Environmental and genetic components. *Journal of Applied Psychology, 74,* 187–192.

Ashton, M. C., Esses, V. M., & Maio, G. R. (2001). *Two dimensions of political attitudes and their individual difference correlates.* Manuscript submitted for publication.

Bargh, J. A., Chaiken, S., Govender, R., & Pratto, F. (1992). The generality of the automatic attitude activation effect. *Journal of Personality and Social Psychology, 62,* 893–912.

Bassili, J. N. (1996). Meta-judgmental versus operative indexes of psychological attributes: The case of measures of attitude strength. *Journal of Personality and Social Psychology, 71,* 637–653.

Beck, L., & Ajzen, I. (1991). Predicting dishonest actions using the theory of planned behavior. *Journal of Research in Personality, 25,* 285–301.

Bell, D. W., Esses, V. M., & Maio, G. R. (1996). The utility of open-ended measures to assess intergroup ambivalence. *Canadian Journal of Behavioural Science, 28,* 12–18.

Bem, D. J. (1970). *Beliefs, attitudes, and human affairs*. Belmont, CA: Brooks/Cole.

Bem, D. J. (1972). Self-perception theory. In L. Berkowitz (Ed.), *Advances in experimental social psychology* (Vol. 6, pp. 1–62). San Diego, CA: Academic Press.

Blessum, K. A., Lord, C. G., & Sia, T. L. (1998). Cognitive load and positive mood reduce typicality effects in attitude-behavior consistency. *Personality and Social Psychology Bulletin, 24,* 497–504.

Bornstein, R. F., & D'Agostino, P. R. (1992). Stimulus recognition and the mere exposure effect. *Journal of Personality and Social Psychology, 63,* 545–552.

Boski, P. (1993). Socio-political value orientations among Poles in presidential '90 and '91 elections. *Polish Psychological Bulletin, 20,* 551–567.

Breckler, S. J. (1984). Empirical validation of affect, behavior, and cognition as distinct components of attitude. *Journal of Personality and Social Psychology, 47,* 1191–1205.

Breckler, S. J., & Wiggins, E. C. (1989). Affect versus evaluation in the structure of attitudes. *Journal of Experimental Social Psychology, 25,* 253–271.

Breckler, S. J., & Wiggins, E. C. (1991). Cognitive responses in persuasion: Affective and evaluative determinants. *Journal of Experimental Social Psychology, 27,* 180–200.

Budd, R. J. (1986). Predicting cigarette use: The need to incorporate measures of salience in the theory of reasoned action. *Journal of Applied Social Psychology, 16,* 663–685.

Cacioppo, J. T., Crites, S. L., Jr., & Gardner, W. L. (1996). Attitudes to the right: Evaluative processing is associated with lateralized late positive event-related brain potentials. *Personality and Social Psychology Bulletin, 22,* 1205–1219.

Cacioppo, J. T., Gardner, W. L., & Berntson, G. G. (1997). Beyond bipolar conceptualizations and measures: The case of attitudes and evaluative space. *Personality and Social Psychology Review, 1,* 3–25.

Cacioppo, J. T., Marshall-Goodell, B. S., Tassinary, L. G., & Petty, R. E. (1992). Rudimentary determinants of attitudes: Classical conditioning is more effective when prior knowledge about the attitude stimulus is low than high. *Journal of Experimental Social Psychology, 28,* 207–233.

Cacioppo, J. T., & Petty, R. E. (1987). Stalking rudimentary processes of social influence: A psychophysiological approach. In M. P. Zanna, J. M. Olson, & C. P. Herman (Eds.), *Social influence: The Ontario symposium* (Vol. 5, pp. 41–74). Hillsdale, NJ: Erlbaum.

Cacioppo, J. T., Petty, R. E., Losch, M. E., & Kim, H. S. (1986). Electromyographic activity over facial muscle regions can differentiate the valence and intensity of affective reactions. *Journal of Personality and Social Psychology, 50,* 260–268.

Campbell, A. (1971). *White attitudes toward Black people*. Ann Arbor, MI: Institute for Social Research.

Carstensen, L. L., Isaacowitz, D. M., & Charles, S. T. (1999). Taking time seriously: A theory of socioemotional selectivity. *American Psychologist, 54,* 165–181.

Chaiken, S., & Baldwin, M. W. (1981). Affective-cognitive consistency and the effect of salient behavioral information on the self-perception of attitudes. *Journal of Personality and Social Psychology, 41,* 1–12.

Chaiken, S., Liberman, A., & Eagly, A. H. (1989). Heuristic and systematic processing within and beyond the persuasion context. In J. S. Uleman & J. A. Bargh (Eds.), *Unintended thought* (pp. 212–252). New York: Guilford.

Chaiken, S., Pomerantz, E. M., & Giner-Sorolla, R. (1995). Structural consistency and attitude strength. In R. E. Petty & J. A. Krosnick (Eds.), *Attitude strength: Antecedents and consequences* (pp. 387–412). Hillsdale, NJ: Erlbaum.

Chaiken, S., & Yates, S. (1985). Affective-cognitive consistency and thought-induced attitude polarization. *Journal of Personality and Social Psychology, 49,* 1470–1481.

Cialdini, R. B. (1993). *Influence: Science and practice* (3rd ed.). New York: Harper-Collins.

Cohen, D., & Nisbett, R. E. (1994). Self-protection and the culture of honor: Explaining Southern violence. *Personality and Social Psychology Bulletin, 20,* 551–567.

Conner, M., & Armitage, C. J. (1998). Extending the theory of planned behavior: A review and avenues for further research. *Journal of Applied Social Psychology, 28,* 1429–1464.

Converse, P. E. (1964). The nature of belief systems in mass publics. In D. E. Apter (Ed.), *Ideology and discontent* (pp. 206–261). New York: Free Press.

Cooper, J., & Fazio, R. H. (1984). A new look at dissonance theory. In L. Berkowitz (Ed.), *Advances in experimental social psychology* (Vol. 17, pp. 229–262). New York: Academic Press.

Crites, S. L., Fabrigar, L. R., & Petty, R. E. (1994). Measuring the affective and cognitive properties of attitudes: Conceptual and methodological issues. *Personality and Social Psychology Bulletin, 20,* 619–634.

de St. Aubin, E. (1996). Personal ideology polarity: Its emotional foundation and its manifestation in individual value systems, religiosity, political orientation, and assumptions concerning human nature. *Journal of Personality and Social Psychology, 71,* 152–165.

Doll, J., & Ajzen, I. (1992). Accessibility and stability of predictors in the theory of planned behavior. *Journal of Personality and Social Psychology, 63,* 754–765.

Dovidio, J. F., Kawakami, K., Johnson, C., Johnson, B., & Howard, A. (1997). On the nature of prejudice: Automatic and controlled processes. *Journal of Experimental Social Psychology, 33*(5), 510–540.

Duval, S., & Wicklund, R. A. (1972). *A theory of objective self-awareness*. New York: Academic Press.

Eagly, A. H., & Chaiken, S. (1993). *The psychology of attitudes*. Fort Worth, TX: Harcourt Brace Jovanovich.

Eagly, A. H., & Chaiken, S. (1998). Attitude structure and function. In D. T. Gilbert, S. T. Fiske, & G. Lindzey (Eds.), *The handbook of social psychology* (4th ed., Vol. 1, pp. 269–322). New York: McGraw-Hill.

Eagly, A. H., Chen, S., Chaiken, S., & Shaw-Barnes, K. (1999). The impact of attitudes on memory: An affair to remember. *Psychological Bulletin, 125,* 64–89.

Eaves, L., Eysenck, H. J., & Martin, N. G. (1989). *Genes, culture, and personality: An empirical approach.* London: Academic Press.

Ennis, R., & Zanna, M. P. (2000). Attitude function and the automobile. In G. R. Maio & J. M. Olson (Eds.), *Why we evaluate: Functions of attitudes* (pp. 395–415). Mahwah, NJ: Erlbaum.

Esses, V. M., Haddock, G., & Zanna, M. P. (1993). Values, stereotypes, and emotions as determinants of intergroup attitudes. In D. M. Mackie & D. L. Hamilton (Eds.), *Affect, cognition, and stereotyping: Interactive processes in group perception* (pp. 137–166). New York: Academic Press.

Esses, V. M., & Maio, G. R. (2002). Expanding the assessment of attitude components and structure: The benefits of open-ended measures for assessing attitude structure. In W. Stroebe & M. Hewstone (Eds.), *European review of social psychology, 12,* 71–102. London: Chichester, UK: Wiley.

Esses, V. M., & Zanna, M. P. (1995). Mood and the expression of ethnic stereotypes. *Journal of Personality and Social Psychology, 69,* 1052–1068.

Fazio, R. H. (1990). Multiple processes by which attitudes guide behavior: The MODE model as an integrative framework. In M. P. Zanna (Ed.), *Advances in experimental social psychology* (Vol. 23, pp. 75–109). San Diego, CA: Academic Press.

Fazio, R. H. (1993). Variability in the likelihood of automatic attitude activation: Data re-analysis and commentary on Bargh, Chaiken, Govender, and Pratto (1992). *Journal of Personality and Social Psychology, 64,* 753–758, 764–765.

Fazio, R. H. (1995). Attitudes as object-evaluation associations: Determinants, consequences, and correlates of attitude accessibility. In R. E. Petty & J. A. Krosnick (Eds.), *Attitude strength: Antecedents and consequences* (pp. 247–282). Hillsdale, NJ: Erlbaum.

Fazio, R. H. (2000). Accessible attitudes as tools for object appraisal: Their costs and benefits. In G. R. Maio & J. M. Olson (Eds.), *Why we evaluate: Functions of attitudes* (pp. 1–36). Mahwah, NJ: Erlbaum.

Fazio, R. H., Jackson, J. R., Dunton, B. C., & Williams, C. J. (1995). Variability in automatic activation as an unobtrusive measure of racial attitudes: A bona fide pipeline? *Journal of Personality and Social Psychology, 69,* 1013–1027.

Fazio, R. H., Ledbetter, J. E., & Towles-Schwen, T. (2000). On the costs of accessible attitudes: Detecting that the attitude object has changed. *Journal of Personality and Social Psychology, 78,* 197–210.

Fazio, R. H., Sanbonmatsu, D. M., Powell, M. C., & Kardes, F. R. (1986). On the automatic activation of attitudes. *Journal of Personality and Social Psychology, 50,* 229–238.

Fazio, R. H., & Williams, C. J. (1986). Attitude accessibility as a moderator of the attitude-perception and attitude-behavior relations: An investigation of the 1984 presidential election. *Journal of Personality and Social Psychology, 51,* 505–514.

Fazio, R. H., & Zanna, M. P. (1978). Attitudinal qualities relating to the strength of the attitude-behavior relationship. *Journal of Experimental Social Psychology, 14,* 398–408.

Fazio, R. H., & Zanna, M. P. (1981). Direct experience and attitude-behavior consistency. In L. Berkowitz (Ed.), *Advances in experimental social psychology* (Vol. 14, pp. 161–202). San Diego, CA: Academic Press.

Feather, N. (1995). Values, valences, and choice: The influence of values on the perceived attractiveness and choice of alternatives. *Journal of Personality and Social Psychology, 68,* 1135–1151.

Fenigstein, A., Scheier, M. F., & Buss, A. H. (1975). Public and private self-consciousness: Assessment and theory. *Journal of Applied Psychology, 43,* 522–527.

Festinger, L. (1957). *A theory of cognitive dissonance.* Evanston, IL: Row, Peterson.

Fishbein, M., & Ajzen, I. (1975). *Belief, attitude, intention, and behavior: An introduction to theory and research.* Reading, MA: Addison-Wesley.

Fleishman, J. A. (1986). Types of political attitude structure: Results of a cluster analysis. *Public Opinion Quarterly, 50,* 371–386.

Freedman, J. L., & Sears, D. O. (1965). Selective exposure. In L. Berkowitz (Ed.), *Advances in experimental social psychology* (Vol. 2, pp. 57–97). San Diego, CA: Academic Press.

Frey, D. (1986). Recent research on selective exposure to information. In L. Berkowitz (Ed.), *Advances in experimental social psychology* (Vol. 19, pp. 41–80). San Diego, CA: Academic Press.

Frey, D., & Rosch, M. (1984). Information seeking after decisions: The roles of novelty of information and decision reversibility. *Personality and Social Psychology Bulletin, 10,* 91–98.

Gardner, W., Cacioppo, J. T., Crites, S., & Berntson, G. (1994). A late positive brain potential indexes between participant differences in evaluative categorizations. *Psychophysiology, 31,* S49.

Giner-Sorolla, R., & Chaiken, S. (1994). The causes of hostile media judgments. *Journal of Experimental Social Psychology, 30,* 165–180.

Glaser, J., & Salovey, P. (1998). Affect in electoral politics. *Personality and Social Psychology Review, 2,* 156–172.

Gold, J. A., & Robbins, M. A. (1979). Attitudes and values: A further test of the semantic memory model. *Journal of Social Psychology, 108,* 75–81.

Gollwitzer, P. M., & Moskowitz, G. B. (1996). Goal effects on action and cognition. In E. T. Higgins & A. W. Kruglanski (Eds.), *Social psychology: Handbook of basic principles* (pp. 361–399). New York: Guilford.

Goodstadt, M. (1971). Helping and refusal to help: A test of balance and reactance theories. *Journal of Experimental Social Psychology, 7,* 610–622.

Green, D. P., Goldman, S. L., & Salovey, P. (1993). Measurement error masks bipolarity in affect ratings. *Journal of Personality and Social Psychology, 64,* 1029–1041.

Greenwald, A. G., & Banaji, M. R. (1995). Implicit social cognition: Attitudes, self-esteem, and stereotypes. *Psychological Review, 102,* 4–27.

Greenwald, A. G., McGhee, D. E., & Schwartz, J. L. K. (1998). Measuring individual differences in implicit cognition: The implicit association test. *Journal of Personality and Social Psychology, 74,* 1464–1480.

Greenwald, A. G., & Sakumura, J. S. (1967). Attitude and selective learning: Where are the phenomena of yesteryear? *Journal of Personality and Social Psychology, 7,* 387–397.

Guglielmi, R. S. (1999). Psychophysiological assessment of prejudice: Past research, current status, and future directions. *Personality and Social Psychology Review, 3,* 123–157.

Haddock, G., & Zanna, M. P. (1998). On the use of open-ended measures to assess attitudinal components. *British Journal of Social Psychology, 37,* 129–149.

Haddock, G., Zanna, M. P., & Esses, V. M. (1993). Assessing the structure of prejudicial attitudes: The case of attitudes toward homosexuals. *Journal of Personality and Social Psychology, 65,* 1105–1118.

Heider, F. (1958). *The psychology of interpersonal relations.* New York: Wiley.

Herek, G. M. (1986). The instrumentality of attitudes: Toward a neofunctional theory. *Journal of Social Issues, 42*(2), 99–114.

Herek, G. M. (2000). The social construction of attitudes: Functional consensus and divergence in the U.S. public's reactions to AIDS. In G. R. Maio & J. M. Olson (Eds.), *Why we evaluate: Functions of attitudes* (pp. 325–364). Mahwah, NJ: Erlbaum.

Higgins, E. T. (1996). Knowledge activation: Accessibility, applicability, and salience. In E. T. Higgins & A. W. Kruglanski (Eds.), *Social psychology: Handbook of basic principles* (pp. 133–168). New York: Guilford.

Houston, D. A., & Fazio, R. H. (1989). Biased processing as a function of attitude accessibility: Making objective judgments subjectively. *Social Cognition, 7,* 51–66.

Jonas, K., Diehl, M., & Brömer, P. (1997). Effects of attitude ambivalence on information processing and attitude-intention consistency. *Journal of Experimental Social Psychology, 33,* 190–210.

Jones, E. E., & Sigall, H. (1971). The bogus pipeline: A new paradigm for measuring affect and attitude. *Psychological Bulletin, 76,* 349–364.

Jordon, N. (1953). Behavioral forces that are a function of attitudes and cognitive organization. *Human Relations, 6,* 273–287.

Judd, C. M., & Kulik, J. A. (1980). Schematic effects of social attitudes on information processing and recall. *Journal of Personality and Social Psychology, 38,* 569–578.

Jussim, L., Nelson, T. E., Manis, M., & Soffin, S. (1995). Prejudice, stereotypes, and labeling effects: Sources of bias in person perception. *Journal of Personality and Social Psychology, 68,* 228–246.

Kallgren, C. A., & Wood, W. (1986). Access to attitude-relevant information in memory as a determinant of attitude-behavior consistency. *Journal of Experimental Social Psychology, 22,* 328–338.

Kaplan, K. J. (1972). On the ambivalence-indifference problem in attitude theory and measurement: A suggested modification of the semantic differential technique. *Psychological Bulletin, 77,* 361–372.

Kardes, F. R., Sanbonmatsu, D. M., Voss, R. T., & Fazio, R. H. (1986). Self-monitoring and attitude accessibility. *Personality and Social Psychology Bulletin, 12,* 468–474.

Katz, D. (1960). The functional approach to the study of attitudes. *Public Opinion Quarterly, 24,* 163–204.

Katz, I., & Hass, R. G. (1988). Racial ambivalence and American value conflict: Correlational and priming studies of dual cognitive structures. *Journal of Personality and Social Psychology, 55,* 893–905.

Kempf, D. S. (1999). Attitude formation from product trial: Distinct roles of cognition and affect for hedonic and functional products. *Psychology and Marketing, 16,* 35–50.

Kerlinger, F. N. (1984). *Liberalism and conservatism: The nature and structure of social attitudes.* Hillsdale, NJ: Erlbaum.

Kinder, D. R., & Sears, D. O. (1985). Public opinion and political action. In G. Lindzey & E. Aronson (Eds.), *Handbook of social psychology* (3rd ed., Vol. 2, pp. 659–741). New York: Random House.

Kraus, S. J. (1995). Attitudes and the prediction of behavior: A meta-analysis of the empirical literature. *Personality and Social Psychology Bulletin, 21,* 58–75.

Kristiansen, C. M., & Zanna, M. P. (1988). Justifying attitudes by appealing to values: A functional perspective. *British Journal of Social Psychology, 27,* 247–256.

Krosnick, J. A. (1989). Attitude importance and attitude accessibility. *Personality and Social Psychology Bulletin, 15,* 297–308.

Krosnick, J. A., & Abelson, R. P. (1992). The case for measuring attitude strength in surveys. In J. Tanur (Ed.), *Questions about questions* (pp. 177–203). New York: Sage.

Krosnick, J. A., Boninger, D. S., Chuang, Y. C., Berent, M. K., & Carnot, C. G. (1993). Attitude strength: One construct or many related constructs? *Journal of Personality and Social Psychology, 65,* 1132–1151.

Kruglanski, A. W. (1989). *Lay epistemics and human knowledge: Cognitive and motivational bases.* New York: Plenum.

Kruglanski, A. W. (1996). Motivated social cognition: Principles of the interface. In E. T. Higgins & A. W. Kruglanski (Eds.), *Social psychology: Handbook of basic principles* (pp. 493–520). New York: Guilford.

Lavine, H., & Snyder, M. (2000). Cognitive processes and the functional matching effect in persuasion: Studies of personality and political behavior. In G. R. Maio & J. M. Olson (Eds.), *Why we evaluate: Functions of attitudes* (pp. 97–131). Mahwah, NJ: Erlbaum.

Lavine, H., Thomsen, C. J., & Gonzales, M. H. (1997). The development of interattitudinal consistency: The shared-consequences model. *Journal of Personality and Social Psychology, 72,* 735–749.

Lavine, H., Thomsen, C. J., Zanna, M. P., & Borgida, E. (1998). On the primacy of affect in the determination of attitudes and behavior: The moderating role of affective-cognitive ambivalence. *Journal of Experimental Social Psychology, 34,* 398–421.

Levine, J. M., & Murphy, G. (1943). The learning and forgetting of controversial material. *Journal of Abnormal and Social Psychology, 38,* 507–517.

Lord, C. G., & Lepper, M. R. (1999). Attitude representation theory. In M. P. Zanna (Ed.), *Advances in experimental social psychology* (Vol. 31, pp. 265–343). San Diego, CA: Academic Press.

Lord, C. G., Lepper, M. R., & Mackie, D. M. (1984). Attitude prototypes as determinants of attitude-behavior consistency. *Journal of Personality and Social Psychology, 46,* 1254–1266.

Lord, C. G., Ross, L., & Lepper, M. R. (1979). Biased assimilation and attitude polarization: The effects of prior theories on subsequently considered evidence. *Journal of Personality and Social Psychology, 37,* 2098–2109.

Lusk, C. M., & Judd, C. M. (1988). Political expertise and the structural mediators of candidate evaluations. *Journal of Experimental Social Psychology, 24,* 105–126.

MacDonald, T. K., & Zanna, M. P. (1998). Cross-dimension ambivalence toward social groups: Can ambivalence affect intentions to hire feminists? *Personality and Social Psychology Bulletin, 24,* 427–441.

MacDonald, T. K., Zanna, M. P., & Fong, G. T. (1996). Why common sense goes out the window: The effects of alcohol on intentions to use condoms. *Personality and Social Psychology Bulletin, 22,* 763–775.

Maio, G. R., Bell, D. W., & Esses, V. M. (1996). Ambivalence and persuasion: The processing of messages about immigrant groups. *Journal of Experimental Social Psychology, 32,* 513–536.

Maio, G. R., Esses, V. M., & Bell, D. W. (2000). Examining conflict between components of attitudes: Ambivalence and inconsistency are distinct constructs. *Canadian Journal of Behavioural Science, 32,* 58–70.

Maio, G. R., & Olson, J. M. (1994). Value-attitude-behavior relations: The moderating role of attitude functions. *British Journal of Social Psychology, 33,* 301–312.

Maio, G. R., & Olson, J. M. (1995). Relations between values, attitudes, and behavioral intentions: The moderating role of attitude

function. *Journal of Experimental Social Psychology, 31,* 266–285.

Maio, G. R., & Olson, J. M. (1998). Values as truisms: Evidence and implications. *Journal of Personality and Social Psychology, 74,* 294–311.

Maio, G. R., & Olson, J. M. (2000). What *is* a value-expressive attitude? In G. R. Maio & J. M. Olson (Eds.), *Why we evaluate: Functions of attitudes* (pp. 249–269). Mahwah, NJ: Erlbaum.

Maio, G. R., Roese, N. J., Seligman, C., & Katz, A. (1996). Ratings, rankings, and the measurement of values: Evidence for the superior validity of ratings. *Basic and Applied Social Psychology, 18,* 171–181.

McGuire, W. J. (1960). A syllogistic analysis of cognitive relationships. In C. I. Hovland & M. J. Rosenberg (Eds.), *Attitude organization and change: An analysis of consistency among attitude components* (pp. 65–111). New Haven, CT: Yale University Press.

McGuire, W. J. (1985). Attitudes and attitude change. In G. Lindzey & E. Aronson (Eds.), *Handbook of social psychology* (3rd ed., Vol. 2, pp. 233–346). New York: Random House.

Moreland, R. L., & Beach, S. R. (1992). Exposure effects in the classroom: The development of affinity among students. *Journal of Experimental Social Psychology, 28,* 255–276.

Ohira, H., Winton, W. M., & Oyama, M. (1998). Effects of stimulus valence on recognition memory and endogenous eyeblinks: Further evidence for positive-negative asymmetry. *Personality and Social Psychology Bulletin, 24,* 986–993.

Olson, J. M. (1992). Self-perception of humor: Evidence for discounting and augmentation effects. *Journal of Personality and Social Psychology, 62,* 369–377.

Olson, J. M., Roese, N. J., & Zanna, M. P. (1996). Expectancies. In E. T. Higgins & A. W. Kruglanski (Eds.), *Social psychology: Handbook of basic principles* (pp. 211–238). New York: Guilford.

Olson, J. M., Vernon, P. A., Harris, J. A., & Jang, K. L. (2001). The heritability of attitudes: A study of twins. *Journal of Personality and Social Psychology, 80.*

Olson, J. M., & Zanna, M. P. (1979). A new look at selective exposure. *Journal of Experimental Social Psychology, 15,* 1–15.

Olson, J. M., & Zanna, M. P. (1993). Attitudes and attitude change. *Annual Review of Psychology, 44,* 117–154.

Osgood, C. E., & Tannenbaum, P. H. (1955). The principle of congruity in the prediction of attitude change. *Psychological Review, 62,* 42–55.

Ouellette, J. A., & Wood, W. (1998). Habit and intention in everyday life: The multiple processes by which past behavior predicts future behavior. *Psychological Bulletin, 124,* 54–74.

Paulhus, D. L. (1991). Measurement and control of response bias. In J. P. Robinson, P. R. Shaver, & L. S. Wrightsman (Eds.), *Measures of personality and social psychological attitudes* (Vol. 1, pp. 17–59). San Diego, CA: Academic Press.

Petty, R. E., & Cacioppo, J. T. (1983). The role of bodily responses in attitude measurement and change. In J. T. Cacioppo & R. E. Petty (Eds.), *Social psychophysiology: A sourcebook* (pp. 51–101). New York: Guilford.

Petty, R. E., & Cacioppo, J. T. (1986). The elaboration likelihood model of persuasion. In L. Berkowitz (Ed.), *Advances in experimental social psychology* (Vol. 19, pp. 123–205). San Diego, CA: Academic Press.

Petty, R. E., & Krosnick, J. A. (Eds.). (1995). *Attitude strength: Antecedents and consequences.* Mahwah, NJ: Erlbaum.

Petty, R. E., & Wegener, D. T. (1998). Matching versus mismatching attitude functions: Implications for scrutiny of persuasive messages. *Personality and Social Psychology Bulletin, 24,* 227–240.

Petty, R. E., Wegener, D. T., & Fabrigar, L. R. (1997). Attitudes and attitude change. *Annual Review of Psychology, 48,* 609–647.

Plomin, R. DeFries, J. C., & Loehlin, J. C. (1977). Genotype-environment interaction and correlation in the analysis of human behavior. *Psychological Bulletin, 84,* 309–322.

Prentice, D. A. (1987). Psychological correspondence of possessions, attitudes, and values. *Journal of Personality and Social Psychology, 53,* 993–1003.

Priester, J. R., & Petty, R. E. (1996). The gradual threshold model of ambivalence: Relating the positive and negative bases of attitudes to subjective ambivalence. *Journal of Personality and Social Psychology, 71,* 431–449.

Quinn, D. M., & Crocker, J. (1999). When ideology hurts: Effects of belief in the Protestant Ethic and feeling overweight on the psychological well-being of women. *Journal of Personality and Social Psychology, 77,* 402–414.

Raden, D. (1985). Strength-related attitude dimensions. *Social Psychology Quarterly, 48,* 312–330.

Reardon, K. K. (1991). *Persuasion in practice.* Newbury Park, CA: Sage.

Reeder, G. D., & Pryor, J. B. (2000). Attitudes toward persons with HIV/AIDS: Linking a functional approach with underlying process. In G. R. Maio & J. M. Olson (Eds.), *Why we evaluate: Functions of attitudes* (pp. 295–323). Mahwah, NJ: Erlbaum.

Roberts, J. V. (1985). The attitude-memory relationship after 40 years: A meta-analysis of the literature. *Basic and Applied Social Psychology, 6,* 221–241.

Roese, N. J., & Jamieson, D. W. (1993). Twenty years of bogus pipeline research: A critical review and meta-analysis. *Psychological Bulletin, 114,* 363–375.

Rokeach, M. (1973). *The nature of human values.* New York: Free Press.

Rosenberg, M. J. (1960). An analysis of affective-cognitive consistency. In C. I. Hovland & M. J. Rosenberg (Eds.), *Attitude organization and change: An analysis of consistency among attitude components* (pp. 15–64). New Haven, CT: Yale University Press.

Rosenberg, M. J. (1968). Hedonism, inauthenticity, and other goals toward expansion of a consistency theory. In R. P. Abelson, E. Aronson, W. J. McGuire, T. M. Newcomb, M. J. Rosenberg, & P. H. Tannenbaum (Eds.), *Theories of cognitive consistency: A sourcebook* (pp. 827–833). Chicago: Rand-McNally.

Roskos-Ewoldsen, D. R., & Fazio, R. H. (1992). The accessibility of source likability as a determinant of persuasion. *Personality and Social Psychology Bulletin, 18,* 19–25.

Ross, M. (1989). Relation of implicit theories to the construction of personal histories. *Psychological Review, 96,* 341–357.

Ross, M., McFarland, C., & Fletcher, G. J. O. (1981). The effect of attitude on the recall of personal histories. *Journal of Personality and Social Psychology, 40,* 627–634.

Russell-McCloud, P. (1999). *A is for attitude: An alphabet for living.* New York: Harper Collins.

Ryan, M. J. (1999). *Attitudes of gratitude: How to give and receive joy every day of your life.* Berkeley, CA: Conari Press.

Scheier, M. F., Buss, A. H., & Buss, D. M. (1978). Self-consciousness, self-report of aggressiveness, and aggression. *Journal of Research in Personality, 12,* 133–140.

Schwartz, S. H. (1992). Universals in the content and structure of values: Theoretical advances and empirical tests in 20 countries. In M. P. Zanna (Ed.), *Advances in experimental social psychology* (Vol. 25, pp. 1–65). San Diego, CA: Academic Press.

Schwartz, S. H., & Struch, N. (1989). Values, stereotypes, and intergroup antagonism. In D. Bar-Tal, C. F. Graumann, A. W. Kruglanski, & W. Stroebe (Eds.), *Stereotyping and prejudice.* New York: Springer.

Schuette, R. A., & Fazio, R. H. (1995). Attitude accessibility and motivation as determinants of biased processing: A test of the MODE model. *Personality and Social Psychology Bulletin, 21,* 704–710.

Scott, W. A. (1968). Attitude measurement. In G. Lindzey & E. Aronson (Eds.), *Handbook of social psychology* (2nd ed., Vol. 2, pp. 204–273). Reading, MA: Addison-Wesley.

Sears, D. O. (1988). Symbolic racism. In P. A. Katz & D. A. Taylor (Eds.), *Eliminating racism: Profiles in controversy* (pp. 53–84). New York: Plenum.

Shavitt, S. (1990). The role of attitude objects in attitude functions. *Journal of Experimental Social Psychology, 26,* 124–148.

Smith, M. B., Bruner, J. S., & White, R. W. (1956). *Opinions and personality.* New York: Wiley.

Snyder, M. (1987). *Public appearances, private realities.* New York: Freeman.

Snyder, M., Clary, E. G., & Stukas, A. A. (2000). The functional approach to volunteerism. In G. R. Maio & J. M. Olson (Eds.), *Why we evaluate: Functions of attitudes* (pp. 365–393). Mahwah, NJ: Erlbaum.

Snyder, M., & DeBono, K. G. (1985). Appeals to image and claims about quality: Understanding the psychology of advertising. *Journal of Personality and Social Psychology, 49,* 586–597.

Snyder, M., & Kendzierski, D. (1982). Acting on one's attitudes: Procedures for linking attitudes and behavior. *Journal of Experimental Social Psychology, 18,* 165–183.

CHAPTER 14

The Social Self

ROY F. BAUMEISTER AND JEAN M. TWENGE

It is difficult to think about the self without referring to other people. Although the very concept of the self seems to denote individualism, the self is nevertheless incomplete without acknowledging our interactions with others. People often describe themselves in terms of relationships (husband, son, mother) or as a member of a profession (and thus as a member of a social group). Even personality traits are usually conceptualized in comparison to other people (one is not extraverted per se, but extraverted compared to others). Self-esteem reflects what others think (Leary, Tambor, Terdal, & Downs, 1995). Attempts at self-control can benefit or harm others (e.g., smoking and drinking; Baumeister, Heatherton, & Tice, 1994). People's behavior can be radically affected by social rejection or exclusion (Twenge, Baumeister, Tice, & Stucke, 2001; K. D. Williams, Cheung, & Choi, 2000). Selves do not develop and flourish in isolation. People learn who and what they are from other people, and they always have identities as members of social groups. By the same token, close personal relationships are potent and probably crucial to the development of selfhood. A human being who spent his or

her entire life in social isolation would have a stunted and deficient self.

In addition, the self is inherently interpersonal because relating to others is part of what the self is *for*. The self is constructed, used, altered, and maintained as a way of connecting the individual organism to other members of its species. By this we are not positing a mysterious homunculus that creates the self to serve its own purposes. Instead, we begin by acknowledging that the need to belong is a fundamental human need that serves the innate biological goals of survival and reproduction (see Baumeister & Leary, 1995), and so psychological mechanisms such as the self are likely to be shaped to foster interpersonal connection. The biological evolution of the species presumably established the cognitive and motivational basis of self, and the experiences of the individual within an immediate social context builds on these bases to shape the self in ways that lead to establishing and maintaining some important social bonds. If no one likes you, the odds are that you will start asking "What's wrong with me?"—and making changes to the self when you reach some answers. In this chapter, we will explore how individual selves affect others and how others affect individual selves.

The *interpersonal self* is one of three major facets of the self (Baumeister, 1998). The other two main aspects are the experience of *reflexive consciousness,* which involves being aware of oneself and constructing knowledge structures (including self-concept and self-esteem) about the self, and the *executive function,* which controls the decisions and actions of the self. As argued previously, the social self provides a crucial piece of this puzzle.

BELONGINGNESS, SOCIAL EXCLUSION, AND OSTRACISM

Theoretical Background

Meaningful human relationships are a crucial part of the self. Baumeister and Leary (1995) have proposed that the *need to belong* is one of the most fundamental human motivations, underlying many emotions, actions, and decisions throughout life. Belongingness theory predicts that people seek to have close and meaningful relationships with others, perhaps because such relationships increase the likelihood of survival and reproduction (Shaver, Hazan, & Bradshaw, 1988). Social exclusion may have hampered reproductive success; it is difficult to find a mate when one is isolated from others or devalued by others. Likewise, social exclusion probably lowered chances of survival during hunter-gatherer times due to lack of food sharing, the difficulty of hunting alone, and lack of protection from animal and human enemies (e.g., Ainsworth, 1989; Hogan, Jones, & Cheek, 1985; Moreland, 1987).

Several motivational and cognitive patterns support the view that people are innately oriented toward interpersonal belongingness (see Baumeister & Leary, 1995, for review). People form relationships readily and with minimal external impetus. They are reluctant to break off a relationship even when its practical purpose has ended. They also seem to categorize others based on their relationships. In general, humans are social animals, and people seek relationships with others as a fundamental need. What happens, however, when this need is not met—when people feel disconnected from social groups and lonely from a lack of close relationships? That is, how does the lack or loss of interpersonal relationships affect the self and behavior?

Previous research suggests that social exclusion is correlated with a variety of negative circumstances, including poor physical and mental health (Bloom, White, & Asher, 1979; D. R. Williams, Takeuchi, & Adair, 1992), crime and antisocial behavior (Sampson & Laub, 1993), alcohol and drug abuse (D. R. Williams et al., 1992), and even reckless driving (Harano, Peck, & McBride, 1975; Harrington & McBride, 1970; Richman, 1985). People who are ostracized by others report negative emotions and a feeling of losing control (K. D. Williams et al., 2000). In general, social exclusion leads to negative emotional experiences such as anxiety, depression, loneliness, and feelings of isolation (Baumeister & Leary, 1995; Baumeister & Tice, 1990; Gardner, Pickett, & Brewer, 2000). Leary et al. (1995) showed that social rejection leads to considerable decreases in feelings of self-esteem. Their *sociometer theory* posits that self-esteem is primarily a measure of the health of social relationships. That is, high self-esteem comes from believing that other people will want to spend time with you and maintain long-term relationships with you. Low self-esteem arises when people experience rejection or fear that they will end up alone in life.

Conversely, fulfilled belongingness needs seem to serve as an inoculation against negative outcomes and a predictor of positive ones. An influential review by Cohen and Wills (1985) concluded that high social support is correlated with lower self-reports of anxiety and depression. Baumeister (1991) and Myers (1992) both reviewed the empirical literature on happiness and concluded that the strongest predictor of happiness was social connectedness. People who are relatively alone in the world are much less happy than people who have close connections with others. All other objective predictors of happiness, including money, education, health, and place of residence, are only weakly correlated with happiness. The importance of social ties for positive life outcomes suggests that social connection carries considerable explanatory power. Social exclusion may be connected to many of the personal and social problems that trouble modern citizens, including aggression and lack of prosocial behavior. In addition, it may be linked to many self-defeating behaviors (such as overeating and taking excessive risks). Last, social exclusion may cause cognitive impairment.

Aggressive Behavior and Prosocial Behavior

During the late 1990s, a series of shootings occurred at American schools, leading to the deaths of a number of young people and the serious injury of many others. In almost every case, the perpetrators were boys who felt rejected by their peers (Leary, 2000). Apparently these young men responded to this rejection with violence, walking into their schools with guns and shooting their fellow students. These tragedies were consistent with several broader patterns of correlation between antisocial, violent behavior and lack of social connections. Garbarino's (1999) studies confirmed that many perpetrators of violence are young men who feel rejected from family and peer groups (see also Leary, 2000; Walsh, Beyer, & Petee, 1987).

Prior research provides partial support for a connection between social exclusion and aggressive behavior. Rejected children are more physically aggressive and more disruptive, and issue more verbal threats than other children (Coie, 1990; Newcomb, Bukowski, & Pattee, 1993). Compared to married men, single men are more likely to speed and drive recklessly, two antisocial behaviors that can lead to injury and death (Harano et al., 1975; Harrington & McBride, 1970). Marital status also correlates with criminal behavior. Stable relationships in adulthood (especially good marriages) are connected to lower incidence of crime and delinquency (Sampson & Laub, 1990, 1993). On the other hand, Wright and Wright (1992) found no link between criminality and marital status in itself. Apparently only a happy (or reasonably happy) marriage is incompatible with criminal behavior.

However, these findings are correlational, so the direction of causation is not clear. For example, men with criminal tendencies may be less likely to find someone to marry. Children who are aggressive are not likely to keep friends. Even third-variable causal explanations are plausible. For example, perhaps lack of money makes poor men both more prone to criminal activity and less desirable as potential husbands.

In order to determine the direction of causation between social exclusion and aggressive behavior, we performed a series of experimental studies (Twenge, Baumeister, et al., 2001). We manipulated social exclusion either by false feedback on a personality test (in the crucial condition, participants heard they would end up alone later in life) or by peer rejection (participants heard either that everyone or no one in a group of their peers chose them as a desirable partner for further interaction). Consistent across several studies, rejected participants were more aggressive toward other people. First, rejected participants issued negative written evaluations of a target when the target had insulted them. Rejected participants also chose to blast the target with higher levels of stressful, aversive noise during a reaction time game after a target issued an insult. In the last study, however, the participant had no interaction (positive or negative) with the target. Even under these conditions, rejected participants were more aggressive toward the target. Thus rejected participants were willing to aggress more even against an innocent third party.

In another series of studies, we examined the effect of social exclusion on prosocial behavior (Twenge, Ciarocco, & Baumeister, 2001). Across five studies, socially excluded people were less prosocial than others. They donated less money to a student fund, were less willing to volunteer for more experiments, were less helpful to the experimenter after a mishap, and were less cooperative in a prisoner's dilemma game. This effect held regardless of whether the prosocial behavior involved a cost to the self, no cost or benefit to the self, or even a benefit to the self. Combined with the aggression studies, the implication of these findings is that social exclusion leads to a reduction in prosocial behavior and an increase in antisocial behavior.

Self-reports of mood consistently failed to mediate the relationship between social exclusion and aggressive or prosocial behavior. In addition, the effects were not due to simply hearing bad news. A misfortune control group heard that they would be accident prone in the future. This group demonstrated significantly less aggressive behavior and more prosocial behavior compared to the social exclusion group. These manipulations of social exclusion are weak compared to real-life experiences such as romantic breakups or ostracism by friends. This makes it less surprising that rejections outside the laboratory can sometimes lead to lethally violent reactions.

These results linking exclusion to more antisocial behavior and less prosocial behavior are especially interesting given some previous studies. A recent paper (K. D. Williams et al., 2000) examined ostracism (being ignored by others) during an Internet ball-tossing game. Participants who were ostracized were subsequently more likely to conform to others' judgments in a line-judging task. The authors suggest that the ostracized participants were thus more willing to make amends and conform in exchange for social acceptance. A previous study also found that female participants who were ostracized socially compensated by working harder on a group task (K. D. Williams & Sommer, 1997). One interpretation of these results is that social exclusion leads to prosocial behavior—thus the opposite results to the Twenge et al. studies. However, there are several explanations for this discrepancy. First, the ostracized participants in the K. D. Williams et al. (2000) studies may have conformed out of passivity rather than out of a desire to rejoin the group. Another difference lies in motivation: the participants in the K. D. Williams et al. (2000) study and the Williams and Sommer (1997) study might have felt more confident that they could regain the favor of the group members in further interaction. In our studies, rejected participants were interacting with someone they did not expect to meet in person. This may have reduced their desire to act prosocially and encouraged them to indulge their antisocial, aggressive impulses. In other words, they might have felt that there was no clear route back to social acceptance.

Could it be that socially rejected people simply lose interest in connecting with others? There is some evidence against this view. Gardner et al. (2000) presented participants with acceptance and rejection experiences. Rejected participants later demonstrated better memory for the social aspects and events in a diary they had read earlier. Thus the experience of rejection seems to make people focus on social events to a greater extent.

Self-Defeating Behavior

Psychologists have often been fascinated with self-defeating behavior because of its fundamental and paradoxical nature (for reviews, see Baumeister, 1997; Baumeister & Scher, 1988). It seems irrational for people to act in ways that are ultimately self-defeating. Why do people do things that bring them suffering, failure, and other misfortunes? A broad range of social problems (e.g., drug addiction, overeating, underachievement, excessive risk-taking) can be regarded as self-defeating acts. Many of these problems are caused by failures of *self-control* or *self-regulation* (Baumeister, Heatherton, et al., 1994), which occur when people find it difficult to resist tempting impulses. In addition, a loss of self-control can lead to taking self-defeating risks (Leith & Baumeister, 1996), which in turn may cause undesirable outcomes such as poor health, drug and alcohol abuse, and harmful accidents.

Self-control loss is also detrimental for relationships. Living together with other people requires some degree of accommodation and compromise, because the self-interest of the individual is sometimes in conflict with the best interests of the group. Sharing, showing humility, respecting the rights and property of others, and other socially desirable acts require some degree of self-control. Few people want to live with someone who continually exploits others, breaks promises, abuses drugs, lashes out in anger, and takes stupid risks. Hence people must use their self-control to curb these impulses, if they want to maintain good interpersonal relationships.

Evidence from the sociological literature suggests that *marriage* (which is one important form of belongingness) inoculates against many self-defeating behaviors. When compared to unmarried or divorced individuals, married people are less likely to abuse alcohol and drugs (D. R. Williams et al., 1992). As mentioned earlier, married men are less likely to be arrested for speeding or reckless driving (Harrington & McBride, 1970) and are less likely to be involved in car accidents (Harano et al., 1975), especially in those related to alcohol (Richman, 1985). In one of the first works of modern sociology, Durkheim (1897/1951) found that suicide—perhaps the ultimate self-defeating behavior—was more common among people who were unmarried or otherwise socially unconnected. These correlational studies suggest a relationship between belongingness and self-defeating behaviors,

including loss of self-control and risk taking. As noted previously, however, these studies are limited due to their correlational design and their exclusive focus on marriage.

In addition, married people are often mentally and physically healthier than single, divorced or widowed individuals. The correlation between marital status and health may have several causes. First, it is possible that spouses provide practical support for health behaviors, such as by reminding their partners to keep physicians' appointments, eat well, and exercise regularly. The social interaction of a marital relationship may also directly increase mental health, which may increase physical health in turn. Third, and most relevant here, not being involved in a close relationship may encourage risky, self-defeating behaviors. Just as single and divorced people are more likely to take risks while driving, they may also take more risks with their health. We have already established that unmarried people are more likely to abuse alcohol and drugs. The same risk-taking, self-defeating tendency may also lead the unmarried to neglect their health by missing appointments, declining to seek health information, and taking a passive role toward health maintenance. It seems that many people feel that life is not worth living (or not as worth living) without close relationships. However, the causation may work the other way; it is certainly plausible that unhealthy people are not as likely to marry or have as many close social relationships.

Like the previous evidence on antisocial behavior, the evidence on social exclusion and self-defeating acts is primarily correlational. We performed a series of experiments to determine the causal path between social exclusion and self-defeating behavior (Twenge, Catanese, & Baumeister, 2001). We manipulated social exclusion using the same methods employed in the research on aggressive and prosocial behaviors (future prediction of a life devoid of social relationships, or rejection by peers). These experiments found that excluded participants consistently displayed more self-defeating behavior. Compared to the other groups, excluded participants procrastinated longer, took irrational risks in a lottery choice, and made more unhealthy choices. These effects were not mediated by mood, no matter how mood was measured (we used three different mood measures). The misfortune control group, who heard that they would be accident prone later in life, did not show significant increases in self-defeating behavior. Thus it appears to be specifically social exclusion that makes people self-destructive.

Cognitive Impairment

If mood does not mediate the relationship between social exclusion and negative outcomes, what does? One possibility is *cognitive impairment*. Social exclusion may impair the ability to reason effectively, and this in turn could lead to self-defeating behavior (which is usually a failure to rationally consider the outcomes of one's actions: Leith & Baumeister, 1996). Cognitive impairment could also lead to antisocial behavior, as socially excluded individuals may give in to aggressive impulses without considering the consequences. This decrease in the ability to reason may result from numbness or excessive rumination.

Our research has found that social exclusion does reduce the ability to reason effectively (Baumeister, Twenge, & Nuss, 2001). Socially excluded participants obtained lower scores on a timed test of intelligence. In a reading comprehension task, social exclusion led to impairments in the ability to retrieve information. Participants read a passage under normal conditions, received the exclusion feedback, and were then asked to recall what they had read. Excluded participants did not answer as many questions correctly as compared with participants in the other conditions. However, their ability to store information was apparently intact. Because the recall questions were difficult, the results could have been due to deficits in either recall or reasoning. We tested pure recall by asking participants to memorize a list of nonsense syllables. They then received the belongingness feedback and were asked to recall the syllables. Social exclusion did not affect the retrieval of simple information; however, we found that it did affect reasoning. Participants were given a timed reasoning test (taken from a Graduate Record Exam analytical section). Those in the excluded condition answered fewer questions correctly than those in the other groups. Thus social exclusion does not affect the storage of information or the retrieval of simple information, but it does affect higher reasoning.

Larger Social Trends in Belongingness and Negative Outcomes

Social exclusion may be important for understanding recent changes in American society. Several authors have argued that the changes of the last 40 years have led to a society in which people lack stable relationships and feel disconnected from each other. Putnam (1995, 2000) found that Americans are now less likely to join community organizations and visit friends than they were in the 1950s and 1960s. The proportion of the population living alone has nearly doubled in recent decades, from 13% in 1960 to 25% in 1997 (U.S. Bureau of the Census, 1998). The substantially increased divorce rate, another indicator of unstable social relations, accounts for a large part of this change. The later age of first marriage has also contributed to the increase in living alone. At the

same time, violent crime has skyrocketed, property crime has increased, and people trust and help each other less than they once did (Fukuyama, 1999).

This breakdown in relationships has occurred alongside several negative social trends. Depression rates (Klerman & Weissman, 1989; Lewinsohn, Rohde, Seeley, & Fischer, 1993) and feelings of anxiety (Twenge, 2000) have increased markedly. The increase in anxiety is directly linked to decreases in social connectedness such as divorce rates, levels of trust, and the percentage of people living alone (Twenge). In addition, crime and antisocial behavior have increased; violent crime is more than 4 times as common as it was in 1960 (6 times as common as in 1950). In fact, Lester (1994) found that statistics measuring social integration (divorce, marriage, and birth rates) were almost perfectly correlated with homicide rates when examined in a time-series analysis. Self-defeating behaviors have also escalated in the last few decades (see Baumeister, Heatherton, et al., 1994). Although it is notoriously difficult to prove which causal processes are operating at the macrosocial level in the complex world, we think that the declines in social integration and belongingness have contributed to the rise of negative social indicators and social problems.

THE SELF AS AN INTERPERSONAL ACTOR

Once people have social relationships, how do these relationships influence their selves, and vice versa? One reason people have selves is to facilitate interactions and relationships with others. For example, it is difficult to go out on a first date if one is in the middle of an identity crisis. Accordingly, Erik Erikson (1950, 1968) famously asserted that identity is a prerequisite for intimacy. People must settle the problems of identity before they are developmentally ready for intimate relations. The sequence may not be that simple, because identity and intimacy seem to develop together, but the link between the two is hard to deny (Orlofksy, Marcia, & Lesser, 1973; Tesch & Whitbourne, 1982).

Identity is also constructed out of social roles. A series of cluster analyses by Deaux, Reid, Mizrahi, and Ethier (1995) revealed five main types of social identities: *relationships* (husband, sibling), *vocational or avocational role* (coin collector, teacher), *political affiliation* (Republican, feminist), *stigmatized identity* (homeless person, fat person), and *religion or ethnicity* (Jewish, Hispanic). As products of the culture and society, roles again reveal the interpersonal dimension of selfhood. To fulfill a relationship-oriented role (such as mother or police officer), one must make the self fit a script that is collectively defined. Each person may interpret a given role in a slightly different way, but the role is nonetheless understood by the social group and is a way of relating to others.

Reflexive consciousness itself may depend partly on interpersonal contact. Sartre's (1953) famous analysis of consciousness emphasized what he called "the look," that is, the subjective experience of looking at someone else and knowing that that person is looking at you. The rise in adolescent self-consciousness and social awkwardness is in part a result of the increased cognitive ability to understand how one appears to others. Teenagers feel self-conscious because they are beginning to fully realize how they are being judged by other people.

How do interpersonal interactions shape the self? The *tabula rasa view* of human nature holds that selves are the products of interpersonal relations. That is, people start off as blank slates, and experiences gradually produce the unique individuality of the complex adult self. Although such views are elegant and sometimes politically appealing, they may suggest too passive or simple a role of the self. The self plays an active role in how it is influenced by others. The broader issue is how selfhood is maintained in an interpersonal environment. For example, part of the self exists in other people's minds; other people know about us and what we are like. Selfhood cannot be achieved or constructed in solitude.

Self-Esteem and Interpersonal Relationships

Self-esteem may be defined as a person's evaluation of self. Thus, self-esteem is a value judgment based on self-knowledge. Because much self-knowledge concerns the person's relations with others, it is not surprising that self-esteem is heavily influenced by interpersonal relationships.

Sociometer Theory

Leary et al. (1995) proposed that self-esteem is a sociometer: that is, an internal measure of how an individual is succeeding at social inclusion (see also Leary & Baumeister, 2000). In their experimental studies, participants are told that no one has chosen them as a partner for further interaction. This experience causes a decline in state self-esteem. In contrast, being chosen by group members increases state self-esteem. Leary et al. (1995) compare self-esteem to a car's gas gauge. The gas gauge itself does not affect the mechanical functioning of the car, but it serves a crucial function by showing the driver how much fuel is in the tank. Leary et al. (1995) suggest that human drivers are strongly motivated to keep their automobiles' gas gauges from reading "*empty*," because most people seek out relationships whenever they see the needle moving in that direction. Self-esteem lets people know when they need "refueling" in the form of human interaction.

The sociometer theory is important for an interpersonal view of the self, because it takes one of the best-known and most prominent intrapsychic variables (self-esteem) and recasts it in interpersonal terms. Concern with self-esteem can easily seem like a private, inner matter. It is easy to assume that self-esteem goes up and down in the person's own inner world with only minimal connection to the environment, and that people accept or reject environmental input according their own choices (e.g., one can either be in denial about a problem, or acknowledge and deal with the problem). Yet the sociometer theory proposes that self-esteem is not purely personal but instead fundamentally relies on interpersonal connection.

There is abundant evidence that people are consistently concerned with the need to form and maintain interpersonal connections (Baumeister & Leary, 1995), and so it seems quite likely that there would be a strong set of internal monitors (possibly including self-esteem) to help the person remain oriented toward that goal. The sociometer view can also readily explain why so much emotion is linked to self-esteem, because strong emotional responses are generally associated with interpersonal relationships. In addition, people tend to derive their self-esteem from the same traits that lead to social acceptance (e.g., competence, likability, attractiveness). When people feel socially anxious, however, self-esteem suffers. A review of multiple studies concluded that the average correlation between social anxiety and self-esteem is about $-.50$ (Leary & Kowalski, 1995). That is, there is a substantial and robust link between worrying about social rejection and having low self-esteem.

Why, then, do people need self-esteem to register changes in social connection, when emotion seems to serve the same purpose? Leary and Baumeister (2000) argue that self-esteem registers long-term eligibility for relationships, rather than just responding to current events. Hence someone might have low self-esteem despite being socially connected—if, for example, she believed that she has managed to deceive people about her true self and personality. If people were to find out what she is really like, she thinks, they might abandon her. Conversely, someone might have high self-esteem despite having no close friends at the moment, because he might attribute this dearth of friendships to the situation or to the lack of suitable people. He might believe that he will have plenty of friends as soon as there are enough people around who can appreciate his good qualities.

There are several possible objections to the sociometer view. It does seem that people can have high self-esteem without having any close relationship at that moment. There is also no direct and simple link between one's immediate social status and self-esteem. Self-esteem seems more stable than social-inclusion status. Shifting the emphasis from current relationships to perceived eligibility for such relationships is one way to address this problem, but more research is needed to verify whether that solution is correct.

Social and Interpersonal Patterns

Self-esteem is also associated with different patterns of social behavior. Indeed, such differences constituted one of the original sources of research interest in self-esteem. Janis (1954) hypothesized that people with low self-esteem are more easily persuaded than people with high self-esteem. One of the most influential and popular measures of self-esteem was developed specifically for use in studies of attitude change (Janis & Field, 1959). This measure, usually known as the Janis-Field Feelings of Inadequacy scale, cemented the view that individuals with low self-esteem feel little self-confidence and are easily swayed by other people's arguments.

The view that low self-esteem is associated with greater persuasibility was supported in those early studies, and subsequent work built upon those studies to link low self-esteem to a broad range of susceptibility to influence and manipulation. A seminal review article by Brockner (1984) concluded that low self-esteem is marked by what he called *"behavioral plasticity"*—the idea that people with low self-esteem are broadly malleable and easily influenced by others. For example, anxiety-provoking stimuli produce stronger and more reliable effects in people with low self-esteem; their reactions are more influenced by the anxiety-provoking situation than are those of people with high self-esteem. People with low self-esteem also show stronger responses to expectancy effects and self-focus inductions.

Self-esteem also effects choices between self-enhancement and self-protection. Many self-esteem differences occur more frequently (or only) in interpersonal situations, and self-esteem may be fundamentally tied toward self-presentational patterns (see Baumeister, Tice, & Hutton, 1989, for review). In general, people with high self-esteem are oriented toward self-enhancement, whereas people with low self-esteem tend toward self-protection. People with high self-esteem want to capitalize on their strengths and virtues and are willing to take chances in order to stand out in a positive way. On the other hand, people with low self-esteem want to remedy their deficiencies and seek to avoid standing out in a negative way.

High self-esteem people's tendency toward self-enhancement can sometimes make them less likable to others. After receiving a negative evaluation, people high in self-esteem emphasized their independence and separateness from others, whereas people with low self-esteem emphasized their interdependence and connectedness with others (Vohs & Heatherton, 2001). These self-construals had direct consequences for interpersonal perceptions. Interaction partners saw independent people as less likable and interdependent people as more likable. Given the differences in behavior based on level of self-esteem, this meant that partners saw low self-esteem individuals as more likable than high self-esteem individuals. However, these differences occurred only after the individuals being perceived had received negative evaluations; presumably self-esteem moderates reactions to ego threat.

The evidence reviewed thus far does not paint an entirely consistent picture of people with low self-esteem. On the one hand, people with low self-esteem seem to desire success, acceptance, and approval, but on the other hand they seem skeptical about it and less willing to pursue it openly. Work by Brown (e.g., 1993) has addressed this conflict directly by proposing that people with low self-esteem suffer from a motivational conflict. Brown and McGill (1989) found that positive, pleasant life events had adverse effects on the physical health of people with low self-esteem; such people actually became ill when too many good things happened. In contrast, people with high self-esteem are healthier when life treats them well. It may be that positive events exceed the expectations of people with low self-esteem. This may force them to revise their self-concepts in a positive direction, and these self-concept changes may be sufficiently stressful to make them sick.

Social Identity Theory

Another way that interpersonal relationships influence self-esteem is through group memberships. *Social identity theory* (e.g., Tajfel, 1982; Tajfel & Turner, 1979; Turner, 1982) argues that the self-concept contains both personal and social attributes. Self-esteem usually focuses on personal attributes, but group memberships are also important. A person will experience higher self-esteem when his or her important social groups are valued and compare favorably to other groups (see also Rosenberg, 1979). Empirical research has confirmed this theory; *collective self-esteem* (feeling that one's social groups are positive) is correlated with global personal self-esteem (Luhtanen & Crocker, 1992). This is particularly true for members of racial or ethnic minorities (Crocker, Luhtanen, Blaine, & Broadnax, 1994). This most likely occurs because minority group members identify more strongly with their ethnic groups, and these groups are obvious and salient to others. In addition, improving the status of the group tends to increase personal self-esteem. For example, favoring in-groups over out-groups in allocation of points or rewards can enhance self-esteem, even when the self does not personally benefit from those allocations (e.g., Lemyre & Smith, 1985;

Oakes & Turner, 1980). Thus self-esteem is not only personal: It also includes a person's evaluations of the groups to which he or she belongs.

Is High Self-Esteem Always Good

To place the findings about self-esteem in perspective, it is useful to ask how important and beneficial high self-esteem actually is. In America today, many people seem to believe that high self-esteem is extremely beneficial. The strong belief in the benefits of self-esteem is a major reason it remains a popular topic of discussion and research. By one count, there are almost 7,000 books and articles about self-esteem (Mruk, 1995). The belief that high self-esteem is a vital aspect of mental health and good adjustment is strong and widespread (e.g., Bednar, Wells, & Peterson, 1989; Mruk, 1995; Taylor & Brown, 1988). In many studies, in fact, self-esteem is measured as an index of good adjustment, so that even the operational definition of healthy functioning involves self-esteem (e.g., Kahle, Kulka, & Klingel, 1980; Whitley, 1983).

However, there is a "dark side" to high self-esteem, especially concerning interactions with others. In one study, people with high self-esteem were more likely than most people to aggress against others and to be interpersonally violent (Baumeister, Smart, & Boden, 1996). Aggression seems to be most common among people who think well of themselves but then interact with someone who disputes their favorable self-appraisal. In particular, inflated, unrealistic, or fluctuating forms of high self-esteem predict outbursts of violence and aggression. This most likely occurs because these types of self-esteem are the most vulnerable to ego threats (e.g., Blaine & Crocker, 1993; Kernis, Granneman, & Barclay, 1989). People appear to lash out at others who criticize them as a way of avoiding any decrease in their self-esteem and the accompanying negative emotion (especially shame; see Tangney, Wagner, Fletcher, & Gramzow, 1992). Normally, people with high self-esteem do not seem defensive, but that may be because they usually think highly of themselves and expect to succeed at most things. When they do fail or are rejected, they are very surprised and thus may respond dramatically.

Inflated self-esteem also predicts social maladjustment. In one study, researchers compared people's self-descriptions with the descriptions of their friends (Colvin, Block, & Funder, 1995). This identified a group of people who thought more highly of themselves than warranted by the opinions of their friends. When followed over time in a longitudinal design, these self-enhancing people displayed poor social skills and decreased psychological adjustment. In a laboratory study, the people in this group tended to express hostility, interrupt others, be socially awkward, irritate others, talk at people instead of talking with them, and perform a variety of other negatively evaluated behaviors. The composite picture is one of a self-centered, conceited person who lacks genuine regard for others. This picture is quite consistent with the literal meaning of high self-esteem, even though it does not fit the popular stereotype.

Narcissism and Interpersonal Relationships

Another individual difference likely to affect interpersonal relationships is *narcissism,* usually defined as an exaggerated view of one's importance, influence, and entitlements. People high in self-esteem are more likely to be high in narcissism, although the correlation is low to moderate rather than high. The imperfect correlation probably reflects the fact that high self-esteem is a very heterogeneous category, including plenty of arrogant, narcissistic people as well as others who simply accept themselves without assuming they are superior to others. Put another way, narcissism is a subcategory of high self-esteem; very few people score high in narcissism but low in self-esteem.

Generally, narcissists tend not only to feel good about themselves, but also to expect deference and recognition from others. Thus, in some ways narcissism is more interpersonally relevant than self-esteem. Campbell (1999) found that narcissists were more interpersonally attracted to highly positive and highly admiring individuals. Narcissists were less attracted to people who offered greater amounts of emotional intimacy. This occurred because narcissists preferred partners who were more self-oriented rather than other-oriented, as part of a strategy to enhance self-esteem. Thus, narcissists found it more important to be with someone who made them look good rather than to be with someone who truly cared for them. This overall strategy for self-enhancement is linked to a noncaring, nonintimate experience of interpersonal relationships in general. Compared to non-narcissists, narcissists report lower levels of empathy (Watson, Grisham, Trotter, & Biderman, 1984), intimacy (Carroll, 1987), communion (Bradlee & Emmons, 1992), caring (Campbell, 1999), and selflessness (Campbell, Foster, & Finkel, 2000). It seems that a narcissist's first question in a relationship is "What can you do for *me?*"

Narcissists also tend to react badly when they are criticized or challenged by others. In laboratory experiments, Bushman and Baumeister (1998) found that narcissists were considerably more aggressive toward someone who had insulted them, as compared to non-narcissists. When the researchers controlled for narcissism statistically, self-esteem did not predict aggressive behavior. Thus it appears that narcissism is the better predictor of interpersonal hostility. This fits the view that aggression comes from only a subset of people with high self-esteem, while other people with high self-esteem are not aggressive.

Other research has found that narcissists are willing to derogate others after receiving threatening feedback (e.g., Kernis & Sun, 1994). They react with hostility, denigration, and aggression when they feel threatened (Rhodewalt & Morf, 1998). In fact, a recent study found that men incarcerated in prisons scored significantly higher in narcissism than samples of male college students (Bushman, Baumeister, Phillips, & Gilligan, 2001). Levels of self-esteem, however, did not differ between the two groups. Thus narcissists tend to be more personally sensitive to criticism, but insensitive to how their behavior affects others. Like the research on self-esteem presented earlier, these results suggest that inflated self-views can often lead to poor consequences for interpersonal relationships.

Reflected Appraisals

The *reflected appraisals* model suggests that people learn about themselves by interacting with others. People find out what other people think of them and then internalize these opinions into their self-views. In addition, information about the self often is meaningful only in comparison to others, as *social comparison theory* emphasizes. One is only fat or thin, intelligent or stupid, friendly or hostile in comparison to other people. In these cases and many others, self-knowledge can grow only when people make these implicit comparisons. Much of reflected appraisals theory stems from symbolic interactionism (e.g., Mead, 1934). Mead's theory argues that most self-knowledge comes from social interactions. The process of reflected appraisals (i.e., how other people's appraisals of you shape your self-understanding) is often described with Cooley's (1902) term the *looking-glass self.* Using an antiquated term for a mirror, the looking-glass self posits that other people provide the mirror through which individuals see and understand themselves.

Cooley (1902) argued that the self-concept consists of "the imagination of our appearance to the other person; the imagination of his judgment of that appearance, and some sort of self-feeling, such as pride or mortification" (p. 184). Thus our self-esteem is also heavily influenced by what others think of us. Mead (1934) elaborated on this notion by suggesting that the self is also shaped by our vision of how a generalized other perceives us. The *generalized other* is

basically the person's whole sociocultural environment. If a society has a negative view of children at a given time, for example, children are likely to internalize this negative view of the generalized other.

An influential literature review by Shrauger and Schoeneman (1979) concluded that *symbolic interactionism* was partially supported by data. The review gathered data comparing self-concepts with the views of others. Although these correlations were positive, they were rather small. Subsequent studies have confirmed that symbolic interaction effects are significant but small (Edwards & Klockars, 1981; Malloy & Albright, 1990). Even some of these weak links can be questioned on methodological grounds, as noted by Felson (1989).

On the other hand, Shrauger and Shoeneman (1979) found that self-concepts were highly correlated with how people *believed* that others perceived them (and subsequent work has replicated this conclusion). Therefore, there is a meaningful link between self-perceptions and other-perceptions (although the causal direction is unclear and probably bidirectional). The discrepancy arises between how people actually perceive Bob and how Bob thinks other people perceive him—but Bob's view of himself is quite similar to how he thinks others see him. Thus others do shape self-views, even though people are not always accurate about how others perceive them.

There seem to be two major reasons for these inaccuracies (see Felson, 1989). First, people do not generally tell someone precisely what they think of him or her. The exchange of interpersonal evaluations is highly distorted. People do not want to offend or distress someone by an honest, negative evaluation, and they are often afraid that the person they criticize will no longer like them. (This is a legitimate fear; most humans tend to like people who like them, and distrust those who criticize them.) When refusing a date, for example, people tend to give false and misleading explanations, often resulting in their being unable to discourage further invitations from the same person (e.g., Folkes, 1982—although some of these explanations have become so popular that they are now more easily understood as a genuine brush-off: "It's not you, it's me." Translated: "It's totally you. You are the big problem. I'm fine."). Even when people are engaging in deliberate self-presentation, they are not very accurate at estimating the impression they actually make on others (e.g., DePaulo, Kenny, Hoover, Webb, & Oliver, 1987). Given the dearth of honest and precise negative feedback from others, it is not surprising that people's self-views remain blissfully unaffected by those concealed opinions and appraisals.

The other source of distortion is self-deception. Often, people do not accept information directly into their views of

to think that they come across the same way to everyone, but they do not.

Baumeister, Hutton, and Tice (1989) studied the cognitive processes behind self-presentation. In this study, subjects were interviewed in pairs. An experimenter instructed one member of each pair to self-present in either a modest or a self-enhancing fashion. After the interview, subjects were given surprise recall tests for both their own and their partners' self-presentations, as well as for their impressions of their partners. Subjects who had been instructed to be modest and self-effacing showed impaired memory for the interaction. Apparently, acting modestly (which is an unusual way to act with strangers) causes greater cognitive load and interferes with the memory storage process during the interaction. In addition, subjects seemed unaware of the influence they had on others (see Gilbert & Jones, 1986). Thus, for example, if John presents himself by saying highly favorable things about himself, Bill may also begin to boast. This might lead John to conclude that Bill must be rather conceited (or at least very self-confident). In fact, Bill's self-promotion was merely a response to John's.

The increase in cognitive load caused by effortful self-presentation may explain some of the findings of DePaulo et al. (1987). When one is concentrating on trying to make a certain impression, he or she may not be fully able to attend to how the other person is responding. After a series of interactions, people may remember merely that they tried to make roughly the same good impression on each interaction partner. However, they might not remember that the partners responded to them differently. Thus, self-presentation is not always successful because it is difficult cognitive work. Making a good impression consumes so many resources that people find it hard to attend to other people's responses and adjust that impression.

Harmful Aspects of Self-Presentation

Through various means, self-presentation can lead to health risks (Leary, Tchividjian, & Kraxberger, 1994). For example, concern about the impression one is making can lead to risky and harmful behaviors; at times, the drive to impress others can outweigh self-preservation. How does this occur? Appearance concerns are a relevant example. On the one hand, people believe that having a suntan is attractive; on the other, most people have heard the warnings about skin cancer. Leary and Jones (1993) showed that the risky behaviors of sunbathing were mainly linked to concern over physical appearance and to the lack of concern about health. People sunbathe to make themselves attractive, often ignoring the physical danger involved. High-heeled and platform shoes are another example: many women wear them because they think it makes them look attractive despite the pain, back problems, and lack of coordination that such shoes often cause. Risky sexual behavior is also influenced by self-presentation. Condoms are generally regarded as the safest method for having intercourse outside of stable, monogamous relationships, but many people do not use them. People often cite self-presentational concerns when explaining their lack of protection, such as embarrassment when buying them and the fear of making a bad impression on an anticipated sexual partner (Leary, 1995). Other risks reviewed by Leary et al. (1994) include hazardous dieting and eating patterns, use of alcohol and illegal drugs, cigarette smoking, steroid use, not wearing safety equipment and other behaviors that may cause accidental injury and even death, and submitting to cosmetic surgery and risk of its subsequent complications. Taken together, these provide strong evidence that self-presentational concerns often take precedence over concerns with maintaining health and even protecting life.

INTERPERSONAL CONSEQUENCES OF SELF-VIEWS

Clearly, characteristics of the self exert an influence on interpersonal relations. One of the best-known findings in social psychology is the link between similarity and attraction (Byrne, 1971; Smeaton, Byrne, & Murnen, 1989); that is, people like those who resemble them (or at least, they avoid and dislike people who are different from them; Rosenbaum, 1986). Similarities on important, heritable traits are especially potent bases for liking and disliking others (Crelia & Tesser, 1996; Tesser, 1993).

Self-Views Alter Person Perception

Evidence suggests that self-views affect how people understand others. Markus, Smith, and Moreland (1985; see also Fong & Markus, 1982) examined the role of self-schemas in person perception. They proposed that someone who has a self-schema in a particular domain will behave like an expert in that domain. For example, schematic people will spot domain-relevant information faster, integrate it into existing information better, and fill in gaps in information more thoroughly. In Markus et al.'s research, people who were schematic for masculinity tended to group more items together when judging the masculinity-relevant behavior of a stimulus person. They also saw the stimulus person as more masculine and more like themselves than did aschematic individuals.

Thus, aspects of self-concept can influence the perception of others (however, it is also possible that greater interest in the area relevant to the self leads to the expertise). The key point appears to be that a particularly well developed aspect of self-knowledge makes one act like an expert in that sphere. If your view of yourself emphasizes loyalty, for example, you will probably be more sensitive to loyalty or disloyalty in others.

One mechanism driving the link between self-views and person perception is the *self-image bias* (Lewicki, 1983, 1984). According to this bias, people tend to judge others on the basis of traits in their own areas of strength. Thus there is a correlation between the favorability and the centrality of self-ratings (Lewicki, 1983). That is, people's most favorable traits are also those that are most central and important for their judgments of others—people judge others by a standard that favors them (the perceiver). For example, students who did well in a computer science course tended to place more emphasis on computer skills when judging others than did students who did not perform well in the computer course (Hill, Smith, & Lewicki, 1989). Lewicki (1984) showed that the self-image bias serves a defensive function: When people receive negative feedback, the effect of self-image bias on perception of others is increased. Along these lines, Dunning, Perie, and Story (1991) found that people construct prototypes of social categories such as intelligence, creativity, and leadership in ways that emphasize their own traits. Thus, inquisitive people think inquisitiveness is a valuable aid to creativity, but noninquisitive people do not believe that inquisitiveness has any far-reaching implications for other outcomes. These prototypes thus influence how people evaluate others.

Rejecting a view of self through a defensive process also affects person perception. Newman, Duff, and Baumeister (1997) proposed a new model of the Freudian defense mechanism of *projection* (basically, seeing one's faults in other people rather than in oneself). This model builds on evidence that suggests that when people try not to think about something, it instead becomes highly accessible in memory (Wegner & Erber, 1992). Newman et al. showed that when people tried to suppress thoughts about a bad trait that had been attributed to them, they then interpreted other people's behavior in terms of that bad trait. Thus, person perception can be shaped by the traits you are trying to deny in yourself, just as much as by the traits that you do see in yourself.

All of these effects can be explained by accessibility. The attributes the self emphasizes, and those the self seeks to deny, operate as highly accessible categories for interpreting others' behavior (Higgins, King, & Mavin, 1982). Social perception thus tends to be self-centered and self-biased. Still, these effects appear to be specific and limited; not all interpersonal perception is wildly distorted by self-appraisals. In particular, these effects seem to be limited to situations in which information about the target person is ambiguous (Lambert & Wedell, 1991; Sedikides & Skowronski, 1993).

Self-Evaluation Maintenance

Several important links between self-esteem and interpersonal relations have been elaborated in Tesser's (1988) self-evaluation maintenance theory. Among other consequences, this theory explains how people may become closer to or more distant from relationship partners as a result of pressures to maintain self-esteem. According to Tesser, two main processes link self-views to interpersonal outcomes. First is the process of *reflection;* one can gain esteem when a close other achieves something. One's self-esteem may get a boost simply from having an uncle who is a Congressman or a child who is quarterback of the football team; from sleeping with a movie star, or from learning one's college basketball team has won a championship. Cialdini and his colleagues have shown how people bask in reflected glory of institutions, for example, by wearing school colors more frequently following a team victory than following a defeat (Cialdini & Richardson, 1980).

The other process is one of *comparison* (see Festinger, 1954; Wills, 1981); this process can instead lead to a decrease in self-esteem. People may compare themselves with others close to them and feel bad if the other person is outperforming them. If your sibling gets better grades than you, if your dimwit brother-in-law earns double your salary, or if your friend wins a scholarship or a job you wanted, you may lose esteem.

Thus, the processes of reflection and comparison with close others produce opposite effects on self-esteem. Tesser's work has therefore gone on to look for factors that determine which process will operate in a given situation. One factor is the *relevance* of the accomplishment to one's self-concept. Thus, a friend's football victory may bring you esteem, as the reflection process predicts—but only if your own football-playing ability is not highly relevant to your own self-esteem. If you played in the same football game and performed terribly, your friend's success would make you look that much worse by comparison. For this reason, people sometimes prefer to see strangers succeed rather than close friends, because the stranger's success does not invite comparison and is less humiliating. Tesser and Smith (1980) showed that people will do more to help a stranger than a friend to succeed at a task that is relevant to the person's own self-esteem.

Meanwhile, the closer the relationship, the greater the effect. You gain (or lose) more esteem if your spouse wins a major award than if your hairdresser wins it. Thus the comparison process may be especially disruptive to close relationships. If a romantic partner succeeds on something irrelevant to your self-esteem, you may feel closer to that partner. If he or she succeeds at something highly relevant to your own goals, then you may feel jealous or threatened, and the intimate relationship may be damaged (Beach, 1992). When the comparison process makes you look bad, the only way to limit the damage may be to reduce closeness. Research confirms that people distance themselves from someone who performs too well on something that is highly relevant to their own self-concepts (Pleban & Tesser, 1981).

Self-Monitoring

Snyder (1974, 1987) proposed an early and influential theory about individual differences in how the self structures interpersonal processes. He was first interested in cross-situational consistency, stimulated by Bem and Allen's (1974) suggestion that some people are more consistent in their traits than others. Snyder introduced the concept of *self-monitoring* as an individual difference, distinguishing between high self-monitors and low self-monitors. A high self-monitor looks to others for cues, modifying his or her behavior to fit the situation and the people in it. A low self-monitor, on the other hand, is more consistent and does not try to alter behavior very much across situations. Subsequent research (Snyder & Swann, 1976) showed that low self-monitors had high attitude-behavior consistency: Their attitudes predicted their verdicts in a simulated jury case. In contrast, high self-monitors' attitudes did not predict their behavior very well, probably because they modified their statements on the jury case to fit the immediate situational demands and cues. It seems that high self-monitors do not see any necessary relation between their private beliefs and their public actions, and so discrepancies do not bother them (Snyder, 1987). Thus, there is a basic difference in how these two types of people regard themselves. Low self-monitors believe that they have strong principles, and they consistently strive to uphold them. High self-monitors see themselves as pragmatic and flexible rather than principled. They respond to the situation and do what they regard as appropriate, which often includes altering their own self-presentations.

Further research addressed the interaction patterns associated with the different levels of self-monitoring. Low self-monitors base friendships on emotional bonds, and they prefer to spend most of their time with the people they like best. In contrast, high self-monitors base friendships on shared activities. Thus they spend time with the people who are best suited to the relevant activity. For example, the low self-monitor would prefer to play tennis with his or her best friend, regardless of how well the friend plays. The high self-monitor would rather play tennis with the best tennis player among his or her acquaintances (or the one best matched to his or her own abilities). Consequently, the social worlds of high self-monitors are very compartmentalized, with different friends and partners linked to specific activities. On the other hand, the social worlds of low self-monitors are relatively uncategorized by activities, with friends chosen instead on the basis of emotional bonds.

These interpersonal patterns carry over into romantic relationships (Snyder & Simpson, 1984; Snyder, 1987). For example, high self-monitoring males choose dating patterns based mainly on physical appearance, whereas low self-monitors place more emphasis on personality and other inner qualities. High self-monitors tend to have more romantic and sexual partners than lows. When it comes to marriage, high self-monitors again look for shared activities and interests, whereas low self-monitors emphasize mainly the pleasures and satisfactions of simply being together.

Partner Views of Self

Swann (1996) advanced a simpler theory of how interpersonal relationships are shaped by self-views. Extending self-verification theory, Swann argued that people prefer romantic partners who see them as they see themselves. People are sometimes torn between a desire to see themselves favorably and a desire to confirm what they already think of themselves (as we discussed earlier). If love is truly blind, a person in love would see the beloved partner in an idealized way. Would that be helpful or harmful?

Swann and his colleagues (Swann, Hixon, & De La Ronde, 1992) have examined such dilemmas in various relationships, ranging from roommates to spouses. On a variety of measures, they found that people would rather be with someone who confirms their self-views (as opposed to someone who saw them favorably). People choose, like, and retain partners who see them accurately. This research might explain why some people have partner after partner who treats them badly: They somehow feel that they do not deserve to be treated well. In this view, the idealizing effects of love are dangerous and harmful to the relationship. Apparently people want their friends and lovers to see all their faults.

However, a large independent investigation found that favorability is more important than consistency with self-views. Murray, Holmes, and Griffin (1996a) found that favorable views of one's partner were associated with better relationships. Idealization was associated with greater satisfaction and happiness about the relationship. A follow-up study (Murray, Holmes, & Griffin, 1996b) found that favorable views of one's partner predicted greater stability and durability of the relationship. This research suggests that perhaps love should be blind (or at least nearsighted enough to wear rose-colored glasses when looking at the loved one). The authors argue that idealized love is not blind, but instead farsighted; partners who idealized each other created the relationships they wanted. Idealization and positive illusions about one's partner seem to strengthen the relationship, making it more pleasant and more likely to last. Seeing the real person beneath the facade is not always the beginning of real intimacy: Sometimes it is the beginning of the end.

These somewhat discrepant results do at least agree that it is quite important for people to believe that their friends and lovers appreciate their good points. It is less clear whether people want their partners to also see their faults and flaws. One possible explanation for the discrepant results of the two authors is that most of Swann's self-consistency work has emphasized traits that the person is highly certain of and committed to having. On the other hand, Murray's favorability effects tend to emphasize a broader spectrum of less certain traits. People might want their close relationship partners to recognize one or two favorite faults but otherwise maintain a highly favorable view of them.

There is also intriguing but preliminary evidence that relationship partners can help sustain consistency. Swann and Predmore (1985) gave people feedback that was discrepant from their self-views and watched how they and their romantic partners responded. When the subject and his or her partner agreed that the feedback was wrong, the pair then joined forces to reject it: They discussed its flaws and decided how best to refute or dismiss it. In contrast, when the partner's view of the subject differed from the subject's self-view, the discrepant feedback led to further disagreements between the subject and partner. It may be that one vital function of close relationship partners is to help maintain and defend one's self-concept against the attacks of the outer world (see also De La Ronde & Swann, 1998).

Sedikides, Campbell, Reeder, and Elliott (1998) explored another important link between self-deception and the interpersonal self. They examined the *self-serving bias,* a classic pattern of self-deception that occurs when people take credit for success but deny blame for failure. When people work in groups, the self-serving bias produces the tendency to claim all the credit for success at joint tasks but to dump the blame for failure on the other group members. However, the authors found that self-serving bias is mitigated when the group members feel a close interpersonal bond with each other.

Thus, people will flatter themselves at their partner's expense—but only when they do not care much about the partner. The interpersonal context dictates whether people will display the self-serving bias.

Self-Handicapping

When someone self-handicaps, he or she tries to explain away failure (or even possible failure) by attributing it to external causes (often external causes of his or her own making). Self-handicapping is usually studied within the context of individual performance, but it has a strong interpersonal aspect as well. One study manipulated whether several crucial aspects of the situation were public (known to others) or private (known only to the subject; Kolditz & Arkin, 1982). Self-handicapping emerged mainly in the public conditions, when the subject's handicap and subsequent performance would be seen by others. In contrast, subjects did not self-handicap when the experimenter was unaware of the handicap. Apparently, self-handicapping is primarily a self-presentational strategy used to control the impression one makes on other people. Self-handicapping rarely occurs when people are concerned only with their private self-views.

EMOTIONS AND THE INTERPERSONAL SELF

Emotions often reflect value judgments relevant to the self. Recent work has increasingly emphasized interpersonal determinants and processes of emotion (Tangney & Fischer, 1995).

Shame and Guilt

Both shame and guilt have strong interpersonal components. The two terms were used in varying ways for decades, but in recent decades a consensus has emerged about how to define the two. The distinction was first proposed in the theoretical work by Lewis (1971), based on clinical observations, and it received considerable elaboration and further support from factor analytic and scale-development studies by researchers such as Tangney (1992, 1995). The difference between the two lies in how much of the self is affected: *Guilt* denounces a specific action by the self, whereas *shame* condemns the entire self.

Shame is usually the more destructive of the two emotions. Because shame signifies that the entire self is bad, simple reparations or constructive responses seem pointless. This absence of constructive solutions probably leads to many of the pathological outcomes connected with shame, such as suicide and major depression (Tangney, Burggraf, & Wagner, 1995). Shame also seems to produce socially undesirable outcomes such as, for some people, a complete withdrawal from others. Other people, however, respond to shame with anger (Tangney et al., 1992). The shift from shame into anger may be a defensive effort to negate the global negative evaluation. There is some evidence that this shift in emotions can lead to violent outbursts (Baumeister et al., 1996). Kitayama, Markus, and Matsumoto (1995) have proposed that the movement from shame to anger reflects the independent selfhood model common to Western cultures and may not occur in cultures that emphasize more interdependent selves.

In contrast, guilt is more reparable and less socially disruptive than shame. Guilt has a strong basis in relationships even when no transgression is involved. For example, some people feel survivor guilt because they have survived when others have died or suffered. The term originated in studies of survivors of the Holocaust and the Hiroshima bombing (Lifton, 1967). More recently, survivor guilt emerged during episodes of corporate downsizing, when people who kept their jobs felt guilty while others were fired (Brockner, Davy, & Carter, 1985). In general, people may feel guilty when they outperform others (Exline & Lobel, 1999).

According to Baumeister, Stillwell, and Heatherton (1994), guilt is mainly interpersonal and seems designed to strengthen relationships. People may try to avoid hurting close others because it makes them feel guilty. After a transgression, guilt makes people seek to make amends or rectify the situation in an attempt to repair the damage to the relationship. It makes people change their behavior so that they will not repeat the damaging behavior. It makes them try to live up to the expectations of others. Feeling guilty is sometimes beneficial to the relationship in and of itself, because guilty feelings confirm that the person cares about the relationship (even if the transgression made it appear that he or she did not care). In addition, people sometimes exaggerate how hurt or upset they are by another person's actions, in order to make that person feel guilty. The guilt makes the other person more willing to comply with the wishes of the person who felt hurt. This tactic can be used to redistribute power in a relationship: Guilt enables otherwise powerless people to sometimes get their way. Usually, the person who is hurt makes his or her feelings and disappointment clear. If the other person cares about your welfare, he or she will want to avoid hurting you, because hurting you will make him or her feel guilty. Hence the person will do what you want.

Baumeister, Reis, and Delespaul (1995) confirmed that guilt plays an important role in close relationships. The authors asked participants to describe their most recent experiences of six different emotions, including guilt. These were then coded for the level of interpersonal connection. Guilt scored the highest of the six major emotions on interpersonal connection. That is, hardly any guilt stories referred to solitary experiences or interactions with strangers; the overwhelming majority of guilt stories involved partners in close relationships, such as family members or romantic partners.

Embarrassment

Similar to shame and guilt, embarrassment seems to be a mixture of self and interpersonal concerns. Modigliani (1971) linked embarrassment to the public self by showing that the best predictor of embarrassment was a situational, perceived loss of others' good opinion. In addition, embarrassability correlates more highly with public self-consciousness than with private self-consciousness (Edelmann, 1985).

In an influential review, Miller (1995) argued that two theoretical perspectives on embarrassment are predominant. The first theory emphasizes concern over being evaluated by others; to be embarrassed, you must first be concerned about others' evaluations. The alternative view invokes the unpleasant nature of awkward social interactions. In one study, Parrott, Sabini, and Silver (1988) presented participants with a hypothetical scenario in which someone refused a date. People reported they would feel less embarrassed if the rejector used an obvious excuse than if the rejector bluntly rejected them, even if the person's rejection was equally negative. However, making an excuse may itself convey a positive evaluation, such as concern for the rejected person's feelings (Miller, 1995). Miller concluded that both perspectives are valid; nevertheless, the concern over social evaluation is the more common cause of embarrassment.

Blushing is one common sign of embarrassment, but people sometimes blush even when there is no obvious social evaluation. Leary, Britt, Cutlip, and Templeton (1992) concluded that unwanted social attention is the most common cause of blushing. In general, people blush as an appeasement to others after violating social norms. People hope that looking embarrassed after a transgression will inform other people that they feel remorseful. Apparently, embarrassment is effective in minimizing negative evaluations. Semin and Manstead (1982) found that subjects expressed greater liking toward someone who was embarrassed after an accidental transgression. When the target person was not embarrassed, subjects did not like the person as much.

Social Anxiety

Schlenker and Leary (1982) argued that social anxiety is directly linked to self-presentation. In their view, social anxiety arises when someone wants to make a particular, desired impression but fears that he or she will fail to do so. As Leary and Kowalski (1995) describe it, social anxiety is essentially a concern about controlling public impressions. Making a particular impression is important for gaining the acceptance of others and for achieving status (two important interpersonal goals). Given the importance of being perceived positively by others, it is hardly surprising that some people become extremely concerned and anxious during social situations.

Disclosing Emotion and Personal Information

So far, we have discussed the interpersonal roots of emotion. In what way do interpersonal situations, however, affect the expression of these emotions? Clark, Pataki, and Carver (1995) found that people are careful about how much happiness they express when they are concerned about the impression they are making on others. As an influential review showed, people are concerned that their success will create feelings of jealousy and dislike (Exline & Lobel, 1999). Clark et al. (1995) also found that people express anger in an attempt to get their own way. Sadness, too, can be used as an interpersonal lever; people show sadness when they want others to see them as dependent in order to gain their help. These strategies correspond to the self-presentational tactics of ingratiation, intimidation, and supplication (E. E. Jones & Pittman, 1982). A more general statement was provided by DePaulo (1992): People can either exaggerate or downplay their emotional reactions in order to meet their self-presentational goals. That is, sometimes it is best to pretend to be having a strong emotional reaction, and other times it is advantageous to conceal one's emotions.

Levels of self-disclosure are also affected by self-control. When one's self-control is depleted by a self-regulatory task, one is less able to maintain an appropriate level of self-disclosure. People with an avoidant attachment style withdraw too much during interactions after being depleted, whereas those with an anxious attachment style disclose too much (Vohs, Ciarocco, & Baumeister, 2002). Because a moderate amount of self-disclosure is best for smooth interaction, self-regulatory depletion affects the quality of interactions through disrupting self-disclosure.

CULTURAL AND HISTORICAL VARIATIONS IN SELFHOOD

Most of the research presented so far has studied North American college students at specific points in time (usually between 1975 and 2000). Although this research is informative, it does not capture the variations in selfhood across the

cultures of the world and the decades of the century. Given that the self is an inherently social construct, there should be considerable cultural and historical variation.

Culture and Society

The past 15 years have brought much interest in the cultural determinants of selfhood. By way of summary, it is useful to draw from an influential review article by Triandis (1989). This review identified several key features of selfhood that vary across different cultures. First, cultures vary in conceptions of the *private self,* or how people understand themselves (e.g., self-regard, self-esteem, introspection, and individual decision making). Second, the *public self* refers to how the individual is perceived by other people, thus including issues such as reputation, specific expectations of others, and impression management. Third, the *collective self* involves memberships in various social groups, from the family to an employing organization or ethnic group. Triandis argues that individualistic societies such as that in much of the United States emphasize the private and public selves and downplay the collective self, whereas other (e.g., Asian) societies tend to emphasize the collective self while downplaying the private self. Variation in these conceptions may also occur within a society. For example, some authors have argued that African Americans show more collectivistic tendencies compared to White Americans (e.g., Baldwin & Hopkins, 1990).

Triandis (1989) also proposed several important cultural dimensions that have important implications for the self. One dimension is *individualism versus collectivism.* Individualistic societies support diversity, self-expression, and the rights of individuals, whereas collectivistic societies promote conformity and a sense of obligation to the group. As a general rule, Western societies such as the United States are more individualistic, whereas Asian and African societies are more collectivistic. In general, relationships are closer in collectivistic societies. The concept of an independent, individual self is not as common; rather, a person sees his or her self as overlapping with the selves of close others.

Another dimension that varies between societies is *tightness,* or the amount of social pressure on individuals. Tight societies demand that individuals conform to the group's values, role definitions, and norms. In contrast, loose societies allow people more freedom to do what they want. (For that reason, tight societies tend to promote the public and collective selves, whereas loose ones allow more scope for the private self to flourish.)

A third dimension of cultural variation proposed by Triandis (1989) is *societal complexity.* In a complex society, an individual tends to belong to many different groups; thus it is less imperative to stay on good terms with any one of these groups. The collective self is therefore not so crucially important. In addition, complex societies allow greater development of the private self (because of the greater availability of many social relationships). The public self is also quite important because it is the common feature of all one's social relations. In contrast, in a simple society people belong to relatively few groups, each of which is then quite important in defining the self. The collective self flourishes in adapting to these memberships, and the need to conform to the group tends to stifle the private self.

Triandis (1989) illustrated some of his central ideas by contrasting American and Japanese societies. Japan tends to be tighter and more collectivistic than the United States, and as a result there is much greater homogeneity: Japanese citizens tend to eat the same foods, whereas Americans use the prerogative of the private self and choose from a broad assortment. Certain Asian traditions, such as having the oldest male order the same food for the entire table, would be unthinkable in the United States, where each individual's special preferences are honored.

Furthermore, Americans place a premium on sincerity. At its base, sincerity is the congruency between public and private selves: You are supposed to say what you mean and mean what you say. In Japan, however, public actions are more important than private sentiments. For example, Americans object to hypothetical dilemmas in which people think one thing and say another, whereas Japanese respondents approve of these options.

Markus and Kitayama (1991) proposed that Asian and Western cultures primarily vary in *independence versus interdependence.* Western cultures, they argue, emphasize the independent self: People are supposed to attend to themselves, to discover and express their unique attributes, and to try to stand out in important ways. In the West, as they say, the squeaky wheel gets the grease. In contrast, Asian cultures emphasize interdependence. Asians are expected to attend to others, to conform to group demands and role obligations, and to try to fit into the group. In Asia, "the nail that stands out gets pounded down." To the Western mind, the self is an autonomous unit that is essentially separate and unique, whereas the Asian view begins with an assumption of the basic and pervasive connectedness of people.

Multiple consequences flow from this idea. As might be expected in an interdependent culture, relationship harmony was more important to self-esteem for students in Hong Kong compared to students in the United States (Kwan, Bond, & Singelis, 1997). Because relationships are more intertwined with the self in these cultures, they are more important to self-esteem and life satisfaction. Self-enhancing biases also differ

between the two types of cultures. In general, Americans tend to self-enhance, whereas the Japanese tend to self-criticize (Kitayama, Markus, Matsumoto, & Norasakkunkit, 1997).

People from independent cultures also tend to describe others in terms of cross-situational, person-centered traits (e.g., "He is stingy"). In contrast, people from interdependent cultures tend to describe others more in terms of specific contexts (e.g., "He behaves properly with guests but feels sorry if money is spent on them"; Markus & Kitayama, 1991, p. 232). Self-descriptions also vary between cultures (Bond & Cheung, 1983; Cousins, 1989). Japanese college students asked to finish a sentence beginning with "I am..." were more likely to respond with social roles ("brother," "student at Tokyo University"), whereas American college students were more likely to respond in terms of personal attributes ("outgoing," "blonde"). Thus, members of independent societies see themselves and others in terms of relatively constant personality traits, whereas members of interdependent societies see personality and behavior as more dependent on the situation.

In addition, interdependent societies do not emphasize consistency among private thoughts and feelings as much as independent societies do. In an interdependent society, it is more important to be accommodating and kind than to be internally consistent. Among independent selves, politeness means giving the other person the maximum freedom to express unique, special, and changing wants. Among interdependent selves, however, politeness means anticipating what the other might want and showing appreciation for their actions. There are also emotional consequences, as Markus and Kitayama (1991) explain. In the West, the expression versus suppression of anger has long been a point of controversy; anger is socially disruptive, but it also expresses the needs of the individual. In Asian cultures, however, there is no controversy: Anger is to be avoided at all costs.

Thus it is important to consider culture when studying the self. Most research on the self, like that on most psychological topics, has involved participants from Western countries. As a result, it may exaggerate the fundamental nature and pervasiveness of the independent self. Although cultures share many conceptions of selfhood, many others show striking differences.

Historical Evolution of Self

It is not necessary to visit multiple cultures to find variations in selfhood. There is often ample variation within a single culture, because cultural change over time modifies the society. This is the root of research on birth cohort differences (e.g., Caspi, 1987; Stewart & Healy, 1989; Twenge, 2000, 2001a, 2001b): Your generation influences the culture you are exposed to and thus your individual characteristics. Western culture's dominant ideas about selfhood have changed and evolved dramatically over the past few centuries (see Baumeister, 1987; Twenge & Campbell, 2001). Thus, the special nature of the modern Western form of selfhood can be understood in a historical context as well as in the context of cross-cultural comparisons. These changes are important for the interpersonal self because many of these trends have affected personal relationships and the independent-interdependent nature of the self. Just as some cultures (such as the West) are more independent, so are some time periods (such as 1970–2000). In addition, shifts in self-views due to societal trends demonstrate the inherently social nature of the self: It changes in response to the larger society and one's generational peers.

Medieval Times to the Twentieth Century

During medieval times, people did not have identity crises the way we do today (see Baumeister, 1987, for a review). In earlier times, age, gender, and family were the decisive determinants of life outcomes and thus of identity. There were set patterns for life, depending on the constraints of these ascribed attributes; if you were born a peasant worker, you remained a peasant worker. Upward mobility was almost nonexistent, and most men entered their father's professions or were apprenticed to professions chosen by their parents. Religion dictated strict standards for behavior and worship. Many marriages were arranged. To put it crudely, a rigid society told our ancestors who they were, and there was not much they could do about it. In general, these societies were tighter and more collectivistic than Western societies are today.

Over the course of several centuries, Western societies became looser and more individualistic. For example, modern selves are based on changing rather than stable attributes. Gender and family background slowly became less important than more changeable attributes such as ability, diligence, and personality. The modern Western self can be defined and redefined much more than the self of earlier eras. This greater freedom has also shifted the burden of defining the self onto the individual; today everyone can choose from a wide spectrum of possible identities. This freedom can cause anxiety, however, because these choices can be overwhelming in their scope and direction. It also requires great self-knowledge, because decisions about careers and romantic partners are based on suitability (What is the best job for me? Is this person the one I'm supposed to marry?) The burden falls most heavily on adolescents, because adolescence ends with the formation of adult identity (e.g., Erikson, 1968). Hence, in the twentieth century adolescence has become a period of in-

decision, uncertainty, experimentation, and identity crisis (see Baumeister & Tice, 1986).

The 1960s to the Present

The trend toward greater focus on the self has accelerated in recent decades. Over the last 30 years, the self has become increasingly more individualized and autonomous. During the late 1960s and 1970s, popular culture promoted self-fulfillment, self-love, and "being your own best friend" (Ehrenreich & English, 1978). Pollsters noted that "the rage for self-fulfillment" had spread everywhere (Yankelovich, 1981). At one time, duty and modesty were the most favorable traits; during the 1970s, however, self-help books advised "a philosophy of ruthless self-centeredness" that informed people that "selfishness is not a dirty word" (Ehrenreich & English, 1978, p. 303). The preoccupation with self so permeated the society that Lasch (1978) called it "The Culture of Narcissism"; L. Y. Jones (1980, p. 260) spoke of the decade's "orgy of self-gratification"; and the young adults of the 1970s acquired the label "The 'Me' Generation." Increasingly, proclaiming that you loved, cherished, and valued yourself was no longer an immodest proposition (L. Y. Jones, 1980; Rosen, 1998; Swann, 1996). By the 1980s, Whitney Houston could sing (without irony) that "the greatest love of all" was for oneself.

This emphasis on individualism had specific consequences for many interpersonal relationships. Because spouses and children necessarily hindered the expression of unfettered individualism, writers and commentators increasingly portrayed marriage and children as "a drag" (Ehrenreich & English, 1978, p. 295). For example, if there was a conflict between what is best for the marriage and what is best for the self, earlier generations often placed the obligation to marriage as the supreme duty, but more recent generations placed the self higher (Zube, 1972). "From now on, Americans would live *for themselves,*" notes David Frum in his cultural history of the 1970s (2000; p. 58). "If anyone or anything else got in the way—well, so much the worse for them." It is probably not a coincidence that divorce rates began to rise substantially during the late 1960s and early 1970s, just as this new individualism was taking hold (Frum).

In addition, many authors have argued that the 1970s promoted negative attitudes toward children—what the Germans call *Kinderfeindlichkeit,* or hostility toward children (see, e.g., Holtz, 1995; Strauss & Howe, 1991). According to some authors, the growing emphasis on individualism tended to decrease the priority parents placed on children's needs as opposed to their own (Ehrenreich & English, 1978). At the same time, the birth rate declined during the 1970s, reaching historic lows that have not been equaled since. Children did not fit into the picture of individual self-fulfillment—after all, what could they really do for their parents?

Not only did the general societal ethos promote the self, but a *self-esteem movement* (an offshoot of the human-potential and self-growth movements) gained prevalence, arguing that "the basis for *everything* we do is self-esteem" (MacDonald, 1986, p. 27; quoted in Seligman, 1995). During the early 1980s, educators began to actively promote self-esteem in school children. This was partially accomplished by affirmation (children were given T-shirts that said "I'm lovable and capable" or sang songs about self-love; e.g., Swann, 1996). In addition, many schools discouraged criticism, telling teachers not to correct misspellings or grammar mistakes, so as not to harm a child's self-esteem (Sykes, 1995). Thus the culture increasingly promoted self-esteem as an end unto itself, rather than as an outcome of accomplishment or meaningful personal relationships.

This popular interest in the self also meant that young people became increasingly exposed to self-esteem as a desirable goal. Gergen (1973) argued that the popularization of psychological concepts often creates changes in the responses of the subject populations. Self-esteem is a prime candidate for changes based on popularization. Not only has self-esteem been directly trumpeted by social movements and promoters, but the concept has received wide media attention in newspapers, magazines, television programs, and popular music (Whitney Houston sings about it, and a popular song in the mid-1990s explained the singer's misguided actions as resulting from "low self-esteem"). If anything, this attention increased during the 1980s; while the self-esteem and human potential movements reached only some people in the 1970s, the 1980s and 1990s saw talk about self-esteem enter the mainstream.

Empirical searches show that coverage of self-esteem has increased substantially in the popular press (these searches were originally performed for Twenge & Campbell, 2001). In 1965, the *Reader's Guide to Periodical Literature* did not even include a listing for *self-esteem* (nor did it list any articles under *self-respect* or *self-love*). In 1995, the *Reader's Guide* listed 27 magazine articles devoted solely to the topic of self-esteem. In addition, a search of the Lexis-Nexus database for 1995 articles mentioning self-esteem exceeded the search limit of 1,000 articles; the 1,000-article limit was still exceeded even when the search was limited to a single month (June 1995). In the academic literature, PsycLit also shows a steady increase in articles mentioning self-esteem. From 1970 to 1974, .6% of all articles in the database mentioned self-esteem. This number increased steadily, reaching .10% from

1975 to 1979 and .12% from 1980 to 1984; the number has since leveled off at .12% to .13%. Thus, over the time period in question, academic publications examining self-esteem have doubled.

One consequence of these cultural changes has been increases in self-esteem as measured by popular questionnaires. Twenge and Campbell (2001) found that college students' scores on the Rosenberg Self-Esteem Scale rose more than a half a standard deviation between the late 1960s and the early 1990s. Children's scores on the Coopersmith Self-Esteem Inventory also increased from the early 1980s to the early 1990s. The authors argued that much of this change can be traced to the self-esteem movement and the general emphasis on the individual self in the larger society. Increases in assertiveness (Twenge, 2001b) and extraversion (Twenge, 2001a) complete the picture of a generation increasingly concerned with the self, individual rights, and self-expression.

To sum up: The self cannot be fully understood without reference to culture, whether that culture differs with respect to region or with respect to time. Research on cultural differences has blossomed into an extensive and growing subfield, while research on birth cohort and change over time is just beginning to be conducted. As Caspi (1987) argued, many aspects of development and personality must be understood within the context of time, because the larger sociocultural environment changes so much from decade to decade (also see Gergen, 1973). When we are born, grow up, and discover our adolescent and adult identities has a substantial effect on how we see the self as an entity.

REFERENCES

Ainsworth, M. D. (1989). Attachments beyond infancy. *American Psychologist, 44,* 709–716.

Baldwin, J. A., & Hopkins, R. (1990). African-American and European-American cultural differences as assessed by the worldviews paradigm: An empirical analysis. *Western Journal of Black Studies, 14,* 38–52.

Baumeister, R. F. (1982). A self-presentational view of social phenomena. *Psychological Bulletin, 91,* 3–26.

Baumeister, R. F. (1987). How the self became a problem: A psychological review of historical research. *Journal of Personality and Social Psychology, 52,* 163–176.

Baumeister, R. F. (1991). *Meanings of life.* New York: Guilford Press.

Baumeister, R. F. (1997). Esteem threat, self-regulatory breakdown, and emotional distress as factors in self-defeating behavior. *Review of General Psychology, 1,* 145–174.

Baumeister, R. F. (1998). The self. In D. T. Gilbert, S. T. Fiske, & G. Lindzey (Eds.), *Handbook of social psychology* (4th ed., pp. 680–740). New York: McGraw Hill.

Baumeister, R. F., Heatherton, T. F., & Tice, D. M. (1994). *Losing control: How and why people fail at self-regulation.* San Diego, CA: Academic Press.

Baumeister, R. F., Hutton, D. G., & Tice, D. M. (1989). Cognitive processes during deliberate self-presentation: How self-presenters alter and misinterpret the behavior of their interaction partners. *Journal of Experimental Social Psychology, 25,* 59–78.

Baumeister, R. F., & Jones, E. E. (1978). When self-presentation is constrained by the target's knowledge: Consistency and compensation. *Journal of Personality and Social Psychology, 36,* 608–618.

Baumeister, R. F., & Leary, M. R. (1995). The need to belong: Desire for interpersonal attachments as a fundamental human motivation. *Psychological Bulletin, 117,* 497–529.

Baumeister, R. F., Reis, H. T., & Delespaul, P. A. E. G. (1995). Subjective and experiential correlates of guilt in everyday life. *Personality and Social Psychology Bulletin, 21,* 1256–1268.

Baumeister, R. F., & Scher, S. J. (1988). Self-defeating behavior patterns among normal individuals: Review and analysis of common self-destructive tendencies. *Psychological Bulletin, 104,* 3–22.

Baumeister, R. F., Smart, L., & Boden, J. M. (1996). Relation of threatened egotism to violence and aggression: The dark side of high self-esteem. *Psychological Review, 103,* 5–33.

Baumeister, R. F., Stillwell, A. M., & Heatherton, T. F. (1994). Guilt: An interpersonal approach. *Psychological Bulletin, 115,* 243–267.

Baumeister, R. F., & Tice, D. M. (1986). How adolescence became the struggle for self: A historical transformation of psychological development. In J. Suls & A. G. Greenwald (Eds.), *Psychological perspectives on the self: Vol. 3.* (pp. 183–201). Hillsdale, NJ: Erlbaum.

Baumeister, R. F., & Tice, D. M. (1990). Anxiety and social exclusion. *Journal of Social and Clinical Psychology, 9,* 165–195.

Baumeister, R. F., Tice, D. M., & Hutton, D. G. (1989). Self-presentational motivations and personality differences in self-esteem. *Journal of Personality, 57,* 547–579.

Baumeister, R. F., Twenge, J. M., & Nuss, C. K. (in press). *Effects of social exclusion on cognitive processes: Journal of personality and social psychology.*

Beach, S. R. H. (1992, May). *Self-evaluation maintenance and marital functioning.* Presented at the conference of the Midwestern Psychological Association, Chicago.

Bednar, R., Wells, G., & Peterson, S. (1989). *Self-esteem: Paradoxes and innovations in clinical theory and practice.* Washington, DC: American Psychological Association.

Bem, D. J., & Allen, A. (1974). On predicting some of the people some of the time: The search for cross-situational consistencies in behavior. *Psychological Review, 81,* 506–520.

Blaine, B., & Crocker, J. (1993). Self-esteem and self-serving biases in reactions to positive and negative events: An integrative review. In R. Baumeister (Ed.), *Self-esteem: The puzzle of low self-regard* (pp. 55–85). New York: Plenum.

Bloom, B. L., White, S. W. & Asher, S. L. (1979). Marital disruption as a stressor: A review and analysis. *Psychological Bulletin, 85,* 867–894.

Bond, M. H., & Cheung, T. (1983). College students' spontaneous self-concept: The effect of culture among respondents in Hong Kong, Japan, and the United States. *Journal of Cross-Cultural Psychology, 14,* 153–171.

Bradlee, P. M., & Emmons, R. A. (1992). Locating narcissism within the interpersonal circumplex and the five-factor model. *Personality and Individual Differences, 13,* 821–830.

Brockner, J. (1984). Low self-esteem and behavioral plasticity: Some implications for personality and social psychology. In L. Wheeler (Ed.), *Review of personality and social psychology: Vol. 4.* (pp. 237–271). Beverly Hills, CA: Sage.

Brockner, J., Davy, J., & Carter, C. (1985). Layoffs, self-esteem, and survivor guilt: Motivational, affective and attitudinal consequences. *Organizational Behavior and Human Decision Processes, 36,* 229–244.

Brown, J. D. (1993). Motivational conflict and the self: The double-bind of low self-esteem. In R. Baumeister (Ed.), *Self-esteem: The puzzle of low self-regard* (pp. 117–130). New York: Plenum.

Brown, J. D., & McGill, K. L. (1989). The cost of good fortune: When positive life events produce negative health consequences. *Journal of Personality and Social Psychology, 57,* 1103–1110.

Bushman, B. J., & Baumeister, R. F. (1998). Threatened egotism, narcissism, self-esteem, and direct and displaced aggression: Does self-love or self-hate lead to violence? *Journal of Personality and Social Psychology, 75,* 219–229.

Bushman, B. J., Baumeister, R. F., Phillips, C. M., & Gilligan, J. (2002). Self-love and self-loathing behind bars: Narcissism and self-esteem among violent offenders in a prison sample. Unpublished manuscript.

Byrne, D. (1971). *The attraction paradigm.* New York: Academic Press.

Campbell, W. K. (1999). Narcissism and romantic attraction. *Journal of Personality and Social Psychology, 77,* 1254–1270.

Campbell, W. K., Foster, C. A., & Finkel, E. J. (2000). *Narcissism and love.* Unpublished manuscript. Cleveland, Ohio: Case Western Reserve University.

Carroll, L. (1987). A study of narcissism, affiliation, intimacy, and power motives among students in business administration. *Psychological Reports, 61,* 355–358.

Caspi, A. (1987). Personality in the life course. *Journal of Personality and Social Psychology, 53,* 1203–1213.

Luhtanen, R. K., & Crocker, J. (1992). A collective self-esteem scale: Self-evaluation of one's social identity. *Personality and Social Psychology Bulletin, 18,* 302–318.

MacDonald, S. (1986, April 28). Political priority #1: Teaching kids to like themselves. *New Opinions.*

Malloy, T. E., & Albright, L. (1990). Interpersonal perception in a social context. *Journal of Personality and Social Psychology, 58,* 419–428.

Markus, H. R., & Kitayama, S. (1991). Culture and the self: Implications for cognition, emotion, and motivation. *Psychological Review, 98,* 224–253.

Markus, H. R., Smith, J., & Moreland, R. (1985). Role of the self-concept in the perception of others. *Journal of Personality and Social Psychology, 49,* 1494–1512.

Mead, G. H. (1934). *Mind, self, and society.* Chicago, IL: University of Chicago Press.

Miller, R. S. (1995). Embarrassment and social behavior. In J. Tangney & K. Fischer (Eds.), *The self-conscious emotions* (pp. 322–339). New York: Guilford.

Modigliani, A. (1971). Embarrassment, facework, and eye contact: Testing a theory of embarrassment. *Journal of Personality and Social Psychology, 17,* 15–24.

Moreland, R. L. (1987). The formation of small groups. In C. Hendrick (Ed.), *Group processes: Review of personality and social psychology: Vol. 8.* (pp. 80–110). Newberry Park, CA: Sage.

Mruk, C. (1995). *Self-esteem: Research, theory, and practice.* New York: Springer.

Murray, S. L., Holmes, J. G., & Griffin, D. W. (1996a). The benefits of positive illusions: Idealization and the construction of satisfaction in close relationships. *Journal of Personality and Social Psychology, 70,* 79–98.

Murray, S. L., Holmes, J. G., Griffin, D. W. (1996b). The self-fulfilling nature of positive illusions in romantic relationships: Love is not blind, but prescient. *Journal of Personality and Social Psychology, 71,* 1155–1180.

Myers, D. (1992). *The pursuit of happiness.* New York: Morrow.

Newcomb, A. F., Bukowski, W. M., & Pattee, L. (1993). Children's peer relations: A meta-analytic review of popular, rejected, neglected, controversial, and average sociometric status. *Psychological Bulletin, 113,* 99–128.

Newman, L. S., Duff, K., & Baumeister, R. F. (1997). A new look at defensive projection: Suppression, accessibility, and biased person perception. *Journal of Personality and Social Psychology, 72,* 980–1001.

Oakes, P. J., & Turner, J. (1980). Social categorization and intergroup behavior: Does minimal intergroup discrimination make social identity more positive? *European Journal of Social Psychology, 10,* 295–301.

Orlofsky, J. L., Marcia, J. E., & Lesser, I. M. (1973). Ego identity status and the intimacy versus isolation crisis of young adulthood. *Journal of Personality and Social Psychology, 27,* 211–219.

Parrott, W. G., Sabini, J., & Silver, M. (1988). The roles of self-esteem and social interaction in embarrassment. *Personality and Social Psychology Bulletin, 14,* 191–202.

Pleban, R., & Tesser, A. (1981). The effects of relevance and quality of another's performance on interpersonal closeness. *Social Psychology Quarterly, 44,* 278–285.

Putnam, R. D. (1995). Bowling alone: America's declining social capital. *Journal of Democracy, 6,* 65–78.

Putnam, R. D. (2000). *Bowling alone: The collapse and revival of American community.* New York: Simon & Schuster.

Rhodewalt, F., & Morf, C. C. (1998). On self-aggrandizement and anger: A temporal analysis of narcissism and affective reactions to success and failure. *Journal of Personality and Social Psychology, 74,* 672–685.

Richman, A. (1985). Human risk factors in alcohol-related crashes. *Journal of Studies on Alcohol, 10,* 21–31.

Rosen, B. C. (1998). *Winners and losers of the information revolution: Psychosocial change and its discontents.* Westport, CN: Praeger.

Rosenbaum, M. E. (1986). The repulsion hypothesis: On the nondevelopment of relationships. *Journal of Personality and Social Psychology, 51,* 1156–1166.

Rosenberg, M. (1979). *Conceiving the self.* New York: Basic Books.

Rosenthal, R., & Jacobson, L. (1968). *Pygmalion in the classroom.* New York: Holt.

Sampson, R. J., & Laub, J. H. (1990). Crime and deviance over the life course: The salience of adult social bonds. *American Sociological Review, 55,* 609–627.

Sampson, R. J., & Laub, J. H. (1993). *Crime in the making: Pathways and turning points through life.* Cambridge, MA: Harvard University Press.

Sartre, J.-P. (1953). *The existential psychoanalysis* (H. E. Barnes, Trans.). New York: Philosophical Library.

Schlenker, B. R. (1975). Self-presentation: Managing the impression of consistency when reality interferes with self-enhancement. *Journal of Personality and Social Psychology, 32,* 1030–1037.

Schlenker, B. R. (1980). Impression management: The self-concept, social identity, and interpersonal relations. Monterey, CA: Brooks/Cole.

Schlenker, B. R. (1986). Self-identification: Toward an integration of the private and public self. In R. Baumeister (Ed.), *Public self and private self* (pp. 21–62). New York: Springer-Verlag.

Schlenker, B. R., & Leary, M. R. (1982). Social anxiety and self-presentation: A conceptualization and model. *Psychological Bulletin, 92,* 641–669.

Sedikides, C., Campbell, W. K., Reeder, G. D., & Elliot, A. J. (1998). The self-serving bias in relational context. *Journal of Personality and Social Psychology, 74,* 378–386.

Sedikides, C., & Skowronski, J. J. (1993). The self in impression formation: Trait centrality and social perception. *Journal of Experimental Social Psychology, 29*, 347–357.

Seligman, M. (1995). *The optimistic child.* New York: Houghton Mifflin.

Semin, G. R., & Manstead, A. S. R. (1982). The social implications of embarrassment displays and restitution behavior. *European Journal of Social Psychology, 12*, 367–377.

Shaver, P., Hazan, C., & Bradshaw, D. (1988). Love as attachment: The integration of three behavioral systems. In R. J. Sternberg & M. L. Barnes (Eds.), *The psychology of love* (pp. 68–99). New Haven, CT: Yale University Press.

Shrauger, J. S., & Schoeneman, T. J. (1979). Symbolic interactionist view of self-concept: Through the looking glass darkly. *Psychological Bulletin, 86*, 549–573.

Smeaton, G., Byrne, D., & Murnen, S. K. (1989). The repulsion hypothesis revisited: Similarity irrelevance or dissimilarity bias? *Journal of Personality and Social Psychology, 56*, 54–59.

Snyder, M. (1974). The self-monitoring of expressive behavior. *Journal of Personality and Social Psychology, 30*, 526–537.

Snyder, M. (1987). *Public appearances, private realities: The psychology of self-monitoring.* New York: Freeman.

Snyder, M., & Simpson, J. (1984). Self-monitoring and dating relationships. *Journal of Personality and Social Psychology, 47*, 1281–1291.

Snyder, M., & Swann, W. B. (1976). When actions reflect attitudes: The politics of impression management. *Journal of Personality and Social Psychology, 34*, 1034–1042.

Snyder, M., & Swann, W. B. (1978). Behavioral confirmation in social interaction: From social perception to social reality. *Journal of Experimental Social Psychology, 14*, 148–162.

Snyder, M., Tanke, E. D., & Berscheid, E. (1977). Social perception and interpersonal behavior: On the self-fulfilling nature of social stereotypes. *Journal of Personality and Social Psychology, 35*, 656–666.

Stewart, A. J., & Healy, J. M. (1989). Linking individual development and social changes. *American Psychologist, 44*, 30–42.

Strauss, W., & Howe, N. (1991). *Generations: The history of America's future, 1584 to 2069.* New York: Morrow.

Swann, W. B. (1996). *Self-traps: The elusive quest for higher self-esteem.* New York: Freeman.

Swann, W. B., Hixon, J. G., & De La Ronde, C. (1992). Embracing the bitter "truth": Negative self-concepts and marital commitment. *Psychological Science, 3*, 118–121.

Swann, W. B., & Predmore, S. C. (1985). Intimates as agents of social support: Sources of consolation or despair? *Journal of Personality and Social Psychology, 49*, 1609–1617.

Sykes, C. J. (1995). *Dumbing down our kids: Why American children feel good about themselves but can't read, write, or add.* New York: St. Martin's Griffin.

Tajfel, H. (1982). Social psychology of intergroup relations. *Annual Review of Psychology, 33*, 1–59.

Tajfel, H., & Turner, J. C. (1979). An integrative theory of intergroup conflict. In S. Worchel & W. Austin (Eds), *Psychology of intergroup relations* (2nd ed., pp. 7–24). Chicago: Nelson-Hall.

Tangney, J. P. (1992). Situational determinants of shame and guilt in young adulthood. *Personality and Social Psychology Bulletin, 18*, 199–206.

Tangney, J. P. (1995). Shame and guilt in interpersonal relationships. In J. Tangney & K. Fischer (Eds.), *The self-conscious emotions* (pp. 114–139). New York: Guilford.

Tangney, J. P., Burggraf, S. A., & Wagner, P. E. (1995). Shame-proneness, guilt-proneness, and psychological symptoms. In J. Tangney & K. Fischer (Eds.), *The self-conscious emotions* (pp. 343–367). New York: Guilford.

Tangney, J. P., & Fischer, K. W. (Eds.), (1995). *The self-conscious emotions: The psychology of shame, guilt, embarrassment, and pride.* New York: Guilford.

Tangney, J. P., Wagner, P. E., Fletcher, C., & Gramzow, R. (1992). Shamed into anger? The relation of shame and guilt to anger and self-reported aggression. *Journal of Personality and Social Psychology, 62*, 669–675.

Taylor, S. E., & Brown, J. D. (1988). Illusion and well-being: A social psychological perspective on mental health. *Psychological Bulletin, 103*, 193–210.

Tesch, S. A., & Whitbourne, S. K. (1982). Intimacy and identity status in young adults. *Journal of Personality and Social Psychology, 43*, 1041–1051.

Tesser, A. (1988). Toward a self-evaluation maintenance model of social behavior. In L. Berkowitz (Ed.), *Advances in experimental social psychology: Vol. 21.* (pp. 181–227). San Diego, CA: Academic Press.

Tesser, A. (1993). The importance of heritability in psychological research: The case of attitudes. *Psychological Review, 100*, 129–142.

Tesser, A., & Smith, J. (1980). Some effects of friendship and task relevance on helping: You don't always help the one you like. *Journal of Experimental Social Psychology, 16*, 582–590.

Tice, D. M., Butler, J. L., Muraven, M. B., & Stillwell, A. M. (1995). When modesty prevails: Differential favorability of self-presentation to friends and strangers. *Journal of Personality and Social Psychology, 69*, 1120–1138.

Triandis, H. C. (1989). The self and social behavior in differing cultural contexts. *Psychological Review, 96*, 506–520.

Turner, J. C. (1982). Towards a cognitive redefinition of the social group. In H. Tajfel (Ed.), *Social identity and intergroup relations* (pp. 15–40). Cambridge: Cambridge University Press.

Twenge, J. M. (2000). The age of anxiety? Birth cohort change in anxiety and neuroticism, 1952–1993. *Journal of Personality and Social Psychology, 79*, 1007–1021.

Twenge, J. M. (2001a). Birth cohort changes in extraversion: A cross-temporal meta-analysis, 1966–1993. *Personality and Individual Differences, 30*, 735–748.

Twenge, J. M. (2001b). Changes in women's assertiveness in response to status and roles: A cross-temporal meta-analysis, 1931–1993. *Journal of Personality and Social Psychology, 81,* 133–145.

Twenge, J. M., Baumeister, B. F., Tice, D. M., & Stucke, T. S. (2001). If you can't join them, beat them: The effects of social exclusion on antisocial behavior. *Journal of Personality and Social Psychology, 81.*

Twenge, J. M., & Campbell, W. K. (2001). Age and birth cohort differences in self-esteem: A cross-temporal meta-analysis. *Personality and Social Psychology Review, 5,* 321–344.

Twenge, J. M., Catanese, K., & Baumeister, R. F. (2001). *If no one will ever love you . . . The effect of social rejection on self-defeating behavior.* Unpublished manuscript.

Twenge, J. M., Ciarocco, N. J., & Baumeister, R. F. (2001). *Help! I need somebody: Effects of social exclusion on prosocial behavior.* Unpublished manuscript.

U.S. Bureau of the Census. (1998). *Statistical abstract of the United States.* Washington, DC: U.S. Government Printing Office.

Vohs, K. D., Ciarocco, N. J., & Baumeister, R. F. (2002). *Interpersonal functioning uses self-regulatory resources.* Manuscript in progress.

Vohs, K. D., & Heatherton, T. F. (2001). Self-esteem and threats to self: Implications for self-construals and interpersonal perceptions. *Journal of Personality and Social Psychology, 81,* 1103–1118.

Walsh, A., Beyer, J. A., & Petee, T. A. (1987). Violent delinquency: An examination of psychopathic typologies. *Journal of Genetic Psychology, 148,* 385–392.

Watson, P. J., Grisham, S. O., Trotter, M. V., & Biderman, M. D. (1984). Narcissism and empathy: Validity evidence for the narcissistic personality inventory. *Journal of Personality Assessment, 45,* 159–162.

Wegner, D. M., & Erber, R. (1992). The hyperaccessibility of suppressed thoughts. *Journal of Personality and Social Psychology, 63,* 903–912.

Whitley, B. E. (1983). Sex role orientation and self-esteem: A critical meta-analytic review. *Journal of Personality and Social Psychology, 44,* 765–778.

Williams, D. R., Takeuchi, R. L., & Adair, R. K. (1992). Marital status and psychiatric disorders among blacks and whites. *Journal of Health and Social Behavior, 33,* 140–157.

Williams, K. D., Cheung, C. K. T., & Choi, W. (2000). Cyberostracism: Effects of being ignored over the Internet. *Journal of Personality and Social Psychology, 79,* 748–762.

Williams, K. D., & Sommer, K. L. (1997). Social ostracism by coworkers: Does rejection lead to loafing or compensation? *Personality and Social Psychology Bulletin, 23,* 693–706.

Wills, T. A. (1981). Downward comparison principles in social psychology. *Psychological Bulletin, 90,* 245–271.

Wright, K. N., & Wright, K. E. (1992). Does getting married reduce the likelihood of criminality? A review of the literature. *Federal Probation, 56,* 50–56.

Yankelovich, D. (1981). *New rules: Searching for self-fulfillment in a world turned upside-down.* New York: Random House.

Zube, M. J. (1972). Changing concepts of morality: 1948–1969. *Social Forces, 50,* 385–393.

CHAPTER 15

Persuasion and Attitude Change

RICHARD E. PETTY, S. CHRISTIAN WHEELER, AND ZAKARY L. TORMALA

Attitudes refer to the general and relatively enduring evaluations people have of other people, objects, or ideas. These overall evaluations can be positive, negative, or neutral, and they can vary in their extremity. For example, one individual might view jazz music in a mildly positive way, whereas another might be wildly positive and another might be somewhat negative. Individuals can hold attitudes about very broad or hypothetical constructs (e.g., anarchy) as well as about very concrete and specific things (e.g., a particular brand of chewing gum). Before turning to our primary focus on the processes involved in changing attitudes, we address some important background issues on the nature and structure of attitudes. Following this background discussion, we describe ways to change attitudes that involve relatively high versus low amounts of cognitive effort and the consequences of these different strategies.

BACKGROUND ISSUES

Bases of Attitudes

Attitudes can be based on different types of information. One popular conceptualization of the attitude construct, the *tripartite theory,* holds that there are three primary types of information on which attitudes can be based (Breckler, 1984; Rosenberg & Hovland, 1960; Zanna & Rempel, 1988): cognitions or beliefs (e.g., *This car gets 10 miles per gallon*), affect or feelings (e.g., *Owning this car makes me happy*), and actions or behavior (e.g., *I have always driven this brand of car*). The basis of the attitude object can have important implications for attitude change (see also the chapter by Olson & Maio in this volume). For example, it may generally be more effective to change attitudes that are based on emotion with emotional strategies rather than with more cognitive or rational ones (Edwards, 1990; Fabrigar & Petty, 1999).

Attitude Storage Versus Construction

Implied in our definition of attitudes is the notion that attitudes are stored memorial constructs. Some researchers have argued that attitudes may in fact not be stored in memory and instead be newly constructed, based upon salient beliefs, emotions, and behaviors each time the individual is asked to report his or her attitude (Schwarz & Bohner, 2001; Wilson & Hodges, 1992). This perspective seems rooted primarily in the finding that attitude reports are susceptible to a variety of contextual biases that can contaminate attitude reports (see Schwarz, 1999).

Although attitude reports are clearly influenced by the immediate context, a strict constructivist view of attitudes seems implausible for a variety of reasons. First, as we review later in this chapter, research has demonstrated that individuals experience aversive arousal when they violate their existing attitudes (e.g., Elliot & Devine, 1994; Elkin & Leippe, 1986; Losch & Cacioppo, 1990), and individuals are often motivated to defend their attitudes in the face of counterattitudinal appeals (e.g., Ditto & Lopez, 1992; Ditto, Scepansky, Munro, Apanovitch, & Lockhart, 1998; Edwards & Smith, 1996; Kunda, 1990; Petty & Cacioppo, 1979a). These findings are consistent with the view that some attitudinal representation exists in memory. Furthermore, research has delineated the conditions under which motivated defense versus attitude construction processes will operate (e.g., Fazio, Zanna, & Cooper, 1977). Second, attitudes can be automatically activated under response conditions that would make spontaneous construction seem unlikely (Bargh, Chaiken, Govender, & Pratto, 1992; Bargh, Chaiken, Raymond, & Hymes, 1996; Fazio, Sanbonmatsu, Powell, & Kardes, 1986). Third, it would seem to be functionally maladaptive for individuals to store a lot of attitude-relevant beliefs for attitude reconstruction in the absence of summary evaluative representations (see also Lingle & Ostrom, 1981). Fourth, research has uncovered structural properties of attitudes that can influence their persistence across a variety of contexts (see Petty & Krosnick, 1995).

If there were no stored attitudes, and evaluations were simply constructed anew each time the attitude object was encountered, many of the processes described in this chapter would have little theoretical utility. Instead, attitude change researchers would better spend their time focusing solely on context effects rather than procedures aimed at changing memorial evaluative representations. In our view, the strict constructivist approach does not seem prudent. In this chapter, attitudes are conceptualized as stored memorial constructs that may or may not be retrieved upon encountering the attitude object (see Fazio, 1990).

In using this conceptualization, we do not mean to imply that attitudes are not susceptible to context effects or are *never* constructed from scratch. Most obviously, when individuals do not have attitudes about a particular attitude object, they may simply construct an attitude when asked for one (Converse, 1970). Also, when individuals are instructed to think about their attitude before reporting it, they may sometimes selectively focus on a subset of attitude-relevant information and this salient information would influence the attitude reported (e.g., Wilson & Kraft, 1993). Similarly, individuals may report different attitudes when contextual variables like conversational norms or social desirability concerns operate (e.g., Fazio, Jackson, Dunton, & Williams, 1995; Schwarz, 1999). However, the fact that contextual variables can sometimes influence attitude reports is not tantamount to establishing that there are no stored evaluations for any attitude objects. Rather, attitude construction processes probably occur mostly when no stored evaluation is readily accessible or when contextual factors contribute to current attitude reports by modifying or shading a retrieved global evaluation (Petty, Priester, & Wegener, 1994).

Attitude Strength

Although we define attitudes as relatively enduring constructs (i.e., stored representations), attitudes can certainly change over time. Attitudes can change from being nonexistent to having some valence, or they can change from one valence to another. Most of this chapter focuses on the processes responsible for changes in attitudes. *Polarization* refers to instances in which an existing attitude maintains the same valence but becomes more extreme. *Moderation* refers to those instances in which an individual's existing attitude becomes less extreme and moves toward the point of neutrality. One's attitude can also cross the neutral point and change valence.

Attitudes may be fruitfully conceptualized as falling along a continuum ranging from nonattitudes to strong attitudes (see Converse, 1970). Strong attitudes are those that influence thought and behavior, are persistent over time, and are resistant to change (Krosnick & Petty, 1995). A large variety of strength indicators have been identified and studied empirically, including attitude accessibility (e.g., Bassili, 1995; Fazio, 1995), certainty (e.g., Gross, Holtz, & Miller, 1995), importance (Krosnick, 1988), and elaboration (Petty, Haugtvedt, & Smith, 1995; see Petty & Krosnick, 1995, for a review of attitude strength variables). Although it is intuitively appealing to assume that attitude strength variables are manifestations of a single latent construct, intercorrelations among the various attitude strength variables are often somewhat low (e.g., Krosnick, Boninger, Chuang, Berent, & Carnot, 1993; Raden, 1985). Furthermore, the search for a limited number of underlying attitude strength factors has yielded inconclusive results so far (see Eagly & Chaiken, 1998, for a review). Nevertheless, it seems reasonable that the many strength variables ultimately boil down to a relatively few critical dimensions that are most important for producing the major strength consequences (e.g., making the attitude resistant to change).

Implicit Versus Explicit Attitudes

Although most research on attitudes concerns people's explicit likes and dislikes, in recent years a good deal of research interest has been generated by the idea of implicit attitudes. In an influential review of implicit attitude effects, Greenwald and Banaji (1995) referred to implicit attitudes as "introspectively unidentified (or inaccurately identified) traces of past experience that mediate favorable or unfavorable feeling, thought, or action toward social objects" (p. 8). This definition suggests that people are unaware of some past experiences (implicit attitudes) that mediate current responses. Wilson, Lindsey, and Schooler (2000) expanded this definition by suggesting that implicit attitudes are "evaluations that (a) have an unknown origin . . . (b) are activated automatically; and (c) influence implicit responses . . ." (p. 104). This definition suggests that people may be unaware of the origin of their past attitudes, although they may be aware of the attitudes themselves. Greenwald, McGhee, and Schwartz (1998) stated that "implicit attitudes are manifest as actions or judgments that are under the control of automatically activated evaluation without the performer's awareness of that causation" (p. 1464). This definition suggests that people are unaware of the effects of implicit attitudes. The implicit attitudes construct has been applied to a growing body of research and can have important implications for how researchers conceptualize attitude change. Although the various definitions of implicit attitudes have significant overlap, their application in practice is sometimes characterized by substantial ambiguity.

As the above definitions imply, one dimension on which implicit attitudes are thought to differ from explicit attitudes is awareness. That is, implicit attitudes are viewed as ones for which people are unaware of what the attitude is, where it comes from, or what effects it has. It is perhaps important to note that these types of awareness are not mutually exclusive. Any attitude can be characterized by all or none of these types of awareness. We discuss each of these features next.

Awareness of the Attitude Itself

The first type of awareness concerns an awareness of the attitude itself—that is, does the person consciously acknowledge that he or she holds an evaluative predisposition toward some person, object, or issue? If so, the attitude is said to be *explicit*. On the other hand, individuals sometimes have stored evaluative associations of which they are unaware. This type of awareness corresponds to the meaning of *implicit* as employed in other psychological research domains.

For example, in many demonstrations of implicit memory, an individual shows evidence of having memorized a piece of information, yet is unable to consciously retrieve the information when desired (see Schacter, 1987, for a review). Similarly, evidence for implicit learning is found when an individual acquires some knowledge or skill that is evidenced on task performance, but the individual is unable to verbalize the underlying rule or basis for the skill (see Seger, 1994, for a review). Thus, according to this criterion, to the extent that people have evaluative predispositions of which they are not consciously aware and are unable to consciously report when asked, these attitudes are said to be implicit.

Awareness of the Basis of the Attitude

Another type of awareness mentioned in some discussions of implicit attitudes concerns awareness of the basis of the attitude. If people are not aware of the attitude itself, it is unlikely that they would be aware of its basis (i.e., where it comes from). However, people are often unaware of the basis of their explicit attitudes as well. For example, repeated subliminal exposures to a stimulus can increase liking of the stimulus (Bornstein & D'Agostino, 1992) without awareness. Although the individual can explicitly report his or her preference for the previously seen stimulus, he or she has no access to the source of the liking (i.e., the previous subliminal exposures). Similarly, a consciously reported attitude (e.g., one's life satisfaction) may be unknowingly biased by extraneous inputs (e.g., the good weather; Schwarz & Clore, 1983). Even if the source of an attitude seems quite explicit (e.g., exposure to a persuasive message), people may be unaware that the message has influenced their attitudes. People sometimes recall having had their new attitude all along (Ross & McFarland, 1988). People can also think that their attitudes have changed when they have not.

Thus, using awareness of an attitude's basis or source as a defining criterion for implicit attitudes is problematic in part because individuals rarely (if ever) have complete access to all of the influences on their judgments (see Nisbett & Wilson, 1977; Wilson & Hodges, 1992). Therefore we do not think that this criterion is a useful one for distinguishing implicit from explicit attitudes. Stated simply, if an attitude is implicit, the basis may be unknown—but not knowing the basis of an attitude does not make it implicit.

Awareness of the Attitude's Influence

A third type of awareness concerns awareness of the extent of an attitude's influence on other judgments and behaviors. For example, Greenwald and Banaji (1995) indicated that halo effects are one example of the operation of implicit attitudes. Halo effects refer to instances in which information about one attribute influences judgments about other unrelated attributes. For example, Johnny may judge Sue to be intelligent because he believes her to be attractive. To the extent that Johnny is unaware that his conscious beliefs concerning her attractiveness influence his judgments of her intelligence, his attitude toward her attractiveness may be labeled *implicit* by this criterion (Greenwald & Banaji, 1995). This view is problematic, however. Individuals are unlikely to be aware of all of the consequences of their attitudes for judgment and behavior, and thus this criterion would render nearly every attitude implicit. Furthermore, whether the attitude was considered implicit could vary from context to context (i.e., the person could be aware that a negative attitude was influencing him or her in one situation but not in another). Consequently, this feature does not appear to be an optimal criterion for defining implicit attitudes. As with the previous criterion, if people are unaware of the attitude itself (i.e., the attitude is implicit) they are unlikely to be aware of the effects of the attitude. But not knowing the effects of an attitude does not make it implicit.

Summary

In considering the three types of awareness, it is awareness or acknowledgement of holding the attitude itself that is the distinguishing feature of implicit versus explicit attitudes. People are aware of holding their explicit attitudes; they are not aware of holding their implicit attitudes. Our use of the phrase *acknowledging one's attitude* is not meant to imply that people like or are comfortable with their attitudes—only that they recognize that they have these attitudes. For example, a person might acknowledge some prejudice for or liking of cigarettes, but the same person might also wish that these attitudes could change. People tend to be happy with and want to defend their attitudes, but this is not always the case. In addition, an implicit attitude may enter consciousness in a variety of ways. For example, therapy may reveal hidden attitudes, or an experimenter may reveal such attitudes to participants in a study. The person's own behavior (e.g., a slip of the tongue) may also provide a clue to an implicit attitude. When presented with such information, a person can acknowledge the implicit attitude, thereby making it explicit—or the person can deny having this reaction (i.e., *the therapist is wrong*), keeping it implicit. Regarding the other dimensions, we note that implicit attitudes generally have an *implicit basis* and have *implicit effects,* but these attributes per se do not make the attitudes implicit because explicit

attitudes can also have an implicit basis and have implicit effects (see also Wegener & Petty, 1998).

Measurement of Attitudes

Researchers have developed a multitude of attitude measurement instruments (see Eagly & Chaiken, 1993; also see the chapter by Olson & Maio in this volume). Measurement of attitudes is important for determining whether attitude change has occurred. A long-standing distinction between attitude measures has been drawn concerning whether the measure is a direct or an indirect one (Petty & Cacioppo, 1981). Direct attitude measures are those that simply ask the respondent to report his or her attitude. Because these measures are transparent and make it obvious that attitudes are being assessed, they can be considered *explicit measures* of attitudes. Included in this category are attitude measurement devices such as the semantic differential (Osgood, Suci, & Tannenbaum, 1957), the one-item rating scale, the Likert scale (Likert, 1932), and the Thurstone scale (Thurstone, 1928). Indirect attitude measures on the other hand are those that do not directly ask the individual to report his or her attitude. Instead, the individual's attitude is inferred from his or her judgments, reactions, or behaviors. Because these measures do not make it obvious that attitudes are being assessed, they can be considered *implicit measures* of attitudes. A person completing an implicit measure is presumably unaware that the measure is assessing attitudes. Included in this category are a wide variety of methods such as the Thematic Apperception Test (Proshansky, 1943), the Information Error Test (Hammond, 1948), the Implicit Association Test (IAT; Greenwald et al., 1998), the automatic evaluation task (e.g., Fazio et al., 1995), physiological measures such as the facial electromyograph (EMG; e.g., Cacioppo & Petty, 1979a) or electroencephalogram (EEG; e.g., Cacioppo, Crites, Bernston, & Coles, 1993), and physical behaviors like nonverbal gestures, eye contact, or seating distance (e.g., Argyle & Dean, 1965; Dovidio, Kawakami, Johnson, Johnson, & Howard, 1997; Macrae, Bodenhausen, Milne, & Jetten, 1994; Word, Zanna, & Cooper, 1974). Direct and indirect measurement methods typically exhibit modest positive correlations (Dovidio, Kawakami, & Beach, 2000).

It is important to note that direct and indirect measurement methods can differ in the extent to which they permit deliberative responding (Vargas, von Hippel, & Petty, 2001). For example, experimenters could require individuals to report their attitudes on a direct one-item rating scale very quickly with no time for deliberation, or they could permit individuals to make the judgment after some minimal or extensive reflection. Similarly, some indirect attitude measures permit relatively slow and deliberate responding (e.g., the Thematic Apperception Test; Information Error Test), whereas others require very fast responses (e.g., the IAT or automatic evaluation task).

Researchers make two common assumptions about direct (explicit) and indirect (implicit) measures of attitudes, and we discuss each assumption in turn.

What Do Implicit and Explicit Measures Assess?

One assumption is that explicit attitude measures tap explicit attitudes, whereas implicit measures tap implicit attitudes (e.g., Dovidio et al., 2000; Greenwald & Banaji, 1995). This assumption is tidy but seems ill-advised for a number of reasons. First, even if it were the case that implicit attitudes could be assessed only with implicit measures, this would not mean that implicit measures assessed only implicit attitudes. In fact, implicit measuring devices have long been used to tap explicit attitudes that people were simply unwilling to report due to social desirability concerns, and such measures do tap explicit attitudes if there is no competing implicit attitude. For example, an attitude measure like eye contact or seating distance could tap primarily implicit attitudes to the extent that the individual is not aware that he or she holds that attitude. Hence, an individual may sit farther away from members of a stigmatized social category despite professing (and believing) that he or she harbors no animosity or dislike towards the group. However, behaviors like eye contact or seating distance can often also be manifestations of quite explicit attitudes. One may sit closer to one's spouse than to a complete stranger and also be quite aware that one prefers the company of one's spouse. Contemporary measures of automatic responding (e.g., Fazio, 1995) also assess primarily explicit attitudes if there is no competing implicit one.

On the other hand, if there is a competing implicit attitude, measures of automatic evaluation might be used to assess it. Thus, discrepancies between nondeliberative implicit measures and deliberative explicit measures can sometimes be attributed to social desirability contaminants (e.g., Fazio et al., 1995; Greenwald et al., 1998), but they can also be due to competing implicit and explicit attitudes (Wilson, Lindsey, & Schooler, 2000).

Second, it does not appear to be the case that implicit attitudes can only be assessed with implicit measures. This is because implicit measures, like explicit ones, vary in the extent to which they allow controlled versus automatic responding (Vargas et al., 2001). For example, if a direct measure is administered quickly with little time for reflection, implicit attitudes might well influence responses (see also Wilson et al., 2000). Thus, if time pressure is high, a fast direct scale might assess a prior and now-rejected attitude because it was

more accessible than was the new attitude (Petty & Jarvis, 1998). Perhaps a simple generalization that can be made is that explicit attitudes are most confidently assessed with deliberative direct attitude assessments. Of course, this statement rests on the assumption that self-presentational concerns or other biasing factors are not contaminating the attitude report. To the extent that such biasing factors (e.g., an unusually positive mood) are at work, the measure may tap the influence of the biasing agents rather than solely the underlying attitude. When direct attitude reports do not permit deliberative responding, however, the direct measure could tap either explicit or implicit attitudes.

Most of the time explicit and implicit measures should assess the same underlying attitude. It is in the interesting case in which the two types of assessments produce different outcomes that one might conclude that the implicit measure has tapped an implicit attitude. Of course, before one reaches this conclusion, it is important to rule out the possibility that the person is actually aware of the conflicting attitude but simply does not report it for purposes of self-presentation.

What Do Implicit and Explicit Measures Predict?

A second assumption is that explicit attitudes predict deliberative behaviors (e.g., jury voting), whereas implicit attitudes predict spontaneous behavior (e.g., seating distances; Dovidio et al., 1997). If implicit attitudes are always more accessible than are explicit attitudes, one might expect this to be the case (Dovidio, et al, 2000; Wilson et al., 2000). For example, Fazio (1990) suggested that highly accessible attitudes influence behavior when motivation and opportunity to evaluate the consequences of one's actions are low, but that less accessible or newly constructed attitudes can influence behavior when motivation and opportunity are high. However, the conclusion that implicit attitudes predict spontaneous behavior whereas explicit attitudes predict deliberative behavior may be premature. Vargas et al. (2001) argued that this conclusion was reached because the prominent contemporary implicit measures have relied on quick and spontaneous reactions (e.g., speeded response task; Wilson et al., 2000; automatic evaluation task; Fazio, 1995), whereas explicit measures have relied on deliberative responses. That is, the information-processing conditions of attitude measurement (spontaneous or deliberate) matched the information-processing conditions of behavioral assessment, and this assessment compatibility fostered higher correlations (Ajzen & Fishbein, 1977). To test this notion, Vargas et al. developed a deliberative implicit measure of attitudes and demonstrated that it could predict deliberative behavior over and above a series of deliberative explicit attitude measures. Although not demonstrated yet, it presumably would be the case that a spontaneous explicit measure could predict spontaneous behavior above and beyond that predicted by a spontaneous implicit measure. To the extent that these effects hold, it suggests that both dimensions of attitudes (implicit-explicit, spontaneous-deliberate) are important to consider in predicting behavior. After discussing the major approaches to attitude change in the next section, we return to the implicit-explicit attitude distinction and discuss some implications of this distinction for understanding attitude change.

ATTITUDE CHANGE: AN OVERVIEW

Now that we have examined some important conceptual issues surrounding the attitude concept, we turn to a discussion of attitude change processes. In the remainder of this chapter we describe the fundamental processes of attitude change that have been proposed by social psychologists in the modern era. The study of attitude change is one of the oldest in social psychology, and so many different theories and effects have been uncovered over the past 50 years that it can be challenging to understand them all.

The focus of theories of attitude change to date has been on producing and changing explicit attitudes. That is, an attitude change technique is deemed effective to the extent that it modifies a person's self-report of attitudes. For example, if a person is neutral toward an abstract symbol prior to the change treatment but is explicitly more favorable afterward, attitude change was successful. Although some recent research has demonstrated that attitude change can be produced on implicit attitude measures (Dasgupta & Greenwald, 2001), these change techniques probably also introduced change that could have been measured with explicit measures (see also Olson & Fazio, 2001). To date, there are no persuasion techniques that have proven to be effective in changing implicit but not explicit attitudes; thus, our review focuses on changing explicit attitudes. The topic of implicit attitude change will likely occupy considerable research attention in the coming decade (e.g., Kawakami, Dovidio, Moll, Hermsen, & Russin, 2000).

To organize the different theories of attitude change, we rely on the key ideas from contemporary dual process models of social judgment (Chaiken & Trope, 1999). The two such models that are most popular for understanding attitude change are the elaboration likelihood model (ELM; Petty & Cacioppo, 1986) and the heuristic-systematic model (HSM; Chaiken, Liberman, & Eagly, 1989). These models provide a metaframework from which to understand the moderation and mediation of attitude change effects, and they explain how the same variable (e.g., source credibility, mood) can have different effects on attitude change in different situations (e.g., increasing attitude change in one situation but decreasing it in another) and produce the same effect by different processes in different situations. Perhaps the key idea in the dual process models is that some processes of attitude change require relatively high amounts of mental effort, whereas other processes of attitude change require relatively little mental effort. Thus, Petty and Cacioppo (1981) reasoned that most of the major theories of attitude change were not necessarily competitive or contradictory, but rather operative in different circumstances. Later in this chapter we use this notion to organize the major processes of persuasion. Although the ELM and HSM stem from somewhat different traditions, today the models have many similarities and can generally accommodate the same empirical results, although the explanatory language and sometimes the assumed mediating processes vary (Eagly & Chaiken, 1993; Petty & Wegener, 1998).

Contemporary persuasion theorists endorse the fundamental dual process notion that different processes lead to attitude change in different circumstances (cf., Kruglanski & Thompson, 1999). Some of these processes require diligent and effortful information-processing activity, whereas others proceed with relatively little mental effort. In this section, we first describe the elaboration likelihood model of persuasion and review some prominent factors that determine whether people exert high or low amounts of mental effort in a persuasion situation (the HSM points to similar factors). Next, we describe in more detail the persuasion processes that tend to require relatively low amounts of mental effort. Following this, we describe the persuasion processes that tend to require relatively high amounts of mental effort.

The Elaboration Likelihood Model of Persuasion

The *elaboration likelihood model* of persuasion (ELM; Petty & Cacioppo, 1981, 1986; Petty & Wegener, 1999) is a theory about the processes responsible for attitude change and the strength of the attitudes that result from those processes. A key construct in the ELM is the *elaboration likelihood continuum*. This continuum is defined by how motivated and able people are to assess the central merits of an issue or a position. The more motivated and able people are to assess the central merits of an issue or position, the more likely they are to effortfully scrutinize all available issue-relevant information. Thus, when the elaboration likelihood is high, people assess issue-relevant information in relation to knowledge that they already possess, and they arrive at a reasoned (although not necessarily unbiased) attitude that is well articulated and bolstered by supporting information (central route). When the elaboration likelihood is low, however, then information scrutiny is reduced and attitude change can result from a number of less resource-demanding processes that do not require as much effortful evaluation of the issue-relevant information (peripheral route). Attitudes that are changed by low-effort processes are postulated to be weaker than are attitudes that are changed the same amount by high-effort processes (see prior discussion of attitude strength).

The elaboration likelihood continuum incorporates both a quantitative and a qualitative distinction (see Petty, 1997; Petty, Wheeler, & Bizer, 1999). That is, as one goes higher on the elaboration continuum, central route processes increase in magnitude (cognitive effort increases), and as one goes down the continuum, central route processes diminish in magnitude (cognitive effort decreases). This quantitative variation suggests that at high levels of elaboration, people's attitudes are determined by their effortful examination of all relevant information, but at lower levels of elaboration, attitudes can be determined by effortful examination of less information (e.g., the person critically examines only the first argument in a message but not the remaining arguments), or less effortful examination of all of the information. In addition, however, the ELM incorporates a qualitative distinction—that is, the ELM holds that not all change processes are the same. For example, consider a person who is exposed to a message with 10 arguments. The high elaboration (central route) processor tends to think carefully about much or all of the information. If motivation or ability to think were reduced, the recipient might think about each argument less carefully or think about fewer arguments (quantitative difference). However, the ELM holds that when the elaboration likelihood is low, people might also process the arguments in a qualitatively different way. For example, rather than assessing the substantive merits of the arguments, they might simply count them and reason, "there are so many arguments, it must be good" (Petty & Cacioppo, 1984). In the section of this chapter entitled "Relatively Low-Effort Processes of Attitude Change," we describe a variety of relatively low-effort processes that can modify attitudes.

In addition to the elaboration continuum and the various processes that operate along it, two other ELM notions are worth explaining. The first is that the ELM postulates a trade-off between the impact of high- and low-effort processes on judgments along the elaboration continuum—that is, as the impact of high-effort processes on judgments increases, the impact of low-effort processes on judgments decreases. This trade-off hypothesis implies a number of things. First is that at most points along the continuum, various change processes can co-occur and jointly influence judgments. Second, however, is that movement in either direction along the continuum tends to enhance the *relative* impact of one or the other family of *processes* (e.g., effortful scrutiny for merit vs. reliance on a counting heuristic) on judgments.

Another important ELM notion is called the *multiple roles hypothesis;* this is the idea that any given variable can influence attitudes by different processes at different points along the elaboration continuum. For example, if a pleasant television show makes you feel happy, this happiness might make you develop a positive attitude toward the products featured in the commercials shown during the show. The mechanism by which this happens can vary, however, depending on the overall elaboration likelihood. When the elaboration likelihood is low (e.g., high distraction), happiness could affect judgments by serving as a simple associative cue (e.g., *if I feel good, I must like it*). On the other hand, if the elaboration likelihood is high, happiness could affect judgments by biasing the thoughts that come to mind (Petty, Schumann, Richman, & Strathman, 1993). If the elaboration likelihood is not constrained to be high or low, being happy can affect the extent of processing of the message arguments. In particular, if the message is counterattitudinal or unpleasant in some way, being happy reduces message processing (Bless, Bohner, Schwarz, & Strack, 1990). If the message is uplifting and pleasant, however, happiness can increase message processing over neutrality (Wegener, Petty, & Smith, 1995). Other variables can also play different roles depending on the overall elaboration likelihood.

Determinants and Dimensions of Elaboration

According to the ELM, in order for high-effort processes to influence attitudes, people must be both motivated to think (i.e., have the desire to exert a high level of mental effort) and have the ability to think (i.e., have the necessary skills and opportunity to engage in thought). There are many variables capable of affecting the elaboration likelihood and thereby influencing whether attitude change is likely to occur by the high- or low-effort processes we describe in more detail shortly. Some of these motivational and ability variables are part of the persuasion situation, whereas others are part of the individual. Some variables affect mostly the amount of information processing activity, whereas others tend to influence the direction or valence of the thinking.

One of the most important variables influencing a person's motivation to think is the perceived personal relevance or importance of the communication (Johnson & Eagly, 1989; Petty & Cacioppo, 1979b, 1990; Petty, Cacioppo, & Haugtvedt, 1992; Thomsen, Borgida, & Lavine, 1995). When personal relevance is high, people are more influenced by the substantive arguments in a message and are less affected by peripheral processes (e.g., Petty, Cacioppo, & Goldman, 1981). There are many ways to render a message self-relevant, such as including many first-person pronouns (Burnkrant & Unnava, 1989) or matching the message in some way to a person's self-conceptions (Petty, Wheeler, & Bizer, 2000). In addition, people are more motivated to scrutinize information when they believe that they are solely responsible for message evaluation (Petty, Harkins, & Williams, 1980), when they are individually accountable (Tetlock, 1983), when they recently have been deprived of control (Pittman, 1994), and when they expect to discuss the issue with a partner (Chaiken, 1980). Increasing the number of message sources can enhance information-processing activity (e.g., Harkins & Petty, 1981; Moore & Reardon, 1987), especially when the sources are viewed as providing independent assessments of the issue (Harkins & Petty, 1987). Various incongruities can increase information-processing activity, such as when an expert source presents surprisingly weak arguments (Maheshwaran & Chaiken, 1991), when the message does not present the information in a form that was expected (S. M. Smith & Petty, 1996), and when people feel ambivalent rather than certain about some issue (Maio, Bell, & Esses, 1996).

In addition to factors associated with the persuasive message or the persuasion context, there are individual differences in people's motivation to think about persuasive communications. For example, people who enjoy thinking (i.e., those high in need for cognition; Cacioppo & Petty, 1982) tend to form attitudes on the basis of the quality of the arguments in a message rather than on peripheral cues (see Cacioppo, Petty, & Morris, 1983). Factors associated with the attitude itself can also influence the extent of information processing. For example, people tend to think more about messages relevant to their accessible attitudes rather than to their relatively inaccessible attitudes (Fabrigar, Priester, Petty, & Wegener, 1998).

Among the important variables influencing a person's ability to process issue-relevant arguments is message repetition. Moderate message repetition provides more opportunities for argument scrutiny (e.g., Cacioppo & Petty, 1979b; Gorn & Goldberg, 1980), which is beneficial for processing as long as tedium is not induced (Cacioppo & Petty, 1989; Cox & Cox, 1988). External distractions (e.g., Petty, Wells, & Brock, 1976), fast presentations (S. M. Smith & Shaffer, 1991) external pacing of messages (such as those on radio or TV rather than in print; Chaiken & Eagly, 1976; Wright, 1981), time pressures on processing (e.g., Kruglanski & Freund, 1983), enhancing recipients' physiological arousal via exercise (e.g., Sanbonmatsu & Kardes, 1988), placing recipients in an uncomfortable posture (Petty, Wells, Heesacker, Brock, & Cacioppo, 1983), and rendering the message difficult to understand (e.g., Ratneshwar & Chaiken, 1991) all decrease substantive message processing and should increase the impact of peripheral processes. Interestingly, even though a number of studies have examined differences in the actual ability of recipients to process a persuasion message, little

work has examined differences in perceived ability to process. For example, a message that appears technical or overly quantitative (Yalch & Elmore-Yalch, 1984) may reduce processing not because it interferes with actual ability, but rather because it interferes with a person's perceived ability to process (e.g., *it's probably too complicated for me, so why bother*).

Individual differences also exist in the ability of people to think about a persuasive communication. For example, as general knowledge about a topic increases, people can become more able (and perhaps more motivated) to think about issue-relevant information (Wood, Rhodes, & Biek, 1995). Knowledge is only effective to the extent that it is accessible, however (e.g., Brucks, Armstrong, & Goldberg, 1988). When knowledge is low or inaccessible, people are more reliant on simple cues (e.g., Wood & Kallgren, 1988).

Of course, in most communication settings, a confluence of factors rather than one variable acting in isolation determines the nature of information processing. Although the effects of single variables on information processing have been studied extensively, there is relatively little work examining possible interactions among variables (cf. Petty, Cacioppo, & Heesacker, 1981).

Relatively Objective Versus Biased Information Processing

The variables we have discussed, such as distraction or need for cognition, tend to influence information-processing activity in a relatively objective manner—that is, all else being equal, distraction tends to disrupt whatever thoughts a person is thinking (Petty et al., 1976). The distraction per se does not specifically target one type of thought (e.g., favorable or unfavorable) to impede. Similarly, individuals with high need for cognition are more motivated to think in general than are people low in need for cognition (Cacioppo, Petty, Feinstein, & Jarvis, 1996). They are not more motivated to think certain kinds of thoughts over others. Some variables, however, are selective in their effects on thinking. For example, when people are highly motivated to think, a positive mood tends to encourage positive thoughts, discourage negative thoughts, or both (Petty et al., 1993), and expert sources tend to encourage favorable rather than unfavorable interpretations of message arguments (Chaiken & Maheswaran, 1994).

The ELM accommodates both relatively objective and relatively biased information processing by pointing to the motivational and ability factors involved. The ELM assumes that motivation is relatively objective when no a priori judgment is preferred and a person's implicit or explicit goal is to seek the truth, wherever it might lead (Petty & Cacioppo, 1986). In contrast, a motivated bias can occur whenever people implicitly or explicitly prefer one judgment over another (see also Kruglanski, 1990). A wide variety of motivations can determine which particular judgment is preferred in any given situation. For example, if the reactance motive (Brehm, 1966) is aroused, people prefer to hold whatever judgment is forbidden. If balance motives (Heider, 1958) are operating, people prefer to adopt the position of a liked source but distance themselves from a disliked source. If impression management motives (Tedeschi, Schlenker, & Bonoma, 1971) are operating, people prefer to hold whatever position they think would be ingratiating. Importantly, many of these biasing motives could have an impact on judgments by either the central or the peripheral route. For example, invocation of reactance could lead to simple rejection of the forbidden position without much thought or through active counterarguing of the position.

The ELM holds that biased processing can occur even if no specific judgment is preferred (i.e., if based on motivational factors alone, processing would be relatively objective)—this is because ability factors can also introduce bias. For example, some people might simply possess a biased store of knowledge compared to other people. If so, their ability to process the message objectively can be compromised. That is, recipients with a biased store of knowledge might be better able to see the flaws in opposition arguments and the merits in their own side compared to recipients with a more balanced store of knowledge (cf. Lord, Ross, & Lepper, 1979). In addition, variables in the persuasion situation can bias retrieval of information even if what is stored is completely balanced and no motivational biases are operating. For example, a positive mood can increase access to positive material in memory (e.g., Bower, 1981). In general, biases in processing a persuasive message are fostered when the message contains information that is ambiguous or mixed rather than clearly strong or weak (Chaiken & Maheswaran, 1994).

Finally, just because some motivational or ability factor results in biased information processing, this does not mean that a biased judgment will result because people sometimes attempt to correct for factors they believe might have unduly biased their evaluations (e.g., Martin, Seta, & Crelia, 1990; Petty & Wegener, 1993; Wilson & Brekke, 1994). The available research suggests that corrections can proceed in different directions depending on recipients' theories of how the biasing event or stimulus (e.g., an attractive source) was likely to have influenced their views. According to the flexible correction model (Petty & Wegener, 1993; Wegener & Petty, 1997), in order for corrections to occur, people should (a) be motivated and able to identify potentially biasing factors, (b) possess or generate a naive theory about the magnitude and direction of the bias, and (c) be motivated and able to make the theory-based correction.

Assessing Information Processing

Persuasion researchers have identified a number of ways to assess the extent to which persuasion is based on effortful consideration of information. Perhaps the most popular procedure to assess the amount of objective information processing that takes place has been to vary the quality of the arguments contained in a message and examine the size of the argument quality effect on attitudes and valenced thoughts (e.g., Petty et al., 1976). Greater argument quality effects suggest greater objective scrutiny. Because strong arguments elicit more favorable thoughts and become more persuasive with thought, but weak arguments elicit more unfavorable thoughts and become less persuasive with thought, thinking enhances the argument quality effect on attitudes and valenced thoughts. If the message processing is biased, however, the size of the argument quality effect on these variables can be attenuated over what it is with objective processing (Nienhuis, Manstead, & Spears, 2001; Petty & Cacioppo, 1986); this is because when engaged in biased processing, people may fail to appreciate the merits or demerits of the arguments (e.g., seeing strengths in even weak arguments and finding some flaws in strong ones).

When biased processing is an issue, there are other means to gauge the extent of thinking. In particular, one can assess the mere number of issue-relevant thoughts generated (Petty, Ostrom, & Brock, 1981). High elaboration conditions are associated with more thoughts (e.g., Burnkrant & Howard, 1984). Also, correlations between message-relevant thoughts and postmessage attitudes tend to be greater when argument scrutiny is high (e.g., Chaiken, 1980; Petty & Cacioppo, 1979b), although other variables, such as the confidence people have in their thoughts, can affect this correlation (Petty, Briñol, & Tormala, 2002). Finally, high message elaboration can produce reading or exposure times longer than more cursory analyses (Mackie & Worth, 1989), although longer reading times might also reflect daydreaming rather than careful message scrutiny (see Wegener, Downing, Krosnick, & Petty, 1995, for a discussion of these measures).

RELATIVELY LOW-EFFORT PROCESSES OF ATTITUDE CHANGE

We have now seen that a multitude of variables can determine whether the attitude change context is likely to be one of relatively high or low cognitive effort. First we focus on the specific low-effort processes that can determine whether attitudes will change, and then we turn to high-effort processes.

The low-effort mechanisms of attitude change vary in the extent to which they require conscious processing, ranging from those relying on automatic associations to those positing simple inferences. Thus, some peripheral processes require somewhat more cognitive effort than do others (Petty & Cacioppo, 1986). Nevertheless, these processes have in common the fact that none of them requires extensive and effortful scrutiny of the central merits of the attitudinal advocacy or position.

Associative Processes

Some low-effort attitude change processes are associative in nature—that is, attitudes are often impacted by associations that develop between attitude objects and positive or negative stimuli (i.e., objects and feelings), or even by observations of those associations. Examples of these processes include classical conditioning, affective priming, mere exposure, and balance.

Classical Conditioning

One way to produce attitude change in the absence of effortful scrutiny is to associate an attitude object that is initially neutral (e.g., a new product) with stimuli that already have positive or negative meaning. Considerable research has demonstrated that when an initially neutral stimulus immediately precedes another stimulus that already has positive or negative associations, the neutral stimulus can come to be positively or negatively evaluated itself. For example, attitudes toward words (e.g., Staats & Staats, 1958), people (e.g., Griffitt, 1970), and products (e.g., Gresham & Shimp, 1985) have been influenced by their association with pleasant or unpleasant odors, temperatures, sounds, shock, photographs, and so on (e.g., Gouaux, 1971; Staats, Staats, & Crawford, 1962; Zanna, Kiesler, & Pilkonis, 1970). Furthermore, attitudes have been shown to be influenced by the contraction of certain muscles associated with positive and negative experiences (e.g., Cacioppo, Priester, & Bernston, 1993; Priester, Cacioppo, & Petty, 1996; Strack, Martin, & Stepper, 1988). Consistent with the classification of classical conditioning as a low-effort process, conditioning effects have been found to be particularly likely when effortful processing is at a minimum (Field, 2000). Specifically, these effects are enhanced when the stimuli are presented subliminally (DeHouwer, Baeyens, & Eelen, 1994) and when the stimuli have no a priori meaning attached to them (Cacioppo, Marshall-Goodell, Tassinary, & Petty, 1992; Priester et al., 1996; Shimp, Stuart, & Engle, 1991).

Affective Priming

Another process that relies on associations between stimuli is affective priming. In this method, also known as *backward*

conditioning, presentation of positively or negatively valenced stimuli immediately precedes rather than follows presentation of target stimuli. These presentations have been found to influence evaluations of the target stimuli. For example, Krosnick, Betz, Jussim, and Lynn (1992) found that subliminal presentation of positive or negative pictures (e.g., smiling people vs. snakes) made subsequent evaluations of target individuals more favorable or less favorable, respectively. Consistent with classification of this change mechanism as a low effort process, these effects have been found to be unaffected by cognitive load (e.g., Hermans, Crombez, & Eelen, 2000) and more likely to occur when the initial affective stimuli can be processed only minimally (DeHouwer, Hermans, & Eelen, 1998) or not at all (e.g., when they have been presented subliminally; Murphy, Monahan, & Zajonc, 1995; Murphy & Zajonc, 1993).

Mere Exposure

Research has also shown that the mere repeated exposure of an object can make one's attitude toward that object more favorable even if one does not recognize the object as having been encountered previously (Zajonc, 1968). Kunst-Wilson and Zajonc (1980), for instance, repeatedly presented participants with a series of polygon images and found that even though participants could not recognize which images they had seen before and which they had not, they expressed significantly greater preferences for those they had seen. Additionally, mere exposure effects also occur in patients suffering from Alzheimer's disease (Winograd, Goldstein, Monarch, Peluso, & Goldman, 1999). Some researchers have argued that even when a stimulus cannot be consciously identified as having been encountered, its previous exposure might make it easier to process. This could create a kind of *perceptual fluency* (Bornstein, 1989; Jacoby, Kelley, Brown, & Jasechko, 1989) that becomes attached to the stimulus or confused with a positive evaluation of the stimulus. This process only occurs, however, to the extent that the feeling of familiarity is not directly attributed to the repeated exposure. If people attribute the experience of familiarity to the repeated exposure of a stimulus, the mere exposure effect is attenuated (Bornstein & D'Agostino, 1994). Moreover, as with other low-effort processes, the influence of mere exposure on attitudes appears to be increased when the repeated object is low in meaning (see Bornstein, 1989, for a review) or presented subliminally (Bornstein & D'Agostino, 1992), thus reducing or eliminating conscious processing. Similarly, the effect appears to be *decreased* as conscious processing increases, such as when evaluation apprehension is induced (Kruglanski, Freund, & Bar-Tal, 1996). When meaningful stimuli are presented (e.g., familiar words or persuasive messages), repeated exposure has been found to accentuate the dominant reaction (e.g., Cacioppo & Petty, 1989; Brickman, Redfield, Harrison, & Crandall, 1972) regardless of whether the reaction is positive or negative. With meaningful stimuli, deliberative analyses can enhance the dominant response, at least until tedium sets in.

Balance

According to balance theory (Heider, 1958), certain cognitive states are associated with pleasantness, whereas other states are associated with unpleasantness. More specifically, balance (harmony) within the elements of an attitudinal system exists when people agree with others they like (or with whom they are closely associated) and disagree with others they dislike (or with whom they are dissociated). Because imbalance is an uncomfortable state (Heider, 1958), people should seek to eliminate it as quickly and easily as possible. In many cases, the easiest way to restore balance is to alter one's evaluation of one of the elements in the attitude system (Rosenberg & Abelson, 1960; see also Visser, 1994). Unlike the effortful restoration of cognitive consistency associated with dissonance reduction (Festinger, 1957; see subsequent discussion), the alteration of evaluations need not be effortful according to balance theory. In addition to the general preference for balanced relationships among people, objects, and attitudes, research has also shown that people prefer positivity in these relationships (Miller & Norman, 1976). Importantly, the changes people make to ensure balance and positivity do not require thoughtful consideration of the central merits of the attitude objects in the system (see Insko, 1984; Newcomb, 1968, for further discussion).

Inference-Based Processes

Low-effort attitude change processes can also be more inferential in nature rather than a result of the operation of affective or associative processes. In other words, people sometimes base attitudes on simple inferences that do not require considerable cognitive processing. The use of balance principles can be considered inferential if people reason that they will feel better if they adopt the attitude of a liked other. Two other inferential rules are to infer one's attitude from one's own behavior and to rely on simple heuristics, or decision rules, that circumvent effortful scrutiny of information.

Attribution

At a general level, attribution theory addresses the inferences people make about themselves and others after witnessing

behaviors and the situational constraints surrounding those behaviors (e.g., Bem, 1965; Jones & Davis, 1965). In some cases, these inferences involve attitudes, such as when individuals infer their own or someone else's attitudes on the basis of their behavior with respect to some attitude object (e.g., if a person donates money to a candidate, it is reasonable to infer that that person favors the candidate). Although some attributional processes require effortful cognitive activity (see Gilbert, 1998, for a review), others result in relatively quick and simple inferences (e.g., inferring that you like a certain TV program because you smile when you watch it).

According to Bem's (1965, 1972) self-perception theory, when people are not attuned to their internal states, they can infer their own attitudes from their behaviors just as they might do when inferring the attitudes of others. Self-perception may be more likely to operate under relatively low-effort conditions. For example, Taylor (1975) conducted a study in which women evaluated the photographs of men under high or low personal relevance conditions. Participants also received false physiological feedback about their responses toward some of the men (see Valins, 1966). Taylor found that the women inferred attitudes from their ostensible physiological reactions to a greater extent when personal relevance was low than when it was high (see also Chaiken & Baldwin, 1981; Wood, 1982). This implies that self-perception processes are more likely to operate when the likelihood of thinking about the attitude object is relatively low rather than high.

Attribution theory has also contributed to attitude change research in other ways. In one application called the overjustification effect, people come to devalue previously enjoyed activities (e.g., running) when they are given overly sufficient rewards for engaging in them (e.g., Lepper, Greene, & Nisbett, 1973). If someone is given an extrinsic reward for promoting a proattitudinal advocacy, for instance, their attitude may become less favorable to the extent that they view their behavior as stemming from the reward rather than from the merits of the position they are endorsing (e.g., Scott & Yalch, 1978). Furthermore, attribution theory has shed light on the processes by which inferences about a message source impact attitudes. For example, Eagly, Chaiken, and Wood (1981) argued that when people are exposed to a persuasive communication, their expectancies regarding the source of the communication have an important impact on their acceptance of that source's position. If the communicator advocates a position that violates his or her own self-interest, he or she is perceived as more trustworthy and the position as more valid. If the communicator takes a position consistent with self-interest, however, he or she is perceived as less trustworthy and the position as less valid. When the position is viewed as valid, it can be accepted with relatively little scrutiny. However, when the position is seen as possibly invalid, effortful scrutiny of the information is increased (Priester & Petty, 1995). We find it interesting that when a source takes a position that violates his or her group's interest (rather than individual self-interest) the source is not seen as more trustworthy—perhaps because violating group interest is seen as disloyal. As a result, when an individual advocates a position that violates group interest, people are surprised and this leads to enhanced message scrutiny (Petty, Fleming, Priester, & Feinstein, 2001).

Heuristics

The heuristic-systematic model of persuasion (HSM; Chaiken et al., 1989) suggests that when people are engaged in relatively little information-processing activity, they typically evaluate persuasive information in terms of stored heuristics, or simple decision rules based on prior experiences or observations. One such heuristic might be that *length implies strength.* In several studies (e.g., Chaiken, 1987; Petty & Cacioppo, 1984) it has been found that people are more persuaded by messages containing large numbers of examples or arguments, but only when recipients of such messages are relatively unmotivated to engage in extensive thought (e.g., low need for cognition or low personal relevance). Similarly, some people might have stored heuristics pertaining to source credibility, such as *experts are usually correct,* and use of these heuristics is especially potent when personal relevance is relatively low (e.g., Petty, Cacioppo, & Goldman, 1981), distraction is high (e.g., Kiesler & Mathog, 1968), or elaboration likelihood is low for some other reason (see Andreoli & Worchel, 1978; Wood & Kallgren, 1988).

As noted earlier, according to dual process models, source expertise, like other variables, can serve in other roles when the elaboration likelihood is moderate or high—such as affecting the extent of processing or biasing argument processing. If source expertise takes on other roles, its impact under high elaboration conditions can be equivalent to or even exceed its impact under low elaboration conditions (Chaiken & Maheswaran, 1994; Kruglanski & Thompson, 1999; Petty, 1994).

A variety of additional variables have been shown to operate as cues when the elaboration likelihood is low—such as source attractiveness (e.g., Chaiken, 1980) and speed of speech (e.g., S. M. Smith & Shaffer, 1995). These variables also can serve in other roles as the likelihood of elaboration is increased (see Petty & Wegener, 1998, for a review). Chaiken et al. (1989) propose that the use of heuristics depends on their availability (i.e., the heuristic must be stored in memory), accessibility (i.e., it must be activated from memory),

and applicability to the judgment at hand (see Chaiken, Wood, & Eagly, 1996). Although this proposition is intriguing, little research has been conducted examining these aspects of heuristics (but see Chaiken & Eagly, 1983). Thus, the operation of some variables that have been attributed to heuristics under low elaboration conditions (e.g., a person's mood state; Schwarz, 1990; Schwarz & Clore, 1983) might instead have impact on attitudes through some other peripheral process (e.g., classical conditioning). Nevertheless, the heuristic concept has been very useful and has sparked a great deal of persuasion research.

RELATIVELY HIGH-EFFORT PROCESSES OF ATTITUDE CHANGE

In addition to the low-effort attitude change mechanisms described previously, attitudes can also be formed and changed through relatively high-effort processes. According to dual-process formulations, these high-effort processes tend to influence persuasive outcomes when motivation and ability to think are relatively high, such as when the issue is of high personal relevance, when people are accountable for their judgments, when they have high knowledge on the topic, when few distractions are present, and so forth.

Message Learning and Reception

Early information-processing theories of attitude change held that persuasion was contingent upon a sequence of stages, including attention, comprehension, learning, acceptance, and retention of the information in a persuasive communication (Hovland, Janis, & Kelley, 1953). Thus, a given persuasive appeal would be successful to the extent that the message and its conclusion were processed, understood, accepted, and later recalled. McGuire (1968) later modified this model and focused on two core processes—reception and yielding. According to McGuire, variables could influence persuasive outcomes by affecting either of these processes, and variables might affect each process in different ways. For example, increasing intelligence might increase the likelihood of reception but decrease the likelihood of yielding. Although some research has examined the role of literal comprehension or reception of a message in attitude change (Eagly, 1974), a majority of the research in this domain has addressed the reception-yielding hypothesis by assessing the relationship between attitude change and message recall. Despite the intuitive appeal of the model, considerable research has demonstrated that attitudes and message recall are often weakly related at best (e.g., Anderson & Hubert, 1963; Watts & McGuire, 1964; see Eagly & Chaiken, 1993, for a review).

A number of factors have been proposed to account for the relatively low correlation between attitude change and information recall. One argument, for example, has been that simple learning theories do not account for the fact that different people form different evaluations of information contained in persuasive messages—that is, although one person may be convinced by an argument, someone else might find it to be ludicrous (see Petty, Ostrom, et al., 1981). Yet both might be able to recall the argument. Attitude change has been found to correspond more closely with information recall when individuals' unique assessments of the information recalled is accounted for (Chattopadhyay & Alba, 1988). Furthermore, attitudes have been found to correlate more strongly with learning and recall when people are not evaluating information on-line at the time of exposure. For example, when processing is made difficult (e.g., Bargh & Thein, 1985; Bodenhausen & Lichtenstein, 1987), when people are given nonevaluative processing goals (e.g., Chartrand & Bargh, 1996; Hastie & Park, 1986; Lichtenstein & Srull, 1987; Mackie & Asuncion, 1990), or when they are the type of people who do not spontaneously engage in evaluation (low in their *need to evaluate;* Tormala & Petty, 2001), the attitude-recall correlation is higher. Under these conditions, when people are asked to report their attitudes, they are forced to first retrieve what they can from memory, and then base their attitudes on the evaluative implications of this information.

Cognitive Response Approach

Following a series of early findings that attitude change and information recall were not consistently related, researchers developed the cognitive response approach to persuasion (e.g., Brock, 1967; Greenwald, 1968; Petty, Ostrom, et al., 1981). According to this approach, attitudes and message argument recall are not always related because persuasion typically depends largely on an individual's idiosyncratic thoughts in response to a persuasive message (i.e., thoughts about message arguments or other factors such as the tone, source, or context of the message). According to the cognitive response view, when exposed to a persuasive message, people reflect on the message with respect to their preexisting knowledge and prior attitude (if they have one), considering information not contained in the message itself. Three aspects of people's cognitive responses have proven important.

Extent of Thought

First, investigators have explored determinants of the extent of issue-relevant thinking. As noted earlier in our discussion of the elaboration likelihood model, a number of variables have been found to affect how much people are motivated (e.g., personal relevance) or able (e.g., distraction) to think about a persuasive communication.

Content of Thought

Another aspect of thinking that has garnered considerable research attention is the content of thought. Perhaps the most important dimension in this regard is the overall valence of the thinking that occurs. Researchers typically categorize thoughts as favorable, unfavorable, or neutral, and then compute an overall valence index (e.g., positive thoughts minus negative thoughts; see Mackie, 1987). According to the cognitive response approach, persuasion can be increased to the extent that the message elicits mostly favorable thoughts (e.g., *If we raise taxes, the roads will improve and reduce my commute time*) and few unfavorable thoughts (e.g., *If we raise taxes, I'll have less money to go out to dinner*). On the other hand, people can resist messages to the extent that they generate mostly unfavorable thoughts and few favorable thoughts.

As noted earlier, people can be motivated to generate particular thoughts by external variables such as their mood (Petty et al., 1993) or the message source (Chaiken & Maheswaran, 1994). In a series of studies on resistance to change, McGuire (1964) demonstrated that counterarguing of persuasive messages could be increased by giving people weak attacking messages prior to a stronger attack. The underlying logic of this inoculation approach to resistance is that a small dose of an attacking virus (i.e., a weak challenge to the person's attitude that is refuted) motivates the person to build up antibodies (i.e., counterarguments) that can be used against subsequent attacks. Even if an exact defense is not anticipated, people are presumably motivated by the inoculation treatment (i.e., the initial attack and refutation) to defend their attitudes by counterarguing opposition messages in the future. Recent research has shown that having people experience a successful defense of their attitudes can produce greater confidence in the initial attitude. This enhanced confidence renders the attitude not only more resistant to change in the future, but also more predictive of future behavior (Tormala & Petty, in press).

Confidence in Thoughts

In addition to extent and content of thinking, recent research has uncovered a third aspect of thought that influences persuasion—the confidence people have in their own cognitive responses. According to the *self-validation hypothesis* (Petty, Briñol, & Tormala, in press), people vary in the extent to which they have confidence in or doubt the validity of the thoughts that they generate to a persuasive message. Although thoughts in which people have confidence have a large impact on attitude change, thoughts in which people have low confidence do not. Thus, this research suggests that favorable thoughts increase persuasion primarily when people have confidence in them. Similarly, unfavorable thoughts decrease persuasion mostly when people have confidence in them. When confidence in thoughts is low, thoughts do not predict attitudes very well even under high elaboration conditions.

Several variables have been shown to affect the confidence people have in their thoughts and thereby to influence the extent of attitude change. For example, in one study (Briñol & Petty, 2001), people who were nodding their head in a *yes* (vertical) fashion while listening to a message reported more confidence in their thoughts than did people who were nodding their heads in a *no* (horizontal) fashion. As a result, when processing a compelling message that elicited mostly favorable thoughts, people nodding yes were more persuaded than were people nodding no (see also Wells & Petty, 1980). However, when processing a specious message that elicited mostly unfavorable thoughts, people nodding yes were less persuaded than were people nodding no. In addition to head nodding, the ease of generating thoughts affects the confidence people have in them (Tormala, Petty, & Briñol, in press). When people are asked to generate a small and easy number of cognitive responses (e.g., counterarguments or favorable thoughts), they have more confidence in the responses and rely on them to a greater extent in determining their attitudes than when they are asked to generate a higher and more difficult number of thoughts.

Self-Persuasion with No Message

The importance of one's own thoughts in producing persuasion outcomes is highlighted in research showing that self-persuasion can occur even in the absence of an external message. For example, research has demonstrated that persuasion in the absence of a message can occur when individuals are asked to actively present or generate their own messages or even when individuals are simply permitted to engage in thought about an attitude object.

Role Playing

Early research on role playing in persuasion found it to be an effective tool to increase persuasion as well as the resistance and persistence of the resulting attitudes. In one of the earliest role-playing demonstrations, Janis and King (1954) examined the differential effects of having people actively present persuasive arguments versus passively hear arguments presented by others. Results indicated that participants who actively generated and presented messages were typically more persuaded than were those who passively listened to messages. This effect has been replicated numerous times (e.g., Elms, 1966; Greenwald & Albert, 1968; Janis & Mann, 1965).

A number of mechanisms have been proposed to account for these role-playing effects. Janis (1968) proposed a *biased scanning* explanation whereby individuals, in the process of supporting an attitudinal position, recruit consistent beliefs and inhibit inconsistent beliefs (see also, Kunda, 1990). This interpretation is based in part on the finding that improvisation is an important element in eliciting role-playing effects. King and Janis (1956) showed that a process of active argument generation was necessary to elicit role-playing persuasion effects. Simply reading a set of persuasive arguments to others did not elicit as much persuasion as did extemporaneously elaborating on the message. Presumably, actively generating arguments in favor of a given position leads to the active retrieval of supportive information that is uniquely persuasive to the individual and to the inhibition of nonsupporting information (Greenwald & Albert, 1968; Janis & King, 1954). The information that people self-generate might seem particularly compelling to the generator because of the enhanced effort involved in generation over passive exposure (Festinger, 1957)—or the arguments might seem more compelling simply because they are associated with the self (i.e., an *ownness bias;* Perloff & Brock, 1980). People might also have more confidence in the thoughts that they generate, leading them to be more influential than are arguments received by others (Petty, et al., 2002).

Mere Thought

Some research has indicated that attitude polarization can sometimes occur when individuals simply engage in extensive thought about an attitude object (see Tesser, Martin, & Mendolia, 1995, for a review). Attitude polarization following thought requires a well-integrated and consistent attitude schema (e.g., Chaiken & Yates, 1985; Tesser & Leone, 1977); otherwise, thought leads to attitude moderation. This relationship appears to be bidirectional—that is, just as having a consistent schema fosters attitude polarization with thought, simply thinking about an issue also tends to increase schema consistency via the generation of schema-consistent cognitions and the reinterpretation of inconsistent cognitions (e.g.,

Millar & Tesser, 1986; Sadler & Tesser, 1973; Tesser & Cowan, 1975).

The attitudinal consequences of mere thought are dependent upon the salient subset of information that is the focus of the thought (Tesser, 1978). Attitude change can sometimes occur following thought because individuals focus on selective subsets of information (e.g., Levine, Halberstadt, & Goldstone, 1996; Wilson, Dunn, Kraft, & Lisle, 1989). For example, when participants are instructed to analyze the reasons for their attitudes, they often focus on those that are easiest to verbalize (Wilson et al., 1989). Consequently, they may often overemphasize the cognitive component of their attitudes to the neglect of the affective component, leading to a momentary attitude shift. Selective focus on a subset of attitude-relevant information increases the impact of that limited subset of information on attitude judgments and can consequently lead to suboptimal decision making (e.g., Wilson et al., 1993; Wilson & Schooler, 1991).

Self-Persuasion as a Result of Dissonance Processes

We have seen that self-persuasion can occur when people are prompted to think by receiving a persuasive message, by doing a role-playing exercise, or by simply being asked to think. Attitude change can also occur when a person's own behavior motivates him or her to think. A common assumption of many persuasion theories is that individuals have a default motivation of accuracy—that is, people want to hold correct attitudes. However, the elaboration likelihood model and other persuasion theories acknowledge that a variety of biasing motivations can sometimes distort objective information processing. Although a number of these motivations exist, the motive to be consistent is the most studied, and the theory of cognitive dissonance is the most influential of the consistency theories. In its original formulation (Festinger, 1957), dissonance was described as a feeling of aversive arousal akin to a drive state experienced by an individual when he or she simultaneously held two conflicting cognitions. The resulting aversive arousal was hypothesized to instigate attempts to restore consonance among the relevant cognitions. Attempts to restore consistency typically involved very active thinking about the attitude object, and the end result of this thinking was often a change in the person's attitude.

Dissonance Effects

A large body of research using different experimental paradigms has supported the essence of dissonance theory (see Brehm & Cohen, 1962; Cooper & Fazio, 1984; Harmon-Jones & Mills, 1999; for reviews). Some experimental procedures used to induce dissonance include coaxing people to write counterattitudinal essays under the illusion of free choice (e.g., Losch & Cacioppo, 1990), undergoing harsh initiations to join an uninteresting group (e.g., Aronson & Mills, 1959), selecting between two different but equally desirable products (e.g., Brehm, 1956), and eating grasshoppers after a request from a dislikable person (Zimbardo, Weisenberg, Firestone, & Levy, 1965). In these instances, people become more favorable toward the initially counterattitudinal position, the uninteresting group, the chosen product, and the initially distasteful grasshoppers.

Early work in dissonance theory suggested that individuals must directly resolve the cognitive inconsistency by changing their attitudes—generating cognitions to make the dissonant elements more consistent (i.e., bolstering)—or by minimizing the importance of the dissonant cognitions (i.e., trivializing; see Simon, Greenberg, & Brehm, 1995). However, some research has suggested that dissonance can be reduced (at least temporarily) by engaging in virtually any activity that distracts one from the dissonance. For example, individuals appear to successfully reduce their dissonance by affirming even unrelated aspects of their self-concepts (Steele, 1988; Tesser & Cornell, 1991), by consuming alcohol (Steele, Southwick, & Critchlow, 1981), or by watching a comedy film (Cooper, Fazio, & Rhodewalt, 1978). By contrast, individuals avoid receiving even positive information about themselves if it is highly related to the dissonance-arousing event, and when such exposure is forced, the amount of experienced dissonance increases (Blanton, Cooper, Skurnik, & Aronson, 1997).

A number of research studies have supported the hypothesis that physiological arousal follows from situations thought to induce cognitive dissonance (e.g., Elkin & Leippe, 1986; Losch & Cacioppo, 1990), and such arousal has been shown to be subjectively unpleasant (Elliot & Devine, 1994). When the arousal can be plausibly misattributed to some unrelated environmental agent (rather than to the true dissonance-arousing event), dissonance-based attitude change fails to occur (e.g., Fazio et al., 1977; Zanna & Cooper, 1974). However, evidence for the mediational role of arousal in eliciting dissonance-based attitude change is equivocal. Some work, for example, suggests that the experience of dissonance has less to do with arousal per se and more to do with feeling unpleasant (e.g., Higgins, Rhodewalt, & Zanna, 1979; Losch & Cacioppo, 1990). Additionally, in contrast to the predictions of dissonance theory, attitude change following a dissonance induction can sometimes fail to reduce dissonance-based arousal (Elkin & Leippe, 1986; Harmon-Jones, Brehm, Greenberg, Simon, & Nelson, 1996).

Limiting Conditions

Early research supported the hypothesis that dissonance was experienced when a person had insufficient justification for violating a belief or attitude (Festinger, 1957; Festinger & Carlsmith, 1959). Since the original formulation of the dissonance construct, however, many researchers have imposed limiting conditions on the basic dissonance predictions. For example, some researchers asserted that commitment to the behavior was necessary to elicit dissonance (e.g., Brehm & Cohen, 1962). Additionally, some research indicates that cognitive inconsistency per se is neither necessary nor sufficient to generate dissonance. In an influential new look at dissonance research, Cooper and Fazio (1984) concluded that for dissonance to be aroused, an individual must be responsible for engaging in an action that has negative or undesired consequences. If an individual engages in a counterattitudinal action that has no apparent effect (e.g., Collins & Hoyt, 1972; Cooper & Worchel, 1970) or a positive effect (Scher & Cooper, 1989), dissonance effects do not occur. Similarly, even a proattitudinal behavior can arouse dissonance if it has unintended, aversive consequences (Scher & Cooper, 1989). Moreover, if the individual does not feel responsibility for the discrepant action because the consequences were unforeseeable (e.g., Cooper, 1971; Hoyt, Henley, & Collins, 1972), dissonance likewise fails to obtain.

Alternative Views

Two additional alternatives implicate the self as the essential component in eliciting dissonance. Steele's self-affirmation theory suggests that dissonance results from any threat to viewing oneself as "adaptively and morally adequate" (Steele, 1988, p. 262). Alternately, Aronson (1969) has argued that dissonance is based on inconsistency between one's self-view and one's actions (e.g., *I am a good person and did a bad deed*). These two alternatives differ in their predictions of whether individuals prefer self-verification or self-enhancement. Steele's self-affirmation theory predicts that people prefer positive feedback even if it is inconsistent with their self-view, whereas Aronson's self-inconsistency view postulates that people will prefer self-consistent feedback even if it is negative. The views also differ in whether people high or low in self-esteem should be more susceptible to dissonance effects. The self-inconsistency view holds that individuals high in self-esteem should show greater dissonance effects because it is more inconsistent for a person with high

self-esteem to engage in bad deeds. The self-affirmation view holds that high self-esteem individuals should show reduced dissonance effects because they have more self-affirmational resources to use to protect against dissonance. Unfortunately, the research evidence on this question is mixed, with some studies showing greater dissonance effects for individuals with low self-esteem (Steele, Spencer, & Lynch, 1993) and other studies showing greater dissonance effects for persons with high self-esteem (Gerard, Blevans, & Malcolm, 1964).

A final alternative is the self-standards model of dissonance (Stone & Cooper, 2001). This model attempts to put the new look, self-consistency, and self-affirmation theories under a single conceptual umbrella by suggesting that dissonance results from the violation of salient normative or idiographic self-standards. According to this model, when dissonant-relevant self-attributes are salient, higher dissonance should result in persons with high than low self-esteem. This is because high self-esteem individuals have higher personal standards and the dissonant behavior is more likely to be inconsistent with these standards. When irrelevant self-attributes are salient, however, the opposite pattern is predicted to occur; this is because the positive irrelevant self-attributes should provide high self-esteem individuals with greater self-affirmational resources to draw upon and therefore reduce the need to engage in self-justification via attitude change. Last, when normative standards are more salient, dissonance should be equal between high and low self-esteem individuals because the same normative standard is determining dissonance arousal for everyone (see Stone & Cooper, 2001, for more detail regarding these predictions).

The true distinctions between the original dissonance theory, the new look formulation, the self-approaches, and the self-standards model are sometimes nebulous, however, and findings consistent with one approach can often be incorporated by another. For example, results that could be inconsistent with the new look formulation include the finding that engaging in counterattitudinal behaviors with no apparent consequences to others (Harmon-Jones, 2000; Harmon-Jones et al., 1996) or engaging in proattitudinal behaviors with positive consequences to others (Dickerson, Thibodeau, Aronson, & Miller, 1992; Prislin & Pool, 1996; Stone, Aronson, Crain, Winslow, & Fried, 1994) can elicit dissonance-based attitude change. However, when aversive consequences are considered to be "anything that blocks one's self-interest or an event that one would rather have not occur" (Cooper & Fazio, 1984, p. 232; Cooper, 1992) or the violation of some standard (Cooper, 1999), the new look approach can accommodate such results (Cooper, 1992; cf. Harmon-Jones, 2000; Harmon-Jones et al., 1996; Stone & Cooper, 2001).

Results that might be inconsistent with the original disso nance formulation include the finding that proattitudinal behaviors can elicit dissonance when aversive consequences result (e.g., Scher & Cooper, 1989) and that inconsistency might fail to arouse dissonance if the individual has low consistency needs (e.g., Cialdini, Trost, & Newsom, 1995; Snyder & Tanke, 1976). The original dissonance formulation might account for such results by considering the importance of the cognitions creating the inconsistency (Harmon-Jones et al., 1996). Important cognitions should have greater weight in determining dissonance magnitude than should unimportant cognitions. Therefore, if aversive (and inconsistent) consequences are highly important, they could override the effect of the proattitudinal act itself (Harmon-Jones et al., 1996). Similarly, individual differences in consistency needs might be accounted for by differential importance weights across individuals.

As should be apparent, the original dissonance formulation and its alternatives appear to be quite flexible in accounting for the wide variety of effects one's behavior can have on one's attitude. The flexibility associated with these different ways of interpreting dissonance findings affords greater explanatory breadth, but it comes with a cost. Specifically, this flexibility makes it difficult to accurately predict when any given individual will experience dissonance—a criticism that has often been leveled at dissonance theory (Aronson, 1992, 1999).

Nondissonance Alternatives

In addition to the dissonance modifications described previously, two nondissonance alternatives have been proposed to account for the findings of dissonance researchers. One such alternative is self-perception theory. As described earlier, self-perception theory (Bem, 1965) holds that individuals often infer their attitudes from their own behavior. Self-perception theory was a formidable opponent to the dissonance view because it was able to account for many of the results attributed to dissonance mechanisms (Greenwald, 1975). It later became apparent that self-perception was a different phenomenon that functioned in different settings and was not simply an alternative explanation for cognitive dissonance (e.g., Beauvois, Bungert, & Mariette, 1995). For instance, in contrast to dissonance processes, self-perception processes appear to operate when one's behavior falls in one's latitude of acceptance and thus elicits little aversive arousal (Fazio et al., 1977). In addition, whereas dissonance reduction has been proposed to require considerable cognitive effort (Festinger, 1957), self-perception processes appear to involve simpler attributional decisions that operate under relatively low effort circumstances (see attribution section in this chapter).

A second alternative mechanism is impression management. Proponents of this view believe that the attitude change observed in dissonance experiments results not from aversive arousal associated with cognitive inconsistency, but instead from the desire to *appear* consistent to others (e.g., Tedeschi et al., 1971). Although impression management is a motivational variable that can affect attitude reports, it cannot account for all dissonance phenomena. For example, dissonance-based attitude change can also occur in situations in which attitude reports are private and anonymous and should therefore arouse no impression management concerns (e.g., Baumeister & Tice, 1984; Hoyt et al., 1972).

Combinatory Approaches

Combinatory approaches emphasize the different ways in which individuals assign value to pieces of information and integrate them into a structure of beliefs and attitudes. These models differ in their emphasis on the types of information individuals consider, as well as the means by which the information is integrated. Three different types of models have received the most research attention.

Probabilogical Model

The probabilogical model (McGuire, 1960, 1981; Wyer, 1970, 1974) suggests that beliefs are represented in memory in a network of syllogistic structures that have both horizontal and vertical dimensions. Each syllogism contains two premises that logically imply a conclusion.
Consider the following syllogism:

Premise 1: Drinking Brand X beer makes one popular.
Premise 2: Being popular is desirable.
Conclusion: Drinking Brand X beer is desirable.

The conclusion of this syllogism relies on Premises 1 and 2. The vertical structure of the network is formed by related syllogisms. For example, Premises 1 and 2 could each be the conclusion of other syllogisms, and the premises that lead to these conclusions could each be the conclusions of yet other syllogisms. The vertical structure of the network has important implications for attitude change because changing beliefs at one point in the vertical structure can lead to logical change in other elements within the vertical structure.

The network of syllogisms also has a horizontal structure. The horizontal dimension incorporates other syllogisms that share the same conclusion and can also have important implications for attitude change. In particular, the probabilogical model specifies that belief in the conclusion of a syllogism should be resistant to the extent that many other syllogisms imply the same conclusion. Hence, if a conclusion that Brand X beer is desirable rests on a single syllogism, undermining one belief in the syllogism should easily undermine one's belief that Brand X beer is desirable. However, if multiple premises support Brand X's virtues, undermining a single syllogism should have less of an effect—that is, the more information on which an attitude is based, the more difficult it should be to change the attitude.

Importantly, the models of McGuire (1960, 1981) and Wyer (1970, 1974) do not assume that beliefs in premises or conclusions are all or none. Rather, people can hold beliefs with differing degrees of likelihood. A number of studies have shown that the probability one assigns to a conclusion follows closely what it should based on the laws of probability (Henninger & Wyer, 1976; Rosen & Wyer, 1972; Wyer, 1973). More important is that *changes* in the belief of a conclusion based a change in belief in one of the premises can also be predicted to a good extent by the laws of probability (McGuire, 1981). However, logical consistency is not the only factor that determines the strength of people's beliefs. The desirability of the beliefs is also important. This *hedonic consistency* (McGuire, 1960) leads to a bias such that people tend to see as likely things that are good, and to see as good things that are likely.

One of the most interesting elements of the probabilogical model is its ability to describe how some attitudes or judgments affect others. The model offers one explanation for how attitude change on one issue such as abortion can affect related attitudes such as one's attitude toward contraception (Mugny & Perez, 1991; see also Dillehay, Insko, & Smith, 1966). Changing one attitude can lead to a change in another if the attitudes are somehow related in the syllogistic network (e.g., being derived from common premises; see also Crano & Chen, 1998).

Expectancy-Value Formulations

Expectancy-value theories propose that attitudes reflect an individual's subjective assessment of the likelihood that an attitude object will be associated with positive or negative consequences or related to important values (Peak, 1955; Rosenberg, 1956; see Bagozzi, 1985, for a review). A particularly influential model, the *theory of reasoned action* (Fishbein & Ajzen, 1975, 1981), posits that attitudes are a multiplicative function of the desirability of an individual's salient beliefs about an attitude object and the likelihood that

those beliefs are true. For example, one's attitude towards a political candidate could be predicted by the expectancy that the candidate will enact certain policies if elected and the value or desirability the individual places on those policies.

Although studied primarily within the framework of behavioral prediction rather than that of attitude change, this formulation has clear implications for the successful developments of persuasive communications. Specifically, the theory of reasoned action implies that attitude change should follow changes in perceptions of the likelihood or desirability of the consequences associated with a position (see Albarracín, in press; Petty & Wegener, 1991, for discussion). And, in fact, a number of studies have indicated that persuasive messages and contextual variables such as a person's mood can produce attitude change by changing the perceived likelihood or desirability of salient beliefs (e.g., Albarracín & Wyer, 2001; Fishbein, Ajzen, & McArdle, 1980; Lutz, 1975; MacKenzie, 1986; Wegener, Petty, & Klein, 1994).

Although some researchers have proposed that virtually all attitude change occurs via the thoughtful consideration of likelihood and desirability assessment (Fishbein & Middlestadt, 1995; McGuire & McGuire, 1991), as we described previously, attitude change can also occur via multiple low-effort processes. Additionally, even likelihood and desirability assessments could be made via low-effort processes. For example, under low-elaboration conditions, individuals are prone to believing whatever they hear (Gilbert, 1991; Gilbert, Tafarodi, & Malone, 1993) and perceiving stimuli positively (Cacioppo & Berntson, 1994; Peeters & Czapinski, 1990). Repeated exposure appears to magnify these propensities. For example, repeated exposure to a piece of information increases perceptions of its validity (e.g., Arkes, Boehm, & Xu, 1991), and as noted earlier, repeated mere exposure to a stimulus increases its desirability (Zajonc, 1968), even when the exposure is subliminal (Bornstein & D'Agostino, 1992).

However, it seems likely that the retrieval and integration of likelihood and desirability assessments of multiple salient beliefs would require effort and would occur only when individuals have the ability and motivation to do so. In support of this reasoning, expectancy-value processes tend to account for more variance in attitudes when motivation (e.g., the need for cognition; Wegener et al., 1994) and ability (e.g., topic-relevant knowledge; Lutz, 1977) to think are high.

Information Integration

In addition to specifying the primary components of attitudes, attitude theorists have also attempted to specify the means by which these components are combined to influence attitudes. As just noted, the expectancy-value formulation of

Fishbein and Ajzen predicts that the information is combined additively to form attitudes—that is, attitudes are postulated to be the sum of the likelihood × desirability products for each salient attribute associated with the attitude object. However, other theorists such as Anderson (1971) have proposed that beliefs are combined by an averaging function. In this formulation, each salient belief is weighted by the individual's assessment of the importance of that piece of information.

Anderson's averaging model has proven efficacious in explaining the impact of different information on resulting attitudes or summary judgments. The flexibility of the averaging account in accommodating the data is simultaneously its greatest strength and weakness (see Eagly & Chaiken, 1984; Petty & Cacioppo, 1981). By adjusting the weighting parameter of the initial attitude or beliefs in a post hoc fashion, the model can accommodate nearly any finding, but an a priori basis for different combinatory patterns is not well specified by the model. Distinguishing the averaging account from additive accounts can be exceedingly difficult, and crucial tests have yet to emerge. At present, there is some suggestion that people are more likely to use an adding integration rule when thinking is at the low end of the elaboration continuum (Betsch, Plessner, Schwieren, & Gütig, 2001), but they use an averaging rule when elaboration is higher (Petty & Cacioppo, 1984).

WHAT HAPPENS WHEN ATTITUDES CHANGE?

We have now discussed the major low- and high-effort approaches to understanding attitude change. As we noted earlier, all of these approaches focus on changing a person's explicit attitude—but what role do implicit attitudes play in attitude change? Our previous discussion of implicit and explicit attitudes suggested that a given individual might hold more than one attitude toward the same attitude object—one explicit and one implicit. It has been demonstrated, for instance, that although people tend to report favorable attitudes toward minority group members on some explicit measures, they may simultaneously show evidence of unfavorable attitudes on more implicit measures (e.g., Banaji & Greenwald, 1995; Devine, 1989; Dovidio et al., 1997; Fazio et al., 1995; Wittenbrink, Judd, & Park, 1997). A common explanation for this finding (e.g., Devine, 1989) has been that negative associations develop early in life and remain accessible in memory even after more positive attitudes are later formed. This explanation is consistent with the dual-memory system articulated by E. R. Smith and DeCoster (2000). According to this model, people have two memory systems—a slow-learning system that detects regularities in the environment over time and a

fast-learning system designed more for the memory of single events or one-time experiences. Based on this formulation, conflicting attitudes might coexist in different systems.

The possibility of people having both implicit and explicit attitudes has a number of important implications. Perhaps the most relevant implication for attitude change is that it suggests that on some occasions when attitudes appear to change (e.g., when initial negative racial attitudes become more positive), the new attitude might not literally replace the old attitude, but may instead coexist in such a way that the old attitude can resurface under specifiable circumstances (Cacioppo et al., 1992; Jarvis, Petty, & Tormala, 1999; Petty, Baker, & Gleicher, 1991; Wilson et al., 2000). This notion is a radical departure from previous treatments of attitude change—that is, the prevailing assumption of prior models was that when attitude change occurred, the prior attitude was incorporated into the new attitude such that the old attitude ceased to exist and was replaced by the new one. In his information integration theory discussed earlier, Anderson (1971) represented this mathematically as

$$A_n = \left(w_0 A_0 + \sum w_i s_i \right) \Big/ \left(w_0 + \sum w_i \right) \quad (15.1)$$

This formula says that a person's new attitude (A_n) following some new information (s) is a weighted (w) average of the new information and the old attitude (A_0). Stated differently, the old attitude is weighted by its importance along with the importance of the new information, each piece of which has some scale value (s). After the integration has taken place, the old attitude is replaced by the new one.

In contrast to the information integration approach, the notion of implicit attitudes suggests that people can have different attitudes toward the same object: one that is explicit and one that is implicit. According to the dual attitude model (Wilson et al., 2000), two attitudes can form when one attitude, A_0, changes to another, A_n. When this occurs, the original attitude A_0 does not actually disappear. Instead, according to this model, it becomes implicit and persists in memory along with A_n, which is considered the explicit attitude. The dual attitude model is depicted schematically in the top panel of Figure 15.1. This model represents a case in which a person with an initially negative attitude toward a racial group subsequently becomes positive. Wilson et al. posit that both attitudes can influence responding. Whereas the newer (explicit) attitude affects controlled responses (e.g., direct attitude measures; deliberative behaviors), the older (now implicit) attitude affects responses that individuals are not motivated or able to control (e.g., indirect attitude measures; spontaneous behaviors; see Dovidio et al., 1997; and Greenwald & Banaji, 1995, for similar views).

Dual Attitudes Model

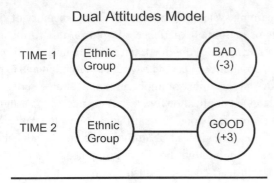

PAST Model

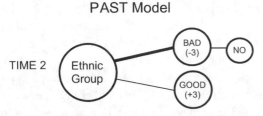

Figure 15.1 *What happens when attitudes change?* (Top panel). In the dual attitudes model, when attitudes change from Time 1 to Time 2, the old attitude becomes implicit and the new attitude is the explicit attitude (Wilson et al., 2000). (Bottom panel). In the PAST model, when attitudes change, the old attitude acquires a "false" tag which allows for the possibility of ambivalent responding (Jarvis et al., 1999; Petty & Jarvis, 1998).

An alternative to the dual attitude model, the PAST (prior attitudes are still there; Jarvis et al., 1999; Petty & Jarvis, 1998) model was also proposed to account for what happens to the old attitude when attitudes change. The PAST model differs, however, in that it presents a more dynamic picture of the relationship between the old and new attitude, suggesting that both can simultaneously influence responding under certain circumstances. In short, the PAST model, like the dual attitudes model, holds that the prior attitude remains in memory, and because it is consciously rejected can be considered implicit (i.e., people are unaware of currently holding this attitude). However, the PAST model proposes that when a new attitude is acquired, the old attitude takes on a *false* or "low confidence" tag that must also be activated if the old attitude is to be suppressed (see Gilbert et al., 1993). The bottom panel of Figure 15.1 presents a schematic depiction according to the PAST model of a person who was initially unfavorable toward a minority group and then became favorable. According to the PAST model, to the degree that the false tag is accessible, the newer attitude will guide responses (see also Kawakami et al., 2000). The prior attitude will have an impact, however, if it was never fully rejected (i.e., no false tag or a weak one), if the false tag cannot be retrieved, or if the tag is retrieved but one is still unable to inhibit the prior

attitude's influence for some other reason. According to the PAST model, when current and prior attitudes conflict and both are accessible, they should produce ambivalent responding. Thus, the PAST model, unlike the dual attitude model, suggests that current and prior attitudes do not always operate in an either-or fashion. Rather, depending on the circumstances, either one or the other or both could exert some impact. Over the coming years, the viability of dual attitude models for understanding attitude change is likely to receive considerable research attention.

CONCLUSIONS

Our goal in this chapter has been to present an organizing framework for understanding the psychological processes responsible for attitude change. Since the earliest empirical studies of attitude change in the 1920s, much has been learned about the underlying determinants and consequences of different attitude change processes. We divided the theoretical processes responsible for modifying attitudes into those that emphasize effortful thinking about the central merits of the attitude object and those that rely on less cognitively demanding processes. This framework allows understanding and prediction of what variables affect attitudes and in what general situations they do so. In addition, this framework helps to place the various minitheories of attitude change in their proper domain of operation. For example, high-effort processes like cognitive responses should account for attitude change in those contexts in which thinking is expected to be high, whereas a lower-effort process such as balance or use of simple heuristics should be more likely to account for empirical effects in those contexts in which thinking is expected to be low. Finally, recognition of an elaboration continuum permits understanding and prediction of the strength of attitudes changed by different processes. Attitudes that are changed as a result of considerable mental effort tend to be more persistent, resistant to counterpersuasion, and predictive of behavior than are attitudes that are changed by a process invoking little mental effort in assessing the central merits of the object.

Although a multitude of processes are involved in changing attitudes, we have a reasonably good handle on what these processes are and when they operate. Yet despite the considerable progress that has been made in understanding attitude change, much work remains to be done. The next decade will likely bring advances in a number of areas. First, greater appreciation is needed for the view that any one variable is capable of multiple roles in the persuasion process. At present, most studies still focus on the one process by which a variable has an impact on attitudes. More research is needed on the multiple ways in which variables can influence attitudes in different situations. Second, one of the most exciting new domains of inquiry is the interplay between explicit and implicit attitudes. For example, what is the best way to conceptualize and assess implicit attitudes? Under what conditions are implicit and explicit attitudes likely to guide action? Are some attitude change processes more likely to influence implicit attitudes, whereas others are more likely to change explicit attitudes? Work on the topic of implicit attitudes is in its infancy, but the next decade promises to provide more definitive answers to these and other questions.

REFERENCES

Ajzen, I., & Fishbein, M. (1977). Attitude-behavior relations: A theoretical analysis and review of empirical research. *Psychological Bulletin, 84*, 888–918.

Albarracín, D. (in press). Cognition in persuasion: An analysis of information processing in response to persuasive communications. In M. P. Zanna (Ed.), *Advances in experimental social psychology*. New York: Academic.

Albarracín, D., & Wyer, R. S. (2001). Elaborative and nonelaborative processing of a behavior-related communication. *Personality and Social Psychology Bulletin, 27*, 691–705.

Anderson, N. H. (1971). Integration theory and attitude change. *Psychological Review, 78*, 171–206.

Anderson, N. H., & Hubert, S. (1963). Effects of concomitant verbal recall on order effects in personality impression formation. *Journal of Verbal Learning and Verbal Behavior, 2*, 379–391.

Andreoli, V., & Worchel, S. (1978). Effects of media, communicator, and message position on attitude change. *Public Opinion Quarterly, 42*, 59–70.

Argyle, M., & Dean, J. (1965). Eye-contact, distance and affiliation. *Sociometry, 28*, 289–304.

Arkes, H. R., Boehm, L. E., & Xu, G. (1991). Determinants of judged validity. *Journal of Experimental Social Psychology, 27*, 576–605.

Aronson, E. (1969). The theory of cognitive dissonance: A current perspective. In L. Berkowitz (Ed.), *Advances in experimental social psychology* (Vol. 4, pp. 1–34). San Diego, CA: Academic.

Aronson, E. (1992). The return of the repressed: Dissonance theory makes a comeback. *Psychological Inquiry, 3*, 303–311.

Aronson, E. (1999). Dissonance, hypocrisy, and the self-concept. In E. Harmon-Jones & J. Mills (Eds.), *Cognitive dissonance: Progress on a pivotal theory in social psychology* (pp. 103–126). Washington, DC: American Psychological Association.

Aronson, E., & Mills, J. (1959). The effects of severity of initiation on liking for a group. *Journal of Abnormal and Social Psychology, 59*, 177–181.

Bagozzi, R. P. (1985). Expectancy-value attitude models: An analysis of critical theoretical issues. *International Journal of Research in Marketing, 2*, 43–60.

Banaji, M. R., & Greenwald, A. G. (1995). Implicit gender stereotyping in judgments of fame. *Journal of Personality and Social Psychology, 68*, 181–198.

Bargh, J. A., Chaiken, S., Govender, R., & Pratto, F. (1992). The generality of the automatic attitude activation effect. *Journal of Personality and Social Psychology, 62*, 893–912.

Bargh, J. A., Chaiken, S., Raymond, P., & Hymes, C. (1996). The automatic evaluation effect: Unconditional automatic attitude activation with a pronunciation task. *Journal of Experimental Social Psychology, 31*, 104–128.

Bargh, J. A., & Thein, R. D. (1985). Individual construct accessibility, person memory, and the recall-judgment link: The case of information overload. *Journal of Personality and Social Psychology, 49*, 1129–1146.

Bassili, J. N. (1995). Response latency and the accessibility of voting intentions: What contributes to accessibility and how it affects vote choice. *Personality and Social Psychology Bulletin, 21*, 686–695.

Baumeister, R. F., & Tice, D. M. (1984). Role of self-presentation and choice in cognitive dissonance under forced compliance: Necessary or sufficient causes? *Journal of Personality and Social Psychology, 46*, 5–13.

Beauvois, J. L., Bungert, M., & Mariette, P. (1995). Forced compliance: Commitment to compliance and commitment to activity. *European Journal of Social Psychology, 25*, 17–26.

Bem, D. J. (1965). An experimental analysis of self-persuasion. *Journal of Experimental Social Psychology, 1*, 199–218.

Bem, D. J. (1972). Self-perception theory. In L. Berkowitz (Ed.), *Advances in experimental social psychology* (Vol. 6, pp. 1–62). New York: Academic.

Betsch, T., Plessner, H., Schwieren, C., & Gütig, R. (2001). I like it but I don't know why: A value-account approach to implicit attitude formation. *Personality and Social Psychology Bulletin, 27*, 242–253.

Blanton, H., Cooper, J., Skurnik, I., & Aronson, J. (1997). When bad things happen to good feedback: Exacerbating the need for self-justification with self-affirmations. *Personality and Social Psychology Bulletin, 23*, 684–692.

Bless, H., Bohner, G., Schwarz, N., & Strack, F. (1990). Mood and persuasion: A cognitive response analysis. *Personality and Social Psychology Bulletin, 16*, 331–345.

Bodenhausen, G. V., & Lichtenstein, M. (1987). Social stereotypes and information-processing strategies: The impact of task complexity. *Journal of Personality and Social Psychology, 52*, 871–880.

Bornstein, R. F. (1989). Exposure and affect: Overview and meta-analysis of research, 1968–1987. *Psychological Bulletin, 106*, 265–289.

Bornstein, R. F., & D'Agostino, P. R. (1992). Stimulus recognition and the mere exposure effect. *Journal of Personality and Social Psychology, 63,* 545–552.

Bornstein, R. F., & D'Agostino, P. R. (1994). The attribution and discounting of perceptual fluency: Preliminary tests of a perceptual fluency/attributional model of the mere exposure effect. *Social Cognition, 12,* 103–128.

Bower, G. H. (1981). Mood and memory. *American Psychologist, 36,* 129–148.

Breckler, S. J. (1984). Empirical validation of affect, behavior, and cognition as distinct components of attitude. *Journal of Personality and Social Psychology, 47,* 1191–1205.

Brehm, J. W. (1956). Postdecision changes in the desirability of alternatives. *Journal of Abnormal and Social Psychology, 52,* 384–389.

Brehm, J. W. (1966). *A theory of psychological reactance.* San Diego, CA: Academic.

Brehm, J. W., & Cohen, A. R. (1962). *Explorations in cognitive dissonance.* New York: Wiley.

Brickman, P., Redfield, J., Harrison, A., & Crandall, R. (1972). Drive and predisposition as factors in the attitudinal effects of mere exposure. *Journal of Experimental Social Psychology, 8,* 31–44.

Briñol, P., & Petty, R. E. (2001). *Overt head movements and persuasion: A self-validation analysis.* Unpublished manuscript, Ohio State University, Columbus.

Brock, T. C. (1967). Communication discrepancy and intent to persuade as determinants of counterargument production. *Journal of Experimental Social Psychology, 3,* 296–309.

Brucks, M., Armstrong, G. M., & Goldberg, M. E. (1988). Children's use of cognitive defenses against television advertising: A cognitive response approach. *Journal of Consumer Research, 14,* 471–482.

Burnkrant, R. E., & Howard, D. J. (1984). Effects of the use of introductory rhetorical questions versus statements on information processing. *Journal of Personality and Social Psychology, 47,* 1218–1230.

Burnkrant, R. E., & Unnava, R. (1989). Self-referencing: A strategy for increasing processing of message content. *Personality and Social Psychology Bulletin, 15,* 628–638.

Cacioppo, J. T., & Berntson, G. G. (1994). Relationship between attitudes and evaluative space: A critical review with emphasis on the separability of positive and negative substrates. *Psychological Bulletin, 115,* 401–423.

Cacioppo, J. T., Crites, S. L., Jr., Bernston, G. G., & Coles, M. G. H. (1993). If attitudes affect how stimuli are processed, should they not affect the event-related brain potential? *Psychological Science, 4,* 108–112.

Cacioppo, J. T., Marshall-Goodell, B. S., Tassinary, L. G., & Petty, R. E. (1992). Rudimentary determinants of attitudes: Classical conditioning is more effective when prior knowledge about the attitude stimulus is low than high. *Journal of Experimental Social Psychology, 28,* 207–233.

Cacioppo, J. T., & Petty, R. E. (1979a). Attitudes and cognitive response: An electro-physiological approach. *Journal of Personality and Social Psychology, 37,* 2181–2199.

Cacioppo, J. T., & Petty, R. E. (1979b). Effects of message repetition and position on cognitive response, recall, and persuasion. *Journal of Personality and Social Psychology, 37,* 97–109.

Cacioppo, J. T., & Petty, R. E. (1982). The need for cognition. *Journal of Personality and Social Psychology, 42,* 116–131.

Cacioppo, J. T., & Petty, R. E. (1989). Effects of message repetition on argument processing, recall, and persuasion. *Basic and Applied Social Psychology, 10,* 3–12.

Cacioppo, J. T., Petty, R. E., Feinstein, J., & Jarvis, B. (1996). Individual differences in cognitive motivation: The life and times of people varying in need for cognition. *Psychological Bulletin, 119,* 197–253.

Cacioppo, J. T., Petty, R. E., & Morris, K. J. (1983). Effects of need for cognition on message evaluation, recall, and persuasion. *Journal of Personality and Social Psychology, 45,* 805–818.

Cacioppo, J. T., Priester, J. R., & Berntson, G. G. (1993). Rudimentary determinants of attitudes: II Arm flexion and extension have differential effects on attitudes. *Journal of Personality and Social Psychology, 65,* 5–17.

Chaiken, S. (1980). Heuristic versus systematic information processing in the use of source versus message cues in persuasion. *Journal of Personality and Social Psychology, 39,* 752–766.

Chaiken, S. (1987). The heuristic model of persuasion. In M. P. Zanna, J. M. Olson, & C. P. Herman (Eds.), *Social influence: The Ontario symposium* (Vol. 5, pp. 3–39). Hillsdale, NJ: Erlbaum.

Chaiken, S., & Baldwin, M. W. (1981). Affective-cognitive consistency and the effect of salient behavioral information on the self-perception of attitudes. *Journal of Personality and Social Psychology, 41,* 1–12.

Chaiken, S., & Eagly, A. H. (1976). Communication modality as a determinant of message persuasiveness and message comprehensibility. *Journal of Personality and Social Psychology, 34,* 605–614.

Chaiken, S., & Eagly, A. H. (1983). Communication modality as a determinant of persuasion: The role of communicator salience. *Journal of Personality and Social Psychology, 45,* 241–256.

Chaiken, S., Liberman, A., & Eagly, A. H. (1989). Heuristic and systematic processing within and beyond the persuasion context. In J. S. Uleman, & J. A. Bargh (Eds.), *Unintended thought* (pp. 212–252). New York: Guilford.

Chaiken, S., & Maheswaran, D. (1994). Heuristic processing can bias systematic processing: Effects of source credibility, argument ambiguity, and task importance on attitude judgment. *Journal of Personality and Social Psychology, 66,* 460–473.

Chaiken, S., & Trope, Y. (1999). *Dual-process theories in social psychology.* New York: Guilford.

Chaiken, S., Wood, W., & Eagly, A. H. (1996). Principles of persuasion. In E. T. Higgins & A. W. Kruglanski (Eds.), *Social psychology: Handbook of basic principles* (pp. 702–742). New York: Guilford.

Chaiken, S., & Yates, S. M. (1985). Affective-cognitive consistency and thought-induced attitude polarization. *Journal of Personality and Social Psychology, 49,* 1470–1481.

Chartrand, T. L., & Bargh, J. A. (1996). Automatic activation of impression formation and memorization goals: Nonconscious goal priming reproduces effects of explicit task instructions. *Journal of Personality and Social Psychology, 71,* 464–478.

Chattopadhyay, A., & Alba, J. W. (1988). The situational importance of recall and inference in consumer decision making. *Journal of Consumer Research, 15,* 1–12.

Cialdini, R. B., Trost, M. R., & Newsom, J. T. (1995). Preference for consistency: The development of a valid measure and the discovery of surprising behavioral implications. *Journal of Personality and Social Psychology, 69,* 318–328.

Collins, B. E., & Hoyt, M. F. (1972). Personal responsibility-for-consequences: An integration and extension of the "forced compliance" literature. *Journal of Experimental Social Psychology, 8,* 558–593.

Converse, P. E. (1970). Attitudes and non-attitudes: Continuation of a dialogue. In E. R. Tufte (Ed.), *The quantitative analysis of social problems* (pp. 168–189). Reading, MA: Addison-Wesley.

Cooper, J. (1971). Personal responsibility and dissonance: The role of foreseen consequences. *Journal of Personality and Social Psychology, 18,* 354–363.

Cooper, J. (1992). Dissonance and the return of the self-concept. *Psychological Inquiry, 3,* 320–323.

Cooper, J. (1999). Unwanted consequences and the self: In search of the motivation for dissonance reduction. In E. Harmon-Jones & J. Mills (Eds.), *Cognitive dissonance: Progress on a pivotal theory in social psychology* (pp. 149–174). Washington DC: American Psychological Association.

Cooper, J., & Fazio, R. H. (1984). A new look at dissonance theory. In L. Berkowitz (Ed.), *Advances in experimental social psychology* (Vol. 17, pp. 229–266). New York: Academic Press.

Cooper, J., Fazio, R. H., & Rhodewalt, F. (1978). Dissonance and humor: Evidence for the undifferentiated nature of dissonance arousal. *Journal of Personality and Social Psychology, 36,* 280–285.

Cooper, J., & Worchel, S. (1970). Role of undesired consequences in arousing cognitive dissonance. *Journal of Personality and Social Psychology, 16,* 199–206.

Cox, D. S., & Cox, A. D. (1988). What does familiarity breed: Complexity as a moderator of repetition effects in advertisement evaluation. *Journal of Consumer Research, 15,* 111–116.

Crano, W. D., & Chen, X. (1998). The leniency contract and persistence of majority and minority influence. *Journal of Personality and Social Psychology, 74,* 1437–1450.

Dasgupta, N., & Greenwald, A. G. (2001). On the malleability of automatic attitudes: Combating automatic prejudice with images of admired and disliked individuals. *Journal of Personality and Social Psychology, 81,* 800–814.

DeHouwer, J., Baeyens, F., & Eelen, P. (1994). Verbal evaluative conditioning with undetected US presentations. *Behaviour Research & Therapy, 32,* 629–633.

DeHouwer, J., Hermans, D., & Eelen, P. (1998). Affective and identity priming with episodically associated stimuli. *Cognition & Emotion, 12,* 145–169.

Devine, P. G. (1989). Stereotypes and prejudice: Their automatic and controlled components. *Journal of Personality and Social Psychology, 56,* 5–18.

Dickerson, C. A., Thibodeau, R., Aronson, E., & Miller, D. (1992). Using cognitive dissonance to encourage water conservation. *Journal of Applied Social Psychology, 22,* 841–854.

Dillehay, R. C., Insko, C. A., & Smith, M. B. (1966). Logical consistency and attitude change. *Journal of Personality and Social Psychology, 3,* 646–654.

Ditto, P. H., & Lopez, D. F. (1992). Motivated skepticism: Use of differential decision criteria for preferred and nonpreferred conclusions. *Journal of Personality and Social Psychology, 63,* 568–584.

Ditto, P. H., Scepansky, J. A., Munro, G. D., Apanovitch, A. M., & Lockhart, L. K. (1998). Motivated sensitivity to preference-inconsistent information. *Journal of Personality and Social Psychology, 75,* 53–69.

Dovidio, J. F., Kawakami, K., & Beach, K. R. (2000). Implicit and explicit attitudes: Examination of the relationship between measures of intergroup bias. In A. Tesser & N. Schwarz (Eds.), *Blackwell handbook of social psychology: Intrapersonal processes.* Oxford, UK: Blackwell.

Dovidio, J. F., Kawakami, K., Johnson, C., Johnson, B., & Howard, A. (1997). On the nature of prejudice: Automatic and controlled processes. *Journal of Experimental Social Psychology, 33,* 510–540.

Eagly, A. H. (1974). Comprehensibility of persuasive arguments as a determinant of opinion change. *Journal of Personality and Social Psychology, 29,* 758–773.

Eagly, A. H., & Chaiken, S. (1984). Cognitive theories of persuasion. In L. Berkowitz (Ed.), *Advances in experimental social psychology* (Vol. 17, pp. 268–361). New York: Academic Press.

Eagly, A. H., & Chaiken, S. (1993). *The psychology of attitudes.* Forth Worth, TX: Harcourt Brace Jovanovich.

Eagly, A. H., & Chaiken, S. (1998). Attitude structure and function. In D. T. Gilbert, S. T. Fiske, & G. Lindzey (Eds.), *The handbook of social psychology* (Vol. 1, pp. 269–322). New York: McGraw-Hill.

Eagly, A. H., Chaiken, S., & Wood, W. (1981). An attribution analysis of persuasion. In J. H. Harvey, W. J. Ickes, & R. F. Kidd (Eds.), *New direction in attribution research* (Vol. 3, pp. 37–62). Hillsdale, NJ: Erlbaum.

Edwards, K. (1990). The interplay of affect and cognition in attitude formation and change. *Journal of Personality and Social Psychology, 59,* 202–216.

Edwards, K., & Smith, E. E. (1996). A disconfirmation bias in the evaluation of arguments. *Journal of Personality and Social Psychology, 71,* 5–24.

Elkin, R. A., & Leippe, M. R. (1986). Physiological arousal, dissonance, and attitude change: Evidence for a dissonance-arousal link and a "Don't remind me" effect. *Journal of Personality and Social Psychology, 51,* 55–65.

Elliot, A. J., & Devine, P. G. (1994). On the motivational nature of cognitive dissonance: Dissonance as psychological discomfort. *Journal of Personality and Social Psychology, 67,* 382–394.

Elms, A. C. (1966). Influence of fantasy ability on attitude change through role-playing. *Journal of Personality and Social Psychology, 4,* 36–43.

Fabrigar, L. R., & Petty, R. E. (1999). The role of the affective and cognitive bases of attitudes in susceptibility to affectively and cognitively based persuasion. *Personality and Social Psychology Bulletin, 25,* 363–381.

Fabrigar, L. R., Priester, J. R., Petty, R. E., & Wegener, D. T. (1998). The impact of attitude accessibility on elaboration of persuasive messages. *Personality and Social Psychology Bulletin, 24,* 339–352.

Fazio, R. H. (1990). Multiple processes by which attitudes guide behavior: The MODE model as an integrative framework. In M. P. Zanna (Ed.), *Advances in experimental social psychology* (Vol. 23, pp. 75–109). San Diego, CA: Academic Press.

Fazio, R. H. (1995). Attitudes as object-evaluation associations: Determinants, consequences, and correlates of attitude accessibility. In R. E. Petty & J. A. Krosnick (Eds.), *Attitude strength: Antecedents and consequences* (pp. 247–282). Mahwah, NJ: Erlbaum.

Fazio, R. H., Jackson, J. R., Dunton, B. C., & Williams, C. J. (1995). Variability in automatic activation as an unobtrusive measure of racial attitudes: A bona fide pipeline? *Journal of Personality and Social Psychology, 69,* 1013–1027.

Fazio, R. H., Sanbonmatsu, D. M., Powell, M. C., & Kardes, F. R. (1986). On the automatic activation of attitudes. *Journal of Personality and Social Psychology, 50,* 229–238.

Fazio, R. H., Zanna, M. P., & Cooper, J. (1977). Dissonance and self-perception: An integrative view of each theory's proper domain of application. *Journal of Experimental Social Psychology, 13,* 464–479.

Festinger, L. (1957). *A theory of cognitive dissonance.* Evanston, IL: Row, Peterson.

Festinger, L., & Carlsmith, J. M. (1959). Cognitive consequences of forced compliance. *Journal of Abnormal and Social Psychology, 58,* 203–210.

Field, A. P. (2000). I like it, but I'm not sure why: Can evaluative conditioning occur without conscious awareness? *Consciousness & Cognition, 9,* 13–36.

Fishbein, M., & Ajzen, I. (1975). *Belief, attitude, intention, and behavior.* Reading, MA: Addison-Wesley.

Fishbein, M., & Ajzen, I. (1981). Acceptance, yielding, and impact: Cognitive processes in persuasion. In R. E. Petty, T. M. Ostrom, & T. C. Brock (Eds.), *Cognitive responses in persuasion* (pp. 339–359). Hillsdale, NJ: Erlbaum.

Fishbein, M., Ajzen, I., & McArdle, J. (1980). Changing the behavior of alcoholics: Effects of persuasive communication. In I. Ajzen & M. Fishbein (Eds.), *Understanding attitudes and predicting social behavior* (pp. 217–242). Englewood Cliffs, NJ: Prentice Hall.

Fishbein, M., & Middlestadt, S. (1995). Noncognitive effects on attitude formation and change: Fact or artifact? *Journal of Consumer Psychology, 4,* 181–202.

Gerard, H. B., Blevans, S. A., & Malcolm T. (1964). Self-evaluation and the evaluation of choice alternatives. *Journal of Personality, 32,* 395–410.

Gilbert, D. T. (1991). How mental systems believe. *American Psychologist, 46,* 107–119.

Gilbert, D. T. (1998). Person perception. In D. Gilbert, S. Fiske, & G. Lindzey (Eds.), *Handbook of social psychology* (Vol. 2, pp. 89–150). New York: McGraw-Hill.

Gilbert, D. T., Tafarodi, R. W., & Malone, P. S. (1993). You can't not believe everything you read. *Journal of Personality and Social Psychology, 65,* 221–233.

Gorn, G. J., & Goldberg, M. E. (1980). Children's responses to repetitive television commercials. *Journal of Consumer Research, 6,* 421–424.

Gouaux, C. (1971). Induced affective states and interpersonal attraction. *Journal of Personality and Social Psychology, 20,* 687–695.

Greenwald, A. G. (1968). Cognitive learning, cognitive response to persuasion, and attitude change. In A. G. Greenwald, T. C. Brock, & T. M. Ostrom (Eds.), *Psychological foundations of attitudes* (pp. 147–170). New York: Academic Press.

Greenwald, A. G. (1975). On the inconclusiveness of crucial cognitive tests of dissonance versus self-perception theories. *Journal of Experimental Social Psychology, 11,* 490–499.

Greenwald, A. G., & Albert, R. D. (1968). Acceptance and recall of improvised arguments. *Journal of Personality and Social Psychology, 8,* 31–34.

Greenwald, A. G., & Banaji, M. R. (1995). Implicit social cognition: Attitudes, self-esteem, and stereotypes. *Psychological Review, 102,* 4–27.

Greenwald, A. G., McGhee, D. E., & Schwartz, J. L. K. (1998). Measuring individual differences in implicit cognition: The implicit association test. *Journal of Personality and Social Psychology, 74,* 1464–1480.

Gresham, L. G., & Shimp, T. A. (1985). Attitude toward the advertisement and brand attitude: A classical conditioning perspective. *Journal of Advertising, 14,* 10–17.

Griffitt, W. B. (1970). Environmental effects on interpersonal affective behavior: Ambient effective temperature and attraction. *Journal of Personality and Social Psychology, 15,* 240–244.

Gross, S., Holtz, R., & Miller, N. (1995). Attitude certainty. In R. E. Petty & J. A. Krosnick (Eds.), *Attitude strength: Antecedents and consequences* (pp. 215–245). Mahwah, NJ: Erlbaum.

Hammond, K. R. (1948). Measuring attitudes by error-choice: an indirect method. *Journal of Abnormal and Social Psychology, 43,* 38–48.

Harkins, S. G., & Petty, R. E., (1981). The multiple source effect in persuasion: The effects of distraction. *Personality and Social Psychology Bulletin, 7,* 627–635.

Harkins, S. G., & Petty, R. E. (1987). Information utility and the multiple source effect. *Journal of Personality and Social Psychology, 52,* 260–268.

Harmon-Jones, E. (2000). Cognitive dissonance and experienced negative affect: Evidence that dissonance increases experienced negative affect even in the absence of aversive consequences. *Personality and Social Psychology Bulletin, 26,* 1490–1501.

Harmon-Jones, E., Brehm, J. W., Greenberg, J., Simon, L., & Nelson, D. E. (1996). Evidence that the production of aversive consequences is not necessary to create cognitive dissonance. *Journal of Personality and Social Psychology, 70,* 5–16.

Harmon-Jones, E., & Mills, J. (1999). *Cognitive dissonance: Progress on a pivotal theory in social psychology.* Washington, DC: American Psychological Association.

Hastie, R., & Park, B. (1986). The relationship between memory and judgment depends on whether the judgment task is memory-based or on-line. *Psychological Review, 93,* 258–268.

Heider, F. (1958). *The psychology of interpersonal relations.* New York: Wiley.

Hermans, D., Crombez, G., & Eelen, P. (2000). Automatic attitude activation and efficiency: The fourth horseman of automaticity. *Psychologica Belgica, 40,* 403–422.

Henninger, M., & Wyer, R. S. (1976). The recognition and elimination of inconsistencies among syllogistically related beliefs: Some new light on the "Socratic effect." *Journal of Personality and Social Psychology, 34,* 680–693.

Higgins, E. T., Rhodewalt, F., & Zanna, M. P. (1979). Dissonance motivation: Its nature, persistence, and reinstatement. *Journal of Experimental Social Psychology, 15,* 16–34.

Hovland, C. I., Janis, I. L., & Kelley, H. H. (1953). *Communication and persuasion: Psychological studies of opinion change.* New Haven, CT: Yale University Press.

Hoyt, M. F., Henley, M. D., & Collins, B. E. (1972). Studies in forced compliance: The confluence of choice and consequences on attitude change. *Journal of Personality and Social Psychology, 23,* 205–210.

Insko, C. A. (1984). Balance theory, the Jordan paradigm, and the Wiest tetrahedron. In L. Berkowitz (Ed.), *Advances in experimental social psychology* (Vol. 18, pp. 89–140). Orlando, FL: Academic Press.

Jacoby, L. L., Kelley, C. M., Brown, J., & Jasechko, J. (1989). Becoming famous overnight: Limits on the ability to avoid unconscious influences of the past. *Journal of Personality and Social Psychology, 56,* 326–338.

Janis, I. L. (1968). Attitude change via role playing. In R. P. Abelson, E. Aronson, W. J. McGuire, T. M. Newcomb, M. J. Rosenberg, & P. H. Tannenbaum (Eds.), *Theories of cognitive consistency: A sourcebook* (pp. 810–818). Chicago: Rand-McNally.

Janis, I. L., & King, B. T. (1954). The influence of role playing on opinion change. *Journal of Abnormal and Social Psychology, 49,* 211–218.

Janis, I. L., & Mann, L. (1965). Effectiveness of emotional role-playing in modifying smoking habits and attitudes. *Journal of Experimental Research in Personality, 1,* 84–90.

Jarvis, W. B. G., Petty, R. E., & Tormala, Z. L. (1999). *Do attitudes really change? An exploration of the PAST model.* Unpublished manuscript, Columbus, OH.

Johnson, B. T., & Eagly, A. H. (1989). Effects of involvement on persuasion: A meta-analysis. *Psychological Bulletin, 106,* 290–314.

Jones, E. E., & Davis, K. E. (1965). From acts to dispositions: The attribution process in person perception. In L. Berkowitz (Ed.), *Advances in experimental social psychology* (Vol. 2, pp. 219–266). New York: Academic Press.

Kawakami, K., Dovidio, J. F., Moll, J., Hermsen, S., & Russin, A. (2000). Just say no (to stereotyping): Effects of training in the negation of stereotypic associations on stereotype activation. *Journal of Personality and Social Psychology, 78,* 871–888.

Kiesler, S. B., & Mathog, R. (1968). The distraction hypothesis in attitude change. *Psychological Reports, 23,* 1123–1133.

King, B. T., & Janis, I. L. (1956). Comparison of the effectiveness of improvised versus non-improvised role-playing in producing opinion changes. *Human Relations, 9,* 177–186.

Krosnick, J. A. (1988). Attitude importance and attitude change. *Journal of Experimental Social Psychology, 24,* 240–255.

Krosnick, J. A., Betz, A. L., Jussim, L. J., & Lynn, A. R. (1992). Subliminal conditioning of attitudes. *Personality and Social Psychology Bulletin, 18,* 152–162.

Krosnick, J. A., Boninger, D. S., Chuang, Y. C., Berent, M., & Carnot, C. G. (1993). Attitude strength: One construct or many related constructs? *Journal of Personality and Social Psychology, 65,* 1132–1151.

Krosnick, J. A., & Petty, R. E. (1995). Attitude strength: An overview. In R. E. Petty & J. A. Krosnick (Eds.), *Attitude strength: Antecedents and consequences* (pp. 1–24). Hillsdale, NJ: Erlbaum.

Kruglanski, A. W. (1990). Motivations for judging and knowing: Implications for causal attribution. In E. T. Higgins & R. M. Sorrentino (Eds.), *Handbook of motivation and cognition: Foundations of social behavior* (Vol. 2, pp. 333–368). New York: Guilford.

Kruglanski, A. W., & Freund, T. (1983). The freezing and unfreezing of lay-inferences: Effects on impressional primacy, ethnic stereotyping, and numerical anchoring. *Journal of Experimental Social Psychology, 19,* 448–468.

Kruglanski, A. W., Freund, T., & Bar-Tal, D. (1996). Motivational effects in the mere-exposure paradigm. *European Journal of Social Psychology, 26,* 479–499.

Kruglanski, A. W., & Thompson, E. P. (1999). Persuasion by a single route: A view from the Unimodel. *Psychological Inquiry, 10,* 83–109.

Kunda, Z. (1990). The case for motivated reasoning. *Psychological Bulletin, 108,* 480–498.

Kunst-Wilson, W. R., & Zajonc, R. B. (1980). Affective discrimination of stimuli that cannot be recognized. *Science, 207,* 557–558.

Lepper, M. R., Greene, D., & Nisbett, R. E. (1973). Undermining children's intrinsic interest with extrinsic reward: A test of the "overjustification" hypothesis. *Journal of Personality and Social Psychology, 28,* 129–137.

Levine, G. L., Halberstadt, J. B., & Goldstone, R. L. (1996). Reasoning and the weighting of attributes in attitude judgments. *Journal of Personality and Social Psychology, 70,* 230–240.

Lichtenstein, M., & Srull, T. K. (1987). Processing objectives as a determinant of the relationship between recall and judgment. *Journal of Experimental Social Psychology, 23,* 93–118.

Likert, R. (1932). A technique for the measurement of attitudes. *Archives of Psychology, 140,* 55.

Lingle, J. H., & Ostrom, T. M. (1981). Principles of memory and cognition in attitude formation. In R. E. Petty, T. M. Ostrom, & T. C. Brock (Eds.), *Cognitive responses in persuasion* (pp. 399–420). Hillsdale, NJ: Erlbaum.

Lord, C. G., Ross, L., & Lepper, M. R. (1979). Biased assimilation and attitude polarization: The effects of prior theories on subsequently considered evidence. *Journal of Personality and Social Psychology, 37,* 2098–2109.

Losch, M. E., & Cacioppo, J. T. (1990). Cognitive dissonance may enhance sympathetic tonus, but attitudes are changed to reduce negative affect rather than arousal. *Journal of Experimental Social Psychology, 26,* 289–304.

Lutz, R. J. (1975). Changing brand attitudes through modification of cognitive structure. *Journal of Consumer Research, 1,* 49–59.

Lutz, R. J. (1977). An experimental investigation of causal relations among cognitions, affect, and behavioral intention. *Journal of Consumer Research, 3,* 197–208.

MacKenzie, S. B. (1986). The role of attention in mediating the effect of advertising on attribute importance. *Journal of Consumer Research, 13,* 174–195.

Mackie, D. M. (1987). Systematic and nonsystematic processing of majority and minority persuasive communications. *Journal of Personality and Social Psychology, 53,* 41–52.

Mackie, D. M., & Asuncion, A. G. (1990). On-line and memory-based modification of attitudes: Determinants of message recall-attitude change correspondence. *Journal of Personality and Social Psychology, 59,* 5–16.

Mackie, D. M., & Worth, L. T. (1989). Processing deficits and the mediation of positive affect in persuasion. *Journal of Personality and Social Psychology, 57,* 27–40.

Macrae, C. N., Bodenhausen, G. V., Milne, A. B., & Jetten, J. (1994). Out of mind but back in sight: Stereotypes on the rebound. *Journal of Personality and Social Psychology, 67,* 808–817.

Maheswaran, D., & Chaiken, S. (1991). Promoting systematic processing in low-motivation settings: Effect of incongruent information on processing and judgment. *Journal of Personality and Social Psychology, 61,* 13–33.

Maio, G. R., Bell, D. W., & Esses, V. M. (1996). Ambivalence in persuasion: The processing of messages about immigrant groups. *Journal of Experimental Social Psychology, 32,* 513–536.

Martin, L. L., Seta, J. J., & Crelia, R. A. (1990). Assimilation and contrast as a function of people's willingness and ability to expend effort in forming an impression. *Journal of Personality and Social Psychology, 59,* 27–37.

McGuire, W. J. (1960). A syllogistic analysis of cognitive relationships. In C. I. Hovland & M. J. Rosenberg (Eds.), *Attitude organization and change: An analysis of consistency among attitude components* (pp. 65–111). New Haven, CT: Yale University Press.

McGuire, W. J. (1964). Inducing resistance to persuasion: Some contemporary approaches. In L. Berkowitz (Ed.), *Advances in experimental social psychology* (Vol. 1, pp. 191–229). New York: Academic.

McGuire, W. J. (1968). Personality and attitude change: An information-processing theory. In A. G. Greenwald, T. C. Brock, & T. M. Ostrom (Eds.), *Psychological foundations of attitudes* (pp. 171–196). New York: Academic.

McGuire, W. J. (1981). The probabilogical model of cognitive structure and attitude change. In R. E. Petty, T. M. Ostrom, & T. C. Brock (Eds.), *Cognitive responses in persuasion* (pp. 291–307). Hillsdale, NJ: Erlbaum.

McGuire, W. J., & McGuire, C. V. (1991). The content, structure, and operation of thought systems. In R. S. Wyer Jr. & T. Srull (Eds.), *Advances in social cognition* (Vol. 4, pp. 1–78). Hillsdale, NJ: Erlbaum.

Millar, M. G., & Tesser, A. (1986). Thought-induced attitude change: The effects of schema structure and commitment. *Journal of Personality and Social Psychology, 51,* 259–269.

Miller, C. E., & Norman, R. M. G. (1976). Balance, agreement, and attraction in hypothetical social situations. *Journal of Experimental Social Psychology, 12,* 109–119.

Moore, D. L., & Reardon, R. (1987). Source magnification: The role of multiple sources in the processing of advertising appeals. *Journal of Marketing Research, 24,* 412–417.

Mugny, G., & Perez, J. A. (1991). *The social psychology of minority influence.* New York: Cambridge University Press.

Murphy, S. T., Monahan, J. L., & Zajonc, R. B. (1995). Additivity of nonconscious affect: Combined effects of priming and exposure. *Journal of Personality and Social Psychology, 69,* 589–602.

Murphy, S. T., & Zajonc, R. B. (1993). Affect, cognition, and awareness: Affective priming with optimal and suboptimal exposures. *Journal of Personality and Social Psychology, 64*, 723–739.

Newcomb, T. M. (1968). Interpersonal balance. In R. P. Abelson, E. Aronson, W. J. McGuire, T. M. Newcomb, M. J. Rosenberg, & P. H. Tannenbaum (Eds.), *Theories of cognitive consistency: A sourcebook* (pp. 28–51). Chicago: Rand-McNally.

Nienhuis, A. E., Manstead, A. S. R., & Spears, R. (2001). Multiple motives and persuasive communication: Creative elaboration as a result of impression motivation and accuracy motivation. *Personality and Social Psychology Bulletin, 27*, 118–132.

Nisbett, R. E., & Wilson, T. D. (1977). Telling more than we can know: Verbal reports on mental processes. *Psychological Review, 84*, 231–259.

Olson, T. M., & Fazio, R. H. (2001). Implicit attitude formation through classical conditioning. *Psychological Science, 12*, 413–417.

Osgood, C. E., Suci, G. J., & Tannenbaum, P. H. (1957). *The measurement of meaning.* Urbana: University of Illinois Press.

Peak, H. (1955). Attitude and motivation. In M. R. Jones (Ed.), *Nebraska Symposium on Motivation* (Vol. 3, pp. 149–188). Lincoln: University of Nebraska Press.

Peeters, G., & Czapinski, J. (1990). Positive-negative asymmetry in evaluations: The distinction between affective and informational negativity effects. *European Review of Social Psychology, 1*, 33–60.

Perloff, R. M., & Brock, T. C. (1980). And thinking makes it so: Cognitive responses to persuasion. In M. Roloff & G. Miller (Eds.), *Persuasion: New directions in theory and research* (pp. 67–100). Beverly Hills, CA: Sage.

Petty, R. E. (1994). Two routes to persuasion: State of the art. In G. d'Ydewalle, P. Eelen, & P. Bertelson (Eds.), *International perspectives on psychological science* (Vol. 2, pp. 229–247). Hillsdale, NJ: Erlbaum.

Petty, R. E. (1997). The evolution of theory and research in social psychology: From single to multiple effect and process models of persuasion. In C. McGarty & S. A. Haslam (Eds.), *The message of social psychology: Perspectives on mind in society* (pp. 268–290). Oxford, UK: Basil Blackwell.

Petty, R. E., Baker, S. M., & Gleicher, S. M. (1991). Attitudes and drug abuse prevention: Implications of the Elaboration Likelihood Model. In L. Donohew, H. E. Sypher, & W. J. Bukoski (Eds.), *Persuasive communication and drug abuse prevention* (pp. 72–90). Hillsdale, NJ: Erlbaum.

Petty, R. E., Briñol, P., & Tormala, Z. L. (in press). Thought confidence as a determinant of persuasion: The self-validation hypothesis. *Journal of Personality and Social Psychology.*

Petty, R. E., & Cacioppo, J. T. (1979a). Effects of forewarning of persuasive intent and involvement on cognitive responses. *Personality and Social Psychology Bulletin, 5*, 173–176.

Petty, R. E., & Cacioppo, J. T. (1979b). Issue-involvement can increase or decrease persuasion by enhancing message-relevant cognitive responses. *Journal of Personality and Social Psychology, 37*, 1915–1926.

Petty, R. E., & Cacioppo, J. T. (1981). *Attitudes and persuasion: Classic and contemporary approaches.* Dubuque, IA: Wm. C. Brown.

Petty, R. E., & Cacioppo, J. T. (1984). The effects of involvement on responses to argument quantity and quality: Central and peripheral routes to persuasion. *Journal of Personality and Social Psychology, 46*, 69–81.

Petty, R. E., & Cacioppo, J. T. (1986). The Elaboration Likelihood Model of persuasion. In L. Berkowitz (Ed.), *Advances in experimental social psychology* (Vol. 19, pp. 123–205). New York: Academic.

Petty, R. E., & Cacioppo, J. T. (1990). Involvement and persuasion: Tradition versus integration. *Psychological Bulletin, 107*, 367–374.

Petty, R. E., Cacioppo, J. T., & Goldman, R. (1981). Personal involvement as a determinant of argument-based persuasion. *Journal of Personality and Social Psychology, 41*, 847–855.

Petty, R. E., Cacioppo, J. T., & Haugtvedt, C. (1992). Involvement and persuasion: An appreciative look at the Sherifs' contribution to the study of self-relevance and attitude change. In D. Granberg & G. Sarup (Eds.), *A social judgment and intergroup relations: Essays in honor of Muzifer Sherif* (pp. 147–175). New York: Springer-Verlag.

Petty, R. E., Cacioppo, J. T., & Heesacker, M. (1981). Effects of rhetorical questions on persuasion: A cognitive response analysis. *Journal of Personality and Social Psychology, 40*, 432–440.

Petty, R. E., Fleming, M. A., Priester, J. R., & Feinstein, A. H. (2001). Violation of individual versus group self-interest: Implications for message processing and persuasion. *Social Cognition, 19*, 418–442.

Petty, R. E., Harkins, S. G., & Williams, K. D. (1980). The effects of group diffusion of cognitive effort on attitudes: An information processing view. *Journal of Personality and Social Psychology, 38*, 81–92.

Petty, R. E., Haugtvedt, C. P., & Smith, S. M. (1995). Elaboration as a determinant of attitude strength. In R. E. Petty & J. A. Krosnick (Eds.), *Attitude strength: Antecedents and consequences* (pp. 93–130). Mahwah, NJ: Erlbaum.

Petty, R. E., & Jarvis, W. B. G. (1998, October). *What happens to the "old" attitude when attitudes change?* Presented at the annual meeting of the Society for Experimental Social Psychology, Lexington, KY.

Petty, R. E., & Krosnick, J. A. (1995). *Attitude strength: Antecedents and consequences.* Mahwah, NJ: Erlbaum.

Petty, R. E., Ostrom, T. M., & Brock, T. C. (1981). *Cognitive responses in persuasion.* Hillsdale, NJ: Erlbaum.

Petty, R. E., Priester, J. R., & Wegener, D. T. (1994). Cognitive processes in attitude change. In R. S. Wyer & T. K. Srull (Eds.), *Handbook of social cognition* (2nd ed., Vol. 2, 69–142). Hillsdale, NJ: Erlbaum.

Visser, M. (1994). Policy voting, projection, and persuasion: An application of balance theory to electoral behavior. *Political Psychology, 15,* 699–711.

Watts, W. A., & McGuire, W. J. (1964). Persistence of induced opinion change and retention of the inducing message contents. *Journal of Abnormal and Social Psychology, 68,* 233–241.

Wegener, D. T., Downing, J., Krosnick, J. A., & Petty, R. E. (1995). Measures and manipulations of strength-related properties of attitudes: Current practice and future directions. In R. E. Petty & J. A. Krosnick (Eds.), *Attitude strength: Antecedents and consequences* (pp. 455–487). Mahwah, NJ: Erlbaum.

Wegener, D. T., & Petty, R. E. (1997). The flexible correction model: The role of naive theories of bias in bias correction. In M. P. Zanna (Ed.), *Advances in experimental social psychology* (Vol., 29, pp. 141–208). San Diego: Academic.

Wegener, D. T., & Petty, R. E. (1998). The naive scientist revisited: Naive theories and social judgment. *Social Cognition, 16,* 1–7.

Wegener, D. T., Petty, R. E., & Klein, D. J. (1994). Effects of mood on high elaboration attitude change: The mediating role of likelihood judgments. *European Journal of Social Psychology, 24,* 25–43.

Wegener, D. T., Petty, R. E., & Smith, S. M. (1995). Positive mood can increase or decrease message scrutiny: The hedonic contingency view of mood and message processing. *Journal of Personality and Social Psychology, 69,* 5–15.

Wells, G. L., & Petty, R. E. (1980). The effects of overt head movement on persuasion: Compatibility and incompatibility of responses. *Basic and Applied Social Psychology, 1,* 219–230.

Wilson, T. D., & Brekke, N. (1994). Mental contamination and mental correction: Unwanted influences on judgments and evaluations. *Psychological Bulletin, 116,* 117–142.

Wilson, T. D., Dunn, D. S., Kraft, D., & Lisle, D. J. (1989). Introspection, attitude change, and attitude-behavior consistency: The disrupting effects of explaining why we feel the way we do. *Advances in Experimental Social Psychology, 22,* 287–343.

Wilson, T. D., & Hodges, S. D. (1992). Attitudes as temporary constructions. In L. L. Martin & A. Tesser (Eds.), *The construction of social judgments* (pp. 37–65). Hillsdale, NJ: Erlbaum.

Wilson, T. D., & Kraft, D. (1993). Why do I love thee?: Effects of repeated introspections about a dating relationship on attitudes toward the relationship. *Personality and Social Psychology Bulletin, 19,* 409–418.

Wilson, T. D., Lindsey, S., & Schooler, T. Y. (2000). A model of dual attitudes. *Psychological Review, 107,* 101–126.

Wilson, T. D., Lisle, D. J., Schooler, J., Hodges, S. D., Klaaren, K. J., & LaFleur, S. J. (1993). Introspecting about reasons can reduce post-choice satisfaction. *Personality and Social Psychology Bulletin, 19,* 331–339.

Wilson, T. D., & Schooler, J. W. (1991). Thinking too much: Introspection can reduce the quality of preferences and decisions. *Journal of Personality and Social Psychology, 60,* 181–192.

Winograd, E., Goldstein, F. C., Monarch, E. S., Peluso, J. P., & Goldman, W. P. (1999). The mere exposure effect in patients with Alzheimer's disease. *Neuropsychology, 13,* 41–46.

Wittenbrink, B., Judd, C. M., & Park, B. (1997). Evidence for racial prejudice at the implicit level and its relationship with questionnaire measures. *Journal of Personality and Social Psychology, 72,* 262–274.

Wood, W. (1982). Retrieval of attitude-relevant information from memory: Effects on susceptibility to persuasion and on intrinsic motivation. *Journal of Personality and Social Psychology, 42,* 798–910.

Wood, W., & Kallgren, C. A. (1988). Communicator attributes and persuasion: Recipients access to attitude-relevant information in memory. *Personality and Social Psychology Bulletin, 14,* 172–182.

Wood, W., Rhodes, N., & Biek, M. (1995). Working knowledge and attitude strength: An information processing analysis. In R. E. Petty & J. A. Krosnick (Eds.), *Attitude strength: Antecedents and consequences* (pp. 283–313). Mahwah, NJ: Erlbaum.

Word, C. O., Zanna, M. P., & Cooper, J. (1974). The nonverbal mediation of self-fulfilling prophecies in interracial interaction. *Journal of Experimental Social Psychology, 10,* 109–120.

Wright, P. L. (1981). Cognitive responses to mass media advocacy. In R. E. Petty, T. M. Ostrom, & T. C. Brock (Eds.), *Cognitive responses in persuasion* (pp. 263–282). Hillsdale, NJ: Erlbaum.

Wyer, R. S., Jr. (1970). Quantitative prediction of belief and opinion change: A further test of a subjective probability model. *Journal of Personality and Social Psychology, 16,* 559–570.

Wyer, R. S., Jr. (1973). Further test of a subjective probability model of social inference. *Journal of Research in Personality, 7,* 237–253.

Wyer, R. S., Jr. (1974). *Cognitive organization and change: An information-processing approach.* Hillsdale, NJ: Erlbaum.

Yalch, R. F., & Elmore-Yalch, R. (1984). The effect of numbers on the route to persuasion. *Journal of Consumer Research, 11,* 522–527.

Zajonc, R. B. (1968). Attitudinal effects of mere exposure. *Journal of Personality and Social Psychology Monograph Supplements, 9,* 1–27.

Zanna, M. P., & Cooper, J. (1974). Dissonance and the pill: An attribution approach to studying the arousal properties of dissonance. *Journal of Personality and Social Psychology, 29,* 703–709.

Zanna, M. P., Kiesler, C. A., & Pilkonis, P. A. (1970). Positive and negative attitudinal affect established by classical conditioning. *Journal of Personality and Social Psychology, 14,* 321–328.

Zanna, M. P., & Rempel, J. K. (1988). Attitudes: A new look at an old concept. In D. Bar-Tal & A. W. Kruglanski (Eds.), *The social psychology of knowledge* (pp. 315–334). Cambridge, UK: Cambridge University Press.

Zimbardo, P. G., Weisenberg, M., Firestone, I., & Levy, B. (1965). Communicator effectiveness in producing public conformity and private attitude change. *Journal of Personality, 33,* 233–255.

CHAPTER 16

Social Influence and Group Dynamics

ANDRZEJ NOWAK, ROBIN R. VALLACHER, AND MANDY E. MILLER

The belief that we are the masters of our own destiny surely ranks among the most fundamental of human conceits. This overarching self-perception is viewed by many scholars as a prerequisite to personal adjustment, enabling us to face uncertainty with conviction and challenges with perseverance (cf. Alloy & Abramson, 1979; Deci & Ryan, 1985; Kofta, Weary, & Sedek, 1998; Seligman, 1975; Taylor & Brown, 1988), and as equally central to the maintenance of social order because of its direct link to the attribution of personal responsibility (cf. Baumeister, Stillwell, & Heatherton, 1994; Shaver, 1985). Its adaptive significance notwithstanding, the sense that one's actions are autonomous, self-generated, and largely impervious to external forces is routinely exaggerated in daily life (e.g., Langer, 1978; Taylor & Brown, 1988), and ultimately can be dismissed as philosophically untenable to the extent that it reflects naive assumptions about personal freedom (cf. Bargh & Chartrand, 1999; Skinner, 1971). Social psychologists know better, and in their pursuit of the true causal underpinnings of behavior, they have routinely

placed the individual at the intersection of various and sundry social forces. In this view, people represent interdependent elements that together comprise larger social entities, be they familial, romantic, or societal in nature. Against this backdrop, people continually influence and in turn are influenced by one another in myriad ways. Social influence is the currency of human interaction, and although its operation may be subtle and sometimes transparent to the individuals involved, its effects are pervasive.

In recognition of the primacy of influence in the social landscape, G. W. Allport (1968) defined the field of social psychology as "an attempt to understand . . . how the thought, feeling, and behavior of the individual are influenced by the actual, imagined, or implied presence of others." No other topic in social psychology can lay claim to such centrality. After all, no one has defined social psychology as the study of impression formation or self-concept, nor have researchers investigating such topics done so without assigning a prominent role to social influence processes. The belief in self-determination may well be important for personal and societal function, but the reality of social influence is equally significant—and for many of the same reasons. Our aim in this chapter is to outline the fundamental features of social influence and to illustrate the manifestations of influence in different contexts. In so doing, we emphasize the various functions served by social influence, both for the individual and for society.

Preparation of this chapter was supported in part by Grant SBR-11657 from the National Science Foundation and Grant 1H01F07310 from the Polish Committee for Scientific Research. The constructive comments of Irving Weiner and Melvin Lerner on an earlier draft are greatly appreciated.

OVERVIEW OF CHAPTER

Because social influence is deeply embedded in every aspect of interpersonal functioning, any attempt to discuss it apart from all the topics and research traditions defining social psychology is necessarily incomplete and potentially misleading. How can one divorce a depiction of basic influence processes from such phenomena as attitude change, self-concept malleability, or the development of close relationships? As it happens, of course, any field of scientific inquiry is differentiated into relatively self-contained regions, and social psychology is no exception. Although it can be argued that one person's practical differentiation is another person's unnecessary fragmentation (see, e.g., Gergen, 1985; Vallacher & Nowak, 1994), it is nonetheless the case that distinct theoretical and research traditions have emerged over the years to create a workable taxonomy of social psychological phenomena. Despite the pervasive nature of social influence, then, it is commonly treated as a separate topic in textbooks and secondary source summaries of relevant theory and research. To an extent, our treatment of social influence works within the accepted boundary conditions. Thus, we discuss such agreed-upon subtopics as compliance, conformity, and obedience to authority. At the same time, however, we attempt to impose a semblance of theoretical order on the broad assortment of relevant processes. So although each manifestation of influence—whether in advertising, the military, or intimate relationships—taps correspondingly distinct psychological mechanisms, there are certain invariant features that transcend the surface structure of social influence phenomena.

We begin by discussing the exercise of external control to influence people's thoughts and behaviors. Rewards and punishments have self-evident efficacy in controlling behavior across the animal kingdom, so their incorporation into influence techniques in human affairs is hardly surprising. We then turn our attention to less blatant strategies of influence that typically fare better in inducing sustained changes in people's thought and behavior. It is noteworthy in this regard that the lion's share of the literature subsumed under the social influence label emphasizes subtle manipulation rather than direct attempts at control. We provide an overview of the principal manipulation techniques and abstract from them common features that are responsible for their relative success. This theme provides the foundation for an even less blatant approach to influence, one centering on the coordination of people's internal states and overt behaviors. People have a natural tendency to bring their beliefs, preferences, and actions in line with those of the people around them, and

this tendency becomes manifest in the absence of overt or subtle manipulation strategies. This penchant for interpersonal synchronization is what enables a mere collection of individuals to become a functional unit defining a higher level of social reality.

We then turn our attention to the manifestation of social influence at the level of society. A central theme here is that the emergence and maintenance of macrolevel properties in a social system can be understood in terms of the microlevel influence processes described in the preceding sections. We describe the results of computer simulations demonstrating this linkage between different levels of social reality. In a concluding section, we abstract what appear to be the common features of influence across different topics and relate them to fundamental psychological processes, chief among them the coordination of individual elements to create a coherent higher-order unit. Our suggestions in this regard are as much heuristic as integrative, and we offer suggestions for future lines of theoretical work to forward this agenda.

EXTERNAL CONTROL

The most elemental way to influence someone's behavior is make rewards and punishments contingent on the enactment of the behavior. For the better part of the twentieth century, experimental psychology was essentially defined in terms of this perspective, and during this era a wide variety of reinforcement principles were generated and validated. Attempts to extend these principles to social psychology were always complicated by the undeniable cognitive capacities of humans and the role of such capacities in regulating behavior (cf. Bandura, 1986; Zajonc, 1980). Nonetheless, several lines of research based on behaviorist assumptions are represented in social psychology (e.g., Byrne, 1971; Staats, 1975). With respect to social influence, this perspective suggests simply that people are motivated to do things that are associated with the attainment of pleasant consequences or the avoidance of unpleasant consequences. Thus, people adopt new attitudes, develop preferences for one another, change the frequency of certain behaviors, or take on new activities because they in effect have been trained to do so. It's fair to say this perspective never achieved mainstream status in social psychology, but one might think that social influence would be an exception. Reinforcement, after all, is defined in terms of the control of behavior, and to the extent that a self-interest premise underlies virtually all social psychological theories (cf. Miller, 1999), it is hard to imagine how the promise of reward or threat of punishment could fail to influence people's thoughts, feelings, and actions.

Bases of Social Power

The ability to control someone's behavior, whether by carrot or stick, is synonymous with having power over that person. Presumably, then, successful influence agents are those who are seen—by the target at least—as possessing social power. In contemporary society, power reflects more than physical strength, immense wealth, or the capacity and readiness to harm others—although having such attributes certainly wouldn't hurt under some circumstances. Social power instead derives from a variety of different sources, each providing a correspondingly distinct form of behavior control. The work of French and Raven (1959; Raven, 1992, 1993) is commonly considered the definitive statement on the various bases of social power and their respective manifestations in everyday life. They identify six such bases: reward, coercion, expertise, information, referent power, and legitimate authority.

Reward power derives, as the term implies, from the ability to provide desired outcomes to someone. The rewards may be tangible and material (e.g., money, a nice gift), but often they are more subtle and nonmaterial in nature (e.g., approval, affection). The compliance-for-reward exchange may be direct and explicit, of course, as when a parent offers an economic incentive to a child for doing his or her homework. But the transaction is often tacit or implicit in the relationship rather than directly stated. The salesperson who pushes used cars with special zeal, for example, may do so because he or she knows the company gives raises to those who meet a certain sales quota. *Coercive power* derives from the ability to provide aversive or otherwise undesired outcomes to someone. As with rewards, coercion can revolve around tangible and concrete outcomes, such as the use or threat of physical force, or instead involve outcomes that are nonmaterial and acquire their valence by virtue of less tangible features. The parent concerned with a child's study habits might express disapproval for the child's shortcomings in this regard, for example, and the salesperson might redouble his or her efforts at moving stock for fear of losing his or her job.

Expert power is accorded those who are perceived to have superior knowledge or skills relevant to the target's goals. Deference to such individuals is common when the target lacks direct personal knowledge regarding a topic or course of action. In the physician-patient relationship, for example, the patient typically complies with the physician's instructions to take a certain medicine, even when the patient has no

idea how the purported remedy will cure him or her. Knowledge, in other words, is power. *Information power* is related to expert power, except that it relates to the specific information conveyed by the source, not to the source's expertise per se. A person could stumble on a piece of useful gossip, for example, and despite his or her general ignorance in virtually every aspect of his or her life, this person might wield considerable power for a time over those who would benefit from this information. Knowledge is power, it seems, even in the hands of someone who doesn't know what he or she is talking about.

Referent power derives from people's tendency to identify with someone they respect or otherwise admire. "Be like Mike" and "I am Tiger Woods," for example, are successful advertising slogans that play on consumers' desire to be similar to a cultural icon. The hoped-for similarity in such cases, of course, is stunningly superficial—all the overpriced shoes in the world won't enable a teenager to defy gravity while putting a basketball through a net or drive a small white ball 300 yards to the green in one stroke. Referent power is rarely asserted in the form of a direct request, operating instead through the pull of a desirable person, and can be manifest without the physical presence or surveillance of the influence agent. A young boy might shadow his older brother's every move, for example, even if the brother hardly notices, and an aspiring writer might emulate Hemingway's sparse writing style even though it is fair to say this earnest adulation is totally lost on Hemingway.

Legitimate power derives from societal norms that accord behavior control to individuals occupying certain roles. The flight attendant who instructs 300 passengers to put their tables in an upright position does not have a great deal of reward or coercive power, nor is he or she seen as necessarily possessing deep expertise pertaining to the request, and it is even more unlikely that he or she is the subject of identification fantasies for most of the passengers. Yet this person wields enormous influence over the passengers because of the legitimate authority he or she is accorded during the flight. Legitimate power is often quite limited in scope. A professor, for example, has the legitimate authority to schedule exams but not to tell students how to conduct their personal lives—unless, of course, he or she also has referent power for them. Legitimate power is clearly essential to societal coordination—imagine how traffic at a four-way intersection would fare if the signal lights failed and the police on the scene had to rely on gifts or their personal charisma to gain the cooperation of each driver. But blind obedience to those in positions of legitimate authority also has enormous potential for unleashing the worst in people, sometimes to the detriment of themselves or others. In recognition of this potential, social psychologists have devoted considerable attention to the nature of legitimate power, with special emphasis on obedience to authority. Not wanting to question this scholarly norm, we highlight this topic in the following section.

Obedience to Authority

Guards herding millions of innocent people into gas chambers, soldiers mowing down dozens of farmers and villagers with machine guns, and hundreds of cult members waiting in line for lethal Kool-Aid that is certain to kill themselves and their children: These images may be unthinkable, but they are part of the legacy of the twentieth century. Nestled in the security of our homes, we are nonetheless affected by such undeniable examples of mass abdications of personal responsibility and decision making; they can keep us up nights, not to mention undermine our sense of control. Although recent times have no monopoly on genocide, the abominations of World War II intensified the drive to plumb the depths of social influence, especially influence over the many by the few in the name of legitimate authority.

The best-known and most provocative line of research on this topic is that of Stanley Milgram (1965, 1974), who conducted a set of controversial laboratory experiments in the early 1960s. Milgram wanted to document the extent to which ordinary people will take orders from a legitimate authority figure when compliance with the orders entails another person's suffering. The idea was to replicate in a relatively benign setting the dynamics at work during wartime, when soldiers are given orders to kill enemy soldiers and citizens. In his experimental situation, ostensibly concerned with the psychology of learning, participant "teachers" were asked to deliver electric shocks to "learners" (who were actually accomplices of Milgram) if the learners produced an incorrect response to an item on a simple learning task. In the initial study, Milgram (1965) found that 65% of the subjects cast in the teacher role obeyed the experimenter's demand to proceed, ultimately administering 450 volts of electricity to a learner (a mild-mannered, middle-aged man with a self-described heart condition) in an adjoining room, despite hearing the learner's protests, screams, and pleas to stop emanating from the other room. Milgram subsequently performed several variations on this procedure, each designed to identify the factors responsible for the striking level of obedience initially observed. In one of the most intriguing variations, subjects were cast in the learner role as well as the teacher role, and the experimenter eventually told the teacher to cease administering shocks. Remarkably, some learners in this situation insisted that the teacher continue "teaching"

them for the good of the experiment. Because the learner did not have the same degree of legitimacy as the experimenter did, however, none of the teachers acceded to the learner's demand to continue shocking them.

Milgram's findings proved unsettling to scholars and laypeople alike. With the horrors of World War II still fairly fresh in people's memories, Milgram's research suggested that Hitler's final solution was not only fathomable, but perhaps also likely to occur again under the right circumstances. After all, these findings were produced by people from a nation of self-professed mavericks whose ancestors had risen up against the motherland's authority less than two centuries earlier. Subsequent research employing Milgram's basic paradigm has demonstrated comparable levels of obedience in many other countries, including Australia, Germany, Spain, and Jordan (Kilham & Mann, 1974; Meeus & Raaijmakers, 1986). The tendency to defer to legitimate authority, even when the demands of authority run counter to one's personal beliefs and inhibitions, appears to be robust, representing perhaps an integral part of human nature.

The power of authority can derive from purely symbolic manifestations, such as titles or clothing, even when the ostensible authority has no credible claim to his or her role as a legitimate authority figure. A man wearing a security guard's uniform, for example, can secure compliance with a request to pick up litter, even when the requests are made in a context outside the guard's purview (Bickman, 1974). Even fictional symbols of authority can produce compliance. Television advertising trades on this tendency with astonishing commercial success. For example, the actor Robert Young, who played the part of Dr. Marcus Welby in a popular TV doctor series in the 1960s, wore a white lab coat in a commercial for Sanka (a brand of decaffeinated coffee). He was not an expert on coffee and certainly not a real doctor, yet the symbols of his authority (the white lab coat, the association with Dr. Welby) were sufficient to increase dramatically the sales of Sanka. Even when an actor states at the outset of a commercial pitch that *I am not a doctor, but I play one on TV,* his recommendations regarding cold remedies are followed by a significant portion of the viewing audience. This deference to titles and uniforms can have devastating effects. A study performed in a medical context, for example, found that 95% of nurses who received a phone call from a "doctor" agreed to administer a dangerous level of a drug to a patient (Hofling, Brotzman, Dalrymple, Graves, & Pierce, 1966).

Although pressures to obey authority are compelling, obedience is not inevitable. Research has shown, for example, that obedience to authority is tempered when the victim's suffering is highly salient and when the authority figure is made to feel personally responsible for his or her actions (Taylor, Peplau, & Sears, 1997). Resistance to authority is enhanced, moreover, when the resister receives social support and in situations in which he or she is encouraged to question the motives, expertise, or judgments of the authority figure (Taylor et al., 1997). It should be reiterated, however, that legitimate authority serves important social functions and should not be viewed with a jaundiced eye only as a necessary evil in the human condition. Policeman, judges, elected representatives, and school crossing guards could not perform their duties if their power were not based on an aura of legitimacy. And as much as teachers like to be liked and to be seen as experts, their power over students in the classroom hinges to a large extent on students' perceiving them as legitimate authority figures. Even parents, who wield virtually every other kind of power (reward, coercion, expertise, information) over their children, must occasionally remind their offspring who is ultimately in charge in order to exact compliance from them. Obedience to authority, in sum, is pervasive in informal and formal social relations, and is neither intrinsically good nor intrinsically bad. Like many features of the human condition, its potential for good or evil is dependent on the restraint and judgment of those who exercise it.

Limitations of External Control

If the exercise of power always had its intended effect, both scholarly and lay interest in social influence would be minimal. Why bother obsessing over something as obvious as the tendency of people to defer to people in a position to offer rewards or threaten punishment? Is detailed experimentation really necessary to figure out why we listen to experts or model the behavior and attitudes of people we admire? And what could be more obvious than the observation that we typically comply with the demands and requests of those who are perceived as entitled to influence us in this way? Fortunately for social psychologists—and perhaps for intellectually curious laypeople as well—the story of social influence does not end with such self-evident conclusions, but rather unfolds with a far more interesting plotline. There is reason to think, in fact, that the general approach to influence outlined previously is among the least effective ways of implementing true change in people's thoughts and feelings relevant to the behavior in question. Indeed, a fair portion of theoretical and research attention over the last 40 years has focused on the tendency for heavy-handed efforts at influence to boomerang, promoting effects opposite to those intended. This is especially the case for attempted influence that trades on reward and coercive power, although the assumptions underlying

this line of theory and research would seem to hold true for legitimate power as well.

Psychological Reactance

To a certain extent, the failure of power-based approaches to induce change in people's action preferences can be traced to the fundamental human conceit noted at the outset. People want to feel like they are the directors of their own fate (cf. Deci & Ryan, 1985), and accordingly are sensitive to attempts by others to diminish this self-perceived role. No one really likes to be told what to do, and influence attempts that are seen in this light run the risk of producing resistance rather than compliance. Reactance theory (J. W. Brehm, 1966; S. S. Brehm & Brehm, 1981) trades on the assumption that people like to feel free, specifying how people react when this feeling is undermined. The basic idea is that when personal freedoms are threatened, people act to reassert their autonomy and control. Commanding a child not to do something runs the risk of eliciting an *I won't!* rebuttal, for example, or reluctant compliance that disappears as soon as the surveillance is lifted (e.g., Aronson & Carlsmith, 1963). In effect, all the bases of power at the parent's disposal—reward, coercion, referent, expert, legitimate—pale in comparison to the child's distaste for having his or her tacit agreement removed from the parent-child exchange.

Considerable evidence has been accumulated over the years in support of the basic tenets of reactance theory (cf. Burger, 1992). Research by Burger and Cooper (1979), for example, found that even something as basic and spontaneous as humor appreciation is subject to reactance effects. Male and female college students were asked to rate ten cartoons in terms of funniness. Some participants rated the cartoons when alone, but others provided the ratings after receiving instructions from confederates to give the cartoons high ratings. Results revealed that pressure by the confederates tended to backfire, producing funniness ratings lower than those produced by participants not subject to the pressure. This effect was pronounced among individuals who had scored high on a preexperimental personality assessment of need for personal control.

Some studies have produced rather counterintuitive findings that call into question the basis for certain public policy initiatives. In a study investigating attempts to reduce alcohol consumption, for example, participants who received a strongly worded antidrinking message subsequently drank more than did those who received a moderately worded message (Bensley & Wu, 1991). The strongly worded message presumably was perceived by participants as a threat to their personal freedom, to which they reacted by drinking more rather than less in an effort to assert their sense of control. Findings such as these cast into doubt the wisdom of the *Just say no* mantra of many contemporary drug education programs aimed at young people. The slogan itself may promote the very behavior it is intended to discourage, because it represents a rather direct short-circuiting of targets' personal decision-making machinery. There is evidence, in fact, that the *Just say no* approach has backfired in some instances, producing increased rather than decreased consumption of illegal substances—although it is not entirely clear that this effect is due primarily to reactance (Donaldson, Graham, Piccinin, & Hansen, 1995).

The experience of psychological reactance is not limited to influence techniques that trade on power per se. Indeed, the concern with protecting one's self-perceived freedom can curtail the effectiveness of any influence attempt that is seen as such. The use of flattery to seduce a target into a new course of action, for example, can backfire if the target is aware—or simply suspicious—that the flattery is being strategically employed for manipulative purposes (e.g., Jones & Wortman, 1973). Indeed, any attempt to gain influence over another person by becoming attractive to him or her runs a serious risk of failure if the attempted ingratiation is transparent to the person. Jones (1964) has referred to this stumbling block to interpersonal influence as the "ingratiator's dilemma." Normally, we like to hear compliments, to have others agree with our opinions, and to interact with people who are desirable by some criterion. As intrinsically rewarding as these experiences are, they also make us correspondingly vulnerable to requests and other forms of influence from the people in question. When their compliments become obsequious or if their desirability is buttressed by a little too much name-dropping, we become suspicious that they are playing on this vulnerability with a particular agenda in mind. The result is resistance rather than assent to their subsequent requests, even requests that might otherwise seem quite reasonable.

Reactance, in short, is a pervasive human tendency that sets clear limits on the effectiveness of all manner of social influence. Power-based forms of influence are particularly vulnerable to reactance effects, not only because they are linked to a restriction of freedom for targets, but also because they tend to be explicit and thus transparent to targets. Letting someone know that you are trying to influence him or her is a decidedly poor strategy—unless, of course, your real goal is to get him or her to do the opposite.

Reverse Incentive Effects

Twentieth-century social psychology is a story of two seemingly incompatible perspectives on human nature. For the first half of the century, social psychology accepted as received wisdom the notion that the behavior of organisms, humans included, is ultimately under the control of external reinforcement. The mindless S-R models invoked by radical behaviorists may not have been most theorists' cup of tea, but no one seriously challenged the assumption that contingencies of positive and negative reinforcement play a pervasive role in shaping people's psychological development as well as their specific behavior in different contexts. People's concern over personal freedom was certainly recognized by social psychologists, but more often than not this penchant was considered an independent force that competed with reinforcement for the hearts and minds of people in their daily lives. Thus, people struggled to control their impulses, resist temptation, delay gratification, and maintain their dignity in the face of incentives to do otherwise.

After mid-century, something akin to a phase transition began to take place in social psychology. Fueled in large part by an emerging emphasis on the importance of cognitive mediation, theory and research began to question the imperial role of rewards and punishments in shaping personal and interpersonal behavior. People's latent preoccupation with self-determination, for example, came to be seen not simply as a force that competed with reinforcement, but rather as a concern that was *activated* by explicit reinforcement contingencies (cf. de Charms, 1968; Deci & Ryan, 1985). Thus, the awareness of a contingency was said to sensitize people to the potential loss of self-determination if they were to adjust their behavior in accordance with the contingency. In effect, awareness of a contingent relation between behavior and reward weakened the power of the contingency, leaving the desire for self-determination the dominant casual force. This reasoning, of course, is consistent with the assumptions of reactance theory, described above. The dethroning of reinforcement theory, however, went far beyond a recognition of people's need for autonomy, freedom, and the like. Two major perspectives in particular captured the academic spotlight for extended periods of time, and today they still stand as basic insights into human motivation—including motivation relevant to social influence.

The first of these, cognitive dissonance theory (Festinger, 1957), sparked psychologists' imagination in large part because of its seemingly counterintuitive take on the role of rewards in shaping thought and behavior. The essence of the theory is a purported drive for consistency in people's thoughts and feelings regarding a course of action. When inconsistency arises, it is experienced as aversive arousal, which motivates efforts to eliminate or at least reduce the inconsistency so as to reestablish affective equilibrium. This sounds straightforward enough, but under the right conditions a concern for restoring consistency can produce what can be described as *reverse incentive* effects (cf. Aronson, 1992; Wicklund & Brehm, 1976). In a prototypical experimental arrangement, subjects are induced to perform an action that they are unlikely to enjoy (e.g., a repetitive or boring task) or one that conflicts with an attitude they are likely to hold (e.g., writing an essay in support of raising tuition at their university). At this point, varying amounts of monetary incentive are offered for the action's performance; some subjects are offered a quite reasonable sum (e.g., $20), others are offered a mere pittance (e.g., $1). Virtually all subjects agree to participate regardless of the incentive value, so technically they all perform a counterattitudinal task (i.e., a task that conflicts with their attitude concerning the task).

According to Festinger, the dissonance experienced as a result of such counterattitudinal behavior can be reduced by changing one of the cognitive elements to make it consistent with the other element. In this situation, the relevant cognitive elements for subjects presumably are their feelings about the action and their awareness they have performed the action. Because the latter thought cannot be changed (i.e., the damage is done), the only cognitive element open to revision is their attitude toward the action (which conveniently had not been assessed yet). So, the theory holds, subjects faced with this cognitive dilemma will adjust their attitude toward the action to make it consistent with the fact that they have engaged in the action. Subjects who performed a boring task now consider it interesting or important. Subjects who wrote an essay espousing an unpopular position now indicate they hold that position themselves. In effect, subjects rationalize their behavior by indicating that it really reflected their true feelings all along.

At this point, one might assume that all subjects would follow this scenario. But revising one's attitude is not the only potential means of reducing the dissonance brought on by counterattitudinal behavior. Festinger suggested that a person can maintain his original attitude if he or she can justify the counterattitudinal behavior with other salient and reasonable cognitive elements. This is where the large versus small reward manipulation enters the picture. A subject offered a large incentive (e.g., $20) for performing the act can use that fact to justify what he or she has done. Who wouldn't do something boring or even write an essay one doesn't believe if the price were right? The reward, in other words, obviates the psychological need to change one's feelings about what one has done. A subject offered a token incentive (e.g., $1), on the other hand, cannot plausibly argue that the reward justified engaging in the boring activity or writing the disingenuous essay. The only recourse in this situation is to revise one's own attitude and indicate liking for the activity or belief in the essay's position.

Note the upshot here: The smaller the contingent reward, the more positive one's resultant attitude toward the behavior; or conversely, the larger the contingent reward, the more negative one's attitude toward the rewarded behavior. This represents a rather stunning reversal of the conventional wisdom regarding the use of rewards to influence people's behavior. To be sure, large rewards are useful—often necessary—to get a person to perform an otherwise undesirable activity or to express an unpopular attitude. But the effect is likely to be transitory, lasting only as long as the reward contingency is in place. To influence the person's underlying thoughts and feelings regarding the action, and thereby bring about a lasting change in his or her behavioral orientation, it is best to employ the minimal amount of reward. In effect, lasting social influence requires reconstruction within the person rather than inducements from the outside.

Mental processes are notoriously hard to pin down objectively, of course, and this fact of experimental psychology has always been a problem for dissonance theory. Festinger and his colleagues did not attempt to measure what they assumed to be the salient cognitions at work in the reward paradigm, nor have subsequent researchers fared much better in providing definitive evidence regarding the stream of thought presumably underlying the experience and reduction of psychological tension. With this gaping empirical hole in the center of the theory, it is not surprising that other theorists soon rushed in to fill the gap with their own inferences about the true mental processes at work. In effect, the results observed in cognitive dissonance research served as something of a Rorschach for subsequent theorists, each of whom saw the same picture but imparted somewhat idiosyncratic interpretations of its meaning. Not all interpretations have fared well, however, and among those that have, there is sufficient common ground to characterize (in general terms at least) a viable alternative to the dissonance formulation.

Central to the alternative depiction of reverse incentive effects is the assumption that people's minds are first and foremost interpretive devices, designed to impose coherence on the sometimes diverse and often ambiguous elements of personal experience. In analogy to Gestalt principles of perception, cognitive processes "go beyond the information given" (Bruner & Tagiuri, 1954) to impart higher-order meaning that links the information in a stable and viable structure. With respect to the dissonance paradigm, subjects' cognitive playing field is presumably populated with an abundance of salient or otherwise relevant information. These cognitive elements include the nature of the task (the activity or essay) and the money received, of course, but they no doubt encompass an assortment of other thoughts and feelings as well. Thus, subjects may be sensitized to their sense of personal freedom and control in that context, for example, or perhaps to their sense of personal competence in performing the task. For that matter, subjects might also be considering their feelings about the experimenter, pondering the value of the experiment, or rethinking the value of psychological research in general. In view of the plethora of likely cognitive elements and the potential for these elements to come in and out of focus in the stream of thought, the achievement of coherence is anything but a trivial task. What processes are at work to impart coherence to this complex and dynamic array of information? And what psychological dimensions capture the resultant coherence?

There is hardly a shortage of relevant theories. Several early models, for example, emphasized processes of causal attribution (cf. Bem, 1972; Jones & Davis, 1965; Kelley, 1967) that were said to promote personal interpretations favoring either internal causation (e.g., personal beliefs and desires) or external causation (most notably, the monetary incentive). In this view, a large incentive provides a reasonable and sufficient cause for engaging in the activity, short-circuiting the need to make inferences about the causal role of one's beliefs or desires. A small incentive, on the other hand, is not perceived as a credible cause for taking the time and expending the effort to engage in the activity, so one instead invokes relevant beliefs and desires as causal forces for the behavior. In effect, the counterintuitive influence of rewards is a testament to their perceived efficacy in causing people to do things they might not otherwise do. Causal attribution, of course, is not the only plausible endpoint of coherence concerns. Other well-documented dimensions relevant to higher-order integrative understanding include evaluative consistency (cf. Abelson et al., 1968), explanatory coherence (cf. Thagard & Kunda, 1998), narrative structure (cf. Hastie, Penrod, & Pennington, 1983), and level of action identification (cf. Vallacher & Wegner, 1987). It is hardly surprising, then, that a number of other models have been fashioned and tested in an attempt to explain why rewards sometimes fail to influence people's beliefs and desires in the intended direction (e.g., Csikszentmihalyi, 1990; Deci & Ryan, 1985; Kruglanski, 1975; Harackiewicz, Abrahams, & Wageman, 1987; Trope, 1986; Vallacher, 1993).

Taken together, the various models emphasizing inference and interpretation have a noteworthy advantage over the standard dissonance reduction model in that they predict reverse incentive effects for any action, not just those that are likely to be viewed in a context-free manner as aversive by some criterion (e.g., repetitive, boring, pointless, time-consuming, etc.). Indeed, some of the most interesting research has established conditions under which otherwise enjoyable or interesting activities can seemingly lose their

intrinsic interest by virtue of their association with material rewards (cf. Lepper & Greene, 1978). Rewards do not always have this effect, however, a point that has been incorporated with varying degrees of success into many of these models. Still, the theoretical preoccupation with the effects of rewards has generated an unequivocal lesson: The success or failure of attempted influence depends on how the attempt engages the mental machinery of the target. Rewards can be perceived as bribery and aversive consequences can mobilize resistance, for example, and both can activate concerns about one's freedom of action and self-determination. Social influence does not operate on blank minds, but rather encounters an active set of interpretative processes that operate according to their own dynamics to make sense of incoming information (Vallacher, Nowak, Markus, & Strauss, 1998).

MANIPULATION

Change in people's behavior can be imposed from the outside by the exercise of power, but this approach to influence may prove effective only as long as the relevant contingencies (reward, punishment, expertise, information) are in place. To influence people in a more fundamental sense, it is necessary to include them as accomplices in the process. A self-sustaining change in behavior requires a resetting of the person's internal state—her or his beliefs, preferences, goals, and so on—in a way that preserves the person's sense of freedom and control. Assuming the influence agent has an agenda that does not coincide with the target's initial preferences and concerns, the agent may then find it necessary to employ subtle strategies designed to manipulate the relevant internal states of the target. Couched in these terms, social influence boils down to various means by which an agent can obtain voluntary compliance from targets in response to his or her requests, offers, or other forms of overture. Research has identified several compliance-inducing strategies, some of which rely on basic interpersonal dynamics, others of which reflect the operation of basic social norms. We discuss specific manifestations of these general approaches in the following sections.

Manipulation Through Affinity

Could you pass the broccoli? Will you marry me? Whether the agenda at issue is mundane or life-altering, requests provide the primary medium by which people seek compliance from one another. Requests are a fairly routine feature of everyday social interaction and have been examined for their effectiveness under experimental arrangements designed to identify basic principles. However, requests are also central to businesses, charitable organizations, political parties, and other societal entities that depend on contributions of money, effort, or time from the citizenry. Accordingly, much of the knowledge concerning compliance has been gleaned from observation—sometimes participant observation—of professional influence agents operating in charitable, commercial, or political contexts (cf. Cialdini, 2001). Experimentation and real-world observation provide cross-validation for one another, and together have generated a useful taxonomy of effective strategies for obtaining compliance. Many of these strategies are based on what can be called the *affinity principle*—the tendency to be more compliant in the hands of an influence agent we like as opposed to dislike.

The Affinity Principle

Whoever suggested caution in the face of friends bearing gifts may not have been advocating cynicism, but rather self-preservation. Extensive research supports the commonsense notion that personal affinity motivates compliance. From sales professionals, the consummate chameleons of the commercial world, to con artists preying on the elderly and college students calling home for cash, several effective influence strategies rest on the influence agent's being liked, known by, or similar to the target. When such affinity exists between agent and target, ruse is not necessarily a prerequisite for compliance. Quite the opposite, in fact, can be true.

Consider, for example, the Tupperware Corporation, which has exploited the power of friendship in an unprecedented fashion. It has been reported that a Tupperware party occurs somewhere every 2.7 seconds (Cialdini, 1995)—although they typically last much longer than that, which suggests the sobering possibility that there is never a moment without one. The format is as follows: A host invites friends and relatives over to his or her home to participate in a gathering at which Tupperware products are demonstrated by a company representative. Armed with the knowledge that their friend and host will receive a percentage of sales, the attendees tend to buy willingly, because they are purchasing from someone they know and like rather than from a stranger. As confirmation for the pivotal role of "liking" in this context, Frenzen and Davis (1990) found that 67% of the variance in purchase likelihood was accounted for by socials ties between the hostess and the guest and only 33% by product preference.

Personal affinity has been shown to be a potent compliance inducer even in the absence of the liked individual. Anecdotal evidence of this phenomenon abounds in our daily lives. It is the rare parent who has not sent his or her child around to friends and neighbors to collect for a school walkathon or raffle. The child, hardly the embodiment of a "compliance professional" (Cialdini, 2001), represents the parent who is (one would hope) liked by the target. In the same vein, Cialdini (1993) discovered that door-to-door salespersons commonly ask customers for names of friends upon whom they might call. Although we may wonder what kind of friends a person might surrender in this way, rejecting the salesperson under these circumstances apparently is seen as a rejection of the referring friend—the person for whom affinity is felt. The potency of the affinity principle per se may be diminished by the physical absence of the liked person, but the allusion appears nonetheless to render the target more susceptible to other compliance tactics.

The affinity principle is not limited to influence seekers and their surrogates, but applies as well to those who are known or at least recognized by the target. During elections, for example, voters have been shown to cast their ballots for candidates with familiar-sounding names (Grush, 1980; Grush, McKeough, & Ahlering, 1978). In similar fashion, survey response rates sometimes double if the sender's name is phonetically similar to the recipient's (Garner, 1999). Physical attractiveness represents another extension of the affinity principle. A total stranger blessed with good looks has a distinct advantage over his or her less attractive counterparts in securing behavioral compliance (Benson, Karabenick, & Lerner, 1976) and attitude change (Chaiken, 1979). Good grooming, for example, accounts for greater variance in hiring decisions than does the applicant's job qualifications, although interviewers deny the impact of attractiveness (Mack & Rainey, 1990). In political campaigns, meanwhile, there is evidence that a candidate's attractiveness can substantially influence voters' perceptions of him or her and affect their voting behavior as well (Budesheim & DePaola, 1994; Efran & Patterson, 1976). Even criminal justice is not immune to the power of physical attractiveness. Better-looking defendants generally receive more favorable treatment in the criminal justice system (Castellow, Wuensch, & Moore, 1990) and often receive lighter sentences when found guilty (Stewart, 1980).

Similarity and Affinity

Similarity between influence agent and target represents a special case of the affinity principle. It is rarely a coincidence when a car salesperson claims to hail from a customer's home state or when an apparel salesperson claims to have purchased the very same outfit the vacillating customer is sporting. People like those who are similar to them (cf. Byrne, 1971; Byrne, Clore, & Smeaton, 1980; Newcomb,

1961), and in accordance with the affinity principle, they are inclined to respond affirmatively to requests from similar others as well. The similarity effect encompasses a wide range of dimensions, including opinions, background, lifestyle, and personality traits (Cialdini & Trost, 1998). Even similarity in nonverbal cues, such as posture, mood, and verbal style, has been observed to increase compliance (LaFrance, 1985; Locke & Horowitz, 1990; Woodside & Davenport, 1974). The effect of similarity is quite pervasive, having been demonstrated across a wide range of variation in age, cultural background, socioeconomic status, opinion topics, and relationship types (cf. Baron & Byrne, 1994).

The power of similarity to elicit compliance has been observed even when the dimension of similarity is decidedly superficial in nature. Sometimes outward manifestations of similarity such as clothing are all that are required. Emswiller, Deaux, and Willits (1971), for example, arranged for confederates to dress as either "straight" or "hippie" and had them ask fellow college students for a dime to make a phone call. When the confederate and target subject were similar in their respective attire, compliance was observed over two thirds of the time. When the confederate-target pair differed in clothing type, however, less than half of the students volunteered the dime. In a related vein, Suedfeld, Bochner, and Matas (1971) observed that if antiwar protestors were asked by a similarly dressed confederate to sign a petition, they tended to do so without even reading the petition. Automatic compliance to the requests of others perceived to be similar has a decidedly nonthinking quality to it. The very automaticity of the similarity principle, however, may have important adaptive significance. By using this heuristic to make quick decisions regarding compliance requests, people can allocate their valuable but limited mental resources to other types of judgment and decision-making situations defined in terms of ambiguous, conflicting, or complex information.

Esteem and Affinity

Perhaps even more basic than our propensity to do things for those we like is our need to be liked by those we know (cf. G. W. Allport, 1939; Baumeister, 1982; Tesser, 1988). To be sure, for some people the desire to be liked can be overridden by other motives, such as the need for acceptance (Rudich & Vallacher, 1999) or desires to be seen accurately (Trope, 1986) or in accordance with one's personal self-view (Swann, 1990). For most people most of the time, however, it is hard to resist the allure of flattery. Receiving positive feedback from someone is highly rewarding and tends to promote a reciprocal exchange with the source. In other words, we like others who seem to like us. When activated in this way,

the affinity principle makes the recipient of flattery a potential target for influence by the flatterer.

Flattery has a long history as an effective compliance technique, both inside and outside the laboratory (cf. Carnegie, 1936/1981; Cialdini, 2001). Drachman, DeCarufel, and Insko (1978), for example, arranged for men to receive positive or negative comments from a person in need of a favor. The person offering praise alone was liked most, even if the targets knew that the flatterer stood to gain from their liking them. Moreover, inaccurate compliments were just as effective as accurate compliments in promoting the target's affinity for the flatterer. So influence agents need not bother gathering facts to support their complimentary onslaught; simply expressing positive comments may be sufficient to woo the target and thereby gain his or her compliance. At the same time, however, the ingratiator's dilemma (Jones, 1964) discussed earlier sets limits on the effectiveness of the esteem principle. In particular, praise and other forms of ingratiation (e.g., opinion conformity with the target) can backfire if the ingratiator's ulterior motives are readily transparent and the praise is seen as solely manipulative. And, of course, the influence agent can simply overdo the flattery and come across as disingenuous and obsequious.

Manipulation Through Scarcity

From childhood on, we want what we lack—be it toys, money, fancy cars, or greener grass. The cache of the unattainable, for example, is a sure bet to spark competition and fuel sales in commercial settings. Cries of *today and today only* and *in limited quantities* have been known to drive shoppers like lemmings toward the blue-light special, and convenient Christmastime shortages of Tickle Me Elmos or Furbees stoke the fires of demand for such toys. We may see ourselves as impervious to such base tactics, but the power of the human tendency to view scarcity as an indicator of worth or desirability is undeniable, well-documented—and routinely exploited as a method of securing compliance (cf. Cialdini, 2001).

It's interesting in this regard to consider the tendency for efforts at censorship to backfire, creating a stronger demand than ever for the forbidden fruit. The prohibition of alcohol in the 1920s, for example, only whetted people's appetite for liquor and spawned the rise of secret establishments (the speakeasy) that provided access to the scarce commodity. Antipornography crusades typically have the same effect, increasing interest in the banned books and magazines, even among people who might not otherwise consider this particular genre. Telling people they cannot read or see something can increase—or even create—a desire to take a proverbial peek at the hard-to-find commodity. By the same token, after the censorship or prohibition is lifted, interest in the object in question tends to wane.

Surprisingly, there is a paucity of research on the psychology of scarcity. The enhanced desirability of scarce items may reflect a perceived loss of freedom to attain the items, in line with reactance theory. The censorship example certainly suggests that people value an object in proportion to the injunction against having it. People don't like having their freedom threatened, and making an item difficult to obtain or forbidding an activity clearly restricts people's options with respect to the item and the activity. Reactance is a reasonable model, but one can envision other theoretical contenders. Simple supply-and-demand economics, for example, has a direct connection to the scarcity phenomenon. The lower the supply-demand ratio with respect to almost any item, the more those who control the resource can jack up the price and still count on willing customers. Perhaps there are viable evolutionary reasons for the heightened interest in scarce resources. The conditions under which we evolved were harsh and uncertain, after all, and there may have been selection pressures favoring our hominid ancestors who were successful at securing and hording valuable but limited food supplies and other resources.

Yet another possibility centers on people's simultaneous desires to belong and to individuate themselves from the groups to which they belong (e.g., Brewer, 1991). Scarcity has a way of focusing collective attention on a particular object, and there may be a sense of social connectedness in sharing the fascination with others. Waiting in line with throngs of shoppers hoping to secure one of the limited copies of the latest Harry Potter volume, for example, is arguably an annoying and irrational experience, but it does make the person feel as though he or she is on the same wavelength as people who would otherwise be considered total strangers. At the same time, if the person is one of the lucky few who manages to secure a copy before the shelves are cleared, he or she has effectively individuated him- or herself from the masses. In essence, influence appeals based on scarcity may be effective because they provide a way for people to belong to and yet stand out from the crowd in a world where he or she may routinely feel both alienated and homogenized.

Manipulation Through Norms

Human behavior, compliance included, is driven to a large extent by social *norms*—context-dependent standards of behavior that exert psychological pressure toward conformity. At the group level, norms provide continuity, stability, and coordination of behavior among individuals. At the individual level, norms provide a moral compass for deciding how to behave in situations that might offer a number of action alternatives. The norm of social responsibility (e.g., Berkowitz & Daniels, 1964), for example, compels us to help those less fortunate than ourselves, and the norm of equity prevents us from claiming excessive compensation for minimal contribution to a group task (cf. Berkowitz & Walster, 1976). Norms pervade social life, and thus provide raw material for social influence agents. By tapping into agreed-upon and internalized rules for behavior, those who are so inclined can extract costly commitments to behavior from prospective targets without having to flatter them.

The Norm of Reciprocity

The obligation to repay what others provide us appears to be a universal and defining feature of social life. All human societies subscribe to the *norm of reciprocity* (Gouldner, 1960), which is understandable in light of the norm's adaptive value (Axelrod, 1984). The sense of future obligation engendered by this norm promotes and maintains both personal and formal relationships. And when widely embraced by people as a shared standard, the reciprocity norm lends predictability, interpersonal trust, and stability to the larger social system. Transactions involving tangible assets are only a subset of the social interactions regulated by reciprocity. Favors and invitations are returned, Christmas cards are sent to those who send them, and compliments are rarely accepted without finding something nice to say in return (Cialdini, 2001).

The social obligation that there be a give for every take is well-documented (DePaulo, Brittingham, & Kaiser, 1983; Eisenberger, Cotterell, & Marvel, 1987; Regan, 1971). Even when gifts and favors are unsolicited (or unwanted), the recipient feels compelled to provide something in return. The ability of uninvited gifts to produce feelings of obligation in the recipient is successfully exploited by many organizations, both charitable and commercial. People may not need personalized address labels, key rings, or hackneyed Christmas cards, but after they have been received, it is difficult not to respond to the organization's request for a "modest contribution" (e.g., Berry & Kanouse, 1987; Smolowe, 1990). A particularly vivid example of this tendency is provided by the Hare Krishna Society (Cialdini, 2001). The members of this religious sect found that they could dramatically increase the success of their solicitations in airports simply by giving travelers a free flower before asking for donations. People find it hard to turn down a request for money after receiving an unsolicited gift, even something as irrelevant to one's current needs as a flower. That receiving a flower is not exactly the high point of the recipients' day is confirmed by Cialdini's observation that the flower more often than not winds up in a nearby waste container shortly after the flower-for-money transaction has been completed.

Reciprocity can have the subsidiary effect of increasing the recipient's liking for the gift- or favor-giver, but the norm can be exploited successfully without implicit application of the affinity principle (e.g., Regan, 1971). Affect does enter the picture, however, when people *fail* to uphold the norm. Nonreciprocation runs the risk of damaging an exchange relationship (Cotterell, Eisenberger, & Speicher, 1992; Meleshko & Alden, 1993) and may promote reputational damage for the offender (e.g., *moocher, ingrate*) that can haunt him or her in future transactions. Somewhat more surprising is evidence that negative feelings can be engendered when the reciprocity norm is violated in the reverse direction. One might think that someone who provides a gift but does not allow the recipient to repay would be viewed as generous, unselfish, or altruistic (although perhaps somewhat misguided or naive). But under some circumstances, such a person is disliked for his or her violation of exchange etiquette (Gergen, Ellsworth, Maslach, & Seipel, 1975). This tendency appears to be universal, having been demonstrated in U.S., Swedish, and Japanese samples.

Cooperation is an interesting manifestation of the reciprocity norm. Just as the act of providing a gift or a favor prompts repayment, cooperative behavior tends to elicit cooperation in return (Braver, 1975; Cialdini, Green, & Rusch, 1992; Rosenbaum, 1980) and can promote compliance with subsequent requests as well (Bettencourt, Brewer, Croak, & Miller, 1992). This notion is not lost on the car salesperson who declares that he or she and the customer are on "the same side" during price negotiations, and then appears to take up the customer's fight against their common enemy, the sales manager. Even if this newly formed alliance comes up short and the demonized sales manager purportedly holds fast on the car's price, the customer may feel sufficiently obligated to repay the salesperson's cooperative overture with a purchase.

A related form of reciprocity is the tactical use of concessions to extract compliance from those who might otherwise be resistant to influence. The strategy is to make a request that is certain to meet with a resounding *no,* if not a rhetorical *are you kidding?* The request might call for a large investment of time and energy, or perhaps for a substantial amount of money. After this request is turned down, the influence agent follows up with a more reasonable request. In effect, the influence agent is making a concession and, in line with the reciprocity norm, the target now feels obligated to make a concession of his or her own. A study by Cialdini et al. (1975) illustrates the effectiveness of what has come to be known as the *door-in-the-face* technique. Posing as representatives of a youth counseling program, Cialdini et al. approached college students to see if they would agree to chaperon a group of juvenile delinquents for several hours at the local zoo. Not surprisingly, most of them (83%) refused. The results were quite different, though, if Cialdini et al. had first asked the students to do something even more unreasonable—spending 2 hours per week as counselors to juvenile delinquents for a minimum of 2 years. After students refused this request—all of them did—the smaller zoo-trip request was agreed to by 50% of the students, a tripling of the compliance rate. The empirical evidence for the door-in-the face technique is impressive (cf. Cialdini & Trost, 1998) and largely supports the reciprocity of concessions interpretation.

The power of reciprocal concessions is also apparent in the *that's not all* technique, which is a familiar trick of the trade among salespeople (Cialdini, 2001). The tactic involves making an offer or providing a come-on to a customer, then following up with an even better offer before the target has had time to respond to the initial offer. This technique is used fairly routinely to push big-ticket commercial items. A salesperson, for example, quotes a price for a large-screen TV, and while the interested but skeptical couple is thinking it over, he or she adds, "but that's not all—if you buy today, I'm authorized to throw in a free VCR." Research confirms that the effectiveness of the that's not all technique is indeed attributable in part to the creation of a felt need in the target to reciprocate the agent's apparent concession (e.g., Burger, 1986), although the contrast between the initial and follow-up concession plays a role as well. In the real world, the knowledge that people tend to reciprocate concessions provides a cornerstone of negotiation and dispute resolution. The bargaining necessary to reach a compromise solution in such instances invariably hinges on one party's making a concession with the assumption that the other party will follow suit with a concession of his or her own. This phenomenon can be seen at work in a wide variety of contexts, including business, politics, international diplomacy, and marriage.

Reciprocity in Personal Relationships

The norm of reciprocity is not limited to transactions between people who otherwise would have little to do with one another (e.g., salespeople and consumers), but rather provides a foundation for virtually every kind of social relationship. The reciprocity norm even plays a role in personal relationships, serving to calibrate the fairness in people's ongoing interactions with friends and lovers. The trust and warmth necessary to maintain a personal relationship would be impossible to maintain if either partner felt that his or her overtures of affection, self disclosures, offers of assistance, and birthday gifts went unreciprocated (cf. Lerner & Mikula, 1994). There are two complications here, however. First, the partners to a relationship are not always equally invested in or dependent on the relationship (e.g., Rusbult & Martz, 1995). In terms of social exchange theory (Kelley & Thibaut, 1978; Thibaut & Kelley, 1959), the comparison level for alternatives (CL_{alt}) for each partner may be substantially different, and this differential dependency can promote exploitative behavior by the less dependent person. In effect, the person who feels more confident that he or she could establish desirable alternative relationships (i.e., the person with the higher CL_{alt}) can set the terms of exchange in the relationship. This power asymmetry need not be discussed explicitly in order for it to promote inequality in overt expressions of affection, the allocation of duties and responsibilities, and decision making.

The second complication arises in relationships that achieve a certain threshold of closeness. Intimate partners are somewhat loathe to think about their union in economic, tit-for-tat terms, preferring instead to emphasize the communal aspect of their relationship (cf. M. S. Clark & Mills, 1979). They feel they operate on the basis of need rather than equity or reciprocity, and this perspective enables them to make sacrifices for one another without expecting compensation or repayment. The apparent suspension of reciprocity may be more apparent than real, however. The issue is not reciprocity per se, but rather the time scale on which reciprocity and other exchange metrics are calculated. What looks like selfless and unrequited sacrifice by one person in the short run can be viewed as inputs that are eventually compensated by the other person in one form or another (cf. Foa & Foa, 1974). Depending on the sacrifice (e.g., fixing dinner vs. taking on a second job), the time scale for repayment can vary considerably (e.g., hours or days vs. weeks or even years), but at some point the scales need to be balanced. The sense that one has been treated unfairly or exploited—or simply that one's assistance and affection have not been duly reciprocated—can ultimately spoil a relationship and bring about its dissolution.

Commitment

Although it is not usually listed as a social norm, *commitment* can influence behavior as much as do reciprocity, equity, responsibility, and other basic social rules and expectations (Kiesler, 1971). After people have committed themselves to an opinion or course of action, it is difficult for them to change their minds, recant, or otherwise fail to stay the course. Commitment does not derive its power solely from the anger and disappointment that breaking of a commitment would engender in others—although this certainly counts for something—but also from a basic desire to act consistently with one's point of view. A commitment that is expressed publicly, whether in front of a crowd or to a single individual, is especially effective in locking in a person's opinion or promise, making it resistant to change despite the availability of good reasons for reconsideration (cf. Deutsch & Gerard, 1955; Schlenker, 1980).

Agents of influence play on this seemingly noble tendency, often for decidedly nonnoble purposes of their own. Several specific techniques have been observed in real-world settings and confirmed in research (Cialdini & Trost, 1998). Perhaps the best-known tactic is referred to as *the foot-in-the-door,* which is essentially the mirror image of the door-in-the-face tactic. Rather than starting out with a large request and then appearing to make a concession by making a smaller request, the foot-in-the-door specialist begins with a minor request that is unlikely to meet with resistance. After securing committing with this request, the influence agent ups the ante by making a far more costly request that is consistent with the initial request. Because of commitment concerns, it can be very difficult at this point for the target to refuse compliance. A series of clever field experiments (Freedman & Fraser, 1966) provide compelling evidence for the effectiveness of this tactic. In one study, suburban housewives were contacted and asked to do something that most of them (78%) refused to do: allow a team of six men from a consumer group to come into their respective homes for 2 hours to "enumerate and classify all the household products you have." Another group of housewives was contacted and presented with a much less inconvenience-producing request—simply answering a few questions about their household soaps (e.g., "What brand of soap do you use in your kitchen sink?"). Nearly everyone complied with this minor request. These women were contacted again three days later, but this time with the larger home-visit request. In this case, over half the women (52%) complied with the request and allowed the men to rummage through their closets and cupboards for 2 hours.

The commitment process underlying this tactic goes beyond the target's concern with maintaining consistency with the action per se. It also engages the target's self-concept with respect to the values made salient by the action. Thus, the women who complied with the initial request in the Freedman and Fraser (1966) studies were presumably sensitized to their self-image as helpful, public-spirited individuals. To maintain consistency with this suddenly salient (and perhaps newly enhanced) self-image, they felt compelled to comply with the later, more invasive request. Assuming this to be the case, the foot-in-the-door tactic holds potential for influencing people's thought and behavior long after the tactic has run its course. Freedman and Fraser (1966) themselves noted a parallel between their approach and the approach employed by the Chinese military on U.S. prisoners of war captured during the Korean War in the early 1950s. A prisoner, approached individually, might be asked to indicate his agreement with mild statements like *The United States is not perfect.* After the prisoner agreed with such minor anti-American statements, he might be asked by the interrogator to elaborate a little on why the United States is not perfect. This, in turn, might be followed by a request to make a list of the "problems with America" he had identified, which he was expected to sign. The Chinese might then incorporate the prisoner's statement in an anti-American broadcast. As a consequence of this ratcheting up of an initially mild anti-American statement, a number of prisoners came to label themselves as collaborators and to act in ways that were consistent with this self-image (cf. Schein, 1956).

Commitment underlies a related tactic known as *throwing a lowball,* which is routinely employed by salespeople to gain the upper hand over customers in price negotiations (Cialdini, 2001). Automobile salespeople, for example, will seduce customers into deciding on a particular car by offering it at a very attractive price. To enhance the customer's commitment to the car, the salesperson might allow the customer to arrange for bank financing or even take the car home overnight. But just before the final papers are signed, something happens that requires changing the price or other terms of the deal. Perhaps the finance department has caught a calculation error or the sales manager has disallowed the deal because the company would lose money at that price. At this point, one might think that the customer would back out of the deal—after all, he or she has made a commitment to a particular exchange, not simply to a car. Many customers do not back out, however, but rather accept the new terms and proceed with the purchase. Apparently, in making the initial commitment, the customer takes mental possession of the object and is reluctant to let it go (Burger & Petty, 1981; Cioffi & Garner, 1996).

Changing the terms of the deal without undermining the target's commitment is not limited to shady business practices. Indeed, lowball tactics underlie transactions having nothing to do with economics, and can be used to gain people's cooperation to do things that center on prosocial concerns rather than personal self-interest (e.g., Pallak, Cook, & Sullivan, 1980). In an interesting application of the lowball approach, Cialdini, Cacioppo, Bassett, and Miller (1978) played on college students' potential commitment to psychological research. Students in Introductory Psychology were contacted to see if they would agree to participate in a study on "thinking processes" that began at 7:00 a.m. Because this would entail waking up before the crack of dawn, few students (24%) expressed willingness to participate in the study. For another group of students, however, the investigators threw a lowball by not mentioning the 7:00 a.m. element until after the students had indicated their willingness to take part in the study. A majority of the students (56%) did in fact agree to participate, and *none* of them backed out of this commitment when informed of the starting time. After an individual has committed to a course of action, new details associated with the action—even aversive details that entail unanticipated sacrifice—can be added without undermining the psychological foundations of the commitment.

Like the lowball tactic, the *bait-and-switch* tactic works by first seducing people with an attractive offer. But whereas the lowball approach changes the rules by which the exchange can be completed, the bait-and-switch tactic nixes the exchange altogether, with the expectation that the target will accept an alternative that is more advantageous to the influence agent. Car salespeople once again unwittingly have furthered the cause of psychological science by their shrewd application of this technique (Cialdini, 2001). They get the customer to the showroom by advertising a car at a special low price. Taking the time to visit the showroom constitutes a tentative commitment to purchase a car. Upon arrival, the customer learns that the advertised special is sold, or that because of its low price, the car doesn't come with all the features the customer wants. Because of his or her commitment to purchase a car, however, the customer typically expresses willingness to examine and purchase a more expensive model—even though he or she wouldn't have made the trip to look at these models in the first place.

SOCIAL COORDINATION

To this point, social influence has been described as if it were a one-way street. One person (the influence agent) has an agenda that he or she wishes to impose upon another person (the influence target). Although influence strategies certainly are employed for purposes of control and manipulation, social influence broadly defined serves far loftier functions in everyday life. Indeed, as noted at the outset, it is hard to discuss any aspect of social relations without acceding a prominent role to influence processes. Social influence is what enables individuals to coordinate their opinions, moods, evaluations, and behaviors at all levels of social reality, from dyads to social groups to societies. The process of social coordination is a thus a two-way street, with all parties to the exchange influencing and receiving influence from one another. The ways and means of coordination are discussed in this section, as are the functions—both adaptive and maladaptive—of this fundamental human tendency.

Conformity

People go to a lot trouble to influence one another. Yet for all the effort expended in service of manipulation, sometimes all it takes to influence a person is to convey one's own attitude or action preference. People take solace from the expressions of like-minded people and develop new ways of interpreting reality from those with different perspectives. In both cases, simply expressing an opinion—no tricks, strategies, or power plays—may be sufficient to bring someone into line with one's point of view. This form of influence captures the essence of conformity, a phenomenon that is commonly counted as evidence for people's herdlike mentality. There is a nonreflective quality to many instances of conformity, but this property enables people to coordinate their thoughts in an efficient manner and attain the social consensus necessary to engage in collective action. We consider first what constitutes conformity, and then we develop both the positive and negative consequences of this manifestation of social influence.

Group Pressure and Conformity

Conformity represents a "change in behavior or belief toward a group as a result of real or imagined group pressure" (Kiesler & Kiesler, 1976). Defined in this way, conformity would seem to be a defining feature of group dynamics. Festinger (1950), for example, suggested that pressures toward uniformity invariably exist in groups and are brought to bear on the individual so that over time, he or she will tend to conform to the opinions and behavior patterns of the other group members. If one of two diners at a table for two says that he or she finds the food distasteful and the other person expresses a more favorable opinion, the first person is unlikely to change his or her views to match those of his or her companion. However, the addition of several more dinner companions, each holding the contrary position, may well cause the person to rethink his or her position and establish common ground with the others. If he or she has yet to express an opinion, the likelihood of conforming to the others' opinions is all the greater. To investigate the variables at work in this sort of context—group size, unanimity of group opinion, and the timing of the person's expressed judgment—Solomon Asch (1951, 1956) performed a series of experiments that became viewed unanimously by social psychologists as classics.

Asch's original intention actually was to demonstrate that people do *not* conform slavishly and uncritically in a group setting (Levine, 1996). Asch put his hope for humanity to a test in a simple and elegant way. Participants thought they were participating in a study on perception. They sat facing a pair of white cardboards on which vertical lines were drawn. One card had a single line, which provided the standard for subjects' perceptual judgments. The second card had three lines of varying length, one of which was clearly the same length as the standard. Participants were simply asked to indicate which of the three lines matched the standard. The correct answer was always obvious, and in fact when participants were tested individually, they rarely made a mistake. To give conformity a chance, Asch (1951) placed a naive participant in a group setting with six other people, who were actually experimental accomplices pretending to be naive participants. By arrangement, the participant always made his judgment after hearing the bogus participants make their judgments. For the first two trials, the accomplices (and, of course, the participant) gave the obviously correct answers. After creating this group consensus, the accomplices gave a unanimous but incorrect answer on the third trial—and again on trials 4, 6, 7, 9, 10, and 12. To Asch's surprise, the typical participant conformed to the incorrect group response one third of the time. Over 80% of the participants conformed to the incorrect majority on at least one trial, and 7% conformed on all seven of the critical trials. Although it was not his intent, Asch had demonstrated that even when there is a clear reality, people are still inclined to go along with the crowd.

Informational and Normative Influence

Presumably, Asch's participants conformed because they wanted the other group members to like them or because they were fearful of ridicule if they failed to go along. During postexperimental interviews, participants typically mentioned these concerns as their motivation for concurring with obviously inaccurate judgments. And when Asch allowed participants to make their responses privately in writing as opposed to publicly by voice, the extent to which participants conformed showed a marked decrease. Because people are obviously less concerned about the approval of others when the others cannot monitor their behavior, these findings suggest that participants' conformity did in fact reflect a desire to win approval or avoid disapproval.

Social approval does not exhaust the possible motives for conformity, however. Indeed, several years prior to Asch's research, Muzafer Sherif (1936) had concocted an equally compelling experimental situation relevant to conformity, but one that played on the often ambiguous nature of physical reality rather than concerns with acceptance, rejection, and the like. Sherif felt that groups provide important information for individuals—and more important, interpretative frameworks for making coherent judgments about information. People have a need for cognitive clarity (Schachter, 1959), but sometimes they lack an objective yardstick for determining the true nature of their experiences. In such instances, people turn to others, not to gain approval but rather to obtain social clues to reality. People are highly prone to rumors, for example, even from unreliable sources, when they hear about goings-on for which no official explanation has been provided. A sudden noise or a hard-to-read message can similarly make people prone to the assessments of others in an attempt to clarify what has happened.

To test this motivation for conformity, Sherif (1936) needed a situation in which the physical environment lacked ready-made yardsticks for understanding, so that the operation of social standards could be observed. His solution was to take advantage of the *autokinetic effect*—the apparent motion of a stationary spot of light in a dark room. The idea was to place a group of participants in this type of situation and ask them to make estimates of the light's movement. Participants, of course, were not informed that the light's movement was illusory. When tested individually, participants varied considerably in their estimates, from virtually no movement to more than 10 inches. He then brought together three participants who had previously made estimates in private, and asked them to announce their individual judgments aloud and in succession. Despite their initial differences, participants converged fairly quickly (often within three trials) on a single estimate that functioned as a group standard for the light's movement. Sherif went on to show that after a group defined reality for participants, they continued to adhere to the group judgment even after they left the group (see also Alexander, Zucker, & Brody, 1970).

Deutsch and Gerard (1955) recognized that people can conform for different reasons and formally distinguished between *normative influence,* which captures the essence of the Asch situation, and *informational influence,* which reflects participants' motivation in the Sherif situation. Normative influence refers to conformity in an attempt to gain approval, whereas informational influence refers to conformity in an attempt to gain clear knowledge about reality. Sometimes it is difficult to determine which basis of conformity is operative in a given situation. Imagine, for example, that you observe someone following the lead of others at a classical music concert. When they sit, he or she sits. When they give a standing ovation, the person follows suit. The group influence in this case could be normative, informational, or perhaps both, depending on the person's primary source of uncertainty. If the person is unsure of his or her standing among the fellow concert-goers, the person's conformity could be driven by desires for approval or fears of ridicule. If the person is unfamiliar with classical music, however, the behavior of others might provide all-important clues about the quality of the performance.

Normative influence is especially salient when the group controls material or psychological rewards important to the person (e.g., Crutchfield, 1955), when the behavior is public rather than private (e.g., Insko, Drenan, Solomon, Smith, & Wade, 1983), or when the person is especially eager for approval (Crowne & Marlowe, 1964). Someone attending the concert with prospective colleagues, for instance, may be especially inclined to match their behavior, particularly if he or she is uncertain about their interest in his or her job candidacy and the concert hall has good lighting. The salience of informational influence in turn depends on the person's confidence in his or her own judgment, and on the person's judgment of how well-informed the group is. Thus, a classical music neophyte who sees tuxedo-clad audience members leap to their feet upon completion of the Rach 3 (Rachmaninoff's third piano concerto) is more likely to follow suit than if he or she instead sees the same behavior by school children. A graduate of Julliard, meanwhile, is unlikely to mimic such behavior in either case. Informational influence tends also to take precedence, not surprisingly, when the judgment task is particularly difficult or ambiguous (e.g., Coleman, Blake, & Mouton, 1958). Even in the Asch situation, conformity is increased when the lines are closer in length and thus harder to judge (Asch, 1952), and when judgments are made from memory rather than from direct perception of the lines (Deutsch & Gerard, 1955), presumably because our memories are considered more fallible than are our immediate perceptions.

Groupthink

Conformity clearly serves important functions, but like every other adaptation, there are downsides as well. A particularly troublesome aspect of conformity is *groupthink* (Janis, 1982). Janis borrowed this term from George Orwell's *1984* to refer to a mode of thinking dominated by a concern for reaching and maintaining consensus, as opposed to making the best decision under the circumstances. Groupthink essentially entails "a deterioration of mental efficiency, reality testing, and moral judgment that results from group pressure" (Janis, 1982, p. 9). Rather than examining all possible courses of action, people in the grips of groupthink expend their mental energy on achieving and maintaining group solidarity and opinion unanimity.

The potential for groupthink exists in any group context, informal as well as formal, but the most intriguing examples concern decisions with far-reaching consequences by people normally considered the best and the brightest. Janis (1982) analyzed several such situations, including the Bay of Pigs invasion during the Kennedy administration, the bombing of Pearl Harbor, and the Vietnam War. Janis identified several common factors in these instances. In each case, crucial decisions were made in small groups whose members had considerable respect and liking for one another. Positive regard is certainly preferable to disinterest or disrespect, of course, but it can also serve to inhibit criticism and close examination of one another's suggestions. The group members also tended to exhibit collective rationalization, systematically discrediting or ignoring all information contrary to the prevailing group sentiment. They also tended to develop strong feelings that their mission (e.g., invading Cuba, implementing a massive troop build-up in South Vietnam) was moral and that the opposite side was not only immoral but also stupid. To further cocoon the group, self-appointed "mind-guards" precluded members from accessing information that was inconsistent with the party line. The upshot is something akin to tunnel vision, in which a single perspective is seen as the only viable perspective—not because of a rational assessment of the facts but because of the group's irrational espirit de corps.

Group Polarization

The groupthink phenomenon has rather straightforward implications for another phenomenon—*group polarization*—that was nonetheless considered surprising when first noted by researchers (e.g., Stoner, 1961; Wallach, Kogan, & Bem, 1962). The conventional wisdom was that individuals in groups avoid going out on the proverbial limb, and thus tend to produce more common or popular opinions and recommendations (cf. F. H. Allport, 1924). It followed from this that a group decision is usually more conservative than the average of the decisions generated by group members individually. This assumption regarding group decision making is reflected in critics' laments about the bland and often timid recommendations generated by committees in bureaucratic environments. When faced with making a decision, groups were assumed to inhibit boldness, subjugating the creative mind to the lowest common denominator of the group. What the research began to reveal, however, was quite the opposite tendency—greater endorsement of risky decisions as a result of group discussion.

This so-called risky shift is not surprising in light of theory and research on groupthink. If anything, the sense of superiority and certainty fostered by an emphasis on cohesiveness as opposed to rationality would seem to be a breeding ground for bold decisions that go beyond what an individual alone would contemplate. The shift toward risky decisions, however, was observed in contexts that didn't involve the intellectual and emotional incest displayed by highly cohesive groups of self-important people. Even groups of strangers brought together for a one-shot encounter in a laboratory setting were found to advocate courses of action with less guarantee of success than the recommendations volunteered by the group members prior to their discussion. Because this observation flew in the face of conventional wisdom, it cried out for both replication and explanation. During the 1960s, neither proved to be in short supply. This burgeoning literature demonstrated greater risk-taking with respect to a wide variety of domains, including bargaining and negotiations (Lamm & Sauer, 1974), gambling behavior (Blascovich, Ginsberg, & Howe, 1975; Lamm & Ochssmann, 1972), and jury decisions (Myers, 1982). The risky shift was observed, moreover, when the consequences of a group's decision involved real as well as hypothetical consequences (Wallach et al., 1962). The research also demonstrated that the risky shift was not limited to recommendations regarding possible courses of action. Indeed, group discussion—again, even among strangers—seemed to intensify all sorts of attitudes, beliefs, values, judgments, and perceptions (Myers, 1982). Such shifts were observed for both sexes, in different populations and cultures (e.g., United States, Canada, England, France, Germany, New Zealand), and with many kinds of group participants (Pruitt, 1971).

Several explanations for the risky shift achieved currency (Forsyth, 1990). The *diffusion of responsibility* perspective suggested that people are less averse to risk in groups because they feel less responsibility for—and hence less anxious about—the potential negative outcomes of risky decisions. The *leadership* account held that risk takers tend to emerge as leaders because of their greater confidence, assertiveness, and involvement in the task, and that their leadership status makes them more influential in group discussions. *Familiarization* theory maintained that group discussion increases members' familiarity with the issue, which reduces their uncertainty and increases their willingness to advocate more risky alternatives. The *value* perspective proposed that taking risks is positively valued (in our culture, at least) and that group members like to be perceived as willing to take a chance; when group members discover that others in the group favor riskier alternatives, they change their original position to agree with the riskiest member.

During this same period, however, some research hinted at the opposite effect of group discussion—a *cautious shift*. To complicate matters even further, research began to find evidence of movement in *both* directions after a group discussion (Doise, 1969; Moscovici & Zavalloni, 1969), suggesting that both risky and cautious shifts were different manifestations of a more basic phenomenon. Based on a review of this research, Myers and Lamm (1976) identified what they felt was the underlying process. According to their group-polarization hypothesis, the "average postgroup response will tend to be more extreme in the same direction as the average of the pregroup responses" (p. 603). Imagine two groups, each consisting of four individuals whose opinions vary in their respective preferences for risk. The average choice of members is closer to the risky end of the caution-risk dimension in one group, but closer to the cautious end of this dimension in the other group. The group-polarization effect predicts that the first group should become riskier as a result of group discussion (i.e., a risky shift), but that the second group should become more cautious during its deliberations (i.e., a cautious shift). The evidence cited by Myers and Lamm (1976) is consistent with this prediction and is widely accepted today as a valid empirical generalization regarding group dynamics.

This straightforward generalization proved to be resistant to a simple theoretical account. Most theorists eventually endorsed the value account (e.g., Myers & Lamm, 1976; Pruitt, 1971; Vinokur, 1971), although it didn't take long for different variations on this general theme to emerge. Of these, two have stood the test of time (thus far). Social comparison theory holds that people attempt to accomplish two goals during group discussion: evaluating the accuracy of their position by comparing it with the positions of other group members, and creating a favorable impression of themselves within the group. The confluence of these two motives results in a tendency to describe one's own position in somewhat more extreme terms (e.g., Goethals & Zanna, 1979; Myers & Lamm, 1976). Persuasive-arguments theory, meanwhile, stresses the importance of the information obtained during group discussion. Whether there is a shift toward risk or toward caution depends on the relative persuasiveness of the arguments favoring each position (e.g., Burnstein & Vinokur, 1977; Vinokur & Burnstein, 1974). The distinction between these two accounts corresponds to the distinction introduced earlier between normative and informational influence. Social comparison theory, with its emphasis on self-presentation attempts to match the perceived group norm, can be understood in terms of normative influence. The persuasive-arguments perspective, meanwhile, is practically synonymous with the rationale of informational influence. As noted in our earlier discussion, these two forms of influence often co-occur,

so it should come as no surprise that social comparison and persuasive arguments often work together to promote polarization in groups (cf. Forsyth, 1990).

Minority Influence

In the film *Twelve Angry Men,* the character played by Henry Fonda turned his one-man minority into a unanimous majority during jury deliberations so that an innocent man could go free. In the face of virulent opposition, Galileo struggled for acceptance of his proof of Copernican theory that the planets revolve around the sun. This acceptance did not come during his lifetime, but his influence lived on and eventually turned the intellectual tide for subsequent generations. Martin Luther King Jr. and Mahatma Gandhi both defied the prevailing norms of their respective cultures and brought about significant social and political change. And in everyday life, people with opinions or lifestyles out of step with those of the majority often manage to preserve their personal perspective, sometimes even overcoming the majority's disapproval and winning acceptance. If conformity were the only dynamic at work in social groups, these examples could be dismissed as aberrations with no implications for our understanding of social influence processes. One can envision groupthink and group polarization carried to the extreme, with the complete suppression of minority opinion and a resultant interpersonal homogeneity.

Far from representing aberrations, these examples suggest that there is more to social life than accommodation by the minority to majority influence. Even in small social groups, it is possible for a lone dissenter to be heard and to convert others to his or her point of view. At a societal level, minority interests and opinions manage to survive in the face of majority disapproval and hostility, and can sometimes manage to become dominant forces in the culture. In recognition of these facts of social life, *minority influence* has emerged as an important topic in social psychology (cf. Moscovici, 1976). Much of this research attempts to identify factors that enable minority opinions to persist in groups. Experiments in the Asch tradition, for example, have found that both group size and unanimity of the majority have important effects on conformity. The relation between group size and conformity appears to be logarithmic, such that conformity increases with increasing group size up to a point, after which the addition of more group members has diminishing impact (Latané, 1981). Asch's own research showed that conformity is reduced if the group opposing the subject is not unanimous. Even one dissenter among the confederates emboldens the naive subject to resist group pressure and express his or her own judgment. This is true even if the dissenting confederate disagrees with the subject as well as the rest of the group (Allen & Levine, 1971). The key factor is not agreement with the subject, but rather the recognition that nonconformity is possible and acceptable.

Other lines of research have explored the conditions under which minority opinions not only survive, but also become influential to varying degrees in the group. A primary conclusion is that minority members must marshal high-quality arguments and come across as credible. In other words, minorities must rely on informational influence to counter the normative influence associated with the majority position. Against this backdrop, research has revealed a variety of more specific factors that foster minority influence. Thus, minorities are persuasive when they hold steadily to their views (Maass & Clark, 1984; Moscovici, Lage, & Naffrechoux, 1969), originally held the majority opinion (e.g., R. D. Clark, 1990; Levine & Ranelli, 1978), are willing to compromise a bit (Mugny, 1982), have at least some support from others (e.g., Asch, 1955; Tanford & Penrod, 1984; Wolf & Latané, 1985), appear to have little personal stake in the issue (Maass, Clark, & Haberkorn, 1982), and present their views as compatible with the majority but just a bit ahead of the curve, so to speak (e.g., Kiesler & Pallak, 1975; Maass et al., 1982; Volpato, Maass, Mucchi-Faina, & Vitti, 1990). Minority influence also has a better chance if the majority wants to make an accurate decision, because this situation gives the advantage to informational over normative influence (Laughlin & Ellis, 1986). The conditions associated with effective minority influence enable groups (and societies) to embrace new ideas, fashions, and action preferences.

Accountability

The notion of conformity conveys an image of nameless automatons who surrender their personal identity to the group. Ironically, however, the coordination function served by mutual influence in a group setting requires rather than negates a sense of personal identity and responsibility among group members. To achieve social coordination, people must feel that they are part of a larger social entity, of course, but they also must feel that this part is uniquely their own. Two research traditions are relevant to the role of accountability in achieving social coordination. The first concerns the conditions under which people abrogate personal responsibility for doing their part to achieve a common goal or for taking the initiative in a group setting in which their involvement would be helpful. The second concerns the conditions under which people in a sense become *overly* sensitized to the group goal

to the point that they lose sight of their personal identity and unique role in the group.

Social Loafing

Sometimes the whole is less than the sum of its parts. This feature of group dynamics was first observed in an experimental setting by Max Ringelman in the 1920s. Using a gauge to measure effort exerted by tug-of-war participants, Ringelman found that the collective effort was always greater than that of any single participant, but less than the sum of all participants (Kravitz & Martin, 1986). If two people working alone could each pull 100 units, for example, their combined output was only 186—not the 200 one would expect if each pulled as hard as he or she could. Similarly, a three-person group did not produce 300 units, but only 255, and an eight-person group managed only 392 units—less than half the 800 possible.

Ringelman suggested that two mechanisms were responsible for this phenomenon. The first, *coordination loss,* reflects difficulties individuals have in combining their efforts in a maximally effective fashion. On a rope-pulling task, for example, people may not synchronize their respective pulls and pauses, and this can prevent each person from reaching his or her full potential. The second mechanism, commonly referred to today as *social loafing* (Latané, 1981), refers to diminished effort by group members. People may simply not work as hard when they feel other people can pick up the load. Latané, Williams, and Harkins (1979) attempted to replicate the Ringelman effect and to determine which of his proposed mechanisms accounted for it. Participants in one study, for example, were simply asked to shout or clap as loud or as hard as they could, while wearing blindfolds and headsets that played a stream of loud noise. When tested alone, participants averaged a rousing 9.22 dynes/cm^2— about as loud as a pneumatic drill or a teenager's stereo system. But in dyads, subjects performed at only 66% capacity, and in six-person groups, their performance dropped to 36% capacity. The results, in other words, revealed an inverse relationship between the number of coperformers and the output each one generated.

To separate the relative impact of coordination loss and social loafing, Latané et al. (1979) tested noise production in pseudogroups. Participants thought that either one other participant or five other participants were cheering with them, although they were actually cheering alone (the blindfolds and headsets came in handy here). Because there were not any other group members, any drop in individual production could not be due to coordination loss, but instead would reflect social loafing. Results revealed that social loafing was the operative mechanism. If participants thought they were cheering with one other person, they shouted at 82% of their individual capacity. Their productivity dropped to 74% if they thought five others were working with them.

Social loafing is not limited to group tasks involving shouting, or even to tasks involving physical effort of some kind. The decrement in personal contribution with increasing group size has been documented in groups working on a variety of tasks, including maze performance, typing, swimming, vigilance exercises, creativity problems, job-selection decisions, and even brainstorming (e.g., Weldon & Mustari, 1988; cf. Forsyth, 1990). Social loafing applies equally well to men and women, to people of all ages, and to groups in many different cultures (e.g., Brickner, Harkins, & Ostrom, 1986; Harkins & Petty, 1982). There may be polarization of attitudes and other mental states in social groups, but this intensification effect apparently does not apply to group member's efforts in accomplishing a group task.

Social loafing varies in accordance with a set of specific factors. Group members loaf less when they are working on interesting or challenging tasks (e.g., Brickner et al., 1986). Loafing is also minimized when each member's contribution to a group project can be clearly identified, presumably because identification creates the potential for evaluation by other group members (e.g., Harkins & Jackson, 1985; Jackson & Latané, 1981; Williams, Harkins, & Latané, 1981). Social loafing is also partly attributable to the diffusion of responsibility that takes place in groups and crowds (cf. Latané & Darley, 1970). Bystanders to emergency situations feel less compelled to intervene if there are other potential helpers (Darley & Latané, 1968), for example, and restaurant patrons leave pitiful tips when there are many people in the dinner party (Latané & Darley, 1970). Diminished personal responsibility reflects members' feeling that someone else will make up the difference, and also reflects their assessment that they can get away with not helping because the blame is shared by everyone in the group.

The research on social loafing has focused primarily on additive group tasks in which each member's performance is redundant with that of every other member. This hardly exhausts the possible relationships among group members. In situations emphasizing individual rather than group performance, for example, there is a tendency for individual energy expenditure and effort to increase rather than decrease when others are physically present (cf. Triplett, 1898; Zajonc, 1965). Whether this *social facilitation* effect (cf. Cotterell, 1972) translates into better performance, however, depends on features of the task and the contingencies surrounding its occurrence. The presence of others typically enhances performance

on overlearned tasks, for example, but tends to hinder performance on novel or difficult tasks (Zajonc, 1965). There is some controversy regarding the social influence processes at work in such contexts, although there is a fair degree of consensus that the presence of others increases a performer's physiological arousal, which in turn activates his or her dominant responses on the task. This is consistent with the empirical generalization noted by Zajonc (1965), because correct responses are dominant for well-learned tasks and incorrect responses are dominant for unfamiliar tasks.

Even in groups mandating cooperation among group members, the nature of the task may entail forms of coordination that go beyond the simple additive criterion employed in social loafing research (cf. Steiner, 1972). Neither simultaneous shouting nor tug-of-war, after all, captures the essence of groups that build machines or solve human relations problems. Many group goals are defined in terms of distinct subacts that must be accomplished by different group members. For such activities, the quality of the group's performance depends on how well members' respective contributions are synchronized in time. Assembling a car on a production line requires such role differentiation, as does maintaining a household, moving heavy pieces of furniture, or implementing plans to manually recount votes in a close election. Coordination is every bit as critical as individual effort per se in such instances, and a particular blend of normative and informational influence may be necessary for the action to unfold smoothly and effectively. Identifying these blends of influence is an agenda for future research.

Deindividuation

Festinger, Pepitone, and Newcomb (1952) coined the term *deindividuation* to describe a mental state defined by total submergence in a group. A deindividuated person feels he or she does not stand out as a unique individual, and this feeling leads to a reduction of inner restraints that can result in impulsive acts or other behaviors that might otherwise be inhibited. Although these behaviors may be benign or even desirable (e.g., spontaneous expression of feelings, laughing and dancing at a boisterous party), researchers have typically focused on the potential for antisocial and aggressive actions under conditions that promote deindividuation (cf. Diener, 1980; Zimbardo, 1970). Soccer hooligans committing random acts of violence, mobs rioting and looting stores, and gangs terrorizing their enemies are disturbing manifestations of this potential.

Several preconditions for deindividuation have been identified (Zimbardo, 1970). Being part of a large, unstructured group, for example, increases one's anonymity and thus can reduce feelings of personal responsibility for one's actions. The same can be said for clothing that conceals one's identity, the cover of darkness, sensory overload, the use of drugs or alcohol, and collective action of a simple, repetitive (or rhythmic) nature (e.g., marching, clapping, dancing). Diener (1980) suggested that the anonymity associated with deindividuating conditions is tantamount to a loss of self-awareness (Duval & Wicklund, 1972) and hence to diminished salience of personal standards for acceptable conduct (e.g., Carver & Scheier, 1999; Higgins, 1987; Vallacher & Solodky, 1979). Lacking the usual self-regulatory mechanisms for enacting and inhibiting behavior, the deindividuated person becomes highly susceptible to influence from the group and the context in which the group is acting. The nature of this influence, however, does not map onto either normative or informational influence in a straightforward manner. Thus, the person is not consciously modifying his or her behavior to court approval from others, nor is he or she gaining a great deal of insight into physical reality from fellow group members.

One likely dynamic at work is akin to what Le Bon (1895/1960) referred to as *behavioral contagion,* the rapid spread of behavior in a group context. Contagion occurs through simple imitation of others' behavior or through the adoption of others' emotional state, and thus is not particularly taxing on people's mental processes. A related possibility follows from emergent norm theory (Turner & Killian, 1972), which holds that people in unstructured group settings without clear a priori group goals are highly susceptible to cues to higher-order meaning and guides to action that develop in the situation. Consider, for example, the experience of walking down New Orleans' Bourbon Street at 2 a.m. during Mardi Gras. This situation is ripe for deindividuation—maybe even prototypical. You are part of a large, unstructured group consisting of unfamiliar people, it's dark and no one is paying attention to you anyway, music is coming from all angles to overwhelm your powers of sensory integration, and there may have been a couple of hurricane specials consumed by this time. But despite the complex array of sights and sounds, there is no plan dictating your movements and shifts in attention. At this point, if others in the throng spontaneously broke into a rhythmic chant or began throwing plastic beads at a passing float, you might be tempted to follow suit. The collective action you observe provides temporary integration for the ensemble of your specific experiences and thus functions as an emergent norm. The norm doesn't imply acceptance or rejection by others—you could keep on walking and no one would care—but it does provide a guide that allows you to engage in concerted action rather than mere movement (cf. Goldman, 1970; Vallacher & Wegner, 1985).

Viewed in this way, it is easy to appreciate how a state of deindividuation can promote widely divergent action trajectories—moral versus immoral, prosocial versus antisocial, effusive versus sullen, and so on. In effect, the deindividuated person is behaving in accordance with rudimentary moment-to-moment action guides that are devoid of higher-level meaning. This mental state is a precondition for emergent understanding (Vallacher & Wegner, 1987), making the person highly susceptible to whatever goals and plans are rendered salient as the situation evolves. Should the situation resolve itself as an occasion for social camaraderie, the person might be inclined to laugh and dance with everyone he or she encounters. But should the opportunity for personal gain at the expense of others suddenly arise, the same person could just as easily behave in a decidedly unfriendly, even aggressive manner toward those who provide the opportunity. Social influence in this context provides personal (if somewhat transient) coherence and direction for individuals' otherwise disassembled and unregulated actions.

THE INDIVIDUAL AND SOCIETY

One of the most challenging problems in social psychology centers on the relation between micro- and macrolevels of description. Social psychological theories are typically couched in terms of a single level of description, with little explicit coordination with theories defined at different levels. Thus, the processes at the level of the individual tend to be independent of group-level processes. Yet it is unreasonable to expect any level of structure and function to operate in isolation. An individual's behavior is influenced by the social context in which he or she functions, and each individual in turn creates the social context for other individuals through his or her interactions with them. The nature of this mutual dependency is difficult to capture, but recent advances in the study of complex systems (cf. Schuster, 1984) are proving useful in linking different levels of social reality (e.g., Nowak & Vallacher, 1998a, 1998b; Nowak, Vallacher, & Burnstein, 1998; Nowak, Vallacher, & Zochowski, 2002). In this section, we describe one relevant approach—*cellular automata*—that has established a track record in this regard in recent years. Other approaches (neural networks, coupled dynamical systems) are showing promise as well, and the reader is referred to the sources cited above for a description of them.

The Cellular Automata Approach

Cellular automata models (Gutowitz, 1991; Ulam, 1952; von Neumann, 1966; Wolfram, 1986) capture important features of complex systems and are widely used in physics and various domains of biology, including neuroscience (Amit, 1989) and population dynamics (May, 1981). A set of elements is specified to represent the basic units (e.g., neurons, people) in the process under consideration. Each element can adopt a finite number of discrete states (e.g., activated vs. inhibited, pro- vs. antiabortion). The elements are arranged in a spatial configuration, the most common of which is a two-dimensional grid. The state of an element at $t + 1$ depends on the states of the neighboring elements at time t. The exact form of this dependence is specified by so-called updating rules. The dynamics of cellular automata depend on the nature of the updating rule and on the format of the grid dictating the neighborhood structure.

Two classes of cellular automata models are used to characterize social processes. In both, elements represent individuals in a social system. In one, personal characteristics change as a result of updating rules. This approach explores changes in attitudes and opinions that occur as a result of social interaction. In the other class, individuals maintain stable characteristics but may change their physical location. This approach has revealed the emergence of spatial patterns on the basis of stable values and preferences. Shelling (1969, 1971), for instance, developed an updating rule specifying that an individual who has more dissimilar than similar neighbors will move to a different random location. Simulations based on this simple rule demonstrated the emergence of spatial patterns corresponding to social segregation. Both classes of models reveal the emergence of regularities and patterns on a global level that were not directly programmed into the individual elements. These regularities and patterns typically take the form of spatial configurations, such as coherent minority opinion clusters that emerge from an initial random distribution of opinions. Regularities may also appear as temporal patterns, including such basic trajectories as the development of a stable equilibrium (fixed-point attractor), alternation between different states (periodic attractor), and apparent randomness (deterministic chaos).

Cellular Automata and Social Processes

Cellular automata models are useful for exploring different social interaction rules and the generation of societal level phenomena as a result of such rules (cf. Hegselman, 1998; Messick & Liebrand, 1995; Nowak, Szamrej, & Latané, 1990). In these applications, the neighborhood structure is intended to capture the structure of interdependence among individuals (Thibaut & Kelley, 1959). *Indirect interdependence* exists when an individual's actions have consequences, intended or unintended, for other people. This form of interdependence is often examined in the context of social

dilemmas, in which an action intended to maximize personal gain has negative consequences for others (cf. Schulz, Alberts, & Mueller, 1994). In the tragedy of the commons (Hardin, 1968), for instance, a farmer is motivated to overgraze an area of land shared with other farmers. In the short run, the farmer gains advantage over his neighbors, but in the long run, everyone—the farmer included—suffers. *Direct interdependence* reflects what we normally think of as social influence: One person directly influences the state or behavior of another person. Power, manipulation, and coordination thus represent direct interdependence. Both indirect and direct forms of interdependence have been examined in cellular automata models.

Interdependence and Social Dilemmas

How can altruistic behavior can emerge against the backdrop of self-interest? Insight into this puzzle derives from cellular automata models that simulate the short- and long-term effects of behavior in the Prisoner's Dilemma Game (PDG). In pioneering this approach, Axelrod (1984) demonstrated that cooperation often emerges among individuals trying to maximize their respective self-interest. Essentially, Axelrod found that cooperators survived by forming clusters with one another, so that they could engage in mutual help without risking exploitation.

In an extension of this approach, Messick and Liebrand (1995) modeled the consequences of different strategies in the PDG. Each interactant occupied a fixed position in a two-dimensional lattice and played a PDG with one of his or her nearest neighbors. On each trial, the interactant chose whether to cooperate or defect according to one of several updating rules, each reflecting a specific social strategy. In a given simulation, everyone used the same strategy. In the tit-for-tat strategy, individuals imitated the choice made on the preceding trial by their neighbor. In the win-cooperate–lose-defect strategy, the interactant with the greater outcome cooperated, whereas the interactant with the smaller outcome defected. In the win-stay–lose-shift strategy, meanwhile, interactants who perceived themselves to be winning behaved in the same fashion on the next trial, whereas interactants who perceived themselves as losing changed their behavior on the next trial. The results of simulations employing these updating rules reveal different effects depending on the size of the group. In relatively small groups, an equilibrium tends to be reached fairly quickly, with all interactants converging on a particular choice. In larger groups, however, each strategy leads to continuous dynamics characterized by the coexistence of different behavioral choices. Eventually, however, each strategy leads to specific proportions of cooperating individuals. These proportions tend to be maintained at the group level, with the interactants themselves continuing to change their choices throughout the simulation.

In a different approach, Hegselman (1998) explored the emergence of social support networks in a society. Individuals lived on a two-dimensional grid containing some unoccupied sites and played a two-person "support game" with all of their immediate neighbors. Each individual was characterized by some probability of needing help. A needy individual clearly benefited, of course, if he or she received help from a neighbor, but providing help to a neighbor was clearly costly. With this trade-off in mind, each individual's preferred neighborhood was one in which he or she could obtain the degree of help needed while minimizing the help he or she provided. Individuals were sometimes provided a migration option that enabled them to move to a more desirable location within a certain radius. The results reveal how support networks can evolve in a world of rational egoists who are differentially needy, but similarly motivated to choose partners in an opportunistic manner. Although social support inevitably develops, the social networks that emerge tend to be highly segregated. Individuals with a moderate probability of becoming needy tend to form relationships with one another, and also with individuals from somewhat higher and lower risk classes. Interestingly, individuals at the extremes of neediness—those with very high or very low probabilities of needing help—tend to have the most difficulty in establishing support relations. If they do manage to form such relationships, their partners tend to be from the same risk class.

Social Influence and the Emergence of Social Structure

The cellular automata model of social process that has been analyzed most thoroughly concerns social influence (e.g., Lewenstein, Nowak, & Latané, 1993; Nowak, Lewenstein, & Frejlak, 1996). The initial formulation of this model (Nowak et al., 1990) focused on the emergence of public opinion in a society characterized by a diversity of attitudes. The model assumes that in the course of social interaction, individuals are motivated to sample the degree of social support for their position on a given topic. The model also assumes, in line with social impact theory (Latané, 1981), that each individual gives the greatest weight to the opinions of others who are spatially closest to him or her and who have the greatest strength (e.g., who are most influential or persuasive). An individual's own opinion is also taken into consideration and is weighted most heavily by virtue of spatial immediacy (i.e., distance is 0). After each round of interaction, the individual compares the degree of support for each attitude position and adopts the one with the strongest support in preparation for the next round of interaction.

In the simulations, one individual is chosen (usually at random), and influence is computed for each opinion in the group. (The strength of influence of each opinion is expressed by the following formula.

$$I_i = \left(\sum_1^N \left(\frac{s_j}{d_{ij}^2} \right)^2 \right)^{1/2}$$

where I_i denotes total influence, s_j corresponds to the strength of each individual, and d_{ij} corresponds to the distance between individuals i and j.) If the resultant strength for an opinion position is greater than the strength of the individual's current position, his or her opinion changes to match the prevailing position. This process is performed for each individual. This procedure is repeated until there are no further changes, which typically requires several rounds of simulation, because a person who had previously changed his or her position to match that of his or her neighbors may revert to the original position if the neighbors change their opinions. Figures 16.1 and 16.2 present representative results of the computer simulations. Each box corresponds to an individual. The color of the box (light vs. dark gray) denotes the individual's position, and the height of the box corresponds to the individual's strength. In Figure 16.1, there is a majority of 60% (light gray) and a minority of 40% (dark gray). The majority and minority members are randomly distributed,

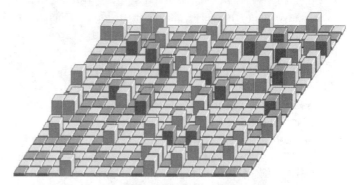

Figure 16.1   Initial distribution of opinions in the simulated group.

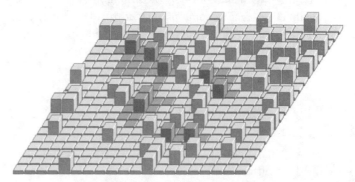

Figure 16.2   Final equilibrium of opinions in the simulated group.

and each group has the same relative proportions of strong and weak members (high vs. low boxes). Figure 16.2 shows the equilibrium reached after six rounds of simulated discussion. Now the majority is 90% and the minority is 10%. Note that the minority opinion has survived by forming clusters of like-minded people and that these clusters are largely formed around strong individuals.

These two group-level outcomes—*polarization and clustering*—are commonly observed in computer simulations (cf. Nowak et al., 1996; Latané, Nowak, & Liu, 1994) and are reminiscent of well-documented social processes. As noted earlier in this chapter, the average attitude in a group becomes polarized in the direction of the prevailing attitude as a result of group discussion (e.g., Moscovici & Zavalloni, 1969; Myers & Lamm, 1976). In the simulations, polarization reflects the greater influence of the majority opinion. In the initial random configuration (Figure 16.1), the average proportion of neighbors holding a given opinion corresponds to the proportion of this opinion in the total group. The average group member, then, is surrounded by more majority than minority members, a difference that results in more minority members' being converted to the majority position than vice versa. Some majority members are converted to the minority position, however, because they happen to be located close to an especially influential minority member, or because by pure accident, more minority members happen to be at this location.

Clustering is also pervasive in social life. Attitudes, for example, have been shown to cluster in residential neighborhoods (Festinger, Schachter, & Back, 1950). Pronounced clustering also characterizes political beliefs, religions, clothing fashions, and farming techniques. Clustering reflects the relatively strong influence exerted by an individual's neighbors. When opinions are distributed randomly, the sampling of opinions through social interaction provides a reasonably accurate portrait of the distribution of opinions in the larger society. When opinions are clustered, however, the same sampling process will yield a highly biased result. Because the opinions of those in the nearby vicinity are weighted the most heavily, the prevalence of one's own opinion is likely to be overestimated. Hence, opinions that are in the minority in global terms can form a local majority. Individuals who hold a minority opinion are therefore likely to maintain this opinion in the belief that it represents a majority position.

Control Factors for Social Influence

The results concerning polarization and clustering have been confirmed analytically (Lewenstein et al., 1993) and have received empirical support as well (Latané, Liu, Nowak,

Bonavento, & Zheng, 1995; Latané & Nowak, 1997). This research has also identified several control factors that are responsible for the emergence of these macroscopic properties (Latané & Nowak, 1997; Lewenstein et al., 1993; Nowak et al., 1996). Individual differences in strength, first of all, are indispensable to the survival of minority clusters. This conclusion is consistent with evidence demonstrating the importance of leaders for maintaining the viability of minority opinions. The literature on brainwashing, for example, documents that natural leaders were commonly removed from the group before attempts were made to brainwash prisoners of war (cf. Schein, 1956). By counteracting the sheer number of majority opinions, the strength of leaders stops minority clusters from decaying. It is worth noting that as a result of social influence, individual differences in strength tend to become correlated with opinions. This is because the weakest minority members are most likely to adopt the majority position, so that over time the average strength of the remaining minority members will grow at the expense of the majority. This scenario is consistent with the observation that individuals advocating minority positions are often more influential than those advocating majority positions.

A second critical control factor is nonlinearity in attitude change. Abelson (1979) demonstrated that when individuals move incrementally toward the opinions of interaction partners as a result of social influence, the invariable outcome of simulations is uniformity and the complete loss of minority clusters. In the model depicted here, however, attitudes are assumed to be categorical in nature (Latané & Nowak, 1994). This means that individuals hold a fixed position and actively resist influence attempts until a critical threshold of influence is reached, at which point they switch dramatically from one category to another rather than incrementally on a dimension of judgment. There is empirical evidence in support of the nonlinearity assumption for attitude topics that are personally important (cf. Latané & Nowak, 1994). Such attitudes display a bimodal distribution, with almost no individuals occupying the intermediate points on the attitude dimension. This suggests, incidentally, that one way to achieve consensus in a group is to decrease the subjective importance of the topic in question.

A third critical feature concerns the geometry of the social space (Nowak, Latané, & Lewenstein, 1994). People do not communicate equally with everyone in a group, nor are their interactions random. Specific communication patterns can be approximated with different geometries of social space. In most of the simulations, social space is portrayed as a two-dimensional matrix of n rows and n columns. This geometry reflects the assumption that interactions typically occur in two-dimensional spaces, such as neighborhoods, town squares, and rooms. One can envision other geometries, however, to capture different communication structures (Nowak et al., 1996). A one-dimensional geometry in which people interact mainly with neighbors to their left and right corresponds to a row of houses along a river or a village stretching along a road. In this case, strong clustering occurs because of well-pronounced local interactions between nearest neighbors. Polarization, however, is inhibited because members of the majority cannot encircle members of the minority and overwhelm them. Far more elaborate geometries of social space can also be envisioned. In the real world, many different geometries no doubt co-occur and thus determine the dynamics of social influence. The availability of telephones, e-mail, and common areas for shopping and recreation clearly add many dimensions to the effective geometry in which interactions occur. The combined effects of such geometries play a significant role in determining the form and outcome of social influence.

A fourth critical factor represents the weight an individual attaches to his or her own opinion as compared to the opinions of others. This variable, referred to as *self-influence,* corresponds to psychological states like self-confidence, strength of conviction, and belief certainty. An individual's self-influence is correlated with his or her strength, although the absolute value of self-influence varies as a function of topic or social setting. When an issue is new or confusing, for example, self-influence is correspondingly lower, reflecting the fact that no strong opinion has formed and everyone is relatively open to external influence. When an issue is familiar and personally important, however, self-influence attains its maximum value for everyone, reflecting the greater importance of one's own opinion compared to others' opinions. Because issue familiarity is assumed to be the same for all individuals in a given simulation, variation in self-influence is a direct reflection of variation among individuals in their respective strength.

The dynamics of social influence are determined by the value of self-influence relative to the total influence of other individuals. When self-influence is low, individuals may switch their opinions several times during the course of simulations. This has the effect of destabilizing clusters. For topics that are unfamiliar, then, one observes heightened dynamics that promote unification based on the majority opinion. However, if self-influence is greater than the combined influence of others, dynamics tend to be dampened altogether, unless sources of noise (random external factors) are present. Because noise works jointly with social influence, noise-induced changes are typically in the same direction as majority influence. Introducing a random factor that by itself would not favor any position can thus neutralize the effect of self-influence and enhance the effect of majority opinion. Very high values of noise, however, can dilute the effects of social interaction as well, producing random changes in opinion.

Social Change and Societal Transitions

This general approach to the modeling of social processes has proven useful in generating insight into the dynamics of social change, including major societal transformations (Nowak & Lewenstein, 1996; Nowak, Lewenstein, & Szamrej, 1993; Nowak & Vallacher, 2001). This approach successfully models social change when a source of bias is introduced that makes the minority opinion more attractive than the majority opinion. The results of simulations reveal that rapid social change occurs in a manner that is remarkably similar to phase transitions in physical phenomena. Expressed metaphorically, changes enter as bubbles of new within the sea of old, and social transitions occur as these bubbles expand and become connected. Thus, for example, a new political ideology or lifestyle fashion that resonates with existing values or interests is introduced into a social system and is immediately embraced by pockets of people in different areas. These pockets become increasingly connected over time, until at some point the new idea achieves widespread dominance over the old idea.

Computer simulations also indicate, however, that the bubbles of the old manage to stay entrenched in the sea of the new. The strongest and best-supported individuals holding the old position, moreover, are the most likely to survive pressures associated with the new position. This, in turn, means that the old position is likely to display a rebound effect when the bias toward the new position disappears or is somehow reversed. This scenario provides an explanation for the return of leftist governments in Eastern Europe after their overwhelming defeat in the elections in the late 1980s.

This model of societal transition stands in marked contrast to the conventional view of social change, which holds that individuals gradually switch from an old set of attitudes or preferences to a new set of ideas. From that perspective, new ideas spread more or less uniformly through a society at a constant and relatively slow rate. The simulation model allows for this mode of social change as long as the social system is near a relatively stable equilibrium and noise is not a significant factor in dictating the system's dynamics (Nowak et al., 1993). The incremental scenario, in other words, may effectively characterize how change occurs in a stable society (e.g., a gradual shift from liberalism to conservatism or vice versa), but it does not capture the nature of change defining periods of rapid social transition.

Two sources of data provide empirical support for this perspective on social transition: the development of the private sector of the Polish economy and the emergence of voting preferences in the Polish parliamentary elections during the transition from socialism to private enterprise in the late 1980s and early 1990s (Nowak, Urbaniak, & Zienkowski, 1994). For a description of these data, as well as a comprehensive depiction of the cellular automata model and its implications for societal transition, the reader is referred to Nowak and Vallacher (2001).

Implications for Cultural Differences

The cellular automata model is useful in understanding and predicting differences among cultures in the dynamics of social influence and societal organization. A primary theme in cross-cultural comparisons centers on collectivism versus individualism (cf. Markus & Kitayama, 1991). In so-called *collectivist* cultures—China and Japan, for example—interdependence among individuals is stressed at the expense of personal independence, so that individuals are readily influenced by the beliefs, attitudes, and expectations of other people. In so-called *individualistic* cultures—the United States, for example—greater emphasis is placed on independence, with individuals maintaining a relatively strong degree of autonomy in their self-concept, attitudes, and lifestyle. This dimension of cultural variation maps directly onto the variable of self-influence in the cellular automata model. In a society that values independence in decision-making and judgment, the magnitude of self-influence is correspondingly strong and operates at the expense of the opinions and expectations of others. Computer simulations have revealed that as self-influence increases in magnitude, the number of individuals changing their opinion on a given issue decreases, there is less polarization and clustering, and the average cluster is smaller in size (Latané & Nowak, 1997; Lewenstein et al., 1993).

Societies also differ in their relative stability. In less modernized societies, which are predominantly rural and agrarian rather than industrial in nature, the social context for individuals is relatively stable over time. In contrast, relatively modernized and industrial societies tend to be characterized by greater social mobility (e.g., travel, permanent relocation) and greater frequency of communication over large distances (by means of phone, e-mail, and fax). These features disturb the stability of social influence exerted by the social context on the individual. At different times, in other words, the individual is exposed to a broad range of opinions that go beyond those expressed in the immediate social context. This aspect of modernized society can be represented in the model as

noise, which reflects the sum of influences (e.g., exposure to mass media, contact with people from other cultures) not accounted for by local influence. The greater the magnitude of noise in a society, the weaker the relative role played by the individual's local context. The opinions of someone in a different part of the country, for example, may have a greater impact on an individual's opinions than do the opinions of his or her immediate neighbors. This is clearly not the case in a stable society, in which everyone is exposed to the same local contacts throughout much of his or her life.

Computer simulations of the model have demonstrated a nonlinear relationship between noise and the distribution of opinions in a society (Latané & Nowak, 1997; Lewenstein et al., 1993). Small values of noise tend to destabilize weak clusters (e.g., Nowak, Vallacher, Tesser, & Borkowski, 2000). Because weak clusters tend also to be small, low-level noise has the effect of increasing the average size of clusters in the society, which is reflected in higher overall clustering and polarization. Higher values of noise, however, can destabilize all minority clusters and thus promote unification of opinions in the society. At very high levels of noise, however, individuals are likely to adopt opinions that are independent of their immediate social context. This not only disrupts clusters, but it also prevents unification of opinions in the society. In effect, everyone switches his or her opinions in a more-or-less random fashion.

In a stable society characterized by low levels of noise, then, a stable pattern of relatively small clusters is to be expected, whereas in a somewhat less stable society characterized by moderate levels of noise, larger clusters and greater opinion polarization is to be expected. With further increases in societal instability, one might expect a breakdown in minority opinion clusters and a tendency toward societal unification in opinion. Finally, in a highly modernized and unstable society, one would expect the pattern of opinions to be largely independent of the pattern of social ties (e.g., neighborhood influence), demonstrating instead the influence of other factors, such as selective exposure to the media and contact with other cultures.

Cultures also differ in their respective values and preferences regarding everything from clothing to religion. This feature is represented in the model as bias. If a new idea resonates well with a culture's prevailing values and preferences, it will take somewhat less social influence for the idea to take hold in the society. But if the idea runs counter to cultural values, it is likely to be resisted even if it is supported by considerable influence. Communist ideology was never fully embraced in Poland, for example, despite the considerable influence exerted by the government, because communist values ran counter to strong Polish traditions of independence and Catholicism. As noted above, research exploring the social change implications of the model has verified that cultural bias is indeed a significant factor in determining the extent to which a new idea or ideology can take hold in a society (cf. Nowak & Vallacher, 2001).

It is interesting to consider cultural differences in terms of the specific combinations of self-influence, noise, and bias. Two industrialized societies may both have high levels of self-influence (i.e., an individualistic orientation), for example, but they may differ considerably in their respective levels of noise (e.g., selective exposure to mass media) or their bias toward various positions (e.g., religious beliefs). Because each of these variables plays a unique role in social influence, the interaction among them is likely to be decisive in shaping the predominant form of social influence characterizing a given society. Cultural variation in social influence processes, in other words, conceivably can be traced to the specific blend of variables in the cellular automata model. The investigation of this possibility provides an important agenda for future research concerning the relationship between micro- and macrolevels of social reality.

TOWARD COHERENCE IN SOCIAL INFLUENCE

Social influence is clearly a big topic, a fact that reflects its centrality to the field of social psychology. The enormous range of ideas and principles associated with this topic, however, is a mixed blessing. On the one hand, the diversity of social influence phenomena and processes attests to the undeniable complexity of human social experience. But on the negative side of the ledger, this very diversity can prove vexing for those—laypeople and theorists alike—who seek integration and synthesis in their understanding. Several hundred studies and dozens of distinct mechanisms may well be necessary to capture the nuances of such a wide-ranging topic, but this state of affairs does little to inspire a feeling of coherent understanding. Like the field of social psychology as a whole (cf. Vallacher & Nowak, 1994), the subfield of social influence is highly fragmented, with poorly defined connections among the separate elements that define it.

Ironically, if there is a basis for theoretical coherence in social influence, it may reflect what psychologists have learned about the dynamics of coherence in recent years. Despite the enormous complexity of human minds and social groups—or perhaps because of such complexity—psychological systems at different levels of personal and social reality display self-organization and the emergence of higher-level properties. The mutual influences among the elements in each system promote such emergence, and the resultant properties in turn provide functional integration and coordination for the component elements. This reciprocal feedback between lower-level elements and higher-level properties may constitute an invariant principle common to all social psychological processes—or to all complex systems, for that matter (cf. Nowak & Vallacher, 1998a). Thus, the specific cognitive elements defining the stream of thought become self-organized with respect to higher-order judgments and values (Vallacher, Nowak, & Kaufman, 1994), specific movements and perceptions become coordinated to produce meaningful action (cf. Vallacher et al., 1998), individuals become integrated into higher-order functional units such as dyads and social groups (e.g., Nowak et al., 2002), and social groups become coordinated with respect to larger goals and values that define the social system in which they are embedded (cf. Nowak & Vallacher, 2001).

With this in mind, it is tempting to consider whether a press for higher-order coherence provides a common denominator for the otherwise dizzying array of specific social influence processes. Perhaps seemingly distinct means of influencing people prove effective or ineffective depending on how well each taps into established rules regarding coherence in thought and action. If so, many of the phenomena discussed in this chapter could be reframed so as to underscore their common features, and new predictions could be generated about the factors that determine whether a given influence strategy will prove successful in a particular context for a particular target. The central idea is that influence involves resynchronization of the elements in the target's relevant cognitive structure. Achieving resynchronization is difficult, however, when the cognitive structure in question is well-integrated and stable. To promote a change in behavior in this case, it is necessary to disassemble or otherwise destabilize the associated cognitive structure. After the structure is destabilized, the person is primed for resynchronization in line with cues to higher-order meaning provided by the influence agent.

A basic strategy for resynchronizing people's thoughts and desires follows from the emergence process of action identification theory (cf. Vallacher & Wegner, 1987; Vallacher et al., 1998). Research on this process has revealed that when people do not have an integrated representation of what they are doing, they become highly sensitive to coherent perspectives on their behavior provided by others. The extrapolation of this process to social influence is straightforward. In this scenario, the influence agent first induces the target to consider the relevant topic or action in concrete, low-level terms. Getting the target to engage in topic-relevant behavior has this effect, provided the behavior is sufficiently novel or complex that it requires attention to detail. Simply describing an action in terms of its details can also induce low-level identification, as can presenting the target with a surplus of concrete information regarding the attitude object. From this disassembled state, the target experiences a heightened press for integration. Left to his or her own devices, the target might emerge with a higher-level frame for the action or topic that reflects past positions or perhaps one that reflects a new integration altogether (Vallacher & Nowak, 1997; Vallacher et al., 1998). If, however, the influence agent offers a message that provides the missing integration before the target has demonstrated emergence on his or her own, the target is likely to embrace this message as an avenue of emergent understanding, even if it conflicts with his or her prior conception.

This general approach to influence is effective in changing people's understanding of their own behavior, but with few exceptions (e.g., Davis & Knowles, 1999; Vallacher & Selz, 1991) this approach has not been extended to other domains of influence. Nonetheless, a wide variety of established influence strategies can be reframed as the disassembly of a coherent state into its lower-level elements, setting the stage for a reconfiguration of the elements in line with the influence agent's agenda. Thus, any strategy that involves inducing the target to engage in acts that are at least somewhat novel or time-consuming can create the necessary precondition for guided emergence, as can providing the target with ambiguous or conflicting information that is open to different higher-level interpretations. Placing the target in a situation that lacks a priori structure and coherence can similarly make him or her vulnerable to emergent norms for how to act. Certain dimensions of individual difference are also associated with vulnerability to social influence, and these too can be considered in light of the emergence scenario. Self-uncertainty (e.g., Swann & Ely, 1984; Vallacher, 1980), low levels of personal agency (Vallacher & Wegner, 1989), field dependence (Witkin, Dyk, Faterson, Goodenough, & Karp, 1962), low cognitive differentiation (Bieri, Atkins, Briar, Leaman, Miller, & Tripodi, 1966), and external locus of control (Rotter, 1966) are clearly distinct constructs, but each can be seen as a manifestation of weak cognitive structure concerning a relevant domain of judgment and self regulation (i.e., the self, action, other people, society). Lacking internal coherence, a person characterized in this fashion utilizes information provided by others as a frame around which he or she can achieve a sense of personal integration.

The failure of influence strategies, meanwhile, may reflect a corresponding failure to disrupt or otherwise disassemble the target's prevailing understanding of the action or topic at issue. Thus, resistance to influence (e.g., psychological reactance) may be enhanced when the target's prevailing perspective is not sufficiently deconstructed for him or her to embrace the influence agent's alternative perspective. In essence, the emergence scenario suggests that all manner of influence, from compliance with requests to brainwashing, are built on a shared platform emphasizing people's inherent press for coherent understanding.

We should note, however, that complete integration is rarely attained in complex systems. The cellular automata model of social influence, for example, commonly produces a highly clustered rather than unified social structure, even though the underlying dynamics are in service of self-organization and coherence (e.g., Nowak et al., 1990, 1998; Nowak & Vallacher, 1998b). Differentiation as opposed to unification is commonly observed as well in people's self-structure (Nowak et al., 2000), despite a sustained press for integration in self-understanding. It is unreasonable, then, to expect the voluminous literature on social influence to admit to a single higher-order principle. Nor should we expect the field to reach a static equilibrium, with an immutable set of conclusions concerning the ways in which people influence one another. Complex systems are inherently dynamic, continually evolving and becoming reconfigured in response to new influences from the outside. Because interest in social influence shows no sign of letting up, we can expect this defining area of social psychology to display repeated episodes of disassembly and reconfiguration in the years to come.

REFERENCES

Abelson, R. P. (1979). Social clusters and opinion clusters. In P. W. Holland & S. Leinhardt (Eds.), *Perspectives in social network research* (pp. 239–256). New York: Academic.

Abelson, R. P., Aronson, E., McGuire, W. J., Newcomb, T. M., Rosenberg, M. J., & Tannenbaum, P. H. (Eds.). (1968). *Theories of cognitive consistency: A sourcebook.* Chicago: Rand-McNally.

Alexander, C. N., Zucker, L. G., & Brody, C. L. (1970). Experimental expectations and autokinetic experiences: Consistency theories and judgmental convergence. *Sociometry, 33,* 108–122.

Allen, V. L., & Levine, J. M. (1971). Social support and conformity: The role of independent assessment of reality. *Journal of Experimental Social Psychology, 4,* 48–58.

Alloy, L. B., & Abramson, L. Y. (1979). Judgment of contingency in depressed and non-depressed students: Sadder but wiser? *Journal of Experimental Psychology: General, 108,* 441–485.

Allport, F. H. (1924). *Social psychology.* Boston: Riverside Editions/Houghton Mifflin.

Allport, G. W. (1939). *Personality: A psychological interpretation.* New York: Holt.

Allport, G. W. (1968). The historical background of modern social psychology. In G. A. Lindzey & E. Aronson (Eds.), *The handbook of social psychology* (Vol. 1, pp. 1–46). Reading, Mass.: Addison-Wesley.

Amit, D. J. (1989). *Modeling brain function: The world of attractor neural networks.* Cambridge, UK: Cambridge University Press.

Aronson, E. (1992). The return of the oppressed: Dissonance theory makes a comeback. *Psychological Inquiry, 3,* 303–311.

Aronson, E., & Carlsmith, J. M. (1963). Effect of the severity of threat on the devaluation of forbidden behavior. *Journal of Abnormal and Social Psychology, 66,* 583–588.

Asch, S. E. (1951). Effects of group pressure upon the modification and distortion of judgment. In H. Guetzow (Ed.), *Groups, leadership, and men* (pp. 177–190). Pittsburgh, PA: Carnegie.

Asch, S. E. (1952). *Social psychology.* Englewood Cliffs, NJ: Prentice-Hall.

Asch, S. E. (1955). Opinions and social pressure. *Scientific American, 19,* 31–35.

Asch, S. E. (1956). Studies of independence and conformity: A minority of one against a unanimous majority. *Psychological Monographs, 70* (9, Whole No. 416).

Axelrod, R. (1984). *The evolution of cooperation.* New York: Basic Books.

Bandura, A. (1986). *Social foundations of thought and action.* Englewood Cliffs, NJ: Prentice-Hall.

Bargh, J. A., & Chartrand, T. L. (1999). The unbearable automaticity of being. *American Psychologist, 54,* 462–479.

Baron, R. A., & Byrne, D. (1994). *Social psychology: Understanding human interaction* (7th ed.). Needham Heights, MA: Allyn & Bacon.

Baumeister, R. F. (1982). A self-presentational view of social phenomena. *Psychological Bulletin, 91,* 3–26.

Baumeister, R. F., Stillwell, A. M., & Heatherton, T. F. (1994). Guilt: An interpersonal approach. *Psychological Bulletin, 115,* 243–267.

Bem, D. J. (1972). Self-perception theory. In L. Berkowitz (Ed.), *Advances in experimental social psychology* (Vol. 6, pp. 1–62). New York: Academic.

Bensley, L. S., & Wu, R. (1991). The role of psychological reactance in drinking following alcohol prevention messages. *Journal of Applied Psychology, 21,* 1111–1124.

Benson, H., Karabenick, S. A., & Lerner, M. (1976). The effects of physical attractiveness, race, and sex on receiving help. *Journal of Experimental and Social Psychology, 12,* 409–415.

Berkowitz, L., & Daniels, L. R. (1964). Affecting the salience of the social responsibility norm: Effects of past help on the response to dependency relationships. *Journal of Abnormal and Social Psychology, 68,* 275–281.

Berkowitz, L. (Series Ed.), & Walster, E. (Vol. Eds.). (1976). *Advances in experimental social psychology: Vol. 9. Equity theory: Toward a general theory of social interaction.* New York: Academic.

Berry, S. H., & Kanouse, D. E. (1987). Physician response to a mailed survey: An experiment in timing of payment. *Public Opinion Quarterly, 51,* 102–114.

Bettencourt, B. A., Brewer, M. B., Croak, M. R., & Miller, N. (1992). Cooperation and the reduction of intergroup bias. *Journal of Experimental Social Psychology, 28,* 301–319.

Bickman, L. (1974). The power of a uniform. *Journal of Applied Social Psychology, 4,* 61–77.

Bieri, J., Atkins, A. L., Briar, S., Leaman, R. L., Miller, H., & Tripodi, T. (1966). *Clinical and social judgment.* New York: Wiley.

Blascovich, J., Ginsberg, G. P., & Howe, R. C. (1975). Blackjack and the risky shift: Pt. 2. Monetary stakes. *Journal of Experimental Psychology, 11,* 224–232.

Braver, S. L. (1975). Reciprocity, cohesiveness, and cooperation in two-person games. *Psychological Reports, 36,* 371–378.

Brehm, J. W. (1966). *A theory of psychological reactance.* New York: Academic.

Brehm, S. S., & Brehm, J. W. (1981). *Psychological reactance: A theory of freedom and control.* New York: Academic.

Brewer, M. B. (1991). The social self: On being the same and different at the same time. *Personality and Social Psychology Bulletin, 17,* 475–482.

Brickner, M., Harkins, S., & Ostrom, T. (1986). Personal involvement: Thought-provoking implications for social loafing. *Journal of Personality and Social Psychology, 51,* 763–760.

Bruner, J. S., & Tagiuri, R. (1954). The perception of people. In G. Lindzey (Ed.), *Handbook of social psychology* (Vol. 2, pp. 634–654). Reading, MA: Addison-Wesley.

Budesheim, T. L., & DePaola, S. J. (1994). Beauty or the beast? The effects of appearance, personality, and issue formation on evaluations of political candidates. *Personality and Social Psychology Bulletin, 20,* 339–348.

Burger, J. M. (1986). Increasing compliance by improving the deal: The that's-not-all technique. *Journal of Personality and Social Psychology, 51,* 277–283.

Burger, J. M. (1992). *Desire for control: Personality, social, and clinical perspectives.* New York: Plenum.

Burger, J. M., & Cooper, H. N. (1979). The desirability of control. *Motivation and Emotion, 3,* 381–393.

Burger, J. M., & Petty, R. E. (1981). The low-ball compliance technique: Task or person commitment? *Journal of Personality and Social Psychology, 40,* 492–500.

Burnstein, E., & Vinokur, A. (1977). Persuasive argumentation and social comparison as determinants of attitude polarization. *Journal of Experimental Social Psychology, 13,* 315–332.

Byrne, D. (1971). *The attraction paradigm.* New York: Academic.

Byrne, D., Clore, G. L., & Smeaton, G. (1980). The attraction hypothesis: Do similar attitudes affect anything? *Journal of Personality and Social Psychology, 51,* 1167–1170.

Carnegie, D. (1981). *How to win friends and influence people.* New York: Pocket Books. (Original work published 1936)

Carver, C. S., & Scheier, M. F. (1999). Themes and issues in the self-regulation of behavior. In R. S. Wyer, Jr. (Ed.), *Advances in social cognition* (Vol. 12, pp. 1–105). Mahwah, NJ: Erlbaum.

Castellow, W. A., Wuensch, K. L., & Moore, C. H. (1990). Effects of physical attractiveness of the plaintiff and defendant in sexual harassment judgments. *Journal of Social Behavior and Personality, 5,* 547–562.

Chaiken, S. (1979). Communicator physical attractiveness and persuasion. *Journal of Personality and Social Psychology, 37,* 1387–1397.

Cialdini, R. B. (1993). *Influence: Science and practice* (3rd ed.). New York: HarperCollins.

Cialdini, R. B. (1995). Principles and techniques of social influence. In A. Tesser (Ed.), *Advanced social psychology* (pp. 257–281). New York: McGraw-Hill.

Cialdini, R. B. (2001). *Influence: Science and practice* (4th ed.). Needham Heights, MA: Allyn & Bacon.

Cialdini, R. B., Cacioppo, J. T., Bassett, R., & Miller, J. A. (1978). Low-ball procedure for producing compliance: Commitment then cost. *Journal of Personality and Social Psychology, 36,* 463–476.

Cialdini, R. B., Green, B. L., & Rusch, A. J. (1992). When tactical pronouncements of change become real change: The case of reciprocal persuasion. *Journal of Personality and Social Psychology, 63,* 30–40.

Cialdini, R. B., & Trost, M. R. (1998). Social influence: Social norms, conformity, and compliance. In D. T. Gilbert, S. T. Fiske, & G. Lindzey (Eds.), *The handbook of social psychology* (Vol. 2, pp. 151–192). New York: McGraw-Hill.

Cialdini, R. B., Vincent, J. E., Lewis, S. K., Catalan, J., Wheeler, D., & Darby, B. L. (1975). Reciprocal concessions procedure for inducing compliance: The door-in-the-face technique. *Journal of Personality and Social Psychology, 31,* 206–215.

Cioffi, D., & Garner, R. (1996). On doing the decision: the effects of active versus passive choice on commitment and self-perception. *Personality and Social Psychology Bulletin, 22,* 133–147.

Clark, M. S., & Mills, J. (1979). Interpersonal attraction in exchange and communal relationships. *Journal of Personality and Social Psychology, 37,* 12–24.

Clark, R. D. (1990). Minority influence: The role of argument refutation of the minority position and social support for the minority position. *European Journal of Social Psychology, 20,* 489–497.

Coleman, J. F., Blake, R. R., & Mouton, J. S. (1958). Task difficulty and conformity pressures. *Journal of Abnormal Social Psychology, 57,* 120–122.

Cotterell, N. B. (1972). Social facilitation. In C. G. McClintock (Ed.), *Experimental social psychology* (pp. 185–236). New York: Holt, Reinhart & Winston.

Cotterell, N. B., Eisenberger, R., & Speicher, H. (1992). Inhibiting effects of reciprocation wariness on interpersonal relationships. *Journal of Personality and Social Psychology, 62,* 658–668.

Crowne, D. P., & Marlowe, D. (1964). *The approval motive: Studies in evaluative dependence.* New York: Wiley.

Crutchfield, R. (1955). Conforming and character. *American Psychologist, 10,* 191–198.

Csikszentmihalyi, M. (1990). *Flow: The psychology of optimal experience.* New York: Harper & Row.

Darley, J. M., & Latané, B. (1968). Bystander intervention in emergencies: Diffusion of responsibility. *Journal of Personality and Social Psychology, 8,* 377–383.

Davis, B. P., & Knowles, E. S. (1999). A disrupt-then-reframe technique of social influence. *Journal of Personality and Social Psychology, 76,* 192–199.

de Charms, R. (1968). *Personal causation.* New York: Academic.

Deci, E. L., & Ryan, R. M. (1985). *Intrinsic motivation and self-determination in human behavior.* New York: Plenum.

DePaulo, B. M., Brittingham, G. L., & Kaiser, M. K. (1983). Receiving competence-relevant help. *Journal of Personality and Social Psychology, 45,* 1046–1060.

Deutsch, M., & Gerard, H. G. (1955). A study of normative and informational social influence upon individual judgment. *Journal of Abnormal Social Psychology, 51,* 629–636.

Diener, E. (1980). Deindividuation: The absence of self-awareness and self-regulation in group members. In P. B. Paulus (Ed.), *Psychology of group influence* (pp. 209–242). Hillsdale, NJ: Erlbaum.

Donaldson, S. I., Graham, J. W., Piccinin, A. M., & Hansen, W. B. (1995). Resistance-training skills and onset of alcohol use. *Health Psychology, 14,* 291–300.

Doise, W. (1969). Intergroup relations and polarization of individual and collective judgments. *Journal of Personality and Social Psychology, 12,* 136–143.

Drachman, D., De Carufel, A., & Insko, C. A. (1978). The extra credit effect in interpersonal attraction. *Journal of Personality and Social Psychology, 14,* 458–467.

Duval, S., & Wicklund, R. A. (1972). *A theory of objective self awareness.* New York: Academic.

Efran, M. G., & Patterson, E. W. J. (1976). *The politics of appearance.* Unpublished manuscript, University of Toronto, Canada.

Eisenberger, R., Cotterell, N., & Marvel, J. (1987). Reciprocation ideology. *Journal of Personality and Social Psychology, 53,* 743–750.

Emswiller, T., Deaux, K., & Willits, J. E. (1971). Similarity, sex, and requests for small favors. *Journal of Applied Social Psychology, 1,* 284–291.

Festinger, L. (1950). Informal social communication. *Psychological Review, 57,* 271–282.

Festinger, L. (1957). *A theory of cognitive dissonance.* Evanston, IL: Row, Peterson.

Festinger, L., Pepitone, A., & Newcomb, T. (1952). Some consequences of de-individuation in a group. *Journal of Abnormal psychology, 47,* 382–389.

Festinger, L., Schachter, S., & Back, K. (1950). *Social pressures in informal groups.* Stanford, CA: Stanford University Press.

Foa, E. B., & Foa, U. G. (1974). *Societal structures of the mind.* Springfield, IL: Thomas.

Forsyth, D. R. (1990). *Group dynamics* (2nd ed.). Pacific Grove, CA: Brooks/Cole.

Freedman, J. L., & Fraser, S. C. (1966). Compliance without pressure: The foot-in-the-door technique. *Journal of Personality and Social Psychology, 4,* 195–202.

French, J., & Raven, B. (1959). The bases of social power. In D. Cartwright (Ed.), *Studies in social power* (pp. 150–167). Ann Arbor, MI: Institute for Social Research.

Frenzen, J. R., & Davis, H. L. (1990). Purchasing behavior in embedded markets. *Journal of Consumer Research, 17,* 1–12.

Garner, R. L. (1999). What's in a name: Persuasion perhaps? Unpublished manuscript, Sam Houston State University. Huntsville, Texas.

Gergen, K. J. (1985). The social constructionist movement in modern psychology. *American Psychologist, 40,* 266–275.

Gergen, K. J., Ellsworth, P., Maslach, C., & Seipel, M. (1975). Obligation, donor resources, and reactions to aid in three cultures. *Journal of Personality and Social Psychology, 31,* 390–400.

Goethals, G. R., & Zanna, M. P. (1979). The role of social comparison in choice shifts. *Journal of Personality and Social Psychology, 37,* 1469–1476.

Goldman, A. I. (1970). *A theory of human action.* Princeton, NJ: Princeton University Press.

Gouldner, A. (1960). The norm of reciprocity: A preliminary statement. *American Sociological Review, 25,* 161–178.

Grush, J. E. (1980). Impact of candidate expenditures, regionality, and prior outcomes on the 1976 Democratic presidential primaries. *Journal of Personality and Social Psychology, 38,* 337–347.

Grush, J. E., McKeough, K. L., & Ahlering, R. F. (1978). Extrapolating laboratory exposure experiments to actual political elections. *Journal of Personality and Social Psychology, 36,* 257–270.

Gutowitz, H. (1991). *Cellular automata: Theory and experiment.* Cambridge, MA: MIT Press.

Harackiewicz, J., Abrahams, S., & Wageman, R. (1987). Performance evaluation and intrinsic motivation: the effects of evaluative focus, rewards, and achievement motivation. *Journal of Personality and Social Psychology, 53,* 1015–1023.

Hardin, G. (1968). The tragedy of the commons. *Science, 162,* 1243–1248.

Harkins, S. G., & Jackson, J. M. (1985). The role of evaluation in eliminating social loafing. *Personality and Social Psychology Bulletin, 11,* 457–465.

Harkins, S. G., & Petty, R. (1982). Effects of task difficulty and task uniqueness on social loafing. *Journal of Personality and Social Psychology, 42,* 1214–1229.

Hastie, R., Penrod, S. D., & Pennington, N. (1983). *Inside the jury.* Cambridge, MA: Harvard University Press.

Hegselman, R. (1998). Modeling social dynamics by cellular automata. In W. B. G. Liebrand, A. Nowak, & R. Hegselman (Eds.), *Computer modeling of social processes* (pp. 37–64). London: Sage.

Higgins, E. T. (1987). Self-discrepancy: A theory relating self and affect. *Psychological Review, 94,* 319–340.

Hofling, C. K., Brotzman, E., Dalrymple, S., Graves, N., & Pierce, C. M. (1966). An experimental study of nurse-physician relationships. *Journal of Nervous and Mental Disease, 143,* 171–180.

Insko, C. A., Drenan, S., Solomon, M. R., Smith, R., & Wade, T. J. (1983). Conformity as a function of the consistency of positive self-evaluation with being liked and being right. *Journal of Experimental Social Psychology, 19,* 341–358.

Jackson, J. M., & Latané, B. (1981). All alone in front of all those people: Stage fright as a function of number and type of co-performers and audience. *Journal of Personality and Social Psychology, 40,* 73–85.

Janis, I. L. (1982). *Victims of groupthink* (2nd ed.). Boston: Houghton Mifflin.

Jones, E. E. (1964). *Ingratiation.* New York: Appleton-Century.

Jones, E. E., & Davis, K. E. (1965). From acts to dispositions: The attribution process in person perception. In L. Berkowitz (Ed.), *Advances in experimental social psychology* (Vol. 2, pp. 220–266). New York: Academic.

Jones, E. E., & Wortman, C. (1973). *Ingratiation: An attributional approach.* Morristown, NJ: General Learning Corporation.

Kelley, H. H. (1967). Attribution in social psychology. *Nebraska Symposium on Motivation, 15,* 419–422.

Kelley, H. H., & Thibaut, J. W. (1978). *Interpersonal relations: A theory of interdependence.* New York: Wiley Inter-Science.

Kiesler, C. A. (1971). *The psychology of commitment.* New York: Academic.

Kiesler, C. A., & Kiesler, S. B. (1976). *Conformity* (2nd ed.). Reading, MA: Addison-Wesley.

Kiesler, C. A., & Pallak, M. S. (1975). Minority influence: The effect of majority reactionaries and defectors, and minority and majority compromisers, upon majority opinion and attraction. *European Journal of Social Psychology, 5,* 237–256.

Kilham, W., & Mann, L. (1974). Level of destructive obedience as function of transmitter and executant roles in the Milgram obedience paradigm. *Journal of Personality and Social Psychology, 29,* 696–702.

Kofta, M., Weary, G., & Sedek, G. (Eds.). (1998). *Personal control in action.* New York: Plenum.

Kravitz, D. A., & Martin, B. (1986). Ringelman rediscovered: The original article. *Journal of Personality and Social Psychology, 50,* 936–941.

Kruglanski, A. W. (1975). The endogenous-exogenous partition in attribution theory. *Psychological Review, 82,* 387–406.

LaFrance, M. (1985). Postural mirroring and intergroup relations. *Personality and Social Psychology Bulletin, 11,* 207–217.

Lamm, H., & Ochssmann, R. (1972). Factors limiting the generality of the risky-shift phenomenon. *European Journal of Social Psychology, 2,* 99–102.

Lamm, H., & Sauer, C. (1974). Discussion-induced shift towards higher demands in negotiation. *European Journal of Social Psychology, 4,* 85–88.

Langer, E. J. (1978). Rethinking the role of thought in social interaction. In J. H. Harvey, W. Ickes, & R. F. Kidd (Eds.), *New directions in attribution research* (Vol. 2, pp. 35–58). Hillsdale, NJ: Erlbaum.

Latané, B. (1981). The psychology of social impact. *American Psychologist, 36,* 343–356.

Latané, B., & Darley, J. M. (1970). *The unresponsive bystander: Why doesn't he help?* New York: Appleton-Century-Crofts.

Latané, B., Liu, J., Nowak, A., Bonavento, M., & Zheng, L. (1995). Distance matters: Physical space and social influence. *Personality and Social Psychology Bulletin, 21,* 795–805.

Latané, B., & Nowak, A. (1994). Attitudes as catastrophes: From dimensions to categories with increasing involvement. In R. R. Vallacher & A. Nowak (Eds.), *Dynamical systems in social psychology* (pp. 219–249). San Diego, CA: Academic.

Latané, B., & Nowak, A. (1997). The causes of polarization and clustering in social groups. *Progress in Communication Sciences, 13,* 43–75.

Latané, B., Nowak, A., & Liu, J. (1994). Measuring emergent social phenomena: Dynamism, polarization and clustering as order parameters of social systems. *Behavioral Science, 39,* 1–24.

Latané, B., Williams, K., & Harkins, S. (1979). Many hands make light work: The causes and consequences of social loafing. *Journal of Personality and Social Psychology, 37,* 822–832.

Laughlin, P. R., & Ellis, A. L. (1986). Demonstrability and social combination processes on mathematical intellective tasks. *Journal of Experimental Social Psychology, 22,* 177–189.

Le Bon, G. (1960). *The crowd.* New York: Viking.

Lepper, M. R., & Greene, D. (Eds.). (1978). *The hidden costs of reward.* Hillsdale, NJ: Erlbaum.

Lerner, M. J., & Mikula, G. (Eds.). (1994). *Entitlement and the affectional bond: Justice in close relationships.* New York: Plenum.

Levine, J. M. (1996, October). *Solomon Asch's legacy for group research.* Paper presented in Plenary Session (S. Fiske, Chair) Honoring the Memory of Solomon Asch. Society for Experimental Social Psychology, Toronto, Canada.

Levine, J. M., & Ranelli, C. J. (1978). Majority reaction to shifting and stable attitudinal deviates. *European Journal of Social Psychology, 8,* 55–70.

Lewenstein, M., Nowak, A., & Latané, B. (1993). Statistical mechanics of social impact. *Physics Review A, 45,* 703–716.

Locke, K. S., & Horowitz, L. M. (1990). Satisfaction in interpersonal interactions as a function of similarity level in dysphoria. *Journal of Personality and Social Psychology, 58,* 823–831.

Maass, A., & Clark, R. D. (1984). Hidden impact of minorities: Fifteen years of minority influence research. *Psychological Bulletin, 95,* 428–450.

Maass, A., Clark, R. K., & Haberkorn, G. (1982). The effects of differential ascribed category membership and norms on minority influence. *European Journal of Social Psychology, 12,* 89–104.

Mack, D., & Rainey, D. (1990). Female applicants' grooming and personnel selection. *Journal of Personality and Social Psychology, 5,* 399–407.

Markus, H. R., & Kitayama, S. (1991). Culture and the self: Implications for cognition, emotion, and motivation. *Psychological Review, 98,* 224–253.

May, R. M. (Ed.). (1981). *Theoretical ecology: Principles and applications.* Oxford, UK: Blackwell Scientific.

Meeus, W. H. J., & Raaijmakers, Q. A. W. (1986). Administrative obedience: Carrying out orders to use psychological-administrative violence. *European Journal of Social Psychology, 16,* 311–324.

Meleshko, K. G. A., & Alden, L. E. (1993). Anxiety and self-disclosure: Toward a motivational model. *Journal of Personality and Social Psychology, 64,* 1000–1009.

Messick, D. M., & Liebrand, V. B. G. (1995). Individual heuristics and the dynamics of cooperation in large groups. *Psychological Review, 102,* 131–145.

Milgram S. (1965). Some conditions of obedience and disobedience to authority. *Human Relations, 18,* 57–75.

Milgram, S. (1974). *Obedience to authority: An experimental view.* New York: Harper & Row.

Miller, D. T. (1999). The norm of self-interest. *American Psychologist, 54,* 1053–1060.

Moscovici, S. (1976). *Social influence and social change.* London: Academic.

Moscovici, S., Lage, E., & Naffrechoux, M. (1969). Influence of a consistent minority on responses of a majority in a color perception task. *Sociometry, 32,* 365–379.

Moscovici, S., & Zavalloni, M. (1969). The group as a polarizer of attitudes. *Journal of Personality and Social Psychology, 12,* 125–135.

Mugny, G. (1982). *The power of minorities.* London: Academic.

Myers, D. G. (1982). Polarizing effects of social interaction. In H. Brandstatter, J. H. Davis, & G. Stocker-Kreichgauer (Eds.), *Group decision making* (pp. 125–161). New York: Academic.

Myers, D. G., & Lamm, H. (1976). The group polarization phenomenon. *Psychological Bulletin, 83,* 602–627.

Newcomb, T. M. (1961). *The acquaintance process.* New York: Holt, Reinhart, & Winston.

Nowak, A., Latané, B., & Lewenstein, M. (1994). Social dilemmas exist in space. In U. Schulz, W. Albers, & U. Mueller (Eds.),

Social dilemmas and cooperation (pp. 114–131). Heidelberg, Germany: Springer-Verlag.

Nowak, A., & Lewenstein, M. (1996). Modeling social change with cellular automata. In R. Hegselman, K. Troitzch, & U. Muller (Eds.), *Modeling and simulation in the social sciences from the philosophy of science point of view* (pp. 249–285). Dordrecht, The Netherlands: Kluwer Academic.

Nowak, A., Lewenstein, M., & Frejlak, P. (1996). Dynamics of public opinion and social change. In R. Hegselman & H. O. Pietgen (Eds.), *Modeling social dynamics: Order, chaos, and complexity* (pp. 54–78). Vienna, Austria: Helbin.

Nowak, A., Lewenstein, M., & Szamrej, J. (1993). Social transitions occur through bubbles. *Scientific American* (Polish version), *12*, 16–25.

Nowak, A., Szamrej, J., & Latané, B. (1990). From private attitude to public opinion: A dynamic theory of social impact. *Psychological Review, 97,* 362–376.

Nowak, A., Urbaniak, J., & Zienkowski, L. (1994). Clustering processes in economic transition. *RECESS Research Bulletin, 3,* 43–61.

Nowak, A., & Vallacher, R. R. (1998a). *Dynamical social psychology.* New York: Guilford.

Nowak, A., & Vallacher, R. R. (1998b). Toward computational social psychology: Cellular automata and neural network models of interpersonal dynamics. In S. J. Read & L. C. Miller (Eds.), *Connectionist models of social reasoning and social behavior* (pp. 277–311). Mahwah, NJ: Erlbaum.

Nowak, A., & Vallacher, R. R. (2001). Societal transition: Toward a dynamical model of social change. In W. Wosinska, R. B. Cialdini, D. W. Barrett, & J. Reykowski (Eds.), *The practice of social influence in multiple cultures* (pp. 151–171). Mahwah, NJ: Erlbaum.

Nowak, A., Vallacher, R. R., & Burnstein, E. (1998). Computational social psychology: A neural network approach to interpersonal dynamics. In W. B. G. Liebrand, A. Nowak, & R. Hegselman (Eds.), *Computer modeling of social processes* (pp. 97–125). London: Sage.

Nowak, A., Vallacher, R. R., Tesser, A., & Borkowski, W. (2000). Society of self: The emergence of collective properties in self-structure. *Psychological Review, 102,* 39–61.

Nowak, A., Vallacher, R. R., & Zochowski, M. (2002). The emergence of personality: Personal stability through interpersonal synchronization. In D. Cervone & W. Mischel (Eds.), *Advances in personality science* (Vol. 1, pp. 292–331). New York: Guilford.

Pallak, M. S., Cook, D. A., & Sullivan, J. J. (1980). Commitment and energy conservation. *Applied Social Psychology Annual, 1,* 235–253.

Pruitt, D. G. (1971). Choice shifts in discussion: An introductory view. *Journal of Personality and Social Psychology, 20,* 339–360.

Raven, B. H. (1992). A power/interaction model of interpersonal influence: French and Raven thirty years later. *Journal of Social Behavior and Personality, 7,* 217–244.

Raven, B. H. (1993). The bases of power: Origins and recent developments. *Journal of Social Issues, 49,* 227–251.

Regan, D. T. (1971). Effects of a favor and liking on compliance. *Journal of Experimental Social Psychology, 7,* 627–639.

Rosenbaum, M. E. (1980). Cooperation and competition. In P. B. Paulus (Ed.), *The psychology of group influence* (pp. 23–41). Hillsdale, NJ: Erlbaum.

Rotter, J. B. (1966). Generalized expectancies for internal versus external control of reinforcement. *Psychological Monographs, 80* (1, Whole No. 609).

Rudich, E. A., & Vallacher, R. R. (1999). To belong or to self-enhance? Motivational bases for choosing interaction partners. *Personality and Social Psychology Bulletin, 25,* 1387–1404.

Rusbult, C. E., & Martz, J. M. (1995). Remaining in an abusive relationship: An investment model analysis of nonvoluntary dependence. *Personality and Social Psychology Bulletin, 21,* 558–571.

Schachter, S. (1959). *The psychology of affiliation: Experimental studies of the sources of gregariousness.* Stanford, CA: Stanford University Press.

Schein, E. (1956). The Chinese indoctrination program for prisoners of war: A study of attempted "brainwashing." *Psychiatry, 19,* 149–172.

Schlenker, B. R. (1980). *Impression management.* Monterey, CA: Brooks/Cole.

Schulz, U., Alberts, W., & Mueller, U. (Eds.). (1994). *Social dilemmas and cooperation.* Heidelberg, Germany: Springer.

Schuster, H. G. (1984). *Deterministic chaos.* Vienna, Austria: Physik Verlag.

Seligman, M. E. P. (1975). *On depression, development, and death.* San Francisco: Freeman.

Shaver, K. G. (1985). *The attribution of blame.* New York: Springer-Verlag.

Shelling, T. (1969). Models of segregation. *American Economic Review, 59,* 488–493.

Shelling, T. (1971). Dynamic models of segregation. *Journal of Mathematical Sociology, 1,* 143–186.

Sherif, M. (1936). *The psychology of social norms.* New York: Harper.

Skinner, B. F. (1971). *Beyond freedom and dignity.* New York: Knopf.

Smolowe, J. (1990, November 26). Contents require immediate attention. *Time,* p. 64.

Staats, A. W. (1975). *Social behaviorism.* Homewood, IL: Dorsey.

Steiner, I. D. (1972). *Group process and productivity.* New York: Academic.

Stewart, J. E. (1980). Defendant's attractiveness as a factor in the outcome of criminal trials: An observational study. *Journal of Applied Psychology, 10,* 348–361.

Stoner, J. A. F. (1961). *A comparison of individual and group decisions involving risk.* Unpublished master's thesis, Massachusetts Institute of Technology, Cambridge.

Suedfeld, P., Bochner, S., & Matas, C. (1971). Petitioner's attire and petition signing by peace demonstrators: A field experiment. *Journal of Applied Social Psychology, 58,* 171–181.

Swann, W. B., Jr. (1990). To be adored or to be known? The interplay of self-enhancement and self-verification. In E. T. Higgins & R. M. Sorrentino (Eds.), *Handbook of motivation and cognition: Foundations of social behavior* (Vol. 2, pp. 408–448). New York: Guilford.

Swann, W. B., Jr., & Ely, R. J. (1984). A battle of wills: Self-verification versus behavioral confirmation. *Journal of Personality and Social Psychology, 46,* 1287–1302.

Tanford, S., & Penrod, S. (1984). Social influence model: A formal integration of research on majority and minority influence processes. *Psychological Bulletin, 95,* 189–225.

Taylor, S. E., & Brown, J. D. (1988). Illusion and well-being: A social psychological perspective on mental health. *Psychological Bulletin, 103,* 193–210.

Taylor, S. E., Peplau, L. A., & Sears, D. O. (1997). *Social psychology* (9th ed.). Upper Saddle River, NJ: Prentice-Hall.

Tesser, A. (1988). Toward a self-evaluation maintenance model of social behavior. In L. Berkowitz (Ed.), *Advances in experimental social psychology* (Vol. 21, pp. 181–227). New York: Academic.

Thagard, P., & Kunda, Z. (1998). Making sense of people: Coherence mechanisms. In S. J. Read & L. C. Miller (Eds.), *Connectionist models of social reasoning and social behavior* (pp. 3–26). Mahwah, NJ: Erlbaum.

Thibaut, J. W., & Kelley, H. H. (1959). *The social psychology of groups.* New York: Wiley.

Triplett, H. (1898). The dynamogenic factors in pace making and competition. *American Journal of Psychology, 9,* 507–533.

Trope, Y. (1986). Identification an inferential processes in dispositional attribution. *Psychological Review, 93,* 239–257.

Turner, R. H., & Killian, L. M. (1972). *Collective behavior* (2nd ed.). Englewood Cliffs, NJ: Prentice-Hall.

Ulam, S. (1952). Random processes and transformations. *Proceedings of International Congress of Mathematics, 2,* 264–275.

Vallacher, R. R. (1980). An introduction to self theory. In D. M. Wegner & R. R. Vallacher (Eds.), The self in social psychology (pp. 3–30). New York: Oxford University Press.

Vallacher, R. R. (1993). Mental calibration: Forging a working relationship between mind and action. In D. M. Wegner & J. W. Pennebaker (Eds.), *Handbook of mental control* (pp. 443–472). Englewood Cliffs, NJ: Prentice-Hall.

Vallacher, R. R., & Nowak, A. (1994). The chaos in social psychology. In R. R. Vallacher & A. Nowak (Eds.), *Dynamical systems in social psychology* (pp. 1–16). San Diego, CA: Academic.

Vallacher, R. R., & Nowak, A. (1997). The emergence of dynamical social psychology. *Psychological Inquiry, 8,* 73–99.

Vallacher, R. R., Nowak, A., & Kaufman, J. (1994). Intrinsic dynamics of social judgment. *Journal of Personality and Social Psychology, 67,* 20–34.

Vallacher, R. R., Nowak, A., Markus, J., & Strauss, J. (1998). Dynamics in the coordination of mind and action. In M. Kofta, G. Weary, & G. Sedek (Eds.), *Personal control in action* (pp. 27–59). New York: Plenum.

Vallacher, R. R., & Selz, K. (1991). Who's to blame? Action identification in allocating responsibility for alleged rape. *Social Cognition, 9,* 194–219.

Vallacher, R. R., & Solodky, M. (1979). Objective self awareness, standards of evaluation, and moral behavior. *Journal of Experimental Social Psychology, 15,* 254–262.

Vallacher, R. R., & Wegner, D. M. (1985). *A theory of action identification.* Hillsdale, NJ: Erlbaum.

Vallacher, R. R., & Wegner, D. M. (1987). What do people think they're doing? Action identification and human behavior. *Psychological Review, 94,* 3–15.

Vallacher, R. R., & Wegner, D. M. (1989). Levels of personal agency: Individual variation in action identification. *Journal of Personality and Social Psychology, 57,* 660–671.

Vinokur, A. (1971). A review and theoretical analysis of the effects of group processes upon individual and group decisions involving risk. *Psychological Bulletin, 76,* 231–250.

Vinokur, A., & Burnstein, E. (1974). Effects of partially shared persuasive arguments on group-induced shifts: A group problem-solving approach. *Journal of Personality and Social Psychology, 29,* 305–315.

Volpato, C., Maass, A., Mucchi-Faina, A., & Vitti, E. (1990). Minority influence and categorization. *European Journal of Social Psychology, 20,* 119–132.

von Neumann, J. (1966). *Theory of self-reproducing automata.* Champaign: University of Illinois Press.

Wallach, M. A., Kogan, N., & Bem, D. J. (1962). Group influence on individual risk taking. *Journal of Abnormal Social Psychology, 1,* 1–19.

Weldon, E., & Mustari, L. (1988). Felt dispensability in groups of coactors: The effects of shared responsibility and explicit anonymity on cognitive effort. *Organizational Behavior and Human Decision Processes, 41,* 330–351.

Wicklund, R. A., & Brehm, J. W. (1976). *Perspectives on cognitive dissonance.* Hillsdale, NJ: Erlbaum.

Williams, K., Harkins, S., & Latané, B. (1981). Identifiably as a deterrent to social loafing: Two cheering experiments. *Journal of Personality and Social Psychology, 40,* 303–311.

Witkin, H. A., Dyk, R. B., Faterson, H. F., Goodenough, D. R., & Karp, S. A. (1962). *Psychological differentiation.* New York: Wiley.

Wolf, S., & Latané, B. (1985). Conformity, innovation, and the psycho-social laws. In S. Moscovici, G. Mugny, & E. Van

Avermaet (Eds.), *Perspectives on minority influence* (pp. 201–215). Cambridge, UK: Cambridge University Press.

Wolfram, S. (Ed.) (1986). *Theory and applications of cellular automata.* Singapore: World Scientific.

Woodside, A. G., & Davenport, J. W. (1974). Effects of salesman similarity and expertise on consumer purchasing behavior. *Journal of Marketing Research, 11,* 198–202.

Zajonc, R. B. (1965). Social facilitation. *Science, 149,* 269–274.

Zajonc, R. B. (1980). Cognition and social cognition: A historical perspective. In L. Festinger (Ed.), *Retrospections on social psychology* (pp. 180–204). New York: Oxford University Press.

Zimbardo, P. G. (1970). The human choice: Individuation, reason, and order versus deindividuation, impulse, and chaos. In W. J. Arnold & D. Levine (Eds.), *Nebraska Symposium on Motivation, 1969* (pp. 237–307). Lincoln: University of Nebraska Press.

CHAPTER 17

Environmental Psychology

GABRIEL MOSER AND DAVID UZZELL

WHY PSYCHOLOGY NEEDS
ENVIRONMENTAL PSYCHOLOGY

Introduction

This review, like the model of psychology we advocate, looks to the past, present, and future of environmental psychology. The chapter begins with a discussion of the importance of the socioenvironmental context for human behavior. Having demonstrated that the environment, far from being a silent witness to human actions, is an integral part of the plot, the chapter continues with an examination of the nature and scope of environmental psychology. Both its interdisciplinary origins and its applied emphasis have conspired to prevent a straightforward and uncontentious definition of environmental psychology. We review some of these and suggest how recent definitions are beginning to adopt a more inclusive, holistic, and transactional perspective on people-environment relations. The next section discusses the various spatial scales at which environmental psychologists operate—from the micro level such as personal space and individual rooms, public/ private spaces, and public spaces to the macro level of the global environment. This incorporates research on the home, the workplace, the visual impact of buildings, the negative effects of cities, the restorative role of nature, and

environmental attitudes and sustainable behaviors. The third section takes three key theoretical perspectives that have informed environmental psychology—determinism, interactionism, and transactionalism—and uses these as an organizing framework to examine various theories used by environmental psychologists: arousal theory, environmental load, and adaptation level theory within a behaviorist and determinist paradigm; control, stress adaptation, behavioral elasticity, cognitive mapping, and environmental evaluation within an interactionist paradigm; and behavior settings, affordance theory and theories of place, place identity, and place attachment within transactionalism.

The fourth section looks to the future of environmental psychology by challenging the assumptions and limiting perspectives of present research. The issues at the forefront of the political and environmental agenda at the beginning of the twenty-first century—human rights, well-being and quality of life, globalization, and sustainability—need to be addressed and tackled by environmental psychologists in a way that incorporates both cross-cultural and temporal dimensions. The impact of environmental psychology may be enhanced if researchers work within the larger cultural and temporal context that conditions people's perceptions and behaviors within any given environment. This concluding section discusses some of the work being undertaken by

unearthed in research in the real world. Kurt Lewin's advocacy of theory-driven practical research ought to have a resonance with environmental psychologists.

The conceptual model by which our perceptions, representations, and behaviors are interdependent with the physical and social environment has frequently been mentioned in psychology. In their work on perception, Brunswik (1959) and Gibson (1950) referred to the role of the environment; Tolman (1948) used the concept of the *mental map* to describe the cognitive mechanisms that accompany maze learning; and in the domain of the psychology of form Lewin (1951) elaborated the theory of the environmental field, conceived as a series of forces that operate on the individual. Lynch's study of *The Image of the City* (1960), although by an urban planner, was another major landmark in the early years of environment-behavior research. The first milestones of environmental psychology date from the late 1960s (Barker, 1968; Craik, 1970; Lee, 1968; Proshansky, Ittelson, & Rivlin, 1970). The intellectual and international origins of environmental psychology are considerably broader than many, typically North American, textbooks suggest (Bonnes & Secchiaroli, 1995).

Although environmental psychology can justly claim to be a subdiscipline in its own right, it clearly has an affinity with other branches of psychology, especially social psychology, but also cognitive, organizational, and developmental psychology. Examples of where environmental psychology has been informed by and contributed to social psychology are intergroup relations, group functioning, performance, identity, conflict, and bystander behavior. However, social psychology often minimizes the role of the environment as a physical and social setting and treats it as simply the stage on which individuals and groups act rather than as an integral part of the plot. Environmental psychology adds an important dimension to social psychology by making sense of differences in behavior and perception according to contextual variables—differences that can be explained only by reference to environmental contingencies.

Although there are strong links to other areas of psychology, environmental psychology is unique among the psychological sciences in terms of the relationship it has forged with the social (e.g., sociology, human ecology, demography), environmental (e.g., environmental sciences, geography), and design (e.g., architecture, planning, landscape architecture, interior design) disciplines.

Because of the difficulties of defining environmental psychology, many writers have sought instead to characterize or describe it, as we ourselves did in part earlier. The most recent of these can be found in the fifth edition of Bell, Greene, Fisher, and Baum's (2001) textbook *Environmental Psychology*. They suggested that (a) environmental psychology studies environment-behavior relationships as a unit, rather than separating them into distinct and self-contained elements; (b) environment-behavior relationships are really interrelationships; (c) there is unlikely to be a sharp distinction between applied and basic research; (d) it is part of an international and interdisciplinary field of study; and (e) it employs an eclectic range of methodologies. But description is not a substitute for definition. Leaving aside Proshansky et al.'s (1970, p. 5) oft-quoted "environmental psychology is what environmental psychologists do," the same authors suggested that "in the long run, the only really satisfactory way . . . is in terms of theory. And the simple fact is that as yet there is no adequate theory, or even the beginnings of a theory, of environmental psychology on which such a definition might be based" (p. 5). By 1978, Bell, Fisher, and Loomis, in the first edition of *Environmental Psychology*, cautiously suggested that it is "the study of the interrelationship between behavior and the built and natural environment," although they preferred to opt for the initial Proshansky et al. conclusion. Other, not dissimilar, definitions followed: "an area of psychology whose focus of investigation is the interrelationship between the physical environment and human behavior and experience" (Holahan, 1982, p. 3); "is concerned with the interactions and relationships between people and their environment" (Proshansky, 1990); "the discipline that is concerned with the interactions and relationships between people and their environments" (McAndrew, 1993, p. 2).

The problem with some of these definitions is that although they describe what environmental psychologists do, unfortunately they also hint at what other disciplines do as well. For example, many (human) geographers could probably live quite comfortably with these definitions. By 1995, Veitch and Arkkelin were no less specific and perhaps even enigmatic with the introduction of the word "enhancing": "a behavioural science that investigates, with an eye towards enhancing, the interrelationships between the physical environment and human behaviour."

These are clearly not the only definitions of environmental psychology, but they are reasonably representative. The definitions have various noteworthy features. First, because the area is necessarily interdisciplinary, the core theoretical perspectives that should inform our approaches have sometimes been minimized. Thus Bonnes and Secchiaroli (1995) drew attention to the need to define the field as a function of the psychological processes studied. Most definitions of environmental psychology focus on the relationship between the environment and behavior, yet paradoxically most of the research in environmental psychology has not been about behavior but perceptions of and attitudes toward the environment and attitudes toward behavior in the environment. Second, many of the definitions refer to relationships between people and the physical or built environment. Proshansky acknowledged that this was problematic because it fails to recognize the importance of the social environment. The distinction between built and natural environments is becoming increasing untenable given the mutual dependency and reciprocity that exist between them, especially within the context of the sustainability debate. Finally, many of the definitions talk about the individual interacting with the environment. Unfortunately, this ignores or minimizes the social dimension of environmental experience and behavior. This is a strange omission given the strong influence of social psychology on the area, although it is perhaps a reflection of the individualistic nature of much social psychology.

Gifford (1997) more usefully offered the following: "Environmental psychology is the study of transactions between individuals and their physical settings. In these transactions, individuals change the environment and their behaviour and experiences are changed by the environment. Environmental psychology includes research and practice aimed at making buildings more humane and improving our relationship with the natural environment" (p. 1). This far more inclusive definition captures key concepts such as experience, change, people-environment interactions and transactions, and natural versus built environments. As long ago as 1987, Stokols (1987) suggested that "the translation of a transactional world view into operational strategies for theory development and research . . . poses an ambitious but promising agenda for future work in environmental psychology" (p. 41). The essence of a transactional approach, Stokols continued, is "its emphasis on the dynamic interplay between people and their everyday environmental settings, or 'contexts'" (p. 42).

DOMAINS OF ENVIRONMENTAL PSYCHOLOGY

Environmental psychology deals with the relationship between individuals and their life spaces. That includes not only the environment to provide us with all what we need to survive but also the spaces in which to appreciate, understand, and act to fulfill higher needs and aspirations.

The individual's cognitions and behaviors gain meaning in relation to the environment in which these cognitions or behaviors are developed. Consequently, environmental psychologists are confronted with the same issues that concern all psychologists. The basic domains of environmental psychology include (a) environmental perceptions and cognitions, (b) environmental values, attitudes, and assessment, and (c) behavioral issues. It studies these processes in relation to the environmental settings and situations in which they occur. For instance, environmental perceptions are not typically studied with the aim of identifying general laws concerning different aspects of the perceived object. Environmental perception deals with built or natural landscape perception with an emphasis on sites treated as entities (Ittelson, 1973); the perceiver is considered part of the scene and projects onto it his or her aspirations and goals, which will have an aesthetic dimension as well as a utilitarian function. The question the perceiver asks in appraising a landscape is not just "Do I like the appearance of this landscape?" but also "What can this landscape do for me (i.e., what function does it serve)?" (Lee, 2001). Likewise, interpersonal behavior within an environmental psychology context is studied in order that we might better understand how environmental settings influence these relationships (e.g., urban constraints on the frequency of relational behavior with friends or relatives; Moser, 1992).

Because of its very focus, environmental psychology has been and remains above all a *psychology of space* to the extent that it analyzes individuals' and communities' perceptions, attitudes, and behaviors in explicit relation to the physical and social contexts within which people and communities exist. Notions of space and place occupy a central position. The discipline operates, then, at several levels of spatial reference, enabling the investigation of people-environment interactions (at the individual, group, or societal level) at each level. Reference to the spatial dimension makes it possible to take into account different levels of analysis:

1. *Private spaces (individual level):* personal and private space, dwelling, housing, workplace, office
2. *Public/private environments (neighborhood-community level):* semipublic spaces, blocks of flats, the neighborhood, parks, green spaces
3. *Public environments (individual-community level, inhabitants):* involving both built spaces (villages, towns, cities) as well as the natural environment (the countryside, landscape, etc.)
4. *The global environment (societal level):* the environment in its totality, both the built and the natural environment, natural resources

Environmental psychology analyzes and characterizes *people-environment interactions and/or transactions* at these different environmental levels. These relations can best be understood through perception, needs, opportunities, and means of control.

Private Spaces

Personal space and privacy are important for individual and community well-being and quality of life. Altman (1975, p. 18) defined privacy as the "selective control of access to the self or one's group." Thus, privacy implicates control over the immediate environment. It is important for the individual to be able to organize and personalize space. Privacy represents a dynamic process of openness and closeness to others (Altman & Chemers, 1980). Thus, privacy adjustments may be established with physical or even psychological barriers wherever individuals seek to isolate or protect themselves from the intrusion of others. This may be important in one's home, but also in the work environment or during leisure activities (e.g., on the beach). Privacy involves not only visual but also auditory exclusivity (Sundstrom, Town, Rice, Osborn, & Brill, 1994). Steady or transitionally occupied places produce place attachment and are often accompanied with ties to personal objects such as furniture, pictures, and souvenirs that mark the appropriation (Korosec-Serfaty, 1976). Appropriation can be defined as a particular affective relation to an object. The appropriated object may become part of the identity of the individual (Barbey, 1976). The appropriation of space has essentially a social function in the sense that the individual or the group marks control over the space (Proshansky, 1976), which in turn produces a feeling of security. When appropriation is not shared with others, or only with one's group, control is absolute.

The use of space in the home or the office environment has produced a variety of studies. The intended function of a room (e.g., kitchen, dormitory, etc.) implies a specific design and determines how the space will be used. There are considerable individual and cultural differences in the use of space in one's home (Kent, 1991; Newell, 1998; Rapoport, 1969).

Personal space is defined as the invisible boundary surrounding each individual into which others may not intrude without causing discomfort (Hall, 1966). Personal space regulates interactions, and its extension depends on environmental variables. Its functions are twofold: protection, in which it acts as a buffer against various interpersonal threats, and communication purpose, in which it determines which sensory communication-channel (touch, visual, or verbal) can and should be used. Thus, interpersonal distances are cues for understanding the specific relationship of two individuals. Research has looked at various social determinants of personal space such as culture and ethnicity, age and gender (e.g., Aiello, 1987; Crawford & Unger, 2000), psychological

factors (Srivastava & Mandal, 1990), and physical factors (Altman & Vinsel, 1977; Evans, Lepore, Shejwal, & Palsane, 1998; Jain, 1993).

In contrast to personal space, territoriality is visibly delimited by boundaries and tends to be home or workplace centered. It is a demarcated and defended space and invariably is an expression of identity and attachment to a place (Sommer, 1969). Territories are controlled spaces that serve to enable the personalization and regularization of intrusion. Therefore, territoriality has an essential function in providing and promoting security, predictability, order, and stability in one's life. Altman and Chemers (1980) identified three types or levels of territory: primary territories (e.g., home or office space), where control is permanent and high and personalization is manifest; secondary territories (e.g., the classroom or open plan office), where control, ownership, and personalization are temporary; and public territories (e.g., the street, the mall), where there is competition for use, intrusion is difficult to control, and personalization is largely absent.

Public/Private Environments

The Home Environment

Analyses at this level deal with the immediate environment of the individual's living space. These could be rows of houses or apartment blocks, the immediate neighborhood, the workplace, or the leisure areas in the immediate surroundings of the home (e.g., parks and green areas). These areas are referred to as *semipublic* or *semiprivate* spaces, which means that the control over them is shared within a community.

A great deal of research in environmental psychology concerns the immediate home environment. Concepts like attachment to place and sense of community contribute to our understanding of how individuals and groups create bonds to a specific place. Although the size of the habitable space is essential for residential satisfaction, other aspects of the living conditions modulate its importance as well. Residents enhance the value of their neighborhood through the transactional relationships they establish with their place of residence. For those who have already acquired basic living conditions and who have an income that allows them to achieve a good quality of life, the agreeable character of the neighborhood has a modulating effect on satisfaction concerning available space in the dwelling. The affective relationship with the dwelling and anchorage in childhood seem to play an important role. Giuliani (1991) found that affective feelings toward the home were attributable to changing conceptions of the self in relation to the home over the life span.

The feeling of being at home is closely connected to a feeling of well-being and varies with the extent of the spatial representation of the neighborhood. A spatially narrow representation is correlated with a weak affective investment in the neighborhood (Fleury-Bahi, 1997, 1998). The degree of satisfaction felt with three of a neighborhood's environmental attributes (green spaces, aesthetics of the built framework, and degree of noise) has an effect on the intensity of the affectivity developed toward it, as well as feelings of well-being. The feeling of being at home in one's neighborhood is linked to the frequency of encounters, the extent of the sphere of close relations, the nature of local relationships, and satisfaction with them. Low and Altman (1992) argued that the origin and development of place attachment is varied and complex, being influenced by biological, environmental, psychological, and sociocultural processes. Furthermore, the social relations that a place signifies may be more important to feelings of attachment than the place itself.

Besides the home and neighborhood environments, other domains involve a problematic congruence between people and their environment (e.g., work, classroom, and institutional environments such as hospitals, prisons, and homes for children or the elderly). How can these environments be designed to meet the needs of their occupants? We illustrate this by examining one setting—the workplace.

Environmental Psychology in the Workplace

Increasing attention is being paid to the design of the workplace so that it matches more effectively the organization's goals and cultural aspirations as well as employee needs and job demands and performance. There has been a long history of research into the workplace (Becker, 1981; Becker and Steele, 1995; Sundstrom, 1987; Wineman, 1986). Indeed, the famous *Hawthorne effect* first noted in the 1920s emerged from a study of the effect of illumination on productivity. Since then there have been many studies examining the ambient work environment and investigating the impact of sound, light, furniture layout, and design on performance and job satisfaction. It is now recognized that the environment, space, and design can operate at a subtler level and have an impact on issues such as status, reward, and the promotion of corporate culture.

Decisions about space use and design should be examined for their embedded assumptions regarding how they will enhance or detract from the organization's goals and values. In other words, whose assumptions underlie the design and management of space, and what are the implications of space-planning decisions? The relationship between the organization's culture, the physical planning of the buildings or offices, and the feel, look, and use of the facilities becomes most apparent especially when there is a mismatch. A mismatch often occurs when a new building is planned according to criteria such as these: How many people should it accommodate? How many square feet should it occupy? How much equipment should it have? How should it look to visitors? Questions typically posed and addressed by environmental psychologists have a different emphasis: Will the designs and space layout enhance or detract from the desired corporate work styles? Is the organization prepared to accept that employees have different working styles and that these should be catered to in the provision of space and facilities? How much control does the organization currently exert over its employees' use of time and space? To what extent are employees permitted to modify their own environment so that it enables them to do their job more effectively? In what way, for whom, and how does the management and design permit, encourage, or enhance the following: personal and group recognition, environmental control (heating, lighting, ventilation, amount and type of furniture, personalized space), social integration and identity, communication within the working group, communication with other working groups, and appropriate levels of privacy? How are issues such as individual and group identity; individual capacities, needs, and preferences; and working patterns reflected in space planning and the allocation of environmental resources? Is space and resource allocation used as a means of reflecting and rewarding status and marking distinctions between job classifications? Is the organization prepared to redefine its understanding of equity and provide space and facilities on the basis of need rather than status?

There are many ways of looking at the relationship between corporate culture and physical facilities. The effective use of the organization's resources lies not in fitting the staff to the workplace but in recognizing that there will be a transaction between staff and workplace so that if the employee cannot or will not be forced into the setting, they will either attempt to modify the setting so that it does approximate more closely their working needs and preferences or become dissatisfied, disaffected, and unproductive. For example, instead of assigning an employee just one space, consideration should be given to permitting if not encouraging. Instead of working in just one place (e.g., a desk), some companies are giving employees access to a number of spaces (e.g., hot desking) that will allow them to undertake their tasks and with more satisfaction and effectiveness. Within such an arrangement staff cannot claim territorial rights over specific spaces but are regarded as temporary lodgers for as long as they need that space: informal privacy spaces for talking to clients and colleagues; quiet, comfortable spaces for writing reports; workstations for undertaking word processing and data analysis; meeting rooms for discussing issues with colleagues; small refreshment areas for informal socializing; and quiet, private telephone suites for confidential matters. There are various possibilities—the type of spaces will depend on the type of work and how it can be undertaken effectively.

Public Environments

Cities are a human creation. They concentrate novelty, intensity, and choice more so than do smaller towns and villages. They provide a variety of cultural, recreational, and educational facilities. Equally, it is argued that cities have become more dangerous because they concentrate all sorts of crime and delinquency and are noisy, overcrowded, and polluted. Three topics addressed at this environmental level are discussed here: the negative effects of cities, the visual impact of buildings, and the restorative role of nature.

The Negative Effects of Cities

Living in metropolitan areas is considered to be stressful. The analysis of behavior in cities has concentrated on noise, density, living conditions (difficulty of access to services), high crime, and delinquency rates. A series of conceptual considerations have been proposed to understand the consequences of these stressors for typical urban behavior, such as paying less attention to others and being less affiliative and less helpful. Environmental overload, environmental stress, and behavioral constraint all point to the potentially negative effects of living in cities as compared with living in small towns. Environmental conditions like noise and crowding not only affect general urban conditions but also have a specific effect on behavior. A comparison of behavior at the same site but under different environmental conditions (noisy-quiet, high-low density) shows a more marked negative effect in the case of high noise and high density (Moser, 1992). Higher crime and delinquency rates are commonly explained by the numerous opportunities that the city offers, along with deindividuation (Zimbardo, 1969). The probability of being recognized is lower, and the criminal can escape without being identified. Fear of crime (which is not necessarily correlated with objective crime rates) restricts people's behavior by making them feel vulnerable. It is exacerbated by an environment that appears to be uncared for (e.g., through littering and vandalism).

Whereas the effect of air pollution on health (e.g., respiratory problems for children and the elderly) is well documented (Godlee & Walker, 1992; Lewis, Baddeley, Bonham, & Lovett, 1970), it has little direct effect on the behavior of urban residents. The relationship between exposure to air pollution and health is mediated by perceptions of the exposure (Elliot, Cole, Krueger, Voorberg, & Wakefield, 1999). The extent to which people feel that they can control the source of air pollution, for instance, influences their response to this pollution. Perceptions of air pollution are also important because they influence people's responses to certain strategies for air pollution management. Whether people perceive air pollution as a problem is of course related to the actual existence of the problem. Generally, people are more likely to perceive environmental problems when they can hear (noise), see (smoke), smell, or feel them. Another important source of information is the media because the media's interpretation of pollution levels may have a social amplification effect and influence public perceptions and attitudes (Kasperson et al., 1988). People believe that heavy-goods vehicles, commuters, and business traffic are the principal sources of urban air pollution. On the other hand, school traffic is often seen as one of the most important causes of transport problems. It is often argued that reducing school trips by car would make a significant difference to urban transportation problems. Paradoxically, although considered to be a major source of congestion, school traffic is not seen as a major source of pollution (Gatersleben & Uzzell, 2000).

The Visual Impact of Buildings

Most of us live in cities. The architecture that surrounds us is more than public sculpture. Research on the visual impact of buildings demonstrates perhaps more than any other area that different user groups perceive and evaluate the environment dissimilarly. The criteria used most widely by the public to assess the visual impact of a building is how contextually compatible it appears to be with the surrounding environment (Uzzell, 2000b). Architects and their clients, however, tend to value more highly the distinctiveness and contrast of buildings. Although there is a place for both, the indication is that there are diverging points of view on what constitutes a desirable building between groups of people (Hubbard, 1994, 1996). Groat (1994) found differences of opinion to be greatest between the public and architects and most similar between the public and planners. Several studies (e.g., Purcell & Nasar, 1992; Nasar, 1993) have demonstrated that architects and educated laypeople differ in their preferences for building styles and in the meanings that they infer from various styles. For example, Devlin and Nasar (1989) found that architects rated more unusual and distinctive residential architecture as more meaningful, clear, coherent, pleasant, and relaxing, whereas nonarchitects judged more conventional and popular residential architecture as such. Similarly, Nasar

(1993) found that not only did architects differ from the public in their preferences and in the meanings that they inferred from different styles, but they also misjudged the preferences of the public.

Individual design features such as color, texture, illumination, and the shape and placement of windows can have a significant impact on evaluations. Overall, such research findings regarding order (including coherence, compatibility, congruity, legibility, and clarity) have been reasonably consistent; increases in order have been found to enhance the evaluative quality of cities (Nasar, 1979), downtown street scenes (Nasar, 1984), and residential scenes (Nasar, 1981, 1983).

The Restorative Role of Nature

Despite city living, many urban residents desire a private house with garden or at least to be able to visit urban parks and recreational areas. Urban residents often seek nature, and research points consistently to its positive psychological function (Staats, Gatersleben, & Hartig, 1997; Staats, Hartig, & Kieviets, 2000). Green spaces and the natural environment can provide not only an aesthetically pleasing setting but also restorative experiences (Kaplan, 1995), including a positive effect on health (Ulrich, 1984; E. O. Moore, 1982). Gifford (1987) summarized this research and identified the following main benefits of nature: cognitive freedom, escape, the experience of nature, ecosystem connectedness, growth, challenge, guidance, sociability, health, and self-control. What seems to be important is the sense of freedom and control felt in nature, in contrast to an urban environment, which is perceived as constraining.

The Global Environment

Local agendas are increasingly informed by global perspectives and processes (Lechner & Boli, 1999). The interaction between the local and the global is crucial and is the essence of globalization (Bauman, 1998; Beck, 1999). Although environmental issues are increasingly seen as international in terms of extent, impact, and necessary response, social psychological studies have traditionally treated many environmental problems as locally centered and limited to a single country. Thus they have been decontextualised in that not only has the local-global environmental dimension been minimized, but perhaps more significantly the local-global social psychological effects have also been minimized. This is well illustrated by Bonaiuto, Breakwell, and Cano (1996), who examined the role of social identity processes as they manifest themselves in place (i.e., local) and national identity in

the perception and evaluation of beach pollution. It was found that subjects who were more attracted to their town or their nation tended to perceive their local and national beaches as being less polluted.

Three phenomena—mass media coverage of environmental issues, the growth in environmental organizations, and the placing of environmental issues on international political agendas—have, intentionally or unintentionally, emphasized the seriousness of global as opposed to local or even national environmental problems. On the other hand, it has been suggested that people are only able to relate to environmental issues if they are concrete, immediate, and local. Consequently, it might be hypothesized that people will consider environmental problems to be more serious at a local rather than global level. If this is the case, then what is the effect of the public's perceptions of the seriousness of environmental problems on their sense of responsibility for taking action? In a series of cross-cultural studies undertaken in Australia, Ireland, Slovakia, and the United Kingdom, members of the public and environmental groups, environmental science students, and children were asked about the seriousness of various environmental problems in terms of their impact on the individual, the local area, the country, the continent, and the world (Uzzell, 2000b). It was consistently found that respondents were able to conceptualize problems at a global level, and an inverse distance effect was found such that environmental problems were perceived to be more serious the farther away they are from the perceiver. This phenomenon repeatedly occurred in each country for all groups. An inverse relationship was also found between a sense of responsibility for environmental problems and spatial scale resulting in feelings of powerlessness at the global level.

We are increasingly conscious of the effect of global environmental processes on local climate. The effects of extreme weather conditions—wind, heat or extreme cold—as, for example, investigated by Suedfeld and others in Antarctic survey stations, have demonstrated various impacts on individuals (Suedfeld, 1998; Weiss, Suedfeld, Steel, & Tanaka, 2000). The effect of seasonal daylight availability on mood has been described as seasonal affective disorder (Rosenthal et al., 1984). Likewise, sunlight has been found to enhance positive mood (Cunningham, 1979).

The most significant topic analyzed at the level of global environment is without doubt individuals' attitudes toward and support of sustainable development. A major challenge for environmental psychology is to enable the understanding and development of strategies to encourage environmentally friendly behavior. There is consistent field research in environmental psychology about the ways to encourage environmentally responsible behavior concerning resources conservation (e.g., energy and water), littering, and recycling. Environmental education, commitment, modeling, feedback, rewards, and disincentives are on the whole effective only if such behavior is reinforced and if opportunities are provided that encourage environmentally friendly behavior.

Growing ecological concern in our societies is attributed to a series of beliefs and attitudes favorable to the environment originally conceptualized by Dunlap (1980) and Dunlap and Van Liere (1984) as the *new environmental paradigm* and now superseded by the New Ecological Paradigm Scale (Dunlap, Van Liere, Mertig, & Jones, 2000). But it is clear from research that proenvironmental attitudes do not necessarily lead to proenvironmental behaviors. Environmental problems can often be conceptualized as *commons dilemma* problems (Van Lange, Van Vugt, Meertens, & Ruiter, 1998; Vlek, Hendrickx, & Steg, 1993). In psychology this is referred to as a social dilemma. The defining characteristics of such dilemmas are that (a) each participant receives more benefits and less costs for a self-interest choice (e.g., going by car) than for a public interest choice (e.g., cycling) and (b) all participants, as a group, would benefit more if they all choose to act in the public interest (e.g., cycling) than if they all choose to act in self-interest (e.g., going by car; Gatersleben & Uzzell, in press). The social dilemma paradigm can explain why many people prefer to travel by car even though they are aware of the environmental costs of car use and believe that more sustainable transport options are necessary. It is in the self-interest of every individual to use cars. Nevertheless, it is in the common interest to use other modes of transport. However, single individuals do not cause the problems of car use; nor can they solve them. They are typically collective problems. People therefore feel neither personally responsible for the problems nor in control of the solutions.

THEORETICAL PERSPECTIVES ON KEY QUESTIONS IN ENVIRONMENTAL PSYCHOLOGY

It was suggested at the beginning of this chapter that the context—the environment—in which people act out their lives is a critical factor in understanding human perceptions, attitudes, and behavior. Psychologists have largely ignored this context, assuming that most explanations for behavior are largely person centered rather than person-in-environment centered. Because environmental psychologists are in a position to understand person-in-environment questions, the history of environmental psychology has been strongly influenced by the need to answer questions posed by the

practical concerns of architects, planners, and other professions responsible for the planning, design, and management of the environment (Uzzell, 2000a). These questions include the following: How does the environment stimulate behavior, and what happens with excessive stimulation? How does the environment constrain and cause stress? How do we form maps of the environment in our heads and use them to navigate through the environment? What factors are important in people's evaluations of the built and natural environment, and how satisfied are they with different environments and environmental conditions? What is the influence of the environment or behavior setting on people? What physical properties of the environment facilitate some behaviors and discourage others? Do we have a sense of place? What effect does this have on our identity? In this section we outline some of the approaches that have been taken to answer these questions.

Typically, within environmental psychology these questions have been addressed from one of three perspectives. The first is a determinist and essentially behaviorist perspective that argues that the environment has a direct impact on people's perceptions, attitudes, and behaviors. The second approach has been referred to as interactionism: The environment has an impact on individuals and groups, who in turn respond by having an impact on the environment. The third perspective is transactional in that neither the person nor the environment has priority and neither one be defined without reference to the other. Bonnes and Secchiaroli (1995) suggested that transactionalism has two primary features: the continuous exchange and reciprocity between the individual and the environment, and the primarily active and intentional role of the individual to the environment.

It is impossible in a chapter of this length to discuss all the theories that have driven environmental psychology research. The varying scales at which environmental psychologists work, as we have seen, assume different models of man, make different assumptions about people-environment and environment-behavior relations, require different methodologies, and involve different interpretive frameworks. In this section we discuss the three principal approaches that have been employed in environmental psychology to account for people's behavioral responses to their environmental settings.

Determinist and Behaviorist Approaches

Arousal theory, environmental load, and adaptation level provide good illustrations of theories that are essentially behaviorist in their assumptions and determinist in their environment-behavior orientation.

Arousal Theory

Arousal theory stipulates that the environment provides a certain amount of physiological stimulation that, depending on the individual's interpretation and attribution of the causes, has particular behavioral effects. Each particular behavior is best performed at a definite level of arousal. The relation between levels of arousal and optimal performance or behavior is curvilinear (Yerkes-Dodson law). Whereas individuals seek stimulation when arousal is too low, too-high levels of arousal produced by either pleasant or unpleasant stimulation or experiences have negative effects on performance and behavior. Anomic behavior in urban environments is attributed to high stimulation levels due to environmental conditions such as excessive noise or crowding (Cohen & Spacapan, 1984). On the other hand, understimulation may occur in certain environments such as the Arctic that cause unease and depression (Suedfeld & Steel, 2000).

The Environmental Load or Overstimulation Approach

According to this model people have a limited capacity to process incoming stimuli, and overload occurs when the incoming stimuli exceed the individual's capacity to process them. Individuals deal with an overloaded situation by concentrating their attention on the most important aspects of a task or by focusing on a fixed goal, ignoring peripheral stimulation in order to avoid distraction. Paying attention to a particular task in an overloaded situation is very demanding and produces fatigue (Kaplan & Kaplan, 1989). Typical aftereffects of being exposed to an overload situation are, according to the overload model, less tolerance to frustration, less attention, and reduced capacity to react in an adaptive way. Milgram (1970) attributed the deterioration of social life in cities to the wide variety of demands on citizens causing a reduced capacity to pay attention to others. The overload approach explains why certain environmental conditions lead to undesirable behavioral consequences such as aggression, lack of helping behavior, and selfishness in urban environments.

Adaptation Level Theory

Adaptation level theory (Wohlwill, 1974) is in certain ways a logical extension of arousal theory and the overload approach. It assumes that there is an intermediate level of stimulation that is individually optimal. Three categories of stimulation can be distinguished: sensory stimulation, social stimulation, and movement. These categories can be described along three dimensions of stimulation: intensity, diversity, and patterning (i.e., the structure and degree of uncertainty of the stimulation). In ideal circumstances a stimulus has to be of average intensity and reasonably diverse, and it must be structured with a reasonable degree of uncertainty. The level of stimulation at which an individual feels comfortable depends on his or her past experience, or, more precisely, on the environmental conditions under which he or she has grown up. This reference level is nevertheless subject to adaptation when individuals change their life environments. If rural people can be very unsettled by urban environments, they may also adapt to this new situation after a certain period of residence. Adaptation level theory postulates an active and dynamic relation of the individual with his or her environment.

Interactionist Approaches

Analyses of the individual's exposure to environmental stressors in terms of control and of behavioral elasticity, on one hand, and environmental cognition (cognitive mapping, environmental evaluations, etc.), on the other hand, refer typically to an interactionist rationale of individual-environment relations.

Stress and Control

Some authors (Proshansky et al., 1970; Stokols, 1978; Zlutnick & Altman, 1972) consider certain environmental conditions to be constraining to the individual. Similarly, others (Baum, Singer, & Baum, 1981; Evans & Cohen, 1987; Lazarus & Folkman, 1984) describe such situations as being stressful. Both approaches lead to conditions as being potentially constraining or stressful and introduce the concept of *control*. Individuals exposed to such situations engage in coping processes. Coping is an attempt to reestablish or gain control over the situation identified as stressing or constraining. According to the psychological stress model, environmental conditions such as noise, crowding, or daily hassles provoke physiological, emotional, and behavioral reactions identified as stress (Lazarus, 1966). Three types of stressors can be distinguished: cataclysmic events (e.g., volcanic eruptions, floods, earthquakes), personal life events (e.g., illness, death, family or work problems), and background conditions (e.g., transportation difficulties, access to services, noise, crowding). Such conditions are potentially stressful according to their nature provided that the individual identifies them as such (Cohen, Evans, Stokols, & Krantz, 1986).

An environment is constraining when something is limiting or prevents individuals from achieving their intentions. This may occur with environmental conditions or stressors like noise or crowding, but also with specific environmental features like fences, barriers, or bad weather. The constraining situation is interpreted by the individual as being out of his or her control. The feeling of not being able to master the situation produces psychological reactance (Brehm, 1966). Unpleasant feelings of being constrained lead the individual to attempt to recover his or her freedom of action in controlling the situation. Having freedom of action or controlling one's environment seems to be an important aspect of everyday life and individuals' well-being. When people perceive control in a noisy situation, their performance is improved (Glass & Singer, 1972); they are less aggressive (Donnerstein & Wilson, 1976; Moser & Lévy-Leboyer, 1985); and they are more often helpful (Sherrod & Dowes, 1974). On the contrary, the perception of loss of control produced by a stressful situation or constraints has several negative consequences on behavior (Barnes, 1981) as well as on well-being and health.

Confronted with a potentially stressful condition, the individual appraises the situation. Appraisals involve both assessing the situation (primary appraisal) and evaluating the possibilities of coping with it (secondary appraisal). The identification of a situation as being stressful depends on cognitive appraisal. Cognitive appraisal of a situation as being potentially disturbing or threatening or even harmful involves an interaction between the objective characteristics of the situation as well as the individual's interpretation of the situation in light of past experience. The secondary appraisal leads to considering the situation as challenging with reference to a coping strategy. Coping strategies depend on individual and situational factors. They consist of problem-focused, direct action such as fleeing the situation, trying to stop, removing or reducing the identified stressor, or reacting with a cognitive or emotional focus such as reevaluating the threatening aspects of the situation. Reaction to a stressful situation may lead the individual to concentrate on the task, focus on the goals, or ignore or even deny the distracting stimuli. Repeated or steady exposure to stressors may result in adaptation and therefore weaker reactions to this type of situation. If the threatening character of the situation exceeds the coping capacities of the individual, this may cause fatigue and a sense of helplessness (Garber & Seligman, 1981; Seligman, 1975).

The Stress-Adaptation Model

In everyday life the individual is exposed to both background stressors and occasionally to excessive environmental stimulation. Consequently, the individual's behavior can only be appreciated when considered in a context perceived and evaluated by the persons themselves and in reference to baseline exposure (Moser, 1992). Any exposure to a constraining or disagreeable stimulus invokes a neuro-vegetative reaction. Confronted with such stimulation, the individual mobilizes cognitive strategies and evaluates the aversive situation with reference to her or his threshold of individual and situational tolerance, as well as the context in which exposure occurs. This evaluation creates a stimulation level that is judged against a personal norm of exposure. In response the individual judges the stimulus as being weak, average and tolerable, or strong. Cognitive processes intervene to permit the individual to engage in adaptive behavior to control the situation. A situation in which the constraints are too high or in which stimulation is excessive produces increased physiological arousal, thereby preventing any cognitive intervention and therefore also control of the situation.

Behavioral Elasticity

This model introduces the temporal dimension of exposure to environmental conditions and refers to individual norms of exposure (Moser, in press). The influence of stressors is well documented, but the findings are rarely analyzed in terms of adaptation to long-term or before-after comparisons. Yet one can assume that where there are no constraining factors, individuals will revert to their own set of norms, which are elaborated through their history of exposure. The principle of elasticity provides a good illustration of individual behavior in the context of environmental conditions. Using the principle of elasticity from solids mechanics to characterize the adaptive capacities of individuals exposed to environmental constraints, three essential behavioral specificities as a consequence of changing environmental contingencies can be distinguished: (a) a return to an earlier state (a point of reference) in which constraints were not present, (b) the ability to adapt to a state of constraint as long as the constraint is permanent, and (c) the existence of limits on one's flexibility. The latter becomes manifest through reduced flexibility in the face of increased constraints, the existence of a breaking point (when the constraints are too great), and the progressive reduction of elasticity as a function of both continuous constraints and of aging.

Returning to an Earlier Baseline.   While attention is mostly given to attitude change and modifying behavior in particular situations, the stability over time of these behaviors is rarely analyzed. Yet longitudinal research often shows that proenvironmental behavior re-sorts to the initial state before the constraints were encountered. This has been shown, for instance, in the context of encouraging people to sort their domestic waste (Moser & Matheau, in press) or in levels of concern about global environmental issues (Uzzell, 2000b). Exposure to constraints creates a disequilibrium, and the individual, having a tendency to reincorporate initial behavior, reverts to the earlier state of equilibrium.

Adaptation: The Ability to Put Up With a Constraining Situation in so Far as It Is Continuous.

Observing behavior in the urban environment provides evidence of the constraining conditions of the urban context. Residents of large cities walk faster in the street and demonstrate greater withdrawal than do those living in small towns: They look straight ahead, only rarely maintain eye contact with others, and respond less frequently to the various requests for help from other people. In other words, faced with an overstimulating urban environment, people use a filtering process by which they focus their attention on those requests that they evaluate as important, disregarding peripheral stimulation. The constant expression of this type of adaptive behavior suggests that it has become normative. The walking speed of inhabitants of small towns is slower that the walking speed of inhabitants in large cities (Bornstein, 1979). So we can assert that such behavior provides evidence of the individual's capacity to respond to particular environmentally constraining conditions.

The Extent and Limits of Flexibility.

The limits of flexibility and, more particularly, the breakdown following constraints that are too great are best seen in aggressive behavior. The distinction between instrumental and hostile aggression (Feshbach, 1964) recalls the distinction between adaptive behavior aimed at effectively confronting a threat and a reactive and impulsive behavior ineffectual for adaptation. Three limits of flexibility can be identified. First is *reduced flexibility in the face of increased constraints*. When exposure to accustomed constraints is relatively high, there is a lower probability of performing an adaptive response, and therefore an increase in reactive behaviors. There is decreased flexibility in the face of constraint, more so if the constraint is added onto already-existing constraints affecting the individual. This is most clearly evident in aggressive behaviors (Moser, 1984). People react more strongly to the same stimulation in the urban environment than in small towns. Hostile aggression thus becomes more frequent. This results in a decrease in adaptive capacities and therefore of flexibility if additional constraints are grafted onto those already present. The second limit is the *existence of a breaking point when the constraints are too great:* Intervention by cognitive processes is prevented if stimulation produces a neuro-vegetative reaction that is too extreme (Moser, 1992; Zillmann, 1978). This is most evident with violent or hostile aggressive behavior. This

involves nonadaptive reactive behavior that is clearly of a different order. As a consequence, breakdown and a limit on flexibility result. Contrary to what occurs when there is elasticity, however, this breakdown fortunately occurs only occasionally and on an ad hoc basis. The third limit is the *progressive loss of elasticity as a function of the persistence of exposure to constraints:* This has been examined under laboratory conditions in the form of postexposure effects. Outside the laboratory, the constant mobilization of coping processes, for example, for those living near airports produces fatigue and lowers the capacity to face new stressful situations (Altman, 1975). One encounters, in particular, greater vulnerability and irritability as well as a significant decrease in the ability to resist stressful events. These effects demonstrate that there is a decreased tolerance threshold, and so a decreased flexibility following prolonged exposure to different environmental constraints.

The elasticity model is an appropriate framework to illustrate the mechanisms and limits of behavioral plasticity. It may perhaps stimulate the generation of a model of behavioral adjustments by placing an emphasis on the temporal dimension and the cognitive processes governing behavior. Environmental cognition, cognitive mapping, and environmental appraisals are likely to fall within an interactionist framework. While they can be individualistic, they are invariably set within a social context. Environmental cognition would be enriched by more research in terms of social representations (Moscovici, 1989) providing the opportunity to emphasize the role of cultural values, aspirations, and needs as a frame of reference for environmental behavior.

Cognitive Mapping

How do we form maps of the environment in our heads and use them to navigate through the environment? Cognition and memory of places produce mental images of our environment. The individual has an organized mental representation of his or her environment (e.g., neighborhood, district, city, specific places), which environmental psychologist call *cognitive maps*. Cities need to be legible so that people can "read" and navigate them. The study of cognitive maps has its origin in the work of Tolman (1948), who studied the way in which rats find their ways in mazes. Lynch (1960), an urban planner, introduced the topic and a methodology to study the ways in which people perceive the urban environment. Lynch established a simple but effective method to collect and analyze mental maps. He suggested that people categorize the city according to five key elements: paths (e.g., streets, lanes), edges (e.g., spatial limits such as rivers and rail tracks), districts (e.g., larger spatial areas or neighborhoods that have specific characteristics and are typically named, such as Soho), nodes (e.g., intersections, plazas), and landmarks (e.g., reference points for the majority of people).

Furthermore, one can distinguish sequential representations (i.e., elements that the individual encounters when traveling from one point of the city to another, rich in paths and nodes) and spatial representations emphasizing landmarks and districts (Appleyard, 1970). Cognitive maps will vary, for example, as a function of familiarity with the city and stage in the life cycle. Such maps can be used to characterize either an individual's specific environment interests or preferences (Milgram & Jodelet, 1976) or the qualities and legibility of a particular environment (Gärling & Evans, 1991; Kitchen, Blades, & Golledge, 1997). Way finding is a complex process involving a variety of cognitive operations such as localization of the target and choosing the route and the type of transportation to reach the goal (Gärling, Böök, & Lindberg, 1986). Sketch maps often carry typical errors that point to the cognitive elaboration of the individual's environmental representation: nonexhaustive, spatial distortions (too close, too apart), simplification of paths and spaces, and overestimation of the size of familiar places.

Environmental Evaluations

What factors are important in people's evaluation of the built and natural environment, and how satisfied are they with different environments and environmental conditions? Some environmental evaluations, called the *place-centered method,* focus on the objective physical properties of the environment such as pollution levels or the amount of urban development over the previous 10 years. The aim is to measure the qualities of an environment by experts or by actual or potential users. Such evaluations are done without taking into account the referential framework of the evaluator (i.e. the values, preferences, or significations attached to the place). These kinds of appraisals are important, but when it is remembered that what may be an environmental problem for one person may be of no consequence to another, it is clear that environmental assessment has an important subjective dimension as well. This person-centered method focuses on the feelings, subjective appreciation of, and satisfaction with a particular environment (Craik & Zube, 1976; Russell & Lanius, 1984).

Some environmental appraisals take the form of contrasting social categories such as architects versus the public (Groat, 1994; Hubbard, 1994) or scientists versus laypeople (Mertz, Slovic, & Purchase, 1998) or of categorizing people who hold particular attitudes (e.g., pro- vs. anticonservation; Nord, Luloff, & Bridger, 1998). The focus of attention is on the role the individual occupies or the attitudes held and the

consequent effect that this has on environmental attitudes and behavior.

Evaluations can be carried out either in the environment that is being evaluated or through simulations. Horswill and McKenna (1999) developed a video-based technique for measuring drivers' speed choice, and their technique has the advantage of maintaining experimental control and ensuring external and ecological validity. They found that speed choice during video simulation related highly to real driving experiences. Research consistently confirms color photographs as a valid measure of on-site response, especially for visual issues (Bateson & Hui, 1992; Brown, Daniel, Richards, & King, 1988; Nasar & Hong, 1999; Stamps, 1990). Stamps (1990) conducted a meta-analysis of research that had previously used simulated environments to measure perceptions of real versus photographed environments (e.g., presented as slides, color prints, and black-and-white prints). He demonstrated that there is highly significant correlation between evaluations of real and simulated (photographed) environments. The advent of digital imaging means that it is now possible to manipulate photographs so that environments can be changed in a systematic and highly convincing way in order to assess public preferences and reactions. The photographs in Figure 17.1 were manipulated with the intention of assessing the impact of different traffic calming measures on drivers' estimates of speed (Uzzell & Leach, 2001).

The research demonstrated that drivers clearly were able to discriminate between the different conditions presented in manipulated photographs. When estimated speeds were correlated against actual speeds along the road as it exists at present, this suggested which design solutions would lead to an increase or decrease in speeding behavior.

Transactional Approaches

Three approaches are discussed here as examples of transactional approaches in environmental psychology: Barker's behavior setting approach; affordances; and place theory, identity, and attachment.

Barker's Behavior Settings

Barker's behavior settings approach has both a theoretical and methodological importance because it provides a framework for analyzing the logic of behavior in particular settings. Barker (1968, 1990) considered the environment as a place where prescribed patterns of behavior, called programs, occur. There is a correspondence between the nature of the physical milieu and a determined number and type of collective behavior taking place in it. According to ecological

Figure 17.1 Digitally manipulated photographs used to assess the impact of alternative traffic-calming measures on drivers' estimates of speed.

psychology, knowing the setting will provide information about the number of programs (i.e., behaviors) in it. Such programs are recurrent activities, regularly performed by persons holding specific roles. A church, for instance, induces behaviors like explaining, listening, praying, singing, and so on, but each type of activity is performed by persons endorsing specific roles. According to his or her role, the priest is a performer and the congregation members are nonperformers. This setting also has a layout and particular furniture that fits that purpose and fixes the program (i.e., what type of behavior should happen in it). The so-called behavior setting (i.e., the physical place and the behaviors) determines what type of behavior is appropriate and therefore can or should occur. Patterns of behavior (e.g., worshipping) as well as settings (e.g., churches) are nevertheless independent: A religious office can be held in the open air, and the church can be used for a concert. It is their role-environment structure or synomorphology that create the behavior setting. Barker's analysis supposes an interdependency between collective patterns of behavior, the program, and the physical space or milieu in which these behaviors take place. Behaviors are supposed to be unique in the specific setting and dependent on the setting in which they occur. *Settings* are delimited places such as within walls, fences, or symbolic barriers. They can be

identified and described. Barriers between settings also delimit programs. Knowing about the setting (e.g., its purpose or intention) infers the typical behaviors of the people in that setting. Barker's conceptualization permits an understanding of environment-behavior relationships such that space might be organized in a certain way in order to meet its various purposes. Behavior settings are dynamic structures that evolve over time (Wicker, 1979, 1987).

Staffing (formerly *manning*) *theory* completes Barker's approach by proposing a set of concepts related to the number of people that the behavior setting needs in order to be functional (Barker, 1960; Wicker & Kirkmeyer, 1976). Besides key concepts like performers who carry out the primary tasks and the nonperformers who observe, the minimum number of people needed to maintain the functioning of a behavior setting is called the *maintenance minimum,* and the maximum is called its *capacity. Applicants* are people seeking to become part of the behavior setting. Overstaffing or understaffing is a consequence of too few or too many applicants for a behavior setting. The consequence of understaffing is that people have to work harder and must endorse a greater range of different roles in order to maintain the functioning of the setting. They will also feel more committed to the group and endorse more important roles. On the other hand, overstaffing requires the fulfillment of adaptive measures to maintain the functioning, such as increasing the size of the setting.

Behavior settings and staffing theory are helpful tools to solve environmental design problems and to improve the functioning of environments. Barker's approach has been applied successfully to the analyses of work environments, schools, and small towns. It helps to document community life and enables the evaluation of the structure of organizations in terms of efficiency and responsibility.

Affordance Theory

Gibson (1979) argued that, contrary to the orthodox view held in the design professions, people do not see form and shape when perceiving a place. Rather, the environment can be seen as offering a set of *affordances;* that is, the environment is assessed in terms of what it can do for us. The design professions are typically taught that the building blocks of perception comprise shape, color, and form. This stems from the view that architecture and landscape architecture are often taught as visual arts rather than as ways of providing functional space in which people can work, live, and engage in recreation. Gibson argues that "the affordances of the environment are what it offers the animal, what it provides or furnishes either for good or ill" (p. 127). Affordances are ecological resources from a functional point of view. They are an objectively specifiable and psychologically meaningful taxonomy of the environment. The environment offers opportunities for use and manipulation. How we use the environment as children, parents, or senior citizens will vary depending on our needs and interests, values, and aspirations.

This perspective suggests that the degree to which built or natural environments are utilized changes as people's roles, relationships, and activities in the environment change. Therefore, the environment can be seen to have a developmental dimension to it. As people develop their cognitive, affective, and behavioral capacities, the resources that the environment offers change. Furthermore, the environment can be designed to facilitate, support, and encourage this. Heft (1988) argued that utilizing Gibson's theory of affordances allows us to describe environmental features in terms of their functional significance for an individual or group. He postulated that to arrive at a functional description of an environment, one requires three sorts of information: the characteristics of the person, the characteristics of the environment, and the behavior of the individual in question. Heft (1988) was interested in children's environment-behavior interactions, with the aim of creating a taxonomy that would describe the functionally significant properties of children's

environments. Based on his analysis of three significant books on children's use of their environment (Barker & Wright, 1951; Hart, 1979; R. Moore, 1986), Heft created a functional taxonomy of children's outdoor environments in terms of the environmental features and activities that they afford the child. The 10 environmental features were flat, relatively smooth surface; relatively smooth slope; graspable/detached object; attached object; nonrigid, attached object; climbable feature; aperture; shelter; moldable materials; and water.

Heft also pointed out that as there is a developmental aspect to the taxonomy, the value of the environment will change for the developing child. As children move from pre-teenagers through to adolescence, so the affordances of different types of environments change in response to their need for social interaction and privacy (Woolley, Spencer, Dunn, & Rowley, 1999). Clark and Uzzell (in press) found that the use of the neighborhood for interaction decreased with age and that by the time the young people had reached 11 years old the number of affordances was significantly lower than for those aged 7 years old. There was no decrease in the use of the neighborhood for retreat. Therefore, the neighborhood retains its importance for retreat behaviors.

Exemplifying the assertion by Bonaiuto and Bonnes (1996) that the experience of small- and large-city living is notably different, Kyttä (1995) examined children's activities in the city, in a small town, and in a rural area in Finland. Using the affordance approach but including categories on social affordances and nature, Kyttä found that the number of positive affordances was highest in the rural area and lowest in the city. However, when the quality of affordances was analyzed, there were no differences between the areas for 8 out of the 11 affordance categories. The attitudes of parents play a significant role in how children perceive affordances. Children with a limited autonomy over their spatial range, due to parental restrictions through fears about safety, see little of the environment and therefore of its affordances.

Theories of Place, Place Identity, and Place Attachment

One of the earliest theories of place was proposed by Canter (1977), whose conceptual, as opposed to behavioral, model proposed that the cognitive system contains information about where places are, what is likely to happen there, and who is likely to be present. Canter defined place as a unit of environmental experience and postulated that the unit of place was the result of the relationships between actions (i.e., behavior is associated or anticipated), conceptions, and physical attributes.

A second influential theory of place is the transactional theory of Stokols and Shumaker (1981), who defined place as the entity between aspects of meaning, physical properties, and relative activity. This is not so dissimilar from Canter's notions of actions, conceptions, and physical properties. Stokols and Shumaker emphasize the collective perceptions of place and propose that a place has a *social imageability*. This imageability is the collectively held social meanings that the place has among its occupants or users. Within social psychology these would be called social representations (Farr & Moscovici, 1984; Moscovici, 1989). Stokols proposed that three dimensions contribute to a group's social imageability of place: functions, goals, and evaluations. *Functions* are individual or group activities that occur within the place regularly and include the norms associated with the activities and the identity and social roles of the occupants/users of the place; *goals* can be either personal or collective and relate to the purpose of the place; *evaluations* include the occupants, physical features, and social functions associated with the place.

Thus, Stokols and Shumaker concluded that the perceived social imageability of a place is the result of the functional, motivational, and evaluative meanings conveyed by the environment. Stokols places particular emphasis on the functional dimension of place and the need to explore the affective and motivational processes in the relationship between people and place. As Bonnes and Secchiaroli (1995) pointed out, to live in an environment does not mean structuring experiences only with respect to its physical reality. Places carry a role in the fulfillment of biological, cultural, psychological, and social needs of the person in the many situations that they will face over their lifetimes.

One such role is their contribution to personal and group identity. Place has been related to identity in two ways. The first could be referred to as *place identification*. This refers to a person's expressed identification with a place. For example, a person from London may refer to himself as a Londoner. In this sense, "Londoner" can be considered to be a social category that is subject to the same rules as is a social identification within social identity theory. Hogg and Abrams (1988) suggested that social identity comprises different social identifications, any one of which will become salient depending on the context. Taking this position suggests that the concept of place identity is subsumed into and becomes a part of social identity.

The second way in which place has been related to identity is through the term *place identity*, a construct promoted by Proshansky, Fabian, and Kaminoff (1983; Proshansky, 1987) that calls for a more radical reevaluation of the construct of identity. Proshansky et al. (1983) proposed that place identity is another aspect of identity comparable to social identity that describes the person's socialization with the physical world. This understanding sets place identity alongside and independent of self-identity, rather than subsumed within it.

Although it may be possible to discuss the relationship between the physical environment and identity without reference to a group, to have two forms of identity would focus discussion on whether identity was more "social" or more "place." This would not seem to be useful in explanatory terms. In addition, it contradicts environmental psychologists' transactional perspective on place (Saegert & Winkel, 1990). Although we agree with Proshansky that self theorists have neglected the physical environment, we would suggest that rather than there being a separate part of identity concerned with place, all aspects of identity will, to a greater or lesser extent, have place-related implications. Although place identity is seen to be a crucial part of the relationship between self and environment, Proshansky never really operationalized the concept. Breakwell's (1986) identity process model, with its constructs of distinctiveness, continuity, self-esteem, and self-efficacy, provides such an investigatory and analytical framework. Although these constructs have a particularly social orientation in Breakwell's formulation, they nevertheless would seem to have useful transfer relevance to other dimensions of identity, including place (Bonaiuto, Breakwell, & Cano, 1996; Uzzell, 1995). For example, distinctiveness and continuity are essential elements in Korpela (1989) and Lalli's (1992) conceptualizations of place identity.

One important mechanism through which place identity is supported is place attachment. Spencer and Woolley (2000), for example, argued that children gain their personal identity through place attachment. Place attachment refers to an emotional bonding between individuals and their life spaces, which could be the home, the neighborhood, or places and spaces at a larger scale (Altman & Low, 1992; Giuliani, 1991; Giuliani & Feldman, 1993).

TIME, SPACE, AND THE FUTURE OF ENVIRONMENTAL PSYCHOLOGY

Needs and Rights in Environmental Psychology

The emphasis of much environmental psychology has been on identifying and then assisting in the process of providing for and satisfying people's needs. It is assumed within the philosophy of Brandt and Bruntland that environmental needs should be defined by those in power (i.e., the West), not by the people whose needs are supposedly being satisfied. This form of donor benevolence as a strategy for tackling environmental deficits operates at the local, national, and international level. Thus, it is argued, we need to prevent pollution and conserve the rainforests, wildlife, energy, and water supplies. The West finds it difficult to understand why those experiencing environmental degradation—but also suffering poverty, malnutrition, poor housing, unemployment, and high mortality rates—have different priorities. The needs-based approach is often carried through to be an assumption that guides environmental psychology research.

An alternative approach focuses on *environmental rights* in which those without power define their needs themselves and try to secure the rightful access to resources to satisfy those needs. There is a difficulty with trying to integrate a bottom-up rights approach with a top-down needs-driven approach because one is faced with the problem of who sets the agenda. Groups will have difficulties asserting their rights when the allocation processes and agendas are structured by others. A rights approach does not mean that neither help nor resources are required or given. Clearly it is essential that the haves of the world continue to provide for the have nots—but within a context of participation, self-determination, transparency in decision-making, and accountability by all concerned. The essential factor is that the starting point for discussing the allocation of resources is different.

Long-term change and development will come about only through informed community action, rather than a dependency relationship on experts and technological-fix solutions. The development of environmental consciousness and capacities without the simultaneous development of opportunities for action leads to a feeling of powerlessness (Uzzell, 1999). For this reason cooperation between all agencies and institutions is necessary in order to secure action opportunities. Psychologists in general and environmental psychologists in particular have the expertise and experience to play an important role in this process. It is here that we can see the value of research in suggesting prescriptive roles and functions for an environmental psychology that should be taken seriously by policy makers and practitioners alike. Some have suggested that the implementation of sustainable development through, for example, Local Agenda 21 initiatives will be possible only with local community consensus (Robinson, 1997). Petts (1995) argued that traditional participatory approaches have been reactive in that the public is expected simply to respond to previously formulated plans. The trend now is for proactive, consensus-building approaches that attempt to involve people in the decision-making process itself.

Cultural Differences and Temporal Processes

Environmental psychology, like other areas of psychology, has focused almost exclusively on topics, theories, and methodologies that have been oriented toward Western assumptions and worldviews. Two topics seem to have been neglected in environmental psychology as they have in other areas of psychology: *cultural differences* and *temporal processes*. Both approaches are even more important at the beginning of the twenty-first century because on the one hand the processes of *globalization* have the effect of destroying cultural differences, and on the other hand, *sustainable development* is seen as a way of ensuring the long-term integrity of biocultural systems.

By defining sustainable development as "development that meets the need of the present without compromising the ability of future generations to meet their own needs," Bruntland (1987) opened the way to concerns related to quality of life. The reference to needs allows not only the requirement that development be harmonious toward and respectful of the environment, but equally for the recognition of the individual's own well-being. Of course, the issue just posed requires us to consider whether we should be thinking in terms of needs or rights, and, indeed, whose needs and whose rights.

Globalization and its corollary, global trade and communications, create pressure toward cultural uniformity in lifestyles. The progressive deployment of globalization has brought on, with reason, fear of a standardization of values and increased anonymity threatening both individual and group identity. It gives rise to movements demanding recognition of local, regional, and national priorities and cultural differences and therefore also specific needs. This search for identity finds its expression spatially. Furthermore, the increase in regional, national, and international forced or voluntary mobility (e.g., political refugees and asylum seekers, economic migration of job-seeking populations, and executives dislocated by their companies) exacerbates confrontations between cultures with different needs, values, and customs. Globalization provides the impetus to situate environmental psychology in a more globally—and, at the same time, culturally—relative framework. The traditional concepts of local community, environmental appropriation, and identity take on new meanings in the context of sustainable development and globalization.

The Cultural Dimension

Quality of life standards are culturally determined. Needs concerning personal space, social life in the neighborhood, and urban experience are different from one culture to another. Furthermore, acting in sustainable ways depends on culturally marked values concerning the environment. From a globalization perspective, how universal is the need for personal space and privacy? Are they the same everywhere? Research in environmental psychology has taught us that, for instance, spatial needs vary both from one culture to another and also on one's stage in the life cycle (Altman, 1975; Sundstrom, 1978). Some studies, such as Nasar and Min (1984), show that people living in the Mediterranean region and in Asia react very differently to confined spatial arrangements. But many such studies are conducted in a culturally homogeneous environment and therefore allow only for conclusions concerning interpersonal differences related to the cultural origins of the research participants (see, e.g., Loo & Ong, 1984). We need more longitudinal research and intercultural studies such as those undertaken to study reactions to density and spatial needs.

The norms, needs, and strategies for adapting to conditions very different from our own are likely to provide us with insights on the dynamics of how people relate to the physical and social dimensions of both their and our environments. Such studies should be able to answer these questions more systematically. Privacy may signify and represent very different conditions not only at the individual level, but also between different cultures (Altman & Chemers, 1980). Individual versus collective housing preferences, as well as the use of different facilities inside and around the dwelling, are all culturally defined. While individual dwelling units appear as an ideal in Anglo-Saxon cultural settings, in some Latin American societies there is a stronger preference for collective housing units, particularly in Brazil, mainly for reasons of increased security. More systematic research in this area should be able to provide guidelines for architects and designers, allowing them to take account of culturally dependent needs beyond the simplistic notions of conception and layout (e.g., kitchens clearly separated from dining rooms). Kent (1991) proposed a classification of different cultural groups according to their use of domestic space. Such a distinction is particularly relevant to the functional segmentation of spatial arrangements. Kent noted that occupants remodel their domestic environment to fit their own cultural imperatives if they find themselves in an environment that fails to correspond to their own cultural standards. Well-being has different meanings in different cultures, and instead of imposing Western standards, environmental psychology should contribute more to identifying culturally specific standards to enable the construction of modular spaces to satisfy diversified needs. This becomes more important than ever in the context of an increasingly mobile (forced or voluntary) society.

At the neighborhood level, well-being depends on how the immediate environment is able to satisfy the specific needs of culturally different people, thereby providing opportunities

for appropriation. Currently there is a preference for homogenization of populations within neighborhoods. Arguably, however, such a strategy may pose more risks for the future than encouraging a process of heterogeneity in terms of the impact on how we perceive others and how we perceive space occupied by foreigners. These are classic lessons to be learned from social psychology (Tajfel, 1982). Neighborhoods not directly controlled or appropriated by the individual can lead to antagonism between culturally different communities. More sociocultural research on living in areas with heterogeneous populations and transcultural relations should be undertaken in order to identify barriers to integration.

Environmental psychology has repeatedly pointed to the negative consequences of living conditions in large urban centers: anonymity, insecurity, indifference to others, and exposure to various types of stress (Moser, 1992). This presents a rather dark portrait of urban living conditions. An environmental psychology has emerged that has deprecated urban centers and lauded the virtues of supposedly more attractive suburban residential environments (Lindberg, Hartig, Garvill, & Gärling, 1992). Taking the Anglo-Saxon single-family house as its model (Cooper, 1972; Thorne, Hall, & Munro-Clark, 1982), this approach has failed to account for what is happening in cities such as Paris where the city center is invariably highly valued as a thriving, attractive, and lively residential as well as commercial and cultural environment. Two thirds of those living in the Paris region indicate that they would prefer to live within Paris proper, whereas one fifth would prefer to live in a small provincial town and only 15% show a preference for the Parisian suburbs (Moser, Ratiu, & Fleury-Bahi, 2002). Such results are in direct contrast to those found in the United States. The American experience cannot be taken as the norm; unfortunately, this is often the case in environmental psychology and other branches of psychology. These differences go beyond merely the characteristics of urban and suburban environments and raise questions concerning the aspirations and needs of city dwellers and the processes that are generating the transformation of cities. Inhabitants of large cities are increasingly culturally diverse; as a consequence, so are their needs. How do cities manage the influx of foreign populations, some of them culturally very different? What are the conditions of territorial appropriation of ethnic and cultural minorities, and what is the territorial behavior of these populations (e.g., segregation, assimilation, or integration in respect of the wider community)?

Over the last few years environmental psychologists have made tentative steps toward building models of the conditions necessary for generating behavior favorable to the global environment, as a function of both values and human well-being (Vlek, Skolnik, & Gattersleben, 1998). How are intercultural differences, particularly with respect to values, compatible with proenvironmental benefits for future generations? Many studies point to individualistic behavior in the face of limited resources (i.e., "the tragedy of the commons"; Hardin, 1968; Thompson & Stoutemyer, 1991), which can be interpreted in more familiar social psychological terms as a social dilemma problem (Van Lange et al., 1998). Other studies focus on the different ways of envisaging our relationship with the environment, such as the *new environmental paradigm* (Arcury & Christianson, 1990; Dunlap et al., 2000). Perception, attitudes, and behavior concerning the environment differ from one culture to another to the extent that they are modulated by environmental variations, the resources available, and the societal context, including values, regulations, infrastructure, and opportunities for action (Lévy-Leboyer, Bonnes, Chase, Ferreira-Marques, & Pawlik, 1996). For instance, the different cultural representations of water form interpretative filters of the objective conditions and normative references orienting individual and collective behavior (Moser, in press). The resolution of the dilemma between individual short-term behavior and collective action that is common in these types of problematic situations depends on cultural values, accessibility to resources, and the perception of these resources. The representation of water is shaped by the values attached to water: Affective and aesthetic values lead to a dynamic, global-ecological vision, whereas functional values and spatial and temporal proximity constitute a limited representation of the same phenomenon.

The Temporal Dimension

There has been a growing interest in recent years in the historicity of psychological processes (Gergen & Gergen, 1984). Too often in psychology, time, like the environment, has been treated as noise rather than as a valid process in itself. Even in areas that have an integral temporal dimension (e.g., social representations), little account is given of either the origins or the development of the representations (Herzlich, 1973; Moscovici, 1976; Uzzell & Blud, 1993). There are clearly difficulties in accessing the past from a psychological point of view (Lowenthal, 1985; Uzzell, 1998). Social structures and social processes change over time, and this in turn has an effect on spatial structures and processes. If psychological processes are molded and influenced by their social context, then changing social structures and regulatory mechanisms will affect those processes and have a consequent effect on the individual, the group, and the environment. Although environmental psychology often hints at the temporal dimension of people-environment relations with the physical and social environment, the temporal dimension has in general been neglected (Altman & Rogoff, 1987; Proshansky, 1987; Werner, Altman, & Brown, 1992).

First, the temporal dimension intervenes in different ways in terms of spatial anchoring and individual well-being. Anchoring is always a process that occurs within a time dimension. It reflects the individual's motivations, social status, family situation, and projects for the future. Well-being has to be set within a time reference, within a time horizon and the life cycle.

Second, the temporal dimension intervenes as a reference in the individual's construction of his or her own identity. Appropriating one's place of residence is conditioned by the individual's residential history. A sense of neighborliness in the immediate environment can compensate for mediocre living conditions, but such compensation does not occur if the person looks back with nostalgia to his or her childhood residence (Lévy-Leboyer & Ratiu, 1993; Ratiu & Lévy-Leboyer, 1993). Furthermore, environmental appropriation revolves around forming social and interpersonal relationships that depend largely on the duration of the person's residence. Those who make emotional investments in their neighborhood and develop a sense of well-being tend to be more satisfied with their interpersonal relations in their neighborhood. This takes the form of relationships that go beyond simple politeness (Fleury-Bahi, 1997, 1998). On the other hand, the lack of free time available to people living in suburbs has an impact on residents' relationships with neighbors (Moser, 1997).

Third, how do interindividual differences, and particularly gender differences, express themselves in relation to the temporal dimension in terms of spatial investment and environmental needs? How are these two variables interrelated? What is their impact on our perceptions, needs, and behaviors? The division of time between leisure and nonleisure activities (e.g., activities involving imposed time constraints and activities) is fundamentally different when we compare urban and non-urban settings. Commuting time, due to the greater distance between home and work, reduces the free time of commuters in large urban areas in an obvious way. This has not been systematically considered with respect to its impact on the appropriation of space. One might assume that people who appropriate their environment and feel at home where they live will also care more about the environment in general and exhibit more frequent ecologically beneficial behaviors as predicted in the Cities, Identity, and Sustainability model (Pol, Guardia, Valera, Wiesenfeld, & Uzzell, 2001; Uzzell, Pol, & Badenes, 2002).

The cognitive and affective evaluation of the environment is contingent on temporal, historical, and cultural factors.

Analyses of the perception, evaluation, and representations of the environment, both built and natural, generally only make implicit reference to the cultural and temporal dimensions. It has been found, for example, that the cognitive image of the city of Paris not only develops and is conditioned by the culture of origin and the sociospatial familiarity but also goes through well-defined representational stages before becoming more or less stable (Ramadier & Moser, 1998).

Increasing population mobility also raises questions concerning the rhythm of life and its consequential territorial implications. All places have a life rhythm. For some it may be shortlived—a period of high-intensity use either by day, week, or season. Many leisure settings fall into this category. Others may be 24-7 environments such as shopping malls and airports that are open and used every hour of the day, every day of the year. What differentiates the rhythm is the different types of groups that occupy the spaces for different reasons at different times. We know from research on leisure and recreation that what makes a recreation place is the social meanings ascribed to the recreational setting rather than the particularities of the activities undertaken (Cheek, Field, & Burdge, 1976). An integral component of this is time. With the development of new technologies, the notion of proximity takes on new meanings that have not been fully explored by environmental psychologists. Finally, the temporal dimension resurfaces in the context of the preservation of the environment and natural resources. One of the conditions for adopting proenvironmental behaviors is the ability to project oneself into the future and to step outside one's own life cycle and act in the interests of future generations.

Both temporal and cultural dimensions have to be taken into account when addressing quality of life issues. Well-being depends on the satisfaction of culturally determined needs. Environmental anchoring and appropriation leading to identity are progressive processes and are essential for individual and group behavior in respect of a sustainable development. The relationship to the environment (at every spatial level—home, neighborhood, city, nation, planet) is mediated by the individual's and the group's sense of control. Each individual has a personal history, a representation of the past, and an anticipatory representation of the future (Doise, 1976) that condition how he or she relates to the environment. This means abandoning the atemporal orientation of environmental psychology in favor of a more dynamic approach. Analyses of proenvironmental behavior have demonstrated the importance of a temporal horizon, yet few research studies explicitly incorporate this dimension. It is only by refocusing analysis on the person and the social group and their relation with the environment in its spatial, cultural, and temporal

dimensions that the discipline will be able to develop its own metatheories. It is in this context that the perspectives of sustainable development and the consequences of globalization can give a new impetus to environmental psychology and help to generate theories with wider applications.

CONCLUSION: APPLYING ENVIRONMENTAL PSYCHOLOGY

Gärling and Hartig (2000) suggested that one of the shortcomings of environmental psychology is that environmental psychologists have only been able to provide general principles in response to the specific needs of practitioners. In short, it is suggested that there is an applications gap. While this may be a valid criticism of science in general, its validity in relation to environmental psychology should be challenged. If there is a gap, is it because environmental psychologists have failed to communicate with or convince other scientists and practitioners of the value of their work? Or is it because environmental psychologists have not delivered the kind of answers that practitioners such as architects and designers have required or were expecting or wanted? Perhaps environmental psychologists have been asking the wrong questions? Or does environmental psychology suffer from a shortage of data? Some might argue that we need better theoretical ways of understanding the data that we have already. It may also be that those who have the task of drawing upon and implementing the results of environmental psychological and other behavioral science research become frustrated at the amount of time, financial resources, and effort that go into generating marginal increases in the amount of variance explained in a set of data. Increasing the amount of variance explained from 33% to 35% is important, but we really need to be far more imaginative in our theoretical and conceptual approaches in order to make serious inroads into the 65% of the variance unaccounted for.

Gifford (2000) argued that we need more challenging, bolder theories. Environmental psychology has an important role to play in providing conceptual guidelines of how to look at and analyze a given setting with reference to its contextual framework. As we suggested at the outset, the essence of environmental psychology is the context. Context is an inseparable part of the explanation of people's transactions with the environment. One way of responding to Gifford's plea for bolder theories is to extend our understanding of context. In the last section we argued that the cultural and temporal dimension of people-environment relations needs to be incorporated into our analytical framework. There is every reason to argue that this should be the new thrust in environmental psychology research because the study of globalization and sustainable development—two crucial issues that we have identified in this chapter—with their implications for people-environment relations will necessitate the incorporation of cross-cultural and temporal analyses if we are to find solutions to the challenges that they pose.

REFERENCES

Aiello, J. R. (1987). Human spatial behaviour. In D. Stokols & I. Altman (Eds.), *Handbook of environmental psychology* (Vol. 1, pp. 505–531). New York: Wiley.

Altman, I. (1975). *The environment and social behavior.* Monterey, CA.: Brooks/Cole.

Altman, I., & Chemers, M. (1980). *Culture and environment.* Monterey, CA: Brooks/Cole.

Altman, I., & Low, S. M. (1992). *Place attachment: Vol. 12. Human behaviour and environment: Advances in theory and research.* New York: Plenum.

Altman, I., & Rogoff, B. (1987). World-views in psychology: Trait, interactional, organismic and transactional perspectives. In D. Stokols & I. Altman (Eds.), *Handbook of environmental psychology* (Vol. 1, pp. 7–40). New York: Wiley.

Altman, I., & Vinsel, A. M. (1977). Personal space: An analysis of E. T. Hall's Proxemic Framework. In I. Altman & J. F. Wohlwill (Eds.), *Human behaviour and environment* (Vol. 2, pp. 181–259). New York: Plenum.

Appleyard, D. (1970). Styles and methods of structuring a city. *Environment and Behaviour, 2,* 10–117.

Arcury, T. A., & Christianson, E. H. (1990). Environmental worldview in response to environmental problems: Kentucky 1984 and 1988 compared. *Environment and Behavior, 22*(3), 387–407.

Barbey, G. (1976). L'appropriation des espaces du logement: Tentative de cadrage théorique. In P. Korosec-Serfaty (Ed.), *Actes de la 3ème Conférence Internationale de Psychologie de l'Espace Construit* (pp. 215–218). Strasbourg, France: Université de Strasbourg Press.

Barker, R. G. (1960). Ecology and motivation. In M. R. Jones (Ed.), *Nebraska symposium on motivation* (Vol. 8, pp. 1–50). Lincoln: University of Nebraska Press.

Barker, R. G. (1968). *Ecological psychology: Concepts and methods for studying the environment of human behavior.* Stanford, CA: Stanford University Press.

Barker, R. G. (1990). Recollections of the Midwest Psychological Field station. *Environment and Behavior, 22,* 503–513.

Barker, R. G., & Wright, H. F. (1951). *One boy's day.* New York: Row, Paterson.

Barnes, R. D. (1981). Perceived freedom and control in the built environment. In J. H. Harvey (Ed.), *Cognition, social behavior and the environment* (pp. 409–422). Hillsdale, NJ: Erlbaum.

Bateson, J. E. G., & Hui, M. K. (1992). The ecological validity of photographic slices and videotapes in simulating the service setting. *Journal of Consumer Research, 19,* 271–281.

Baum, A., Singer, J. E., & Baum, C. S. (1981). Stress and the environment. *Journal of Social Issues, 37,* 4–35

Bauman, Z. (1998). *Globalization.* London: Polity Press.

Beck, U. (1999). *What is Globalization?* London: Polity Press.

Becker, F. D. (1981). *Workplace: Creating environments in organisations.* New York: CBS Educational as Professional Publishing.

Becker, F. D., & Steele, F. (1995). *Workplace by design: Mapping the high-performance workscape.* San Francisco: Jossey-Bass.

Bell, P. A., Fisher, J. D., & Loomis, R. J. (1978). *Environmental psychology* (1st ed.). Philadelphia: Saunders.

Bell, P. A., Greene, T. C., Fisher, J. D., & Baum, A. (2001). *Environmental psychology* (5th ed.). Fort Worth, TX: Harcourt.

Bonaiuto, M., Breakwell, G. M., & Cano, I. (1996). Identity processes and environmental threat: The effects of nationalism and local identity upon perception of beach pollution. *Journal of Community and Applied Social Psychology, 6,* 157–175.

Bonnes, M., & Secchiaroli, G. (1995) *Environmental psychology: A psycho-social introduction.* London: Sage.

Bornstein, M. H. (1979). The pace of life revisited. *International Journal of Psychology, 259,* 83–90.

Breakwell, G. M. (1986) *Coping with threatened identities.* London: Methuen.

Brehm, J. W. (1966). *A theory of psychological reactance.* New York: Academic Press.

Brown, T. C., Daniel, T. C., Richards, M. T., & King, D. A. (1988). Recreation participation and the validity of photo-based preference judgements. *Journal of Leisure Research, 20*(4), 40–60.

Brunswik, E. (1956). *Perception and the representative design of psychological experiments.* Berkeley: University of California Press

Bruntland, G. H. (1987). *Our common future: Report of the World Commission on Environment and Development.* Oxford, UK: Oxford University Press.

Canter, D. (1977). *The psychology of place.* London: Architectural Press.

Cheek, N. H., Field, D., & Burdge, R. (1976). *Leisure and recreation places.* Ann Arbor, MI: Ann Arbor Science.

Clark, C., & Uzzell, D. L. (in press). The affordances of the home, neighbourhood, school and town centre for adolescents. *Journal of Environmental Psychology.*

Cohen, S., & Spacapan, S. (1984). The social psychology of noise. In D. Jones & A. J. Chapman (Eds.), *Noise and society* (pp. 221–245). New York: Wiley

Cohen, S., Evans, G. W., Stokols, D., & Krantz, D. S. (1986). *Behavior, health and environment stress.* New York: Plenum.

Cooper, C. (1972). The house as symbol. *Design and Environment, 14,* 178–182.

Craik, K. H. (1970). Environmental psychology. In K. H. Craik (Ed.), *New directions in psychology* (Vol. 4, pp. 1–121). New York: Holt, Rinehart, and Winston.

Craik, K. H., & Zube, E. H. (1976). *Perceiving environmental quality: Research applications.* New York: Plenum.

Crawford, M., & Unger, R. (2000) *Women and gender: A feminist psychology.* New York: McGraw-Hill.

Cunningham, M. R. (1979). Weather, mood, and helping behavior: Quasi experiments with the sunshine Samaritan. *Journal of Personality and Social Psychology, 37,* 1947–1956.

Devlin, K., & Nasar, J. L. (1989). The beauty and the beast: Some preliminary comparisons of 'high' versus 'popular' residential architecture and public versus architect judgements of same. *Journal of Environmental Psychology, 9,* 333–344.

Doise, W. (1976). *Groups and individuals.* Cambridge, UK: Cambridge University Press.

Donnerstein, E., & Wilson, D. W. (1976). Effects of noise and perceived control on ongoing and subsequent aggressive behavior. *Journal of Personality and Social Psychology, 34,* 774–781.

Dunlap, R. E. (1980). Ecology and the social sciences: An emerging paradigm. *American Behavioral Scientist, 24,* 1–149

Dunlap, R. E., & Van Liere, K. D. (1984). Commitment to the dominant social paradigm and concern for environmental quality. *Social Science Quarterly, 65,* 1013–1028.

Dunlap, R. E., Van Liere, K. D., Mertig, A. G., & Jones, R. E. (2000). Measuring endorsement of the new ecological paradigm: A revised NEP Scale. *Journal of Social Issues, 56,* 425–442.

Elliot, S. J., Cole, D. C., Krueger, P., Voorberg, N., & Wakefield, S. (1999). The power of risk perception: Health risk attributed to air pollution in an urban industrial neighbourhood. *Risk Analysis, 19*(4), 621–634.

Evans, G., & Cohen, S. (1987). Environmental stress. In D. Stokols & I. Altman (Eds.), *Handbook of environmental psychology* (Vol. 1, pp. 571–610). New York: Wiley.

Evans, G. W., Lepore, S. J., Shejwal, B. R., & Palsane, M. N. (1998). Chronic residential crowding and children's well-being: An ecological perspective. *Child Development, 69*(6), 1514–1523.

Farr, R., & Moscovici, S. (1984). *Social representations.* Cambridge, UK: Cambridge University Press.

Feshbach, S. (1964). The function of aggression and the regulation of aggressive drive. *Psychological Review, 71,* 257–272.

Festinger, L. A., Schachter, S., & Back, K. (1950). *Social pressures in informal groups.* New York: Harper and Row.

Fleury-Bahi, G. (1997). Histoire, identité résidentielle et attachement au quartier actuel: Étude sur les habitants de la ville de Paris (History, residential identity and attachment to the residential environment: Study on the inhabitants of Paris). *Psychologie Française, 42*(2), 183–184.

Fleury-Bahi, G. (1998). Paris et ses habitants: Identité résidentielle et attachement au quartier (Paris and its inhabitants: Residential identity and neighborhood attachment). *Revue des Etudes Urbaines, 25,* 49–71.

Garber, J., & Seligman, M. E. P. (Eds.). (1981). *Human helplessness: Theory and applications.* New York: Academic Press.

Gärling, T., Böök, A., & Lindberg, E. (1986). Spatial orientation and wayfinding in the designed environment: A conceptual analysis and some suggestions for post-occupancy evaluation. *Journal for Architectural and Planning Research, 3,* 55–64.

Gärling, T., & Evans, G. W. (1991). *Environmental cognition and action.* New York: Oxford University Press.

Gärling, T., & Hartig, T. (2000). Environmental psychology and the environmental (design) professions. *Newsletter of the International Association of Applied Psychology, 121*(1), 30–32.

Gatersleben, B., & Uzzell, D. L. (2000). The risk perception of transport-generated air pollution. *Journal of the International Association of Traffic and Safety Science, 24*(1), 30–38.

Gatersleben, B., & Uzzell, D. (in press). Social dilemmas and changing travel behaviour: Becoming the public and private citizen. In C. L. Spash & A. Biel (Eds.), *Social psychology and economics in environmental research (SPEER).*

Gergen, K. J., & Gergen, M. M. (1984). *Historical social psychology,* Hillsdale, NJ: Erlbaum.

Getzels, J. W. (1975). Images of the classroom and visions of the learner. In T. G. David & B. D. Wright (Eds.), *Learning environments.* Chicago: University of Chicago Press.

Gibson, J. J. (1950). *The perception of the visual world.* Boston: Houghton Mifflin.

Gibson, J. J. (1979). *The ecological approach to visual perception.* Boston: Houghton Mifflin.

Gifford, R. (1987). *The motivation of park users.* Victoria, British Columbia: Optimal Environments.

Gifford, R. (1997). *Environmental psychology: Principles and practice* (2nd ed.). London: Allyn & Bacon.

Gifford, R. (2000). Environmental psychology and the frog pond. *IAAP Newsletter, 11*(2), 28–30.

Giuliani, V. (1991). Towards an analysis of mental representations of attachment to the home. *Journal of Architectural and Planning Research, 8*(2), 133–146.

Giuliani, V., & Feldman, R. (1993). Place attachment in a developmental and cultural context. *Journal of Environmental Psychology, 13,* 267–274.

Glass, D. C., & Singer, J. E. (1972). *Urban stress: Experiments on noise and social stressors.* New York: Academic Press.

Godlee, F., & Walker, A. (1992). *Health and the environment.* British Medical Journal. London: Tavistock Square.

Groat, L. (1994). Carbuncles, columns and pyramids, lay and expert evaluations of contextual design strategies. In B. C. Scheer & W. F. E. Preiser (Eds.), *Design review: Challenging urban aesthetic control* (pp. 156–164). New York: Chapman and Hall.

Hall, E. T. (1966). *The hidden dimension.* New York: Doubleday.

Hammond, S. (1993). The descriptive analyses of shared representations. In G. Breakwell & D. Canter (Eds.), *Empirical approaches to social representations* (pp. 205–222). Oxford: Clarendon.

Hardin, G. (1968). The tragedy of the commons. *Science, 162,* 1243–1248.

Hart, R. (1979). *Children's experience of place.* New York: Irvington.

Heft, H. (1988). Affordances of children's environments: A functional approach to environmental description. *Children's Environmental Quarterly, 5*(3), 29–27.

Herzlich, C. (1973). *Health and illness: A social psychological analysis.* London: Academic Press.

Hogg, M., & Abrams, D. (1988). *Social identifications A social psychology of intergroup relations and group processes.* London: Routledge.

Holahan, C. J. (1982). *Environmental psychology.* New York: Random House.

Horswill, M. S., & McKenna, F. P. (1999). The development, validation and application of a video-based technique for measuring an everyday risk-taking behaviour: Drivers' speed choice. *Journal of Applied Psychology, 84*(6), 977–985.

Hubbard, P. (1994). Professional vs. lay tastes in design control: An empirical investigation. *Planning Practice and Research, 3,* 271–287.

Hubbard, P. (1996). Conflicting interpretations of architecture: An empirical investigation. *Journal of Environmental Psychology, 16*(2), 75–92.

Ittelson, W. H. (1973). *Environment and cognition.* New York: Seminar.

Jain, U. (1993). Cocommitants of population density in India. *Journal of Social Psychology, 133,* 331–336.

Kaplan, S. (1995). The restorative benefits of nature: Toward an integrative framework. *Journal of Environmental Psychology, 15*(3), 169–182.

Kaplan, S., & Kaplan, R. (1989). The visual environment: Public participation in design and planning. *Journal of Social Issues, 45,* 59–85.

Kasperson, R. E., Renn, O., Slovic, P., Brown, H. S., Emel, J., Goble, R., Kasperson, J. X., & Ratick, S. (1988). The social amplification of risk: A conceptual framework. *Risk Analysis, 8*(2), 177–187.

Kent, S. (1991). Partitioning space: Cross-cultural factors influencing domestic spatial segmentation. *Environment and Behavior, 23,* 438–473

Kitchen, R., Blades, M., & Golledge, R. G. (1997) Relations between psychology and geography. *Environment and Behaviour, 29,* 554–573.

Korosec-Serfaty, P. (Ed.). (1976, June). *Appropriation of space.* Proceedings of the third International Architectural Psychology Conference, Louis Pasteur University, Strasbourg, France.

Korpela, K. (1989). Place identity as a product of environmental self regulation. *Journal of Environmental Psychology, 9,* 241–256.

Korte, C. (1980). Urban non-urban differences in social behavior and social psychological models of urban impact. *Journal of Social Issues, 36,* 29–51.

Korte, C., & Kerr, N. (1975). Responses to altruistic opportunities under urban and rural conditions. *Journal of Social Psychology, 95,* 183–184.

Krupat, E. (1985). *People in cities: The urban environment and its effects.* Cambridge, MA: Cambridge University Press.

Kyttä, M. (1995). *The affordances of urban, small town and rural environments for children.* Paper presented at the international conference Building Identities: Gender Perspectives on Children and Urban Space, Amsterdam, April 1995.

Lalli, M. (1992). Urban-related identity: Theory, measurement, and empirical findings. *Journal of Environmental Psychology, 12,* 285–305.

Lazarus, R. S. (1966). *Psychological stress and the coping process.* New York: McGraw-Hill.

Lazarus, R. S., & Folkman, S. (1984). *Stress, appraisal and coping.* New York: Springer.

Lechner, F., & Boli, J. (1999). *The globalization reader.* Oxford, UK: Blackwell.

Lee, T. R. (1968). Urban neighbourhood as socio-spatial schema. *Human Relations, 20*(3), 240–267.

Lee, T. R. (2001). *Perceptions, attitudes and preferences in forests and woodlands* (Technical Paper No. 18). Edinburgh, Scotland: Forestry Commission.

Lévy-Leboyer, C., Bonnes, M., Chase, J., Ferreira-Marques, J., & Pawlik, K. (1996). Determinants of pro-environmental behaviors: A five-countries comparison. *European Psychologist, 1*(2), 123–129.

Lévy-Leboyer, C., & Ratiu, E. (1993). The need for space and residential satisfaction. *Architecture et Comportement, 9,* 475–490.

Lewin, K. (1951). Formalization and progress in psychology. In D. Cartwright (Ed.), *Field theory in social science.* New York: Harper.

Lewis, J., Baddeley, A. D., Bonham, K. G., & Lovett, D. (1970). Traffic pollution and mental efficiency. *Nature, 225,* 95–97.

Lindberg, E., Hartig, T., Garvill, J., & Gärling, T. (1992). Residential-location preferences across the lifespan. *Journal of Environmental Psychology, 12,* 187–198.

Loo, C. M., & Ong, P. (1984). Crowding, perception and attitudes, consequences of crowding among the Chinese. *Environment and Behavior, 16,* 55–67.

Low, S. M., & Altman, I. (1992). *Place attachment.* New York: Plenum.

Lowenthal, D. (1985). *The past is a foreign country.* Cambridge, UK: Cambridge University Press.

Lynch, K. (1960). *The image of the city.* Cambridge, MA: MIT Press.

McAndrew, T. (1993). *Environmental psychology*. Pacific Grove, CA: Brooks/Cole.

Merrens, M. (1973). Non-emergency helping behaviour in various sized communities. *Journal of Social Psychology, 90*, 327–328.

Mertz, C., Slovic, P., & Purchase, I. (1998). Judgments of chemical risks: Comparisons among senior managers, toxicologists, and the public. *Risk Analysis, 18*, 391–404.

Milgram, S. (1977). The experience of living in cities. In S. Milgram (Ed), *The Individual in a Social World: Essays and Experiments, Reading* (pp. 24–41) MA: Addison Wesley.

Milgram, S., & Jodelet, D. (1976). Psychological maps of Paris. In H. M. Proshansky, W. H. Ittelson, & L. G. Rivlin (Eds.), *Environmental psychology* (pp. 104–124). New York: Holt, Rinehart, and Winston.

Moore, E. O. (1982). A prison environment's effect on health care and service demands. *Journal of Environmental Systems, 11*, 17–34.

Moore, R. (1986). *Childhood's domain*. London: Croom Helm.

Moscovici, S. (1976). *La psychanalyse: Son image et son public* (2nd ed.). Paris: Presses Universitaires de France.

Moscovici, S. (1989). Des représentations collectives aux représentations sociales. In D. Jodelet (Ed.), *Les représentations sociales* (pp. 62–86). Paris: Presses Universitaires de France.

Moser, G. (1984). Everyday vandalism: User behavior in malfunctioning public phones. In C. Lévy-Leboyer (Ed.), *Vandalism* (pp. 167–174). Amsterdam: North-Holland.

Moser, G. (1988). Urban stress and helping behavior: Effects of environmental overload and noise on behavior. *Journal of Environmental Psychology, 8*, 287–298.

Moser, G. (1992). *Les stress urbains*. Paris: A. Colin.

Moser, G. (1997). L'univers relationnel des citadins: Modalités d'ajustement aux contraintes urbaines. *Psychologie Française, 42*, 2.

Moser, G. (in press). Environmental psychology for the new millennium: Towards an integration of cultural and temporal dynamics. In UNESCO (Ed.), *The encyclopedia of life support systems*. Oxford: Eolls.

Moser, G., & Corroyer, D. (2001). Politeness in an urban environment: Is city life still synonymous with civility? *Environment and Behavior, 33*(3), 611–625.

Moser, G., & Lévy-Leboyer, C. (1985). Inadequate environment and situation control. *Environment and Behavior, 17*(4), 520–533.

Moser, G., & Matheau, A. (in press). Promoting selective littering: The effect of the feeling of personal responsibility and the awareness of consequences. In A. Kantas, Th. Velli, & A. Hantzi (Eds.), *Societally significant applications of psychological knowledge*. Athens, Greece: Ellinika Grammata.

Moser, G., Ratiu, E., & Fleury-Bahi, G. (2002). Appropriation and interpersonal relationships: From dwelling to city through the neighborhood. *Environment and Behavior, 34*(1), 122–136.

Nasar, J. L. (1979). The evaluative image of the city. In A. D. Seidel & S. Danford (Eds.), *Environmental design: Research, theory, and application* (pp. 38–45). Washington, DC: Environmental Design Research Association.

Nasar, J. L. (1981). Visual preferences of elderly public housing residents: Residential street scenes. *Journal of Environmental Psychology, 1*, 303–313.

Nasar, J. L. (1983). Adult viewers' preferences in residential scenes. *Environment and Behavior, 15*(5), 589–614.

Nasar, J. L. (1984). Cognition in relation to downtown street-scenes: A comparison between Japan and the United States. In D. Duerk & D. Campbell (Eds.), *The challenge of diversity* (pp. 122–128). Washington, DC: Environmental Design Research Association.

Nasar, J. L. (1993). Connotative meanings of house styles. In G. Arias (Ed.), *The meaning and use of housing: Ethnoscapes* (Vol. 7, pp. 143–167). Avebury: Gower.

Nasar, J. L., & Hong, X. (1999). Visual preferences in urban signscapes. *Environment and behavior, 31*(5), 671–691.

Nasar, J. L., & Min, M. S. (1984). *Modifiers of perceived spaciousness and crowding: A cross-cultural study*. Toronto, Canada: American Psychological Association.

Newell, P. B. (1998). A cross-cultural comparison of privacy definitions and functions: A systems approach. *Journal of Environmental Psychology, 18*, 357–371.

Nord, M., Luloff, A., & Bridger, J. (1998). The association of forest recreation with environmentalism. *Environment and Behavior, 30*, 235–246.

Petts, J. (1995). Waste management strategy development: A case study of community involvement and consensus building in Hampshire. *Journal of Environmental Planning and Management, 38*(4), 519–536.

Pol, E., Guardia, J., Valera, S., Wiesenfeld, E., & Uzzell, D. (2001). Cohesión e identificación en la construcción de la identidad social: La relación entre ciudad, identidad y sostenibilidad (Social cohesion and identification in the construction of social identity). *Revista Universidad de Guadalajara: Dossier, 19*, 40–48.

Proshansky, H. M. (1976, September). *City and self identity*. Paper presented at the Annual Meeting of the American Psychological Association, Washington, DC.

Proshansky, H. M. (1987). The field of environmental psychology: Securing the future. In D. Stokols & I. Altman (Eds.), *Handbook of environmental psychology* (Vol. 2, pp. 1467–1488). New York: Wiley.

Proshansky, H. M. (1990). The pursuit of understanding: An intellectual history. In I. Altman & K. Christensen (Eds.), *Environment and behaviour studies: Emergence of intellectual traditions*, pp. 9–30. New York: Plenum.

Proshansky, H. M., Fabian, A. K., & Kaminoff, R. (1983). Place identity: Physical world socialisation of the self. *Journal of Environmental Psychology, 3*, 57–83.

Proshansky, H. M., Ittelson, W. H., & Rivlin, L. G. (1970). *Environmental psychology: Man and his physical setting*. New York: Holt, Rinehart, and Winston.

Purcell, A., & Nasar, J. L. (1992). Experiencing other peoples houses: A model of similarities and differences in environmental experience. *Journal of Environmental Psychology, 12,* 199–211.

Ramadier, T., & Moser, G. (1998). Social legibility, the cognitive map and urban behaviour. *Journal of Environmental Psychology, 18*(3), 307–319.

Rapoport, A. (1969). *House form and culture*. Englewood Cliffs, NJ: Prentice Hall.

Ratiu, E., & Lévy-Leboyer, C. (1993). Besoin d'espace et satisfaction résidentielle. In M. Segaud (Ed.), *Evolution des modes de vie et architecture du logement: Recherches* (Vol. 42, pp. 59–70). Paris: Cité-Projets, Plan Construction et Architecture.

Robinson, G. M. (1997). Community-based planning: Canada's Atlantic coastal action program (ACAP). *Geographical Journal, 163*(1), 25–37.

Rosengren, W. R., & DeVault, S. (1970). The sociology of time and space in an obstetrical hospital. In H. Proshansky, W. Ittelson, & L. Rivlin (Eds.), *Environmental psychology,* 439–453. New York: Holt, Rinehart, and Winston.

Rosenthal, N. E., Sack, D. A., Gillen, J. C., Levy, A. J., Goodwin, F. K., Davenport, Y., Mueller, P. S., Newssome, D. A., & Wehr, T. A. (1984). Seasonal Affective Disorder: A description of the syndrome and preliminary findings with light therapy. *Archives of General Psychiatry, 41,* 72–80.

Russell, J. A., & Lanius, U. F. (1984). Adaptation level and the affective appraisal of environments. *Journal of Environmental Psychology, 4,* 119–135.

Saegert, S., & Winkel, G. (1990). Environmental psychology. *Annual Review of Psychology, 41,* 441–477.

Seligman, M. E. P. (1975). *Helplessness*. San Francisco: W. F. Freeman.

Sherrod, D. R., & Dowes, R. (1974). Environmental determinants of altruism: The effects of stimulus overload and perceived control on helping, *Journal of Experimental Social Psychology, 10,* 14–27.

Simmel, G. (1957). The metropolis and mental life. In K. H. Wolff (Ed. & Trans.), *The sociology of Georges Simmel*. Glencoe, IL: Free Press. (Original work published 1903)

Sommer, R. (1969). *Personal space*. Englewood Cliffs, NJ: Prentice Hall.

Spencer, C., & Woolley, H. (2000). Children and the city: A summary of recent environmental psychology research. *Child: Care, Health and Development, 26*(3), 181–197.

Srivastava, P., & Mandal, M. K. (1990). Proximal facings to spatial affect expressions in schizophrenia. *Comprehensive Psychiatry, 31,* 119–124.

Staats, H., Gatersleben, B., & Hartig, T. (1997). Change in mood as a function of environmental design: Arousal and pleasure on a simulated forest hike. *Journal of Environmental Psychology, 17*(4), 283–300.

Staats, H., Hartig, T., & Kieviets, A. (2000). Restorative effects of outdoor environments. *International Journal of Psychology, 35*(3–4), 126–126.

Stamps, A. E. (1990). Use of photographs to simulate environments: A meta-analysis. *Perceptual and Motor Skills, 71,* 907–913

Stokols, D. (1978). A typology of crowding experiences. In A. Baum & Y. Epstein (Eds.), *Human response to crowding,* 219–255. Hillsdale, NJ: Erlbaum.

Stokols, D. (1987). Conceptual strategies of environmental psychology. In D. Stokols & I. Altman (Eds.), *Handbook of environmental psychology* (Vol. 1, pp. 41–70). New York: Wiley.

Stokols, D., & Shumaker, S. (1981). People in place: A transactional view of settings. In J. Harvey (Ed.), *Cognition, social behaviour and the environment* (pp. 441–488). Hillsdale, NJ: Erlbaum.

Suedfeld, P. (1998). What can abnormal environments tell us about normal people? Polar stations as natural psychology laboratories. *Journal of Environmental Psychology, 18*(1), 95–102.

Suedfeld, P., & Steel, G. D. (2000). The environmental psychology of capsule habitats. *Annual Review of Psychology, 51,* 227–253.

Sundstrom, E. (1978). Crowding as a sequential process: Review of research of the effects of population density on humans. In A. Baum & Y. M. Epstein (Eds.), *Human response to crowding* (pp. 31–116). Hillsdale, NJ: Erlbaum.

Sundstrom, E. (1987). Work environments: offices and factories. In D. Stokols & I. Altman (Eds.), *Handbook of environmental psychology* (Vol. 2, pp. 733–782). New York: Wiley.

Sundstrom, E., Town, J. P., Rice, R. W., Osborn, D. P., & Brill, M. (1994). Office noise, satisfaction and performance. *Environment and Behavior, 26,* 195–222.

Tajfel, H. (1982). *Social identity and inter-group relations*. Cambridge, UK: Cambridge University Press.

Thompson, S. C., & Stoutemyer, K. (1991). Water use as a commons dilemma: The effects of education that focuses on long-term consequences and individual action. *Environment and Behavior, 23*(3), 314–333.

Thorne, R., Hall, R., & Munro-Clark, M. (1982). Attitudes towards detached houses, terraces, and apartments: Some current pressures towards less preferred but more accessible alternatives. In P. Bart, A. Cheng, & G. Francescato (Eds.), *Knowledge for design* (pp. 435–438). Washington, DC: Environmental Design Research Association.

Tolman, E. C. (1948). Cognitive maps in rats and men. *Psychological Review, 55,* 189–208.

Ulrich, R. S. (1984). View through a window may influence recovery from surgery. *Science, 224,* 420–421.

Uzzell, D. L. (1995). Creating place identity through heritage interpretation. *International Journal of Heritage Studies, 1*(4), 219–228.

Uzzell, D. L. (1998). Interpreting our heritage: A theoretical interpretation. In D. L. Uzzell & R. Ballantyne (Eds.), *Contemporary issues in heritage and environmental interpretation: Problems and prospects* (pp. 11–25). London: The Stationery Office.

Uzzell, D. L. (1999). Education for environmental action in the community: New roles and relationships. *Cambridge Journal of Education, 29*(3), 397–413.

Uzzell, D. L. (2000a). Environmental psychology and the environmental (design) professions: A comment on Gärling and Hartig. *Newsletter of the International Association of Applied Psychology, 121*(1), 32–34.

Uzzell, D. L. (2000b). The psycho-spatial dimension to global environmental problems. *Journal of Environmental Psychology, 20*(3), 307–318.

Uzzell, D. L., & Blud, L. (1993). Vikings! Children's social representations of history. In G. Breakwell & D. Canter (Eds.), *Empirical approaches to social representations* (pp. 110–133). Oxford, UK: Oxford University Press.

Uzzell, D. L., & Leach, R. (2001). *Engineering quiet lanes in the Surrey Hills AONB: Predicting drivers' speed.* Report to the Surrey County Council, Guildford: University of Surrey.

Uzzell, D. L., Pol, E., & Badenes, D. (2002). Place identification, social cohesion and environmental sustainability. *Environment and Behavior, 34*(1), 26–53.

Van Lange, P. A. M., Van Vugt, M., Meertens, R. M., & Ruiter, R. A. (1998). A social dilemma analysis of commuting preferences: The roles of social value orientations and trust. *Journal of Applied Social Psychology, 28*(9), 796–820.

Veitch, R., & Arkkelin, D. (1995). *Environmental psychology: An interdisciplinary perspective.* Englewood Cliffs, NJ: Prentice Hall.

Vlek, C., Skolnik, M., & Gaterslcbcn, B. (1998). Sustainablc dcvclopment and quality of life: Expected effects of prospective changes in economic and environmental conditions. *Zeitschrift für experimentelle Psychologie, 45*(4), 319–333.

Vlek, Ch., Hendrickx, L., & Steg, L. (1993). A social dilemmas analysis of motorised-transport problems and six general strategies for social behaviour change. In ECMT (Ed.), *Transport policy and global warming* (pp. 209–225). Paris: European Conference of Ministers of Transport (ECMT).

Weiss, K., Suedfeld, P., Steel, G. D., & Tanaka, M. (2000). Psychological adjustment during three Japanese Antarctic research expeditions. *Environment and Behavior, 32*(1), 142–156.

Werner, C. M., Altman, I., & Brown, B. B. (1992). A transactional approach to interpersonal relations: Physical environment, social context and temporal qualities. *Journal of Social and Personal Relationships, 9,* 297–323.

Wicker, A. W. (1979). *An introduction to ecological psychology.* Monterey, CA: Brooks/Cole.

Wicker, A. W. (1987). Behavior settings reconsidered: Temporal stages, resources, internal dynamics, context. In D. Stokols & I. Altman (Eds.), *Handbook of environmental psychology* (Vol. 2, pp. 613–653). New York: Wiley.

Wicker, A. W., & Kirkmeyer, S. (1976). From church to laboratory to national park: A program of research on excess and insufficient populations in behavior settings. In S. Wapner, S. B. Cohen, & B. Kaplan (Eds.), *Experiencing the environment,* 157–185. New York: Plenum.

Wineman, J. D. (1986). *Behavioural issues in office design.* New York: Van Nostrand Reinhold.

Wohlwill, J. F. (1974). Human response to levels of environmental stimulation. *Human Ecology, 2,* 127–147.

Wohlwill, J. F., & Heft, H. (1987). The physical environment and development of the child. In D. Stokols & I. Altman (Eds.), *Handbook of environmental psychology* (Vol. 1, 281–328). New York: Wiley.

Woolley, H., Spencer, C. P., Dunn, J., & Rowley, G. (1999). The child as citizen: Experiences of British town and city centres. *Journal of Urban Design, 4,* 255–282.

Zillmann, D. (1978). *Hostility and aggression.* Hillsdalc NJ: Erlbaum.

Zimbardo P. G. (1969). The human choices: Individuation, reason, and order versus deindividuation, impulse, and chaos. In W. J. Arnold & D. Levine (Eds.), *Nebraska symposium on motivation,* 237–307. Lincoln: University of Nebraska Press.

Zlutnick, S., & Altman, I. (1972). Crowding and human behavior. In J. F. Wohlwill & D. H. Carson (Eds.), *Environment and the social sciences* (pp. 44–60). Washington, DC: American Psychological Association.

CHAPTER 18

Close Relationships

MARGARET S. CLARK AND NANCY K. GROTE

In this chapter we draw links between well-being in close relationships and the application of fairness rules in those relationships. In doing so we discuss and link two literatures: a large (and growing) literature on close relationships and a far smaller (and increasingly less active) literature dealing with distributive justice rules and perceptions of fairness in intimate relationships. In sketching out links we set forth some theoretical ideas both about what constitutes a high-quality relationship and about how use of fairness norms relates to the quality of what are often called *close relationships*—friendships, romantic relationships, marriages, and family relationships.

DEFINING QUALITY RELATIONSHIPS

What constitutes a good, high-quality friendship, dating relationship, marriage, or family relationship? What differentiates a high-quality close relationship from one of lower quality? Surprisingly, until quite recently most social and even clinical psychologists had not tackled this question. We attempt to do so in this chapter. First, though, because relationship quality often has been equated with relationship stability, with relationship satisfaction, or with the lack of conflict in a relationship, we begin with arguments *against* using those relationship characteristics as indexes of the overall quality of a relationship.

Stability Is Not Enough

Although at first blush equating relationship stability and relationship quality seems reasonable, making this general assumption is unwise. After all, many stable relationships are

Preparation of this chapter and of some of the empirical work cited within the chapter was supported by the National Science Foundation under grant 9983417. The second author's participation was supported by B/Start Grant 1-R03 MH57914 from the National Institute of Mental Health. Any opinions, findings, conclusions, or recommendations expressed in this material are those of the authors and do not necessarily reflect the views of the National Science Foundation or the National Institute of Mental Health. The authors thank Kristin Boyd, Brooke Feeney, Patricia Jennings, and R. Virginia Fraser for comments on earlier versions of this manuscript.

characterized by unhappiness. Interdependence theorists provide straightforward explanations as to why this is sometimes the case (Kelley & Thibaut, 1978; Rusbult, Arriaga, & Agnew, 2001; Rusbult & Van Lange, 1996). Satisfaction, they point out, is just one determinant of commitment to stay in relationships. Other powerful determinants of relationship stability can keep people in relationships despite unhappiness with that relationship.

First, the more one has *invested* in a relationship, the less likely one is to leave that relationship (Rusbult, 1983). Investments include such things as joint memories, financial investments, friends, possessions, and children. Second, the poorer one's *alternatives* to a relationship, including the alternative of being on one's own, the less likely one is to leave the relationship (Kelley & Thibaut, 1978; Rusbult & Martz, 1995). A woman might stay in an abusive relationship if she perceives her alternatives to be worse, including the option of being alone with no job skills and no financial resources. Finally, *personal and social prescriptives* against leaving relationships can keep a person within a relationship in which satisfaction is low (Cox, Wesler, Rusbult, & Gaines, 1997). A person may have a quite miserable relationship with his or her child yet stay due to very strong personal and societal beliefs that one should never abandon one's child.

Satisfaction Is Not Enough

What about satisfaction? Are relationship members' ratings of their own satisfaction with their relationship valid indexes of the existence of a good relationship? Such ratings often have been used in this way, and we do believe that these are better indexes of the existence of a good relationship than is relationship stability. Problems remain, however, and interdependence theorists again provide us with good reasons not to accept satisfaction as the sine qua non of a good relationship.

They point out that satisfaction is only partially determined by the rewards and costs associated with our relationships. A person's *comparison level* for a relationship is another important determinant of satisfaction (Kelley & Thibaut, 1978). A person's comparison level for a particular relationship is what that person expects (or feels he or she deserves) from that relationship. It is the person's set of standards for the relationship. If a person has had poor-quality relationships in the past, a current relationship that objective observers judge to be a bad relationship might, to that person, seem quite good compared to his or her expectations. In contrast, if a person has had terrific-quality relationships in the past, a current relationship that objective observers judge to be quite good might seem, to that person, to be quite unsatisfactory by comparison.

Another reason satisfaction ratings are not terrific measures of relationship quality is that they are generally collected from a single individual or, at best, from each member of a relationship independently. However, relationship quality is the characteristic of a dyad. It is certainly possible for one person to report being very satisfied with a relationship and his or her partner to report being very unsatisfied with the relationship. What would we then say the quality of the relationship was? For these reasons we do not believe that member satisfaction is the ideal way to judge the quality of a relationship.

Lack of Conflict Is Not Enough

Although many researchers have used the absence of conflict as an index of high-quality relationships and the presence of conflict as an index of low-quality relationships, we believe that such measures are flawed for two reasons. First, it is certainly possible for a relationship to be characterized by low conflict and, simultaneously, by low mutual sharing of concerns and low mutual support. We would not consider this to be a high-quality relationship. For instance, two spouses may lead largely independent lives while sharing the same home. Each may go about his or her business with little or no reliance on the other. Conflict in such a relationship would be quite low, but so too would mutual sharing of concerns, comfort, and support. Indeed, many researchers define interdependence as the very essence of a relationship. They would not view such a relationship as being much of a relationship at all, much less a high-quality one.

Second, we would not consider all conflict to be bad for relationships. Conflict often arises when one person in a relationship feels that his or her needs have been neglected. Raising this as a concern and working it out with a partner may give rise to conflict. However, at the same time, if the conflict is resolved to both persons' satisfaction, the relationship is likely to have been improved relative to what it had been prior to the conflict. This logic suggests that the presence of some conflict in a close relationship (as long as it is dealt with in a constructive fashion) may actually be a positive indicator of relationship quality.

Good Relationships Foster Members' Well-Being

Having rejected stability and satisfaction as valid indexes of good relationships, we suggest that high-quality relationships are ones in which members behave in such a manner as to foster the well-being of their partners. We define *well-being*, in turn, as each member's good physical and mental health and each member's being able to strive toward and reach desired individual and joint goals.

We further suggest that the best way to define such relationships is in terms of the interpersonal processes (and their impact on individual well-being) that characterize relationships. By identifying interpersonal processes likely to foster well-being in relationships, not only can we define high-quality relationships, but, simultaneously, we can also come to understand just *why* such relationships are of high quality.

This said, recent research suggests that good relationships are those in which each member (a) feels an ongoing responsibility for the other member's welfare and acts on that feeling by noncontingently meeting the needs of the partner and (b) feels comfortable and happy about that responsibility; in addition, in most mutual, adult, equal-status relationships each member (c) firmly believes that his or her partner feels a similar sense of responsibility for his or her own welfare and relies on that feeling by turning to the other for support without feeling obligated to repay and (d) believes that the other feels comfortable and happy about that responsibility.

Members of high-quality mutual friendships, romantic relationships, and family relationships trust each other, feel secure with each other, and derive satisfaction from nurturing each other. They understand, validate, and care for each other. They keep track of each other's needs (Clark, Mills, & Powell, 1986), help each other (Clark, Ouellette, Powell, & Milberg, 1987), and feel good about doing so (Williamson & Clark, 1989, 1992). They feel bad when they fail to help (Williamson, Pegalis, Behan, & Clark, 1996). They respond to one another's distress and even anger with accommodation and support (Finkel & Campbell, 2001; Rusbult, Verette, Whitney, Slovik, & Lipkus, 1991) rather than with reciprocal expressions of distress and anger or with defensiveness (Gottman, 1979). They express their emotions to their partners (Clark, Fitness, & Brissette, 2001; Feeney, 1995, 1999). They turn to one another for help (Simpson, Rholes, & Nelligan, 1992). They are willing to forgive one another's transgressions (McCullough, 2000). Further, members of such relationships are likely to hold positive illusions about partners that, in turn, bring out the best in those partners (Murray & Holmes, 1997; Murray, Holmes, & Griffin, 1996a, 1996b; Murray, Holmes, Dolderman, & Griffin, 2000) and to possess cognitive structures in which even their partner's apparent faults are linked to virtues (Murray & Holmes, 1993). Finally, members of such relationships appear ready to engage in some active relationship-protecting processes such as viewing their own relationship as being better than those of others (Johnson & Rusbult, 1989; Simpson, Gangestad, & Lerma, 1990; Van Lange & Rusbult, 1995). All these things contribute to a sense of intimacy between partners (Reis & Patrick, 1996; Reis & Shaver, 1988) and relationship members' having the sense that their relationship is a safe haven (Collins & Feeney, 2000).

Relationship researchers do not have a single name for what we are describing as a high-quality relationship. Rather, several terms currently in use describe different aspects of such a relationship. We have called relationships in which people assume responsibility for another's well-being and that benefit that person without expecting repayments *communal relationships* (Clark & Mills, 1979, 1993). However, assuming responsibility for another person's needs and striving to meet those needs on a noncontingent basis does not necessarily imply that one is competent or successful at so doing. Other terms in the literature for relationships imply success at following such norms. For example, relationships in which members successfully attend to, understand, validate, and effectively care for one another have been called *intimate relationships* by Reis and Shaver (1988; Reis & Patrick, 1996). Relationships in which members view the other as one who does care for their welfare and themselves as worthy of such are have been called *secure relationships* by attachment researchers (Ainsworth, Blehar, Waters, & Wall, 1978; Collins & Allard, 2001; Hazan & Shaver, 1987; Simpson et al., 1992). From our perspective, the exact terminology is not that important—an understanding of the interpersonal processes characterizing these relationships *is* important.

Agreement on Levels of Responsibility Matters

It is not sufficient just to characterize high-quality friendships, romantic relationships, marriages, and family relationships as those in which members assume responsibility for a partner's welfare. It is also important, in our opinion, for members to assume the "right" levels of such responsibility. Of course, it is possible and easy to understand that a relationship might be of low quality because members of a relationship do too little to foster the other's welfare. That seems obvious. A parent who fails to feed his or her child adequately clearly does not have a high-quality relationship with that child. Spouses who ignore one another's needs clearly do not have a high-quality relationship. Less obviously, it is also possible for members to do too much to foster the other's welfare. A person who receives an extravagant, expensive present from a casual friend is likely to feel quite uncomfortable and indebted and is unlikely to describe the relationship as high quality. A very young child might feel as if he must comfort his constantly distressed mother and do so. Objective observers would not consider this to be a sign of a high-quality relationship. Indeed, they are likely to consider this to be a sign of poor parenting. So, how are we to understand what degree of responsiveness to another's needs is right for a relationship?

We suspect that almost everyone has a hierarchy of what we call communal relationships. By this we mean that people have a set of relationships with others about whose needs they believe they *ought* to care and to whose needs they believe they *ought* to strive to be responsive in a noncontingent fashion (Clark & Mills, 1993; Mills & Clark, 1982). These relationships vary from weak to strong, with strength referring to the degree of responsibility the person believes he or she ought to assume for the other's welfare. One end of the hierarchy is anchored by relationships in which the person feels a very low degree of responsibility for the partner's needs (e.g., a relationship with an acquaintance for whom the person might provide directions or the time of day with no expectation of compensation). The other end of the hierarchy is anchored by relationships in which the person assumes tremendous responsibility for the other's needs (e.g., a parent-child relationship in which the parent would do just about anything at any cost to ensure the child's welfare.)

Figure 18.1 depicts one hypothetical person's hierarchy of communal relationships. Communal relationships, from weak to strong, are depicted on the x-axis. The costs one is willing to incur to meet the other's needs (noncontingently) are depicted on the y-axis. The dashed line in the figure depicts the costs the person is willing to incur in order to benefit the other on a communal basis.

Beneath the implicit cost line benefits will be given and accepted on a communal, need, basis. Thus, for instance, strangers give one another the time of day, neighbors take in one another's mail on a temporary basis, friends throw birthday parties for one another and travel to one another's weddings, and parents spend years raising children and tremendous amounts of money to support those children.

Above the cost line benefits are generally not given or even considered. When they are given, they are given on an exchange basis. Consider, for instance, a relationship partner who needs a car. This is a costly benefit and one that falls above the cost line for most relationships, such as those with acquaintances, neighbors, or friends. Under most circumstances this means that this benefit will not be given (or asked for) in such relationships. The topic simply will not come up. However, a person might *sell* his car to a friend (an economic exchange in which the parties agree that the money and the care of equal value). Neighbors might agree to provide each other's child with rides to and from soccer practice following a rule of equality (half the days one person drives, half the days the other drives), and so forth.

Recognizing the existence of hierarchies of communal relationships should help to understand the nature of high-quality personal (communal) relationships. As we said earlier, these relationships are characterized by assumed, noncontingent responsibility for a partner's needs. Here we add that the level of responsibility actually assumed on the part of a caregiver or expected on the part of a person in need (in the absence of true emergencies) ought also to be appropriate to the location of that relationship in its members' hierarchy of relationships. If the costs involved in meeting the need fall beneath the implicit cost boundary shown in Figure 18.1, the responsiveness ought to be present. If costs exceed the boundary, benefits should *not* be given, except for emergencies or in instances in which both members wish to strengthen the communal nature of the relationship. Indeed, giving a benefit that falls above the implicit cost boundary might harm the quality of the relationship. So too may asking for too costly a benefit or implying the existence of too strong a communal relationship by self-disclosing too much (Chaiken & Derlega, 1974; Kaplan, Firestone, Degnore, & Morre, 1974) be likely to hurt the relationship.

This should help to explain why responsiveness must be within appropriate bounds even though responsiveness to needs is a hallmark of good relationships. A casual friend should not give one an extravagant present. It exceeds the appropriate level of responsiveness to needs. A young child is not supposed to assume a great deal of communal responsibility for his or her parent. Thus, a child consistently comforting a troubled parent is not a sign of a high-quality relationship. In contrast, a parent *is* supposed to assume great communal responsibility for his or her child. Thus, a parent

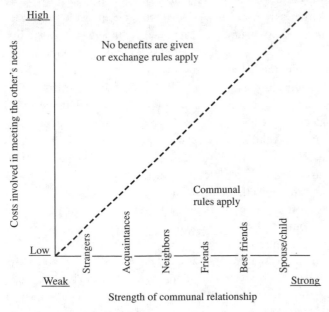

Figure 18.1   The costs one hypothetical person is willing to incur to meet the needs of members of his or her social network on a communal basis.

consistently comforting his or her troubled child is a sign of a high-quality relationship.

NECESSARY ABILITIES AND FORTITUDES

Having a hierarchy of communal relationships in which one believes one *should* behave communally (up to an implicit cost level) is one thing. Actually pulling off the task of appropriately and skillfully attending to one another's needs in such relationships is quite another thing. For mutually supportive, trusting, secure, and intimate communal relationships to exist and to thrive, members must have three distinct sets of skills. One set allows for responding to one's partner's needs effectively. A second set allows for eliciting a partner's attention to one's own needs. The third set involves being able to distinguish successfully when one ought to behave in accord with communal rules and when the application of such rules is socially inappropriate.

Responding Effectively to a Partner's Needs

Skills and fortitudes necessary to respond effectively to a partner's needs include empathic accuracy (Ickes, 1993) and the ability to draw out one's partner's worries and emotional states (Miller, Berg, & Archer, 1983; Purvis, Dabbs, & Hopper, 1984). Many studies support the idea that understanding a spouse's thoughts, beliefs, and feelings is linked with good marital adjustment (e.g., Christensen & Wallace, 1976; Noller, 1980, 1981; Gottman & Porterfield, 1981; Guthrie & Noller, 1988). Another skill important to meeting a partner's needs is knowing when and how to offer help in such a way that it will not threaten the potential recipient's self-esteem or make the potential recipient feel indebted, but will be accepted. Still another skill important to meeting a partner's needs is the ability to give help that the partner (*not* the self) desires and from which the partner (*not* the self) will benefit. To do so requires accurate perception of differences in needs between the self and the partner. Many parents go wrong in this regard. They may impose their needs on the child and may be seen by outsiders as living "through their child," often to the detriment of the child.

Some of these abilities require learning, practice, and intelligence (e.g., the ability to draw a partner out, empathic accuracy, and provision of emotional support). The keys to others may lie more in emotional fortitudes. A person may wish to express empathy or offer help but fail to do so out of fear of appearing awkward or being rejected. One's history of personal relationships in general and one's history within the

particular relationship in question provide explanations for a lack of emotional fortitude in providing help. If one's past partners (or current partner) have not been open to accepting help in the past, then the person is likely to be reluctant to offer care. A lack of fortitude may also stem from temporary factors. When temporarily stressed or in a bad mood, people may not feel that they have the energy to help because they may be especially likely to anticipate that negative outcomes will be associated with helping (Clark & Waddell, 1983).

Alerting Partners to Your Needs

Next consider skills and fortitudes necessary for *eliciting* needed support for the self from one's partner. In this regard, freely expressing one's own need states to the partner through self-disclosure and emotional expression should be important. After all, a partner cannot respond to needs without knowing what they are. Given this, it is not surprising to us that self-disclosure has been found to increase positive affect (Vittengl & Holt, 2000), liking (Collins & Miller, 1994), and satisfaction in dating relationships (Fitzpatrick & Sollie, 1999), marriages (Meeks, Hendrick, & Hendrick, 1998), and sibling relationships (Howe, Aquan-Assee, Bukowski, Rinaldi, & Lenoux, 2000). Of course, one ought also to be able to ask outright for help and accept it when it is offered. Perhaps less obviously, possessing the ability to say "no" to requests from the partner that interfere with one's needs ought to be crucial to the partner's being attentive and responsive to one's needs. It should also be important that, over time, one demonstrates that one does not exaggerate needs or constantly seek help when it is not needed (Mills & Clark, 1986). This ought to increase a partner's sense that one is appropriately, and not overly, dependent.

Although help-seeking skills might seem easy, enacting them requires certain emotional fortitudes. In particular, exercising all these skills probably requires having the firm sense that one's partner truly cares for one and will, indeed, meet one's needs to the best of his or her ability. Otherwise, self-disclosure, emotional expression, and asking for help seem inadvisable. Under such circumstances, one risks being rebuffed, rejected, or evaluated negatively. The partner may even use information to mock or exploit the other. Negative assertion on one's own behalf may also be frightening, as it too many provide a basis for rejection. Thus it may seem best not to seek help and not to assert oneself. However, if one does not do so, keeping the relationship on a communal basis becomes difficult. It is for just these reasons that we believe that a sense of trust and security in relationships is key to following communal norms.

Knowing When to Be Communal

Applying communal rules effectively within appropriate bounds requires the skills and fortitudes just mentioned. Avoiding their use in nonemergency situations outside those bounds may require additional fortitudes. One must be able to detect whether the other desires a communal relationship and, if so, at what strength. Being too anxious for intimate communal relationships may lead one to behave communally in inappropriate situations. Work by attachment researchers suggests that this is something that anxious, ambivalent, or preoccupied people often do (Hazan & Shaver, 1987; Simpson & Rholes, 1998).

LINKING RELATIONSHIP AND JUSTICE RESEARCH

Having reviewed some relationship work suggesting what interpersonal processes and interpersonal skills make a personal relationship such as a friendship, romantic relationship, marriage, or family relationship a high-quality relationship, we turn to linking this work to work on the use of distributive justice rules. In this regard we have already made clear that we believe that benefits are ideally distributed according to needs (and not inputs) in relationships such as friendships, romantic relationships, marriages, and family relationships. We have also made clear that we believe such responsiveness should be noncontingent.

Our views fit well with some past work on distributive justice. Specifically, our views fit well with work supporting the idea that use of a needs-based norm governing the giving and receiving of benefits is preferred to using other distributive justice norms in personal relationships (Clark et al., 1986; Clark et al., 1987; Deutsch, 1975, 1985, for family relationships; Lamm & Schwinger, 1980, 1983). At the same time, our views conflict with the arguments of many other distributive justice researchers who have claimed that following other rules—rules such as equity (Walster, Walster, & Berscheid, 1978; Sabatelli & Cecil-Pigo, 1985; Sprecher, 1986; Utne, Hatfield, Traupman, & Greenberger, 1984) or equality (Austin, 1980; Deutsch, 1975, 1985, for friendships)—are best for friendships, romantic relationships, and family relationships. It also conflicts with the view that an individual solely watching out for his or her own welfare is best in such relationships (Cate, Lloyd, & Henton, 1985; Huston & Burgess, 1979).

Are we right? Is following a noncontingent, responsiveness-to-needs rule best for personal relationships? Is it better than rules of equality or equity? If so, why? We think it is best, and

we make the following theoretical and empirical case for this viewpoint.

Following Communal Norms Affords Security; Following Contingent Norms Undermines Security

The reason we believe that following a communal rule is ideal for ongoing intimate relationships is that it is the only rule that can afford members of the relationship the sense that the other truly cares for their welfare. If another responds to one's needs on a noncontingent basis, the logical inference is that the other truly cares for oneself. This, in turn should heighten trust in the other and promote a sense of security. Instances in which the other benefits a person at some cost to him- or herself should be especially likely to heighten trust (Holmes & Rempel, 1989).

Note that, by definition, contingent distributive justice norms (equity, equality, exchange) involve receiving benefits as conditions of benefiting a person. In contrast, a need-based or communal norm dictates noncontingent giving and acceptance of benefits. Thus, communal responsiveness should be uniquely valuable in terms of providing recipients of care with a sense of being valued and cared for—two of the components Reis and Shaver (1988) pointed out as essential for attaining a sense of intimacy in relationships.

Looking at this from the perspective of the person who gives help also provides insight into the importance of following a communal norm in friendships, romantic relationships, and family relationships. At the same time that noncontingent provision of benefits should cause a recipient to feel valued and cared for, so too should it cause the donor of the benefit to see him- or herself as a nurturant, caring individual. This is simply a matter of self-perception. Both feeling cared for and judging oneself to be a nurturant individual are, we suspect, deeply satisfying. It is just these feelings, we believe, that form the essence of what people desire from their friendships, family relationships, and romantic relationships.

People Advocate and Follow Communal Norms

Not only do we believe that—ideally and often in practice—people follow a communal rule in their intimate relationships and do not keep track of individual inputs and outcomes from a relationship, participants in our studies share our belief (Grote & Clark, 1998; Clark & Grote, 2001). What we did to examine this is straightforward: We asked people. First, we came up with prototype descriptions of a number of ways in which people might choose to distribute benefits within their intimate relationships. That is, we made up descriptions of communal rule, an exchange rule, an equity rule, and an equality rule. Then we had people in a number of different types of close, personal relationships (i.e., friendships, dating relationships, marriages) rate the extent to which they viewed these rules to be ideal for their relationship (from -3 indicating "not at all ideal" to $+3$ indicating "extremely ideal"). They also rated each rule according to the extent to which they thought it was realistic on a similar scale.

In each case the communal rule was rated as ideal for these relationships and as substantially more ideal than were any of the remaining rules (the ratings generally fell on the "not ideal" ends of the scales). In each case the communal rule also was rated as being on the realistic side of the scales and as being more realistic than any of the remaining rules.

Use of Communal Norms and Relationship Satisfaction

Some evidence that a tendency to follow contingent, record-keeping norms is associated with lower marital satisfaction comes from studies by Murstein, Cerreto, and MacDonald (1977) and by Buunk and VanYperen (1991). Murstein et al. (1977) measured the "exchange orientation" of one member of a group of married couples with a scale including items such as, "If I do dishes three times a week, I expect my spouse to do them three times a week." They also administered a marital adjustment scale to research participants. Among both men and women, an exchange orientation toward marriage was negatively correlated with marital adjustment. (We would note, however, that they did not find an analogous negative correlation between exchange orientation and satisfaction in friendships, perhaps because the friendships were weak ones.)

Buunk and VanYperen (1991) had individuals fill out an eight-item measure of exchange orientation and a Global Measure of Equity (see Walster et al., 1978). The latter measure asks, "Considering what you put into your relationship relative to what you get out of it and what your partner puts in compared to what he gets out of it, how does your relationship 'stack up'?" Respondents could indicate that they were getting a much better or better deal, an equitable deal, or a much worse or worse deal than their partner. Buunk and VanYperen also measured satisfaction with the relationship with an eight-item Likert-type scale that measures the frequency with which the interaction with the partner in an intimate relationship is experienced as rewarding and not as aversive.

As these researchers expected, perceiving oneself to be over- or underbenefited relative to one's spouse was linked with lower relationship satisfaction among those high in exchange orientation but not among those low in exchange

orientation. More important for the present point, however, there was a main effect of being high in exchange orientation on marital satisfaction. Those high in exchange orientation reported substantially lower marital satisfaction than did those low in exchange orientation. They did so regardless of whether they reported being underbenefited, equitably benefited, or overbenefited (Buunk & VanYperen, 1991).

Can We Follow Contingent Rules Anyway?

Still another reason we believe that people do not keep track of inputs and calculate fairness on some sort of contingent basis in well-functioning close relationships is simply that following any contingent rule in relationships in which levels of interdependence are high is virtually impossible. Even to make a substantial effort to do so day to day and week to week would be so effortful as to be tremendously irritating and painful to the relationship members involved. Consider the impossibility of accurately keeping track of benefits first.

Think of the sheer number and variety of benefits that are likely to be given and received in an intimate relationship for example, between a husband and wife living together in the same home. Each day a very large number of household tasks (e.g., making beds, doing laundry, picking up clutter, preparing food, shopping for food, putting groceries away, vacuuming, dusting, taking the mail in, feeding pets, changing light bulbs and toilet paper, etc.) are done. So too are a variety of nonhousehold services (e.g., dropping a spouse off at work, picking up take-out food, dropping off dry cleaning, having something framed, visiting relatives, etc.). Then there are benefits that fall within the categories of verbal affection, physical affection, information, instructions, and goods that are given and received. Furthermore, things such as restrained behavioral impulses might be considered benefits. How in the world can two people in a relationship accurately track these things and still accomplish anything else in their lives? The answer is, we think, that they cannot.

To make matters worse, one must keep in mind that tracking the equality or equity of benefits given and benefits received involves far more than simply keeping track of what has been given by each member of a relationship. To compute equality or equality one must place values or weights on the diverse benefits given and received and compute the equality, equity, or evenness of repeated specific exchanges. What is taking the garbage out worth? Does it matter if it is cold and rainy outside? How does it compare with another simple service such as putting the laundry in the machine or unloading the dishwasher? Tougher yet, how does it compare with giving a hug (and does the hug get discounted because both people benefit)?

To push this even further, consider these questions. How does the ability and enjoyment of giving a benefit figure into the calculations? If one partner enjoys doing laundry and the other does not, is laundry done by the latter weighted higher than laundry done by the former? If one partner does not care if the living room is cluttered but the other one does, does it count at all if the latter person cleans up the clutter? These questions are difficult, and they probably seem silly. We suggest that the reason they may seem silly is precisely that people simply do not try to calculate these things in their day-to-day lives, primarily because in good times issues of fairness do not occur to them. Moreover, in times of more stress, when people may have some desire to compute such things, they realize the futility of trying to compute objective equality or equity across diverse domains of inputs and outcomes. (Later we address what we suspect they actually do in times of stress.)

Even If We Could Follow Contingent Norms, Do We Have Access to the Necessary Information?

Imagine that one did have the cognitive capacity to keep track of all benefits given and received in a relationship. Does one have access to all the relevant input? We do not think so. Again, consider a husband and wife who live together—a husband and wife who can surmount the obstacles to record keeping just discussed. We still think it would be an impossible task to track everything that ought to be tracked simply because each person has better access to contributions that he or she has made to the relationship than to contributions that the other has made for a number of reasons. The most straightforward reason is that many contributions one partner makes to the relationship are made in the absence of the other partner.

Picture the husband arriving home prior to the wife. He stops at the mailbox and brings the mail into the house. He throws out the junk and leaves the rest on the table. He notices that the cat has tipped over a plant and cleans up the mess. He listens to three solicitation messages left on the answering machine and deletes them. Although tired, he chats pleasantly when his mother-in-law calls in order to make her feel good and keep her company. He starts dinner. His wife arrives. She notices the mail on the table and the dinner cooking, but does she know anything about the other contributions to the relationship that her spouse has made? No, and he may well not mention them. The general point is that because of the lopsided accessibility of information about contributions to a relationship, there will always be a bias to perceive that the self has made more contributions than the partner has made.

ARE CONTINGENT RULES EVER USED IN CLOSE RELATIONSHIPS?

To recap, we argued that the ideal norm for giving and receiving benefits in close relationships (within an implicit cost boundary) is a need-based, or communal, norm. We further noted that when such relationships are functioning well, issues of fairness tend not to arise. This is not, however, to say that complaints and distress never arise. A need may be neglected, and the neglected person may become distressed and complain. Ideally, the partner responds to that distress and complaint in such a manner as to address the need at hand, soothe the partner, and maintain the relationship on an even, communal keel. However, perhaps the need will not be addressed. It is then, we contend, that processes leading to concerns about fairness may begin to unfold.

Imagine that a person neglects his or her partner's needs; the latter complains, but the former does not respond by adequately addressing the need. Even then, we suspect, the situation may unfold in such a manner that issues of fairness do not arise. Specifically, sometimes the partner will respond with a benign interpretation of the behavior. For instance, that partner may respond by blaming unstable, situational causes rather than the partner (cf. Bradbury & Fincham, 1990), and the behavior may simply be tolerated. Rusbult et al. (1991) described this action as accommodation, generally, and as an instance of reacting with loyalty, more specifically.

For instance, consider a woman who lives far from her family of origin and misses them terribly. She tells her husband of her desire to visit them during their next vacation. He refuses, countering that he would rather take a relaxing trip, perhaps one to the beach. She then suggests that they could go for just a weekend, and he refuses again, saying that he really wants her to stay home and get some work done and that he really needs her company. In other words, he does not respond to her needs. In the face of this his wife may interpret his behavior benignly by attributing it to the situation ("He's very stressed. It's not that he doesn't love me; he just needs to relax"). She may then behave constructively by continuing on with her own communal behavior (acting loyally). She may even go beyond benignly attributing her partner's behavior to the nonstable, situational factors and actually connect her partner's faults (as evidenced by the poor behavior) to virtues, as Murray and Holmes (1993) observed. For instance, his reluctance to visit relatives and his desire to be with her alone on vacation or at home might be taken as evidence of his love for her and of his sensible nature—he does not want to take too much on. In any case, she continues on, maintaining her faith in the overall communal nature of their relationship.

But sometimes spouses do not respond in such an accommodating manner or by connecting their partner's faults to virtues. Instead, they may conclude that their partner really is not a good partner or that they themselves are not worthy of care. In such instances, people may well experience an inclination to switch to contingent rules of distributive justice, and they may actually do so. Doing so, we believe, is triggered by the judgment that one's partner has not met one's need combined with a judgment that this is due to a lack of true caring for the self. One might say that trust in the partner has evaporated. At such times, the adoption of a contingent distributive justice rule in place of a communal rule is likely to seem adaptive. It seems adaptive, we contend, because it is judged to be a more effective means of getting what one needs from one's partner than is trusting that partner to be noncontingently responsive to one's needs.

Consider once again the woman who lives far from her family of origin and misses them terribly. This time, after she suggests that they could go just for a weekend and he refuses again, saying that he really wants her to stay home and that he needs her company, she becomes increasingly distressed at her husband's refusal to respond in any way to her needs. She may attribute his behavior to himself rather than to the situation ("He's selfish"). Alternatively, or perhaps additionally, she may attribute his behavior to herself ("I'm not loveable"). His faults may also bring other faults to mind ("He's selfish; he's often inconsiderate"). He is really not very insightful or intelligent. In general, he is an embarrassment to be around.

In any case, the wife may conclude that the only way her husband is going to respond to her needs is if he *must* do so in order to receive benefits himself (a contingent, exchange perspective). Thus, she may counter his responses by thinking, "Well, OK, if that's the way he's going to be," and saying, "Look, if you're not willing to visit my family, then you certainly can't expect me to go visit yours next May when we were planning on going. I'm only going to go if you do the same for me."

This threat may well work in that the spouse agrees to go visit her family. Unfortunately, we propose, it works with some costs. Switching from a communal to an exchange norm sacrifices important things. First, the donor of a benefit will no longer be able to derive the same sense of nurturing the other. He or she must attribute at least part (or maybe all) of their motivation to their own selfish interests. Second, the recipient of the benefit no longer derives the same sense of being cared for and security from acquiring the benefit. He or she must attribute at least part (or maybe all) of the donor's motivation to the donor's own self-interest rather than to the donor's sense of caring for them. Trust is also likely to deteriorate.

When Will People Switch?

We already suggested that switches from communal to exchange norms are likely to be triggered when a person feels that his or her needs have not been met. We have also suggested, however, that this will not always occur. Thus, an important question becomes when it will and will not occur. We have two answers to this question, one having to do with the situation in which a person finds him- or herself and one having to do with the personality of the person whose needs have been neglected and who is, therefore, vulnerable to switching.

The Situation Matters

Our first answer is straightforward. We predict that people will be more likely to switch from communal to exchange equality or equity norms when they perceive that their needs are being neglected. This may occur because a partner who has normally been quite responsive to the person's needs ceases to be so responsive to that person's needs. This could occur because the partner has become interested in someone or something else or because the partner is under considerable stress or is distracted from the partner's needs. It also may occur because the person who needs help has experienced a large increase in needs that the partner cannot meet. If this is the case, and if the partner continues to neglect needs despite any attempts on the person's part to rectify the situation, the person *might* switch to an exchange norm.

Of course, there are other options available to the person who has lost faith in the communal norm. The person could leave the relationship altogether or switch immediately to simply watching out for his or her own needs without adopting a norm such as equity or equality.

How are decisions between these options made? We can only speculate at this point, but it seems to us that certain variables that have long been discussed by interdependence theorists are relevant to making these decisions. If there are few barriers to leaving (i.e., in interdependence terms, if the person has good alternative options, such as being alone or forming alternative relationships), if investments in the relationship are low, and if there are few social or personal prescriptives to leaving, the person whose needs are being neglected might simply leave. A switch to contingent, record-keeping norms might never take place. We suspect this often happens in friendships. If a friend neglects one's needs, people usually have other friends (or potential friends) to whom they can turn. There are typically not great social or personal prescriptives against letting a friendship lapse, and investments in friendships tend to be lower than those in other close relationships (e.g., romantic relationships, marriages, or parent-child relationships).

On the other hand, sometimes there are considerable barriers to leaving a close relationship. Investments may be high, alternatives may not seem attractive, and there may be strong social and personal pressures working against a person's leaving the relationship. We suspect that when such barriers are high, people whose needs have been seriously neglected will stay in the relationship but switch from adherence to a communal norm to adherence to a contingent record-keeping norm such as equity, equality, or exchange. This may happen in many marriages in which investments that cannot be recouped have been made (e.g., children, a joint house, financial success, joint friends), alternatives seem poor (being poorer, living alone, leaving the house), and strong prescriptions against leaving exist (one's church or parents would disapprove). In such circumstances, the best option may seem to be to continue relationship but to switch the basis on which benefits are given in such a way that one feels more certain that one's needs will be met. This may seem most workable even if one has to sacrifice a sense of being nurtured and of nurturing.

Individual Differences Matter

We believe that it is the situation that triggers people to switch from communal to contingent, record-keeping distributive justice norms, but we also believe that personality matters. People differ from one another in terms of their chronic tendencies to believe that others will be responsive to their needs and that they are worthy of such responsiveness. This has been a major theme in recent relationship literature. It is especially evident in the attachment theory and the empirical work that has been based on that theory. Secure individuals are assumed to view close others as likely to respond to their needs on a consistent basis, and they feel comfortable depending on others for support. Insecure people do not. However, attachment theorists are not the only ones who have emphasized differences in how people tend to view their partners. Others have talked about people differing in their chronic tendencies to trust other people in close relationships without necessarily referring to attachment theory (Holmes & Rempel, 1989), or about how chronic levels of self-esteem may relate to views of, and reactions to, close partners (Murray, Holmes, MacDonald, & Ellsworth, 1998). For our own part, we have discussed chronic individual differences in communal orientation, which refers to the tendency to respond to the needs of others and to expect others to respond to one's own needs on a noncontingent basis (Clark et al., 1987).

We suspect that these chronic individual differences that people bring to their close relationships will be important determinants of switching from communal to exchange norms in the face of evidence that one's partner is neglecting one's needs. We suspect that almost everyone (regardless of attachment style, trust, self-esteem, or communal orientation) understands communal norms as we have discussed them. Moreover, we would assert that almost everyone believes that communal norms are ideal for friendships, romantic relationships, and marriages and that people start off such relationships following such norms. Indeed, it is by following such norms in the first place that people signal to potential partners that they want a friendship or romantic relationship with another person.

However, we also suspect that people who are insecure, have low trust in others, are low in self-esteem, or are low in chronic communal orientation (variables that we suspect co-occur) will be especially vulnerable to switching from a communal to an exchange norm in the face of real or imagined evidence that the other is neglecting their needs. They are the people, we assert, who react to the slightest evidence of such neglect with conclusions that the evidence indicates that the other is selfish and does not care for them or that they are unworthy of care. Further, we suggest that such conclusions, in turn, lead them to back away from the relationship. Alternatively (perhaps because they also are likely to perceive that they have fewer good alternatives than others do), these insecure individuals might be led to switch to a contingent, record-keeping norm such as equality, equity, or exchange as a basis for giving and receiving benefits in their relationship.

Evidence

The arguments we have just made suggest something that, to date, has not received attention in the distributive justice literature. Researchers in that tradition have typically advocated that there is one real rule that governs the giving and receiving of benefits within close relationships. Some suggest it is equality (Austin, 1980; Deutsch, 1975, 1985, for friendships); some suggest it is equity (Sabatelli & Cecil-Pigo, 1985; Utne et al., 1984; Walster et al., 1978); and some say it is a need-based rule (Deutsch, 1975, 1985, for family relationships; Lamm & Schwinger, 1980, 1983; Mills & Clark, 1982). Whatever rule they advocate, though, it has tended to be a single rule, and they have suggested that people in close relationships generally follow *that* rule. If a person does a good job following the particular rule, all is well. If the rule is violated, unhappiness results, and either the distress must be resolved or the relationship may end. We are suggesting something quite different.

We are suggesting that people in general start off their close relationships believing in a communal norm and doing their best to follow it. Such a norm requires mutual responsiveness to needs. However, it is inevitable that needs will be neglected. When this happens or when it is perceived to have happened, distress will occur, as we have argued. The distress, in turn, sets the stage for a possible switch to a contingent, record-keeping norm such as equity or exchange. Thus, it is likely that it is *distress* that—in most relationships some of the time and in some relationships very often—leads to record keeping. Such record keeping will, however, necessarily be retrospective at first. As such, it is very likely that it will be biased in such a manner as to result in evidence of inequity. Perceptions of inequity will, in turn, lead to judgments of unfairness. Then, in an iterative fashion, these perceptions will lead to further distress. Note that this is the reverse of what has typically been argued in the past, which is that record keeping and calculations of equity come first and that distress results when inequities are detected (Walster et al., 1978).

Is there any evidence for our proposal that distress precedes perception of unfairness in close relationships (rather than vice versa)? The answer is yes (Grote & Clark, 2001). In a recent study we tracked both conflict and perceptions of unfairness in a sample of about 200 married couples. These couples were enrolled in the study at a time when the wife was in the third trimester of her first pregnancy. Marital conflict (distress) was tapped at that time, again a few months after the baby was born, and a third time when the baby was about 1 year old. We also asked many questions about the division of household labor at all three points in time and about how fair the husband and wife felt that division of labor to be. (Notably, the division of labor was almost always judged to be unfair, with the wife performing more whether she stayed at home, worked part time or worked full time, and with both spouses agreeing that this was unfair.)

The longitudinal panel design of this study allowed us to conduct path analyses on the data in order to ascertain whether conflict at Time 1 predicted perceptions of unfairness at Time 2 (controlling for perceptions of unfairness at Time 1). Our theoretical position led us to the prediction that it would. We were also able to test whether perceptions of unfairness at Time 1 would predict conflict at Time 2 (controlling for conflict at Time 1). Traditional perspectives would lead to the prediction that it would. However, our theoretical perspective led us to predict that that would not necessarily be the case. That is, we believed that the division of labor could be inequitable and could be judged to be unfair when a social scientist came along and asked about it but still might not disrupt the relationship if both partners felt that their needs were being met and did not feel stressed.

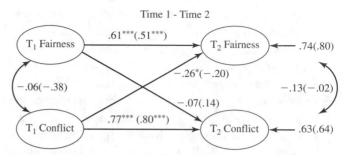

Figure 18.2 Links between relationship conflict and perceptions of fairness in relationships across time.

The results, which are shown in Figure 18.2, were as we expected. Conflict at Time 1 (which we felt was indicative of situations in which at least one person was feeling that his or her needs were not being met) prospectively and significantly predicted perceptions of unfairness at Time 2 controlling for perceptions of unfairness at Time 1. Perceptions of unfairness at Time 1, however, were not significant prospective predictors of conflict at Time 2 controlling for perceptions of conflict at Time 1. This occurs, we assert, because in low-stress times when partners' needs are being met (as we suspected was the case for most couples prior to the birth of an eagerly anticipated first child), people are not keeping track of inputs and outcomes day to day and are not calculating fairness. Whereas they can report on inequities in housework when a social scientist asks them to do so, we believe that most of our couples were not doing this on their own. That is why our measures of perceived unfairness did not predict conflict. In contrast, the early measures of conflict, we suspect, did pick up on those couples including at least one member who felt that his or her needs were being neglected. It is among these couples, we suspect, that record keeping (much of it retrospective and biased) emerged, resulting in perceptions of unfairness.

Once record keeping does emerge and unfairness is perceived, we have predicted that those perceptions of unfairness will increase unhappiness further. Evidence for this subsequent process emerged in the Grote and Clark data as well. Specifically, when changes in the patterns of data from Time 2 until Time 3 were examined, it was found that perceptions of unfairness at Time 2 (shortly after the baby had been born) until Time 3 (when the baby was about 1 year old) did significantly predict increases in conflict, controlling for conflict at Time 2. This occurred, we believe, because once couples were stressed and record keeping commenced, finding evidence of inequities increased distress still further. One interesting result was that conflict measured at Time 2 did not predict further increases in perceptions of unfairness as Time 3 (controlling for perceptions of unfairness at Time 2).

Thus, we have acquired and reported evidence consistent with the notion that the existence of inequities in a marriage will not necessarily lead to distress. We have also acquired and reported evidence consistent with the notions that distress might be what triggers contingent record keeping and perceptions of unfairness. We do not yet have hard empirical evidence that there are individual differences in people's tendencies to feel that their needs have been neglected and, in turn, to switch from adherence to a communal norm to adherence to some sort of record keeping, contingent, distributive justice norm. However, we are currently collecting and beginning to analyze data relevant to just that question.

Permanent or Temporary Switches?

A final issue we wish to address in this chapter is whether the change will be permanent or temporary once people switch from a communal to a contingent, record-keeping norm for distributing benefits within their relationship. We propose that most such switches will be temporary. These changes will occur when a person is dissatisfied with how a relationship is going, wishes to ensure that his or her needs are met by the partner, and (not incidentally) wishes to signal his or her distress to the partner. Indeed, *communicating* displeasure may be just as important a motivator of the switch as is ensuring that one gets what one wants. Once the switch has been made and communicated, the protest function of having done so is largely accomplished. So, too, may the person have accomplished the short-term goal of having one immediate need addressed.

However, once a contingent, record-keeping distributive justice norm begins to be used, all the disadvantages of following such a norm will emerge. That is, record keeping will have to be done. It is tedious; it is virtually impossible to do competently; and given all the sorts of biases already discussed in this chapter, there will inevitably be disagreements over whether equity, equality, or fair exchange have been achieved. Moreover, the advantages of following a communal norm will evaporate. The recipient of benefits will not feel that the other cares for him or her, and the donor of benefits will not derive satisfaction for having nurtured a partner. These things combined with the strong societal norm that communal rules ought to characterize marriages and other close relationships will combine to push couples back to following a communal norm. Moreover, stresses in relationships themselves will often dissipate, and reminders of a partner's true caring attitudes will reemerge. Thus, we would predict that couples will often bounce back to using communal norms.

On the other hand, there should also be cases when couples do not bounce back. Chronic neglect of at least one partner's needs by the other may predict this. So too may either partner's long-term, pessimistic views of the likelihood of the other being caring (and of the self being worthy of care) predict such a lack of resilience. These two things, in combination, may be especially likely to predict that a switch to contingent norms will be longer term. Such a switch, as we have already noted, is unlikely to constitute a satisfying solution. Therefore, we believe that it will likely be followed by a further switch to purely self-interested behavior or to the dissolution of the relationship. Whether the relationship persists long term (and perhaps happily), given the use of contingent record-keeping norms, or whether it ends will depend on the presence or absence of the sorts of barriers to leaving that interdependence theorists have discussed. That is, having poor alternatives, high investments, and feeling prescriptions against leaving are factors likely to keep couples together despite giving and receiving benefits on what we consider to be nonoptimal bases. Good alternatives, low investments, and low prescriptions to leaving are likely to predict relationship dissolution.

CONCLUSIONS

In this chapter we described what we believe to be the characteristics of a high-quality friendship, dating relationship, marriage, or family relationship. We suggested that quality ought not be defined in terms of stability, satisfaction, or conflict but rather in terms of the presence of interpersonal processes that facilitate the well-being of its members. We also suggested that members ought to agree implicitly on the degree of responsiveness to needs that is expected in the relationship and that relationships can go bad not only if responsiveness to needs is not present when expected but also if it is present when it is not called for.

Next we pointed out that viewing close relationships in this way suggests taking a new approach to understanding the use (and nonuse) of contingent, record-keeping distributive justice norms in intimate relationships. In well-functioning intimate relationships people should respond to one another's needs in a noncontingent fashion as those needs arise. Record keeping should not be an issue, and fairness should not be discussed. Fairness simply should not be a salient issue for people in such relationships. (Of course, if some social scientist comes along and asks participants to judge the fairness of the giving and receiving of benefits in that relationship, we have no doubt that members will come up with such ratings. We just do not think they do this spontaneously on their own.) Members of such relationships appear to be following a communal rule, and we believe that following such a rule promotes a sense of intimacy, security, and well-being in the relationship.

However, we argued further, record keeping may become an issue in relationships that members would like to see operate on a communal basis. It becomes an issue if and when needs are perceived to have been neglected and attributions of a lack of caring are made. In such cases, partners in a relationship may switch to record-keeping norms such as exchange, equity, or equality in an effort to ensure that their needs are met. Once this is done, it is very likely that unfairness will be perceived (whether it objectively exists or not), and distress is likely to increase. However, we do believe that many couples are resilient and will "bounce back" to following communal norms with time. Others will not be resilient, and members of such relationships will continue, often times unhappily, to use record-keeping rules to give and receive benefits or even to rely on pure self-interest. Depending on barriers to exiting the relationship, it may or may not dissolve.

REFERENCES

Ainsworth, M. D., Blehar, M. C., Waters, C., & Wall, S. (1978). *Patterns of attachment: A psychological study of the strange situation.* Hillsdale, NJ: Erlbaum.

Austin, W. (1980). Friendship and fairness: Effects of type of relationship and task performance on choice of distribution rules. *Personality and Social Psychology Bulletin, 6,* 402–408.

Bradbury, T. N., & Fincham, F. D. (1990). Attributions in marriage: Review and critique. *Psychological Bulletin, 107,* 3–33.

Buunk, B. P., & Van Yperen, N. W. (1991). Referential comparisons, relational comparisons, and exchange orientation: Their relation to marital satisfaction. *Personality and Social Psychology Bulletin, 17,* 709–717.

Cate, R. M., Lloyd, S. A., & Henton, J. M. (1985). The effect of equity, equality and reward level on the stability of students' premarital relationships. *Journal of Social Psychology, 125,* 175–725.

Chaiken, A. L., & Derlega, V. J. (1974). Liking for the norm-breaker in self-disclosure. *Journal of Personality, 42,* 117–129.

Christensen, L., & Wallace, L. (1976). Perceptual accuracy as a variable in marital adjustment. *Journal of Sex and Marital Therapy, 2,* 130–136.

Clark, M. S., Fitness, J., & Brissette, I. (2001). Understanding people's perceptions of relationships is crucial to understanding their emotional lives. In G. Fletcher & M. S. Clark (Eds.), *Blackwell handbook of social psychology: Interpersonal processes* (pp. 253–278). London: Blackwell.

Clark, M. S. & Grote, N. K. (2001). Manuscript in preparation.

Clark, M. S., & Mills, J. (1979). Interpersonal attraction in exchange and communal relationships. *Journal of Personality and Social Psychology, 37,* 12–24.

Clark, M. S., & Mills, J. (1993). The difference between communal and exchange relationships: What it is and is not. *Personality and Social Psychology Bulletin, 19,* 684–691.

Clark, M. S., Mills, J., & Powell, M. C. (1986). Keeping track of needs in communal and exchange relationships. *Journal of Personality and Social Psychology, 51,* 333–338.

Clark, M. S., Ouellette, R., Powell, M. C., & Milberg, S. (1987). Recipient's mood, relationship type and helping. *Journal of Personality and Social Psychology, 53,* 94–103.

Clark, M. S., & Waddell, B. (1983). Effects of moods on thoughts about helping, attraction, and information acquisition. *Social Psychology Quarterly, 46,* 31–35.

Collins, N. L., & Allard, L. M. (2001). Cognitive representations of attachment: The content and function of working models. In G. J. O. Fletcher & M. S. Clark (Eds.), *Blackwell handbook of social psychology: Interpersonal processes* (pp. 60–85). London: Blackwell.

Collins, N. L., & Feeney, B. C. (2000). A safe haven: An attachment theory perspective on support seeking and caregiving in intimate relationships. *Journal of Personality and Social Psychology, 78,* 1053–1073.

Collins, N. L., & Miller, L. C. (1994). Self-disclosure and liking: A meta-analytic view. *Psychological Bulletin, 116,* 457–475.

Cox, C. L., Wesler, M. O., Rusbult, C. E., & Gaines, S. O. (1997). Prescriptive support and commitment processes in close relationships. *Social Psychology Quarterly, 60,* 79–90.

Deutsch, M. (1975). Equity, equality and need: What determines which value will be used as the basis of distributive justice? *Journal of Social Issues, 31,* 137–148.

Deutsch, M. (1985). Distributive justice: A socio-psychological perspective. New Haven: Yale University Press.

Feeney, J. A. (1995). Adult attachment and emotional control. *Personal Relationships, 2,* 143–159.

Feeney, J. A. (1999). Adult attachment, emotional control, and marital satisfaction. *Personal Relationships, 6,* 169–185.

Finkel, E. J., & Campbell, W. K. (2001). Self-control and accomodation in close relationships: An interdependence analysis. *Journal of Personality and Social Psychology, 81,* 263–277.

Fitzpatrick, J., & Sollie, D. L. (1999). Influence of individual and interpersonal factors on satisfaction and stability in romantic relationships. *Personal Relationships, 6,* 337–350.

Gottman, J. M. (1979). *Marital interaction: Experimental investigations.* New York: Academic Press.

Gottman, J. M., & Porterfield, A. L. (1981). Communicative competence in the nonverbal behavior of married couples. *Journal of Marriage and the Family, 43,* 817–824.

Grote, N. K., & Clark, M. S. (1998). Distributive justice norms and family work: What is perceived as ideal, what is applied, and what predicts perceived fairness? *Social Justice Research, 11,* 243–269.

Grote, N. K., & Clark, M. S. (2001). Does conflict drive perceptions of unfairness or do perceptions of unfairness drive conflict? *Journal of Personality and Social Psychology, 80, 2,* 281–293.

Guthrie, D. M., & Noller, P. (1988). Married couples' perceptions of one another in emotional situations. In P. Noller & M. A. Fitzpatrick (Eds.), *Perspectives on marital interaction* (pp. 153–181). Cleveland, OH: Multilingual Matters.

Hazan, C., & Shaver, P. (1987). Romantic love conceptualized as an attachment process. *Journal of Personality and Social Psychology, 52,* 511–524.

Holmes, J. G., & Rempel, K. (1989). Trust in close relationships. In C. Hendrick (Ed.), *Review of personality and social psychology: Vol. 10. Close relationships* (pp. 187–219). Newbury Park, CA: Sage.

Howe, N., Aquan-Assee, J., Bukowski, W. M., Rinaldi, C. M., & Lenoux, P. M. (2000). Sibling self-disclosure in early adolescence. *Merrill-Palmer Quarterly, 46,* 653–671.

Huston, T. L., & Burgess, T. L. (1979). Social exchange in developing relations: An overview. In R. Burgess & T. Huston (Eds.), *Social exchange in developing relations.* New York: Academic Press.

Ickes, W. (1993). Empathic accuracy. *Journal of Personality, 61,* 587–610.

Johnson, D. J., & Rusbult, C. E. (1989). Resisting temptation: Devaluation of alternative partners as a means of maintaining commitment in close relationships. *Journal of Personality and Social Psychology, 57,* 967–980.

Kaplan, K. J., Firestone, I. J., Degnore, R., & Morre, M. (1974). Gradients of attraction as a function of disclosure probe intimacy and setting formality: On distinguishing attitude oscillation from attitude change—Study one. *Journal of Personality and Social Psychology, 30,* 638–646.

Kelley, H. H., & Thibaut, J. (1978). *Interpersonal relations: A theory of interdependence.* New York: Wiley.

Lamm, H., & Schwinger, T. (1980). Norms concerning distributive justice: Are needs taken into consideration in allocation decisions? *Social Psychology Quarterly, 43,* 425–429.

Lamm, H., & Schwinger, T. (1983). Need consideration in allocation decisions: Is it just? *Journal of Social Psychology, 119,* 205–209.

McCullough, M. E. (2000). Forgiveness as human strength: Theory, measurement, and links to well-being. *Journal of Social and Clinical Psychology, 19,* 43–55.

Meeks, B. S., Hendrick, S. S., & Hendrick, C. (1998). Communication, love and relationship satisfaction. *Journal of Social and Personal Relationships, 15,* 755–773.

Miller, L. C., Berg, J., & Archer, R. L. (1983). Openers: Individuals who elicit intimate self-disclosure. *Journal of Personality and Social Psychology, 44,* 1234–1244.

Mills, J., & Clark, M. S. (1982). Exchange and communal relationships. In L. Wheeler (Ed.), *Review of personality and social psychology* (pp. 121–144). Beverly Hills, CA: Sage.

Mills, J., & Clark, M. S. (1986). Communications that should lead to perceived exploitation in communal and exchange relationships. *Journal of Social and Clinical Psychology, 4,* 225–234.

Murray, S. L., & Holmes, J. G. (1993). Seeing virtues in faults: Negativity of the transformation of interpersonal narratives in close relationships. *Journal of Personality and Social Psychology, 65,* 707–722.

Murray, S. L., & Holmes, J. G. (1997). A leap of faith? Positive illusions in romantic relationships. *Personality and Social Psychology Bulletin, 23,* 586–604.

Murray, S. L., Holmes, J .G., Dolderman, D., Griffin, D. W. (2000). What the motivated mind sees: Comparing friends' perspectives to married partners' views of each other. *Journal of Experimental Social Psychology.*

Murray, S. L., Holmes, J. G., & Griffin, D. (1996a). The benefits of positive illusions: Idealization and the construction of satisfaction in close relationship. *Journal of Personality and Social Psychology, 70,* 79–98.

Murray, S. L., Holmes, J. G., & Griffin, D. (1996b). The self-fulfilling nature of positive illusions in romantic relationships: Love is not blind, but prescient. *Journal of Personality and Social Psychology, 71,* 1155–1180.

Murray, S. L., Holmes, J. G., MacDonald, G., & Ellsworth, P. (1998). Through the looking glass darkly? When self-doubts turn into relationship insecurities. *Journal of Personality and Social Psychology, 75,* 1459–1480.

Murstein, B. I., Cerreto, M., & MacDonald, M. G. (1977). A theory and investigation of the effect of exchange-orientation on marriage and friendships. *Journal of Marriage and the Family, 39,* 543–548.

Noller, P. (1980). Misunderstandings in marital communication: A study of couples' nonverbal communication. *Journal of Personality and Social Psychology, 39,* 1135–1148.

Noller, P. (1981). Gender and marital adjustment level differences in decoding messages from spouses and strangers. *Journal of Personality and Social Psychology, 41,* 272–278.

Purvis, J. A., Dabbs, J. M., & Hopper, C. H. (1984). The "Opener": Skilled user of facial expression and speech pattern. *Personality and Social Psychology Bulletin, 10,* 61–66.

Reis, H. T., & Patrick, B. C. (1996). Attachment and intimacy: Component processes. In E. T. Higgins & A. W. Kruglanski (Eds.), *Social psychology: Handbook of basic principles.* New York: Guilford Press.

Reis, H. T., & Shaver, P. (1988). Intimacy as an interpersonal process. In S. W. Duck (Ed.), *Handbook of personal relationships* (pp. 367–391). New York: Wiley.

Rusbult, C. E. (1983). A longitudinal test of the investment model: The development (and deterioration) of satisfaction and commitment in heterosexual relationships. *Journal of Personality and Social Psychology, 45,* 101–117.

Rusbult, C. E., Arriaga, X. B., & Agnew, C. R. (2001). Interdependence in close relationships. In G. Fletcher & M. S. Clark (Eds.),

Blackwell handbook of social psychology: Interpersonal processes (pp. 359–387). London: Blackwell.

Rusbult, C. E., & Martz, J. M. (1995). Remaining in an abusive relationship: An investment model analysis of nonvoluntary commitment. *Personality and Social Psychology Bulletin, 21,* 558–571.

Rusbult, C. E., & Van Lange, P. A. M. (1996). Interdependence processes. In E. T. Higgins & A. Kruglanski (Eds.), *Social psychology: Handbook of basic principles.* New York: Guilford Press.

Rusbult, C. E., Verette, J., Whitney, G., Slovik, L., & Lipkus, I. (1991). Accomodation processes in close relationships: Theory and preliminary empirical evidence. *Journal of Personality and Social Psychology, 60,* 53–78.

Sabatelli, R. M., & Cecil-Pigo, E. F. (1985). Relational interdependence and commitment in marriage. *Journal of Marriage and the Family, 47,* 931–937.

Simpson, J. A., Gangestad, S. W., & Lerma, M. (1990). Perception of physical attractiveness: Mechanisms involved in the maintenance of romantic relationships. *Journal of Personality and Social Psychology, 59,* 1192–1201.

Simpson, J. A., & Rholes, W. S. (1998). *Attachment theory and close relationships.* New York: Guilford Press.

Simpson, J. A., Rholes, W. S., & Nelligan, J. S. (1992). Support seeking and support giving within couples in an anxiety-provoking situation: The role of attachment styles. *Journal of Personality and Social Psychology, 62,* 434–446.

Sprecher, S. (1986). The relation between inequity and emotions in close relationships. *Social Psychology Quarterly, 51,* 318–328.

Utne, M. K., Hatfield, E., Traupmann, J., & Greenberger, D. (1984). Equity, marital satisfaction, and stability. *Journal of Social and Personal Relationships, 1,* 323–332.

Van Lange, P. A. M., & Rusbult, C. E. (1995). My relationship is better than—and not as bad as—yours is: The perception of superiority in close relationships. *Personality and Social Psychology Bulletin, 21,* 32–44.

Vittengl, J. R., & Holt, C. S. (2000). Getting acquainted: The relationship of self-disclosure and social attraction to positive affect. *Journal of Personality and Social Psychology, 17,* 53–66.

Walster, E., Walster, G. W., & Berscheid, E. (1978). *Equity: Theory and research.* Boston: Allyn & Bacon.

Williamson, G. M., & Clark, M. S. (1989). Providing help and desired relationship type as determinants of changes in moods and self-evaluations. *Journal of Personality and Social Psychology, 56,* 722–734.

Williamson, G. M., & Clark, M. S. (1992). Impact of desired relationship type on affective reactions to choosing and being required to help. *Personality and Social Psychology Bulletin, 18,* 10–18.

Williamson, G. M., Pegalis, L., Behan, A., & Clark, M. S. (1996). Affective consequences of refusing to help in communal and exchange relationships. *Personality and Social Psychology Bulletin, 22,* 34–47.

CHAPTER 19

Altruism and Prosocial Behavior

C. DANIEL BATSON AND ADAM A. POWELL

The word *prosocial* does not appear in most dictionaries; it was created by social scientists as an antonym for *antisocial*. *Prosocial behavior* covers the broad range of actions intended to benefit one or more people other than oneself—behaviors such as helping, comforting, sharing, and cooperating. The word *altruism* has at times been used to refer to a subset of these behaviors—for example, self-sacrificial helping or helping in the absence of obvious, external rewards. Such usage seems inappropriate, however, because altruism is a motivational concept. Altruism is the motivation to increase another person's welfare; it is contrasted to *egoism,* the motivation to increase one's own welfare (MacIntyre, 1967). There is no one-to-one correspondence between prosocial behavior and altruism. Prosocial behavior need not be motivated by altruism; altruistic motivation need not produce prosocial behavior.

WHY DO—AND DON'T—PEOPLE ACT PROSOCIALLY?

Addressing the question of why people act prosocially may seem natural and necessary for social psychologists. Indeed, in the field's first text William McDougall (1908) made this

question focal: "The fundamental problem of social psychology is the moralization of the individual by the society into which he is born as a creature in which the non-moral and purely egoistic tendencies are so much stronger than any altruistic tendencies" (p. 16). When Kurt Lewin, his students, and his colleagues ushered in modern social psychology in the 1930s and 1940s, however, other questions took precedence. These were the pressing social-problem questions provoked by the rise of Nazism, two world wars, the Holocaust, the advent of the nuclear age, the Cold War, and racial injustice. Attention was directed to totalitarian and autocratic leadership, conformity and obedience to authority, aggression, prejudice, ethnocentrism, interpersonal and intergroup conflict, propaganda, persuasion, and attitude formation and change.

The 1960s brought the question of why people act prosocially to the fore once again. This question did not replace the social-problem questions; it was added to the list. Several shocking cases in which bystanders failed to help persons in desperate need raised concern about the breakdown of social structure and social decency, especially in urban environments. Best known is the case of Kitty Genovese, whose brutal stabbing and eventual death was witnessed by 38 of her neighbors in the Kew Gardens area of Queens, New York. Her murder took more than half an hour, and despite her pleading screams, no one intervened; no one even called the police. More heartening were the courageous acts of Freedom Riders and other civil rights workers, Black and White, who suffered beatings, imprisonment, and in some cases death to further the cause of racial equality in the American South. Youth were in the streets to protest the Vietnam War and to proclaim the dawning of the Age of Aquarius. The times they were a-changin'. Social psychologists were asked, Why do—and don't—people act prosocially?

Before attempting to offer an answer to this question, one should probably inquire of the questioner, "Why do you ask?" This response is necessary because the question has been asked for two very different reasons. Some have asked in order to reach the practical goal of encouraging prosocial behavior; others, in order to challenge currently dominant theories of social motivation. The dominant motivational theories in psychology, sociology, economics, and political science are firmly founded on assumptions of universal egoism (Mansbridge, 1990; Wallach & Wallach, 1983). Can one account for all prosocial behavior in terms of egoism, or must one make room for altruism as well? Might there be other forms of prosocial motivation besides egoism and altruism?

These two reasons for asking why people act prosocially beg for very different answers. So, if one is not clear which reason lies behind the question, the answer provided may appear irrelevant and the research on which it is based misguided. To avoid such confusion, this chapter addresses the two concerns in turn—first the practical, then the theoretical.

VARIANCE-ACCOUNTED-FOR EMPIRICAL ANALYSIS

Psychologists pursuing the practical concern of promoting prosocial behavior usually employ one of two strategies: (a) a variance-accounted-for empirical analysis or (b) application and extension of existing social psychological theory. One view of science that has long been popular among psychologists, especially psychologists with an applied orientation, is empirical prediction and control. From this perspective, promoting prosocial behavior requires, first, identification of its most powerful predictors. Then one can engage in social engineering, creating an environment that optimizes these predictors and, thereby, prosocial behavior. The logic seems straightforward. Its apparent simplicity has, however, proved deceptive.

Dispositional Versus Situational Determinants

Operating with an implicit variance-accounted-for model, several investigators around 1970 attempted to determine whether

dispositional or situational factors were better predictors of prosocial behavior. The dispositional variables studied include anomie, authoritarianism, autonomy, deference, intelligence, Machiavellianism, nurturance, religiosity, self-esteem, social desirability, social responsibility, submissiveness, and succorance. Not one of these, by itself, was a clear predictor. In contrast, situational factors—ambiguity of need, severity of need, physical appearance of victim, similarity to victim, friendship, number of bystanders, location (urban vs. rural), cost of helping, and so on—seemed powerful. These results led several reviewers (e.g., Huston & Korte, 1976; J. A. Piliavin, Dovidio, Gaertner, & Clark, 1981) to conclude that situational variables are better predictors of prosocial behavior than are dispositional variables.

Soon, however, this conclusion was challenged as part of the general counterattack by personality researchers against situationist critiques. Staub (1974) found that an aggregate dispositional measure, a prosocial orientation index (combining measures of feelings of personal responsibility, social responsibility, moral reasoning, prosocial values, and a low level of Machiavellianism), was a reasonably good predictor of helping across several different measures. Rushton (1980) reanalyzed previous research (notably, the classic studies by Hartshorne and May in the late 1920s) by computing aggregate measures of prosocial behavior and found far better evidence of cross-situation consistency than had analyses based on individual measures.

Other researchers pointed to the greater predictive potential of dispositional factors for the higher cost, nonspontaneous, longer term helping that occurs in the natural stream of behavior outside the psychological laboratory. For example, Oliner and Oliner (1988) conducted a major study using interviews and questionnaires to identify predictors of acting to rescue Jews in Nazi Europe. They claimed evidence for the predictive power of three dispositional factors: (a) a proclivity to feel empathy for those in need, (b) sensitivity to normative pressure from social groups, and (c) adherence to inclusive, universal moral principles such as justice or care. Presumably, better prediction is possible outside the laboratory because the more reflective decision process involved in planned (nonspontaneous) helping permits more chance for personal values, attitudes, and dispositions to come into play.

Still other researchers argued that it was an oversimplification to expect a personality variable to relate to helping in all situations. Many pointed to the greater success of predicting prosocial behavior using disposition-situation interactions (e.g., Romer, Gruder, & Lizzardo, 1986). For example, self-confidence and independence seem to correlate with helping in emergency situations, especially dangerous ones, but not in response to a request to contribute to the United Way (Wilson, 1976). Snyder and Ickes (1985) suggested that the predictive power of dispositional factors should be manifest only when situational pressure is weak, not when it is strong. Carlo, Eisenberg, Troyer, Switzer, and Speer (1991) claimed support for this distinction between weak and strong pressure when predicting prosocial behavior. Within these more recent studies, then, dispositional predictors have fared better than in earlier work. Still, correlations between personality measures and prosocial behavior—however measured—rarely rise above .30 to .40, leaving 85% to 90% of the variance unaccounted for.

At the same time that dispositional predictors were being revived, the health of situational predictors took a turn for the worse: Their ecological validity was questioned (Bar-Tal, 1984). Could one expect a situational predictor of single-act helping by college students in a controlled laboratory experiment to be equally powerful in predicting naturally occurring prosocial behavior outside the lab, such as volunteerism (Clary & Snyder, 1991)?

Proliferating Predictors and Predictions

Since 1970, proposed predictors of prosocial behavior have proliferated well beyond the initial dichotomy between dispositional and situational factors. Krebs and Miller (1985) presented an interlocking three-tier classification. Most distal from the specific prosocial behavior are biological and cultural predictors (see also Fiske, 1992). These predictors combine to produce enduring dispositional characteristics, which are more proximal. Dispositional factors then combine with situational factors to produce cognitive and affective reactions, which are considered the most proximal predictors of prosocial behavior. Within each of these broad classes, numerous specific variables can be identified.

In additions to proliferating predictors, there are also many different forms of prosocial behavior to be predicted, and the variables that predict one form may not predict another. For example, within the domain of helping are rescuing, donating, assisting, volunteering, and giving social support (Pearce & Amato, 1980). Moreover, each of these categories includes a wide range of specific behaviors. One can assist by holding a door, answering a request for directions, splinting a broken leg at the scene of an automobile accident, securing false papers for a Jew in Nazi Europe, or enabling a suicide. One can volunteer to serve on the board of directors for the local symphony, to call potential blood donors, to be a buddy for someone who has AIDS, or to join the rescue squad. Critics claim—and research supports the claim (Levine, Martinez, Brase, & Sorenson, 1994; Omoto & Snyder, 1995)—that variables accounting for variance in one form of prosocial behavior in one setting are not likely to account for the same amount of variance (if any) in other forms of behavior or in

other settings. Talk of prediction based on interactions among person, situation, and behavior has become common (e.g., Bandura, 1991; Carlo et al., 1991).

One need not pursue this logic very far—adding predictors, behaviors to be predicted, situations in which prediction can be made, and populations for which predictions can be made—to realize that a general variance-accounted-for answer to the question of why people act prosocially is impossible. All one can hope for is the identification of predictors that account for a specific prosocial behavior in a specific situation for a specific population at a specific time (Snyder, 1993). Although useful to address some applied questions, such research is apt to become ideographic rather than nomothetic (Allport, 1961), with very little generalizability.

APPLICATION AND EXTENSION OF EXISTING THEORY

Well aware of the limited, ad hoc nature of a variance-accounted-for approach, Lewin (1951) reminded us, "There is nothing so practical as a good theory" (p. 169). In opposition to the Aristotelian approach to science that guides the variance-accounted-for strategy, in which the scientist's goal is to identify essential features to predict outcomes, Lewin advocated a Galilean approach. Galileo's goal was to identify underlying genotypic (conditional-genetic) constructs and the highly general—even universal—relations among them that account for observable phenotypic events. Lewin was convinced that explanatory theories developed and tested following Galileo are of far more practical value than are explanations developed following Aristotle, even though the Galilean model relies on contrived laboratory experiments rather than on direct, real-world observation.

Psychologists approaching the study of prosocial behavior from Lewin's Galilean perspective are not likely to look to empirical research to identify predictors accounting for the most variance. They are likely instead to look to existing theory about genotypic psychological processes, using research to illustrate and document the relevance of these processes to understanding prosocial behavior. At least seven broad theoretical perspectives have been applied in this way: social learning, tension reduction, norms and roles, exchange or equity, attribution, esteem enhancement/maintenance, and moral reasoning. Let us briefly consider each of these.

Social Learning

Social learning theory suggests that if you want to know why people act prosocially, you should consider their learning history. You should consider not only the rewards and punishments received following helping (or not), but also the relative rewards—the benefits minus the costs. You should consider observational learning or modeling that comes from watching the actions of others. You should consider self-rewards. Much research has supported a social learning explanation of prosocial behavior (for reviews, see Bandura, 1977; Rushton, 1980). Integrating and coordinating social learning principles, Cialdini, Baumann, and Kenrick (1981) proposed a three-step developmental sequence: (a) In the young child prosocial behavior is a product of material rewards and punishments; (b) in the preadolescent it is a product of social as well as material rewards and punishments; and (c) in the adolescent and adult it is a product of internalized self-reward, as well as social and material rewards and punishments.

Mood Effects

Building on the idea that helping can be a basis for self-reward, Cialdini, Darby, and Vincent (1973) proposed a *negative-state relief hypothesis:* that adults are more likely to help when they feel bad. The reason is that adults have learned that they can reward themselves for helping and so feel better.

Not only does helping have reward value for people who feel bad, but it also seems rewarding for people who feel good. Indeed, the effect is even clearer for good mood. Across a range of studies (e.g., Isen & Levin, 1972; Weyant, 1978), people induced to feel good have been more likely to give help to good causes.

What accounts for this pervasive reward value of helping for people in a good mood? One possibility is a desire to maintain the good mood. Seeing another person in need can throw a wet blanket on a good mood, so one may help in order to shed this blanket and maintain the mood (Wegener & Petty, 1994). Isen, Shalker, Clark, and Karp (1978) suggested a second possibility: Being in a good mood may bias one's memories about and attention to the positive and negative aspects of various activities, including helping. When in a good mood, a person is more likely to recall and attend to positive rather than negative aspects of life. Applied to helping, a good mood makes people more likely to remember and attend to the positive, rewarding features and less likely to attend to the negative features, such as the costs involved.

General Assessment

Social learning theory finds itself in an awkward position in contemporary social psychology. There seems little doubt that the theory is in large measure correct. However, perhaps because of its relatively straightforward explanation of behavior, without the ironic twists and the revelations of subtle faux pas for which cognitive explanations have become renown, social learning theory generates little excitement. The direct focus on behavior and reinforcement history seems almost unpsychological in its lack of nuance. Even with the added emphasis on self-reward, cognitive representation, self-regulation, and reciprocal determinism (Bandura, 1977, 1991), social learning theory seems bland. Still, were one forced to choose a single theory to explain why people do—and do not—act prosocially, social learning theory should almost certainly be the choice. "As Einstein has emphasized, the goal is to account for the most facts with the fewest principles" (Dollard & Miller, 1950, p. 6). Social learning theory has probably come closer to this goal than has any other theory in the history of social psychology.

Tension Reduction

Tension reduction has long been a popular explanation of why people help others in need, especially others in obvious pain or distress. The general idea is that people find it upsetting to see another person suffer and that preferring not to be upset, they relieve the other's suffering.

Perhaps the best way to describe the relationship between tension reduction, which is a form of motivation, and social learning is to say that they are related by marriage. Social learning can exist without tension reduction, as in the pure operant theories descendant from Watson and Skinner. Tension reduction can exist without social learning, as in reactions to pain, extreme temperatures, hunger, thirst, and other physiological needs. Yet social learning and tension reduction lived together for many years in relative harmony, housed within Hull's (1943) general learning theory and its descendants, including Dollard and Miller's (1950) version of social learning theory. In response to the current cognitive zeitgeist, social learning theory has of late been less attached to tension reduction, showing more interest in cognitive processes (Bandura, 1977, 1991). Whether this philandering is grounds for divorce is hard to say. In any case, tension reduction has also been seen stepping out without operant processes by its side, most notably in dissonance theory—at least as originally conceived by Festinger (1957).

Why should the suffering of others upset someone? Most straightforward is the answer proposed by J. A. Piliavin et al. (1981), among others. They suggested that witnessing another's distress evokes vicarious distress that has much the same character as the victim's distress, and the witness is motivated to escape his or her own distress. One way to escape is to help because helping terminates the stimulus causing the distress. Of course, running away may enable the witness to escape just as well and at less cost, as long as the old adage "out of sight, out of mind" works.

Variations on the theme of aversive-arousal reduction have been provided by Hornstein (1982), Reykowski (1982), and Lerner (1982). Focusing on the self-other relationship, Hornstein suggested that when certain others are in need—specifically, those whom one cognitively links to self as "us" and "we" rather than "them" and "they"—one experiences a state of promotive tension in which one is "aroused by *another's* needs almost as if they were one's own" (Hornstein, 1982, p. 230). Once so aroused, one is motivated to reduce this tension by aiding the fellow "we-grouper."

Reykowski's (1982) proposed explanation, though quite different, also involves reduction of aversive tension: "The sheer discrepancy between information about the real or possible state of an object and standards of its normal or desirable state will evoke motivation" (p. 361). Reykowski applied this general principle to prosocial motivation as follows: If a person perceives a discrepancy between the current state and the expected or ideal state of another person (i.e., perceives the other to be in need), cognitive inconsistency and motivation to reduce this aversive inconsistency will result. Relieving the other's need is one way to remove the inconsistency and escape the situation. Another, less prosocial way is to change one's perception and decide that the other's suffering is acceptable, even desirable.

Lerner's (1980, 1982) just-world hypothesis led him to an explanation similar to but more specific than Reykowski's. Lerner suggested that most people believe in a just world—a world in which people get what they deserve and deserve what they get. The existence of a victim of innocent suffering is inconsistent with this belief. In order to reduce the arousal produced by this inconsistency, a person may help another in need. Alternatively, the person may derogate the innocent victim, making the suffering appear deserved.

At first glance, Cialdini's negative-state relief model may appear to be another example of aversive-arousal reduction. In fact, it is not. Although it too begins with the proposition that seeing someone in need evokes a negative affective state, from this common starting point the two explanations diverge. The negative-state relief explanation claims that the goal of helping is to obtain mood-enhancing self-rewards that one has learned are associated with helping; aversive-arousal reduction explanations claim that the goal of helping is to eliminate the mood-depressing stimulus. Negative-state relief is a social learning explanation that assumes that the increased need for some type—any type—of mood-enhancing reward motivates helping; aversive-arousal reduction explanations make no assumptions about prior learning history but focus instead on reduction of current tension.

Norms and Roles

Theories that seek to explain prosocial behavior in terms of norms and roles often make heavy use of social learning principles. Yet norm and role theories are not direct descendants of classic learning theory and behaviorism. Instead, they trace their ancestry to symbolic interactionism and its analysis of social behavior using a dramaturgical metaphor (cf. Goffman, 1959; Mead, 1934). Within this metaphor, norms provide the script of the social drama, specifying what should be done and said when; roles are the parts to be played. (More formally, *norms* are a group's written or unwritten rules of appropriate behavior for those occupying particular roles; *roles* are behavior patterns that are characteristic, and expected, of a person who occupies a particular position in a social structure.)

In both developmental and social psychology, norms and roles have been adopted into the social learning family; it is assumed that people learn the norms and roles appropriate to a given situation through social reinforcement and modeling. At the same time that people are learning that acting prosocially can bring rewards, they are also learning the norms for prosocial behaviors that should be performed by individuals in various roles in different social situations. These norms dictate that one should help people in need—at least some people under some circumstances—to avoid social or self-administered sanctions.

Reciprocity

One prosocial norm that has been studied extensively is reciprocity. Gouldner (1960) suggested that this norm tells people both that they should help people who help them and that they should not injure these people. He believed that this norm was universal, an important part of the moral code of every culture. He also believed that the pressure on a person to comply with the norm of reciprocity depends on the circumstances under which the initial help was given—including (a) how badly one needed help, (b) one's perception of how much the other person gave relative to his or her total resources, (c) one's perception of the other person's motives for helping (was it a bribe?), and (d) whether the other person helped voluntarily or was pressured into it. Much evidence supports the claim that people are motivated to comply with the norm of reciprocity (e.g., Wilke & Lanzetta, 1982).

Social Responsibility

A second norm that psychologists have suggested motivates helping is social responsibility. This norm dictates that one person should help another in need when the latter is dependent on the former—that is, when others are not available to help and thus the second person is counting specifically on the first. Although this norm does seem to exist, its effect on helping has been surprisingly difficult to demonstrate. After more than a decade of research attempts to do so, Berkowitz (1972) concluded, "The findings do not provide any clear-cut support for the normative analysis of help-giving. . . . The potency of the conjectured 'social responsibility norm' was greatly exaggerated" (pp. 68, 77).

Why has evidence that the norm of social responsibility leads to prosocial behavior been so elusive? Darley and Latané (1970) suggested that this norm may be at once too general and too specific. The norm may be too general in that everyone in our society adheres to it. If this is true, it cannot account for why one person helps and another does not. On the other hand, the norm may be too specific in that it comes with a complex pattern of exceptions, situations in which an individual may feel exempt from acting in accordance with the norm. The norm may be characterized not simply by a rule that says, "If someone is dependent on you for help, then help," but by a more complex rule that says, "If someone is dependent on you for help, then help, *except when . . .*" There may be individual differences in readiness to accept exceptions—that is, to deny responsibility (Schwartz, 1977). Moreover, exceptions may vary for individuals in different roles and in different social situations. One advantage of remembering the dramaturgical roots of the concept of norms is that it makes explicit their role specificity.

Darley and Latané (1970) also pointed out that in addition to norms for helping, there are norms for not helping. A person may be taught, "Help those in need," and at the same time, "Mind your own business." Which norm is the one to follow? If the former, one may help; if the latter, probably not.

Effects of Race and Sex

Exceptions to and conflicts among norms may account for the highly inconsistent effects on prosocial behavior of demographic variables such as race and sex. It has sometimes been found that same-race helping is more frequent (e.g., Gaertner & Bickman, 1971), sometimes that cross-race helping is more frequent (Katz, Cohen, & Glass, 1975), and sometimes that the race of the victim or helper makes no difference (Wispé & Freshley, 1971). Similarly, sometimes men help more than women (West, Whitney, & Schnedler, 1975), sometimes women help more than men (Wegner & Crano, 1975), and sometimes the sex of the helper makes no difference (J. A. Piliavin & Piliavin, 1972). It does appear, however, that women are generally more likely to be helped than are men (Gruder & Cook, 1971).

How can we account for these seemingly contradictory findings? One possibility is that given their different social roles in different situations, Blacks and Whites—and men and women—may feel more or less obligated to help a dependent other. For example, Black students on a predominantly White campus, acutely aware of their minority status, may feel strong responsibility for helping a fellow Black student but very little responsibility for helping a White student; White students may be more likely to help a Black student when failure to do so clearly violates norms proscribing racial prejudice. Helping may be more normative for men than for women in one situation—for example, intervening in a potentially dangerous emergency. Helping may be more normative for women than for men in another situation—for example, providing sympathy and support after a friend's breakup with her fiancé (Eagly & Crowley, 1986). A role-sensitive normative analysis renders the apparent inconsistencies comprehensible.

Norm Salience

Some researchers have suggested that the problem with social norms lies in norm salience and focus of attention. Only when attention is focused on the norm as a standard for behavior is concern about violating it likely to affect behavior (Cialdini, Kallgren, & Reno, 1991). Consistent with this suggestion, Gibbons and Wicklund (1982) found that if normative standards of helpfulness were salient and thus a focus of attention, then focusing on oneself increased helping. Presumably, being self-focused when the norm was salient highlighted the threat of sanctions for failing to act in line with personal standards. In the absence of salient standards for helpfulness, however, self-focus led to less helping; it seemed to inhibit attention to others' needs (see also Karylowski, 1984).

Personal Norms

Because broad social norms like social responsibility have limited ability to predict whether a person will help, Schwartz (1977) proposed a change of focus in thinking about norms. Rather than thinking about social norms, Schwartz suggested that we should think of more specific, personal norms. By personal norms he meant internalized rules of conduct that are socially learned, that vary among individuals within the same society, and that direct behavior in particular situations.

Applied to helping, a personal norm involves a sense of obligation to perform a specific helping act. For example, people may say (either publicly or to themselves), "I ought to give a pint of blood in the blood drive." Such statements appear to be far more predictive of whether a person will give blood than are statements of agreement with broad social norms like the norm of social responsibility—at least if the person in question is one who believes in acting responsibly (Schwartz & Howard, 1981). Specific statements like this are particularly powerful as predictors when one also takes into account extenuating circumstances, such as whether an individual was in town during the blood drive, had no major scheduling conflicts, and was physically able to give blood (Zuckerman & Reis, 1978). At this level of specificity, however, it is not clear whether the statement about giving blood reflects a sense of personal obligation stemming from an internalized rule of conduct (i.e., a personal norm) or simply an intention to act in a particular way.

Exchange or Equity

Perhaps the most direct extension of social learning principles into interpersonal relations is exchange or equity theory. When developing exchange theory, Homans (1961) explicitly and proudly declared his agenda to be the reduction of social relations—including cooperation, helping, and other prosocial behaviors—to reinforcement principles operating within the individual. Equity theorists were not so reductionist. They considered social relations to have emergent properties that were irreducible to the benefits and costs for the individuals involved. In their view, social learning teaches one to value equitable relations, in which the ratio of outcomes to inputs is equal for the relating individuals. Walster, Berscheid, and Walster (1973) claimed that equity theory was a general theory that subsumed social learning theory (and psychoanalytic theory). Although this may seem a myopic inversion, equity theory does add an important dimension to the understanding of prosocial behavior by introducing both social comparison and distributive justice. Needs and benefits are no longer defined by looking at the individual alone; the definition is broadened to include needs based on relative deprivation (Adams, 1965).

Homans (1961) pointed out that if a recipient of help cannot return the favor in a tangible way, then he or she must return esteem and deference. Otherwise, the relationship will not remain beneficial to both parties and thus will not continue. Walster et al. (1973) argued that not only the relatively underbenefited but also the relatively overbenefited are motivated to restore equity (although they acknowledged that inequity in one's favor is more tolerable than the reverse). Acting prosocially to redistribute resources more fairly is one way to restore equity—but only one. Equity may also be restored psychologically by enhancing the perceived inputs of the advantaged or devaluing the inputs of the disadvantaged, thereby justifying the difference in outcomes.

Attribution

Attribution theory concerns inferences drawn about the causes of events (Heider, 1958; Jones & Davis, 1965). Attributions can affect prosocial behavior in two major ways. First, attributions about why a person is in need are made not only by potential helpers and bystanders but also by the person in need, with consequences for each. Second, attributions about the character of a person who helps are made not only by the helpers themselves but also by the persons helped, again with consequences for each.

Attributing the Cause of Others' Needs

People are far more likely to help innocent victims than to help those who bring their troubles on themselves (Weiner, 1980). Although this relationship is no surprise, the reason for it is not entirely clear. Perhaps causing one's own need (or not working to prevent it) violates ingrained standards for self-sufficiency and prudence; perhaps causing one's own need but not suffering the consequences violates our sense of justice; perhaps it seems inequitable to those who perceive themselves to have exerted effort to avoid need. In any case, people *are* less likely to help those who bring their troubles on themselves, even though the explanation for this behavior has never been carefully explored.

Attributing the Cause of One's Own Need

People in need may be predisposed to attribute their need to situational causes, as something thrust upon them by unavoidable circumstances and carrying no implications about personal ability or worth. This attribution may, however, be hard to sustain when the need is produced by failure on a task that one expected to perform successfully, especially when comparable peers succeed (Fisher, Nadler, & Whitcher-Alagna, 1982). To avoid an esteem-damaging dispositional attribution, the person in need may attempt to deny the failure and not seek or appreciate help (Nadler, 1991).

Attributing the Cause of Help

Helpers make attributions about the nature and cause not only of others' needs but also of their own helping. A helper may ask, "Why did I help in this situation?" Possible answers include the following: (a) because I am a kind, caring, helpful person—a dispositional attribution likely to be self-rewarding and encourage one to help in a range of situations in the future; (b) because I am the kind of person who helps in this particular situation (e.g., I am a blood donor; J. A. Piliavin, Callero, & Evans, 1982)—a dispositional attribution likely to encourage one to help again in this situation; (c) because of situational pressure—a situational attribution not likely to increase helping in the future, at least not when situational pressure is absent; and (d) because I am a compliant schnook and a pushover who cannot say no—a dispositional attribution likely to be self-punishing and to discourage future helping. Grusec (1991) traced the development and demonstrated the prosocial benefits of children attributing their helping to a broad disposition to be helpful.

An attributional analysis suggests a complicating limit on the effects of social learning. To the extent that subsequent helping is mediated by self-attributions of helpfulness, inducing help by providing material or social rewards in the form of incentives or salient models, norms, and so on may actually diminish rather than increase subsequent helping, much as providing extrinsic incentives can diminish activity based on intrinsic motivation (Lepper, Greene, & Nisbett, 1973). Consistent with this possibility, research suggests that providing incentives—whether money, models, or norms—reduces self-perceived altruism following helping (e.g., Thomas, Batson, & Coke, 1981).

These results reveal a dilemma. One important source of motivation to help, the external reward that comes from payment or praise for helping, actually undermines a second important source of motivation to help, the self-reward that comes from seeing oneself as a good, kind, caring person. Consider the long-term consequences. As self-reward is undermined, additional external pressure may be necessary to coerce the person to help. This additional external pressure further erodes the helper's chances for self-reward. Over time, the result may be a slide toward a more and more cynical self-concept, in which personal kindness plays an increasingly minor role and help is offered only for a price.

The person helped is also likely to make attributions about why the helper acted. The most obvious and most frequently studied attributions for helping are that the helper acted (a) out of concern, with no strings attached, or (b) in order to indebt, control, or demean the recipient. Attributions of the second kind may be especially problematic when made by recipients of international aid. Research by Greenberg and his colleagues (e.g., Greenberg & Frisch, 1972) demonstrated, as expected, that aid is not appreciated to the degree that it is perceived as an attempt to control. In return, the benefactor is likely to receive hostility rather than gratitude (Tesser, Gatewood, & Driver, 1968).

Esteem Enhancement/Maintenance

Models of esteem enhancement/maintenance have been both popular and numerous in social psychology since about 1980.

As an explanation for prosocial behavior, these models generally assume that people act prosocially to enhance or recover self-esteem (Brown & Smart, 1991).

One might expect perceptions of the esteem-enhancing potential of helping to follow the same three-step developmental sequence outlined by Cialdini et al. (1981). For the young child, gaining material rewards for doing good enhances esteem; for the middle child, social approval enhances esteem; by adolescence, self-directed and uncoerced—even anonymous—help may be necessary to feel good about oneself.

Not only benefactors, but also recipients, may act and react with an eye to their self-esteem. Fisher et al. (1982) proposed an esteem-loss explanation for recipients' negative reactions to receiving aid. Consistent with the comparative aspects of self-esteem, Nadler, Fisher, and Ben-Itzhak (1983) found that when individuals were having trouble on a task that reflected on their abilities, receipt of help from a friend produced more negative self-evaluation than did receipt of help from a stranger.

DePaulo, Nadler, and Fisher (1983) pointed out that concern over loss of esteem both in others' and in one's own eyes may go a long way toward explaining reticence to seek help when in need. To seek help is to admit that you lack the competence, knowledge, or other valuable resources necessary to cope and, moreover, that the person from whom you seek help has these resources. Consistent with this analysis, people are less likely to seek help to the degree that they hold themselves in high esteem and do not anticipate a chance to reciprocate the help (Nadler, 1991).

This analysis must be qualified by roles and norms, however. For the young child, seeking help from his or her parents is not likely to be upsetting or damaging to self-esteem. For a middle-level executive who finds himself out of a job, the thought of applying for welfare assistance to feed his family may be devastating.

Moral Reasoning

Moral reasoning theories (also called cognitive developmental or rational developmental theories of morality) build on the classic work of Piaget. Typically, they accept his account of intellectual development as a process of adaptation through assimilation and accommodation proceeding in an invariant developmental sequence from sensorimotor to preoperational to concrete operational to formal operational thought (Piaget, 1926). They also accept Piaget's (1932) application of this model of intellectual development to moral judgment. Moral reasoning theories, of which Kohlberg's (1976) is the best known, treat situations in which one person might act to benefit another as problems or puzzles to be solved, much like the problems in volume conservation that Piaget gave his children. The key to prosocial action is the level of moral reasoning used to solve the puzzle or dilemma. In Kohlberg's (1976) words, "To act in a morally high way requires a high stage of moral reasoning. . . . Moral stage is a good predictor of action" (p. 32).

Kohlberg claimed to have identified a universal and invariant sequence of six stages in moral reasoning, grouped in pairs into three levels: (a) preconventional (judgment based on immediate consequences for self), (b) conventional (judgment based on social norms, rules, and laws), and (c) post-conventional (judgment based on universal moral principles that at once transcend and undergird the moral conventions of society). The moral principle that Kohlberg considered most important was a neo-Kantian principle of justice whereby each individual is accorded equal rights and dignity in a Kingdom of Ends.

Controversy has surrounded moral reasoning theories from the start. First, evidence that moral reasoning develops universally in the invariant sequence of stages that Kohlberg described is equivocal at best (Kurtines & Greif, 1974). Second, the link between level of moral reasoning and prosocial behavior is far less clear than one might expect (Blasi, 1980; Eisenberg, 1991). In defense, supporters of moral reasoning models have pointed out that (a) adequate measurement of moral reasoning is difficult and (b) in almost any moral dilemma one may justify a given course of action in different ways, using different levels of moral reasoning. Both points seem true, but they reduce the explanatory power of moral reasoning theories, casting doubt on Kohlberg's claim that moral stage is a good predictor of prosocial action. Modified models of moral reasoning that incorporate social learning principles offer better explanatory power (e.g., Eisenberg, 1986). One must ask of these models, however, whether the social learning principles do all the explanatory work.

In addition to being challenged from outside by researchers who question the value of moral reasoning as a sufficient or even necessary explanation of prosocial behavior, Kohlberg's focus on justice as the capstone of moral maturity has been challenged from inside the moral-reasoning camp. The most notable challenge has come from his former student and colleague Carol Gilligan. In addition to an ethic of justice and fairness, Gilligan (1982) called for recognition of an ethic of care. Although she believed that both men and women display reasoning based on justice and reasoning based on care, she claimed that the former is more characteristic of men and the latter more characteristic of women. She also claimed that Kohlberg's exclusive focus on justice led to a perception that men are superior to women in moral reasoning. Finally, she claimed that this apparent superiority will disappear if one listens to the moral voice of women, who speak more of care than of justice.

Evidence for the claimed sex difference in use of perspectives of justice and care has been limited and weak (Walker, 1991). But research has supported Gilligan's claim that moral dilemmas can be approached from a perspective of care rather than justice (Gilligan, Ward, & Taylor, 1988; Walker, 1991). It remains unclear, however, what a care perspective is. Is it (a) a reflection of Kohlberg's conventional stage of morality, (b) an alternative mode of moral reasoning with its own developmental sequence, or (c) not a form of moral reasoning at all but an emotional reaction or bond? In sum, although the distinction between justice and care seems to have value, considerably more conceptual precision is needed to know the nature and significance of this distinction.

Amalgamated Models

One need not rely on just one of these seven theoretical perspectives to explain prosocial behavior. It is possible to invoke more than one in a given situation or to invoke one in one situation and another in a different situation. It is also possible to combine perspectives into an amalgamated model. Sometimes, such an amalgamation has been created by the integration of different theoretical perspectives (e.g., social learning and norm theories); more often, it has resulted from arranging perspectives in sequence, adding boxes and arrows to a flowchart of steps that lead ultimately to prosocial behavior. The impetus for creating amalgamated models seems to be the desire to be comprehensive, a desire that stems from the same aspirations for prediction and control that underlie the more ad hoc variance-accounted-for approach. But in amalgamated models, this desire takes advantage of existing theories to pull together and organize a range of explanations.

Perhaps the best known and most enduring amalgamated model is the arousal/cost-reward model originally proposed by I. M. Piliavin, Rodin, and Piliavin (1969) and developed and elaborated by J. A. Piliavin et al. (1981), Dovidio (1984), and Dovidio, Piliavin, Gaertner, Schroeder, and Clark (1991). Originally, this model combined a tension-reduction motivational component with a cost-reward assessment of the various behavioral means to reduce the tension. Over the years, norms, equity concerns, and attribution processes have been incorporated as well, producing a flowchart with 8 boxes and 17 arrows that is too complex to describe here. Other amalgamated models include those developed by Bar-Tal (1982), who relies most heavily on social learning and moral-reasoning perspectives, and by Schwartz (1977), who relies most heavily on norms, especially personal norms.

Amalgamated models make three useful contributions. First, they remind us of the complexity of prosocial behavior and thereby caution against simplistic explanations. Second, they sketch a causal ordering of the various psychological processes assumed to be operating—although these orderings are rarely tested. Third, they provide a mnemonic for relevant psychological processes and theoretical perspectives.

Amalgamated models have potential liabilities too. First, the desire to be comprehensive exerts pressure toward proliferation of boxes and arrows. As more intervening steps are added and more arrows are drawn, multiple paths connect postulated antecedent and consequent variables. This makes achieving clear causal prediction increasingly difficult. The models become less explanatory and more purely descriptive. It seems to be a general and ironic rule in science that the greater the number of different explanatory models combined, the less the resulting explanatory power (recall Einstein's admonition to account for the most facts with the fewest principles).

Second, having accepted the goal of making an amalgamated model comprehensive, one can expend much energy trying to make anomalous data fit. The breadth and complexity of these models make success almost inevitable. With effort, data can be made to fit even when they do not. The consequence is that opportunities for new insight and understanding are lost—or at least discouraged. This is a very serious liability if, as we wish to suggest in the next section of this chapter, the anomalous aspects of prosocial behavior are what have contributed the most to psychology.

The seven perspectives reviewed thus far reveal the scope and power of existing psychological theory available to explain why people act prosocially. Yet in spite of this scope and power, these existing theories sometimes seem inadequate. Even after hearing their explanations, one may experience a nagging sense of "yes, but" when faced with a dramatic display of concern for another's welfare—or a dramatic display of callousness. Such displays have long intrigued and puzzled not only psychologists but also philosophers and other behavioral and social scientists. They call for a rethinking of our existing theories about why people do and do not act prosocially, even a rethinking of our assumptions about human nature.

By attending to these anomalies, researchers have extended and altered our theories of social motivation. Attempts to explain prosocial anomalies have not caused a total rewrite of our theories, of course, but they have caused some rewriting, and likely there will be more.

ANOMALOUS FAILURES TO ACT PROSOCIALLY

The anomalous aspects of prosocial behavior have been of particular interest to those concerned with the theoretical rather than practical implications of why people do—and don't—act prosocially. At times, a failure to act prosocially can be baffling. How can individuals who were raised in caring and nurturing homes, whose parents rewarded them for showing concern, who become upset when they hear about suffering in remote corners of the world, who have a well-developed sense of duty, justice, and social responsibility, and who are highly sensitive to how they look in others' eyes as well as in their own fail to respond to the needs of others, even when it would cost little to do so? Given all the pressure that society brings to bear, failures to act prosocially can seem quite anomalous, almost amazing. Yet they happen.

Let's return to the murder of Kitty Genovese. At the time, explanations bandied about in the media focused on the breakdown in modern urban society of moral fiber, social norms, and sense of community. Her death was said to be a product of apathy, alienation, anomie, and angst.

Effect of Others on Decisions Under Pressure

Bibb Latané and John Darley (1970) came up with an ingenious alternative to these dispositional explanations. Their explanation was based in part on existing psychological theory and in part on new theoretical insights. They observed that once we notice a possible emergency situation, we must make several decisions in order to help. We must decide that an emergency exists, that it is our personal responsibility to act, and that there is something we can do to help. To complicate matters, these decisions must be made under pressure; emergencies involve threat, ambiguity, urgency, and stress. The presence of other bystanders can influence this pressure-packed decision sequence at each step, tipping the scales toward inaction.

Is a scream in the night a woman being attacked or harmless high-spirited play? Uncertain, bystanders may turn to others present, seeking cues to help them decide. No one wishes to appear foolishly excited over an event that is not an emergency, so each individual reacts initially with a calm outward demeanor, while looking at other people's reactions. Others do the same. No one appears upset, creating a state of pluralistic ignorance (Miller & McFarland, 1987). Everyone decides that since no one else is upset, the event must not be an emergency (Latané & Darley, 1968; Latané & Rodin, 1969).

Even if one decides that the situation is an emergency and that someone is in dire need of help, the presence of others can still discourage action. To explain how, Darley and Latané (1968) moved beyond existing theory and proposed a diffusion of responsibility. If others are available, each individual may feel less personal obligation to come forward and help. One call to the police is as helpful, if not more helpful, than 20 calls. In the Kitty Genovese case, her neighbors may have seen lights in other windows and assumed that other neighbors had heard the screams and that someone else had already called. Some may have thought, "Something should be done, but why should I be the one to do it?" Thoughts like these, made possible by awareness of other bystanders without knowing what the others are doing, diffuses the responsibility to help among all the bystanders present and makes it less likely that any one bystander will help.

Latané and Darley's (1970) answer to the question of why none of the 38 witnesses to the murder of Kitty Genovese helped has stood up remarkably well to experimental test (see Latané & Nida, 1981). Still, the psychological process that underlies diffusion of responsibility remains unclear. Do the costs of helping lead to a motivated, optimistic redefinition of the situation ("I'm sure someone else has already helped, so there is no longer a need")? Is there a recognition of continuing need but denial of personal responsibility, either by reasoning that others present are better qualified to act ("Somebody's got to do something, but not me; they're the ones who know what to do") or shifting from a prescriptive to a descriptive norm ("I can't be blamed; no one else is doing anything either")? Might some people fail to act out of deference or modesty ("I'll let someone else be the hero")? Each of these processes involves the effect of others on decision making under pressure, and they are often confounded in research; yet these processes are distinct. Any or all could operate, suggesting that more research is needed.

Blaming the Victim

Another important theoretical development stimulated by reflection on bystander "apathy" was Melvin Lerner's (1970, 1980) just-world hypothesis. The anomaly on which Lerner focused was not the failure to help victims of accidents, attacks, or other emergencies, but rather the more pervasive and pernicious tendency for the haves in society to be unresponsive to the needs of the have-nots. Lerner observed, as did Ryan (1971), that people often not only fail to notice need or to show concern for victims, but that they actively derogate and blame victims.

To explain this apparent anomaly, Lerner turned to the seemingly prosocial principle of justice. He reasoned as follows. If children are to delay gratification and pursue long-term goals, they must develop a belief that effort brings results. For most of us, this belief in contingency leads in turn to a belief in a just world, a sense of appropriateness—that people get what they deserve (and deserve what they get)—necessary for trust, hope, and confidence in our future. Witnessing the suffering of innocent victims violates the belief in a just world. In order to reduce the discomfort produced by this threat, we may help. But there is an alternative: We may derogate or blame the victims (if they have less, they must deserve less; that is, they must be less deserving). Lerner and his associates provided extensive evidence that witnessing an innocent victim suffer can lead to derogation (see Lerner, 1980, for a review). The insight that a natural—even noble—belief in justice, when carried into an unjust world, can itself become a source of injustice has proved major.

ANOMALOUS PROSOCIAL ACTS

In the 1960s, heightened social conscience focused attention on anomalous failures to act prosocially. In the broader sweep of Western thought, this focus is itself anomalous. Through the centuries, the puzzle that has intrigued those contemplating the human condition has not been why people fail to care for others in need; the puzzle has been why people care.

From Aristotle and Aquinas through Hobbes and Bentham to Nietzsche and Freud, the dominant view in Western thought has been that people are, at heart, exclusively self-interested. Given this view, what explains the enormous effort and energy directed toward benefiting others? At times, what people do for others can be spectacular. Soldiers have thrown themselves on live grenades to protect their comrades. Crews worked around the clock in extreme danger to free the trapped victims of the Oklahoma City bombing. Firemen died directing others to safety when the World Trade Center towers collapsed. Surviving an airline crash, Arland Williams lost his life in the icy waters of the Potomac because he repeatedly gave others his place in the rescue helicopter. Mother Teresa dedicated her life to the dying of Calcutta, the poorest of the poor, bringing care and comfort to thousands. Rescuers of Jews in Nazi Europe, such as Miep Gies (1987), who helped hide Anne Frank and her parents, and Oskar Schindler, risked their own lives—and often the lives of their loved ones—day after day for months, or even years.

How can we reconcile these actions with a view that people are exclusively self-interested? Could some people, to some degree, under some circumstances, be capable of having another person's interest at heart? Is it possible for one person to have another person's welfare as an ultimate goal (altruism), or is all helping simply an instrumental means of obtaining one or another form of self-benefit (egoism)? This has been called the altruism question (Batson, 1991).

The Altruism Question

One easy answer to the altruism question that can quickly be laid to rest goes like this: Even if it were possible for a person to be motivated to increase another's welfare, such a person would be pleased by attaining this desired goal, so even this apparent altruism would be a product of egoism. In the words of Tolman's (1923) well-turned epithet, this argument is "more brilliant than cogent" (p. 203). Philosophers have shown it to be flawed by pointing out that it involves a confusion between two different forms of psychological hedonism. The *strong* form of hedonism asserts that the ultimate goal of human action is always the attainment of personal pleasure; the *weak* form asserts only that goal attainment always brings pleasure. The weak form is not inconsistent with the altruistic claim that the ultimate goal of some action is to benefit another rather than to benefit oneself; the pleasure obtained can be a consequence of reaching this goal without being the goal itself. The strong form of psychological hedonism is inconsistent with the possibility of altruism, but to affirm this form is simply to assert that altruism does not exist, an empirical assertion that may or may not be true (see MacIntyre, 1967, for discussion of these philosophical arguments).

More serious advocates of universal egoism argue that some specific self-benefit is always the ultimate goal of helping; benefiting the other is simply an instrumental goal on the way to one or another ultimately self-serving end. They point to all the self-benefits of helping: the material, social, and self-rewards received; the material, social, and self-punishments avoided; and aversive-arousal reduction. Advocates of altruism counter that simply because self-benefits follow from benefiting another, this does not prove that the self-benefits were the helper's ultimate goal. These self-benefits may be unintended consequences of reaching the ultimate goal of benefiting the other. If so, the motivation would be altruistic, not egoistic.

Advocates of altruism claim more than possibility, of course. They claim that altruistic motivation exists, that at least some people under some circumstances act with the ultimate goal of increasing another person's welfare.

The Empathy-Altruism Hypothesis

Over the centuries, the most frequently proposed source of altruistic motivation has been an other-oriented emotional response congruent with the perceived welfare of another person—today usually called *empathy* (Batson, 1987) or *sympathy* (Wispé, 1986). If another person is in need, these empathic emotions include sympathy, compassion, tenderness, and the like. The *empathy-altruism hypothesis* claims that these emotions evoke motivation with an ultimate goal of benefiting the person for whom the empathy is felt—that is, altruistic motivation. Various forms of this hypothesis have been espoused by Thomas Aquinas, David Hume, Adam Smith, Charles Darwin, Herbert Spencer, and William McDougall, as well as in contemporary psychology by Hoffman (1975), Krebs (1975), and Batson (1987).

Considerable evidence supports the idea that feeling empathy for a person in need leads to increased helping of that person (see Batson, 1991; Eisenberg & Miller, 1987, for reviews). Observing an empathy-helping relationship, however, tells us nothing about the nature of the motivation that underlies this relationship. Increasing the other person's welfare could be (a) an ultimate goal, producing self-benefits as unintended consequences; (b) an instrumental goal on the way to the ultimate goal of gaining one or more self-benefits; or (c) both. That is, the motivation could be altruistic, egoistic, or both.

Egoistic Alternatives to the Empathy-Altruism Hypothesis

Three general classes of self-benefits can result from helping a person for whom one feels empathy. Such help can (a) reduce one's empathic arousal, which may be experienced as aversive; (b) enable one to avoid possible social and self-punishments for failing to help; and (c) enable one to gain social and self-rewards for doing what is good and right. The empathy-altruism hypothesis does not deny that these self-benefits of empathy-induced helping exist. It claims that they are unintended consequences of the empathically aroused helper reaching the ultimate goal of reducing the other's suffering. Proponents of egoistic alternatives to the empathy-altruism hypothesis disagree. They claim that one or more of these self-benefits are the ultimate goal of empathy-induced helping. In the past two decades more than 30 experiments have tested these three egoistic alternatives against the empathy-altruism hypothesis.

The most frequently proposed egoistic explanation of the empathy-helping relationship is *aversive-arousal reduction*. This explanation claims that feeling empathy for someone who is suffering is unpleasant, and empathically aroused individuals help in order to benefit themselves by eliminating their empathic feelings. Benefiting the victim is simply a means to this self-serving end.

Over half a dozen experiments have tested the aversive-arousal reduction explanation against the empathy-altruism hypothesis by varying the ease of escape from further exposure to the empathy-evoking need without helping. Because empathic arousal is a result of witnessing the need, either terminating this need by helping or terminating exposure to it by escaping should reduce one's own empathic arousal. Escape does not, however, enable one to reach the altruistic goal of relieving the victim's need. Therefore, the aversive-arousal explanation predicts elimination of the empathy-helping relationship when escape is easy; the empathy-altruism hypothesis does not. Results of these experiments have consistently patterned as predicted by the empathy-altruism hypothesis and not by the aversive-arousal reduction explanation, casting doubt on this popular egoistic account (see Batson, 1991, for a review).

A second egoistic explanation invokes *empathy-specific punishment*. It claims that people learn through socialization that additional obligation to help, and thus additional shame and guilt for failure to help, is attendant on feeling empathy for someone in need. As a result, when people feel empathy, they are faced with impending social or self-censure beyond any general punishment associated with not helping. They say to themselves, "What will others think—or what will I think of myself—if I don't help when I feel like this?" and then they help out of an egoistic desire to avoid these empathy-specific punishments. Once again, experiments designed to test this explanation have failed to support it; the results have consistently supported the empathy-altruism hypothesis instead (Batson, 1991).

The third major egoistic explanation invokes *empathy-specific reward*. It claims that people learn through socialization that special rewards in the form of praise and pride are attendant on helping a person for whom they feel empathy. As a result, when people feel empathy, they think of these rewards and help out of an egoistic desire to gain them.

The general form of this explanation has been tested in several experiments and received no support (Batson et al., 1988, Studies 1 & 5; Batson & Weeks, 1996), but two variations have also been proposed. Best known is the negative-state relief explanation proposed by Cialdini et al. (1987). Cialdini et al. suggested that the empathy experienced when witnessing another person's suffering is a negative affective state—a state of temporary sadness or sorrow—and the person feeling empathy helps in order to gain self-rewards to counteract this negative state.

Although this egoistic alternative received some initial support (Cialdini et al., 1987; Schaller & Cialdini, 1988), subsequent research has revealed that this was likely due to procedural artifacts. Experiments avoiding these artifacts have instead supported the empathy-altruism hypothesis (Batson et al., 1989; Dovidio, Allen, & Schroeder, 1990; Schroeder, Dovidio, Sibicky, Matthews, & Allen, 1988). It now seems clear that the motivation to help evoked by empathy is not directed toward the egoistic goal of negative-state relief.

A second interesting variation on an empathy-specific reward explanation was proposed by Smith, Keating, and Stotland (1989). They claimed that rather than helping to gain the rewards of seeing oneself or being seen by others as a helpful person, empathically aroused individuals help in order to feel joy at the needy individual's relief: "It is proposed that the prospect of empathic joy, conveyed by feedback from the help recipient, is essential to the special tendency of empathic witnesses to help. . . . The empathically concerned witness to the distress of others helps in order to be happy" (Smith et al., 1989, p. 641).

Some early self-report data were supportive, but more rigorous experimental evidence has failed to support this empathic-joy hypothesis. Instead, experimental results have once again consistently supported the empathy-altruism hypothesis (Batson et al., 1991; Smith et al., 1989). The empathic-joy hypothesis, like other versions of the empathy-specific reward explanation, seems unable to account for the empathy-helping relationship.

A Tentative Conclusion

Reviewing the empathy-altruism research, as well as related literature in sociology, economics, political science, and biology, J. A. Piliavin and Charng (1990) concluded that

> There appears to be a "paradigm shift" away from the earlier position that behavior that appears to be altruistic must, under closer scrutiny, be revealed as reflecting egoistic motives. Rather, theory and data now being advanced are more compatible with the view that true altruism—acting with the goal of benefiting another—does exist and is a part of human nature. (p. 27)

Pending new evidence or a plausible new egoistic explanation of the existing evidence, this conclusion seems correct. It appears that the empathy-altruism hypothesis should—tentatively—be accepted as true.

Implications of the Empathy-Altruism Hypothesis

If the empathy-altruism hypothesis is true, the implications are wide ranging. Universal egoism—the assumption that all human behavior is ultimately directed toward self-benefit—has long dominated not only psychology but other social and behavioral sciences as well (Campbell, 1975; Mansbridge, 1990; Wallach & Wallach, 1983). If individuals feeling empathy act, at least in part, with an ultimate goal of increasing the welfare of another, then the assumption of universal egoism must be replaced by a more complex view of motivation that allows for altruism as well as egoism. Such a shift in our view of motivation requires, in turn, a revision of our underlying assumptions about human nature and human potential. It implies that we humans may be more social than we have thought—that other people can be more to us than sources of information, stimulation, and reward as we each seek our own welfare. To some degree and under some circumstances, we can care about their welfare as an end in itself.

The evidence for the empathy-altruism hypothesis also forces us to face the question of why empathic feelings exist. What evolutionary function do they serve? Admittedly speculative, the most plausible answer relates empathic feelings to parenting among higher mammals, in which offspring live for some time in a very vulnerable state (de Waal, 1996; Hoffman, 1981; McDougall, 1908; Zahn-Waxler & Radke-Yarrow, 1990). Were parents not intensely interested in the welfare of their progeny, these species would quickly die out. Empathic feelings for offspring, and the resulting altruistic motivation, may promote one's reproductive potential not by increasing the number of offspring but by increasing the chance of their survival.

Clearly, however, empathic feelings extend well beyond one's own children. People can feel empathy for a wide range of individuals (including nonhumans) as long as there is no preexisting antipathy (Batson, 1991; Krebs, 1975; Shelton & Rogers, 1981). From an evolutionary perspective, this extension may be attributed to cognitive generalization whereby one "adopts" others, making it possible to evoke the primitive and fundamental impulse to care for progeny when these adopted others are in need (Batson, 1987; MacLean, 1973). Such cognitive generalization may be possible because of (a) human cognitive capacity, including symbolic thought, and (b) the lack of evolutionary advantage for sharp discrimination of empathic feelings in the small hunter-gatherer bands of early humans. In these bands, those in need were often one's children or close kin, and one's own welfare was tightly tied to the welfare even of those who were not close kin (Hoffman, 1981).

The empathy-altruism hypothesis also may have wide-ranging practical implications. Given the power of empathic feelings to evoke altruistic motivation, people may sometimes suppress or avoid these feelings. Loss of the capacity to feel empathy for clients may be a factor, possibly a central one, in the experience of burnout among case workers in the helping professions (Maslach, 1982). Aware of the extreme effort involved in helping or the impossibility of helping effectively, these case workers—as well as nurses caring for terminal patients, and even pedestrians confronted by the homeless—may try to avoid feeling empathy in order to avoid the resulting altruistic motivation (Shaw, Batson, &

Todd, 1994; Stotland, Mathews, Sherman, Hansson, & Richardson, 1978). There seems to be, then, egoistic motivation to avoid altruistic motivation.

More positively, experiments have tested the possibility that empathy-induced altruism can be used to improve attitudes toward stigmatized out-groups. Thus far, results look quite encouraging. Inducing empathy has improved racial attitudes, as well as attitudes toward people with AIDS, the homeless, and even convicted murderers (Batson, Polycarpou, et al., 1997; Dovidio, Gaertner, & Johnson, 1999). Empathy-induced altruism has also been found to increase cooperation in a competitive situation (a *prisoner's dilemma*), even when one knows that the person for whom one feels empathy has acted competitively (Batson & Ahmad, 2001; Batson & Moran, 1999).

Other Possible Sources of Altruistic Motivation

Might there be sources of altruistic motivation other than empathic emotion? Several have been proposed, including an altruistic personality (Oliner & Oliner, 1988), principled moral reasoning (Kohlberg, 1976), and internalized prosocial values (Staub, 1974). There is some evidence that each of these potential sources is associated with increased prosocial motivation, but as yet, it is not clear whether this motivation is altruistic. It may instead be an instrumental means to the egoistic ultimate goals of (a) maintaining one's positive self-concept or (b) avoiding guilt (Batson, 1991; Batson, Bolen, Cross, & Neuringer-Benefiel, 1986; Carlo et al., 1991; Eisenberg et al., 1989). More and better research exploring these possibilities is needed.

Beyond the Egoism-Altruism Debate: Other Prosocial Motives

Thinking more broadly, beyond the egoism-altruism debate that has been the focus of attention and contention for the past two decades, might there be other forms of prosocial motivation—forms in which the ultimate goal is neither to benefit oneself nor to benefit another individual? Two possibilities seem especially worthy of consideration: collectivism and principlism.

Collectivism: Benefiting a Group

Collectivism involves motivation to benefit a particular group as a whole. The ultimate goal is not to increase one's own welfare or the welfare of the specific others who are benefited; the ultimate goal is to increase the welfare of the group. Robyn Dawes and his colleagues put it succinctly: "Not me or thee but we" (Dawes, van de Kragt, & Orbell, 1988). They also suggested that collectivist prosocial motivation is a product of group identity (Brewer & Kramer, 1986; Tajfel, 1981; Turner, 1987).

As with altruism, however, what looks like collectivism may actually be a subtle form of egoism. Perhaps attention to group welfare is simply an expression of enlightened self-interest. After all, if one recognizes that ignoring group needs and the common good in a headlong pursuit of self-benefit will only lead to less self-benefit in the long run, then one may decide to benefit the group as a means to maximize overall self-benefit. Appeals to enlightened self-interest are often used by politicians and social activists trying to encourage prosocial response to societal needs. They warn of the long-term consequences for oneself and one's children of pollution and squandering natural resources. They remind that if the plight of the poor becomes too severe, those who are well off may face revolution. Such appeals seem to assume that collectivism is simply a form of egoism.

The most direct evidence that collectivism is independent of egoism comes from research by Dawes, van de Kragt, and Orbell (1990). They examined the responses of individuals who had been given a choice between allocating money to themselves or to a group. Allocation to oneself maximized individual but not group profit, whereas allocation to the group maximized collective but not individual profit.

Dawes et al. (1990) found that if individuals faced with this dilemma made their allocation after discussing it with other members of the group, they gave more to the group than if they had no prior discussion. Moreover, this effect was specific to the in-group with whom the discussion occurred; allocation to an out-group was not enhanced. Based on this research, Dawes et al. claimed evidence for collectivist motivation independent of egoism, arguing that their procedure ruled out the two most plausible egoistic explanations: (a) enlightened self-interest (by having no future contact and only one allocation round) and (b) socially instilled conscience (a norm to share, if evoked, should increase sharing with the out-group as well as the in-group). There is reason to doubt, however, that their procedure effectively ruled out self-rewards and self-punishments associated with conscience. The research on norms reviewed earlier suggests that norms can be more refined than Dawes and his coworkers allowed. We may have a norm that says "share with your buddies" rather than a norm that simply says "share." So, although this research is important and suggestive, more and better evidence is needed to justify the conclusion that collectivist prosocial motivation is not reducible to egoism.

Principlism: Upholding a Moral Principle

Not only have most moral philosophers argued for the importance of a prosocial motive other than egoism, but most since Kant (1724–1804) have shunned altruism and collectivism as well. They reject appeals to altruism, especially empathy-induced altruism, because feelings of empathy, sympathy, and compassion are too fickle and too circumscribed. Empathy is not felt for everyone in need, at least not to the same degree. They reject appeals to collectivism because group interest is bounded by the limits of the group; it may even encourage doing harm to those outside the group. Given these problems with altruism and collectivism, moral philosophers have typically advocated prosocial motivation with an ultimate goal of upholding a universal and impartial moral principle, such as justice (Rawls, 1971). We shall call this moral motivation *principlism.*

Is acting with an ultimate goal of upholding a moral principle really possible? When Kant (1785/1898) briefly shifted from his analysis of what ought to be to what is, he was ready to admit that even when the concern we show for others appears to be prompted by duty to principle, it may actually be prompted by self-love (pp. 23–24). The goal of upholding a moral principle may be only an instrumental goal pursued as a means to reach the ultimate goal of self-benefit. If so, then principle-based motivation is actually egoistic.

The self-benefits of upholding a moral principle are conspicuous. One can gain the social and self-rewards of being seen and seeing oneself as a good person. One can also avoid the social and self-punishments of shame and guilt for failing to do the right thing. As Freud (1930) suggested, society may inculcate such principles in the young in order to bridle their antisocial impulses by making it in their best personal interest to act morally (see also Campbell, 1975). Alternatively, through internalization (Staub, 1989) or development of moral reasoning (Kohlberg, 1976), principles may come to be valued in their own right and not simply as instrumental means to self-serving ends.

The issue here is the same one faced with altruism and collectivism. We need to know the nature of the underlying motive. Is the desire to uphold justice (or some other moral principle) an instrumental goal on the way to the ultimate goal of self-benefit? If so, this desire is a form of egoism. Is upholding the principle an ultimate goal, and the ensuing self-benefits merely unintended consequences? If so, principlism is a fourth type of prosocial motivation, independent of egoism, altruism, and collectivism.

Recent research suggests that people often act so as to appear moral while, if possible, avoiding the cost of actually being moral (Batson, Kobrynowicz, Dinnerstein, Kampf, & Wilson, 1997; Batson, Thompson, Seuferling, Whitney, & Strongman, 1999). This research also suggests that if moral motivation exists, it is easily overpowered by self-interest. Many of us are, it seems, quite adept at moral rationalization.

We are good at justifying to ourselves (if not to others) why a situation that benefits us or those we care about does not violate our moral principles—for example, why storing our nuclear waste in someone else's backyard is fair, why terrorist attacks by our side are regrettable but necessary evils whereas terrorist attacks by the other side are atrocities, and why we must obey orders even if it means killing innocent people. The abstractness of most moral principles, and their multiplicity, makes rationalization all too easy (see Bandura, 1991; Bersoff, 1999; Staub, 1990).

But this may be only part of the story. Perhaps in some cases upholding a moral principle *can* serve as an ultimate goal, defining a form of motivation independent of egoism. If so, perhaps these principles can provide a basis for responding to the needs of others that transcends reliance on self-interest or on vested interest in and feeling for the welfare of certain other individuals or groups. Quite an "if," but it seems well worth conducting research to find out.

Conflict and Cooperation of Prosocial Motives

To recognize the range of possible prosocial motives makes available more resources to those seeking to produce a more humane, caring society. At the same time, a multiplicity of prosocial motives complicates matters. These different motives for helping others do not always work in harmony. They can undercut or compete with one another.

Well-intentioned appeals to extended or enlightened self-interest can backfire by undermining other prosocial motives. Providing people with money or other tangible incentives for showing concern may lead people to interpret their motivation as egoistic even when it is not (Batson, Coke, Jasnoski, & Hanson, 1978). In this way, the assumption that there is only one answer to the question of why we act for the common good—egoism—may become a self-fulfilling prophecy (Batson, Fultz, Schoenrade, & Paduano, 1987) and may create a self-perpetuating norm of self-interest (Miller, 1999; Miller & Ratner, 1998).

Nor do the other three prosocial motives always work in harmony. They can conflict with one another. For example, altruism can—and often does—conflict with collectivism or principlism. We may ignore the larger social good, or we may compromise our principles, not only to benefit ourselves but also to benefit those individuals about whom we especially care (Batson, Batson, et al., 1995; Batson, Klein, Highberger, & Shaw, 1995). Indeed, whereas there are clear social sanctions against unbridled self-interest, there are not clear sanctions against altruism. Batson, Ahmad, et al. (1999) found that altruism can at times be a greater threat to the common good than is egoism.

Each of the four possible prosocial motives that we have identified has its strengths. Each also has its weaknesses. The potential for the greatest good may come from strategies that orchestrate these motives so that the strengths of one can overcome the weaknesses of another. Strategies that combine appeals to either altruism or collectivism with appeals to principle seem especially promising. For example, think about the principle of justice. Upholding justice is a powerful motive, but it is vulnerable to rationalization. Empathy-induced altruism and collectivism are also powerful motives, but they are limited in scope. They produce partiality—special concern for a particular person or persons or for a particular group. If we can lead people to feel empathy for the victims of injustice or to perceive themselves in a common group with them, we may be able to get these motives working together rather than at odds. Desire for justice may provide perspective and reason; empathy-induced altruism or collectivism may provide emotional fire and a force directed specifically toward relief of the victims' suffering, preventing rationalization.

Something of this sort occurred, we believe, in a number of rescuers of Jews in Nazi Europe. A careful look at data collected by the Oliners and their colleagues (Oliner & Oliner, 1988) suggests that involvement in rescue activity frequently began with concern for a specific individual or individuals for whom compassion was felt—often individuals known previously. This initial involvement subsequently led to further contacts and rescue activity and to a concern for justice that extended well beyond the bound of the initial empathic concern. Something of this sort also lay at the heart of Gandhi's and Martin Luther King's practice of nonviolent protest. The sight on the TV news of a small Black child in Birmingham being literally rolled down the street by water from a fire hose under the direction of Police Chief Bull Connor, and the emotions this sight evoked, seemed to do more to arouse a concern for justice than did hours of reasoned argument and appeals for equal civil rights.

Something of this sort also can be found in the writing of Jonathan Kozol. Deeply concerned about the "savage inequalities" in public education between rich and poor communities in the United States, Kozol (1991) does not simply document the inequity. He takes us into the lives of individual children. We come to care deeply for them and, as a result, about the injustice.

RESEARCH METHOD MATTERS

Efforts to explain prosocial behavior, especially its seemingly anomalous aspects, have raised thorny issues about research methods that, though not specific to this area, flourish here.

Most of these issues are rooted in mire produced by two features. First, psychologists are not the only ones who care about prosocial behavior. Most research participants see themselves as good, kind, caring people, and they want to be seen that way by others. Second, although cool, cognitive analysis and inference are often involved, theory and research on prosocial behavior focuses on relatively hot, active processes—the interplay of values, emotions, motives, and behavior. These processes may not be accessible to cool introspection.

To reap a fruitful harvest from the mire that these two features create, researchers need to avoid the pitfalls of demand characteristics, evaluation apprehension, social desirability, self-presentation, and reactive measures. Consequently, research on prosocial behavior still relies heavily on high-impact deception procedures of the sort made famous in the social psychology of the 1960s (Aronson, Brewer, & Carlsmith, 1985). The currently popular procedure of presenting research participants with descriptions of hypothetical situations and asking them to report what they would do is of limited use when studying prosocial behavior. Commitment to actual behavior—if not the behavior itself—is almost always required (Lerner, 1987). Rather than relying heavily on self-reports, thought listing, or retrospective analysis to reveal mediating psychological processes, we must often study these processes indirectly by designing research that allows the effect of mediators to be inferred from observable behavior. Typically, this means one must successfully deceive participants, run the experiments on each participant individually, use between-group designs, and so on. Clearly, such research is difficult. Equally clearly, it requires careful sensitivity to and protection of the welfare and dignity of participants.

Deeming care and sensitivity insufficient, some universities have instituted a blanket prohibition on the use of high-impact deceptions of the kind needed to address key research questions concerning prosocial behavior. It is ironic that the study of prosocial, ethical behavior is one of the areas to suffer most from restrictions imposed in response to concerns about research ethics.

Few would disagree that society could benefit from increased prosocial behavior. Rage and hate crimes, terrorist attacks, child and spouse abuse, neglect of the homeless, the plight of people with AIDS, and the growing disparity between rich and poor (and smug callousness toward the latter) provide all-too-frequent reminders of crying need. Given the societal importance of understanding why people act to benefit others, given the apparent necessity of using high-impact deception research to provide this understanding, and given the dangers of obtaining misleading information using other methods, it is not the use of these methods, but rather a blanket prohibition of them, that seems unethical.

CONCLUSION

Over the past 30 years the practical concern to promote prosocial behavior has led to both a variance-accounted-for empirical approach and the application of existing psychological theories. In addition, existing theory has been challenged and new theoretical perspectives developed by a focus on anomalous aspects of why people do—and don't—act prosocially. Research has challenged currently dominant theories of social motivation and even of human nature—views that limit the human capacity to care to self-interest. This research has raised the possibility of a multiplicity of social motives—altruism, collectivism, and principlism, as well as egoism. It also has raised important theoretical questions—as yet unanswered—about how these motives might be most effectively orchestrated to increase prosocial behavior. More broadly, research in this area takes exception to the currently dominant focus in social psychology on cognitive representation of the social environment and processing of social information, calling for increased attention to motives, emotions, and values.

Research on prosocial behavior provides evidence that in addition to our all-too-apparent failing and fallibilities, we humans are, at times, capable of caring, and caring deeply, for people and issues other than ourselves. This possibility has wide-ranging theoretical implications, suggesting that we are more social than even our most social theories have led us to believe. It also has wide-ranging practical implications, suggesting untapped resources for social change. At present, however, these theoretical and practical implications are only partly realized, providing a pressing—and daunting—agenda.

REFERENCES

Adams, J. S. (1965). Inequity in social exchange. In L. Berkowitz (Ed.), *Advances in experimental social psychology* (Vol. 1, pp. 267–299). New York: Academic.

Allport, G. W. (1961). *Pattern and growth in personality.* New York: Holt, Rinehart, and Winston.

Aronson, E., Brewer, M., & Carlsmith, J. M. (1985). Experimentation in social psychology. In G. Lindzey & E. Aronson (Eds.), *The handbook of social psychology: Vol. 1. Theory and method* (3rd ed., pp. 441–486). New York: Random House.

Bandura, A. (1977). *Social learning theory.* Englewood Cliffs, NJ: Prentice-Hall.

Bandura, A. (1991). Social cognitive theory of moral thought and action. In W. M. Kurtines & W. M. Gewirtz (Eds.), *Handbook of moral behavior and development: Vol. 1. Theory* (pp. 45–103). Hillsdale, NJ: Erlbaum.

Bar-Tal, D. (1982). Sequential development of helping behavior: A cognitive-learning model. *Developmental Review, 2,* 101–124.

Bar-Tal, D. (1984). American study of helping behavior: What? why? and where? In E. Staub, D. Bar-Tal, J. Karylowski, & J. Reykowski (Eds.), *Development and maintenance of prosocial behavior: International perspectives on positive morality* (pp. 5–27). New York: Plenum.

Batson, C. D. (1987). Prosocial motivation: Is it ever truly altruistic? In L. Berkowitz (Ed.), *Advances in experimental social psychology* (Vol. 20, pp. 65–122). New York: Academic.

Batson, C. D. (1991). *The altruism question: Toward a social-psychological answer.* Hillsdale, NJ: Erlbaum.

Batson, C. D., & Ahmad, N. (2001). Empathy-induced altruism in a Prisoner's Dilemma: II. What if the target of empathy has defected? *European Journal of Social Psychology, 31,* 25–36.

Batson, C. D., Ahmad, N., Yin, J., Bedell, S. J., Johnson, J. W., Templin, C. M., & Whiteside, A. (1999). Two threats to the common good: Self-interested egoism and empathy-induced altruism. *Personality and Social Psychology Bulletin, 25,* 3–16.

Batson, C. D., Batson, J. G., Griffitt, C. A., Barrientos, S., Brandt, J. R., Sprengelmeyer, P., & Bayly, M. J. (1989). Negative-state relief and the empathy-altruism hypothesis. *Journal of Personality and Social Psychology, 56,* 922–933.

Batson, C. D., Batson, J. G., Slingsby, J. K., Harrell, K. L., Peekna, H. M., & Todd, R. M. (1991). Empathic joy and the empathy-altruism hypothesis. *Journal of Personality and Social Psychology, 61,* 413–426.

Batson, C. D., Batson, J. G., Todd, R. M., Brummett, B. H., Shaw, L. L., & Aldeguer, C. M. R. (1995). Empathy and the collective good: Caring for one of the others in a social dilemma. *Journal of Personality and Social Psychology, 68,* 619–631.

Batson, C. D., Bolen, M. H., Cross, J. A., & Neuringer-Benefiel, H. E. (1986). Where is the altruism in the altruistic personality? *Journal of Personality and Social Psychology, 50,* 212–220.

Batson, C. D., Coke, J. S., Jasnoski, M. L., & Hanson, M. (1978). Buying kindness: Effect of an extrinsic incentive for helping on perceived altruism. *Personality and Social Psychology Bulletin, 4,* 86–91.

Batson, C. D., Dyck, J. L., Brandt, J. R., Batson, J. G., Powell, A. L., McMaster, M. R., & Griffitt, C. (1988). Five studies testing two new egoistic alternatives to the empathy-altruism hypothesis. *Journal of Personality and Social Psychology, 55,* 52–77.

Batson, C. D., Fultz, J., Schoenrade, P. A., & Paduano, A. (1987). Critical self-reflection and self-perceived altruism: When self-reward fails. *Journal of Personality and Social Psychology, 53,* 594–602.

Batson, C. D., Klein, T. R., Highberger, L., & Shaw, L. L. (1995). Immorality from empathy-induced altruism: When compassion and justice conflict. *Journal of Personality and Social Psychology, 68,* 1042–1054.

Batson, C. D., Kobrynowicz, D., Dinnerstein, J. L., Kampf, H. C., & Wilson, A. D. (1997). In a very different voice: Unmasking moral hypocrisy. *Journal of Personality and Social Psychology, 72,* 1335–1348.

Batson, C. D., & Moran, T. (1999). Empathy-induced altruism in a Prisoner's Dilemma. *European Journal of Social Psychology, 29,* 909–924.

Batson, C. D., Polycarpou, M. P., Harmon-Jones, E., Imhoff, H. J., Mitchener, E. C., Bednar, L. L., Klein, T. R., & Highberger, L. (1997). Empathy and attitudes: Can feeling for a member of a stigmatized group improve feelings toward the group? *Journal of Personality and Social Psychology, 72,* 105–118.

Batson, C. D., Thompson, E. R., Seuferling, G., Whitney, H., & Strongman, J. (1999). Moral hypocrisy: Appearing moral to oneself without being so. *Journal of Personality and Social Psychology, 77,* 525–537.

Batson, C. D., & Weeks, J. L. (1996). Mood effects of unsuccessful helping: Another test of the empathy-altruism hypothesis. *Personality and Social Psychology Bulletin, 22,* 148–157.

Berkowitz, L. (1972). Social norms, feelings, and other factors affecting helping and altruism. In L. Berkowitz (Ed.), *Advances in experimental social psychology* (Vol. 6, pp. 63–108). New York: Academic.

Bersoff, D. M. (1999). Why good people sometimes do bad things: Motivated reasoning and unethical behavior. *Personality and Social Psychology Bulletin, 25,* 28–39.

Blasi, A. (1980). Bridging moral cognition and moral action: A critical review of the literature. *Psychological Bulletin, 88,* 1–45.

Brown, J. D., & Smart, S. A. (1991). The self and social conduct: Linking self-representations to prosocial behavior. *Journal of Personality and Social Psychology, 60,* 368–375.

Brewer, M. B., & Kramer, R. M. (1986). Choice behavior in social dilemmas: Effects of social identity, group size, and decision framing. *Journal of Personality and Social Psychology, 50,* 543–549.

Campbell, D. T. (1975). On the conflicts between biological and social evolution and between psychology and moral tradition. *American Psychologist, 30,* 1103–1126.

Carlo, G., Eisenberg, N., Troyer, D., Switzer, G., & Speer, A. L. (1991). The altruistic personality: In what contexts is it apparent? *Journal of Personality and Social Psychology, 61,* 450–458.

Cialdini, R. B., Baumann, D. J., & Kenrick, D. T. (1981). Insights from sadness: A three-step model of the development of altruism as hedonism. *Developmental Review, 1,* 207–223.

Cialdini, R. B., Darby, B. L., & Vincent, J. E. (1973). Transgression and altruism: A case for hedonism. *Journal of Experimental Social Psychology, 9,* 502–516.

Cialdini, R. B., Kallgren, C. A., & Reno, R. R. (1991). A focus theory of normative conduct: A theoretical refinement and reevaluation of the role of norms in human behavior. In M. P. Zanna (Ed.), *Advances in experimental social psychology* (Vol. 24, pp. 201–234). Orlando, FL: Academic.

Cialdini, R. B., Schaller, M., Houlihan, D., Arps, K., Fultz, J., & Beaman, A. L. (1987). Empathy-based helping: Is it selflessly or selfishly motivated? *Journal of Personality and Social Psychology, 52,* 749–758.

Clary, E. G., & Snyder, M. (1991). A functional analysis of altruism and prosocial behavior: The case of volunteerism. In M. S. Clark (Ed.), *Prosocial behavior* (pp. 119–148). Newbury Park, CA: Sage.

Darley, J. M., & Latané, B. (1968). Bystander intervention in emergencies: Diffusion of responsibility. *Journal of Personality and Social Psychology, 10,* 202–214.

Darley, J. M., & Latané, B. (1970). Norms and normative behavior: Field studies of social interdependence. In J. Macaulay & L. Berkowitz (Eds.), *Altruism and helping behavior* (pp. 83–101). New York: Academic.

Dawes, R., van de Kragt, A. J. C., & Orbell, J. M. (1988). Not me or thee but we: The importance of group identity in eliciting cooperation in dilemma situations: Experimental manipulations. *Acta Psychologica, 68,* 83–97.

Dawes, R., van de Kragt, A. J. C., & Orbell, J. M. (1990). Cooperation for the benefit of us—not me, or my conscience. In J. J. Mansbridge (Ed.), *Beyond self-interest* (pp. 97–110). Chicago: University of Chicago Press.

DePaulo, B. M., Nadler, A., & Fisher, J. D. (Eds.). (1983). *New directions in helping: Vol. 2. Help seeking.* New York: Academic.

de Waal, F. (1996). *Good natured: The origins of rights and wrongs in humans and other animals.* Cambridge, MA: Harvard University Press.

Dollard, J., & Miller, N. E. (1950). *Personality and psychotherapy.* New York: McGraw-Hill.

Dovidio, J. (1984). Helping behavior and altruism: An empirical and conceptual overview. In L. Berkowitz (Ed.), *Advances in experimental social psychology* (Vol. 17, pp. 361–427). New York: Academic.

Dovidio, J. F., Allen, J. L., & Schroeder, D. A. (1990). The specificity of empathy-induced helping: Evidence for altruistic motivation. *Journal of Personality and Social Psychology, 59,* 249–260.

Dovidio, J. F., Gaertner, S. L., & Johnson, J. D. (1999, October). *New directions in prejudice and prejudice reduction: The role of cognitive representations and affect.* Paper presented at the annual meeting of the Society of Experimental Social Psychology, St. Louis, MO.

Dovidio, J. F., Piliavin, J. A., Gaertner, S. L., Schroeder, D. A., & Clark, R. D., III (1991). The arousal/cost-reward model and the process of intervention: A review of the evidence. In M. S. Clark (Ed.), *Prosocial behavior* (pp. 86–118). Newbury Park, CA: Sage.

Eagly, A. H., & Crowley, M. (1986). Gender and helping behavior: A meta-analytic review of the social psychological literature. *Psychological Bulletin, 100,* 283–308.

Eisenberg, N. (1986). *Altruistic emotion, cognition, and behavior.* Hillsdale, NJ: Erlbaum.

Eisenberg, N. (1991). Meta-analytic contributions to the literature on prosocial behavior. *Personality and Social Psychology Bulletin, 17,* 273–282.

Eisenberg, N., & Miller, P. (1987). Empathy and prosocial behavior. *Psychological Bulletin, 101,* 91–119.

Eisenberg, N., Miller, P. A., Schaller, M., Fabes, R. A., Fultz, J., Shell, R., & Shea, C. L. (1989). The role of sympathy and altruistic personality traits in helping: A re-examination. *Journal of Personality, 57,* 41–67.

Festinger, L. (1957). *A theory of cognitive dissonance.* Stanford, CA: Stanford University Press.

Fisher, J. D., Nadler, A., & Whitcher-Alagna, S. J. (1982). Recipient reactions to aid: A conceptual review and a new theoretical framework. *Psychological Bulletin, 91,* 27–54.

Fiske, A. P. (1992). The four elementary forms of sociality: Framework for a unified theory of social relations. *Psychological Review, 99,* 689–723.

Freud, S. (1930). *Civilization and its discontents* (J. Riviere, Trans.). London: Hogarth.

Gaertner, S. L., & Bickman, L. (1971). Effects of race on the elicitation of helping behavior: The wrong number technique. *Journal of Personality and Social Psychology, 20,* 218–222.

Gibbons, F. X., & Wicklund, R. A. (1982). Self-focused attention and helping behavior. *Journal of Personality and Social Psychology, 43,* 462–474.

Gies, M. (1987). *Anne Frank remembered: The story of the woman who helped to hide the Frank family.* New York: Simon & Schuster.

Gilligan, C. (1982). *In a different voice: Psychological theory and women's development.* Cambridge, MA: Harvard University Press.

Gilligan, C., Ward, J. V., & Taylor, J. M. (1988). *Mapping the moral domain: A contribution of women's thinking to psychological theory and education.* Cambridge, MA: Harvard University Press.

Goffman, E. (1959). *The presentation of self in everyday life.* Garden City, NY: Doubleday/Anchor Books.

Gouldner, A. W. (1960). The norm of reciprocity: A preliminary statement. *American Sociological Review, 25,* 161–179.

Greenberg, M. S., & Frisch, D. M. (1972). Effect of intentionality on willingness to reciprocate a favor. *Journal of Experimental Social Psychology, 8,* 99–111.

Gruder, C. L., & Cook, T. D. (1971). Sex, dependency, and helping. *Journal of Personality and Social Psychology, 19,* 290–294.

Grusec, J. (1991). The socialization of altruism. In M. S. Clark (Ed.), *Prosocial behavior* (pp. 9–33). Newbury Park, CA: Sage.

Heider, F. (1958). *The psychology of interpersonal relations.* New York: Wiley.

Hoffman, M. L. (1975). Developmental synthesis of affect and cognition and its implications for altruistic motivation. *Developmental Psychology, 11,* 607–622.

Hoffman, M. L. (1981). Is altruism part of human nature? *Journal of Personality and Social Psychology, 40,* 121–137.

Homans, G. C. (1961). *Social behavior: Its elementary forms.* New York: Harcourt.

Hornstein, H. A. (1982). Promotive tension: Theory and research. In V. Derlega & J. Grzelak (Eds.), *Cooperation and helping behavior: Theories and research* (pp. 229–248). New York: Academic.

Hull, C. L. (1943). *Principles of behavior.* New York: Appleton-Century.

Huston, T. L., & Korte, C. (1976). The responsive bystander: Why he helps. In T. Lickona (Ed.), *Moral development and behavior: Theory, research, and social issues* (pp. 269–283). New York: Holt, Rinehart, & Winston.

Isen, A. M., & Levin, P. F. (1972). Effect of feeling good on helping: Cookies and kindness. *Journal of Personality and Social Psychology, 21,* 344–348.

Isen, A. M., Shalker, T. E., Clark, M., & Karp, L. (1978). Affect, accessibility of material in memory, and behavior: A cognitive loop? *Journal of Personality and Social Psychology, 36,* 1–13.

Jones, E. E., & Davis, K. E. (1965). From acts to dispositions: The attribution process in person perception. In L. Berkowitz (Ed.), *Advances in experimental social psychology* (Vol. 2, pp. 219–266). New York: Academic.

Kant, I. (1898). *Kant's Critique of Practical Reason and other works on the theory of ethics* (T. K. Abbott, Trans.) (4th ed.). New York: Longmans, Green. (Original work published 1785)

Karylowski, J. (1984). Focus of attention and altruism: Endocentric and exocentric sources of altruistic behavior. In E. Staub, D. Bar-Tal, J. Karylowski, & J. Reykowski (Eds.), *Development and maintenance of prosocial behavior: International perspectives on positive morality* (pp. 139–154). New York: Plenum.

Katz, I., Cohen, S., & Glass, D. (1975). Some determinants of cross-racial helping. *Journal of Personality and Social Psychology, 32,* 964–970.

Kohlberg, L. (1976). Moral stages and moralization: The cognitive-developmental approach. In T. Lickona (Ed.), *Moral development and behavior: Theory, research, and social issues* (pp. 31–53). New York: Holt, Rinehart, & Winston.

Kozol, J. (1991). *Savage inequalities: Children in America's schools.* New York: Crown.

Krebs, D. L. (1975). Empathy and altruism. *Journal of Personality and Social Psychology, 32,* 1134–1146.

Krebs, D. L., & Miller, D. T. (1985). Altruism and aggression. In G. Lindzey & E. Aronson (Eds.), *Handbook of social psychology: Vol. 2. Special fields and applications* (3rd ed., pp. 1–71). New York: Random House.

Kurtines, W. M., & Greif, E. B. (1974). The development of moral thought: Review and evaluation of Kohlberg's approach. *Psychological Bulletin, 81,* 453–470.

Latané, B., & Darley, J. M. (1968). Group inhibition of bystander intervention. *Journal of Personality and Social Psychology, 10,* 215–221.

Latané, B., & Darley, J. M. (1970). *The unresponsive bystander: Why doesn't he help?* New York: Appleton-Crofts.

Latané, B., & Nida, S. A. (1981). Ten years of research on group size and helping. *Psychological Bulletin, 89,* 308–324.

Latané, B., & Rodin, J. A. (1969). A lady in distress: Inhibiting effects of friends and strangers on bystander intervention. *Journal of Experimental Social Psychology, 5,* 189–202.

Lepper, M. R., Greene, D., & Nisbett, R. E. (1973). Undermining children's intrinsic interest with extrinsic reward: A test of the "overjustification" hypothesis. *Journal of Personality and Social Psychology, 28,* 129–137.

Lerner, M. J. (1970). The desire for justice and reactions to victims. In J. Macaulay & L. Berkowitz (Eds.), *Altruism and helping behavior* (pp. 205–229). New York: Academic.

Lerner, M. J. (1980). *The belief in a just world: A fundamental delusion.* New York: Plenum.

Lerner, M. J. (1982). The justice motive in human relations and the economic model of man: A radical analysis of facts and fictions. In V. J. Derlega & J. Grzelak (Eds.), *Cooperation and helping behavior: Theories and research* (pp. 249–278). New York: Academic.

Lerner, M. J. (1987). Integrating societal and psychological rules of entitlement: The basic task of each social actor and fundamental problem for the social sciences. *Social Justice Research, 1,* 107–125.

Levine, R. V., Martinez, T. S., Brase, G., & Sorenson, K. (1994). Helping in 36 U.S. cities. *Journal of Personality and Social Psychology, 67,* 69–82.

Lewin, K. (1951). *Field theory in social science: Selected theoretical papers.* New York: Harper.

MacIntyre, A. (1967). Egoism and altruism. In P. Edwards (Ed.), *The encyclopedia of philosophy* (Vol. 2, pp. 462–466). New York: Macmillan.

MacLean, P. D. (1973). *A triune concept of the brain and behavior.* Toronto, Canada: University of Toronto Press.

Mansbridge, J. J. (1990). *Beyond self-interest.* Chicago: University of Chicago Press.

Maslach, C. (1982). *Burnout: The cost of caring.* Englewood Cliffs, NJ: Prentice-Hall.

McDougall, W. (1908). *An introduction to social psychology.* London: Methuen.

Mead, G. H. (1934). *Mind, self, and society* (posthumous; C. M. Morris, Ed.). Chicago: University of Chicago Press.

Miller, D. T. (1999). The norm of self-interest. *American Psychologist, 54,* 1053–1060.

Miller, D. T., & McFarland, C. (1987). Pluralistic ignorance: When similarity is interpreted as dissimilarity. *Journal of Personality and Social Psychology, 53,* 298–305.

Miller, D. T., & Ratner, R. K. (1998). The disparity between the actual and assumed power of self-interest. *Journal of Personality and Social Psychology, 74,* 53–62.

Nadler, A. (1991). Help-seeking behavior: Psychological costs and instrumental benefits. In M. S. Clark (Ed.), *Prosocial behavior* (pp. 290–311). Newbury, CA: Sage.

Nadler, A., Fisher, J. D., & Ben-Itzhak, S. (1983). With a little help from my friend: Effect of single or multiple act aid as a function of donor and task characteristics. *Journal of Personality and Social Psychology, 44,* 310–321.

Oliner, S. P., & Oliner, P. M. (1988). *The altruistic personality: Rescuers of Jews in Nazi Europe.* New York: Free.

Omoto, A. M., & Snyder, M. (1995). Sustained helping without obligation: Motivation, longevity of service, and perceived attitude change among AIDS volunteers. *Journal of Personality and Social Psychology, 68,* 671–686.

Pearce, P. L., & Amato, P. R. (1980). A taxonomy of helping: A multidimensional scaling analysis. *Social Psychology Quarterly, 43,* 363–371.

Piaget, J. (1926). *The language and thought of the child.* New York: Harcourt.

Piaget, J. (1932). *The moral judgment of the child.* London: Kegan Paul.

Piliavin, I. M., Rodin, J., & Piliavin, J. A. (1969). Good Samaritanism: An underground phenomenon. *Journal of Personality and Social Psychology, 13,* 289–299.

Piliavin, J. A., Callero, P. L., & Evans, D. E. (1982). Addiction to altruism?: Opponent-process theory and habitual blood donation. *Journal of Personality and Social Psychology, 43,* 1200–1213.

Piliavin, J. A., & Charng, H.-W. (1990). Altruism: A review of recent theory and research. *American Sociological Review, 16,* 27–65.

Piliavin, J. A., Dovidio, J. F., Gaertner, S. L., & Clark, R. D., III (1981). *Emergency intervention.* New York: Academic Press.

Piliavin, J. A., & Piliavin, I. M. (1972). Effect of blood on reactions to a victim. *Journal of Personality and Social Psychology, 23,* 353–362.

Rawls, J. (1971). *A theory of justice.* Cambridge, MA: Harvard University Press.

Reykowski, J. (1982). Motivation of prosocial behavior. In V. J. Derlega & J. Grzelak (Eds.), *Cooperation and helping behavior: Theories and research* (pp. 352–375). New York: Academic.

Romer, D., Gruder, C. L., & Lizzardo, T. (1986). A person-situation approach to altruistic behavior. *Journal of Personality and Social Psychology, 51,* 1001–1012.

Rushton, J. P. (1980). *Altruism, socialization and society.* Englewood Cliffs, NJ: Prentice-Hall.

Ryan, W. (1971). *Blaming the victim.* New York: Random House.

Schaller, M., & Cialdini, R. B. (1988). The economics of empathic helping: Support for a mood-management motive. *Journal of Experimental Social Psychology, 24,* 163–181.

Schroeder, D. A., Dovidio, J. F., Sibicky, M. E., Matthews, L. L., & Allen, J. L. (1988). Empathy and helping behavior: Egoism or altruism? *Journal of Experimental Social Psychology, 24,* 333–353.

Schwartz, S. H. (1977). Normative influences on altruism. In L. Berkowitz (Ed.), *Advances in experimental social psychology* (Vol. 10, pp. 221–279). New York: Academic.

Schwartz, S. H., & Howard, J. (1981). A normative decision-making model of altruism. In J. P. Rushton & R. M. Sorrentino (Eds.), *Altruism and helping behavior* (pp. 189–211). Hillsdale, NJ: Erlbaum.

Shaw, L. L., Batson, C. D., & Todd, R. M. (1994). Empathy avoidance: Forestalling feeling for another in order to escape the motivational consequences. *Journal of Personality and Social Psychology, 67,* 879–887.

Shelton, M. L., & Rogers, R. W. (1981). Fear-arousing and empathy-arousing appeals to help: The pathos of persuasion. *Journal of Applied Social Psychology, 11,* 366–378.

Smith, K. D., Keating, J. P., & Stotland, E. (1989). Altruism reconsidered: The effect of denying feedback on a victim's status to empathic witnesses. *Journal of Personality and Social Psychology, 57,* 641–650.

Snyder, M. (1993). Basic research and practical problems: The promise of a "functional" personality and social psychology. *Personality and Social Psychology Bulletin, 19,* 251–264.

Snyder, M., & Ickes, W. (1985). Personality and social behavior. In G. Lindzey & E. Aronson (Eds.), *Handbook of social psychology: Vol. 2. Special fields and applications* (3rd ed., pp. 883–948). New York: Random House.

Staub, E. (1974). Helping a distressed person: Social, personality, and stimulus determinants. In L. Berkowitz (Ed.), *Advances in experimental social psychology* (Vol. 7, pp. 293–341). New York: Academic.

Staub, E. (1989). Individual and societal (group) values in a motivational perspective and their role in benevolence and harmdoing. In N. Eisenberg, J. Reykowski, & E. Staub (Eds.), *Social and moral values: Individual and societal perspectives* (pp. 45–61). Hillsdale, NJ: Erlbaum.

Staub, E. (1990). Moral exclusion, personal goal theory, and extreme destructiveness. *Journal of Social Issues, 46*(1), 47–64.

Stotland, E., Mathews, K. E., Sherman, S. E., Hansson, R. O., & Richardson, B. Z. (1978). *Empathy, fantasy, and helping.* Beverly Hills, CA: Sage.

Tajfel, H. (1981). *Human groups and social categories: Studies in social psychology.* Cambridge, UK: Cambridge University Press.

Tesser, A., Gatewood, R., & Driver, M. S. (1968). Some determinants of gratitude. *Journal of Personality and Social Psychology, 9,* 233–236.

Thomas, G. C., Batson, C. D., & Coke, J. S. (1981). Do good samaritans discourage helpfulness? Self-perceived altruism after exposure to highly helpful others. *Journal of Personality and Social Psychology, 40,* 194–200.

Tolman, E. C. (1923). The nature of instinct. *Psychological Bulletin, 20,* 200–218.

Turner, J. C. (1987). *Rediscovering the social group: A self-categorization theory.* London: Basil Blackwell.

Walker, L. J. (1991). Sex differences in moral reasoning. In W. M. Kurtines & J. L. Gewirtz (Eds.), *Handbook of moral behavior and development: Vol. 2. Research* (pp. 333–364). Hillsdale, NJ: Erlbaum.

Wallach, M. A., & Wallach, L. (1983). *Psychology's sanction for selfishness: The error of egoism in theory and therapy.* San Francisco: W. H. Freeman.

Walster, E., Berscheid, E., & Walster, G. W. (1973). New directions in equity research. *Journal of Personality and Social Psychology, 25,* 151–176.

Wegener, D. T., & Petty, R. E. (1994). Mood management across affective states: The hedonic contingency hypothesis. *Journal of Personality and Social Psychology, 66,* 1034–1048.

Wegner, D. M., & Crano, W. D. (1975). Racial factors in helping behavior: An unobtrusive field experiment. *Journal of Personality and Social Psychology, 32,* 901–905.

Weiner, B. (1980). A cognitive (attribution)-emotion-action model of motivated behavior: An analysis of judgments of help giving. *Journal of Personality and Social Psychology, 39,* 186–200.

West, S. G., Whitney, G., & Schnedler, R. (1975). Helping a motorist in distress: The effects of sex, race, and neighborhood. *Journal of Personality and Social Psychology, 31,* 691–698.

Weyant, J. M. (1978). Effects of mood states, costs, and benefits on helping. *Journal of Personality and Social Psychology, 36,* 1169–1176.

Wilke, H., & Lanzetta, J. T. (1982). The obligation to help: Factors affecting response to help received. *European Journal of Social Psychology, 12,* 315–319.

Wilson, J. P. (1976). Motivation, modeling, and altruism: A Person x Situation analysis. *Journal of Personality and Social Psychology, 34,* 1078–1086.

Wispé, L. (1986). The distinction between sympathy and empathy: To call forth a concept, a word is needed. *Journal of Personality and Social Psychology, 50,* 314–321.

Wispé, L., & Freshley, H. (1971). Race, sex, and sympathetic helping behavior: The broken bag caper. *Journal of Personality and Social Psychology, 17,* 59–65.

Zahn-Waxler, C., & Radke-Yarrow, M. (1990). The origins of empathic concern. *Motivation and Emotion, 14,* 107–130.

Zuckerman, M., & Reis, H. T. (1978). Comparison of three models for predicting altruistic behavior. *Journal of Personality and Social Psychology, 36,* 498–510.

CHAPTER 20

Social Conflict, Harmony, and Integration

JOHN F. DOVIDIO, SAMUEL L. GAERTNER, VICTORIA M. ESSES, AND MARILYNN B. BREWER

SOCIAL CONFLICT AND INTEGRATION

Humans are fundamentally social animals. Not only is group living of obvious contemporary importance (see Spears, Oakes, Ellemers, & Haslam, 1997), but also it represents the fundamental survival strategy that has likely characterized the human species from the beginning (see Simpson & Kenrick, 1997). The ways in which people understand their group membership thus play a critical role in social conflict and harmony and in intergroup integration. This chapter examines psychological perspectives on intergroup relations and their implications for reducing bias and conflict and for enhancing social integration. First, we review social psychological theories on the nature of individual and collective identities and their relation to social harmony and conflict. Then, we examine theoretical perspectives on reducing intergroup bias and promoting social harmony. Next, we explore the importance of considering majority and minority perspectives on intergroup relations, social conflict, and integration. The chapter concludes by considering future directions and practical implications.

Preparation of this chapter was supported by NIMH Grant MH 48721 to the first two authors and an SSHRC Grant to the third author. We gratefully acknowledge the helpful guidance, suggestions, and support provided by Mel Lerner and Irv Weiner on earlier versions of the work.

INDIVIDUAL AND COLLECTIVE IDENTITY

Perspectives on social conflict, harmony, and integration have reflected a variety of disciplinary orientations. For instance, psychological theories of intergroup attitudes have commonly emphasized the role of the individual, in terms of personality and attitude, in social biases and discrimination (see Duckitt, 1992; Jones, 1997). Traditional psychological theories, such as the work on the authoritarian personality (Adorno, Frenkel-Brunswik, Levinson, & Sanford, 1950), have considered the role of *dysfunctional* processes in the overt expression of social biases. More contemporary approaches to race relations, such as aversive racism and symbolic racism perspectives, have considered the contributions of *normal* processes (e.g., socialization and social cognition) to the expression of subtle, and often unconscious, biases (Dovidio & Gaertner, 1998; S. Gaertner & Dovidio, 1986; Kovel, 1970; Sears, 1988; Sears & Henry, 2000). In addition, the role of social norms and standards is emphasized in recent reconceptualizations of older measures, such as authoritarianism. Right-wing authoritarianism (Altemeyer, 1996, 1998) has been found to be associated with negative attitudes toward a number of groups, particularly those socially stigmatized by society (e.g., Altemeyer, 1996; Esses, Haddock, & Zanna, 1993).

Recent approaches to intergroup relations within psychology have also considered the role of individual differences in representations of group hierarchy. *Social dominance theory* (Pratto & Lemieux, 2001; Pratto, Sidanius, Stallworth, & Malle, 1994; see also Sidanius & Pratto, 1999) assumes that people who are strongly identified with high-status groups and who see intergroup relations in terms of group competition will be especially prejudiced and discriminatory toward out-groups. These biases occur spontaneously as a function of individual differences in social dominance orientation, in contexts in which in-group–out-group distinctions are salient (Pratto & Shih, 2000). Scales developed to measure social dominance orientation pit the values of group dominance and equality against each other (see Pratto et al., 1994; Sidanius & Pratto, 1999). People high in social dominance orientation believe that group hierarchies are inevitable and desirable, and they may thus see the world as involving competition between groups for resources. They endorse items such as, "Some groups of people are simply inferior to other groups" and "Sometimes other groups must be kept in their place." Individuals high in social dominance orientation believe that unequal social outcomes and social hierarchies are appropriate and therefore support an unequal distribution of resources among groups in ways that usually benefit their own group (see Pratto et al., 1994; Sidanius, Levin, & Pratto, 1996). Individuals low in social dominance orientation, in contrast, are generally concerned about the welfare of others and are empathic and tolerant of other individuals and groups (Pratto et al., 1994). They tend to endorse items such as, "Group equality should be our ideal" and "We would have fewer problems if we treated people more equally."

Sociological theories, in contrast, have frequently emphasized the role of large-scale social and structural dynamics in intergroup relations in general and in race relations in particular (Blauner, 1972; Bonacich, 1972; Wilson, 1978). These theories have considered the dynamics of race relations largely in economic and class-based terms—and often to the exclusion of individual influences (see Bobo, 1999).

Despite the existence of such divergent views, both sociological and psychological approaches have converged to recognize the importance of understanding the impact of group functions and collective identities on race relations (see Bobo, 1999). In terms of group functions, Blumer (1958a, 1958b, 1965a, 1965b), for instance, offered a sociologically based approach focusing on defense of group position, in which group competition and threat were considered fundamental processes in the development and maintenance of social biases. With respect to race relations, Blumer (1958a) wrote, "Race prejudice is a defensive reaction to such challenging of the sense of group position. . . . As such, race prejudice is a protective device. It functions, however shortsightedly, to preserve the integrity and position of the dominant group" (p. 5).

From a psychological orientation, Sherif, Harvey, White, Hood, and Sherif (1961) similarly proposed that the functional relations between groups are critical in determining intergroup attitudes. According to this position, competition between groups produces prejudice and discrimination, whereas intergroup interdependence and cooperative interaction that result in successful outcomes reduce intergroup bias (see also Bobo, 1988; Bobo & Hutchings, 1996; Campbell, 1965; Sherif, 1966).

With respect to the importance of collective identity, psychological research has emphasized how the salience of group versus individual identity can influence the way in which people process social information. In particular, the operation of group-level processes has been hypothesized to be dynamically distinct from the influence of individual-level processes. Different modes of functioning are involved, and these modes critically influence how people perceive others and experience their own sense of identity. In terms of perceptions of others, for example, Brewer (1988) proposed a *dual process model of impression formation* (see also the continuum model; Fiske & Neuberg, 1990; see also Fiske, Lin, & Neuberg, 1999). The primary distinction in Brewer's model is between two types of processing: person based and category based. Person-based processing is bottom up and data driven, involving the piecemeal acquisition of information that begins "at the most concrete level and stops at the lowest level of abstraction required by the prevailing processing objectives" (Brewer, 1988, p. 6). Category-based processing, in contrast, proceeds from global to specific; it is top-down. In top-down processing, how the external reality is perceived and experienced is influenced by category-based, subjective impressions. According to Brewer, category-based processing is more likely to occur than is person-based processing because social information is typically organized around social categories.

With respect to one's sense of identity, *social identity theory* (Tajfel & Turner, 1979) and *self-categorization theory* (Turner, 1985; see also Onorato & Turner, 2001) view the distinction between personal identity and social identity as a critical one (see Spears, 2001). When personal identity is salient, a person's individual needs, standards, beliefs, and motives primarily determine behavior. In contrast, when social identity is salient, "people come to perceive themselves as more interchangeable exemplars of a social category than as unique personalities defined by their individual differences from others" (Turner, Hogg, Oakes, Reicher, & Wetherell, 1987, p. 50). Under these conditions, collective needs, goals, and standards are primary.

This perspective also proposes that a person defines or categorizes the self along a continuum that ranges at one extreme from the self as a separate individual with personal motives, goals, and achievements to the self as the embodiment of a social collective or group. At the individual level, one's personal welfare and goals are most salient and important. At the group level, the goals and achievements of the group are merged with one's own (see Brown & Turner, 1981), and the group's welfare is paramount. At each extreme, self-interest fully is represented by the pronouns "I" and "We," respectively. Intergroup relations begin when people think about themselves as group members rather than solely as distinct individuals.

Illustrating the dynamics of this distinction, Verkuyten and Hagendoorn (1998) found that when individual identity was primed, individual differences in authoritarianism were the major predictor of the prejudice of Dutch students toward Turkish migrants. In contrast, when social identity (i.e., national identity) was made salient, in-group stereotypes and standards primarily predicted prejudiced attitudes. Thus, whether personal or collective identity is more salient critically shapes how a person perceives, interprets, evaluates, and responds to situations and to others (Kawakami & Dion, 1993, 1995).

Although the categorization process may place the person at either extreme of the continuum from personal identity to social identity, people often seek an intermediate point to balance their need to be different from others and their need to belong and share a sense of similarity to others (Brewer, 1991). This balance enhances one's feelings of connection to the group and increases group cohesiveness and social harmony (Hogg, 1996). However, social categorization into in-groups and out-groups also lays the foundation for the development of intergroup bias or ethnocentrism. In addition, intergroup relations tend to be less positive than interpersonal relations. Insko, Schopler, and their colleagues have demonstrated a fundamental *individual-group discontinuity effect* in which groups are greedier and less trustworthy than individuals (Insko et al., 2001; Schopler & Insko, 1992). As a consequence, relations between groups tend to be more competitive and less cooperative than those between individuals. In general, then, the social categorization of others and oneself plays a significant role in prejudice and discrimination.

Although social categorization generally leads to intergroup bias, the nature of that bias—whether it is based on in-group favoritism or extends to derogation and negative treatment of the out-group—depends on a number of factors, such as whether the structural relations between groups and associated social norms foster and justify hostility or contempt (Mummendey & Otten, 2001; Otten & Mummendey, 2000). However, different treatment of in-group versus out-group members, whether rooted in favoritism for one group or derogation of another, can lead to different expectations, perceptions, and behavior toward in-group versus out-group members that can ultimately create a self-fulfilling prophecy. Initial in-group favoritism can also provide a foundation for embracing more negative intergroup feelings and beliefs that result from intrapersonal, cultural, economic, and political factors. In the next section we describe alternative, and ultimately complementary, theoretical approaches to intergroup conflict and integration.

Perspectives on Intergroup Relations and Conflict

In general, research on social conflict, harmony, and integration has adopted one of two perspectives, one with an emphasis on the functional relations between groups and the other on the role of collective identities.

Functional Relations Between Groups

Theories based on functional relations often point to competition and consequent perceived threat as a fundamental cause of intergroup prejudice and conflict. *Realistic group conflict theory* (Campbell, 1965; Sherif, 1966), for example, posits that perceived group competition for resources produces efforts to reduce the access of other groups to the resources. This process was illustrated in classic work by Muzafer Sherif and his colleagues (Sherif et al., 1961). In 1954 Sherif and his colleagues conducted a field study on intergroup conflict in an area adjacent to Robbers Cave State Park in Oklahoma. In this study 22 12-year-old boys attending summer camp were randomly assigned to two groups (who subsequently named themselves Eagles and Rattlers). Over a period of weeks they became aware of the other group's existence, engaged in a series of competitive activities that generated overt intergroup conflict, and ultimately participated in a series of cooperative activities designed to ameliorate conflict and bias.

To permit time for group formation (e.g., norms and a leadership structure), the two groups were kept completely apart for one week. During the second week the investigators introduced competitive relations between the groups in the form of repeated competitive athletic activities centering around tug-of-war, baseball, and touch football, with the winning group receiving prizes. As expected, the introduction of competitive activities generated derogatory stereotypes and conflict among these groups. These boys, however, did not simply show in-group favoritism as we frequently see in laboratory studies. Rather, there was genuine hostility between these groups. Each group conducted raids on the other's cabins that resulted in the destruction and theft of property. The boys carried sticks, baseball bats, and socks filled with rocks as potential weapons. Fistfights broke out between members of the groups, and food and garbage fights erupted in the dinning hall. In addition, group members regularly exchanged verbal insults (e.g., "ladies first") and name-calling (e.g., "sissies," "stinkers," "pigs," "bums," "cheaters," and "communists").

During the third week, Sherif and his colleagues arranged intergroup contact under neutral, noncompetitive conditions. These interventions did not calm the ferocity of the exchanges, however. Mere intergroup contact was not sufficient to change the nature of the relations between the groups. Only after the investigators altered the functional relations between the groups by introducing a series of superordinate goals—ones that could not be achieved without the full cooperation of both groups and which were successfully achieved—did the relations between the two groups become more harmonious.

Sherif et al. (1961) proposed that functional relations between groups are critical in determining intergroup attitudes. When groups are competitively interdependent, the interplay between the actions of each group results in positive outcomes for one group and negative outcomes for the other. Thus, in the attempt to obtain favorable outcomes for themselves, the actions of the members of each group are also realistically perceived to be calculated to frustrate the goals of the other group. Therefore, a win-lose, zero-sum competitive relation between groups can initiate mutually negative feelings and stereotypes toward the members of the other group. In contrast, a cooperatively interdependent relation between members of different groups can reduce bias (Worchel, 1986).

Functional relations do not have to involve explicit competition with members of other groups to generate biases. In the absence of any direct evidence, people typically presume that members of other groups are competitive and will hinder the attainment of one's goals (Fiske & Ruscher, 1993). Moreover, feelings of interdependence on members of one's own group may be sufficient to produce bias. Rabbie's behavioral interaction model (see Rabbie & Lodewijkx, 1996; Rabbie & Schot, 1990; cf. Bourhis, Turner, & Gagnon, 1997), for example, argues that either intragroup cooperation or intergroup competition can stimulate intergroup bias. Similarly, L. Gaertner and Insko (2000), who unconfounded the effects of categorization and outcome dependence, demonstrated that dependence on in-group members could independently generate intergroup bias among men. Perhaps as a consequence of feelings of outcome dependence, allowing opportunities for greater interaction among in-group members increases intergroup bias (L. Gaertner & Schopler, 1998), whereas increasing interaction between members of different groups (S. Gaertner et al., 1999) or even the anticipation of future interaction with other groups (Insko et al., 2001) decreases intergroup bias.

Recently, Esses and her colleagues (Esses, Dovidio, Jackson, & Armstrong, 2001; Esses, Jackson, & Armstrong, 1998; Jackson & Esses, 2000) have integrated work on realistic group conflict theory (Campbell, 1965; LeVine & Campbell, 1972; Sherif, 1966; see also Bobo, 1988) and social dominance theory (Pratto, 1999; Sidanius & Pratto, 1999) within the framework of the *instrumental model of group conflict*. This model proposes that resource stress (the perception that access to a desired resource, such as wealth or political power, is limited) and the salience of a potentially competitive out-group lead to perceived group competition for resources. Several factors may determine the degree of perceived resource stress, with the primary ones including perceived scarcity of resources and individual or group support for an unequal distribution of resources, which is closely related to social dominance orientation (Pratto et al., 1994). Moreover, resource stress is likely to lead to perceived group competition when a relevant out-group is present. Some groups are more likely to be perceived as competitors than are others. Out-groups that are salient and distinct from one's own group are especially likely to stand out as potential competitors. However, potential competitors must also be similar to the in-group on dimensions that make them likely to take resources. That is, they must be interested in similar resources and in a position to potentially take these resources.

The combination of resource stress and the presence of a potentially competitive out-group leads to perceived group competition. Such perceived group competition is likely to take the form of zero-sum beliefs: beliefs that the more the other group obtains, the less is available for one's own group. There is a perception that any gains that the other group might make must be at the expense of one's own group. The model is termed the *instrumental model of group conflict* because attitudes and behaviors toward the competitor out-group are hypothesized to reflect strategic attempts to remove the source of competition. Efforts to remove the other group from competition may include out-group derogation, discrimination, and avoidance of the other group. One may express negative attitudes and attributions about members of the other group in an attempt to convince both one's own group and other groups of the competitors' lack of worth. Attempts to eliminate the competition may also entail discrimination and opposition to policies and programs that may benefit the other group. Limiting the other group's access to the resources also reduces competition. Consistent with this model, Esses and her colleagues have found that individuals in Canada and the United States perceive greater threat, are more biased against, and are more motivated to exclude immigrant groups that are seen as involved in a zero-sum competition for resources with nonimmigrants (Esses et al., 1998, 2001; Jackson & Esses, 2000).

Discrimination can serve less tangible collective functions as well as concrete instrumental objectives. Blumer (1958a) acknowledged that the processes for establishing group position may involve goals such as gaining economic advantage, but they may also be associated with the acquisition of intangible resources such as prestige. Taylor (2000), in fact, suggested that symbolic, psychological factors are typically more important in intergroup bias than are tangible resources. Theoretical developments in social psychology, stimulated by social identity theory (Tajfel & Turner, 1979), further highlight the role of group categorization, independent of actual realistic group conflict, in motivations to achieve favorable group identities ("positive distinctiveness") and consequently on the arousal of intergroup bias and discrimination.

Collective Identity

Human activity is rooted in interdependence. Group systems involving greater mutual cooperation have substantial survival advantages for individual group members over those systems without reciprocally positive social relations (Trivers, 1971). However, the decision to cooperate with nonrelatives (i.e., to expend resources for another's benefit) is a dilemma of trust because the ultimate benefit for the provider depends on others' willingness to reciprocate. Indiscriminate trust and altruism that are not reciprocated are not effective survival strategies.

Social categorization and group boundaries provide a basis for achieving the benefits of cooperative interdependence without the risk of excessive costs. In-group membership is a form of contingent cooperation. By limiting aid to mutually acknowledged in-group members, total costs and risks of nonreciprocation can be contained. Thus, in-groups can be defined as bounded communities of mutual trust and obligation that delimit mutual interdependence and cooperation. The ways in which people understand their group membership thus play a critical role in social harmony and conflict.

Models of category-based processing (Brewer, 1988; see also Fiske et al., 1999) assume that "the mere presentation of a stimulus person activates certain classification processes that occur automatically and without conscious intent. . . . The process is one of 'placing' the individual social object along well-established stimulus dimensions such as age, gender, and skin color" (Brewer, 1988, pp. 5–6). We have further hypothesized that "a primitive type of categorization may also have a high probability of spontaneously occurring, perhaps in parallel process. This is the categorization of individuals as members of one's ingroup or not" (Dovidio & Gaertner, 1993,

p. 170). Because of the centrality of the self in social perception (Higgins & Bargh, 1987; Kihlstrom et al., 1988), we propose that social categorization involves most fundamentally a distinction between the group containing the self (the in-group) and other groups (the out-groups) between the "we's" and the "they's" (see also Tajfel & Turner, 1979; Turner et al., 1987). This distinction has a profound influence on evaluations, cognitions, and behavior.

Social identity theory (Tajfel & Turner, 1979) and, more recently, self-categorization theory (Turner, 1985; Turner et al., 1987) address the fundamental process of social categorization. From a social categorization perspective, when people or objects are categorized into groups, actual differences between members of the same category tend to be perceptually minimized (Tajfel, 1969) and often ignored in making decisions or forming impressions. Members of the same category seem to be more similar than they actually are, and more similar than they were before they were categorized together. In addition, although members of a social category may be different in some ways from members of other categories, these differences tend to become exaggerated and overgeneralized. Thus, categorization enhances perceptions of similarities within groups and differences between groups—emphasizing social difference and group distinctiveness. This process is not benign because these within- and between-group distortions have a tendency to generalize to additional dimensions (e.g., character traits) beyond those that differentiated the categories originally (Allport, 1954, 1958). Furthermore, as the salience of the categorization increases, the magnitude of these distortions also increases (Abrams, 1985; Brewer, 1979; Brewer & Miller, 1996; Dechamps & Doise, 1978; Dion, 1974; Doise, 1978; Skinner & Stephenson, 1981; Turner, 1981, 1985).

Moreover, in the process of categorizing people into two different groups, people typically classify themselves *into* one of the social categories and *out of* the other. The insertion of the self into the social categorization process increases the emotional significance of group differences and thus leads to further perceptual distortion and to evaluative biases that reflect favorably on the in-group (Sumner, 1906), and consequently on the self (Tajfel & Turner, 1979). Tajfel and Turner (1979), in their social identity theory, proposed that a person's need for positive identity may be satisfied by membership in prestigious social groups. This need also motivates social comparisons that favorably differentiate in-group from out-group members, particularly when self-esteem has been challenged (Hogg & Abrams, 1990). For example, Meindl and Lerner (1984) found that experiencing an esteem-lowering experience (committing an unintentional transgression) motivated people to reject an opportunity for equal status contact between the in-group and an out-group in favor of interaction that implied the more positive status of the in-group. Within social identity theory, successful intergroup discrimination is then presumed to restore, enhance, or elevate one's self-esteem (see Rubin & Hewstone, 1998).

As we noted earlier, the social identity perspective (see also self-categorization theory; Turner et al., 1987) also proposes that a person defines or categorizes the self along a continuum that ranges at one extreme from the self as the embodiment of a social collective or group to the self as a separate individual with personal motives, goals, and achievements. Self-categorization in terms of collective identity, in turn, increases the likelihood of the development of intergroup biases and conflict (Schopler & Insko, 1992). As Sherif et al.'s (1961) initial observations revealed, intergroup relations begin to sour soon after people categorize others in terms of in-group and out-group members: "Discovery of another group of campers brought heightened awareness of 'us' and 'ours' as contrasted with 'outsiders' and 'intruders,' [and] an intense desire to compete with the other group in team games" (Sherif et al., 1961, p. 95). Thus, social categorization lays the foundation for intergroup bias and conflict that can lead to, and be further exacerbated by, competition between these groups.

Additional research has demonstrated just how powerfully mere social categorization can influence differential thinking, feeling and behaving toward in-group versus out-group members. Upon social categorization of individuals into in-groups and out-groups, people spontaneously experience more positive affect toward the in-group (Otten & Moskowitz, 2000; Otten & Wentura, 1999). They also favor in-group members directly in terms of evaluations and resource allocations (Mullen, Brown, & Smith, 1992; Tajfel, Billig, Bundy, & Flament, 1971), as well as indirectly in valuing the products of their work (Ferguson & Kelley, 1964). In addition, in-group membership increases the psychological bond and feelings of "oneness" that facilitate the arousal of promotive tension or empathy in response to others' needs or problems (Hornstein, 1976). In part as a consequence, prosocial behavior is offered more readily to in-group than to out-group members (Dovidio et al., 1997; Piliavin, Dovidio, Gaertner, & Clark, 1981). People are also more likely to initiate "heroic" action on behalf of an in-group member than another person, for example by directly confronting a transgressor who insults the person (Meindl & Lerner, 1983). Moreover, people are more likely to be cooperative and exercise more personal restraint when using endangered common resources when these are shared with in-group members than with others (Kramer & Brewer, 1984), and they work harder for groups they identify more as their in-group (Worchel, Rothgerber, Day, Hart, & Butemeyer, 1998).

In terms of information processing, people retain more information in a more detailed fashion for in-group members than for out-group members (Park & Rothbart, 1982), have better memory for information about ways in which in-group members are similar and out-group members are dissimilar to the self (Wilder, 1981), and remember less positive information about out-group members (Howard & Rothbart, 1980). Perhaps because of the greater self-other overlap in representations for people defined as in-group members (E. R. Smith & Henry, 1996), people process information about and make attributions to in-group members more on the basis of self-congruency than they do for out-group members (Gramzow, Gaertner, & Sedikides, 2001).

People are also more generous and forgiving in their explanations for the behaviors of in-group relative to out-group members. Positive behaviors and successful outcomes are more likely to be attributed to internal, stable characteristics (the personality) of in-group than out-group members, whereas negative outcomes are more likely to be ascribed to the personalities of out-group members than of in-group members (Hewstone, 1990; Pettigrew, 1979). Observed behaviors of in-group and out-group members are encoded in memory at different levels of abstraction (Maass, Ceccarelli, & Rudin, 1996). Undesirable actions of out-group members are encoded at more abstract levels that presume intentionality and dispositional origin (e.g., she is hostile) than identical behaviors of in-group members (e.g., she slapped the girl). Desirable actions of out-group members, however, are encoded at more concrete levels (e.g., she walked across the street holding the old man's hand) relative to the same behaviors of in-group members (e.g., she is helpful).

Language plays another role in intergroup bias through associations with collective pronouns. Collective pronouns such as "we" or "they" that are used to define people's in-group or out-group status are frequently paired with stimuli having strong affective connotations. As a consequence, these pronouns may acquire powerful evaluative properties of their own. These words (we, they) can potentially increase the availability of positive or negative associations and thereby influence beliefs about, evaluations of, and behaviors toward other people—often automatically and unconsciously (Perdue, Dovidio, Gurtman, & Tyler, 1990).

The process of social categorization, however, is not completely unalterable. Categories are hierarchically organized, and higher level categories (e.g., nations) are more inclusive of lower level ones (e.g., cities or towns). By modifying a perceiver's goals, motives, past experiences, and expectations, as well as factors within the perceptual field and the situational context more broadly, there is opportunity to alter the level of category inclusiveness that will be primary in a given situation. Although perceiving people in terms of a social category is easiest and most common in forming impressions, particularly during bitter intergroup conflict, appropriate goals, motivation, and effort can produce more individuated impressions of others (Brewer, 1988; Fiske et al., 1999). This malleability of the level at which impressions are formed—from broad to more specific categories to individuated responses— is important because of its implications for altering the way people think about members of other groups, and consequently about the nature of intergroup relations.

Although functional and social categorization theories of intergroup conflict and social harmony suggest different psychological mechanisms, these approaches may offer complementary rather than necessarily competing explanations. For instance, realistic threats and symbolic threats reflect different hypothesized causes of discrimination, but they can operate jointly to motivate discriminatory behavior. W. Stephan and his colleagues (Stephan, Diaz-Loving, & Duran, 2000; Stephan & Stephan, 2000; Stephan, Ybarra, Martinez, Schwarzwald, & Tur-Kaspa, 1998) have found that personal negative stereotypes, realistic group threat, and symbolic group threat all predict discrimination against other groups (e.g., immigrants), and each accounts for a unique portion of the effect. In addition, personal-level biases and collective biases may also have separate and additive influences. Bobo and his colleagues (see Bobo, 1999) have demonstrated that group threat and personal prejudice can contribute independently to discrimination against other groups. The independence of these effects points to the importance of considering each of these perspectives for a comprehensive understanding of social conflict and integration, while at the same time reinforcing the theoretical distinctions among the hypothesized underlying mechanisms.

Given the centrality and spontaneity of the social categorization of people into in-group and out-group members, and given the important role of functional relations between groups in a world of limited resources that depend on differentiation between in-group and out-group members, how can bias be reduced? Because categorization is a basic process that is fundamental to prejudice and intergroup conflict, some contemporary work has targeted this process as a place to begin to improve intergroup relations. This work also considers the functional relations among groups. In the next section we explore how the forces of categorization may be disarmed or redirected to promote more positive intergroup attitudes—and potentially begin to penetrate the barriers to reconciliation among groups with a history of antagonistic relations. One of the most influential strategies involves creating and structuring intergroup contact.

INTERGROUP CONTACT AND THE REDUCTION OF BIAS

For the past 50 years the *contact hypothesis* (Allport, 1954; Amir, 1969; Cook, 1985; Watson, 1947; Williams, 1947; see also Pettigrew, 1998a; Pettigrew & Tropp, 2000) has represented a promising and popular strategy for reducing intergroup bias and conflict. This hypothesis proposes that simple contact between groups is not automatically sufficient to improve intergroup relations. Rather, for contact between groups to reduce bias successfully, certain prerequisite features must be present. These characteristics of contact include equal status between the groups, cooperative (rather than competitive) intergroup interaction, opportunities for personal acquaintance between the members (especially with those whose personal characteristics do not support stereotypic expectations), and supportive norms by authorities within and outside of the contact situation (Cook, 1985; Pettigrew, 1998a). Research in laboratory and field settings generally supports the efficacy of the list of prerequisite conditions for achieving improved intergroup relations (see Pettigrew & Tropp, 2000).

Contact and Functional Relations

Consistent with functional theories of intergroup relations, changing the nature of interdependence between members of different groups from perceived competition to cooperation significantly improves intergroup attitudes (Blanchard, Weigel, & Cook, 1975; Cook, 1985; Deutsch & Collins, 1951; Green, Adams, & Turner, 1988; Stephan, 1987; Weigel, Wiser, & Cook, 1975). Cooperative learning (Slavin, 1985), jigsaw classroom interventions in which students are interdependent on one another in problem-solving exercises (Aronson & Patnoe, 1997), and more comprehensive approaches in schools that involve establishing a cooperative community, resolving conflicts, and internalizing civic values (e.g., Peacekeepers; Johnson & Johnson, 2000) also support the fundamental principles outside of the laboratory. Although it is difficult to establish all of these conditions in intergroup contact situations, the formula is effective when these conditions are met (Cook, 1984; Johnson, Johnson, & Maruyama, 1983; Pettigrew, 1998a).

Structurally, however, the contact hypothesis has represented a list of loosely connected, diverse conditions rather than a unifying conceptual framework that explains *how* these prerequisite features achieve their effects. This is problematic because political and socioeconomic circumstances (e.g., real or perceived competitive, zero-sum outcomes) often preclude introducing these features (e.g., cooperative interdependence, equal status) into many contact settings. Despite substantial documentation that intergroup cooperative interaction reduces bias (Allport, 1954; Aronson, Blaney, Stephan, Sikes, & Snapp, 1978; Cook, 1985; Deutsch, 1973; Johnson et al., 1983; Sherif et al., 1961; Slavin, 1985; Worchel, 1979), it is not clear how cooperation achieves this effect. One basic issue involves the psychological processes that mediate this change.

The classic functional relations perspective by Sherif et al. (1961) views cooperative interdependence as a direct mediator of attitudinal and behavioral changes. However, recent approaches have extended research on the contact hypothesis by attempting to understand the potential common processes and mechanisms that these diverse factors engage to reduce bias. Several additional explanations have been proposed (see Brewer & Miller, 1984; Miller & Davidson-Podgorny, 1987; Worchel, 1979, 1986). For example, cooperation may induce greater intergroup acceptance as a result of dissonance reduction serving to justify this type of interaction with the other group (Miller & Brewer, 1986). It is also possible that cooperation can have positive, reinforcing outcomes. When intergroup contact is favorable and has successful consequences, psychological processes that restore cognitive balance or reduce dissonance produce more favorable attitudes toward members of the other group and toward the group as a whole to be consistent with the positive nature of the interaction. In addition, the rewarding properties of achieving success may become associated with members of other groups (Lott & Lott, 1965), thereby increasing attraction (S. Gaertner et al., 1999). Also, cooperative experiences can reduce intergroup anxiety (Stephan & Stephan, 1984).

Intergroup contact can also influence how interactants conceive of the groups and how the members are socially categorized. Cooperative learning and jigsaw classroom interventions (Aronson & Patnoe, 1997), which are designed to increase interdependence between members of different groups and to enhance appreciation for the resources they bring to the task, may reduce bias in part by altering how interactants conceive of the group boundaries and memberships. In the next section we consider how the effects of intergroup contact can be mediated by changes in personal and collective identity.

Contact, Categorization, and Identity

From the social categorization perspective, the issue to be addressed is how intergroup contact can be structured to alter cognitive representations in ways that eliminate one or more of the basic features of the negative intergroup schema. Based on the premises of social identity theory, three alternative models for contact effects have been developed and tested in experimental and field settings: decategorization, recategorization, and mutual differentiation.

Each of these models can be described in terms of recommendations for how to structure cognitive representations of situations in which there is contact between the groups, the psychological processes that promote attitude change, and the mechanisms by which contact experiences are generalized to change attitudes toward the out-group as a whole. Each of these strategies targets the social categorization process as the place to begin to understand and to combat intergroup biases. *Decategorization* encourages members to deemphasize the original group boundaries and to conceive of themselves as separate individuals rather than as members of different groups. *Mutual differentiation* maintains the original group boundaries, maintaining perceptions as different groups, but in the context of intergroup cooperation during which similarities and differences between the memberships are recognized and valued. *Recategorization* encourages the members of both groups to regard themselves as belonging to a common, superordinate group—one group that is inclusive of both memberships.

Rather than viewing these as competing positions and arguing which one is correct, we suggest that these are complementary approaches and propose that it is more productive to consider *when* each strategy is most effective. To the extent that it is possible for these strategies, either singly or in concert, to alter perceptions of the "Us versus Them" that are reflected in conflictive intergroup relations, reductions in bias and social harmony may be accomplished. Moreover, decategorization and recategorization strategies may increase the willingness of group representatives to view the meaning of the intergroup conflict from the other group's perspective and to offer solutions that recognize both groups' needs and concerns.

Decategorization: The Personalization Model

The first model is essentially a formalization and elaboration of the assumptions implicit in Allport's contact hypothesis (Brewer & Miller, 1984). A primary consequence of salient in-group–out-group categorization is the deindividuation of members of the out-group. Social behavior in category-based interactions is characterized by a tendency to treat individual members of the out-group as undifferentiated representatives of a unified social category, ignoring individual differences within the group. The personalization perspective on the contact situation implies that intergroup interactions should be structured to reduce the salience of category distinctions and promote opportunities to get to know out-group members as individual persons, thereby disarming the forces of categorization.

The conditional specifications of the contact hypothesis (e.g., cooperative interaction) can be interpreted as features of the situation that reduce category salience and promote more differentiated and personalized representations of the participants in the contact setting. Interdependence typically motivates people to focus more on the individual characteristics of a person, with whom their outcomes are linked, than more general category representations (Fiske, 2000). Attending to personal characteristics of group members not only provides the opportunity to disconfirm category stereotypes, but it also breaks down the monolithic perception of the out-group as a homogeneous unit (Wilder, 1978). In this scheme, the contact situation encourages attention to information at the individual level that replaces category identity as the most useful basis for classifying participants.

With a more differentiated representation of out-group members, there is the recognition that there are different types of out-group members (e.g., sensitive as well as tough professional hockey players), thereby weakening the effects of categorization and the tendency to minimize and ignore differences between category members. When personalized interactions occur, in-group and out-group members slide even further toward the individual side of the self as individual versus group member continuum. Members "attend to information that replaces category identity as the most useful basis for classifying each other" (Brewer & Miller, 1984, p. 288) as they engage in personalized interactions. Repeated personalized contacts with a variety of out-group members should, over time, undermine the value and meaningfulness of the social category stereotype as a source of information about members of that group. This is the process by which contact experiences are expected to generalize—via reducing the salience and meaning of social categorization in the long run (Brewer & Miller, 1996).

A number of studies provide evidence supporting this perspective on contact effects (Bettencourt, Brewer, Croak, & Miller, 1992; Marcus-Newhall, Miller, Holtz, & Brewer, 1993). Miller, Brewer, and Edwards (1985), for instance, demonstrated that a cooperative task that required personalized interaction with members of the out-group resulted not only in more positive attitudes toward out-group members in the cooperative setting but also toward other out-group members shown on a videotape, compared to cooperative contact that was task focused rather than person focused.

During personalization, members focus on information about an out-group member that is relevant to the self (as an individual rather than as a group member). Repeated personalized interactions with a variety of out-group members should over time undermine the value of the category stereotype as a source of information about members of that group. Thus, the effects of personalization should generalize to new situations as well as to heretofore unfamiliar out-group members. For the benefits of personalization to generalize, however, it is of course necessary for the identities of out-group members to be salient—at least somewhat—during the interaction to allow the group stereotype to be weakened.

Further evidence of the value of personalized interactions for reducing intergroup bias comes from data on the effects of intergroup friendships (Hamberger & Hewstone, 1997; Pettigrew, 1997; Pettigrew & Meertens, 1995). For example, across samples in France, Great Britain, the Netherlands, and Germany, Europeans with out-group friends were lower on measures of prejudice, particularly affective prejudice (Pettigrew, 1998a). This positive relation did not hold for other types of acquaintance relationships in work or residential settings that did not involve formation of close interpersonal relationships with members of the out-group. In terms of the direction of causality, although having more positive intergroup attitudes can increase the willingness to have cross-group friendships, path analyses indicate that the path *from* friendship *to* reduction in prejudice is stronger than the other way around (Pettigrew, 1998a).

Other research reveals three valuable extensions of the personalized contact effect. One is evidence that personal friendships with members of one out-group may lead to tolerance toward out-groups in general and reduced nationalistic pride, a process that Pettigrew (1997) refers to as *deprovincialization*. Thus, decategorization based on developing cross-group friendships that decrease the relative attractiveness of a person's in-group provides increased appreciation of the relative attractiveness of other out-groups more generally.

A second extension is represented by evidence that contact effects may operate indirectly or vicariously. Although interpersonal friendship across group lines leads to reduced prejudice, even knowledge that an in-group member has befriended an out-group member has the potential to reduce bias while the salience of group identities remains high for the observer (Wright, Aron, McLaughlin-Volpe, & Ropp, 1997). A third extension relates to interpersonal processes involving the arousal of empathic feelings for an out-group member, which can increase positive attitudes toward members of that group more widely (Batson et al., 1997). Thus, personalized interaction and interpersonal processes more generally can directly and indirectly increase positive feelings for out-group members through a variety of processes that can lead to more generalized types of harmony and integration at the group level.

Recategorization: The Common In-Group Identity Model

The second social categorization model of intergroup contact and conflict reduction is also based on the premise that reducing the salience of in-group–out-group category distinctions is key to positive effects. In contrast to the decategorization approaches described earlier, however, recategorization is not designed to reduce or eliminate categorization, but rather to structure a definition of group categorization at a higher level of category inclusiveness in ways that reduce intergroup bias and conflict (Allport, 1954, p. 43).

Allport (1954, 1958) was aware of the benefits of a common in-group identity, although he regarded it as a catalyst rather than as a product of the conditions of contact:

> To be maximally effective, contact and acquaintance programs should lead to a sense of equality in social status, should occur in ordinary purposeful pursuits, avoid artificiality, and if possible enjoy the sanction of the community in which they occur. While it may help somewhat to place members of different ethnic groups side by side on a job, the gain is greater if these members regard themselves as part of a *team* [italics added]. (Allport, 1958, p. 489)

In contrast, the *common in-group identity model* (S. Gaertner, Dovidio, Anastasio, Bachman, & Rust, 1993; S. Gaertner & Dovidio, 2000) proposes that group identity can be a critical mediating factor. According to this model, intergroup bias and conflict can be reduced by factors that transform participants' representations of memberships from two groups to one, more inclusive group. With common in-group identity, the cognitive and motivational processes that initially produced in-group favoritism are redirected to benefit the common in-group, including former out-group members.

Allport's (1954, 1958) description of widening circles of inclusion, hierarchically organized, depicts a person's various in-group memberships from one's family to one's neighborhood, to one's city, to one's nation, to one's race, to all of humankind. Recognizing that racial group identity had become the dominant allegiance among many White racists, Allport questioned the accuracy of the common belief that in-group loyalties always grow weaker the larger their circle of inclusion, which might prevent loyalty to a group more inclusive than race. Rather, Allport proposed the potential value of shifting the level of category inclusiveness from race to humankind. He recognized that the "clash between the idea of race and of One World . . . is shaping into an issue that may well be the most decisive in human history. The important question is, Can a loyalty to mankind be fashioned before interracial warfare breaks out?" (pp. 43–44). But is it too difficult and unrealistic for people to identify with humankind? Allport proposed that this level of common in-group identification is difficult for most people primarily because there are few symbols that make this more ephemeral in-group real or concrete. That is, groups such as nations have symbols that include flags, buildings, and holidays, but at the international level there are few icons that help serve as anchors for unity and world loyalty. Attempts to forge superordinate cooperative alliances, therefore, would more likely engage identification processes if symbols were adopted to affirm the joint venture.

Among the antecedent factors proposed by the common in-group identity model are the features of contact situations that are necessary for intergroup contact to be successful (e.g., interdependence between groups, equal status, equalitarian norms; Allport, 1954). From this perspective, intergroup cooperative interaction, for example, enhances positive evaluations of out-group members, at least in part, because cooperation transforms members' representations of the memberships from "Us" versus "Them" to a more inclusive "We." In a laboratory experiment, S. Gaertner, Mann, Dovidio, Murrell, and Pomare (1990) directly tested and found strong support for the hypotheses that the relation between intergroup cooperation and enhanced favorable evaluations of out-group members was mediated by the extent to which members of both groups perceived themselves as one group. In addition, the generalizability of this effect was supported by a series of survey studies conducted in natural settings across very different intergroup contexts: bankers experiencing corporate mergers, students in a multiethnic high school, and college students from blended families (see S. Gaertner, Dovidio, & Bachman, 1996). Moreover, appeals that emphasize the common group membership of nonimmigrants and immigrants have been shown to improve attitudes toward immigrants and to increase support for immigration among people in Canada and the United States, and particularly among those high in social dominance orientation for whom group hierarchy is important (Esses et al., 2001).

These effects of recategorization on behaviors, such as helping and self-disclosure (see Dovidio et al., 1997; Nier et al., 2001), as well as on attitudes, have some extended, practical implications. Recategorization can stimulate interactions among group members in the contact situation that can in turn activate other processes, which subsequently promote more positive intergroup behaviors and attitudes. For example, both self-disclosure and helping typically produce reciprocity. More intimate self-disclosure by one person normally encourages more intimate disclosure by the other (Archer & Berg, 1978; Derlega, Metts, Petronio, & Margulis, 1993). As we discussed earlier, the work of Miller, Brewer, and their colleagues (e.g., Brewer & Miller, 1984; Miller et al., 1985) has demonstrated that personalized and self-disclosing interaction can be a significant factor in reducing intergroup bias.

Considerable cross-cultural evidence also indicates the powerful influence of the norm of reciprocity on helping (Schroeder, Penner, Dovidio & Piliavin, 1995). According to this norm, people should help those who have helped them, and they should not help those who have denied them help for no legitimate reason (Gouldner, 1960). Thus, the development of a common in-group identity can motivate interpersonal behaviors between members of initially different groups that can initiate reciprocal actions and concessions (see Deutsch, 1993; Osgood, 1962). These reciprocal actions and concessions not only will reduce immediate tensions but also can produce more harmonious intergroup relations beyond the contact situation.

Although finely differentiated impressions of out-group members may not be an automatic consequence of forming a common in-group identity, these more elaborated, differentiated, and personalized impressions can quickly develop because the newly formed positivity bias is likely to encourage more open communication (S. Gaertner et al., 1993). The development of a common in-group identity creates a motivational foundation for constructive intergroup relations that can act as a catalyst for positive reciprocal interpersonal actions. Thus, the recategorization strategy proposed in our model as well as decategorization strategies, such as individuating (Wilder, 1984) and personalizing (Brewer & Miller, 1984) interactions, can potentially operate complementarily and sequentially to improve intergroup relations in lasting and meaningful ways.

Challenges to the Decategorization and Recategorization Models

Although the structural representations of the contact situation advocated by the decategorization (personalization) and recategorization (common in-group identity) models are different, the two approaches share common assumptions about the need to reduce category differentiation and associated processes. Because both models rely on reducing or eliminating the salience of intergroup differentiation, they involve structuring contact in a way that will challenge or threaten existing social identities. However, both cognitive and motivational factors conspire to create resistance to the dissolution of category boundaries or to reestablish category distinctions over time. Although the salience of a common superordinate identity or personalized representations may be enhanced in the short run, then, these may be difficult to maintain across time and social situations.

Brewer's (1991) *optimal distinctiveness model* of the motives underlying group identification provides one explanation for why category distinctions are difficult to change. The theory postulates that social identity is driven by two opposing social motives: the need for inclusion and the need for differentiation. Human beings strive to belong to groups that transcend their own personal identity, but at the same time they need to feel special and distinct from others. In order to satisfy both of these motives simultaneously, individuals seek inclusion in distinctive social groups where the boundaries between those who are members of the in-group category and those who are excluded can be drawn clearly. On the one hand, highly inclusive superordinate categories do not satisfy distinctiveness needs. Thus, inclusive identities, which may not be readily accepted, may be limited in their capacity to reduce bias (Hornsey & Hogg, 2000a, 2000b). On the other hand, high degrees of individuation fail to meet needs for belonging and for cognitive simplicity and uncertainty reduction (Hogg & Abrams, 1993). These motives are likely to make either personalization or common in-group identity temporally unstable solutions to intergroup discrimination and prejudice.

Preexisting social-structural relations between groups may also create strong forces of resistance to changes in category boundaries. Even in the absence of overt conflict, asymmetries between social groups in size, power, or status create additional sources of resistance. When one group is substantially smaller than the other in the contact situation, the minority category is especially salient, and minority group members may be particularly reluctant to accept a superordinate category identity that is dominated by the other group. Another major challenge is created by preexisting status differences between groups, where members of both high- and low-status groups may be threatened by contact and assimilation (Mottola, 1996).

The Mutual Differentiation Model

These challenges to processes of decategorization/recategorization led Hewstone and Brown (1986) to recommend an alternative approach to intergroup contact in which cooperative interactions between groups are introduced without degrading the original in-group–out-group categorization. More specifically, this model favors encouraging groups working together to perceive complementarity by recognizing and valuing mutual assets and weaknesses within the context of an interdependent cooperative task or common, superordinate goals. This strategy allows group members to maintain their social identities and positive distinctiveness while avoiding insidious intergroup comparisons. Thus, the *mutual intergroup differentiation model* does not seek to change the basic category structure of the intergroup contact situation, but to change the intergroup affect from negative to positive interdependence and evaluation.

In order to promote positive intergroup experience, Hewstone and Brown (1986) recommended that the contact situation be structured so that members of the respective groups have distinct but complementary roles to contribute toward common goals. In this way, both groups can maintain positive distinctiveness within a cooperative framework. Evidence in support of this approach comes from the results of an experiment by Brown and Wade (1987) in which work teams composed of students from two different faculties engaged in a cooperative effort to produce a two-page magazine article. When the representatives of the two groups were assigned separate roles in the team task (one group working on figures and layout, the other working on text), the contact experience had a more positive effect on intergroup attitudes than when the two groups were not provided with distinctive roles (see also Deschamps & Brown, 1983; Dovidio, Gaertner, & Validzic, 1998).

Hewstone and Brown (1986) argued that generalization of positive contact experiences is more likely when the contact situation is defined as an intergroup situation rather than as an interpersonal interaction. Generalization in this case is direct rather than requiring additional cognitive links between positive affect toward individuals and toward representations of the group as a whole. This position is supported by evidence, reviewed earlier, that cooperative contact with a member of an out-group leads to more favorable generalized attitudes toward the group as a whole when category membership is made salient during contact (e.g., Brown, Vivian, & Hewstone, 1999; van Oudenhoven, Groenewoud, & Hewstone, 1996).

Although in-group–out-group category salience is usually associated with in-group bias and the negative side of intergroup attitudes, cooperative interdependence is assumed to override the negative intergroup schema, particularly if the two groups have differentiated, complementary roles to play. Because it capitalizes on needs for distinctive social identities, the mutual intergroup differentiation model provides a solution that is highly stable in terms of the cognitive-structural aspects of the intergroup situation. The affective component of the model, however, is likely to be less stable. Salient intergroup boundaries are associated with mutual distrust (Schopler & Insko, 1992), which undermines the potential for cooperative interdependence and mutual liking over any length of time. By reinforcing perceptions of group differences, this differentiation model risks reinforcing negative beliefs about the out-group in the long run; intergroup anxiety (Greenland & Brown, 1999; Islam & Hewstone, 1993)

and the potential for fission and conflict along group lines remain high.

In addition, theoretical approaches and interventions are often guided by the perspective of the majority group. Indeed, because the majority group typically possesses the resources, focusing strategies for reducing conflict and enhancing social harmony on the majority group have considerable potential. However, it is not enough, and without considering all of the groups involved, these strategies can be counterproductive. Intergroup relations need to be understood from the perspective of each of the groups involved. We consider the issue of multiple perspectives in the next section.

HARMONY AND INTEGRATION: MAJORITY AND MINORITY PERSPECTIVES

The perspectives that majority and minority group members take on particular interactions and on intergroup relations in general may differ in fundamental ways. The attributions and experiences of people in seemingly identical or comparable situations may be affected by ethnic or racial group membership (see Crocker & Quinn, 2001). In the United States, Blacks perceive less social and economic opportunity than do Whites (Schuman, Steeh, Bobo, & Krysan, 1997). Cross-culturally, the generally nonstigmatized ethnic and racial majorities perceive intergroup contact more positively than do minorities (S. Gaertner, Rust, Dovidio, Bachman, & Anastasio, 1996; Islam & Hewstone, 1993). Distinctiveness, associated with numerical minority status or the salience of physical or social characteristics, can exacerbate feelings of stigmatization among members of traditionally disadvantaged groups (e.g., Kanter, 1977; Niemann & Dovidio, 1998).

More generally, group status has profound implications for the experience of individuals, their motivations and aspirations, and their orientations to members of their own group and of other groups. As Ellemers and Barreto (2001) outlined, responses to the status of one's group depend on whether one is a member of a low- or high-status group, the importance of the group to the individual (i.e., strength of identification), the perceived legitimacy of the status differences, and the prospects for change at the individual or group level (see also Branscombe & Ellemers, 1998). Wright (2001; see also Tajfel & Turner, 1979) further proposed that people in low-status groups will be motivated to pursue collective action on behalf of their group, rather than seek personal mobility, when they identify strongly with the group or when possibilities for individual mobility are limited, when intergroup comparisons produce perceptions of disadvantage and that disadvantage is viewed as illegitimate, and when people believe that the intergroup hierarchy can change and the in-group has the resources to change it. Although collective action may have long-term benefits in achieving justice and equality, in the short-term the conditions that facilitate collective action may intensify social categorization of members of the in-group and out-groups, temporarily increase conflict, and reduce the likelihood of harmony or integration between groups.

Racial and ethnic identities are unlikely to be readily abandoned because they are frequently fundamental aspects of individuals' self-concepts and esteem and are often associated with perceptions of collective injustice. Moreover, when such identities are threatened, for example by attempts to produce a single superordinate identity at the expense of one's racial or ethnic group identity, members of these groups may respond in ways that reassert the value of the group (e.g., with disassociation from the norms and values of the larger society; see Branscombe, Schmitt, & Harvey, 1999; Steele, 1997) and adversely affect social harmony.

In addition, efforts to incorporate minority groups within the context of a superordinate identity may also produce negative responses from the majority group. Mummendey and Wenzel (1999) argued that because the standards of the superordinate group will primarily reflect those of the majority subgroup, the minority out-group will tend to be viewed as nonnormative and inferior by those standards, which can exacerbate intergroup bias among majority group members and increase group conflict. In contrast, S. Gaertner and Dovidio (2000) have proposed that the simultaneous existence of superordinate and subordinate group representations (i.e., dual- or multiple-identities) may not only improve intergroup relations (see also Hornsey & Hogg, 2000a, 2000b) but also may contribute to the social adjustment, psychological adaptation, and overall well-being of minority group members (LaFromboise, Coleman, & Gerton, 1993). Therefore, identifying the conditions under which a dual identity serves to increase or diffuse intergroup conflict is an issue actively being pursued by contemporary researchers.

There is evidence that intergroup benefits of a strong superordinate identity can be achieved for both majority and minority group members when the strength of the subordinate identity is high, regardless of the strength of subordinate group identities. For example, in a survey study of White adults, H. J. Smith and Tyler (1996, Study 1) measured the strengths of respondents' superordinate identity as "American" and also the strengths of their subordinate identification as "White." Respondents with a strong American identity, independent of the degree to which they identified with being White, were more likely to base their support for affirmative action policies that would benefit Blacks and other minorities on relational

concerns regarding the fairness of congressional representatives than on concerns about whether these policies would increase or decrease their own well-being. However, for those who had weak identification with being American and primarily identified themselves with being White, their position on affirmative action was determined more strongly by concerns regarding the instrumental value of these policies for themselves. This pattern of findings suggests that a strong superordinate identity (such as being American) allows individuals to support policies that would benefit members of other racial subgroups without giving primary consideration to their own instrumental needs.

Among minorities, even when racial or ethnic identity is strong, perceptions of a superordinate connection enhance interracial trust and acceptance of authority within an organization. Huo, Smith, Tyler, and Lind (1996) surveyed White, Black, Latino, and Asian employees of a public-sector organization. Identification with the organization (superordinate identity) and racial-ethnic identity (subgroup identity) were independently assessed. Regardless of the strength of racial-ethnic identity, respondents who had a strong organizational identity perceived that they were treated fairly within the organization, and consequently they had favorable attitudes toward authority. Huo et al. (1996) concluded that having a strong identification with a superordinate group can redirect people from focusing on their personal outcomes to concerns about "achieving the greater good and maintaining social stability" (pp. 44–45), while also maintaining important racial and ethnic identities.

S. Gaertner et al. (1996) found converging evidence in a survey of students in a multiethnic high school. In particular, they compared students who identified themselves on the survey using a dual identity (e.g., indicating they were Korean and American) with those who used only a single subgroup identity (e.g., Korean). Supportive of the role of a dual identity, students who described themselves *both* as Americans and as members of their racial or ethnic group had less bias toward other groups in the school than did those who described themselves only in terms of their subgroup identity. Also, the minority students who identified themselves using a dual identity reported lower levels of intergroup bias in general relative to those who used only their ethnic or racial group identity.

Not only do Whites and racial and ethnic minorities bring different values, identities, and experiences to intergroup contact situations, but also these different perspectives can shape perceptions of and reactions to the nature of the contact. Blumer (1958a) proposed that group status is a fundamental factor in the extent of and type of threat that different groups experience. Recent surveys reveal, for example, that Blacks show higher levels of distrust and greater pessimism about intergroup relations than do Whites (Dovidio & Gaertner, 1998; Hochschild, 1995). Majority group members tend to perceive intergroup interactions as more harmonious and productive than do minority group members (S. Gaertner et al., 1996; Islam & Hewstone, 1993; see also the survey of college students discussed earlier), but they also tend to perceive subordinate and minority groups as encroaching on their rights and prerogatives (Bobo, 1999). In addition, majority and minority group members have different preferences for the ultimate outcomes of intergroup contact. Whereas minority group members often tend to want to retain their cultural identity, majority group members may favor the assimilation of minority groups into one single culture (a traditional melting pot orientation): the dominant culture (e.g., Horenczyk, 1996).

Berry (1984; Berry, Poortinga, Segall, & Dasen, 1992) presented four forms of cultural relations in pluralistic societies that represent the intersection of "yes–no" responses to two relevant questions: (a) Is cultural identity of value, and to be retained? (b) Are positive relations with the larger society of value, and to be sought? These combinations reflect four adaptation strategies for intergroup relations: (a) integration, when cultural identities are retained and positive relations with the larger society are sought; (b) separation, when cultural identities are retained but positive relations with the larger society are not sought; (c) assimilation, when cultural identities are abandoned and positive relations with the larger society are desired; and (d) marginalization, when cultural identities are abandoned and are not replaced by positive identification with the larger society.

Research in the area of immigration suggests that immigrant groups and majority groups have different preferences for these different types of group relations. Van Oudenhoven, Prins, and Buunk (1998) found in the Netherlands that Dutch majority group members preferred an assimilation of minority groups (in which minority group identity was abandoned and replaced by identification with the dominant Dutch culture), whereas Turkish and Moroccan immigrants most strongly endorsed integration (in which they would retain their own cultural identity while also valuing the dominant Dutch culture).

These preferences also apply to the preferences of Whites and minorities about racial and ethnic group relations in the United States. Dovidio, Gaertner, and Kafati (2000) have found that Whites prefer assimilation most, whereas racial and ethnic minorities favor pluralistic integration. Moreover, these preferred types of intergroup relations for majority and minority groups—a one-group representation (assimilation) for Whites and dual representation (pluralistic integration) for racial and ethnic minorities—differentially mediated the consequences of intergroup contact for the different groups. Specifically, for Whites, more positive perceptions of intergroup contact related to stronger superordinate (i.e., common group) representations, which in turn mediated more positive attitudes to their school and other groups at the school. In contrast, for minority students, a dual-identity (integration) representation—but not the one-group representation—predicted more positive attitudes toward their school and to other groups. In general, these effects were stronger for people higher in racial-ethnic identification, both for Whites and minorities.

These findings have practical as well as theoretical implications for reducing intergroup conflict and enhancing social harmony. Although correlational data should be interpreted cautiously, it appears that for both Whites and racial and ethnic minorities, favorable intergroup contact may contribute to their commitment to their institution. However, strategies and interventions designed to enhance satisfaction need to recognize that Whites and minorities may have different ideals and motivations. Because White values and culture have been the traditionally dominant ones in the United States, American Whites may see an assimilation model—in which members of other cultural groups are absorbed into the mainstream—as the most comfortable and effective strategy. For racial and ethnic minorities, this model, which denies the value of their culture and traditions, may be perceived not only as less desirable but also as threatening to their personal and social identity—particularly for people who strongly identify with their group. Thus, efforts to create a single superordinate identity, though well intentioned, may threaten one's social identity, which in turn can intensify intergroup bias and conflict. As Bourhis, Moise, Perrault, and Sebecal (1997) argued with respect to the nature of immigrant and host community relations, conflict is likely to be minimized and social harmony fostered when these groups have consonant acculturation ideals and objectives.

CONCLUSIONS

In this chapter we have examined the fundamental psychological processes related to intergroup relations, group conflict, social harmony, and intergroup integration. Intergroup bias and conflict are complex phenomena having historical, cultural, economic, and psychological roots. In addition, these are dynamic phenomena that can evolve to different forms and manifestations over time. A debate about whether a societal, institutional, intergroup, or individual level of analysis is most appropriate, or a concern about which model of bias or bias reduction accounts for the most variance, not only may thus be futile but may also distract scholars from a more fundamental mission: developing a comprehensive model of social conflict, harmony, and integration.

We propose that understanding how structural, social, and psychological mechanisms *jointly* shape intergroup relations can have both valuable theoretical and practical implications. Theoretically, individual difference (e.g., social dominance orientation; Sidanius & Pratto, 1999), functional (e.g., Sherif & Sherif, 1969), and collective identity (e.g., Tajfel & Turner, 1979; Turner et al., 1987) approaches can be viewed as complementary rather than competing explanations for social conflict and harmony (see Figure 20.1). Conceptually, intergroup relations are significantly influenced by structural factors as well as by individual orientations toward intergroup relations (e.g., social dominance orientation; Sidanius & Pratto, 1999) and toward group membership (e.g., strength of identification) and by the nature of collective identity. Functional relations within and between groups and social identity can influence perceptions of intra- and intergroup support or threat as well as the nature of group representations (see Figure 20.1). For instance, greater dependence on in-group members can strengthen the perceived boundaries, fostering representations as members of different groups and increasing perceptions of threat (L. Gaertner & Insko, 2000). Empirically, self-interest, realistic group threat, and identity threat have been shown independently to affect intergroup relations adversely (Bobo, 1999; Esses et al., 1998; Stephan & Stephan, 2000). Perceptions of intergroup threat or support and group representations can also mutually influence one another. Perceptions of competition or threat increase the salience of different group representations and decrease the salience of superordinate group connections, whereas stronger inclusive representations of the

groups can decrease perceptions of intergroup competition (S. L. Gaertner et al., 1990).

Similarly, within the social categorization approach, researchers have posited not only that decategorization, recategorization, and mutual intergroup differentiation processes can each play a role in the reduction of bias over time (Pettigrew, 1998a), but also that these processes can facilitate each other reciprocally (S. L. Gaertner et al., 2000; Hewstone, 1996). Within an alternating sequence of categorization processes, mutual differentiation may emerge initially to neutralize threats to original group identities posed by the recategorization and decategorization processes. Once established, mutual differentiation can facilitate the subsequent recognition and acceptance of a salient superordinate identity and recategorization, which would have previously stimulated threats to the distinctiveness of group identities (S. Gaertner & Dovidio, 2000).

Reductions in perceived threat, increased perceptions of intergroup support, and more inclusive representations (either as a superordinate group or as a dual identity), in turn, can activate group- and individual-level processes that can reduce intergroup conflict (see Figure 20.1). These processes may also operate sequentially. For example, once people identify with a common group identity, they may be more trusting of former out-group members and consequently be willing to engage in the type of personalized, self-disclosing interaction that can further promote social harmony (Brewer & Miller, 1984; Dovidio et al., 1997). Thus, factors related to structural and functional relations between groups and those associated with collective representations (e.g., involving mutual intergroup differentiation, recategorization, and decategorization

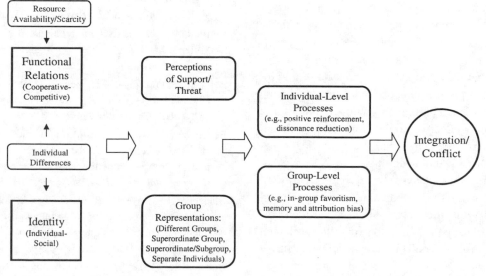

Figure 20.1   The roles of functional and identity relations in social conflict and integration.

processes) can operate in a complementary and reciprocal fashion.

Pragmatically, understanding the nature of bias and conflict can suggest ways in which these forces can be harnessed and redirected to promote social harmony. Given the different perspectives, needs, and motivations of majority (high status) and minority (low status) groups, interventions based on these principles need to be considered carefully. Nevertheless, understanding the multilevel nature of prejudice and discrimination is an essential step for finding solutions—which may need to be similarly multifaceted. These principles may be applied to reduce social conflict and facilitate the integration of groups as disparate as corporations and stepfamilies (S. Gaertner, Bachman, Dovidio, & Banker, 2001), to improve race relations in the workplace (Dovidio, Gaertner, & Bachman, 2001) and more generally (Dovidio & Gaertner, 1998), and to meet the challenge of managing immigration successfully—in ways that facilitate the achievement and well-being of immigrants and that produce the cooperation and support of residents of the receiving country (Esses et al., 2001).

In addition, these approaches may be applied integratively to reduce international tensions and improve national relations (Pettigrew, 1998b). Rouhana and Kelman (1994), for example, described the activities and outcomes of a program of workshops designed to improve Palestinian-Israeli relations and to contribute to peace in the Middle East. These workshops required Palestinian and Israeli participants to search for solutions that satisfy the needs of both parties. Rouhana and Kelman (1994) explained that this enterprise "can contribute to a creative redefinition of the conflict, to joint discovery of win-win solutions, and to transformation of the relationship between the parties" (p. 160). Conceptually, this orientation changes the structural relations between the groups from competition to cooperation, facilitates the development of mutually differentiated national identities within a common workshop identity, and permits the type of personalized interaction that can enhance social harmony. Pettigrew (1998b) proposed that these workshops serve as a setting for direct interaction that provides opportunities for developing coalitions of peace-minded participants across conflict lines. Thus, a strategic and reflective application of basic social-psychological principles can have significant practical benefits in situations of long-standing conflict.

In conclusion, the issues related to social conflict, harmony, and integration are complex indeed. As a consequence, approaches to understanding these processes need to address the issues at different levels of analysis and to consider structural as well as psychological factors. This diversity of perspectives produces a complicated and sometimes apparently inconsistent picture of the nature of intergroup relations. However, rather than viewing these approaches as competing positions, we suggest that they often reflect different perspectives on a very large issue. No single position is definitive, but jointly they present a relatively comprehensive picture of the multifaceted nature of intergroup relations.

REFERENCES

Abrams, D. (1985). Focus of attention in minimal intergroup discrimination. *British Journal of Social Psychology, 24,* 65–74.

Adorno, T. W., Frenkel-Brunswik, E., Levinson, D. J., & Sanford, R. N. (1950). *The authoritarian personality.* New York: Harper.

Allport, G. W. (1954). *The nature of prejudice.* Cambridge, MA: Addison-Wesley.

Allport, G. W. (1958). *The nature of prejudice* (abridged). Garden City, NY: Doubleday.

Altemeyer, B. (1996). *The authoritarian specter.* Cambridge, MA: Harvard University Press.

Altemeyer, B. (1998). The "other authoritarian personality." In M. P. Zanna (Ed.), *Advances in experimental social psychology* (Vol. 30, pp. 47–92). San Diego, CA: Academic.

Amir, Y. (1969). Contact hypothesis in ethnic relations. *Psychological Bulletin, 71,* 319–342.

Archer, R. L., & Berg, J. H. (1978). Disclosure reciprocity and its limits: A reactance analysis. *Journal of Experimental Social Psychology, 14,* 527–540.

Aronson, E., & Patnoe, S. (1997). *The jigsaw classroom.* New York: Longman.

Aronson, E., Blaney, N., Stephan, C., Sikes, J., & Snapp, M. (1978). *The jigsaw classroom.* Beverly Hills, CA: Sage.

Batson, C. D., Polycarpou, M. P., Harmon-Jones, E., Imhoff, H. J., Mitchener, E. C., Bednar, L. L., Klein, T. R., & Highberger, L. (1997). Empathy and attitudes: Can feeling for a member of a stigmatized group improve feelings toward the group? *Journal of Personality and Social Psychology, 72,* 105–118.

Berry, J. W. (1984). Cultural relations in plural societies. In N. Miller & M. B. Brewer (Eds.), *Groups in contact: The psychology of desegregation* (pp. 11–27). Orlando, FL: Academic.

Berry, J. W., Poortinga, Y. H., Segall, M. H., & Dasen, P. R. (1992). *Cross-cultural psychology: Research and applications.* Cambridge, UK: Cambridge University Press.

Bettencourt, B. A., Brewer, M. B., Croak, M. R., & Miller, N. (1992). Cooperation and the reduction of intergroup bias: The roles of reward structure and social orientation. *Journal of Experimental Social Psychology, 28,* 301–319.

Blanchard, F. A., Weigel, R. H., & Cook, S. W. (1975). The effects of relative competence of group members upon interpersonal attraction in cooperating interracial groups. *Journal of Personality and Social Psychology, 32,* 519–530.

Blauner, R. (1972). *Race oppression in America.* New York: Harper & Row.

Blumer, H. (1958a). Race prejudice as a sense of group position. *Pacific Sociological Review, 1,* 3–7.

Blumer, H. (1958b). Recent research on race relations in the United States of America. *International Social Science Bulletin, 10,* 403–477.

Blumer, H. (1965a). Industrialization and race relations. In G. Hunter (Ed.), *Industrialization and race relations: A symposium* (pp. 228–229). New York: Oxford University Press.

Blumer, H. (1965b). The future of the Color Line. In J. C. McKinney & E. T. Thompson (Eds.), *The South in continuity and change* (pp. 322–336). Durham, NC: Seeman.

Bobo, L. (1988). Group conflict, prejudice, and the paradox of contemporary racial attitudes. In P. A. Katz & D. A. Taylor (Eds.), *Eliminating racism: Profiles in controversy* (pp. 85–114). New York: Plenum.

Bobo, L. (1999). Prejudice as group position: Micro-foundations of a sociological approach to racism and race relations. *Journal of Social Issues, 55*(3). 445–472.

Bobo, L., & Huchings, V. L. (1996). Perceptions of racial group competition: Extending Blumer's theory of group position to a multiracial context. *American Sociological Review, 61,* 951–972.

Bonacich, E. (1972). A theory of ethnic antagonism. *American Sociological Review, 77,* 547–559.

Bourhis, R. Y., Moise, L. C., Perreault, S., & Senecal, S. (1997). Towards an interactive acculturation model: A social psychological approach. *International Journal of Psychology, 32,* 369–386.

Bourhis, R. Y., Turner, J. C., & Gagnon, A. (1997). Interdependence, social identity, and social discrimination. In R. Spears, P. J. Oakes, N. Ellemers, & S. A. Haslam (Eds.), *The social psychology of stereotyping and group life* (pp. 273–295). Malden, MA: Blackwell.

Branscombe, N. R., Schmitt, M. T., & Harvey, R. D. (1999). Perceiving pervasive discrimination among African Americans: Implications for group identification and well-being. *Journal of Personality and Social Psychology, 77,* 135–149.

Branscombe, N. R., & Ellemers, N. (1998). Coping with group-based discrimination: Individualistic versus group-level strategies. In J. K. Swim & C. Stangor (Eds.), *Prejudice: The target's perspective* (pp. 243–266). San Diego, CA: Academic.

Brewer, M. B. (1979). Ingroup bias in the minimal intergroup situation: A cognitive motivational analysis. *Psychological Bulletin, 86,* 307–324.

Brewer, M. B. (1988). A dual process model of impression formation. In T. S. Srull & R. S. Wyer (Eds.), *Advances in social cognition: Vol. 1. A dual process model of impression formation* (pp. 1–36). Hillsdale, NJ: Erlbaum.

Brewer, M. B. (1991). The social self: On being the same and different at the same time. *Personality and Social Psychology Bulletin, 17,* 475–482.

Brewer, M. B., & Miller, N. (1984). Beyond the contact hypothesis: Theoretical perspectives on desegregation. In N. Miller & M. B. Brewer (Eds.), *Groups in contact: The psychology of desegregation* (pp. 281–302). Orlando, FL: Academic.

Brewer, M. B., & Miller, N. (1996), *Intergroup relations.* Buckingham, UK: Open University Press.

Brown, R. J., & Turner, J. C. (1981). Interpersonal and intergroup behavior. In J. C. Turner & H. Giles (Eds.), *Intergroup behavior* (pp. 33–64). Chicago: University of Chicago Press.

Brown, R. J., Vivian, J., & Hewstone, M. (1999). Changing attitudes through intergroup contact: The effects of group membership salience. *European Journal of Social Psychology, 29,* 741–764.

Brown, R. J., & Wade, G. (1987). Superordinate goals and intergroup behavior: The effect of role ambiguity and status on intergroup attitudes and task performance. *European Journal of Social Psychology, 17,* 131–142.

Campbell, D. T. (1965). Ethnocentric and other altruistic motives. In D. Levine (Ed.), *Nebraska symposium on motivation* (Vol. 13, pp. 283–311). Lincoln: University of Nebraska Press.

Cook, S. W. (1984). Cooperative interaction in multiethnic contexts. In N. Miller & M. B. Brewer (Eds.), *Groups in contact: The psychology of desegregation* (pp. 291–302). Orlando, FL: Academic.

Cook, S. W. (1985). Experimenting on social issues: The case of school desegregation. *American Psychologist, 40,* 452–460.

Crocker, J., & Quinn, D. M. (2001). Psychological consequences of devalued identities. In R. J. Brown & S. L. Gaertner (Eds.), *Blackwell handbook of social psychology: Intergroup processes* (pp. 238–257). Oxford, UK: Blackwell.

Derlega, V. J., Metts, S., Petronio, S., & Margulis, S. T. (1993). *Self-disclosure.* Newbury Park, CA: Sage.

Deschamps, J. C., & Brown, R. (1983). Superordinate goals and intergroup conflict. *British Journal of Social Psychology, 22,* 189–195.

Deschamps J. C., & Doise, W. (1978). Crossed-category membership in intergroup relations. In H. Tajfel (Ed.), *Differentiation between social groups* (pp. 141–158). London: Academic.

Deutsch, M. (1973). *The resolution of social conflict.* New Haven, CT: Yale University Press.

Deutsch, M. (1993). Educating for a peaceful world. *American Psychologist, 48,* 510–517.

Deutsch, M., & Collins, M. (1951). *Interracial housing: A psychological evaluation of a social experiment.* Minneapolis: University of Minnesota Press.

Doise, W. (1978). *Groups and individuals: Explanations in social psychology.* Cambridge, UK: Cambridge University Press.

Dovidio, J. F., & Gaertner, S. L. (1993). Stereotypes and evaluative intergroup bias. In D. M. Mackie & D. L. Hamilton (Eds.), *Affect, cognition, and stereotyping: Interactive processes in intergroup perception* (pp. 167–193). Orlando, FL: Academic.

Dovidio, J. F., & Gaertner, S. L. (1998). On the nature of contemporary prejudice: The causes, consequences, and challenges of aversive racism. In J. Eberhardt & S. T. Fiske (Eds.),

Confronting racism: The problem and the response (pp. 3–32). Newbury Park, CA: Sage.

Dovidio, J. F., Gaertner, S. L., & Bachman, B. A. (2001). Racial bias in organizations: The role of group processes in its causes and cures. In M. E. Turner (Ed.), *Groups at work: Theory and research* (pp. 415–444). Mahwah, NJ: Erlbaum.

Dovidio, J. F., Gaertner, S. L., & Kafati, G. (2000). Group identity and intergroup relations: The Common In-Group Identity Model. In S. R. Thye, E. J. Lawler, M. W. Macy, & H. A. Walker (Eds.), *Advances in group processes* (Vol. 17, pp. 1–34). Stamford, CT: JAI.

Dovidio, J. F., Gaertner, S. L., & Validzic, A. (1998). Intergroup bias: Status, differentiation, and a common in-group identity. *Journal of Personality and Social Psychology, 75,* 109–120.

Dovidio, J. F., Gaertner, S. L., Validzic, A., Matoka, K., Johnson, B., & Frazier, S. (1997). Extending the benefits of re-categorization: Evaluations, self-disclosure and helping. *Journal of Experimental Social Psychology, 33,* 401–420.

Duckitt, J. (1992). Psychology and prejudice: A historical analysis and integrative framework. *American Psychologist, 47,* 1182–1193.

Ellemers, N., & Barreto, M. (2001). The impact of relative group status: Affective, perceptual, and behavioral consequences. In R. Brown & S. L. Gaertner (Eds.), *Blackwell handbook of social psychology: Intergroup processes* (pp. 324–343). Malden, MA: Blackwell.

Esses, V. M., Dovidio, J. F., Jackson, L. M., & Armstrong, T. L. (2001). The immigration dilemma: The role of perceived group competition, ethnic prejudice, and national identity. *Journal of Social Issues, 57,* 389–412.

Esses, V. M., Haddock, G., & Zanna, M. (1993). Values, stereotypes, and emotions as determinants of intergroup attitudes. In D. Mackie & D. Hamilton (Eds.), *Affect, cognition and stereotyping: Interactive processes in group perception* (pp. 137–166). San Diego, CA: Academic.

Esses, V. M., Jackson, L. M., & Armstrong, T. L. (1998). Intergroup competition and attitudes toward immigrants and immigration: An instrumental model of group conflict. *Journal of Social Issues, 54,* 699–724.

Ferguson, C. K., & Kelley, H. H. (1964). Significant factors in over-evaluation of own groups' products. *Journal of Abnormal and Social Psychology, 69,* 223–228.

Fiske, S. T. (2000). Interdependence and the reduction of prejudice. In S. Oskamp (Ed.), *Reducing prejudice and discrimination* (pp. 115–135). Hillsdale, NJ: Erlbaum.

Fiske, S. T., Lin, M., & Neuberg, S. L. (1999). The continuum model: Ten years later. In S. Chaiken & Y. Trope (Eds.), *Dual process theories in social psychology* (pp. 231–254). New York: Guilford.

Fiske, S. T., & Neuberg, S. L. (1990). A continuum model of impression formation: From category based to individuating processes as a function of information, motivation, and attention.

In M. P. Zanna (Ed.), *Advances in experimental social psychology* (Vol. 23, pp. 1–74). San Diego, CA: Academic.

Fiske, S. T., & Ruscher, J. B. (1993). Negative interdependence and prejudice: Whence the affect? In D. M. Mackie & D. L. Hamilton (Eds.), *Affect, cognition, and stereotyping: Interactive processes in group perception* (pp. 239–268). New York: Academic.

Gaertner, L., & Insko, C. A. (2000). Intergroup discrimination in the minimal group paradigm: Categorization, reciprocation, or fear? *Journal of Personality and Social Psychology, 79,* 77–94.

Gaertner, L., & Schopler, J. (1998). Perceived ingroup entitativity and intergroup bias: An interconnection of self and others. *European Journal of Social Psychology, 28,* 963–980.

Gaertner, S. L., Bachman, B. A., Dovidio, J. D., & Banker, B. S. (2001). Corporate mergers and stepfamily marriages: Identity, harmony, and commitment. In M. A. Hogg & D. Terry (Eds.), *Social identity in organizations* (pp. 265–282). Oxford, UK: Blackwell.

Gaertner, S. L., & Dovidio, J. F. (1986). The aversive form of racism. In J. F. Dovidio & S. L. Gaertner (Eds.), *Prejudice, discrimination, and racism* (pp. 61–89). Orlando, FL: Academic.

Gaertner, S. L., & Dovidio, J. F. (2000). *Reducing intergroup bias: The Common Ingroup Identity Model.* Philadelphia, PA: Psychology Press.

Gaertner, S. L., Dovidio, J. F., Anastasio, P. A., Bachman, B. A., & Rust, M. C. (1993). The common ingroup identity model: Recategorization and the reduction of intergroup bias. In W. Stroebe & M. Hewstone (Eds.), *European review of social psychology* (Vol. 4. pp. 1–26). New York: Wiley.

Gaertner, S. L., Dovidio, J. F., & Bachman, B. A. (1996). Revisiting the Contact Hypothesis: The induction of a common ingroup identity. *International Journal of Intercultural Relations, 20*(3&4), 271–290.

Gaertner, S. L., Dovidio, J. F., Banker, B., Houlette, M., Johnson, K., & McGlynn, E. (2000). Reducing intergroup conflict: From superordinate goals to decategorization, recategorization, and mutual differentiation. *Group Dynamics, 4,* 98–114.

Gaertner, S. L., Dovidio, J. F., Rust, M. C., Nier, J., Banker, B., Ward, C. M., Mottola, G. R., & Houlette, M. (1999). Reducing intergroup bias: Elements of intergroup cooperation. *Journal of Personality and Social Psychology, 76,* 388–402.

Gaertner, S. L., Mann, J. A., Dovidio, J. F., Murrell, A. J., & Pomare, M. (1990). How does cooperation reduce intergroup bias? *Journal of Personality and Social Psychology, 59,* 692–704.

Gaertner, S. L., Rust, M. C., Dovidio, J. F., Bachman, B. A., & Anastasio, P. A. (1996). The Contact Hypothesis: The role of a common ingroup identity on reducing intergroup bias among majority and minority group members. In J. L. Nye & A. M. Brower (Eds.), *What's social about social cognition?* (pp. 230–360). Newbury Park, CA: Sage.

Gouldner, A. (1960). The norm of reciprocity: A preliminary statement. *American Sociological Review, 25,* 161–178.

Gramzow, R. H., Gaertner, L., & Sedikides, C. (2001). Memory for in-group and out-group information in a minimal group context: The self as an informational base. *Journal of Personality and Social Psychology, 80,* 188–205.

Green, C. W., Adams, A. M., & Turner, C. W. (1988). Development and validation of the School Interracial Climate Scale. *American Journal of Community Psychology, 16,* 241–259.

Greenland, K., & Brown, R. J. (1999). Categorization and intergroup anxiety in contact between British and Japanese nationals. *European Journal of Social Psychology, 29,* 503–521.

Hamberger, J., & Hewstone, M. (1997). Inter-ethnic contact as a predictor of blatant and subtle prejudice: Tests of a model in four West European nations. *British Journal of Social Psychology, 36,* 173–190.

Hewstone, M. (1990). The "ultimate attribution error"? A review of the literature on intergroup attributions. *European Journal of Social Psychology, 20,* 311–335.

Hewstone, M. (1996). Contact and categorization: Social psychological interventions to change intergroup relations. In N. Macrae, M. Hewstone, & C. Stangor (Eds.), *Foundations of stereotypes and stereotyping* (pp. 323–368). New York: Guilford.

Hewstone, M., & Brown, R. J. (1986). Contact is not enough: An intergroup perspective on the "Contact Hypothesis." In M. Hewstone & R. Brown (Eds.), *Contact and conflict in intergroup encounters* (pp. 1–44). Oxford, UK: Basil Blackwell.

Higgins, E. T., & Bargh, J. A. (1987). Social cognition and social perception. *Annual Review of Psychology, 38,* 369–425.

Hochschild, J. L. (1995). *Facing up to the American dream: Race, class, and the soul of the nation.* Princeton, NJ: Princeton University Press.

Hogg, M. A. (1996). Social identity, self-categorization, and the small group. In E. H. Witte & J. H. Davis (Eds.), *Understanding group behavior: Vol. 2. Small group processes and interpersonal relations. Understanding group behavior* (pp. 227–253). Hillsdale, NJ: Erlbaum.

Hogg, M. A., & Abrams, D. (1990). Social motivation, self-esteem and social identity. In D. Abrams & M. A. Hogg (Eds.), *Social identity theory: Constructive and critical advances* (pp. 28–47). New York: Harvester Wheatsheaf.

Hogg, M. A., & Abrams, D. (1993). Towards a single-process uncertainty-reduction model of social motivation in groups. In M. Hogg & D. Abrams (Eds.), *Group motivation: Social psychological perspectives* (pp. 173–190). London: Harvester Wheatsheaf.

Horenczyk, G. (1996). Migrant identities in conflict: Acculturation attitudes and perceived acculturation ideologies. In G. Breakwell & E. Lyons (Eds.), *Changing European identities: Social psychological analyses of social change* (pp. 241–250). Woburn, MA: Butterworth-Heinemann.

Hornsey, M. J., & Hogg, M. A. (2000a). Assimilation and diversity: An interactive model of subgroup relations. *Personality and Social Psychology Review, 4,* 143–156.

Hornsey, M. J., & Hogg, M. A. (2000b). Intergroup similarity and subgroup relations: Some implications for assimilation. *Personality and Social Psychology Bulletin, 26,* 948–958.

Hornstein, H. A. (1976). *Cruelty and kindness: A new look at aggression and altruism.* Englewood Cliffs, NJ: Prentice-Hall.

Howard, J. M., & Rothbart, M. (1980). Social categorization for in-group and out-group behavior. *Journal of Personality and Social Psychology, 38,* 301–310.

Huo, Y. J., Smith, H. H., Tyler, T. R., & Lind, A. E. (1996). Superordinate identification, subgroup identification, and justice concerns: Is separatism the problem. Is assimilation the answer? *Psychological Science, 7,* 40–45.

Insko, C. A., Schopler, J., Gaertner, L., Wildschut, T., Kozar, R., Pinter, B., Finkel, E. J., Brazil, D. M., Cecil, C. L., & Montoya, M. R. (2001). Interindividual-Intergroup discontinuity reduction through the anticipation of future interaction. *Journal of Personality and Social Psychology, 80,* 95–111.

Islam, M. R., & Hewstone, M. (1993). Dimensions of contact as predictors of intergroup anxiety, perceived outgroup variability and outgroup attitude: An integrative model. *Personality and Social Psychology Bulletin, 19,* 700–710.

Jackson, L. M., & Esses, V. M. (2000). Effects of perceived economic competition on people's willingness to help empower immigrants. *Group Processes and Intergroup Relations, 3,* 419–435.

Johnson, D. W., Johnson, F. P., & Maruyama, G. (1983). Interdependence and interpersonal attraction among heterogeneous and homogeneous individuals: A theoretical formulation and a meta-analysis of the research. *Review of Educational Research, 52,* 5–54.

Johnson, D. W., & Johnson, R. T. (2000). The three Cs of reducing prejudice and discrimination. In S. Oskamp (Ed.), *Reducing prejudice and discrimination* (pp. 239–268). Hillsdale, NJ: Erlbaum.

Jones, J. M. (1997). *Prejudice and racism* (2nd ed.). New York: McGraw-Hill.

Kanter, R. M. (1977). *Men and women of the corporation.* New York: Basic Books.

Kawakami, K., & Dion, K. L. (1993). The impact of salient self-identities on relative deprivation and action intentions. *European Journal of Social Psychology, 23,* 525–540.

Kawakami, K., & Dion, K. L. (1995). Social identity and affect as determinants of collective action. *Theory and Psychology, 5,* 551–577.

Kihlstrom, J. F., Cantor, N., Albright, J. S., Chew, B. R., Klein, S. B., & Niedenthal, P. M. (1988). Information processing and the study of the self. In L. Berkowitz (Ed.), *Advances in experimental social psychology* (Vol. 21, pp. 145–180). Orlando, FL: Academic.

Kovel, J. (1970). *White racism: A psychohistory.* New York: Pantheon.

Kramer, R. M., & Brewer, M. B. (1984). Effects of group identity on resource utilization in a simulated commons dilemma. *Journal of Personality and Social Psychology, 46,* 1044–1057.

Sumner, W. G. (1906). *Folkways*. New York: Ginn.

Tajfel, H. (1969). Cognitive aspects of prejudice. *Journal of Social Issues, 25*(4), 79–97.

Tajfel, H., Billig, M. G., Bundy, R. F., & Flament, C. (1971). Social categorisation and intergroup behavior. *European Journal of Social Psychology, 1,* 149–177.

Tajfel, H., & Turner, J. C. (1979). An integrative theory of intergroup conflict. In W. G. Austin & S. Worchel (Eds.), *The social psychology of intergroup relations* (pp. 33–48). Monterey, CA: Brooks/Cole.

Taylor, M. C. (2000). Social contextual strategies for reducing racial discrimination. In S. Oskamp (Ed.), *Reducing prejudice and discrimination* (pp. 71–89). Hillsdale, NJ: Erlbaum.

Trivers, R. L. (1971). The evolution of reciprocal altruism. *Quarterly Review of Biology, 46,* 35–37.

Turner, J. C. (1981). The experimental social psychology of intergroup behavior. In J. C. Turner & H. Giles (Eds.), *Intergroup behavior* (pp. 66–101). Chicago: University of Chicago Press.

Turner, J. C. (1985). Social categorization and the self-concept: A social cognitive theory of group behavior. In E. J. Lawler (Ed.), *Advances in group processes* (Vol. 2, pp. 77–122). Greenwich, CT: JAI.

Turner, J. C., Hogg, M. A., Oakes, P. J., Reicher, S. D., & Wetherell, M. S. (1987). *Rediscovering the social group: A self-categorization theory.* Oxford, UK: Basil Blackwell.

van Oudenhoven, J. P., Groenewoud, J. T., & Hewstone, M. (1996). Cooperation, ethnic salience and generalization of interethnic attitudes. *European Journal of Social Psychology, 26,* 649–661.

van Oudenhoven, J. P., Prins, K. S., & Buunk, B. (1998). Attitudes of minority and majority members towards adaptation of immigrants. *European Journal of Social Psychology, 28,* 995–1013.

Verkuyten, M., & Hagendoorn, L. (1998). Prejudice and self-categorization: The variable role of authoritarianism and ingroup stereotypes. *Personality and Social Psychology Bulletin, 24,* 99–110.

Watson, G. (1947). *Action for unity.* New York: Harper.

Weigel, R. H., Wiser, P. I., & Cook, S. W. (1975). The impact of cooperative learning experiences on cross-ethnic relations and attitudes. *Journal of Social Issues, 31,* 219–244.

Wilder, D. A. (1978). Reducing intergroup discrimination through individuation of the outgroup. *Journal of Personality and Social Psychology, 36,* 1361–1374.

Wilder, D. A. (1981). Perceiving persons as a group: Categorization and intergroup relations. In D. L. Hamilton (Ed.), *Cognitive processes in stereotyping and intergroup behavior* (pp. 213–257). Hillsdale, NJ: Erlbaum.

Wilder, D. A. (1984). Predictions of belief homogeneity and similarity following social categorization. *British Journal of Social Psychology, 23,* 323–333.

Williams, R. M., Jr. (1947). *The reduction of intergroup tensions.* New York: Social Science Research Council.

Wilson, W. J. (1978). *The declining significance of race.* Chicago: University of Chicago Press.

Worchel, S. (1979). Cooperation and the reduction of intergroup conflict: Some determining factors. In W. Austin & S. Worchel (Eds.), *The social psychology of intergroup relations* (pp. 262–273). Monterey, CA: Brooks/Cole.

Worchel, S. (1986). The role of cooperation in reducing intergroup conflict. In S. Worchel & W. Austin (Eds.), *The psychology of intergroup relations* (pp. 288–304). Chicago: Nelson-Hall.

Worchel, S., Rothgerber, H., Day, E. A., Hart, D., & Butemeyer, J. (1998). Social identity and individual productivity with groups. *British Journal of Social Psychology, 37,* 389–413.

Wright, S. C. (2001). Strategic collective action: Social psychology and social change. In R. Brown & S. L. Gaertner (Eds.), *Blackwell handbook of social psychology: Intergroup processes* (pp. 409–430). Malden, MA: Blackwell.

Wright, S. C., Aron, A., McLaughlin-Volpe, T., & Ropp, S. A. (1997). The extended contact effect: Knowledge of cross-group friendships and prejudice. *Journal of Personality and Social Psychology, 73,* 73–90.

CHAPTER 21

Prejudice, Racism, and Discrimination

KENNETH L. DION

Prejudice (i.e., biased and usually negative *attitudes* toward social groups and their members), racism (a negatively oriented prejudice toward certain groups seen as biologically different and inferior to one's own), and discrimination (unfair *behavior* or unequal treatment accorded others on the basis of their group membership or possession of an arbitrary trait, such as skin color) have been favored topics of research and theorizing for many years by psychologists—especially social and personality psychologists—around the world. Of these three concepts, prejudice is perhaps the most central and important. Prejudice underlies racism and is also believed to motivate acts of discrimination. Between 1887 and 2000, nearly 4,000 papers were published on prejudice in journals covered by the American Psychological Association's electronic database of published psychological literature. Since the 1950s, in particular, the pace of psychological research on prejudice has steadily increased.

Much like prejudice as a topic in international prose and poetry (Larson, 1971), the psychology of prejudice reflects two main themes: (a) *the psychology of the bigot,* which seeks to understand why some people are prejudiced toward

certain groups and their members, and (b) *the psychology of the victim of prejudice and discrimination,* which focuses on the psychological correlates and consequences of experiencing or perceiving oneself to be an object or target of prejudice or discrimination. These two principal themes likewise provide the basic organization for this chapter.

Research on the psychology of the bigot far exceeds that on the psychology of the victim of prejudice and discrimination. One reason for this differential emphasis undoubtedly stems from the optimistic view that if the psychology of bigotry could be truly understood, scientifically based remedial efforts could then be devised and deployed to reduce, if not eliminate, prejudice at its source within the bigot. Yet, even if we suddenly possessed a magic bullet that instantly turned bigots into tolerant people, a strong case could be made for a psychology of the victim. Among other reasons, some of the prejudice and discrimination confronting members of oppressed groups comes from structural and institutional forms of racism, sexism, and all other "isms" rather than being solely due to intolerant and bigoted individuals. The task of addressing the social structural bases of prejudice within society and its institutions is apt to be far more daunting and difficult than reducing prejudices in individuals with psychological or other means—a formidable enough challenge in its own right (see the chapter on reducing prejudice by Dovidio in this volume).

Preparation of this chapter was made possible by a research grant to Kenneth L. Dion and Karen K. Dion from the Social Sciences and Humanities Research Council of Canada.

The extant literature on prejudice is also so vast and diverse that one chapter cannot realistically suffice to capture it all. Accordingly, this chapter's goal is to survey major perspectives and research foci on the aforementioned two themes underlying the psychology of prejudice at the turn of the twenty-first century. The amount of psychological research on prejudice has, to some extent, waxed and waned over the last five decades of the twentieth century. The prejudice literature has also been characterized by different emphases or waves, such as whether prejudice is conceptualized as a form of psychopathology or is instead viewed as being the product of normal cognitive processes (Duckitt, 1994). The present chapter focuses on the historical continuity of key ideas and psychological explanations about prejudice over the past several decades and emphasizes links between classic and contemporary research on prejudice.

We begin, then, with the psychology of bigotry. Under this principal theme, the classic perspectives of authoritarian personality, just world, and belief congruence theories are considered first. Though proposed in the 1950s and 1960s, these perspectives are still with us and remain important to our contemporary understanding of prejudice. For example, by focusing on beliefs and values, belief congruence theory presaged and anticipated more recent theories of racism (considered later under the rubric of ambivalence approaches to prejudice) and also has links to more recent perspectives on prejudice and impression formation. After considering ambivalence approaches, our focus shifts to automatic and controlled processing approaches to prejudice, especially the dissociation model and recent innovations in measuring prejudice with automatic activation procedures. The final section under the psychology of bigotry highlights integrative approaches (viz., social dominance theory, integrated threat theory, and the multicomponent approach to intergroup attitudes), each of which incorporates insights from multiple perspectives in seeking to understand prejudice better.

The psychology of the victim of prejudice and discrimination—the second principal theme of this chapter—begins with a consideration of attributional ambiguity perspectives, focusing on the complex but important issue of whether and when attributing a rejection or failure to prejudice can buffer one's sense of well-being and self-esteem. Following that, the stressfulness of perceiving oneself to be a target of prejudice or discrimination and the consequences of stereotype threat for task performance, respectively, are considered. Finally, the relationship of relative deprivation and perceived discrimination to protest and desires to take corrective action is considered. I begin, though, with the psychology of bigotry.

THE PSYCHOLOGY OF BIGOTRY

Authoritarian Personality Theories

The Original Theory of the Authoritarian Personality

The original theory of the authoritarian personality (OTAP), proposed by Adorno, Frenkel-Brunswik, Levinson, and Sanford (1950), was the first comprehensive and systematic attempt by psychologists to understand theoretically the roots of prejudice and to link ethnic, racial, religious, and ethnocentric prejudices to personality. Adopting the research methodologies of mid-twentieth-century social and clinical psychology along with a guiding psychoanalytic theoretical perspective, Adorno et al. (1950) postulated that the origins of the prejudice-prone authoritarian personality stemmed from a particular pattern of childhood influences and parental practices (see Brown, 1967, for an excellent in-depth analysis of the OTAP). Specifically, the authoritarian personality was the presumed result of an upbringing by parents who, among other things, (a) disciplined their child harshly, (b) emphasized duties and obligations instead of affection in child-parent relations, (c) made their love dependent on the child's unquestioning obedience, and (d) were status-oriented by being ingratiating toward those of higher social status but contemptuous toward those of lesser social status.

According to the OTAP, the child in such a family develops hostility but cannot express it toward the harsh, frustrating, but feared parents. This submission leads the child to develop a sense of itself as dependent upon its parents and unable to defy their authority. Moreover, the child in an authoritarian family presumably deploys an array of defense mechanisms to deal with the repressed hostility felt toward its parents. By identifying with the aggressor and following a strategy of "if you can't beat them, join them," the child comes to idealize its parents and to identify with established authority in general. Repressed hostility and other impulses unacceptable to its parents, such as aggression and sex, are displaced and projected by the child onto minority and subordinate groups as safe, alternative outlets. As a result, the child in an authoritarian family presumably develops a rigid personality organization characterized by a moralistic attitude toward unconventional people and practices, prejudice toward minority and other out-groups, and a tendency to idealize power, status, strength, and toughness but to disdain tenderness, weakness, and self-introspection.

The OTAP has several implications flowing from the central idea that prejudice toward ethnic and racial minorities and other target groups reflects an underlying, deep-seated personality structure in the bigot. First, prejudice should relate to attitudes toward a variety of issues and objects (e.g., attitudes toward sex, power, and political-economic issues) that would otherwise appear unrelated to prejudice and to one another because their interrelations reflect deeper, unconscious processes and connections. (OTAP's tenet that prejudice is rooted in unconscious processes is clearly echoed in contemporary theories of prejudice emphasizing automatic cognitive processing, described later, as an important feature of individuals' prejudicial beliefs and their expression.) Second, the authoritarian personality would be prejudiced toward a wide variety of target groups. If an authoritarian person's prejudice toward one group were somehow blocked, it would presumably be expressed, in a process of symptom substitution, toward other groups. Third, if prejudice is indeed deeply rooted in a personality structure, it should be difficult to change and would require depth-oriented techniques, such as psychotherapy and insight, that promote and produce profound personality change in the bigoted individual.

Adorno et al. (1950) attempted to validate the OTAP, in good part, by developing a personality scale, the California *F* (for fascism) scale, whose items were constructed to tap the right-wing political ideology and belief syndrome that they theorized as comprising the authoritarian personality. U.S. respondents' *F* scale scores correlated positively, as hypothesized, with their scores on other attitude scales designed to assess anti-Semitism, negative attitudes toward Blacks and other U.S. minority groups, and U.S. ethnocentrism. The *F* scale was subsequently incorporated into numerous studies in the 1950s and 1960s. Though criticized at the time of its initial appearance and later for keying all its items in one direction and not correcting for acquiescence response set, the *F* scale was still sporadically used by psychological and survey researchers well up to the 1980s. It remained for Altemeyer (1981, 1988, 1996), in a trilogy of books reflecting often painstaking psychometric research, to demonstrate conclusively the California *F* scale's serious inadequacies as a measure of proneness to prejudice and to refocus the conceptualization of the authoritarian personality into a more rigorously defined construct and scale of right-wing authoritarianism.

The Theory of Right-Wing Authoritarianism

Altemeyer (1981) persuasively detailed the inadequacies of the California *F* scale, most notably its lack of scale homogeneity and its saturation with response sets, especially acquiescence. Even more important, however, he created a psychometrically and conceptually appropriate scale of *right-wing authoritarianism* (RWA) that he has continued to

refine (see Altemeyer, 1996). Altemeyer defined RWA as the covariation of three attitudes: (a) *authoritarian submission* (i.e., ready submission to societally established authorities), (b) *authoritarian aggression* (i.e., aggression sanctioned by established authorities toward defined targets or social groups), and (c) *conventionalism* (i.e., adherence to conventions endorsed by societally established authorities). Altemeyer (1981, 1988, 1996) has extensively documented RWA's correlates, often with numerous replications. For example, RWA is concentrated more among politicians of the right, fundamentalist Protestants, and the poorly educated. Also, parents outscore their university-age offspring in RWA.

Altemeyer's approach to RWA differs from the OTAP in several important regards (Dion, 1990). By contrast to the OTAP's psychoanalytic perspective, Altemeyer has favored social learning theory as an explanation for the development of RWA in individuals, especially Bandura's versions with their emphases on vicarious learning and self-regulation by cognitive processes. Social learning theory has provided Altemeyer with a heuristic framework for explaining the contribution to RWA of personal experiences in one's adolescence, of parents and peers, of university education and parenthood, and the paradoxical role of religion in fostering RWA by creating a sense of self-righteousness. Second, whereas the OTAP portrayed authoritarianism as a personality dimension with its developmental roots in infancy and early childhood, Altemeyer has viewed RWA as an attitudinal orientation that emerges and crystallizes in early adolescence, suggesting that it may be more readily amenable to change within the individual.

Finally, in addition to documenting its empirical links to prejudice, Altemeyer (1988, 1996) has particularly focused on the political correlates of RWA. He has shown repeatedly that individuals (usually university students) scoring high on the RWA scale are reportedly more than willing and ready to punish others and to infringe upon and curtail their civil rights, especially those who threaten the social order. RWA scale scores have also been found to discriminate well between provincial and state legislators in Canada and the United States belonging to right- and left-wing political parties. Knowing politicians' RWA scale scores appears to be a useful piece of information for predicting their attitudes and behaviors.

Research by Altemeyer and others indicates that the RWA scale correlates between .30 and .50 with measures of prejudice toward racial and ethnic minorities and ethnocentrism scales. RWA correlates negatively with internal motivation (e.g., personal standards) and positively with external motivation (e.g., social or peer pressure) by White people to respond without prejudice toward Black people (Plant & Devine, 1998). RWA consistently correlates more highly, between .5 and .6, with homophobia and negative attitudes toward homosexuals. Indeed, Altemeyer (1996) contended that RWA is the single individual difference variable most relevant for predicting attitudes toward homosexuals, especially negative ones.

Studies by other investigators have likewise documented a consistently negative relationship between RWA and attitudes toward homosexuals and homosexuality (e.g., Haddock, Zanna, & Esses, 1993; Lippa & Arad, 1999; Whitley, 1999), strongly reinforcing Altemeyer's conclusion in this regard. The negative attitudes toward homosexuals by those scoring high in RWA are due to perceived impediments of homosexuals and homosexuality to one's values (Haddock et al., 1993) or to religiousness. Finally, a recent lexical approach to mapping the structure of social attitudes by Saucier (2000) showed that authoritarianism and RWA (along with conservatism and religiousness) defined the first and largest of three factors in the domain of social attitudes and beliefs. Clearly, the authoritarianism construct, especially RWA, remains important in psychological research on prejudice and in linking prejudice to individuals' personality and attitudes.

Just World Theory

An individual's belief in a just world (BJW) is another psychological dimension relevant for understanding individuals' reactions to ethnic and racial minorities and victims of ill fortune. According to Lerner's (1980) just world theory, we all believe, to a varying extent, in a just world where people get what they deserve and also deserve what they get. The BJW presumably enables us to view our world as a safe, predictable place where we can expect to obtain desired rewards and to avoid unpleasant outcomes. Becoming aware of an innocent victim who does not deserve to suffer, however, threatens one's BJW. Individuals go to considerable lengths to maintain and protect their BJW in the face of contrary information. For example, classic experiments by Lerner and his colleagues have demonstrated that when unable to prevent or compensate for an innocent victim's suffering, observers preserved their BJW by derogating the victim and seeing the suffering as deserved (see Lerner, 1980).

Questionnaire measures of the BJW consistently correlate with the tendency to blame visible victims (e.g., ethnic and racial minorities, the unemployed, and immigrants and asylum seekers) with samples of university and community respondents in the United States, Canada, and Europe (see Montada & Lerner, 1998). However, the BJW construct is conceptually and empirically distinguishable from authoritarianism. Using factor analyses of questionnaire measures from a sample of Canadian university students in Ontario, Lerner (1978) showed that authoritarianism (as measured by Rokeach's 1960 F scale) and BJW loaded on separate, independent factors. Authoritarianism loaded on a xenophobia factor characterized by high loading for authoritarianism, adherence to the Protestant ethic (a belief in the virtues of hard work and effort), attitudes toward social changes, and negative attitudes toward both minority groups and out-groups (e.g., Americans). By contrast, the BJW loaded on a win-lose view of the world, in which winners (e.g., Americans) were viewed positively, while losers (e.g., Native Indians and Métis) were negatively appraised. The BJW also correlates positively, but only modestly (i.e., between .1 and .3) with RWA (Lambert, Burroughs, & Chasteen, 1998).

It is interesting that blaming victims for their ill fate strengthens the observer's BJW (see Lerner & Montada, 1998). In turn, believing oneself to have been victimized as a target of prejudice or discrimination also appears to affect the BJW adversely. Birt and Dion (1987) found that in Toronto, the greater the perceived discrimination against homosexuals as a group, the weaker was the BJW among gay and lesbian respondents. Thus, just world theory and the BJW have relevance for the psychology of being a victim of prejudice and discrimination as well as the psychology of bigotry.

Belief Congruence Theory

Rokeach (1960) criticized the OTAP for focusing on right-wing authoritarianism, contending that authoritarianism need not be tied inextricably to either right- or left-wing political views. As an alternative, he proposed the construct of *closed-mindedness* or dogmatism and developed several Dogmatism Scales in an attempt to measure authoritarianism and to assess general authoritarianism of the political left as well as the political right. Unfortunately, his Dogmatism Scales possess serious psychometric limitations and are relatively little used today. Moreover, if it exists, left-wing authoritarianism would involve resisting and opposing conventional and established authorities (see Altemeyer, 1996, for an interesting discussion of dogmatism and left-wing authoritarianism and some new prospective scales for measuring these dimensions).

In the same book on the open and closed mind, however, Rokeach, Smith, and Evans (1960) also proposed an important perspective on prejudice: belief congruence theory (BCT). According to BCT, individuals cognitively organize their psychological world along the lines of belief congruence, liking those with similar beliefs and disliking those with dissimilar beliefs. Although the link between attitude similarity and interpersonal attraction had already been well demonstrated by that point, Rokeach et al.'s provocative contribution was to extent it to the domain of prejudice and to argue that *all* forms of prejudice were essentially different forms of belief prejudice. Thus, according to BCT, the racial conflict between Blacks and Whites in the United States is not due to race per se but rather to opposite or conflicting stands on key issues such as affirmative action in employment and education. Likewise, the antipathies between English and French in Canada are not due to ethnicity per se, but rather to conflict over the issue of Quebec's role, and the place of the French language, within Canada. In other words, racial and ethnic prejudice, as two examples, presumably reflect belief prejudice.

BCT clearly suggests research in which belief is pitted against group membership characteristics such as race or ethnicity. Rokeach et al. (1960), for example, had samples of White university students from northern and southern parts of the United States rate their desires to be friends with members of pairs of stimulus persons whose races and beliefs, both race-relevant and -irrelevant, were specified. For example, Type R pairs varied in race but kept belief constant (e.g., a White person who believes in God vs. a Black person who believes in God). Type B pairs kept race constant but varied belief (a Black person who believes in God vs. a Black person who is an atheist). Type RB pairs varied both race and belief simultaneously. Differences in friendliness ratings for members of a stimulus person pair were taken as reflecting discrimination. A critical comparison suggested by BCT involved a choice between an in-group member with dissimilar beliefs versus an out-group member with beliefs similar to one's own. For this pair comparison, individuals' preference typically goes to the latter, consistent with BCT. Likewise, Rokeach and Mezei (1966) showed that belief similarity excels race in predicting preferences for work partners among employment applicants following actual interpersonal interaction and discussion between Black and White participants with similar and dissimilar beliefs on an issue.

BCT remains as relevant a theory of prejudice in the twenty-first century as it was in the latter half of the twentieth century, largely due to the research over the past several decades of Insko and his colleagues (e.g., Cox, Smith, & Insko, 1996; Insko, Nacoste, & Moe, 1983) as well as recent contributions by Biernat and her colleagues (Biernat, Vescio, & Theno, 1996; Biernat, Vescio, Theno, & Crandall, 1996). For example, Insko et al. (1983) reviewed the literature and compared the strong version of BCT (when social pressure is absent, only belief determines racial-ethnic discrimination) to a weak version (when social pressure is absent, belief is more important than race in determining discrimination or prejudice). They concluded that the weak version of BCT was clearly supported by the evidence, whereas the strong version was more problematic (e.g., race effects in the form of in-group favoritism occur even in the absence of social pressure).

Cox et al. (1996) reported results of three cross-sectional surveys conducted over several decades of Black and White teenagers sampled from a North Carolina school system who had responded to stimulus persons varying in race and belief, using a belief discrepancy manipulation in which dissimilar beliefs were ones that respondents themselves had previously attributed to the other race. For White respondents, race effects (i.e., preferring their own race to Blacks on social distance and other attitude measures) steadily declined across three points in time from 1966 to 1993, as did perceived disapproval of interracial contacts and relationships. The effects of belief similarity affected all of their dependent variables and were constant across decades for White respondents. For Black respondents, more complex findings were obtained: Specifically, race effects (i.e., in-group preference) did not decline between 1979 and 1993 (the only two time periods including Black respondents), and belief similarity primarily influenced same-race rather than interracial evaluations.

BCT has clear links to contemporary perspectives on impression formation and prejudice. For example, Cox et al. (1996) noted that BCT is very similar to Fiske and Neuberg's (1990) temporal-continuum model of impression formation. In the latter model, a perceiver begins with categorical information (viz., race, ethnicity, sex, age, etc.) about a person but proceeds, if time permits and circumstances require, to process individuating information (e.g., beliefs of the stimulus person). Like Fiske and Neuberg's model, BCT deals with the issue of when individuating information (viz., beliefs and values) about a stimulus person overcomes competing categorical information (viz., group membership) in the impressions we form of others. Likewise, the importance that BCT accords to perceived belief dissimilarity in eliciting prejudice is shared today by terror management theory, a perspective focusing on the psychological consequences of being aware of, or sensitized to, one's mortality (Solomon, Greenberg, & Pyszczynski, 2000).

BCT has also been extended to the value domain. Schwartz and Struch (1989) proposed that perceptions of value dissimilarities between groups underlie intergroup antagonisms and undercut feelings of shared humanity. Likewise, Biernat, Vescio, Theno, and Crandall (1996) reported studies in which group membership cues (race and sexual orientation, respectively, in separate studies) were crossed with value violation (e.g., a lazy vs. dependable worker in the race study or a good vs. bad parental example in the sexual orientation study).

Value similarity had a strong effect on stimulus person ratings in both studies and a stronger effect than group membership characteristics (i.e., whether the stimulus person being evaluated was an in-group or out-group member from the perspective of the respondent).

When only group membership cues are available, perceivers infer that an out-group member has dissimilar beliefs, triggering a discriminatory or prejudicial response toward her or him, whether the out-group is defined by race or sexual orientation (see Stein, Hardyck, & Smith, 1965; Pilkington & Lydon, 1997). When belief similarity or dissimilarity is crossed with group membership, belief effects (i.e., preferring the individual with similar beliefs to one with dissimilar beliefs) are stronger. Race effects, however, usually remain evident in interpersonally intimate domains such as eating together, dating, and marriage. Insko et al. (1983; Cox et al., 1996) have suggested that race effects in these particular domains reflect perceived disapproval of interracial contact by reference persons such as parents and peers rather than intimacy per se.

In sum, as a perspective on prejudice, BCT anticipated the subsequent focus on the importance of values in prejudice, an idea pivotal to ambivalence approaches to prejudice that emerged in the 1970s and 1980s. I now turn to ambivalence approaches to prejudice.

Ambivalence Approaches

Myrdal (1994) was perhaps first to suggest that ambivalence underlies White Americans' attitudes and behaviors toward Blacks. This idea lay fallow in U.S. psychology until the late 1970s (see Crosby, Bromley, & Saxe, 1980; Pettigrew, 1979). By that point, though, it had become increasingly apparent that White Americans were less prone to strident racism asserting White superiority, Black inferiority, and racial segregation but instead inclined toward subtler expressions of racism. Although attitude surveys suggested growing racial tolerance among White Americans from the 1960s onward, the evidence was much less clear on indirect indicators (e.g., nonverbal behavior and helping behavior) that feelings of White Americans toward Blacks had truly become more tolerant.

In the last few decades, several groups of researchers concerned with prejudice, racism, and discrimination in the United States have characterized White Americans' attitudes toward Black Americans in the latter twentieth and early twenty-first centuries as being ambivalent in nature, that is, consisting of both positive and negative elements (see Jones, 1997). They differ, however, in the nature of the positive and negative elements comprising this ambivalence and other aspects of their models. These ambivalence approaches include

theories of aversive racism, symbolic and modern racism, response amplification, ambivalent sexism, and blatant versus subtle prejudice.

Aversive Racism

Dovidio and Gaertner (1986), for example, proposed a theory of *aversive racism,* in which they characterized the racial attitudes of most liberal, White Americans today as a subtler and less obviously bigoted view of Black Americans than the *dominative racism* (i.e., old-fashioned, "redneck" views of White superiority and Black inferiority) of previous generations. According to the aversive racism perspective, prejudice in the United States of the later twentieth century became a subtler, less direct, and perhaps more pernicious form than before, although dominative racism has not disappeared altogether.

Aversive racism theory suggests that on one hand, most White Americans subscribe strongly to an egalitarian value system, inclining them to sympathize with victims of injustice, such as Black Americans and other racial minorities, and to support policies promoting racial equality. This strong adherence to egalitarianism enables White Americans to regard themselves as being unprejudiced and nondiscriminatory. This positive component of the ambivalence comprising aversive racism is not assumed, however, to include genuinely pro-Black attitudes or sentiments of true friendship between Whites and Blacks in the United States.

On the other hand, owing to a historically racist culture in the United States and certain feelings of negative affect (e.g., uneasiness, disgust, fear, and discomfort, though not necessarily hostility or hate) toward Black Americans, most White Americans are assumed to avoid Black-White interracial interactions and to be biased and discriminatory toward Black Americans in situations in which they can do so without appearing to be prejudiced or in which it may be justified under a rationale preserving their erstwhile egalitarian values. Aversive racism is not assumed to be a psychopathological phenomenon but rather to reflect normal cognitive processes and the influence of sociocultural and historical processes on White Americans.

Several implications flow from aversive racism theory and the idea that aversive racists are strongly motivated and vigilant to avoid appearing racially bigoted. First, traditional prejudice measures in the form of standard attitude scales would presumably be difficult and perhaps of limited use for assessing aversive racism, according to Dovidio and Gaertner (1986). Nevertheless, based on survey research up to the 1990s, Dovidio and Gaertner (1991) estimated that perhaps a fifth of White U.S. citizens were overtly racist. The other 80%

of White Americans would presumably be, to varying extent, ambivalent toward Black Americans. White Americans who espouse a political philosophy of liberalism should be especially prone to aversive racism (Biernat, Vescio, Theno, & Crandall, 1996).

As noted earlier, a second implication of aversive racism theory is that in situations where discrimination would be blatant and where the appropriate behavior is normative and well-defined, White Americans would be unlikely to discriminate against Black Americans because doing so would contradict their allegedly nonprejudiced, egalitarian ideals and self-images. However, in ambiguous situations where the discrimination is less blatant or obvious, White Americans should be more likely to be biased against Black Americans because in that case they can do so without necessarily threatening their self-images. This feature of aversive racism theory—emphasizing the normative structure of situations as a moderator variable for predicting when racially ambivalent White Americans will or will not discriminate against Black Americans—is perhaps its most unique and distinctive feature among ambivalence approaches (Biernat, Vescio, Theno, & Crandall, 1996). These predictions have been amply supported in studies of White Americans, mostly college students, by Dovidio, Gaertner, and their colleagues.

This supportive research has included studies of helping, social cognition studies measuring reaction times linking the words "white" and "black" to positive and negative stereotype characteristics, studies where pictures of Black and White individuals' faces are presented as primes (Dovidio & Gaertner, 1986), research on juridic recommendations of the death penalty in a capital case (Dovidio, Smith, Gershenfeld Donnella, & Gaertner, 1997), and personnel selection recommendations in 1989 and 1999 (Dovidio & Gaertner, 2000), among others. In all of these studies, findings supported aversive racism theory and were unaffected by whether the participants had scored low or high on standard prejudice measures, though high scorers on such scales often showed greater bias toward Blacks than did low scorers.

What remains to be demonstrated by aversive racism theorists is that it is actually the conflict or tension between the positive element of egalitarianism, or one hand, and negative feelings toward Blacks, on the other, that constitutes the underlying basis of ambivalence for White Americans' attitudes and behaviors toward Blacks and is the driving force behind their discrimination of Blacks in ambiguous situations. Indeed, egalitarianism is the value that perhaps most strongly promotes tolerance and mitigates negative feelings toward Blacks by White Americans. Presenting liberal-oriented U.S. university students with an egalitarian message has been shown by Biernat, Vescio, and Theno (1996) to elicit more

positive ratings of a Black stimulus person than a White one. Whether egalitarianism promotes tolerance among individuals in countries other than the United States, however, remains to be seen. With White participants from Portugal and Brazil, Vala and Lima (2001) found that activating an egalitarian norm affected perceptions and evaluations of a White but not a Black stimulus person.

Although aversive racism theory has an excellent track record in predicting a variety of cognitions and behaviors in the social psychological laboratory, documenting the precise nature of White Americans' ambivalence toward Blacks remains a task to be completed. Using recently developed automatic processing techniques (described later) to assess nonconscious feelings of antipathy toward Blacks (or other oppressed group members) in conjunction with standard value measures to assess egalitarianism and other potentially race-relevant values may provide some useful leverage for assessing aversive racism in White participants and for testing the theory directly.

Symbolic and Modern Racism

Closely related to aversive racism theory are the constructs of *symbolic* and *modern racism* that have been suggested by several researchers, such as McConahay (1986) and Sears (1988; Sears & Funk, 1991). The symbolic and modern racism constructs originated because standard prejudice scales of the 1950s and 1960s became increasingly problematic for U.S. survey researchers in the 1960s and 1970s, owing to social desirability issues (i.e., the transparency of what they were measuring) and because they failed to predict racially relevant political behavior, such as voting intentions for capable Black candidates in elections where candidates of both races were running and racism likely played a role in the outcome (see Kinder & Sears, 1981).

What did predict voting and support for progressive racial policies were attitude items reflecting an abstract, moral tone that Black Americans were violating cherished White American values such as individualism and the Protestant ethic extolling the virtues of individual effort and hard work—qualities White Americans often felt were lacking among Black Americans. Ambivalence, then, arises because many White Americans want to maintain a nonprejudiced image even though they privately resent and dislike Blacks and feel the racial discrimination toward Blacks in the United States no longer exists. In protecting themselves from the appearance of being prejudiced, symbolic or modern racists justify their negative attitudes and behaviors toward Blacks by invoking nonprejudiced explanations in the form of American values or ideals. A symbolic or modern racist, for example, might justify opposition to affirmative action programs benefiting Blacks by saying that they violate the value of equality by favoring one group over others.

The constructs of symbolic and modern racism are similar to aversive racism. In both cases, the ambivalence arises from negative feelings toward Black people versus core American values. In both cases, White Americans dislike and avoid racial prejudice but seek indirect ways to manifest their negative feelings toward Black Americans. All three racism constructs are interested in predicting interpersonal behavior, with symbolic and modern racism being used mainly to predict political attitudes and behavior, typically in surveys. Symbolic and modern racism are assumed to emerge from early political socialization and not to be based on personal experience, personal competition, or direct, personal, economic threats to Whites from Blacks. Unlike aversive racism, however, items and scales to assess symbolic and modern racism have been constructed by their adherents and have proven very popular in survey and experimental research on prejudice by psychologists in the late twentieth century.

McConahay (1986), for example, presented a Modern Racism Scale (MRS) and an Old-Fashioned Racism Scale (OFRS), with moderate, positive correlations between the two, and items loading on one or the other factor in exploratory factor analyses. Whereas the OFRS was reactive (i.e., White U.S. respondents' scores were lower when it was administered by a Black experimenter than by a White one), the MRS was nonreactive (at least in the 1980s). Items from symbolic or modern racism scales became the standard measure of prejudice toward Blacks in the United States in the 1980s and 1990s and are still frequently used in this regard. In the twenty-first century, newer scales such as the Blatant and Subtle Prejudice Scales (Pettigrew & Meertens, 1995) or the Social Dominance Orientation Scale (Pratto, Sidanius, Stallworth, & Malle, 1994), both of which are discussed later, are perhaps more apt to become the preferred, "paper-and-pencil" measures of prejudice.

Sniderman and Tetlock (1986), themselves prominent political psychologists, have strongly criticized the constructs and measurement of symbolic and modern racism. Among other things, they criticized symbolic and modern racism for being unclear as to the causal relation between anti-Black affect and core American values, for equating political policy preferences (e.g., opposition to busing school children or affirmative action) with racism itself, and for suggesting that old-fashioned racism no longer existed in the United States. Sniderman and Tetlock even contended that symbolic racism theory was unfalsifiable and therefore unscientific. The MRS, they also charged, was confounded with political conservatism. Sniderman and his colleagues showed that political

conservatism related not to rejection and prejudice toward out-group members but rather to greater support for those, whether from the in-group or out-group, who behaved in a manner consistent with politically conservative principles (e.g., Sniderman, Piazza, Tetlock, & Kendrick, 1991).

Although proponents of symbolic and modern racism have not thoroughly explored the presumed link to values, Biernat, Vescio, and Theno (1996) did so in a series of studies. For example, after completing Rokeach's Value Survey, White U.S. undergraduates were asked to rate the extent to which four target groups, including Black Americans, supported or violated their values. Whether considering their top value or their hierarchy of values, Black Americans were perceived as less supportive of their values than were White Americans; however, there was no difference in perceived violation of values for these two target groups. Likewise, differences in ratings of White versus Black support and violation of values correlated with measures of modern racism as well as pro- and anti-Black attitudes, although these correlations were consistently modest in magnitude. Consistent with theories of symbolic and modern racism, Biernat et al. showed that White individuals who scored high on the Protestant work ethic and had their values made salient rated a Black employee less positively than a White employee when they violated the work ethic.

Thus, Biernat, Vescio, and Theno's (1996) research partially supported models of symbolic and modern racism. However, if violating core American values is indeed one of the two key components of symbolic and modern racism, one would expect to find much stronger relationships than they did. Biernat et al. also questioned the assumption that modern-symbolic racism is a *blending* of negative affect toward Blacks and core American values, such as individualism. Their analyses suggested that egalitarianism is a stronger predictor than individualism of intergroup attitudes and that combining negative affect with value measures added little beyond the separate components in predicting responses to an out-group member in their studies of race and sexual orientation.

In the ambivalence approach presented next the focus shifts to conflict between pro- and anti-Black attitudes linked to values as the determinant of positive and negative reactions to Blacks by White Americans.

Ambivalence Amplification

Katz and Hass (1988) contended that most White Americans hold both positive and negative attitudes about Black Americans that are relatively independent of one another. A White American who endorses positive statements about Blacks on a "Pro-Black scale" is neither more nor less likely to agree with anti-Black statements from a separate "Anti-Black scale." Moreover, for White American respondents, these racial beliefs relate to different and conflicting value systems. Pro-Black attitudes (e.g., beliefs that Blacks have a disadvantaged position in society) are linked to humanitarian-egalitarian values. By contrast, anti-Black attitudes (e.g., beliefs that Black people lack the drive or skills necessary to improve their socioeconomic position) related to White respondents' beliefs in individualism and the Protestant ethic.

Katz and his colleagues proposed that when these conflicting beliefs are salient to a White person holding them and who also becomes aware of the ambivalence, he or she experiences negative arousal and is motivated to reduce this tension. Indeed, Hass, Katz, Rizzo, Bailey, and Moore (1992) have demonstrated that White American participants experienced negative mood change when their racial ambivalence toward Black people was stimulated by reading a vivid description of an ugly racial incident in which gangs of young Whites in New York City viciously beat some Black Americans whose car had broken down in their neighborhood. This discomfort can be reduced, according to these theorists, by intensifying either the positive or negative component of the conflicted attitude toward Blacks—an idea defining *response amplification theory*.

Response amplification theory suggests that for ambivalent White Americans attitudes and behavior will be more polarized or amplified toward Black Americans than toward fellow White Americans. Experimental evidence for response amplification theory, as applied to Black Americans and other socially stigmatized groups such as the handicapped, was presented by Katz and Glass (1979). For example, White U.S. undergraduates who had been led to believe that they had delivered a series of strong shocks to a victim derogated a Black victim more than a White victim, and this derogation was a function of the extent of ambivalence as reflected by measures of prejudice and sympathy toward Blacks. Whether racial ambivalence potentiates positive or negative responses depends on the situational context and the ambivalent person's behavioral options.

Ambivalent Sexism

Sexism, like racism, reflects ambivalence. Glick and Fiske (1996) viewed sexism as a multidimensional construct involving ambivalence. They proposed that *ambivalent sexism* comprises two positively correlated components: hostile sexism (HS) and benevolent sexism (BS). The former consists of hostility, negative attitudes, and negative stereotypes of women. By contrast, BS is a set of interrelated sexist attitudes that portray women stereotypically and in restricted roles but

that are subjectively positive in affective tone from the perceiver's viewpoint and elicit prosocial behaviors (e.g., helping) or intimacy seeking (e.g., self-disclosure). Benevolent sexism reflects a positive attitude toward women and positive stereotypes about women, although Glick and Fiske do not view it as a good thing. Although both HS and BS were originally postulated to include three underlying components, this conjecture was supported only for BS, while HS was found to be a unidimensional construct.

Both HS and BS relate, as one would expect, to other measures of modern sexism (Swim, Aikin, Hall, & Hunter, 1995) and neo-sexism (Tougas, Brown, Beaton, & Joly, 1995). Benevolent sexism, however, relates to subtler forms of sexism than HS, masked as it is in a veil of positive sentiment toward women. Glick and Fiske (1996) suggested that among women, BS reflects a tendency to adopt as one's own the prevalent forms of sexist prejudice in U.S. society. They also suggested that while modern- and neo-sexism measures excel in predicting gender-related political attitudes, HS and BS scales together (comprising the Ambivalent Sexism Inventory, or ASI) would be better at predicting attitudes and behavior in the realm of interpersonal and romantic relationships between women and men. As well, sexist ambivalence—the combination of scoring high on both BS and HS—is believed to polarize attitudes and behaviors toward women, in a process like that proposed by Katz, Haas, and their colleagues for amplified responses toward Black Americans and the physically handicapped as induced by ambivalence.

Blatant and Subtle Prejudice

The preceding ambivalence approaches differ in whether they assume that old-fashioned prejudice still exists or whether it is seen to be as potent as its modern or symbolic variants. For example, advocates of symbolic and modern racism suggest that it is the more dominant form of prejudice today. Other ambivalence approaches assume that both forms are prevalent and require assessment by researchers interested in prejudice. For example, Pettigrew and Meertens (1995) postulated the existence of both blatant and subtle prejudice toward out-groups today. They characterized blatant prejudice (the traditional form) as "hot, close, and direct" and suggested that it consisted of two components: (a) perceived threat and rejection of the out-group and (b) avoidance of intimacy (especially sex and marriage). By contrast, subtle prejudice (the modern variant) is "cool, distant, and indirect" and includes three components: (a) defense of traditional values, (b) exaggeration of cultural differences, and (c) denial of positive emotional responses toward out-groups.

Pettigrew and Meertens (1995) created separate multi-item scales for blatant and subtle prejudice toward immigrants and administered them to survey respondents from four European countries with regard to several different target groups. Across countries, confirmatory factor analyses suggested that two-factor models surpassed a one-factor model, but that a correlated two-factor model and a hierarchical model in which blatant and subtle prejudice were first-order factors subsumed under a general second-order factor were equally viable models to account for the pattern of scale scores.

An advantage of using both subtle and blatant prejudice scales is that a threefold typology emerged that yielded different patterns of responses to immigrants in Pettigrew and Meertens's (1995) research. Respondents who scored low on both blatant and subtle prejudice scales were called "equalitarians," a group who were most in favor of maintaining and enhancing immigrants' rights in their countries and who presumably have internalized most strongly contemporary norms of tolerance in their societies. Respondents scoring high on both scales comprised "bigots," who were most in favor of returning immigrants to their home countries and restricting immigrants' rights and were assumed to have rejected current norms against blatant prejudice. "Subtles" were respondents scoring low on blatant prejudice but high on subtle prejudice and were assumed to have only partially and incompletely internalized norms against blatant prejudice. On immigration issues, "subtles" adopted a middling, nonprejudicial stance between bigots and equalitarians and required justification for restricting immigrants' rights. The "subtles" category, of course, is the analogue to symbolic, modern, and aversive racism in that these people strive to appear nonprejudiced and are assumed to express their biases against immigrants in ways that do not violate current norms against blatant prejudice.

Automatic and Controlled Processing

The Dissociation Model

As noted earlier in discussing ambivalence approaches to prejudice, some prejudice researchers (e.g., Crosby et al., 1980; Dovidio & Gaertner, 1986) have suggested that most White Americans are prejudiced toward Black people and that subtle behaviors that individuals can less readily monitor and censor (e.g., helping, nonverbal behavior, reaction times to briefly presented stimuli) are better gauges of White Americans' true racial attitudes. In an influential contribution to the prejudice literature, Devine (1989) strongly challenged and countered this view. She claimed that it implied that

prejudiced beliefs and attitudes were unamenable to change, as well as that prejudice is an inevitable, unavoidable product of normal cognitive processes.

As an alternative, Devine (1989) proposed a dissociation model that emphasizes the importance of distinguishing between automatic versus controlled cognitive processing and the differentiation of stereotype activation versus personal beliefs. The automatic versus controlled processing distinction emerged in cognitive psychology during the 1970s and subsequently has become an increasingly important construct in social and personality psychology (see Bargh, 1989). Automatic processing refers to unintentional, nonconscious cognitive processing that occurs without effort or intention and is unlimited by cognitive capacity. By contrast, controlled cognitive processing refers to intentional, effortful, and goal-directed processing of information that is assumed to be under the person's awareness and control but subject to limitation by cognitive capacity (e.g., attentional limits). Applying this distinction to the relationship between stereotyping and prejudice, Devine (1989) suggested that *stereotype activation* was an automatic process that did not require intention, attention, or cognitive capacity on the part of a perceiver. Instead, whenever an appropriate cue is present, such as the appearance of a Black person or a symbolic representation of one, a White U.S. perceiver's stereotype of Black people should be activated automatically.

Devine (1989) proposed that common socialization experiences in late-20th-century America have led White people in the U.S. to become equally knowledgeable about the prevalent and generally negative stereotype of Black people, regardless of their personal levels of prejudice. As a consequence of this common knowledge, her dissociation model predicted that automatic activation of the stereotype would be equally strong and unavoidable for White U.S. perceivers, regardless of the extent of their personal prejudice toward Blacks.

Prejudiced and nonprejudiced White persons, however, were expected in the dissociation model to differ in their *personal beliefs* concerning Black people, and this difference in personal beliefs regarding Blacks should be manifested on cognitive tasks involving deliberate, controlled cognitive processing. Specifically, on such a task, nonprejudiced White persons should inhibit and override their negative cultural stereotype of Blacks because it conflicts with their egalitarian values and their personal beliefs and to replace the pejorative, Black stereotype with more positive perceptions and attributions of Black persons. On this latter point, Devine's (1989) analysis of nonprejudiced perceivers agrees with aversive racism and modern-symbolic racism theories in positing a conflict between core American values, on one hand, and a desire to avoid appearing prejudiced, on the other.

For prejudiced White persons, on the other hand, the cultural stereotype of Blacks and their personal beliefs about them are congruent with one another. Because they do not conflict, there would be little need for them to censor their negative personal beliefs concerning Black people. Thus, according to the dissociation model, White persons varying in prejudice toward Black people should differ on cognitive tasks involving controlled processing but not on tasks involving automatic processing.

Devine (1989) supported her dissociation model with three studies, in which the MRS served as the measure used to define high versus low levels of prejudice in White participants. One study demonstrated that on an open-ended measure, both high- and low-prejudice White participants listed very similar characteristics, and predominantly negative ones, when asked to describe the cultural stereotype of Black people—an effect since replicated by other investigators in the United States and the United Kingdom (e.g., Lepore & Brown, 1997). Another study deployed a controlled processing task by giving participants ample time to list alternative labels for "Black Americans" and then asking them to list all of their thoughts in response to this label. Thoughts on this listing task were categorized by judges as being positive beliefs, negative beliefs, or traits. Highly prejudiced White participants listed negative traits most often, while less prejudiced ones were more likely to list thoughts reflecting positive beliefs—uncontroverisal and unsurprising results.

In what has since become a more controversial study, however, Devine (1989) also compared reactions of White persons varying in prejudice on an automatic processing task in which participants were subliminally presented with word primes parafoveally (i.e., outside the central visual field) while performing a perceptual vigilance task. Word primes were related to the Black stereotype either 20% or 80% of the time and included reference both to the category Blacks and to stereotypic traits for Black Americans (e.g., lazy, poor, oppressed, etc.). Following this automatic processing task in which participants had been primed to varying extent with racially relevant stimuli, they read an ambiguous story about a male person of unspecified race performing various assertive behaviors and then rendered their impressions of him. As predicted by the dissociation model, impressions of the stimulus person were affected by the automatic processing task in that attributions of hostility were more likely when primes from the preceding automatic processing task had been proportionally more stereotypically oriented (i.e., in the 80% condition instead of the 20% one), with no difference as a function of the participants' level of prejudice.

From the preceding research, Devine (1989) concluded that controlled processing rather than automatic processing differentiates the highly prejudiced from their less prejudiced White counterparts. Moreover, White people with egalitarian ideals employ controlled processing to try to behave and think in an unprejudiced manner toward Black people. Both high- and low-prejudiced White Americans have the same stereotypic knowledge of Black people and are presumably both susceptible to having this stereotypic knowledge that is presumably elicited automatically beneath their awareness. However, stereotypic and prejudicial responses can be overridden by intentional and flexible controlled processing.

Deciding to be unprejudiced is, according to the dissociation model, a conscious, intentional act of controlled processing. Inhibiting and overriding stereotypic and prejudicial responses elicited by automatic activation processes and replacing them with more appropriate and positive beliefs toward Blacks and other minorities held by individuals seeking to be unprejudiced is akin, Devine has argued, to their "breaking a bad habit." That is, the White person trying to be unprejudiced toward Black people must consciously and deliberately decide to forego prejudicial beliefs and actions (the bad, old habit) and to replace them with new attitudes and behaviors consistent with an egalitarian outlook (the new, good habit). In essence, Devine's (1989) dissociation model suggests that for those seeking to be (or actually being) unprejudiced, automatic and controlled processes must become *dissociated* from one another, with the good habit of tolerance strengthened at the expense of the bad habit of prejudice.

Monteith (1993; Monteith, Devine, & Zuwerink, 1993; Monteith & Walters, 1998) and her colleagues (Devine & Monteith, 1999; Devine, Monteith, Zuwerink, & Elliot, 1991) have explored in depth the self-regulatory processes by which low-prejudice White Americans (i.e., those who score low on prejudice measures, such as the MRS) inhibit prejudiced responses and maintain egalitarian standards. First, low-prejudice Whites do indeed have personal beliefs and standards against expressing prejudice toward oppressed groups, such as Black people and homosexuals, but many of the former also acknowledge responding from time to time in ways that are more prejudiced than their personal beliefs would warrant. Second, when they do find themselves exhibiting a biased response toward an oppressed group member (i.e., what Monteith and her colleagues term a *prejudice-related discrepancy*), low-prejudice White Americans experience emotional responses in the form of guilt and negative, self-directed affect as well as increased self-focus and self-attention, and they subsequently monitor their behavior more carefully to ensure that it conforms more closely to their personal beliefs.

Critique of the Dissociation Model

The dissociation model's contention that prejudiced and unprejudiced perceivers would be equally responsive to priming by an automatic processing task has, however, been recently criticized and questioned by several investigators. Lepore and Brown (1997), for example, criticized Devine's (1989) automatic processing study for including both categorical cues referring to Blacks as a social group and stereotypic traits of Black people among the subliminal primes. As an alternative to the dissociation model, Lepore and Brown argued that the link between the category and the stereotypic features relating to Blacks differentiates White perceivers varying in prejudice, with the link being much stronger and more chronically accessible for highly prejudiced White persons than for less prejudiced ones. If only categorical cues referring to Blacks as a group comprise the subliminal primes on an automatic processing task, one should observe highly prejudiced White persons subsequently forming more negative impressions than less prejudiced ones—a result that Lepore and Brown (1997, Study 2), in fact, have obtained.

By contrast, subliminal cues that include stereotypic attributes along with the categorical label also prime the stereotypic knowledge of both high- and low-prejudice White perceivers, which has been shown to be highly similar. Thus, subliminal cues containing both category references and stereotypic attributes on an automatic processing task would *not* be expected to reveal differences between White persons varying in prejudice, a prediction that Lepore and Brown (1997, Study 3) also supported in a conceptual replication of Devine's (1989) automatic processing study. Null hypothesis predictions have been rife on the issue of automatic processing effects on impression formation as a function of the White participants' prejudice toward Blacks. Predicting the null hypothesis, however, is problematic because tests of such hypotheses often lack sufficient statistical power (see Cohen, 1992).

Kawakami, Dion, and Dovidio (1998) further reinforced Lepore and Brown's conceptual analysis in two ways. They found that high-prejudice White persons were more responsive to primes on a single task where automatic and controlled processing could both be experimentally manipulated by varying stimulus onset asynchrony (i.e., the difference in time between presentation of the prime and a subsequent, to-be-responded-to stimulus). Second, individual differences in stereotype attribution as assessed by a separate measure

correlated with stereotypic activation on the experimental task when it allowed automatic processing.

With regard to Devine's automatic processing findings, Fazio, Jackson, Dunton, and Williams (1995) have suggested that the MRS has become a reactive and insensitive measure of racial prejudice. Consistent with this point, they showed that the levels of modern racism in White American participants failed to moderate priming effects on a procedure (described later) that was designed to elicit automatic activation of racial attitudes.

Taken together, the preceding critiques of the dissociation model have important implications for prejudice and its reduction. According to Lepore and Brown's (1997) alternative perspective, low-prejudice White persons have never established the bad habit of prejudice toward Black people in the first place or established it much less firmly than their highly prejudiced White counterparts. For low-prejudice White persons, the link between the social category, Blacks, and the culturally stereotypic information about them is already weak and tenuous. Rather than unlearning a bad habit, those interested in reducing prejudice in White people presumably need to focus on the highly prejudiced Whites and on weakening the associative strength of the links between the category of Blacks as a social group and negative stereotypic information and content about them.

Automatic Activation as Prejudice Measures

Automatic activation techniques are a means of unobtrusively measuring racial and other intergroup attitudes and an alternative to traditional attitude scales, which are often compromised by social desirability and transparency regarding the goal of assessing prejudice. Even the MRS has recently been shown to be sensitive to social desirability, yielding lower scores from White participants when administered by a Black experimenter than by a White one (Fazio et al., 1995, Study 3). From their findings in several studies, Fazio et al. (1995) have styled the MRS as a measure of White Americans' "willingness to express" negative feelings or opinions about Blacks, one that also confounds racism with political conservatism. Other researchers have noted that correlations between old-fashioned and modern and symbolic racism are higher than would be expected if these were truly two separate constructs rather than different aspects of a single construct (see Dovidio et al., 1997; Swim et al., 1995).

As an alternative, Fazio et al. (1995) proposed a priming paradigm using automatic activation of attitudes from memory as an unobtrusive measure of racial attitudes that is demonstrably superior to the MRS. The priming procedure consists of multiple trials on a computer in which the prime consists of a symbolic representation of the attitude object, such as digitized photos of stimulus persons from one or more racial groups. Immediately following the prime, a target in the form of a positive or negative evaluative adjective is displayed, and the participant is required to indicate its connotation as either good or bad by pressing different computer keys. When the prime and target are evaluatively congruent for the participant, responding should be facilitated as manifested in a faster, more efficient reaction time. By contrast, when prime and target are evaluatively incongruent with one another from the viewpoint of the participant, responding should be slowed, as reflected by a longer reaction time.

Using this priming procedure, Fazio et al. (1995) showed in several studies that White U.S. university students showed greater facilitation when negative adjectives were preceded by photos of Black people. By contrast, a small sample of Black participants showed response facilitation on the priming task when photos of Blacks preceded positive adjectives and when White photos were preceded by negative adjectives. Moreover, scores on this unobtrusive measure of racial attitudes had predictive validity for a Black experimenter's ratings of the participant's friendliness and interest when interacting with her, to which MRS scores were unrelated.

Along similar lines, Greenwald, McGhee, and Schwartz (1998) suggested the Implicit Association Test (IAT) as a related procedure for assessing implicit attitudes, defined as behaviors, feelings, or thoughts elicited outside the participant's awareness by automatically activated evaluation procedures (see Greenwald & Banaji, 1995). The IAT consists of a series of five discrimination tasks, conducted on computer, in which the participants differentiate between two categories of stimuli by responding as quickly as possible on different computer keys.

If one were assessing White attitudes toward Black people with the IAT, the first task would be an initial target-concept discrimination in which they might be asked to differentiate between White and Black American first names by pressing different keys on the computer. The second task is an associated attribute discrimination in which the participant differentiates pleasant from unpleasant words. The third step is the initial combined task in which the two prior tasks are now superimposed or mapped onto one another, such as using one key for individual stimuli that are either White or pleasant and another key for stimuli that are either Black or unpleasant. In the fourth step, the response keys from the first task are reversed. The fifth and final step, the reverse combined task, reverses the response key contingencies from the third step (e.g., one key for stimuli that are either White or unpleasant or either Black or pleasant. The difference in speed of responding to the two combined tasks on the IAT

provides the measure of implicit attitudes. Following the earlier example, a latency shorter for the first combined task than for the reverse combined task would suggest a less positive or more negative implicit attitude toward Blacks by a White participant.

Using the IAT, Greenwald and Banaji (1998) found evidence that it may reveal the existence of prejudice that is not evident on paper-and-pencil attitude measures such as the semantic differential scale. Whereas a majority of a sample of White American participants in one study indicated no Black-White difference or even a pro-Black preference on paper-and-pencil ratings, all but one had IAT scores indicating a White preference, presumably a nonconscious one. Greenwald and his colleagues have also found modest positive correlations between IAT scores and some "explicit" attitude measures such as the feeling thermometer (in which social groups are rated on a 100-point thermometer scale) and a diversity index but not others, especially semantic differential scales. IAT scores, they suggested, do not merely reflect greater familiarity with one's in-group (e.g., naming practices, facial stimuli) compared to an out-group. The IAT procedure, they also proposed, yields stronger effect sizes and is therefore more sensitive than the priming procedure devised by Fazio et al. (1995) and by other investigators.

One would not necessarily expect implicit and explicit measures of racial attitudes to correlate highly with one another. Demonstrating this point, Dovidio, Kawakami, Johnson, Johnson, and Howard (1997) showed that the predictive validity of implicit (i.e., elicited by automatic processing techniques, such as priming or the IAT) and explicit measures of racial attitudes (i.e., elicited by self-report measures such as scales of modern and old-fashioned racism) of White participants toward Black people diverges in a predictable manner. Specifically, implicit prejudice measures predicted spontaneous cognitions and behaviors that are not easily monitored but reflect automatic processing, such as performance on a word-completion task in which answers may be racially tinged or nonverbal behavior such as eye blinking or direct gaze when interacting with a Black person. By contrast, explicit prejudice measures possessed predictive validity for deliberative thoughts and actions that reflect controlled processing, such as judgments of a Black defendant's guilt in a juridic decision-making task and evaluations.

Fazio et al. (1995) had previously obtained a similar pattern of findings. Their unobtrusive priming measure of prejudice in Whites had predictive validity for rated quality of interaction with a Black experimenter, whereas explicit measures predicted deliberative acts such as attractiveness ratings of photos and evaluations of the fairness of the Rodney King verdict (in which White police officers in Los Angeles were exonerated from charges of using excessive force with a Black defendant). Both explicit and implicit measures predicted attributions of responsibility for the causes of rioting following the Rodney King verdict. Thus, implicit attitude measures add an important, new, and separate dimension to the conceptual and methodological toolbox that psychologists have to assess prejudice.

To summarize, both automatic and controlled cognitive processing play an important role in the social psychology of bigotry. Racial stimuli presented below or just above the threshold of awareness operate as primes that influence thinking and behavior by White persons toward members of a stereotyped group such as Blacks. If the racial prime includes only reference to the social category, automatic activation will activate stronger stereotypes among the more highly prejudiced Whites than among the less prejudiced. If the racial prime includes both categorical reference as well as stereotypic trait information, differences on dependent measures (e.g., impression formation) between participants differing in levels of prejudice by Whites will usually no longer be apparent.

An important development for automatic processing techniques has been their utilization for assessing prejudice, avoiding problems with standard attitude measures of prejudice such as social desirability, and deliberately masking one's negative feelings toward specific groups. These techniques, such as the priming methodology as well as the IAT, will undoubtedly be increasingly utilized to assess individuals' nonconscious prejudices, with the resulting measures being especially helpful in predicting behaviors and cognitions toward out-group members that an individual cannot easily monitor and censor.

Integrative Approaches

The rubric of integrative approaches includes perspectives on prejudice that include the insights of multiple theoretical viewpoints concerning the psychology of bigotry that their advocates have organized into a single, coherent, explanatory framework. By incorporating multiple perspectives, each integrative approach becomes a broad, comprehensive explanation of prejudice. Social dominance theory, integrated threat theory, and a multicomponent approach to intergroup attitudes exemplify integrative approaches to prejudice.

Social Dominance Theory

Social dominance theory (SDT) assumes that societies are structured as group-based social hierarchies, with one or a small number of dominant or hegemonic groups at the top of the social structure and at least one subordinate group below them (Sidanius, Levin, Rabinowitz, & Federico, 1999; Sidanius & Pratto, 1999). In general, dominant group members disproportionately enjoy society's goods and benefits (i.e., wealth, status, and power), whereas subordinate group members suffer a disproportionate share of society's miseries and inequities (i.e., poverty, low prestige, and relative powerlessness).

In group-based social hierarchies, individual's stations in life are determined largely by their membership in socially constructed groups defined by race, gender, age, religion, social class, and so on. Group-based hierarchies are assumed to be highly stable, often reflecting consensus as to which groups are dominant and subordinate, respectively. For example, perceived social standing of U.S. ethnic groups in 1964 and later in 1989 correlated almost perfectly across the quarter century (Sidanius & Pratto, 1999). SDT defines three types of social stratification systems: an age system where adults and older individuals command more resources and power than the younger, a gender system in which men possess greater status and power than women, and an arbitrary set system in which socially constructed, arbitrarily defined categories (e.g., races, occupations, social classes, nationalities) enjoy disproportionately more status and power over other socially constructed categories. SDT concentrates especially on gender and arbitrary set systems of group-based hierarchy.

Whereas age and gender systems of group hierarchy are assumed by SDT to be universal across human societies, arbitrary set hierarchies differ in several regards. First, they display more definitional fluidity across time period and countries. Sidanius and Pratto (1999), the principal architects of SDT, claimed that arbitrary set hierarchies emerge only in societies that produce an economic surplus. Arbitrary set hierarchies tend to be dynastic with social status passing on to one's children. Finally, arbitrary set hierarchies are presumably maintained more by terror, violence, and brutality than by age- and gender-based hierarchies.

Three basic assumptions of SDT are as follows: (a) Most intergroup conflict and oppression reflect a predisposition toward forming group-based social hierarchy; (b) social systems are prone to hierarchy-enhancing (HE) forces pushing toward greater inequality, and opposing effects of hierarchy-attenuating (HA) forces toward greater equality; and (c) conflict between HE and HA forces produces relatively stable social systems.

From these assumptions SDT concerns itself with the mechanisms that contribute to group-based social hierarchy and with how hierarchies affect these mechanisms. Behavioral asymmetry is one mechanism. The notion of behavioral asymmetry is that the behavioral repertoires of dominant and subordinate group members differ and that these differences contribute to the hierarchical relationships among these groups. Four types of behavioral asymmetries are asymmetrical in-group bias, systematic out-group favoritism or deference, self-debilitating behavior, and ideological asymmetry.

Regarding in-group bias (i.e., favoring one's own group over other groups), dominants show more than do subordinates. This asymmetrical in-group bias reinforces the hegemonic group's dominance over the subordinate group. By contrast, deference, or out-group favoritism, is more apt to be shown by members of the subordinate group, again reinforcing the dominant group's hegemony. Self-debilitation occurs when subordinate group members engage in more self-defeating and self-destructive behavior, such as criminal activity or drugs, than do dominant group members. Ideological asymmetry refers to the idea the antiegalitarian values lead one to endorse policies and ideologies promoting group-based inequality, such as support for the death penalty in the United States, which dominant group members endorse more strongly than do subordinate group members.

The degree of group-based social inequality is also influenced by support for various legitimizing myths (LMs). These are ideologies that provide moral or intellectual justifications for group-based social hierarchies within all three hierarchical systems (age, gender, or arbitrary set). SDT defines two types of LMs based on whether they facilitate social inequality and are HE or facilitate social equality and are HA. Racism, sexism, and ageism exemplify HE-LMs, while feminism, socialism, and universalism are HA-LM examples.

The psychological aspect of SDT is the construct of social dominance orientation (SDO) as assessed by an eponymous scale. SDO is a personality dimension defined as an attitude toward intergroup relations reflecting antiegalitarianism and intolerance, at one end, to support for group-based hierarchy and the domination of inferior groups by superior groups, at the opposite end. A high score on the SDO scale reflects a willingness to accept inequalities between and among groups in society. Items in the SDO scale refer to groups in the abstract and thus tap the respondent's acceptance of intergroup inequalities for whatever group distinctions are salient to the respondent in a given sociopolitical or national context.

SDO scale scores have been shown to relate to many political attitudes (e.g., political conservatism, nationalism, patriotism), legitimizing ideologies (e.g., racism, sexism, belief in fate), social attributions (e.g., internal vs. external attributions for the fate of the poor), HE/HA career choices (e.g., police officers vs. teachers), and group evaluations (see Sidanius et al., 1999; Sidanius & Pratto, 1999). In Saucier's (2000, p. 378) study of the structure of social attitudes, SDO

loaded with Machiavellianism on a dimension defined as "favoring whatever is immediately beneficial to me and mine, disregarding wider concerns of fairness or morality," which was separate from the factor on which authoritarianism loaded on.

Focusing on prejudice specifically, Whitley (1999) has shown that (a) SDO predicted most forms of prejudice toward Black Americans and homosexuals in a sample of White, heterosexual U.S. university students and (b) SDO also mediated gender differences in those prejudices in that sample. According to Sidanius, Pratto, and their colleagues, SDO also shows discriminant validity in being relatively independent of other constructs such as conservatism, interpersonal dominance, and right-wing authoritarianism, although Altemeyer (1996) reported a moderate, positive correlation between RWA and SDO. Consistent with the notion that attitudes toward group hierarchy reflected in the SDO scale are culturally universal, Pratto et al. (2000) showed that with proper translation and back translation, SDO can be reliably measured cross-culturally, and its scores related in theoretically predicted ways to sexism, prejudice toward oppressed groups by majority group members, and related attitudes (e.g., support for the military) for samples of respondents in several countries outside North America, including Israel, Taiwan, and the People's Republic of China (Shanghai), as well as Canada.

Advocates of SDT have suggested that the SDO construct can account for the relationships between conservatism and racism and between conservatism and antimiscegenation (i.e., a disdain for interracial marriages) in terms of their mutual dependence on SDO (see Sidanius & Pratto, 1999). Advocates of SDT also believe that individual differences in SDO are determined by four factors: group status, gender, socialization, and temperament. First, the greater the social status of one's in-group in a given society, the higher is one's level of SDO. In the United States, for example, White Americans outscore Black Americans in SDO. In Israel, Ashkenazi (European ancestry) Jews have higher SDOs than Sephardic (North-African or Middle Eastern ancestry) Jews. Second, the single most reliable finding of SDT research is that with a few exceptions in cultures outside North America (see Pratto et al., 2000), males outscore females on SDO. Socialization experiences, such as education, are also assumed to affect SDO, with higher educational levels relating inversely to SDO. Finally, higher SDO scores correlate with lower empathy levels and greater aggressivity—temperamental features that are presumably heritable and that promote out-group prejudice.

Advocates of SDT view it as a theoretical perspective linking the individual and the social structure together in the explanation of prejudice, and one that provides a comprehensive explanation for the oppression of subordinate groups by dominant ones in human societies around the world. As such, its advocates claim that SDT complements and integrates theories of prejudice focusing on the individual, such as the right-wing authoritarianism theory (see Altemeyer, 1996; Whitley, 1999), and those focusing on the role of social structure and elites, such as Marxism, as well as providing a theoretical bridge between these micro and macro levels of analysis.

Proponents of SDT have also noted some differences between their perspective and other theories of prejudice and racism. Sidanius et al. (1999) suggested that symbolic racism is limited to focusing on racism toward Black Americans in one historical and cultural context (viz., the United States in the late 20th century), whereas SDT claims a much wider historical and cross-cultural focus as well as a broader sweep regarding oppressed groups around the world to which it presumably applies. In fact, however, some evidence suggests that U.S.-derived measures of prejudice, especially blatant and subtle prejudice, work as well in Europe as they do in the United States (Pettigrew et al., 1998). Similarly, while symbolic and modern racism theories focus on values such as individualism and the Protestant ethic, SDT instead emphasizes *anti*egalitarianism as crucial to prejudice.

Its proponents also suggest that SDT complements intergroup theories, such as social identity theory (SIT), by taking into account the attitudes and behaviors of subordinate group members as well as those from the dominant group, focusing on out-group derogation as well as in-group favoritism, and differentiating status and power in intergroup relations. Indeed, researchers have profitably used both SDT and SIT (e.g., Levin & Sidanius, 1999; Levin, Sidanius, Rabinowitz, & Federico, 1998) to yield insights into intergroup processes, such as the relationship between in-group identification and SDO in high-status versus low-status groups in a society. Clearly, SDT is presently one of the most prominent and promising contemporary theories of prejudice, and the SDO measure is apt to become a scale of choice among those who wish to use an explicit prejudice measure instead of, or along with, implicit prejudice measures.

Integrated Threat Theory

Without claiming to incorporate all possible causes of prejudice, Walter Stephan, Cookie Stephan, and their colleagues have nevertheless proposed that threat is certainly one major class of its causes and arguably its principal one. Their integrated threat theory (ITT) identifies and combines four major types of threat that they and other investigators have previously documented as relevant to understanding and predicting prejudice: (a) realistic threats, (b) symbolic threats, (c) intergroup anxiety, and (d) stereotyping (e.g., Stephan & Stephan, 1996; Stephan, Ybarra, & Bachman, 1999). Although other theories and investigators have emphasized one or another of these threats, the Stephans and their associates provide a distinctive twist or interpretation of each threat in the overall context of ITT.

Realistic threats include any perceived threats from another group to the welfare, well-being, or survival of one's in-group and its members. Symbolic threats are perceived group differences in beliefs, values, or norms that may threaten the in-group's way of life. Unlike symbolic racism, ITT's symbolic threats apply to a wider array of groups, both dominant and subordinate, and to value differences in general, rather than those typifying only U.S. society, such as the Protestant ethic. The intergroup anxiety construct derives from prior research by Stephan and Stephan (1985), referring to the negative emotions occurring when one interacts with members of another group, especially an antagonistic or competitive out-group. Beliefs about the characteristics of groups and the traits of group members (i.e., stereotypes) constitute yet another threat by creating expectancies about the type of interactions that can be anticipated with out-group members, with negative expectancies reflecting prejudice. Finally, in addition to the four types of threat, ITT also assumes that the history and nature of prior contact between groups (e.g., negative, positive, or mixed) and the status of groups relative to one another also needs to be taken into account for predicting prejudice.

Immigrants are assumed by ITT to elicit all four types of threat in members of immigrant-receiving societies, such as the United States, Spain, and Israel. For that reason, attitudes toward immigrant groups have figured prominently as a criterion of particular interest in ITT research. Using samples of university students at several locales throughout the United States, Stephan, Ybarra, and Bachman (1999) showed that all four threats were relevant for predicting prejudice toward Cubans (in Miami), Mexicans (in New Mexico), and Asians (in Hawaii), accounting for 50% or more of the variance in attitudes toward each of these different immigrant groups. Stephan, Ybarra, Martinez, Schwarzwald, and Tur-Kaspa (1998) likewise showed that each of the four threats was a reliable predictor of attitudes held by Spanish university students toward Moroccan immigrants and by Israeli students toward Ethiopian and Russian immigrants to Israel.

Structural equation modeling (SEM) analyses by Stephan et al. (1998) indicated that the four threats comprised a single, unitary dimension of threat. Schwarzwald and Tur-Kaspa (1997) showed that realistic, symbolic, and interpersonal threats were significant predictors of Israeli university students' attitudes toward Ethiopian and Russian immigrants, whereas individual differences in SDO predicted prejudice toward Ethiopian immigrants only. By exploring women's attitudes toward men, Stephan, Stephan, Demitrakis, Yamada, and Clason (2000) showed that ITT is useful for target groups other than immigrants and for attitudes of members of subordinate or oppressed groups as well as dominant ones. Stephan et al. found that for women, symbolic threat, intergroup anxiety, and negative contact were predictors of negative attitudes toward men; however, contrary to prediction, realistic threats failed to emerge as a reliable predictor.

Because the preceding research on ITT is correlational in nature, it does not and cannot conclusively document that the causal sequence goes only from perceived threat to prejudice and not the other way or in both directions. However, Maio, Esses, and Bell (1994) experimentally manipulated perceived realistic and symbolic threats and found increased prejudice toward immigrants, thus validating at least the proposed causal sequence of threats heightening prejudice that lies at the core of ITT, at least for that target group.

Assessment of different types of threat has potential utility for those interested in improving intergroup relations. In studies in which attitudes toward more than one target group are assessed from an ITT perspective, one may explore which target group may deserve more attention in ameliorative efforts (for an example, see Schwarzwald & Tur-Kaspa, 1997). Similarly, in the aforementioned studies of ITT, some but usually not all types of threat emerged as significant predictors, suggesting where change attempts might profitably focus. For example, in attitudes of U.S. university students toward Mexican immigrants, intergroup anxiety has emerged as the most reliable predictor (Stephan & Stephan, 1996; Ybarra & Stephan, 1994). ITT is, therefore, especially useful for those interested in reducing as well as understanding prejudice (see the chapter on reducing prejudice by Dovidio in this volume).

The Multicomponent Approach to Intergroup Attitudes

The multicomponent approach to intergroup attitudes (MAIA), proposed by Esses, Haddock, and Zanna (1993; see also Haddock et al., 1993; Zanna, 1994), is the final example of an integrative theoretical approach to be considered. Although MAIA was derived independently from ITT, the two perspectives clearly resemble one another in their mutual emphases on symbolic beliefs and emotional reactions to out-groups as important predictors of prejudice and also in a shared interest in determining if and when stereotypes of out-groups will relate to prejudice toward them.

MAIA presumes that an intergroup attitude, like the attitude concept in general, has several components (viz., evaluations, cognitions, and affect). An attitude toward a social group is an overall evaluation, either positive or negative.

Esses and her colleagues use the feeling thermometer as their preferred measure of an intergroup attitude as a global evaluation. The goal of MAIA is to predict prejudice and intergroup attitudes, relying mainly on cognitive and affective factors as the key predictors. Stereotypes and symbolic beliefs constitute MAIA's cognitive factors. Stereotypes are beliefs about the characteristics of groups, both those shared with other perceivers (i.e., a consensual stereotype) and those unique to a given perceiver (a personal stereotype), with personal stereotypes assumed by MAIA researchers to be more useful to predict prejudice than consensual stereotypes. Symbolic beliefs are a person's ideas as to how a social group hinders or facilitates her or his core values and norms. In the MAIA the affective component consists of the specific feelings and emotions evoked by a social group (see also Esses, Haddock, & Zanna, 1994). To assess personal stereotypes, symbolic beliefs, and emotions toward one or more groups, MAIA researchers typically employ open-ended measures in which respondents first list their thoughts and feelings toward a specified group and then go over their lists in order to rate the valence of each entry and the percentage of the social group believed to be characterized by it.

In their initial studies MAIA researchers explored attitudes among English-Canadian university respondents in Ontario toward several social groups: English-Canadians, French-Canadians, Native Indians, Pakistanis, and homosexuals (see Esses et al., 1993). The MAIA model successfully predicted attitudes toward the out-groups. Attitudes toward Pakistanis and homosexuals were best predicted by symbolic beliefs, a component of intergroup attitudes believed to be important for assessing prejudice toward disliked or unfavorable groups. By contrast, out-groups more favorably regarded by the English-Canadian respondents (viz., French-Canadians and Native Indians) were best predicted by emotions.

Esses et al. (1993) also showed that RWA is an important moderator of out-group attitudes and their subcomponents. English-Canadian respondents scoring high on RWA had consistently more negative attitudes toward all four out-groups, especially the disfavored groups, and symbolic beliefs were their single best predictor of attitudes toward different groups, including French-Canadians. By contrast, emotions best predicted the more favorable out-group attitudes of those scoring low on RWA.

These conclusions, particularly regarding homosexuals as a target group, were further reinforced in two studies by Haddock et al. (1993). Their first study confirmed the more negative attitude of high RWA scorers toward homosexuals and the importance of symbolic beliefs in predicting prejudice toward homosexuals. Their second study replicated and extended these findings by showing that for those scoring high on RWA, past experience and perceived value dissimilarity were additional factors along with symbolic beliefs that were useful in predicting their prejudicial attitude toward homosexuals.

Because intergroup attitudes can be ambivalent rather than uniformly positive or negative, Esses and her colleagues extended their open-ended techniques to assess attitudinal ambivalence toward various social groups. In one study, Bell, Esses, and Maio (1996) assessed evaluations, stereotypes, symbolic beliefs, and emotions that a sample of English-Canadian university students in Ontario felt toward Native People, French-Canadians, Canadians, and Oriental immigrants. Respondents were more ambivalent toward Native People than Canadians or Oriental immigrants, with French-Canadians in between. Correlations between average ambivalence scores and an overall summary evaluation of each group showed that ambivalence was unrelated to attitude toward Native Peoples but negatively related to attitudes for the other groups, especially French-Canadians. Because MAIA takes into account ambivalence in intergroup attitudes, it could also qualify as an ambivalence approach to prejudice.

Conclusion

As perhaps the ultimate form of an integrative approach to the psychology of bigotry, one could ask what a general theory of prejudice would look like. In reviewing the literature on theories of racism and their own research on values and prejudice, Biernat, Vescio, Theno, and Crandall (1996) outlined just such a general theory of prejudice. A general theory, they suggested, should seek to predict or explain prejudice by oppressors toward an array of potential target groups, such as Blacks, homosexuals, ethnic groups, women, and so on in the United States and in other countries. They also generated a list of factors that promote prejudice. From racism and belief congruence theories (as well as SDT, ITT, and MAIA, it might be added), these prejudice-promoting factors include negative affect toward Blacks (and other groups), prototypic values such as antiegalitarianism, individualism, and the Protestant ethic, the perception that members of groups who are the target of prejudice violate cherished beliefs and values, as well as normative and contextual cues that condone or permit prejudice and discrimination. Other contributing factors, they noted, would include known correlates of prejudice, such as an authoritarian personality (especially RWA) and attributional styles in perceivers that lead them to attribute negative outcomes confronting oppressed people to internal, controllable causes rather than external ones.

To their list of factors promoting prejudice should also be added individual differences in aggressiveness and social dominance orientation, realistic threats, and situational cues that prime and stimulate negative out-group attitudes, both subliminally and supraliminally. In addition, unconscious processes of the types specified by the OTAP and automatic processing approaches to prejudice would also need to be taken into account. On the other hand, humanitarian and egalitarian values, internal motivation to avoid prejudice, and empathy and sympathetic identification with the underdog would help to counteract prejudice and its expression.

This outline for a general theory of prejudice summarizes well the insights of psychology's best theories for understanding prejudice at the dawn of the twenty-first century. It highlights ambiguities that future research might try to resolve, such as whether egalitarian values promote or counter prejudice or both, depending on yet other factors. Finally, it is perhaps useful as a heuristic device for designing and executing studies of prejudice, with an eye to evaluating the relative power of promotive and counteractive factors and assessing their unique predictive power and interactions. Illustrating just such an approach is the research by Biernat, Vescio, Theno, and Crandall (1996), which (among other things) included measures of core American values, prejudice scales, supraliminal priming of values, and experimental variations in value violation by attitude targets representing (in different studies) variations in race, sexual orientation, and weight status.

Having completed a review of prejudice from the perspective of the bigot, I now consider the psychology of prejudice from the viewpoint of the victim or target.

THE PSYCHOLOGY OF THE VICTIM OF PREJUDICE AND DISCRIMINATION

Psychologists have long been interested in the effects of discrimination on members of oppressed groups. One early approach to exploring this question was to assess samples of oppressed individuals on psychological measures as a means of exploring the impact of oppression. Kardiner and Ovesey (1951), for example, used psychoanalytic interviews and responses to projective tests such as the thematic apperception test (TAT) and the Rorschach to assess the "mark of oppression" among Black Americans. Similarly, Karon (1975) compared samples of White respondents and northern versus southern Black respondents in the United States on a modified version of the Tomkins-Horn Picture Arrangement Test (PAT), a projective test for assessing personality. Although both studies showed evidence of the stigma of being Black in the United States, they did not link it clearly to experiences of discrimination encountered by their respondents.

Attributional Ambiguity Perspectives

Beginning in the 1970s, research on the psychology of being a victim of prejudice and discrimination changed in several important ways (see Dion, Earn, & Yee, 1978). First, it shifted toward an experimental approach in which discrimination experiences were manipulated by investigators in the psychological laboratory by creating conditions in which participants from stigmatized groups either could or could not attribute a negative outcome to prejudice on the part of others (an attributional ambiguity paradigm) or were explicitly given the odds that their failure was due to discrimination by allegedly biased judges of their performance (the base rate paradigm). Second, these experimentally oriented researchers often adopted a viewpoint stressing the attributional ambiguity of being a target of prejudice (see Crocker & Major, 1989; Crocker, Major, & Steele, 1998; Dion, 1975, 1986; Dion & Earn, 1975; Dion et al., 1978).

According to an attributional ambiguity perspective, instances of encountering prejudice or discrimination are often ambiguous. For example, Black Americans who encounter a rejection from a White American confront an attributional dilemma to explain the situation and must decide whether the rejection is due to something about themselves (i.e., a personal characteristic) or to something about the person rejecting them (e.g., a prejudicial bias or a discriminatory reaction against Blacks). Attributional ambiguity perspectives emphasize that the type of attributions that a victim of prejudice or discrimination makes in such a situation (i.e., an internal attribution to the self, an external attribution of perceived prejudice or discrimination, or perhaps both) has a psychological impact on the victim's self-evaluations and affective reactions.

Attributions of Prejudice and Self-Esteem

Dion (1975) provided the first suggestive evidence for a link between attributions of prejudice and self-esteem in an experiment where university women competed against several opponents in a laboratory setting, who they were led to believe were either all male or all female; and the women themselves were made to fail either mildly or severely. Following experimentally induced failure, the women rated themselves on positive and negative traits comprising the female stereotype and self-esteem traits and indicated to what extent their opponents were biased and prejudiced against them. From this latter measure, women were further categorized into high- versus low-perceived prejudice groups, with perceived prejudice taken as an additional independent variable along with the experimental variables of alleged sex of the opponents and severity of failure (i.e., an internal analysis).

Unsurprisingly, the greater the failure, the lower was the women's subsequent self-esteem. However, perceived prejudice moderated this effect and apparently mitigated the impact of severe failure in decreasing women's self-esteem. Specifically, women who experienced severe failure with male opponents and perceived it as reflecting sexist prejudice showed higher self-regard than did those who did not see their putative male opponents as prejudiced. Dion (1975) interpreted this finding as suggesting that perceived prejudice or discrimination may not inevitably lower self-esteem in the victim. Rather, under some circumstances the attribution of prejudice may sustain self-esteem by enabling the minority or subordinate group member to attribute a negative experience to prejudice by others toward an arbitrary trait (i.e., their group membership) rather than to their own personal qualities as an individual.

In an important theoretical statement and elaboration of the attributional ambiguity perspective, Crocker and Major (1989) reviewed the then-existing literature and outlined several ways that members of stigmatized groups could protect their self-concepts in the face of a negative experience. For example, a stigmatized group member could interpret the negative encounter as due to prejudice or discrimination toward their group. Alternatively, they could protect themselves from invidious comparisons with privileged majority group members by comparing their outcomes to their own in-group rather than to the out-group and by focusing on those dimensions on which their group exceeds the dominant out-group. Major and Schmader (1998) have added psychological disengagement to the list of ways in which stigmatized group members may psychologically insulate and protect themselves from prejudice and discrimination. Miller and Kaiser (2001a, 2001b) recently outlined the wide variety of responses that those who are discriminated against may employ to protect themselves, drawing from the literature on coping and stress as well as attachment theory for insights.

Crocker and Major (1993) qualified the conditions under which attributing negative outcomes to prejudice could buttress one's self-esteem: namely, when the stigma was perceived as legitimate, justifiable, or controllable and legitimizing beliefs supported the stigmatized group's lower status, or when other important beliefs were threatened by attributions of prejudice. Crocker, Cornwell, and Major (1993) supported this reasoning in a subsequent experiment in which obese women were rejected by an attractive male confederate as a potential date. Although the obese women attributed the negative outcome to their weight, they did not attribute it to the male rater or to his prejudice. Crocker et al. interpreted the lower self-esteem by obese women to the fact that obesity is widely seen as a controllable stigma, which legitimizes and justifies prejudice and bias toward the overweight. The stigma of obesity, however, applies more to White than to Black American women (Hebl & Heatherton, 1998).

Crocker, Major, and their colleagues have also conducted experimental tests of the attributional ambiguity perspective with groups that regard prejudice and discrimination toward them as illegitimate. Crocker, Voelkl, Testa, and Major (1991) focused on sex and race in separate experiments in order to explore the potential buffering effects of perceived prejudice on self-esteem. Their study with White U.S. university women as participants succeeded in experimentally varying their attributions to prejudice on the part of a sexist man evaluating an essay of theirs negatively; however, the trait measure of global self-esteem failed to yield reliable differences as a function of perceived prejudice, though the mood measure followed the prediction of a self-protective function for attributions of prejudice.

Crocker et al. (1991) reported finding evidence for the buffering effects of perceived prejudice on self-esteem with Black American participants who had received either positive or negative interpersonal feedback from a White evaluator. These participants believed that the White evaluator either could see them from another room and was thus aware of their race or could not see them because of a drawn blind and hence was unaware of their race. Black participants who thought they could be seen by a White evaluator and had attributed the evaluator's feedback to prejudice showed less of a pretest-posttest difference in self-esteem than when they thought that the White evaluator could not see them. In other words, in the condition where prejudice was attributed, Black participants appeared to discount the negative feedback from a White evaluator, with the consequence that their self-esteem was left unchanged. They also discounted positive feedback when the White evaluator could allegedly see them and showed decreased self-esteem in that condition.

The classic book *Black Like Me,* in which White author James Griffin (1961) described his experiences posing as a Black man in the U.S. South of the 1950s, had suggested a similar process among Black Americans. Recalling an instance of racial discrimination he had experience, he noted, "The Negro's only salvation . . . lies in his belief, the old belief of his fore fathers, that these things are not directed against him personally, but against his race, his pigmentation. His mother or aunt or teacher long ago carefully prepared him, explaining that '. . . they don't do it to you because you're Johnny—they don't even know you. They do it against your Negro-ness'" (p. 48). In the United States, Black Americans are considerably more likely to be targets of prejudice and discrimination than are members of other minority or subordinate groups. Perhaps as a consequence of this greater victimization now and in the past, Black Americans have developed through ethnic group socialization the strategy of discounting negative (and perhaps positive) feedback from White majority group members and attributing negative feedback to prejudice as a means of coping and sustaining their self-esteem.

Some investigators (e.g., Branscombe & Ellemers, 1998; Kobrynowicz & Branscombe, 1997), however, have questioned whether Crocker et al. (1991) actually succeeded in demonstrating the buffering effects of attributing prejudice on self-esteem with their Black participants. Branscombe and Ellemers (1998) have instead suggested that in-group identification is a necessary mediator between the attribution of prejudice for experiences of oppression and self-esteem for Black American men and women as well as other minority groups in the United States, such as Native Americans and Hispanic-Americans. The greater the in-group identification, the more likely that attributions of prejudice for experiences of discrimination or oppression will be associated with the maintenance and retention of high self-esteem.

Protective Benefits for Majority Group Members

Of course, even members of dominant, hegemonic groups can and sometimes do avail themselves of the self-protective benefits of perceiving themselves and their group as being discriminated against, but apparently without the same psychological dilemma and tradeoff confronting members of oppressed groups. Kobrynowicz and Branscombe (1997) argued that certain members of structurally privileged groups, such as White American men whose self-esteem may be low or otherwise vulnerable, may exaggerate estimates of perceived discrimination against their group as a means of bolstering their self-esteem. Consistent with this perspective, a sample of White men scoring low in self-esteem were especially prone to perceive themselves and their group as having been discriminated against on the basis of gender. Likewise, Branscombe (1998) showed that asking men to contemplate their group's disadvantage on the basis of gender led to *higher* self-esteem, whereas thinking about their group's advantages produced decreases on group-related well-being. By contrast, women contemplating their group's disadvantages scored *lower* in reported self-esteem. Thus, the self-protective effect of attributing one's failure to discrimination is apparently even more evident among dominant majority group members and has positive benefits for both their self-esteem and their sense of control.

The Personal-Group Discrimination Discrepancy

Research originally conducted in the tradition of relative deprivation theory has suggested that individuals in subordinate and oppressed groups typically perceive more group discrimination than personal discrimination. Specifically, in testing models of egoistic relative deprivation (defined later), Crosby (1982) observed that members of a sample of working women in Massachusetts believed that they, as individual women, were personally less deprived and discriminated against in terms of income and employment opportunities than were women as a group. Crosby (1984) subsequently attributed the tendency for women to perceive less personal than group discrimination to a process of denial of their personal disadvantage.

This phenomenon has since been observed among ethnic and racial groups in the United States, Canada, and elsewhere and has been labeled the personal-group discrimination discrepancy (PGDD; Taylor, Wright, Moghaddam, & Lalonde, 1990; Taylor, Wright, & Porter, 1994). Much like Crosby (1982), Taylor et al. (1990) found that Haitian and East Indian women in Montreal reported more group than personal discrimination across four sources of potential discrimination (viz., race, culture, status as newcomers to Canada, and sex). Dion and Kawakami (1996) likewise found a PGDD across a variety of domains for six ethnic groups in Toronto, three of them visible minorities and the other three White or nonvisible minorities, although the PGDD was consistently stronger among the visible minorities.

Explanations for the Personal-Group Discrimination Discrepancy

One reason that people from oppressed groups may be reluctant to claim that they have personally experienced prejudice or discrimination is that there are social costs to attributing a setback to discrimination. In two studies, Kaiser and Miller (2001) showed that a Black person who attributed a failing grade on a test to discrimination was perceived by Whites as being a complainer and was evaluated less positively than was a Black person attributing the failure to the low quality of his answers on the test.

Perhaps the most comprehensive explanation of the PGDD, at present, has been suggested by Postmes, Branscombe, Spears, and Young (1999). Postmes and his colleagues argued that the PGDD is not an intentional comparison between oneself and one's group as regards experienced discrimination. If the latter were the case, the difference between separate ratings of perceived discrimination for self and for group (i.e., the standard way of assessing the PGDD) should relate highly to a single direct comparison for self (compared to others of one's group, e.g., a gender group) or in-group (compared to a comparison out-group, e.g., the other gender group). In fact, standard PGDD scores correlated only modestly with direct comparisons for self and for group.

Instead, Postmes et al. (1999) proposed and showed that ratings of personal discrimination and of group discrimination are based on two separate judgments: an interpersonal judgment comparing self and other in-group members for ratings of personal discrimination and an intergroup judgment comparing one's in-group to an out-group for ratings of group discrimination. Consistent with this emphasis on different types of judgment and comparison referents, they also demonstrated that ratings of personal discrimination or advantage reflect personal, self-serving motives; whereas ratings of group discrimination or advantage are influenced by social identity motives and in-group identification. Other researchers' analyses of the PGDD converge with Postmes et al.'s conclusions (Dion & Kawakami, 1996; Kessler, Mummendey, & Leisse, 2000; Quinn, Roese, Pennington, & Olson, 1999).

Perceived Prejudice and Discrimination as Stressors

A Stress Model

A number of investigators have independently proposed that perceiving oneself to be a target of prejudice or discrimination is a psychosocial stressor. For example, Dion, Dion, and Pak (1992) contended that perceived prejudice or discrimination is a social stressor because it elicits cognitive appraisals of threat such that its victims see themselves as being deliberate targets of negative behavior by one or more out-group antagonists and impute stable, malevolent motives and intentions to them. Moreover, prejudice and discrimination are often unpredictable stressors, entailing greater adaptational costs for the victim than a predictable or controllable stressor (see Allison, 1998, for an excellent discussion of other stress models).

If perceived prejudice and discrimination are indeed stressors, they should produce in individuals various social-psychological consequences known to result from stress, such as negative affect, reported stress, psychological or psychiatric symptoms, and lowered sense of well-being, as well as heightened in-group identification (a frequent response to external threat to one's group). Dion et al.'s stress model of perceived discrimination has now been amply supported by both experimental and correlational studies. In an experiment varying perceived prejudice in an attributional ambiguity paradigm, Dion and Earn (1975) found that when they made attributions to prejudice for a severe failure, Jewish men showed evidence of heightened in-group identification as well as a stress response on mood measures: namely, feeling more aggression, greater sadness, higher anxiety, and heightened self-consciousness. Similar, Crocker et al. (1993) found that women, especially obese ones, reported more negative moods when they received negative feedback from an attractive man as opposed to positive feedback.

Correlational studies concur strongly with experimental studies in documenting a link between perceived discrimination and stress. Perceptions of discrimination in Black Americans correlate with psychiatric symptoms. Landrine and Klonoff (1996; Klonoff & Landrine, 1999) developed a reliable 18-item measure of perceived racial discrimination called the Schedule of Racist Events (SRE) and validated it in two separate studies with samples of Black American community respondents. In the most recent study with more than 500 respondents sampled from middle- and lower-class sections of San Bernardino, California, they found that 96% reported discrimination in the past year and 98% at some time during their lives. For 95% of the respondents, these discrimination experiences were labeled as stressful. Black American men reported more experiences of discrimination than did their female counterparts. In both studies, frequency of discrimination experiences correlated positively with psychiatric symptoms, accounting for about 10% of the variance. In the 1996 study, the frequency of discrimination experiences was also linked to cigarette smoking.

Other researchers have highlighted the cumulative and chronic stressfulness of perceived discrimination among Black Americans. Feagin (1991) emphasized that for Black Americans, even those well ensconced in the middle class, the cumulative effect of racist encounters over a lifetime becomes potentially more potent than a simple sum of frequency count of such experiences might suggest. Branscombe, Schmitt, and Harvey (1999) showed the negative effects upon well-being of chronic perceptions of discrimination in Black American respondents. Branscombe and her colleagues emphasized that chronic perceptions of discrimination and stable attributions of pervasive prejudice have quite different effects on self-esteem and well-being than do attributions to prejudice for a single event, such as is typically explored in laboratory studies of perceived prejudice or discrimination.

A Biopsychosocial Model

Clark, Anderson, Clark, and Williams (1999) proposed a biopsychosocial model of racism as a stressor for Black Americans. Its underlying assumption is that perceived racism leads to heightened psychological and physiological stress responses from Black Americans. In this model, constitutional, sociodemographic, psychological, and behavioral factors are proposed to moderate the relationship between an environmental stimulus and its perception as being racist. Perceptions of racism are then linked to coping responses, psychological and physiological stress responses, and health outcomes.

The links between perceived racism and health outcomes among Black Americans are perhaps the most intriguing and important aspect of Clark et al.'s (1999) model. The authors suggested that racism and its perception (or denial) relate to cardiovascular, neuroendocrine, and immune system responses by Black Americans. Hypertension among Black Americans may well be associated, albeit in complex ways, with experiences of racism and methods of coping with them. For example, Krieger (1990) found that Black American women who indicated that they passively accepted racist experiences were over four times more likely to report hypertension than were those indicating a more active response to unfair treatment. Moreover, those Black American women reporting no instances of unfair treatment were more than $2\frac{1}{2}$ times more likely to report hypertension than were those reporting one or more experiences of racism. If one assumes that Black women reporting no instances were denying or internalizing racist experiences, this finding and other studies (Krieger & Sidney, 1996) suggest that as a coping mechanism, denial may have unfortunate health correlates or consequences for Black Americans. The specific links between perceptions and experiences of racism and hypertension in Black Americans of both sexes, however, remain to be firmly established and better understood.

Like racism, sexism also has pernicious consequences for individuals experiencing and perceiving it. Landrine, Klonoff, Gibbs, Manning, and Lund (1995) correlated lifetime and recent experiences of sexist events from their Schedule of Sexist Events (SSE) with scores from anxiety and depression scales, the Hopkins Symptom Checklist (HSC), and a measure of premenstrual tension syndrome (PMTS). Hierarchical regression analyses were performed in which generic stress measures for life events and hassles were entered at the first step, followed by lifetime and recent SSE scores in the second step. SSE scores accounted for additional variance beyond the generic stress indexes. Sexist discrimination emerged as an especially important and better predictor than generic stress for symptoms from the PMTS and HSC measures including premenstrual, somatization, obsessive-compulsive, depressive, and total psychiatric symptoms. Moreover, the ability of SSE scores to predict symptoms varied as a function of the U.S. women's ages and ethnicities. Lifetime SSE scores enhanced prediction (over and above generic stress measures) of total HSC symptoms for older women but not for younger ones.

Buffers for Discrimination-Related Stress

Not all members of oppressed groups will suffer the stress of discrimination in the same way or to the same extent. The personality construct of hardiness—a composite of self-esteem and sense of control—may be one factor that buffers the stress of experiencing or perceiving discrimination toward oneself and one's group. Dion et al. (1992) explored the role of personality-based hardiness in a study of Toronto's Chinese community. As they predicted, the relationship of discrimination to psychological symptoms was markedly higher among Chinese community respondents who were low in hardiness than among those high in hardiness. Indeed, for those scoring high in hardiness, discrimination and reported psychological symptoms were effectively unrelated, whereas they related reasonably strongly for those low in hardiness. In addition, alternative interpretations in terms of differential life stresses or differential exposure to discrimination in the two hardiness groups were ruled out as rival explanations (see Dion et al., 1992).

Foster and Dion (2001) explored whether the beneficial relationship of personality-based hardiness to discrimination-related stress is due to buffering or denial in an experiment in which women confronted gender discrimination on an examination. The findings favored a buffering interpretation and suggested that the buffering was due to the types of attributions that hardy women made relative to their less hardy counterparts. Specifically, hardy women made specific, unstable attributions rather than global, stable ones; that is, they tended to see the gender discrimination as a unique and unusual occurrence, even though there were no differences between the hardy and nonhardy women in perceived unfairness of the discrimination.

Whereas hardiness may provide a personality-based buffer and coping dimension, in-group identification has been hypothesized to be important in predicting reliance on group-based responses to coping with discrimination and buffering self-esteem. Branscombe and Ellemers (1998) proposed a *rejection-identification model* suggesting that greater willingness to make attributions to prejudice among Black Americans heightens their minority-group identification as well as hostility toward the dominant White group but has a negative effect on personal and collective sense of well-being. Minority-group identification, however, has a buffering effect in sustaining well-being. Branscombe and her colleagues tested and supported this model with SEM

procedures. Some alternative theoretical models failed to receive support.

Stereotype Threat

Not only do women and minority members confront prejudice and discrimination, but they also must deal with broadly shared, negative stereotypes about their groups by majority group members, which can have pernicious and deleterious effects upon their academic and athletic performance. Black Americans, for example, confront low expectations in the realm of academic ability, whereas women in the United States, Canada, and some other societies are presumed by consensually shared stereotypes to be inferior in mathematics compared to men.

Steele (1997; Steele & Aronson, 1995) and his colleagues contended that negative stereotypes impugning the abilities of stigmatized group members constitute a powerful situational threat with two notable consequences. First, in a testing situation involving an ability where one's group is negatively stereotyped, the performance of those members who care about the ability and doing well on the test can be adversely affected. Second, chronic experiences of stereotype threat can lead members of stigmatized groups to disidentify by denying the importance of the ability for themselves. At the college level, this disidentification can lead to academic dropouts among Black Americans and proportionally fewer women enrolling in math, science, and engineering programs where mathematical ability is prerequisite.

Initial Studies

Steele and Aronson (1995) reported the first set of four experiments documenting the impact of stereotype threat on the performance of Black American university students, relative to their White American counterparts, at Stanford University, an elite U.S. university. These investigators told participants that difficult and challenging items from the Graduate Record Examination (GRE) either were diagnostic of their intellectual ability (the diagnostic or stereotype threat condition) or were a test of problem-solving with no implications for diagnosing their intellectual ability (the nondiagnostic or no-stereotype-threat condition). In all four studies, participants' previous Scholastic Achievement Test (SAT) scores in high school were statistically controlled in the analyses by means of analysis of covariance (ANCOVA) procedures.

The first two studies by Steele and Aronson (1995) demonstrated that Black American participants in the diagnostic or stereotype threat condition completed fewer items and attained lower accuracy (i.e., number of items correct relative to the number attempted) than did either Black or White participants in the other conditions. Steele and Aronson's third experiment demonstrated that the diagnostic ability manipulation elicited among Black participants who were expecting to take a difficult test (but did not do so) the racial stereotype of Blacks held by Whites as well as an avoidance of self-characterization in terms of this stereotype, and even an avoidance of indicating one's racial status on a demographic postquestionnaire, relative to nondiagnostic and control conditions. In Study 4, priming race by merely having participants indicate their race on a demographic questionnaire before attempting a challenging intellectual test served to inhibit performance by Black participants and presumably to elicit stereotype threat. Steele and Aronson proposed that the mechanism underlying the impact of stereotype threat on the test performance of their Black American participants was probably an inefficiency of cognitive processing, not unlike that produced by other evaluative pressures.

Croizet and Claire (1998) extended the applicability of the stereotype threat concept to those of low socioeconomic status (SES) outside the United States. Using a predominantly female sample of French university students, these investigators likewise found that under stereotype threat, students of low SES obtained fewer correct answers, attempted fewer items, and had lower overall accuracy on verbal GRE items. By contrast, much like Steele and Aronson (1995) had previously found in comparing Black and White American participants, there was no difference in test performance between participants of low and high SES when the same test was described as nondiagnostic of one's intellectual ability. Varying the salience of SES before the test by having participants indicate their parents' occupation and educational level, however, had no effect in this study.

Recent Studies

Spencer, Steele, and Quinn (1999) themselves applied stereotype threat theory to U.S. women's math performance in three studies including math-oriented students who had taken calculus and had performed highly on the high-school mathematics section of the SAT. Their first experiment demonstrated that a gender difference, with women underperforming men, occurred only when the math GRE items used to assess math performance were difficult rather than easy. Spencer and his colleagues varied stereotype threat in the next two studies by informing participants either that there was a gender difference previously obtained with the math GRE items they were to solve (threat condition) or not (no stereotype threat). In the no threat condition, women's performance on the math

GRE test equalled that of men. By contrast, in the threat condition, women underperformed men. Finally, their third experiment demonstrated that the stereotype threat effect was obtainable at a state university in the U.S. whose academic standards were less rigorous and selective than the elite university samples in prior studies and further explored possible mediating processes. The mediational tests excluded evaluation apprehension and self-efficacy as a basis for the impact of stereotype threat on women's math performance. Anxiety emerged as a weak mediator of stereotype threat.

Finally, recent studies by different sets of investigators show that stereotype threat can affect the performance of White majority group members and does not require that one be a member of a historically stigmatized group. Aronson et al. (1999) conducted two experiments in which White students of high math ability at an elite U.S. university were presented information that Asian Americans outperform Whites in math (stereotype threat condition) or not (no threat condition). Additionally, in the second study they selected math-oriented students who scored on the bottom and top tertiles of rated importance of mathematics ability to their self-concept as a means of assessing low versus high identification with this domain. Their first study showed that White students performed less well on a challenging math test when threatened with a racial stereotype indicating their inferiority relative to Asians. Their second study showed that this stereotype effect occurred only when the White students were math-identified and that evaluation apprehension was a weak, potential mediator.

Stone, Lynch, Sjomeling, and Darley (1999) took advantage of a golf test that they presented to Black and White Princeton University participants as indicating their "natural athletic ability" or their "sports intelligence." Their first study showed that performance by Black students on the golf test suffered more when it constituted a stereotype threat (an indication of sports intelligence—a negative stereotype for Whites) than when it did not (an indication of natural athletic ability—a positive stereotype for Blacks). By contrast, for White participants for whom the opposite was true (i.e., sports intelligence is a positive stereotype, and natural athletic ability is a negative or less positive stereotype than for Blacks), the reverse pattern was obtained, as predicted from stereotype threat theory. Their second study, focusing on White participants only, showed that the detrimental effects of stereotype threat on performance on the golf test occurred only for "engaged" participants for whom performance in the athletic domain was important to their self-worth and not for those who were "disengaged." In addition to showing the importance of engagement for the stereotype threat effect, their explorations of mediators for White participants implicated performance anxiety and lowered expectations when the task's difficulty became apparent.

In sum, accumulating evidence suggests that the stereotype threat effect is real and that its effects can be demonstrated among historically stigmatized groups such as Black Americans and White women as well as nonstigmatized groups. Also, apart from the obvious importance of a person being engaged and identified with the domain (e.g., math, athletics, etc.), the precise mechanisms responsible for the stereotype threat effect remain somewhat ambiguous. The preceding studies have assessed an array of potential mediators—such as self-handicapping and situational and trait anxiety, as well as test anxiety, evaluation apprehension; self-concept, and so on—with self-report measures. Weak evidence of potential mediators has emerged, though not the same ones across studies and groups. Perhaps different mechanisms will ultimately be shown to be important for different target groups. What seems clear at present is that the stereotype threat effect is not due to a lowering of effort, as stereotype-threatened individuals typically work or try harder than their nonthreatened counterparts. On the other hand, stereotype threat seems to act as a distractor and an additional pressure that reduces one's effectiveness for successfully completing challenging tasks at the limit of one's ability in a given domain.

Advocates of stereotype threat theory suggest that their perspective is optimistic in that it points to a situational stressor as a key factor in underperformance by negatively stereotyped and stigmatized groups, in contrast to dispositional interpretations of innate inferiority in ability, genetic factors, and so on. Stereotype threat theory also provides a viable explanation for why academic achievement tests have lower criterion validity for stigmatized groups in the U.S. and elsewhere than for nonstigmatized ones. Once the deleterious effects of stereotype threat are identified and understood, steps to counteract them in standardized testing and in academic learning environments can be developed—a process that Steele and his colleagues have already begun with some notable success (see Aronson, Quinn, & Spencer, 1998; Steele, 1997; see also the chapter on reducing prejudice by Dovidio in this volume).

Relative Deprivation, Perceived Discrimination, and Desire for Corrective Action

Paradoxically, members of oppressed groups do not always, or even often, respond to stereotypes, disadvantage, deprivation, and discrimination by seeking redress or social change. Relative deprivation theory (RDT) is one conceptual

framework that tries to predict when and why members of an oppressed group will respond to their disadvantage with attempts to instigate social change, such as political protest. As its name implies, RDT assumes that one's feelings of deprivation are not absolute but instead depend on the individual or group with whom one compares.

RDT proposes different types of deprivation as defined by two dimensions. One dimension concerns the focus of comparison and defines the distinction between egoistic and fraternalistic relative deprivation (RD). Egoistic RD occurs when an individual feels deprived relative to others in their membership group. Fraternalistic RD (also called collectivistic RD by those of us preferring a gender-neutral label) occurs when one's group is perceived to be at a disadvantage to one or more out-groups. The second dimension concerns the cognitive-affective distinction. Cognitive RD concerns the perception of inequality, whereas affective RD refers to resentment over inequalities. Taken together, these two dimensions define four types of RD. Reviews of RDT (e.g., Dion, 1986) indicate that of these four types, it is primarily affective, collectivistic RD (i.e., resentment over poorer treatment of one's group compared to other groups) that best predicts desires and attempts at social change.

In a series of studies, I and my colleagues have pitted perceived discrimination against measures of RD types to assess their relative efficacy at predicting attitudinal measures of desires to take corrective action (Dion, 2002). With groups in Canada such as lesbians and gays, Chinese university students, and women, we have consistently found that perceived discrimination is a more powerful and consistent predictor of reported desires to corrective action than are the different RD types, with the notable exception of affective, collectivistic RD (e.g., Birt & Dion, 1987; Dion & Kawakami, 2000). Together, perceived discrimination and affective, collectivistic RD predict desires to take corrective action in response to group disadvantage quite well. Relatedly, Foster (2000) has shown that global attributions of gender discrimination (i.e., seeing gender discrimination as affecting many situations in one's life) was also associated with greater proneness to support collective action in U.S. college women. Thus, the victim's perceptions of discrimination—whether it is seen as being global in its effects, whether it affects one's group, and whether it evokes a negative affective response—make a difference in stimulating desires to take corrective action and to mobilize one's efforts with others to create social change.

Conclusion

Perceived prejudice and discrimination are pivotal in the psychology of ethnic and intergroup relations. The literature on the psychology of being a victim of prejudice and discrimination that was reviewed earlier suggests several conclusions. First, for some groups and for some individuals within oppressed groups, perceptions of prejudice and attributions of setbacks to prejudice may buffer self-esteem and maintain well-being. However, the buffering effect of attributed prejudice is probably a weak one, may occur for only some groups, involves a tradeoff between types of self-esteem and perceived control, and is mediated or moderated by in-group identification. Somewhat perversely, the buffering effects of perceived discrimination on self-esteem seem to be more straightforward and clearer for members of dominant than of subordinate groups. Second, the experience or perception of prejudice and discrimination toward oneself and one's group is unquestionably stressful, although personality-based hardiness and in-group identification may moderate discrimination-related stress to some extent. Discrimination-related stress has been linked to mental and physical health outcomes for both American women and Black Americans. Stereotype threat—the perception of being negatively stereotyped by others in academic and other domains—is also a stressor whose deleterious effects on achievement task performance are now established, although the mediators are unclear. Finally, Some evidence suggests that perceived prejudice and discrimination, along with feelings of resentment about in-group disadvantage relative to other groups, instigate desires to take corrective social action. These conclusions demonstrate that our knowledge of the psychology of victimization has advanced appreciably in the last several decades of the twentieth century.

A FINAL THOUGHT

Having considered the psychology of bigotry as well as the psychology of being a victim of prejudice and discrimination, a next step for future psychological research on prejudice may be to explore the reciprocal interaction between bigot and victim. To date, the psychology of bigotry and the psychology of being a victim of prejudice and discrimination have been investigated separately from one another and have focused heavily on intrapersonal dynamics (e.g., the effects of automatic processing on a person's cognitions and behaviors). Yet, some previous theorists (e.g., Dion et al., 1978) have suggested that the bigot and the victim of prejudice form a complementary role relationship with one another. Understanding the interpersonal dynamics of prejudice may require investigating situations in the laboratory and the community where victims of prejudice confront the bigotry, whether from one or more persons or an institution, directly. As always, psychological researchers interested in prejudice will rise to the methodological and theoretical challenges of exploring the reciprocal interactions between bigot and victim.

REFERENCES

Adorno, T. W., Frenkel-Brunswik, E., Levinson, D. J., & Sanford, R. N. (1950). *The authoritarian personality.* New York: Harper & Row.

Allison, K. W. (1998). Stress and oppressed social category membership. In J. K. Swim & C. Stangor (Eds.), *Prejudice: The target's perspective* (pp. 145–170). Orlando, FL: Academic.

Altemeyer, B. (1981). *Right-wing authoritarianism.* Winnipeg, Canada: University of Manitoba Press.

Altemeyer, B. (1988). *Enemies of freedom: Understanding right-wing authoritarianism.* San Francisco: Jossey-Bass.

Altemeyer, B. (1996). *The authoritarian specter.* Cambridge, MA: Harvard University Press.

Aronson, J., Lustina, M. J., Good, C., Keough, K., Steele, C. M., & Brown, J. (1999). When white men can't do math: Necessary and sufficient factors in stereotype threat. *Journal of Experimental Social Psychology, 35,* 29–46.

Aronson, J., Quinn, D. M., & Spencer, S. J. (1998). Stereotype threat and the academic underperformance of minorities and women. In C. Stangor & J. Swim (Eds.), *Prejudice: The target's perspective* (pp. 83–103). Orlando, FL: Academic.

Bargh, J. (1989). *Unintended thought.* New York: Guilford.

Bell, D. W., Esses, V. M., & Maio, G. R. (1996). The utility of open-ended measures to assess intergroup ambivalence. *Canadian Journal of Behavioural Science, 28,* 12–18.

Biernat, M., Vescio, T. K., & Theno, S. A. (1996). Violating American values: A "value congruence" approach to understanding out-group attitudes. *Journal of Experimental Social Psychology, 32,* 387–410.

Biernat, M., Vescio, T. K., Theno, S. A., & Crandall, C. S. (1996). Values and prejudice: Toward understanding the impact of American values on out-group attitudes. In C. Seligman, J. M. Olson, & M. P. Zanna (Eds.), *The psychology of values: The Ontario Symposium* (Vol. 8, pp. 153–189). Mahwah, NJ: Erlbaum.

Birt, C. M., & Dion, K. L. (1987). Relative deprivation theory and responses to discrimination in a gay male and lesbian sample. *British Journal of Social Psychology, 26,* 139–145.

Branscombe, N. R. (1998). Thinking about one's gender group's privileges or disadvantages: Consequences for well-being in women and men. *British Journal of Social Psychology, 37,* 167–184.

Branscombe, N. R., & Ellemers, N. (1998). Coping with group-based discrimination. In J. K. Swim & C. Stangor (Eds.), *Prejudice: The target's perspective* (pp. 243–266). Orlando, FL: Academic.

Branscombe, N. R., Schmitt, M. T., & Harvey, R. D. (1999). Perceiving pervasive discrimination among African-Americans: Implications for group identification and well-being. *Journal of Personality and Social Psychology, 77,* 135–149.

Brown, R. (1967). *Social psychology*. New York: Free Press.

Clark, R., Anderson, N. B., Clark, V. R., & Williams, D. R. (1999). Racism as a stressor for African-Americans. *American Psychologist, 54*, 805–816.

Cohen, J. (1992). A power primer. *Psychological Bulletin, 112*, 155–159.

Cox, C. L., Smith, S. L., & Insko, C. A. (1996). Categorical race versus individuating belief as determinants of discrimination: A study of southern adolescents in 1966, 1979, and 1993. *Journal of Experimental Social Psychology, 32*, 39–70.

Crocker, J., Cornwell, B., & Major, B. (1993). The stigma of overweight: Affective consequences of attributional ambiguity. *Journal of Personality and Social Psychology, 64*, 60–70.

Crocker, J., & Major, B. (1989). Social stigma and self-esteem: The self-protective function. *Psychological Review, 96*, 608–630.

Crocker, J., & Major, B. (1993). Reactions to stigma. The moderating role of justifications. In M. P. Zanna & J. M. Olson (Eds.), *The psychology of prejudice: The Ontario Symposium* (Vol. 7, pp. 289–314). Mahwah, NJ: Erlbaum.

Crocker, J., Major, B., & Steele, C. (1998). Social stigma. In D. T. Gilbert, S. T. Fiske, & G. Lindzey (Eds.), *The handbook of social psychology* (4th ed., Vol. 2, pp. 504–553). New York: McGraw-Hill.

Crocker, J., Voelkl, K., Testa, M., & Major, B. (1991). Social Stigma: The affective consequences of attributional ambiguity. *Journal of Personality and Social Psychology, 60*, 218–228.

Croizet, J.-C., & Claire, T. (1998). Extending the concept of stereotype threat to social class: The intellectual underperformance of students from low socioeconomic backgrounds. *Personality and Social Psychology Bulletin, 24*, 588–594.

Crosby, F. (1982). *Relative deprivation and working women*. New York: Oxford University Press.

Crosby, F. (1984). The denial of personal discrimination. *American Behavioral Scientist, 27*, 371–386.

Crosby, F., Bromley, S., & Saxe, L. (1980). Recent unobtrusive studies of black and white discrimination and prejudice: A literature review. *Psychological Bulletin, 87*, 546–563.

Devine, P. G. (1989). Stereotypes and prejudice: Their automatic and controlled components. *Journal of Personality and Social Psychology, 56*, 5–18.

Devine, P. G., & Monteith, M. J. (1999). Automaticity and control in stereotyping. In S. Chaiken & Y. Trope (Eds.), *Dual-process theories in social psychology* (pp. 339–360). New York: Guilford.

Devine, P. G., Monteith, M. J., Zuwerink, J. R., & Elliot, A. J. (1991). Prejudice with and without compunction. *Journal of Personality and Social Psychology, 60*, 817–830.

Dion, K. L. (1975). Women's reactions to discrimination from members of the same or the opposite sex. *Journal of Research in Personality, 9*, 294–306.

Dion, K. L. (1986). Responses to perceived discrimination and relative deprivation. In J. M. Olson, C. P. Herman, & M. P. Zanna (Eds.), *Relative deprivation and social comparison: The Ontario Symposium* (Vol. 4, pp. 159–179). Mahwah, NJ: Erlbaum.

Dion, K. L. (1990). Review of the book *Enemies of freedom: Understanding right-wing authoritarianism*. *Canadian Psychology, 31*, 374–376.

Dion, K. L. (2002). The social psychology of perceived prejudice and discrimination. *Canadian Psychology, 43*, 1–10.

Dion, K. L., Dion, K. K., & Pak, A. W.-p. (1992). Personality-based hardiness as a buffer for discrimination-related stress in members of Toronto's Chinese community. *Canadian Journal of Behavioural Science, 24*, 517–536.

Dion, K. L., & Earn, B. M. (1975). The phenomenology of being a target of prejudice. *Journal of Personality and Social Psychology, 32*, 944–950.

Dion, K. L., Earn, B. M., & Yee, P. H. N. (1978). The experience of being a victim of prejudice: An experimental approach. *International Journal of Psychology, 13*, 197–214.

Dion, K. L., & Kawakami, K. (1996). Ethnicity and perceived discrimination in Toronto: Another look at the personal/group discrimination discrepancy. *Canadian Journal of Behavioural Science, 28*, 203–213.

Dion, K. L., & Kawakami, K. (2000, June 18). *Predictors of collective action among women*. Symposium presentation to the Third Biennial Meeting of the Society for the Psychological Study of Social Issues, Minneapolis, MN.

Dovidio, J. F., & Gaertner, S. L. (1986). The aversive form of racism. In J. F. Dovidio & S. L. Gaertner (Eds.), *Prejudice, discrimination, and racism* (pp. 61–89). Orlando, FL: Academic.

Dovidio, J. F., & Gaertner, S. L. (1991). Changes in the expression and assessment of racial prejudice. In H. J. Knopke, R. J. Norrell, & R. W. Rogers (Eds.), *Opening doors: Perspectives on race relations in contemporary America* (pp. 119–148). Tuscaloosa: University of Alabama Press.

Dovidio, J. F., & Gaertner, S. L. (2000). Aversive racism and selection decisions: 1989 and 1999. *Psychological Science, 11*, 315–319.

Dovidio, J. F., Kawakami, K., Johnson, C., Johnson, B., & Howard, A. (1997). On the nature of prejudice: Automatic and controlled processes. *Journal of Experimental Social Psychology, 33*, 510–540.

Dovidio, J. F., Smith, J. K., Gershenfeld Donnella, A. G., & Gaertner, S. L. (1997). Racial attitudes and the death penalty. *Journal of Applied Social Psychology, 27*, 1466–1487.

Duckitt, J. (1994). *The social psychology of prejudice*. Westport, CT: Praeger.

Esses, V. M., Haddock, G., & Zanna, M. P. (1993). Values, stereotypes, and emotions as determinants of intergroup attitudes. In D. M. Mackie & D. L. Hamilton (Eds.), *Affect, cognition, and stereotyping: Interactive processes in group perception* (pp. 137–166). Orlando, FL: Academic.

Esses, V. M., Haddock, G., & Zanna, M. P. (1994). The role of mood in the expression of intergroup stereotypes. In M. P. Zanna & J. M. Olson (Eds.), *The psychology of prejudice: The Ontario Symposium*. (Vol. 7, pp. 77–101). Mahwah, NJ: Erlbaum.

Fazio, R. H., Jackson, J. R., Dunton, B. C., & Williams, C. J. (1995). Variability in automatic activation as an unobtrusive measure of racial attitudes: A bona fide pipeline? *Journal of Personality and Social Psychology, 69*, 1013–1027.

Feagin, J. R. (1991). The continuing significance of race: AntiBlack discrimination in public places. *American Sociological Review, 56*, 101–116.

Fiske, S. T., & Neuberg, S. L. (1990). A continuum of impression formation from category-based to individuating processes: Influences of information and motivation on attention and interpretation. In M. P. Zanna (Ed.), *Advances in experimental social psychology* (Vol. 23, pp. 1–74). Mahwah, NJ: Erlbaum.

Foster, M. D. (2000). Utilization of global attributions in recognizing and responding to gender discrimination among college women. *Current Psychology: Developmental, Learning, Personality, Social, 19*, 57–69.

Foster, M. D., & Dion, K. L. (2001, June). *Hardiness and responses to perceived discrimination: Buffer or denial?* Symposium conducted at the 13th Annual Convention of the American Psychological Society, Toronto, Ontario, Canada.

Glick, P., & Fiske, S. (1996). The Ambivalent Sexism Inventory: Differentiating hostile and benevolent sexism. *Journal of Personality and Social Psychology, 70*, 491–512.

Greenwald, A. G., & Banaji, M. R. (1995). Implicit social cognition: Attitudes, self-esteem, and stereotypes. *Psychological Review, 102*, 4–27.

Greenwald, A. G., McGhee, D. E., & Schwartz, J. L. K. (1998). Measuring individual differences in implicit cognition: The Implicit Association Test. *Journal of Personality and Social Psychology, 74*, 1464–1480.

Griffin, J. H. (1961). *Black like me.* Boston: Houghton Mifflin.

Haddock, G., Zanna, M. P., & Esses, V. M. (1993). Assessing the structure of prejudicial attitudes: The case of attitudes toward homosexuals. *Journal of Personality and Social Psychology, 65*, 105–118.

Hass, R. G., Katz, I., Rizzo, N., Bailey, J., & Moore, L. (1992). When racial ambivalence evokes negative affect, using a disguised measure of mood. *Personality and Social Psychology Bulletin, 18*, 786–797.

Hebl, M. R., & Heatherton, T. F. (1998). The stigma of obesity in women: The difference is black and white. *Personality and Social Psychology Bulletin, 24*, 417–426.

Insko, C. A., Nacoste, R. W., & Moe, J. L. (1983). Belief congruence and racial discrimination: Review of the evidence and critical evaluation. *European Journal of Social Psychology, 13*, 153–174.

Jones, J. M. (1997). *Prejudice and racism* (2nd ed.). New York: McGraw-Hill.

Kaiser, C. R., & Miller, C. T. (2001). Stop complaining! The social costs of making attributions to discrimination. *Personality and Social Psychology Bulletin, 27*, 254–263.

Kardiner, A., & Ovesey, L. (1951). *The mark of oppression.* New York: Norton.

Karon, B. P. (1975). *Black scars: A rigorous investigation of the effects of discrimination.* New York: Springer.

Katz, I., & Glass, D. C. (1979). An ambivalence-amplification theory of behavior toward the stigmatized. In W. G. Austin & S. Worchel (Eds.), *The social psychology of intergroup relations* (pp. 55–70). Monterey, CA: Brooks/Cole.

Katz, I., & Hass, R. G. (1988). Racial ambivalence and American value conflict: Correlational and priming studies of dual cognitive structures. *Journal of Personality and Social Psychology, 55*, 893–905.

Kawakami, K., Dion, K. L., & Dovidio, J. F. (1998). Racial prejudice and stereotype activation. *Personality and Social Psychology Bulletin, 24*, 407–416.

Kessler, T., Mummendey, A., & Leisse, U.-K. (2000). The personal-group discrepancy: Is there a common information basis for personal and group judgment? *Journal of Personality and Social Psychology, 79*, 95–109.

Kinder, D. R., & Sears, D. O. (1981). Prejudice and politics: Symbolic racism versus racial threats to the good life. *Journal of Personality and Social Psychology, 40*, 414–431.

Klonoff, E. A., & Landrine, H. (1999). Cross-validation of the Schedule of Racist Events. *Journal of Black Psychology, 25*, 231–254.

Kobrynowicz, D., & Branscombe, N. R. (1997). Who considers themselves victims of discrimination? Individual difference predictors of perceived gender discrimination in women and men. *Psychology of Women Quarterly, 21*, 347–363.

Krieger, N. (1990). Racial and gender discrimination: Risk factors for high blood pressure? *Social Science & Medicine, 30*, 1273–1281.

Krieger, N., & Sidney, S. (1996). Racial discrimination and blood pressure: The CARDIA Study of young black and white adults. *American Journal of Public Health, 86*, 1370–1378.

Lambert, A. J., Burroughs, T., & Chasteen, A. L. (1998). Belief in a just world and right-wing authoritarianism as moderators of perceived risk. In L. Montada & M. J. Lerner (Eds.), *Responses to victimizations and belief in a just world* (pp. 107–125). New York: Plenum.

Landrine, H., & Klonoff, E. A. (1996). The Schedule of Racist Events: A measure of racial discrimination and a study of its negative and physical and mental health consequences. *Journal of Black Psychology, 22*, 144–168.

Landrine, H., Klonoff, E. A., Gibbs, J., Manning, V., & Lund, M. (1995). Physical and psychiatric correlates of gender discrimination: An application of the Schedule of Sexist Events. *Psychology of Women Quarterly, 19*, 473–492.

Larson, C. R. (Ed.). (1971). *Prejudice.* New York: Signet.

Lepore, L., & Brown, R. (1997). Category and stereotype activation: Is prejudice inevitable? *Journal of Personality and Social Psychology, 72*, 275–287.

Lerner, M. J. (1978). "Belief in a just world" versus the "authoritarian" syndrome . . . but nobody liked the Indians. *Ethnicity, 8*, 229–237.

Lerner, M. J. (1980). *The belief in a just world: A fundamental delusion.* New York: Plenum.

Lerner, M. J., & Montada, L. (1998). An overview: Advances in belief in a just world theory and methods. In L. Montada & M. J. Lerner (Eds.), *Responses to victimizations and belief in a just world* (pp. 1–7). New York: Plenum.

Levin, S., Sidanius, J. (1999). Social dominance and social identity in the United States and Israel: In-group favoritism and out-group derogation. *Political Psychology, 20,* 99–126.

Levin, S., Sidanius, J., Rabinowitz, J. L., & Federico, C. (1998). Ethnic identity, legitimizing ideologies, and social status: A matter of ideological asymmetry. *Political Psychology, 19,* 373–404.

Lippa, R., & Arad, S. (1999). Gender, personality, and prejudice: The display of authoritarianism and social dominance in interviews with college men and women. *Journal of Research in Personality, 33,* 463–493.

Maio, G. R., Esses, V. M., & Bell, D. W. (1994). The formation of attitudes toward new immigrant groups. *Journal of Applied Social Psychology, 24,* 1762–1776.

Major, B., & Schmader, T. (1998). Coping with stigma through psychological disengagement. In J. K. Swim & C. Stangor (Eds.), *Prejudice: The target's perspective* (pp. 219–241). Orlando, FL: Academic.

McConahay, J. B. (1986). Modern racism, ambivalence, and the Modern Racism Scale. In J. F. Dovidio & S. L. Gaertner (Eds.), *Prejudice, discrimination, and racism* (pp. 91–125). Orlando, FL: Academic.

Miller, C. T., & Kaiser, C. R. (2001a). A theoretical perspective on coping with stigma. *The Journal of Social Issues, 57*(1), 73–92.

Miller, C. T., & Kaiser, C. R. (2001b). Implications of mental models of self and others for the targets of discrimination. In M. R. Leary (Ed.) *Interpersonal rejection* (pp. 189–212). New York: Oxford University Press.

Montada, L., & Lerner, M. J. (Eds.). (1998). *Responses to victimizations and belief in a just world.* New York: Plenum.

Monteith, M. J. (1993). Self-regulation of prejudiced responses: Implications for progress in prejudice reduction efforts. *Journal of Personality and Social Psychology, 65,* 469–485.

Monteith, M. J., Devine, P. G., & Zuwerink, J. R. (1993). Self-directed versus other-directed affect as a consequence of prejudice-related discrepancies. *Journal of Personality and Social Psychology, 64,* 198–210.

Monteith, M. J., & Walters, G. L. (1998). Egalitarianism, moral obligation, and prejudice-related standards. *Personality and Social Psychology Bulletin, 24,* 186–199.

Myrdal, G. (1944). *The American dilemma: The Negro problem and modern democracy.* New York: Harper.

Pettigrew, T. F. (1979). Racial change and social policy. *Annals of the Academy of Political and Social Science, 441,* 114–131.

Pettigrew, T. F., Jackson, J. S., Ben Brika, J., Lemaine, G., Meertens, R. W., Wagner, U., & Zick, A. (1998). Out-group prejudice in Western Europe. In W. Stroebe & M. Hewstone (Eds.), *European review of social psychology* (Vol. 8, pp. 241–273). London: Wiley.

Pettigrew, T. F., & Meertens, R. W. (1995). Subtle and blatant prejudice in Western Europe. *European Journal of Social Psychology, 25,* 57–75.

Pilkington, N. W., & Lydon, J. E. (1997). The relative effect of attitude similarity and attitude dissimilarity on interpersonal attraction: Investigating the moderating roles of prejudice and group membership. *Personality and Social Psychology Bulletin, 23,* 107–122.

Plant, E. A., & Devine, P. G. (1998). Internal and external motivation to respond without prejudice. *Journal of Personality and Social Psychology, 75,* 811–832.

Postmes, T., Branscombe, N. R., Spears, R., & Young, H. (1999). Comparative processes in personal and group judgments: Resolving the discrepancy. *Journal of Personality and Social Psychology, 76,* 320–338.

Pratto, F., Liu, J. H., Levin, S., Sidanius, J., Shih, M., Bachrach, H., & Hegarty, P. (2000). Social dominance orientation and the legitimization of inequality across cultures. *Journal of Cross-Cultural Psychology, 31,* 369–409.

Pratto, F., Sidanius, J., Stallworth, L. M., & Malle, B. F. (1994). Social dominance orientation: A personality variable predicting social and political attitudes. *Journal of Personality and Social Psychology, 67,* 741–763.

Quinn, K. A., Roese, N. J., Pennington, G. L., & Olson, J. M. (1999). The personal/group discrimination discrepancy: The role of information complexity. *Personality and Social Psychology Bulletin, 25,* 1430–1440.

Rokeach, M. (Ed.). (1960). *The open and closed mind.* New York: Basic Books.

Rokeach, M., & Mezei, L. (1966). Race and shared belief as factors in social distance. *Science, 151,* 167–172.

Rokeach, M., Smith, P. W., & Evans, R. I. (1960). Two kinds of prejudice or one? In M. Rokeach (Ed.), *The open and closed mind* (pp. 132–168). New York; Basic Books.

Saucier, G. (2000). Isms and the structure of social attitudes. *Journal of Personality and Social Psychology, 78,* 366–385.

Schwartz, S., & Struch, N. (1989). Values, stereotypes, and intergroup antagonism. In D. Bar-Tal, C. F. Graumann, A. W. Kruglanski, & W. Stroebe (Eds.), *Stereotyping and prejudice: Changing conceptions* (pp. 151–168). New York: Springer-Verlag.

Schwarzwald, J., & Tur-Kaspa, M. (1997). Perceived threat and social dominance as determinants of prejudice toward Russian and Ethiopian immigrants in Israel. *Megamot, 38,* 504–527.

Sears, D. O. (1988). Symbolic racism. In P. A. Katz & D. A. Taylor (Eds.), *Eliminating racism* (pp. 53–84). New York: Plenum.

Sears, D. O., & Funk, C. L. (1991). The role of self-interest in social and political attitudes. In M. P. Zanna (Ed.), *Advances in experimental social psychology* (Vol. 24, pp. 2–91). San Diego, CA: Academic.

traditions, acculturation, information about the implications of applying specific rules of justice, personal and socially shared values, the impact of social roles and positions (for reviews, see Tyler, Boeckman, Smith, & Huo, 1997), personality traits, and basic belief systems (cf. Schmitt, 1994, for a review). It is not the aim of this chapter to review and discuss this kind of research. Rather, the influential theory that the concern for justice has the instrumental function of maximizing self-interest is disputed.

Justice: A Means to Serve Self-Interest?

The view that people care about justice purely as a means to pursue their own self-interest is prominent in social psychology (a review is provided by Tyler et al., 1997). It forms the core assumption in the equity theory of social exchange (Adams, 1965; Homans, 1961; Walster, Berscheid, & Walster, 1978), which states that people prefer equity as a strategic choice to maximize their individual gains within social exchanges on either the short or the long term.

Thibault and Walker (1975) took a similar approach to explain people's preference rankings for different ways of settling conflicts with others—by negotiation, mediation, arbitration, or court decisions. They supposed that people's preferences were guided by their personal self-interests. The best strategy is to keep control over the outcome. In situations in which people have only limited control over the outcome because authorities have decisional power, people seek procedural control and attempt to influence the outcome by having a voice and by presenting arguments, their views, and evidence. Therefore, people view those procedures in which they have voice and influence as fairer than others. That means that the fairness ratings given to procedures are dependent on the indirect control over the outcome that these procedures allow.

The reasons given for this reduction of the concern for justice to a concern for self-interest mirror social contract theories in political philosophy. Philosophers—from Hobbes (1648/1970) to Rawls (1971)—have tackled the question of why individuals living in a fictional "original" prestate situation consented to build a state with powerful institutions, laws, and rules of justice. The basic answer is that it was to their best mutual advantage to restrict their egoistic fight for their own interests by establishing a system of social norms which would and could regulate their rights and obligations in competition as well as in cooperation. If this idea is generalized slightly, informal social norms (like most justice norms) can also be regarded as serving the mutual advantage of all (Hardin, 1996). Both the establishment of a state with a system of rules and of powerful institutions to ensure their

observation can be considered to be rational choices in the well-understood self-interest of individuals, especially when the social system is structured in a way that even the weak, less fortunate, and less able individuals participate in the common wealth (Rawls, 1971).

For several reasons, this rational choice modeling of the justice motive is disputable.

- What is missing in these theoretical accounts is the normative, prescriptive core of justice. Justice is an *ought,* a moral imperative for social life. It is not a means to achieve personal aims, but rather an end in itself (Montada, 1998a). People are obligated to observe the norms of justice regardless of whether this is in their self-interest. Moreover, they are entitled to claim justice from other actors, organizations, state institutions, and so on, not only for themselves but also for others.

- The model does not fit to empirical data showing that justice concerns are not reducible to self-interests and may in fact conflict with self-interests.

- There is no empirical proof of the reductionistic view of the model; it is merely an anthropological assumption. As such, it is part of a belief system and is not a testable scientific hypothesis. These three arguments are elaborated in more detail in this section.

Justice as an End in Itself

In every rational-choice explanation of the justice motive, it is not the concern for justice that is the primary motivational factor—rather, it is concerns for one's self-interests. If justice matters at all, then it matters only insofar as it serves these other concerns. This implies that justice is not acknowledged as a prescriptive normative standard.

When the equity principle is applied, inequity is unjust and needs to be rectified. The disadvantaged are entitled to claim equity, and anybody observing inequity is entitled or even obligated to claim equity for the disadvantaged. Those who are overbenefited within an exchange relation are morally obligated to reestablish equity.

The prescriptive nature of justice norms is not dependent on the actors' self-interest or on observers' sympathies with the advantaged or disadvantaged party in a social exchange relationship. Of course, self-interest may motivate actors to interpret and to balance the investments and benefits to their own advantage, and observers' sympathies with advantaged actors, for instance, may motivate them to discount the investments or overestimate the benefits of the disadvantaged in order to avoid or cope with feelings of injustice. Such biased distortions of so-called objective justice, however, do not mean that justice and its standards are disregarded. They can perhaps be interpreted as trade-offs between self-interest and justice motives, but not as a reduction of the justice motive to self-interest; this is not what Walster et al. (1978) and others wanted to explain by referring to self-interest. What they wanted to explain was why people care about justice in the first place.

Concern for justice may mean that people claim justice for themselves—for example, equitable shares in their social exchanges, voice in disputes, and so forth; it is incontestable that this serves self-interest. But concern for justice means also that people claim or (at least) that they concede justice for all parties involved, equitable shares for all actors, or equal voice for all. Equal justice for all involved does not and must not result in maximum benefits for the subject who raises these claims: Equitable shares are usually less than the maximum share, and voice may benefit the other party if he or she has the better arguments. There is consensus among philosophers of justice that the crucial test of whether actions are based on a concern for justice is whether the actor not only claims justice for him- or herself, but at least concedes justice for others, if not claiming it for them.

Of course, the rules of justice may be applied for reasons other than establishing justice. Self-interest and further concerns may provide the motivation.

- Politicians may fight for more justice merely in order to win the votes of those whose claims they are voicing.
- In business exchanges, equity rules may be observed because the actors expect that this will pay off in the long run.
- Companies may expect just wages to increase efficiency by stabilizing the motivation and performance of their employees.
- Retaliation may be used for the rational reason that it will stop continued defection (egoistical behavior) by another party.
- Applying the rule of parity in allocations within a group may be a rational choice aimed at furthering the social cohesion of the group.
- Responsiveness to needs of one's spouse may express one's sympathy and love (and may not be an application of the need principle of justice).

In these cases, justice is not the primary concern—if it is a concern at all—but rather comes into play as a means of pursuing the actors' other concerns. This is a tactical use of justice that does not require that the actors have internalized the relevant justice principles, that they believe in their validity, or that they are convinced that these principles should be applied by everyone in similar cases. It can be assumed that concerns for justice—if they exist at all—will be trumped by the actors' primary concerns if there ever were a conflict between the two motives.

This is not the case when justice is the actors' primary concern or at least one of his or her main concerns. In these cases, actors are committed to establishing, reestablishing, or maintaining justice—whatever they may hold to be just. In such cases, concerns for justice are not easily trumped by other concerns.

It is well known in psychology that actors usually have more than one concern in a given situation and that different concerns may come into conflict. We need to use valid diagnostic measures to show that justice was one of the concerns taken into consideration in a given situation, even if it was ultimately trumped by other concerns. If justice was only considered for tactical reasons, actors who neglected justice in order to achieve the desired outcomes should not be expected to show signs of moral disquiet about their behavior.

In cases in which justice is a concern in itself, its neglect causes *feelings of guilt* and possibly also efforts to correct one's actions, compensate for the resulting injustice, beg for pardon, excuse or justify one's actions, minimize the unjust consequences mentally, deny the injustice by blaming the victims or the disadvantaged, and so on. These are possible indicators for the neglect of justice concerns by acting subjects.

In social interactions, the rules of justice may be neglected or violated by others. In this case, subjects' concern for justice may be indicated by explicit claims for justice, *resentment of others' behavior,* criticism of this behavior, punishment, or retaliation; but this concern may also be indicated by mental reconstructions aiming at minimizing or denying the perceived injustices, as shown in the literature on belief in a just world and observed injustices (cf. Lerner, 1977, 1980; Montada & Lerner, 1998, for overviews), as well as by coping with suffered injustice (cf. Montada, 1994). Both victims of injustices and observers who are not directly affected may have concerns for justice and have to cope with experienced or perceived injustice in one way or the other.

Empirical Evidence for the Justice Motive as a Primary Motive

Looking at empirical research, we find much evidence that does not fit the rational-choice modeling of the justice concern. Instances of resentment in which the resenting subjects do not have any vested interests of their own but nonetheless commit themselves to costly and potentially risky attempts to restore justice are especially significant in this respect. It is not unusual for social movements to be initiated and supported by people without any vested interests of their own. Think of Keniston's (1970) study of young radicals involved in the anti–Vietnam-war movement, and of the studies Haan, Smith, and Block (1968) and Fishkin, Keniston, and McKinnon (1973) have conducted about activists in the 1960s civil rights movement. Moral orientations and social responsibility were the motivational bases identified here. Phenomena such as the survivor guilt described for Holocaust survivors (L. Baron, 1987), Hiroshima survivors (Lifton, 1967), and released prisoners of war (Lifton, 1954) demonstrate that not all people who have been favorably advantaged are able to enjoy their good fortune.

They perceive the disadvantaged victims as belonging to their own community of solidarity (Deutsch, 1985), whereby equality and need are postulated to be the preferred justice principles (Deutsch, 1975) and communal orientations are prevalent (Clark & Chrisman, 1994; Lerner & Whitehead, 1980). Managers' feelings of guilt after layoff decisions (Lerner, 1996) indicate that members of the management feel more obligations toward the staff than expected. Guilt felt by survivors of layoffs (Brockner, 1994) is another example. As Cohen (1986) has pointed out, the application of standards of justice depends on the psychological boundaries of the community one has in mind. Susan Opotow (1996) uses the term *scope of justice* to depict the fact that some people draw their personal boundaries much wider than do others. Those who are concerned about global inequalities (Olson, 1997) have a wide scope of justice. If self-interest is the dominant concern, the scope of justice will not be extended to include those who are disadvantaged relative to oneself.

We have studied the ways in which relatively privileged people respond to the misery, the problems, and the poor life conditions of less fortunate others: poor people in developing countries, unemployed individuals in their own countries, physically handicapped people, and foreign guest workers with unfavorable working and living conditions (Montada, Schmitt, & Dalbert, 1986; Montada & Schneider, 1989, 1991; Montada, Schneider, & Reichle, 1988). How do people in relatively privileged life situations respond emotionally when confronted with the hardships and the misery of the disadvantaged? Do they respond with sympathy or angry reproaches, pride in their own achievements, satisfaction about their higher standards of living, feelings of guilt about their relatively privileged situations (which they may not consider to be entirely deserved), or resentment about the unjust treatment of the disadvantaged? We found large interindividual differences in these emotional responses. Guilt feelings—which in this case we called *existential guilt* and *resentment*—were with respect to their intensity normally distributed

emotions in large heterogeneous samples, rather than being rare or exotic abnormalities. Guilt and resentment have meaningful correlates; some examples include perception of the existing inequalities as unjust, cognitions that one's own higher standard of living and the lower standard of living of others are causally related, or cognitions that the inequalities could be reduced by redistribution—and preference for the need-based principle of distributive justice (over the contribution-proportional principle). It has been shown that both guilt and resentment dispose people to perform prosocial activities in favor of the disadvantaged (guilt is more closely associated with personal sacrifices, resentment with political protest). It could also be proved that guilt and resentment were not reducible to self-interests of the privileged which was also assessed in these studies—namely, in terms of fear of losses through forced redistribution and anger at the disadvantaged because of their lack of self-help. Guilt and resentment proved to be not reducible to fear of loss or to anger at the disadvantaged.

In these studies, we tried to disentangle justice and self-interest by looking more closely at people who are better off than others are, consider their views and standards of justice violated to their own advantage, and feel morally uneasy about this situation. They feel responsible for helping to correct the injustice. Other researchers (De Rivera, Gerstman, & Maisels, 1994; Edelstein & Krettenauer, 1996) have come to similar conclusions. Such findings recall those of equity research, in which distress was observed in people who were overbenefited.

Whereas justice claims arising from a position of relative deprivation can easily be interpreted to be self-interested, this is not the case when justice is claimed for the disadvantaged by those in a more privileged position. From the perspective of rational choice theory, one could of course ask *Isn't it a rational choice, serving self-interest in the long run, to correct the gross inequalities existing all over the world, for instance, to prevent violent rebellion by the disadvantaged?* The counterquestion to this would be *Why guilt and resentment instead of fear of their violent efforts to restore equality—or instead of cool, strategic deliberation how to prevent their violent attacks at the status quo?*

Whenever self-interest has been assessed and factor analyzed together with justice scales, the independence of these variables was demonstrated (e.g., Montada & Schneider, 1990; Moschner, 1998).

Traps of Reductionism

Reducing the number of human motives seems to correspond to the ideal of parsimony in theory construction. Of two theories, the one with fewer postulates is the more parsimonious. Such a comparison presupposes that both theories explain the same empirical phenomena and allow the same predictions. A motivation theory that posits only a small number of motives—or even a single one—would seem to be more parsimonious than would one that offers a larger number of motives.

The parsimony argument may have added to the reductionistic stance that the justice motive (as well as other motives such as altruism, social responsibility, love, etc.) can in fact be reduced to or unmasked, so to speak, as self-interest. The economic analysis of behavior (Ramb & Tietzel, 1993) suggests that a great variety of behavior (if not all) can be explained by assuming some degree of self-interest as the basic motivation. This idea is illustrated in the following examples (cf. Montada, 1998a):

- Hypothetically, caring for disabled parents can easily be traced back to selfish motivations such as the desire to cultivate a favorable public image or to ensure that the parents do not withdraw their love or financial support.
- Hypothetically, improvements in community or state care for the poor can be interpreted as enhancing political leaders' chances of being elected by these less privileged voters.
- As mentioned previously, the avoidance of opportunistic and selfish behavior can reasonably be interpreted as self-serving in the context of continued social exchanges.

The economic theory of behavior allows elegant so-called explanations of every action by tracing a path to some basic hypothetical self-interest (e.g., Baurmann & Kliemt, 1995). With some ingenuity, it is possible to generate hypotheses reducing every surface motive to an underlying self-interest, or to unmask it as ultimately serving self-interest. This kind of hypothesizing may be creative, but it clearly does not constitute valid scientific proof of the hypotheses proposed. Instead of asking the scientific question *What explains X?*, rational-choice theorists ask *How might a rational-choice theory explain X?* (Green & Shapiro, 1994, p. 203). Bunge has therefore criticized rational-choice modeling, arguing that it has "inhibited the search for alternatives" (1989, p. 210).

Approaching the scientific task of explaining the interindividual and intra-individual variance of human behavior with a single-motive model is counterproductive because this single motive (maximizing one's self-interest) does not contribute to the explanation of the behavioral variance. The statement that a person's behavior is motivated by self-interest has no informational value and no scientific validity as long as alternative motives such as altruism, social responsibility, the justice

motive, and moral obligation are not tested and excluded by empirical data. Furthermore, the seeming parsimony of a single-motive model is offset by the necessary increase in the number of corollary hypotheses needed to predict and explain the behavioral variance and the diversity of behaviors observed. Single-motive conceptions may best be understood as anthropological predecisions without scientific validity or utility. They are part of a belief system, not of a scientific knowledge system.

Trade-Offs Between the Justice Motive and Other Motives

Lerner (1977, 1980, 1998) has stressed the categorical normative quality of the justice motive as a primary motive and as an aim in itself. After it is internalized as a normative standard, justice imposes itself as an *ought*—valid for oneself and for others, not as an option that can be rationally deliberated and chosen when it seems functional for a particular goal or disregarded without moral disquiet if other options arise. Defining justice as an ought implies that unjustified violations evoke moral emotions—guilt when the subject him- or herself has failed to meet the requirements of the ought by action or omission, and resentment when others have done so (Montada, 1993).

We agree that the justice motive may come into conflict with other motives such as self-interest, but can it be trumped by egoism without remorse (cf. Lerner, 1996, on managers' guilt after layoff decisions)? Lerner doubts whether humans can give up the fundamental delusive belief that the world is a place where everybody gets what he or she deserves—ultimately, at least. This motivated belief in a just world (BJW) is supported by what Lerner has called the *personal contract* to observe the rule of justice.

Lerner has contributed and instigated a wealth of empirical studies showing that the justice motive does not always appear as a straightforward application of standards of justice. Trade-offs between what one deserves and what others deserve are elaborated in specific situations, as are trade-offs between justice concerns and other concerns such as self-interest (Montada, 1998b). The three psychologically fascinating phenomena described in the following passage can be interpreted as examples of *trade-offs between justice concerns and self-interests.*

Blaming innocent victims is a phenomenon observed in many experiments conducted by Lerner and his students (cf. Lerner, 1980), as well as in studies carried out elsewhere (cf. Furnham, 1998; Maes, 1998; Montada, 1998b). Blaming victims is plausibly interpreted as subjects' doing an injustice in an attempt to preserve their belief in a just world, which is or would be threatened by the victimization of innocent people. Belief in a just world can be assumed to be a psychological resource that may be defended by attributing responsibility and blame to the victims themselves, thus reframing the injustice of their victimization.

Another exciting phenomenon is the *exchange fiction,* discussed in more detail in works by Holmes, Miller, and Lerner (cited in Lerner, 1977) and Lerner (1980). It has been observed that many people tend to prefer buying an over-priced article when they know that the profits will go to needy people, rather than directly donating an amount of money corresponding to the price difference. The explanation for this phenomenon is that helping a needy person establishes a commitment and personal responsibility for this and other needy persons. Thus, any act of helping is problematic in several respects: It implies an acknowledgment of undeserved neediness which is threatening the belief in a just world; it creates a continuing and generalized responsibility for needy people, a responsibility that may interfere with personal concerns; and finally, it creates further injustices with respect to all other similarly needy people who have not been helped. Yet provided that they are not to blame for having inflicted their hardships upon themselves, needy people deserve to be helped. This conflict is best solved by an exchange fiction that allows the donation to be masked as a purchase.

The third phenomenon is called the *free riding dilemma.* Everyone will agree that free riding—profiting without investing—serves self-interests. Those who do invest resent free riders for their selfishness. A relevant observation here is that opinion polls conducted in Europe during the 1990s revealed that two thirds of employees were in principle willing to reduce their working hours and income (on average by 10% to 20%), if this would result in the creation of new jobs for unemployed persons. However, this willingness was very rarely translated into action. At least two hypotheses explain this discrepancy: (a) Self-interest (preserving one's level of income) finally outweighs the justice motive, and (b) moving the targets of social comparison changes the objects and contents of the justice motive. When considering mass unemployment and its undeserved sequelae, it would be a just decision for the relatively privileged to share their working time and income. When comparing themselves with free riders (other full-time employees who are not willing to share their privileges), however, subjects who do choose to share would feel relatively deprived. Thus, not sharing can be justified as long as free riding is not prevented at the societal level. What at first glance appears to be selfish behavior may well be motivated by justice concerns (Montada, 1998b).

JUSTICE: A UNIVERSAL CONCERN WITH DIVERGING VIEWS

The concern for justice seems to be an anthropological universal. However, there does not appear to be a universal consensus on what is considered to be just or unjust. We speak of justice in the singular as if there were only one single, just solution for every social system and for every problem or conflict; yet frequently, there are diverging views about what would be just, which criteria should be applied, and how they should be applied in order to establish justice. This is true for all domains of social life in which justice is critical: distributions, social exchanges, and the retribution and acknowledgement of deeds. The application of different standards of justice results in diverging and conflicting outcomes. A common view about what is just and what is unjust would be helpful to avoid and to settle social conflicts in private and business contexts, as well as in the political arena within and between societies.

The normative nature of justice is obvious. The aim of *normative disciplines* is to analyze and account for normative standards, to elaborate reasonable and just solutions for specific cases, and to conceive criteria and procedures for just decision-making. The ultimate challenge for normative approaches may be to find universally valid solutions. In view of the difficulty of that task, the focus may be displaced from the concrete solutions to the procedures of finding a solution—precisely as in discourse ethics (Ackerman, 1980) in which ideal rules of discourse are considered a guarantee for the ethical truth of the result.

It is not the aim of *empirical approaches* to propose the best standards of justice and the best solutions for justice problems. Instead, the following questions are investigated: What do people consider to be just and unjust? How divergent or convergent are the views about justice? Which are the belief systems and dispositions that influence people's perceptions of justice and injustice? What is the motivational impact of experienced or observed injustice? How do people cope with experienced or observed injustices? How can justice conflicts be settled? How can one-sided views of justice be qualified? What is the impact of procedures on the appraisal of decisions?

There are interfaces between normative and empirical approaches: Philosophical theories of justice imply anthropological assumptions that need to be tested empirically (e.g., Frohlich & Oppenheimer, 1990, on Rawls' theory of justice), and the ethical validity of empirically assessed views about justice and injustice as well as the claims for justice has to be examined normatively and cannot be taken for granted.

THE JUSTICE OF DISTRIBUTIONS

Standards of Distributive Justice

In *the domain of distributions*—that is, the allocation or the existing distribution of material resources or symbolic goods, rights, duties, positions, power, opportunities, taxes, and so on, within as well as between groups and populations—*equality* certainly constitutes the basic idea of justice. However, equality can be specified in many different ways. It may mean *equal shares for all human beings* or—if that is impossible or dysfunctional—*equal opportunities.* Alternatively, according to Aristotle, it may mean *equal shares or equal opportunities for all equal human beings.* This second view implies that human beings differ and that specific individual differences justify unequal allocations and given inequalities in the distribution of resources, rights, duties, and so forth (e.g., according to citizenship, social status, specific merits, professional qualifications, productivity, age, conventional rights, gender, neediness). In this sense, equality means equal shares for all those with the same status, for all those with the same kinds of merits, needs, conventional rights, and so forth. That implies unequal shares for people with different status, merits, and so forth. A particular variant of the equal opportunity rule is the equal chance rule, in which a lottery procedure is used when it is impossible for goods to be split up (e.g., in the allocation of organs for transplantation), or the rotation schedule, which may be appropriate when it would be dysfunctional for a position to be split. Equal opportunity may also mean providing similar material, physical, and social conditions for development, for a good life, for health, and so on.

Walzer (1983) somewhat neutralized the justice problems with inequalities in allocations and existing distributions by his concept of *complex equality,* which postulates that distributions in different *spheres of justice* (material wealth, social recognition in various contexts, political power, education, kinship and love, recreation time, etc.) are not perfectly correlated. Thus, a lower rank in one sphere may be compensated by a higher ranking in another. Moreover, the subjective importance of the different spheres of justice varies within a population, so that the perceived overall inequalities may be reduced further.

However, the question of which differences between people justify which inequalities in allocations and distributions remains open. In the ongoing discussions, arguments are inspired by cultural traditions and social philosophies such as egalitarianism, liberalism, social welfarism, utilitarianism, and the human and civil rights movements. We are far from having reached a general consensus on this question;

the preferred standards of distributive justice vary between and within cultures and they are subject to historical changes.

This fact applies across all fields of distributive justice. For instance, the populations of postcommunist states are less tolerant of inequalities, and they claim more responsibility for individual welfare from the governments than do the populations of states with a liberal tradition (Kluegel, Mason, & Wegener, 1995). The rules of justice for the allocation and withdrawal of scarce goods such as scholarships, state-subsidized housing, jobs, and so on vary largely within and across states (Elster, 1992). In the dismissal of employees, for instance, the criteria applied include the employees' seniority, acquired skills, current productivity, neediness, responsibility for a family, age, and gender. Although it may be possible to justify the application of each of these criteria, each could result in different decisions—not a single just solution. Therefore, the application of different justice principles can result in grossly diverging outcomes. Given this multitude of justice criteria, conflicts about which ones would be appropriate in which cases are not surprising.

Although a long list of justice principles has been identified empirically (Reis, 1984), psychological research has largely been limited to three of them: *equality* (equal shares for all those within specified social boundaries), *allocation according to merit or to contributions* (achievements, investments, etc.), and *allocation according to needs.* Moreover, most empirical research has focused on the application of these principles in single concrete allocations of material goods. Fewer psychological studies are available on the allocation of symbolic goods, rights, and positions, on the withdrawal of positions, or on the allocation of loads (e.g., tasks, taxes; for a comprehensive review, see Törnblom, 1992). Data have been gathered on individual preferences for a particular justice principle in specific cases and contexts (e.g., Schmitt & Montada, 1981), and for culturally shared preferences (e.g., Bierbrauer, 2000; Schwinger, 1980).

The Choice of a Principle

Viewing the application of a justice principle as a choice raises a question as to the goals of a specific choice: Is the objective merely to act or evaluate justly, or to avoid disharmony, to strengthen solidarity, to demonstrate solidarity, to motivate performances or effort, to punish laziness, to enhance productivity within a social system by stimulating competitiveness, or perhaps to further the health and growth of the recipients? Deutsch (1975), for instance, has argued that people who pursue economic productivity should use proportionality to contributions as the allocation principle (because this kind of allocation can be expected to motivate recipients to give their best), whereas people trying to foster enjoyable and harmonious social relationships should use the equality principle, and those aiming to foster personal growth and welfare may well consider the need principle to be appropriate.

However, as is discussed later in greater detail, these goals per se have little to do with justice. Justice as a set of social norms creates entitlements and duties (cf. Lerner, 1987). Which goals allocators pursue has nothing to do with justice unless they are actively trying to discharge their own duty to observe rules of justice, to observe the entitlements of recipients, or—in the case that they have to impose tasks, loads, and risks—the legal and moral obligations of the addressees. The relevant question, which was also posed by Deutsch (1975), is not what choice is functional for which goal, but what *ought* to be chosen for the reason of justice. Although equality, equity, and need are principles of distributive justice, not every allocation according to one of these criteria is for doing justice. In many empirical studies the aim of applying a specific principle of distribution— doing justice or pursuing another goal—is not adequately assessed.

For instance, Barrett-Howard and Tyler (1986) found that proportionality to contributions is more likely to be used as an allocation principle when productivity is the goal, whereas the equality and the need principles are preferred when harmony and welfare are the goals. In experimental studies, Mikula and Schwinger observed that most participants are polite when asked to propose a way of distributing joint earnings. Those who (were made believe to) have contributed more to the joint undertaking tended to propose equal shares, and those who (were made believe to) have contributed less propose that the earnings should be allocated according to the respective contributions (Schwinger, 1980). It is open to question, however, whether the participants in these studies considered their allocation proposals to be a *just* solution or to be functional for some other goal like social harmony.

It may well be that justice counts less in some social contexts (e.g., in intimate relationships) and situations (e.g., in emergencies) than in others. But it should be assessed whether justice is at stake or some other goal. When respondents are explicitly asked to rate several alternative criteria for allocations with respect to their justice, it emerges that the equality and the need principles are more frequently applied within close relationships (e.g., between friends or within stable cooperative working groups), the need principle is more frequently applied in health care and welfare

contexts, and the contribution principle is more often used in economic contexts (e.g., Schmitt & Montada, 1981).

Social Comparisons as a Basis for Justice Appraisals

Equity Theory

Much attention has been paid to the *equity theory* of distributive justice—equity as a criterion in the valuation of social exchange relationships is tackled later in this chapter—which was originally developed in the context of work organizations to explore employees' reactions to their wages and promotions (Adams, 1965). The basic components are (a) proportionality of contributions (performance, effort, invested time, expertise, etc.) and outcomes (benefits, grades, acknowledgements etc.), and (b) equal ratios of contributions and outcomes for similar actors.

Later on, the concept of equity was used in an inflationary manner and was taken as a synonym for what people subjectively considered to be just or fair, regardless of the criterion they may apply to judge whether their outcomes were equitable: contributions, status, membership, need, or others. The assumption was that *equity is in the eye of the beholder* (Walster & Walster, 1975). Used this broadly, equity is no longer conceived as one justice criterion or principle among others, but rather is synonymous with the justice of outcomes. The criteria used by the beholders were not assessed, probably because the authors were only interested in the prediction and explanation of the emotional and behavioral consequences of the experience of injustice, and not in the prediction of experienced injustice on the basis of specific criteria (Mikula, 1980).

Equity theory predicts that people will be satisfied when they consider their outcomes (e.g., their wages) to be equitable. They resent receiving too little and feel uneasy about receiving too much. Many studies have supported the basic assumptions of equity theory. People feel satisfied with equitable outcomes and those who feel underbenefited are angry—but also those who feel overbenefited feel uneasy (for a review, see Tyler et al., 1997). This has been demonstrated by subjects' self reports, by physiological measures of the emotional arousal (Markowski, 1988), and by observation of behaviors aimed at restoring justice (e.g., adjusting one's job performance, cf. Greenberg, 1988). The first finding that people are dissatisfied when receiving less than would be equitable does not allow any discrimination between a justice motive and self-interest. The second finding, that people feel distressed when overbenefited, is stronger evidence for the justice motive, which is discussed in the next section.

The conclusion that equity and inequity are in the eye of the beholder does not only mean that various criteria of justice may be applied. Rather, subjects may view the values of their own contributions and benefits in an entirely different way from the way they see the contributions and benefits of others. A self-serving bias in appraisals of contributions and benefits has been identified in a few studies (Lerner, Somers, Reid, Chiriboga, & Tierney, 1991; Schlenker & Miller, 1977). Therefore, justice conflicts may also arise in cases in which all parties apply the equity principle (Montada, 2000).

The Theory of Relative Deprivation

Research on distributive justice was instigated by the concept of relative deprivation developed by Stouffer, Suchman, DeVinney, Star, and Williams (1949). These authors observed that soldiers' satisfaction with the promotion system within their section of the army was not determined by their current position nor by the objective probability of promotion. (In fact, dissatisfaction was more prevalent in the air force than in military police although the air force had a higher promotion rate.) Rather, comparisons with similar others had a considerable impact on their level of satisfaction. They were dissatisfied when they felt that they were disadvantaged (deprived) in relation to similar others. Depending on the availability and the choice of comparison referents, people in the same objective situation may be either satisfied or dissatisfied. In most studies, the objective social situation correlates only weakly with feelings of personal deprivation. What are the circumstances leading to feelings of relative deprivation?

Crosby (1976) proposed five necessary and sufficient preconditions that can be illustrated using the example of wages. A person must (a) see that someone else has a higher wage, (b) want to have this higher wage as well, (c) feel entitled to this higher wage, (d) think it is feasible to be paid a higher wage, and (e) lack a sense of personal responsibility for not receiving this higher wage. The denial of any personal responsibility for one's relatively disadvantaged situation is a necessary condition for feeling entitled to claim the wanted good. Feasibility can be defined by using one of the postulates in Folger's referent cognition theory (1986): Resentment will occur when persons can easily imagine obtaining the wanted good, implying that they do not perceive any serious objective restrictions or barriers. If they do not, some actor or agency must be responsible for withholding the wanted good.

Runciman (1966) has distinguished between egoistical (personal) and fraternal (group) deprivation. The latter

implies that a person views his or her social group or the social category to which he or she belongs as disadvantaged compared with another social group or category. It is remarkable that in Western societies with a liberal tradition, even large inequalities in material wealth between social groups or categories are not viewed as being unjust by the majority of the population, and consequently do not cause feelings of group deprivation (Shepelak & Alwin, 1986). This can be explained by the dominant liberal ideology that everybody is personally responsible for his or her success and welfare. When discrimination is made salient and is clearly perceived, however, feelings of group deprivation may become more prevalent.

Conceptually, group deprivation does not imply personal deprivation: The two have different comparison targets. Personal deprivation occurs when individuals perceive that they are disadvantaged compared with others of similar social status. Group deprivation is based on comparisons with groups of dissimilar status. However, high levels of group deprivation are less frequent among individuals ranking at the lower end of their group's objective deprivation range— that is, among those who are (objectively speaking) the most deprived. In fact, the more advantaged members of disadvantaged groups are, the more likely it is that they will resent the difference between their group and more advantaged groups and engage in protest actions (e.g., Pettigrew, 1964). An explanatory hypothesis is that they compare themselves with members of the more advantaged group and feel personal deprivation in relation to them (D. M. Taylor & Moghaddam, 1994). For instance, women in higher-status positions who earn significantly more money than does the average woman resent the gender-bound inequalities in earnings more than do women in low-wage groups (Crosby, 1982). Thus, relative group deprivation may be mediated by a perceived personal deprivation because the choice of comparison target may cross the borderline between social groups (Zanna, Crosby, & Lowenstein, 1987).

The 1960s civil rights movement in the United States emerged during a period in which the disadvantaged were making economic social gains. The observation that protest against discrimination becomes more probable within upward economic and social development can be explained by the hypotheses (a) that comparisons with advantaged groups become more likely (Pettigrew, 1972), and (b) that reality cannot keep pace with raised expectations and feelings of entitlement to further improvement (Gurr, 1970).

Fraternal (group, collective) deprivation has different consequences from those of personal deprivation. People are more likely to admit the existence of an unjust discrimination and disadvantaging of their group than of themselves. This corresponds to the well-known *better-than-average* phenomenon: *I am personally better off than the average member of my group* (e.g., Crosby, 1982, for women's appraisal of justice in wages). People are more likely to engage in protest when they perceive their group as relatively deprived (e.g., Dion, 1986; Dubé & Guimond, 1986). One explanatory hypothesis is that personal deprivation is more likely to be associated with symptoms of depression than with outrage against an unjust system (Hafer & Olson, 1993). Another hypothesis is that protest against personal relative deprivations can be attributed to envy, an emotion and motive that has negative connotations. Protest against fraternal relative deprivation means both solidarity with one's group and a fight for more social justice: Both motivations are respectable. If oneself is better off than the average of one's group, one's protest even has a prosocial—not an egotistical—touch (Montada, 2001a).

Relative deprivation theory emphasizes the role of perceived injustice in comparison to referents in the emergence of resentment and assertive actions both in the personal context or in the political arena. But the theory does not specify which standards of justice are applied, nor which referents are chosen for comparison by whom—nor does it specify any other antecedents. Therefore, relative deprivation theory works well as a post hoc framework for interpretation. It is less suited to predict resentment and protest. For instance, the spectrum of options for choosing comparison referents and standards of justice is large, and these choices are motivated whether they are deliberated or spontaneous. Those who are motivated to avoid or reduce feelings of unjust discrimination have the option of downward comparisons. Findings revealing that the majority of subjects state that they are personally better off than the average member of their social group demonstrates the motivated nature of this choice (Crosby, 1982; S. E. Taylor & Brown, 1988). The majority of those belonging to disadvantaged groups tend to avoid comparisons with advantaged groups (Major & Testa, 1988), or to underestimate the size of the inequality (Wegener, 1987). These and further coping strategies may help them to keep an emotional balance by controlling feelings of injustice.

The question of how an active movement against injustice arises has led to many explanatory hypotheses (Major, 1994; J. Martin & Murray, 1986). Latent feelings of relative deprivation may be made conscious as a result of public condemnations of existing discrimination and injustice. Participation in public protests may be dependent on a rational calculation of the expected personal costs and benefits, on the strength of one's feelings of solidarity with one's group, and of moral obligations to support it. Participation may be triggered by outrage. Outrage against group relative deprivation may be inflamed by unexpected and noticeably unjust losses and loads decreed by those in power (Moore, 1978), especially when losses were preceded by upward economic and social development that has set higher standards for the appraisal of the present unsatisfactory state (Davies, 1962). The justice principle violated is the right to preserve the status quo and to preserve the present conditions of life and the acquired rights, an issue that is referred to very frequently in political disputes. Latent feelings of group relative deprivation may flare up as a reaction to events of enraging victimization of members of the own minority group; such reactions may explode collectively in riots, especially when the state authorities violate their duties by contributing to the unjust action or by failing to intervene in ongoing victimization (Lieberson & Silverman, 1965): The withholding of basic civil rights by representatives of the state is especially enraging.

The cases referred to by Moore (1978) and by Lieberson and Silverman (1965) are characterized by an unequal distribution of power. If the disadvantaged groups do not see the possibility to push through their claims by taking legal action, outrage may bring the empowerment to take collective action to correct disadvantageous decisions, to change the power structure, or to retaliate the victimization.

JUSTICE IN SOCIAL RELATIONS

Justice in social relations means justice with respect to the exchanges between the members of social systems, the exchanges between social groups, corporations, and organizations, and between individuals and institutions—but it also concerns the exchanges of casual encounters.

Forms and Contents of Social Exchanges

Exchanges are ubiquitous in social life—between individuals, groups, organizations, and states, between individuals and groups, individuals and organizations, and so forth. Exchanges may be direct, for instance, when two individuals express their liking for one another, conclude a contract, or attack one another. Exchanges may also be indirect, for instance, when an individual donates money to a charity that provides help to people in need, or when the state collects taxes from its citizens, using this income to pay for education, law and order, and so on. Exchange relationships may be sequentially chained. For instance, each adult generation cares for the welfare and development of the younger generation, as well as the welfare of the aged parent generation. The next generation will in turn do the same, thus abiding by the terms of the generation contract.

What are the contents of social exchanges? Not only products and money, but also status (e.g., by a marriage or by granting citizenship), commitment to a relationship, attentiveness, information, services, support, good mood, love, loyalty, and—on a less positive note—burdens (such as health problems, addictions, and depression), criticism, blame, harm, mistrust, and hostility.

What Is Fair and Just in Social Exchanges?

Fair Contracts

The *contract* is a prototypical form of social exchange. Contracts are regarded as just when the partners are equally informed and equally free to consent (Nozick, 1974). Justice is threatened if relevant information is withheld, if pressure is exerted, or if one party is not free to refuse to enter into the contract because of a certain predicament.

Because contracts are of eminent importance in social life, many legal norms have been established that specify the obligations of the partners to provide all relevant information, to observe the contractual agreements, to respect social norms in the contents of the contract, and so forth. A contract only has to be fair *ex ante:* Valid contracts have to be fulfilled, even if they turn out to be unfavorable for one party because of circumstances beyond the control of the contractual partner (e.g., unexpected significant changes in market prices). Moreover, specific legal regulations have been established to protect the supposedly less powerful parties—with respect to rent control, industrial law, and product liability.

Laws and Social Role Norms

Legal regulations have also been established for many noncontractual relationships, specifying the rights and duties of the exchange partners (e.g., married couples, parents and children, administrations and citizens, police and citizens, etc.). Most important is, of course, the criminal law (addressed in this chapter's section on retributive justice) containing negative exchanges that are banned by law in a society.

Many exchange relationships are regulated not by laws but by informal social norms, for example, by the system of reciprocal social roles. Many normative scripts for social roles are conventional in character. They prescribe the rights and obligations of the actors, and they shape the normative expectations held by the actors and by the public with respect to the reciprocally related roles. Further regulations are found in the behavioral codes of professional associations, in public conventions regarding politically correct behavior, in the rule systems of sports, in the bylaws of organizations, and so forth. These legal and conventional rule systems correspond to and are shaping the sense of justice within the population.

Justice Principles

Many social exchanges are not subjected to legal or role-bound norms but still have to be fair and just. Which standards of justice are operating here? Modified forms of the equality criterion are standards for appraising *the fairness of exchange relationships,* especially the principles of *reciprocity* and *equity.* Social exchanges are regarded as just if reciprocity is established. This is true for positive exchanges, in which equal mutual advantage is the normative standard, as well as for negative exchanges, as portrayed in the biblical rule of "an eye for an eye and a tooth for a tooth."

Equal mutual advantages have also been postulated in Hobbes' (1648/1970) social contract conception of the state and in the sociological theory of role-bound exchanges (teacher-student, physician-patient, employer-employee, leader-follower; cf. Parsons, 1951). However, the general truth of Parson's equal–mutual-advantage assumption for reciprocal social roles has been criticized with good reason (Gouldner, 1960): Some social roles or positions are certainly more attractive, powerful, prestigious, and profitable than others. And the equal opportunity assumption, which means that all citizens have equal opportunities to receive the more favorable positions, is illusory.

Equity has been proposed as the normative standard for social exchanges, implying equal ratios of investments/costs and outcomes/benefits for all parties involved (Homans, 1961). Equity is to assess easily only when the investments and outcomes are quantifiable—for instance, in money equivalents. This is possible for market exchanges.

The claim that equity is *the* general justice principle in exchange relationships (Walster et al., 1978) is exaggerated. One reason is that equity theory is too vaguely defined to be applicable in qualitatively and structurally different relationships. How should the ratio of contributions to benefits be calculated, for example, for the employer and the employee, the mother and the child, the players in a tennis match, or the victim of an accident and his or her rescuer? All actors in these relationships have obligations or entitlements, but they are not entitled an equal ratio of contributions to benefits. The entitlements are based on contracts, on particular social and moral norms, or on the norms of fair play. Every citizen maintains an exchange relationship with the state. The citizens and the state (in the same way as the insured and their insurance companies) have reciprocal rights and obligations that cannot be represented in the equity formula. Nevertheless, the relationships can be evaluated as just if all parties meet their obligations.

The equity principle is less precise than it was contended to be in more informal social exchanges, in which its assessment is based on subjectively focused and subjectively valued exchanges (of goods, services, love, respect, trust, loyalty, harm, negligence, hostilities, etc.), and indirect and chained exchanges (e.g., services to third parties or to the community that are of indirect benefit to the exchange partner) may or may not be included in subjective evaluations. Nevertheless, it has been proposed as *the* justice principle in social relations, even in close personal relationships. As it is worthwhile to have a closer look at close relationships this issue will be taken up in a later section.

Implicit Contracts Within Social Relationships

Not every aspect of a relationship can be explicitly articulated in a contract. For instance, employment contracts imply that employees use working time for the employer and not for private interests, that they are conscientious, that they do not misuse the contract by spying for a competitor, and so on. In return, the employer does not require employees to perform inappropriate tasks (e.g., those that are below the employee's qualification level) and also takes care to ensure a safe working environment.

Moreover, existing, practiced relationships create new, contract-like expectations. For instance, significant changes in the task structure that was practiced for a long time by an employee cannot simply be assigned by the employer to the employee; rather, they have to be negotiated. People believe that employers have obligations to their current employees but not to those requesting employment (Kahneman, Knetsch, & Thaler, 1986). There is a widespread view that seniority (defined here as the length of continuous employment with an employer) is an important factor protecting against layoff in the case of workforce reduction (Elster, 1992; Engelstad, 1998). The period of notice that tenants must be given is dependent on the length of the tenancy; in many countries, this issue is regulated by law. People are expected to keep to existing exchange relationships, even if the prevailing market situation would allow one party to make more profit elsewhere. Rousseau has investigated the implicit psychological contracts (and the entitlements derived from them) that are built up in ongoing relationships (Rousseau & Anton, 1988; Rousseau & Parks, 1993). Respectful treatment, meaningful work, and a safe working environment constitute important parts of these implicit contracts.

It may well be that the perceived quality of an existing relationship shapes the expectations of what would be an appropriate reciprocal treatment. And these expectations have a normative character; violations may be valuated as undeserved. One limit, however, is that people, as mentioned previously, consider different justice rules as appropriate depending on the kind of the relationship (e.g., equal distribution or distribution according to needs within close relationships but equitable distributions in market exchange). Relationship issues are also an important topic of procedural justice research (Tyler et al., 1997) and are addressed later in this chapter. The way people are treated by authorities—as representatives of social systems, communities, or social groups—is informative with respect to their social status. If the treatment is not felt to be in accordance with their subjective entitlements, it is considered unjust. These entitlements are part of implicit psychological contracts.

Entitlement to Respectful Treatment

One aspect of social interactions has attracted much attention in justice research—respect. Miller (2001) has recently provided an excellent review. A few examples are mentioned here. Lind and Tyler (1988) have stressed the eminent importance of respectful and decent treatment in their group value theory of procedural justice. Mikula (1986) studied unjust experiences of students in daily life and found frequently mentioned unjustified accusation and blame, the giving of orders in an inappropriate form, and ruthless misuses of status and power (see also Clayton, 1992). Bies and Tripp (1996) found that humiliation and wrongful accusation by superiors were instances of reported injustices. Insult and disrespectful treatment have been identified as powerful instigators of resentment and aggression (R. A. Baron, 1993; Bettencourt & Miller, 1996; Folger & Skarlicki, 1998; Heider, 1958). People in general seem to expect respect from others in social interactions, and they seem to feel entitled to respectful treatment and interaction. The right of being treated with dignity is the first of the human rights. However, what *respect* and *disrespect* mean in concrete social encounters may vary a lot between individuals, settings, kinds of relationships, social groups, subcultures, and cultures. Nevertheless, what has been named *interactional justice* (Bies & Moag, 1986) seems to be agreed upon in psychological contracts about a code of conduct (Robinson, Kraatz, & Rousseau, 1994; Rousseau, 1995) defining what is and what is not acceptable in a relationship. As the code of conduct frequently is neither explicitly articulated nor negotiated between interaction partners, the normative expectations have to be derived from observed resentment and reproaches, from aggressive responses, and from further behavioral manifestations of feeling violated (e.g., withdrawal, reduced commitment, cf. Miller,

2001). These responses function also as a measures to educate the offender whose apologies and remorse are healing the relationship (Ohbuchi, Kameda, & Agarie, 1989; Montada & Kirchhoff, 2000). The range of normative expectations may encompass the acknowledgement of expertise, performances and efforts, granted supports, loyalty, consideration of one's preferences, sympathies, aversions, fears, handicaps, and vulnerabilities: All these have to be respected. Moreover, codes of politically correct behavior and language that have to be respected have gained much attention.

Disrespect is experienced as an offence to the personal and social identity. Some of the victims' responses to disrespect are meant as a defense or restoration of their violated self (Vidmar, 2000). In case of public disrespect, the aim of responses may be to restore social status in the eyes of others. Violent acts may have these functions to restore the self-esteem and social status (Megargee & Bohn, 1979; Toch, 1969; for a review, see Streng, 1995)—evening the score by retaliation (Greenberg & Scott, 1996).

The motive to even the score may also be given in responses like reduction of commitment at the workplace or in close relationships, reduction of trust, and silent or explicit rejection of proposals. The positive effects of respectful treatment by authorities on the acceptance of their decisions and on generalized trust in them (Lind & Tyler, 1988) mirror this hypothesis in positive terms.

Justice Within Close Relationships

"The rule most frequently advocated as *the* rule governing all relationships, including intimate ones, is equity" (Clark & Chrisman, 1994, p. 17). Participants are expected to be more satisfied with the relationship, which is in turn expected to be more stable when equity is realized. Participants strive to make inequitable relationships equitable by changing their contributions, their expected outcomes, or both by requesting change in the contributions made by their partners or by reappraising their own or their partners' contributions and outcomes (Walster et al., 1978). Because equity is in the eye of the beholder, so to speak, reappraisals may be functional for establishing subjective equity.

It is indisputable that exchanges can be balanced on various dimensions (e.g., those emphasized by Foa and Foa (1980)—love, status, money, material goods, services, and information): Information can be compensated by money, services by love, and so on. In our culture, parents typically do not expect that their investments into their children's care, development, and education would be reciprocated by the children. Instead, they feel more than compensated when they are loved by their children. To assess whether a relationship is

considered just, one has to look at the balances that are actually made. The global measure of equity generally used in research—that is, asking subjects what they contribute to a relationship and what they get out of it—relative to their partner(s) is unsatisfactory. The precise balances have to be specified if we are to learn how appraisals of equity and inequity are generated.

One major problem is the validity of global measures of equity. Respondents who do not really balance contributions and outcomes for themselves and for their partners may use the terms equity and justice synonymously. Detailed measures across numerous exchange dimensions—which may additionally be weighted according to personal importance—are possible, however (e.g., Lujansky & Mikula, 1983; Van Yperen & Buunk, 1994). The correlations between detailed and global measures are generally modest or near zero (Sprecher & Schwartz, 1994). Thus, using global measures of equity does not really clarify which justice standards are actually used by respondents.

Nevertheless, in accordance with hypotheses derived from equity theory, some studies have found that not only respondents who feel deprived compared to their partner but also those who feel advantaged are less satisfied with their relationship than are respondents who perceive their relationship as equitable (Buunk & van Yperen, 1991). The effects of equity ratings on satisfaction in the partnership and the stability of the relationship are, however, generally weak or nonexistent (Sprecher & Schwartz, 1994).

Thus, we do not have robust evidence in favor of the equity model in close relationships, such as those between family members, in intimate partnerships, and best friendships. Research about justice in close relationships is reported and reviewed in a volume edited by Lerner and Mikula (1994) and a special issue of *Social Justice Research* (Vol. 11, 3) edited by Mikula (1998). One might question whether justice actually matters at all in these kinds of relationships, which ideally are characterized by mutual love, trust, and caring. However, as Desmarais and Lerner (1994) argue, the degree of "closeness" is not the same at all times and for all parties, and it may vary from an *identity* relationship (in which the parties' identities are merged), to a *unit* relationship (in which equal but independent partners cooperate), and even to a *nonunit* relationship (in which the parties compete with one another). According to Desmarais and Lerner (1994), strong effects of equity ratings on satisfaction are not to be expected within identity relationships—"where meeting a partners' needs is most likely to create harmonious relations, while equal and reciprocal treatment may be alienating in close relationships" (p. 45)—in which the partners are not looking for long-term reciprocity. In a study with married couples, Desmarais and

Lerner found that, for respondents who believe that they are in an identity relation with their partner, satisfaction with the relationship correlates higher with the partner's outcomes than with the respondent's own outcomes.

Lerner's distinction of an identity relationship from a unit and a nonunit relationship (Lerner & Whitehead, 1980) corresponds to Clark and Mills' distinction between the communal- versus the exchange-norm orientation in intimate partnerships (1979). The communal-norm orientation means feeling responsible for and being responsive to the other's needs without expecting repayment. It is satisfying enough to meet the other's needs. The partner's outcomes are no less important than one's own outcomes; on the contrary, they take precedence. Extending the authors' argumentation slightly, the following could be stated: Whereas with exchange-norm orientations, outcomes (benefits) are balanced against inputs (costs), in communal-norm orientations the ratio between outcomes and costs is not decisive because one's own inputs are viewed not as costs, but rather as welcome opportunities to meet the partner's needs. Any ensuing rewards are interpreted not as profits on one's own investments, but rather as an expression of the partner's affection and love.

However, conflicts are not unusual in close relationships, and because these conflicts are essentially justice conflicts, it is worthwhile to examine which justice principles are applied when conflicts occur. As long as an identity relation exists, all investments, all self-sacrifices, and all burdens are not balanced with one's outcomes, but the balances may be made when the partner withdraws his or her love (Montada & Kals, 2001).

Research by Cate and colleagues (Cate, Lloyd, Henton, & Larson, 1982; Cate, Lloyd, & Henton, 1985) and Desmarais and Lerner (1989) has shown that the level of received rewards (e.g., in the six resource areas of love, status, services, goods, money, and information) predicts relationship satisfaction better than does global equity (and equality as well), regardless of whether the relationship is traditional or modern in terms of gender-role orientation (M. W. Martin, 1985). Do these findings mean that self-interest is the dominant motive in close relationships? To answer this question, the partner's rewards (stemming from the respondents' own responses to their partner's needs) also need to be assessed. It may well be that those relationships that both partners experience as rewarding are satisfying. One kind of empirical findings seems to support this interpretation: Rusbult (1987) and Hays (1985) found that own rewards minus costs (investments) predict relationship success less well than own rewards *plus* costs (which may mean the partner's rewards). The latter index may reflect the mutual responsiveness of the partners to each other's needs (Clark & Chrisman, 1994).

An exchange orientation implies the normative expectation that one's own investments (definable as the material, social, and personality resources one brings into the relationship) will be repaid or yield profits—if not immediately, then in the long run. This economic view of close relationships would suggest that partners keep track of their own investments and outcomes and—in the equity version of the model—of their partner's as well. The few studies investigating this aspect have found that respondents who desire or already have communal relationships do not tend to keep track of the respective investments and outcomes (Clark & Chrisman, 1994). Furthermore, as shown by Grote and Clark (1998), communal relationships represent the widely preferred ideal for partnerships. In the same study, these authors found the perceived fairness of the distribution of housework and child-care responsibilities to be positively related to adherence to communal norms in the partnership (for women) and negatively related to an adherence to exchange norms (for men and women).

However, it is open to question whether the responsiveness to the other's needs, which is typical for a communal orientation, is motivated by love, sympathy, altruism, or justice. The justice motive implies an awareness of the partner's entitlements and of one's own perceived obligations. Love and sympathy, same as altruism, may motivate to satisfy the other's desires and needs without conceiving these as entitlements and without feeling obliged to do that. In social relationships, applying the need principle of justice, feeling sympathy with the needs of the loved one, and being altruistic may motivate an actor to choose the same behavioral commitments. Nevertheless, the justice motive and sympathy, altruism, and love are distinct motives, and conflicts between them may occur or be induced (cf. Batson, 1996). The behavioral commitments are not informative with respect to the question how they are motivated. We need valid assessments of the actors' motives behind their responses to the needs of a loved one. To assume a justice motive, one has, at least, to ask respondents explicitly about the others' entitlements or their deservingness. Another approach is to observe or ask respondents about their emotions that imply perceived own violations of justice norms, namely feelings of guilt or of indebtedness—and to explore the justice appraisals assumed to be necessary components of these emotions.

The justice motive may also be inferred from resentment of the partner. Freudenthaler and Mikula (1998) offer an example of this approach with their investigation of women's sense of injustice regarding the unbalanced division of housework. In their interview study with employed women living in a partnership, perceived violations of entitlement are predicted by four variables related to household chores: unfulfilled wants, social comparisons of their partner's with other men's commitments, normative social expectations of partner's commitments, and lack of justification as to why their partner is contributing less than expected. Perceived violations of entitlement together with attributions of responsibility to the partner and lack of justification predicted 53% of the criterion variable *blaming the partner*. This set of variables includes the key variables for the perception of injustice: entitlements on the basis of some justice norm and violation of these entitlements by a responsible actor who does not have convincing justification (cf. Lerner, 1987; Montada, 1991). To predict perceptions of violated entitlements, it is necessary to assess the justice norms applied by the individual.

Another example based on a similar conceptual model offers a questionnaire study conducted by Reichle (1996) about losses and restrictions experienced by spouses after the birth of their first child. Anger (resentment) toward the spouse was predicted by attributing responsibility for one's own losses and restrictions to the spouse, which was moderated by the perceived injustice of the losses and a negative balance of perceived gains and losses (explained variance = 74%). Marital dissatisfaction was explained by anger toward the spouse, extent of the experienced losses, number of losses attributed to the spouse, and attribution of responsibility for the losses to the spouse (explained variance = 77%). Within this sample, strong preferences for using the equality and the need principle in distributions of tasks, opportunities, and restrictions (in contrast to gender specific traditional norms) and strong preferences for negotiations as the just way to proceed in cases of disagreement were observed (Reichle & Gefke, 1998).

The Effects of Social Exchanges on Third Parties

Assessing the justice of social exchange relationships would be incomplete without examining the effects of exchanges on third parties. Adverse effects of exchange relationships on third parties raise justice problems—but to my knowledge, they have not yet been an object of psychological research.

Contracts that are fair to the contractual parties may incur serious disadvantages for others. For instance, cartel contracts may be fair for the contract parties, but they are made at the expense of others. Exclusive contracts of sale put other suppliers at a disadvantage. Granting government subsidies to a big company in financial trouble may be viewed as fair by its employees but as unfair by its competitors. Labor contracts between employers' organizations and unions may be viewed as a fair distribution of profits but may cause rationalization measures leading to the dismissal of part of the workforce, or they may prevent the expansion of the workforce, which

would have provided jobs for the unemployed. Even in close relationships, adverse effects on third parties are not unusual. Parents may enjoy the loyal support of their partner in cases of conflict with their adolescent child who in turn considers this loyalty to be a coalition at his or her own cost.

Therefore, it is adequate to expand the view from the directly concerned exchange parties and to examine the consequences for others and for the social system.

THE JUSTICE OF RETRIBUTIONS

The phrase *retributive justice* normally means the justice of retribution for crimes and negligence, as well as the justice of compensations for caused damages and harm. However, special achievements (intellectual, artistic, moral, etc.), especially those that go beyond the call of duty, are also to be repaid or acknowledged. Because the justice of acknowledgement of special achievements has received little research attention thus far, it is only mentioned here; the retribution for crimes and negligence is treated in more detail.

Just Retribution and Punishment

Though just retribution for crimes is anchored in criminal law, in criminal justice proceedings, and in precedents in court judgments, empirical social and behavioral sciences can contribute significant insights, because the sense of justice held by the general public does not perfectly coincide with that reflected by the legal code and court decisions.

What is just retribution for the violation of criminal law? A first answer could be *reparation for the damages* caused, analogous to the equity principle of social exchanges. Such regulations exist in the civil code, as can be seen in liability laws: The defective product must be replaced; the damage must be compensated; the price must be reduced if services are insufficient; the caused secondary costs (expenses, opportunity costs) are to be balanced out. Compensation for damages is not a prevalent goal in criminal justice.

For most people's sense of justice, equitable compensation would be an *inadequate atonement for a crime*. This is true not only for crimes which have caused irreversible losses: How could, for example, the murder of a person, permanent health impairments following a physical injury, or psychological damage caused by terror or humiliation be compensated? This is generally true because the violation of criminal law means a violation of the moral consensus without which the social community cannot survive (Miller & Vidmar, 1981). Regardless of the amount of damage, this injury to the moral code of society demands punishment. The violation of the basic values of the community, those which make up its identity and its self-esteem, as well as violation of the sacred symbols of a society (e.g., its religious tenets, its flag) demand retribution. The primary purpose of retribution is atonement.

The rational-choice model also offers an explanation of why compensation alone is insufficient. If the bank robber could compensate the crime simply by returning the money, there would be no deterrent: He or she could attempt it again and again without risk, in the hopes of one day not being caught. Therefore, retribution must be independent of compensation for damages. Alongside atonement and compensation for damages, a third purpose in legal punishment is deterrence, which is supposed to have an effect on the perpetrator as well as on the public at large. Additional functions of legal punishment are considered: building up or reinforcing a sense of justice in the population, resocializing the perpetrator, and protecting the community by incapacitation of the offender (e.g., by imprisonment or death penalty).

Analyzing the valuations of the various *functions of legal punishment,* Vidmar & Miller (1980) identified two main motives: a controlling and a retaliation motive. The retaliation motive emphasizes the perpetrator's guilt and the severity of the crime. The function of atonement is placed in the foreground. The controlling motive aims at keeping the criminal in check and protecting society. Of importance are the dangerousness of the criminal and the degree of harmfulness of the crime. Miller and Vidmar also differentiate the motives according to whether they are directed at the perpetrator or at a third party: A motive for retaliation can also be to dampen public outcry. We should take this psychological analysis a step further and distinguish between deterring the perpetrators and resocializing them because different measures seem to be appropriate for those two goals.

It is remarkable that the victims of crimes are only marginally considered in the functions of retribution, if at all. In fact, in the historical development of criminal justice in the modern age, the main focus was protecting society and guaranteeing fairness to the perpetrator, not to providing justice to the victim. For a long time, the victim played exclusively the role of a witness in criminal proceedings. The witness does not have a powerful role: He or she does not control the procedure, and his or her credibility and reputation may be doubted. Only recently have victims had the right to function as joint plaintiffs in such crimes as rape and bodily injury, thereby gaining a bit more control in the course of the trial; this should be relevant for their assessment of procedural justice, according to hypotheses forwarded by Thibault and Walker (1975). Whether the victim received justice was of no concern to the criminal justice system. Victimology has

finally taken the rights of victims seriously—for example, their need for acknowledgement of their status as victims, which will be documented by the conviction of the perpetrator (Fischer, Becker-Fischer, & Düchting, 1998).

The various goals of legal punishment may conflict with one another and thus create their own problems of justice: Is the retributive sentencing of a young offender for robbery with grievous bodily harm to the victim just, or is a mild sentence with an attempt at his resocialization more just? When general deterrence is the objection, the mitigating factors associated with the individual offense may easily be overlooked.

Perpetrator's Responsibility and Blameworthiness

In criminal law the severity of the crime is the first decisive factor in determining the degree of guilt and blameworthiness of the offender (recognizable by the range of penalties for a crime). Moreover, mitigating and aggravating circumstances are considered. Special importance is given to the assessment of the offender's responsibility for the criminal act and to potential justifications of this act. This practice coincides with the sense of retributive justice in the public.

A guilty verdict presupposes the *attribution of responsibility* to the perpetrator. The assessment of the defendant's responsibility is a core problem in jurisprudence. Defendants may use any of eight arguments to deny or to diminish their responsibility for their behavior and its consequences (cf. Hamilton & Hagiwara, 1992; Heider, 1958; Montada, 2001b; Semin & Manstead, 1983):

1. *Denial of agency.* Persons may deny that their behavior was under their voluntary control. Reasons given for the lack of volitional control include lack of competence, fatigue, external influences, effects of drugs, intense affects, and so on. In the courtroom, for instance, insanity, intense emotional states, or being under the influence of drugs are sometimes accepted as factors that exclude or reduce actors' responsibility for their deeds.

2. *Lack of foreseeability of consequences.* Persons may deny that the consequences of their actions could have been foreseen.

3. *Lack of intent.* Persons may deny that the negative effects of their actions were intentional; this may lower the degree of responsibility assigned to them, but does not free them of responsibility in every case (Heider, 1958). The person may be judged not to be malevolent, but he or she may still be blamed for carelessness.

4. *Assigning coresponsibility to others.* Persons may try to reduce their own responsibility by attributing responsibility to coactors.

5. *Displacing responsibility.* Persons may deny their own responsibility by ascribing the responsibility for their actions or omissions to others, asserting that they were seduced, persuaded, misinformed, or forced by these third parties. A special subcategory of this type is the displacement of responsibility to authorities who have given orders for the action to be taken.

6. *Mental retardation and developmental immaturity.*

7. *Lack of adequate socialization and education.* Disadvantaged childhood and adolescence, deficient socialization, and a lack of education are arguments frequently used by lawyers to deny the defendant's responsibility, because these factors are widely believed to cause behavior disorders.

8. *Denial of having caused damages or harm.* Even if the person does not deny responsibility for an action or omission, he or she may deny the presumed effects of that action, either by doubting the existence of any harm or damage or by denying that harm or damage was caused by the action or omission in question.

Apart from arguments to deny or diminish responsibility, blameworthiness can be reduced by justifications of one's action or omission. Justifications do not deny responsibility. Rather, they offer reasons such as the following that are expected to reduce their blameworthiness and liability for compensation:

1. Persons may make reference to their benevolent intent or to the positive effects or benefits of their actions or omissions. They may claim that any negative effects are balanced out by positive ones.

2. Persons may assert that the victim had been informed and had consented (e.g., to participate in a high-risk medical research program or to engage in sexual contact).

3. Persons may legitimize their action as a just retaliation or punishment. The victim is viewed as an offender who deserves to be punished.

4. Persons may derogate the victim as being inferior or dangerous, and may assert that their own actions are appropriate for this kind of person (cf. Bandura, 1990, on dehumanization of victims).

5. Persons may justify their actions by referring to legitimate self-interests, whether personal or communal.

6. Persons may legitimize their actions by referring to their normative obligations or higher-order values (e.g., group norms, obligations of obedience, religious norms).

7. Persons may interpret their action as defense of their reputation (e.g., their face, so to speak).

8. Persons may legitimize their action by referring to consensus information, either that "most people act or would have acted the same way" or that "most people approve of the legitimacy of the action."

Arguments to deny or diminish responsibility on the one hand and justifying arguments on the other may be presented by defendants (cf. Sykes & Matza, 1957, on the defense pleas of criminals in general; Deegener, 1997, on men charged with sexual child abuse), or by the defendants' representatives. Even victims trying to cope with intense outrage and hatred against the offender may use such arguments to calm down their emotions.

There is much empirical proof suggesting that the punitiveness of victims as well as that of observers who were not directly affected is dependent on the attributed level of offenders' responsibility; this also holds true outside the courtroom.

In people's sense of justice, responsibility and justifications do have much weight (Burnstein & Worchel, 1969; Kolik & Brown, 1979; Shklar, 1990; Zillmann & Cantor, 1977; and others). In a vignette study, Schmitt, Hoser, and Schwenkmezger (1991) distinguished six grades of responsibility for an injury: (a) intended injury; (b) awareness and acceptance of possible injury; (c) careless action; (d) impulsive action, forced action, or unforeseeable effects; (e) benevolent action performed in a clumsy manner; and (f) behavior not under volitional control. They found a high correlation between these levels of responsibility and the mean state-anger scores of respondents taking the perspective of victims in the vignettes. The perceived blameworthiness of actors may be inferred from these state-anger scores. Montada and Kirchhoff (2000) have demonstrated that credible justifications substantially reduce victims' anger at the offender, as well as the degree of punishment the victims regard as appropriate.

Retributive justice *requires* a valid assessment of the offender's responsibility and blameworthiness. The offender's own views of his or her blameworthiness must be given a careful hearing. Giving voice to the offender is a central principle of procedural justice; yet other's views and information by others also need to be included in the decision-making process.

Blameworthiness, Apologies, and Retribution

According to the concept of retribution as atonement, a penalty is just when it is proportionate to the degree of guilt. The penalty is reduced, however, if sincere apologies by the offender are offered. Goffman (1971) named the following components for honest apologies in a private context: The perpetrator must (a) express remorse and emotional distress because he or she has violated a legal and moral norm and has harmed the victim; (b) he or she accepts responsibility for the violation and liability for blame; (c) he or she credibly expresses willingness to observe the moral rule in the future; and (d) acknowledges that it is up to the victim to accept or to refuse the apology, and that forgiveness is a grace granted by the victim which cannot be claimed by the perpetrator.

It has been empirically proven that sincere apologies reconcile victims and judges (as well as observers not directly involved) and reduce their desire for retribution and their punitiveness (Miller & Vidmar, 1981; Montada & Kirchhoff, 2000). Goffman (1971) explained this phenomenon as follows: By showing remorse, the perpetrator accepts the validity of the violated norm, accepts his or her own guilt and blameworthiness, brings him- or herself once again back to the normative consensus of the community, and confirms the views of the victim. Therefore, apologies attenuate the retributive counteraggression of victims as well as of the punitiveness of the broader public (Ohbuchi et al., 1989). The perpetrator's attempt at reparation has similar effects (Darley & Shultz, 1990). Some courts also reduce the penalties if in perpetrator-victim compensation an agreement was reached (Rössner, 1998).

Victims' Need for Retribution

Whereas the assessment of appropriate penalties has been widely studied, only a few studies exist of the victim's needs for retribution. It is known, however, that for the victims of violent crimes, retributive reactions by the state are more important than are reparations (Baurmann & Schädler, 1991; Pfeiffer, 1993). The large majority of victims assess sentences as too mild in their own cases (Richter, 1997).

A study of victims of violent crimes (rape, physical injury, attempted murder, robbery, kidnapping) done by Orth (2000)—on the average 4 years after the crime and 2 years after the court trial—pointed out that two thirds of the sample were dissatisfied with the court's judgment; and those who were dissatisfied tended to react with pronounced feelings of indignation, disappointment, helplessness, mistrust in the legal system, a diminished belief in a just world, reduced self-esteem, and reduced trust in the future. The effects of dissatisfaction, however, were moderated by victims' appraisal of the proceedings as just. Procedural justice was assessed by some of Leventhal's (1980) criteria and by the relational criteria proposed by Lind and Tyler (1988) that will be discussed in a following section.

THE JUSTICE OF SOCIAL SYSTEMS AND POLITICS

The justice of allocations and existing distributions in general can be assessed for different levels, for instance, within primary groups, within casual social formations as realized in most laboratory experiments, within organizations and institutions (Elster, 1992, speaks of *local* justice), at the level of the society (Brickman, Folger, Goode, & Schul, 1981, speak of macrojustice), and at the international level.

It is important to note that for assessing the justice of allocations and distributions, one needs to determine *social borderlines* that specify who is principally entitled to receive a share of the resources to distribute, who is obligated to bear a share of the tasks and loads to be allocated, and so on (Cohen, 1986). However, the determined borderlines may be criticized as unjust. Should the inheritance of a deceased person who has not made his or her will be distributed only among his or her descendants, or should those persons be included who have self-sacrificingly cared for him or her for years? Should the profits of a business be distributed exclusively to the shareholders or should the stakeholders participate? Who has to bear the losses? Should the tax revenues of rich states be distributed exclusively within the state or should developing states also participate?

Because the constitution, the legal system, and the institutions of a society have an impact on distributions, these components of the societal system are also the objects of justice appraisals—for example, the economic system, the labor laws, the health and welfare system, the educational system, environmental protection laws, immigration rules, the generation contract; all of these may be valued as basically just or may be criticized as unjust, as well as the politics responsible for their implementation and adaptation. Constitutions may be criticized for failing to guarantee human rights, the protection of the environment, or animal welfare; the economic and tax systems may be criticized for allowing the development of huge inequalities in wealth or for demotivating individual productivity; the educational system may be blamed for failing to provide equal opportunities for the socially disadvantaged or failing to meet the needs of gifted students. Justice arguments can be found to support or censure any given policy, and all parties concerned usually seem convinced that their view is the only valid one; this is how normative standards are conceived—as generally valid and as binding for all concerned.

Imbalances of Justice at the Societal Level

Not every claim, not every evaluation of social conditions, and not every protest against injustice is justified. Claims and protests are often based on a one-sided subjective concept of justice: Unbalanced claims—for the preservation of the status quo, of freedom rights, of the equality principle, of the need or the equity principle, and so on—lead to unjust solutions because all other principles of justice have been violated. This idea may be illustrated by a few case examples that are currently disputed.

Affirmative Action

Not seldom, efforts to correct one injustice result in the creation of another. A prominent example is the affirmative action taken to correct the indisputable historical disadvantages of women in the labor market, problems that still persist to this day. For instance, women are still underrepresented in top-level positions. Interpreting this fact as unjust discrimination against women, various types of affirmative action have been taken to give preference to female applicants over their male competitors. The justice problem with this policy is that it aims to correct a historical problem by reversing gender privileges in today's generation of students and young professionals. Today's young women have certainly suffered fewer injustices in education and in the labor market than have earlier generations of women, and today's young men are less privileged than were their male predecessors. Therefore, it is problematic for these historical injustices to be corrected by affirmative action's affecting only the present generation of young women and men, with no impact on preceding generations. The question is whether it is just that the costs of this measure have to be borne exclusively by young men. Moreover, justice—at least in terms of equity—is more frequently valuated at the level of individuals, not at the level of groups or collectives. Therefore, as D. M. Taylor and Moghaddam (1994) argue, many people have justice problems with affirmative action policies.

This approach to correcting a historical injustice is based on an implicit assumption advanced by the new feminist movement—namely, that the gender categories *male* and *female* were in fact social groups. Would it not be a mistake to believe that the whole group of women will vicariously participate in and profit from the success of some—mostly already privileged—young women? Women are not a social group, but rather a social category. This distinction is psychologically an important one (cf. Griffith, Parker, & Törnblom, 1993). Individually, most women are members of gender-mixed social groups such as families, where they are bound not only to daughters, sisters, and mothers, but also to sons, husbands, brothers, and fathers. They may be proud of the careers of the male as well as of the female members of their family.

This is not to deny the continuing existence of unjust gender inequalities in the labor markets. Unjust gender inequalities are recognized by many of those who doubt that the concrete policy of affirmative action will result in new injustices. This is also true for affirmative action in the realm of ethnic inequalities in education and in the job market (cf., for instance, Bobocel, SonHing, Holmvoll, & Zanna, 2002).

Environmental Protection Policies

There is little doubt that current and future environmental pollution entails not only health risks, but also the risk of climate changes with incalculable consequences. There is also little doubt that the current pollution of air, soil, and water entails gross injustices. Because pollution is a side effect of productive processes in agriculture, industry, and business, and of traffic, air conditioning, and so on, the justice concern is about the allocation of the profits, costs, and risks resulting from these processes and activities. Some people and some populations benefit more than do others from these processes, and those who profit most are unlikely to be those who have most to lose from the risks and disadvantages of pollution (cf. the concept of environmental racism, Clayton, 1996).

The costs of pollution are still typically externalized—that is to say, the costs and risks are mainly borne not by those who have caused them, nor by those who have most to gain from the processes in question. The externalization of costs bears always the risk of an injustice. One of the policies for reducing pollution injustices is the internalization of the costs by means of pollution taxes. However, pollution taxes may result in new justice problems.

First, there is no guarantee that the taxes raised will be used to compensate the victims of pollution. In fact, not even all of the victims of pollution can be identified because its harmful effects are long lasting, interact with many other factors, and are cumulative. Furthermore, air and water pollution extend across regional and state boundaries, and such pollution may involve delayed risks for the future when coming generations may be affected by the greenhouse effect.

Second, pollution taxes may intensify social inequalities. They may be ruinous for poorer firms, but not for richer ones; they may be prohibitive for poorer car owners, but not for more affluent drivers who can easily afford to pay the new taxes. The result may be the bankruptcy of some firms, the consequent dismissal of employees, and the aggravation of social inequalities (Montada & Kals, 2000; Russell, 2000). Looking at the branched systemic effects of every intervention, it is not easy to avoid new injustices.

Justice for the Defendant Versus Justice for the Victim

The principle of giving defendants the benefit of the doubt is uncontested in criminal law, but the practice violates the victims' claims to retribution, at least in the case of those victims who have no doubts as to the guilt of the defendant. Many such victims experience an acquittal or a light sentence by the judges as a secondary victimization (Orth, 2000) after the state was not able to protect them from primary victimization by the crime.

Underserved Welfare Benefits

The fact that an ostensibly indolent unemployed father profits from the generous welfare benefits accorded to his family is unjust. It may be justified, however, by the constitutional guarantee of equal opportunity for all citizens: The children's opportunities have to be safeguarded, and they are not responsible for their father's unemployment. Furthermore, the economic system does not allow the father to be forcibly employed. The assessment of justice requires looking at the social system as a whole, and (frequently) considering which of several injustices is to be less tolerable.

State Subsidies to Business

Subsidizing uncompetitive business sectors aids those employed in these sectors and thus can be justified by the principle of need; but it may hinder modernization. Subsidies for preservation instead of investment in the future can place a mortgage on the future and a burden on the next generation. Every instance of subsidization by means of public funds that has no sustainable effect is an injustice to the needs of the next generation. The concerns of the next generation should carry the same weight as those of the present generation.

In political conflicts, the principle of preserving acquired rights is frequently asserted. In the spring of 1997, coal miners in Germany took to the streets to force a continuation of the hitherto-granted government subsidies, which consisted of about LSD 55000-per job position per year. If an equal amount of subsidy had been demanded to create new jobs for all the four million unemployed persons searching for jobs (the unemployment rate was 10.4%), that would have required the entire federal budget. Applying the equality principle of justice in this conflict would have demonstrated the injustice of a one-sided application of the principle of acquired rights preservation and would have undercut the miners' demands.

Pension Systems on a Transfer Basis

The current pension system in Germany raises at least two justice problems. First, with the current shift in the age pyramid, the younger generations can no longer be guaranteed that they will receive a pension of an equal ratio to their contributions as currently is paid to the pensioners; this is tantamount to an exploitation of the younger generation. Second, parents with children are exploited by the pension system insofar as their investments in time and money in the development and education of their children represent an essential contribution for the future performance capabilities of the pension system, but the parents do not receive equitable financial compensation for their investments. In addition, if they reduce their paid work to save time for caring for their children, as mothers frequently do, their own pensions will be lowered.

What Is Unjust and What Would Be Just?

It is much easier to reveal injustices than it is to establish justice within complex social systems. Pointing to imbalances is not yet a generally accepted solution. As justice conflicts and justice dilemmas become apparent, the question is how they may be resolved. There are several approaches to avoid or to settle justice conflicts and to resolve justice dilemmas:

- Just procedures in decision making help to avoid creating feelings and perceptions of injustice.
- When more than one principle of justice is valid in a case, a mixed application of principles would be helpful to avoid gross imbalances.
- Mediation methods can settle justice conflicts in which (ideally) all concerned have a guided discourse about all issues and perspectives at stake and have a chance to find a mutually accepted solution.

These approaches are outlined next. It should become obvious that justice is a personal and social construction.

AVOIDING AND SETTLING JUSTICE CONFLICTS

Procedural Justice

Given the broad spectrum of options for appraising, constructing, and realizing justice in the various fields of social life, conflicts about justice are unavoidable. How can these conflicts be settled? How can peace be preserved? One answer is to ensure fair decision-making—using procedures that are broadly accepted as just within the population (Luhmann, 1983). This solution holds for parliamentary procedures, elections, institutional decisions, decisions of courts, arbitration, and decisions of other authorities. The separation of powers is a crucial element in the appraisal of justice in a given society—this includes the right to appeal against decisions of authorities, also against institutional and parliamentary decisions in administrative and constitutional courts.

Extensive empirical research has confirmed the impact of fair procedures on conflict resolution and on the acceptance of authoritative decision-making. From a normative perspective, the question of which procedures are just is a crucial one. Although Thibaut and Walker's (1975) book is entitled *Procedural Justice,* the authors address the issue of control more than they do that of justice. Preferences for procedures of conflict resolution that give more control over to the parties involved may well be motivated by self-interest—as Thibaut and Walker have argued—and not by a justice motive. Therefore, it is crucial to ask whether the parties involved claim to have control by voice only for themselves or equally for the other party. Leventhal (1980) has drawn up a set of justice rules for the procedures of decision making—for example, impartiality of the authorities, consistent use of arguments, consideration of relevant information, objectivity in the review of information, and revision of decisions if new information becomes available. The granting of a voice to all concerned is also essential—all concerned should be given the opportunity to present their views and claims and to take influence on the decision-making process by having their views and claims considered by the authorities. These are criteria that have emerged in Western cultures as procedural rights to be claimed by everyone. There is ample general evidence of what has been dubbed the *fair procedure effect,* which refers to the phenomenon that perceived procedural fairness helps the parties involved to accept even those decisions or outcomes that are less favorable than they had expected or hoped for (Greenberg & Folger, 1983).

However, a higher level of education is probably required for individuals to understand exactly what is actually meant by Leventhal's list of criteria—and to determine whether authorities observe these rules or violate them. Intellectually less demanding criteria for procedural fairness would therefore be helpful. The concept of respectful and decent treatment by authorities is easy to grasp. In their group value theory of procedural justice, Lind and Tyler (1988) emphasize the way people are treated by authorities. According to their theory, people care about their valuation and status in their group, community, company, or society, and they infer this status from the way they are treated by authorities. Because the way one is treated by authorities is informative with respect to one's social status and has an impact on one's self-esteem—as is assumed by political theorists such as Lane (1988) and Rawls (1971), as well as by psychologists (cf. Tyler, Degouey, & Smith, 1996; Van den Bos, Lind, Vermunt, & Wilke, 1997)—the concern for respectful and decent treatment in conflict-resolution procedures would appear to be motivated by the striving to gain or to maintain high self-esteem and a positive self-concept. Lind and Tyler's (1988) group value theory of

procedural justice has inspired a wide range of research activities and has generated an impressive body of knowledge about the favorable impact that perceived respectful and decent treatment by authorities has on one's own perceived status, on one's self-esteem, on the acceptance of decisions, and on one's trust in authorities' fairness and the legitimacy of institutions (Tyler et al., 1997; Vermunt & Törnblom, 1996).

One question as to the justice component of group value theory remains open, however: Is everyone entitled to claim decent, respectful treatment by authorities? Even those who have seriously violated the law and social norms? Respectful treatment by benevolent authorities may enhance self-esteem, and it may produce further beneficial effects, including the willingness to accept the authorities' decisions, but that alone does not imply that justice is involved. Only if authorities were obliged to treat everyone in a respectful or even friendly manner, everybody would be entitled to claim this kind of treatment, regardless of whether they deserve it. But is everyone truly entitled to receive respectful treatment? Or is this kind of treatment only deserved and claimable by certain people—for example, by law-abiding citizens, by people who have accumulated merits, by employees who always have given their best?

Brockner et al. (1998) and Heuer, Blumenthal, Douglas, and Weinblatt (1999) have made first steps to approach this question empirically. They could identify subjects' self-esteem as a moderator variable: Specifically, having a voice and influential informational input into an ongoing dispute is correlated more closely with perceived procedural fairness among people with high self-esteem than it is among those with low self-esteem. Respondents with high self-esteem seem to assume that they deserve and are entitled to respectful treatment as well as to being given a voice. Consequently, they and only they tend to associate respectful treatment with fairness to resent unfairness if they do not get what they expect.

Nevertheless, positive effects that are analogous to the fair procedure effect may well be observable also in cases in which perpetrators are benevolently treated respectfully and decently by legal authorities: Such defendants may gain trust that the sentence is fair, may accept the authority of the judges instead of opposing them, may feel accepted as members of the community, and may reciprocally accept the rules of that community. Benevolence and grace may well have significant integrating power, even if they are not to be claimed.

Settling Justice Conflicts by Mediation

There is good reason to assume that at their core, all hot social conflicts are conflicts of justice (Montada, 2000). Insights into procedural justice—as well as insights into the prevalence of justice dilemmas and knowledge of how to deal with justice dilemmas—are helpful to settle social conflicts. We can differentiate several strategies for dealing with conflicts of justice in a mediation setting; they are outlined in the following discussion.

Articulating Conflicting Concepts of Justice

Existing justice conflicts are often not clearly articulated at the beginning of a mediation. The conflicts manifest themselves as emotions, specifically as resentment of the opposing party. It happens on occasion that the parties *cannot clearly articulate* their views of justice and require assistance with this articulation. To be able to assist, the mediators need an repertory of hypotheses concerning the principles of justice. Only clearly articulated concepts of justice can be communicated and reflected.

Mediators must keep in mind that the *manifest objects of a conflict* are not necessarily identical with the *underlying deep structure* of the conflict—an example can be found, for instance, in the many conflicts between parents and their adolescent children: the demands of the children for autonomy and the demands of the parents for maintaining authority and the acceptance of their norms and values by the children. The manifest conflicts about dress, hairstyle, neatness, contacts with peers, and so on do not directly reflect their deep structure. Thus, solutions to the manifest conflicts do not always lead to a lasting settlement because the deep structure of conflicting demands is not articulated and not addressed in the agreement.

Imparting Understanding for the Other Party's Concepts of Justice

After the proper articulation of the conflicts, the second step in the process is imparting an understanding of the respective demands and normative concepts of the other party. Understanding does not mean that their demands and normative concepts were adopted and accepted as justified. Each party should, however, reformulate the other party's views of justice and injustice in such a way that this party feels itself to be correctly understood; this is analogous to giving and having a voice in decision making, and it is a sign of reciprocal respect. If, in addition, each party can be induced to formulate arguments for the views of the respective opposing party, then a great deal has been achieved; this is in line with principles of discourse ethics and the ideal communication situation (Habermas, 1990).

Imparting Insight Into the Dilemma Structure of Conflicts of Justice

Settling conflicts is made easier when insight is gained that divergent principles of justice do exist and may be valid and that justice dilemmas result from this fact (Montada & Kals, 2001). The normative character of justice implies that everyone is convinced that his or her own conception of justice is valid for everyone else. Each party involved draws the unreflected conclusion that others are either in error in their differing viewpoints or are egoistic, perhaps even maliciously violating justice. If the person, however, recognizes that a justice dilemma exists, then he or she no longer views the position of the other parties as completely illegitimate and his or her own position as the only legitimate one. In conflict mediation, the questioning of the exclusive validity of every single principle of justice by pointing to the concurrent validity of competing principles is an important strategy (Montada & Kals, 2001).

The justification of the validity of a moral rule or principle is to be distinguished from the justification of decisions in concrete cases in which competing principles are relevant (Habermas, 1993). This step requires concrete attempts to qualify all conflicting claims for justice. Does this mean general relativism of values, a questioning of their validity? No! Not one of the aforementioned principles of justice is unfounded. Their validity can be established with good arguments. As this applies, however, to all conflicting principles, this implies that none of these principles is valid exclusively. We must counter a *negative relativism* that states *Nothing is valid* with the *positive relativism No principle is valid absolutely; many principles are valid.* Making one principle absolute and applying it to the exclusion of others would violate all other principles.

It is the wisdom of institutions to consider various principles of justice in their regulations and decisions. The social market economy, for instance, is an attempt to harmonize the rights of the individual citizen to free economic activity with the maxims of the social welfare state. Rawls' *maximin-principle* is also a suggestion toward integration of the freedom of all citizens to economic activity (which ensures best collective wealth) with the rights of every citizen to participate in the general prosperity (1971).

Regulations for decision making and individual decisions seem to find rather broad acceptance when several principles of justice are considered at the same time; this can be seen in the research on the distribution of scarce goods such as university study places, subsidized housing, and transplant organs, as well as in the research on the layoff of employees

(Elster, 1992). If the decision *procedures* are, moreover, judged as being just, then their acceptance can be expected.

Qualifying Norms of Justice Empirically

If the parties are claiming different principles to apply in the pending conflict, it can be helpful to show that each party is applying completely different standards of justice in different situations and contexts; this shall demonstrate that the parties accept more then one standard as valid and the debate can be focused on the reasons that one principle is preferred in the specific case at conflict. A further possibility of qualifying principles empirically consists of pointing to the application of a multitude of principles and their intermixing in various areas of society. Here we can also point to empirical studies on institutional distribution procedures in the allocation or withdrawal of goods in short supply (Elster, 1992) as well as to Walzer's (1983) observations that various norms of justice are used in different spheres of justice.

Communicating the Subjective Implementations of Justice Principles

If the conflict is not about which principle of justice is to be applied—that is, if the parties to the conflict apply the same principle but think they have contradicting justifiable claims—the justifications of these claims must be finely analyzed. As an example may few cases of divorce mediation in which at least one party claims a fair balancing of the former exchanges. That means that everything must be disclosed—all resources, all achievements, all sacrifices, all the love and loyalty invested in the marriage, all burdens borne, and also all returns. There can be no guarantee that a proper balance will be reached in a divorce settlement. But just communicating an understanding for the subjective assessments of the other party may be a step toward improving the relationship.

Adhering to Principles of Procedural Justice

Mediation requires that the rules of procedural justice will be observed—the impartiality of the mediators, extensive probing into personal perspectives and demands, careful consideration of information presented, a respectful and polite interaction, and so on. In mediation, the decision is made not by a third party (e.g., a judge), but rather by the parties themselves. For the mediation proceedings to be judged as fair, the mediators' behavior is important. The mediation is conflict settlement worked out in common by the parties and the mediators; therefore, the fairness of the proceedings depends also on the parties' behavior.

It is true that one cannot oblige parties to the conflict to be impartial—an essential principle of procedural justice. But one can oblige them not only to listen to the positions and arguments of the opposing party, but also to show with their own reformulation of those arguments that they have understood the other party's position. When this action is coupled with a respectful and appreciative attitude, shown by Lind, Tyler, and others to be significant, a proper precondition is created to judge the mediation as fair proceedings. It is easier to come to an agreement under this precondition, and the lasting acceptance of this agreement is more probable.

JUSTICE AS A PERSONAL AND SOCIAL CONSTRUCTION

Although the justice motive is universal, divergent views about justice are indisputable. This becomes evident in historical changes, cultural differences, and the ubiquitous debates and conflicts in the private sphere—in the political arenas as well as in the courtrooms. The debates and conflicts have two different topics: (a) Which principle or rule of justice is the right one to be applied?, and (b) What is the right application of a principle? With respect to the distribution of a scarce good, it may (a) be debated whether the equality, the equity, the need, or some other principle is the right one to apply; and it may (b) be debated who at all is entitled to be considered for the distribution, who is more or less needy, who has contributed more, and so forth. The first topic is the choice of a principle (or a set of principles); the second topic is its implementation.

Justice Appraisals: Intuitions or Moral Reasoning?

In many situations we experience and perceive injustices spontaneously and emotionally (Lerner, 1998). Those who are outraged have no doubts that justice was violated; that means they have a sense of justice telling them what is just and unjust in the specific case at stake. This is not a deliberated, reflected, thoroughly proofed judgment, but rather is an intuitive appraisal. It may well be that the outrage will disappear when the case is reappraised, when new hypotheses about the facts are formed and tested (Bernhardt, 2000) or are offered by credible others, by the offender (Montada & Kirchhoff, 2000), or by observers (e.g., Zillmann & Cantor, 1977).

Observers whose belief in a just world is shattered by being confronted with victims of injustice either commit themselves to restore justice if that would be feasible (e.g., Lerner & Simmons, 1966); claim justice from powerful others as the state (e.g. Schmitt, 1998); or they deny the injustices by derogating the victims (Lerner & Simmons, 1966), blaming the victims for having caused their own fate, or denying that harm and losses are serious (e.g., Montada, 1998a).

CONCLUSIONS AND OUTLOOK

We have good reasons to assume that the concern for justice is universal, and we have ample empirical evidence that a universal consensus on what is to be considered as just or unjust is the exception rather than the rule. We can observe diverging views between individuals, groups, and cultures, and we know of significant historical changes. This is not to say that no cases would exist in which views about justice are shared in a culture: Experimental social psychology has no problems finding and arranging cases that are considered unjust by nearly everybody. But the omnipresence of conflicts and debates about what is unjust and what would be just—in private lives, in public debates, and in the political arena on the local, national, and international levels—gives evidence of diverging views.

Two kinds of social conflicts and debates should be distinguished: (a) conflicts about the standards or principles of justice to be applied, and (b) conflicts about facts that are relevant when a specific standard of justice is applied. For instance, in conflicts about the layoff of employees, the choice and the weight of different standards or criteria of justice may be disputed (seniority, merit, current productivity, or neediness of the employees vs. equal chances of all or an equal cutback of wages and working time for all, an alternative to layoffs). Otherwise it may be disputed who has more or fewer merits, who is more or less productive, or needy, and so forth. The first kind of conflict is obviously a justice conflict, but the latter is also a justice conflict, insofar as criteria of procedural justice may subjectively seem violated when one's own view of the facts is not shared by everybody—namely, the criteria of voice, impartiality, or objectivity.

It is an important task of empirical research to identify the standards of justice that are applied and to describe the cultural and individual preferences that may be specific to contexts and cases. On the basis of such information, a reliable assessment of the conflicting views in actual disputes is possible; such an assessment is a precondition for a discourse and for conflict settlement. Until now, research has focused on only a few standards of justice and has not paid attention to the whole spectrum of criteria.

An enlightened discourse has to take several perspectives at a problematic case or a justice conflict. Being aware of the prevalence of justice dilemmas—meaning that two or more valid principles of justice are conflicting—should help to avoid and to overcome one-sided views.

Looking at the character of justice appraisals, Lerner's distinction between preconscious, intuitive, and experiential versus rational processes in coming to judgments about justice and injustice is a very important one (Lerner, 1998). Many appraisals of injustice are intuitive and not consciously reflected upon. Furthermore, the parties of justice conflicts have primarily intuitive beliefs about justice and rarely have founded their positions on reflected moral reasoning. What is the problem with that? Experienced and observed injustices may motivate actions that have good and productive consequences: Protest may assert the validity of a justice norm, stop further violations, motivate compensation for the victims, and so forth. But it is also true that experienced and observed injustices may motivate terrible actions, up to homicide, war, and genocide. Moreover, they may mean a serious impairment of the well-being and mental health of individuals. Therefore, it might be well-advised to subject these intuitions of justice and injustice to reflected moral reasoning.

For this purpose, the typical use of the singular form when speaking of justice may be counterproductive because it may suggest that a single view of justice is valid: Which view should be valid other than the own intuitively compelling one? Whenever views of justice and injustice instigate emotions or motivate actions that have negative effects for the subjects, for others, or for the social systems, moral reasoning may help to demonstrate that no single view can claim absolute validity: Accepting one view, one principle absolute would violate all others. Trying to integrate and to balance various principles of justice in their decisions and regulations is the wisdom of institutions and authorities.

Moral reasoning and discourses about justice are one way that views about justice are built up or changed; these are not the only ways, however. The socialization and adoption of views of justice takes many more ways. Social facts as well as the dominant ideologies and traditions have a coining effect on people's minds, at least as long as they are not criticized by trustworthy people as unjust.

A look at social movements and the psychological processes and strategies used to change the public awareness about entitlements and obligations is informative, as Major (1994) has shown. It is no less informative to examine psychological barriers against changes of the worldview—a consolidated belief in a just world, the conviction that the status quo is justified or deserved, self-serving biases, or prejudices.

At the individual level, the construction of justice can also be observed in victims of injustice, in observers, and in perpetrators. The coping strategies of victims who try to avoid or to reduce burning outrage and hatred against their victimizers or who search for answers to the question *Why me?* are well described. Observers who are not able or not willing to bear the costs of correcting undeserved victimizations of others reconstruct a case in order to preserve their belief in a just world (Lerner, 1980), which is to be considered a personal resource (Dalbert, 2001). And the perpetrators try to justify their deeds as Sykes and Matza (1957) and others have described; these are examples of the motivated malleability of justice views.

On the other side, we have many examples that justice views can impose themselves compellingly and uncontrollably to individuals, leading to intensive emotions of resentment of a perpetrator or of guilt when the victim him- or herself has failed. Such justice views function psychologically as categorical (unconditional) imperatives. This is not proof of their indisputable exclusive validity, but it is proof of the moral character of justice norms, and it supports the thesis that the justice motive is a primordial motive that is not instrumental and cannot be reduced to some other motive like self-interest.

In psychological research on this topic, it is crucial to make sure that concern for justice is the object of investigation and not some other concern. Entitlements and corresponding obligations shall be the focus and participants' concern can be seen by looking at the emotional reactions to violations of justice norms like guilt and resentments.

REFERENCES

Ackerman, B. A. (1980). *Justice in the liberal state*. New Haven, CT: Yale University Press.

Adams, J. S. (1965). Inequity in social exchange. In L. Berkowitz (Ed.), *Advances in experimental social psychology* (Vol. 2, pp. 267–289). New York: Academic Press.

Bandura, A. (1990). Selective activation and disengagement of moral control. *Journal of Social Issues, 46,* 27–46.

Baron, L. (1987). The holocaust and human decency: A review of research on the rescue of Jews in Nazi-occupied Europe. *Humboldt Journal of Social Relations, 13,* 237–251.

Baron, R. A. (1993). Criticism (informal negative feedback) as a source of perceived unfairness in organizations: effects, mechanisms, and countermeasures. In R. Cropanzano (Ed.), *Justice in the workplace: Approaching fairness in human resource management* (pp. 155–170). Hillsdale, NJ: Erlbaum.

Barrett-Howard, E., & Tyler, T. R. (1986). Procedural justice as a criterion in allocation decisions. *Journal of Personality and Social Psychology, 50,* 296–304.

Baurmann, M. C., & Kliemt, H. (1995). Zur Ökonomie der Tugend [About the economy of virtue]. *Ökonomie und Gesellschaft, 11,* 13–44.

Baurmann, M. C., & Schädler, W. (1991). *Das Opfer nach der Straftat—seine Erwartungen und Perspektiven* [The victims of crime—their expectations and perspectives]. Wiesbaden, Germany: Bundeskriminalamt: BKA-Forschungsreihe, Bd. 22.

Batson, C. D. (1996). Empathy, altruism, and justice: Another perspective on partiality. In L. Montada & M. J. Lerner (Eds.), *Current societal concerns about justice* (pp. 49–66). New York: Plenum Press.

Bernhardt, K. (2000). *Steuerung der Emotion Empörung durch Umwandlung assertorischer Urteile in hypothetische Urteile und Fragen: Ein Trainingsprogramm* [The regulation of the emotion resentment through replacing assertive judgements by hypotheses and questions: A training program]. Doctoral dissertation, Trier, Germany: Universität Trier.

Bettencourt, B. A., & Miller, N. (1996). Sex differences in aggression as a function of provocation: a meta-analysis. *Psychological Bulletin, 119,* 422–447.

Bierbrauer, G. (2000). Legitimität und Verfahrensgerechtigkeit in ethnopluralen Gesellschaften [Legitimity and procedural justice in ethnoplural societies]. In A. Dieter, L. Montada, & A. Schulze (Eds.), *Gerechtigkeit im Konfliktmanagement und in der Mediation* (pp. 63–80). Frankfurt am Main, Germany: Campus.

Bies, R. J., & Moag, J. (1986). Interactional justice: Communication criteria of fairness. In R. J. Lewicki, B. M. Sheppard, & M. H. Bazermann (Eds.), *Research on negotiations in organizations* (Vol. 1, pp. 43–55). Greenwich, CT: JAI Press.

Bies, R. J., & Tripp, T. M. (1996). Beyond distrust: "Getting even" and the need for revenge. In R. Kramer & T. R. Tyler (Eds.), *Trust in organizations*. Beverly Hills, CA: Sage.

Bobocel, D. R., SonHing, L. S., Holmvoll, C. M., & Zanna, M. P. (2002). Policies to redress social injustice: Is the concern for justice a cause of support and of opposition? In M. Ross & D. Miller (Eds.), *The justice motive in social life: Essays in honor of Melvin Lerner* (pp. 204–225). New York: Cambridge University Press.

Brickman, P., Folger, R., Goode, E., & Schul, Y. (1981). Microjustice and macrojustice. In M. J. Lerner & S. C. Lerner (Eds.), *The justice motive in social behavior* (pp. 173–201). New York: Plenum Press.

Brockner, J. (1994). Perceived fairness and survivors' reactions to layoffs, or how downsizing organizations can do well by doing good. *Social Justice Research, 7,* 345–363.

Brockner, J., Siegel, P. A., Martin, C., Reed, T., Heuer, L., Wiesenfeld, B., Grover, S., & Bjorgvinsson, S. (1998). The moderating effect of self-esteem in reaction to voice: Converging evidence from five studies. *Journal of Personality and Social Psychology, 75,* 394–487.

Bulman, R. J., & Wortman, C. B. (1977). Attributions of blame and coping in the "real world": Severe accident victims react to their lot. *Journal of Personality and Social Psychology, 51,* 277–283.

Bunge, M. (1989). Game theory is not a useful tool for the political scientist. *Epistemologia, 12,* 195–212.

Burnstein, E., & Worchel, P. (1969). Arbitrariness of frustration and its consequences for aggression in a social situation. In L. Berkowitz (Ed.), *Roots of aggression* (pp. 75–91). New York: Atherton Press.

Buunk, B. P., & van Yperen, N. W. (1991). Referential comparisons, relational comparisons, and exchange orientation: Their relation to marital satisfaction. *Personality and Social Psychology Bulletin, 17,* 709–717.

Cate, R. M., Lloyd, S. A., & Henton, J. M. (1985). The effect of equity, equality and reward level on the stability of students' premarital relationships. *Journal of Social Psychology, 125,* 715–725.

Cate, R. M., Lloyd, S. A., Henton, J. M., & Larson, J. H. (1982). Fairness and reward level as predictors of relationship satisfaction. *Social Psychology Quarterly, 45,* 177–181.

Clark, M. S., & Chrisman, K. (1994). Resource allocation in intimate relationships: Trying to make sense of a confusing literature. In M. J. Lerner & G. Mikula (Eds.), *Entitlement and the affectional bond* (pp. 65–88). New York: Plenum Press.

Clark, M. S., & Mills, K. (1979). Interpersonal attraction in exchange and communal relationships. *Journal of Personality, 37,* 12–24.

Clayton, S. D. (1992). The experience of injustice: Some characteristics and correlates. *Social Justice Research, 5,* 71–92.

Clayton, S. D. (1996). What is fair in the environmental debate. In L. Montada & M. J. Lerner (Eds.), *Current societal concerns about justice* (pp. 195–211). New York: Plenum Press.

Cohen, R. L. (1986). Membership, intergroup relations, and justice. In M. J. Lerner & R. Vermunt (Eds.), *Social justice in human relations* (Vol. 1, pp. 239–258). New York: Plenum Press.

Cohen, R. L. (1989). Fabrications of justice. *Social Justice Research, 3,* 31–46.

Crosby, F. A. (1976). A model of egoistical relative deprivation. *Psychological Review, 83,* 85–131.

Crosby, F. A. (1982). *Relative deprivation and working women.* New York: Oxford University Press.

Dalbert, C. (2001). *The justice motive as a personal resource: Dealing with challenges and critical life events.* New York: Kluwer.

Darley, J., & Shultz, T. (1990). Moral rules: Their content and acquisition. *Annual Review of Psychology, 41,* 525–556.

Davies, J. C. (1962). Toward a theory of revolution. *American Sociological Review, 27,* 5–19.

Deegener, G. (1997). Das Verantwortungs—Abwehr—System sexueller Missbraucher [The system of responsibility denial of sexual abusers]. In G. Amann & R. Wipplinger (Eds.), *Sexueller Missbrauch: Ein Handbuch* (pp. 310–329). Tübingen, Germany: Deutsche Gesellschaft für Verhaltenstherapie.

De Rivera, J., Gerstman, E., & Maisels, L. (1994). The emotional motivation of righteous behavior. *Social Justice Research, 7,* 91–106.

Desmarais, S., & Lerner, M. J. (1989). A new look at equity and outcomes as determinants of satisfaction in close personal relationships. *Social Justice Research, 3,* 137–109.

Desmarais, S., & Lerner, M. J. (1994). Entitlement in close relationships: A justice motive analysis. In M. J. Lerner & G. Mikula (Eds.), *Entitlement and the affectional bond* (pp. 43–64). New York: Plenum Press.

Deutsch, M. (1975). Equity, equality, and need: What determines which value will be used as the basis for distributive justice? *Journal of Social Issues, 31,* 137–149.

Deutsch, M. (1985). *Distributive justice: A social psychological perspective.* New Haven, CT: Yale University Press.

Dion, K. L. (1986). Responses to perceived discrimination and relative deprivation. In J. Olson, C. P. Herman, & M. Zanna (Eds.), *Relative deprivation and social comparison* (pp. 159–180). Hillsdale, NJ: Erlbaum.

Dubé, L., & Guimond, S. (1986). Relative deprivation and social protest: The personal group issue. In J. Olson, C. P. Herman, & M. Zanna (Eds.), *Relative deprivation and social comparison* (pp. 201–216). Hillsdale, NJ: Erlbaum.

Edelstein, W., & Krettenauer, T. (1996). Justice as solidarity: A study of political socialization of adolescents from East and West Germany within the theoretical framework of Durckheim's sociology of morality. *Social Justice Research, 9,* 281–304.

Elster, J. (1992). *Local justice.* New York: Sage.

Engelstad, F. (1998). The significance of seniority in layoffs: A comparative analysis. *Social Justice Research, 11,* 103–120.

Epstein, S. (1984). Controversial issues in emotion theory. In P. Shaver (Ed.), *Review of personality and social psychology* (pp. 64–88). Beverly Hills, CA: Sage.

Fischer, G., Becker-Fischer, M., & Düchting, C. (1998). *Neue Wege in der Hilfe für Gewaltopfer* [New ways in helping victims of violence]. Düsseldorf, Germany: Ministerium für Arbeit, Gesundheit und Soziales des Landes Nordrhein-Westfalen.

Fishkin, J., Keniston, K., & McKinnon, C. (1973). Moral reasoning and political ideology. *Journal of Personality and Social Psychology, 27,* 109–119.

Foa, E. B., & Foa, U. G. (1980). Resource theory: Interpersonal behaviour as exchange. In K. J. Gergen, M. S. Greenberg, & R. H. Willis (Eds.), *Social exchange* (pp. 70–94). New York: Plenum Press.

Folger, R. (1986). A referent cognitions theory of relative deprivation. In J. M. Olson, C. P. Herman, & M. P. Zanna (Eds.), *Relative deprivation and social comparison: The Ontario symposium* (pp. 33–55). Hillsdale, NJ: Erlbaum.

Folger, R., & Skarlicki, D. P. (1998). A popcorn metaphor for employee aggression. In R. Griffin, A. O'Leary-Kelly, & J. Collins (Eds.), *Dysfunctional behavior in organizations: Violent and deviant behavior. Monographs in organizational behavior and industrial relations* (pp. 43–81). Stanford, CT: JAI Press.

Freudenthaler, H. H., & Mikula, G. (1998). From unfulfilled wants to the experience of injustice regarding the lopsided division of household labor. *Social Justice Research, 11*(3), 289–312.

Frohlich, N., & Oppenheimer, J. A. (1990). Choosing justice in experimental democracies with production. *American Political Science Review, 84,* 461–477.

Furnham, A. (1998). Measuring the Beliefs in a Just World. In L. Montada & M. J. Lerner (Eds.), *Responses to victimizations and belief in a just world* (pp. 141–162). New York: Plenum Press.

Goffman, E. (1971). *Relations in public: Microstudies of the public order.* Harmondsworth, United Kingdom: Penguin.

Gouldner, A. (1960). The norm of reciprocity. *American Review, 25,* 1611–1078.

Green, D. P., & Shapiro, I. (1994). *Pathologies of rational choice theory: A critique of applications in political science.* New Haven, CT: Yale University Press.

Greenberg, J. (1988). Equity and workplace status: A field experiment. *Journal of Applied Psychology, 72,* 606–613.

Greenberg, J., & Folger, R. (1983). Procedural Justice, participation, and the fair process effect in groups and organizations. In P. Paulus (Ed.), *Basic group process* (pp. 235–266). New York: Springer.

Greenberg, J., & Scott, K. S. (1996). Why do workers bite the hands that feed them? Employee theft as a social exchange process. In B. M. Staw & L. L. Cummings (Eds.), *Research in organizational behavior* (pp. 111–156). Greenwich, CT: JAI Press.

Griffith, W. J., Parker, M. J., & Törnblom, K. Y. (1993). Putting the group back into intergroup justice studies. *Social Justice Research, 6,* 331–342.

Grote, N. K., & Clark, M. S. (1998). Distributive justice norms and family work: What is perceived as ideal, what is applied, and what predicts perceived fairness. *Social Justice Research, 11*(3), 243–270.

Gurr, T. R. (1970). *Why men rebel.* Princeton, NJ: Princeton University Press.

Haan, N., Smith, M. B., & Block, J. (1968). Moral reasoning of young adults: Political-social behavior, family background, and personality correlates. *Journal of Personality and Social Psychology, 10,* 183–201.

Hafer, C. L., & Olson, J. M. (1993). Beliefs in a just world, discontent, and assertive actions by working women. *Personality and Social Psychology Bulletin, 19,* 30–38.

Hamilton, V. L., & Hagiwara, S. (1992). Roles, responsibility, and accounts across cultures. *International Journal of Psychology, 27*(2), 157–179.

Hardin, R. (1996). Distributive justice in a real world. In L. Montada & M. J. Lerner (Eds.), *Current societal problems about justice* (pp. 9–24). New York: Plenum Press.

Hays, R. B. (1985). A longitudinal study of friendship development. *Journal of Personality and Social Psychology, 48,* 909–924.

Heider, F. (1958). *The psychology of interpersonal relations.* New York: Wiley.

Heuer, L., Blumenthal, E., Douglas, A., & Weinblatt, T. (1999). A deservingness approach to respect as a relationally based fairness judgement. *Personality and Social Psychology Bulletin, 25,* 1279–1292.

Hobbes, T. (1970). *Leviathan.* London: Dent. (Original work published 1648)

Homans, G. C. (1961). *Social behaviour: Its elementary forms.* New York: Harcourt, Brace, and World.

Kahneman, D., Knetsch, J. L., & Thaler, R. H. (1986). Fairness and the assumptions of economics. *Journal of Business, 59,* 5285–5300.

Keniston, K. (1970). Student activism, moral development, and morality. *American Journal of Orthopsychiatry, 40,* 577–592.

Kluegel, J. R., Mason, D. S., & Wegener, B. (Eds.). (1995). *Social justice and political change. Political opinion in capitalist and post-communist states.* New York: de Gruyter.

Kolik, J. A., & Brown, R. (1979). Frustration, attribution of blame, and aggression. *Journal of Experimental Social Psychology, 15,* 183–194.

Lane, R. E. (1988). Procedural goods in a democracy: How one is treated versus what one gets. *Social Justice Research, 2,* 177–192.

Lerner, M. J. (1977). The justice motive. Some hypotheses as to its origins and forms. *Journal of Personality, 45,* 1–32.

Lerner, M. J. (1980). *The belief in a just world: A fundamental delusion.* New York: Plenum Press.

Lerner, M. J. (1987). Integrating societal and psychological rules of entitlement: The basic tasks of each social actor and for the social sciences. *Social Justice Research, 1,* 107–125.

Lerner, M. J. (1996). Doing justice to the justice motive. In L. Montada & M. J. Lerner (Eds.), *Current societal concerns about justice* (pp. 1–8). New York: Plenum Press.

Lerner, M. J. (1998). The two forms of Belief in a Just World: Some thoughts on why and how people care about justice. In L. Montada & M. J. Lerner (Eds.), *Responses to victimizations and Belief in a Just World* (pp. 247–269). New York: Plenum Press.

Lerner, M. J., & Mikula, G. (Eds.). (1994). *Entitlement and the affectional bond.* New York: Plenum Press.

Lerner, M. J., & Simmons, C. H. (1966). Observer's reactions to the "innocent victim": Compassion or rejection? *Journal of Personality and Social Psychology, 4,* 203–210.

Lerner, M. J., Somers, D., Reid, D., Chiriboga, D., & Tierney, M. (1991). Adult children as caregivers: Egocentric biases in judgments of sibling contributions. *Gerontologist, 31,* 746–755.

Lerner, M. J., & Whitehead, L. A. (1980). Procedural justice viewed in the context of justice motive theory. In G. Mikula (Ed.), *Justice and social interaction* (pp. 219–256). Bern, Switzerland: Hans Huber.

Leventhal, G. S. (1980). What should be done with equity theory? New approaches to the study of fairness in social relationships. In K. J. Gergen, M. S. Greenberg, & R. H. Willis (Eds.), *Social exchange: Advances in theory and research* (pp. 27–55). New York: Plenum Press.

Lieberson, S., & Silverman, R. A. (1965). The precipitants and underlying conditions of race riots. *American Sociological Review, 30,* 887–898.

Lifton, R. J. (1954). "Home by Ship": Reaction patterns of American prisoners of war repatriated North Korea. *American Journal of Psychiatry, 110,* 733–751.

Lifton, R. J. (1967). *Death in life: Survivors of Hiroshima.* New York: Random House.

Lind, A. E., & Tyler, T. R. (1988). *The social psychology of procedural justice.* New York: Plenum Press.

Luhmann, N. (1983). *Legitimation durch Verfahren* [Legitimation by procedures]. Frankfurt am Main, Germany: Suhrkamp.

Lujansky, H., & Mikula, G. (1983). Can equity explain the quality and stability of romantic relationships? *British Journal of Social Psychology, 22,* 101–112.

Maes, J. (1998). Eight stages in the development of research on the construct of Belief in a Just World. In L. Montada & M. J. Lerner (Eds.), *Responses to victimizations and belief in a just world* (pp. 163–185). New York: Plenum Press.

Major, B. (1994). From social inequality to personal entitlement: The role of social comparisons, legitimacy appraisals, and group membership. In M. Zanna (Ed.), *Advances in experimental social psychology* (Vol. 26, pp. 293–355). New York: Academic Press.

Major, B., & Testa, M. (1988). Social comparison processes and judgments of entitlement and satisfaction. *Journal of Experimental Social Psychology, 25,* 101–120.

Markowski, B. (1988). Injustice and arousal. *Social Justice Research, 2,* 223–233.

Martin, M. W. (1985). Satisfaction with intimate exchange: Gender-role differences and impact of equity, equality, and rewards. *Sex Roles, 13,* 597–605.

Martin, J., & Murray, A. (1986). Catalysts for collective violence. In R. Folger (Ed.), *The sense of injustice: Social psychological perspectives.* New York: Plenum Press.

Megargee, E. I., & Bohn, M. J. (1979). *Classifying criminal offenders: a new system based on the MMPI.* Beverly Hills, CA: Sage.

Mikula, G. (1980). On the role of justice in allocation decisions. In G. Mikula (Ed.), *Justice and Social Interaction* (pp. 127–166). Bern, Switzerland: Hans Huber.

Mikula, G. (1986). The experience of injustice: Toward a better understanding of its phenomenology. In H. W. Bierhoff,

R. L. Cohen, & J. Greenberg (Eds.), *Justice in social relations* (pp. 103–124). New York: Plenum Press.

Mikula, G. (Ed.). (1998). Justice in the family: Multiple perspectives on the division of labor [Special issue]. *Social Justice Research, 11*(3).

Miller, D. T. (2001) Disrespect and the experience of injustice. *Annual Reviews Psychology, 52,* 527–553.

Miller, D. T., & Vidmar, N. (1981). The social psychology of punishment reactions. In M. J. Lerner & S. C. Lerner (Eds.), *The justice motive in social behavior.* New York: Academic Press.

Montada, L. (1991). Coping with life stress: Injustice and the question "Who is responsible?" In H. Steensma & R. Vermunt (Eds.), *Social justice in human relations* (Vol. 2, pp. 9–30). New York: Plenum Press.

Montada, L. (1992). Attribution of responsibility for losses and perceived injustice. In L. Montada, S.-H. Filipp, & M. J. Lerner (Eds.), *Life crises and the experience of loss in adulthood* (pp. 133–162). Hillsdale, NJ: Erlbaum.

Montada, L. (1993). Understanding oughts by assessing moral reasoning or moral emotions? In G. Noam & T. Wren (Eds.), *The moral self* (pp. 292–309). Boston: MIT Press.

Montada, L. (1994). Injustice in harm and loss. *Social Justice Research, 7,* 5–28.

Montada, L. (1998a). Justice: Just a rational choice? *Social Justice Research, 12,* 81–101.

Montada, L. (1998b). Belief in a Just World: A hybrid of justice motive and self-interest? In L. Montada & M. J. Lerner (Eds.), *Responses to victimizations and belief in a just world* (pp. 217–246). New York: Plenum Press.

Montada, L. (2000). Mediation bei Gerechtigkeitskonflikten [Mediation in justice conflicts]. In A. Dieter, L. Montada, & A. Schulze (Eds.), *Gerechtigkeit im Konfliktmanagement und in der Mediation* (pp. 37–62). Frankfurt, Germany: Campus.

Montada, L. (2001a). Gerechtigkeit und Neid [Justice and envy]. *Berliner Debatte, 3,* 48–58.

Montada, L. (2001b). Denial of responsibility. In A. E. Auhagen & H. W. Bierhoff, *Responsibility: The many faces of a social phenomenon* (pp. 79–92). London: Routledge.

Montada, L., & Kals, E. (2000). Political implications of psychological research on ecological justice and proenvironmental behaviors. *International Journal of Psychology, 35,* 168–176.

Montada, L., & Kals, E. (2001). *Mediation. Lehrbuch für Psychologen und Juristen* [Mediation. Textbook for psychologists and jurists]. Weinheim, Germany: PVU.

Montada, L., & Kirchhoff, S. (2000). *Bitte um Verzeihung, Rechtfertigungen und Ausreden: Ihre Wirkungen auf soziale Beziehungen* [Apologies, justifications and excuses: Their effects on social relations]. (Berichte aus der Arbeitsgruppe "Verantwortung, Gerechtigkeit, Moral" Nr. 130). Trier, Germany: Universität Trier, Fachbereich I—Psychologie.

Montada, L., & Lerner, M. J. (1998). *Responses to victimization and Belief in a Just World.* New York: Plenum Press.

Montada, L., Schmitt, M., & Dalbert, C. (1986). Thinking about justice and dealing with one's own privileges: A study of existential guilt. In H. W. Bierhoff, R. Cohen, & J. Greenberg (Eds.), *Justice in social relations* (pp. 125–143). New York: Plenum Press.

Montada, L. & Schneider, A. (1989). Justice and emotional reactions to the disadvantaged. *Social Justice Research, 3,* 313–344.

Montada, L., & Schneider, A. (1990). *Coping mit Problemen sozial Schwacher: Annotierte Ergebnistabellen* [Coping with problems of socially disadvantaged: annotated tables of results]. (Berichte aus der Arbeitsgruppe "Verantwortung, Gerechtigkeit, Moral" Nr. 52). Trier, Germany: Universität Trier, Fachbereich I—Psychologie.

Montada, L., & Schneider, A. (1991). Justice and prosocial commitments. In L. Montada & H. W. Bierhoff (Eds.), *Altruism in social systems* (pp. 58–81). Toronto, Canada: Hogrefe & Huber.

Montada, L., Schneider, A., & Reichle, B. (1988). Emotionen und Hilfsbereitschaft [Emotions and readiness to give support]. In H. W. Bierhoff & L. Montada (Eds.), *Altruismus: Bedingungen der Hilfsbereitschaft* (pp. 130–153). Göttingen, Germany: Hogrefe.

Montada, L., Schneider, A., & Seiler, S. (1999). *Bewältigung emotionaler Belastungen durch Querschnittslähmung mittels Relativierung von Verantwortlichkeitsattributionen* [Coping with emotional distress of paraplegics by qualifying responsibility attributions]. (Berichte aus der Arbeitsgruppe "Verantwortung, Gerechtigkeit, Moral" Nr. 125). Trier, Germany: Universität Trier, Fachbereich I—Psychologie.

Moore, B. (1978). *Injustice: The social bases of obedience and revolt.* White Plains, NY: Sharpe.

Moschner, B. (1998). Ehrenamtliches Engagement und soziale Verantwortung [Volunteering and social responsibility]. In B. Reichle & M. Schmitt (Eds.), *Verantwortung, Gerechtigkeit und Moral* (pp. 73–86). Weinheim, Germany: Juventa Verlag.

Nozick, R. (1974). *Anarchy, state and utopia.* New York: Basic Books.

Ohbuchi, K., Kameda, M., & Agarie, N. (1989). Apology as aggression control: Its role in mediation appraisal of and response to harm. *Journal of Personality and Social Psychology, 56(2),* 219–227.

Olson, J. T. (1997). Perceptions of global inequality: A call for research. *Social Justice Research, 10,* 39–62.

Opotow, S. (1996) Is justice finite? The case of environmental inclusion. In L. Montada & M. J. Lerner (Eds.), *Current societal concerns about justice* (pp. 213–230). New York: Plenum Press.

Orth, U. (2000). *Strafgerechtigkeit und Bewältigung krimineller Viktimisierung: Eine Untersuchung zu den Folgen des Strafverfahrens bei Opfern von Gewalttaten* [Criminal justice and coping with criminal victimization: A study of the consequences of criminal proceeding on crime victims]. Unveröffentlichte dissertation, Trier: Universität Trier, Fachbereich I—Psychologie.

Parsons, T. (1951). *The social system.* Glencoe, IL: Free Press.

Pettigrew, T. F. (1964). *A profile of the Negro American.* Princeton, NJ: Van Nostrand.

Pettigrew, T. F. (1972). *Racially separate or together.* New York: McGraw-Hill.

Pfeiffer, C. (1993). Opferperspektiven: Wiedergutmachung und Strafe aus der Sicht der Bevölkerung [Victim perspectives: Compensation and punishment in the view of the population]. In P. A. Albrecht (Ed.), *Festschrift für Horst Schüler-Springorum zum 65. Geburtstag* (pp. 53–80). Köln, Germany: Heymanns.

Ramb, B.-T., & Tietzel, M. (Eds.) (1993). *Ökonomische Verhaltenstheorie* [Economical theory of behavior]. München, Germany: Franz Vahlen.

Rawls, J. (1971). *A theory of justice.* Cambridge, MA: Belknap.

Reichle, B. (1996). From is to ought and the kitchen sink: On the justice of distributions in close relationships. In L. Montada & M. J. Lerner (Eds.), *Current societal concerns about justice* (pp. 103–136). New York: Plenum Press.

Reichle, B., & Gefke, M. (1998). Justice of conjugal divisions of labor: You can't always get what you want. *Social Justice Research, 3,* 271–287.

Reichle, B., Schneider, A., & Montada, L. (1998). How do observers of victimization preserve their believe in a just world cognitively or actionally? Findings from a longitudinal study. In L. Montada & M. J. Lerner (Eds.), *Responses to victimizations and belief in a just world. Critical issues in social justice* (pp. 55–64). New York: Plenum Press.

Reis, H. T. (1984). The multidimensionality of justice. In R. Folger (Ed.), *The sense of injustice: Social psychological perspectives* (pp. 25–61). New York: Plenum Press.

Richter, H. (1997). *Opfer krimineller Gewalttaten. Individuelle Folgen und ihre Verarbeitung* [Violent crime victims. Individual consequences of and coping with victimization]. Mainz, Germany: Weißer Ring.

Robinson, S. L., Kraatz, M. S., & Rousseau, D. M. (1994). Changing obligations and the psychological contract: a longitudinal study. *Academic Management Journal, 37,* 137–152.

Rössner, D. (1998). Mediation und Strafrecht [Mediation and criminal law]. In D. Strempel (Ed.), *Mediation für die Praxis* (pp. 42–54). Berlin: Haufe.

Rousseau, D. M. (1995). *Psychological contracts in organizations.* Thousand Oaks, CA: Sage.

Rousseau, D. M., & Anton, R. J. (1988). Fairness and implied contract: Obligations in job terminations: A policy-capturing study. *Human Performance, 1,* 273–289.

Rousseau, D. M., & Parks, J. M. (1993). The contracts of individuals and organizations. *Research in Organizational Behavior, 15,* 1–43.

Runciman, W. G. (1966). *Relative deprivation and social justice: A study of attitudes to social inequality in twentieth-century England.* Berkeley: University of California.

Rusbult, C. (1987). Responses to dissatisfaction in close relationships: The exit-voice-loyalty-neglect model. In D. Perlman & S. Duck (Eds.), *Intimate relationships: Development, dynamics, and deterioration* (pp. 209–237). Newbury Park, CA: Sage.

Russell, Y. (2000). *Intergenerationelle Verantwortlichkeit und Gerechtigkeit im globalen Umweltschutz* [Intergenerational responsibility and justice in global environment protection]. Doctoral dissertation, Trier, Germany: Universität Trier.

Schlenker, B. R., & Miller, R. S. (1977). Egocentrism in groups. *Journal of Personality and Social Psychology, 35,* 755–764.

Schmitt, M. (1994). *Gerechtigkeit als innerdeutsches Problem: Skizze eines Forschungsvorhabens* [Justice as inner German problem: Sketch of a research project] (Berichte aus der Arbeitsgruppe "Verantwortung, Gerechtigkeit, Moral" Nr. 75). Trier, Germany: Universität Trier, Fachbereich I—Psychologie.

Schmitt, M. (1998). Gerechtigkeit und Solidarität im wiedervereinigten Deutschland [Justice and solidarity in reunified Germany]. In B. Reichle & M. Schmitt (Eds.), *Verantwortung, Gerechtigkeit und Moral* (pp. 87–98). Weinheim, Germany: Juventa.

Schmitt, M., Hoser, K., & Schwenkmezger, P. (1991). Schadensverantwortlichkeit und Ärger [Responsibility for damage and anger]. *Zeitschrift für Experimentelle und Angewandte Psychologie, 38*(4), 634–647.

Schmitt, M., & Mohiyeddini, C. (1996). Sensitivity to befallen injustice and reactions to a real-life-disadvantage. *Social Justice Research, 9,* 223–238.

Schmitt, M., & Montada, L. (1981). Determinanten der Gerechtigkeit [Determinants of justice]. *Zeitschrift für Sozialpsychologie, 13,* 32–44.

Schwinger, T. (1980). Just allocations of goods: Decisions among three principles. In G. Mikula (Ed.), *Justice and social interaction* (pp. 95–126). Bern, Switzerland: Hans Huber.

Semin, G. R., & Manstead, A. S. R. (1983). *The accountability of conduct. A social psychological analysis.* New York: Academic Press.

Shepelak, N. J., & Alwin, D. (1986). Beliefs about inequality and perceptions of distributive Justice. *American Sociological Review, 51,* 30–46.

Shklar, J. (1990). *The faces of justice.* New Haven, CT: Yale University Press.

Shweder, R. A., & Haidt, J. (1993). The future of moral psychology: Truth, intuition, and the pluralist way. *Psychological Science, 4,* 360–365.

Sprecher, S., & Schwartz, P. (1994). Equity and balance in the exchange of contributions in close relationships. In M. J. Lerner & G. Mikula (Eds.), *Entitlement and the affectional bond* (pp. 11–42). New York: Plenum Press.

Streng, F. (1995). Fremdenfeindliche Gewaltkriminalität als Herausforderung für kriminologische Erklärungsansätze [Violent crimes against strangers as a challenge for criminological explanatory approaches]. *Jura, 17,* 182–190.

Stouffer, S. A., Suchman, E. A., DeVinney, L. C., Star, S. A., & Williams, R. A., Jr. (1949). *The American soldier: Adjustments during army life* (Vol. 1). Princeton, NJ: Princeton University Press.

Sykes, G. M., & Matza, D. (1957). Techniques of neutralization: a theory of delinquency. *American Journal of Sociology, 22,* 664–670.

Taylor, S. E., & Brown, J. D. (1988). Illusion and well-being: Some social psychological contributions to a theory of mental health. *Psychological Bulletin, 103,* 193–210.

Taylor, D. M., & Moghaddam, F. M. (1994). *Theories of intergroup relations.* New York: Preager.

Thibaut, J. W., & Walker, L. (1975). *Procedural justice: A psychological analysis.* Hillsdale, NJ: Erlbaum.

Toch, H. (1969). *Violent men : An inquiry into the psychology of violence.* Chicago: Aldine.

Törnblom, K. Y. (1992). The social psychology of distributive justice. In K. R. Scherer (Ed.), *Justice: Interdisciplinary perspectives* (pp. 177–284). Port Chester, NY: Cambridge University Press.

Tyler, T. R., Boeckman, R. J., Smith, H. J., & Huo, Y. Z. (1997). *Social justice in a diverse society.* Boulder, CO: Westview Press.

Tyler, T. R., Degouey, P., & Smith, H. J. (1996). Understanding why the justice of group procedures matters. *Journal of Personality and Social Psychology, 70,* 913–930.

Van den Bos, K., Lind, E. A., Vermunt, R., & Wilke, H. A. M. (1997). How do I judge my outcome when I do not know the outcome of others? The psychology of the fair process effect. *Journal of Personality and Social Psychology, 72,* 1034–1046.

Van Yperen, N. W., & Buunk, B. P. (1994). Social comparison and social exchange in marital relationships. In M. J. Lerner & G. Mikula (Eds.), *Entitlement and the affectional bond* (pp. 89–116). New York: Plenum Press.

Vermunt, R., & Törnblom, K. (Eds.) (1996). Distributive and procedural justice [Special issue]. *Social Justice Research, 9*(4).

Vidmar, N. (2000). Retribution and revenge. In J. Sanders & V. L. Hamilton (Ed.), *Handbook of justice research in law* (pp. 31–63). New York: Kluwer.

Vidmar, N., & Miller, D. T. (1980). The social psychology of punishment. *Law and Society Review, 14,* 565–602.

Walster, E., & Walster, G. W. (1975). Equity and social justice. *Journal of Social Issues, 31,* 21–43.

Walster, E., Berscheid, E., & Walster, G. W. (1978). *Equity: Theory and research.* Boston: Allyn & Bacon.

Walzer, M. (1983). *Spheres of justice: A defense of pluralism and equality.* New York: Basic Books.

Wegener, B. (1987). The illusion of distributive justice. *European Sociological Review, 3,* 1–13.

Zanna, M., Crosby, F., & Lowenstein, G. (1987). Male reference groups and discontent among female professionals. In B. A. Gutek & L. Larwood (Eds.), *Women's career development* (pp. 28–41). Newbury Park, CA: Sage.

Zillmann, D., & Cantor, J. R. (1977). Affective responses to the emotions of a protagonist. *Journal of Experimental Social Psychology, 13,* 155–165.

CHAPTER 23

Aggression, Violence, Evil, and Peace

JOSEPH DE RIVERA

Although aggression, violence, and evil are interrelated, contemporary research is so specialized that it is unusual to group them together, and this chapter is unique in considering them together with ideas and research on peace. Why place such disparate fields in the same chapter? In part, it is because we study aggression and violence in order to avoid the evil that they occasion and to achieve peace. However, if peace were simply the absence of violence, it would not require separate treatment; and if peace were a completely independent field, it would be better to make use of separate chapters. Typically, there are separate chapters on aggression and prosocial behavior. Here, however, we argue that the achievement of peace rests on an understanding of aggression, violence, and evil, yet requires us to go beyond that material to include not only what is usually conceived as prosocial behavior but the use of aggression in a struggle with violence and evil. Hence, we must consider these topics in conjunction with one another. The attainment of peace requires us to have an understanding of aggression, and the pitfalls of violence and evil, as well as the various paths that may lead toward a peaceful world.

We begin with aggression because although it is often violent, aspects of aggression may be necessary for the achievement of peace. We will then sample the voluminous literature on forms of violence and the ways in which it may be controlled. Although many of these forms are clearly related to aggression, Gandhi asserted that the worst form of

violence is poverty. Such violence is masked and occurs because of unjust economic and political structures. And when we turn to examine evil we find that a difficult moral judgment is involved. Although most contemporary judgment considers violence to be evil, much of our striving for peace and justice involves us in violence that we do not acknowledge as evil. This is one of the facts that requires us to base any quest for peace (valued as good) on a thorough understanding of violence and evil. In this way, we will not be naive when we finally come to consider how peace may be attained.

AGGRESSION

Aggression has different meanings that focus our attention on different aspects of behavior and lead to the creation of different approaches to its understanding. We may distinguish at least three different definitions:

1. Aggression as behavior intended to hurt an *other,* whether this intent is motivated emotionally (as by anger, pain, frustration, or fear) or instrumentally, as a means to an end (as in punishing misbehavior or intimidating an other to attain one's end.) There are two caveats to this definition. First, the intention to hurt may be embedded in larger intentions that have quite different meanings. Although the

definition succeeds in avoiding the inclusion of hurting that is accidental or an unavoidable aspect of helping (as in washing a wound that needs to be cleaned), it does include behaviors as disparate as a swat on the bottom to correct a child and the dropping of a nuclear bomb to win a war. Second, the other who is hurt may be the self (as in suicide) and may include animals.

2. Aggression as assertive, moving-out behavior that is aimed at getting what one desires (sometimes without regard for the wishes of others).

3. Aggression as the assertion of one's power in a relationship and the removal of challenges to what one believes ought to exist.

If we work from the first definition, we may view aggression as behavior that is clearly to be discouraged and socially controlled. However, the second definition is much more positive, at least in an individualistic culture, and we may want to support such behavior as long as it is balanced by a concern for others. The third definition raises a number of evaluative issues. It is morally neutral if one accepts challenges or power as a fact of life, but its presumption of a power relationship between persons or groups may be viewed as morally repugnant. These alternatives may be kept in mind as we examine four major approaches to aggression: as socially learned, as emotion based, as biologically grounded, or as embedded in conflict.

Social Learning Theories

Focusing on aggression as behavior that results in personal injury or property destruction, Bandura (1973) showed how people may learn such behavior by modeling the aggressive behavior of others. Shown an adult striking a large inflatable "Bobo" doll, children learn the observed pattern of behavior. The pattern is then encouraged or inhibited by what happens to the model. If the behavior is rewarded, the model is liked and chosen for emulation. Even when children are critical of the aggressive means that are used, the amount of their aggression increases. If the model is punished, the child's subsequent aggression decreases. Models also function by suggesting the social acceptability of some forms of behavior, thus facilitating patterns of behavior that have already been learned.

Since the direct punishment of aggression is itself aggressive, it models aggression at the same time that it discourages it. Thus, although small amounts of nonabusive spanking can be beneficial in disciplining children between the ages of 2 and 6 years (Larzelere, 1996), physical punishment generally promotes aggression. The frequency of physical punishment is linearly related to the frequency of aggression toward siblings (as well as toward parents) across a wide range of ages (Larzelere, 1986).

The modeling of aggression may occur in families, neighborhoods, or on TV, and in each of these cases numerous studies show that children exposed to aggressive models are more apt to engage in aggressive behavior. Children growing up in abusive families are apt to assault their own children (Silver, Dublin, & Lourie, 1969); higher rates of aggressive behavior occur in neighborhoods where there is a subculture of violence that provides models and rewards aggressive behavior (Wolfgang & Ferracuti, 1967); children exposed to a film depicting police violence show more violence during a subsequent game of floor hockey than do children who had just watched an exciting film on bike racing (Josephson, 1987); the general aggressiveness of teenagers (as rated by teachers and classmates) is correlated to the amount of violence that they watched on TV when they were children (Turner, Hesse, & Peterson-Lewis, 1986); and both self-reported aggression and the seriousness of criminal arrests at age 30 is predicted by the violence level of the TV show persons watched at age 8 (as reported by their mothers 22 years earlier; Eron, Huesmann, Lefkowitz, & Walder, 1972).

From the perspective of social learning theory, aggression is neither instinctive nor produced by frustration. It is a pattern of learned behavior that has been rewarded so that it is efficacious within a given society. Aggressive cultures assume that aggression is innate and natural, without realizing that there are other cultures where aggressive patterns of behavior do not occur or occur with far less frequency. Although emotional conditions often precede aggression, numerous studies have shown that loss, frustration, or anger lead to aggression only when an aggressive pattern of behavior has been learned and reinforced. For example, Nelson, Gelfand, and Hartmann (1969) involved children in competitive or noncompetitive play and then had them observe either an aggressive or a nonaggressive model. Those who had lost in competitive play were most prone to behave aggressively, but only when they were exposed to the aggressive model.

We may see aggression as a pattern of learned behavior, but Huesman (1986) has proposed that we may also conceptualize it as a more general social script, a program of how to act in problematic social situations. Children learn such scripts by observing how others behave in life and on TV. Realistic violence by a perpetrator with whom the child can identify is highly salient and easily leads to fantasy and rehearsal as a way of solving problems. Aggressive scripts may be used in quite different circumstances and provide ways to gain attention and get one's way. Among middle-class peers, the use of such scripts is likely to result in unpopularity. The resulting social isolation may lead to increased television viewing, and an even greater reliance on the use of aggressive scripts, eventually producing the habitual use of violence.

In Huesmann's (1998) informational processing model, people use a heuristic search process to retrieve a script that is relevant for their situation. The use of an aggressive script will depend on how situational cues are interpreted, the availability of aggressive scripts, the normative evaluation of such a script once it is activated, and the interpretation of consequences. Regarding the last factor, Huesmann pointed out that if a child is beaten for aggression, the child may feel disliked rather than interpret his or her behavior as unprofitable.

Although most researchers focus on the use of aggressive scripts by delinquents, the scripts are as available for use in international conflicts as in bullying and gang wars. McCauley (2000) pointed out that while the least socialized are more involved in personal violence, it is the best socialized who are often involved in the intergroup violence of war. In fact, personal scripts are an aspect of the societal myths that we shall consider when we deal with the concept of evil, and Schellenber (1996) pointed out that interpersonal violence may be more influenced by the extent to which a society engages in war than the reverse. Thus, Ember and Ember's (1994) analysis of the relationship between war and interpersonal violence in 186 societies suggested that socialization for aggression and severity of childhood punishment appear to be more a consequence rather than a cause of war, and it is this socialization that is most directly related to interpersonal violence.

Aggressive scripts are available for use in any social conflict, and if aggressive behavior is perceived as justified, an observer is more apt to identify with the aggressor and more apt to model the behavior. In the context of competition, the goal of winning may entail a willingness to hurt, and this is easily conflated with a willingness to hurt in order to win. Paradoxically, the fact that context affects the meaning of a behavior is an argument for Bandura's behavioral definition of aggression as that which results in (rather than intends) harm. For example, bomber pilots often do not intend to hurt civilians. Any intention to harm is embedded in the goal of carrying out a mission, and attention is directed toward mundane means (the pilot who carried the Hiroshima bomb was primarily concerned that added weight might prevent a safe takeoff).

Many social forces inhibit aggression, and Bandura (1999) has extended his earlier work by examining how aggression is more likely to occur when a person is morally disengaged from the victim. Such disengagement may occur by justifying the aggression, by using euphemistic labels, or by using advantageous moral comparison. It is facilitated by displacing responsibility for the damage that is done (as in Milgram's, 1974, experiments), by diffusing responsibility (Zimbardo, 1995), and by increasing the distance between persons and evidence of the pain that they are inflicting (Kilham & Mann, 1974). Finally, moral disengagement occurs when dehumanization prevents empathic responsiveness (see Bandura, Underwood, & Fromson, 1975). Personally, I would argue that we witness the contrast between moral engagement and moral disengagement whenever we either empathize with the struggles of an ant or step on the nuisance. A scale measuring the extent of moral disengagement has been used in different nations and shown to be positively related to support for military action (McAlister, 2001).

Emotional Bases

In Bandura's work on the modeling of aggressive behavior, the meaning of the behavior as intent to harm is implicit. Berkowitz (1993) emphasized that this meaning may be crucial. This becomes apparent if we focus on aggressive ideas and emotions. If one person tackles another in a football game, we may see the skillful, determined act of an athlete, or we may see a deliberate attempt to injure another person. For Berkowitz, it is only in the latter case that the model may activate the aggressive thoughts and emotional reactions that may lead to aggressive behavior. He pointed out that modeling is more apt to occur when a person identifies with the aggressor and when negative emotional states exist. He also distinguishes between instrumental aggression that occurs as a means of achieving some planned end and emotional aggression that is grounded in passion and is typically spontaneous and unplanned. The deliberate "taking out" of a star player is quite different from a blow thrown in temper.

Berkowitz tends to focus on emotional aggression, which he sees as pushed out, impelled from within, although this impulsion can be influenced by external cues. He sees such aggression as having both a motoric component (tightened jaw and fists, striking out, etc.) and an urge to hurt, injure, and destroy. He makes two major points. First, he argues that the emotional state that underlies emotional aggression is not only anger, but all negative affect. He shows that the discomfort produced by heat, cold, noise, overcrowding, frustration, or free-floating annoyance lead to the increased probability or strength of aggressive behavior. For example, when a student makes a mistake, other students behave more aggressively when they are in a hot room (Baron, 1977), and they use more punishment than reward when they are in pain. Riots are more apt to occur in hot spells (Baron & Ransberger, 1978), and domestic assaults occur more frequently when air pollution is high (Rotton & Frey, 1985; see also Berkowitz, 1982; Anderson & Anderson, 1998).

Second, he asserts that the emotional state consists of a network of feelings, ideas, memories, and expressive motor reactions that are associated with one another so that the activation of one part of the net will activate other parts. Unpleasant memories will promote a negative mood, and this will increase the probability of negative thoughts and aggressive behavior. An external cue that has an aggressive meaning (e.g., a weapon) may activate aggressive thoughts and—particularly if negative feelings are present—lead to an increased probability of aggressive behavior. Thus, in the classic experiment by Berkowitz and LePage (1967), angered subjects delivered more shocks to their partner when guns rather than badminton rackets were in the room (for further findings see Turner, Simons, Berkowitz, & Frodi, 1977). Even more disturbing, Berkowitz argued that cues associated with pain, frustration, suffering, and aversive stimuli in general may activate negative affect and increase the probability of aggression. Thus, Berkowitz and Frodi (1979) showed that when women university students were angered and distracted, they were more punitive when the child they were supervising was "funny looking" and stuttered. The activation of negative affect does not necessarily lead to aggression. Such behavior may be inhibited by either fear of punishment or empathic concerns, and a person may learn to respond with other behaviors. However, a person is susceptible to the influence of negative moods and external stimulation, and aggressive behavior is a "natural" response to negative affect that will tend to occur whenever self-control is reduced.

Biological Perspectives

From a biological perspective, many species of animals exhibit aggressive behavior, and we may consider a good deal of this to be instinctually based. Inasmuch as this is so, there are constraints on the ease with which we can modify aggressive behavior. The concept of instinct can be approached from the view of contemporary behavioral evolutionary theory or from its original conception as used by Freud.

Behavioral Evolution

Rather than view aggressive behavior as a learned response, we may conceptualize aggression as the product of evolutionary processes, that is, behavior patterns based on genetic influences that have persisted because they have been adaptive, helping members of a species survive in specific environments. Thus, we may find aggressive patterns of behavior programmed into the nervous system because the genes that served as the basis for these programs were selected by the reproduction of the organisms that possessed them. In its original conception, instinctual behavior was viewed as a sort of drive that, like hunger, was directed toward a goal, building if it were not satisfied and becoming less and less particular about the ideal goal object until it could be satisfied by something that would not ordinarily be chosen. However, it is difficult to imagine the goal of an aggressive drive because there are so many different functions for aggression. There is the aggression involved in predation, in the defense of the young, in the struggle between males for mates, and so on. It may be better to consider instinctual aggression as comprised of particular behavior patterns that can be released by particular cues in the environment. We may then consider both internal and external factors that may influence these aggressive patterns, as well as how the patterns may have adaptive significance. For example, in most species males engage in more intraspecies aggression than females, and this aggression is involved in the competition to fertilize females. In some species the struggle for mates involves the establishment and defense of territory and may function to spread members of a species out over territory, thus preserving food supplies.

When we examine the human species, we find that societies vary widely in the amount of aggression. However, within any given society males always appear more aggressive than females. Observational studies find boys more aggressive than girls (E. E. Maccoby & Jacklin, 1974); teenage males are more apt to offer more violent solutions (Archer & McDaniel, 1995); and violent crimes are more apt to be committed by men (J. Q. Wilson & Herrnstein, 1985). However, Straus and Gelles (1990) suggested that within-family aggression may be as prevalent in females.

The sex differences in aggression that are found appear to be related to testosterone, which seems to influence both the development of the brain and some of the physiology underlying current behavior (R. T. Rubin, 1987). However, the exact relationship between testosterone and aggression is unclear, in part because behaving aggressively appears to affect the release of testosterone and because testosterone levels may be related more to dominance behavior than to aggression as intent to hurt. Mazur and Booth (1998) argued that testosterone both rises in response to a challenge to dominance and increases in winners and decreases in losers. Alternatively, van Creveld (2000) argued that males gravitate toward violence because their bodies are better adapted for aggressive combat and because the exercise of this advantage is a way for men to solve the existential problem posed by the fact that they cannot bear children. They justify their existence by insisting on the necessity of violence and their preeminence in its exercise.

In humans, as in other animals, it is easy to imagine how aggressive behavior in a conflict between males could result in the reproductive advantage of stronger males and, hence, that the genes of aggressive males would be more likely to be reproduced in specific environments (Daly & Wilson, 1985). However, if we imagine early humans as existing in hunter-gatherer groups, it seems clear that cooperative behavior within the group would also contribute to survival. Even when the sacrifices involved in such cooperation might result in a disadvantage for a particular individual and his or her genes, genes related to cooperative behavior might be preserved if the cooperation favored kin or others who reciprocated the cooperation, or if the penalty of not cooperating was high, or (in certain conditions) if the group itself benefited (see D. S. Wilson & Sober, 1994). It seems probable that the genetics favoring cooperative behavior may offset those favoring male in-group aggressiveness. However, this may not be so when we consider intergroup combat. Thus, it has been noted that boys evidence more intragroup cooperation than girls when their group is in competition (Shapira & Madsen, 1974). In his studies on the conflict between Hindus and Muslims, Kakar (1996) observed that when boys and girls were asked to construct an "exciting" scene with toys and dolls identifiable as Hindu or Muslim, the boys constructed scenes of violence whereas the girls created scenes of family life. Further, Thompson (1999) has pointed out that group selection may also have favored the selection of aggressive individuals who are willing to die for their group when it is in combat.

Freudian Theory

Freud's psychoanalytic theory is written from a biological perspective that is based on the older idea of instincts as drives or needs. The development of his thinking about aggression is complex and has been described and critiqued by Fromm (1973). Taken literally, few would agree with Freud's conceptualization. However, on a metaphoric level his theory allows a rather elegant statement of a viable theoretical position, best expressed in his letter to Albert Einstein on the cause of war (Freud, 1933). Working in the manner of evolutionary biologists today, Freud assumed that early humans lived in small groups. He postulated that these groups were initially dominated by the compelling aggression of the strongest male. This dominance could eventually be overcome by an aggressive union of weaker males. However, such a union had to be maintained by the growth of law and feelings of unity. As Freud (1933, p. 276) put it, "Here, I believe we have all the essentials: violence overcome by the transference of power to a larger unity, which is held together by emotional ties between its members." As Freud surveyed history he was not encouraged by what he saw. Although aggression within groups is contained by laws that are enforced by group union, there is no way to contain aggression between groups. Some propose the ideal of a union between groups, but a mere ideal is not sufficient to overcome the aggressive drive of independent groups, and powerful groups are unwilling to grant sufficient power to a superordinate body.

In spite of the apparent cogency of the previous arguments, it should be noted that the consensus of contemporary social scientists is that there is no instinctual press for war per se. Thus, the group gathered at Seville to examine the problem declared, "It is scientifically incorrect when people say that war cannot be ended because it is part of human nature" (UNESCO, 1991, p. 10). The reasoning behind such a statement is well explicated by Fromm (1973). He pointed out that war, like slavery, is a human institution. Early hunter-gatherer groups had no reason to engage in warfare because there were no goods to plunder. Far from being an aspect of "primitive" man, warfare develops along with the development of civilization. Agriculture and animal husbandry lead to surpluses and the development of specializations and hierarchies of power that then become involved in the conquest of other peoples. Fromm pointed out that there were and still are peaceful peoples, as well as evidence for a relatively high degree of civilization in a number of matrilocal societies that existed before warfare began. Of course, these facts do not preclude a possible instinctive base for the in-group biases that are so prevalent whenever groups must share resources. Culture interfaces with a biological base for both cooperation and violence. Although chimpanzees show extensive cooperative behavior, Blanchard and Blanchard (2000) pointed out that they also form raiding parties and that this aggressiveness is inhibited when they are afraid.

Conflict Theories

Rather than focus on aggression as the response of individuals, we may examine the role it plays in the relations between people, as a way of wining conflicts, establishing dominance, or managing impression. This more sociological approach may be linked to both emotion and biology. Regarding emotion, I proposed that anger is best regarded as a response to a challenge to what a person asserts ought to exist (de Rivera, 1977, 1981). I argued that when persons become angry, they are attempting to remove a challenge in a way that is analogous to an animal defending territory. Learned aggressive responses are recruited to serve this end.

Considering aggression as an aspect of conflict is close to the biological perspective in that it considers the function of aggression in a specific cultural environment. In game theory the choice of a competitive or mistrustful, rather than cooperative, strategy may be regarded as involving aggression in the sense that benefits to the self are sought without regard for injury to the other. Research shows how many situations seduce persons to play aggressively even when this is not in their best interest (Deutsch, 1958). And the game theory used in the study of conflict is enriched by utilizing the perspective of evolutionary biology (D. S. Wilson, 1998).

Scheff (1999) asserted that emotional sequences play a crucial role in both interpersonal and intergroup conflict, and he focused on the roles of pride and shame as signals of solidarity and alienation. He argued that if shame is acknowledged, connections of solidarity and trust can be built. However, shame is often unacknowledged. Such unacknowledged shame may involve painful feeling with little ideation and is often signaled by furtiveness. When it is bypassed, it involves rapid thoughts that occur with little feeling and is accompanied by hostility or withdrawal from the other in ways that mask the shame. The unacknowledged shame feeds on itself, and the person becomes ashamed that he or she is ashamed, experiences a panic state, or enters a humiliated fury. A typical pattern is to mask the shame with anger, and Scheff sees such shame-anger loops at the heart of destructive conflicts. He suggested that they account for the need for vengeance and are at the heart of deterrence strategy. The danger of appearing weak, the underlying unacknowledged shame, is euphemistically treated as face-saving and status competition.

Seeing aggression as an aspect of conflict reminds us that at least two parties are involved and that aggression increases as the parties respond to one another. In their examination of conflicts between individuals, groups, and nations, J. Z. Rubin, Pruitt, and Kim (1994) described how conflicts escalate in aggressiveness. This escalation occurs in different ways: Influence attempts move from light to heavy tactics, from persuasive attempts to threats and violence; issues proliferate from small to large so that parties become increasingly involved in the conflict and commit more resources to it; issues move from the specific to the general so that the relationship between parties deteriorates; motivation shifts from simply doing well for the self to winning and then to hurting the other; and participants may grow from few to many. Thus, the strength of the aggressive responses (from a harsh word to a physical threat), the generalization of the attack (from one aspect of behavior to a description of character), and the extensity of the conflict (from a disagreement over one thing to disagreements over many) all may increase.

Fortunately, such conflicts often subside, decreasing as forbearance prevails, tempers cool, and apologies are made. This is particularly true when the parties to the conflict have common interests and a history of cooperation. However, conflicts that spiral and escalate may lead to structural changes that make it difficult for the conflict to subside. These involve psychological transformations. When groups are involved, there are changes in group and community dynamics. The psychological changes that occur involve the development of negative attitudes and beliefs about the other, the development of competitive and hostile goals, and the deindividuation and dehumanization discussed earlier. As R. K. White (1984) described, an intensely negative image of the other begins to develop, and the other becomes regarded as immoral, inhuman, and evil. When groups are involved, they become polarized. They become increasingly extreme in hostile attitudes and develop norms that resist compromise as well as contentious group goals that contribute to in-group solidarity at the expense of the out-group. They select militant leaders, become more liable to the problems of *groupthink* (Janis, 1983), and initiate the development of militant subgroups. The entire community may become polarized as members are forced to choose sides and neutrality becomes impossible without one's loyalty becoming questioned.

VIOLENCE AND ITS CONTROL

Violence seems to imply a damaging of the other, a hurting that is more than temporary pain. However, what is considered to be violent often seems to depend on one's side. Thus, Blumenthal, Kahn, Andrews, and Head (1972) found that persons tend to distinguish between the violence of those they dislike and the "justified force" of groups they favor. Further, the violence that is ordinarily considered is the *direct* violence involved in using force to injure, damage, or destroy a person or to violate unjustly a person's rights. We tend to overlook indirect violence. In this section on violence we consider the many forms of direct violence that occur between persons, within communities, and in and between societies. However, we also consider the violence that is done when human beings are distorted and prevented from developing their potential, the *structural* violence described by Galtung (1969).

Personal Violence

Violence often occurs in an interpersonal context. We first consider men who are particularly prone to violence, and then examine family violence, rape, and bullying.

Violent Men

Men committed about 90% of the violent crimes between 1960 and 1980 in the United States (J. Q. Wilson &

Herrnstein, 1985). Although this percentage is changing (it is now 83%), men are more apt to be involved, and some are particularly prone to violence. Thus, Berkowitz (1993) cited a number of studies that present evidence for a degree of violent consistency across situations and across time. For example, Farrington (1989) reported on a longitudinal study of 400 working-class males that lived in a section of London. Youths and their parents were periodically interviewed; teachers rated their behavior; and court records were examined. Of the 100 youths who were most aggressive at age 9, 14% had been convicted of a violent offense by age 21 as compared with 4% of the other boys.

Aggressive scripts appear to be much more prevalent in some subcultures, are available to groups, and are promoted by negative affect. Thus, Dunning, Murphy, and Williams (1988) documented how the British football hooligans, who "have an aggro" and violently attack strangers, are working-class males who grow up in families where they witness, receive, and are coached in violence until many enjoy the skills and thrills involved. However, it should also be noted that the studies showing how particular people are prone to violence also reveal the inaccuracy of prediction over time. Many people change to become more or less aggressive as they age. And it must also be realized that the reactions of others can amplify initial marginal deviance so that greater problems develop (Caprara & Zimbardo, 1996).

What are the motivations behind violent crime? Using peer interviews of 69 men who had records for repeated violence, Toch (1969/1993) distinguished nine types of motivational processes. His most frequent classification (used to describe 28 cases) involved the promoting or defending of a self-image that seemed to be constructed as a compensation for the fact that the person was not convinced of his own worth. By contrast, another 16 cases involved a basic egocentrism that evidenced a complete lack of empathy with others, who were simply seen as objects. Although Toch demonstrated that his classification can be used with some reliability, it is clear that often more than one process is involved, and his main concern was to point out that violence should not be treated as homogeneous. He also pointed out that once a man has been involved in violence, he may develop a habit of using violence. Violence creates its own needs and reinforces the very insecurities and egocentricity that was its source, and a person may define the self in a way that makes violence more probable in the future.

Baumeister and Campbell (1999) distinguished three distinct processes that they believe may be involved in an intrinsic appeal to commit violent acts (as opposed to instrumental motives for either selfish or idealistic ends). They differentiated sadism (the pleasure of inflicting suffering or terror involved in Toch's bullying category) from violent thrill seeking. They argued that the former is an addictive process, while the latter is more the sporadic sensation seeking of the bored (and often drunk and impulsive). They estimated that sadism may develop in about 5% of persons who are repeatedly violent and possibly explained by Solomon's (1980) opponent process theory. By contrast, they saw violent thrill seeking as motivated by boredom combined with high sensation seeking and low impulse control (and more likely to occur under the influence of alcohol). Both processes are, of course, opposed by any guilt feelings an individual may have.

A third process involves threatened egoism and, at first glance, appears to be related to Toch's category of self-image promoting and defending. However, Toch views his category as involving persons who are not convinced of their own worth, while Baumeister and Campbell feel that the process they are describing is more a reaction when a narcissistic view of the self is threatened. This disparity may involve some important distinctions (along with some semantic and measurement issues). Baumeister, Smart, and Boden's (1996) literature review seemed to show that aggressors tend to have favorable, even grandiose, views of the self, and Bushman and Baumeister's (1998) laboratory study showed the highest aggression coming from the injured self-esteem of insulted narcissists. However, the review article often involved the aggression of psychopaths and rapists whom Toch would classify as egocentric, and narcissism also implies egocentricity. We may need to distinguish the inflated (and narcissistic) self-esteem of the bully from the poor self-esteem of other violent persons.

The previous analyses are useful in understanding persons whose violence is not condoned by the society in which they live, but how may we understand the tolerated violence of leaders such as Hitler, Stalin, or Pol Pot, lieutenants such as Himmler or Goering, or the masses involved in publicly sponsored killings such as those that occurred in the Roman coliseum or any number of blatant purges and massacres? Although we may assume a certain amount of egocentricity, objectification, and lack of empathy, there appear to be deeper motivational reasons, the sort of instinctual tendency for destruction postulated by Freud. An alternative is suggested by Fromm's (1973) analysis of destructive character structure. Fromm distinguished between a biologically adaptive aggression that humans share with other animals and a malignant aggression that is distinctly human and maladaptively destructive, a point discussed more fully when we consider the nature of evil. One of the character structures he describes involves the worship of technique and the fusion of technique with the destructiveness seen in modern warfare. This may be objectively measured and related to political attitudes that favor military power and the repression of dissent (see M. Maccoby, 1972).

Family Violence

Although there are obvious differences between child abuse and domestic violence, it seems important to relate these two types of violence to each other and to the rather neglected topic of sibling abuse. For example, Patterson (1982) showed that the families of antisocial and abused children fail to provide consistent and effective discipline when children are aggressive, fail to monitor their whereabouts, and do not provide positive reinforcement for prosocial skills. He suggested that in such families, a problem child learns to be aggressive by attacking and dominating siblings, and a sample of such children shows that they attack siblings at almost 10 times the normal rate, as well as being involved in hitting their fathers and mothers and being hit by them (Patterson, 1986).

One often thinks of child abuse as involving physical or sexual abuse. However, by far the most prevalent form of abuse involves neglect. Thus, Sedlak (1990) reported an incidence rate of 14.6 per 1,000 as contrasted with rates of 4.9 for physical abuse and 2.1 for sexual abuse. Parental neglect usually occurs in situations of low family income and education and often where there is a high level of stress and a lack of social support (Garbarino, 1991). In such situations there is probably less parental maturity, less knowledge about child development, and a greater degree of attachment disturbances. Further, mothers (and one presumes fathers) may be quite depressed, and this may contribute to the neglect of children (see Pianta, Egeland, & Erickson, 1989). Poverty and the lack of social support also appear to be a factor in both physical and sexual abuse.

Azar (1991) pointed out that in order to understand fully how abuse occurs we must look at the interpersonal dynamics that occur within the social context. Her investigations of abusive mothers reveal that they often misperceive a child's behavior. If a 3-year-old spills a glass of milk, the mother may perceive willful disobedience and may lack the skills to cope with what she perceives as a challenge to her authority. Learned patterns of aggression that occur in a situation perceived as a struggle for dominance may account for a good deal of physical abuse. In any case, in their review of theories of child abuse, Azar, Povilaitis, Lauretti, and Pouquette (1998) argued that the best way to understand child abuse is to focus on how a parent interacts with a child in a social situation that is influenced by both societal and cultural factors. The interaction will be influenced by a child who may be more or less pleasing and difficult and by a mother who may

have more or less parental and social skills, impulse control, and ability to manage stress. And the interaction occurs in a context that may or may not provide helpful or aggressive models, be stressful, or lend social support. To some extent this overall model for understanding may also be applicable to sexual abuse. However, sexual abuse seems less dependent on societal stress and more on personality factors such as high familial dependence, psychopathy, or pedophilic tendencies (Rist, 1979), or, more generally, as having its origin within perpetrators rather than in the interaction between perpetrator and victim (Haugaard, 1988).

Domestic abuse in the sense of partner abuse is often attributed to male batterers, and the U.S. Department of Justice (1995) reported about twice as many wives and girlfriends killed by husbands and boyfriends as the converse (1,500:700). However, a telephone survey of 6,000 married or cohabiting couples found that as many females as males appeared to be involved in partner violence (Straus & Gelles, 1990). In many cases of extreme violence the superior physical strength of the males was offset by the more frequent use of weapons by females. In a similar vein, surveys of lesbian couples have found as much or more violence as in heterosexual couples (Waldner-Haugrud, Gratch, & Magruder, 1997).

Regardless of the degree to which violence in perpetrated by males, it seems important to distinguish between different sorts of perpetrators. Holtzworth-Munroe (2000) distinguished between three groups of men involved in marital violence: Those who become violent within the family only as a result of an inability to manage conflict escalation; those who have difficulty with trust issues and become overly dependent on their wives, resorting to violence when their needs are not met; and those who are antisocial and violent in all relationships. Clearly, the management of domestic abuse in each of these cases requires quite different strategies. In some cases couples therapy seems appropriate, but in others it would simply prolong abuse. In some cases separation offers a solution. However, Hart (1992) reported that about 75% of emergency room visits and calls to law enforcement, and 50% of the homicides, occur after separation.

Intervention programs attempting to teach men anger management and conflict resolution skills in small groups typically report a 53% to 83% success rate (Edleson, 1996). Although these rates are encouraging, the lower percentages occur when there is a longer follow-up time and when success is based on the reports of the victims or on arrest rates. Further, the rates are based on men who complete the programs (which last from 10 to 36 sessions) and appear to ignore differences in different types of abusers. In one evaluation, of about 500 men who contacted the program, only 283 attended the first session, and only 153 completed the sessions. Programs are also available for the treatment of aggressive women (see Leisring, Dowd, & Rosenbaum, in press), although these may face the same attendance problems as do the men's programs.

Rape

Estimation of the prevalence of rape depends a great deal on how it is defined and how the statistics are collected (Muehlenhard, Powch, Phelps, & Giusti, 1992). In a well-designed study involving over 3,000 college women, 15% reported that they had experienced unwanted sexual penetration because a man had used physical force or given them alcohol or drugs, and an additional 12% reported having had to resist physical force (Koss, Gigycz, & Wisniewski, 1987). Few of these instances were reported, and many may not have been termed "rape" or recognized as such.

After years of study, Malamuth (1998) presented data showing that coercive sex is most apt to be perpetrated by males who have both an orientation toward impersonal sex (often related to a violent childhood) and a hostile masculinity (involving feelings of rejection and a desire to dominate women). To some extent these risk factors may be mitigated by the ability to empathize.

If the problem of sexual aggression were only a problem of restraining a relatively small percentage of males, it might be fairly easily addressed. Unfortunately, it seems clear that larger percentages can be influenced by subcultural norms in some gangs, military units, sports teams, and fraternities. These subcultures suggest that what seems like rape to some is merely normal masculine action. Such norms encourage the objectification of women as sexual objects and the reinforcement of rape myths (O'Toole, 1997). Fortunately, it appears that it may be possible to create intervention programs that decrease the acceptance of such norms (Flores & Hartlaub, 1998). However, it may also be possible to create conditions such as war that lead men to rape.

Although we have been examining rape as a form of personal violence, rape may also be used impersonally as an instrument of war (Copelon, 1995). Enloe (2000) pointed out the different ways in which such militarized rape may be used to achieve political objectives and may become institutionalized. The brutality of such rape is particularly devastating because victims are often subsequently rejected by their own communities (Turshen, 2000).

Bullying and Malicious Gossip

A defining aspect of bullying is that the behavior occurs repeatedly so that there is a pattern of abuse and intimidation

(Boulton & Underwood, 1992). So defined, Bernstein and Watson (1997) reported that from 7% to 10 % of U.S. school children are victimized by about another 7% of the children who are active bullies. Similar percentages are found in Great Britain (Atlas & Pepler, 1998), with prevalence highest in the middle-school years. The average bully appears to have normal self-esteem (see Bernstein & Watson, 1997), and the average victim has less self-perceived social competence compared with other members of their peer group (Egan & Perry, 1998). There are a number of detrimental aspects to bullying. Those who are bullied feel unsafe at school and appear to be at risk for illness, failure, and depression (Wylie, 2000). The bullies begin to think that they can get what they want by using power to dominate others, something that often fails to work in adult life (Oliver, Hoover, & Hazler, 1994). In addition, the majority of children who witness the bullying typically feel fear and fail to intervene. Thus, they may be being trained to be ineffective bystanders. Fortunately, it is possible to train teachers, students, and parents in ways to intervene. Such training, involving the entire community, has proven effective in Scandinavia, where programs have reduced bullying by 50% (Olweus, 1991, 1993).

Community Violence

Although it sometimes takes personal forms, some types of violence are more communal than interpersonal. Among such forms are riots, gang extortion and warfare, and police violence. Although space considerations prevent an adequate discussion of these forms of violence, some contemporary work may be noted.

Riots

The failure of structural factors in predicting which cities would have the most commodity riots, together with difficulties in satisfactorily predicting which individuals would participate in them, has led McPhail (1994) to abandon both structural strain and relative deprivation as predictors and to advocate extending Snyder's (1979) work of examining the factors that affect the interpersonal processes that assemble a riot. Such an approach inquires into communication patterns and the motives of individuals as they assemble to engage in collective goals. McPhail argued that it is important to distinguish between collective goals that do not intend violence (although violence may result) and collective goals that do intend violence (as is the case with England's football hooligans). It would also seem wise to consider the group emotions that can occur when group members share attitudes and have a common sentience (see K. K. Smith & Crandell,

1984). Such group emotion may play a role in the generation of crowd violence in cases where police suppositions of violence may create a self-fulfilling prophecy of violence in sports fans (Stott & Reicher, 1998).

A nuanced account of the group emotions involved in riots is provided by Kakar's (2000) description of the protracted communal clashes between Hindus and Muslims in Hyderabad, India. After a skillful delineation of economic, political, historical, demographic, social-psychological, and psychoanalytic accounts, he focused on the psychological shifts that occur at the outbreak of violence. He noted how the character of rumors begins to change from general threats to rumors that the body is threatened by previously benign substances, how the boundaries of individuals with peaceful religious identities and a basic sense of trust become replaced by a transcendent communal identity with a propensity for anxiety and violence, how individual behavior becomes governed by a different sort of morality, and how a history of coexistence is replaced by a history of violence. Of course, these shifts are perpetrated by demagogues, and much of the violence is perpetrated by gangs of young people, but Kakar's point is that the entire community is caught up in altered identities and that certain norms are still in existence that enable people to return to their traditional religious identities and live in relative harmony after the violence subsides.

Gangs and Gang Warfare

In 1996 there were about 31,000 gangs with approximately 846,000 members in the United States (Office of Juvenile Justice and Delinquency Prevention, 1998). It seems likely that gangs develop whenever societies fragment and lower-class males lack access to legitimate sources of power and prestige. It might be interesting to study gangs as quasi states. Certainly, delinquent gangs involve symbols of identification for group membership, territorial claims, leadership power struggles, in-group protection, and out-group antagonism (Capozzoli & McVey, 2000). When the Soviet Union collapsed, hundreds of violent groups emerged who, as Volkov (2000, p. 709) noted, "intimidated, protected, gathered information, settled disputes, gave guaranties, enforced contracts and taxed." He argued that these entrepreneurs of violence created organizations that were essentially "violence-managing agencies." The more successful gradually became legitimized by becoming involved in prosocial activities and absorbed in the process of state formation.

Hill, Howell, Hawkins, and Battin-Pearson (1999) noted four risk factors that predict adolescent involvement in gangs. On the community level these include poverty, high rates of mobility, and dysfunctional norms. A crucial problem created by gang warfare (and by civil war in general) is the impact that violence has on children. Kostelny and Garbarino (2001) pointed out that in some Chicago neighborhoods, 38% of elementary school children have seen a dead body outside, and 21% have had someone threaten to shoot them. They have noted how repeated violence often leads to regression, a loss of trust, sense of no future, and increased aggressive behavior. They propose a series of measures to counteract these affects, including home visiting and early education programs, as well as specific violence prevention programs at both the elementary- and middle-school levels.

One might think that children who have suffered the sort of violence that occurs when civil society has disintegrated would themselves become violent. However, this is not necessarily so. What sort of moral character might develop in South Africa, where, after the violence of apartheid, children were subjected to criminal, domestic, and vigilante violence, often with a lack of clarity about the reasons for the violence? Dawes (1994) reported that the majority of children do not appear to have become violent or even to seek retaliation. In fact, many evidence an increased empathy. He points out that moral behavior is learned in a sociocultural context. People construct their identities and reputations as members of groups and learn moral conduct in settings that assign responsibility to the roles that people chose to play. Hence, children may learn that violence is called for in one situation but immoral in another. Although a culture may arise and lead some to assume violent roles, such violence is not automatically produced by being exposed to violence but is subject to the rhetoric and morality developed by a group in a situation.

Merely increasing the number of police in an area high in gang crime does not seem to be effective, but a study by Fritsch, Caeti, and Taylor (1999) suggested that if the additional police focus on curfew and truancy enforcement, it is possible to reduce gang-related crime. However, many investigators argue that suppression is less effective than social interventions that offer centers of activity for at-risk youth before they become involved in gangs (Spergel & Grossman, 1997), and there is some evidence that such centers are effective alternatives (Thurman, Giacomazzi, Reisig, & Mueller, 1996).

The Use of Violence in Social Control

Unfortunately, the process of maintaining social control often involves violence and far more violence than appears justifiable. In fact, it may be argued that punishment and the use of any violence, as opposed to an aggressive use of force and physical restraint, fails to deter violence and cannot be justified (Gilligan, 2000). When violence is used, it may occur in the form of police violence in the streets or violence within prisons in the form of torture or cruel and unusual punishment. In the United States the reported instances of death from police violence are relatively low, about 300 deaths per year. It seems evident that laws and strong civilian control must demand a professional force that minimizes the use of violence and that excellent training is crucial. Toch, Grant, and Galvin (1974) argued that the best way to achieve control over unacceptable police violence is to have peer review panels who review all arrest reports, tally deployed violence, and work with those officers who exceed a predefined number of incidents. Such officers are helped to understand their behavior and create alternative approaches to handling the situations that provoked their violence. When their incidents decrease, they themselves are enlisted to become members of the panel.

In the United States an increasing number of persons are being imprisoned: The prison population in maximum-security prisons more than doubled from 1987 to 1997. There are now over 1.6 million persons in federal and state prisons, and inmates outnumber guards 38 to 1 (U.S. Department of Justice, 1999). Note that this figure does not include persons in county and city jails. Much of this increase is due to non-violent drug offenders and targets African American and Black men. As Haney and Zimbardo (1998) pointed out, the increased use of imprisonment reflects a policy choice to imprison individual lawbreakers rather than to correct the social conditions that contribute to crime. There are troubling indications that the increased privatization of prisons is leading to abusive practices such as the increased use of stun belts and solitary confinement. Further, there is every indication that prisons are failing to rehabilitate a majority of those who are incarcerated. Thus, Beck and Shipley (1997) reported that an estimated 62.5% of the prisoners released from 11 state prisons were rearrested for a felony or serious misdemeanor within three years of their release and that 41.4% were returned to prison or jail. Many prisons appear to be dominated by gangs (Lerner, 1984), and violence and domination occur between inmates and are often used by guards. It is evident that most prisons are providing an environment that encourages learning violence rather than responsibility (Haney & Zimbardo, 1998).

There are managerial approaches that reduce violence (Reisig, 1998), vocational programs that offer structure and reduce assault rates (McCorkle, Miethe, & Drass, 1995), and educational programs that reduce violence and recidivism (Matthews & Pitts, 1998). However, neither governmental officials nor the American public seems willing to spend money on what is often seen as coddling prisoners. There appears to be a general attitude that favors punishment over re-habilitation, a general failure to distinguish between what might help different types of prisoners, and a general lack of compassion for those who find themselves in prison.

Torture is the most troublesome form of police violence, and it often leaves its victims crippled both physically and psychologically. This is particularly true when, as is often the case, the aim of the torture was not to obtain information but to intimidate and destroy a person so that he or she could no longer function as a leader of resistance to those in authority. While victims differ widely in their posttorture symptoms and some have demonstrated an incredible capacity to forgive and heal, many need both physical and psychological treatment. Elsass (1997) has described effective treatment methods, and the journal *Torture* is devoted to the prevention of torture and the rehabilitation of its victims.

As defined in the 1984 United Nations Convention Against Torture, torture involves the intentional infliction of severe pain or suffering, by or with the agreement of a public official, in order to obtain information or a confession, or to punish, intimidate, or coerce. Perhaps the most evident indication of the extent of the problem is that by the year 2000 only 119 of the 188 member states had endorsed the rules against torture promulgated by the UN convention.

Amnesty International (2000) enumerated a 12-point program to eliminate torture. These include calling for every nation to officially condemn and enact laws against torture, refuse evidence obtained under torture, make the location of all prisoners known, allow prisoners to communicate, have all allegations of torture investigated by an authority independent of the prison system, have authorities clearly state their opposition to the use of torture, punish torturers, and compensate victims.

Societal Violence

Although community violence often reflects what is happening within a society, there are forms of violence that occur throughout the society in which communities are embedded. This include the violence in its media and the violence that occurs when a society engages in war, is subjected to civil war, ethnic violence, and genocide, or must deal with terrorism.

Media Violence

We saw how aggressive behavior can be learned by following the models provided on film and TV. Hence, it is troubling to note that Hepburn (1997) reported that 57% of the TV programs monitored at four different locations in the United States contained some sort of violence, whereas only 4% presented an antiviolence theme. American children are exposed to vast amounts of violence on TV; Signorelli, Gerber, and Morgan (1995) estimated that the average 12-year-old has seen over a 100,000 acts of violence. There is little doubt that this sort of exposure contributes to violence (see Eron, Heusmann, Lefkowitz, & Walder, 1996). The violence is most apt to be learned when an attractive perpetrator with whom the viewer can identify engages in justified and rewarded violence that fails to depict the harm suffered by the victim of the violence (S. L. Smith & Donnerstein, 1998).

Media violence appears to promote violence in a number of different ways (see Berry, Giles, & Williams, 1999). Besides modeling violent behavior and weakening inhibitions about violence, it numbs or desensitizes reactions to violence and decreases empathy for victims. Similar negative effects occur as a consequence of playing violent video games (Anderson & Bushman, 2001). Although the evidence for the danger of viewing violence is increasing, warnings against viewing such violence appear to be decreasing in the U.S. mass media (Bushman & Anderson, 2001).

Interstate Warfare

Richardson (1960a) began the statistical study of war when his concern for human life led him to define war in terms of human deaths rather than in terms of declarations or historical significance. Setting 1,000 deaths as a lower limit and the log of deaths as a scale of magnitude (thus 1,000 deaths is a magnitude-3 war), he argued that counting was the best antiseptic for prejudice and proceeded to count the wars between 1820 and 1945. He showed that many magnitude-6 wars (about a million deaths) were not remembered because they lacked political significance (e.g., the Taiping rebellion, the war in La Plata), and many of the 188 magnitude-3 wars were completely overlooked. He also established that the nation responsible for the most wars keeps changing in different periods so that focusing on containing any given aggressor cannot prevent war.

Richardson proposed a sort of molecular model of war that imagined nations as bumping up against each other, with some of these conflicts resulting in war. Those with more borders and energy have a greater chance of collisions. In accord with such a model, he shows that the number of wars that a nation fights correlates highly with its number of borders (he includes colonies in this count), and the number of wars breaking out in any given year follows a Poisson (chance) distribution. Factors we might think of as lessening the probability of war, such as common language or religion, do not. What does lessen the probability of war between peoples is the number of years in which they live under a common gov-

ernment. The probability of war decreases geometrically with each decade of common government.

Which disputes result in war? Vasquez and Henehan (2001) showed that the probability of war is greater when there is a territorial dispute than when there is a policy dispute. Wallace (1979), who investigated 99 serious international disputes occurring between 1815 and 1965, reported that 26 resulted in war and that in 23 of these cases the war was preceded by an arms race. There were only five cases where an arms race did not lead to war, and we are probably fortunate that the arms race between the United States and the Soviet Union proved to be in this category.

When arms races occur, there is instability in the balance of power, and the race accelerates exponentially in a way that Richardson (1960b) can describe with a simple pair of differential equations. Basically, this elegant mathematical model reveals that races occur when a pair of nations are more afraid of each other than they are concerned with the cost to their own economy. A more complex model dealing with more than two nations and chaotic transitions is described by Behrens, Feichtinger, and Prskawetz (1997). Richardson's model stresses deterministic factors, and Rapoport (1960) has pointed out how such an approach may be contrasted with an approach that involves strategic gaming over interests or struggles involving different ideologies. Applying this latter approach, R. Smith, Sola, and Spagnolo (2000) demonstrated that in the conflict between Greece and Turkey, the amount each nation spends on arms does *not* depend on what the other is spending but is a function of bureaucratic and political inertia. Current spending by the United States also appears to evidence this pattern.

Subsequent to Richardson's work, the Stockholm International Peace Research Institute has kept an ongoing account of wars that focuses on number of deaths. Their statistics reveal millions of largely overlooked deaths, with 10 magnitude-6 wars that have occurred since 1945 and about 30 wars going on in any given year. Over recent years the number of interstate wars has decreased while the number of intrastate (civil) wars has increased. There have also been an increasingly large percentage of civilian deaths, which now account for about 85% of the casualties. One ray of hope for decreasing interstate conflict is offered by statistics that demonstrate that fewer militarized disputes occur when nations have important trade relations and when nations are democracies (Oneal, Oneal, Maoz, & Russett, 1996). Under such conditions war is not in the interest of those in power. However, these statistics do not consider support for covert interference, as in the U.S. involvement in overthrowing the democratically elected governments of Guatemala and Chile. Nor do they consider that the number of reasonably democratic nations is not high and that the conditions for democracy may be difficult to achieve (see de Rivera, in press). Nevertheless, we are reminded that interstate war is not inevitable.

Civil War, Ethnic Violence, and Genocide

Although civil wars sometimes simply reflect a struggle for power within a dominant group, they often involve ethnic group interests or ideological differences that become involved in a struggle for power. Their complexity is nicely captured in a series of case studies that deal with the wars in Central America, Ireland, Israel, Rwanda, and Sri Lanka from a psychological point of view. In Ireland (Cairns & Darby, 1998), Sri Lanka (J. D. Rogers, Spencer, & Uyangoda, 1998), and many other nations, important ethnic groups have both inflicted and experienced the sort of prejudicial treatment so aptly demonstrated in Tajfel's (1982) studies. Niens and Cairns (2001) applied social identity theory to the understanding of ethnic conflict and have concluded that overcoming the stereotypes that are involved requires contact situations in which people's group memberships are *more* rather than *less* emphasized.

In considering these disputes it is important to note that there are often many people within each group who are willing to treat the other group fairly. However, extremists within each group oppose any efforts to take the interests of the other group into consideration. Rather than creating a common intergroup political front, the moderates appear constrained by their intragroup identity with their extremists so that rational compromises that would be in the interest of both groups are impossible to achieve. Some methods that may be helpful in resolving these conflicts will be discussed when techniques of negotiation are considered.

Gurr (1996) identified 268 politically significant national and minority peoples (about 18% of the world's population), three fourths of whom experienced political disadvantages. Almost 100 of these groups participated in violent conflict between 1945 and 1990. He argued that it is important to recognize the grievances of minorities, the fact that cultural identities are important aspects of human being, and that it is not always possible to assimilate a minority culture. A critical problem is posed by the fact that conflicting parties often find it difficult to create a common historical narrative. An example is furnished by Rouhana and Bar-Tal's (1998) balanced account of the Israeli-Palestinian conflict.

Gottlieb (1993) argued that some conflicts may be managed by allowing people to have two identities, a formal national identity and a state identity. The national identity could control some language use in education, local law, and marriage rites. The state identity could control currency, border defense, and other factors necessary for a nation-state to survive in a global economy. Psychologically, such an arrangement makes sense because, as Brewer (1999) notes, it is quite possible to have a positive in-group identity that is independent of negative attitudes toward out-group members. Such in-group identities may be less threatened when clear boundaries between groups are recognized within the bounds of a common state.

In some nation-states, such as in Turkey in 1915, Germany in the 1930s, Iraq in the 1980s, and Rwanda in the 1990s, political decisions lead to genocide. Most students of genocide argue that genocides are not the inevitable results of ethnic differences. They point to the fact that people often have lived together peacefully for years, often with a considerable amount of intermarriage. The genocide occurs when leaders emphasize group identity, often in order to consolidate power or mobilize support in a power struggle. Yet the genocide is only possible when rapidly arousing fear and hatred. In the case of Rwanda, D. N. Smith (1998) argued that official hate propaganda combined with projective sexual envy, a belief in sorcery, authoritarianism, and a breakdown in traditional restraints and opportunities.

Staub (1989) examined a number of genocides in an attempt to conceptualize the common processes involved. He finds that they occur under circumstances of material deprivation and social disorganization that frustrate basic human needs. In such circumstances, individuals feel helpless and increasingly rely on their group membership. The seeds of genocide are sown if the group develops a destructive ideology in which an enemy group is perceived to stand in the way of the fulfillment of a hopeful vision. The conditions for the genocide evolve as violence begins to occur and is justified by an increasing devaluation of the enemy group, a devaluation that may easily be mobilized for political purposes. Although Staub emphasized that genocide is the outcome of normal group processes, he noted that there appear to be cultural preconditions. These include prejudices that become part of a cultural background, an ideology of antagonism, and the lack of a pluralistic culture. In many cases there also appears to be a particularly strong respect for authority that makes it difficult to resist immoral orders and may contribute to the threat and anxiety experienced when authority is unable to fulfill basic needs.

Once civil war has occurred, processes of reconciliation must restore the fabric of the society. The difficulties are immense, requiring a balance between needs for justice, the saving of face, and the support of sources of power that may be implicated by revelations of human rights abuses. Above all, as Lederach (1997) observed, the relationship between groups must change so that out-group members are no longer excluded from one's moral framework, and this must occur at the grassroots level as well as at the level of top leadership. Lederach stressed the need for years of work in rebuilding trust in teams from different strata of the society. He showed that such reconciliation requires the assistance of third parties who can accompany disputants with an attitude of humility as they, both individuals and communities, wrestle with the problems of combining truth, justice, and mercy.

Governmental initiative is often required, and certainly the most successful effort to date has been the South African government's establishment of its Truth and Reconciliation Commission. Rather than attempting to punish those responsible for the torture and murders that occurred during the maintenance of apartheid, the commission was charged with establishing what happened—making known the fate of victims and providing them with the opportunity to relate their accounts and achieve some measure of reparation, facilitating the amnesty of offenders who made full disclosure, and recommending measures to prevent future violations (de la Rey, 2001). Although justice was not achieved in the sense of adequate reparations, of punishment of the guilty, or even of an adequate admission of guilt or request for forgiveness, the public hearings held by the commission provided a forum that allowed a public acknowledgment of what had happened and the establishment of a common moral framework. In contrast to the situation in Argentina, where there is still no public recognition for the abuses under the military dictatorship or condemnation of those involved in torture and disappearances, the South African public can speak of what occurred and move on with a new public identity and history.

Terrorism

Terrorism may be distinguished from the guerilla tactics of rebels who are fighting a military opponent within their own territory. Terrorism involves random attacks on civilians as a means of gaining political ends and has been used by both states and revolutionaries (J. R. White, 1998). In the former case, a government that is engaged in a war attempts to destroy its opponent's will to fight, or a despotic government maintains its power by creating an emotional climate of terror that prevents the organization needed for political opposition (de Rivera, 1992). In the latter case, groups without access to political power use terror to publicize their grievances, extort concessions, or overthrow a regime that is experienced as repressive. All cases involve the training for aggression and moral desensitization described in the section

on aggression. However, terrorism is situated in historical circumstances that have interesting and largely unexplored psychological aspects.

An example is provided by the September 11, 2001, attack on the United States. Most of the terrorists were from Saudi Arabia. Although the government is repressive in that there are no ways to express discontent, the United States supports the regime in exchange for access to oil. The alternative to the king Monarchy would probably be an Islamic state rather than a secular democracy. Such a state is fundamentally religious and is conceived hierarchically rather than democratically. Vatikiotis (1986) noted that it is not based on the skepticism, experimentation, and tolerance essential to pluralistic politics. It is based on a different psychology, and its stability would require the cultivation of a different set of emotional relationships and customs (de Rivera, in press). Hence, we are dealing with the problems of psychological identity and the ambiguous role of religion that will be considered when we discuss the nature of evil. An examination of past attempts to deal with revolutionary terrorism suggests that the more successful have involved meeting the underlying needs that fuel the terrorism, as well as the suppression of terrorist elements.

Structural Violence

The concept of structural violence has been articulated by Galtung (1969, 1975/1980, 1996) to capture how economic and political structures may place constraints on the human potential. It sees violence as present when humans are diminished and points to the fact that this occurs when social structures prevent the meeting of human needs. Galtung pointed out that modern society is organized hierarchically and that those on top often use their position in ways that exploit those below, preventing them from having the resources they need. The top dogs are in control of resource distribution, and their decisions determine who has access to education, health care, and good jobs. Further, he argued that the top dogs maintain their power by a series of devices that work against the underdogs organizing a resistance.

One measure of structural violence is furnished by the human poverty index (HPI; United Nations Development Programme, 1999). This index uses five variables that reflect the loss of potentials that could be resolved by public policies. These are the percentage of the population dying before age 40, the percentage of underweight children (under age 5), the percentages of the population without access to potable water and without health care, and the percentage of illiterate adults.

It is important to realize that the hierarchies of power and privilege that exist within each society are connected to those in other societies in ways that support one another. The top dogs in a poor nation are often quite wealthy and well connected to the top dogs in other nations, so they are positioned to use aid in ways that maintain their power. Although Galtung does not deny that domestic problems may generate international conflict, he stresses that many domestic problems are exacerbated by the policies of exploitation of the elites in powerful countries. The entire system—the hierarchies and the connections between them—completely masks the responsibility for the terrible violence that it occasions. For specific examples from Sub-Saharan Africa see Nathan (2000) and Tandon (2000).

While we have discussed both direct violence and the structural violence that can be attributed to greed and the fear of losing power, a considerable amount of violence on both the personal and state level is motivated by what can only be considered as "good" motives. As Butigan (1999, p. 13) pointed out, "Violence is often motivated by fear, unrestrained anger, or greed to increase domination or power over others. It can also be motivated by a desire for justice in the face of injustice: a longing to put things right, to overcome an imbalance of power, or end victimization or oppression." This fact requires us to look at the nature of evil.

EVIL

While aggression and violence are largely matters of fact, evil involves a moral judgment. We must consider how it is conceptualized and how religions attempt to contain it.

Conceptions of Evil and Its Experience

What is meant by *evil?* Berkowitz (1999) argued that it should be distinguished from mundane badness and that there is a commonly shared prototype for evil. This prototype reflects action that not only is morally wrong but also reveals an excessive departure from social norms. The judgment of evil has to do with the helplessness of victims, the responsibility of the perpetrator, and the imbalance between the great wrong that is done for a relatively small gain.

Staub (1999) argued that a conscious intention to destroy is not a necessary aspect of evil. Rather, the word *evil* is appropriately used to categorize the repetition of intensely harmful actions that are not commensurate with instigating conditions. He recognizes that the term communicates horror, and although he is opposed to romanticizing evil as mythic and incomprehensible, he believes that the concept of evil may be a useful way to mobilize prosocial group norms. As an example of evil and the need for the concept, he discusses

the evil involved in bystanders who allow genocides to occur. Stohl (1987) showed that nations are typically bystanders, and this is reflected in the minimal news devoted to accounts of genocidal actions. However, the judgment that genocide is evil is reflected by the development of an international norm against genocide that may eventually be enforced by the establishment of a permanent international court.

Without the concept of evil it might be easy for people to avoid making judgments that need to be made. In this regard, Miller, Gordon, and Buddie (1999) have evinced concern that situational explanations of criminal actions may result in persons' condoning such actions. They demonstrate that when persons make judgments after situational explanations, they have less unfavorable attitudes and punitive responses toward the perpetrator. However, they do not show that the criminal action is condoned, and many would argue that the action rather than the person should be considered evil. To consider a person or group evil may evade an examination of the situational conditions.

Although psychologists have considered the concept of evil, they have not yet addressed evil as an experience. The concept of evil implies an objective judgment; the evil is experienced as "real." Of course, one may argue that evil and all values are really subjective and relative—simply what a person likes or wants. *Value* in this view is reduced to what someone is willing to pay. Yet we continue to *experience* value as existing apart from ourselves and as different from mere taste. As F. Heider (1958) asserted, value differs from what we want. It is characterized by what an objective order wants. We experience goodness and evil as objective in nature, as existing apart from our judgment of them, although we may recognize that our judgment may be faulty and may change with time. In the latter regard, Rozin, Markwith, and Stoess (1997) pointed out that smoking has recently become moralized. That is, smoking is now regarded by many as bad in a moral sense, an object of disgust. Note that the process of moralization involves emotional responses that help constitute the very value that is perceived as objective.

Evil exists in relation to what is Good, and the latter is what is necessary for life, for fertility, health, and success in getting food and outwitting enemies. In any society that is not completely secularized, Goodness exists because humans exist and could not exist without it. Evil is more problematic. Although some persons and religions regard Evil as essential and in primary opposition to the Good, others view it as secondary and existing because of the actions of humans; still others view it as illusory, as existing only as an object of our perception. Likewise, the relationship between Good and Evil may be seen in different ways. Evil may be viewed as a malevolent force or as ignorance, as repellant to Goodness or as the simple absence of Goodness. Thus, it may be symbolized as an active Devil or as darkness, as destructive choice or as the obstacles between humans and Goodness. Ricoeur (1967) pointed out that humans have symbolized evil in three quite different ways that reflect different experiences and conceptualizations. As *stain*, evil is contagious, and one may unintentionally become contaminated by its impurity. As *sin*, evil is a ruptured relationship with God, a departure from a path or missing of the mark that may be affected by the actions of one's people. As *guilt*, evil is a personal responsibility that occurs because of one's intentions. In all cases, one is removed from Goodness and must be relived of the stain, sin, or guilt in order to reconnect with Goodness.

K. G. Heider (1991) argued that in some cultures the basic moral conflict of life is more between order and disorder than between good and evil. Thus, in Indonesian and Japanese films the dominant concern appears to be the restoration of order rather than the triumph of the good over the bad. This may be related to a cultural tendency to see persons as more socially embedded than individually autonomous. The "villain" is not inherently bad but is more an agent of disorder who is easily welcomed back into the fold once order is restored. However, the restoration of order may involve the recognition of evil and its removal. Thus, Wessells and Monteiro (2001) described how child soldiers who have engaged in unjustified killings may participate in purification ceremonies to be reintegrated into the community.

Every society, and certainly our own, appears to have myths about evil, perhaps because we humans seem to need to give meaning to our suffering. In Western society, Ricoeur (1967) distinguished four such myths that continue to influence our thinking: the Greek tragic and Platonic myths and the Babylonian and Judaic creation myths. Each views the source of evil quite differently. In the Babylonian myth, the world is created in the process of a power struggle between the gods; violence is used to create the order that prevents the agony of chaos; and humans must serve the state in order to prevent chaos. By contrast, in the Judaic myth a God peacefully creates an essentially good world in which evil enters when people do what they are not supposed to do. Both of these myths are operative in our contemporary society. On the one hand, Wink (1992) has pointed out that much of the violence portrayed on TV exemplifies the Babylonian myth. That is, there is a power struggle between bad chaotic forces and good order, and the good guys use violence to restore order. Likewise, the strategic policy of the (putatively Christian) United States is actually based on the use of violence to maintain peace. On the other hand, the nation as a whole still subscribes to Judeo-Christian ideals of justice and believes in the freedom to choose between good and evil.

The Ambiguous Role of Religion

Taking Otto's (1923) idea of the Holy as a starting point, Appleby (2000) argued that the sacred can either be the locus of violence as a sacred duty or a militant nonviolence dedicated to peace. Defining religion as a response to a reality that is perceived as sacred, he showed that it gives the authority to kill or to heal and argued that religious leadership determines which course is taken, appealing to religious identity either to exploit or to transcend ethnic animosities. On the one hand, Appleby showed how religion was an important element in the destruction of Bosnia and the development of Islamic terrorism. He distinguished fundamentalism as a response to secularization (describing the terrorist violence that developed in 2 of 10 such movements) from the ethnonationalistic use of religion (and often violence) to unify a state and discussed how both differ from cult violence. On the other hand, he gave concrete examples of dozens of Gandhi-like figures who have worked for peace and discussed the role that religious organizations have played in peace meditations. He convincingly demonstrated that religion is always a construction of a sacred past and has the potential to inculcate nonviolence as the religious norm. He argued that religious education should be devoted to this end and supported with the technical skills and material resources it needs to organize peace.

The choice between good and evil is central to Fromm's (1955, 1973) analysis of evil. He pointed out that human beings, as distinct from all other animals, are aware of themselves as apart from nature and aware of their ultimate death. This existential dilemma creates common needs that must be met. These include needs for an object of devotion and for affective ties, unity, effectiveness and stimulation. Each can be met in either life-enhancing or life-destroying ways. An object of devotion can be an ideal or an idol; affective ties can be of love or sadomasochism; unity can be achieved by practicing an open religion or by losing the self in a trance state or a social role, effectiveness by creating or destroying, stimulation by active or passive excitation. Fromm sees these choices as determining whether a society and individual will become good or evil.

While Fromm emphasized the role of choice in determining how to meet basic needs, both Staub (1999) and Burton (1990) saw evil as stemming from the *frustration* of basic needs such as security, identity, connective ties to others, effectiveness, control, and autonomy. They believe that if persons cannot fulfill these constructively, they will engage in destructive behavior. Such an analysis lies in our understanding of some of the conditions that promote destructive behavior and in encouraging those with power to consider the needs of others. However, the emphasis on need fulfillment appears to neglect the role of personal responsibility and the fact that a large amount of violence stems from greed. It reflects a liberal view of basic human goodness (if only needs were met by the state) as opposed to a conservative view that sees everyone as basically selfish (and needing the state to enforce law and order).

The previous analyses begin with the needs of individuals. By contrast, Macmurray (1961) argued that individuals exist only in relationships with others. He sees these relations as composed of two strands: a love (caring) for the other and a fear (concern) for the self. Although both strands are always present, one always dominates. When a caring for the other dominates, the person is unified. However, any real or perceived hurt, betrayal, or abandonment causes the fear for the self to dominate, and when this occurs a person suffers dualistic splits (mind from body, reason from emotion, the practical from the ideal, the self from the other). At this point a person (or society) may focus either on individualism ("if the other doesn't care for me, I'd better care for myself") or on a conforming collectivism ("if I'm good, then they will care for me"). Because people assume that others are similar, the former leads to a Hobbesian analysis (the need for a strong state to enforce contracts between basically selfish people), whereas the latter leads to Rousseau, Marx, and the idea that people are basically good and will agree about basic needs. However, Macmurray asserted that people must continually wrestle with the choice as to whether concern for the other or concern for the self will dominate action. In his view, self-development occurs only when acceptance, understanding, forbearance, and forgiveness lead to the restoration of the dominance of caring for the other. Then, a person's unity is restored and, with it, the ability for genuine freedom and cooperation (see de Rivera, 1989).

How may we relate aggression to values of good and evil? In an attempt to distinguish between a "good" aggressive audacity, necessary for human progress, and an aggression that intends to destroy, Kelly (1965) proposed that the latter involves hostility. Hostility occurs when there is a threat to a person's belief system and the person extorts evidence in an attempt to maintain beliefs and the way that one is living one's life in the face of contrary evidence. Examples include fundamentalist terrorists or the middle-class Germans who became Nazis. Kelly might assert that the latter were not simply frustrated by inflation. Rather, they saw their belief system—their commitment to the value of hard work and thrift—crumple as the savings from their hard work were wiped away by inflation (see Moore, 1978). For Kelly, the alternative to hostility is to allow the experience of tragedy.

It is this experience, rather than the certainty that one's beliefs are valid, that is the basis of hope.

Kelly's analysis is supported by aspects of Peck's (1983) examination of the "group evil" involved in the MyLai massacre. On one level, Peck pointed out that it is easier for groups to commit atrocities because of the diffusion of responsibility and the normal narcissistic influences of group pride and out-group denigration. However, on a societal level, Peck argued that the group that killed innocent villagers manifested a broader societal problem. The group contained men who had been rejected from the broader society to do the dirty work that others did not want to see. The war itself was an attempt to defend a narcissistic image of American perfection, and when the situation in Vietnam presented evidence of the fallibility of the American worldview, the government was willing to destroy Vietnam rather than acknowledge this error. It may be noted that the research that was recommended to prevent future atrocities was rejected on the grounds that it might prove embarrassing.

The unwillingness to admit the tragic is an aspect of refusing to acknowledge evil, and Macmurray (1944) argued that a major problem is posed by the fact that one may do what one ought to do and yet still be involved in evil. A "just war" may be necessary; but when thousands of innocents are killed, the war is still evil, and the morally correct action of participating in the war does not absolve a person from having participated in that evil. Note that a person holding such a point of view is protected from the sort of dissonance reduction that is involved when a person hurts another and then justifies the aggression by devaluating the other. This suggests that public ceremonies of atonement might protect a society from becoming involved in any more evil than is necessary. Perhaps if Americans had the opportunity to mourn the deaths of all the Koreans and Chinese killed in the Korean War, there would have been less readiness to become involved in Vietnam or continuing sanctions against Iraq. In any case it seems desirable to confront the evil that is within as well as without. Such a confrontation leads us to examine the possibility of peace.

PEACE

By peace we do not mean the "negative" peace that is the absence of war but a "positive" peace (Barash, 1991) that is the opposite of evil—not the absence of conflict but the resolution of conflict in creative rather than destructive ways. We may imagine different aspects of this peace: the personal peace of inner harmony and compassion, the communal peace that exists when social norms and institutions promote a concern for the welfare of others and a peaceful resolution of conflict, and the peace that results from an environment that allows people to satisfy their basic needs. There are at least four different paths to peace: paths of strength, negotiation, justice, and personal transformation. Each may be viewed as involving types of aggression.

Peace Through Strength

It is said that the sword is the olive leaf's brother, and it seems self-evident that weakness invites attack while strength discourages it. Bullies pick on the insecure; criminals flourish in the absence of police; and history is filled with one people's expanding at the expense of another. Few would argue against the idea that some sort of strength is necessary for peace, and some, like Sumner (1911), would argue that peace is attained only by the imposition of order that occurs when states use their strength to expand their dominion. However, there are some problems with conventional interpretations of this path or with relying on it to produce positive or even negative peace. Empirically, Singer and Small's (1979) statistics, examining 59 recent wars, fail to show a significant relationship between strength and the probability of being attacked. Consider three problems:

First, it is not clear how much strength is sufficient to provide a sense of security. Surveys repeatedly show that a majority of the American public feels secure against foreign attack and favor nuclear disarmament (Kay, 1998), and in 1997 U.S. military expenditures were 172% of *all* its possible enemies combined (Council for a Livable World Education Fund, 1998). However, the government continues to spend far more than appears necessary (Defense Monitor, 2000). In part, the excess funding is due to economic pressure from the military-industrial complex (Fogarty, 2000), the need to maintain a weapons industry, and the desire to export weapons to maintain a favorable balance of trade. However, to a large extent the extraordinary funding seems driven by an underlying insecurity that was not present before the beginning of the Cold War.

Second, if we assume that the weak will be attacked, the obvious converse is that the strong will expand and attack. Hence, those who build strength will become involved in using power to impose their will. This appears to be true of the United States.

Third, when two powers come into conflict with each other, they each build strength so that the other will not dominate them, and the resulting conflict is simply more deadly. History gives us Athens versus Sparta, Rome versus Carthage, the United States versus the Soviet Union, and dozens of other examples, and we saw earlier that structural changes in conflict spirals often have disastrous outcomes. In the future we may witness a race to dominate space weaponry.

These problems have given rise to two quite different solutions: the development of nonviolent defense systems and the strengthening of the United Nations so that it could begin to function as a world government with an international police force.

Nonviolent Defense

Nonviolent defense may not be as impracticable as one might imagine. There are effective nonviolent self-defense forms such as aikido and tai chi, in which the defense maintains a calm center of gravity to take advantage of the momentum of an attack and the fact that the attacker is likely to be unbalanced. The defender gains control of the attack and turns it aside (Ueshiba, 1921). There are forms of community policing in which the community prevents violence by maintaining civilized norms (J. Q. Wilson & Kelling, 1989), and Canada (1995) has called for the use of unarmed peace officers trained and organized by local colleges. Finally, there are many examples of the successful use of nonviolent resistance against dictatorial governments. Sharp (1973) published the results of a historical survey that carefully examines the methods and dynamics of nonviolent action to influence political decisions. He gives specific examples of 198 techniques that have been used, ranging from public assemblies and marches, through boycotts and strikes, to noncooperation, civil disobedience, and the establishment of alternative structures of government, including successful uses against the Russian and British empires, the Nazis, Latin American dictators, and the Soviet Union. Sharp's (1990) pragmatic examination of when nonviolent defense has worked and what factors make such resistance possible distinguishes between situations conducive and nonconducive to nonviolent resistance. Relative power is not as important as one might imagine. The contest is really one of wills, and a central factor is the cohesiveness of the nonviolent group and the ability to maintain communications so that tactics can be adapted to the changing situation.

Although civilian defense may be an alternative to military might, it may be argued that any defense that is organized by the state will be used to maintain structural violence. Citizens give the state a monopoly of violence so that it may maintain order and curb crime. And it may be argued that a democratically run state succeeds in having adequate police control and adequate control over its police. However, from an anarchist standpoint, states—at least nation-states based on centralized power—commit far more violence than their citizens do. Hence, Martin (1984) argued that working with state systems will never abolish war because states themselves are the problem. His anarchist solution is to use grassroots strategies to build alternative institutions to the state and its existing bureaucracies.

Developing the United Nations

To some extent we already have the rudiments of a democratic world police force. The United Nations forces have been engaged in over 50 missions. These have included the monitoring of elections, the provision of the international police presence needed after civil turmoil, the maintenance of buffer zones between former combatants, and armed interventions needed to prevent extensive civilian casualties.

Clearly, the last case, armed interventions, is the most problematic form of intervention. Studies of the military interventions in northern Iraq, Somalia, Bosnia, Rwanda, and Haiti (Weiss, 1999) have attempted to assess the degree of the civilian costs incurred before intervention, the cost of military intervention, and the civilian benefits of the intervention. Weiss discussed the quandaries faced by those hoping to use military forces to achieve humanitarian assistance and recommended careful "conflict impact assessment" before attempting to use military force in situations where a presence is not desired by both sides of the conflict.

Although many problems are posed by military intervention once armed conflict has erupted, it may be argued that to have the possibility of military intervention may be helpful in influencing decisions in the early stages of a conflict that threatens to degenerate into military struggle. This is the position taken by Jentleson (2000) in his analysis of the possibilities of preventative diplomacy. He argued that the parties to a conflict are often driven to military action by the uncertainty of a situation in which the other side may strike first. In such situations, diplomacy—with the possibility of intervention and rewards—may be used to influence the calculus of whether to attack or negotiate. The participants in the volume edited by Jentleson present 10 cases where preventative diplomacy either succeeded in averting potential disaster (as in the Baltics and North Korea) or missed opportunities (as in Chechnya and Yugoslavia). They discuss the use and misuse of intelligence; the strategy of using mixes of deterrents, inducements, and reassurances; and the necessity for fast action.

Unfortunately, fast action is currently limited by the fact that there is no permanent UN military force so that each UN action requires the new recruitment of troops, equipment, and money from whatever nations are willing to donate (Holt, 1995). It would be easy to create a small standing force, but the major powers are reluctant to set a precedent and begin an international force that could conceivably challenge their military preeminence. Given the fact that the United States has a veto power in the Security Council (which must concur

in the use of any UN forces), an interesting psychological problem is posed by why conservative representatives feel the need to maintain tight national control by blocking *any* permanent UN forces. This need for the maintenance of control is manifested also in the reluctance to endorse a nuclear test ban treaty or an international criminal court for war crimes.

Peace Through Negotiation

Instead of regarding the other as an enemy, it is often possible to search for mutual gains, and trade has often been an alternative to war. While horse trading has been known for millennia, there have been a number of advances in the tactics and strategies of negotiation. One promising approach that has been advanced by Fisher and Ury (1981) is "principled" negotiation. Rather than either strongly maintaining a bargaining position or softly compromising in order to maintain a valued relationship, they argue that one should search for the interests that underlie the bargaining positions. The negotiator than attempts to create a solution that meets the interests of both parties and searches for objective criteria to determine what is fair. Note that this approach uses aggression in the sense of attempting to get what one wants and insisting on fairness.

Although principled negotiation is a practical approach that can often be used, it assumes that the conflict to be negotiated is essentially a conflict about interests. However, some conflicts involve past wounds, different values, and the very identities of the parties to the conflict. This is often true when ethnic conflicts are involved. The Israelis and Palestinians, for example, do not simply have conflicting interests concerning security and sovereignty, but issues about the identity of the Jewish and Palestinian peoples as well. To deal with these sorts of conflicts, Burton (1990) advanced a form of "transformative" negotiation in which the negotiating process deals with the sharing of underlying needs and identities as well as interests. Such negotiations require a deeper level of trust and, when successful, involve a transformation of identities so that definitions that reflect enmity or involve devaluations of the other are no longer aspects of identity. A discussion of such needs may be helpful in intractable conflicts. For example, Cross and Rosenthal (1999) randomly paired 20 Jewish and 20 Arab students to discuss the dispute over the control of Jerusalem, and they contrasted different methods of negotiation. Participants who used a method in which they identified needs and fears about identity, recognition, and security before they attempted to generate ideas for mutual satisfaction became less pessimistic about the conflict and showed a more positive attitude change toward the other.

In order to deal with the pain and shame of past injuries and the conflicts between identity needs, C. R. Rogers and Ryback (1984) and Kelman (1996) used problem-solving workshops in which people may share underlying pains, fears, and needs. In the approach used by Rogers and Ryback, a facilitator models the role of respectfully listening and accepting the initial hostility expressed by both parties. Without the accepting presence of the mediator, the hostility would be responded to defensively, but the authors write that after the mediator accepts the hostility, the underlying pain is expressed, and this is responded to sympathetically. This approach should be contrasted with the reframing of hostile statements in couples therapy, in order to avoid shame-hostility cycles, which is advocated by Scheff (1999).

Kelman's workshops are carefully structured in ways that lead both parties to share their underlying needs. Since political leaders are usually hindered by the demands of their position and constituency, he attempted to work with opinion leaders and those who may come into political power in the future. These workshops are quite effective in getting participants to understand and empathize with opposing views. However, the participants are then confronted with the problem of explaining their new tolerance to their compatriots in ways that avoid an accusation of being traitors. From my outsider perspective it appears that these sorts of workshops need to occur between the liberal and conservative parties within the opposing sides of a conflict. It would be fascinating to see the extent to which transformative negotiation could be used to arrive at creative solutions to the sort of classic problems that have divided political parties.

Differences in values are usually expressed in the rhetoric of political parties and typically are debated by having opponents state their conflicting views and then rebut the views of their opponent as both attempt to create a rhetoric that will influence third parties and capture their support. However, Rapoport (1960) has advocated another strategy, which he believes is more apt to produce creative solutions and minimize devaluation of the opponent. He suggested that each opponent should state the *other's* point of view until the other agrees that it has been correctly presented. Then, rather than rebutting the other's view, the opponent should create ways to *agree* with the other's view, not by role playing the other side but by honestly finding points of agreement. Rapoport pointed out that any statement has a region of validity. Thus, if the other says, "11 plus 2 is 1," a person may respond by agreeing to the extent that one is referring to clock time. Preliminary studies (de Rivera, 1968) have shown that the technique is usable, and it would be interesting to see if it could be used to create acceptable public policies for divisive issues such as legalized abortion.

When a negotiation between parties can be arranged, it is more successful than third-party mediation. Jackson (2000) studied 295 conflicts that occurred between 1945 and 1995 and found 1,154 negotiation efforts, with 47% success (82% lasting more than 8 weeks), and 1,666 mediations, with 39.4% success (51.7% lasting). Of course, mediation is probably more often attempted when the level of hostility is high and interferes with negotiation, but it seems clear that third parties should first encourage direct negotiation. When hostility is high, there are innovative approaches to conflict management that stress the use of third parties as go-betweens. Galtung and Tschudi (2001) argued that when emotions hinder the ability of conflicting parties to dialogue with one another, it is often possible to create better dialogue with neutral conflict workers who can then work separately with the conflicting parties to create a solution that transcends deep differences. Patai (1973) pointed out that in Arabic cultures a mutually respected third party may be used to request solutions that conflicting parties can grant out of generosity and respect, without appearing to give in to the other party with whom they are in conflict, and Pedersen (2001) reminded conflict workers that collectivistic cultures may manage conflicts in ways that are substantially different from those favored in the West.

Negotiation is increasingly being used to settle civil disputes, and in the future it may be used increasingly in criminal cases. Zehr (1990) convincingly argued that many crimes rupture human relationships and that it is these relationships that need to be repaired. Currently, crime is viewed as contrary to the state, and the state punishes an offender (who is made into a "criminal," who often attempts to avoid responsibility by offering a defense) and largely ignores the victim. Zehr suggested that, as an alternative, the state ask the victim if he or she would like to meet the offender and see what the offender could do to restore the human relationship between them. Studies of trial programs of such "restorative justice" have found that about 50% of victims want to meet the person who wronged them, that it is usually possible to negotiate a way to restore the human relationship, and that in such cases there is much less recidivism. Justice has been attained nonviolently, by restoration rather than retribution.

Peace Through Justice

There are times when repressive forces are so strong that a completely unjust "peace" may exist for years. However, situations inevitably change, and when opportunities arise, rebellion and revolution occur, often killing some who opposed the injustice that existed. Yet the path of peace through justice is much more than an attempt to stave off violent revolution.

It is an attempt to achieve a positive peace, a fundamentally just world.

The conflict between those desiring justice and those resisting it could be achieved by negotiation. However, this can only occur if parties are willing to negotiate, and there are many situations in which people with property and power do not wish to negotiate, particularly when oppression and exploitation are involved. Hence, the building of structural peace often requires the creation of social strain and disequilibria (Montiel, 2001). Attempts at organization are often met with violence, and this may result in counter violence. Even when the oppressed succeed in using counter violence, it often happens that the success only replaces one system of exploitation with another. Knowing these facts and facing injustice within the context of the British colonialism led Gandhi to create his method of nonviolent resistance.

By nonviolence (literally, *satyagrha* or "truth power") Gandhi (1983) did not mean either passivity or the use of socially acceptable nonviolent tactics to coerce his opponent to give in. He meant asserting the truth as one saw it while being open to the perceptions of opponents and their interests, treating them with respect and attempting to convince them, and accepting suffering rather than inflicting it or giving in to injustice. Inherent in his approach are the unity of means and end and the unity of all life. Gandhi's approach is aggressive in the sense of asserting one's will, and some have argued that his methods were coercive. However, Burrowes (1996, chap. 7) established that he always attempted to change the heart of his opponent and that any coercion that existed was a coercion for a negotiation that could satisfy the needs of both parties. Several of his nonviolent campaigns have been described and evaluated by Bondurant (1965); a general history of nonviolent methods and the dynamics of how they influence political decisions has been presented by Sharp (1973); and the psychology of nonviolence, in both its positive and problematic aspects, has been discussed by Pelton (1974). A recent history of nonviolent social movements since 1970 may be found in the volume by Zunes, Kurtz, and Asher (1999), and Sutherland and Meyer (2000) contrasted the role played by both nonviolence and violence in the struggle for freedom and social justice in Africa.

Peace Brigades International (PBI) is an example of current nonviolence in practice. This nonhierarchical organization furnishes unarmed volunteers who accompany human rights workers who are committed to nonviolence but have received death threats because of their work. Working in a nonpartisan way with the government of the nation where atrocities are being committed, and backed by an international emergency response network that communicates with embassies throughout the world, PBI has been successful in the effort to open the political space essential for democracy (see Mahony & Egeren, 1997). Building on such efforts, Hartsough and Duncan (2001) are attempting to organize a volunteer nonviolent global peace force that could be used in situations where unarmed peacekeepers could function as neutral observers.

Peace Through Personal Transformation

Although each of the previous paths toward peace have merit, it may be argued that correctly following any of them requires a sort of personal development that can only be called transformational. This is perhaps most evident in the person who commits to Gandhi's path of nonviolent action and develops a willingness to suffer rather than inflict injury as he or she acts to further justice. However, it is also required in the negotiator who develops an ability to acknowledge shame and refuses to allow egoistic needs to interfere with the skillful conduct of a negotiation, or the practitioner of defense who remains centered and balanced in dealing with a situation of potential violence, the type of self required if we are to have a more peaceful world (de Rivera, 1989). Forming such a self constitutes another path toward peace that takes personal transformation as its means. Rather than focusing on strength, negotiation, or justice, it emphasizes the development of an inner peacefulness that may spread outward to influence the conduct of others. An exemplar is the Vietnamese monk Thich Nhat Hanh (1991).

Thich Nhat Hanh, who has helped thousands of refugees and has established a number of meditation centers, is committed to living in the sacredness of each moment and developing a compassion for all being. He and dozens of other activists who have published accounts, along with hundreds of less well known activists (see True, 1985), have dedicated their lives to a practical living of nonviolence that they assume will influence the people around them and gradually create an atmosphere of peace that will affect the communities in which they live and, eventually, national policy. Although there are numerous anecdotal accounts of the sorts of effects they have generated, there has been little systematic study of their influence. The personal transformations involved in the development of nonviolence may be examined in the context of character development or in uses of the imagination to promote the development of peaceful action.

Character Development

Although the public is acquainted only with a few well-known peace activists, there are many persons who have risked or devoted their lives to working for peace and justice, and one may ask how such commitment develops. Oliner and

Oliner's (1988) inquiry into the background of people who risked helping Jews during the Holocaust reveals a family background that combined both warmth and caring within the family with the welcoming of people from different groups into the family. Both these factors seem important in Hannon's (1990) study of a sample of 21 Boston peace activists. He found that many had some sort of religious socialization that provided a moral basis that was challenged by radicalizing college experiences. He argued for an identity crisis that could in part be understood in terms of Erikson's (1963) fifth stage, in which the adolescent seeks an ideology that can be affirmed by peers and that defines what is good and evil. However, in these activists the resolution of the crisis also involved a transition to Kohlberg's (1973) postconventional moral reasoning and Fowler's (1981) transition from conventional to individualistic/reflective faith. This was often influenced by one or more adults who served as a sort of sponsor to the new identity, which usually also involved participation in a network of like-minded peers. In their study of 28 moral exemplars, Colby and Damon (1999) reported that the exemplars did not begin as exceptional people but became increasingly caring as their goals were transformed by their interactions with others. They found that the exemplars were characterized by an absence of conflict between selfish and moral goals. In accord with Macmurray's (1961) conceptualization, the absence of the more typical split between self and other coincided with a faith in the eventual triumph of goodness for humanity.

The Use of Imagination

Boulding (1988) pointed out that action is guided by a vision of the future and that many people lack a vision of what a peaceful world would be like. (In my own experience, students find it much easier to imagine alien abductions than a peaceful world.) Accordingly, she has experimented with workshops in which people are asked to imagine a future world that is peaceful. She has found that such a world needs to be placed about 30 years in the future so that it seems possible but not too remote. After imagining some of the details of a peaceful world, participants are asked to imagine the steps that enabled such a world to come into being and, finally, to come up with a plan for the steps they might personally take.

Working from a neo-Jungian perspective, Watkins (1988) postulated that the imagination needed to work for peace is checked by a conflict with other aspects of the self. She asked persons to imagine the part of them that wants to work for peace and to construct a character to represent that part (Is it a man or a woman, rich or poor, how old, how dressed?). Similarly, persons create a character to represent the part of them that has other interests and things to do. Watkins postu-

lated that it is the relationship between these characters that governs whether a person's energy is available for peace work. Accordingly, she asked her subjects to imagine the two characters meeting each other and attempts to structure these meetings so that the two accept rather than reject one another. Preliminary evidence suggests that when persons are able to imagine a friendly meeting, they are more likely to engage in actions that promote peace.

Macy (1983) used imagination in still other ways in the course of the workshops she has created to deal with the despair that she believes prevents many persons from taking action to stop the use of nuclear weapons. After exercises designed to help people feel and express pain and despair, she involved participants in empowering exercises. For example, persons may be asked to imagine themselves before they were born, looking at the earth and deciding to help. They evidently choose a particular time to be born, a nation and family to be born into, and a specific gender and personality so that they could act for peace. Next, they were asked to remember why they made the choices they did. What are they here to do? Although Macy's and Boulding's workshops have clear immediate effects, we lack data on whether they affect long-term commitments.

Developing Cultures of Peace

Each of the four paths toward peace may be seen as ways to develop cultures of peace that could replace the cultures of violence that exist in many contemporary societies. Although such a goal is idealistic, it is not unrealistic. Peaceful cultures have existed in the past, and there are small peaceful cultures that exist today. An examination of such cultures reveals a number of interesting characteristics. Bonta's (1993) annotated bibliography describes over 60 traditional peoples and contemporary subcultures. Although they differ in many ways, they all emphasize cooperative rather than competitive relationships, dislike power and downplay individual recognition and wealth, have many ways to prevent and resolve conflict, value group harmony over abstract concepts of justice, and think of themselves as essentially peaceful.

Ross (1993), who has contrasted the extent of conflict in a sample of 90 preindustrial societies, showed that the level of conflict is related to socialization practices. Cultures without much conflict tend to place a high value on children, are high in warmth and affection, and are low in male gender identity conflict. These psycho-cultural roots of peace are orthogonal with the way a society is structured, and Ross showed that the extent to which aggression is directed out at external targets, rather than expressed within the society, depends on the extent to which there are strong cross-cutting interest ties within the society.

Turning to modern societies, the Peace Forum's (2000) sophisticated index of the peacefulness of contemporary nations is based on a combination of measures of external and internal conflict and measures of domestic justice. The index reveals the relative peacefulness of the developed but small nations such as Denmark, the Netherlands, and Portugal, as contrasted with many of the less developed nations and the powerful permanent members of the Security Council (the United States ranks 51st among the 74 nations for which data are available). The people of these smaller nations may feel more secure because their life is more predictable. People can trust one another and their social institutions (Fogarty, 2000), and they may find it easier to accept the need for the mutual obligations and responsibilities stressed by Hearn (1997).

Although powerful societies are often relatively violent, Boulding (2000) has described how there are always many peaceful elements mixed in with the violent components. In religion, for example, there is the idea of a holy war but also the image of the peaceful garden. And it may be noted that after the putatively Islamic terrorist attack on the United States, the president of Iran phoned the pope to discuss the importance of Christian-Muslim dialogue (Catholic Free Press, 2001). Boulding argued that these peaceful elements make it possible to conceive realistically of developing peaceful cultures in modern society.

How might we conceptualize what such cultures could be like? One way is to consider the transformations that would be involved in moving from the culture of violence to which many of us have become accustomed to a culture of peace. Adams and True (1997) suggested that these transformations might be characterized as follows:

1. The redefinition of power so that it was understood to involve joint problem solving and active nonviolence rather than the use of hierarchies that require violent domination.

2. The mobilization of people and the attainment of solidarity by building relationships of understanding and trust between groups rather than having one group dominate another or by achieving solidarity by focusing on the defeat of a common enemy.

3. The participation of all people in the decisions that affect their lives.

4. The open sharing of information in the press and in civic society.

5. The development and empowerment of the caring and nurturing qualities traditionally associated with the role of women.

6. The development of a cooperative and sustainable (rather than exploitative) economies.

We may imagine a global culture of peace involving the previous transformations along with an environment in which armaments were controlled and human rights were ensured. Such a culture has been advocated by 20 Nobel peace laureates and promoted by UNESCO. To assist this development, the General Assembly of the United Nations has launched a decade of initiatives to achieve a culture of peace and requested a progress report from the secretary general (see Adams, 2000). Current research is attempting to develop indicators for the eight aspects of such a culture so that it will be possible to assess progress toward its development.

Of course, a global culture of peace both influences and is dependent upon the specific cultures of peace developed by different societies. Each nation has its own particular challenges, and it seems clear that peace, like human rights, must be developed by a discourse between groups from within each society as theses groups dialogue with groups from without (An-Nàim, 1992). The movement toward a culture of peace is the first social movement that includes nation states as well as people. However, progress toward its goal cannot depend on the initiative of those powerful states whose interest is in maintaining the status quo. Rather, the development of each of the components of cultures of peace will depend on the less powerful nations and on the hundreds of grassroots initiatives by nongovernmental organizations that are constructing the paths of peace described previously. Each of these paths, along with an understanding of aggression, violence, and evil, is critical to developing the aspects of peaceful culture.

International arms control and the maintenance of human rights require some system of international security. Given the current state of human development, this security must rest on the strength of some international authority that can take aggressive action when it is required, but whose violence is checked by a division of power and civilian control. Whenever that system of authority is reduced to the use of violent means, this must be publicly acknowledged as an evil. Such an authority will develop only when the strengthening of emotional ties leads powerful nations to surrender their monopoly of violence. NATO and other regional forces are steps in this direction, and we may see a strengthening of UN police forces in an effort to control terrorism.

The challenges to achieving a consensus about international norms on terrorism involve issues that must be aggressively negotiated. The path of negotiation, as well as an understanding of the structural changes that perpetrate conflict, is also involved in attempts to increase democratic participation, the sharing of information, and intergroup trust. The latter rests on a mastery of transformative as well as principled negotiation. Such negotiation will be much easier if synergistic societal structures lead those who want power to meet the needs of those without it.

The transformation of hierarchies of power and the attainment of an equitable and sustainable economy require the development of justice by nonviolent action. The evil of structural violence can only be overcome by methods that employ the creative use of aggression pioneered by Gandhi. This will require a learning of a different set of scripts and myths, heroes, and heroines who overcome negative emotions and moral disengagement, as well as the development of norms for intervening when violence occurs.

Gender equality and the development of the nurturance and caring that is required for domestic and civil peace will require personal transformations. This path will also be needed to develop the sense of security that constrains the desire for power of those in authority, to restrict the egoism that can hinder negotiation, and to develop the compassionate nonviolence needed to attain justice. These personal transformation need not depend solely on individual efforts. If a culture of peace develops, there will be ceremonies that remember all of the victims of war, a honoring of tragedy will replace claims of goodness, and signs will ask God to bless the world. These will help develop the sorts of persons required by the culture.

REFERENCES

Adams, D. (2000). Toward a global movement for a culture of peace. *Peace & Conflict, 6*(3), 259–266.

Adams, D., & True, M. (1997). UNESCO's culture of peace program: An introduction. *International Peace Research Newsletter, 35,* 15–18.

Amnesty International. (2000). *Torture worldwide: An affront to human dignity.* New York: Amnesty International.

Anderson, C. A., & Anderson, K. B. (1998). Temperature and aggression: Paradox, controversy, and a (fairly) clear picture. In R. G. Geen & E. Donnerstein (Eds.), *Human aggression: Theories, research, and implicators for social policy* (pp. 248–298). San Diego, CA: Academic Press.

Anderson, C. A., & Bushman, B. J. (2001). Effects of violent video games on aggressive behavior, aggressive cognition, aggressive affect, physiological arousal, and prosocial behavior: A meta-analytic review of the scientific literature. *Psychological Science, 12,* 353–359.

An-Naim, A. A. (1992). Toward a cross-cultural approach at defining an international standard of human rights: The meaning of cruel, inhuman, or degrading treatment or punishment. *Human rights in cross cultural perspectives: A quest for consensus.* Philadelphia: University of Pennsylvania Press.

Appleby, R. S. (2000). *The ambivalence of the sacred: Religion, violence, and reconciliation.* Lanham, MD: Rowman & Littlefield.

Archer, D., & McDaniel, P. (1995). Violence and gender: Differences and similarities across societies. In R. B. Ruback & N. A. Weiner (Eds.), *Interpersonal violent behaviors: Social and cultural aspects* (pp. 63–88). New York: Springer.

Atlas, R. S., & Pepler, D. J. (1998). Observation of bullying in the classroom. *The Journal of Educational Research, 92,* 86–98.

Azar, S. T. (1991). Models of child abuse: A metatheoretical analysis. *Criminal Justice & Behavior Special Issue: Physical child abuse, 18*(1), 30–46.

Azar, S. T., Povilaitis, Y. T., Lauretti, F. A., & Pouquette, L. C. (1998). The current status of etiological theories in intrafamilial child maltreatment. In J. R. Lutzker (Ed.), *Handbook of child abuse research and treatment* (pp. 3–30). New York: Plenum Press.

Bandura, A. (1973). *Aggression: A social learning analysis.* Englewood Cliffs, NJ: Prentice Hall.

Bandura, A. (1999). Moral disengagement in the perpetration of inhumanities. *Personality and Social Psychology Review, 3*(3), 193–209.

Bandura, A., Underwood, B., & Fromson, M. E. (1975). Disinhibition of aggression through diffusion of responsibility and dehumanization of victims. *Journal of Research in Personality, 9,* 253–269.

Barash, D. P. (1991). *Introduction to peace studies.* Belmont, CA: Wadsworth.

Baron, R. A. (1977). *Human aggression.* New York: Plenum Press.

Baron, R. A., & Ransberger, V. M. (1978). Ambient temperature and the occurrence of collective violence: The "long, hot summer" revisited. *Journal of Personality and Social Psychology, 36,* 351–360.

Baumeister, R. F., & Campbell, W. K. (1999). The intrinsic appeal of evil: Sadism, sensational thrills, and threatened egotism. *Personality and Social Psychology Review, 3*(3), 210–221.

Baumeister, R. F., Smart, L., & Boden, J. M. (1996). Relation of threatened egotism to violence and aggression: The dark side of high self-esteem. *Psychological Review, 103,* 5–33.

Beck, A. J., & Shipley, B. E. (1997). *Recidivism of prisoners released in 1983: Special report.* Washington, DC: Bureau of Justice Statistics.

Behrens, D. A., Feichtinger, G., & Prskawetz, A. (1997). Complex dynamics and control of arms race. *European Journal of Operational Research, 100,* 192–215.

Berkowitz, L. (1982). Aversive conditions as stimuli to aggression. In I. Berkowitz (Ed.), *Advances in experimental social psychology* (Vol. 15, pp. 249–288). New York: Academic Press.

Berkowitz, L. (1993). *Aggression: Its causes, consequences, and control.* New York: McGraw-Hill.

Berkowitz, L. (1999). Evil is more than banal: Situationism and the concept of evil. *Personality and Social Psychology Review, 3*(3), 246–253.

Berkowitz, L., & Frodi, A. (1979). Reactions to a child's mistakes as affected by her/his looks and speech. *Social Psychology Quarterly, 42,* 420–425.

Berkowitz, L., & LePage, A. (1967). Weapons as aggression-eliciting stimuli. *Journal of Personality and Social Psychology, 7,* 202–207.

Bernstein, J. Y., & Watson, M. W. (1997). Children who are targets of bullying. *Journal of Interpersonal Violence, 12,* 483–498.

Berry, M., Giles, H., & Williams, A. (1999). Communication studies: Overview. *Encyclopedia of Violence, Peace, and Conflict, 1,* 375–388.

Blanchard, D. C., & Blanchard, R. J. (2000). Emotions as mediators and modulators of violence: Some reflections on the "Seville statement on violence." *Social Research, 67*(3), 683–708.

Blumenthal, M. D., Kahn, R. L., Andrews, F. M., & Head, K. B. (1972). *Justifying violence: Attitudes of American men.* Ann Arbor, MI: Institute for Social Research.

Bondurant, J. V. (1965). *Conquest of violence: The Gandhian philosophy of conflict* (Rev. ed.). Berkeley: University of California Press.

Bonta, B. D. (1993). *Peaceful peoples: An annotated bibliography.* Metuchen, NJ: Scarecrow.

Boulding, E. (1988). Image and action in peace building. *Journal of Social Issues, 44*(2), 17–37.

Boulding, E. (2000). *Cultures of peace: The hidden side of history.* Syracuse, NY: Syracuse University Press.

Boulton, M. J., & Underwood, K. (1992). Bully/victim problems among middle school children. *British Journal of Educational Psychology, 62,* 73–87.

Brewer, M. B. (1999). The psychology of prejudice: Ingroup love or outgroup hate? *Journal of Social Issues, 55*(3), 429–444.

Burrowes, R. J. (1996). *The strategy of nonviolent defense: Canadian approach.* Albany: State University of New York Press.

Burton, J. W. (1990). *Conflict: Resolution and prevention.* London: Macmillan.

Bushman, B. J., & Anderson, C. A. (2001). Media violence and the American public: Scientific facts versus media misinformation. *American Psychologist, 56*(6/7), 477–489.

Bushman, B. J., & Baumeister, R. F. (1998). Threatened egotism, narcissism, self-esteem, and direct and displaced aggression: Does self-love or self-hate lead to violence? *Journal of Personality and Social Psychology, 75,* 219–229.

Butigan, K. (1999). *From violence to wholeness: A ten part program in the spirituality and practice of active nonviolence.* Las Vegas, NV: Pace e Bene Franciscan Nonviolence Center.

Cairns, E., & Darby, J. (1998). The conflict in Northern Ireland: Causes, consequences, and controls. *American Psychologist, 53*(7), 754–760.

Canada, G. (1995). *Fist stick knife gun: A personal history of violence in America.* Boston, MA: Beacon Press.

Capozzoli, T. K., & McVey, S. R. (2000). *Kids killing kids: Managing violence and gangs in schools.* New York: St. Lucie Press.

Caprara, G., & Zimbardo, P. (1996). Aggregation and amplification of marginal deviations in the social construction of personality and maladjustment. *European Journal of Personality, 10,* 79–110.

Center for Defense Information. (2000). *The Defense Monitor, 29*(2).

Colby, A., & Damon, W. (1999). The development of extraordinary moral commitment. In M. Killen & D. Hart (Eds.), *Morality in everyday life: Developmental perspectives* (pp. 342–370). New York: Cambridge University Press.

Copelon, R. (1995). Gendered war crimes: Reconceptualizing rape in time of war. In J. Peters & A. Wolper (Eds.), *Women's rights, human rights* (pp. 197–214). New York: Routledge.

Council for a Livable World Education Fund. (1998, December). *Caution: Military-industrial complex at work.* Washington, DC: Author.

Cross, S., & Rosenthal, R. (1999). Three models of conflict resolution: Effects on intergroup expectancies and attitudes. *Journal of Social Issues, 55*(3), 561–580.

Daly, M., & Wilson, M. (1985). Competitiveness, risk taking, and violence: The young male syndrome. *Ethology and Sociobiology, 6,* 59–73.

Dawes, A. (1994). The emotional impact of political violence. In A. Dawes & D. Donald (Eds.), *Childhood and adversity.* Capetown, South Africa: David Philip.

de la Rey, C. (2001). Reconciliation of divided societies. In D. J. Christie, R. V. Wagner, & D. D. N. Winter (Eds.), *Peace, conflict, and violence: Peace psychology for the 21st century* (pp. 251–261). Upper Saddle River, NJ: Prentice Hall.

de Rivera, J. H. (1968). *The psychological dimension of foreign policy.* Columbus, OH: Charles E. Merrill.

de Rivera, J. H. (1977). A structural theory of the emotions. *Psychological Issues Monograph.* New York: International Universities Press.

de Rivera, J. H. (1981). *Conceptual encounter: A method for the exploration of human experience.* Lanham, MD: University Press of America.

de Rivera, J. H. (1989). Love, fear, and justice: Transforming selves for the new world. *Social Justice Research, 3,* 387–426.

de Rivera, J. H. (1992). Emotional climate: Social structure and emotional dynamics. In K. T. Strongman (Ed.), *International review of studies on emotion* (Vol. 2). New York: Wiley.

de Rivera, J. H. (in press). Emotion and the formation of social identities. In J. Barbolet & M. L. Lyon (Eds.), *Emotion in social theory: Cross-disciplinary perspectives.*

Deutsch, M. (1958). Trust and suspicion. *Journal of Conflict Resolution, 2,* 265–279.

Dunning, E., Murphy, P., & Williams, J. (1988). *The roots of football hooliganism: An historical and sociological study.* London: Routledge & Kegan Paul.

Edleson, J. L. (1996). Controversy and changes in batterer's programs. In J. Edleson & Z. C. Eisikovits (Eds.), *Future interventions with battered women and their families* (pp. 154–169). Thousand Oaks, CA: Sage.

Egan, S. K., & Perry, D. G. (1998). Does low self-regard invite victimization? *Developmental Psychology, 34,* 299–309.

Elsass, P. (1997). *Treating victims of torture and violence.* New York: New York University Press.

Ember, C. R., & Ember, M. (1994). War, socialization, and interpersonal violence: A cross-cultural study. *Journal of Conflict Resolution, 38,* 620–646.

Enloe, C. (2000). *Maneuvers: The international politics of women's lives.* Berkeley: University of California Press.

Erikson, E. (1963). *Childhood and society* (2nd ed.). New York: W. W. Norton.

Eron, L. D., Huesmann, L. R., Lefkowitz, M. M., & Walder, L. O. (1972). Does television violence cause aggression? *American Psychologist, 27,* 253–263.

Eron, L. D., Huesmann, L. R., Lefkowitz, M. M., & Walder, L. O. (1996). Does television violence cause aggression? In D. Greenberg (Ed.), *Criminal careers* (Vol. 2, pp. 311–321). Aldershot, Hampshire, England: Ashgate Publishing.

Farrington, D. P. (1989). Long-term prediction of offending and other life outcomes. In H. Wegener, F. Losel, & J. Haisch (Eds.), *Criminal behavior and the justice system* (pp. 26–39). New York: Springer-Verlag.

Fisher, R., & Ury, W. (1981). *Getting to yes: Negotiating agreement without giving in* (2nd ed.). New York: Penguin.

Flores, S. A., & Hartlaub, M. G. (1998). Reducing rape-myth acceptance in male college students: A meta-analysis of intervention studies. *Journal of College Student Development, 39*(5), 438–448.

Fogarty, B. E. (2000). *War, peace, and the social order.* Boulder, CO: Westview Press.

Fowler, J. (1981). *Stages of faith.* San Francisco: Harper and Row.

Freud, S. (1933). Why war? In J. Strachey (Ed.), *Standard edition of the complete psychological works of Sigmund Freud* (Vol. 22, pp. 199–215). London: Hogarth Press.

Fritsch, E. J., Caeti, T. J., & Taylor, R. W. (1999). Gang suppression through saturation patrol, aggressive curfew, and truancy enforcement: A quasi-experimental test of the Dallas anti-gang initiative. *Crime and Delinquency, 45*(1), 122–139.

Fromm, E. (1955). *The sane society.* New York: Holt, Rinehart, and Winston.

Fromm, E. (1973). *The anatomy of human destructiveness.* New York: Holt, Rinehart, and Winston.

Galtung, J. (1969). Violence, peace and peace research. *Journal of Peace Research, 3,* 176–191.

Galtung, J. (1980). *Essays in peace research: Peace, research, education, and action* (Vol. 1). Copenhagen: Christian Ejlers. (Original work published 1975)

Galtung, J. (1996). *Peace by peaceful means: Peace, conflict, development, and civilization.* Copenhagen: Christian Ejlers.

Galtung, J., & Tschudi, F. (2001). Crafting peace: On the psychology of the TRANSCEND approach. In D. J. Christie, R. V. Wagner, & D. D. N. Winter (Eds.), *Peace, conflict, and violence: Peace psychology for the 21st century* (pp. 210–222). Upper Saddle River, NJ: Prentice Hall.

Gandhi, M. K. (1983). *Non-violent resistance (Satyagraha).* New York: Schocken.

Garbarino, J. (1991). Not all bad developmental outcomes are the result of child abuse. *Development and Psychopathology, 3,* 45–50.

Gilligan, J. (2000). Punishment and violence: Is the criminal law based on one huge mistake. *Social Research, 67*(3), 745–772.

Gottlieb, G. (1993). *Nation against state.* New York: Council on Foreign Relations Press.

Gurr, T. R. (1996). Minorities, nationalists and ethnopolitical conflict. In C. A. Crocker (Ed.), *Managing global chaos: Sources of and response to international conflict* (pp. 53–78). Washington, DC: United States Institute of Peace.

Haney, C., & Zimbardo, P. (1998). The past and future of the U.S. prison policy: Twenty-five years after the Stanford prison experiment. *American Psychologist, 53*(7), 709–727.

Hanh, T. N. (1991). *Peace is every step: The path of mindfulness in everyday life.* New York: Bantam Books.

Hannon, J. T. (1990). Becoming a peace activist: A life course perspective. In J. Lofland & S. Marullo (Eds.), *Peace movements of the '80's: Sociological perspectives.* Piscataway, New Brunswick: Rutgers University Press.

Hart, B. (1992). *Remarks to the task force on child abuse and neglect.* Retrieved April 1992 from home.cybergrrl.com/dv/stat

Hartsough, D., & Duncan, M. (2001). Creating a global nonviolent peace force. *Fellowship, 67*(1-2), 14–15.

Haugaard, J. J. (1988). The use of theories about the etiology of incest as guidelines for legal and therapeutic interventions. *Behavioral Sciences and the Law, 6*(2), 221–238.

Hearn, F. (1997). *Moral order and social disorder: The American search for a civil society.* New York: Aldine de Gruyter.

Heider, F. (1958). *The psychology of interpersonal relations.* New York: Wiley.

Heider, K. G. (1991). *Indonesian cinema: National culture on screen.* Honolulu: University of Hawaii Press.

Hepburn, M. A. (1997). A medium's effects under scrutiny. *Social Education, 61*(5), 244–249.

Hill, K. G., Howell, J. C., Hawkins, D. J., & Battin-Pearson, S. R. (1999). Childhood risk factors for adolescent gang membership: results from the Seattle social development project. *Journal of Research in Crime and Delinquency, 36,* 300–322.

Holt, V. K. (1995). *Briefing book on peacekeeping: The U.S. role in United Nations peace operations* (2nd ed.). New York: Council for a Livable World Education Fund.

Holtzworth-Munroe, A. (2000). A typology of men who are violent towards their female partners: Making sense of the heterogeneity in husband violence. *Current Directions in Psychological Science, 9*(4), 140–143.

Huesmann, L. R. (1998). The role of social information processing and cognitive schema in the acquisition and maintenance of habitual aggressive behavior. In R. G. Geen & E. Donnerstein (Eds.), *Human aggression: Theories, research, and implicators for social policy* (pp. 73–110). San Diego, CA: Academic Press.

Jackson, R. (2000). Managing Africa's violent conflicts. *Peace & Change, 25*(2), 208–224.

Janis, I. L. (1983). *Groupthink: Psychological studies of policy decisions and fiascoes.* Boston: South End Press.

Jentleson, B. W. (Ed.). (2000). *Opportunities missed, opportunities seized: Preventive diplomacy in the post-Cold War world.* Lanham, MD: Rowman & Littlefield.

Josephson, W. L. (1987). Television violence and children's aggression: Testing and priming, social script, and disinhibition predictions. *Journal of Personality and Social Psychology, 53,* 882–890.

Kakar, S. (1996). *The colors of violence.* Chicago: University of Chicago Press.

Kakar, S. (2000). The time of Kali: Violence between religious groups in India. *Social Research, 67*(3), 877–899.

Kay, A. F. (1998). *Locating consensus for democracy: A ten-year U.S. experiment.* St. Augustine, FL: Americans Talk Issues.

Kelman, H. C. (1996). The interactive problem-solving approach. In C. A. Crocker, F. O. Hampson, & P. Aall (Eds.), *Managing global chaos* (pp. 501–520). Washington, DC: United States Institute of Peace Press.

Kelly, G. A. (1965). The threat of aggression. *Journal of Humanistic Psychology, 5,* 195–201.

Kilham, W., & Mann, L. (1974). Level of destructive obedience as a function of transmitter and executant roles in the Milgram obedience paradigm. *Journal of Personality and Social Psychology, 29,* 696–702.

Kohlberg, L. (1973). Continuities in childhood and adult moral development revisited. In P. B. Baltes & K. W. Schaie (Eds.), *Lifespan development psychology* (2nd ed.). New York: Academic Press.

Koss, M. P., Gigycz, C. A., & Wisniewski, N. (1987). The scope of rape: Incidence and prevalence of sexual aggression and victimization in a national sample of higher education students. *Journal of Consulting and Clinical Psychology, 55*(2), 162–170.

Kostelny, K., & Garbarino, J. (2001). The war close to home: Children and violence in the United States. In D. J. Christie, R. V. Wagner, & D. D. N. Winter (Eds.), *Peace, conflict, and violence: Peace psychology for the 21st century* (pp. 110–119). Upper Saddle River, NJ: Prentice Hall.

Larzelere, R. E. (1986). Moderate spanking: Model or deterrent of children's aggression in the family? *Journal of Family Violence, 1,* 27–36

Larzelere, R. E. (1996). A review of the outcomes of parental use of nonabusive or customary physical punishment. *Pediatrics, 98,* 824–828.

Lederach, J. P. (1997). *Building peace: Sustainable reconciliation in divided societies.* Washington, DC: United States Institute of Peace Press.

Leisring, P. A., Dowd, L., & Rosenbaum, A. (in press). Treatment of partner aggressive women. *Journal of Aggression, Maltreatment and Trauma.*

Lerner, S. (1984, October 15). Rule of the cruel: How violence is built into America's prisons. *The New Republic, 191,* 17–21.

Maccoby, E. E., & Jacklin, C. N. (1974). *The psychology of sex differences.* Stanford, CA: Stanford University Press.

Maccoby, M. (1972). Emotional attitude and political choices. *Politics and Society, (Winter),* 209–239.

Macmurray, J. (1944). *Upton lectures.* Unpublished presentation, Manchester College, Oxford University, Oxford, UK.

Macmurray, J. (1961). *Persons in relation.* Atlantic Highlands, NJ: Humanities Press.

Macy, J. (1983). *Despair and personal power in the nuclear age.* Philadelphia: New Society.

Malamuth, N. M. (1998). The conference model as an organizing framework for research on sexually aggressive men: Risk moderators, imagined aggression, and pornographic consumption. In R. G. Geen & E. Donnerstein (Eds.), *Human aggression: Theories, research, and implicators for social policy* (pp. 230–249). San Diego, CA: Academic Press.

Martin, B. (1984). *Uprooting war.* London: Freedom Press.

Matthews, R., & Pitts, J. (1998). Rehabilitation, recidivism, and realism: Evaluating violence reduction programs in prison. *Prison Journal, 78,* 390.

Mazur, A., & Booth, A. (1998). Testosterone and dominance in men. *Behavioral & Brain Sciences, 21*(3), 353–397.

McAlister, A. (2001). Moral disengagement: Measurement and modification. *Journal of Peace Research, 38*(1), 87–99.

McCauley, C. (2000). Some psychologists think they know about aggression and violence. *The HFG Review, 4*(1), 39–44.

McCorkle, R. C., Miethe, T. D., & Drass, K. A. (1995, July). The roots of prison violence: A test of the deprivation, management, and 'not-so-total' institution models. *Crime & Delinquency, 41,* 317–331.

McPhail, C. J. (1994). Presidential address: The dark side of purpose: Individual and collective violence in riots. *The Sociological Quarterly, 35*(1), 1–32.

Milgram, S. (1974). *Obedience to authority: An experimental view.* New York: Harper & Row.

Miller, A. G., Gordon, A. K., & Buddie, A. M. (1999). Accounting for evil and cruelty: Is to explain to condone. *Personality and Social Psychology Review, 3*(3), 254–268.

Montiel, C. J. (2001). Toward a psychology of structural peacebuilding. In D. J. Christie, R. V. Wagner, & D. D. N. Winter (Eds.), *Peace, conflict, and violence: Peace psychology for the 21st century* (pp. 282–294). Upper Saddle River, NJ: Prentice Hall.

Moore, B. (1978). *Injustice: The social bases of obedience and revolt.* London: Macmillan.

Muehlenhard, C. L., Powch, I. G., Phelps, J. L., & Giusti, L. M. (1992). Definitions of rape: Scientific and political implications. *Journal of Social Issues: Adult Sexual Assault, 48*(1), 23–44.

Murray, A. (2000). Under the palaver tree: A moratorium on the importation, exportation, and manufacture of light weapons. *Peace & Change, 25*(2), 265–281.

Nathan, L. (2000). The four horsemen of the apocalypse: The structural cause of crisis and violence in Africa. *Peace and Change, 25,* 188–207.

Nelson, J. D., Gelfand, D. M., & Hartmann, D. P. (1969). Children's aggression following competition and exposure to an aggressive model. *Child Development, 40,* 1085–1097.

Niens, U., & Cairns, E. (2001). Intrastate violence. In D. J. Christie, R. V. Wagner, & D. D. N. Winter (Eds.), *Peace, conflict, and violence: Peace psychology for the 21st century* (pp. 39–48). Upper Saddle River, NJ: Prentice Hall.

Office of Juvenile Justice and Delinquency Prevention. (1998). *Youth gangs: An overview.* Washington, DC: United States Department of Justice.

Oliner, S. P., & Oliner, P. M. (1988). *The altruistic personality.* New York: Free Press.

Oliver, R., Hoover, J. H., & Hazler, R. (1994). The perceived roles of bullying in small-town midwestern schools. *Journal of Counseling & Development, 72,* 416–420.

Olweus, D. (1991). Bully-victim problems among school children: Basic facts and effects of a school-based intervention program. In D. Pepler & K. Rubin (Eds.), *The development and treatment of childhood aggression* (pp. 411–448). Hillsdale, NJ: Erlbaum.

Olweus, D. (1993). *Bullying at school: What we know and what we can do.* Cambridge, MA: Blackwell.

Oneal, J. R., Oneal, F. H., Maoz, Z., & Russett, B. (1996). The liberal peace: Interdependence, democracy, and international conflict, 1950–85. *Journal Peace Research, 33*(1), 11–28.

O'Toole, L. L. (1997). Subcultural theory of rape revisited. In L. L. O'Toole & J. R. Schiffman (Eds.), *Gender violence* (pp. 215–222). New York: New York Clement Press.

Otto, R. (1923). *The idea of holy.* New York: Oxford University Press.

Patai, R. (1973). *The Arab mind.* New York: Scribner's.

Patterson, G. R. (1982). *Coercive family process: Vol. 3. A social learning approach.* Eugene, OR: Castalia.

Patterson, G. R. (1986). The contribution of siblings to training for fighting: A microsocial analysis. In D. Olweus, J. Block, & M. Radke-Yarrow (Eds.), *Development of antisocial and prosocial behavior: Research, theories, and issues* (pp. 235–262). Orlando, FL: Academic Press.

Peck, M. S. (1983). *People of the lie: The hope for healing human evil.* New York: Simon and Schuster.

Pedersen, P. B. (2001). The cultural context of peacemaking. In D. J. Christie, R. V. Wagner, & D. D. N. Winter (Eds.), *Peace, conflict, and violence: Peace psychology for the 21st century* (pp. 183–192). Upper Saddle River, NJ: Prentice Hall.

Pelton, L. H. (1974). *The psychology of nonviolence.* New York: Pergamon Press.

Pianta, R., Egeland, B., & Erickson, M. F. (1989). The antecedents of maltreatment: Results of the mother-child interaction research project. In D. Cicchetti & V. Carlson (Eds.), *Child maltreatment* (pp. 203–253). New York: Cambridge University Press.

Rapoport, A. (1960). *Fights, games, and debates.* Ann Arbor: University of Michigan Press.

Reisig, M. D. (1998, April). Rates of disorder in higher-custody prisons: A comparative analysis of managerial practices. *Crime and Delinquency,* 229–244.

Richardson, L. F. (1960a). *Arms and insecurity: A mathematical study of the causes and origins of war.* Pittsburgh, PA: Boxwood Press.

Richardson, L. F. (1960b). *The statistics of deadly quarrels.* Pittsburgh, PA: Boxwood Press.

Ricoeur, P. (1967). *The symbolism of evil.* Boston: Beacon Press.

Rist, K. (1979). Incest: Theoretical and clinical views. *American Journal of Orthopsychiatry, 49*(4), 680–691.

Rogers, C. R., & Ryback, D. (1984). One alternative to nuclear planetary suicide. *The Counseling Psychologist, 12,* 3–12.

Rogers, J. D., Spencer, J., & Uyangoda, J. (1998). Sri Lanka: Political violence and ethnic conflict. *Journal of the American Psychological Association, 53*(7), 771–777.

Ross, M. H. (1993). *The culture of conflict: Interpretations and interests in comparative perspective.* New Haven, CT: Yale University Press.

Rotton, J., & Frey, J. (1985). Air pollution, weather, and violent crime: Concomitant time-series analysis of archival data. *Journal of Personality and Social Psychology, 49,* 1207–1220.

Rouhana, N. M., & Bar-Tal, D. (1998). Psychological dynamics of intractable ethnonational conflicts: The Israeli-Palestinian case. *Journal of the American Psychological Association, 53*(7), 761–770.

Rozin, P., Markwith, M., & Stoess, C. (1997, March). Moralization and becoming a vegetarian: The transformation of preference into values and the recruitment of disgust. *Psychological Science, 8*(2), 67–73.

Rubin, J. Z., Pruitt, D. G., & Kim, S. H. (1994). *Social conflict: Escalation, stalemate, and settlement* (2nd ed.). New York: McGraw-Hill.

Rubin, R. T. (1987). The neuroendocrinology and neurochemistry of anitsocial behavior. In S. A. Mednick, T. E. Moffitt, & S. A. Stack (Eds.), *The causes of crime* (pp. 239–262). Cambridge, UK: Cambridge University Press.

Scheff, T. J. (1999). Collective emotions in warfare. *Encyclopedia of violence, peace, and conflict, 1,* 331–341.

Schellenber, J. A. (1996). *Conflict resolution: Theory, research, and practice.* Albany: State University of New York Press.

Sedlak, A. (1990). *Technical amendments to the study findings: National incidence and prevalence of child abuse and neglect, 1988.* Rockville, MD: Westat.

Shapira, A., & Madsen, M. C. (1974). Between and within-group cooperation and competition among kibbutz and non-kibbutz children. *Developmental Psychology, 10,* 140–245.

Sharp, G. (1973). *The politics of nonviolent action* (Vols. 1–3). Boston: Porter Sargent.

Sharp, G. (1990). *Civilian-based defense: A post-military weapons system.* Princeton, NJ: Princeton University Press.

Signorelli, N., Gerber, G., & Morgan, M. (1995). Violence on television: The cultural indicators project. *Journal of Broadcasting and Electronic Media, 39*(2), 278–283.

Silver, L. B., Dublin, C. C., & Lourie, R. S. (1969). Does violence breed violence? Contributions from a study of the child abuse syndrome. *American Journal of Psychiatry, 126,* 404–407.

Singer, J. D., & Small, M. (1979). Foreign policy indicators: Predictors of war in history and in the state of the world message. In J. D. Singer, *The correlates of war: Vol. 1. Research origins and rationale* (pp. 298–330). New York: Free Press.

Smith, D. N. (1998). The psychocultural roots of genocide: Legitimacy and crisis in Rwanda. *Journal of the American Psychological Association, 53*(7), 743–753.

Smith, K. K., & Crandell, S. D. (1984). Exploring collective emotion. *American Behavioral Scientist, 27*(6), 813–828.

Smith, R., Sola, M., & Spagnolo, F. (2000). The person's dilemma and regime-switching in the Greek-Turkish arms race. *Journal of Peace Research, 37,* 737–750.

Smith, S. L., & Donnerstein, E. (1998). Harmful effects of exposure to media violence: Learning of aggression, emotional desensitization, and fear. In R. G. Geen & E. Donnerstein (Eds.), *Human aggression: Theories, research, and implicators for social policy* (pp. 168–204). San Diego, CA: Academic Press.

Snyder, D. (1979). Collective violence processes: Implications for disaggregated theory and research. In L. Kriesberg (Ed.), *Research in social movements, conflicts and change* (Vol. 2, pp. 35–61). Greenwich, CT: JAI Press.

Solomon, R. L. (1980). The opponent-process theory of acquired motivations: The costs of pleasure and the benefits of pain. *American Psychologist, 35,* 691–712.

Spergel, I. A., & Grossman, S. F. (1997). The little village project: A community approach to the gang problem. *Social Work, 42,* 456–470.

Staub, E. (1989). *The roots of evil: The origins of genocide and other group violence.* New York: Cambridge University Press.

Staub, E. (1999). The roots of evil: Social conditions, culture, personality, and basic human needs. *Personality and Social Psychology Review, 3*(3), 179–192.

Stohl, M. (1987). Outside of a small circle of friends: States, genocide, mass killing and the role of bystanders. *Journal of Peace Research, 24*(2), 151–166.

Stott, C., & Reicher, S. (1998). How conflict escalates: The intergroup dynamics of collective football crowd "violence." *Sociology, 32*(2), 353–377.

Straus, M. A., & Gelles, R. J. (1990). *Physical violence in American families: Risk factors and adaptions to violence in 8,145 families.* New Brunswick, NJ: Transaction.

Sutherland, B., & Meyer, M. (2000). *Guns and Gandhi in Africa: Pan African insights on nonviolence, armed struggle and liberation in Africa.* Trenton, NJ: Africa World Press.

Tajfel, H. (1982). Introduction. In H. Tajfel (Ed.), *Social identity and intergroup relations* (pp. 1–11). Cambridge, UK: Cambridge University Press.

Tandon, Y. (2000, April). Root causes of peacelessness and approaches to peace in Africa. *Peace & Change, 25*(2), 166–187.

Thompson, N. S. (1999). Group selection and the origins of evil. *Skeptic, 7*(2), 70–73.

Thurman, Q. C., Giacomazzi, A. L., Reisig, M. D., & Mueller, D. G. (1996). Community-based gang prevention and intervention: An evaluation of the neutral zone. *Crime & Delinquency, 42*(2), 279–295.

Toch, H. H. (1993). *Violent men: An inquiry into the psychology of violence.* Chicago: Aldine. (Original work published 1969)

Toch, H., Grant, J. D., & Galvin, R. T. (1974). *Agents of change: A study in police reform.* New York: Wiley.

True, M. (1985). *Justice-seekers, peacemakers: 32 portraits of courage.* Mystic, CT: XXIII Publications.

Turner, C. W., Hesse, B. W., & Peterson-Lewis, S. (1986). Naturalistic studies of the long-term effects of television violence. *Journal of Social Issues, 42,* 51–74.

Turner, C. W., Simons, L. S., Berkowitz, L., & Frodi, A. (1977). The stimulating and inhibiting effects of weapons of aggressive behavior. *Aggressive Behavior, 3,* 355–378.

Turshen, M. (2000). The political economy of violence against women during armed conflicts in Uganda. *Social Research, 67*(3), 803–824.

Ueshiba, K. (1921). *The spirit of Aikido* (T. Unno, Trans.). Tokyo: Hoslanska International.

UNESCO. (1991). *The Seville statement on violence: Preparing the ground for the constructing of peace.* Report disseminated at the 25th session of the General Conference of UNESCO, November, 1989, Paris.

United Nations Development Programme (UNDP). (1999). *Human development report 1999.* New York: Oxford University Press.

United States Department of Justice. (1995). *Uniform crime reports for the United States, 1994.* Washington, DC: Author.

United States Department of Justice. (1999). *Annual bulletin of prisoners in 1999.* Washington, DC: Bureau of Justice Statistics.

van Creveld, M. (2000). A woman's place: Reflections on the origins of violence. *Social Research, 67*(3), 825–848.

Vasquez, J., & Henehan, M. T. (2001). Territorial disputes and the probability of war, 1816–1992. *Journal of Peace Research, 38*(2), 123–138.

Vatikiotis, P. J. (1986). The spread of Islamic terrorism. In B. Netanyahu (Ed.), *Terrorism: How the West can win* (pp. 77–83). New York: Avon Books.

Volkov, V. (2000). The political economy of protection rackets in the past and present. *Social Research, 67*(3), 709–744.

Waldner-Haugrud, L. K., Gratch, L. V., & Magruder, B. (1997). Victimization and perpetration rates of violence in gay and lesbian relationships: Gender issues explored. *Violence and Victims, 12*(2), 173–184.

Wallace, M. D. (1979). Arms race and escalation. *Journal of Conflict Resolution, 23,* 3–16.

Watkins, M. (1988). Imagination and peace: On the inner dynamics of promoting peace activism. *Journal of Social Issues, 44*(2), 39–57.

Weiss, T. G. (1999). *Military-civilian interactions: Intervening in humanitarian crises.* Lanham, MD: Rowman & Littlefield.

Wessells, M., & Monteiro, C. (2001). Psychological interventions and post-war reconstruction in Angola: Interweaving western and traditional approaches. In D. J. Christie, R. V. Wagne & D. D. N. Winter (Eds.), *Peace, conflict, and violence: Peace psychology for the 21st century* (pp. 262–275). Upper Saddle River, NJ: Prentice Hall.

White, J. R. (1998). *Terrorism: An introduction.* Belmont, CA: Wadsworth.

White, R. K. (1984). *Fearful warriors: A psychological profile of U.S.-Soviet relations.* New York: Free Press.

Wilson, D. S. (1998). Game theory and animal behavior. In L. A. Dugatkin & H. K. Reeve (Eds.), *Game theory and human behavior* (pp. 261–282). New York: Oxford University Press.

Wilson, D. S., & Sober, E. (1994). Reintroducing group selection to the human behavioral science. *Behavioral and Brain Sciences, 17,* 585–654.

Wilson, J. Q., & Herrnstein, R. J. (1985). *Crime and human nature.* New York: Simon and Schuster.

Wilson, J. Q., & Kelling, G. L. (1989, February). Making neighborhoods safe. *The Atlantic Monthly,* 46–52.

Wink, W. (1992). *Engaging the powers.* Minneapolis, MN: Fortress Press.

Wolfgang, M. E., & Farracuti, F. (1967). *The subculture of violence: Toward an integrated theory of criminology.* London: Social Science Paperbacks.

Wylie, M. S. (2000). Teaching kids to care. *Family Therapy Networker.* Retrieved from http://www.familytherapynetwork.com/so00feat.html

Zehr, H. (1990) *Changing lenses: A new focus for crime and justice.* Scottdale, PA: Herald Press.

Zimbardo, P. G. (1995). The psychology of evil: A situationist perspective on recruiting good people to engage in anti-social acts. *Research in Social Psychology, 11,* 125–133.

Zunes, S., Kurtz, L. R., & Asher, S. B. (Eds.). (1999). *Nonviolent social movements: A geographical perspective.* Malden, MA: Blackwell.

CHAPTER 24

Personality in Political Psychology

AUBREY IMMELMAN

Portions of this chapter draw extensively from the author's earlier
publications cited in the references, especially Immelman (1993,
1998, 2002). Preparation of this chapter was supported in part by a
Faculty Development and Research grant from St. John's University
and the College of St. Benedict. I wish to thank Richard Wielkiewicz
and Sara Wonderlich for their careful reading of the manuscript and
their critical comments.

PERSONALITY IN POLITICAL PSYCHOLOGY

Political psychology "has a long past, but as an organized discipline, it has a short history," wrote William F. Stone in *The Psychology of Politics* (Stone & Schaffner, 1988, p. v). Niccolò Machiavelli's political treatise, *The Prince* (1513/1995), an early precursor of the field, has modern-day echoes in Richard Christie and Florence Geis's *Studies in Machiavellianism* (1970). The formal establishment of political psychology as an interdisciplinary scholarly endeavor was anticipated by notable precursors in the twentieth century with a focus on personality, among them Graham Wallas's *Human Nature in Politics* (1908); Harold Lasswell's *Psychopathology and Politics* (1930) and *Power and Personality* (1948); Hans Eysenck's *The Psychology of Politics* (1954); Fred Greenstein's *Personality and Politics* (1969); and the *Handbook of Political Psychology* (1973) edited by Jeanne Knutson, who founded the International Society of Political Psychology in 1978.

The purpose of this chapter is to sketch the rich history of personality in political psychology, to take stock of the current state of personality-in-politics inquiry, and to map out new directions for this emerging application of personality theory informed by the rich possibilities of contextually adjacent scientific fields such as evolution, of which Theodore Millon wrote in the opening chapter of this volume.

THE EMERGENCE OF PERSONALITY INQUIRY IN POLITICAL PSYCHOLOGY

In the present chapter, the terms *personality* and *politics* are employed in Greenstein's (1992) narrowly construed sense. Politics, by this definition, "refers to the politics most often studied by political scientists—that of civil government and of the extra-governmental processes that more or less directly impinge upon government, such as political parties" and campaigns. Personality, as narrowly construed in political psychology, "excludes political attitudes and opinions . . . and applies only to nonpolitical personal differences" (p. 107).

Origins of Personality-in-Politics Inquiry

Knutson's 1973 *Handbook,* most notably the chapter "From Where and Where To?" by James Davies, defined the field at the time of its publication (Stone & Schaffner, 1988, p. v). Davies (1973) credits political scientist Charles Merriam of the University of Chicago with stimulating "the first notable liaisons between psychology and political science" (p. 18) in the 1920s and 1930s. Though Merriam did not personally

exploit the fruitful possibilities he saw for a productive union of the two disciplines, his "intellectual progeny," Harold Lasswell, "was the first to enter boldly into the psychological house of ill repute, establish a liaison, and sire a set of ideas and influences of great vitality" (p. 18).

Machiavelli's famous treatise serves as testimony that, from the beginning, the study of personality in politics constituted an integral part of political-psychological inquiry. In the modern era, the tradition dates back to Sigmund Freud, who collaborated with William Bullitt on a psychological study of U.S. president Woodrow Wilson (Freud & Bullitt, 1967).

Types of Personality-in-Politics Inquiry

In examining the state of the personality-in-politics literature, Greenstein (1969) proposed three types of personality-in-politics inquiry: individual, typological, and aggregate.

Individual inquiry (Greenstein, 1969, pp. 63–93), which is idiographic in orientation, involves single-case psychological analyses of individual political actors. Although the single-case literature historically comprised mostly psychological biographies of public figures, such as Alexander and Juliette George's *Woodrow Wilson and Colonel House* (1956) and Erik Erikson's *Gandhi's Truth* (1969), it also encompassed in-depth studies of members of the general population, such as Robert Lane's *Political Ideology* (1962). With increasing specialization in political psychology since the 1960s, the focus has shifted progressively to the psychological examination of political leaders, while single-case studies of ordinary citizens have become increasingly peripheral to the main focus of contemporary political personality research.

Typological inquiry (Greenstein, 1969, pp. 94–119), which is nomothetic in orientation, concerns multicase analyses of political actors. This line of inquiry encompasses the main body of work in political personality, including the influential work of Harold Lasswell (1930, 1948), James David Barber (1965, 1972/1992), Margaret Hermann (1974, 1980, 1986, 1987), and David Winter (1987, 1998) with respect to high-level political leaders; however, part of this literature focuses more on followers (i.e., mass politics) than on leaders (i.e., elite politics)—for example, Theodor Adorno, Else Frenkel-Brunswik, Daniel Levinson, and Nevitt Sanford's classic *The Authoritarian Personality* (1950) and Milton Rokeach's *The Open and Closed Mind* (1960). Greenstein (1992) has submitted that typological study "is of potentially great importance: if political actors fall into types with known characteristics and propensities, the laborious task of analyzing them *de novo* can be obviated, and uncertainty is reduced about how they will perform in particular circumstances" (p. 120).

Aggregate inquiry (Greenstein, 1969, pp. 120–140) includes a large and diverse body of work on national character, conflict among nations, behavior in groups, and global psychologizing about humanity and society (pp. 15–16). Greenstein (1992) has written that the impact of mass publics on politics, except for elections and drastic shifts in public opinion, "is partial and often elusive," in contrast to the political impact of leaders, which tends to be "direct, readily evident, and potentially momentous in its repercussions" (p. 122).

In his review of "Personality and Politics" in the *Handbook of Personality* (Pervin, 1990), Dean Keith Simonton (1990) observed that the psychometric examination of political leaders represents the leading edge of current personality-in-politics research (p. 671). Moreover, by 1990 the dominant paradigm in the psychological examination of leaders had undergone a shift from the earlier preponderance of qualitative, idiographic, psychobiographic analysis, to more quantitative and nomothetic methods—in other words, Greenstein's (1969) typological inquiry. Simonton's assessment is as valid now as it was more than a decade ago. Contemporary personality-in-politics inquiry focuses almost exclusively on the psychological examination of high-level political leaders and the impact of personal characteristics on leadership performance and policy orientation.

Its other principal avenue of inquiry, the study of ordinary citizens, has retreated from the political personality landscape, although it left a legacy of momentous works such as Adorno et al. (1950), Rokeach (1960), and others. As Simonton (1990) has noted, "the heyday of personality studies conducted on the typical citizen is past; the personality traits germane to citizen ideology and candidate preferences have been inventoried many times" (p. 671). This trend represents a distinct shift from the personality-and-culture era of the 1940s and 1950s (McGuire, 1993), in which psychobiography, studies of national character, and research involving the authoritarian personality syndrome flourished (Levin, 2000, p. 605). In this regard, Greenstein (1992) pointed to "the vexed post–World War II national character literature in which often ill-documented ethnographic reports and cultural artifacts . . . were used to draw sweeping conclusions about modal national character traits," with the result that by the 1950s, "there was broad scholarly consensus that it is inappropriate simply to attribute psychological characteristics to mass populations on the basis of anecdotal or indirect evidence" (p. 122). Accordingly, political personality inquiry became more leadership oriented in emphasis, with the study of followers (or mass publics) in the domain of political psychology increasingly shifting to cognate areas such as political socialization, political attitudes, prejudice and intergroup conflict, political

participation, party identification, voting behavior, and public opinion, which could be studied more systematically than the impalpable notion of national character.

THE EVOLUTION OF PERSONALITY INQUIRY IN POLITICAL PSYCHOLOGY

Political psychology, as much as any social-scientific endeavor, has evolved in sociohistoric context. Accordingly, the evolution of personality-in-politics inquiry in the second half of the twentieth century can be viewed against the backdrop of three defining events: the legacy of the Nazi Holocaust and World War II; the Cold War and the threat of nuclear annihilation; and the collapse of communism in Central and Eastern Europe and the Soviet Union, with its attendant new world order.

The Postwar Era

The rise of Hitler and the Nazi Holocaust stimulated personality research in the areas of authoritarianism, belief systems, and ideology, as represented in the work of Adorno et al. (1950) and Rokeach (1960), noted previously—precisely the historical juncture that in the domain of social psychology stimulated vigorous research programs in conformity (e.g., Asch, 1955) and obedience (e.g., Milgram, 1963).

In a definitive 1973 review of research developments in political psychology since Lasswell (1951), Davies identified four distinct lines of inquiry in post–World War II political psychology: (a) the study of voting behavior in stable democracies, the dominant trend, which had become "increasingly dull, repetitious, and a precious picking of nits"; (b) cross-national comparative research in relatively stable, democratic polities (which included "the vexed post–World War II national character literature" noted by Greenstein, 1992, (p. 122); (c) the genesis of behavioral patterns established in childhood (i.e., political socialization), which, along with cross-national research, "provided some relief from the [dominant trend's] rather static study of behavior under stable circumstances"; and (d) psychological political biography (p. 21). Concerning the latter, which is most closely allied to contemporary political personality inquiry, Davies (1973) noted the futility of attempting to ascertain the psychological determinants of *why* some individuals emerge as leaders, given the rudimentary nature of available conceptual tools and measuring devices. More useful, according to Davies, would be analysis and description of leadership *style,* which had become increasingly sophisticated, as evidenced by the work of Barber (1972–1992)—"the boldest step yet in establishing a typology applicable to all American presidents," successfully making a case for "the predictability of. . . . how presidents will act" (Davies, 1973, p. 25).

The Cold War Era

By the 1960s, the Cold War, punctuated by the 1962 Cuban missile crisis, brought about an important shift in the direction of political personality research. In the shadow of the nuclear sword, the focus of interest shifted from the mass politics of followers to the elite politics of foreign-policy decision making. In social psychology, this trend was paralleled by research endeavors such as Charles Osgood's (1962) explication of graduated reciprocation in tension-reduction (GRIT) and Irving Janis's (1972/1982; Janis & Mann, 1977) influential work on groupthink and decision-making fiascoes. In his review of advances in the study of personality and politics, Greenstein (1992) noted that the 1970s and 1980s were marked by "burgeoning inquiry into political perception and cognitive psychology more generally" (p. 112), as represented by Robert Jervis's (1976) text on threat perception and deterrence and Richard Lau and David Sears's (1986) edited collection of papers on political cognition.

As a field, political psychology thrived in the sociohistoric environment of the Cold War, as witnessed by the publication of the *Handbook of Political Psychology* in 1973, with an important chapter on "Personality in the Study of Politics" by its editor, Jeanne Knutson; William F. Stone's (1974) groundbreaking introductory political psychology textbook; and the founding of the International Society of Political Psychology in 1978. Greenstein, in his now classic *Personality and Politics* (1969), set about the task of clearing a path "through the tangle of intellectual underbrush" (Greenstein, 1987, p. v) of conflicting perspectives on whether personality in politics was amenable to, and worthy of, disciplined inquiry.

Well into the 1980s, however, three powerful influences would subdue the impact of Greenstein's (1969) and Knutson's (1973) important work in mapping out a conceptual framework conferring figural status upon the *personality* construct in the evolving study of personality in politics: the dominant interest in foreign-policy decision making against the backdrop of the Soviet-U.S. struggle for superpower supremacy; the cognitive revolution (see McGraw, 2000; Simon, 1985), which extended its reach from its parent discipline of psychology into mainstream political science; and the person–situation debate (see Mischel, 1990) then raging in personality psychology.

In a preface to the new edition (1987) of *Personality and Politics,* Greenstein observed that "one kind of political psychology—the cognitive psychology of perception and misperception—has found a respected niche in a political science field, namely international relations" (p. vi). Ole Holsti (1989) asserted that the psychological perspective constituted a basic necessity in the study of international politics. As the 1980s drew to a close, Jervis (1989), in a paper outlining major challenges to the field of political psychology, wrote, "The study of individual personalities and personality types has fallen out of favor in psychology and political science, but this does not mean the topics are unimportant" (p. 491). Significantly, two decades earlier George (1969) and Holsti (1970) had published influential papers that revived the World War II–era operational code construct, in part because perception and beliefs were viewed as more easily inferred than personality—given "the kinds of data, observational opportunities, and methods generally available to political scientists" (George, 1969, p. 195).

The renewed focus on *operational codes*—beliefs about the fundamental nature of politics, which shape one's worldview, and hence, one's choice of political objectives—steered political personality in a distinctly cognitive direction. Stephen Walker (1990, 2000) and his associates (Dille & Young, 2000; Schafer, 2000) would carry this line of inquiry forward to the present day. Moreover, Hermann (1974) initiated a research agenda that accorded cognitive variables a prominent role in the study of political personality. Hermann's (1980) conceptual scheme accommodated four kinds of personal characteristics hypothesized to play a central role in political behavior: *beliefs* and *motives,* which shape a leader's view of the world, and *decision style* and *interpersonal style,* which shape the leader's personal political style. Hermann's model warrants particular attention because of the degree to which it integrated existing perspectives at the time, and because of its enduring influence on the study of personality in politics.

Conceptually, Hermann's notion of *beliefs* is anchored to the philosophical beliefs component of the operational code construct. Her interest in *motives* stems from Lasswell's *Power and Personality* (1948) and Winter's *The Power Motive* (1973)—an approach to political personality that Winter (1991) would elaborate into a major political personality assessment methodology in its own right. Hermann's construal of *decision style* overlaps with the instrumental beliefs component of George's (1969) operational code construct and aspects of Barber's (1972/1992) formulation of presidential character, focusing particularly on conceptual complexity (see Dille & Young, 2000)—once again, an approach to political personality that would later develop into a major branch of political personality assessment, as represented in the work of Suedfeld (1994) on integrative complexity. Finally, Hermann's *interpersonal style* domain encompasses a number of politically relevant personality traits such as suspiciousness, Machiavellianism, and task versus relationship orientation in leadership (see Hermann, 1980, pp. 8–10).

Methodologically, a common strand of cognitively and motivationally oriented trait approaches—such as those of Hermann (1987), Suedfeld (1994), Walker (1990), and Winter (1998)—is their reliance on content analysis of public documents (typically speeches and other prepared remarks or interviews and spontaneous remarks) for the indirect assessment of political personality (see Schafer, 2000, for a recent overview of issues in at-a-distance methods of psychological assessment).

As Simonton (1990) has noted, "The attributes of character that leave the biggest impression on political affairs involve both cognitive inclinations, which govern how an individual perceives and thinks about the world, and motivational dispositions, which energize and channel individual actions in the world" (pp. 671–672). Hermann's model, in capturing cognition (including beliefs or attitudes) and motivation (recognizing the importance of affect in politics and checking the tendency in political psychology toward overemphasis of human rationality), clearly fills Simonton's prescription. On the other hand, Hermann's construal of decision style as a personality (or input) variable is problematic. Renshon's (1996b) integrative theory of character and political performance, for example, specifies political and policy judgments and decision making, along with leadership, as performance (output) variables. Finally, Hermann's construal of personality in terms of interpersonal style is too restrictive for a comprehensive theory of personality in politics.

The New World Order

Epochal events such as the fall of the Berlin Wall in 1989, the collapse of communist rule in Central and Eastern Europe in 1989–1990, the disintegration of the Soviet Union in 1991–1992, South Africa's transition from apartheid state to nonracial democracy in 1994 following Nelson Mandela's release from prison in 1990, and the Persian Gulf War in 1991 marked the beginning of a *new world order*, which stimulated renewed research interest in psychometric inquiry—an area that contemporaneously began to emerge as a new paradigm for the study of personality in politics (Immelman, 1988, 1993; Simonton, 1990). In psychometric personality-in-politics inquiry, standard psychometric instruments were adapted to "derive personality measures from biographical data rather than through content analysis of primary materials" (Simonton, 1990, p. 678), although some investigators (e.g., Kowert, 1996; Rubenzer, Faschingbauer, & Ones, 2002), though similar in intent, opted for indirect expert ratings

instead of direct analysis of biographical data. The focus of psychometric inquiry is less on cognitive variables and foreign-policy decision making and more on a personological understanding of the person in politics, his or her personality attributes, and the implications of personality for leadership performance and generalized policy orientation.

George and George's (1956) psychoanalytically framed study of Woodrow Wilson, which relied on clinical insights rather than psychometric evaluation of biographical data, is the best known precursor of the personological trend in political personality research. In Simonton's (1990) judgment, qualitative, nonpsychometric psychobiographical analyses "have leaned heavily on both theoretical perspectives and methodological approaches that cannot be considered a central current in mainstream personality research" (p. 671). Although some highly informative personological studies (e.g., Glad, 1996; Post, 1991; Renshon, 1996a, 1998) continued in the older psychobiographic tradition, the twentieth century closed with a distinct shift in a psychometric direction (Immelman, 1998, 2002; Kowert, 1996; Lyons, 1997; Rubenzer et al., 2002).

Although some contemporary psychobiographically oriented studies are theoretically eclectic (e.g., Betty Glad's 1996 study of the transfer of power from Gorbachev to Yeltsin in Russia and from De Klerk to Mandela in South Africa), the modern psychoanalytic reformulations of Heinz Kohut (1971, 1977) and Otto Kernberg (1984) have acquired considerable cachet in political psychology. Swansbrough (1994), for instance, conducted a Kohutian analysis of George Bush's personality and leadership style in the Persian Gulf war. Similarly, Stanley Renshon's (1996a) psychobiography of Bill Clinton is informed primarily by Kohutian self psychology. Jerrold Post's (1991) psychobiographical analysis of Saddam Hussein is more indebted to Kernberg's notion of narcissistic personality organization (see Post, 1993). Despite Simonton's (1990) grim prognostication and Jervis's (1989) observation that "Freudian analysis and psychobiographies are out of fashion" (p. 482), the psychobiographic tradition has been revitalized by the analytic insights of scholars such as Post and Renshon.

OBSTACLES TO THE ADVANCEMENT OF THE PERSONALITY-IN-POLITICS ENTERPRISE

Greenstein (1992) has formulated what may be the most concise statement of the case for studying personality in politics: "Political institutions and processes operate through human agency. It would be remarkable if they were *not* influenced by the properties that distinguish one individual from another"

(p. 124). Yet, specialists in the study of politics "tend to concentrate on impersonal determinants of political events and outcomes" or define away personal characteristics, "positing rationality . . . and presuming that the behavior of actors can be deduced from the logic of their situation" (p. 106). The relevance of the study of personality with respect to political leadership is nicely captured in Renshon's (1996b) contention that

> many of the most important aspects of presidential performance rely on the personal characteristics and skills of the president. . . . It is his views, his goals, his bargaining skills . . . , his judgments, his choices of response to arising circumstance that set the levers of administrative, constitutional, and institutional structures into motion. (p. 7)

In this regard, Glad (1996), writing about the collapse of the communist state in the Soviet Union and the apartheid state in South Africa, has shown convincingly that the personal qualities of leaders can play a critical role at turning points in history.

Scholarly Skepticism and Inadequate Conceptual and Methodological Tools

Despite the conviction of personality-in-politics practitioners in the worth of their endeavor, the study of personality in politics is not without controversy (see Lyons, 1997, pp. 792–793, for a concise review of "controversies over the presidential personality approach"). Greenstein (1969, pp. 33–62) offered an incisive critique of "two erroneous" and "three partially correct" objections to the study of personality in politics, lamenting that the study of personality in politics was "*not* a thriving scholarly endeavor," principally because "scholars who study politics do not feel equipped to analyze personality in ways that meet their intellectual standards. . . . [thus rendering it primarily] the preserve of journalists" (p. 2). The optimistic verdict more than three decades later is that political personality has taken root and come of age as a scholarly endeavor, as evidenced by the inclusion of the present chapter in this volume.

Inadequate Transposition From Source to Target Discipline

Although the enterprise of studying personality in politics has largely succeeded in countering common objections to its usefulness, it has been hampered by inadequate transposition from the source discipline of personality assessment to the target discipline of political psychology. For political personality inquiry to remain a thriving scholarly endeavor *and*

have an impact beyond the narrow confines of academic political psychology, it will need to account, at a minimum, for the patterning of personality variables "across the entire matrix of the person" (Millon & Davis, 2000, pp. 2, 65). Only then will political personality assessment provide an adequate basis for explaining, predicting, and understanding political outcomes. Moreover, political personologists will need to advance an integrative theory, not only of personality and of political leadership, but also of the personality-politics nexus. In *The Psychological Assessment of Presidential Candidates* (1996b), Stanley Renshon provides a partial blueprint for this daunting task.

Inadequate Progress From Description of Observable Phenomena to Theoretical Systematization

Ultimately, scholarly progress in personality-in-politics inquiry hinges on its success in advancing from the "natural history stage of inquiry" to a "stage of deductively formulated theory" (Northrop, 1947). The intuitive psychologist's "ability to 'sense' the correctness of psychological insight" (chapter by Millon in this volume) presents an easily overlooked obstacle to progress in political-personological inquiry. Early in the development of a scientific discipline, according to philosopher of science Carl Hempel (1965), investigators primarily strive "to describe the phenomena under study and to establish simple empirical generalizations concerning them," using terms that "permit the description of those aspects of the subject matter which are ascertainable fairly directly by observation" (p. 140). Hermann's (1974, 1980) early work illustrates this initial stage of scientific development. In the words of Hempel (1965),

> The shift toward theoretical systematization is marked by the introduction of new, "theoretical" terms, which refer to various theoretically postulated entities, their characteristics, and the processes in which they are involved; all of these are more or less removed from the level of directly observable things and events. (p. 140)

Hermann's (1987) proposal of a model suggesting how leaders' observable personal characteristics "link to form role orientations to foreign affairs" (p. 162) represents considerable progress in this direction; however, it lacks systematic import.

A Lack of Systematic Import

Theoretical systematization and empirical import (operational definitions) are necessary but not sufficient for scientific progress.

> To be scientifically useful a concept must lend itself to the formulation of general laws or theoretical principles which reflect uniformities in the subject matter under study, and which thus provide a basis for explanation, prediction, and generally scientific understanding. (Hempel, 1965, p. 146)

The most striking instance of this principle of systematic import, according to Hempel (1965), "is the periodic system of the elements, on which Mendeleev based a set of highly specific predictions, which were impressively confirmed by subsequent research" (p. 147). Hempel chronicled similar scientific progress in biological taxonomic systems, which proceeded from primitive classification based on observable characteristics to a more advanced phylogenetic-evolutionary basis. Thus, "two phenomenally very similar specimens may be assigned to species far removed from each other in the evolutionary hierarchy, such as the species Wolf (*Canis*) and Tasmanian Wolf (*Thylacinus*)" (Hempel, 1965, p. 149).

For personality-in-politics inquiry to continue advancing as a scholarly discipline, it will have to come to grips with the canon of systematic import. At base, this means that theoretical systematizations cannot be constructed on the foundation of precisely those personal characteristics from which they were originally inferred (see chapter by Millon in this volume). As Kurt Gödel (1931) demonstrated with his incompleteness theorem, no self-contained system can prove or disprove its own propositions while operating within the axioms of that system.

TOWARD A GENERATIVE THEORY OF PERSONALITY AND POLITICAL PERFORMANCE

Ideally, conceptual systems for the study of political personality should constitute a comprehensive, generative, theoretically coherent framework consonant with established principles in the adjacent sciences (particularly the more mature natural sciences; see Millon's chapter in this volume), congenial with respect to accommodating a diversity of politically relevant personal characteristics, and capable of reliably predicting meaningful political outcomes. In this regard, Renshon (1996b) is critical of unitary trait theories of political personality (such as those relying primarily on isolated personality variables, motives, or cognitive variables), noting that "it is a long causal way from an individual trait of presidential personality to a specific performance outcome" and that unitary trait theories fail to contribute to the

development of an integrated psychological theory of leadership performance. He ventures that "more clinically based theories . . . might form the basis of a more comprehensive psychological model of presidential performance" (p. 11).

The problem bedeviling contemporary personality-in-politics inquiry, however, is more profound than the precarious perch of leadership performance theories on a fragmented personological foundation. In his critique of postwar research directions in political psychology, Davies (1973) declared:

> There is . . . a kind of atrophy of theory and research that can help us link observable acts with their deeply and generally antecedent causes in the human organism, notably the nervous and endocrine systems. Aristotle sought such relationships. So did Hobbes, whose *Leviathan* (1651) founded its analysis of political institutions on a theory of human nature. And likewise, Lasswell has sought to relate fundamental determinants to observable effects—and vice versa. (p. 26)

Similarly, but with greater theoretical precision, Millon (1990), in explicating his evolutionary theory of personality, distinguished between "true, theoretically deduced" nosologies and those that provide "a mere explanatory summary of known observations and inferences" (p. 105). He cited Hempel (1965), who proposed that scientific classification ought to have an "objective existence in nature, . . . 'carving nature at the joints,'" in contradistinction to 'artificial' classifications, in which the defining characteristics have few explanatory or predictive connections with other traits" (p. 147). Ultimately, "in the course of scientific development, classifications defined by reference to manifest, observable characteristics will tend to give way to systems based on theoretical concepts" (Hempel, 1965, pp. 148–149).

Greenstein (1987), pointing to the work of Gangestad and Snyder (1985) and Morey (1985), acknowledged the substantial progress since the publication of his seminal *Personality and Politics* (1969) "in grounding complex psychological typologies empirically," yet pessimistically proclaimed that "complex typologies are not easily constructed and documented" (Greenstein, 1987, p. xiv). Although Greenstein was clearly correct on both counts, he failed to report that these typologies had already been constructed and empirically documented (see, for example, Millon, 1986). Greenstein's (1987) conclusion, that the difficulty of constructing a complex typology renders it "productive to classify political actors in terms of single traits that differentiate them in illuminating ways" (p. xiv), is therefore patently founded on a false premise. This pitfall of overlooking parallel developments in clinical science is reminiscent of Barber's (1972/1992) construction, de novo, of a rudimentary 2×2 model for assessing presidential character, which yields little more systematic import or prototypal distinctiveness than the humoral doctrine of Hippocrates, 24 centuries earlier.

Toward a Politically Relevant Theory of Personality in Politics

Renshon (1996b) has argued persuasively that a president's character serves as the foundation for leadership effectiveness, in part because political parties (in the United States) have lost much of their ability to serve as "filters" for evaluating candidates, who are no longer mere standard-bearers of party platforms and ideologies (pp. 38–40). Renshon examines the psychology of presidential candidates using theories of character and personality, theories of presidential leadership and performance, and theories of public psychology. For a concise, schematic outline of Renshon's model, which is anchored to Kohut's (1971, 1977) psychoanalytic self theory, the reader is referred to appendix 2 (pp. 409–411) of his book, *The Psychological Assessment of Presidential Candidates* (1996b).

For the great majority of psychodiagnosticians, who are more familiar with Axis II of the *Diagnostic and Statistical Manual of Mental Disorders* (4th ed.; *DSM-IV*) of the American Psychiatric Association (APA; 1994) than with Kohutian self psychology as a framework for recording personality functioning, Renshon's (1996b) particular clinically based theory of political personality may be somewhat restrictive, if not arcane. Fortunately, the value of Renshon's work with respect to mapping out an integrated theory of character and leadership for political personality assessment is not contingent upon the utility of the personological component of his model; it can easily be molded to the theoretical proclivities of the practitioner, including—perhaps especially—those favoring a theoretical orientation more compatible with the *DSM-IV.*

Toward a Psychologically Grounded Theory of Political Performance

In developing a psychologically grounded theory of political performance, Renshon (1996b) distinguished between two key elements of presidential role performance: "making good policy and political decisions" and "pursuing and realizing policy purposes" (p. 12). With regard to the former, Renshon (1996b) proposed a model of judgment and decision making (pp. 206–223, 411) capable of accommodating those cognitive constructs that became popular in Cold War–era political psychology (e.g., integrative complexity). Concerning the second aspect of political performance, Renshon (1996b) proposes "three distinct aspects" (p. 226) of political leadership

shaped by character: *mobilization,* the ability to arouse, engage, and direct the public; *orchestration,* the organizational skill and ability to craft specific policies; and *consolidation,* the skills and tasks required to preserve the supportive relationships necessary for implementing and institutionalizing one's policy judgments (pp. 227, 411).

However, those seeking to develop a generative theory of personality and political performance confront a conceptual minefield—a problem highlighted previously with respect to the overly restrictive, psychodynamically framed character component of Renshon's model, which limits its integrative potential. This issue is examined more closely in the next section.

CONCEPTUAL PROBLEMS IN THE STUDY OF PERSONALITY IN POLITICS

Unresolved conceptual problems that cloud personality-in-politics inquiry include a lack of agreement about the appropriate levels of analysis; a lack of clarity about the requisite scope of inquiry; theoretical stagnation; and a failure of some approaches to satisfy basic standards for operationalizing the *personality* construct.

Levels of Analysis

In his early efforts to chart a course for the field's development, Greenstein (1969) noted that the personality-in-politics literature was "formidably gnarled—empirically, methodologically, and conceptually" (p. 2). He identified three operational levels for the assessment of personality in politics: phenomenology, dynamics, and genesis. In Greenstein's opinion, these distinctions are useful

> for sorting out the different kinds of operations involved in the psychological diagnosis of political actors, and for ordering diagnostic operations in terms of both the directness of their bearing on explanations of political action and the degree to which they can be carried out in a more or less standardized fashion. (p. 144)

Phenomenology—regularities in the observable behavior of political actors—according to Greenstein, is "the most immediately relevant supplement to situational data in predicting and explaining the actor's behavior" (p. 144), whereas explanations of *genesis* are "remote from the immediate nexus of behavior" and pose "difficult questions of validation" (p. 145). With the increasing dominance of descriptive approaches and the dwindling influence of psychoanalysis in contemporary personality assessment (Jervis, 1989, p. 482; Simonton, 1990, p. 671), preoccupation with personality dynamics can be expected to wane, while psychogenesis already occupies a peripheral role in political personality, of primary interest to psychohistorians.

Millon's (1990) evolutionary model refines Greenstein's three operational levels of analysis (phenomenology, dynamics, and genesis) by redefining genesis as a conceptual construct, relabeling dynamics as the *intrapsychic* level of analysis, disaggregating phenomenology into *phenomenological* and *behavioral* data levels, and adding a fourth, *biophysical,* data level.

The critical operational constructs are the clinical domains (or personality attributes), which provide an explicit basis for personality assessment. Millon's (1990) evolutionary model specifies four *structural* domains (object representations, self-image, morphologic organization, and mood or temperament) and four *functional* domains (expressive behavior, interpersonal conduct, cognitive style, and regulatory mechanisms) encompassing four data levels: *behavioral* (expressive behavior, interpersonal conduct); *phenomenological* (cognitive style, object representations, self-image); *intrapsychic* (regulatory mechanisms, morphological organization); and *biophysical* (mood or temperament).

Scope of Inquiry

Beyond simply refining Greenstein's (1969) specification of operational levels for personality-in-politics inquiry, the scope of this endeavor must be elucidated if political personality is to extricate itself from the "tangled underbrush." The requisite scope of inquiry is implied in the organizational framework of a representative undergraduate personality text (Pervin & John, 2001), which presents theory and research in terms of structure, process, development, psychopathology, and change—a formulation consistent with the organizing framework of structure, dynamics, development, assessment, and change that Gordon Allport employed in his seminal text, *Personality: A Psychological Interpretation* (1937). Millon's (1990, 1996) contemporary clinical model of personality follows this time-honored tradition by construing personality in terms of its structural and functional domains, normal and pathological variants, developmental background (including hypothesized biogenic factors and characteristic developmental history), homeostatic (self-perpetuation) processes, and domain-based modification strategies and tactics.

Theoretical Orientation

In an important recapitulation nearly a quarter-century after his landmark work in *Personality and Politics* (1969),

Greenstein (1992) resolved, "The study of personality and politics is possible and desirable, but systematic intellectual progress is possible only if there is careful attention to problems of evidence, inference, and conceptualization" (p. 105). He went on to assert, however, that "it is not appropriate to recommend a particular personality theory," suggesting that the theories of "Freud, Jung, Allport, Murray, and . . . many others" (p. 117) are all potentially useful. Although there is merit in Greenstein's (1973) counsel to "let many flowers bloom" (p. 469), professional psychodiagnosticians—who tend not to treat the classic schools of personality theory as templates for tailoring their assessment tools—might find this assertion quite striking. Burgeoning scientific and technological progress in clinical science over the past half-century practically dictates that assimilating contemporary approaches to psychodiagnostics and personality assessment provides a less obstacle strewn passage for personality-in-politics practitioners than steering a course illuminated solely by the radiance of the great pioneers of personality theory. Despite major advances in behavioral neuroscience, evolutionary ecology, and personality research in the past two decades (see chapter by Millon in this volume), personality-in-politics inquiry arguably has become insular and stagnant, with few fresh ideas and—with the exception of cognitive science—little indication of meaningful cross-pollination of ideas from adjacent disciplines.

Necessary Conditions for Operationalizing Research Designs

In the original *Handbook of Political Psychology* (1973), Knutson implored that, to be feasible for studying personality in politics, conceptual models should fulfill three critical requirements for operationalizing research designs in political personality: Clearly conceptualize the meaning of the term *personality;* delineate attributes of personality that can be quantified or objectively assessed, thereby rendering them amenable to scientific study; and specify how the personality attributes subjected to scientific inquiry relate to the personality construct (pp. 34–35). As shown next, Millon's (1990, 1996) evolutionary model of personality satisfies all three of Knutson's criteria, making it eminently useful for studying personality in politics.

Defining Personality

From Millon's evolutionary-ecological perspective, personality constitutes ontogenetic, manifest, adaptive styles of thinking, feeling, acting, and relating to others, shaped by interaction of latent, phylogenetic, biologic endowment and social experience (chapter by Millon in this volume). This construal is consistent with the contemporary view of personality as

> a complex pattern of deeply embedded psychological characteristics that are largely nonconscious and not easily altered, expressing themselves automatically in almost every facet of functioning. Intrinsic and pervasive, these traits emerge from a complicated matrix of biological dispositions and experiential learnings, and ultimately comprise the individual's distinctive pattern of perceiving, feeling, thinking, coping, and behaving. (Millon, 1996, p. 4)

Delineating the Core Attributes of Personality

In constructing an integrated personality framework that accounts for "the patterning of characteristics across the entire matrix of the person" (Millon & Davis, 2000, p. 2), Millon (1994b) favors a theoretically grounded "prototypal domain model" (p. 292) that combines quantitative dimensional elements (e.g., the five-factor approach) with a qualitative categorical approach (e.g., *DSM-IV*). The *categorical* aspect of Millon's model is represented by eight universal attribute domains relevant to all personality patterns, namely expressive behavior, interpersonal conduct, cognitive style, mood or temperament, self-image, regulatory mechanisms, object representations, and morphologic organization.

Assessing Personality on the Basis of Variability Across Attributes

Millon specifies prototypal features (diagnostic criteria) within each of the eight attribute domains for each personality style (Millon, 1994a; Millon & Everly, 1985) or disorder (1990, 1996) accommodated in his taxonomy. The *dimensional* aspect of Millon's schema is achieved by evaluating the "prominence or pervasiveness" (1994b, p. 292) of the diagnostic criteria associated with the various personality types.

Additional Considerations

Traditionally, political personality assessment has borne little resemblance to the conceptualization of personality shared by most clinically trained professional psychodiagnosticians, or to their psychodiagnostic procedures. In satisfying Knutson's three criteria, Millon's personological model offers a viable integrative framework for a variety of current approaches to political personality, thus narrowing conceptual and methodological gaps between existing formulations in the source disciplines of personology and personality assessment and the target discipline of contemporary political personality—specifically the psychological examination of political leaders.

Although necessary for operationalizing research designs, Knutson's (1973) three criteria provide an insufficient basis for applied personality-in-politics modeling. A theoretically sound, comprehensive, useful personality-in-politics model with adequate explanatory power and predictive utility must meet additional standards. I propose the following basic standards for personality-in-politics modeling:

1. The meaning of the term *personality* should be clearly defined.
2. Quantifiable personality attributes amenable to objective assessment should be clearly specified.
3. The personality attributes subject to inquiry should be explicitly related to the personality construct as whole.
4. The conceptual model for construing personality in politics should be congruent with personality systems employed with reference to the general population.
5. The conceptual model for construing political personality should be integrative, capable of accommodating diverse, multidisciplinary perspectives on politically relevant personal characteristics.
6. The conceptual model should offer a unified view of normality and psychopathology.
7. The conceptual model should be rooted in personality theory, with clearly specified referents in political leadership theory.
8. The personality-in-politics model should be embedded in a larger conceptual framework that acknowledges cultural contexts and the impact of distal and proximal situational determinants that interact with dispositional variables to shape political behavior.
9. The methodology for assessing political personality should be congruent with standard psychodiagnostic procedures in conventional clinical practice.
10. The assessment methodology should be inferentially valid.
11. The assessment methodology should meet acceptable standards of evidence for reliability.
12. For purposes of predictive utility, the assessment methodology should be practicable during political campaigns.
13. For considerations of efficiency, the assessment methodology should be minimally cumbersome or unwieldy.
14. For optimal utility, the assessment methodology should be remote, indirect, unobtrusive, and nonintrusive.

15. For advancing theoretical systematization, the conceptual model should be nomothetically oriented, permit typological inquiry, and posit a taxonomy of political personality types.

A PERSONALITY-IN-POLITICS AGENDA FOR THE NEW CENTURY

In the new world order of the twenty-first century, personality-in-politics inquiry is poised to reclaim personality as the central organizing principle in the study of political leadership, informed by insights garnered from the cognitive revolution preceding the close of the twentieth century and energized by the quickening evolutionary reconceptualization of personology at the dawn of the new millennium.

From Cognitive Revolution to Evolutionary Psychology

On the crest of major breakthroughs in evolutionary biology during the preceding quarter-century, the emerging evolutionary perspective in psychology since the mid-1980s (see Buss, 1999; Millon, 1990; Millon, this volume) represents the first major theoretical shift in the discipline since the cognitive revolution of the 1950s and 1960s. Conceptually, the integrative capacity of Millon's (1990; Millon, this volume) evolutionary model renders it sufficiently comprehensive to accommodate major tenets of psychodynamic, behavioral, humanistic, interpersonal, cognitive, biogenic, and trait approaches to personality. Methodologically, Millon's framework provides an empirically validated taxonomy of personality patterns compatible with the syndromes described in *DSM-IV*, Axis II (APA, 1994).

No present conceptual system in the field of political personality rivals Millon's model in compatibility with conventional psychodiagnostic methods and standard clinical practice in personality assessment. Moreover, no current system matches the elegance with which Millon's evolutionary model synthesizes normality and psychopathology. In short, Millon offers a theoretically coherent alternative to existing conceptual frameworks and assessment methodologies for the psychological examination of political leaders (see Post, 2003, for an up-to-date collection of current conceptualizations; see Kinder, 1999, for a series of reviews, both critical and laudatory, of "Millon's evolving personality theories and measures").

The Utility of Millon's Model as a Generative Framework for the Study of Personality in Politics

The work of Millon (1990, 1994a, 1996, and his chapter in this volume; Millon & Davis, 2000; Millon, Davis, & Millon, 1996; Millon & Everly, 1985) provides a sound foundation for conceptualizing and assessing political personality, classifying political personality types, and predicting political behavior.

Epistemologically, it synthesizes the formerly disparate fields of psychopathology and normatology and formally connects them to broader spheres of scientific knowledge, most notably their foundations in the natural sciences (Millon, this volume). Diagnostically, it offers an empirically validated taxonomy of personality patterns congruent with the syndromes described on Axis II of *DSM-IV* (APA, 1994), thus rendering it compatible with conventional psychodiagnostic procedures and standard clinical practice in personality assessment.

Millon (1986) uses the concept of the personality *prototype* (paralleling the medical concept of the *syndrome*) as a global formulation for construing and categorizing personality systems, proposing that "each personality prototype should comprise a small and distinct group of primary attributes that persist over time and exhibit a high degree of consistency" (p. 681). To Millon, the essence of personality categorization is the differential identification of these enduring (stable) and pervasive (consistent) primary attributes. This position is consistent with the conventional view of personality in the study of politics (see Knutson, 1973, pp. 29–38). In organizing his attribute schema, Millon (1986) favors "an arrangement that represents the personality system in a manner similar to that of the body system, that is, dividing the components into *structural* and *functional* attributes" (p. 681; see Millon, 1990, pp. 134–135, for a concise summary of these attribute domains).

The Core Characteristics of a Comprehensive Model of Personality in Politics

A comprehensive model for the study of personality in politics (see Fig. 24.1) should account for structural and functional personality attributes, at behavioral, phenomenological, intrapsychic, and biophysical levels of analysis; permit supplementary developmental causal analysis (i.e., genesis or etiology); provide an explicit framework for risk analysis (i.e., account for normal variability as well as personality pathology); and provide an assessment methodology. Furthermore, the personality model should be linked with performance outcomes, recognize the impact of situational variables and the cultural context on political performance, and allow for personological, situational, and contextual filters that may modulate the impact of personality on political performance.

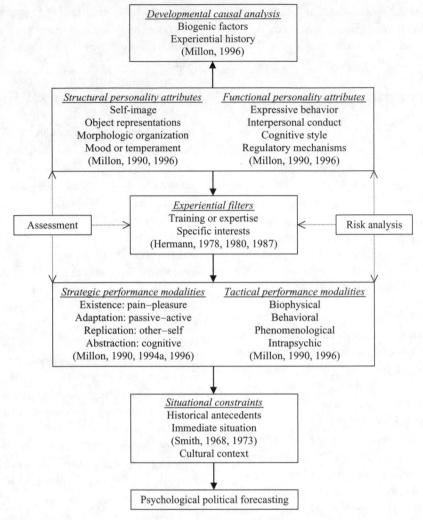

Figure 24.1 A generative conceptual model for assessing personality and political performance.

STRUCTURAL ATTRIBUTES OF PERSONALITY

Structural attributes, according to Millon (1990), "represent a deeply embedded and relatively enduring template of imprinted memories, attitudes, needs, fears, conflicts, and so on, which guide the experience and transform the nature of ongoing life events" (p. 147). Millon (1986, 1990) has specified four structural attributes of personality, outlined in the following subsections. Where relevant, equivalent or compatible formulations in the field of political psychology are noted.

Self-Image

Self-image, located at the phenomenological level of analysis, denotes a person's perception of self-as-object or the manner in which people overtly describe themselves (Millon, 1986; 1990, pp. 148–149).

This domain accommodates *self-confidence,* an element of decision style in Hermann's (1980, 1987) conceptual scheme. It also offers an alternative theoretical basis for construing Renshon's (1996b) character domain of *ambition,* derived from Kohut's (1971, 1977) psychoanalytic self theory.

Object Representations

The domain of *object representations,* located at the phenomenological level of analysis, encompasses the inner imprint left by a person's significant early experiences with others—in other words, the structural residue of significant past experiences, composed of memories, attitudes, and affects, which serves as a substrate of dispositions for perceiving and responding to the social environment (Millon, 1986, 1990, p. 149).

This domain accommodates Renshon's (1996b) character attribute of *relatedness,* which is steeped in object-relations theory, including Kohut's (1971) selfobject construct and Karen Horney's (1937) interpersonal tendencies.

Morphologic Organization

Morphologic organization, located at the intrapsychic level of analysis, embodies the overall architecture that serves as framework for a person's psychic interior—the structural strength, interior congruity, and functional efficacy of the personality system (Millon, 1986, 1990, pp. 149, 157).

This domain, roughly equivalent to the notion of ego strength, provides a good fit for Renshon's (1996b) realm of *character integrity,* derived from Kohut's (1971) self theory and elaborated in terms of Erikson's (1980) notions of ego identity and ego ideal.

Mood or Temperament

Mood or *temperament,* located at the biophysical level of analysis, captures a person's typical manner of displaying emotion and the predominant character of an individual's affect, and the intensity and frequency with which he or she expresses it (Millon, 1986, 1990, p. 157).

This domain provides a suitable fit for Barber's (1972/1992) construal of presidential character along *positive–negative* (i.e., affective) and *active–passive* (i.e., predisposition to activity, or temperamental) dimensions. In conjunction with the domain of cognitive style, mood or temperament also provides a conceptual frame of reference for the so-called *pessimistic explanatory style* of stable (vs. unstable), global (vs. specific), and internal (vs. external) causal attribution with respect to adversity, which, in combination with excessive rumination about problems, has been shown to predict not only susceptibility to helplessness and depression, but the electoral defeat of presidential candidates (Zullow & Seligman, 1990).

FUNCTIONAL ATTRIBUTES OF PERSONALITY

Functional attributes, according to Millon (1990), "represent dynamic processes that transpire within the intrapsychic world and between the individual's self and psychosocial environment" (p. 136). Millon (1986, 1990) has specified four functional attributes of personality, outlined in the next sections. Where relevant, equivalent or compatible formulations in the field of political psychology are noted.

Expressive Behavior

Expressive behavior, located at the behavioral level of analysis, refers to a person's characteristic behavior—how the individual typically appears to others and what the individual knowingly or unknowingly reveals about him- or herself or wishes others to think or to know about him or her (Millon, 1986, 1990, p. 137).

Numerous *personality traits* commonly used to describe political behavior are accommodated by this domain, including assertiveness, confidence, competence, arrogance, suspiciousness, impulsiveness, prudence, and perfectionism.

Interpersonal Conduct

Interpersonal conduct, located at the behavioral level of analysis, includes a person's typical style of interacting with others, the attitudes that underlie, prompt, and give shape to these actions, the methods by which the individual engages others to meet his or her needs, and the typical modes of coping with social tensions and conflicts (Millon, 1986, 1990, pp. 137, 146).

This domain accommodates the personal political characteristic of *interpersonal style* in Hermann's (1980, 1987) conceptual scheme, including its two operational elements, *distrust of others* and *task orientation.* The domain of interpersonal conduct also offers a conceptual niche for Christie and Geis's (1970) operationalization of *Machiavellianism,* which remains popular as a frame of reference for describing political behavior.

Cognitive Style

Cognitive style, located at the phenomenological level of analysis, signifies a person's characteristic manner of focusing and allocating attention, encoding and processing information, organizing thoughts, making attributions, and communicating thoughts and ideas (Millon, 1986, 1990, p. 146).

This domain accommodates the personal political characteristics of *beliefs* and *decision style* in Hermann's (1980, 1987) framework, most notably the *conceptual complexity* component of decision style, and *integrative complexity* (e.g., Suedfeld & Tetlock, 1977; Tetlock, 1985), which rose to prominence during the Cold War era as a major construct for operationalizing personality in politics. The domain of cognitive style is also compatible with the notions of *nationalism* and *belief in one's own ability to control events* (the two key operational elements of beliefs in Hermann's conceptual framework) and her operationalization of several beliefs associated with contemporary reformulations of the operational code construct (George, 1969; Holsti, 1970; Walker, 1990), such as *belief in the predictability of events* and *belief in the inevitability of conflict.*

Regulatory Mechanisms

The domain of *regulatory mechanisms,* located at the intrapsychic level of analysis, involves a person's characteristic mechanisms of self-protection, need gratification, and conflict resolution (Millon, 1986, 1990, pp. 146–147).

The need-gratification facet of the regulatory mechanisms domain provides a potential fit for Winter's (1973, 1987, 1991, 1998) approach to political personality, which emphasizes needs for *power, achievement,* and *affiliation,* and for the related *motives* aspect of the personal characteristics component of Hermann's (1980, 1987) conceptual scheme.

PERSONALITY DESCRIPTION, PSYCHOGENETIC UNDERSTANDING, AND PREDICTIVE POWER

The practical value of conceptual systems for assessing personality in politics is proportionate to their predictive utility in anticipating political behavior. Moreover, there is considerable merit in a personality model's capacity to promote accurate understanding of the developmental antecedents of political personality patterns.

Developmental Causal Analysis

The importance of a developmental component in a comprehensive model of personality is implicit in Millon and Davis's (2000) contention that, "once the subject has been conceptualized in terms of personality prototypes of the classification system, biographical information can be added" to answer questions about the origin and development of the subject's personality characteristics (p. 73). Greenstein (1992) cautions against "the fallacy of observing a pattern of behavior and simply attributing it to a particular developmental pattern, without documenting causality, and perhaps even without providing evidence that the pattern existed" (p. 121).

Millon (1996, chapter 3) frames developmental causal analysis in terms of hypothesized *biogenic factors* and the subject's characteristic *developmental history*. For the majority of present-day personality-in-politics investigators, who generally favor a descriptive approach to personality assessment, developmental questions are of secondary relevance; however, an explicit set of developmental relational statements is invaluable for psychobiographically oriented analysis. Moreover, precisely because each personality pattern has characteristic developmental antecedents, in-depth knowledge of a subject's experiential history can be useful with respect to validating the results of descriptive personality

assessment, or for suggesting alternative hypotheses (Millon & Davis, 2000, p. 74). This benefit notwithstanding, genetic reconstruction does not constitute an optimal basis for personality assessment and description.

A Framework for Risk Analysis

As Sears (1987) has noted, a problem with existing conceptualizations of personality in politics is the dichotomy between pathology-oriented and competence-oriented analyses. Millon's evolutionary theory of personality bridges the gap by offering a unified view of normality and psychopathology: "No sharp line divides normal from pathological behavior; they are relative concepts representing arbitrary points on a continuum or gradient" (Millon, 1994b, p. 283). The synthesis of normality and pathology is an aspect of Millon's principle of *syndromal continuity,* which holds, in part, that personality disorders are simply "exaggerated and pathologically distorted deviations emanating from a normal and healthy distribution of traits" (Millon & Everly, 1985, p. 34). Thus, whereas criteria for normality include "a capacity to function autonomously and competently, a tendency to adjust to one's environment effectively and efficiently, a subjective sense of contentment and satisfaction, and the ability to actualize or to fulfill one's potentials" (Millon, 1994b, p. 283), the presence of psychopathology is established by the degree to which a person is deficient, imbalanced, or conflicted in these areas (Millon, this volume).

At base, then, Millon (1994b) regards pathology as resulting "from the same forces . . . involved in the development of normal functioning . . ., [the determining influence being] the character, timing, and intensity" (p. 283) of these factors (see also Millon, 1996, pp. 12–13). From this perspective, risk analysis would entail the classification of individuals on a range of dimensions, each representing a normal-pathological continuum.

Despite the emphasis of Millon's (1996) clinical model on personality disorders, the absence of a conceptual distinction between normal and abnormal personality—the assertion that personality disorders are merely pathological distortions of normal personality attributes (Millon, 1990; Millon & Everly, 1985)—his theoretical system is particularly well suited for studying the implications of personality for political performance, because implicit in the principle of syndromal continuity is a built-in framework for risk analysis. In short, Millon's system offers an integrated framework for construing normal variability and personality pathology, and suggests the likely nature and direction of personality decompensation under conditions of catastrophic personality breakdown.

ASSESSMENT METHODOLOGIES

Approaches to the indirect assessment of personality in politics can generally be classified into three categories: content analysis, expert ratings, and psychodiagnostic analysis of biographical data.

Content Analysis

The fundamental assumption of content-analytic techniques for at-a-distance (i.e., indirect) measures "is that it is possible to assess psychological characteristics of a leader by systematically analyzing what leaders say and how they say it" (Schafer, 2000, p. 512). Content analysis remains the dominant approach to indirect personality assessment and is widely acknowledged in political psychology as a reliable data-analytic method. It draws on the assumptions and methods of psychology, political science, and speech communication (Schafer, 2000, p. 512) and predates the establishment of political psychology as a discrete field—having been used, for example, to analyze Nazi propaganda during World War II. Holsti's (1977) classic overview of qualitative and quantitative content-analytic approaches in political psychology remains relevant today, including his examination of perennial validity concerns such as the logic of psychological inferences about communicators engaging in persuasive communication (pp. 133–134); the ambiguities of authorship in documentary sources other than interviews and press conferences (p. 134); and problems of coding (e.g., word or symbol vs. theme or sentence coding) and data analysis (e.g., frequency vs. contingency measures; pp. 134–137). Paralleling advances in information technology, a recent development has been "automated content analysis" (Dille & Young, 2000), which "offers a less expensive, quicker, and more reliable alternative to commissioning graduate students to pore over and content-analyze texts" (p. 595).

Schafer (2000) and Walker (2000) provide good overviews of the current state of content-analytic at-a-distance assessment, its major conceptual and methodological issues, and future research directions. Clearly, content analysis can be a useful tool for dissecting political propaganda, examining psychologically relevant images in political rhetoric, and operationalizing important, politically relevant psychological constructs such as motives and conceptual or integrative complexity. However, content analysis does not offer a congenial frame of reference for comprehensive, clinically oriented psychological assessment procedures capable, in the words of Millon and Davis (2000), of capturing the patterning of personality variables "across the entire matrix of the person" (p. 65).

Expert Ratings

Paul Kowert (1996) has endeavored to move beyond the content-analytic methods (e.g., Hermann, 1980; Walker, 1990; Winter, 1987) that dominated political personality inquiry during the Cold War era, by applying Q-sort methodology to single-case analysis. In view of the huge role of public opinion polling, focus groups, professional speech writers, and political spin in contemporary politics, it seems prudent to find alternatives to speeches and interviews as primary sources of data for psychological evaluation.

An important advantage of expert ratings is that it yields coefficients of interrater reliability. However, this is offset by a variety of validity issues. Specifically, ratings by presidential scholars are fundamentally impressionistic and not based on systematic personality assessment (see Etheredge, 1978, p. 438). In some cases, high interrater reliability may merely reflect a convergence of conventional wisdom and shared myths about the personality characteristics of past presidents.

A major disadvantage of the expert-rating approach is that it is uneconomical, cumbersome, and impractical. To gather data for his study of the impact of personality on American presidential leadership, Kowert (1996) solicited 42 experts on American presidents. Rubenzer and his associates (2002), for their ambitious, highly resourceful study of U.S. presidents (employing primarily Big Five personality measures), attempted to contact nearly 1,000 biographers, presidential scholars, journalists, and former White House officials, eventually securing the cooperation of 115 raters who collectively completed 172 assessment packets, each containing 620 items.

A vexing difficulty with expert ratings is that it is impractical for studying candidates in the heat of presidential campaigns, when—as noted by Renshon (1996b, chapter 13)—accurate personality assessment is critical with respect to assessing psychological suitability for office. Historians and presidential scholars are not optimal sources of information under these conditions. Journalists who cover presidential candidates are potentially more reliable, but may be too immersed in their own reporting to offer much assistance. A more practical approach would be to extract personality data directly from the writings of journalists, presidential scholars, biographers, and other experts, which obviates the need for soliciting their active cooperation.

Psychodiagnostic Analysis of Biographical Data

Simonton (1990) credits Lloyd Etheredge (1978) with establishing the diagnostic utility "of abstracting individual traits immediately from biographic data" to uncover the link between personality and political leadership (p. 677). Simonton (1986) argues that "biographical materials [not only] . . . supply a rich set of facts about childhood experiences and career development . . . [but] such secondary sources can offer the basis for personality assessments as well" (p. 150).

Etheredge (1978) used a hybrid psychodiagnostic/expert-rating approach. As subjects he selected 36 U.S. presidents, secretaries of state, and presidential advisors who served between 1898 and 1968 and "assessed personality traits by searching scholarly works, insiders' accounts, biographies, and autobiographies" of his subjects (p. 437). Specifically, Etheredge excerpted passages relevant to two dimensions: dominance–submission and introversion–extroversion. He deleted explicit information and cues regarding the identity of the political figures and then rated them on the two personality dimensions of interest, along with two independent judges who were unaware of the subjects' identities.

Etheredge (1978), in commenting on "troublesome methodological issues" in such "second-hand assessment of historical figures," raises an important problem with respect to atheoretical trait approaches to the study of personality:

> A man like Secretary [John Foster] Dulles could be dominant over his subordinates yet deferential to a superior. This social context must be standardized explicitly. I chose to assess dominance by assessing dominance over nominal subordinates on the assumption that a person's inner desire to dominate would be less inhibited and show itself more clearly in this sector of life. In addition, since America's use of force has often been directed against smaller countries, I felt this was the most relevant tendency of international behavior that would generalize. (p. 437)

Etheredge's concerns highlight the indispensability of systematic import in personality-in-politics theorizing. Theory-driven conceptualization safeguards the psychodiagnostician against several pitfalls in Etheredge's reasoning. Most important, in spuriously identifying a problem where none in fact existed, Etheredge introduced troubling confounds. The pattern that Etheredge observed with respect to Secretary Dulles transparently conveys a prototypical instance of the distinctive interpersonal conduct of highly conscientious (or compulsive) personalities. In stark contrast, highly dominant personalities consistently assert themselves in relation to both superiors and subordinates.

In lacking a prior personality taxonomy and proceeding atheoretically, Etheredge missed an important, politically relevant distinction with respect to dominance. Clearly, a purely dimensional scale can *obscure* important distinctions among disparate personality types. In short, dimensional

prominence provides a necessary but insufficient basis for personality assessment; it must be complemented by categorical distinctiveness—in other words, a comprehensive theory of types.

This concern with categorical distinctiveness is reflected in the work of Lyons (1997), who used the Myers-Briggs Type Indicator (MBTI; Myers & McCaulley, 1985) as a frame of reference for systematically extracting data from secondary-source biographies to construct a typological profile of U.S. president Bill Clinton, which he then used as a framework for analyzing President Clinton's leadership style. However, in applying the Myers-Briggs model qualitatively, Lyons's approach is somewhat impressionistic, lacking the empirical basis essential for assessing dimensional prominence and the nomothetic focus necessary for comparative study.

A noteworthy aspect of Lyons's method is that he used one set of biographies, predating Bill Clinton's election as president, for extracting personality data and another set, focusing on the Clinton presidency, for inferring leadership style (see Lyons, 1997, p. 799). This is consistent with the solution implied in Greenstein's (1992) critique that

> single-case and typological studies alike make inferences about the inner quality of human beings . . . from outer manifestations—their past and present environments . . . and the pattern over time of their political responses. . . . They then use those inferred constructs to account for the same kind of phenomena from which they were inferred—responses in situational contexts. The danger of circularity is obvious, but tautology can be avoided by reconstructing personality from some response patterns and using the reconstruction to explain others. (pp. 120–121)

Greenstein's point is valid insofar as it highlights the inherent danger of pseudoexplanations of leadership behaviors in terms of mere diagnostic labels. However, Lyons's approach seems overly reductionistic and risks reifying the scientific method. At the operational level, it may be useful to view personality as the independent variable and leadership as the dependent variable—*as if* they were causally related. Conceptually, however, the relationship is fundamentally correlational. The fallacy involved in construing personality and leadership as hypothetical cause and effect, respectively, is akin to the so-called third-variable problem in correlational studies: Rather than manifest personality properties (x) *causing* observed leadership style (y), both variables likely express a *common latent structure* (z); to paraphrase Millon (1996), the "opaque or veiled inner traits" undergirding the "surface reality" (p. 4) of both observed variables.

Millon's system offers abundant prospects for psychodiagnostic analysis of biographical data. Several personality inventories have been developed to assess personality from a

Millonian perspective. Best known among these is the widely used Millon Clinical Multiaxial Inventory–III (MCMI-III; Millon, Davis, & Millon, 1996), a standard clinical diagnostic tool employed worldwide. The Millon Index of Personality Styles (MIPS; Millon, 1994a) was developed to assess and classify personality in nonclinical (e.g., corporate) settings. Similarly, Strack (1991) developed the Personality Adjective Check List (PACL) for gauging normal personality styles. Oldham and Morris, in their trade book, *The New Personality Self-Portrait* (1995), offer a self-administered instrument congruent with Millon's model. Immelman (1999; Immelman & Steinberg, 1999) adapted the Millon Inventory of Diagnostic Criteria (MIDC) from Millon's work, specifically for the assessment of personality in politics.

Immelman (1998, 2002) uses the MIDC to synthesize, transform, and systematize diagnostically relevant information collected from the literature on political figures (primarily biographical sources and media reports) into Millon's (1990) four data levels (behavioral, phenomenological, intrapsychic, and biophysical). The next section outlines the Millonian approach to political personality assessment.

A Theory-Driven Psychodiagnostic Assessment Methodology

Favoring the more systematic, quantitative, nomothetic approach advocated by Simonton (1986, 1988, 1990), Immelman (1993, 1998, 2002) adapted Millon's model of personality (1986, 1990, 1994a, 1996; Millon & Davis, 2000; Millon & Everly, 1985) for the indirect assessment of personality in politics. Immelman's (1999) approach is equivalent to Simonton's (1986, 1988) in that it quantifies, reduces, and organizes qualitative data extracted from the public record. It is dedicated to quantitative measurement, but unlike the currently popular five-factor model, which is atheoretical, the Millonian approach is theory driven. The assessment methodology yields a personality profile derived from clinical analysis of diagnostically relevant content in biographical materials and media reports, which provides an empirical basis for predicting the subject's political performance and policy orientation (Immelman, 1998).

Sources of Data

Immelman (1998, 1999, 2002) gathers diagnostic information pertaining to the personal and public lives of political figures from a variety of published materials, selected with a view to securing broadly representative data sets. Pertinent selection criteria include comprehensiveness of scope (e.g., coverage of developmental history as well as political

career), inclusiveness of literary genre (e.g., biography, autobiography, scholarly analysis, and media reports), and the writer's perspective (e.g., a balance between admiring and critical accounts).

Personality Inventory

Greenstein (1992) criticizes analysts who "categorize their subjects without providing the detailed criteria and justifications for doing so" (p. 120). In Immelman's (1999) approach, the diagnostic criteria are documented by means of a structured assessment instrument, the second edition of the MIDC (Immelman & Steinberg, 1999), which was compiled and adapted from Millon's (1990, 1996; Millon & Everly, 1985) prototypal features and diagnostic criteria for normal personality styles and their pathological variants. The justification for classification decisions is provided by documentation from independent biographical sources. The *Millon Inventory of Diagnostic Criteria Manual* (Immelman, 1999) describes the construction, administration, scoring, and interpretation of the MIDC. The 12 MIDC scales (see Immelman, 1999, 2002, for the full MIDC taxonomy) correspond to major personality patterns posited by Millon (e.g., 1994a, 1996) and are coordinated with the normal personality styles described by Oldham and Morris (1995) and Strack (1997).

Diagnostic Procedure

The diagnostic procedure can be summarized as a three-part process: first, an *analysis* phase (data collection) in which source materials are reviewed and analyzed to extract and code diagnostically relevant psychobiographical content; second, a *synthesis* phase (scoring and interpretation) in which the unifying framework provided by the MIDC prototypal features, keyed for attribute domain and personality pattern, is employed to classify the diagnostically relevant information extracted in phase 1; and finally, an *evaluation* phase (inference) in which theoretically grounded descriptions, explanations, inferences, and predictions are extrapolated from Millon's theory of personality, based on the personality profile constructed in phase 2 (Immelman, 1998, 1999, 2002).

SITUATIONAL VARIABLES, EXPERIENTIAL FILTERS, AND POLITICAL PERFORMANCE

Greenstein (1992) cautions against "the psychologizing and clinical fallacies" of explaining behavior in terms of personality while ignoring situational determinants (p. 121). This, of course, is simply the familiar fundamental attribution error (Ross, 1977). Clearly, a comprehensive model of personality in politics should account for the impact of situational variables and the cultural context on political performance and recognize that certain personal characteristics (e.g., training and experience) serve as filters for the political expression of personality.

The best known integrative framework for political psychology is the conceptual map developed by M. Brewster Smith (1968), which illustrates interactions among distal and proximate social antecedents, the social environment, the immediate situation, personality processes and dispositions of political actors, and political behavior. Smith's conceptual map has been exhaustively detailed in the political psychology literature and will not be recapitulated here. The reader is referred to Smith (1968, 1973), Greenstein (1969, pp. 25–31; cf. Greenstein's 1992, pp. 114–116, reformulation), and Stone and Schaffner (1988, pp. 32–43).

Filter Variables That Modulate the Impact of Personality on Political Performance

An important aspect of Hermann's (1980, 1987) model of personality in politics is that it stipulates not only the conditions under which personal characteristics will most directly influence political behavior (e.g., the wide decision latitude of leaders in authoritarian regimes), but also specific filter variables that modulate the impact of personality on political performance. A high-level political leader's *training, experience, or expertise* has "a dampening effect" on the impact of personal characteristics on government behavior because it increases the range or repertoire of policy-relevant, role-related behaviors available to the leader (Hermann, 1987, p. 166). *Sensitivity to the environment* similarly inhibits the impact of personality in politics. According to Hermann (1987), "the more sensitive the leader is to cues from his political environment, the more likely other types of factors are to intervene in this relationship" (p. 166). Hermann's employment of this particular variable as a filter is problematic in that social responsiveness is in essence a personality trait. Finally, *interest* in foreign affairs (or in any aspect of politics for that matter, depending on the political domain of interest) "acts as a motivating force" (Hermann, 1980, p. 13); it "enhances the effect of a leader's [personal] orientation on government policy" by increasing his or her participation in the decision-making process and restricting the delegation of authority in the political domain of interest (Hermann, 1987, p. 166).

It is worth noting that Renshon's construal of "skills and talents" that mediate the relationship between character and political performance (see Renshon, 1996a, p. 47; 1996b, pp. 194–199), stripped of its surplus Kohutian self-psychological significance, is not incompatible with Hermann's notion of experiential filters.

Systematic Import in a Generative Theory of Personality and Political Performance

In his introduction to a special issue of the journal *Leadership Quarterly* devoted to political leadership, guest editor Dean Keith Simonton (1998) asserted that "political leadership has received inadequate attention by researchers who specialize in the study of leadership" (p. 239). To highlight the disproportionate focus of leadership research on small problem-solving groups, Simonton noted that a recent edition of the classic *Bass & Stogdill's Handbook of Leadership* (Bass, 1990) dispensed with the topic of political leadership in only four pages.

Hermann (1986) demarcated the requisite scope of inquiry by specifying five ingredients necessary for understanding political leadership:

> (1) the leader's personality and background, as well as the [leadership] recruitment process . . .; (2) the characteristics of the groups and individuals whom the leader is leading; (3) the nature of the relationship between the leader and those he leads; (4) the context or setting in which the leadership is taking place; and (5) the outcomes of interactions between the leader and those led in specific situations. (p. 169)

Clearly, Hermann accords personality a prominent place in the study of political leadership. She elaborates by specifying seven personal characteristics that influence political leadership: (a) the leader's basic political beliefs, which influence "the kinds of goals and strategies the leader will urge on his [or her] political unit"; (b) the leader's political style, which contributes to the structure and function of the political unit; (c) the leader's motivation for seeking a political leadership position, which shapes "the general focus of attention of the leader's behavior"; (d) the leader's reaction to stress and pressure, which has a bearing on the kinds of issues prone "to cause problems for the leader and how detrimental and pervasive stress is likely to be"; (e) the manner in which the leader was first recruited into a political leadership position, which is instrumental in determining "how free of political debts and obligations" he or she will be and predicts "the rhetoric and practices" that the leader will tend to revert to; (f) the leader's previous political experience, which signifies how qualified he or she is for the position and "what strategies and styles have paid off for the leader" over time; and (g) the unique generational experiences of the leader upon embarking on a political career, in terms of the prevailing political climate that helped "shape the norms and beliefs" of the leader and his or her constituents (pp. 173–180).

Developing a comprehensive model of political leadership is beyond the scope of the present endeavor, which is dedicated primarily to mapping out a generative conceptual framework and methodology for studying personality in politics. Nonetheless, there is heuristic value in broadly stipulating the major tenets for an evolving theory of political leadership synergistically superimposed upon a comprehensive, generative model of personality in politics. Of central relevance in this regard are Hermann's (1986) first two personal characteristics surmised to influence political leadership: political beliefs impinging on a *leader's goals or strategies*, and *stylistic* elements that fashion the structural and functional attributes of political units. These core characteristics are important signposts for a generative theory of personality and political performance compliant with Hempel's (1965) canon of systematic import.

To this end, Millon's evolutionary model of personality provides a practical point of departure. David Buss (1999) has bluntly asserted that "theories of personality inconsistent with evolutionary principles stand little or no chance of being correct" (p. 52). Paralleling Millon's (1996, chapter 5) construal of a personologically based evolutionary model of psychotherapeutic intervention, an applied personologic model of leadership can be construed as encompassing both strategic and tactical modalities. From this frame of reference, *strategic* dimensions of political leadership would consist of generalized, personality-based leadership orientations, including higher-order political aims and long-term policy goals and preferences, whereas *tactical* (stylistic) modalities of political leadership would consist of more concrete, focal leadership objectives and political maneuvers, typically dictated by circumstances but shaped both by the leader's underlying structural and functional personality attributes and by his or her higher order strategic aims and goals. The distinction between strategic and tactical modalities of political performance is equivalent to the distinction between philosophical and instrumental beliefs in George's (1969) operational code construct. *Philosophical* (epistemological) beliefs include a leader's "assumptions and premises" about "the fundamental nature of politics" and "the nature of political conflict," whereas *instrumental* beliefs relate to "ends–means relationships in the context of political action" (p. 199). When reconceptualized in evolutionary terms, this general perspective provides a heuristic basis for an emergent personological interpretation of political performance.

AN EVOLUTIONARY MODEL OF PERSONALITY AND POLITICAL PERFORMANCE: THE STRATEGIC MODALITIES

Paralleling the conceptual foundations of his personological model, Millon's (1996, chapter 5) strategic modalities of applied psychological intervention are derived from three universal, interacting domains or spheres of evolutionary and ecological principles (1990; Millon, this volume): *existence* (the pain–pleasure polarity), *adaptation* (the passive–active polarity), and *replication* (the other–self polarity). A practical operationalization of these three polarities is provided by the Millon Index of Personality Styles (MIPS; Millon, 1994a; cf. Millon, this volume), which assesses them in accordance with six "motivating aims": life enhancement (pleasure seeking) versus life preservation (pain avoidance), ecologic modification (active) versus ecologic accommodation (passive), and reproductive propagation (self-individuating) versus reproductive nurturance (other-nurturing).

The MIPS also assesses four "cognitive modes," or predilections of *abstraction,* consonant with Carl Jung's (1921/1971) theory of types. Unlike the three universal motivating aims, the cognitive modes represent a distinctly human sphere of functioning and were thus redundant with respect to deriving Millon's (1990, 1996) original taxonomy of adaptive and maladaptive personality styles from evolutionary ecology. However, precisely by virtue of the fact that abstraction "concerns the emergence of uniquely human competencies that foster anticipatory planning and reasoned decision making" (Millon, 1999, pp. 442–443; Millon, this volume), the cognitive modes are critical with respect to deducing a synergistic, personological model of political performance. Moreover, the four distinctly human cognitive propensities will likely be at the forefront of future advances in Millon's personality system, judging from his current conviction that predilections of abstraction, the most recent stage of evolution, comprise "central elements in personologic derivations" (Millon, this volume).

It is noteworthy that in terms of evolutionary theory, Osgood's (Osgood, Suci, & Tannenbaum, 1957) three semantic differential dimensions, namely evaluation (good–bad), potency (strong–weak), and activity (active–passive), can be conceptually linked to, respectively, Millon's (1990) pleasure–pain, self–other, and active–passive polarities.

Aims of Existence: The Pain–Pleasure Polarity

The two-dimensional (i.e., two linearly independent vectors) pain–pleasure polarity (Millon, 1990, pp. 51–64; Millon, this volume) is conceptualized in terms of, respectively, life enhancement (pleasure seeking) and life preservation (pain avoidance): "acts that are 'attracted' to what we experientially record as 'pleasurable' events (positive reinforcers) . . . [versus] behaviors oriented to 'repel' events experientially characterized as 'painful' (negative reinforcers)" (Millon, this volume).

Hypothetically, the pain–pleasure polarity could partially account for individual differences in ideological (e.g., liberal–conservative) resonance in politics. In evolutionary terms, liberalism can be construed as a primary concern "with improvement in the quality of life" and "behaviors that improve survival chances," and conservatism as an avoidance of "actions or environments that threaten to jeopardize survival" (Millon & Davis, 2000, p. 58). Thus construed, liberals seek to maximize survival by seeking pleasure (life enhancement, or positive reinforcement), whereas conservatives seek to maximize survival by avoiding pain (life preservation, or negative reinforcement).

The nature of the relationship between personality and ideology has been a perennial concern in political psychology and remains a topic worthy of study. As early as 1907, William James drew a personological distinction between two ideologically relevant philosophical temperaments: optimistic, idealistic tender-mindedness versus pessimistic, materialistic tough-mindedness—a position compatible with Millon's (1990) life-enhancement and life-preservation polarities.

Evolutionary theory also may shed new light on an unresolved controversy in political psychology, namely the debate over authoritarianism as fundamentally a right-wing phenomenon versus authoritarianism as an expression of both right-wing and left-wing ideological extremism. Eysenck (1954) proposed a two-factor theory that among its classifications conceptualized fascists as tough-minded conservatives, communists as tough-minded radicals, and liberals as tender-minded moderates. Paul Sniderman (1975) conjectured that low self-esteem encourages both left-wing and right-wing extremism. More consonant with Millon's pain–pleasure polarity, Silvan Tomkins's (1963) polarity theory posits that people with more humanistic, left-wing, ideo-affective postures (or scripts) both express and are more receptive to positive affect, whereas those with more normative, right-wing scripts tend to be more responsive to negative affect. Stone (1980; Stone & Smith, 1993), a leading critic of what he calls the myth of left-wing authoritarianism, has argued on empirical grounds that the evidence for left-wing authoritarianism is flawed (see Altemeyer, 1996; McFarland, Ageyev, & Abalakina, 1993) and that authoritarianism is, in essence, a right-wing phenomenon.

In Hermann's conceptual scheme, a core belief component shaping a leader's worldview is *nationalism,* which emphasizes "the importance of maintaining national honor and dignity" (Hermann, 1987, p. 167). In Millon's evolutionary terms, the motivating aim of nationalism clearly is a life-preserving (pain-avoidant) orientation.

The pain–pleasure dimension also provides evolutionary underpinnings for Barber's (1972/1992) fourfold (active–passive × positive–negative) categorization of presidential character, in which positivity–negativity is described in terms of enjoyment derived from political office. Positive leaders have a generally optimistic outlook and derive pleasure from the duties of public office, whereas negative leadership has a more pessimistic tone, being oriented toward pain aversion.

Finally, the pain–pleasure dimension suggests a possible evolutionary basis for the three management models proposed by Johnson (1974) and employed by George and Stern (1998) to classify the policy-making structures and advisory systems favored by recent U.S. presidents.

Formalistic chief executives prefer "an orderly policy-making [*sic*] structure, . . . well-defined procedures, hierarchical lines of communication, and a structured staff system" (George & Stern, 1998, p. 203). In evolutionary terms, they seek to *preserve* life by minimizing pain.

Competitive chief executives encourage "more open and uninhibited expression of diverse opinions, analysis, and advice" and tolerate or encourage "organizational ambiguity, overlapping jurisdictions, and multiple channels of communication to and from the president" (George & Stern, 1998, p. 203). In evolutionary terms, they seek to *enhance* life by maximizing pleasure.

Collegial chief executives attempt to benefit from the advantages of both the competitive and formalistic approaches while avoiding their pitfalls. Thus, they strive for "diversity and competition in the policymaking system," balanced by "encouraging cabinet officers and advisers to identify at least partly with the presidential perspective" and "encouraging collegial participation" (George & Stern, 1998, p. 203). In evolutionary terms, collegial executives are intermediate on both the pleasure-seeking and pain-avoidant polarities.

The systematic import of a generative theory is implicit in the suggestion that Johnson's (1974) management model fails to account for at least two additional executive styles: *complex* types high on both the pleasure-seeking and pain-avoidant polarities, and *undifferentiated* types low on both valences.

Modes of Adaptation: The Passive–Active Polarity

The passive–active polarity (Millon, 1990, pp. 64–77; Millon, this volume) is conceptualized in terms of ecologic modification (active) and ecologic accommodation (passive); that is, "whether initiative is taken in altering and shaping life's events or whether behaviors are reactive to and accommodate those events" (Millon, this volume).

The passive–active dimension provides evolutionary underpinnings for Barber's (1972/1992) fourfold (active–passive × positive–negative) categorization of presidential character, in which activity–passivity is described in terms of energy invested in political office. In evolutionary terms, a passive orientation can be construed as "a tendency to accommodate to a given ecological niche and accept what the environment offers," whereas an active orientation can be construed as "a tendency to modify or intervene in the environment, thereby adapting it to oneself" (Millon & Davis, 2000, p. 59).

The passive–active dimension also provides an evolutionary basis for Etheredge's (1978) fourfold (high–low dominance × introversion–extroversion) classification of personality-based differences in foreign-policy operating style and role orientation. High-dominance introverts (*bloc* or *excluding* leaders such as Woodrow Wilson and Herbert Hoover) actively seek to reshape the world, typically by means of containment policies or by tenaciously advancing a personal vision. High-dominance extraverts (*world* or *integrating* leaders such as Theodore Roosevelt, Franklin D. Roosevelt, John F. Kennedy, and Lyndon B. Johnson) actively seek to reshape the world through advocacy and pragmatic leadership on a wide range of foreign-policy fronts. Low-dominance introverts (*maintainers* such as Calvin Coolidge) tend to persevere with the existing order, passively pursuing a foreign policy that amounts to "a holding action for the status quo." Low-dominance extraverts (*conciliators* such as William McKinley, William Taft, Warren Harding, Harry Truman, and Dwight D. Eisenhower), though revealing a preference for accommodating to existing arrangements, are more flexible and open to change, tending "to respond to circumstances with the sympathetic hope that accommodations can be negotiated" (Etheredge, 1978, pp. 449–450).

Finally, in Hermann's (1980, 1987) conceptual scheme, a core belief contributing to a leader's worldview, along with nationalism, is *belief in one's own ability to control events*. In evolutionary terms, a more efficacy-oriented, internal locus of control implies an active-modifying motivating aim, in contrast to a more external locus of control, which suggests a passive-accommodating mode of adaptation. Hermann's (1987) expansionist, active-independent, and influential orientations are more actively oriented, whereas her mediator-integrator, opportunist, and developmental orientations are more passively oriented.

Strategies of Replication: The Other–Self Polarity

The other–self polarity (Millon, 1990, pp. 77–98) is conceptualized in terms of, respectively, reproductive nurturance (other) and reproductive propagation (self): a nurturing tendency to value the needs of others versus an individuating self-orientation that seeks to realize personal potentials before attending to the needs of others (Millon, 1994a, p. 6; Millon, this volume).

In political psychology, three social motives (which in Hermann's conceptual scheme are postulated to contribute to a leader's worldview) are regarded as playing a key role in leader performance: need for power, need for achievement, and need for affiliation (Winter, 1987, 1998). In evolutionary terms, the *need for power*, involving "the desire to control, influence, or have an impact on other persons or groups" (Hermann, 1987, p. 167), suggests a self-individuating replicating strategy, as does the *need for achievement*, which involves "a concern for excellence" and personal accomplishment (Winter, 1998, p. 369). Conversely, the *need for affiliation*, reflecting "concern for establishing, maintaining, or restoring warm and friendly relations with other persons or groups" (Hermann, 1987, p. 167), suggests an other-nurturing replicating strategy. Hermann's (1987) expansionist, active-independent, and influential orientations are more self-oriented, whereas her mediator-integrator, opportunist, and developmental orientations are more other-oriented.

Hermann (1980) also posits two key elements of interpersonal style that, in conjunction with decision style, shape a leader's personal political style: distrust of others and task orientation (see Hermann, 1987, pp. 163, 167). In evolutionary terms, the *trust–distrust* and *task–relationship* dimensions of leadership are easily reconceptualized as surface manifestations of the other–self bipolarity.

The two key elements of decision style in Hermann's (1980) framework are *conceptual complexity* and *self-confidence*, which she construes (following Ziller, Stone, Jackson, & Terbovic, 1977), as jointly determinative of "how ideological or pragmatic a political leader will be" (Hermann, 1987, p. 164). Ziller (1973) developed a social-psychological theory of personality that examines two components of the self-concept—self-esteem and complexity of the self-concept—in the context of responsiveness to the views of others. Ziller et al. (1977) conducted a series of important studies investigating the effects of the four *self–other orientations* (high/low self-esteem × high/low self-complexity) on political behavior. They found that, in terms of political behavior, persons with high self-esteem and high self-complexity (apoliticals) "have difficulty being responsive" to others; persons with low self-esteem and high self-complexity (pragmatists) "are quite responsive" to the opinions of others; persons with high self-esteem and low self-complexity (ideologues) "are generally nonresponsive" to the opinions of others; and persons with low self-esteem and low self-complexity (an indeterminate type) "are highly responsive within a narrow range of social stimuli" (Ziller et al., 1977, pp. 179–180). According to Ziller and his coworkers, low self-esteem/high self-complexity pragmatists and high self-esteem–low self-complexity ideologues "parallel the two leadership roles which have been observed in small groups, the task role (ideologue) and the socio-emotional role (pragmatist)" (p. 193).

Stone and Baril (1979), elaborating on the findings of Ziller et al. (1977), used self–other orientation as a conceptual basis for postulating two distinctive political prototypes, each having a different motivational base. The *pragmatist*—akin to Barber's (1965) active-negative advertiser—is motivated by power seeking to compensate for low self-esteem (as anticipated by Lasswell, 1948), being driven by self-enhancement and self-promotion. The second political personality type, the *ideologue*—akin to Barber's (1965) active-positive lawmaker—is more other oriented, apparently having a sincere interest in good legislation (defined as either pursuing ideological goals or as serving a constituency).

Stone and Baril's (1979) construal of self- and other-oriented political personality types, in concert with Barber's (1965, 1972/1992) scheme, lends empirical and theoretical support for the utility of Millon's (1990) other–self polarity in an overarching theory of political personality and performance. In addition, Ziller et al.'s (1977) explication of four self–other orientations in relation to social responsiveness offers a conceptual substrate for Hermann's (1980, 1987) notion of "sensitivity to the [political] environment" as a filter for modulating the influence of personal characteristics on political behavior.

Predilections of Abstraction: The Cognitive Polarities

The cognitive modes of abstraction (Millon, 1990, pp. 42–43, 1994a, pp. 3–4, 6–7, 21–27), which encompass "the sources employed to gather knowledge about the experience of life and the manner in which this information is gathered and transformed" (Millon, this volume), are conceptualized in terms of four polarities subserving two superordinate functions, namely *information sourcing* and *transformational processing* of cognitive data:

1. The *external–internal orientation polarity* involves extraceptive (extraversing) versus intraceptive (introversing) modes of information gathering or knowledge sourcing.

2. The *tangible–intangible disposition polarity* entails realistic (sensory, concrete) versus intuitive (abstract) modes of attending to, selecting, and perceiving information.

3. The *ideational–emotional preference polarity* pertains to intellective (thinking) versus affective (feeling) modes of information processing.

4. The *integrating–innovative bias polarity* relates to assimilative (systematizing) versus imaginative (innovating) modes of knowledge transformation; that is, knowledge assimilation versus cognitive accommodation.

Implicitly, Choiniere and Keirsey (1992) cross the tangible–intangible cognitive mode with the other–self motivating aim to yield a fourfold (realistic, concrete vs. intuitive, abstract mode of thought and speech × moral sanctioning vs. pragmatic utilitarian value orientation) categorization of U.S. presidents as *Guardians* (concrete sanctioners), *Idealists* (abstract sanctioners), *Artisans* (concrete utilitarians), and *Rationals* (abstract utilitarians; pp. 8–10; see also pp. 598–602). Furthermore, Choiniere and Keirsey's (1992) model of "presidential temperament" distinguishes two variants of each type—*directing* and *reporting* (pp. 11–12)—a distinction that appears to be a surface manifestation of Millon's (1990) active–passive polarity. Thus, when reconceptualized in terms of Millon's (1994a) three universal evolutionary motivating aims and four cognitive modes, there are eight distinct leadership styles: *active-realist utilitarians* (Operator Artisans such as Theodore Roosevelt, Franklin D. Roosevelt, John F. Kennedy, and Lyndon B. Johnson); *passive-realist utilitarians* (Player Artisans such as Warren Harding and Ronald Reagan); *active-intuitive utilitarians* (Organizer Rationals such as Herbert Hoover and Dwight D. Eisenhower); *passive-intuitive utilitarians* (Engineer Rationals such as Thomas Jefferson and Abraham Lincoln); *active-realist sanctioners* (Monitor Guardians such as George Washington, Woodrow Wilson, Calvin Coolidge, Harry Truman, Jimmy Carter, and Richard Nixon); *passive-realist sanctioners* (Conservator Guardians such as William McKinley, William Taft, Gerald Ford, and George H. W. Bush); *active-intuitive sanctioners* (Mentor Idealists); and *passive-intuitive sanctioners* (Advocate Idealists). There have been no Idealist U.S. presidents; however, Choiniere and Keirsey (1992) present Mohandas Gandhi and Eleanor Roosevelt as prototypes of, respectively, the Mentor and Advocate Idealist.

AN EVOLUTIONARY MODEL OF PERSONALITY AND POLITICAL PERFORMANCE: THE TACTICAL MODALITIES

Millon's (1996, chapter 5) tactical modalities of applied psychological intervention are conceptually anchored to his eight structural and functional personality domains, encompassing the behavioral, phenomenological, intrapsychic, and biophysical levels of analysis. Millon (1996) notes that the eight domains "are not themselves the parts of personality, but do serve as a means of classifying the parts or constructs of personality" (p. 183). There is heuristic value in employing a parallel organizational scheme to classify the constructs of political performance (leadership and decision making). At a minimum, such a heuristic model establishes explicit links between the source domain of personality and the target domain of political performance.

Biophysical Level

Fundamentally, Barber's (1972/1992) dimensions of *activity–passivity* and *positive affect/negative affect* constitute a temperamental (i.e., having a predisposition to activity and emotionality) construct. Thus, Barber's construal of "presidential character" offers a congenial framework for deducing biophysical (temperamental and affective) modalities of presidential performance.

The biophysical modality also is capable of accommodating the notion of *emotional intelligence,* one of the six key qualities in Greenstein's (2000) schema for describing presidential leadership style and job performance. The flawed presidencies of Lyndon B. Johnson, Richard Nixon, Jimmy Carter, and Bill Clinton all serve as stark reminders of the pernicious effects that failed emotional management can have on presidential performance. More significant, however, is that this modality offers a congenial framework for accommodating the emerging biopolitical perspective (e.g., Marcus, 2001; Masters, 1989) on the psychology of politics.

Behavioral Level

The ubiquitous *task–relationship* dimension, prevalent in contemporary theories of leadership (including that of Hermann, 1986), presents a clear-cut instance of a personality-based leadership orientation observed at the behavioral level. The behavioral modality also represents the appropriate data level for assessing Renshon's (1996b) "three distinct aspects of presidential and political leadership: mobilization, orchestration, and consolidation" (p. 226). Three of Greenstein's (2000) six stylistic and performance qualities can be assembled at the behavioral level of analysis: *organizational capacity, effectiveness as a public communicator,* and *political skill.*

Phenomenological Level

Numerous personality-based leadership traits and qualities converge on the phenomenological data level, including *conceptual complexity* (Hermann, 1974, 1987), *integrative complexity* (Suedfeld, 1994), *cognitive style* (George & Stern, 1998), *sense of efficacy and competence* (George & Stern, 1998), and *judgment/decision making* (Renshon, 1996b).

Two of Greenstein's (2000) presidential leadership and performance qualities, namely *vision* (which subsumes both the power to inspire and consistency of viewpoint) and *cognitive style,* assemble at this data level.

Intrapsychic Level

Both Hermann's (1987) *trust–distrust* dimension (a component of interpersonal style) and George and Stern's (1998) *orientation toward political conflict* (which influences a leader's choice of policy-making system) lend themselves to analysis at the intrapsychic data level. Indeed, numerous personological and social-psychological perspectives relevant to political leadership, judgment, and decision making converge at the intrapsychic level, including the ego-defensive notion of scapegoating as a form of *displaced aggression* (Adorno et al., 1950; Hovland & Sears, 1940); the belief in a just world and blaming the victim (Lerner, 1970) as a form of *defensive attribution;* and the problem of *defensive avoidance* in political decision making (Janis & Mann, 1977). The intrapsychic modality also offers a heuristic frame of reference for examining psychodynamic aspects of xenophobia, ethnic hatred, and the so-called roots of evil (Staub, 1989) as expressed in political leadership.

CONCLUSION

Political psychologists recognize that political outcomes are governed by a multitude of factors, many of them indeterminate. Nonetheless, the study of personality in politics has advanced sufficiently to permit broad personality-based performance predictions and to pinpoint a political candidate's specific strengths and limitations.

A coherent psychodiagnostic framework capable of capturing the critical personological determinants of political performance, embedded in a broad range of attribute domains across the entire matrix of the person—not just the individual's motives, operational code, integrative complexity, or personality traits—is the one indispensable tool without which the assessment of personality in politics can neither prevail nor prosper.

Although this chapter has but scratched the surface in breaking new ground for the construction of a generative, evolutionary foundation for personality-in-politics inquiry, I join Theodore Millon (coeditor of this volume) in reflecting as he did upon concluding his epoch-making *Toward a New Personology: An Evolutionary Model* (1990):

> Some may very well argue they just struggled through an author's need not only to impose an unnecessary order but to frame

its elements in an overly formalistic sequence; that I, the author, have forced the subject of personology into the procrustean bed of theoretical predilections, drawing on tangential topics of little or no relevance. If such a case be valid, I regret that my habit of seeking bridges between scientific domains has led me to cohere subjects best left disparate. It is hoped that this philosophic prejudice, obviously inspired by a personally driven world view, will yet prove to have a modicum of empirical merit and theoretical value. (p. 177)

REFERENCES

Adorno, T. W., Frenkel-Brunswik, E., Levinson, D. J., & Sanford, N. (1950). *The authoritarian personality*. New York: Harper & Row.

Allport, G. W. (1937). *Personality: A psychological interpretation*. New York: Holt.

Altemeyer, B. (1996). *The authoritarian specter*. Cambridge, MA: Harvard University Press.

American Psychiatric Association. (1994). *Diagnostic and statistical manual of mental disorders* (4th ed.). Washington, DC: Author.

Asch, S. E. (1955). Opinions and social pressure. *Scientific American, 19,* 31–35.

Barber, J. D. (1965). *The lawmakers: Recruitment and adaptation to legislative life*. New Haven, CT: Yale University Press.

Barber, J. D. (1992). *The presidential character: Predicting performance in the White House* (4th ed.). Englewood Cliffs, NJ: Prentice Hall. (Originally published 1972)

Bass, B. M. (1990). *Bass & Stogdill's handbook of leadership: Theory, research, and managerial applications* (3rd ed.). New York: Free Press.

Buss, D. M. (1999). Human nature and individual differences: The evolution of human personality. In L. A. Pervin & O. P. John (Eds.), *Handbook of personality: Theory and research* (2nd ed., pp. 31–56). New York: Guilford.

Choiniere, R., & Keirsey, D. (1992). *Presidential temperament: The unfolding of character in the forty presidents of the United States*. Del Mar, CA: Prometheus Nemesis.

Christie, R., & Geis, F. L. (1970). *Studies in Machiavellianism*. New York: Academic Press.

Davies, J. C. (1973). From where and where to? In J. N. Knutson (Ed.), *Handbook of political psychology* (pp. 1–27). San Francisco: Jossey-Bass.

Dille, B., & Young, M. D. (2000). The conceptual complexity of Presidents Carter and Clinton: An automated content analysis of temporal stability and source bias. *Political Psychology, 21,* 587–596.

Erikson, E. H. (1969). *Gandhi's truth: On the origins of militant nonviolence*. New York: W. W. Norton.

Erikson, E. H. (1980). *Identity and the life cycle*. New York: W. W. Norton.

Etheredge, L. S. (1978). Personality effects on American foreign policy, 1898–1968: A test of interpersonal generalization theory. *American Political Science Review, 72,* 434–451.

Eysenck, H. J. (1954). *The psychology of politics*. London: Routledge.

Freud, S., & Bullitt, W. C. (1967). *Thomas Woodrow Wilson: A psychological study*. Boston: Houghton Mifflin.

Gangestad, S., & Snyder, M. (1985). "To carve at the joints": On the existence of discrete classes in personality. *Psychological Review, 92,* 317–349.

George, A. L. (1969). The "operational code": A neglected approach to the study of political leaders and decision-making. *International Studies Quarterly, 13,* 190–222.

George, A. L., & George, J. L. (1956). *Woodrow Wilson and Colonel House: A personality study*. New York: John Day.

George, A. L., & Stern, E. (1998). Presidential management styles and models. In A. L. George & J. L. George, *Presidential personality and performance* (pp. 199–280). Boulder, CO: Westview Press.

Glad, B. (1996). Passing the baton: Transformational political leadership from Gorbachev to Yeltsin; from De Klerk to Mandela. *Political Psychology, 17,* 1–28.

Gödel, K. (1931). Über formal unentscheidbare Sätze der Principia Mathematica und verwandter Systeme I [On formally undecidable propositions of Principia Mathematica and related systems I]. *Monatshefte für Mathematik und Physik, 38,* 173–198.

Greenstein, F. I. (1969). *Personality and politics: Problems of evidence, inference, and conceptualization*. Chicago: Markham.

Greenstein, F. I. (1973). Political psychology: A pluralistic universe. In J. N. Knutson (Ed.), *Handbook of political psychology* (pp. 438–469). San Francisco: Jossey-Bass.

Greenstein, F. I. (1987). *Personality and politics: Problems of evidence, inference, and conceptualization* (New ed.). Princeton, NJ: Princeton University Press.

Greenstein, F. I. (1992). Can personality and politics be studied systematically? *Political Psychology, 13,* 105–128.

Greenstein, F. I. (2000). *The presidential difference: Leadership style from FDR to Clinton*. New York: Free Press.

Hempel, C. G. (1965). *Aspects of scientific explanation*. New York: Free Press.

Hermann, M. G. (1974). Leader personality and foreign policy behavior. In J. N. Rosenau (Ed.), *Comparing foreign policies: Theories, findings, and methods* (pp. 201–234). New York: Wiley/Sage-Halsted.

Hermann, M. G. (1980). Explaining foreign policy behavior using the personal characteristics of political leaders. *International Studies Quarterly, 24,* 7–46.

Hermann, M. G. (1986). Ingredients of leadership. In M. G. Hermann (Ed.), *Political psychology* (pp. 167–192). San Francisco: Jossey-Bass.

Hermann, M. G. (1987). Assessing the foreign policy role orientations of sub-Saharan African leaders. In S. G. Walker (Ed.), *Role theory and foreign policy analysis* (pp. 161–198). Durham, NC: Duke University Press.

Holsti, O. R. (1970). The "operational code" approach to the study of political leaders: John Foster Dulles' philosophical and instrumental beliefs. *Canadian Journal of Political Science, 3,* 123–157.

Holsti, O. R. (1977). Foreign policy decision makers viewed psychologically: "Cognitive process" approaches. In G. M. Bonham & M. J. Shapiro (Eds.), *Thought and action in foreign policy* (pp. 120–143). Basel, Switzerland: Birkhäuser Verlag.

Holsti, O. R. (1989). The political psychology of international politics: More than a luxury. *Political Psychology, 10,* 495–500.

Horney, K. (1937). *The neurotic personality of our times*. New York: W. W. Norton.

Hovland, C. I., & Sears, R. R. (1940). Minor studies of aggression: Correlation of lynchings with economic indices. *Journal of Psychology, 9,* 301–310.

Immelman, A. (1988, July). *The perception of South African psychologists P. W. Botha's personality style.* Paper prepared for the Eleventh Annual Scientific Meeting of the International Society of Political Psychology, Secaucus, NJ.

Immelman, A. (1993). The assessment of political personality: A psychodiagnostically relevant conceptualization and methodology. *Political Psychology, 14,* 725–741.

Immelman, A. (1998). The political personalities of 1996 U.S. presidential candidates Bill Clinton and Bob Dole. *Leadership Quarterly, 9,* 335–366.

Immelman, A. (1999). *Millon inventory of diagnostic criteria manual* (2nd ed.). Unpublished manuscript, St. John's University, Collegeville, MN.

Immelman, A. (2002). The political personality of U.S. president George W. Bush. In L. O. Valenty & O. Feldman (Eds.), *Political leadership for the new century: Personality and behavior among American leaders* (pp. 81–103). Westport, CT: Praeger.

Immelman, A., & Steinberg, B. S. (Compilers). (1999). *Millon inventory of diagnostic criteria* (2nd ed.). Unpublished research scale, St. John's University, Collegeville, MN.

James, W. (1907). *Pragmatism*. New York: Longmans, Green.

Janis, I. L. (1982). *Groupthink: Psychological study of foreign policy decisions and fiascos* (2nd ed.). Boston: Houghton Mifflin. (Original work published 1972 as *Victims of groupthink: A psychological study of foreign policy decisions and fiascos*)

Janis, I. L., & Mann, L. (1977). *Decision making: A psychological analysis of conflict, choice, and commitment*. New York: Free Press.

Jervis, R. (1976). *Perception and misperception in international politics*. Princeton, NJ: Princeton University Press.

Jervis, R. (1989). Political psychology: Some challenges and opportunities. *Political Psychology, 10,* 481–493.

Johnson, R. T. (1974). *Managing the White House: An intimate study of the presidency*. New York: Harper & Row.

Jung, C. G. (1971). Psychological types (H. G. Baynes, Trans., & R. F. C. Hull, Rev.). (*The collected works of C. G. Jung, Vol. 6.*) Princeton, NJ: Princeton University Press. (Original work published 1921)

Kernberg, O. (1984). *Severe personality disorders: Psychotherapeutic strategies*. New Haven, CT: Yale University Press.

Kinder, B. N. (Ed.). (1999). Millon's evolving personality theories and measures [Special series]. *Journal of Personality Assessment, 72*(3).

Knutson, J. N. (1973). Personality in the study of politics. In J. N. Knutson (Ed.), *Handbook of political psychology* (pp. 28–56). San Francisco: Jossey-Bass.

Kohut, H. (1971). *The analysis of the self*. New York: International Universities Press.

Kohut, H. (1977). *The restoration of the self*. New York: International Universities Press.

Kowert, P. A. (1996). Where *does* the buck stop?: Assessing the impact of presidential personality. *Political Psychology, 17,* 421–452.

Lane, R. E. (1962). *Political ideology: Why the American common man believes what he does*. New York: Free Press.

Lasswell, H. D. (1930). *Psychopathology and politics*. Chicago: University of Chicago Press.

Lasswell, H. D. (1948). *Power and personality*. New York: W. W. Norton.

Lasswell, H. D. (1951). *The political writings of Harold D. Lasswell*. New York: Free Press.

Lau, R. R., & Sears, D. O. (Eds.). (1986). *Political cognition: The 19th Annual Carnegie Symposium on Cognition*. Hillsdale, NJ: Erlbaum.

Lerner, M. J. (1970). *The belief in a just world: The fundamental delusion*. New York: Plenum Press.

Levin, S. (2000). Undergraduate education in political psychology. *Political Psychology, 21,* 603–620.

Lyons, M. (1997). Presidential character revisited. *Political Psychology, 18,* 791–811.

Machiavelli, N. (1995). *The prince* (W. K. Marriott, Trans.). New York: ILTweb. Available online: http://www.ilt.columbia.edu/projects/digitexts/machiavelli/the_prince/title.html (Original work circa 1513)

Marcus, G. E. (2001). Political psychology: A personal view. In K. R. Monroe (Ed.), *Political psychology* (pp. 95–106). Mahwah, NJ: Erlbaum.

Masters, R. D. (1989). *The nature of politics*. New Haven, CT: Yale University Press.

McFarland, S., Ageyev, V., & Abalakina, M. (1993). The authoritarian personality in the United States and the former Soviet Union: Comparative studies. In W. F. Stone, G. Lederer, & R. Christie (Eds.), *Strength and weakness: The authoritarian personality today* (pp. 199–225). New York: Springer-Verlag.

McGraw, K. M. (2000). Contributions of the cognitive approach to political psychology. *Political Psychology, 21,* 805–832.

McGuire, W. J. (1993). The poly-psy relationship: Three phases of a long affair. In S. Iyengar & W. J. McGuire (Eds.), *Explorations in political psychology* (pp. 9–35). Durham: University of North Carolina Press.

Milgram, S. (1963). Behavioral study of obedience. *Journal of Abnormal and Social Psychology, 67,* 371–378.

Millon, T. (1986). Personality prototypes and their diagnostic criteria. In T. Millon & G. L. Klerman (Eds.), *Contemporary directions in psychopathology: Toward the DSM-IV* (pp. 671–712). New York: Guilford.

Millon, T. (1990). *Toward a new personology: An evolutionary model.* New York: Wiley.

Millon, T. (with Weiss, L. G., Millon, C. M., & Davis, R. D.). (1994a). *Millon Index of Personality Styles manual.* San Antonio, TX: Psychological Corporation.

Millon, T. (1994b). Personality disorders: Conceptual distinctions and classification issues. In P. T. Costa, Jr. & T. A. Widiger (Eds.), *Personality disorders and the five-factor model of personality* (pp. 279–301). Washington, DC: American Psychological Association.

Millon, T. (with Davis, R. D.). (1996). *Disorders of personality: DSM-IV and beyond* (2nd ed.). New York: Wiley.

Millon, T. (1999). Reflections on psychosynergy: A model for integrating science, theory, classification, assessment, and therapy. *Journal of Personality Assessment, 72,* 437–456.

Millon, T., & Davis, R. D. (2000). *Personality disorders in modern life.* New York: Wiley.

Millon, T., Davis, R. D., & Millon, C. (1996). *Millon Clinical Multiaxial Inventory–III.* Minnetonka, MN: National Computer Systems.

Millon, T., & Everly, G. S., Jr. (1985). *Personality and its disorders: A biosocial learning approach.* New York: Wiley.

Mischel, W. (1990). Personality dispositions revisited and revised: A view after three decades. In L. A. Pervin (Ed.), *Handbook of personality: Theory and research* (pp. 111–134). New York: Guilford.

Morey, L. C. (1985). An empirical comparison of interpersonal and DSM-III approaches to classification of personality disorders. *Psychiatry, 48,* 358–364.

Myers, I. B., & McCaulley, M. H. (1985). *Manual: A guide to the development and use of the Myers-Briggs Type Indicator.* Palo Alto, CA: Consulting Psychologists Press.

Northrop, F. S. C. (1947). *The logic of the sciences and the humanities.* New York: Macmillan.

Oldham, J. M., & Morris, L. B. (1995). *The new personality self-portrait* (Rev. ed.). New York: Bantam Books.

Osgood, C. E. (1962). *An alternative to war and surrender.* Urbana: University of Illinois Press.

Osgood, C. E., Suci, G. J., & Tannenbaum, P. H. (1957). *The measurement of meaning.* Urbana: University of Illinois Press.

Pervin, L. A. (Ed.). (1990). *Handbook of personality: Theory and research.* New York: Guilford.

Pervin, L. A., & John, O. P. (2001). *Personality: Theory and research* (8th ed.). New York: Wiley.

Post, J. M. (1991). Saddam Hussein of Iraq: A political psychological profile. *Political Psychology, 12,* 279–289.

Post, J. M. (1993). Current concepts of the narcissistic personality: Implications for political psychology. *Political Psychology, 14,* 99–121.

Post, J. M. (Ed.). (2003). *The psychological assessment of political leaders: Method and application.* Ann Arbor: University of Michigan Press.

Renshon, S. A. (1996a). *High hopes: The Clinton presidency and the politics of ambition.* New York: New York University Press.

Renshon, S. A. (1996b). *The psychological assessment of presidential candidates.* New York: New York University Press.

Renshon, S. A. (1998). Analyzing the psychology and performance of presidential candidates at a distance: Bob Dole and the 1996 presidential campaign. *Leadership Quarterly, 9,* 377–395.

Rokeach, M. (1960). *The open and closed mind: Investigations into the nature of belief systems and personality systems.* New York: Basic Books.

Ross, L. (1977). The intuitive psychologist and his shortcomings: Distortions in the attribution process. In L. Berkowitz (Ed.), *Advances in experimental social psychology* (Vol. 10, pp. 174–221). New York: Academic Press.

Rubenzer, S. J., Faschingbauer, T. R., & Ones, D. S. (2002). Assessments of America's chief executives: Insights from biographers and objective personality measures. In L. O. Valenty & O. Feldman (Eds.), *Political leadership for the new century: Personality and behavior among American leaders* (pp. 105–133). Westport, CT: Praeger.

Schafer, M. (2000). Issues in assessing psychological characteristics at a distance: An introduction to the symposium. *Political Psychology, 21,* 511–527.

Sears, D. O. (1987). Political psychology. *Annual Review of Psychology, 38,* 229–255.

Simon, H. (1985). Human nature in politics: The dialogue of psychology with political science. *American Political Science Review, 79,* 293–304.

Simonton, D. K. (1986). Presidential personality: Biographical use of the Gough Adjective Check List. *Journal of Personality and Social Psychology, 51,* 149–160.

Simonton, D. K. (1988). Presidential style: Personality, biography, and performance. *Journal of Personality and Social Psychology, 55,* 928–936.

Simonton, D. K. (1990). Personality and politics. In L. A. Pervin (Ed.), *Handbook of personality: Theory and research* (pp. 670–692). New York: Guilford.

Simonton, D. K. (1998). Introduction. Political leadership: Part I—World heads of state. *Leadership Quarterly, 9,* 239–242.

Smith, M. B. (1968). A map for the analysis of personality and politics. *Journal of Social Issues, 24*(3), 15–28. (Reprinted in F. I. Greenstein & M. Lerner, Eds., *A source book for the study of personality in politics,* pp. 34–44. Chicago: Markham, 1971.)

Smith, M. B. (1973). *Political attitudes.* In J. N. Knutson (Ed.), *Handbook of political psychology* (pp. 57–82). San Francisco: Jossey-Bass.

Sniderman, P. M. (1975). *Personality and democratic politics.* Berkeley: University of California Press.

Staub, E. (1989). *The roots of evil: The origins of genocide and other group violence.* New York: Cambridge University Press.

Stone, W. F. (1974). *The psychology of politics.* New York: Free Press.

Stone, W. F. (1980). The myth of left-wing authoritarianism. *Political Psychology, 2,* 3–19.

Stone, W. F., & Baril, G. L. (1979). Self-other orientation and legislative behavior. *Journal of Personality, 47,* 162–176.

Stone, W. F., & Schaffner, P. E. (1988). *The psychology of politics* (2nd ed.). New York: Springer-Verlag.

Stone, W. F., & Smith, L. D. (1993). Authoritarianism: Left and right. In W. F. Stone, G. Lederer, & R. Christie (Eds.), *Strength and weakness: The authoritarian personality today* (pp. 144–156). New York: Springer-Verlag.

Strack, S. (1991). *Personality Adjective Check List manual* (Rev. ed.). South Pasadena, CA: 21st Century Assessment.

Strack, S. (1997). The PACL: Gauging normal personality styles. In T. Millon (Ed.), *The Millon inventories: Clinical and personality assessment* (pp. 477–497). New York: Guilford.

Suedfeld, P. (1994). President Clinton's policy dilemmas: A cognitive analysis. *Political Psychology, 15,* 337–349.

Suedfeld, P., & Tetlock, P. E. (1977). Integrative complexity of communications in international crises. *Journal of Conflict Resolution, 21,* 169–184.

Swansbrough, R. H. (1994). A Kohutian analysis of President Bush's personality and style in the Persian Gulf crisis. *Political Psychology, 15,* 227–276.

Tetlock, P. E. (1985). Integrative complexity of American and Soviet foreign policy rhetoric: A time-series analysis. *Journal of Personality and Social Psychology, 49,* 1565–1585.

Tomkins, S. S. (1963). Left and right: A basic dimension of ideology and personality. In R. W. White (Ed.), *The study of lives* (pp. 388–411). New York: Atherton Press.

Walker, S. G. (1990). The evolution of operational code analysis. *Political Psychology, 11,* 403–418.

Walker, S. G. (2000). Assessing psychological characteristics at a distance: Symposium lessons and future research directions. *Political Psychology, 21,* 597–602.

Wallas, G. (1908). *Human nature in politics.* London: Archibald Constable. (Reprinted 1981 by Transaction Books, New Brunswick, NJ)

Winter, D. G. (1973). *The power motive.* New York: Free Press.

Winter, D. G. (1987). Leader appeal, leader performance, and the motive profiles of leaders and followers: A study of American presidents and elections. *Journal of Personality and Social Psychology, 52,* 196–202.

Winter, D. G. (1991). Measuring personality at a distance: Development of an integrated system for scoring motives in running text. In A. J. Stewart, J. M. Healy, Jr., & D. J. Ozer (Eds.), *Perspectives in personality: Approaches to understanding lives* (pp. 59–89). London: Jessica Kingsley.

Winter, D. G. (1998). A motivational analysis of the Clinton first term and the 1996 presidential campaign. *Leadership Quarterly, 9,* 367–376.

Ziller, R. C. (1973). *The social self.* Elmsford, NY: Pergamon.

Ziller, R. C., Stone, W. F., Jackson, R. M., & Terbovic, N. J. (1977). Self-other orientations and political behavior. In M. G. Hermann (Ed.), *A psychological examination of political leaders* (pp. 174–204). New York: Free Press.

Zullow, H. M., & Seligman, M. E. P. (1990). Pessimistic rumination predicts defeat of presidential candidates, 1900 to 1984. *Psychological Inquiry, 1,* 52–61.

Author Index

Subject Index